Fodor's

SOUTH AMERICA

SIXTH EDITION

Where to Stay and Eat
for All Budgets

Must-See Sights
and Local Secrets

Ratings You Can T

D1009991

Fodor's Travel Publications   New York, Toronto, London, Sydney, Auckland
www.fodors.com

FODOR'S SOUTH AMERICA
Editor: Diane Mehta

Editorial Production: Ira-Neil Dittersdorf
Editorial Contributors: Eddy Ancinas, Gregory Benchwick, Diego Bigongiari, Carissa Bluestone, Karla Brunet, Brian Byrnes, Joyce Dalton, Michael de Zayas, Ana Lúcia do Vale, Paul Eisenberg, Rhan Flatin, José Fonseca, Denise Garcia, Robin Goldstein, Joan Gonzalez, Satu Hummasti, Deborah Kaufman, Shannon Kelly, Olivia Mollet, Victoria Patience, Holly S. Smith, Mark Sullivan, Carlos Tornquist, Jeffrey Van Fleet
Maps: David Lindroth, *cartographer*; Bob Blake and Rebecca Baer, *map editors*
Design: Fabrizio La Rocca, *creative director*; Guido Caroti, *art director*; Melanie Marin, *senior photo editor*
Production/Manufacturing: Robert B. Shields
Cover Photo (Ccasccara Range, Ausangate Trek, Peru): Nevada Wier/The Image Bank/Getty Images

SPECIAL SALES
This book is available for special discounts for bulk purchases for sales promotions or premiums. Special editions, including personalized covers, excerpts of existing books, and corporate imprints, can be created in large quantities for special needs. For more information, write to Special Markets/Premium Sales, 1745 Broadway, MD 6-2, New York, New York 10019, or e-mail specialmarkets@randomhouse.com.

AN IMPORTANT TIP & AN INVITATION
Although all prices, opening times, and other details in this book are based on information supplied to us at press time, changes occur all the time in the travel world, and Fodor's cannot accept responsibility for facts that become outdated or for inadvertent errors or omissions. So **always confirm information when it matters,** especially if you're making a detour to visit a specific place. Your experiences—positive and negative—matter to us. If we have missed or misstated something, **please write to us.** We follow up on all suggestions. Contact the South America editor at editors@fodors.com or c/o Fodor's, 1745 Broadway, New York, NY 10019.

PRINTED IN THE UNITED STATES OF AMERICA

10 9 8 7 6 5 4 3 2

DESTINATION SOUTH AMERICA

Our tendency to think of everything south of the Río Grande as being "just like Mexico" does grave injustice to the variety that is South America. Perhaps that's why the southern half of the Americas doesn't leap to the collective North American mind as a potential vacation option. But some five centuries ago, of course, Europeans discovered South America as a travel destination; the first European visitors grafted then their culture, religion, and architecture onto already vibrant, developed indigenous societies that thrived long before Christopher Columbus' wanderlust got the best of him. That melding of cultures in large part is responsible for South America's incredible variety. Cities don't get more cosmopolitan than Buenos Aires and Rio de Janeiro, and their denizens have little in common with those of the Bolivian highlands, whose ways have changed little since the Conquest. And as in any country, cities may be their brain and nerve centers, without ever being their soul. You'll be amply rewarded with any attempt to get out of the urban areas and experience the changing landscapes.

Tim Jarrell, Publisher

CONTENTS

Maps

CloseUps

ABOUT THIS BOOK

There's no doubt that the best source for travel advice is a like-minded friend who's just been where you're headed. But with or without that friend, you'll have a better trip with a Fodor's guide in hand. Once you've learned to find your way around its pages, you'll be in great shape to find your way around your destination.

SELECTION

Our goal is to cover the best properties, sights, and activities in their category, as well as the most interesting communities to visit. We make a point of including local food-lovers' hot spots as well as neighborhood options, and we avoid all that's touristy unless it's really worth your time. You can go on the assumption that everything you read about in this book is recommended wholeheartedly by our writers and editors. Flip to On the Road with Fodor's to learn more about who they are. It goes without saying that no property mentioned in the book has paid to be included.

RATINGS

Orange stars ★ denote sights and properties that our editors and writers consider the very best in the area covered by the entire book. These, the best of the best, are listed in the Fodor's Choice section in the front of the book. Black stars ★ highlight the sights and properties we deem Highly Recommended, the don't-miss sights within any region. Use the index to find complete descriptions. In cities, sights pinpointed with numbered map bullets ❶ in the margins tend to be more important than those without bullets.

SPECIAL SPOTS

Pleasures & Pastimes focuses on types of experiences that reveal the spirit of the destination. Watch for Off the Beaten Path sights. Some are out of the way, some are quirky, and all are worth your while. If the munchies hit while you're exploring, look for Need a Break? suggestions.

SEE IT ALL

In cities, Good Walks guide you to important sights in each neighborhood; ▶ indicates the starting points of walks and itineraries in the text and on the map.

BUDGET WELL

Hotel and restaurant price categories from ¢ to $$$$ are defined in the opening pages of each chapter—expect to find a balanced selection for every budget. For attractions, we always give standard adult admission fees; reductions are usually available for children, students, and senior citizens. Look in Discounts & Deals in Smart Travel Tips for information on destination-wide ticket schemes. Want to pay with plastic? AE, D, DC, MC, V following restaurant and hotel listings indicate whether American Express, Discover, Diner's Club, MasterCard, or Visa are accepted.

BASIC INFO

Smart Travel Tips lists travel essentials for the entire area covered by the book; city- and region-specific basics end each chapter. To find the best way to get around, see the transportation section; see individual modes of travel ("Car Travel," "Train Travel") for details. We assume you'll check Web sites or call for particulars.

ON THE MAPS

Maps throughout the book show you what's where and help you find your way around. Black and orange numbered bullets ❶ ❶ in the text correlate to bullets on maps.

BACKGROUND

In general, we give background information within the chapters in the course of explaining sights as well as in CloseUp boxes and in Understanding South America at the end of the book. The Portuguese and Spanish vocabularies can be invaluable.

FIND IT FAST

Within the book, chapters are arranged alphabetically, starting with Argentina, in the south of the continent. City chapters cover an entire city and nearby areas; other chapters are divided into regions, within which towns are covered in logical geographical order and attractive routes and interesting places between towns are flagged as En Route. Heads at the top of each page help you find what you need within a chapter.

DON'T FORGET

Restaurants are open for lunch and dinner daily unless we state otherwise; we mention dress only when there's a specific requirement and reservations only when they're essential or not accepted—it's always best to book ahead. Hotels have private baths, phone, TVs, and air-conditioning and operate on the European Plan (a.k.a. EP, meaning without meals). We always list facilities but not whether you'll be charged extra to use them, so when pricing accommodations, find out what's included.

SYMBOLS

Many Listings

★ Fodor's Choice
★ Highly recommended
⊠ Physical address
✛ Directions
🕮 Mailing address
☎ Telephone
🖷 Fax
⊕ On the Web
✎ E-mail
🖃 Admission fee
☉ Open/closed times
► Start of walk/itinerary
Ⓜ Metro stations
▭ Credit cards

Hotels & Restaurants

🏨 Hotel
↩ Number of rooms
♨ Facilities
🍽 Meal plans
✕ Restaurant
⚓ Reservations
👗 Dress code
↘ Smoking
🍷 BYOB
✕🏨 Hotel with restaurant that warrants a visit

Other

☾ Family-friendly
🛈 Contact information

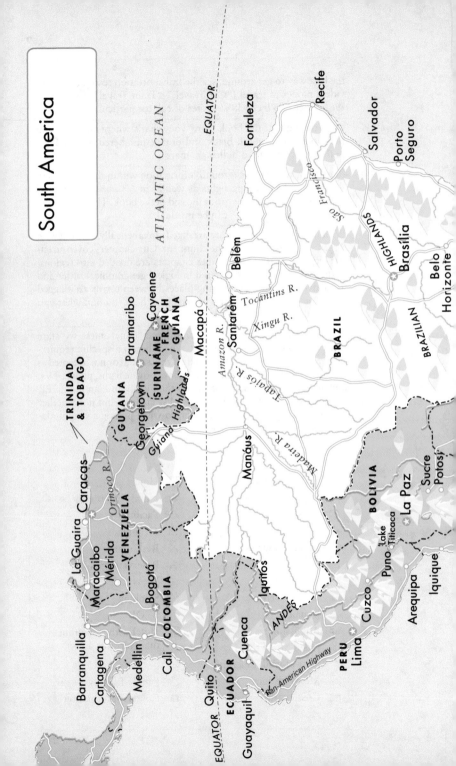

South America

ATLANTIC OCEAN

EQUATOR

TRINIDAD & TOBAGO

Barranquilla
Cartagena
La Guaira
Caracas
Maracaibo
Mérida
Medellín
Bogotá
Cali
COLOMBIA
Quito
ECUADOR
Guayaquil
Cuenca
EQUATOR

VENEZUELA
Orinoco R.
GUYANA
Georgetown
SURINAME
Paramaribo
FRENCH GUIANA
Cayenne
Guiana Highlands
Macapá

Manáus
Iquitos
ANDES
Lima
PERU
Cuzco
Pan-American Highway

Amazon R.
Tapajós R.
Madeira R.
Santarém
Xingu R.
Tocantins R.
Belém

BRAZIL
BRAZILIAN HIGHLANDS
São Francisco

Recife
Fortaleza
Salvador
Porto Seguro
Brasília
Belo Horizonte

BOLIVIA
La Paz
Sucre
Potosí
Lake Titicaca
Puno
Arequipa
Iquique

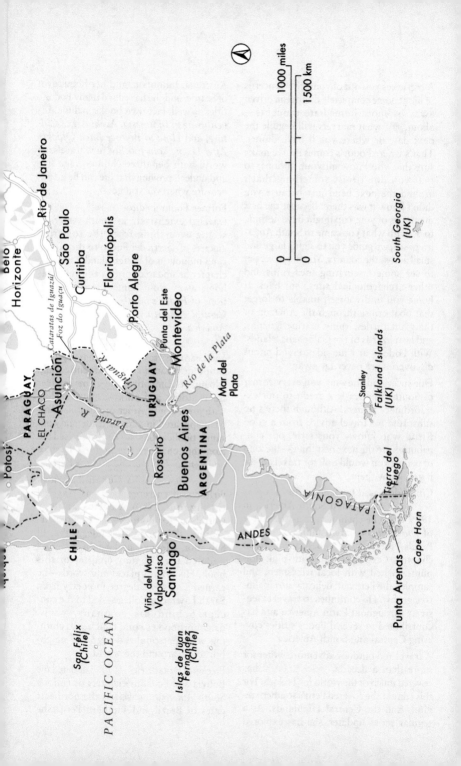

A trip takes you out of yourself. Concerns of life at home completely disappear, driven away by more immediate thoughts—about, say, what marvels will beguile the next day, or where you'll have dinner. That's where Fodor's comes in. We make sure that you know all your options, so that you don't miss something that's around the next bend just because you didn't know it was there. Because the best memories of your trip might have nothing to do with what you came to South America to see, we guide you to sights large and small across the country. You might set out to see some fascinating Inca ruins and other archaeological sites, but back at home you find yourself unable to forget that boat cruise through the Amazon or the giant turtles, spiny marine iguanas, and lava lizards of the Galápagos Islands. With Fodor's at your side, serendipitous discoveries are never far away.

Our success in showing you every corner of South America is a credit to our extraordinary writers. Although there's no substitute for travel advice from a good friend who knows your style, our contributors are the next best thing—the kind of people you would poll for travel advice if you knew them.

Colorado-based freelance writer Gregory Benchwick first visited South America in 1999 when he spent a year as the editor of *The Bolivian Times*. While researching Peru's North Coast and Amazon Basin chapters Gregory swam with pink dolphins, visited with local tribesmen, and sampled the Peruvian delicacy *suri* (palm-tree grubs). He continues to travel extensively throughout Latin America and has contributed to several Fodor's titles covering Central and South America.

A travel and outdoor adventure writer for more than a decade, Holly S. Smith has covered much of the world for Fodor's. For this edition she covered Peru's southern regions and the Central Highlands. As a regular series updater, she has explored Australia, Indonesia, and her hometown of Seattle, and she has edited many Fodor's titles as well. Her own books include *Adventuring in Indonesia, Aceh: Art & Culture,* and *How to Bounce Back Quickly After Losing Your Job.* She now travels the world with her three children (age five and under), proving that life can be an adventure wherever you go.

Former Fodor's editor Mark Sullivan has traveled extensively in South America, seeing everything from the towering glaciers of Tierra del Fuego to the mysterious monoliths of Easter Island. Lima, the chapter he updated for this edition, is his home away from home. He edited editions of *Fodor's South America, Fodor's Central America,* and *UpClose Central America.*

Joyce Dalton, who updated the Adventure and Learning Travel chapter, has explored exotic destinations from Argentina and Albania to Zimbabwe and Zanzibar. Her travel stories and photos, many dealing with great South American destinations, have appeared in various trade and consumer publications. Joyce also revised the Romania chapters for *Fodor's Eastern and Central Europe.* and *Fodor's Europe.*

Michael de Zayas, a Cuban-American writer and entrepreneur, has traveled throughout Latin America and the Caribbean for Fodor's—he covered Argentina, the Bahamas, Chile, Cuba, El Salvador, Mexico, and Spain. Michael updated the Uruguay chapter of this book. His love of places and words—he earned a master's degree in poetry from Sarah Lawrence College—led to the concept behind his company, www.neighborhoodies.com, which sells clothing with personalized logos of neighborhoods around the world.

Freelance writer Joan Gonzalez updated the Bolivia and Ecuador chapters of *Fodor's South America,* as well as the northeast cities of Brazil and southern Peru. She also co-authored the first edition of *Fodor's Los Cabos* pocket guide. She started her journalism career on newspapers in her home state of Ohio, where she was a prize-winning journalist and sports editor before moving to Miami and getting involved with writing about Latin America.

American-born Erik Riesenberg was raised in Colombia and spent more than 15 years in the country. He has toured much of the country, from the cities to the small villages in between to the snow-capped mountain of Nevado de Ruiz near Colombia's Atlantic coast, and the various Carnaval festivities celebrated all over the country. He is always impressed by the warmth and hospitality of the Colombian people who go out of their way to make sure visitors feel welcome. Erik currently lives and works in San Francisco.

Costa Rica–based freelancer writer and pharmacist Jeffrey Van Fleet divides his time between Central America and Wisconsin but always looks for opportunities to enjoy South America's cosmopolitan vibe. He is a regular writer to Costa Rica's English-language *Tico Times*. Jeff updated the Paraguay, Venezuela, and Smart Travel Tips A to Z chapters for this edition, and also contributed to Fodor's guides to Chile, Argentina, Costa Rica, Central America, and Peru.

We'd also like to thank Martin Mosley and the staff of LanChile Airlines, Misty Pinson of MSP Communications, Marisol Cabello of the Embassy of Chile, Anna Cravens at Aerolineas Argentinas in Los Angeles, Alfredo del Giusti of the Chamber of Tourism in Mendoza, and Gustavo Ezquerra at Alunco Travel in Bariloche.

The profusion of fascinating destinations might make choosing just one South American country—or even two or three—seem impossible. The truth is that the jagged spine of the Andes splits the continent into two very distinct regions, which makes planning trips much less daunting. West of this monumental mountain range is the thin strip of land running along the Pacific Ocean. Here you'll find some of the continent's most intriguing port towns, from the colonial splendor of Colombia's Cartagena to the jumble of colorful houses tumbling down the hills surrounding Chile's Valparaíso, and some of the most fascinating archaeological discoveries, from Ingapirca in Ecuador to Machu Picchu in Peru. The topography is remarkably varied, from the high plateaus of Ecuador, Peru, and Bolivia to the sprawling deserts of Chile. Many head to the western side of the continent en route to see the unique creatures of the Galápagos or the stoic stone heads of Easter Island.

East of the Andes, the marvels are no less alluring. The Amazon Basin—extending across parts of nine countries and covering more than 10 million square km (4 million square mi)—eclipses all other natural wonders. But there are many other sights well worth seeing, from the endless plains of the Pantanal in Brazil to the steely blue glaciers of Patagonia. Some of the world's largest and most exciting cities—Rio de Janeiro, São Paulo, Montevideo, and Buenos Aires—are settled along the Atlantic coast.

① Argentina

Romantic notions of gauchos riding the ranges and tango dancers gliding across the floor have given Argentina a mystique, but these images tell only half the story. Duck into the upscale boutiques of Buenos Aires's Recoleta district, drop by for tea at an elegant *confitería,* or attend an opera at the world-famous Teatro Colón, and you'll realize that *Porteños* (the residents of this port city) are educated, sophisticated, and urbane. Like a certain city to the north, Buenos Aires never sleeps: dinner is often taken at midnight, and the streets are still full of people when you leave the restaurant sometime past 2 AM.

Away from the capital, the pace is slower, the people more open, and the landscape striking. North of Buenos Aires are the stunning Iguazú Falls—in all, some 300 separate waterfalls that thunder over a 4-km-wide (2½-mi-wide) precipice on the border of Brazil, Argentina, and Paraguay. In Patagonia to the south, you'll find the ski resort of Bariloche; the icy monoliths of Parque Nacional los Glaciares; and the famous Parque Nacional Tierra del Fuego at the very tip of the country.

② Bolivia

Visitors are often giddy upon arrival in La Paz, perhaps with relief at having landed safely in the world's highest capital city. More likely it's *soroche,* a wooziness caused by the lack of oxygen at high altitudes. But even after you've sipped the local remedy called *mate de coca* you may find that Bolivia still leaves you breathless. Although it lacks a coastline (that was lost to Chile more than a century ago), Bolivia has a bit of everything else, from lofty Andean peaks to lush Amazon rain forests.

Not far from La Paz, the ruins of Tiwanaku are set in the strangely beautiful altiplano, the barren plateau that lies between two branches of the Andes. Here you'll find La Puerta del Sol (Gate of the Sun), an imposing stone fixture believed to be a solar calendar built by a civilization that surfaced around 600 BC and mysteriously disappeared around AD 1200. Another Bolivian sight on everyone's agenda is Lake Titicaca—the highest navigable lake in the world and the legendary birthplace of the Inca empire. Hydrofoils and hovercrafts ply the waters, passing traditional gondola-shape boats made of reeds.

(3) Brazil

Portuguese-speaking Brazil is the fifth-largest country in the world and has an oversized vitality to match. Its high-energy attitude can be seen everywhere—in highways, dams, industrial complexes, and even in the capital city of Brasília, which was constructed from scratch in the wilderness in an effort to promote development of the nation's vast interior.

To most visitors, Brazil is Rio de Janeiro, famous for its spectacular bayside setting, fabulous beaches, skimpy string bikinis, and riotous Carnaval. But Brazil goes far beyond Rio's beaches and hedonistic pleasures. Skyscrapers, stock markets, and agribusiness set the pace in the megalopolis of São Paulo. Far to the southwest is the mighty Foz de Iguaçu (Iguaçu Falls). The massive Pantanal—an untamable mosaic of swamp and forest teeming with wildlife—is the dominant feature of Brazil's far west both in geography and in tourist appeal. A unique Afro-Brazilian culture thrives in tropical Salvador, capital of Bahia State. And then there's the Amazon, a gargantuan waterway flowing for more than 4,000 mi, so wide in places you can't see the shore from a riverboat's deck, and banked by a rainforest that houses the greatest variety of life on earth.

(4) Chile

You're never far from the ocean in this 4,267-km-long (2,650-mi-long) country, as it averages only 177 km (110 mi) in width. Chile is justly famous for its twin resort cities of Valparaíso and Viña del Mar, known for their wide swaths of sand and nonstop nightlife. But this ribbon of country isn't just a string of beautiful beaches—it has everything from desolate salt flats to awe-inspiring glaciers. In the north, you'll find the Atacama Desert, so dry that in some areas no rain has ever been recorded. Next come the copper mines that brought great wealth to the country, followed by the fertile Central Valley region that's home to the sprawling capital of Santiago. The green and aquamarine waters of the Lake District are to the south, offering outstanding fishing and water sports. Finally, in the extreme south lies the forbidding landscape of windswept Tierra del Fuego.

Lauded for its award-winning wines and world-renowned seafood, Chile draws raves for its succulent *centolla* (king crab) and *congrio* (conger eel). Patagonia is known for its tender and moist *cordero asado* (grilled lamb). You'll work up quite an appetite with all the country's outdoor activities, from hiking up smoldering volcanoes to rafting down raging rivers. Jet-set skiers from all over the world prefer the championship slopes at Valle Nevado, not far from Santiago, where they can schuss during summer months when snows melt in the Northern Hemisphere.

5 **Colombia**

Colombia is the continent's only country to touch both the Pacific and the Atlantic. The Andes begin here, which means the topography ranges from chilly mountain peaks to sultry coastal lowlands. The country's major cities sit at different altitudes, and with each comes a different attitude. Bogotá, the sprawling capital, sits at 8,700 ft and has a formal air that recalls its colonial past. The atmosphere grows more relaxed and informal, however, if you descend 2,000 ft to Medellín, a small but vibrant city whose mild climate has earned it the name "city of eternal spring."

Sadly, much of the country is embroiled in bitter battles between the government and factions on the left and right. But some parts of Colombia are far removed from the fighting. The historical port of Cartagena, for example, is a destination for many tourists. It is one of the best-preserved colonial cities in the Americas; it's also a lively, exuberant town with strong Afro-Caribbean influence.

6 **Ecuador**

A patchwork of highland and jungle, this tiny nation claims some of the hemisphere's most impressive landscapes. A living quilt of terraced green plots covers the lower slopes of cloud-capped volcanoes, where corn grows twice as tall as the sturdy peasant farmers. Quito, the capital, lies at the foot of Volcán Pichincha, a mighty volcano that sometimes sputters to life. The city has two distinct faces, the Old City, with its carefully preserved colonial buildings and the New City, where luxury hotels are sprouting as fast as flowers after a spring rain. Just 24 km (15 mi) outside the city, you can have your picture taken as you straddle the equator at a monument indicating the dividing line between the Northern and Southern hemispheres. In Ecuador, if you are patient, you can eventually see all the stars in our universe.

Cuenca, a beautifully preserved colonial city, offers both architectural charm and an outstanding market. No rainbow could possibly compete with the flaming colors worn by the highland women, who adorn their necks with strands of golden beads. The coastal region is home to the bustling metropolis of Guayaquil, a once seedy port city slowly recovering its status. Guayaquil also serves as a departure point for planes and ships to the enchanting Galápagos Islands, home of the remarkable wildlife that sparked naturalist Charles Darwin's theories of evolution.

7 **Paraguay**

In this unspoiled land, time and tradition have stood still for generations. Paraguay may be short on trendy eateries and luxurious accommodations, but it's long on charm. Asunción is a provincial capital whose pleasures are simple: a stroll through the botanical gardens; a leisurely lunch at an outdoor café; or an afternoon of shopping for *ñandutí*, the country's unique, intricate, spiderweb lace. In the countryside, motorcycles and pop music compete with oxcarts and traditional *polca* music in the hearts and minds of the rural people. The country's original inhabitants were the Guaraní, and the ruins of missions near Encarnación are an impressive reminder of their fascinating legacy. Here, Jesuit missionaries converted the native population and organized a unique communal society. Several of the lovely colonial-era buildings, abandoned when the Jesuits were expelled from the region in 1767, are currently being restored.

8 Peru

Peru contains a wealth of history within its borders. Cusco, once the capital of the Inca empire, is one of the hemisphere's most beautiful cities. Although the Spaniards who conquered the region in the 16th century tried to superimpose their culture on the indigenous people, they never really succeeded. When a 1953 earthquake struck the city, it felled much of the convent of Santo Domingo, which had been built over the ruins of the sacred Temple of the Sun. Hidden for so long beneath the facade built by the Spanish, the Inca walls beneath withstood the disaster.

On a hilltop outside of Cusco is the massive fortress of Sacsayhuaman, whose zigzag shape is visible only from the air. It's a great introduction to Inca culture before you head to the unforgettable Machu Picchu. Thought by many archaeologists to have been the last refuge of the Incas, Machu Picchu was never discovered by the Spaniards. The maze of temples, houses, terraces, and stairways lay abandoned in lofty solitude until explorer Hiram Bingham stumbled upon the city in 1911. The three-hour train trip from Cusco to Machu Picchu is exhilarating, passing by dozens of smaller ruins before finally reaching the famed "lost city."

If the gems of Peru's Inca past are locked away on the altiplano, then its capital, Lima, is the safekeeper of colonial treasures. Perhaps no other city in the Americas enjoyed such power and prestige during the height of the colonial era. For an entirely different side of Peru, visit the rain forest near Puerto Maldonado, where the sounds of the Amazon jungle are ever present.

9 Uruguay

Gently rolling hills and grasslands are the hallmarks of Uruguay, one of South America's smallest countries. Ninety percent of the land is used for grazing, and Uruguayans are justifiably proud of their fine beef cattle. A visit to an *estancia* (ranch) is an excellent way to experience both the scenery and the people—well educated yet unpretentious, industrious yet relaxed, they're the most remarkable aspect of Uruguay. Another culture altogether exists along the coasts. The country's beaches are among the best on the continent; without even leaving Montevideo, Uruguay's gracious capital, you can sample more than half a dozen of them. The most fashionable beach, however, is 137 km (85 mi) to the east at Punta del Este, a haven for well-heeled foreign visitors. Often called the South American Riviera, this resort is also a popular site for international conferences and movie festivals.

(10) Venezuela

Just a few hours from the eastern United States, Venezuela is perhaps the continent's most accessible destination for North American travelers. Caracas, the crowded capital, is a futuristic blend of glass office towers and concrete apartment buildings built on the heels of the oil boom. You can find a bit of colonial charm around tree-lined Plaza Bolívar, but Caracas is better known for its selection of world-class restaurants, interesting art galleries, and stylish nightspots.

Venezuela enjoys South America's longest Caribbean coast, with stretches of pristine white sand lapped by warm turquoise waters. Isla Margarita has long been a destination popular with sun-seeking Europeans, and North Americans have been, increasingly, discovering its charms. In the Andean city of Mérida, the world's longest and highest cable car carries you to the foot of glacier-topped Pico Bolívar. In the southeast, huge table-top mountains called *tepuis* tower over the grasslands of Parque Nacional Canaima, a national park the size of Belgium. Here, the spectacular Angel Falls plummet more than 2,647 ft into a bizarre landscape of black lagoons, pink sand beaches, and unique plant life.

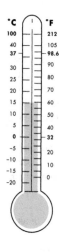

°C °F

100 — 212
40 — 105
37 — 98.6
30 — 90
25 — 80
20 — 70
15 — 60
10 — 50
5 — 40
0 — 32
−5 — 20
−10 — 10
−15 — 0
−20

Seasons below the Equator are the reverse of those in the north—summer in Argentina, Bolivia, Chile, Paraguay, Peru, and Uruguay, and portions of Brazil and Ecuador, runs from December to March and winter from June to September. Prices in beach resorts invariably are higher during the summer months. If you're looking for a bargain, stick to the off-season.

Climate

Because of the great variety of latitudes, altitudes, and climatic zones on the continent, you'll encounter many different kinds of weather in any given month. The highland areas of the Andes—which run north to south down the west coast of South America from Colombia through Ecuador, Peru, Bolivia, Chile, and Argentina—are at their most accessible and most comfortable in the dry season, May–October. July–September is ski season in Chile and Argentina.

An entirely different climate reigns in the Amazon basin, whose tropical and subtropical rain forests spread from Ecuador and Peru across the northern third of Brazil. The dry season runs from May to September—which means it's simply less rainy than at any other time. Contrary to what you may have heard, the rainy season is a great time for an Amazon River trip; the waters are higher then and boats can venture farther upriver into the tributaries.

Certain ocean regions—the Atlantic coast from Brazil all the way down to the famous resort of Punta del Este in Uruguay, as well as the Caribbean shore of Venezuela—are at their hottest and most crowded when it's North America's winter. The sea moderates temperatures in most South American cities year-round, even as far south as Buenos Aires. The Pacific coast is bordered mainly by a strip of desert, where the climate is always hospitable. Argentine and Chilean Patagonia hold countless fjords, perfect for cruising from November to March.

Weather wise, May and June are probably the best months to visit South America, as you can expect both good weather and off-season prices. These months, as well as September and October, are also relatively uncrowded.

⛅ Forecasts **Weather Channel Connection** ☎ 900/932–8437, 95¢ per minute from a Touch-Tone phone ⊕ www.weather.com.

PLEASURES & PASTIMES

Archaeology The mysteries of ancient ruins such as the windswept streets at Tiwanaku in Bolivia and the stately temple at Ingapirca in Ecuador never fail to tantalize. Peru alone has a wealth of pre-Columbian sites that would take weeks to fully explore. Almost every major archaeological site in the country is worth seeing, but the must-see sights include Machu Picchu, the fortresses of Pisac and Ollantaytambo, and the Qorikancha, the temple of the sun, in the imperial city of Cusco. If you have more time, visit the Nazca lines, gigantic, mysterious drawings in the desert; the Chimú city of Chán Chán, outside Trujillo; and the Moche tomb of the warrior priest at Sipán. And while some sites in Colombia are too dangerous to visit, Bogotá's Gold Museum and its Museum of Archaeology have wonderful collections of pre-Columbian gold, artifacts, and ceramics.

Colonial Architecture There's no question that Spain's conquistadors brought a legacy of greed, corruption, and slavery to South America. But they also left the continent with a collection of colonial architecture unmatched in the world. The Spaniards grafted many of their churches and palaces onto the Inca structures of Cusco, an odd juxtaposition that in many ways defines the region's history. Stroll the ramparts of the fortress city of Cartagena, in Colombia, or the cobblestone streets of Quito's Old City, now a UNESCO World Heritage site, a sign of South America's commitment to preserving its pre-independence heritage. But not all was glitter and splendor in the colonial era—in southern Paraguay and the Argentine Litoral are ruins of Jesuit missions, a seamless blending of missionary and indigenous cultures that worked side-by-side. And dozens of wooden Jesuit churches are scattered around Chile's Chiloé island, their function similar to the missions on the opposite side of the continent. All are elegant in their simplicity.

Eating & Drinking Culinary partisans may argue over whether exotic Afro-Brazilian concoctions, delicious Peruvian and Chilean seafood dishes, or sinfully succulent Argentine and Uruguayan grilled meats should claim the title of South America's most delicious regional foods. For most visitors, however, the entire continent is a diner's delight. Expect to eat dinner well after dark, as many restaurants don't even open their doors until 8 or 9. What if you get hungry? The Chileans have solved the problem by creating a late afternoon meal called *onces*, which consists of tea with sandwiches and pastries. Peruvians pass the time with a pisco sour, an intoxicating brew made with a locally produced brandy, while Brazilians kick back with a *caipirinha*, a mixture of lime juice, sugar, and a liquor made from sugar cane.

Festivals It's fun to be in many countries—particularly Brazil and the Caribbean countries—during Carnaval, a raucous festival held the week before Ash Wednesday. In strongly Catholic South America, dozens of saints days are marked by processions and other festivities. Semana Santa, the week between Palm Sunday and Easter Sunday, is particularly important; it's a time for elaborate religious processions through the streets of many towns. (But on an increasingly secularized continent, many anticipate Holy Week as a chance to get away to the beach or the mountains.) In the Andean countries, the time between harvest and the next planting (June to November) is when many folk festivals take place.

Spending the Night

No matter what your travel finances, you won't be priced out of the market when it comes to finding places to stay in South America—though you'll have more trouble stretching your budget in large cities, such as Buenos Aires or Caracas. But everything is here. At one end of the spectrum, you'll find hostels and backpackers' digs. There are many small- or medium-size, independent, family-run inns, where you'll get pampered with equally family-style service. The luxury international chains all have outposts in South America, too, along with some chains local to the continent or to individual countries. Their names may be unfamiliar to you, but they don't lack for service.

Wilderness & Wildlife

Volcanoes, some still smoldering, run the length of the Andes; at their feet lie everything from the desolate, windswept sand dunes of Peru's Reserva Nacional Paracas to the bubbling hot springs of Chile's Parque Nacional Nevado Tres Cruces. The 30,000-year-old Perito Moreno Glacier broods in Argentina's Parque Nacional los Glaciares, while spires of ice slide off the glacier in Chile's Parque Nacional Laguna San Rafael. A mighty roar fills the air as the raging waters of Iguazú Falls—higher and wider than Niagara—plunge over basalt cliffs at the point where Argentina, Paraguay, and Brazil meet. The spectacular Angel Falls crashes nearly two-thirds of a mile down a cliff in a corner of Venezuela so remote that it was unknown to the world until 1937. And simply nothing is more amazing than the Amazon, most closely associated with Brazil, but its watershed, the world's largest rain forest area, extends into eight other South American nations.

If you're a sports enthusiast you'll appreciate the thrills of white-water rafting in Peruvian jungles, bone-fishing along Venezuela's coast, downhill skiing in the Argentine Andes, and hiking and climbing in the pristine wilderness of the Chilean Lake District. If instead you're a sun worshiper, most dedicated of hedonists, you can spend your time mingling with beautiful people on the glittering beaches in Uruguay's posh Punta del Este, Chile's Viña del Mar, Venezuela's Isla Margarita, or, of course, Brazil's Ipanema.

Those looking for more unusual adventures can come nose to nose with sea lions and giant tortoises in the Galápagos Islands or look for pterodactyl-like hoatzins balancing in the branches of trees along Venezuela's more remote rivers. In Argentina, whales and elephant seals frolic at Península Valdés while penguin clans hold reunions on the beaches at Punta Tombo. Flamingos, foxes, and guanacos (cousins of the llama) inhabit Chile's Parque Nacional Torres del Paine.

Photography

Few vacation spots provide better subjects—from landscapes and cityscapes to wildlife and people—for photographers. It's difficult to imagine colors more brilliant, light more intense, or textures more complex than those that meet the eye at every glance: the perfectly shaped cones of Ecuador's volcanoes, the colonial splendor of Peru's cathedrals, and the colorful rooftops of the towns in Chile's southernmost reaches.

Shopping

Savvy shoppers can spend all day at chic boutiques brimming with good buys in Brazilian gemstones, Colombian emeralds, and Argentine or Uruguayan leather. Handicrafts lovers will marvel at the Paraguayan lace, Peruvian textiles, or fine Panama hats (they really come from Ecuador) sold in bustling street-corner *ferias* and covered *mercados*.

FODOR'S CHOICE

The sights, restaurants, hotels, and other travel experiences on these pages are our editors' top picks—our Fodor's Choices. They're the best of their type in the area covered by the book—not to be missed and always worth your time. In the destination chapters that follow, you will find all the details.

LODGING

ARGENTINA

Llao Llao Hotel & Resort, near Bariloche. This first-class resort in Patagonia sits on a hill between two lakes and is surrounded by snow-clad peaks. $$$$

Marriott Plaza Hotel, Buenos Aires. The capital's first grand hotel draws illustrious guests. $$$$

Sheraton Internacional Cataratas de Iguazú. Have breakfast or a drink on a balcony overlooking the falls—and be sure to ask for a room with a view. $$$$

Hotel y Resort Las Hayas, Ushuaia. Pampering amenities abound at this Patagonian hotel and spa nestled in the foothills of the Andes. $$$

BOLIVIA

Hotel Europa, La Paz Outstanding views of snowcapped Mt. Illimani from the rooftop garden set this hotel apart, as does the original artwork in the lobby, and understated, elegant rooms. $$$$

Gran Hotel Paris, La Paz. Stop in for tea at this lovely fin-de-siècle hotel on historic Plaza Murillo. Six Louis XVI–style suites have balconies overlooking the plaza's formal gardens. $$

Inca Utama Hotel & Spa–Andean Roots Eco Village, Huatajata. It's well worth the trip to Lake Titicaca to visit this hotel and museum complex with exhibits, native workshops, an observatory, a spa, and a children's park. $$–$$$

BRAZIL

Copacabana Palace, Rio. Old-world elegance joins contemporary amenities and white-glove service. $$$$

Caiman Ecological Refuge, Pantanal. This deluxe ranch, which promotes ecological awareness, is one of the region's top lodges. $$$–$$$$

Gran Meliá São Paulo. The location is as big a draw as the creature comforts, some of them high-tech. $$$–$$$$

Tropical Cataratas EcoResort, Foz do Iguaçu. Within a nature preserve and with the roar of the falls in the background, these are the finest accommodations near Iguaçu. $$$

Lago Salvador, Manaus. One of several famed jungle lodges offers seclusion and a sense of unity with the forest as well as simple comforts. *$$*

CHILE

Hotel Explora, San Pedro de Atacama. This architecturally forward-thinking hotel has skewed lines and a sleek courtyard. For your all-inclusive stay you can expect the best service and amenities of any lodging in northern Chile. *$$$$*

Hotel Antumalal, Pucón. This Frank Lloyd Wright–inspired masterpiece perched on a cliff feels like a country inn, with cozy rooms and spectacular grounds. *$$$$*

Hotel Del Mar, Viña del Mar. Marble floors, fountains, abundant gardens, and impeccable service make this one of Chile's most luxurious hotels. The exterior is true to the casino's neoclassical design, but spacious guest rooms are pure 21st century. *$$$$*

Lodge Andino Terrantai, San Pedro de Atacama. This architectural beauty with river-stone walls has high-ceilinged rooms and beautiful tile floors, and a tiny, natural-rock plunge pool in the center. *$$$*

COLOMBIA

Santa Clara, Cartagena. Beyond its arched porticos and lush courtyards, this historic hotel in a 17th-century convent holds some of the most stylish rooms in Colombia and the best French food in town. *$$$$*

ECUADOR

Café Cultura hotel, Quito. Bougainvillea over the gate are the first introduction to this unusually cozy colonial-style inn. *$*

Colón Guayaquil Hilton, Guayaquil. Majestic, with a 10-story atrium lobby and an outdoor pool ringed by palm trees, this hotel is a dynamite choice if you're in search of the finer things. *$$$–$$$$*

Hampton Inn Boulevard Hotel & Casino, Guayaquil. Behind the beautiful San Francisco church and close to museums you'll find this delightful inn. *$$*

Hotel Oro Verde, Cuenca. Once named "La Laguna" after the artificial lake at its center, this place will delight animal lovers: ducks swim past your window, three resident alpacas munch on the grassy banks, and peacocks stroll through bushes. *$$$*

Mansion del Angel hotel, Quito. Housed in a lavish fin-de-siècle mansion this luxurious hotel has rooms with antique four-poster beds and a chandelier-lit stairway. *$$*

PARAGUAY

Hotel Las Margaritas, Asunción One of the capital's newest and most lavish hotels—with a lobby overflowing with plants and paintings—will not charge you equally lavish rates. *$–$$*

PERU

Country Club Lima Hotel, Lima. With hand-painted tiles and a stained-glass ceiling in the lobby, this hacienda-style hotel dating from 1927 is a work of art. *$$$$*

ExplorNapo, Iquitos. This rustic lodge deep in the rain forest offers access to a canopy walkway 110 feet above ground. $$$$

Machu Picchu Pueblo Hotel, Aguas Calientes. In this semitropical paradise, the stone bungalows have cathedral ceilings, exposed beams, and flagstone floors, creating an atmosphere of rustic elegance. $$$$

URUGUAY

Casapueblo Club Hotel, Punta Ballena. At this 13-floor surrealist hotel and museum complex perched on a rocky point are allusions to Arab minarets and domes, cathedral vaulting, Grecian whitewash, and continuous sculptural flourishes. $$$$

Four Seasons Carmelo hotel, Colonia del Sacramento. Enjoy a fusion of Asian styles—from tai chi classes to bungalows with private Japanese gardens. In the evening torches illuminate the paths of the resort—through sand dunes. $$$$

VENEZUELA

Arekuna camp, Canaima National Park. Get a stylish cabaña at this luxury camp by the Río Caroni, just outside the strikingly surreal pink beaches, black lagoons, and giant waterfalls of the park. $$$$

Posada Mediterráneo, Isla Gran Roque in Los Roques National Park. Climb the white stone staircase to the rooftop terrace hung with sun-shaded hammocks and enjoy the view from the island over the Caribbean. $$$

Los Frailes Inn. This stylish 17th-century monastery-turned-hotel has unique, sumptuous rooms and the exterior has enough flowers and vines to make the city seem deceptively distant. $$

BUDGET LODGING

BOLIVIA

Hotel Rosario, La Paz. Inside this Spanish-style inn are bright rooms and a sunny courtyard with flowering clay pots; outside are spectacular views of Mt. Chacaltaya. ¢

BRAZIL

Pousada Araras EcoLodge, Transpantaneira Highway, south of Cuiabá. This lodge combines outstanding amenities with ecotours in the northern Pantanal. $

ECUADOR

Casa Grande Hotel, Bahia de Caraquez. In this comfortable, friendly guest house are paintings by the artist Eduardo Kingman, large rooms with picture windows and private baths, a sunny backyard, and home-cooked meals. ¢

PARAGUAY

Hotel Centu Cué, Villa Florida. These bungalows are scattered along the banks of the Río Tebicuary, one of South America's most beautiful rivers. ¢

PERU

Hotel Mossone, Huacachina. In a century-old mansion, the Hotel Mossone offers dining on a veranda overlooking the Huacachina lagoon. $

Sonesta Posada del Inca, Sacred Valley of the Incas. The colonial-style guest rooms at this 300-year-old former convent have balconies that overlook the courtyards overflowing with flowers. $

La Casa de Melgar, Arequipa. Staying at this colonial inn is like traveling back in time, as the suites have the original *sillar* ceilings and vintage cookstoves. ¢

RESTAURANTS

ARGENTINA

Tomo Uno, Buenos Aires. Three decades of imaginative interpretations of classic Argentine dishes have made this restaurant the best known in Buenos Aires. $$$

1884 Restaurante, Mendoza. The gracious stone halls of a century-old bodega provide the backdrop for sensational Argentine haute cuisine. $$–$$$

El Trapiche, Buenos Aires. This friendly neighborhood grill serves up huge portions of traditional Argentine fare. $–$$

BOLIVIA

Aransaya, La Paz. Spectacular views of the city await you at this restaurant on the penthouse of the Radisson Plaza Hotel. International and regional specialties are exquisitely presented. $$–$$$

Wagamama, La Paz. Fresh trout from Lake Titicaca, cooked Japanese style, is the staple and specialty here. $–$$

BRAZIL

Olympe, Rio. Sensitive use of Brazilian ingredients and chefs whose creativity knows no end yield out-of-this-world meals. $$$$

Famiglia Mancini, São Paulo. The atmosphere here is jovial, the decor is unique, and the food is some of the best Italian you'll find in South America's largest city. $$–$$$$

Trapiche Adelaide, Salvador. It's almost impossible to have a bad meal in this city, but this restaurant along the harbor still stands out for its unique blend of French and Bahian cuisines and for its fresh fish. $$–$$$

Porcão, Rio. When in Rio, head here for the churrascaria experience: waiters zip among tables, slicing sizzling chunks of grilled beef, pork, and chicken onto your plate. $$

Fogo Caipira, Campo Grande. The delicious Pantanal fish and western Brazilian beef dishes here are unforgettable. ¢–$$

CHILE

Aquí Está Coco, Santiago. Flotsam and jetsam found on nearby beaches add a whimsical touch to this restaurant cooking up the best fish and shellfish in the capital. $$–$$$

Bristol, Santiago. Try this innovative take on traditional Chilean dishes, with a buffet that includes unlimited access to a wine cart stocked with a dozen quality vintages. $$–$$$

Delicias del Mar, Viña del Mar. Expect such seafood delicacies as Peruvian-style ceviche and the house's own version of paella. Oenophiles: know that there's an extensive, almost exclusively Chilean wine list. *$–$$*

COLOMBIA

Casa Medina, Bogotá. Antiques imported by aristocratic Bogotano families are scattered throughout the dining rooms, each evoking a different European country. Once a private mansion and now a national monument, the restaurant serves elegant French cuisine. *$$$–$$$$*

El Hato Viejo, Medellín. Large portions of delicious roasted meat and freshly grilled seafood have made this second-story restaurant in the heart of town a local hangout. *$–$$*

PARAGUAY

La Paraguayita, Asunción. Paraguayan steaks are turned on the grill while you relax beneath jacaranda trees on this restaurant's lovely terrace. *¢–$*

Peter's Restaurant en Casapueblo, Asunción. Renowned German chef Gato Dumas uses only natural ingredients, as in his delicious filet mignon medallions on a bed of julienned seasonal vegetables. *¢–$*

PERU

Astrid y Gaston, Lima. If you think the restaurant itself is a work of art, it's just a warm-up for the imaginative entrées. The eye-catching *pato asado con mil especies* (roast duck with 1,000 spices) is accompanied by a pepper bubbling over with basil risotto. *$$–$$$$*

La Taberna, Ica. Bodega El Catador outside Ica opened this romantic restaurant serving exquisite local specialties at candlelit tables and with live Peruvian music. *$$*

El Cartujo, Lima. Monks who took a vow of silence gave this place its name, but you won't be able to say enough about the sole stuffed with lobster or the sea bass topped with crab. There's a top-notch wine list, too. *$–$$*

La Posada del Puente, Arequipa. Relax with a glass of excellent Peruvian or Chilean wine at this elegant restaurant overlooking the Río Chili. *$*

Pucará, Cusco. Cusco's best restaurant is always packed with locals who turn out for the tasty, economical lunch special. *$*

VENEZUELA

Lee Hamilton's Steak House, Caracas. Cuts of beef this tasty usually require going south to Argentina. This place is the only restaurant in town that serves real American cuts of beef. *$$$–$$$$*

BUDGET RESTAURANTS

ARGENTINA

Almacen de Ramos Generales, Buenos Aires Province. You won't find a better *bife de chorizo* (sirloin steak) than at this elegant restaurant, which remembers its country-store roots. *¢–$*

El Viejo Molino, Trelew. This converted 1886 mill defines fun, sophisticated dining in a city where you'd never expect to find it. ¢–$

BOLIVIA

Pronto, La Paz. Locals love the delicious pastas here, as well as the top-notch service. ¢–$

San Marcos, Potosí. Come for the trout, the steak doused with cognac and set aflame, or to check out how the ancient machinery from the former silver processing plant is now part of this unusual restaurant's design. ¢–$

BRAZIL

Canto da Peixada, Manaus. This restaurant owes its popularity to masterful preparation of river fish. $

Lá em Casa, Belém. Outstanding interpretations of indigenous Amazon dishes have given this restaurant international renown. $

Braz, São Paulo. Old Italy prevails at this pizzeria with delicious pies. ¢–$

ECUADOR

La Querencia, Quito. The city views and serene gardens are enough reason to go, but wonderful Ecuadorean dishes are the main draw. ¢–$

Villarosa Restaurant, Cuenca. One of the city's best-loved places has tastefully decorated salons and a balcony with an open fireplace to cut the chill and enjoy the grilled trout with almonds or the fruit-and-chocolate fondue. ¢

PERU

Fitzcarraldo, Iquitos. Originally a private home during Iquitos's rubber boom of the late 19th century, the Fitzcarraldo has a sumptuous menu of exotic jungle game dishes and great views of the Amazon River. ¢–$

HISTORIC SITES

ARGENTINA

Calle Museo Caminito, Buenos Aires. Vibrant scenes of colorful buildings, tango dancers, and artisans at work fill this pedestrian-only street.

Cementerio de La Recoleta, Buenos Aires. A veritable who's who of Argentine history, this city of the dead is filled with elaborate mausoleums.

BOLIVIA

Cerro Rico, Potosí. If you don't mind tight spaces, descend into one of the 5,000 tunnels that crisscross Cerro Rico, the "Rich Hill" that filled Spain's coffers with silver until the reserves were exhausted in the early 19th century.

BRAZIL

Palácio Catete, Rio. The former presidential palace's details are as incredible as its history.

Teatro Amazonas, Manaus. No other structure better represents the opulence of the rubber boom.

CHILE	**Cerros Pintados (Painted Hills), Reserva Nacional Pampa del Tamarugal.** Here you'll find the largest group of geoglyphs—more than 400—in the world. Scientists believe these figures of birds, animals, and geometric patterns, which ancient peoples may have used to help them navigate the desert, date from AD 500 to 1400.
ECUADOR	**Temples at Ingapirca, Cuenca.** At this ancient city is an elliptical stone structure acknowledged to be a temple to the sun that was built by the Incas. A small museum houses artifacts found at the ruins.
PARAGUAY	**Trinidad, Southern Paraguay.** The red sandstone structures found here make up the country's most impressive collection of Jesuit ruins. Built between 1712 and 1764, they survey the countryside from a hilltop.
PERU	**Machu Picchu.** The most important archaeological site in South America, the "lost city of the Incas" is rediscovered every day by adventurous travelers.
	Nazca. Twelve miles north of the town of Nazca is one of the world's greatest mysteries, 11 giant engravings of animals and shapes known as the Nazca Lines.
	Sacsayhuaman, Cusco. The massive fortress of Sacsayhuaman, perhaps the most important Inca monument after Machu Picchu, is built of blocks of stones weighing up to 361 tons.
VENEZUELA	**Teleférico cable car, Mérida.** Built in the 1957 by French engineers, the world's longest and highest cable car system ascends in four breathtaking stages to the 15,634-ft Pico Espejo.

MARKETS & CRAFTS

ECUADOR	**Olga Fisch's Folklore, Quito.** This curious shop and small museum is in the colonial home of the late Olga Fisch (1901–1990), who worked with craftspeople to turn folk art into modern works of art. The handwoven textiles and pottery are inspired by indigenous motifs.
PARAGUAY	**Ao P'oí Raity, Asunción.** Excellent *ñandutí* lacework and *ao p'oí* embroidery are sold here.
	Constancio Sanabria, Luque. Paraguayan harps and guitars are made and sold in this workshop just outside Asunción.
PERU	**Plaza de Armas, Cusco.** If you keep your eyes open and bargain hard, you may wind up with a great deal on the attractive sweaters that flood the streets off the central square.
	Sunday market, Pisac. In the Cusco area, this is the place for Andean demon masks and weavings.

Central Market, Chiclayo. Everything you could want or need for your favorite *bruja* (witch) and *curandero* (magical healer) is on hand at this market on the North Coast.

MUSEUMS

ARGENTINA

Museo Paleontológico, Trelew. You can marvel at dinosaur bones and other fossils, and watch archaeologists at work at this impressive paleontology museum.

BOLIVIA

Casa Real de Moneda, Potosí. The Royal Mint was once used to forge coins from the silver mined in the nearby hills. Here you'll find huge wooden presses that fashioned the strips of silver from which the coins were pressed.

Museo Textil Etnográfico, Sucre. The Textile and Ethnographic Museum showcases 4,000-year-old weavings and tapestry art of the Andean world, as well as regional fiesta garb.

BRAZIL

Museu Afro-Brasileiro, Salvador. Africa's strong influence on this region of the country is displayed in a fascinating collection of musical instruments, masks, costumes, and artifacts.

Museu de Arte Naif do Brasil, Rio. The canvases that grace the walls bring to art what Brazilians bring to life: verve, color, and joy.

CHILE

Museo de Arte Precolombino, Santiago. Personal items from Central and South America's indigenous peoples are on display in the city's beautifully restored Royal Customs House.

COLOMBIA

Donación Botero collection, Bogotá. Fernando Botero's artwork interprets his subjects from a distinctly Latin-American standpoint—Colombians affectionately refer to him as "the man who paints fat people." There are also original pieces by Corot, Monet, Matisse, Picasso, Dalí, Chagall, Bacon, and de Kooning.

Museo de Oro, Bogotá. In weight, more than $200 million in gold, gathered from indigenous cultures, and the largest uncut emerald in the world are housed here at the Gold Museum.

Palacio de la Inquisición, Cartagena. This former headquarters of the Spanish Inquisition for much of South America displays racks and thumbscrews, along with other torture devices.

PARAGUAY

Museo Jesuítico, San Ignacio. Paraguay's first Jesuit mission is now a museum of wood carvings by the indigenous Guaraní people.

PERU

Museo Brúning, Lambayeque. The Brúning displays ancient, pre-Incan artifacts from the Chiclayo area, including the fascinating remains from the tomb of the Lord of Sipán.

Museo de Oro, Lima. The gold museum, considered one of the finest in South America, displays a massive collection of metallurgy.

Museo Nacional de Antropología y Arqueología, Lima. This museum's collection of anthropological artifacts from throughout Peru includes Chavín obelisks and Paracas weavings.

Museo Arqueológico Rafael Larco Herrera, Lima. The museum houses an extensive collection of pre-Columbian ceramics, including an extremely popular collection of erotic pieces.

Museo Histórico Regional, Ica. A visit to this museum provides an excellent overview of the area's ancient cultures, with fine displays of Paracas weavings and Nazca ceramic sculptures.

VENEZUELA **Museo de Arte Contemporáneo de Caracas Sofía Imber, Caracas.** With works by Picasso, Miró, and Bacon, this museum has one of the best collections of modern art in South America.

NATURAL WONDERS

ARGENTINA **Bosque Petrificado José Ormaechea, Patagonia.** The wood is 65 million years old in this eerie, wind-swept petrified forest.

Cataratas de Iguazú, Northeast. This set of 275 waterfalls ranks as one of the world's greatest wonders.

Cruce a Chile por Los Lagos, Patagonia. Blue lakes, volcanoes, waterfalls, and forests are all part of this Andean-lake odyssey from Bariloche to Chile.

Glaciar Moreno, Patagonia. One of the few advancing glaciers in the world is also a noisy one—tons of ice peel off and crash into Lago Argentino on a regular basis.

Parque Provincial Aconcagua. As you follow the Mendoza River up to the top of the Andes, the dramatic scenery along the way makes getting there every bit as spectacular as the final destination.

Península Valdés, Patagonia. This is the best place to view southern right whales as they feed, mate, give birth, and nurse their offspring. Seals and penguins will keep you company, too.

Reserva Faunistica Punta Tombo, Patagonia. Visit the largest colony of Magellanic penguins in the world at this nature reserve.

BOLIVIA **Isla del Sol.** According to legend, the Inca Empire was founded on Sun Island, on shimmering Lake Titicaca. Here you'll see beautiful coves sheltering white sandy beaches, steep Inca steps and a sacred fountain at the port of Yumani, and ruins of the Inca palace of Pilkokaina.

Salar de Uyuni. Visit the world's biggest and highest desert of salt near Potosí, where you'll find red and green mineral-tinted lagoons and an island with towering cacti.

BRAZIL	**Pantanal Wetlands.** This vast floodplain is the best place to see wildlife outside sub-Saharan Africa. Its savannas, forests, and swamps are home to more than 600 bird species as well as anacondas, jaguars, monkeys, and other creatures.
	Parque Nacional do Iguaçu. This amazing preserve has one of the world's most fantastic waterfalls.
CHILE	**Parque Nacional Torres del Paine, Patagonia.** Glaciers that swept through the region millions of years ago created the ash-gray spires that dominate this unforgettable national park.
ECUADOR	**Galápagos Islands.** One of the planet's great natural wonders, the islands not only provide close contact with marine and island-bound wildlife, they also provide a unique perspective on Charles Darwin's theory of evolution.
	Mitad del Mundo, Quito. The exact latitudinal center of the earth, determined in 1736, is right here 26 km (16 mi) north of Quito. You can take an elevator up the Middle of the World monument, a tall stone obelisk crowned with a 2.5-ton metal globe.
	Parque Nacional Machalilla. This 136,850-acre park in Puerto López, northwest of Guayaquil, protects patches of endangered tropical dry forests, stretches of spectacular coastline, and the island of Isla de la Plata, a 3,000-acre seabird sanctuary where humpback whales are often sighted.
PARAGUAY	**Río Tebicuary.** Fish for the salmonlike dorado from a launch on the river, whose banks are home to monkeys, capybaras, and the occasional alligator.
PERU	**Manu Biosphere Reserve.** More than 4½ million acres of pristine wilderness, ranging from cloud forest to tropical rain forest, make up this sprawling national park.
VENEZUELA	**Angel Falls, Canaima National Park.** The highest waterfall in the world is the centerpiece of this remarkably beautiful national park the size of Belgium.
	Los Roques National Park. This archipelago of 350 islands with thriving coral reefs and sparkling beaches also has some of the most incredible snorkeling, diving, and fishing in the Caribbean.

QUINTESSENTIAL SOUTH AMERICA

BRAZIL	**Corcovado and Cristo Redentor, Rio.** The city's icon gazes out benevolently from Corcovado Mountain.
URUGUAY	**Colonia del Sacramento.** One of South America's most beautiful colonial cities—on the edge of a peninsula—has wonderfully preserved architecture, rough cobblestone streets, and an easy grace and tranquillity evident in its people and pace.

SPIRITUAL SIGHTS

ARGENTINA	**San Ignacio Miní, Northeast.** These are the most stunning and well-preserved remains of the many Jesuit missions that thrived in Argentina more than 200 years ago.
CHILE	**Iglesia Santa María de Loreto, Achao.** Of the dozens of wonderful wooden churches on the archipelago of Chiloé, this one on the island of Achao is the most fascinating.
COLOMBIA	**Cerro de la Popa, Cartagena.** This colonial monastery on a hill southeast of the walled city affords the best view in Cartagena and has a small museum and a chapel.
	Iglesia Museo Santa Clara, Bogotá. The interior of this 17th-century church is painted with dazzling frescoes and wall reliefs—the work of nuns once cloistered there.
ECUADOR	**Compañía de Jesús, Quito.** Almost 1½ tons of gold were poured into the ceilings, walls, pulpits, and altars during construction here—the wealthiest Jesuit church in South America.
PERU	**Catedral, Cusco.** This Baroque cathedral, located where there once was an Inca palace, is considered one of the most splendid churches in the Americas.
	Convento de Santa Catalina, Arequipa. In the late 1500s, 400 Dominican nuns and their servants walled themselves off from the rest of the city in this complex, a maze of streets and structures where 20 nuns still reside.
	Qorikancha, Cusco. When a 1953 earthquake crumbled the walls of the Convent of Santo Domingo, the foundations of the ancient Inca Temple of the Sun were revealed underneath.
VENEZUELA	**Iglesia de San Francisco, Caracas.** Gilded altarpieces make this one of the country's best examples of colonial architecture.

SMART TRAVEL TIPS

Finding out about your destination before you leave home means you won't squander time organizing everyday minutiae once you've arrived. You'll be more streetwise when you hit the ground as well, better prepared to explore the aspects of South America that drew you here in the first place. The organizations in this section can provide information to supplement this guide; contact them for up-to-the-minute details, and consult the A to Z sections that end each chapter for facts on the various topics as they relate to the region's countries. Happy landings!

ADDRESSES

The most common street terms in Spanish are *calle* (street), *avenida* (avenue), and *bulevar* (boulevard). The latter two terms are often abbreviated (as *Av.* and *Bul.*); calle is either spelled out or, in some countries, dropped entirely so that the street is referred to by proper name only. In Portuguese *avenida* and *travessa* (lane) are abbreviated (as *Av.* and *Tr.*) while other common terms such as *estrada* (highway) and *rua* (street) aren't. Street numbering doesn't enjoy the wide popularity in South America that it has achieved elsewhere. In some of this guide's listings, establishments have necessarily been identified by the street they're on and their nearest cross street—Calle Bolívar and Av. Valdivia, for example. In extreme cases, where neither address nor cross street is available, you may find the notation "s/n," meaning *sin número*, or "no street number."

AIR TRAVEL

As you would expect, major airlines in the United States offer the greatest number of daily nonstop flight departures to South America; major gateways in South America include Buenos Aires, Caracas, Lima, Quito, Rio de Janeiro, Santiago, and São Paulo. Major gateways in the United States include Atlanta, Dallas, Houston, Los Angeles, Miami, New York, Newark, and Washington, D.C. Smaller airlines—including regional, low-cost, and no-frill airlines—usually have a limited number of flights daily. Numerous South American airlines have regularly scheduled flights from North America. Linguistic and cultural connections make Miami the favored gateway for all South American airlines, with Aerolineas Argentinas, Aeropostal, Avianca, LAB Airlines, LanChile, LanEcuador, LanPeru, TAM and Varig flying to their respective national hubs. New York's Kennedy Airport is served by Aerolineas Argentinas, Avianca, LanChile and Varig.

Getting to and from the airport won't be the most pleasant aspect of your South American journey. Subway transit to the airports is nearly nonexistent, and bus service, while often cheap, tends to require a serious time commitment and subjecting yourself to crowded conditions if you have a lot of luggage. Taxi fares to city centers vary from the reasonable to a steep $20–$35 in Buenos Aires, Caracas, Lima, Montevideo, Rio, Santiago, and São Paulo, where airports are long distances from downtowns. If you're concerned about your destination not being understood, write it down on a piece of paper and present it to the bus or taxi driver.

BOOKING

When you book, look for nonstop flights and remember that "direct" flights stop at least once. Try to avoid connecting flights, which require a change of plane. Two airlines may operate a connecting flight jointly, so ask whether your airline operates every segment of the trip; you may find that the carrier you prefer flies you only part of the way. To find more booking tips and to check prices and make online flight reservations, log on to www.fodors.com.

CARRIERS

American Airlines has the greatest frequency of service to South America, flying from Miami to Asunción, Barranquilla, Belo Horizonte, Bogotá, Buenos Aires, Cali, Caracas, Guayaquil, La Paz, Lima, Montevideo, Quito, Rio de Janeiro, Santa Cruz, Santiago, and São Paulo; from Dallas to Lima, Santiago, and São Paulo; from New York to Rio, and São Paulo; and from San Juan to Caracas.

Continental flies from Houston to Bogotá, Caracas, Guayaquil, Lima, Quito, Rio, and São Paulo; and from Newark to Bogotá, Guayaquil, Lima, Quito, and São Paulo. Delta connects Atlanta with Bogotá, Caracas, Lima, Santiago, and São Paulo. United flies from Miami to Buenos Aires, Montevideo, Rio, and São Paulo; from Chicago to Buenos Aires, Montevideo, and São Paulo; and from Washington Dulles to Buenos Aires, Montevideo, and São Paulo.

Air Canada connects Toronto with São Paulo. Canadians will find more choices in destinations and schedules flying via one of the U.S. hubs.

From the United Kingdom, British Airways has service from London Gatwick to Bogotá, Buenos Aires, Caracas, and São Paulo. American, Continental, Delta, and United fly from London to their respective U.S. hubs with connections to South America. With its large network of South American routes, another good bet is Spain's Iberia, connecting London, via Madrid, with Bogotá, Buenos Aires, Caracas, Guayaquil, Lima, Quito, Rio, Santiago, and São Paulo.

From Sydney, you can fly Qantas to Santiago on Sunday and Friday; Aerolíneas Argentinas has flights from Buenos Aires to Sydney on Thursday and Saturday. All transpacific flights stop in Auckland before proceeding on to South America. From Auckland, Air New Zealand offers flights to major Brazilian cities, via Los Angeles, through its partnership with Varig.

Numerous South American airlines have regularly scheduled flights from North America. Many have alliances with larger airlines. These airlines also offer connections to other cities not served by larger airlines. Within South America, there's a lot of flexibility. In Argentina, Aerolíneas Argentinas flies to Buenos Aires with connections to cities throughout the country as well as to Asunción, Bogotá, Caracas, Lima, Montevideo, Rio de Janeiro, Santiago, and São Paulo. Bolivia's LAB Airlines flies to Santa Cruz and La Paz, with connections to all major Bolivian cities as well as to Asunción, Buenos Aires, Montevideo, Rio de Janeiro, Santiago, and São Paulo. TAM Brazilian Airlines flies to São Paulo with connections to major Brazilian cities; its Paraguayan affiliate TAM Mercosur connects to Asunción. Varig flies to Fortaleza, Manaus, Rio, and São Paulo with connections to other cities; its Uruguayan partner Pluna connects to Montevideo. In Colombia, Avianca and its affiliate Aces have flights to Barranquilla, Bogotá, Cali, Cartagena, Medellín, and San Andrés, and connections throughout the country. LanChile flies to Santiago with connections to destinations throughout South America. Its affiliate LanPeru flies to Lima and connects with cities throughout Peru, and its other affiliate, LanEcuador, connects Miami with Quito and Guayaquil. In Venezuela, Avensa flies to Caracas with connections to Canaima, Maracaibo, Porlamar, and Mérida.

🛪 From North America **Air Canada** ☎ 800/776-3000, 800/361-8620 in Canada ⊕ www.aircanada.ca. **American** ☎ 800/433-7300 in North America ⊕ www.aa.com. **Continental** ☎ 800/231-0856, 800/525-0280 in Canada ⊕ www.continental.com. **Delta** ☎ 800/241-4141 in North America ⊕ www.delta.com. **United** ☎ 800/241-6522 in North America ⊕ www.united.com.

🛪 From the U.K. **American** ☎ 0845/778-9789. **Avianca** ☎ 0870/576-7747. **British Airways** ☎ 0845/779-9977 ⊕ www.british-airways.com. **Continental** ☎ 0800/776-464. **Delta** ☎ 0800/414-767. **Iberia** ☎ 0845/601-2854 ⊕ www.iberia.com. **United** ☎ 0845/844-4777. **Varig** ☎ 0800/997-000.

🛪 From Australia & New Zealand **Air New Zealand** ☎ 13-24-76 in Australia, 0800/737-000 in New Zealand ⊕ www.airnz.co.nz. **Qantas** ☎ 13-13-13 in Australia, 0800/808-767 in New Zealand ⊕ www.qantas.com.au.

🛪 South American Airlines **Aerolíneas Argentinas** ☎ 800/333-0276, 800/688-0008 in Canada ⊕ www.aerolineas.com.ar. **Avensa** ☎ 800/428-3672, 800/387-8667 in Canada ⊕ www.avensa.com.ve. **Avianca/Aces** ☎ 800/284-2622, 800/387-8667 in Canada ⊕ www.avianca.com.co. **LanChile/LanPeru/LanEcuador** ☎ 800/735-5526 ⊕ www.lanchile.com. **LAB Airlines** ☎ 800/337-0918 ⊕ www.labairlines.com. **TAM** ☎ 888/235-9826 ⊕ www.tam-usa.com. **Varig/Pluna** ☎ 800/468-2744, 800/468-2744 in Canada ⊕ www.varig.com.

CHECK-IN & BOARDING

Always **find out your carrier's check-in policy.** Plan to arrive at the airport about two hours before your scheduled departure time for domestic flights and 2½ to 3 hours before international flights. You may need to arrive earlier if you're flying from one of the busier airports or during peak air-traffic times. To avoid delays at airport-security checkpoints, try not to wear any metal. Jewelry, belt and other buckles, steel-toe shoes, barrettes, and underwire bras are among the items that can set off detectors.

Assuming that not everyone with a ticket will show up, airlines routinely overbook planes. When everyone does, airlines ask for volunteers to give up their seats. In return, these volunteers usually get a several-hundred-dollar flight voucher, which can be used toward the purchase of another ticket, and are rebooked on the next flight out. If there are not enough volunteers, the airline must choose who will be denied boarding. The first to get bumped are passengers who checked in late and those flying on discounted tickets, so get to the gate and check in as early as possible, especially during peak periods.

Always **bring a government-issued photo I.D.** to the airport; even when it's not required, a passport is best.

Be prepared to show your passport when leaving any South American country and to pay hefty airport taxes. Fees on international flights from Brazil, for example, can run as high as $40; even domestic flights may incur $10 in additional charges. Although some countries accept dollars, you should **plan to pay taxes with local currency.**

CUTTING COSTS

The least expensive airfares to South America are priced for round-trip travel and must usually be purchased in advance. Airlines generally allow you to change your return date for a fee; most low-fare tickets, however, are nonrefundable. It's smart to call a number of airlines and check the Internet; when you are quoted a good price, book it on the spot—the same fare may not be available the next day, or even the next hour. Always check different routings and look into using alternate airports. Also, price off-peak flights, which may be significantly less expensive than others. Travel agents, especially low-fare specialists (⇨ Discounts & Deals), are helpful.

Consolidators are another good source. They buy tickets for scheduled flights at reduced rates from the airlines, then sell them at prices that beat the best fare available directly from the airlines. (Many also offer reduced car-rental and hotel rates.) Sometimes you can even get your money back if you need to return the ticket. Carefully read the fine print detailing penalties for changes and cancellations, purchase the ticket with a credit card, and confirm your consolidator reservation with the airline.One good bet for South American ticketing is the Seattle-based company, Around the World.

Look into discount passes. Country carriers, such Aerolíneas Argentinas or Lan-Chile, often have passes that make flying to several destinations within one country affordable. These must always be purchased before arrival and in conjunction with a flight into and out of the country on that carrier.

When you fly as a courier, you trade your checked-luggage space for a ticket deeply subsidized by a courier service. There are restrictions on when you can book and how long you can stay. Some courier companies list with membership organizations, such as the Air Courier Association and the International Association of Air Travel Couriers; these require you to become a member before you can book a flight.

Many airlines, singly or in collaboration, offer discount air passes that allow foreigners to travel economically in a particular country or region. These visitor passes usually must be reserved and purchased before you leave home. Information about passes often can be found on most airlines' international Web pages, which tend to be aimed at travelers from outside the carrier's home country. Also, try typing the name of the pass into a search engine, or search for "pass" within the carrier's Web site.

🛪 Consolidators**AirlineConsolidator.com** ☎ 888/468-5385 ⊕ www.airlineconsolidator.com; for international tickets. **Best Fares** ☎ 800/880-1234 or 800/576-8255 ⊕ www.bestfares.com; $59.90 annual membership. **Cheap Tickets** ☎ 800/377-1000 or 800/652-4327 ⊕ www.cheaptickets.com. **Expedia** ☎ 800/397-3342 or 404/728-8787 ⊕ www.expedia.com. **Hotwire** ☎ 866/468-9473 or 920/330-9418 ⊕ www.hotwire.com. **Now Voyager Travel** ✉ 45 W. 21st St., Suite 5A New York, NY 10010 ☎ 212/459-1616 🖷 212/243-2711 ⊕ www.nowvoyagertravel.com. **Onetravel.com** ⊕ www.onetravel.com. **Orbitz** ☎ 888/656-4546 ⊕ www.orbitz.com. **Priceline.com** ⊕ www.priceline.com. **Travelocity** ☎ 888/709-5983, 877/282-2925 in Canada, 0870/876-3876 in the U.K. ⊕ www.travelocity.com.

🛪 Courier Resources**Air Courier Association/Cheaptrips** ☎ 800/280-5973 or 800/282-1202 ⊕ www.aircourier.org or www.cheaptrips.com; $34 annual membership. **International Association of Air Travel Couriers** ☎ 308/632-3273 ⊕ www.courier.org; $45 annual membership. **Now Voyager Travel** ✉ 45 W. 21st Street, Suite 5A, New York, NY 10010 ☎ 212/459-1616 🖷 212/243-2711 ⊕ www.nowvoyagertravel.com.

🛪 Discount Passes**Aerolíneas Argentinas** ☎ 800/333-0276, 800/688-0008 in Canada ⊕ www.aerolineas.com.ar. **Boomerang Pass,** Qantas, ☎ 800/227-4500, 0845/774-7767 in the U.K., 131-313 in Australia, 0800/808-767 in New Zealand ⊕ www.qantas.com. **FlightPass,** EuropebyAir, ☎ 888/387-2479 ⊕ www.europebyair.com. **Lan-Chile/LanPeru** ☎ 800/735-5526 ⊕ www.lanchile.com. **SAS Air Passes,** Scandinavian Airlines, ☎ 800/221-2350, 0845/6072-7727 in the U.K., 1300/727-707 in Australia ⊕ www.scandinavian.net.

ENJOYING THE FLIGHT

State your seat preference when purchasing your ticket, and then repeat it when you confirm and when you check in. For more legroom, you can request one of the few emergency-aisle seats at check-in, if you're capable of moving obstacles comparable in weight to an airplane exit door (usually between 35 and 60 pounds)—a Federal Aviation Administration requirement of passengers in these seats. Seats behind a bulkhead also offer more legroom, but they don't have underseat storage. Don't sit in the row in front of the emergency aisle or in front of a bulkhead, where seats may not recline.

Ask the airline whether a snack or meal is served on the flight. If you have dietary concerns, request special meals when booking. These can be vegetarian, low-cholesterol, or kosher, for example. It's a good idea to pack some healthful snacks and a small (plastic) bottle of water in your carry-on bag. On long flights, try to maintain a normal routine, to help fight jet lag. At night, get some sleep. By day, eat light meals, drink water (not alcohol), and **move around the cabin** to stretch your legs. For additional jet-lag tips consult *Fodor's FYI: Travel Fit & Healthy* (available at bookstores everywhere).

International travel between the Americas is less wearying than to Europe or Asia because there's no problem with jet lag. New York, for instance, is in the same time zone as Lima. If you have a choice between day or night flights—and those to southern South America always depart after dark—take a night plane if you sleep well while flying. Especially en route to the Andean countries, you will have lovely sunrises over the mountains. Southbound, the best views are usually out windows on the plane's left side.

Smoking policies vary from carrier to carrier. Many airlines prohibit smoking on all of their flights; others allow smoking only on certain routes or certain departures. Ask your carrier about its policy.

FLYING TIMES

The major North American departure points for South American flights are New York (8½ hours to Rio, 11 hours to Buenos Aires, 4 hours to Caracas) and Miami (7 hours to Rio, 8 hours to Buenos Aires, 3½ hours to Caracas). If you're traveling from Canada and connecting in the United States, the Toronto–New York flight is just over an hour; that to Miami is 3 hours. If you're connecting in the United States from London it's about 6 hours to New York and 9 hours to Miami. Expect some 18–20 hours on Sydney–Buenos Aires flights, including the Auckland stopover. Note that flight times may vary according to the type of plane. Flights between South American capitals can be as long as 6 hours (Buenos Aires–Caracas)

and as short as 40 minutes (Buenos Aires–Montevideo).

HOW TO COMPLAIN

If your baggage goes astray or your flight goes awry, complain right away. Most carriers require that you **file a claim immediately.** The Aviation Consumer Protection Division of the Department of Transportation publishes *Fly-Rights,* which discusses airlines and consumer issues and is available online. You can also find articles and information on mytravelrights.com, the Web site of the nonprofit Consumer Travel Rights Center.

🛂 **Aviation Consumer Protection Division** ✉ U.S. Department of Transportation, Office of Aviation Enforcement and Proceedings, C-75, Room 4107, 400 7th St. SW, Washington, DC 20590 ☎ 202/366-2220 ⊕ airconsumer.ost.dot.gov. **Federal Aviation Administration Consumer Hotline** ✉ for inquiries: FAA, 800 Independence Ave. SW, Washington, DC 20591 ☎ 800/322-7873 ⊕ www.faa.gov.

RECONFIRMING

Check the status of your flight before you leave for the airport. You can do this on your carrier's Web site, by linking to a flight-status checker (many Web booking services offer these), or by calling your carrier or travel agent.

Always **reconfirm your flights 72 hours in advance,** even if you have a ticket and a reservation. This is particularly true for travel within South America, where flights tend to operate at full capacity.

AIRPORTS

Major airports in South America are in Buenos Aires, Argentina (EZE); Caracas, Venezuela (CCS); Lima, Peru (LIM); Quito, Ecuador (UIO); Rio de Janeiro, Brazil (GIG); Santiago, Chile (SCL); and São Paulo, Brazil (GRU). A smaller selection of flights jets into Asunción, Paraguay (ASU); Bogotá, Colombia (BOG); La Paz, Bolivia (LPB); Montevideo, Uruguay (MVD); and Santa Cruz, Bolivia (VVI).

BIKE TRAVEL

The rugged terrain and varying road conditions pose considerable challenges. If you're adventurous enough to try it, consider a mountain bike, since basic touring bikes are too fragile for off-road treks. Better yet, consider a tour operator—many within South America offer bike trips that range in length from a half-day to a week or more. Avoid riding in congested urban areas where it's difficult getting around by car, let alone by bike.

BIKES IN FLIGHT

Most airlines accommodate bikes as luggage, provided they are dismantled and boxed; check with individual airlines about packing requirements. Some airlines sell bike boxes, which are often free at bike shops, for about $20 (bike bags can be considerably more expensive). International travelers often can substitute a bike for a piece of checked luggage at no charge; otherwise, the cost is about $100. Most U.S. and Canadian airlines charge $40–$80 each way.

BUS TRAVEL

Buses are the primary means of transportation for most South Americans, and buses run regularly almost anywhere there are roads—and some places where the term "road" is used charitably. Accordingly, bus-travel options are much greater than in North America. In particular, Brazil, Chile, and Venezuela have good service. In Bolivia, Ecuador, and Peru, washed-out roads can cause delays of several hours, or cancellations during the worst of the rainy season. Almost everywhere you'll find spectacular views. The low cost of bus travel is its greatest advantage; its greatest drawback is the time you need to cover the distances involved and, in some countries, allow for delays due to faulty equipment or poor road conditions. When traveling by bus, pack light and dress comfortably and be sure to **keep a close watch on your belongings,** especially in the terminal itself, and during the commotion of boarding and disembarking from the bus.

Note that the U.S. State Department strongly warns against traveling between Colombian cities by bus due to the risk of robbery, assault, and kidnapping. If you must take the bus, opt for a first-class bus (variously called *pullman, metropolitano, de lujo,* or *directo*) or a deluxe bus with air-conditioning (called *thermo* or *climatizado*), which only run between Bogotá, Medellín, Cali, and the Caribbean Coast.

CLASSES

Various classes of service are offered in every country, with each increase in price buying plusher seats and more leg room. Tickets often include assigned seat numbers for major inter-urban journeys. If you're over 5 feet 10 inches buy the most expensive ticket available and try for front-row seats; otherwise, be prepared for knee pain. In out-of-the-way rural areas, seating is first come, first serve as you board.

Bathrooms, air-conditioning, and in-bus movies or music are common amenities. Chile, on the extreme end of the scale, offers business-class-style sleeper buses with all of the above, plus pillows, blankets, and a bow-tied attendant who serves surprisingly palatable meals. Even in cash-strapped countries, the buses are generally modern and clean. Be prepared, however, to relieve yourself by the side of the road. Food stops are usually made en route, though it's a good idea to bring snacks and water. An additional top layer of clothing comes in handy if it gets cold—or it can serve as a pillow.

FARES & SCHEDULES

Bus fares are substantially cheaper than in North America or Europe. You'll usually pay no more than $2 per hour of travel. Argentina is the more costly exception, with fares about $4–$5 per hour of travel. Competing bus companies serve all major and many minor routes, so it can really pay to shop around. Always speak to the counter clerk, as competition may mean fares are cheaper than the official price posted on the fare board. Don't plan on the clerk speaking much English. Write down your destination on a piece of paper if you don't speak the local language.

PAYING

Tickets are sold at bus-company offices and at city bus terminals. Note that in larger cities there may be different terminals for buses to different destinations, and some small towns may not have a terminal at all. Instead you'll be picked up and dropped off at the bus company's office. You should **expect to pay with cash,** as credit cards aren't always accepted, and traveler's checks, never.

RESERVATIONS

Reservations aren't necessary except for trips to popular destinations during high season. Summer weekends and major holidays are the busiest times. You should arrive at bus stations early for travel during peak seasons.

CAMERAS & PHOTOGRAPHY

South America, with its majestic landscapes and varied cityscapes, will hugely appeal to photographers. Latin Americans seem amenable to having picture-taking tourists in their midst, but you should always ask permission before taking someone's picture. People in remote villages often don't like being photographed. Many of the people in traditional dress hanging around heavily touristed areas expect you to pay them if you take their photo.

To avoid the blurriness caused by your hand shaking, buy a mini tripod—they're available in sizes as small as 6 inches. Get a small beanbag to support your camera on uneven surfaces. If you'll be visiting the Andes, get a skylight (81B or 81C) or polarizing filter to minimize haze and light problems. The higher the altitude, the greater the proportion of ultraviolet rays. Light meters don't read these rays and consequently, except for close-ups or full-frame portraits where the reading is taken directly off the subject, photos may be overexposed. These filters may also help with the glare caused by white adobe buildings, sandy beaches, and so on. Bring high-speed film to compensate for low light under the tree canopy on rain forest trips. Invest in a telephoto lens to photograph wildlife, as even standard zoom lenses of the 35–88 range won't capture a satisfying amount of detail.

Casual photographers should consider using inexpensive disposable cameras to reduce the risks inherent in traveling with sophisticated equipment. One-use cameras with panoramic or underwater functions can be nice supplements to a standard camera and its gear.

The *Kodak Guide to Shooting Great Travel Pictures* (available at bookstores everywhere) is loaded with tips.
📷 Photo Help **Kodak Information Center** ☎ 800/242-2424 ⊕ www.kodak.com.

EQUIPMENT PRECAUTIONS

Don't pack film or equipment in checked luggage, where it is much more susceptible to damage. X-ray machines used to view checked luggage are extremely powerful and therefore are likely to ruin your film. Try to ask for hand inspection of film, which becomes clouded after repeated exposure to airport X-ray machines, and keep videotapes and computer disks away from metal detectors. Always keep film, tape, and computer disks out of the sun. Carry an extra supply of batteries, and be prepared to turn on your camera, camcorder, or laptop to prove to airport security personnel that the device is real.

FILM & DEVELOPING

Bring your own film. In many areas, film is expensive and frequently stored in hot conditions. Plan on shooting a minimum of one 36-exposure roll per week of travel. If you don't want the hassle of keeping a shot log, **make a quick note whenever you start a new roll**—it will make identifying your photos much easier when you get home.

CAR RENTAL

Driving in South America isn't easy. Congested city streets are chaotic at best, life-threatening at worst; country roads aren't as crowded, but the poor conditions and lack of signs are discouraging. Highways are generally well maintained, but sometimes are clogged by construction equipment. That said, many seasoned travelers enjoy driving in South America. Certain areas are best explored on your own in a car: in Venezuela, Isla Margarita and the mountains of Mérida; in Chile, the Central Valley and the Lake District; in Peru, Ica and the Nazca plain on the road from Lima.

Rental costs are high compared to those in the U.S. A mid-sized vehicle might run you between $60 and $100 per day, including insurance.

Alamo 800/522-9696 ⊕ www.alamo.com. **Avis** 800/331-1084, 800/879-2847 in Canada, 0870/606-0100 in the U.K., 02/9353-9000 in Australia, 09/526-2847 in New Zealand ⊕ www.avis.com. **Budget** 800/527-0700, 0870/156-5656 in the U.K. ⊕ www.budget.com. **Dollar** 800/800-6000, 0800/085-4578 in the U.K. ⊕ www.dollar.com. **Hertz** 800/654-3001, 800/263-0600 in Canada, 0870/844-8844 in the U.K., 02/9669-2444 in Australia, 09/256-8690 in New Zealand ⊕ www.hertz.com. **National Car Rental** 800/227-7368, 0870/600-6666 in the U.K. ⊕ www.nationalcar.com.

CUTTING COSTS

For a good deal, book through a travel agent who will shop around. Fly-drive packages, popular in Europe, are rare in South America. To make arrangements before you leave home, **book through a travel agent familiar with the region.** Although international car-rental agencies have better service and maintenance track records than local firms (they also provide better breakdown assistance), your best bet at getting a good rate is to **rent from local companies.** Only reserve ahead (and check that a confirmed reservation guarantees you a car) if you plan to rent during a holiday period.

The continent's major gateway cities are the best place for renting cars, with their city offices offering slightly better rates than airport branches. Plenty of local companies offer good service and lower rates than branches of the major international firms. No matter who you rent from, make sure the agent notes any dents and nicks in the vehicle on your rental form, to avoid you having to pay for the damage when you return the car.

Consider hiring a car and driver through your hotel concierge, or, easier yet, **make a deal with a taxi driver** for some extended sightseeing at a longer-term rate. Drivers often charge an hourly rate, regardless of the distance traveled. You'll have to pay cash, but you'll often spend less than you would for a rental car.

INSURANCE

When driving a rented car you are generally responsible for any damage to or loss of the vehicle. You also may be liable for any property damage or personal injury that you may cause while driving. Before you rent, see what coverage you already have under the terms of your personal auto-insurance policy and credit cards.

In many places, such as Chile's rugged Southern Coast, you are expected to pay out of pocket for common damages such as cracked or broken windshields, and repairing flat tires is your responsibility everywhere.

Always **give the rental car a once-over** to make sure that the headlights, jack, Đand tires (including the spare) are in working condition.

REQUIREMENTS & RESTRICTIONS

Your own driver's license is acceptable in most countries in South America. However, an International Driver's Permit (IDP), available from most national automobile associations, is a good idea, if for no other reason than it provides a document in the local language—more readily recognized by police authorities. Argentina and Colombia require an IDP from those who wish to rent a car. Minimum driving ages vary from country to country. Some countries impose a maximum age of 65 or 70.

SURCHARGES

Before you pick up a car in one city and leave it in another, ask about drop-off charges or one-way service fees, which can be substantial. Also inquire about early-return policies; some rental agencies charge extra if you return the car before the time specified in your contract while others give you a refund for the days not used. To avoid a hefty refueling fee, fill the tank just before you turn in the car, but be aware that gas stations near the rental outlet may overcharge. It's almost never a deal to buy the tank of gas that's in the car when you rent it; the understanding is that you'll return it empty, but some fuel usually remains.

CAR TRAVEL

Your driver's license may not be recognized outside your home country. International driving permits (IDPs) are available from the American and Canadian automobile associations and, in the United Kingdom, from the Automobile Association and Royal Automobile Club. These international permits, valid only in conjunction with your regular driver's license, are universally recognized; having one may save you a problem with local authorities.

Some common-sense rules of the road: before you set out establish an itinerary and **ask about gas stations.** Be sure to plan your daily driving distance conservatively and **avoid driving after dark.** Always **obey speed limits and traffic regulations.** Above all, **if you get a traffic ticket, don't argue**—and plan to spend longer than you want settling it.

AUTO CLUBS

🚗 In Australia **Australian Automobile Association** ☎ 02/6247-7311 ⊕ www.aaa.asn.au.
🚗 In Canada **Canadian Automobile Association (CAA)** ☎ 613/247-0117 ⊕ www.caa.ca.
🚗 In New Zealand **New Zealand Automobile Association** ☎ 09/377-4660 ⊕ www.aa.co.nz.
🚗 In the U.K. **The Automobile Association (AA)** ☎ 0870/600-0371 ⊕ www.theaa.com. **Royal Automobile Club (RAC)** ☎ 0800/092-2222 for membership, 0800/015-4435 for insurance ⊕ www.rac.co.uk.
🚗 In the U.S. **American Automobile Association** ☎ 800/564-6222 ⊕ www.aaa.com.

CHILDREN IN SOUTH AMERICA

South Americans love children, and having yours along may prove to be your special ticket to meeting the locals. Children are welcomed in hotels and in restaurants, especially on weekends, when South American families go out for lunch in droves.

Let older children join in on planning as you outline your trip. Scout your library for picture books, storybooks, and maps about places you'll be going. Try to explain the concept of foreign language; some kids, who may have just learned to talk, are confused when they can't understand strangers and strangers can't understand them. On sightseeing days try to schedule activities of special interest to your children.

Know in advance that if you are renting a car in South America, it's very difficult to arrange for a car seat. For general advice about traveling with children, consult *Fodor's FYI: Travel with Your Baby* (available in bookstores everywhere).

FLYING

If your children are two or older, ask about children's airfares. As a general rule, infants under two not occupying a seat fly at greatly reduced fares or even for free. But if you want to guarantee a seat for an infant, you have to pay full fare. Consider flying during off-peak days and times; most airlines will grant an infant a seat without a ticket if there are available seats. When booking, confirm carry-on allowances if you're traveling with infants. In general, for babies charged 10% to 50% of the adult fare you are allowed one carry-on bag and a collapsible stroller; if the flight is full, the stroller may have to be checked or you may be limited to less.

Experts agree that it's a good idea to use safety seats aloft for children weighing less than 40 pounds. Airlines set their own policies: if you use a safety seat, U.S. carriers usually require that the child be ticketed, even if he or she is young enough to ride free, because the seats must be strapped into regular seats. And even if you pay the full adult fare for the seat, it may be worth it, especially on longer trips. Do **check your airline's policy about using safety seats during takeoff and landing.** Safety seats are not allowed everywhere in the plane, so get your seat assignments as early as possible.

When reserving, request children's meals or a freestanding bassinet (not available at all airlines) if you need them. But note that bulkhead seats, where you must sit to use the bassinet, may lack an overhead bin or storage space on the floor.

LODGING

Most hotels in South America allow children under a certain age to stay in their parents' room at no extra charge, but others charge for them as extra adults; be sure to find out the cutoff age for children's discounts. Some large hotels, often those that are branches of U.S. chains, or those in resort areas, have children's programs, or baby-sitters.

PRECAUTIONS

Children must have all their inoculations up to date before traveling abroad. All South American countries have strict requirements for children traveling alone or with one parent, and insist on documented approval from both parents, whether present or not, for the child to travel. Make sure that health precautions, such as what to drink and eat, are applied to the whole family. A bout of traveler's diarrhea may be an mere inconvenience to you as an adult, but can result in serious dehydration to infants and toddlers. Many pharmacies sell an equivalent to the product Pedialyte to replenish lost fluids and electrolytes. Not cramming too much into each day will keep the whole family healthier while on the road.

SIGHTS & ATTRACTIONS

There's plenty for kids to do in South America. Major cities are filled with interesting museums that will appeal to the entire family. Every town has public parks where parents can relax while their children romp. Places that are especially appealing to children are indicated by a rubber-duckie icon (🐤) in the margin.

SUPPLIES & EQUIPMENT

Pack things to keep your children busy while traveling. For children of reading age, bring books from home; English-language books for kids are hard to find in many places. Disposable diapers are easy to find in supermarkets in metropolitan areas; baby formula is available as well, but not as easy to find.

COMPUTERS ON THE ROAD

If you're traveling with a laptop, carry a spare battery, a universal adapter plug, and a converter if your computer isn't dual voltage. Ask about electrical surges before plugging in your computer. Keep your disks out of the sun and avoid excessive heat for both your computer and disks. In many South American countries, carrying a laptop computer could make you a target for thieves; conceal your laptop in a generic bag, and keep it close to you at all times. Note that South America's luxury hotels typically offer business centers with computers.

CONCIERGES

Concierges, found in many urban hotels, can help you with theater tickets and dinner reservations: a good one with connections—which are always key in South America—may be able to get you seats for a hot show or prime-time dinner reservations at the restaurant of the moment. You can also turn to your hotel's concierge for help with travel arrangements, sightseeing plans, services ranging from aromatherapy to zipper repair, and emergencies. **Always tip** a concierge who has been of assistance. (⇨ Tipping)

CONSUMER PROTECTION

Whether you're shopping for gifts or purchasing travel services, **pay with a major credit card** whenever possible, so you can cancel payment or get reimbursed if there's a problem (and you can provide documentation). If you're doing business with a particular company for the first time, contact your local Better Business Bureau and the attorney general's offices in your state and (for U.S. businesses) the company's home state as well. Have any complaints been filed? Finally, if you're buying a package or tour, always consider travel insurance that includes default coverage (⇨ Insurance).

📁 BBBs **Council of Better Business Bureaus** ✉ 4200 Wilson Blvd., Suite 800, Arlington, VA 22203 ☎ 703/276-0100 📠 703/525-8277 🌐 www.bbb.org.

CRUISE TRAVEL

The continent counts Atlantic, Pacific, and Caribbean coastlines, but cruise travel to and around South America isn't as widespread as you'd expect. Ships do dock at Rio and the colonial city of Cartagena, Colombia, through the fjords of southern Chile, and around the Galápagos Islands.

To learn how to plan, choose, and book a cruise-ship voyage, consult *Fodor's FYI: Plan & Enjoy Your Cruise* (available in bookstores everywhere).

CUSTOMS & DUTIES

When shopping abroad, keep receipts for all purchases. Upon reentering the country, **be ready to show customs officials what you've bought.** Pack purchases together in an easily accessible place. If you think a duty is incorrect, appeal the assessment. If you object to the way your clearance was handled, note the inspector's badge number. In either case, first ask to see a supervisor. If the problem isn't resolved, write to the appropriate authorities, beginning with the port director at your point of entry.

IN AUSTRALIA

Australian residents who are 18 or older may bring home A$400 worth of souvenirs and gifts (including jewelry), 250 cigarettes or 250 grams of cigars or other tobacco products, and 1,125 ml of alcohol (including wine, beer, and spirits). Residents under 18 may bring back A$200 worth of goods. Members of the same family traveling together may pool their allowances. Prohibited items include meat products. Seeds, plants, and fruits need to be declared upon arrival.

📧 **Australian Customs Service** ⬠ Regional Director, Box 8, Sydney, NSW 2001 ☎ 02/9213–2000 or 1300/363263, 02/9364–7222 or 1800/020–504 quarantine-inquiry line 🖷 02/9213–4043 ⊕ www.customs.gov.au.

IN CANADA

Canadian residents who have been out of Canada for at least seven days may bring in C$750 worth of goods duty-free. If you've been away fewer than seven days but more than 48 hours, the duty-free allowance drops to C$200. If your trip lasts 24 to 48 hours, the allowance is C$50. You may not pool allowances with family members. Goods claimed under the C$750 exemption may follow you by mail; those claimed under the lesser exemptions must accompany you. Alcohol and tobacco products may be included in the seven-day and 48-hour exemptions but not in the 24-hour exemption. If you meet the age requirements of the province or territory through which you reenter Canada, you may bring in, duty-free, 1.5 liters of wine or 1.14 liters (40 imperial ounces) of liquor or 24 12-ounce cans or bottles of beer or ale. Also, if you meet the local age requirement for tobacco products, you may bring in, duty-free, 200 cigarettes and 50 cigars. Check ahead of time with the Canada Customs and Revenue Agency or the Department of Agriculture for policies

regarding meat products, seeds, plants, and fruits.

You may send an unlimited number of gifts (only one gift per recipient, however) worth up to C$60 each duty-free to Canada. Label the package UNSOLICITED GIFT—VALUE UNDER $60. Alcohol and tobacco are excluded.

📧 **Canada Customs and Revenue Agency** ⬠ 2265 St. Laurent Blvd., Ottawa, Ontario K1G 4K3 ☎ 800/461-9999 in Canada, 204/983-3500, 506/636-5064 ⊕ www.ccra.gc.ca.

IN NEW ZEALAND

All homeward-bound residents may bring back NZ$700 worth of souvenirs and gifts; passengers may not pool their allowances, and children can claim only the concession on goods intended for their own use. For those 17 or older, the duty-free allowance also includes 4.5 liters of wine or beer; one 1,125-ml bottle of spirits; and either 200 cigarettes, 250 grams of tobacco, 50 cigars, or a combination of the three up to 250 grams. Meat products, seeds, plants, and fruits must be declared upon arrival to the Agricultural Services Department.

📧 **New Zealand Customs** ⬠ Head office: The Customhouse, 17–21 Whitmore St., Box 2218, Wellington ☎ 09/300–5399 or 0800/428–786 ⊕ www.customs.govt.nz.

IN SOUTH AMERICA

The Andean Trade Preference Act exempts from U.S. Customs duty many goods, including artisan works from Bolivia, Colombia, Ecuador, and Peru in an effort to stimulate the economy of those countries. The exemptions are in effect until 2006.

IN THE U.K.

From countries outside the European Union, including South America, you may bring home, duty-free, 200 cigarettes, 50 cigars, 100 cigarillos, or 250 grams of tobacco; 1 liter of spirits or 2 liters of fortified or sparkling wine or liqueurs; 2 liters of still table wine; 60 ml of perfume; 250 ml of toilet water; plus £145 worth of other goods, including gifts and souvenirs. Prohibited items include meat and dairy products, seeds, plants, and fruits.

HM Customs and Excise ☒ Portcullis House, 21 Cowbridge Rd. E, Cardiff CF11 9SS ☎ 0845/010-9000 or 0208/929-0152 advice service, 0208/929-6731 or 0208/910-3602 complaints ⊕ www.hmce.gov.uk.

IN THE U.S.

U.S. residents who have been out of the country for at least 48 hours may bring home, for personal use, $800 worth of foreign goods duty-free, as long as they haven't used the $800 allowance or any part of it in the past 30 days. This exemption may include 1 liter of alcohol (for travelers 21 and older), 200 cigarettes, and 100 non-Cuban cigars. Family members from the same household who are traveling together may pool their $800 personal exemptions. For fewer than 48 hours, the duty-free allowance drops to $200, which may include 50 cigarettes, 10 non-Cuban cigars, and 150 ml of alcohol (or 150 ml of perfume containing alcohol). The $200 allowance cannot be combined with other individuals' exemptions, and if you exceed it, the full value of all the goods will be taxed. Antiques, which the U.S. Bureau of Customs and Border Protection defines as objects more than 100 years old, enter duty-free, as do original works of art done entirely by hand, including paintings, drawings, and sculptures. This doesn't apply to folk art or handicrafts, which are in general dutiable.

You may also send packages home duty-free, with a limit of one parcel per addressee per day (except alcohol or tobacco products or perfume worth more than $5). You can mail up to $200 worth of goods for personal use; label the package PERSONAL USE and attach a list of its contents and their retail value. If the package contains your used personal belongings, mark it AMERICAN GOODS RETURNED to avoid paying duties. You may send up to $100 worth of goods as a gift; mark the package UNSOLICITED GIFT. Mailed items do not affect your duty-free allowance on your return.

To avoid paying duty on foreign-made high-ticket items you already own and will take on your trip, register them with Customs before you leave the country. Consider filing a Certificate of Registration for laptops, cameras, watches, and other digital devices identified with serial numbers or other permanent markings; you can keep the certificate for other trips. Otherwise, bring a sales receipt or insurance form to show that you owned the item before you left the United States.

For more about duties, restricted items, and other information about international travel, check out the U.S. Bureau of Customs and Border Protection's online brochure, *Know Before You Go.*

U.S. Bureau of Customs and Border Protection ☒ for inquiries and equipment registration, 1300 Pennsylvania Ave. NW, Washington, DC 20229 ⊕ www.cbp.gov ☎ 877/287-8667, 202/354-1000 ☒ for complaints, Customer Satisfaction Unit, 1300 Pennsylvania Ave. NW, Room 5.2C, Washington, DC 20229.

DISABILITIES & ACCESSIBILITY

South America isn't very well equipped to handle travelers with disabilities. There are few ramps and curb cuts, and it takes effort and planning to negotiate cobble city streets, get around museums and other buildings, and explore the countryside. Cities such as Rio de Janeiro, Buenos Aires, Santiago, and Caracas are the most comfortable.

LODGING

Despite the Americans with Disabilities Act, the definition of accessibility seems to differ from hotel to hotel. Some properties may be accessible by ADA standards for people with mobility problems but not for people with hearing or vision impairments, for example.

If you have mobility problems, ask for the lowest floor on which accessible services are offered. If you have a hearing impairment, check whether the hotel has devices to alert you visually to the ring of the telephone, a knock at the door, and a fire/emergency alarm. Some hotels provide these devices without charge. Discuss your needs with hotel personnel if this equipment isn't available, so that a staff member can personally alert you in the event of an emergency.

If you're bringing a guide dog, get authorization ahead of time and write down the name of the person with whom you spoke.

International chain hotels, especially those in large cities, are your best bet for accommodations. They are most likely to have elevators, ramps, and wider doorways.

RESERVATIONS

When discussing accessibility with an operator or reservations agent, ask hard questions. Are there any stairs, inside *or* out? Are there grab bars next to the toilet *and* in the shower/tub? How wide is the doorway to the room? To the bathroom? For the most extensive facilities meeting the latest legal specifications, opt for newer accommodations. If you reserve through a toll-free number, consider also calling the hotel's local number to confirm the information from the central reservations office. Get confirmation in writing when you can.

SIGHTS & ATTRACTIONS

Few sights in South America were designed with travelers in wheelchairs in mind, and fewer still have been renovated to meet their needs. Newer destinations may have the necessary facilities, but don't count on it. Call ahead or ask someone who has visited before.

TRANSPORTATION

Buses with wheelchair lifts are nearly unheard of in South America. Taxis are an option, but many are small and difficult to climb into. Hiring a car and driver is often the best way for people with mobility challenges to get around.

🔁 Complaints **Aviation Consumer Protection Division** (⇨ Air Travel) for airline-related problems. **Departmental Office of Civil Rights** ✉ for general inquiries, U.S. Department of Transportation, S-30, 400 7th St. SW, Room 10215, Washington, DC 20590 ☎ 202/366-4648 🖶 202/366-9371 ⊕ www.dot. gov/ost/docr/index.htm. **Disability Rights Section** ✉ NYAV, U.S. Department of Justice, Civil Rights Division, 950 Pennsylvania Ave. NW, Washington, DC 20530 ☎ ADA information line 202/514-0301, 800/514-0301, 202/514-0383 TTY, 800/514-0383 TTY ⊕ www.ada.gov. **U.S. Department of Transportation Hotline** ☎ for disability-related air-travel problems, 800/778-4838 or 800/455-9880 TTY.

TRAVEL AGENCIES

In the United States, the Americans with Disabilities Act requires that travel firms serve the needs of all travelers. Some agencies specialize in working with people with disabilities.

🔁 Travelers with Mobility Problems **Access Adventures/B. Roberts Travel** ✉ 206 Chestnut Ridge Rd., Scottsville, NY 14624 ☎ 585/889-9096 ⊕ www.brobertstravel.com ✎ dltravel@prodigy. net, run by a former physical-rehabilitation counselor. **CareVacations** ✉ No. 5, 5110-50 Ave., Leduc, Alberta, Canada, T9E 6V4 ☎ 780/986-6404 or 877/ 478-7827 🖶 780/986-8332 ⊕ www.carevacations. com, for group tours and cruise vacations. **Flying Wheels Travel** ✉ 143 W. Bridge St., Box 382, Owatonna, MN 55060 ☎ 507/451-5005 🖶 507/451-1685 ⊕ www.flyingwheelstravel.com.

DISCOUNTS & DEALS

Be a smart shopper and compare all your options before making decisions. A plane ticket bought with a promotional coupon from travel clubs, coupon books, and direct-mail offers or purchased on the Internet may not be cheaper than the least expensive fare from a discount ticket agency. And always keep in mind that what you get is just as important as what you save.

DISCOUNT RESERVATIONS

To save money, look into discount reservations services with Web sites and toll-free numbers, which use their buying power to get a better price on hotels, airline tickets (⇨ Air Travel), even car rentals. When booking a room, always **call the hotel's local toll-free number** (if one is available) rather than the central reservations number—you'll often get a better price. Always ask about special packages or corporate rates.

When shopping for the best deal on hotels and car rentals, look for guaranteed exchange rates, which protect you against a falling dollar. With your rate locked in, you won't pay more, even if the price goes up in the local currency.

🔁 Airline Tickets **Air 4 Less** ☎ 800/AIR4LESS; low-fare specialist.

🔁 Hotel Rooms **Accommodations Express** ☎ 800/444-7666 or 800/277-1064 ⊕ www.acex. net. **Hotels.com** ☎ 800/246-8357 ⊕ www.hotels. com. **Steigenberger Reservation Service** ☎ 800/ 223-5652 ⊕ www.srs-worldhotels.com. **Turbotrip. com** ☎ 800/473-7829 ⊕ www.turbotrip.com.

PACKAGE DEALS

Don't confuse packages and guided tours. When you buy a package, you travel on your own, just as though you had planned the trip yourself. Fly/drive packages, which combine airfare and car rental, are often a good deal. In cities, ask the local visitor's bureau about hotel and local transportation packages that include tickets to major museum exhibits or other special events.

EATING & DRINKING

The restaurants (all of which are indicated by a ✕) that we list are the cream of the crop in each price category. Properties indicated by a ✕⌂are lodging establishments whose restaurant warrants a special trip.

MEALS & SPECIALTIES

"Breakfast," "lunch" and "dinner" are *desayuno, almuerzo,* and *cena,* respectively, in Spanish, and *café-da-manhã, almoço,* and *jantar* in Portuguese.

MEALTIMES

During the week, most restaurants in urban and resort areas serve lunch from noon until mid-afternoon, and then open again for dinner from 7 or 8 PM until well into the evening. Buenos Aires is downright legendary for late-night dining, but in most places, you'll be disappointed if you insist on dinner at 6. Restaurants tend to remain open all day on Sundays. Small, basic, family-run restaurants, especially in rural areas, serve lunch, but often not dinner, and might close on Sunday. Lunch is usually the best bargain of the day at any dining establishment, with most restaurants offering a prix-fixe menu, including appetizer, main course, and dessert. Unless otherwise noted, the restaurants listed in this guide are open daily for lunch and dinner.

RESERVATIONS & DRESS

Reservations are always a good idea; we mention them only when they're essential or not accepted. Book as far ahead as you can, and reconfirm as soon as you arrive. (Large parties should always call ahead to check the reservations policy.) We mention dress only when men are required to wear a jacket or a jacket and tie.

WINE, BEER & SPIRITS

Each South American country takes pride in its locally brewed beers, and most are tasty bargains, always lower priced than North American or European imports. Chilean and Argentine wines are world-famous and are drunk all over the continent. High taxes and mark-ups mean you'll pay dearly for spirits.

ECOTOURISM

For ecotourism vacations and details on trips that put you in touch with the great outdoors, *see* Chapter 2, Adventure and Learning Vacations.

ELECTRICITY

Unlike in the United States and Canada—which have a 110- to 120-volt standard—the current in Argentina, Chile, Paraguay, Peru, Uruguay, and the urban areas of Brazil is 220 volts to 240 volts, 50 cycles alternating current (AC). Ecuador, Colombia, Venezuela, and rural Brazil use currents of 110 volts, 60 cycles alternating current. To use 110/120-volt equipment in a 220/240 country, bring a converter. Also, many wall outlets in South America take Continental-type plugs, with two round prongs. To accommodate U.S.-style flat-prong plugs, you'll need an adapter. **Consider buying a universal adapter;** the Swiss-Army-knife of adapters, a universal has several types of plugs in one handy unit.

If your appliances are dual-voltage, you'll need only an adapter. Don't use 110-volt outlets marked FOR SHAVERS ONLY for high-wattage appliances such as blow-dryers. Most laptops operate equally well on 110 and 220 volts and so require only an adapter.

EMBASSIES & CONSULATES

For information on Australian, Canadian, New Zealand, U.K., and U.S. embassies and consulates in South America, *see* the individual country A to Z section at the end of each chapter.

🎏 Embassies in Australia**Argentina** ⊠ 7 National Circuit, Barton, ACT 2600 ☎ 02/6273-9111. **Bolivia (Consulate)** ⊠ 4 Bridge St., Sydney, NSW 2000 ☎ 02/9247-4235. **Brazil** ⌂ Box 1540, Canberra, ACT 2601 ☎ 616/273-2372. **Chile** ⊠ 10 Culgoa Circuit, O'Malley, ACT 2606 ☎ 02/6286-2430.

Colombia ✉ 101 Northbourne Ave., 2nd fl., Turner, ACT 2612 ☎ 02/6257–2027. **Ecuador** ✉ 11 London Circuit, Canberra, ACT 2601 ☎ 02/6262–5282. **Peru** ✉ 40 Brisbane Ave., Barton, ACT 2600 ☎ 02/6273–8752. **Uruguay** ✉ 24 Brisbane Ave., Barton, ACT 2600 ☎ 02/6273–9100. **Venezuela** ✉ 7 Culgoa Circuit, O'Malley, ACT 2606 ☎ 02/6290–2968.

🔢 Embassies in Canada **Argentina** ✉ 90 Sparks St., Suite 910, Ottawa, Ontario K1P 5B4 ☎ 613/236–2351. **Bolivia** ✉ 130 Albert St., Suite 416, Ottawa, Ontario K1P 5G4 ☎ 613/236–5730. **Brazil** ✉ 450 Wilbrod St., Ottawa, Ontario K1N 6M8 ☎ 613/237–1090. **Chile** ✉ 50 O'Connor St., Suite 1413, Ottawa, Ontario K1P 6L2 ☎ 613/235–4402. **Colombia** ✉ 360 Albert St., Suite 1002, Ottawa, Ontario K1R 7X7 ☎ 613/230–3760. **Ecuador** ✉ 50 O'Connor St., Suite 316, Ottawa, Ontario K1P 6L2 ☎ 613/563–8206. **Paraguay** ✉ 151 Slater St., Suite 501, Ottawa, Ontario K1P 5H3 ☎ 613/567–1283. **Peru** ✉ 130 Albert St., Suite 1901, Ottawa, Ontario K1P 5G4 ☎ 613/238–1777. **Uruguay** ✉ 130 Albert St., Suite 1905, Ottawa, Ontario K1P 5G4 ☎ 613/234–2727. **Venezuela** ✉ 32 Range Rd., Ottawa, Ontario K1N 8J4 ☎ 613/235–5151.

🔢 Embassies in New Zealand **Argentina** ✉ 142 Lambton Quay, Wellington ☎ 04/472–8330. **Brazil** ✉ 10 Brandon St., Wellington ☎ 04/473–3516. **Chile** ✉ 19 Bolton St., Wellington ☎ 04/471–6270. **Ecuador** (Consulate) ✉ 2 St. Martins Lane, Auckland ☎ 09/377–4321. **Peru** ✉ 40 Mercer St., Wellington ☎ 04/499–8087. **Uruguay** (Consulate) ✉ 79 Cambridge Terrace, Christchurch ☎ 03/374–6774.

🔢 Embassies in the U.K. **Argentina** ✉ 65 Brook St., London W1Y 1YE ☎ 020/7318–1300. **Bolivia** ✉ 106 Eaton Sq., London SW1W 9AD ☎ 020/7235–4248. **Brazil** ✉ 32 Green St., London W1K 7AT ☎ 020/7499–0877. **Chile** ✉ 12 Devonshire St., London W1N 2DS ☎ 020/7580–6392. **Colombia** ✉ Flat 3A, 3 Hans Crescent, London SW1X 0LR ☎ 020/7589–9177. **Ecuador** ✉ Flat 3B, 3 Hans Crescent, London SW1X 0LS ☎ 020/7584–2648. **Paraguay** ✉ 344 High St., Kensington, London W14 8NS ☎ 020/7937–1253. **Peru** ✉ 52 Sloane St., London SW1X 9SP ☎ 020/7235–1917. **Uruguay** ✉ 2nd fl., 140 Brompton Rd., London SW3 1HY ☎ 020/7589–8835. **Venezuela** ✉ 1 Cromwell Rd., London SW7 2HR ☎ 020/7584–4206.

🔢 Embassies in the U.S. **Argentina** ✉ 1600 New Hampshire Ave. NW, Washington, DC 20009 ☎ 202/238–6400. **Bolivia** ✉ 3014 Massachusetts Ave. NW, Washington, DC 20008 ☎ 202/483–4410. **Brazil** ✉ 3006 Massachusetts Ave. NW, Washington, DC 20008 ☎ 202/238–2700. **Chile** ✉ 1732 Massachusetts Ave. NW, Washington, DC 20036 ☎ 202/785–

1746 Ext. 145. **Colombia** ✉ 2118 Leroy Pl. NW, Washington, DC 20008 ☎ 202/387–8338. **Ecuador** ✉ 2535 15th St. NW, Washington, DC 20009 ☎ 202/234–7200. **Paraguay** ✉ 2400 Massachusetts Ave. NW, Washington, DC 20008 ☎ 202/483–6960. **Peru** ✉ 1700 Massachusetts Ave. NW, Washington, DC 20036 ☎ 202/833–9860. **Uruguay** ✉ 2715 M St. NW, 3rd fl., Washington, DC 20006 ☎ 202/331–1313. **Venezuela** ✉ 1099 30th St. NW, Washington, DC 20007 ☎ 202/342–2214.

ETIQUETTE & BEHAVIOR

Attitudes range from the strict Catholicism of a country like Ecuador to the anything-goes outlook of Brazil. In general, however, Latin Americans lean toward conservative dress and quiet behavior. To feel more comfortable, take a cue from what the locals are wearing. Except in beach cities, men typically don't wear shorts and women don't wear short skirts. Bathing suits are fine on beaches, but cover up before you head back into town. People dress up to enter churches, so you might get dirty looks if you stroll in wearing a T-shirt or halter top.

The conservative dress belies the warmth and friendliness of most all South Americans. Don't be afraid to smile in the streets, ask for directions, or strike up a conversation with a local. Be advised, however, that South Americans consider it impolite not to give you directions, so they may prefer to give you false directions instead of no directions. Unless you're in a fast-paced city like Buenos Aires or Rio, life here is lived at a slower pace than you're probably accustomed to, and there's an unwavering appreciation of family and friendship; a store clerk may place equal importance on chatting with you or her neighbor as on tending to your business needs. Knowing this will help you understand why things may take a little longer to get done.

GAY & LESBIAN TRAVEL

Brazil is South America's most popular destination for gay and lesbian travelers, and major cities—such as Rio, São Paulo, and Salvador—have numerous gay bars, organizations, and publications. Argentines hold a liberal attitude toward homosexuality, and Buenos Aires enjoys an active gay scene. In Uruguay and Venezuela, gay rights are increasingly discussed, with gay communities in Montevideo and Caracas leading the way. Outside these destinations, however, you may encounter difficulties due to conservative political and religious norms. In Ecuador and Peru, for example, gay acts are illegal and public attitudes toward homosexuality are generally negative. Be discreet. Police harassment still occurs. The local gay scene, if you can find it, is still quite underground.

🖪 Gay- & Lesbian-Friendly Travel Agencies **Different Roads Travel** ✉ 8383 Wilshire Blvd., Suite 520, Beverly Hills, CA 90211 ☎ 323/651-5557 or 800/429-8747 (Ext. 14 for both) 🖷 323/651-5454 ✎ lgernert@tzell.com. **Kennedy Travel** ✉ 130 W. 42nd St., Suite 401, New York, NY 10036 ☎ 212/840-8659, 800/237-7433 🖷 212/730-2269 ⊕ www.kennedytravel.com. **Now, Voyager** ✉ 4406 18th St., San Francisco, CA 94114 ☎ 415/626-1169 or 800/255-6951 🖷 415/626-8626 ⊕ www.nowvoyager.com. **Skylink Travel and Tour/Flying Dutchmen Travel** ✉ 1455 N. Dutton Ave., Suite A, Santa Rosa, CA 95401 ☎ 707/546-9888 or 800/225-5759 🖷 707/636-0951; serving lesbian travelers.

GAY & LESBIAN WEB SITES

For information about South America's gay scene, check out the Internet. The best site online for general information about gay travel is Out and About. You can scour though the back issues for information on gay-friendly destinations. You also can try PlanetOut and Gay.Com, two general-interest gay sites.

🖪 Gay & Lesbian Web Sites ⊕ www.planetout.com/travel ⊕ www.outandabout.com ⊕ www.gay.com/travel

HEALTH

ALTITUDE SICKNESS

Altitude sickness, or *soroche,* may be a problem when you visit countries along the Andes—Venezuela, Colombia, Ecuador, Peru, Bolivia, Argentina, and Chile. The symptoms are shortness of breath, nausea, and splitting headaches. The best way to prevent it is to take it slow. Spend a few nights at lower elevations before you head higher. If you must fly directly to higher altitudes, plan on doing next to nothing for the first day or two. If you begin to feel ill, a few cups of herbal tea made from coca leaves will perk you right up. Drinking lots of water, taking frequent naps, and taking over-the-counter analgesics also help. If symptoms persist or become severe, return to lower elevations. Note that if you have high blood pressure or a history of heart trouble, check with your doctor before traveling to such heights as those at Cuzco in Peru and La Paz in Bolivia (both above 11,000 feet) and Quito in Ecuador (above 9,000 feet).

DIVERS' ALERT

Do not fly within 24 hours of scuba diving.

Neophyte divers should have a complete physical exam before undertaking a dive. If you have travel insurance, make sure your policy applies to scuba-related injuries, as not all companies provide this coverage.

FOOD & DRINK

The major health risk in South America is *diarrea,* or traveler's diarrhea, caused by eating contaminated fruit or vegetables or drinking contaminated water. So watch what you eat and stay away from food that is uncooked or has been sitting around. Avoid ice, uncooked food, and unpasteurized milk and milk products, and **drink only bottled water** or water that has been boiled for at least 20 minutes, even when you're brushing your teeth. Eschew ice, often made with unpurified water. Ask for drinks without ice (*sin hielo* in Spanish, *sem gelo* in Portuguese). *Un antidiarreico* is the general Spanish term for antidiarrheal medicine. Drink plenty of purified water or tea—chamomile (*camomila* in Portuguese, *manzanilla* in Spanish) is a good folk remedy. In severe cases, rehydrate yourself with a salt-sugar solution (½ teaspoon salt, *sal* in both languages, and 4 tablespoons sugar, *açúcar* in Portuguese and *azúcar* in Spanish) per quart of water (*agua* in both languages).

MEDICAL PLANS

No one plans to get sick while traveling, but it happens, so consider signing up with a medical-assistance company. Members get doctor referrals, emergency evacuation or repatriation, hotlines for medical consultation, cash for emergencies, and other assistance.

🔢 Medical-Assistance Companies**International SOS Assistance** ⊕ www.internationalsos.com ✉ 8 Neshaminy Interplex, Suite 207, Trevose, PA 19053 ☎ 215/245-4707 or 800/523-6586 🖷 215/244-9617 ✉ Landmark House, Hammersmith Bridge Rd., 6th floor, London, W6 9DP ☎ 20/8762-8008 🖷 20/8748-7744 ✉ 12 Chemin Riant-bosson, 1217 Meyrin 1, Geneva, Switzerland ☎ 22/785-6464 🖷 22/785-6424 ✉ 331 N. Bridge Rd., 17-00, Odeon Towers, Singapore 188720 ☎ 6338-7800 🖷 6338-7611 ✉ Av. Eugenio Mendoza at Calle 1 Transersal Caracas ☎ 0212/263-8591.

OVER-THE-COUNTER REMEDIES

Mild cases of diarrhea may respond to Imodium (known generically as loperamide), Pepto-Bismol (not as strong)—both can be purchased over the counter—and Lomotil, which requires a prescription. Be on the safe side and bring a small supply with you. Aspirin is readily available, as is acetaminophen (sold under the brand names Tylenol and Panadol).

SHOTS & MEDICATIONS

All travelers should have up-to-date tetanus boosters, and a hepatitis A inoculation can prevent one of the most common intestinal infections. If you're heading to tropical regions (including parts of Bolivia, Brazil, Colombia, Ecuador, French Guiana, Guyana, Paraguay, Peru, Suriname, and Venezuela) you should get yellow fever shots. Children traveling to South America should have current inoculations against measles, mumps, rubella, and polio.

According to the Centers for Disease Control (CDC) there's a limited risk of cholera, typhoid, malaria, hepatitis B, dengue, and Chagas' disease. While a few of these you could catch anywhere, most are restricted to jungle areas. If you plan to visit remote regions or stay for more than six weeks, **check with the CDC's International Travelers Hot Line.**

In tropical and subtropical areas with malaria and dengue, which are both carried by mosquitoes, take mosquito nets, wear clothing that covers the body, apply repellent containing DEET, and use a spray against flying insects in living and sleeping areas. Chloroquine is prescribed as a preventative antimalarial agent, though many malarial strains in northern South America are now resistant to chloroquine. Mefloquine, Doxycycline, or Malarone are the preventative drugs of choice in those cases. No vaccine exists against dengue.

🔢 Health Warnings**National Centers for Disease Control and Prevention** (CDC) ✉ Office of Health Communication, National Center for Infectious Diseases, Division of Quarantine, Travelers' Health, 1600 Clifton Rd. NE, Atlanta, GA 30333 ☎ 877/394-8747 international travelers' health line, 800/311-3435 other inquiries, 404/498-1600 Division of Quarantine 🖷 888/232-3299 ⊕ www.cdc.gov/travel. **World Health Organization** (WHO) ⊕ www.who.int.

INSURANCE

The most useful travel-insurance plan is a comprehensive policy that includes coverage for trip cancellation and interruption, default, trip delay, and medical expenses (with a waiver for preexisting conditions).

Without insurance you'll lose all or most of your money if you cancel your trip, regardless of the reason. Default insurance covers you if your tour operator, airline, or cruise line goes out of business—the chances of which have been increasing. Trip-delay covers expenses that arise because of bad weather or mechanical delays. Study the fine print when comparing policies.

If you're traveling internationally, a key component of travel insurance is coverage for medical bills incurred if you get sick on the road. Such expenses aren't generally covered by Medicare or private policies. U.K. residents can buy a travel-insurance policy valid for most vacations taken during the year in which it's purchased (but check preexisting-condition coverage). British and Australian citizens need extra medical coverage when traveling overseas.

Always **buy travel policies directly from the insurance company**; if you buy them from a cruise line, airline, or tour operator that goes out of business you probably won't be covered for the agency or operator's default, a major risk. Before making any purchase, review your existing health and home-owner's policies to find what they cover away from home.

Travel Insurers In the U.S.: **Access America** ✉ 2805 N. Parham Rd., Richmond, VA 23294 ☎ 800/284-8300 🖷 804/673-1491 or 800/346-9265 🌐 www.accessamerica.com. **Travel Guard International** ✉ 1145 Clark St., Stevens Point, WI 54481 ☎ 715/345-0505 or 800/826-1300 🖷 800/955-8785 🌐 www.travelguard.com.

In the U.K.: Association of British Insurers ✉ 51 Gresham St., London EC2V 7HQ ☎ 020/7600-3333 🖷 020/7696-8999 🌐 www.abi.org.uk. In Canada: **RBC Insurance** ✉ 6880 Financial Dr., Mississauga, Ontario L5N 7Y5 ☎ 800/668-4342 or 905/816-2400 🖷 905/813-4704 🌐 www.rbcinsurance.com. In Australia: **Insurance Council of Australia** ✉ Insurance Enquiries and Complaints, Level 12, Box 561, Collins St. W, Melbourne, VIC 8007 ☎ 1300/780808 or 03/9629-4109 🖷 03/9621-2060 🌐 www.iecltd.com.au. In New Zealand: **Insurance Council of New Zealand** ✉ Level 7, 111-115 Customhouse Quay, Box 474, Wellington ☎ 04/472-5230 🖷 04/473-3011 🌐 www.icnz.org.nz.

LANGUAGE

In Brazil, the language is Portuguese; Spanish is spoken in Argentina, Bolivia, Colombia, Chile, Ecuador, Paraguay, Peru, Uruguay, and Venezuela. French is spoken in French Guiana; in Guyana it's English; and in Suriname it's Dutch. In many rural areas, indigenous languages are also spoken. As in many places throughout the world, you're more likely to find English-speaking locals in major cities than in small towns or the countryside.

LANGUAGES FOR TRAVELERS

A phrase book and language-tape set can help get you started. *Fodor's/Living Language Spanish for Travelers* (available at bookstores everywhere) is excellent.

Living Language also sells more comprehensive language programs: *Spanish Complete Course, Ultimate Spanish, All Audio Spanish, Spanish Without the Fuss, Ultimate Portuguese, Portuguese Complete Course, In-Flight Portuguese.*

LODGING

It's always good to take a look at your room before accepting it; if it isn't what you expected, you might have several others from which to choose. Expense is no guarantee of charm or cleanliness, and accommodations can vary dramatically within one hotel. Many older hotels in South America have rooms with charming old-world-style balconies or spacious terraces; ask if there's a room *con balcón* or *con terraza* when checking in.

Unfortunately, a number of South American hotels have electric-powered heaters attached to the shower heads, referred to as a "suicide shower" by some irreverent budget travelers. In theory, you can adjust both the temperature and the pressure. In practice, if you want hot water, you have to turn the water pressure down very low; if you want pressure, expect a brisk rinse. Don't adjust the power when you're under the water—you can get a little shock.

If you ask for a double room, you'll get a room for two people, but you're not guaranteed a double mattress. If you prefer a double bed over a twin bed, ask for a *cama matrimonial* in Spanish or *cama de casal* in Portuguese.

The lodgings (all indicated with 🏠) that we list are the cream of the crop in each price category. We always list the facilities that are available—but we don't specify whether they cost extra: When pricing accommodations, always ask what's included. All hotels listed have private bath unless otherwise noted. Properties indicated by ✕🏠 are lodging establishments whose restaurant warrants a special trip.

APARTMENT & VILLA OR HOUSE RENTALS

If you want a home base that's roomy enough for a family and comes with cooking facilities, consider a furnished rental. These can save you money, especially if you're traveling with a group. Home-exchange directories sometimes list rentals as well as exchanges.

International Agents Hideaways International ✉ 767 Islington St., Portsmouth, NH 03801 ☎ 603/430-4433 or 800/843-4433 🖷 603/430-4444 🌐 www.hideaways.com, annual membership $145. **Villas International** ✉ 4340 Redwood Hwy., Suite D309, San Rafael, CA 94903 ☎ 415/499-9490 or 800/221-2260 🖷 415/499-9491 🌐 www.villasintl.com.

HOME EXCHANGES

If you would like to exchange your home for someone else's, join a home-exchange organization, which will send you its updated listings of available exchanges for a year and will include your own listing in at least one of them. It's up to you to make specific arrangements.

Exchange Clubs **HomeLink International** Box 47747, Tampa, FL 33647 ☎ 813/975-9825 or 800/638-3841 ㊟ 813/910-8144 ⊕ www.homelink. org; $110 yearly for a listing, online access, and catalog; $70 without catalog.

HOSTELS

No matter what your age, you can save on lodging costs by staying at hostels.In some 4,500 locations in more than 70 countries around the world, Hostelling International (HI), the umbrella group for a number of national youth-hostel associations, offers single-sex, dorm-style beds and, at many hostels, rooms for couples and family accommodations. HI affiliates are in Argentina, Bolivia, Brazil, Chile, Colombia, Ecuador, Peru, and Uruguay. Membership in any HI national hostel association, open to travelers of all ages, allows you to stay in HI-affiliated hostels at member rates; one-year membership is about $28 for adults (C$35 for a two-year minimum membership in Canada, £14 in the U.K., A$52 in Australia, and NZ$40 in New Zealand); hostels charge about $10–$30 per night. Members have priority if the hostel is full; they're also eligible for discounts around the world, even on rail and bus travel in some countries.

Organizations **Hostelling International–USA** ✉ 8401 Colesville Rd., Suite 600, Silver Spring, MD 20910 ☎ 301/495-1240 ㊟ 301/495-6697 ⊕ www. hiusa.org. **Hostelling International–Canada** ✉ 205 Catherine St., Suite 400, Ottawa, Ontario K2P 1C3 ☎ 613/237-7884 or 800/663-5777 ㊟ 613/237-7868 ⊕ www.hihostels.ca. **Hostelling International–Latin America** ⊕ www.hostelslatinamerica.org. **YHA England and Wales** ✉ Trevelyan House, Dimple Rd., Matlock, Derbyshire DE4 3YH, U.K. ☎ 0870/870-8808, 0870/ 770-8868, 0162/959-2600 ㊟ 0870/770-6127 ⊕ www.yha.org.uk. **YHA Australia** ✉ 422 Kent St., Sydney, NSW 2001 ☎ 02/9261-1111 ㊟ 02/9261-1969 ⊕ www.yha.com.au. **YHA New Zealand** ✉ Level 1, Moorhouse City, 166 Moorhouse Ave., Box

436, Christchurch ☎ 03/379-9970 or 0800/278-299 ㊟ 03/365-4476 ⊕ www.yha.org.nz.

HOTELS

All hotels listed have private bath unless otherwise noted.

Toll-Free Numbers **Best Western** ☎ 800/528-1234 ⊕ www.bestwestern.com. **Choice** ☎ 800/424-6423 ⊕ www.choicehotels.com. **Clarion** ☎ 800/424-6423 ⊕ www.choicehotels.com. **Comfort Inn** ☎ 800/424-6423 ⊕ www.choicehotels. com. **Days Inn** ☎ 800/325-2525 ⊕ www.daysinn. com. **Four Seasons** ☎ 800/332-3442 ⊕ www. fourseasons.com. **Hilton** ☎ 800/445-8667 ⊕ www.hilton.com. **Holiday Inn** ☎ 800/465-4329 ⊕ www.ichotelsgroup.com. **Howard Johnson** ☎ 800/446-4656 ⊕ www.hojo.com. **Hyatt Hotels & Resorts** ☎ 800/233-1234 ⊕ www.hyatt.com. **Inter-Continental** ☎ 800/327-0200 ⊕ www. ichotelsgroup.com. **Marriott** ☎ 800/228-9290 ⊕ www.marriott.com. **Le Meridien** ☎ 800/543-4300 ⊕ www.lemeridien.com. **Quality Inn** ☎ 800/424-6423 ⊕ www.choicehotels.com. **Radisson** ☎ 800/333-3333 ⊕ www.radisson.com. **Sheraton** ☎ 800/325-3535 ⊕ www.starwood.com/sheraton.

MAIL & SHIPPING

For details on mail service, postal rates, and overnight services, see the A to Z sections throughout each chapter.

MONEY MATTERS

Some South American currencies—Paraguay's for example—are unstable, continually losing value against the dollar. Bolivia and Brazil—two countries with historically volatile currencies—have made moves in recent years to stabilize the value of their money. Ecuador has taken the ultimate step, scrapping the local currency and making the U.S. dollar the coin of the realm. The exchange rate of the Venezuelan currency, the bolívar, is fixed at 1,600 to the U.S. dollar. For information on specific currencies, as well as service charges, taxes, and tipping, see the country A to Z section at the end of each chapter.

Prices throughout this guide are given for adults. Substantially reduced fees are almost always available for children, students, and senior citizens. For information on taxes, see Taxes.

ATMS

ATMs (*cajero automático* in Spanish or *caixa electronico* in Portuguese) are widely available in cities, and you can get cash with a Cirrus- or Plus-linked debit card or with a major credit card. Some bank machines in Argentina, Bolivia, and Chile even offer a choice of local or U.S. currencies.

The bank networks aren't evenly dispersed. American Express ATMs are limited to major cities. MasterCard is welcome in the southernmost countries, while almost all ATMs in Brazil and Peru accept only Visa. To be on the safe side, carry a variety of cards. Note also that if your PIN code is more than four digits long it might not work in some countries. Check with your bank for details of changing the PIN to a four-digit password.

ATM Locations MasterCard Cirrus ☎ 800/424-7787 ⊕ www.mastercard.com/atm. **Visa Plus** ☎ 800/843-7587 ⊕ www.visa.com/atm.

CREDIT CARDS

For costly items, try to use your credit card whenever possible—you'll come out ahead, whether the exchange rate at which your purchase is calculated is the one in effect the day the vendor's bank abroad processes the charge or the one prevailing on the day the charge company's service center processes it at home.

If you're traveling outside major cities, always check to see whether your hotel accepts credit cards. You may have to bring enough cash to pay the bill.

Throughout this guide, the following abbreviations are used: **AE**, American Express; **DC**, Diners Club; **MC**, MasterCard; and **V**, Visa.

CURRENCY EXCHANGE

For the most favorable rates, **change money through banks.** Although ATM transaction fees may be higher abroad than at home, ATM rates are excellent because they're based on wholesale rates offered only by major banks. You won't do as well at exchange booths in airports or rail and bus stations, in hotels, in restaurants, or in stores. To avoid lines at airport exchange booths, get a bit of local currency before you leave home.

Plan ahead, since it's often hard to change large amounts of money at hotels on weekends, even in capital cities. If you're heading for rural areas, you may not be able to change currency at all, so don't leave the city without adequate amounts of local currency in small denominations.

International Currency Express ✉ 427 N. Camden Dr., Suite F, Beverly Hills, CA 90210 ☎ 888/278-6628 orders 🖷 310/278-6410 ⊕ www.foreignmoney.com. **Travel Ex Currency Services** ☎ 800/287-7362 orders and retail locations ⊕ www.travelex.com.

TRAVELER'S CHECKS

Do you need traveler's checks? It depends on where you're headed. If you're going to rural areas and small towns, go with cash; traveler's checks are best used in cities. Lost or stolen checks can usually be replaced within 24 hours. To ensure a speedy refund, buy your own traveler's checks—don't let someone else pay for them: irregularities like this can cause delays. The person who bought the checks should make the call to request a refund. So before you leave, buy checks denominated in U.S. dollars—they're more easily exchanged than other currencies. Traveler's checks are not available in South American currencies.

PACKING

If there's a rule for dressing in South America, it's to **dress more conservatively on the west coast than on the east.** In the Andean countries avoid wearing short shorts or halter tops. Women traveling to Brazil can bring their most risqué outfits—and be prepared for no one to even notice. If you're doing business in South America, you'll need the same attire you would wear in U.S. and European cities: for men, suits and ties; for women, suits for day wear and cocktail dresses or other suitable dinner clothes.

For sightseeing and leisure, casual clothing and good walking shoes are both desirable and appropriate, and most cities don't require very formal clothes, even for evenings. (You'll want to pack something more elegant for dining and dancing in some cities, especially Buenos Aires, Caracas, and Rio.) For beach vacations, you'll need lightweight sportswear, a bathing suit, a sun hat, and lots of sunscreen. Travel in rain forest areas will require long-sleeve shirts, long pants, socks, sneakers, a hat, a light waterproof jacket, a bathing suit, and insect repellent, ideally containing DEET. Light colors are best, since mosquitoes avoid them. You can never have too many large resealable plastic bags (bring a whole box), which are ideal for storing film, protecting things from rain and damp, and quarantining stinky socks.

If you're visiting Patagonia or the Andes, bring a jacket and sweater—wool or gortex are good bets if you hike in mountainous areas—or plan to acquire one of the hand-knit sweaters or ponchos crowding the marketplaces. Evening temperatures in Cuzco, La Paz, and Quito rarely get above the 50s. Southern cities, such as Buenos Aires and Santiago, also become cool during the South American winter (May–September).

You'll have little trouble finding toiletry articles in supermarkets in larger cities, though you might have to set aside that brand loyalty to, say, your favorite deodorant. Contact lens supplies and feminine hygiene products can be more difficult to find. Bring a supply with you. Condoms are openly available—a surprise in such a devoutly Catholic part of the world—but other over-the-counter contraceptives prove more elusive. Carry a supply of toilet paper with you for use in public rest rooms. Lodgings of all stripes supply towels and soap, but few, save the most luxurious ones, offer a washcloth: Bring your own.

Other useful items include a screw-top bottle that you can fill with purified water, a money pouch, a travel flashlight and extra batteries, a Swiss Army knife with a bottle opener, a medical kit, binoculars, and a pocket calculator to help with currency conversions. A sarong or light cotton blanket can have many uses: beach towel, picnic blanket, and cushion for hard seats.

In your carry-on luggage, pack an extra pair of eyeglasses or contact lenses and enough of any medication you take to last a few days longer than the entire trip. You may also ask your doctor to write a spare prescription using the drug's generic name, as brand names may vary from country to country. In luggage to be checked, **never pack prescription drugs, valuables, or undeveloped film.** And don't forget to carry with you the addresses of offices that handle refunds of lost traveler's checks. Check *Fodor's How to Pack* (available at online retailers and bookstores everywhere) for more tips.

To avoid customs and security delays, carry medications in their original packaging. Don't pack any sharp objects in your carry-on luggage, including knives of any size or material, scissors, nail clippers, and corkscrews, or anything else that might arouse suspicion.

To avoid having your checked luggage chosen for hand inspection, don't cram bags full. The U.S. Transportation Security Administration suggests packing shoes on top and placing personal items you don't want touched in clear plastic bags.

CHECKING LUGGAGE

You're allowed to carry aboard one bag and one personal article, such as a purse or a laptop computer. Make sure what you carry on fits under your seat or in the overhead bin. Get to the gate early, so you can board as soon as possible, before the overhead bins fill up.

Baggage allowances vary by carrier, destination, and ticket class. On international flights, you're usually allowed to check two bags weighing up to 70 pounds (32 kilograms) each, although a few airlines allow checked bags of up to 88 pounds (40 kilograms) in first class. Some international carriers don't allow more than 66 pounds (30 kilograms) per bag in business class and 44 pounds (20 kilograms) in economy. On domestic flights, the limit is usually 50 to 70 pounds (23 to 32 kilograms) per bag. In general, carry-on bags shouldn't exceed 40 pounds (18 kilograms). Most airlines won't accept bags that weigh more than 100 pounds (45 kilograms) on domestic or international flights. Expect to pay a fee for baggage that exceeds weight limits.

Check baggage restrictions with your carrier before you pack.

Airline liability for baggage is limited to $2,500 per person on flights within the United States. On international flights it amounts to $9.07 per pound or $20 per kilogram for checked baggage (roughly $640 per 70-pound bag), with a maximum of $634.90 per piece, and $400 per passenger for unchecked baggage. You can buy additional coverage at check-in for about $10 per $1,000 of coverage, but it often excludes a rather extensive list of items, shown on your airline ticket.

Before departure, itemize your bags' contents and their worth, and label the bags with your name, address, and phone number. (If you use your home address, cover it so potential thieves can't see it readily.) Include a label inside each bag and **pack a copy of your itinerary.** At check-in, make sure each bag is correctly tagged with the destination airport's three-letter code. Because some checked bags will be opened for hand inspection, the U.S. Transportation Security Administration recommends that you leave luggage unlocked or use the plastic locks offered at check-in. TSA screeners place an inspection notice inside searched bags, which are re-sealed with a special lock.

If your bag has been searched and contents are missing or damaged, file a claim with the TSA Consumer Response Center as soon as possible. If your bags arrive damaged or fail to arrive at all, file a written report with the airline before leaving the airport.

☐ Complaints **U.S. Transportation Security Administration Contact Center** ☎ 866/289-9673 ⊕ www.tsa.gov.

PASSPORTS & VISAS

When traveling internationally, carry your passport even if you don't need one (it's always the best form of I.D.) and **make two photocopies of the data page** (one for someone at home and another for you, carried separately from your passport). If you lose your passport, promptly call the nearest embassy or consulate and the local police.

U.S. passport applications for children under age 14 require consent from both parents or legal guardians; both parents must appear together to sign the application. If only one parent appears, he or she must submit a written statement from the other parent authorizing passport issuance for the child. A parent with sole authority must present evidence of it when applying; acceptable documentation includes the child's certified birth certificate listing only the applying parent, a court order specifically permitting this parent's travel with the child, or a death certificate for the nonapplying parent. Application forms and instructions are available on the Web site of the U.S. State Department's Bureau of Consular Affairs (⊕ travel.state.gov).

ENTERING SOUTH AMERICA

For details on passport and visa requirements, *see* the country A to Z section at the end of each chapter.

PASSPORT OFFICES

The best time to apply for a passport or to renew is in fall and winter. Before any trip, check your passport's expiration date, and, if necessary, renew it as soon as possible.

☐ Australian Citizens **Passports Australia** Australian Department of Foreign Affairs and Trade ☎ 131-232 ⊕ www.passports.gov.au.

☐ Canadian Citizens **Passport Office** ⊠ to mail in applications: 200 Promenade du Portage, Hull, Québec J8X 4B7 ☎ 819/994-3500 or 800/567-6868 ⊕ www.ppt.gc.ca.

☐ New Zealand Citizens **New Zealand Passports Office** ☎ 0800/22-5050 or 04/474-8100 ⊕ www.passports.govt.nz.

☐ U.K. Citizens **U.K. Passport Service** ☎ 0870/521-0410 ⊕ www.passport.gov.uk.

☐ U.S. Citizens **National Passport Information Center** ☎ 877/487-2778, 888/874-7793 TDD/TTY ⊕ travel.state.gov.

SAFETY

Don't wear a money belt or a waist pack, both of which peg you as a tourist. Distribute your cash and any valuables (including your credit cards and passport) between a deep front pocket, an inside jacket or vest pocket, and a hidden money pouch. Do not reach for the money pouch once you're in public.

Although there has been a real effort to crack down on tourist-related crime throughout South America, petty theft is still prevalent in urban areas, especially around hotels, restaurants, and bars. Wherever you go, don't wear expensive clothing, avoid flashy jewelry, and **never handle money in public places.** It's a good idea to **keep your money in a pocket rather than a wallet,** which is easier to steal. Use extra vigilance when withdrawing cash from ATMs. Opt for a cash machine located inside a bank with a security guard nearby. On buses and in crowded areas, hold handbags close to the body; thieves use knives to slice the bottom of a bag and catch the contents as they fall out. Keep cameras in a secure bag, preferably one with a chain or wire embedded in the strap. Always remain alert for pickpockets, and **don't walk alone at night,** especially in the larger cities.

TRAVEL ADVISORIES

South America has had its share of political struggle and drug-related strife. Before heading to a particular country, **get the latest travel warnings and advisories.** The United States, United Kingdom, Canada, Australia, and New Zealand each maintain hot lines, fax lines, and Internet sites with this information for their citizens.

At press time, Colombia was the subject of the sternest warnings due to violence by drug traffickers and paramilitary groups throughout the country. You should exercise extreme caution when visiting Colombia. The political situation in Venezuela remains volatile in the wake of an early 2003 nationwide strike that paralyzed the country, though life is much calmer outside Caracas. Be aware that regions of Ecuador, Peru, and Venezuela that are close to the Colombian border also see sporadic outbreaks of violence. Be sure to contact your government for up-to-the-minute travel advisories.

WOMEN IN SOUTH AMERICA

If you carry a purse, choose one with a zipper and a thick strap that you can drape across your body; adjust the length so that the purse sits in front of you at or above hip level. (Don't wear a money belt or a waist pack.) Store only enough money in the purse to cover casual spending. Distribute the rest of your cash and any valuables between deep front pockets, inside jacket or vest pockets, and a concealed money pouch.

Women, especially those with light hair, can expect many pointed looks and the occasional hiss or catcall—integral aspects of the "machismo" culture in South America. Ignore the comments. Outright come-ons or grabbing is rare, but do be careful when out at night. Don't go out alone, have your hotel or restaurant call a taxi for you, and watch your drink in crowded bars. The risk of date rape drugs being slipped into a drink is real.

SENIOR-CITIZEN TRAVEL

There's no reason that active, well-traveled senior citizens shouldn't visit South America, whether on an independent vacation, an escorted tour, or an adventure trek. Before you leave home, however, determine what medical services your health insurance will cover outside the United States; note that Medicare doesn't provide for payment of hospital and medical services outside the United States. If you need additional travel insurance, buy it (⇨ Insurance).

The continent is full of good hotels and competent ground operators who will meet your flights and organize your sightseeing. To qualify for age-related discounts, mention your senior-citizen status up front when booking hotel reservations (not when checking out) and before you're seated in restaurants (not when paying the bill). Be sure to have identification on hand. When renting a car, ask about promotional car-rental discounts, which can be cheaper than senior-citizen rates.

🎓 Educational Programs **Elderhostel** ✉ 11 Ave. de Lafayette, Boston, MA 02111-1746 ☎ 877/426-8056, 978/323-4141 international callers, 877/426-2167 TTY 🖷 877/426-2166 ⊕ www.elderhostel.org. **Interhostel** ✉ University of New Hampshire, 6 Garrison Ave., Durham, NH 03824 ☎ 603/862-1147 or 800/733-9753 🖷 603/862-1113 ⊕ www.learn.unh. edu. **Folkways Institute** ✉ 14600 S.E. Aldridge Rd., Portland, OR 97236-6518 ☎ 503/658-6600 🖷 503/658-8672.

STUDENTS IN SOUTH AMERICA

Although airfares to and within the continent are high, you can take buses to most South American destinations for mere dollars, and you can usually find safe, comfortable (if sparse), affordable accommodations for a fraction of what it might cost back home. Hostels exist in Argentina, Bolivia, Brazil, Chile, Colombia, Ecuador, Peru, and Uruguay, and backpacking is popular throughout the continent. Most cities also have vibrant student populations.

▣ IDs & Services **STA Travel** ✉ 10 Downing St., New York, NY 10014 ☎ 212/627-3111, 800/777-0112 24-hr service center 🖷 212/627-3387 ⊕ www.sta.com. **Travel Cuts** ✉ 187 College St., Toronto, Ontario M5T 1P7, Canada ☎ 800/592-2887 in the U.S., 416/979-2406 or 866/246-9762 in Canada 🖷 416/979-8167 ⊕ www.travelcuts.com.

TELEPHONES & THE INTERNET

When dialing a number from abroad, drop the initial 0 from the local area code. For details on country codes, directory and operator assistance, local and long-distance calls, phone cards, pay phones, cell phones, and phone company offices *see* the A to Z section at the end of each country chapter.

Internet access is surprisingly widespread. In addition to full-fledged cyber cafés, look for machines set up in phone offices. Rates range from $1 to $10 an hour. Many upscale hotels catering to business travelers offer Internet access to their guests among their amenities. If you're logging in to one of the Web-based e-mail sites, know that late afternoon is an especially sluggish time because usage is higher.

South American computer keyboards are not identical to, but do resemble, those in English-speaking countries. Your biggest frustration will probably be finding the @ symbol to type an e-mail address. If you need to ask, it's called *arroba* in Spanish and Portuguese.

LONG-DISTANCE SERVICES

AT&T, MCI, and Sprint access codes make calling long-distance relatively convenient, but you may find the local access number blocked in many hotel rooms. First ask the hotel operator to connect

you. If the hotel operator balks, ask for an international operator, or dial the international operator yourself. One way to improve your odds of getting connected to your long-distance carrier is to travel with more than one company's calling card (a hotel may block Sprint, for example, but not MCI). If all else fails, call from a pay phone. The country code is 1 for the United States and Canada, 61 for Australia, 64 for New Zealand, and 44 for the United Kingdom.

TIME

Mainland South America spans three time zones. Colombia, Ecuador, Peru, and a small slice of western Brazil share a time zone with New York and Miami when the U.S. East Coast observes standard time. Bolivia, Chile, Paraguay, Venezuela, and central and western Brazil are one hour later. Argentina, Uruguay, and eastern Brazil (including Rio and São Paulo) are one hour later still. Note that Chile and Paraguay observe daylight savings time and move ahead one hour from October to March; the southern states of Brazil (including Rio and São Paulo) do so from October to February.

TOURS & PACKAGES

Because everything is prearranged on a prepackaged tour or independent vacation, you spend less time planning—and often get it all at a good price.

BOOKING WITH AN AGENT

Travel agents are excellent resources. But it's a good idea to collect brochures from several agencies, as some agents' suggestions may be influenced by relationships with tour and package firms that reward them for volume sales. If you have a special interest, find an agent with expertise in that area; the American Society of Travel Agents (ASTA; ⇨ Travel Agencies) has a database of specialists worldwide. You can log on to the group's Web site to find an ASTA travel agent in your neighborhood.

Make sure your travel agent knows the accommodations and other services of the place being recommended. Ask about the hotel's location, room size, beds, and whether it has a pool, room service, or programs for children, if you care about these. Has your agent been there in person or sent others whom you can contact?

Do some homework on your own, too: local tourism boards can provide information about lesser-known and small-niche operators, some of which may sell only direct.

BUYER BEWARE

Each year consumers are stranded or lose their money when tour operators—even large ones with excellent reputations—go out of business. So check out the operator. Ask several travel agents about its reputation, and try to **book with a company that has a consumer-protection program.** (Look for information in the company's brochure.) In the United States, members of the United States Tour Operators Association are required to set aside funds ($1 million) to help eligible customers cover payments and travel arrangements in the event that the company defaults. It's also a good idea to choose a company that participates in the American Society of Travel Agents' Tour Operator Program; ASTA will act as mediator in any disputes between you and your tour operator.

Remember that the more your package or tour includes, the better you can predict the ultimate cost of your vacation. Make sure you know exactly what is covered, and **beware of hidden costs.** Are taxes, tips, and transfers included? Entertainment and excursions? These can add up.

🗂 Tour-Operator Recommendations **American Society of Travel Agents (⇨ Travel Agencies). National Tour Association (NTA)** ⊠ 546 E. Main St., Lexington, KY 40508 ☎ 859/226–4444 or 800/682–8886 🖷 859/226–4404 ⊕ www.ntaonline. com. **United States Tour Operators Association (USTOA)** ⊠ 275 Madison Ave., Suite 2014, New York, NY 10016 ☎ 212/599–6599 🖷 212/599–6744 ⊕ www.ustoa.com.

TRAIN TRAVEL

In most South American countries, trains don't play an important role in the transportation system. Venezuela, for example, has no rail service at all. Those countries that still have trains have service cutbacks with each passing year. Still, there are some excellent rail trips. In Peru, take the three-hour run to Machu Picchu from Cuzco and the all-day ride from Cuzco to Puno on Lake Titicaca. In Ecuador, a worthwhile trip is the dawn-to-dusk run through the Andes down the Avenue of the Volcanoes between Quito and Riobamba.

Chile has a good, though limited, rail system that runs south from the capital to the Lake District. Take the overnight trip from Santiago to Temuco, a route using sleeper cars appointed in faded velvet and wood veneer. Argentina's rail system was built by the British, but service is rapidly shrinking. Trains still operate in metropolitan Buenos Aires and within Patagonia but no longer run between the two. Argentina has a few tourist-only rail excursions: Tierra del Fuego's "Train to the End of the World" and Salta's "Train to the Clouds" are world-famous.

Ticket prices are usually quite reasonable. Chile and some places in Argentina have sleeping and dining cars; the other countries, few services at all. Plan to **buy your train tickets three days ahead,** two weeks in summer months, and **arrive at the station well before departure time.** There are no rail passes, and there's no way of reserving seats before you leave home.

TRAVEL AGENCIES

A good travel agent puts your needs first. Look for an agency that has been in business at least five years, emphasizes customer service, and has someone on staff who specializes in your destination.

In addition, **make sure the agency belongs to a professional trade organization.** The American Society of Travel Agents (ASTA)—the largest and most influential in the field with more than 20,000 members in some 140 countries—maintains and enforces a strict code of ethics and will step in to help mediate any agent-client disputes involving ASTA members if necessary. ASTA (whose motto is "Without a travel agent, you're on your own") also maintains a Web site that includes a directory of agents. (If a travel agency is also acting as your tour operator, *see* Buyer Beware *in* Tours & Packages.)

Local Agent Referrals **American Society of Travel Agents (ASTA)** ✉ 1101 King St., Suite 200, Alexandria, VA 22314 ☎ 703/739-2782 or 800/965-2782 24-hr hotline 🖷 703/684-8319 🌐 www. astanet.com. **Association of British Travel Agents** ✉ 68-71 Newman St., London W1T 3AH ☎ 020/7637-2444 🖷 020/7637-0713 🌐 www.abta.com. **Association of Canadian Travel Agencies** ✉ 130 Albert St., Suite 1705, Ottawa, Ontario K1P 5G4 ☎ 613/237-3657 🖷 613/237-7052 🌐 www.acta.ca. **Australian Federation of Travel Agents** ✉ Level 3, 309 Pitt St., Sydney, NSW 2000 ☎ 02/9264-3299 or 1300/363-416 🖷 02/9264-1085 🌐 www.afta.com.au. **Travel Agents' Association of New Zealand** ✉ Level 5, Tourism and Travel House, 79 Boulcott St., Box 1888, Wellington 6001 ☎ 04/499-0104 🖷 04/499-0786 🌐 www.taanz.org.nz.

VISITOR INFORMATION

Learn more about foreign destinations by checking government-issued travel advisories and country information. For a broader picture, consider information from more than one country.

Most South American countries offer very little basic travel information. Few countries have tourist offices overseas, though there are a few travel sections in some embassies and consulates (and some cultural attachés will mail brochures and the like). Often your best bets are the airlines and tour operators with programs to South America (⇨ Air Travel *and* Tours & Packages).

Argentina **Argentina Government Tourism Office** ✉ 2655 Le Jeune Rd., Coral Gables, FL 33134 ☎ 305/442-1366.

Bolivia **Embassy of Bolivia** (⇨ Embassies & Consulates).

Brazil **Consulate General of Brazil and Trade Bureau** ✉ 1185 Ave. of the Americas, 21st fl., New York, NY 10036 ☎ 212/827-0976, for general travel and business information on Brazil. **Riotur** ✉ 3601 Aviation Blvd., Suite 2100, Manhattan Beach, CA 90266 ☎ 310/643-2638 ✉ 201 E. 12th St., Suite 509, New York, NY 10003 ☎ 212/375-0801, for information on the city of Rio.

Chile **Embassy of Chile** 🌐 www.chile-usa.org (⇨ Embassies & Consulates).

Colombia **Embassy of Colombia** (⇨ Embassies & Consulates).

Ecuador **Embassy of Ecuador** (⇨ Embassies & Consulates).

Paraguay **Embassy of Paraguay** 🌐 www.paraguayembassy.ca (⇨ Embassies & Consulates).

Peru **Embassy of Peru** 🌐 www.peruemb.org (⇨ Embassies & Consulates).

Uruguay **Embassy of Uruguay** (⇨ Embassies & Consulates).

Venezuela **Embassy of Venezuela** 🌐 www.embavenez-org.us (⇨ Embassies & Consulates, *above*). **Venezuelan Tourism Association** 🖃 Box 3010, Sausalito, CA 94966 ☎ 415/331-0100.

Government Advisories **U.S. Department of State** ✉ Overseas Citizens Services Office, 2100 Pennsylvania Ave. NW, 4th floor, Washington, DC 20520 ☎ 202/647-5225 interactive hotline or 888/407-4747 🌐 www.travel.state.gov. **Consular Affairs Bureau of Canada** ☎ 800/267-6788 or 613/944-6788 🌐 www.voyage.gc.ca. **U.K. Foreign and Commonwealth Office** ✉ Travel Advice Unit, Consular Division, Old Admiralty Building, London SW1A 2PA ☎ 0870/606-0290 or 020/7008-1500 🌐 www.fco.gov.uk/travel. **Australian Department of Foreign Affairs and Trade** ☎ 300/139-281 travel advice, 02/6261-1299 Consular Travel Advice Faxback Service 🌐 www.dfat.gov.au. **New Zealand Ministry of Foreign Affairs and Trade** ☎ 04/439-8000 🌐 www.mft.govt.nz.

WEB SITES

Do check out the World Wide Web when planning your trip. You'll find everything from weather forecasts to virtual tours of famous cities. Be sure to visit Fodors.com (🌐 www.fodors.com), a complete travel-planning site. You can research prices and book plane tickets, hotel rooms, rental cars, vacation packages, and more. In addition, you can post your pressing questions in the Travel Talk section. Other planning tools include a currency converter and weather reports, and there are loads of links to travel resources.

For South American countries, official tourism sites are rare—and the sites that exist aren't always comprehensive. Be prepared to really surf to find the information you need. You may have more luck if you search by region or city. Don't rule out sites in Spanish or Portuguese, as some have links to sites in English.

On Portuguese- or Spanish-language sites, watch for the name of the country, region, state, or city in which you have an interest. (Don't forget that Brazil is spelled *Brasil* in both languages, the only variation you'll encounter.) The search terms for "look," "find," and "get" are *olhar/achar, buscar,* and *pegar* in Portuguese, and *mirar* and *buscar* in Spanish. "Next" and "last" (as in "next/last 10") are *próximo* and *último/ anterior* in both Portuguese and Spanish. Keep an eye out for such words as (where the words are different, Portuguese is provided first, followed by Spanish): *turismo* (tourism), *turístico* (tourist-related), *hoteis/ hoteles* (hotels), *restaurantes* (restaurants), *governo/gobierno* (government), *estado* (state), *província/provincia* (province), *cidade/ciudad* (city).

The following sites, in English unless otherwise noted, are good places to start a search: ⊕ www.lanic.utexas.edu (the Latin American Network Information Center at the University of Texas, with country-specific sections and exhaustive links to tourism, history, culture, business, and academic sites); ⊕ www.turismo.gov.ar (official Argentine tourist board site); ⊕ www. bolivia.com (some tourism information on Bolivia, Spanish only); ⊕ www.embratur. gov.br (the official Brazilian tourist board site, with information in English provided by the Brazilian embassy in London), ⊕ www.brazilny.org (the official consular Web site in New York, with details about other consulates and the embassy as well as travel information and links to other sites), ⊕ www.brazilinfocenter.org (a Washington, D.C.–based organization that promotes political and business issues, rather than tourism, but whose Web site has an incredible number of helpful links), ⊕ www.vivabrazil.com (a site with background and travel info on Brazil's different regions as well as links that will help you arrange your trip); ⊕ www.gochile.cl (tourist and business information on Chile); ⊕ www.winesofchile.com (site for true oenophiles); ⊕ www.colombia.com (business and tourism information on Colombia, Spanish only); ⊕ www.ecuador. org (Ecuador Embassy's official site); ⊕ www.paraguay.com (mostly news, with travel information on Paraguay, including maps and city-specific information on where to eat and sleep and what to see); ⊕ www.peru-explorer.com (with Peruvian geography and cultural history as well as travel facts and photos); ⊕ www.turismo. gub.uy (the Uruguay Ministry of Tourism's site); ⊕ www.embavenez-us.org (the Venezuelan Embassy's site, with news and travel and economic information).

ARGENTINA

1

MOST TRAVELERS THINK THEY'VE STUMBLED ON a long-lost European country when they get to Argentina. Most Argentines, too, are convinced they're more European than South American. A quick look at the people walking down the avenues of any Argentine city confirms the impression. There are more Italian surnames than Spanish and the largest colony of Yugoslavs outside of their fractured homeland. There are tens of thousands of descendants of Jewish immigrants from Eastern Europe, and communities of British, French, and German families enjoy cultural and financial clout far beyond their insignificant numbers.

But in spite of the symbiosis with Europe, the country has had a chaotic past, politically and economically. The pitfalls of Argentine politics weren't inappropriately characterized in the musical *Evita:* "Truth is stranger than fiction" is a maxim confirmed by the musical-chairs–like process that has placed both soldiers and civilians in the country's presidency. Further, Argentina is a me-first society that considers government a thorn in its side and whose citizens avoid paying taxes with the finesse of bullfighters. As a community, it's totally chaotic, but as individuals, Argentines are generous and delightful, full of life, and eager to explain the intricacies of their complex society. They're also philosophers, anxious to justify their often enviable existence. Friendship is a time-consuming priority, and family connections are strong. Argentines work longer hours than New Yorkers—just not so efficiently—and rival Madrileños at dining until dawn.

Argentina's vast territory stretches more than 5,000 km (3,000 mi) from north to south and encompasses everything from snow-covered mountains to subtropical jungle. In the north, in the sultry province of Misiones, nature is raucous and rampant; here the spectacular Iguazú Falls flow amid foliage that is rain-forest–thick. In the pampas, or plains, of central Argentina, the countryside recalls the American West: Gauchos herd the cattle that provide Argentina with the beef it consumes in massive quantities. In the west, the Andean backbone Argentina shares with Chile attracts climbers to Mt. Aconcagua, the Southern Hemisphere's highest peak, and draws skiers to Bariloche and other resorts. Patagonia, in the south, is like no other place on earth. Monumental glaciers tumble into mountain lakes, depositing icebergs like meringue on a floating island. Penguins troop along beaches like invading forces, whales hang out with several yards of their tails emerging from the sea, and at the tip of Patagonia, South America slips into Beagle Channel in Tierra del Fuego.

EXPLORING ARGENTINA

Buenos Aires is the political, economic, and cultural capital of Argentina and the gateway to the rest of the country. The pampas—vast plains of cattle ranches and home of the gauchos—extend south from the capital. The Iguazú Falls lie roughly 1,300 km (800 mi) to the city's northeast on the border with Paraguay and Brazil. Nestled in the shadow of the soaring Andes, the Cuyo was once a desert before irrigation transformed it into the fourth-largest wine-producing region in the world. Below the pampas is Patagonia, the rough and largely uninhab-

Any trip to Argentina should start in Buenos Aires, where you'll develop a strong sense of the peoples' character and culture. However, there's so much more beyond the big city: gauchos work ranches that sprawl over every horizon, Iguazú Falls are perhaps the most spectacular falls in the world, and the lonely, windswept reaches of Patagonia roll on forever and a few miles more. The availability of domestic flights from Buenos Aires to every major city makes sampling the country a snap.

If you have
5 days

Spend most of your visit in **Buenos Aires,** which has more than enough to keep you happily occupied. Break up your exploration of this dynamic city by taking a one- or two-day side trip to the estancias of **The Pampas.**

If you have
7 days

Spend a few days in **Buenos Aires,** with a day trip or overnight stay at a nearby estancia in the **The Pampas.** Then catch a short (1½ hour) flight up to Puerto Iguazú to see the **Cataratas del Iguazú.** You'll need at least two days to fully explore the falls. If you can tear yourself away from nature's spectacle, spend a day or two exploring the nearby missions.

If you have
10 days

Visit **Buenos Aires** for two or three days and then head straight to **Patagonia.** Spend at least a week here—the addition of more flights between the region's major hubs make it easy to get a taste of both the Atlantic and Andean sides.

ited territory that extends south to Tierra del Fuego and consumes a third of Argentina. It's divided into two regions: the Atlantic, with an incomparable variety of marine life, including whales, sea elephants, and penguins, and the Andes, with frozen lakes, glaciers, and thousand-year-old forests.

About the Restaurants

Dining in Argentina is an art, a passion, and a pastime. Whether eaten at home or in a restaurant, meals are events. *Sobremesa* (chatting at the table after the meal) is just as important as the dining ritual itself, and people linger over wine or coffee long after the dishes have been cleared away. Breakfast is usually served until 11 AM; lunch runs from 12:30 to 3:30; dinner is from 8 to around midnight. Several restaurants in Buenos Aires and other large cities stay open all night, or at least well into the morning, catering to the after-theater and nightclub crowd.

About the Hotels

Buenos Aires has an array of hotels, inns, *apart-hotels* (short-term rental apartments), and hostels. Pampas lodgings are best known for their sprawling, secluded, all-inclusive estancias—country mansions complete with an on-site staff of gauchos to lead guests through the grasslands. A visit to the Pampas region isn't complete without a stay at one of these memorable old-world estates. Hotels in the Northwest's major cities tend to be modern and comfortable. The city of Mendoza has many good, small to medium-size hotels. The smaller cities of San Luís, San Juan, and San Rafael have at least one modern hotel, plus others that are more run-of-the-mill. Idyllic lake-view lodges, cozy *cabañas* (cabins), vast *estancias* (ranches), and inexpensive *hospedajes* or *residenciales* (bed-and-breakfasts) are found in towns and in the countryside throughout Patagonia. High season in Argentina includes the summer months of mid-December through February, and the winter holidays that fall in July.

WHAT IT COSTS In Argentina Pesos					
	$$$$	**$$$**	**$$**	**$**	**¢**
RESTAURANTS	over 35	25–35	15–25	8–15	under 8
HOTELS	over 300	220–300	140–220	80–140	under 80

Restaurant prices are for one main course at dinner. Hotel prices are for two people in a standard double room in high season.

BUENOS AIRES

Updated by
Brian Byrnes
and Victoria
Patience

Buenos Aires, the ninth largest city in the world and the hub of the southern cone, is a sprawling metropolis rising from the Río de la Plata and stretching more than 200 square km (75 square mi) to the surrounding pampas, the fertile Argentine plains. With more than one-third of the country's 39 million inhabitants living in or around Buenos Aires, the city is the political, economic, and cultural center of Argentina and the gateway to the rest of the country.

Unlike most other Latin American cities, where the architecture reveals a strong Spanish colonial influence, Buenos Aires has a mix of styles. Modern high-rises sit side by side with ornate buildings from days long gone. At every turn you'll be reminded of the city's European heritage: with their boulevards lined with palatial mansions and spacious parks, the neighborhoods of El Centro, La Recoleta, and Belgrano evoke Rome, Madrid, Paris, and Budapest. The plazas of Palermo and Belgrano mirror those in Paris; Rome's Pantheon inspired the Parroquia de Nuestra Señora; the Avenida de Mayo has been compared to both Madrid and Budapest; and the Vatican Embassy on Avenida Alvear replicates the Jacquemart-André Museum in Paris. San Telmo and La Boca have a distinctly working-class Italian feel, in contrast to the stately aplomb of Plaza de Mayo and Avenida de Mayo.

Buenos Aires locals refer to themselves as *Porteños* because many of them originally arrived by boat from Europe and settled in the port area. Known as thinkers, Porteños delve into philosophical discussions and psychoanalysis (as proven by the large number of psychoanalysts per capita—in fact, the most of any city in the world). With 85% of the Argentine population of European origin, there's a blurred sense of national identity in Buenos Aires—South American or European?—and residents are often concerned with how outsiders perceive them. People here look at one another closely, whether it be a casual, appreciative glance or a curious stare, making many of them deeply image-conscious.

The Distinctive Cuisine

Argentina is basically a steak-and-potatoes country. The beef is so good, most Argentines see little reason to eat anything else, though pork, lamb, and chicken are tasty alternatives, and *civito* (kid), when in season, is outstanding. *Carne asado* (roasted meat) usually means grilled *a la parrilla* (on a grill over hot coals), but it can also be baked in an oven or slowly roasted at an outdoor barbecue (*asado*).

Beyond beef, many Argentine dishes are influenced by other cultures. Pasta, pizza, and Italian specialties are on every menu in almost all restaurants. Fish has not been a favored dish in this meat-loving country, even though trout and salmon from lakes and streams yield both quality and quantity and *centolla* (giant crab) and *mejillones* (mussels) are trapped offshore in Ushuaia.

Not to be missed, when available, is the white asparagus that grows south of Buenos Aires.

Ecotourism

In Argentina, where climates range from tropical to subantarctic and altitudes descend from 22,000 feet to below sea-level, every conceivable environment on Earth is represented: high, low, hot, cold, temperate, dry, wet, and frozen. Because the population (about 40 million) is small relative to its land mass (roughly 2,000 mi long and 900 mi wide), plants, birds, and animals thrive undisturbed in their habitats.

Along the South Atlantic coast, sea mammals mate and give birth on empty beaches and in protected bays. Guanaco, rhea, and native deer travel miles over isolated Andean trails and across windswept plains. Birds are everywhere—passing above in clouds of thousands, descending on a lagoon like a blanket of feathers, or rising in a flutter of pink flamingos.

Sports & the Outdoors

Fishing in the national parks of Patagonia's northern lake district (especially around Bariloche) is legendary. Hiking and mountain biking in Argentina's national and provincial parks—over mountain trails, and through forests to lakes, villages, and campgrounds—provide unique memories of an abundant and vast wilderness. If you're a serious mountaineer, you know the challenges of Aconcagua (in Mendoza Province) and Cerro Fitzroy, Mt. Tronadór, and Lanín Volcano in Patagonia. The Club Andinos (Andean Mountaineering Clubs) in Bariloche, Mendoza, Ushuaia, and other towns organize national and international excursions. Since Argentina's seasons are the opposite of North America's, you can ski or snowboard from June to September.

Wine

Given the high consumption of beef rather than fish, Argentines understandably drink a lot of *vino tinto* (red wine); Malbec and Cabernet are the most popular. If you prefer *vino blanco* (white wine), try a sauvignon blanc or chardonnay from Mendoza, or lesser-known wineries from farther north, such as La Rioja and Salta, where the Torrontés grape thrives. This varietal produces a dry white with a lovely floral bouquet. A popular summer cooler is *clericot*, a white version of sangría (available in some restaurants), made with strawberries, peaches, oranges, or whatever fruits are in season.

Buenos Aires has no Eiffel Tower, no internationally renowned museums, no must-see sights that clearly identify it as a world-class city. Rather, the essence of Buenos Aires resides in singular encounters imbued with intense Latin spirit—a flirtatious glance, a heartfelt chat, a juicy steak, an impassioned tango—to create a vibrant and unforgettable urban experience.

Exploring Buenos Aires

Buenos Aires is a sprawling city, best explored one neighborhood at a time on foot and by public transportation—*colectivo* (bus), *subte* (subway), or relatively inexpensive taxis. Streets are basically laid out in a grid, though a few streets transverse the grid diagonally; these are helpfully called *diagonales*. *Avenidas* are two-way streets, while *calles* are generally one-way. Streets and avenues running north–south change names at Avenida Rivadavía. Each city block is 100 meters (328 feet) long, and addresses are based on the building's measured position from the corner (for instance, 180 Calle Florida is 80 meters from the corner, and 100 meters, or one block, from 80 Calle Florida).

San Telmo

The bohemian San Telmo neighborhood, named after the patron saint of seafarers, sits midway between bustling El Centro and the quiet port area of La Boca. Its cobblestone streets teem with early-19th-century colonial buildings, once inhabited by affluent Spaniards. Upon the outbreak of yellow fever in the late 1800s, the wealthy moved northward, leaving behind opulent mansions that were converted into tenements and occupied by immigrant families in the late 19th century. Thanks to renewed urban planning and government subsidies, the worn sidewalks and formerly crumbling structures have been transformed into quaint streets lined with antiques shops, galleries, chic restaurants, and traditional tango halls. The neighborhood is a cradle of the city's historic and cultural traditions, and all its landmarks have been declared National Historic Monuments.

Numbers in the text correspond to number in the margin and on the Buenos Aires map.

a good walk

To reach San Telmo by subway, take Line E to the Independencia station, and be prepared to walk nine blocks east along Avenida Independencia to Calle Defensa, the oldest street in the city. The sights in this walk are all grouped around this street. Head south down Calle Defensa until you reach **Plaza Dorrego** ❶▶, framed by bars, restaurants, and antiques shops. On Calle Humberto Primero, which borders the south side of Plaza Dorrego, visit the **Museo Penitenciario Antonio Ballvé** ❷ and its

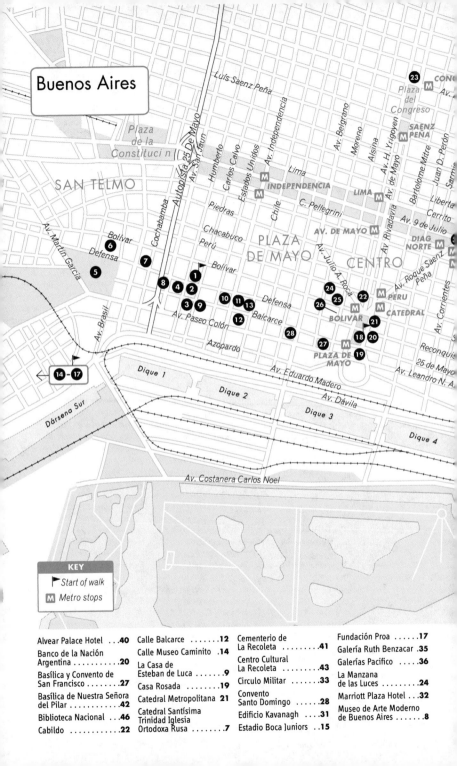

Buenos Aires

KEY

► Start of walk

Ⓜ Metro stops

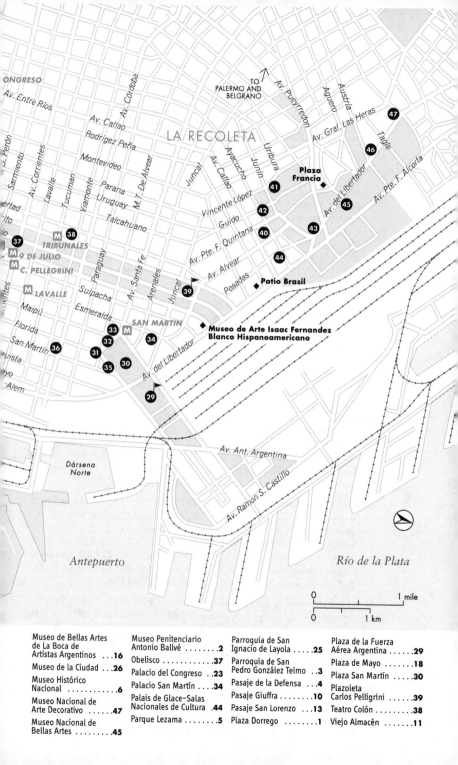

TO PALERMO AND BELGRANO

LA RECOLETA

Plaza Francia

Patio Brasil

Museo de Arte Isaac Fernandez Blanco Hispanoamericano

TRIBUNALES

9 DE JULIO

C. PELLEGRINI

LAVALLE

SAN MARTIN

Dársena Norte

Av. Ant. Argentina

Av. Ramon S. Castillo

Antepuerto

Río de la Plata

0   1 mile

0   1 km

adjoining chapel, Nuestra Señora del Carmen. Next door, a mix of colonial, baroque, neoclassical, and Italianate architecture can be seen in the **Parroquia de San Pedro González Telmo** ❸. Head back to Plaza Dorrego and south again on Defensa toward **Pasaje de la Defensa** ❹, with its hodgepodge of tiny shops selling antiques and curios. Continue down Calle Defensa to the southern edge of San Telmo to reach **Parque Lezama** ❺, home to the **Museo Histórico Nacional** ❻. Overlooking the park, the onion-shape domes of the **Catedral Santísima Trinidad Iglesia Ortodoxa Rusa** ❼ rise above the treetops lining Avenida Brasíl. From here head north again along Calle Defensa to reach Avenida San Juan and the **Museo de Arte Moderno de Buenos Aires** ❽. Remains of the colonial period are found just off Calle Defensa on Calle Carlos Calvo, where you'll see **La Casa de Esteban de Luca** ❾, and down **Pasaje Giuffra** ❿, also off Calle Defensa. The legendary **Viejo Almacén** ⓫, open only for dinner and shows, is on Avenida Independencia. **Calle Balcarce** ⓬, which runs parallel to Calle Defensa, and the intersecting **Pasaje San Lorenzo** ⓭ lead you past unique period architecture.

TIMING & PRECAUTIONS

San Telmo thrives on Sunday, when the art and antiques market in Plaza Dorrego bustles with activity and street performers. A few hours will give you plenty of time to see the sights, but you could easily spend a full day exploring the neighborhood. San Telmo is one of the city's seedier districts, and you should exercise caution when walking here—especially at night. Violent crime is rare, but unemployment in the area, combined with the knowledge that tourists flock here, has led to instances of petty crime.

WHAT TO SEE

⓬ Calle Balcarce (Balcarce Street). Although a stretch of this street is known for its touristy tango dinner shows, it nevertheless leads you past some unique Spanish colonial architecture, such as the Viejo Hotel at No. 1053, and No. 1016, the former home of artist Juan Carlos Castagnino (it now houses his son's art gallery). Stroll down this street to reach one of the first of the quickly vanishing *conventillos* (tenements) of the past, on the corner of Humberto Primero. ⊠ *San Telmo.*

❾ La Casa de Esteban de Luca (Esteban de Luca's House). Distinguished poet and soldier Esteban de Luca, who wrote the country's first national anthem and was a hero of the May Revolution of 1810, once lived in this house, where he entertained the local literati. It now operates as a quaint, if somewhat touristy, restaurant serving international and local cuisine; Antonio Banderas dined here during the filming of *Evita*. ⊠ *Calle Defensa 1000, San Telmo* ☎ *11/4361–4338.*

❼ Catedral Santísima Trinidad Iglesia Ortodoxa Rusa (Holy Trinity Russian Orthodox Church). Five towering sky-blue domes characterize the first Orthodox church built in Latin America, in 1904. Venetian mosaics, stained glass, and icons sent from St. Petersburg by Czar Nicholas II and Czarina Alexandra adorn the church. ⊠ *Av. Brasíl 315, San Telmo* ☎ *11/4361–4274* 🖅 *Free* ⊙ *Sat. 5 PM–8:30 PM, Sun. 10 AM–12:30 PM.*

❽ Museo de Arte Moderno de Buenos Aires (Museum of Modern Art of Buenos Aires). Once the site of a tobacco company, MAMBA retains the original exposed-brick facade and fabulous wooden door with wrought-iron fixtures. Local and international contemporary artists, both prominent and up-and-coming, display their paintings, sculptures, and media arts here. And you can often see the exhibiting artists, either giving lectures or just hanging out. Note that the museum closes one month in summer, usually in February, so it's best to call ahead to confirm. ⊠ *Av. San Juan 350, San Telmo* ☎ *11/4361–1121* ⌨ *1 peso, free Wed.* ⊗ *Tues.–Sat. 10–8, Sun. 11–8.*

★ ❻ **Museo Histórico Nacional** (National History Museum). The Lezama family's stately mansion now houses artifacts and paintings illustrating Argentine history, spanning the 16th through 20th centuries. Ask to see the extensive collection of paintings by Cándido López, who learned to paint with his left hand after losing his right arm in the War of the Triple Alliance of the 1870s. López's panoramic paintings depicting battlefield scenes spearheaded contemporary primitive painting. Also among the displays are articles from General José de San Martín's campaigns during the 1810 War of Independence against Spain. ⊠ *Calle Defensa 1600, San Telmo* ☎ *11/4307–4457* ⌨ *1 peso* ⊗ *Feb.–Dec., weekdays 11–5, Sat. 3–6, Sun. 2–6.*

❷ **Museo Penitenciario Antonio Ballvé** (Antonio Ballvé Penitentiary Museum). Exhibiting artifacts from early-20th-century prison life, this modest museum, once a women's hospice, includes a genuine striped uniform and jail cell. Behind its large courtyard stands **Nuestra Señora del Carmen** chapel, named after the patron saint of the federal penitentiary service. The chapel dates from the Jesuit period. ⊠ *Humberto Primero 378, San Telmo* ☎ *11/4362–0099* ⌨ *1 peso* ⊗ *Wed.–Fri. 2–6, Sun. noon–7.*

❺ **Parque Lezama** (Lezama Park). Enormous magnolia, palm, cedar, and elm trees shade the sloping hillside and winding paths of this park, where families and couples gather. Immortalized by Argentine writer Ernesto Sabato in his novel *Sobre Heroes y Tumbas* (*Of Heroes and Tombs*), the park is steeped in history and is said to be the site on which the city was first founded by Pedro de Mendoza. In the 1700s the Company of Guinea operated its slave trade here. Entrepreneur Gregorio Lezama eventually purchased the large tract of land in 1858, forging his expansive estate. Exotic flora, bronze statues of Greek heroes, enormous urns, and an imposing fountain shipped from Paris decorate the land. Lezama's widow donated the property to the city, enabling the ⇨ **Museo Histórico Nacional** to be housed here. The weekend artisan fair attracts large crowds. ⊠ *Brasíl and Paseo Colón, San Telmo* ⌨ *Free* ⊗ *Daily dawn–dusk.*

❸ **Parroquia de San Pedro González Telmo** (San Pedro González Telmo Parish Church). Abandoned halfway through its construction by the Jesuits in 1767, when the order was expelled from Argentina, this church was finally completed in 1858. The cloisters and domed chapel, designed by Father Andrés Blanqui in 1738, are the only remnants of the original structure. ⊠ *Humberto Primero 340, San Telmo* ☎ *11/4361–1168* ⌨ *Free* ⊗ *Weekdays 10–noon, Sat. 6–8:30, Sun. 9–12:30.*

❹ **Pasaje de la Defensa** (Defense Alley). The long, internal, Roman-style courtyards of this colonial building, known as a *casa chorizo* (sausage home) because of its narrowness, give the structure the feel of a passageway. Centuries ago this was a home for people with hearing impairments. It eventually became a conventillo but is now a picturesque spot for antiques and curio shopping. ⊠ *Calle Defensa 1179, San Telmo* ۞ *Shops daily 10–6.*

⑩ Pasaje Giuffra (Giuffra Alley). A glimpse down this short alley gives you a sense of what the city looked like two centuries ago. ⊠ *Off Calle Defensa, San Telmo.*

⑬ Pasaje San Lorenzo (San Lorenzo Alley). A typical colonial-era alleyway, Pasaje San Lorenzo still retains the charm of its past. At No. 380 stand the ruins of the thinnest building—about 8 feet wide—in the city; it once belonged to a freed slave. ⊠ *Off Calle Balcarce, San Telmo.*

★ ▶ **❶ Plaza Dorrego** (Dorrego Plaza). Stately old trees shade outdoor tables at this square, the second oldest in the city and a peaceful haven on weekdays. On Sunday from 10 to 5 the plaza comes alive with the bustling **Feria de San Pedro Telmo** (San Pedro Telmo Fair), with its street vendors, performers, and tango dancers. Here you'll find tango memorabilia, leather goods, antique silver, brass, jewelry, crystal, and a wide variety of Argentine and European turn-of-the-20th-century curios. The architecture surrounding the plaza provides an overview of the influences—Spanish colonial, French classical, and ornate Italian masonry—that shaped the city in the 19th and 20th centuries. ⊠ *San Telmo.*

⑪ Viejo Almacén (Old General Store). This popular spot for tango is a fine example of colonial architecture. Built in 1798 as a general store, it also served as the British Hospital in the 1840s, and then as a customhouse. Tango artist Edmundo Rivero purchased the building in 1969 and turned it into a hot spot for tango. It's only open for dinner and shows. ⊠ *Av. Independencia 1064, at Calle Balcarce, San Telmo* ☎ *11/4307–6689 or 11/4300–3388* ⊕ *www.viejo-almacen.com.ar.*

La Boca

The vibrant working-class neighborhood of La Boca, just south of San Telmo, served as the first port of Buenos Aires, on the now polluted waters of the Riachuelo River. The imposing Avellaneda Bridge towers over the sunken, decaying ships; humble corrugated-metal dwellings; and brightly painted conventillos (the use of bright colors originated from the custom of using paint left over from the boatyards). Waves of immigrants passed through this area; the most significant and lasting group were Italian immigrants from Genoa, who arrived between 1880 and 1930. Cafés, pubs, and general stores that once catered to passing sailors now dot the renovated port. Note that the subte does not go to La Boca, and the surrounding neighborhoods can be a bit rough, so your safest and easiest option is to take a taxi.

a good walk

The highlight of La Boca is the **Calle Museo Caminito** ⑭ ▶, an open-air art market and museum on a pedestrians-only street off Avenida Pedro de Mendoza. Once you reach the end of Caminito, turn right on Calle Garibaldi. Along the railway, two blocks up, you'll find the **Estadio Boca Juniors** ⑮, home to one of Argentina's most popular soccer teams. Make a right onto Calle Brandsen and another onto Calle del Valle Iberlucea; this will lead you back to Caminito. To your left, on La Vuelta de Rocha, is the **Museo de Bellas Artes de La Boca de Artistas Argentinos** ⑯, a noteworthy neighborhood museum; to your right, the **Fundación Proa** ⑰ houses modern art and design.

TIMING & PRECAUTIONS
A couple of hours should give you enough time to explore La Boca. Visit the area during the weekend daylight hours; although the nightlife here is singular, it's best not to wander about after dark. Stay in the area of the Caminito, which is patrolled by local police, and avoid straying into surrounding areas.

WHAT TO SEE

Fodor'sChoice
★

Calle Museo Caminito (Little Path Museum Street). Since 1959, the pedestrian-only Caminito has been an open-air art museum and market, flanked by colorful, haphazardly constructed dwellings. The two-block walk along the street takes you past local artists, many of whom create their work on-site against a backdrop of tango music and dancers. You may find the perfect souvenir here. ⊠ *Av. Pedro de Mendoza (La Vuelta de Rocha promenade), La Boca* ☞ *Free* ⊙ *Daily 10–6.*

⑮ **Estadio Boca Juniors** (Boca Juniors Stadium). The Boca Juniors, one of Argentina's most popular soccer teams, are the proud owners of this distinctive stadium, with vibrant murals by artists Pérez Celis and Romulo Macció. Should you chance a game, be prepared for throngs, pandemonium, and street revelry—and never wear red and white, the colors of the rival River Plate team. The bordering street shops sell Boca paraphernalia. ⊠ *Brandsen 805, corner of Calle del Valle Iberlucea, La Boca* ☎ *11/4309–4700* ⊕ *www.bocasistemas.com.ar.*

⑰ **Fundación Proa** (Prow Foundation). This thoroughly modern art museum is a refreshing addition to the traditional neighborhood—the building fuses classic Italianate architecture with modern elements to represent the prow of a ship. Choice international exhibits, concerts, and events take place year-round. After you're done looking at the artwork, you can watch the sun set over the river from the terrace. There's also a reading room. ⊠ *Av. Pedro de Mendoza 1929, La Boca* ☎ *11/4303–0909* ⊕ *www.proa.org* ☞ *3 pesos* ⊙ *Tues.–Sun. 11–7.*

⑯ **Museo de Bellas Artes de La Boca de Artistas Argentinos** (La Boca Fine Arts Museum of Argentine Artists). Artist and philanthropist Benito Quinquela Martín donated this building to the state to create a cultural center in 1933. Then he personally set out to fill it from top to bottom with an extensive collection of works by Argentine artists. You'll also find some 800 works by Martín, who was known for his vibrant depictions of the port area. The view from the terrace alone makes the museum worth a visit. ⊠ *Av. Pedro de Mendoza 1835, La Boca* ☎ *11/4301–1080* ☞ *1 peso* ⊙ *Tues.–Fri. 9–6:30, weekends 10–6.*

Plaza de Mayo

Many of the country's most significant historical events transpired around the axis of Plaza de Mayo (May Plaza), though outsiders perhaps best know the square from the balcony scene in the 1996 film *Evita*. Named for the May Revolution of 1810, Plaza de Mayo has witnessed both sociopolitical upheaval and national triumphs and continues to be an emblem of the nation. Its attractions are principally architectural. Government workers and businesspeople crowd the area on weekdays; on weekends it becomes a haven for homing pigeons and migrating swallows, as well as the children who delight in feeding them.

All subway lines lead to **Plaza de Mayo** ☝. The architecturally eclectic Casa de Gobierno, better known as the **Casa Rosada**⑲ , stands at the eastern end of the square, with its back to the river. Two examples of stately neoclassical architecture sit along the northern side of the plaza: the **Banco de la Nación Argentina**⑳ and the **Catedral Metropolitana**㉑ . Directly opposite the Casa Rosada, on the western side of the plaza, the historic town council is housed in the colonial **Cabildo**㉒ . At this point you have two options. Walk west along Avenida de Mayo to admire the architectural wonders of yesteryear—lots of French-inspired domes and towers with Iberian accents—and to stop in at one of the numerous sidewalk cafés. The avenue was built to connect the Casa Rosada to the legislative **Palacio del Congreso**㉓ . Alternatively, you can walk from Plaza de Mayo southwest along Avenida Julio A. Roca (also known as Diagonal Sur) to the Jesuit-constructed cluster of buildings known as **La Manzana de las Luces**㉔ , including catacomblike tunnels and the **Parroquia de San Ignacio de Loyola**㉕ . Walk east on Calle Alsina to the **Museo de la Ciudad**㉖ , exhibiting the city's historic artifacts. Continue east on Calle Alsina; across Calle Defensa are the colonial **Basílica y Convento de San Francisco**㉗ and the smaller San Roque Chapel, to its left. Another of the city's oldest churches, **Convento Santo Domingo**㉘ , is two blocks south on Calle Defensa.

TIMING & PRECAUTIONS

This walk can take the better part of the day if you thoroughly explore each sight. Taxis are best hailed far from financial institutions, as robbers, assuming tourists have extracted money from bank machines, have been known to pose as taxi drivers to search for potential victims in these areas. On weekends this area, aside from the square, is deserted, so take precautions.

WHAT TO SEE

㉕ **Banco de la Nación Argentina** (National Bank of Argentina). The state bank's imposing neoclassic building was designed in 1940 by Alejandro Bustillo, architect of numerous government buildings in the 1930s and 1940s. Its vaulted ceiling is the world's third largest, after those of St. Peter's in Rome and the U.S. Capitol. You can visit its **Museo Numismática** (Coin Museum) at Bartolome Mitre 326. ⊠ *At Reconquista and Rivadavía, Plaza de Mayo* ☎ *11/4347–6277* 🎟 *Free* ⊙ *Weekdays 10–3.*

㉗ **Basílica y Convento de San Francisco** (Convent and Basilica of St. Francis). A 1911 Bavarian baroque facade now fronts this structure, which was originally built in 1754 in a neo–Italian Renaissance style. Its interior was lavishly refurbished after being vandalized in 1955, during the turmoil surrounding the siege of Perón's government. The basilica houses the second-largest tapestry in the world, depicting the Glorification of St. Francis, and a 20,000-volume archive—one of the city's oldest and most treasured, though not always open to the casual bibliophile. ⊠ *Defensa and Alsina, Plaza de Mayo* ☎ *11/4331–0625* 🎟 *Free* ⊙ *Weekdays 8 AM–7 PM, Sat. 6:30 PM–8 PM, Sun. 9:30 AM–11 AM and 5:30 PM–7 PM.*

㉒ Cabildo (Town Hall). The epicenter of the May Revolution of 1810, where patriotic citizens gathered to vote against Spanish rule, the hall is one of Argentina's national shrines. The original building dates from 1765 but has undergone successive renovations, mostly to its detriment. Inside, a small museum exhibits artifacts pertaining to the events of the May Revolution as well as a jail cell. Thursdays and Fridays from 11 to 6, an artisan fair takes place on the **Patio del Cabildo.** You can participate in glassblowing and other crafts; musical performances are held from 1 to 3. ⊠ *Bolívar 65, Plaza de Mayo* ☎ *11/4334–1782* ⌨ *1 peso* ☉ *Tues.–Fri. 11:30–6, Sun. 1–6; tours at 3 and 5.*

⑲ Casa Rosada (Pink House). The Casa de Gobierno (Government House), dubbed the Casa Rosada by President Domingo Fausto Sarmiento in 1873 for its pink color, houses the executive branch of the government. The building was originally constructed in the late 19th century over the foundations of an earlier customhouse and fortress. Swedish, Italian, and French architects have since modified the structure, which accounts for the odd mix of styles. The balcony facing Plaza de Mayo has served as a presidential podium for addressing crowds. Evita rallied the *descamisados* (shirtless working class), the Pope blessed the crowd during a visit in 1998, and Madonna sang her filmed rendition of "Don't Cry for Me Argentina" from this lofty stage. Check for a small banner hoisted alongside the nation's flag, indicating "the president is in." Behind the structure, you can find the brick-wall remains of the 1845 **Taylor Customs House,** discovered after being buried for almost a century. Enter Casa Rosada through the basement level of the **Museo de la Casa Rosada,** the only area open to the public, which exhibits presidential memorabilia along with objects from the original customhouse and fortress. Call ahead to arrange an English-language tour. ⊠ *Hipólito Yrigoyen 219, Plaza de Mayo* ☎ *11/4344–3802 or 11/4344–3600* ⌨ *Free* ☉ *Museum weekdays 10–6, Sun. 2–6; tours at 11 and 4.*

㉑ Catedral Metropolitana (Metropolitan Cathedral). Keep an eye out for eclectic details on the cathedral—from the neoclassic facade and neo-Renaissance vessels to the 12 Corinthian columns representing the apostles. The first building on this site was a 16th-century adobe ranch house; the current structure dates to 1827. The embalmed remains of General José de San Martín, known as the Argentine Liberator for his role in the War of Independence, rest here in a marble mausoleum carved by the French sculptor Carrière Belleuse. Soldiers of the Grenadier Regiment, an elite troop created and trained by San Martín in 1811, permanently guard the tomb. Group tours in English are available, but you need to call ahead. ⊠ *At Rivadavia and San Martín, Plaza de Mayo* ☎ *11/4331–2845* ⌨ *Free* ☉ *Weekdays 8–7, weekends 9–7:30; guided tours in Spanish weekdays at 11:30 and 4 and weekends at 4.*

㉘ Convento Santo Domingo (St. Dominick Convent). Here, at this historic convent from the 1750s, Spanish troops thwarted British attempts to invade the then-Spanish colony in 1807. Bullet holes on the left-hand bell tower and captured British flags testify to the battle. General Manuel Belgrano, a hero from the War of Independence, lies buried in the courtyard's mausoleum. ⊠ *Defensa 422, Plaza de Mayo* ☎ *11/4331–1668*

🍴 *Free* 🕐 *Weekdays 10–7, Sat. 9–noon and 2:30–6:30, Sun. 10:30–12:30 and 2:30–6:30.*

㉔ La Manzana de las Luces (Block of Bright Lights). Constructed by the Jesuits in the early 1800s, prior to their expulsion, La Manzana de las Luces was an enclave meant for higher learning. This was the former colonial administrative headquarters for the Jesuits' vast land holdings in northeastern Argentina and Paraguay. In 1780 the city's first School of Medicine was established here, and this eventually became home to the University of Buenos Aires early in the 19th century. Among the historic buildings still standing are the ➪ **Parroquia de San Ignacio de Loyola** and the neoclassic Colegio Nacional, traditionally the top-notch public school for society's future leaders. You can tour parts of the historic tunnels, still undergoing archaeological excavation, which linked the area to the Cabildo and the port. The original purpose of these tunnels is a source of speculation—were they used for defense or smuggling? ✉ *Perú 272, Plaza de Mayo* 🕿 *11/4342–6973* 🍴 *3 pesos guided tours; free Tues. and Fri.* 🕐 *Guided tours weekdays at 3; weekends at 3, 4:30, and 6.*

㉖ Museo de la Ciudad (City Museum). This museum houses temporary exhibits both whimsical and probing on aspects of domestic and public life in Buenos Aires in times past. The **Farmacia La Estrella** (Star Pharmacy) is a quaint survivor from the 19th century. ✉ *Calle Alsina 412, Plaza de Mayo* 🕿 *11/4331–9855 or 11/4343–2123* 🍴 *1 peso* 🕐 *Weekdays 11–7, Sun. 3–7.*

㉓ Palacio del Congreso (Palace of the Congress). The facade of the congressional building, constructed in 1906, resembles that of the U.S. Congress—except for the trumpet-wielding angels of revelation. The monumental structure stands on the west end of the expansive **Plaza del Congreso**. This spot marks Km 0 for routes leading out of the city. ✉ *Plaza del Congreso, Plaza de Mayo* 🕿 *11/4959–3000* 🍴 *Free* 🕐 *Guided tours in English Mon., Tues., and Fri. at 4; in Spanish at 11 and 5.*

㉕ Parroquia de San Ignacio de Loyola (St. Ignatius of Loyola Parish Church). Dating from 1713, this church is the only one from that era to have a baroque facade. It's part of ➪ **La Manzana de las Luces.** ✉ *Bolívar 225, Plaza de Mayo* 🕿 *11/4331–2458* 🍴 *Free* 🕐 *Daily 9–2 and 5–8:30.*

★ 🏳 **⑱ Plaza de Mayo** (May Square). Dating to 1580, this central square has been the stage for many important events throughout the nation's history, including the uprising against Spain on May 25, 1810—hence its name. The central obelisk, **Pirámide de Mayo,** was erected in 1811 on the anniversary of the Revolution of May; the crowning small bronze statue of liberty was added later. The bronze equestrian statue of General Manuel Belgrano, designer of Argentina's flag, dates from 1873 and stands at the east end of the plaza. The plaza remains the traditional site for ceremonies as well as mass protests, most recently the bloody clashes in December 2001 that led to the resignation of then-President Fernando de la Rua. It's here that the Madres de la Plaza de Mayo (Mothers of May Square) have marched silently for more than two decades, every Thursday at 3:30; they demand justice for *los desaparecidos,* the young people who "disappeared" during the military government's reign from 1976 to 1983. Here, too, you can witness the changing of the Grenadier Regiment guards; it takes place weekdays every two hours from 9 until 7, Saturday at 9 and 11, and Sunday at 9, 11, and 1. ⊠ *Plaza de Mayo.*

El Centro

El Centro is the Porteño's mecca; if you have not visited its urban flux, you have not visited Buenos Aires. Illuminated by flashing billboards, the Obelisk, at the intersection of bustling Avenida Corrientes and Avenida 9 de Julio, rises above this commercial and social hub. If all the activity is too much for you, don't despair: just steps away from the bustling pedestrian Calles Florida and Lavalle are serene, shaded plazas with fountains, monuments, and statues.

a good walk

El Centro can be reached by subte; lines run beneath the main avenues and are worth taking to admire the tiled murals within the stations. Begin your walk at the **Plaza de la Fuerza Aérea Argentina** ㉙ ►, across from the Retiro train station. Cross Avenida Libertador to admire the **Plaza San Martín** ㉚, with its statues and fountains. Walking the square's perimeter, you'll see the surrounding grandiose architecture along the eastern end. The neorationalist **Edificio Kavanagh** ㉛ stands in stark contrast to the opulent **Marriott Plaza Hotel** ㉜. Crowning the plaza's southern tip is the **Círculo Militar** ㉝. At Calle Maipú 994, near the intersection with Calle Marcelo T. de Alvear, Jorge Luis Borges wrote some of his short stories and poems in the sixth-floor corner apartment. Nearby, on Calle Arenales, you'll find the Ministry of Foreign Affairs, housed in the **Palacio San Martín** ㉞. Walk back to Avenida Santa Fe and follow it east around the plaza; the basement-level **Galería Ruth Benzacar** ㉟ stands at the entrance to Calle Florida. Take this pedestrian street, crowded with shops and people, south to the magnificent **Galerías Pacífico** ㊱. Next door, on the corner of Calle Florida and Avenida Córdoba, stop and admire the magnificent facade of the 1914 Versailles-inspired Centro Naval; its intricate iron door was fashioned from the metal and bronze of cannons fired during the War of Independence. Continue south along Calle Florida until you reach bustling Avenida Corrientes, the traditional theater district. Head west on Corrientes, toward Avenida 9 de Julio, to reach the **Obelisco** ㊲. Walk two blocks toward the river along Avenida 9 de Julio, the widest avenue in the world, to the **Teatro Colón** ㊳ for a backstage tour.

TIMING & PRECAUTIONS

Set aside a full day to explore El Centro. It's easy to navigate the area on foot. Avenida Corrientes is jammed during the evening with restaurant- and theatergoers. Weekends, historic areas are relatively deserted, and some stores and restaurants have limited hours. Calle Lavalle, although a shopping and commerce center, is also peppered with adult entertainment and a mega–bingo hall, so take proper precautions at night.

WHAT TO SEE

㉝ **Círculo Militar** (Military Circle). A monument to the nobler historic pursuits of the Argentine armed forces, the Officers' Club was built in 1902 by French architect Louis Sortais in the heavily ornate French style of the period. The **Museo Nacional de Armas** (National Arms Museum), in the basement, is packed with military memorabilia. You can only visit inside the Círculo Militar with a guided tour. ⊠ *Av. Santa Fe 750, El Centro* ☎ *11/4311–1071* 💷 *3.50 pesos* ⊙ *Guided tours Mar.–Dec., Wed. and Thurs. at 3.*

㉛ Edificio Kavanagh (Kavanagh Building). The monolithic 1930s-era Kavanagh apartment building, inaugurated in the same year as Avenida 9 de Julio, was constructed in an imposing neorationalist style, with art deco touches. For a time this was the tallest high-rise in South America, with 31 floors. ⊠ *Florida 1065, El Centro.*

㉟ Galería Ruth Benzacar (Ruth Benzacar Gallery). Monthly exhibits showcase the works of modern Argentine artists. Ask to see the vast collection of paintings in the basement. ⊠ *Florida 1000, El Centro* ☎ *11/4313–8480* 💷 *Free* ⊙ *Weekdays 11:30–8, Sat. 10:30–1:30.*

㊱ Galerías Pacífico (Pacific Gallery). Milan's Galleria Vittorio Emanuele served as the architectural model for this former headquarters of the Buenos Aires–Pacific Railway, designed during Buenos Aires's turn-of-the-20th-century golden age. It's now an upscale shopping mall and cultural center. Noteworthy features include the facade, skylighted dome, and murals. The **Centro Cultural Borges** (⊕ www.ccborges.org.ar), a showcase for young talent, is on the mezzanine level. ⊠ *Florida 753, El Centro* ☎ *11/5555–5100.*

㉜ Marriott Plaza Hotel. In 1908 local financier Ernesto Tornquist commissioned German architect Alfred Zucker to build the city's first luxury hotel. The Plaza, like its namesake in New York City, continues a tradition of old-world elegance and is famous for the illustrious guests who have stayed here. ⊠ *Calle Florida at Plaza San Martín, El Centro.*

㊲ Obelisco (Obelisk). Towering over the city at 221½ feet, the Obelisk is one of Buenos Aires's most prominent landmarks, built in 1936 on the site where the nation's flag was first raised. Open-air concerts are frequently staged in the area surrounding the Obelisk, and during elections or major soccer matches, crowds of Porteños converge here, rejoicing in the outcome of the day's events. ⊠ *Av. 9 de Julio and Corrientes, El Centro.*

㉞ Palacio San Martín (San Martín Palace). Originally the home of the Anchorena family, the palace has housed the Ministry of Foreign Affairs since 1936. The ornate building, designed in 1909 by Alejandro Cristophersen in grandiose French neoclassical style, exemplifies the turn-of-the-20th-century opulence of Buenos Aires. ⊠ *Arenales 761, El Centro* ☎ *11/4819–7000 Ext. 7985* ⊙ *Guided tours in English and Spanish Fri. at 3, 4, and 5.*

▶ **㉙ Plaza de la Fuerza Aérea Argentina** (Argentine Air Force Square). England donated the central brick clock tower in this square, **Torre Monumental,** on the occasion of the 1910 centennial celebration of the May Revolution. Originally known as Plaza Británica (British Square), the plaza was defiantly renamed by the city in 1982 as a result of the Falkland Islands War. ⊠ *Av. Libertador and Calle San Martín, El Centro.*

㉚ Plaza San Martín (San Martín Square). Once a muddy riverbank suburb at the northern end of the city, this plaza gradually evolved, taking its place as the second most important in the city. At one time populated by marginal members of colonial society, the area was transformed in the late 1800s when the aristocratic families of San Telmo fled here to escape yellow fever. Today it's one of the most sumptuous neighborhoods in Buenos Aires. French landscape architect Charles Thays designed the square in the 1800s, juxtaposing local and exotic trees. The imposing bronze equestrian monument to General José de San Martín, designed in 1862 by French artist Louis Daumas, dominates the park, as does the Monumento a los Caídos en las Malvinas. Guarded by a Grenadier, the 25 black marble slabs of the monument are engraved with the names of those who died in the 1982 Falkland Islands War. ⊠ *Av. Libertador and Calle Florida, El Centro.*

★ ㊳ **Teatro Colón** (Colón Theater). Its magnitude, magnificent acoustics, and opulence (grander than Milan's La Scala) position the Colón among the top five opera houses worldwide. Inaugurated in 1908 with Verdi's *Aida,* it has hosted the likes of Maria Callas, Richard Strauss, Arturo Toscanini, Igor Stravinsky, Enrico Caruso, and Luciano Pavarotti. The Italianate building with French interiors is the result of successive modifications by various architects. The seven-tier theater has a grand central chandelier, with 700 lights to illuminate the 2,490 mere mortals in the audience. Many seats are reserved for season-ticket holders, so tickets are hard to come by for choice performances. However, don't forego the opportunity to sit in the lofty upper-tier *paraíso,* which is more economical and an experience in itself (side entrance on Calle Tucuman; no reservation required). Check availability for guided tours in Spanish of the theater, museum, workshops, and rehearsal halls. The season runs from March to December. ⊠ *Toscanini 1180, El Centro* ☎ *11/4378–7100 tickets, 11/4378–7133 tours* ⊕ *www.teatrocolon.org.ar* 🏷 *10 pesos* ☉ *Guided tours Mon.–Sat. hourly 10–5, Sun. 11–3.*

La Recoleta

Open green spaces border this elegant residential and shopping district, replete with boutiques, cafés, handsome old apartment buildings, mansions, plazas, and cultural centers. Named for the barefoot Franciscan Recoleto friars who settled here in the early 1700s, the neighborhood later became home to brothels and seedier activities, including the then-ruffian's tango. The outbreak of yellow fever in 1871 in the south of the city caused the elite to swarm to this area, laying the foundations for a concentration of intellectual and cultural activity.

a good walk

Though a number of buses run through here, a taxi ride is your best bet. No subway route directly serves La Recoleta; the closest station is eight blocks away at Estación Pueyrredón.

Begin at **Plazoleta Carlos Pellegrini**㊴ ☛ on Avenida Alvear. Flanking the square are the imposing embassies of France and Brazil and the Jockey Club. Head west on the elegant Avenida Alvear, lined with French-style architecture and haute couture boutiques, to reach the exquisite **Alvear Palace Hotel**㊵. Continue two blocks along Alvear; the staired sidewalk on the left, called R. M. Ortiz, leads past a gargantuan rubber tree and a string of Parisian-style cafés, pubs, and eateries. Continue in the same direction until you encounter the final resting ground for some of Argentina's most illustrious citizens at the **Cementerio de La Recoleta** ㊶. Next door are the **Basílica de Nuestra Señora del Pilar** ㊷ and the cultural playground, **Centro Cultural La Recoleta** ㊸. Finally, at the end of the *veredita* (little sidewalk), you'll find the Paseo del Pilar lined with places to eat and the Buenos Aires Design Center. The grassy Plaza Intendente Alvear surrounds the area and on weekends hosts the city's largest artisan fair. At the foot of the slope, across Alvear, is the ocher-color **Palais de Glace–Salas Nacionales de Cultura** ㊹. From here walk west along Avenida del Libertador to reach the **Museo Nacional de Bellas Artes** ㊺, the city's fine-arts museum. The enigmatic public library **Biblioteca Nacional** ㊻ towers over the Plaza Ruben Darío. A few blocks farther west, bordering the neighborhood of Palermo, is the opulent **Museo Nacional de Arte Decorativo** ㊼, a decorative arts museum.

TIMING &
PRECAUTIONS
You can explore La Recoleta in half a day, though you could easily spend a full morning or afternoon in the cemetery or cultural centers alone. This area is relatively safe day and night, but always stay aware of your surroundings.

WHAT TO SEE

㊵ **Alvear Palace Hotel.** Old-world elegance characterizes this hotel, opened in 1932. The Porteño elite gather in the lobby piano bar, which is ideal for high tea or cocktails. Visiting presidents, dignitaries, and celebrities often stay here when they are in town. ✉ *Av. Alvear 1891, La Recoleta* ☎ *11/4808–2100* ⊕ *www.alvearpalace.com.*

㊷ **Basílica de Nuestra Señora del Pilar** (Basilica of Our Lady of Pilar). In 1732 the Franciscan Recoleto friars built this colonial-style basilica and adjoining cloister. The church is considered a national treasure for its six German baroque–style altars, the central one overlaid with Peruvian engraved silver, and relics sent by Spain's King Carlos III. Buenos Aires's elite families take pride in celebrating weddings and other religious events here. ✉ *Junín 1904, La Recoleta* ☎ *11/4803–6793* ▭ *Free* ☉ *Daily 8 AM–9 PM.*

㊻ **Biblioteca Nacional** (National Library). Conceived by its director, writer Jorge Luis Borges, and possibly stemming from the infinite labyrinth of books depicted in his novel *El Aleph,* this monolithic structure took three decades to complete. It opened in 1992 after much red tape and now towers over Plaza Ruben Darío. The work of Le Corbusier inspired the modernist structure, which was designed by Clorinda Testa. Check for scheduled cultural activities. You'll need to show an official document like a passport or driver's license to enter. ✉ *Agüero 2502, La Recoleta* ☎ *11/4808–6000* ⊕ *www.bibnal.edu.ar* ▭ *Free* ☉ *Weekdays 9 AM–8 PM, weekends noon–7.*

㊶ **Cementerio de La Recoleta** (La Recoleta Cemetery). The ominous gates, Doric-columned portico, and labyrinthine pathways of the oldest cemetery in Buenos Aires (1822) lend a sense of foreboding to this virtual city of the dead. The cemetery covers 13½ acres of prime property and has more than 6,400 elaborate vaulted tombs and majestic mausoleums, 70 of which have been declared historic monuments. The mausoleums resemble chapels, Greek temples, pyramids, and miniature mansions.

Fodor'sChoice
★

The cemetery is a veritable who's who of Argentine history: this is the final resting place for the nation's most illustrious figures. The administrative offices at the entrance provide a free map, and caretakers throughout the grounds can help you locate the more intriguing tombs, such as the embalmed remains of Eva Perón and her family; Napoléon Bonaparte's granddaughter; the brutal *caudillo* (dictator) Facundo Quiroga, buried standing, at his request; and prominent landowner Dorrego Ortiz Basualdo, in the most monumental sepulchre, complete with chandelier. ⊠ *Junín 1760, La Recoleta* 🕾 *11/4803–1594* ☉ *Daily 8–5:30; free guided tours in Spanish last Sun. of month at 2:45.*

❸ Centro Cultural La Recoleta (La Recoleta Cultural Center). The former cloisters and internal patios of the Franciscan monks have been converted into a dynamic cultural center with exhibits, performances, and workshops. Weekends the entire area teems with artisans and street performers in the city's largest arts-and-crafts market. ⊠ *Junín 1930, La Recoleta* 🕾 *11/4803–1041 or 11/4803–9744* ⊕ *www.centroculturalrecoleta.org* 🕾 *1 peso* ☉ *Tues.–Fri. 2–9, weekends 10–9.*

★ ❹ Museo Nacional de Arte Decorativo (National Museum of Decorative Art). This dignified, harmonious French neoclassic landmark houses a fascinating collection of period furnishings, silver, and objets d'art—but it's worth the price of admission just to enter this breathtaking structure. The museum also contains Asian art as well as the Zubov collection of miniatures from Imperial Russia. Stop in for tea or lunch at the elegant museum café, **Errázuriz.** ⊠ *Av. del Libertador 1902, La Recoleta* 🕾 *11/4801–8248* 🕾 *4 pesos* ☉ *Daily 2–7; free guided tours (in English) weekends at 4:30.*

❹ Museo Nacional de Bellas Artes (National Museum of Fine Arts). Some 11,000 works of art—from drawings and paintings to statues and tapestries—are displayed in a building that used to be the city's waterworks. The museum's exhibits of significant international and local masters range from medieval times to the postmodern era, and the collection of 19th- and 20th-century Argentine art is its crowning achievement. Check out Cándido López's first-hand renderings of soldier life during the War of the Triple Alliance. His work can also be found in the National History Museum. The temporary-exhibit pavilion showcases modern international and Argentine art and photography. You'll also find a gift shop, library, and cafeteria here. ⊠ *Av. del Libertador 1473, La Recoleta* 🕾 *11/4803–0802 tours* ⊕ *www.mnba.org.ar* 🕾 *Free* ☉ *Tues.–Fri. 12:30–7:30, weekends 9:30–7:30.*

❹ Palais de Glace–Salas Nacionales de Cultura (Ice Palace–National Cultural Exhibition Halls). Always worth checking out are the changing exhibits, ranging from fine art to ponchos to national foods to African art, at this exhibition hall, formerly an ice-skating rink. The banner outside will tell you what's going on. ⊠ *Posadas 1725, La Recoleta* 🕾 *11/4805–4354* 🕾 *Free* ☉ *Tues.–Sun. 2–8.*

▶ ❸ Plazoleta Carlos Pellegrini (Carlos Pellegrini Square). Stately mansions, the highbrow Jockey Club, private apartments, and the embassies of France and Brazil frame this square, now primarily used for parking.

The Brazilian Embassy has a stately neoclassic facade; the early-20th-century building of the French Embassy was of such importance that the city decided to loop the continuation of Avenida 9 de Julio around the back of it rather than raze the structure. ⊠ *La Recoleta.*

Palermo

With nearly 350 acres of parks, wooded areas, and lakes, Palermo provides a peaceful escape from the rush of downtown. Families flock here on weekends to picnic, suntan, bicycle, in-line skate, and jog. The polo field and hippodrome make this the city's nerve center for equestrian activities. One of the largest barrios, Palermo is also one of the most dynamic, with several distinct subneighborhoods: Palermo Viejo has classic Spanish-style architecture; Las Cañitas, Palermo Hollywood, and SoHo have trendy shopping, nightlife, and dining. Some of the most exclusive and expensive real estate in Buenos Aires can be found here, in opulent Palermo Chico, an elegant residential area, and in the prime properties lining the Avenida del Libertador and overlooking the parks.

a good walk

The Estación Plaza Italia, on subte Line D, takes you to the entrance of the zoo and botanical gardens in Palermo. Some of the city's biggest parks are found in this neighborhood around the **Plaza Italia,** at the intersection of Avenidas Sarmiento, Santa Fe, and Las Heras: the **Jardín Botánico Carlos Thais,** the **Jardín Zoológico,** and the historic **Sociedad Rural Argentina,** the city's most extensive fairgrounds and exhibition center. **Parque Tres de Febrero** is at the far end of the zoo, along Avenida Sarmiento, past the U.S. Consulate on the left and across Avenida del Libertador. Here you will find the **Paseo del Rosedal,** abloom with more than 1,000 species of roses in season. Head southeast on Avenida del Libertador to the **Jardín Japonés,** a tranquil Japanese garden, or continue north along Sarmiento to the **Planetario Galileo Galilei,** for astronomy buffs. After staring at the stars, head southeast on Avenida Presidente Figueroa Alcorta to reach the superb **Museo MALBA,** for an impressive display of Latin American artwork.

TIMING

An even-pace ramble through Palermo should take no more than two hours, though you could easily spend an entire afternoon at the zoo, Japanese Garden, and the Botanical Garden. If you're up for shopping, visit the Alto Palermo shopping center (at the Bulnes stop on Line D) or the entire length of shops and boutiques along Avenida Santa Fe.

WHAT TO SEE

Jardín Botánico Carlos Thais (Charles Thays Botanical Garden). With 20 acres of gardens and 8,000 varieties of exotic and local flora, the Botanical Garden is a welcome, unexpected oasis in the city. Different sections of the park re-create the environments of Asia, Africa, Oceania, Europe, and the Americas. Among the garden's treasures is the Chinese "tree of gold," purportedly the only one of its kind. Winding paths lead you to hidden statues, a brook, and past the resident cats and dragonflies. The central area contains a greenhouse and the exposed-brick botanical school and library. ⊠ *Av. Santa Fe 3951, Palermo* ☎ *11/4832–1552* ☜ *Free* ☉ *Daily 8–6.*

★ **Jardín Japonés** (Japanese Garden). Arched wooden bridges and walkways traverse still waters in this Japanese oasis. A variety of shrubs and flowers frame the ponds, which brim with golden carp. The traditional teahouse, where you can enjoy adzuki-bean sweets and tea, overlooks the Zen garden. ⊠ *Avs. Casares and Adolfo Berro, Palermo* ☎ *11/ 4804–4922* ⊕ *www.jardinjapones.com.ar* ⊠ *3 pesos* ☉ *Daily 10–6.*

☺ **Jardín Zoológico** (Zoological Garden). You enter through the quasi-Roman triumphal arch into this architecturally eclectic, 45-acre city zoo dating from 1874. The pens, mews, statuary, and fountains themselves are well worth the visit. Among the expected zoo community are a few surprises: a rare albino tiger; indigenous monkeys, known to perform lewd acts for their audiences; and llamas (watch out—they spit). Some smaller animals roam freely, and there are play areas for children, a petting farm, and a seal show. *Mateos* (traditional, decorated horse-drawn carriages) stand poised at the entrance to whisk you around the greens. ⊠ *Avs. General Las Heras and Sarmiento, Palermo* ☎ *11/4806–7412* ⊠ *8 pesos* ☉ *Tues.–Sun. 10–5.*

★ **Museo MALBA** (Museo de Arte de Latinoamericano de Buenos Aires). This fabulous museum has more than 220 works from the private collection of businessman and founder Eduardo Constantini. The sleek, modern structure is home to one of the largest collections of Latin American art in the world, including original works by Frida Kahlo, Fernando Botero, and a slew of Argentine artists. The museum also features seasonal exhibitions, lectures, movies, and live music. The adjoining café is a fashionable place to end your day with a cup of coffee and a piece of cake. ⊠ *Av. Presidente Figueroa Alcorta 3415, Palermo* ☎ *11/4808–6500* ⊕ *www.malba. org.ar* ⊠ *4 pesos, free on Wed.* ☉ *Thurs.–Mon. noon–8, Wed. noon–9.*

☺ **Parque Tres de Febrero** (February 3 Park). With 1,000 acres of woods, lakes, and trails, Parque Tres de Febrero is the city's playground. Here you can take part in organized tai chi and gym classes and impromptu soccer matches or jog, bike, in-line skate, or take a boat out on the lake. If you're looking for something less active, try the park's **Museo de Artes Plásticas Eduardo Sívori** (Eduardo Sívori Art Museum; ⊠ Av. Infanta Isabel 555, Palermo ☎ 11/4774–9452 ⊠ 1 peso), exhibiting 19th- and 20th-century Argentine art; it's open Tuesday–Friday noon–7 and weekends 10–7. Street vendors sell refreshments within the park, as do the many cafés lining the Paseo de la Infanta (running from Libertador toward Sarmiento in the park). ⊠ *Bounded by Avs. del Libertador, Sarmiento, Leopoldo Lugones, and Dorrego, Palermo.*

★ **Paseo del Rosedal** (Rose Garden). Approximately 15,000 rosebushes, representing more than 1,000 different species, bloom seasonally in this garden. A stroll along the clay paths takes you through the Jardín de los Poetas (Poets' Garden), dotted with statues of literary figures, and to the enchanting Patio Andaluz (Andalusian Patio), covered in vines and ideal for picture-taking. ⊠ *Avs. Infanta Isabel and Iraola, Palermo.*

☺ **Planetario Galileo Galilei** (Galileo Galilei Planetarium). The sci-fi exterior of this landmark holds more appeal than its flimsy content. This great orb positioned on a massive concrete tripod looks like something out of *Close Encounters of the Third Kind,* and it seems as though small green men in foil suits could descend from its central staircase at any moment. A highlight is the authentic asteroid at the entrance; the pond with swans, geese, and ducks is a favorite with children. ✉ *Avs. Sarmiento and Belisario Roldán, Palermo* ☎ *11/4771–6629* ⊕ *www.earg.gov.ar/ planetario* 🎫 *4 pesos* ⊙ *Weekdays 9–6, weekends 2–8.*

⚐ **Plaza Italia** (Italian Square). A monument to the Italian general Giuseppe Garibaldi towers over this square at the intersection of avenidas Santa Fe, Las Heras, and Sarmiento. Here you'll also see a fragment of a 2,000-year-old Roman column, donated by Italy to the city in 1955. A landmark in the area, the square is an ideal meeting spot. ✉ *Palermo.*

Ⓒ **Sociedad Rural Argentina** (Rural Society of Argentina). Exhibitions relating to agriculture and cattle raising are often held at the fairgrounds here. The biggest is the annual monthlong summer **Exposición Rural** (Rural Exposition), where you can see livestock such as cows and horses, gaucho shows, and expert horse performances. ✉ *Off Plaza Italia, Palermo* ☎ *11/4324–4700* ⊕ *www.ruralarg.org.ar.*

Belgrano

European-style parks and plazas, Paris-inspired boulevards, shopping strips, residential areas, a fashionable district of mansions and luxury high-rises, and cobblestone streets characterize historic Belgrano. It's also home to the expanding Barrio Chino (China Town).

a good walk

To reach Belgrano by subte, take Line D to Estación Juramento, the next-to-last stop. You can also take the Mitre Line commuter train from Retiro station to Belgrano station.

Head first to the **Museo de Arte Español Enrique Larreta,** on Calle Juramento, for a taste of Spanish colonial art. Across Juramento, on the west side of the plaza, is the **Museo Histórico Sarmiento,** which commemorates Argentina's independence from Spain. From here, walk across the romantic **Plaza Manuel Belgrano** to reach the **Parroquia de Nuestra Señora de la Inmaculada Concepción.** After visiting the church, head two blocks west along Calle Juramento, across busy Avenida Cabildo, to the **Mercado,** a traditional open-air food market.

TIMING & PRECAUTIONS   This walk can be done in two to three hours, though you may want to spend more time wandering around this beautiful barrio. If you want to see all the museums, it's best to visit in the afternoon, when they're all open. The atmospheric cafés are open 24 hours. Patrolled around the clock by private security and city police, Belgrano is relatively safe, though you should still watch your belongings.

WHAT TO SEE   **Mercado.** This open-air local market is a trove of cheeses, fruits, vegetables, sausages, and beef cuts, plus a few surprises. ✉ *Juramento and Ciudad de la Paz, Belgrano* ⊙ *Daily 5 PM–11 PM.*

★ **Museo de Arte Español Enrique Larreta** (Enrique Larreta Museum of Spanish Art). Once the beautiful home of a Spanish governor, the building now houses poet and novelist Enrique Larreta's vast collection of Spanish 13th- through 20th-century art and artifacts. ✉ *Juramento 2291, Belgrano* ☎ *11/4783–2640* 🎫 *1 peso* ⊙ *Mon., Wed.–Fri. 12:30–7:45, weekends 3–7:45.*

Museo Histórico Sarmiento (Sarmiento Museum of History). This 1873 Italianate building showcases historical documents and artifacts relating to the nation's founders. ⊠ *Cuba 2079, Belgrano* 📞 *11/4783-7555* 💵 *1 peso* ⊘ *Tues.–Fri. 2–6:45, Sun. 3–6:45; guided tours in Spanish Sun. at 4.*

Parroquia de Nuestra Señora de la Inmaculada Concepción (Our Lady of the Immaculate Conception Parish Church). Nicknamed *La Redonda* (The Round One), this beautiful church, modeled after Rome's Pantheon, has a relief replica of Da Vinci's *Last Supper.* ⊠ *Vuelta de Obligado 2042, Belgrano* 📞 *11/4783-8008* ⊘ *Daily 7 AM–9 PM.*

Plaza Manuel Belgrano (Manuel Belgrano Square). The square, named after General Belgrano, the War of Independence hero, is the site of a bustling artisan fair on weekends. ⊠ *Juramento and Av. Cuba, Belgrano.*

Where to Eat

Although international cuisine can be found throughout Buenos Aires, it's the traditional *parrilla*—a restaurant serving grilled meat—that Argentines (and most visitors) flock to. These restaurants vary from upscale eateries to local spots. The meal often starts off with *chorizo* (a large, spicy sausage), *morcilla* (blood sausage), and *chinchulines* (tripe), before moving on to the myriad cuts of beef that make Argentina famous. Don't pass up the rich *provoleta* (grilled provolone cheese sprinkled with olive oil and oregano) and garlic-soaked grilled red peppers as garnish.

Cafés are a big part of Buenos Aires culture: open long hours, they constantly brim with locals knocking back a quick *cafecito* (espresso) or taking their time over a *café con leche* (coffee with milk) served with *medialunas* (croissants) or *facturas* (small pastries). Many places have bilingual menus or someone on hand who is eager to practice his or her English.

El Centro

ARGENTINE
$$$
Fodor's Choice
★

✕ **Tomo Uno.** For the last 35 years the famed Concaro sisters have made Tomo Uno a household name with such dishes as spicy squid and quail egg salad or perfectly cooked lamb *en croute* (baked in a pastry shell) with wild mushrooms and garnished with crispy eggplant and spinach. For dessert, try the grapefruit in Riesling with pear ice cream or the chocolate tart that oozes warm, dark *ganache* (semisweet chocolate and whipped cream heated and stirred together). White linen–covered tables are set far apart, making quiet conversation easy, and the service is excellent. The restaurant, on the mezzanine of the Hotel Panamericano, has views over the Obelisco. ⊠ *Carlos Pellegrini 521, El Centro* 📞 *11/4326-6698* ⌖ *Reservations essential* 🖃 *AE, DC, MC, V* ⊘ *Closed Sun. No lunch Sat.* Ⓜ *Line B, Estación Carlos Pellegrini; Line D, Estación 9 de Julio.*

¢–$

✕ **El Palacio de la Papa Frita.** This old standby is popular for its hearty traditional meals—succulent steaks, homemade pastas, and fresh salads. The *papas soufflé* (inflated french fries) reign supreme; try them *a la provençal* (sprinkled with garlic and parsley) along with the classic *bife a medio caballo* (steak topped with a fried egg). ⊠ *Lavalle 735, El*

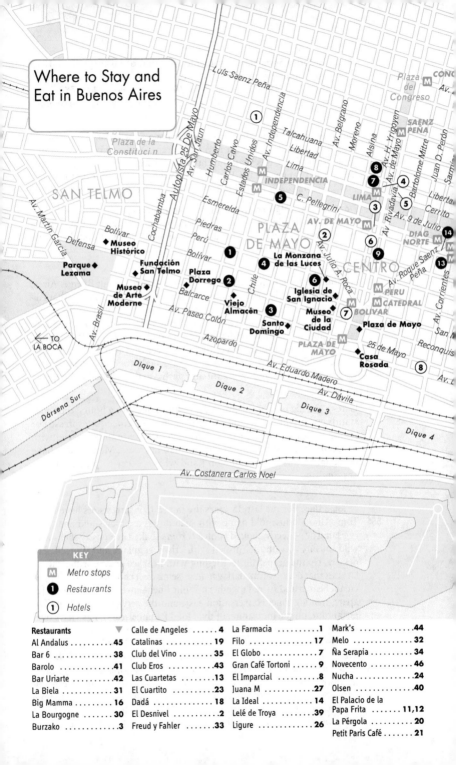

Where to Stay and Eat in Buenos Aires

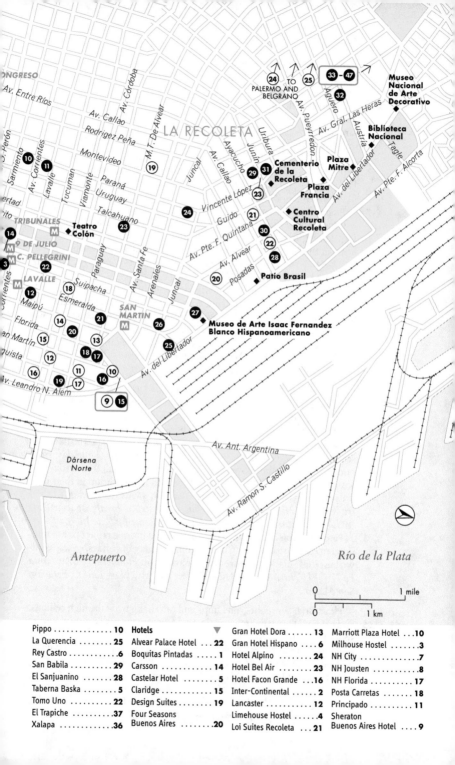

Centro ☎ *11/4393–5849* Ⓜ *Line C, Estación Lavalle* ✉ *Av. Corrientes 1612, El Centro* ☎ *11/4374–8063* Ⓜ *Line B, Estación Callao* 🖃 *AE, DC, MC, V.*

¢–$ ✕ **Juana M.** The minimalist chic decor of this basement restaurant is in stark contrast to what's on the menu: traditional down-to-earth *parilla* fare at prices that are hard to beat. Catch a glimpse of meats sizzling on the grill behind the salmon-colored bar—the only swath of color in the restaurant—then head to your table to devour your steak and *chorizo* (fat, spicy sausage). The staff is young and friendly. ✉ *Carlos Pellegrini 1535, La Recoleta* ☎ *11/4326–0462* ⊘ *No lunch Sat.* Ⓜ *Line C, Estación San Martín.*

¢–$ ✕ **Pippo.** Pippo is known for its simplicity and down-to-earth cooking. Try the *estofado* (beef stew), filled pastas, or *lomo* (sirloin) with fries. For dessert, flan is topped off with cream or dulce de leche. It's in the heart of the Corrientes theater district. ✉ *Paraná 356, El Centro* ☎ *11/4374–6365* Ⓜ *Line B, Estación Uruguay* ✉ *Av. Callao 1077, La Recoleta* ☎ *11/4812–4323* 🖃 *No credit cards.*

¢ ✕ **La Querencia.** Northern Argentinian fare is dished up fast-food style in a rustic setting. Choose from combos that include empanadas and tamales as well as rich local stews such as *locro* (hard corn cooked slowly with meat and vegetables). The *humitas* (ground corn wrapped in a corn husk) are excellent. You can eat in at basic wooden tables, or carry out. ✉ *Esmeralda 1392, El Centro* ☎ *11/4393–3202* Ⓜ *Line C, Estación San Martín* 🖃 *No credit cards* ⊘ *No lunch Sun.*

CAFÉS ✕ **La Ideal.** Part of the charm of this spacious 1918 confitería is its sense
¢–$ of nostalgia: a fleur-de-lis motif prevails, and the timeworn European furnishings and stained glass create an atmosphere of bygone days, which set the tone for scenes filmed here for the 1998 film *The Tango Lesson.* La Ideal is famous for its *palmeritas* (glazed cookies) and tea service. Tango lessons are offered Monday through Thursday from noon to 3, with a full-blown *milonga* (tango dance ball) Wednesday and Saturday from 3 to 8. The waitstaff seem to be caught up in their own dreams—service is listless. ✉ *Suipacha 384, at Av. Corrientes, El Centro* ☎ *11/4326–0521* 🖃 *No credit cards* ⊘ *No breakfast weekends* Ⓜ *Line C, Estación C. Pellegrini; Line D, Estación 9 de Julio.*

¢–$ ✕ **Petit Paris Café.** The crystal chandeliers and marble tabletops are reminiscent of a Parisian café. Choose from a variety of coffees, cakes, sandwiches, and salads, or more filling pastas and *milanesas.* ✉ *Av. Santa Fe 774, El Centro* ☎ *11/4312–5885* 🖃 *AE, MC, V* Ⓜ *Line C, Estación San Martín.*

CONTINENTAL ✕ **Plaza Grill.** Wrought-iron lamps and fans hang from the high ceilings,
$$–$$$$ and original Dutch delft porcelain tiles decorate the walls at this favorite spot of executives and politicians. The wine list is extensive, and the Continental menu includes excellent steak, salmon with basil and red wine, and pheasant with foie gras. ✉ *Marriott Plaza Hotel, Florida 1005, El Centro* ☎ *11/4590–8974* ⌚ *Reservations essential* 🖃 *AE, DC, MC, V* Ⓜ *Line C, Estación San Martín.*

$$ ✕ **La Pérgola.** On the third floor of the Sheraton Libertador hotel, this restaurant serves mouthwatering appetizers such as salmon bisque.

Among the flavorful entrées are pasta; grilled steak; and sole with shrimp, artichoke hearts, shallots, capers, and asparagus, served in a white wine sauce. ⊠ *Sheraton Libertador, Av. Córdoba 680, El Centro* ☏ *11/ 4322–8800 or 11/4322–6622* ⌂ *Reservations essential* ⋔ *Jacket and tie* ⊟ *AE, DC, MC, V* Ⓜ *Line C, Estación Lavalle.*

ECLECTIC ╳ **Dadá.** Eclectic Porteño '60s pop culture characterizes one of the city's
★ $ best-kept secrets, where murals inspired by Dalí, Miró, Lichtenstein, and Mondrian are splashed across the walls and smoky jazz fills the small, intimate space. Seasonal specials are chalked up behind the cluttered bar. The short but inventive menu showcases the best of local produce. ⊠ *San Martín 941, El Centro* ☏ *11/4314–4787* ⊟ *AE, MC, V* ☉ *Closed Sun.* Ⓜ *Line C, Estación San Martín.*

FRENCH ╳ **Catalinas.** Chef Ramiro Pardo's exclusive recipes lend a strong Iberian
★ $$$$ touch to the superb French seafood and game served in this century-old building. Savor the lobster tail with caviar and cream or the *pejerrey* (a kind of mackerel) with king-crab mousse filling. Businesspeople lunch here, and a varied crowd gathers for dinner. Several fixed-price menus make this delight easier on the pocket, but wines and desserts can double the price of your meal. ⊠ *Reconquista 850, El Centro* ☏ *11/ 4313–0182* ⌂ *Reservations essential* ⋔ *Jacket and tie* ⊟ *AE, DC, MC, V* ☉ *Closed Sun. No lunch Sat.* Ⓜ *Line C, Estación Florida.*

$–$$ ╳ **Ligure.** French cuisine adapted to Argentine tastes is the specialty here. Try thistles *al parmesano* with your steak *au poivre* with brandy sauce and the *panqueques* (crepes) de dulce de leche. Despite the busy downtown location, the inside is very quiet. ⊠ *Juncal 855, El Centro* ☏ *11/ 4394–8226* ⊟ *AE, MC, V* Ⓜ *Line C, Estación San Martín.*

PIZZA ╳ **Filo.** Come here for the lively, arty atmosphere, but be prepared for
$–$$ crowds at all hours. The excellent flat-bread pizza is not the only specialty; try the pasta or the spinach salad tossed with mushrooms and bathed in balsamic vinegar. On your way to the rest room, check out the arts space in the basement. ⊠ *San Martín 975, El Centro* ☏ *11/ 4311–0312* ⊟ *AE, MC, V* Ⓜ *Line C, Estación San Martín.*

★ $ ╳ **Las Cuartetas.** Probably the most famous pizzeria in town, Las Cuartetas specializes in huge deep-dish pizzas that are packed with flavor and quite a challenge to finish. The restaurant extends back through three retro-tiled rooms adorned with plastic plants—the Formica-topped tables are usually all full. ⊠ *Corrientes 838, El Centro* ☏ *11/4326–0171* ⊟ *No credit cards* ☉ *No lunch Sun.* Ⓜ *Line B, Estación C. Pellegrini; Line C, Estación Diagonal Norte; Line D, Estación 9 de Julio.*

¢–$ ╳ **El Cuartito.** A true porteño classic, El Cuartito has been doing some of the best pizza in town since 1934 and the surroundings have changed little in the last 40 years. Drop in for a quick couple of slices at the *mostrador* (counter) or make yourself comfortable under the portraits of Argentine sporting greats for fantastic, no-nonsense pizzas and empanadas. Try a slice of *fainá* (chickpea-flour bread), the typical local accompaniment to pizza, and don't miss out on their flan with dulce de leche. ⊠ *Talcahuano 937, El Centro* ☏ *No phone* ⊟ *No credit cards* Ⓜ *Line D, Estación Tribunales.*

Palermo

ARGENTINE
$–$$

✕**Club del Vino.** A wine lover's paradise, this multidimensional eatery has a wine cellar, museum, and shop, along with live entertainment in the downstairs theatre–café. Past the fountain and tall, stained-glass ceiling of the entrance hall is an intimate yellow dining room and a large patio filled with candelit tables. The fixed-price *catador* (wine taster) menu includes *milanesa* (breaded veal cutlet) with sweet potatoes and flan, accompanied by a merlot, malbec, and cabernet. The restaurant is not always open for lunch, so call ahead. ✉ *Cabrera 4737, Palermo* ☎ *11/4833–0048* ▭ *AE, DC, MC, V* ⊘ *Closed Sun.*

$–$$
Fodor'sChoice
★

✕**El Trapiche.** The menu is endless and so are the portions at this busy parrilla on the edge of trendy Palermo Hollywood. High ceilings hung with hams, walls stacked with wine, contain a pleasant racket—Trapiche is always packed with locals who keep coming back for what's arguably the best classic Argentine food in town, with a wine list to match. Share a selection of barbecued meats or have the *sorrentinos de calabaza al scarparo* (squash-filled fresh pasta in a spicy cream sauce) all to yourself. If you have room, finish off with a fruit-filled crepe, flambéed for you at your table. ✉ *Paraguay 5099, Palermo* ☎ *11/4772–7343* ▭ *AE, DC, MC, V* Ⓜ *Line D, Estación Palermo.*

$–$$

✕**Freud y Fahler.** Red walls, colored pane-glass screens, and vintage chandeliers give warmth to this quiet corner restaurant on a peaceful cobbled street in Palermo Viejo. The menu is short but imaginative; try the *pollo dos cocciones* (chicken cooked in two different ways) with sweet-potato pasta, and follow it with spiced white-chocolate cake with plum ice cream and orange sauce. The well-informed young staff give friendly advice on food and wine. The lunch menus are an excellent value. ✉ *Gurruchaga 1750, Palermo* ☎ *11/4833–2153* ▭ *V* ⊘ *Closed Sun.*

¢

✕**Club Eros.** A basic dining room at the back of an old sports club in the heart of Palermo Viejo, Club Eros is a long-kept secret that is beginning to get out. The excellent renditions of classic *criolla* fare at rock-bottom prices have begun to draw young Palermo trendies as well as older customers who have been loyal to the club for decades. There's no menu, but you can confidently order a *bife de chorizo* (steak) and fries, a *milanesa,* or a huge plate of *ravioles de ricotta*; alternatively, ask one of the waiters for advice. The flan con dulce de leche is one of the best (and biggest) in town. ✉ *Uriarte 1609, Palermo* ☎ *11/4832–1313* ▭ *No credit cards.*

¢

✕**Ña Serapia.** Diners come to Ña Serapia for the authentic country food—tamales, locro, empanadas—and inexpensive wines. This is strictly no-frills, but the food is consistently good. ✉ *Av. Las Heras 3357, Palermo* ☎ *11/4801–5307* ▭ *No credit cards* Ⓜ *Line D, Estación Bulnes.*

CONTINENTAL
$$

✕**Bar 6.** The seasonally changing menu at Bar 6 may include risotto, stir-fry, shellfish, salads, *pappardelle* (extra-thick pasta ribbons) served with grilled vegetables and succulent prawns, and duck. If it's available, start with the grilled polenta topped with goat cheese; move on to marinated salmon with dill and cilantro; and finish off with goat-cheese ice cream and candied tomatoes. The waiters are usually too busy being beautiful to attend to you in a hurry, but the food makes up for their indifference. Stone, wood, and glass create a thoroughly modern yet inviting and down-to-earth spot. ⊠ *Armenia 1676, Palermo* ☎ *11/4833–6807* 🚫 *AE, MC, V* ☯ *Closed Sun.*

$$ ✕ **Bar Uriarte.** Don't be fooled by Bar Uriarte's minimalist front: the exposed kitchen gives way to the low lights of a sophisticated bar with two intimate dining spaces. You can simply lounge on the cozy sofas with a drink or have a longer meal at one of the airy dining room's oiled-wood tables. Chef Paula de Felipe's dishes are as sleek as the surroundings: try the martini-lemon chicken and be sure to leave room for a piece of pear-and-almond cake with cinnamon ice cream. Pass by in the afternoon—Uriarte's modern afternoon tea snacks will tide you over until dinner. Discrete live DJs warm things up on the weekend. ⊠ *Uriarte 1572, Palermo* ☎ *11/4834–6004* 🚫 *AE, DC, MC, V* ☯ *Closed Sun.*

$$ ✕ **Barolo.** An old town house done up in bright green and mauve, Barolo offers modern bistro dining on a quiet street in Palermo Hollywood. The lamb in mascarpone is unmissable, as are the sweet potato gnocchi with hazelnut cream sauce. Wines of the month are chalked up on a blackboard over the bar. ⊠ *Bonpland 1612, Palermo* ☎ *11/4772–0841* 🚫 *AE, V* ☯ *Closed Sun. No lunch Sat.*

DELICATESSEN   ✕ **Big Mamma.** This Porteño version of a New York deli has everything
¢–$ you'd expect (except pickles): made-to-order sandwiches, hot pastrami, bagels and lox, and even knishes. Breakfast combos are great value, and there's an eat-everything-on-the-menu deal if you're really hungry. ⊠ *Reconquista 1080, El Centro* ☎ *11/4894–1232* 🚫 *AE, DC, MC, V.*

¢–$ ✕ **Mark's.** The first deli to arrive in Palermo Viejo, Mark's big sandwiches and salads have been steadily drawing crowds for all-day munching (it's open 10:30 AM–8:30 PM). Ingredients are top quality, combinations inventive, and the large variety of breads—the house specialty—are all baked on premise. Tastefully mismatched tables, chairs, and sofas are available if you want to eat in; there's also a small patio if you want some sun. The cheesecake in itself is an excuse for a visit. ⊠ *El Salvador 4701, Palermo* ☎ *11/4832–6244* 🚫 *No credit cards* ☯ *Closed Mon.*

ECLECTIC   ✕ **Lelé de Troya.** Each room of this converted old house is drenched in
$–$$ a different color—from the walls to the chairs and plates—and the food is just as bold. The kitchen is on view from the covered lemon-yellow patio, and you can watch as loaf after loaf of the restaurant's home-made breads is drawn from the clay oven. Follow dishes like salmon ravioli or *mollejas* (a cut of beef) in cognac with one of Lelé's many Middle Eastern and Italian desserts. The restaurant holds tango classes on Monday nights and has a changing art space. ⊠ *Costa Rica 4901, Palermo* ☎ *11/4832–2726* 🚫 *AE, MC, V.*

ITALIAN   ✕ **Novecento.** With the feel of a Little Italy eatery, this bistro, which has
$$–$$$ branches in New York and Miami Beach, is a magnet for young, high-brow Porteños. Snug, candlelit tables offer intimacy. Try the pyramid of green salad, steak, and fries, or shrimp with bacon. Crème brûlée and "Chocolate Delight" are tempting desserts. In summer you can dine outdoors. ⊠ *Báez 199, Palermo* ☎ *11/4778–1900* 🚫 *AE, MC* ☯ *No lunch Mon.* Ⓜ *Line D, Estación Ministro Carranza.*

MEXICAN ✕ **Xalapa.** This kitschtastic tangerine-color corner restaurant serves up
¢–$ reasonably authentic tacos, burritos, and enchiladas, as well as more
complicated dishes such as chicken *con mole* (a rich, spicy, chocolatey
sauce), all at excellent prices. Dishes can be spiced up on request. Things
get chaotic on weekends when Xalapa fills up with returning local diners, but the wait for a table is worth it. ✉ *El Salvador 4800, Palermo*
☎ *11/4833–6102* ▭ *No credit cards* ☽ *No lunch.*

SCANDINAVIAN ✕ **Ølsen.** Ølsen is a showcase for Nordic flavors and contemporary
★ $$ Scandinavian design. Past the rectangular, walled garden filled with
scattered sculptures and white lounge chairs is a cavernous space with
walls of painted-white exposed bricks. Lime-green tables and chairs give
a '70s feel to the place, as do the cowhide barstools and veneer bar, be-
hind which lurks the restaurant's impressive vodka selection. Snack on
smørrebrød (open sandwiches) with different vodka shots, or try the *bifes
gravlax* (beef with specially cured salmon) and *rösti* (sauteed on both
sides until crisp) potatoes. The prix fixe menu is an excellent value, and
this is *the* place for Sunday brunch. ✉ *Gorriti 5870, Palermo* ☎ *11/
4776–7677* ▭ *AE, V* ☽ *Closed Mon.*

SPANISH ✕ **Al Andalus.** The food at this Andalusian restaurant is truly spectacu-
★ $–$$ lar. You'll have trouble choosing between the lamb *tagine* (a rich, dark
stew cooked with plums and almonds), the *Pastel Andalusí* (a sweet-
and-sour filo packed with lamb and chicken), or the goat cheese, saffron, and wild mushroom risotto. The *torta antigua* (chocolate cake) is
a not to be missed. You can eat in a tented dining room, under the ceramic lights of the quieter rust-red bar, or stretch out on sofas draped
with Moroccan rugs beside a tiled fountain in the plant-filled courtyard.
✉ *Godoy Cruz 1823, Palermo* ☎ *11/4832–9286* ▭ *AE, MC, V*
☽ *Closed Sun. and Mon.*

Plaza de Mayo

CAFÉ ✕ **Gran Café Tortoni.** The art nouveau decor and high ceilings transport
★ ¢–$ you to the faded, glorious past of the city's first confitería, established
in 1858. Carlos Gardel, one of Argentina's most famous tango stars;
writer Jorge Luis Borges; local and visiting dignitaries; and intellectuals have all eaten and sipped coffee here. Don't miss the *chocolate con
churros* (thick hot chocolate with baton-shaped donuts for dipping). You
must reserve ahead of time for the nightly tango shows. ✉ *Av. de Mayo
829, Plaza de Mayo* ☎ *11/4342–4328* ▭ *AE, MC, V* Ⓜ *Line A,
Estación Perú.*

CUBAN ✕ **Rey Castro.** A high, stained-glass ceiling and exposed brick walls hung
$ with black-and-white photos of old Havana are the backdrop for this
tasteful tribute to all things Cuban. The efficient service and fixed-price
menus attract businesspeople at lunchtime, but things relax at night when
DJs or live musicians often perform. As well as the usual rice-and-beans
classics are dishes such as *cazuela de mariscos* (a rich seafood casserole);
follow it with a flambéed lime crepe or coconut rice pudding. Alternatively, go straight to the cigar bar for a rum. ✉ *Perú 342, Plaza de Mayo*
☎ *11/4342–9998* ▭ *No credit cards* ☽ *Closed Sun. No lunch Sat.*
Ⓜ *Line A, Estación Perú; Line E, Estación Bolívar.*

SPANISH $\quad$ × **El Globo.** Hearty pucheros, suckling pig, squid, and other Spanish-Ar-
$$ $\quad$ gentine fare are served in a large dining area in a century-old building.
⊠ *Hipólito Yrigoyen 1199, Plaza de Mayo* ☎ *11/4381–3926* ▤ *AE, DC,
MC, V* Ⓜ *Line C, Estación Av. de Mayo; Line A, Estación Lima.*

$–$$ $\quad$ × **El Imparcial.** Founded in 1860, the oldest restaurant in town owes its
name (meaning impartial) to its neutrality in the face of the warring po-
litical factions of Buenos Aires's Spanish immigrants. Hand-painted
tiles, heavy wooden furniture and paintings of Spain are all strong reminders of the restaurant's origins, as are the elderly waiters, many of
whom are from the old country. Talking politics is no longer banned
within, good news for today's Argentines, who keep coming to El Imparcial for the renowned *paellas* and *mariscos* (seafood dishes). ⊠ *Hipólito Irigoyen 1201, Plaza de Mayo* ☎ *11/4383–2919* ▤ *AE, DC, MC,
V* Ⓜ *Line A, Estación Lima.*

La Recoleta

ARGENTINE $\quad$ × **El Sanjuanino.** Authentic Andean fare is served at this long-established
¢–$ $\quad$ spot. El Sanjuanino is especially known for its *pollo a la piedra* (chicken
pressed flat by stones), venison, and antelope stew, but you can also take
out piping-hot empanadas or tamales or *humita* (steamed corn cakes
wrapped in husks) for a picnic in the park. ⊠ *Posadas 1515, La Recoleta* ☎ *11/4804–2909* ▤ *AE, MC, V.*

¢–$ $\quad$ × **Melo.** This popular café in Barrio Norte, a neighborhood bordering La
Recoleta, serves up large portions of juicy steaks, crepes, salads, and pastas. The friendly service makes up for the spartan decor. Try the beef bro-
chettes with vegetables or the spinach crepes with cream sauce. ⊠ *Pacheco
de Melo 1829, La Recoleta* ☎ *11/4801–4251* ▤ *AE, DC, MC, V.*

CAFÉS $\quad$ × **La Biela.** Porteños linger at this quintessential sidewalk café opposite
$–$$ $\quad$ the Recoleta cemetery, sipping espressos, discussing politics, and peo-
ple-watching—all of which are best done at an outdoor table beneath
the shade of an ancient rubber tree. ⊠ *Quintana 596, at Junín, La Recoleta* ☎ *11/4804–0449* ▤ *V.*

¢–$ $\quad$ × **Nucha.** Choosing from the mouthwatering selection of handmade cakes
and pastries on display at this chic but cozy Recoleta café can be difficult. Take your time over cake and fantastic coffee at polished dark-wood
tables looking out onto Plaza Vicente López. Service is very friendly.
⊠ *Paraná 1343, La Recoleta* ☎ *11/4813–9507* ▤ *No credit cards.*

FRENCH $\quad$ × **La Bourgogne.** This French restaurant is generally considered one of
★ $$$$ $\quad$ the best—and most expensive—restaurants in town. White tablecloths
and fresh roses emphasize the restaurant's innate elegance. A sophisticated waitstaff brings you complimentary hors d'oeuvres as you choose
from chef Jean-Paul Bondoux's creations, which include foie gras, rab-
bit, escargots, chateaubriand, *côte de veau* (veal steak), and wild boar
cooked in *cassis* (black-currant liqueur). The fixed-price menu is more
affordable than à la carte selections. ⊠ *Alvear Palace Hotel, Ayacucho
2027, La Recoleta* ☎ *11/4805–3857* ✍ *Reservations essential* 🕱 *Jacket
and tie* ▤ *AE, DC, MC, V* Ⓜ *Line C, Estación San Martín.*

ITALIAN $\quad$ × **San Babila.** This trattoria is known for its excellent handmade pas-
$$$ $\quad$ tas and classic Italian dishes, created from the century-old recipes of the

chef's grandmother. *Cappelletti di formaggio* (cheese-filled round pasta) and *risotto de funghi porcini* (wild mushroom and saffron risotto) are good bets. There are fixed-price menus to choose from, and a friendly English-speaking staff. ☒ *R. M. Ortíz 1815, La Recoleta* ☎ *11/4801–9444* ▤ *AE, DC, MC, V.*

San Telmo

ARGENTINE ✕ **Calle de Ángeles.** Colón Theater's set designers have created a San Telmo
$–$$ alfresco with tree branches overhead and winged angels peering over balconies, justifying the restaurant's name—"Street of Angels." A cobblestone path runs down the middle, dimly lit by street lamps. Chefs prepare Argentine dishes with a Mediterranean slant. Garnish your parrilla with grilled eggplant or bell peppers, or try the juicy lamb. The coffee mousse on almond rings is a perfect ending. Locals gather at the bar to play the Spanish card game *truco*. ☒ *Chile 318, San Telmo* ☎ *11/4361–8822* ▤ *AE, MC, V* ☯ *Closed Sun. No lunch Sat.*

$ ✕ **La Farmacia.** Mismatched tables and chairs, comfy leather sofas, and poptastic colors fill this century-old corner house that used to be a traditional pharmacy. Generous breakfasts and afternoon teas are served on the cozy ground floor, lunch and dinner are in the first-floor dining room, and you can have late-night drinks on the bright-yellow roof terrace, which has a view over San Telmo. Arts and dance workshops are run upstairs, and the building has two boutiques selling local designers' work. The modern Argentine dishes are simple but well done, and the fixed-price lunch and dinner menus get you a lot for a little. ☒ *Bolívar 898, San Telmo* ☎ *11/4300–6151* ▤ *No credit cards* ☯ *Closed Mon.* Ⓜ *Lines C and E, Estación Independencia.*

¢ ✕ **El Desnivel.** Chaotic and always packed with both locals and tourists, this tavernlike San Telmo parrilla does huge portions of steaks and pastas at excellent prices—you can watch your meat being cooked on the huge barbecue at the front. The surly waiters are renowned for their rudeness, but it's all part of the experience. ☒ *Defensa 855, San Telmo* ☎ *11/4300–9081* ▤ *No credit cards* ☯ *Closed Mon.* Ⓜ *Lines C and E, Estación Independencia.*

SPANISH ✕ **Taberna Baska.** Old-world decor and efficient service are hallmarks
$–$$ of this busy, no-nonsense Spanish restaurant. Try such typical dishes as *chiripones en su tinta* (a variety of squid in ink) or *fideua gandiense* (a seafood-packed pasta paella with a saffron-and-pepper sauce). ☒ *Chile 980, San Telmo* ☎ *11/4334–0903* ▤ *AE, DC, MC, V* ☯ *Closed Mon.* Ⓜ *Line C, Estación Independencia.*

★ $ ✕ **Burzako.** Classic Basque dishes reinvented for a young Argentine public are what keep Burzako's tables busy. Dishes such as *rabo de buey* (a rich oxtail-and-wine stew) and seasonally changing fish use only the best and freshest local ingredients, and the huge portions leave you loathe to move. Recover from the meal over another bottle from their savvy, well-priced wine list. Despite the rustic tavern furnishings, Burzako draws a funky crowd, and weekends the basement becomes a bar where local bands often play. ☒ *México 345, San Telmo* ☎ *11/4334–0721* ▤ *AE, DC, MC, V* ☯ *Closed Sun.*

Where to Stay

In general, hotels are not standardized, and although major chains are appearing, they adapt their services and decor to match the personality of the city: most have bidets but not ice makers or vending machines. Smaller hotels have a family-run feel, with all the charming quirks that entails. The rooms in medium-price hotels may be smaller than expected, but the facilities and service are usually of high quality. And posh, exclusive hotels afford world-class comfort and conveniences. Most lodging establishments have Internet and/or e-mail access.

El Centro

$$$$ ⌂**Claridge.** Stylish wood paneling and high ceilings lend a distinctly British feel to this hotel with a traditionally Anglo-Argentine clientele. Rooms are done in shades of blue, with dark-wood furnishings and bronze fittings. The hotel is in the hectic business district, and it's nice to wind down in the spa or heated outdoor pool after a busy day. ☒ *Tucumán 535, El Centro, 1049* ☎ *11/4314–7700, 800/223–5652 in U.S.* ☒ *11/4314–8022* ⊕ *www.claridge.com.ar* ⤼ *155 rooms, 6 suites* ♨ *Restaurant, room service, IDD phones, in-room data ports, in-room safes, minibars, cable TV, pool, gym, health club, massage, spa, bar, laundry service, concierge, Internet, business services, meeting room, airport shuttle, no-smoking floors* ▭ *AE, DC, MC, V* ⓦ *BP* Ⓜ *Line C, Estación San Martín.*

$$$$ ⌂**Inter-Continental.** This luxury hotel may be a modern construction, but it was designed with the elegance of the 1930s in mind. The handsome lobby—in marble, leather, bronze, and wood—leads to an outdoor courtyard with a fountain. Rooms are adorned with large black armoires, marble-top nightstands, sleeper chairs, and black-and-white photos of Buenos Aires. The hotel has convenient access to the bordering city nerve center but is itself in a tranquil area. There's a transit lounge for early arrival and late departure. ☒ *Moreno 809, El Centro, 1091* ☎ *11/4340–7100* ☒ *11/4340–7199* ⊕ *www.buenos-aires.interconti.com* ⤼ *315 rooms, 15 suites* ♨ *2 restaurants, café, room service, IDD phones, in-room data ports, in-room safes, cable TV, indoor pool, gym, hot tub, massage, sauna, Turkish bath, bar, baby-sitting, laundry service, concierge, business services, meeting room, parking (fee), no-smoking floors* ▭ *AE, DC, MC, V* ⓦ *BP* Ⓜ *Line E, Estación Belgrano.*

$$$$ ⌂**Marriott Plaza Hotel.** Crystal chandeliers and Persian carpets decorate the sumptuous public spaces at the city's first grand hotel. The rooms are spacious and elegantly appointed, and some have bay windows overlooking the park. The pool affords views of the park at the health club, a modern oasis. ☒ *Florida 1005, El Centro, 1005* ☎ *11/4318–3000, 800/228–9290 in U.S.* ☒ *11/4318–3008* ⊕ *www.marriott.com* ⤼ *325 rooms, 12 suites* ♨ *2 restaurants, coffee shop, room service, IDD phones, in-room data ports, in-room safes, minibars, cable TV with movies, pool, gym, health club, hair salon, hot tub, sauna, bar, laundry service, concierge, Internet, business services, meeting rooms* ▭ *AE, DC, MC, V* ⓦ *BP* Ⓜ *Line C, Estación San Martín.*

FodorśChoice
★

$$$$ ⌂**Sheraton Buenos Aires Hotel.** The Sheraton is popular with American businesspeople and tour groups seeking familiar comforts. The rooms are standard but afford views of the Río de la Plata, Plaza de la Fuerzas Aérea Argentina and its clock tower, or the glass skyscrapers of the Catalinas area. The separate Park Tower next door, part of Sheraton's Luxury Group, has spacious, expensive rooms with cellular phones, entertainment centers, and 24-hour butler service. ⊠ *San Martín 1225, El Centro, 1104* ☎ *11/4318–9000, 800/325–3535 in U.S.* 🖷 *11/4318–9353* ⇥ *713 rooms, 29 suites* ⌖ *2 restaurants, coffee shop, room service, IDD phones, in-room data ports, in-room fax, in-room safes, minibars, cable TV with movies, 2 tennis courts, 2 pools, fitness classes, gym, health club, hair salon, massage, sauna, bar, lobby lounge, baby-sitting, laundry service, concierge, Internet, business services, convention center, meeting rooms, car rental, travel services, parking (fee), no-smoking rooms* ⊟ *AE, DC, MC, V* ⦿ *BP* Ⓜ *Line C, Estación Retiro.*

$$$ ▦ **Gran Hotel Dorá.** A cozy lobby with a small '50s-style bar greets you at this old-fashioned hotel, located just off Plaza San Martín. Public areas are filled with original Latin American paintings and sculpture, including a mural by Argentine artist Castagnino in the lobby lounge. Simple elegance permeates the comfortable rooms, which are decorated in Louis XVI style. It caters primarily to Europeans and Argentines who prefer a Continental atmosphere. Ask for one of the front-facing rooms, which are larger. ⊠ *Maipú 963, El Centro, 1006* ☎ *11/4312–7391* 🖷 *11/ 4313–8134* ⊕ *www.dorahotel.com.ar* ⇥ *96 rooms, 1 suite* ⌖ *Snack bar, room service, IDD phones, in-room data ports, in-room safes, minibars, cable TV, bar, laundry service, Internet, business center, meeting rooms, free parking* ⊟ *AE, DC, MC, V* ⦿ *CP* Ⓜ *Line C, Estación San Martín.*

★ $$$ ▦ **NH City.** The clean art deco lines of the NH City's facade are mirrored within: in the spacious lobby, molded pillars support an original stained-glass ceiling, which filters sunlight onto the white marble floors. Warm wood paneling and comfy boutique furniture in mocha, russet, and slate invite you to relax from the first step through the door. In the rooms, indulgence takes the form of huge beds made up with masses of white cotton linen, and NH even provides *à la carte* pillows, to make sure you really sleep well. The roof-top pool has spectacular views over the cupolas of nearby historic neighborhood San Telmo. ⊠ *Bolívar 160, El Centro, 1066* ☎ *11/4121–6464* 🖷 *11/4121–6450* ⊕ *www.nh-hotels.com* ⇥ *297 rooms, 6 suites* ⌖ *Restaurant, café, room service, IDD phones, in-room data ports, in-room safes, minibars, cable TV, pool, gym, sauna, bar, laundry service, concierge, Internet, business services, meeting rooms* ⊟ *AE, DC, MC, V* ⦿ *BP* Ⓜ *Line A, Estación Perú, Line E, Estación Bolívar.*

$$$ ▦ **NH Jousten.** From the 1930s on, the Jousten was one of the best-known luxury hotels in town—guests included local deities Perón and Evita— before the building fell into disrepair and eventual abandonment. Thanks to the massive renovation carried out by Spanish hotel group NH, the latest in contemporary boutique design rubs shoulders with the hotel's stunning original architectural features, such as an ornate molded ceiling in the lobby and hand-painted tiles in the Spanish-style bar. The well-appointed rooms are filled with warm grays and deep reds, and furnished with sleek hardwood furniture and big, inviting beds. Suites have pri-

FodorsChoice
★

vate terraces overlooking the River Plate. ⊠ *Corrientes 280, El Centro, 1043* ☎ *11/4321–6750* 🖷 *11/4321–6775* ⊕ *www.nh-hoteles.com* ⇨ *80 rooms, 5 suites* ♨ *Restaurant, room service, IDD phones, in-room data ports, in-room safes, minibars, cable TV, lobby lounge, baby-sitting, concierge, dry cleaning, laundry service, Internet, business services, travel services* ▭ *AE, DC, MC, V* |☉| *BP* Ⓜ *Line B, Estación L. N. Alem.*

$$$ 🏨 **Posta Carretas.** This comfortable *hostería* (inn) has the atmosphere of a mountain lodge. Wood paneling creates a cozy atmosphere, a nice contrast to the bustle outside. Suites are brightly decorated and have whirlpools. The lobby bar overlooks the indoor pool, and there's a small garden where you can relax. ⊠ *Esmeralda 726, El Centro, 1007* ☎ *11/4322–8567* 🖷 *11/4322–8606* ⊕ *www.postacarretas.com.ar* ⇨ *90 rooms, 26 suites* ♨ *Coffee shop, room service, IDD phones, in-room data ports, in-room safes, some in-room hot tubs, minibars, cable TV, indoor pool, gym, sauna, bar, dry cleaning, laundry service, Internet, business services, meeting room, parking (fee)* ▭ *AE, DC, MC, V* |☉| *BP* Ⓜ *Line C, Estación San Martín.*

$$ 🏨 **Design Suites.** With its harmonious minimalist aura, and chrome and pine fittings complemented by tones of beige and gray, this central hotel has been designed to feng shui perfection. Rooms overlook the Plaza Pizurno and are flooded with sunlight. A nightcap is included in the rate, and you can count on professional and friendly service. ⊠ *M. T. de Alvear 1683, El Centro, 1060* ☎☎ *11/4814–8700* ⊕ *www.designsuites.com* ⇨ *40 rooms* ♨ *Restaurant, room service, in-room data ports, some in-room hot tubs, in-room safes, some kitchenettes, cable TV, pool, gym, bar, laundry service, Internet, meeting room* ▭ *AE, DC, MC, V* Ⓜ *Line D, Estación Callao.*

$$ 🏨 **NH Florida.** Although hotel group NH bills this as their no-frills option in Buenos Aires, the boutique chic of this downtown hotel suggests otherwise. The low, '70s-style lobby has a long wood-lined reception area filled with sculpted-looking armchairs in warm neutrals and arresting modern flower arrangements. Upstairs, rooms go easy on the eye with beige, gold, and russet furnishings, fluffy white linen, pale parquet flooring, and white marble bathrooms. The friendly young staff deals quickly with the requests. A few blocks away, the NH Latino has similar decor and services. ⊠*San Martín 839, El Centro, 1004* ☎*11/4321–9850* 🖷*11/4321–9875* ⊕ *www.nh-hoteles.com* ⇨ *148 rooms* ♨ *Restaurant, IDD phones, in-room data ports, in-room safes, minibars, cable TV, bar, laundry service, Internet, business services, free parking* ▭ *AE, DC, MC, V* |☉| *BP* Ⓜ *Line C, Estación San Martín.*

$ 🏨 **Carsson.** A walk down the long, red-carpeted foyer takes you away from the bustle of the city and into a welcoming English-style hotel with first-rate service. The spacious rooms vary in color schemes, but all have Louis XIV–style furniture; request one *contra frente* (room not facing the street) to avoid street noise. ⊠ *Viamonte 650, El Centro, 1053* ☎*11/4322–3601* 🖷*11/4322–3551* ⇨ *108 rooms, 9 suites* ♨ *Restaurant, coffee shop, room service, IDD phones, in-room data ports, in-room safes, minibars, cable TV, bar, baby-sitting, laundry service, Internet, business services, meeting room, parking (fee)* ▭ *AE, DC, MC, V* |☉| *CP* Ⓜ *Line C, Estación Lavalle.*

$ 🏨 **Castelar Hotel.** Classic Spanish lines define the exterior of this 1928 hotel; the French classical interior has Italian marble and handsome furnishings. Though small, rooms are well equipped, and the service is very good. Breakfast is included in the rate, as is partial access to the spa, with its Turkish baths and Finnish saunas, massage, and beauty treatments. ⊠ *Av. de Mayo 1152, El Centro, 1085* 🕾 *11/4383–5000* 🖷 *11/4383–8388* ⊕ *www.castelarhotel.com.ar* 🛏 *153 rooms, 7 suites* ♨ *Coffee shop, restaurant, room service, IDD phones, minibars, health club, hair salon, massage, sauna, spa, Turkish bath, laundry service, business services, meeting room, Internet, parking (fee)* 🖃 *AE, MC, V* ¶⊙¶ *BP* Ⓜ *Line A, Estación Lima.*

$ 🏨 **Hotel Facon Grande.** A lobby filled with Argentine handicrafts and rustic wood and leather furniture remind you that this hotel was named for a Gaucho hero. The Argentine countryside is further invoked in the muted greens and browns of the room furnishings. Guests are mainly from other Latin American countries or the provinces. ⊠ *Reconquista 645, El Centro, 1003* 🕾🖷 *11/4312–6360* ⊕ *www.hotelfacongrande. com* 🛏 *98 rooms, 3 suites* ♨ *Restaurant, room service, IDD phones, minibars, cable TV, bar, laundry service, Internet, meeting room, parking (fee)* 🖃 *AE, DC, MC, V* ¶⊙¶ *CP* Ⓜ *Line B, Estación Alem.*

★ **$** 🏨 **Lancaster.** The countess who decorated this traditional and central hotel made good use of her family heirlooms—old family portraits, marble pillars, and a 200-year-old clock grace the lobby. All rooms have antique mahogany furniture, and some have views of the port of Buenos Aires. You can dine on French cuisine with Iberian accents at the hotel's excellent Catalinas restaurant. ⊠ *Av. Córdoba 405, El Centro, 1054* 🕾 *11/4311–3201* 🖷 *11/4312–4068* ⊕ *www.lancasterhotel-page.com* 🛏 *72 rooms, 18 suites* ♨ *Restaurant, room service, IDD phones, in-room data ports, in-room safes, minibars, cable TV, pool, gym, hair salon, sauna, spa, squash, pub, dry cleaning, laundry service, concierge, Internet, business services, meeting room, travel services* 🖃 *AE, DC, MC, V* ¶⊙¶ *CP* Ⓜ *Line C, Estación San Martín.*

$ 🏨 **Principado.** Rooms are modern and comfortable at this central hotel, built for the World Cup in 1978. Sunlight floods through the large windows in the reception area. The decor is cozy Spanish colonial, with comfortable leather couches in the split-level lobby. The highlight is the friendly coffee shop. ⊠ *Paraguay 481, El Centro, 1057* 🕾 *11/4313–3022* 🖷 *11/4313–3952* ⊕ *www.principado.com.ar* 🛏 *88 rooms* ♨ *Restaurant, coffee shop, room service, IDD phones, in-room data ports, in-room safes, minibars, cable TV, bar, dry cleaning, laundry service, Internet, business services, parking (fee)* 🖃 *AE, DC, MC, V* ¶⊙¶ *CP* Ⓜ *Line C, Estación San Martín.*

★ **¢** 🏨 **Gran Hotel Hispano.** The Spanish colonial architecture and small but charming rooms bordering the central patio of an old-style casa chorizo give this hotel a traditional and friendly feel. Outside, walls are pink, plants abound, and the patio's glass ceiling is opened up on sunny days. Inside, the well-appointed rooms are high-ceilinged yet cozy. The hotel has been owned by the Perreira family for the last 50 years, and the service is efficient and personal. ⊠ *Av. de Mayo 861, El Centro, 1084* 🕾 *11/4345–2020* 🖷 *11/4345–2020* ⊕ *www.hhispano.com.ar* 🛏 *60 rooms*

⚘ *Café, room service, IDD phones, minibars, cable TV, laundry service, Internet, airport shuttle, parking (fee)* ⊟ *AE, DC, MC, V* ⫯◯⫯ *CP* Ⓜ *Line A, Estación Piedras.*

¢ ▦ **Limehouse Hostel.** High ceilings, wooden floors, and exposed brick are part of the charm of this turn-of-the-20th-century corner building that has been completely recycled into a hostel for laid-back young travelers. Dorm rooms are spacious, and communal areas include a pool room, two eating areas, a fully equipped kitchen, and a sofa-filled lounge where beers and home-made pizza are served up at night while guests swap tales. There's also a room with a library of maps, guidebooks, and travel information to help you plan the rest of your trip, and the hip, young staff are always on hand to help. There are a few private rooms, some of which can be rented by the month. The hostel is right on 9 de Julio Avenue, so things can get noisy at night. ⊠ *Lima 11, El Centro, 1073* ☎ *11/4383–4561* ⊕ *www.limehouseargentina.com* ⇱ *10 private rooms, 50 dorm beds* ⚘ *Snack bar, fans, bar, library, laundry facilities, Internet, travel services; no a/c, no room phones, no room TVs* ⊟ *No credit cards* ⫯◯⫯ *CP* Ⓜ *Line A, Estación Lima.*

¢ ▦ **Milhouse Hostel.** Backpackers flock to Milhouse for the low prices and slick service. The cozy private rooms open out on to a terraced walkway overlooking the central plant-filled patio. Dorm rooms are large, with brightly colored walls that offset the high, white ceilings. In addition to a restaurant serving no-frills Argentine fare, there are cooking facilities for guests, and an all-night café-bar to keep you going through marathon pool and Ping-Pong sessions. Milhouse's ultra-efficient staff organize all kinds of social activities, from *asados* (barbecues), visits to the football stadium, and tango lessons to all-night clubbing marathons. ⊠ *Hipólito Irigoyen 959, El Centro, 1086* ☎☎ *11/4345–9605 or 11/4343–5038* ⊕*www.milhousehostel.com* ⇱*13 private rooms, 42 dorm beds* ⚘*Restaurant, fans, Ping-Pong, bar, library, laundry facilities, Internet, travel services, parking (fee); no a/c, no room phones, no room TVs* ⊟ *MC* ⫯◯⫯ *CP* Ⓜ *Line A, Estación Piedras; Line C, Estación Av. de Mayo.*

La Recoleta

★ **$$$$** ▦ **Alvear Palace Hotel.** Built in 1932 as a luxury apartment building, the Alvear retains its old-world opulence and is a preferred reception venue for visiting dignitaries. Decorated in French Empire style, with regal burgundy and deep blue, the rooms have large windows draped in silk, and feather beds with Egyptian cotton linen. Fine shops, museums, and restaurants are all nearby. ⊠ *Av. Alvear 1891, La Recoleta, 1129* ☎ *11/ 4808–2100 or 11/4804–7777, 800/448–8355 in U.S.* 🖷 *11/4804–9246* ⊕ *www.alvearpalace.com* ⇱ *100 rooms, 100 suites* ⚘ *2 restaurants, coffee shop, room service, IDD phones, in-room data ports, in-room safes, some in-room hot tubs, minibars, indoor pool, health club, gym, sauna, lobby bar, laundry service, concierge, Internet, business services, meeting room, no-smoking rooms* ⊟ *AE, DC, MC, V* ⫯◯⫯ *BP.*

★ **$$$$** ▦ **Four Seasons Hotel Buenos Aires.** The luxurious Four Seasons Hotel has a 13-floor marble tower and an adjacent late-19th-century mansion, with private butler service for its handsome suites. In addition to its priceless art collection, the hotel houses a beautiful Roman-style pool, health club, and landscaped garden. Guest rooms are spacious, and outstanding service ensures many repeat visitors. ⊠ *Posadas 1086, La Recoleta, 1011* ☎ *11/4321–1200* 🖷 *11/4321–1201* ⊕ *www.fourseasons.com* ⬦ *138 rooms, 27 suites* ⚭ *Restaurant, room service, IDD phones, in-room data ports, in-room fax, in-room safes, minibars, cable TV, pool, fitness classes, health club, gym, massage, sauna, bar, lobby lounge, baby-sitting, dry cleaning, laundry service, concierge, Internet, business services, meeting rooms, airport shuttle, travel services, parking (fee), no-smoking rooms* ▤ *AE, DC, MC, V* ⊖ *BP.*

$$$$ 🖾 **Loi Suites Recoleta.** The spacious rooms here are decorated with taste-ful beiges and creams. In addition to the usual amenities, all rooms have large-screen TVs, stereo systems, and microwaves. Breakfast and a nightly happy hour take place at the elegant white-stone pool area. Nearby are restaurants, bars, cafés, shopping, cultural centers, and a cinema. Loi Suites also operate two smaller apart-hotels downtown. ⊠ *Vicente López 1955, La Recoleta, 1128* ☎ *11/5777–8950* 🖷 *11/5777–8999* ⊕ *www.loisuites.com.ar* ⬦ *88 rooms, 24 suites* ⚭ *Restaurant, room service, IDD phones, in-room data ports, in-room safes, minibars, microwaves, cable TV, indoor-outdoor pool, gym, sauna, bar, dry clean-ing, laundry service, Internet, business services, meeting rooms, parking (fee)* ▤ *AE, DC, MC, V* ⊖ *CP.*

★ **$$** 🖾 **Hotel Bel Air.** The classic facade of the Bel Air belies the smooth mod-ern lines within. The small lobby has a curving pale-wood bar and a café where trendy Recoleta-ites meet for coffee. The spacious rooms have parquet flooring and simple modern furnishings in beige and cream—you can upgrade at little extra cost to a superior room, which have small terraces. On a quiet street in the heart of Recoleta, the Bel Air is within a few blocks of shops and eateries and the Recoleta cemetery. ⊠ *Are-nales 1462, La Recoleta, 1062* ☎ *11/4021–4000* 🖷 *11/4816–0016* ⊕ *www.hahoteles.com* ⬦ *67 rooms, 15 suites* ⚭ *Restaurant, café, room service, IDD phones, in-room data ports, in-room safes, minibars, cable TV, gym, bar, dry cleaning, laundry service, Internet, business ser-vices, meeting rooms, airport shuttle, travel services, no-smoking rooms* ▤ *AE, DC, MC, V* ⊖ *BP.*

Palermo

★ **$** 🖾 **1555 Malabia House.** A classic turn-of-the-20th-century town house, 1555 Malabia House is a tranquil home-away-from-home in the heart of trendy Palermo SoHo. Pale wood fittings and harmonious white-and-beige furnishings are interrupted by splashes of color from Oriental rugs, original paintings, and bold flower arrangements. You can curl up with a drink on the sofas in the common living room or sit amongst the rich greens of three plant-filled inner patios. Service is highly personalized and the young staff are knowledgeable about the nearby eateries, clubs, and fashionable shops. ⊠ *Malabia 1555, Palermo, 1414* ☎ *11/ 4832–3345 or 11/4833–2410* ⊕ *www.malabiahouse.com.ar* ⬦ *11 rooms, 4 suites* ⚭ *Room service, IDD phones, fans, in-room safes, minibars, cable TV, bar, laundry service, concierge, Internet, meeting room, airport shuttle, parking (fee)* ▤ *AE, DC, MC, V* ⊖ *CP* Ⓜ *Line D, Estación Scalabrini Ortiz.*

¢ 🖾 **Hotel Alpino.** Decorated with leather sofas in the lobby, dark browns, and wood paneling, this hotel has functional, though somber, rooms.

It's close to the Parque Zoológico and the Jardín Botánico. ⊠ *Cabello 3318, Palermo, 1425* 🏢 *11/4802–5151* ⊕ *www.geocities.com/ alpinohotel* 🛏 *35 rooms* ⌂ *Room service, IDD phones, in-room data ports, in-room safes, minibars, cable TV, laundry service, meeting rooms, parking (fee)* ⊟ *AE, DC, MC, V* ⋅○⋅ *CP* Ⓜ *Line D, Estación Plaza Italia.*

San Telmo

★ ¢–$ ⤬⊡ **Boquitas Pintadas.** This petite, self-proclaimed pop hotel—whimsically called "Little Painted Mouths" as a tribute to Manuel Puig's novel of the same name—is as intimate as it is extraordinary. Rooms have names like "Gilda" and "The Chamber of Roses," and the kitschy decor changes every three months. A library features Puig's works, and the hotel hosts ongoing film screenings and art exhibits. A modern restaurant serves unique, eclectic dishes and funky cocktails; weekends there's an all-night party with DJs. Though it's slightly outside the city center, bordering San Telmo, Boquitas Pintadas nevertheless has easy access to the city center. ⊠ *Estados Unidos 1393, San Telmo, 1101* 🏢 *11/ 4381–6064* ⊕ *www.boquitas-pintadas.com.ar* 🛏 *6 rooms, 1 suite* ⌂ *Restaurant, room service, cable TV, library, bar, nightclub, dry cleaning, laundry service, Internet, business services, travel services* ⊟ *No credit cards* Ⓜ *Line E, Estación San José.*

Nightlife & the Arts

Listings of events can be found daily in the English-language *Buenos Aires Herald* as well as in the more comprehensive Friday edition. The tourist office distributes free copies of a helpful guide called "Buenos Aires Day and Night." If you read Spanish, check out the major papers' Friday supplements: *Via Libre* in *La Nación* and *Sí* in *Clarín*. The latter's daily "Espectáculos" section also has listings. Trendier spots can be found in *Wipe*, a pocket-sized magazine distributed in bars, restaurants, and boutiques. On-line, check out www.dondevamos.com for general nightlife suggestions and www.buenosaliens.com for clubbing and electronic music information.

Nightlife

It's good to begin with a basic understanding of the Argentine idea of nightlife: theater performances start at 9 PM or 9:30 PM; the last movie begins after midnight; and nightclubs don't begin filling up until 2 or 3 AM. In fact, even if you wanted to go clubbing early, you might not be allowed in: "early evening" hours (meaning before midnight) are often reserved for teenagers, and no one over 18 may be permitted to enter until after that time. For the most part, Buenos Aires's dance clubs attract young crowds (in the 18–30 age range). Note that the subte closes at 10 PM, so if you go out late, either count on taking a taxi home or waiting until 5 AM for the subte to start running again.

BARS & CLUBS The young and beautiful groove to hip-hop and R&B at **El Codo** (⊠ Guardia Vieja 4085, Almagro 🏢 11/4862–1381). For a quiet drink, head for the wooden tables and exposed brick of **El Imaginario** (⊠ Bulnes 905, Almagro 🏢 11/4866–0672), a converted old corner building in the heart of Almagro. Live bands play the basement on weekends.

THE ART OF TANGO

THE TANGO IS MACHO, THE TANGO IS STRONG. *It smells of wine and tastes like death."*

So goes the famous tango "Why I sing like this," whose mix of nostalgia, violence, and sensuality sum up what is truly the dance of Buenos Aires. The tango was born at the end of the 19th century in the conventillos (tenement houses) of the port neighborhood of La Boca, although its roots are not known for sure: different theories place its origins in Spain, Italy, and even Africa. Nevertheless, the tango swept quickly from the immigrant quarter to the brothels and cabarets of the whole city, and by the 1920s had become respectable enough to fill the salons and drawing rooms of the upper class. In the 1930s, with the advent of Carlos Gardel, tango's great hero, the tango became known outside Argentina. Since then, tango has had its ups and downs in Buenos Aires, but remains a key part of the city's culture.

Today, you can experience tango culture all over Buenos Aires: from street performers on Calle Florida and Plaza Dorrego to glitzy shows at expensive clubs. Opening days and times of tango halls vary greatly, so call ahead to check. Be sure to visit the Chacarita cemetery grave of Carlos Gardel, who died in a plane crash in 1935 at the age of 40.

Both musicians and dancers perform at **Bar Sur** (⊠ Estados Unidos 299, San Telmo ☎ 11/4362–6086), a small, traditional bar in San Telmo. In Boedo, **La Esquina de Homero Manzi** (⊠ San Juan 3601, Boedo ☎ 11/4957–8488) has reasonably priced shows in an opulent café. Consistently excellent, well-attended performances are held at the classic tango café **El Querandi** (⊠ Perú 302, at Moreno, San Telmo ☎ 11/4342–1760 ⊕ www.

querandi.com.ar). Perhaps the glitziest spot in town is **Señor Tango** (⊠ Vieytes 1655, Barracas ☎ 11/4303–0231), whose daily shows are aimed at tourists. A traditional show takes place in a colonial-style house at **Viejo Almacén** (⊠ Balcarce 786, at Independencia, San Telmo ☎ 11/4307–6689).

Celebrated old-guard tango musicians Salgán and De Lío frequently perform at **Club del Vino** (⊠ Cabrera 4737, Palermo ☎ 11/4833–0050). The classic **Gran Café Tortoni** (⊠ Av. de Mayo 829, Plaza de Mayo ☎ 11/4342–4328) is one of the best places to listen to tango music.

Akarense (⊠ Donado 1355 at Av. Los Incas, Villa Ortúzar ☎ 11/4651–2121) draws the best dancers to its beautiful hall. Behind the unmarked doors of **La Catedral** (⊠ Sarmiento 4006, Almagro ☎ No phone) is a contemporary club where you can eat, drink, and hit the floor. Crowds of local regulars gather on Friday night at **Club Gricel** (⊠ La Rioja 1180, San Cristóbal ☎ 11/4957–7517), which sometimes has classes. All ages come to practice at **La Ideal** (⊠ Suipacha 384, Plaza de Mayo ☎ 11/4601–8234). **Sin Rumbo** (⊠ Tamborini 6157, Villa Urquiza ☎ 11/4571–9577 or 11/4574–0972) attracts old milonga dancers and also has some classes. A young crowd gathers at informal club **La Viruta-La Estrella** (⊠ Armenia 1366, Palermo ☎ 11/4774–6357).

For more information contact **Academia Nacional de Tango** (⊠ Av. de Mayo 833, Plaza de Mayo ☎ 11/4345–6968).

Twenty- to thirtysomethings let off steam at relaxed bar **La Diosa** (✉Rafael Obligado 3731 at Salguero, Costanera ☎ 11/4806–1079), where anything from live bands to strippers fills the stage. The best international house, trance, and techno DJs play to crowds of thousands at Buenos Aires's biggest nightclub, **Pachá Clubland** (✉ Costanera Norte and La Pampa, Costanera ☎ 11/4788–4280), which looks out over the river.

The best place downtown for electronic music is **Big One** (✉ Alsina 940, El Centro ☎ 11/4775–4804), where a cool set gathers to listen to local and imported DJs. Trendy thirtysomethings order wine and sushi at fashionable **Gran Bar Danzón** (✉ Libertad 1161, 1st fl., El Centro ☎ 11/4811–1108). For a little rowdy Irish-bar action and some (canned) Guinness, check out **The Kilkenny** (✉ Marcelo T. De Alvear 399, El Centro ☎ 11/4312–7291). **La Cigale** (✉ 25 de Mayo 722, El Centro ☎ 11/4312–8275) has a large turquoise bar where you can sip cocktails while smooth sounds spin. Classic café **La Ideal** (✉ Suipacha 384, El Centro ☎ 11/4326–0521) hosts an electronica club night every Saturday. At converted old mansion **Milín** (✉Paraná 1048, El Centro ☎11/4815–9925) you can sip drinks at the bar or out in the garden while quiet sophisticates chat around you. An older, more refined crowd gathers for drinks and cigars at the Marriott's elegant **Plaza Bar** (✉ Florida 1005, El Centro ☎ 11/4318–3000). An English-speaking expat crowd often gathers at **Shamrock** (✉ Rodríguez Peña 1220, El Centro ☎ 11/4812–3584), an Irish-style bar; late nights head downstairs to the Shamrock Basement where local DJs spin house and techno. A mixed crowd gathers for beer and rock at the only microbrewery in town, **Buller** (✉ R. M. Ortíz 1827, La Recoleta ☎ 11/4808–9061), which has seven house beers.

At former toy store **Acabar** (✉Honduras 5733, Palermo ☎11/4772–0845) you can enjoy board games with your cocktails. You may see a model or rock star at **Buenos Aires News** (✉ Av. Libertador 3883, Palermo ☎ 11/4778–1500), one of the city's hottest nightspots. **El Living** (✉ M. T. de Alvear 1540, Palermo ☎ 11/4811–4730) is a trendy disco and bar with lounge chairs and great drinks. A Palermo classic, **Malas Artes** (✉ Honduras 4999 on Plaza Serrano, Palermo ☎ 11/4831–0743) draws a mixed crowd for Quilmes beer and peanuts at wooden tables. A hip crowd gathers at **Mundo Bizarro** (✉ Guatemala 4802, Palermo ☎ 11/4773–1967), a shrine to '50s bizarre that serves the best cocktails in town.

A varied menu of live music is on offer at laid-back bar **Niceto** (✉ Cnel. Niceto Vega 5510 at Humboldt, Palermo ☎ 11/4779–9396), which also hosts raunchy club night '69 on Thursdays. Classic rock and indie fill the ground floor of Palermo mainstay **El Podestá** (✉ Armenia 1742, Palermo ☎ 11/4832–2776): upstairs a more trendy crowd grooves to electronic beats. The cream of the Argentine rock scene hang out at **The Roxy** (✉ Arcos del Sol, between Casares and Sarmiento, Palermo ☎ 11/4899–0313), a large club with several different theme nights. Palermo Hollywood darlings gather for drinks at **Único** (✉ Honduras 5604, Palermo ☎ 11/4775–6693), a large corner bar that's usually packed.

Students, bohemians, old men, and young trendies all gather to down a beer or a coffee at **Bar El Británico** (✉ Brazil 399 at Defensa, San Telmo

🏠 11/4300–6894), a vintage classic that's open all night. The ground floor of pop hotel **Boquitas Pintadas** (✉ Estados Unidos 1393, San Telmo 🏠 11/4381–6064) starts off the night as a retro-kitsch cocktail bar and segues into all-night weekend dance parties and cool after-hours sessions, finishing with breakfast at dawn.

GAY & LESBIAN CLUBS **Angels** (✉ Viamonte 2168, El Centro) has several dance floors and attracts a primarily gay and transvestite clientele. The most popular gay dance club (men only) is **Contramano** (✉ Rodríguez Peña 1082, El Centro 🏠 No phone); it's open from midnight Wednesday–Saturday and Sunday from 8 PM. The young and hip head to **Glam** (✉ Cabrera 3046, Palermo 🏠 11/4963–2521) for smooth cruising in a classy setting. Utter excess is the idea at **Oxen** (✉ Sarmiento 1662, El Centro 🏠 11/4375–0366), where a mainly male crowd gets down to pumping club anthems. On Friday, the dance club **Palacio** (✉ Alsina 940, near Plaza de Mayo) is the place to be.

JAZZ CLUBS There are particularly good jazz listings in newspaper *Página 12*'s Thursday supplement, *No*.

An older, arty crowd gathers for drinks, philosophy, and live jazz at **Clásica y Moderna** (✉ Callao 892, El Centro 🏠 11/4812–8707). Wine and choice live jazz come together at **Club Del Vino** (✉ Cabrera 4737, Palermo 🏠 11/4833–0050), which has a classic smoky theater–café packed with tables. The 1858 classic **Gran Café Tortoni** (✉ Av. de Mayo 829, near Plaza de Mayo 🏠 11/4342–4328) hosts jazz on weekends. **Notorious** (✉ Av. Callao 966, El Centro 🏠 11/4815–8473) stages jazz shows several times per week, and when there isn't live music, CD players at each table provide the background music. **La Revuelta** (✉ Alvarez Thomas 1368, Chacarita 🏠 11/4553–5530 Ⓜ Line B, Estación F. Lacroze) is a quiet, sophisticated bar that has a varied program of live jazz and blues several times a week. The best of Porteño jazz bands (and occasional imports) play at intimate **Thelonious Bar** (✉ Salguero 1884, La Recoleta 🏠 11/4829–1562).

The Arts

Buenos Aires has a busy schedule of world-class cultural events. Except for some international short-run performances, tickets to most events are surprisingly easy to get. Note that, like most other businesses in Argentina, theaters take a summer vacation (January–February). Men usually wear jackets and ties to theater performances, and women also dress accordingly.

Tickets can be purchased at the box office of the venue or at various ticket outlets. **Entrada Plus** (🏠 11/4324–1010) sells tickets for theater, dance performances, and concerts; tickets can be sent to your hotel or picked up at the box office. **Ticketmaster** (🏠 11/4321–9700) sells tickets for events at the Colón, Luna Park, Teatro Globo, and the Teatro Municipal San Martín and accepts MasterCard and Visa for phone purchases. **Ticketek** (🏠 11/4323–7200) has tickets for concerts, local theaters, and music halls. Tickets for international gigs are often available at branches of **Tower Records** (✉ Florida 770, El Centro 🏠 11/4327–5151).

You can purchase discount tickets for music-hall revues, plays, concerts, and movies through **Cartelera Baires** (⊠ Av. Corrientes 1382, Local 24, El Centro ☎ 11/4372–5058). **Cartelera Vea Más** (⊠ Av. Corrientes 1660, Paseo La Plaza, Local 26 El Centro ☎ 11/4370–5319) sells discount movie and theater tickets.

CLASSICAL MUSIC
& OPERA By any standard, the **Teatro Colón** (⊠ Ticket office, Tucumán 1111, El Centro ☎ 11/4378–7100 or 11/4370–7132) is one of the world's finest opera houses. An ever-changing stream of imported talent bolsters the well-regarded local company. The opera and symphony seasons run from March to December. The **Teatro San Martín** (⊠ Av. Corrientes 1530, El Centro ☎ 11/4374–9680) holds year-round classical music performances by top Argentine performers: many concerts are free.

DANCE When you think dance in Buenos Aires, you think of the tango—and this is the capital of that most passionate of dances. But dance is not only about the tango: Porteños also gather in droves on weekends to dance to the pulsating beats of samba and salsa.

Dance all night to fantastic salsa at relaxed **Calle 24** (⊠ Aráoz 2424, Palermo ☎ 11/4943–7736); some nights feature other Latin rhythms, so call ahead to check what's on. The best salsa dancers in town show off their moves (and their outfits) at **Caribean Salsa** (⊠ Rivadavia 2217, Once ☎ 11/4326–4546). Get into Brazilian rhythms at **Maluco Beleza** (⊠ Sarmiento 1728 Capital Federal, Palermo ☎ 11/4372–1737), where you can learn to samba, lambada, and even *capoeira.* Cuban rhythms fill the floor at **Ron y Son** (⊠ Salta 508, San Telmo ☎ 11/4382–3427)—Friday and Saturday there's a dinner orchestra playing *son* and *boleros,* then things heat up when owner Ibrahim Ferrer Junior (son of the Buena Vista Social Club star) and his band take to the stage. **La Trastienda** (⊠ Balcarce 460, at Belgrano, San Telmo ☎ 11/4342–7650) is a large dance hall hosting salsa classes and energetic crowds; it also occasionally doubles as a performance space for tango shows. The oldest and most important club in the Buenos Aires salsa scene is undoubtedly **La Salsera** (⊠ Yatay 961, Almagro ☎ 11/4866–1829), which has great music in a casual setting.

The **Ballet del Colón** is headquartered at the Teatro Colón but gives open-air performances in Palermo in summer. When world-famous Argentine dancer **Julio Bocca and the Ballet Argentino** perform in Buenos Aires, it's often at unconventional locations such as the rock and sports stadium **Luna Park** (⊠ Bouchard 465, El Centro ☎ 11/4311–1990). Avant-garde contemporary Argentine dance troupes often perform at **Centro Cultural Recoleta** (⊠ Junín 1930, La Recoleta ☎ 11/4803–1040). World-class contemporary dance is performed several times a year at the **Teatro San Martín** (⊠ Av. Corrientes 1530, El Centro ☎ 11/4374–9680).

FILM Buenos Aires is a great city for film lovers, with about 50 movie theaters in the downtown area offering everything from standard Hollywood flicks to Argentine films to world art-house fare. The names of films are generally given in Spanish, but English-language films are shown undubbed, with Spanish subtitles. The stretch of Calle Lavalle between Florida and 9 de Julio is lined with old one- or two-screen cinemas, which, with their plush bucket seats and classic theater architecture, make up in charm for what they lack in audio-visual finesse. The Lavalle theaters charge 4 to 5 pesos for all screenings. There are several art-house theaters on Avenida Corrientes, but be aware that foreign-language films are only subtitled in Spanish. Many museums and cultural centers also have screening rooms for off-beat movies. All of the major shopping malls have large state-of-the-art cinema complexes that charge 8 or 9 pesos, with half-price tickets available for the first show of the day and all day Wednesday. Weekends, there are *trasnoche* show times starting after midnight. Check the *Herald, Clarín,* or *La Nación* for daily listings. Every April, Buenos Aires hosts the *Festival de Cine Independiente,* which showcases the choicest independent films from all over the world.

Cine Lorca (⊠ Corrientes 1428, El Centro ☎ 11/4371–5017) has two screens showing the best of independent and art-house films in classic surroundings. At the 10-screen multiplex **Cinemark Palermo** (⊠ Beruti 3399, Palermo ☎ 11/4827–9500) you can catch the latest from Hollywood in comfort. **Cinemark Puerto Madero** (⊠ Av. M. de Justo 1960, Puerto Madero ☎ 11/4315–3008) has comfortable seating and eight screens. If you know Spanish, check out the **Complejo Cultural Tita Merello** (⊠ Suipacha 442, El Centro ☎ 11/4322–1195), which screens only Argentine cinema. The **Hoyts General Cinema** (⊠ Av. Corrientes 3200, El Centro ☎ 11/4866–4800) complex is inside the Abasto shopping mall and is the main location for films shown in the *Festival de Cine Independiente* (Independent Film Festival). The largest and most luxurious theater in the city is the **Village Recoleta** (⊠ Vicente Lópes and Junín, La Recoleta ☎ 0810–444–66843), inside the entertainment complex next to the Recoleta cemetery.

Sports & the Outdoors

Bicycling, In-Line Skating & Running

You can cover a lot of Buenos Aires on wheels and heels, but cyclists should beware, as Porteño drivers are not known for their tolerance of two-wheelers: expect to be cut off frequently, and to find even marked bicycle routes full of parked cars. Twenty-three kilometers (14 mi) of well-marked bike trails, known as *bicisendas* (⊠ Trailhead: Av. Lugones at General Paz, Núñez, at the edge of Capital Federal), connect the major green spaces within the city. You can rent bikes and in-line skates at the **Circuito KDT** (⊠ Salguero 3450, El Centro ☎ 11/4802–2619). The **Reserva Ecológica** (⊠ Av. Tristán Achával Rodríguez 1550, Puerto Madero ☎ 11/4315–1320) is ideal for running, skating, and cycling, but it's wise to do so with a partner, for safety's sake.

Chess

Pursuing a hobby, especially one with such a universal language as chess, is a good way to meet Argentines. You can pick up a game at the following places. In Palermo Hollywood, funky **Acabar** (⊠ Honduras 5733, Palermo ☎ 11/4772–0845) is dedicated to all things ludic—shelves are stacked with all kinds of board games that diners and drinkers can use. **Gran Café Tortoni** (⊠ Av. de Mayo 829, Plaza de Mayo ☎ 11/4342–4328) offers old-world elegance. Play under chandeliers and to the sounds of tango at the classic *confiteria* **La Ideal** (✉ Suipacha 384, El Centro ☎ 11/4326–1081). If you prefer a game in the sun, **Parque Rivadavia** (✉ Rivadavia between Acoyte and Doblas, Caballito) has dozens of outdoor tables, which fill up afternoons and weekends with local chess and checkers players.

Horse Racing

It is said that the mighty Argentine Thoroughbreds were one of the contributing factors for the British victory in the South African Boer War. Argentines import select stock for breeding swift horses, prized throughout the world. Although the past 40 years of rough economic instability has handicapped the Thoroughbred industry, Argentine horses still win their share of races worldwide. There are two main tracks in Buenos Aires; check the *Buenos Aires Herald* for schedules.

The **Hipódromo Argentino de Palermo** (✉ Av. del Libertador 4101, Palermo ☎ 11/4777–9009), across from the polo fields in Palermo, is 10 minutes from downtown. The 1878 belle epoque architecture of the Tattersall (grandstand) and gardens add an elegant touch to the sport.

Generally, two races per week take place at the **Hipódromo de San Isidro** (✉ Av. Márquez 504, Buenos Aires Province ☎ 11/4743–4010).

Polo

The major Argentine Polo tournaments are played in November. Stunning athletic showmanship is displayed on the two excellent fields of the Palermo **Campo Argentino de Polo** (Argentine Polo Field; ✉ Av. del Libertador 4000 at Dorrego, Palermo), a source of national pride. Admission to autumn (March–May) and spring (September–December) matches is free. The much-heralded Campeonato Argentino Abierto (Argentine Open Championship) takes place in November; admission runs 15–120 pesos. Tickets can be purchased in advance by phone through **Ticketek** (☎ 11/4323–7200) or at the polo field on the day of the event. For match information contact the **Asociación Argentina de Polo** (✉ H. Yrigoyen 636, fl. 1, Apt. A, Plaza de Mayo ☎ 11/4331–4646 ⊕ www.aapolo.com).

Soccer

For most Porteños, *fútbol* (soccer) is a fervent passion. The national team is one of the top five of 203 teams in the FIFA–Coca-Cola World Ranking. The World Cup can bring the country to a standstill. Matches are held year-round and are as exciting as they are dangerous. You're safest in the *platea* (preferred seating area), which cost around 20–60 pesos, rather than in the chaotic 10 pesos *popular* (standing room) section. Passions run especially high when the Boca Juniors take on their arch rivals, the River Plate in the match known as the *supercláisco. Hinchas* (fans) paint their faces accordingly: blue and yellow for Boca Juniors or red and white for the River Plate.

Tickets can be purchased at long lines at the stadiums, through **Ticketek** (☎ 11/4323–7200), or through the teams' official Web sites. The River Plate play at **Estadio Antonio Vespucio Liberti** (✉ Av. Pte. Figueroa Alcorta 7597, Núñez ☎ 11/4788–1200 ⊕ www.cariverplate.com.ar), better known as the Monumental, for its size. Argentina's international football matches also take place here. **Estadio Boca Juniors** (✉ Brandsen 805, La Boca ☎ 11/4362–2152 ⊕ www.bocajuniors.com.ar), also known as *La Bombonera* (meaning candy box, supposedly because the sound of fans' singing reverberates as it would inside a candy box), is the Boca Juniors' home stadium.

Spas

Many of the luxury hotels listed in the lodging section offer spa and health facilities. With more than a century of experience, **Colmegna Spa** (✉ Av. Sarmiento 839, El Centro ☎ 11/4326–1257) is a standout in urban spas. For 150 pesos you can luxuriate for a day with a Turkish bath, body peel, massage, hair treatment, and a healthy light lunch. Reservations are essential. It's open Monday–Saturday 11–8. French-run **Evian Agua Club & Spa** (✉ Cerviño 3626, Palermo ☎ 11/4807–4688) has a variety of day-spa programs, which include massages and hydrotherapy as well as access to their other facilities, with prices ranging 140–240 pesos. Reservations are essential.

Shopping

Porteños are known for their obsession with fashion. As a result, Buenos Aires has a wide range of options for buying clothing and footwear, from shopping malls and commercial strips to cobbled streets with designer boutiques. Open-air markets are a great source for souvenir handicrafts.

Many shops in traditional tourist areas (such as Calle Florida) are taking advantage of the confusion caused by currency devaluation, and may try to charge tourists in dollars for what they charge Argentines for in pesos, so always confirm which currency you're dealing with up front.

When shopping in Buenos Aires, keep your receipts: the 21% VAT tax, included in the sales price, is entirely refundable for purchases exceeding $200 at stores displaying a duty-free sign. When you depart, allow plenty of time to visit the return desk at the airport to obtain your refund.

Art & Antiques

Most antiques shops are grouped together in San Telmo near Plaza Dorrego. One of the city's largest auction houses, **Posadas** (✉ Posadas 1227, La Recoleta ☎ 11/4815–3573), has furnishings and artwork from local estates. Check the *Herald* and *La Nación* for scheduled estate auctions.

Clothing

Head to Avenida Alvear and Calle Quintana for haute couture; ready-to-wear clothing can be found along the shopping strips at Avenida Santa Fe 800–1500, on Calle Florida from Plaza San Martín to Corrientes, and at Belgrano's Avenida Cabildo 1600–2200, with discount and seconds stores on Avenida Córdoba 4400–5000. The following chain stores appear in nearly every mall and shopping strip: **Voss** (funky baby clothes), **Cheeky** (colorful, smart clothing for children from infants to preteens), **Chocolate** (good-quality clothing for women in their twenties), **Cristóbal Colón** (rugged outdoorsy clothes), **Mancini** (clothes for the modern professional man). A wide range of trendy young menswear is available at **Bensimon. Ona Saez** and **Kosiuko** sell edgy women's and men's clothes.

Paula Cahen D'Anvers has a modern, clean line for women and an adorable selection for very young children. **Port Said** does stylish clothes for older women. For young designers, head to Palermo Viejo, and check out the arcades on Santa Fe for vintage and club wear.

Handicrafts

Among the unique crafts you'll come across are traditional ponchos, mates, *boleadoras* (gaucho lassos), wood carvings, leather goods, silver, and alpaca products. With wide selections and good prices, open-air markets are the best places for purchasing crafts, but you can also find them throughout the city in specialty shops. For authentic, top-quality furniture and textiles, try **Arte Étnico Argentino** (⊠ El Salvador 4900, Palermo ☎ 11/4833–6661 ☉ Closed mornings). **Kelly's** (⊠ Paraguay 431, El Centro ☎☎ 11/4311–5712 Ⓜ Line C, Estación San Martín) sells high-quality crafts from all over Argentina. The best silverware in town, including *mates*, gaucho belt buckles, and jewelry, is at **Platería Parodi** (⊠ Av. de Mayo 720, El Centro ☎ 11/4342–2207 Ⓜ Line A, Estación Piedras). The cream of Argentine designers show off unusual contemporary handicrafts, as well as cutting-edge jewelry, clothing, accessories, furniture, and items for the home at **Puro Diseño Argentino** (⊠ Buenos Aires Design Center Shop 1004, Av. Pueyrredón 2501, La Recoleta ⊕ www.purodiseno.com.ar).

Jewelry

You'll find 18- and 20-karat gold and silver in Argentina at competitive prices. The inexpensive gold district is on **Calle Libertad**, between avenidas Corrientes and Rivadavía. Bargaining is expected. Be sure to ask if the stone is real, or you may take home a surprise. You'll find Brazilian emeralds and the semiprecious *rodocrosita*, "rose of the Inca," ranging in color from pink to red and native only to Argentina. **Antonio Belgiorno** (⊠ Av. Santa Fe 1347, La Recoleta ☎ 11/4811–1117), an excellent silversmith, crafts singular quality pieces. Decorated sculptures of birds in flight from **Cousiño** (⊠ in Sheraton Buenos Aires Hotel, San Martín 1225, El Centro ☎ 11/4318–9000 ⊕ www.cousinojewels.com) are exhibited in the National Museum of Decorative Arts. **Guthman** (⊠ Viamonte 597, El Centro ☎ 11/4312–2471) has an acclaimed selection of jewelry. For high-quality classic silver jewelry, and silverware in general, try **Juan Carlos Pallarols Orfebre** (⊠ Defensa 1039, San Telmo ☎ 11/4362–0641), famous locally for having crafted pieces for Máxima, Argentina's export to the Dutch royal family. For unusual handmade contemporary designs, call to visit the workshop of designer **Paula Levy** (☎ 11/4553–9885 or 11/155–607–6135).

Leather

Anything that can be worn is available in leather in Buenos Aires. Items are cut from cowhide, antelope, kidskin, pigskin, sheepskin, lizard, snake, and porcupine in an array of colors and styles. You can often find prices that are cheaper than those abroad, but be sure to check the quality and stitching. The hub of Buenos Aires's leather industry are the dozens of specialist and wholesale stores on Murillo at Scalabrini Ortíz in Villa Crespo (accessible by subway), where some great bargains can be had, but shop carefully as quality and price vary wildly. Leather stores and shopping galleries line Calle Florida, where bargaining is commonplace.

For sheepskin jackets, head to **Arandú** (⊠ Paraguay 1259, El Centro ☎ 11/4816–6191), which also sells fur-lined saddles, boots, and other leather goods for that Marlboro-man look, Argentine-style. For well-designed jackets and other clothing in high-quality leather, try **Breeders** (⊠ Patio Bullrich Posadas 1245, La Recoleta ☎ 11/4814–7495). **Casa López** (⊠ M. T. de Alvear 640, Palermo ☎ 11/4311–3044) is known for classic designs with a modern twist, and is particularly good for jackets and bags. **La Martina** (⊠ Paraguay 661, El Centro ☎ 11/4311–5963) carries items for the discriminating equestrian. **Murillo 666** (⊠ Murillo 666, Villa Crespo ☎ 11/4855–2024 Ⓜ Line B, Estación Malabia), though out of the way, has a selection of women's bags and jackets at bargain prices. Check out **Prune** (⊠ Florida 963, El Centro) for chic, contemporary shoes and handbags. **Rossi y Caruso** (⊠ Av. Santa Fe 1601, La Recoleta ☎ 11/4811–1538) has quality riding equipment and classic handbags, clothing, shoes, and boots; King Juan Carlos of Spain and many other celebrities are customers here.

Markets

The array of open-air markets throughout Buenos Aires testifies to the esteem in which Argentina holds its artists. You'll find unique items while enjoying wonderful street performances. The selections include crafts, art, antiques, and curios. Opening times vary, though most take place on weekends from 10 to 5. Feel free to bargain, but don't expect it always to work. Traditional handicrafts, steak sandwiches, and folkloric dance displays are what makes the **Feria de Mataderos** (⊠ Lisandro de la Torre and Av. de los Corrales, Mataderos ☎ 11/4372–4836) famous. The market is open on Sunday only. **Feria de San Pedro Telmo** (⊠ Plaza Dorrego, Humberto I y Defensa, San Telmo ☎ 11/4331–9855), open Sunday only, packs a small San Telmo square with all kinds of antiques and curios, to the sound of tango, which is danced on the surrounding cobbled streets. Local artisans sell handmade clothes, jewelry, and homeware as well as more traditional crafts at the large **Feria Recoleta** (⊠ Avs. Libertador and Pueyrredón, La Recoleta ☎ 11/4343–0309), open weekends only. In the heart of colorful La Boca, **Vuelta de Rocha handicraft market (Caminito)** (⊠ Av. Pedro de Mendoza and Caminito, La Boca) has a good selection of work from local artists, as well as handicrafts and souvenirs.

Shoes

Guido (⊠ Florida 704, El Centro ☎ 11/4322–7548 ⊠ Av. Quintana 333, La Recoleta ☎ 11/4811–4567) carries men's shoes and loafers in traditional styles. Since 1897 **López Taibo** (⊠ Av. Corrientes 350, El Centro ☎ 11/4328–2132 ⊠ Av. Alvear 1902, La Recoleta ☎ 11/4804–8585) has made refined, durable men's and women's shoes and accessories. **Paruolo** (⊠ Alto Palermo Mall Av. Santa Fe 3251, Palermo ☎ 11/5777–8000 Ext. 8216) does hip, affordable shoes for young women. The weird and wonderful designs of **Ricky Sarcany** (⊠ Paseo Alcorta, Salguero 3172, La Recoleta ☎ 11/4806–5439) are must-haves for local celebrities. For original designs and beautiful finishes, try well-priced **Zapatos de María** (⊠ Showroom: Libertad 1661, La Recoleta ☎ 11/4815–5001); all shoes are handmade.

Shopping Malls

Abasto (⊠ Av. Corrientes 3247, El Centro, ☎ 11/4959–3400 Ⓜ Line B, Estación Carlos Gardel), in a renovated marketplace, has clothing stores, restaurants, cinemas, a children's museum, and several interesting tango spots housed in a huge historic building that used to be the city's main market.

Busy **Alto Palermo** (⊠ Av. Santa Fe 3251, at Av. Colonel Díaz, Palermo ☎ 11/5777–8000 Ⓜ Line D, Estación Bulnes) has three floors with about 130 shops, an extensive food hall, a cinema, and an entertainment center.

Galerías Pacífico (⊠ Calle Florida 753, at Av. Córdoba, El Centro ☎ 11/4319–5100 Ⓜ Line B, Estación Florida) is in a building designed during Buenos Aires's turn-of-the-20th-century golden age in the style of Milan's Galleria Vittorio Emanuele, and features original murals by several Argentine greats. Now a polished, split-level, multipurpose center, it includes refined shops and boutiques, a food court, a cinema, and the Centro Cultural Borges, a showcase for young talent.

Argentine designers show their new lines of ready-to-wear clothing for men and women at **Paseo Alcorta** (⊠ Salguero 3172, at Av. F. Alcorta, Palermo ☎ 11/5777–6500). You'll find international labels, such as Christian Dior, Kenzo, Ralph Lauren, Mozel, and Yves St-Laurent. Also here are an entertainment center, a movie theater, and a food court.

Patio Bullrich (⊠ Enter at Posadas 1245 or Av. del Libertador 750, La Recoleta ☎ 11/4815–3501) has some of the finest and priciest shops in town, as well as a movie theater. The multilevel mall was once the headquarters for the Bullrich family's renowned auction house.

Solar de la Abadía (⊠ Marie Luis Campos at Arcos, Belgrano ☎ 11/4778–5005) has an upbeat feeling and is a great place to pick up souvenirs, buy trendy clothing, or enjoy a snack in the food court or at one of the surrounding bistros and bars.

Wool

Argentina has traditionally been the world's largest exporter of wool. Shopping malls sell quality wool items in a variety of styles. Unusual hand-made knitwear and woven clothing is sold at some Palermo fashion boutiques as well as in the open-air markets. For classic, well-made knitwear try **Alessia** (⊠ Galerías Pacífico, Calle Florida 753, El Centro ☎ 11/5555–5321). High-quality contemporary woolen clothing for men, women, and children is made by **María Aversa** (⊠ El Salvador 4580, Palermo ☎ 11/4833–0073). **Silvia y Mario** (⊠ M. T. de Alvear 550, Palermo) stocks a huge selection of elegant cashmere ensembles.

Buenos Aires A to Z

AIRPORTS & TRANSFERS

All international flights arrive and depart from Aeropuerto Internacional Ministro Pistarini, more widely known as Ezeiza International Airport, 47 km (29 mi) outside of downtown Buenos Aires. Ezeiza is served by a variety of foreign airlines, as well as domestic airlines with international routes. Departure tax is $30.50, or the equivalent in pesos.

Domestic flights within Argentina and flights from Uruguay generally depart from Aeroparque Jorge Newbery, about 15 or 20 minutes from downtown. The airport tax is about $15 for domestic flights and $10 for flights to Uruguay.

🔢 **Aeroparque Jorge Newbery** ☎ 11/5480-6111. **Ezeiza International Airport** ☎ 11/5480-6111.

AIRPORT
TRANSFERS

There are several means of transportation between the airports and Buenos Aires. Information counters within the airports can help you choose among the various licensed transport services; you can also check with the airport's Secretary of Tourism office for additional assistance. Generally, the cheapest transportation is by colectivo (2 pesos), but the trip can take a while—up to two hours from Ezeiza International Airport—and you're only allowed two bags. Privately owned bus or van service is about 15 pesos per passenger to downtown from Ezeiza, with scheduled departures. *Remises* (unmarked taxis with prearranged fixed prices) run 35–45 pesos from Ezeiza and 8–12 pesos from Jorge Newbery Airport; they're limited to four passengers. Metered taxi service, available at the sidewalk, can be a bit steeper depending on traffic.

🔢 **Manuel Tienda León** ☎ 11/4383-4454 or 0810/888-5366 ⊕ www.tiendaleon.com.

BUS TRAVEL

Most long-distance and international buses arrive at and depart from the Estación Terminal de Omnibus. The terminal houses more than 60 bus companies, arranged in order of destinations served, not by name. Rates vary according to distance, services, and season; compare prices before purchasing.

Colectivos (city buses) connect the city's barrios and the Greater Buenos Aires area. You're assured a seat on a *diferencial* bus (indicated by a sign on the front of the bus); they run less frequently than colectivos and are more expensive. Bus stops are on every other block (200 meters [656 feet] apart) and are marked by an easy-to-miss small metal sign with the number of the bus line. Hail your bus and let the driver know your destination; then insert your coins in the machine (exact change is not necessary, but coins are), which will print your ticket. Fares within the perimeter of the city are 65¢ to 80¢; diferencials cost 2 pesos for any destination in the city. Once on board, head for the back, where you'll disembark. A small bell on the grab bar lets you indicate where you'd like to get off to the driver. Don't depend on the drivers for much assistance; they're busy trying to navigate traffic. You can purchase "Lumi Guía de Transporte," a handy guide to the routes, at any news kiosk, or visit the Spanish-language colectivo Web site.

🔢 **Colectivo** ⊕ www.loscolectivos.com.ar. **Estación Terminal de Omnibus** ✉ Av. Ramos Mejía 1680, El Centro ☎ 11/4310-0700.

CAR RENTAL

Note that some reputable local agencies tend to be more affordable than international companies and offer the same quality service.

Hiring a remis—car with driver—is a comfortable and convenient way to tour the city. This service costs about 25–35 pesos per hour, sometimes with a three-hour minimum and an additional charge per kilometer (½ mi) if you drive outside the city limits.

🚖 Local Agencies **Annie Millet** ✉ Av. Santa Fe 883, 1st fl., El Centro ☎ 11/6777-7777 ⊕ www.amillet.com.ar. **GVS** ✉ Leandro N. Alem 699, El Centro ☎ 11/4315-0777. **Localiza** ✉ Maipu 924, El Centro ☎ 0800/999-2999 or 11/4315-8483 ⊕ www.localiza.com.ar. **Rent-a-Sol** ✉ Av. Libertador 6553, Belgrano ☎ 11/4787-2140 or 11/4787-1414.

🚖 Major Agencies **Avis** ✉ Ezeiza International Airport, Ezeiza ☎ 11/4480-9387 ✉ Jorge Newbery Airport, Costanera ☎ 11/4776-3003 ✉ Cerrito 1527, El Centro ☎ 11/4326-5542 ⊕ www.avis.com.ar. **Dollar** ✉ M. T. de Alvear 449, El Centro ☎ 11/4315-8800 ⊕ www.dollar.com.ar.

🚖 Remises **Annie Millet Transfers** ✉ Santa Fe 883, fl. 1, El Centro ☎ 11/6777-7777. **Remises REB** ✉ Billinghurst 68, Palermo ☎ 11/4863-1226 or 11/4862-6271. **Remises Rioja** ✉ Rioja 3023, Olivos ☎ 11/4794-4677. **Remises Universal** ✉ 25 de Mayo 611, fl. 4, El Centro ☎ 11/4315-6555.

CAR TRAVEL

Avenida General Paz completely encircles Buenos Aires. If you're driving into the city from the exterior, you'll know you're in Buenos Aires proper once you've crossed this road. If you're entering the city from the north, chances are you will be on the Ruta Panamericana, which has wide lanes and good lighting. Autopista 25 de Mayo is the quickest way to the airport from downtown. The R2 (Ruta 2) takes you to the Atlantic coastal beach resorts in and around Mar del Plata.

Porteños drive with verve, independence, and a general disdain for traffic rules. A more convenient and comfortable option is to have your travel agent or hotel arrange for a remis, especially for a day's tour of the suburbs or nearby pampas. This service costs about 25–35 pesos per hour, sometimes with a three-hour minimum and an additional charge per kilometer if you drive outside the city limits. Remises usually end up being cheaper than cabs, especially during peak hours.

If you prefer to take the wheel and try your hand at dealing with Buenos Aires road rage, you can rent a car at any agency in the city. Drive defensively and use caution when approaching overpasses and upon exiting, as there have been incidences of *ladrillazos* (brick throwing) for the purpose of theft.

PARKING Parking can be a problem in the city, but there are several underground municipal parking garages and numerous private garages. Look for a blue sign with an E (for *estacionamiento* [parking]). The cost is about 3–4 pesos for the first hour, and 1–1.50 pesos for each additional half hour. Most shopping malls have parking garages, which are usually free or give you a reduced rate with a purchase.

RULES OF THE ROAD Most driving rules in the United States apply here, but keep in mind the following: right turns on red are not allowed; never park on the left side of the street, where there is a yellow line on the curb, or near a bus stop; and left turns are seldom allowed, unless indicated. Where there are no traffic lights, intersections are a free-for-all; vehicles coming from your right have the right-of-way. During the week, Microcentro, the bustling commercial and financial district bounded by Carlos Pellegrini, Avenida Córdoba, Avenida Leandro Alem, and Avenida de Mayo, is off-limits to vehicles other than public transportation.

EMERGENCIES

There's a pharmacy on nearly every block in Buenos Aires, indicated by a green cross. Your hotel will be able to guide you to the nearest one. *Farmacias de turno* rotate 24-hour shifts or remain open 24 hours and will deliver to your hotel, if in the area.

7 Emergency Services **Ambulance** ☎ 107. **Fire** ☎ 100. **Police** ☎ 111 or 114346-5770.

7 Hospital **British Hospital** ✉ Pedriel 74, Barracas ☎ 11/4304-2052, 11/4334-9000 emergencies.

7 24-hour Pharmacies **Farmacia Cabildo** ✉ Cabildo 1971, Belgrano ☎ 11/4781-8788. **Farmacia DeMaria** ✉ F. J. Sta. Maria de Oro 2927, Palermo ☎ 11/4778-7311. **Farmacia Luciani** ✉ Las Heras 2002, La Recoleta ☎ 11/4803-6111.

HEALTH

The city water and sanitation services are optimum, though you may prefer to purchase bottled water for drinking: many find the chlorine in the city's water supply unpleasant.

MONEY MATTERS

Ever since the Argentine peso was devalued in 2002, U.S. dollars have not been as widely accepted. If you arrive in Buenos Aires with dollars or euros, it's best to get them changed at one of the many "casa de cambios" or change houses located in El Centro. Use caution though, as would-be thieves are known to canvas the area. Another option is to ask your hotel to change your money into pesos, although you will likely get a less favorable exchange rate.

CURRENCY EXCHANGE At Ezeiza International Airport you can exchange currency at Casa Piano and Banco Nación, in Terminal A, on the ground level. You may want to use an ATM, also found in Terminal A, to extract local currency for a better rate. You can exchange currency at any of the locations below.

7 Exchange Services **American Express** ✉ Arenales 707, El Centro ☎ 11/4310-3000. **Banco Piano** ✉ San Martín 345, El Centro ☎ 11/4394-2463. **BankBoston** ✉ Florida 99, El Centro ☎ 11/4820-2000. **Cambio America** ✉ Sarmiento 501, El Centro ☎ 11/4393-0054. **Citibank** ✉ Bartolomé Mitre 530, El Centro ☎ 11/4329-1000. **Forex Cambio** ✉ M. T. de Alvear 540, El Centro ☎ 11/4312-7729 or 11/4311-5543. **HSBC Republic** ✉ Florida 201, El Centro ☎ 11/4320-2800. **Western Union** ✉ J. L. Borges 2472, Palermo ☎ 11/4777-1940.

SAFETY

Buenos Aires is generally a safe city. Violent crime is rare, and at any time of night, you'll see young children and old ladies strolling about, apparently unconcerned about the hour or the darkness. Police consistently patrol areas where tourists are likely to be. That said, keep in mind that Buenos Aires is a big city and take precautions: pickpocketing and robberies are not uncommon. Go out at night in pairs or, better yet, in groups.

Though there are still sporadic protests, they have taken on a much calmer and more subdued tone compared to the height of the economic crisis in 2001 and 2002. If you happen upon a demonstration, exercise caution, but don't be overly concerned—there have not been any violent protests in the city for a while.

SUBWAY TRAVEL

The *subte,* the oldest subway system in Latin America, dating to 1913, has five underground lines and the *premetro,* which runs above ground in the General Savio barrio. All begin in El Centro and fan out in different directions. Though not as extensive as the bus system, subte service is efficient and inexpensive. Trains marked with R (for *Rapido*) run express.

Line A travels beneath Avenida Rivadavía from Plaza de Mayo to Primera Junta and is serviced by handsome antique wooden cars. Line B begins at Leandro Alem Station, in the financial district, and runs under Avenida Corrientes to Federico Lacroze Station. Line C, under Avenida 9 de Julio, connects the two major train stations, Retiro and Constitución, making stops along the way in El Centro. Line D runs from Catedral Station on Plaza de Mayo to Congreso de Túcuman in Belgrano. Line E takes you from Bolívar Station, at Plaza de Mayo, to Plaza de los Virreyes, in the neighborhood of Chacabuco.

Cospeles (tokens) and subway passes cost 70¢ and will take you anywhere in the subway system. The subte shuts down around 10 PM and reopens at 5 AM.

📶 **Metrovías** ☎ 11/4553-9214 or 0800/555-1616 ⊕ www.metrovias.com.ar.

TAXIS

Taxis are easy to identify: they're black and have yellow tops. An unoccupied one will indicate LIBRE on the left-hand side of the windshield. Hail it, or call for a radio taxi and wait a few minutes. There's always a slight risk of coming across a thief posing as a taxi driver, and there's no way of identifying one until it's too late. If you telephone for a taxi, you'll have to wait a few minutes, but you can be sure of its origin.

Meters start at 1.12 pesos and charge 14¢ per ¼ km (⅛ mi); you'll also end up paying for standing time spent at a light or in a traffic jam. In the central downtown area, fares average 2–4 pesos out to Recoleta will cost you 5–6 pesos, San Telmo 4–6 pesos, and Belgrano 8 pesos.

📶 Taxi Companies **Blue Way Taxi** ☎ 11/4777-8888. **City Taxi** ☎ 11/4585-5544. **Cirtax Taxi** ☎ 11/4504-8440. **Su Taxi** ☎ 11/4635-2500.

TELEPHONES

Public phones are found on nearly every block and usually operate with a telephone card, which can be purchased at any kiosk. Simply slide the card in, check your card's remaining minutes, then dial. Some public phones are coin operated. To make a long-distance call from a pay phone, go to a *telecentro* or *locutorio*—found throughout the city—providing private booths and fax service, as well as Internet and e-mail services for about 3 pesos per hour. (Note that you may still need a local phone card to make a long-distance call, even if you have your own calling card.)

When calling cellular phone numbers in Buenos Aires, dial 15 before the number (unless calling from another cellular phone with a Buenos Aires number). Local cellular phone charges vary and are charged to the caller, unless made from a public phone. Cellular-phone rentals are available, though pricey; some hotels even rent phones.

VISITOR INFORMATION

Tourist information centers at the airports and in six locations around the city provide maps, though few brochures, and have English-speaking personnel. You'll find the centers on the Caminito; Calle Florida; Centro Cultural General San Martín, at Avenida Sarmiento 1551; at the Obelisk; in Puerto Madero; and at the Retiro Bus Terminal, at the corner of Avenida Antártida Argentina and Calle 10. For friendly guidance and brochures, maps, and even vacation-planning tips, try the information counter on the second floor of the Galerías Pacífico shopping center at Calle Florida 753.

You can get information over the phone, on weekdays from 9 to 5, from the Dirección de Turismo del Gobierno de la Ciudad de Buenos Aires. The Secretaría de Turismo de la Nación runs a telephone information service, which is toll-free from any point in Argentina, 24 hours a day.

🔲 **Dirección de Turismo del Gobierno de la Ciudad de Buenos Aires** ☎ 11/4313–0187 ⊕ www.buenosaires.gov.ar. **Secretaría de Turismo de la Nación** ✉ Av. Santa Fe 883, El Centro ☎ 11/4312–2232 or 0800/555–0016 ⊕ www.turismo.gov.ar.

THE PAMPAS

Updated by Robin Goldstein

The most famous area of Buenos Aires province is the Pampas—an unending sea of grass, occasionally interrupted by winding streams and low hills. The region comprises nearly one-quarter of Argentina (including the provinces of La Pampa and southern Córdoba and Santa Fé, in addition to Buenos Aires Province) and it is deeply infused in the Argentine identity. The name derives from the native Quéchua word for "flat field"—the Pampas's famous fertile grasslands are home to the horses and cattle that make up the mainstay of Argentina's economy. All over are signs of active ranch life, from the cattle grazing to the modern-day gauchos working the wide-open spaces. Some of the Pampas's best sights, each with a distinct draw, are within an hour's drive of the nation's capital, Buenos Aires.

La Plata

50 km (31 mi) southeast of Buenos Aires via R1 and R14.

At the famous 1889 Paris Exposition (think Eiffel Tower), Jules Verne honored La Plata with a gold medal, citing the newly built city as a symbol of resplendent modernity. Accepting the medal was Dardo Rocha, the Buenos Aires governor who a few years prior assembled a team of architects and planners and created the provincial capital from the dust of semi-arid desert.

La Plata succeeds today from that creative genesis, a beautiful city of palatial estates on an ordered grid intersected by wide, diagonal boulevards and a rational scheme of parks and plazas every six blocks. The core of the city's planning is the "monumental axis" between 51st and 53rd streets, which contains most of the attractive churches, and government and cultural buildings.

Catedral de La Plata stands at the south end of Plaza Moreno's tiled walkway. This graceful, pinkish brick building is a jewel of late-19th-century architecture. The neo-Gothic structure, inspired by cathedrals in Amiens and Cologne, was originally inaugurated in 1932 but lacked the long double spires. During the past decade of restoration, the monumental stained-glass window was completed and a museum documenting the church's history was added. Construction wasn't complete until November 19, 2000—118 years to the day after the city's foundation stone was laid. A carillon with 25 bronze bells enlivens the western (51st Street) tower; the eastern (53rd Street) tower has an elevator that rises to a lookout with the city's best views. ⊠ *Calle 14 between Calles 51 and 53* ☎ *221/4224–4184, museum 221/424–0112* ⊕ *www.catedral.laplata.net* ⊙ *Museum Mon.–Sat. 9–7, Sun. 9–1 and 4:30–8:30.*

At the north end of Plaza Moreno is the 1883 German neoclassical **Palacio Municipal,** which is recognizable by its central clock tower. The sumptuous interior is worthy of exploration, especially the Salón Dorado (Golden Salon), with its marble staircase, painted ceilings, and mosaic tile floors. ⊠ *Plaza Moreno s/n* ⊙ *Daily 10–6.*

In the northern portion of the city, the eucalyptus-shaded forest promenade, **Paseo del Bosque,** is a good place to relax. Recreational options include a lake with paddle-boat rentals, an outdoor amphitheater, and an equestrian center.

The **Universidad Nacional de La Plata** (La Plata National University; ⊠ Av. 7 No. 776 ☎ 221/483–3349), in Paseo del Bosque, is one of the most famous universities in Argentina and one of the few with a campus in the style of a North American or European school.

The geographic center of the city is **Plaza Moreno,** where the Piedra Fundacional (La Plata's Founding Stone) was laid in 1882.

The equestrian statue of South American liberator José de San Martín stands in the center of **Plaza San Martín.** On the north side of the square is the black slate roof of the French neoclassic Legislatura (provincial legislature) building. On the west end is the Pasaje Dardo Rocha, a building originally designed as a train station, which was converted into a grand cultural center.

Teatro Argentino—a seven-story concrete behemoth by Le Corbusier—replaced a palace that burned down in 1977. Inside is the country's second-largest theater. ⊠ *Av. 51 s/n* ☎ *221/429–1743.*

☼ Fifteen minutes (7 km/4 mi) outside the city, the Eva Perón–founded **Ciudad de los Niños** (City of Children) is part amusement park, part museum. Children can walk through miniature replicas of historic Argentine buildings. ⊠ *Ruta General Belgrano, Km 7* ☎ *221/484–0194* ⊠ *1 peso* ⊙ *Daily 9 AM–sunset.*

Where to Stay & Eat

★ ¢–$ ✕ **Cervecería Modelo.** This alehouse restaurant opened its doors in 1892—just 10 years after the city was founded. The most interesting tradition is tossing peanut shells to the floor. Pigeons, who have cleverly found a way inside, peck at the jettisoned shells. It's part of an established quirkiness that includes what might be the largest menu in the country (which an exceptionally friendly and fast waitstaff guide you through). The homemade pasta is a good bet; you have a choice of 25 sauces. The restaurant stays open late: until 2 AM weekdays and 3 AM weekends. ☒ *Calle 5 at Calle 54* ☎ *221/421–1321* ☱ *AE, DC, MC, V.*

$$$ ✕ **Estancia Juan Gerónimo.** South of La Plata in the tiny village of Veronica, this estancia, which is said to have once belonged to a shipwrecked English bandit, makes a perfect weekend getaway. The early 1920s ranch is set on a mammoth plot of land—more than 10,000 acres—that has been declared a UNESCO World Natural Biosphere Reserve. Day visits can be arranged. Horse enthusiasts love the grounds. It's said that after choosing from among 150 horses, you can ride around the estancia for three days without covering the same terrain. The working farm has a staff of a half-dozen cattle-handling gauchos. ☒ *In Veronica, 100 km (63 mi) south of La Plata, 165 km (103 mi) south of Buenos Aires* ☝ *Arroyo 873, Buenos Aires, 1007* ☎ *Buenos Aires reservations 11/4937–4326, estancia 222/148–1414* ☎ *11/4327–0105* ⊕ *www.juangeronimo.com.ar* ⤶ *11 rooms* ♻ *Restaurant, fishing, hiking, horseback riding, laundry service* ☱ *AE, MC, V* ⦿ *FAP.*

¢ ⊡ **Benevento Hotel.** This comfortable hotel resulted from the complete restoration of a circa 1890 home, which revealed sumptuous, long-hidden details. The elegant, bright white building has round corner bays on the upper three of its four floors and low, black iron rails on the balconies. Rooms—which have 15-foot ceilings, wood floors, and all-new bathrooms—vary in design, so you might want to look at a few before deciding. The corner rooms are magnificent. ☒ *Calle 2 645, 1900* ☎☎ *221/489–1078 or 221/437–7721* ⊕ *www.hotelbenevento.com.ar* ⤶ *20 rooms, 1 suite* ♻ *Restaurant, room service, in-room safes, bar, laundry service* ☱ *AE, MC, V* ⦿ *BP.*

Máximo Paz

50 km (31 mi) southeast of Buenos Aires, past the Ezeiza airport.

Máximo Paz is nothing more than a little working-class string of provisions stores and tire shops along a dusty strip of dirt—that is, until you reach the sprawling, luxurious Estancia Villa Maria, the town's only draw. It's an easy day trip or overnight from Buenos Aires—van service to the estancia is available if you don't want to drive.

Where to Stay & Eat

$$$$ ⊡ **Estancia Villa Maria.** This incredible Norman-Tudor mansion on 110 acres of countryside is evocative of the estates of English landed gentry. The expansive estate was bought in the 1890s by one of Argentina's wealthiest families. The crops were planted then, but the mansion itself—designed by Argentine architect Alejandro Bustillo—wasn't built until 1923. Whether wandering amidst the grounds, horseback riding, or sitting down

to a formal, family-style lunch in the colonial dining room, you can live out your aristocratic Argentine fantasies here. The omnipresent, attentive service will pamper you at every turn, and the deferential staff speaks English and French. At this writing, some of the breathtaking gardens were slated to be converted into a championship golf course. ⊠ *R205, Km 47, Máximo Paz, 1814* ☎ *Estancia 11/02274–450909, Buenos Aires reservations 11/4322–7785* 🖶 *11/4964–2710* ⊕ *www.estanciavmaria.com.ar* ⇩ *15 rooms* ⚘ *Restaurant, golf course, tennis court, pool, bicycles, horseback riding, laundry service* ⊟ *No credit cards* �“⊙I *FAP.*

Tigre & the Paraná Delta

30 km (19 mi) northwest of Buenos Aires on the Ruta Panamericana, 35 km (22 mi) northwest of Buenos Aires on Avenida Libertador.

A drive through the shady riverside suburbs of Buenos Aires takes you to the river port town of Tigre, the embarkation point for boats that ply the Delta del Paraná. The delta is a vast maze of canals, tributaries, and river expanding out like the veins of a leaf. A boat trip from Tigre through the delta makes a nice day trip from Buenos Aires. For an especially memorable ride, take a sunset cruise. Along the way you'll travel past colorfully painted houses built on stilts to protect them from floods. The most comfortable way to travel the delta's waterways is aboard a large catamaran. The picturesque **Puerto de Frutos** market, in the central part of the port area, is a good place to find handcrafted items at good prices. The market is particularly busy on weekends.

☾ Aside from the river, the main attraction is the **Tren de la Costa** (Coastal Train), originally built in 1895 as a passenger train and refurbished in 1990. Along its way from Estación Retiro in Buenos Aires to Tigre, the train meanders through some of Buenos Aires's most fashionable northern suburbs, stopping at 11 stations.

☾ At the end of the Tren de la Costa is **Parque de la Costa** (Coastal Park), one of Argentina's largest, most modern amusement parks. If you want to combine a visit here with sightseeing, take the ferryboat trip for a half-hour ride on the river delta. There's also an IMAX theater and restaurants with surprisingly good Argentine fare.

San Antonio de Areco

110 km (68 mi) west of Buenos Aires.

If you look around this small town off R8, you can find the most authentic scenes of traditional life in the Pampas. During the early 1700s the town was a regular stop on the route to Peru. Buenos Aires was still a part of the viceroyalty of Peru, and San Antonio de Areco was the last Spanish-populated settlement on the border of the native inhabitants' territory. The town has come to represent cowboy life, most notably at the gaucho museum. Across the street from the museum entrance is a typical *parrilla* (restaurant specializing in grilled meats), run by a local family, where traditional gaucho songs are sung. In summer the Río Areco (Areco River), which runs through town, is teeming with swimmers—especially a short walk from the museum near the center of town, at the Puente Viejo (Old Bridge). The sleepy downtown itself is made up of a couple of shopping streets typical of the small-town life of the Buenos Aires province.

The **Museo Gauchesco Ricardo Güiraldes** (Gaucho Museum) conjures up the gaucho life of the past by letting you explore traditional estancia grounds just outside of town, including a 150-year-old *pulpería* (an old country store from gaucho times) tavern with wax figures, a replica of an 18th-century hacienda, and an old chapel. The museum also documents the life and work of Ricardo Güiraldes (1886–1927), whose gaucho novels fired the popular imagination of the Argentine people. Güiraldes is buried in town. ⊠ *Camino Ricardo Güiraldes* ☎ *232/645–6201* ₪ *2 pesos* ☉ *Wed.–Mon. 11–5.*

Where to Stay & Eat

Note that you can do a day trip from Buenos Aires to one of the estancias listed below, though you will be asked to pay for a whole "ranch day"—which includes activities along with drinks, lunch, and afternoon empanadas—even if you only want to stop by for lunch.

¢–$ × **Almacen de Ramos Generales.** This old general store is airy and charming, with remnants stowed away in every corner. The food here is simply outstanding, and the small-town setting makes this all the more remarkable. The *picada* begins with salami, pork, cheese, eggplant *en escabeche* (pickled), and wondrous french fries with basil. The *bife de chorizo* (sirloin steak), meanwhile, is one of the best anywhere, perfectly juicy, tender, and flavorful. The atmosphere, too, is just right: it's country-store-meets-elegant-restaurant. Pleasant hues of light pour in from the plate-glass windows while you enjoy the impeccable service and memorable food. ⊠ *Zapiola 143, between Lavalle and Sdo. Sombra* ☎ *2326/456376* ⊕ *www.ramosgeneralesareco.com.ar* ▭ *No credit cards.*

FodorsChoice ★

$$$$ ×▥ **Estancia El Ombú de Areco.** This fantastic, faded-glory 1890s house on acres of lush land was built by General Richieri. One of the two relaxing swimming pools, where you'll be brought empanadas and drinks in the afternoon, is set on a miniature hill overlooking the fields. A stay here, complete with gaucho and folkloric shows, participation in daily ranch activities, horseback rides, tours of the nearby town, and four full meals, provides a great taste of the ranching lifestyle. ⊠ *Ruta 32, Cuartel VI, 1609* ☎☎ *Buenos Aires reservations 11/4710–2795; estancia 232/649–2080* ⊕ *www.estanciaelombu.com* ◀ *9 rooms* ♢ *Restaurant, 2 pools, laundry service* ▭ *AE, V* ◯ *FAP.*

$$ ×▥ **Estancia La Bamba.** The main house, owned by the venerable Aldao family, dates from around 1832 and is done in traditional Argentine style with beautiful, roofed verandas and an interior courtyard with a well. The garden is a great place for sunbathing or stargazing. Living and dining rooms ooze aristocratic country splendor. There are lovely views of the surrounding plains and all kinds of ranch activities. Rooms include the full package—four meals per day, eaten family-style with the other guests. Some staff members speak English. ⊠ *Reservations in Buenos Aires: Maipú 859, 4th fl., Buenos Aires, 1006* ☎☎ *Buenos Aires reservations 11/4314–0394; estancia 232/645–6293* ⊕ *www.la-bamba.com.ar* ◀ *8 rooms* ♢ *Restaurant, horseback riding, laundry service* ▭ *AE, V* ◯ *FAP.*

The Pampas A to Z

BOAT & FERRY TRAVEL

Boats are a good way to get around in the Tigre River delta. Fishermen may be willing to take you between coastal towns on their boats; arrangements can be made right at the pier, or your hotel can probably point you in the right direction.

BUS TRAVEL

Traveling by bus to the beach from Buenos Aires is very common. Cóndor is a recommended service from Buenos Aires to La Plata. The bus from Buenos Aires to La Plata costs about 5 pesos one-way and takes 1½ hours. For San Antonio de Areco, bus service is available on companies including Pullman General Belgrano and Chevallier.

🚌 **Chevallier** ✉ Smith and Gral. Paz, San Antonio de Areco ☎ 2326/453904. **Cóndor** ✉ Terminal de Autobuses, La Plata ☎ 221/423-2745. **Pullman General Belgrano** ✉ Segundo Sombra and Smith, San Antonio de Areco ☎ 2326/454059.

CAR TRAVEL

Driving is the best and most convenient option for getting to towns in the region. It's easiest to rent a car in Buenos Aires, but possible to pick up a rental in any of the towns listed.

EMERGENCIES

Emergency phone numbers are nationwide, and most major hospitals have some English-speaking doctors.

🚑 Emergency Services **Ambulance** ☎ 107. **Fire** ☎ 100. **Police** ☎ 101.

MONEY MATTERS

Local banks in all towns have 24-hour ATMs; most banks are on either the NYCE or Cirrus systems.

TRAIN TRAVEL

The Metropolitano rail line serves the southern part of Greater Buenos Aires and extends to the city of La Plata; it runs from Estación Constitución. Estación Once, in the city center, provides train service to some cities in the provinces of Buenos Aires and La Pampa through Ferrobaires. Tickets can be bought at the train station or booked by phone. Within the Pampas, train service is limited. Buses are generally more reliable.

🚆 **Estación Constitución** ✉ Av. General Hornos 11, near San Telmo, San Telmo ☎ 11/4304-0028. **Estación Once** ✉ Av. Pueyrredón and Bartolomé Mitre, Balvanera ☎ 11/4861-0043. **Ferrobaires** ☎ 11/4553-1295. **Metropolitano** ☎ 0800/666-358-736 ⊕ www.tms.com.ar. **Train tickets** ☎ 0800/222-8736.

MISIONES AND CATARATAS DEL IGUAZÚ

Updated by
Diego
Bigongiari

The small banana-shape province of Misiones juts out from the Argentine mass, surrounded by Paraguay to the east and Brazil to the west. Nowhere else in Argentina is there such a gorgeous subtropical landscape: the lush vegetation stunningly contrasts with the rich red tones of the soil, and three minor mountain chains give picturesque texture to the forest. The region also has an abundance of waterfalls—the most famous are the magnificent Cataratas del Iguazú.

Though nature is the main attraction in this province, the area is also known for its Jesuit mission ruins. The Jesuits, who came here in the early 17th century, were the first in a long line of foreigners to make their home in this province.

Posadas

1,060 km (657 mi) northeast of Buenos Aires.

One of the first Jesuit missions in the area, Reducción Nuestra Señora de la Encarnación de Itapúa was established in 1615 at Posadas, which is now the capital of Misiones Province. The mission later moved across the Río Paraná to present-day Encarnación, Paraguay. The area that is now Posadas was later occupied by Paraguayan troops, who used it as a base for doing commerce with Brazil. During the War of the Triple Alliance (1865–70), Argentina took possession of the land and the valuable stockpile of Brazilian products and christened the town Posadas. Of the wave of immigrants who came to the area in the late 19th century, many settled in Posadas. Today many descendants of these immigrants still live here, giving the town of nearly 250,000 a more cosmopolitan feel than other provincial capitals in the region. The tree-lined streets, plazas, and Costanera make the town very pleasant, though there's actually little to do. It's primarily a base for exploring other sights in the area, most notably the Jesuit mission ruins.

Before you visit the Jesuit mission ruins, it helps to get some background at the **Museo Arqueológico Andres Guacurari** (Andres Guacurari Archaeology Museum). You can learn about the unique society created by the missionaries and see objects found at the missions, such as ceramic tiles, a printing press, clothing, a Bible translated into Guaraní, and wooden statues of Christ. ⊠ *General Páz 1865* 🍲 *Free* ☉ *Daily 8–11 and 3–6.*

Where to Stay & Eat

★ $ ✕ **La Rueda.** There's no better place in town for a "running spit" and a "free fork." Less literally translated, *espeto corrido* and *tenedor libre* mean all-you-can-eat meat and salad. The enormous 30-year-old restaurant is a true town establishment. As suggested by the name, there's a wheel motif that pervades everything from the shape of the ceiling to the chairs. Although the restaurant is a bit outside town, the excellent quality of the meat and the very reasonable prices make it a good dining option. ⊠ *Juan Manuel de Rosas 6380* 🕾 *3752/454111* ▤ *MC, V* ☉ *No dinner Sun.*

¢–$ ✕ **El Oriental.** Depending on how long you've been in the region, you may be desperate for a change of cuisine: this is as exotic as it gets. The Chinese food here won't knock you off your feet, but it's generally good and quite inexpensive. Beware: in this carnivorous country, even the spring rolls have meat. ⊠ *Junín 2168* 🕾 *3752/430586* ▤ *DC, MC, V.*

$ 🏨 **Julio César.** Though the hotel doesn't quite live up to its reputation as the most luxurious accommodation in town (the rooms have shoddy rugs and peeling paint), its location is ideal, and the hotel's facilities are

excellent. Note that the superior rooms cost 15 pesos more than standard rooms and are only slightly nicer. ☒ *Entre Ríos 1951, 3300*
☎ *3752/427930* 🖷 *3752/420599* 🖳 *100 rooms, 5 suites* ♢ *Restaurant,
room service, minibars, pool, gym, bar, laundry service, meeting room,
Internet* ▤ *AE, DC, MC, V.*

★ $ 🏨 **La Aventura.** The 30 small cabañas set on stunning grounds have the
feel of a far-away weekend resort, yet they're only 15 minutes from town.
There's a fantastic view of the Río Paraná, just below. You can sunbathe
on the small strip of beach or by the large pool. The cabañas are clean
and modern and have kitchenettes. ☒ *Avs. Urquiza and Zapiola, take
Av. A. Guacurari from north end of town due west to Av. Urquiza, 3300*
☎🖷 *3752/465555* 🖳 *30 cabañas* ♢ *Restaurant, room service, kitchenettes, 2 tennis courts, pool, beach, fishing, volleyball, 2 bars, business
services* ▤ *AE, DC, MC, V.*

¢ 🏨 **Le Petit Hotel.** This small hotel, really more of a house, six blocks from
the town center, is the best bargain in town. Picasso prints hang in the
lobby and halls, and the modest-size guest rooms are cozy and well maintained. ☒ *Santiago del Estero 1630, 3300* ☎ *3752/436031* 🖳 *10
rooms* ♢ *Restaurant, Internet* ▤ *No credit cards.*

San Ignacio Miní

Fodor'sChoice
★   *59 km (37 mi) northeast of Posadas.*

San Ignacio Miní is the best-preserved and most frequently visited of
the Jesuit missions ruins. The mission was originally established in 1610
in Guayrá, a region of present-day Brazil. Seeking refuge from Portuguese
slave traders who were raiding the mission, capturing the native populations living there, and selling them in Brazil, the mission relocated to
a spot near the Río Paraná in 1632. In 1695 it moved again, 3½ km (2
mi) away, to where its ruins are today. At its height, in 1733, the mission had more than 3,300 Guaraní inhabitants; there were never more
than three Jesuits at any one time.

The mission's layout was typical of others in the region: a school, a cemetery, a church, and living quarters surrounded a central green. Where it
stood out was in its dedication to music and the arts. This was one of
the first music conservatories in the region, and the precision with
which instruments were constructed and played here gained the mission
fame throughout the New World and Europe. The facade of the church
provides an excellent example of the stellar artwork created here: both
the Jesuits and Guaranís sculpted Hellenic columns and traditional
Guaraní images into the red sandstone.

Shortly after the expulsion of the Jesuits in 1767, the mission was abandoned and left to the jungle. In the 1940s, however, the National Commission of Historic Monuments began restoring the mission: what you
see today is a mixture of the original buildings and new construction.
One aspect that cannot be reproduced is the surrounding environment:
the jungle was gradually cut down as the town of San Ignacio sprang
up, and now ugly brick buildings peek behind the ruins, and a mess of

restaurants and artisan shops line the outside walls. It's most likely that you'll just stop in San Ignacio for a few hours. Hour-long guided tours (in Spanish) are available throughout the day and are included in the admission fee. Each day after dusk there's a sound-and-light show. The small museum contains a model of the mission, original tiles, and various metal objects unearthed during the restoration. ⊠ *Off R12, San Ignacio* ☎ *3752/470186* ⊠ *2.50 pesos* ☼ *Daily 7–7.*

Where to Stay

¢ ▣ **Hotel San Ignacio.** The only option for an overnight stay in the area is this inexpensive hotel four blocks from the ruins. The majority of lodgers are young backpackers, and the facilities cater to this crowd: a bar, paddleball court, and recreation room with two pool tables and old arcade games. The four simple, clean cabañas all have two rooms and can sleep four to five people. The hotel usually fills up by late afternoon, so it's a good idea to make a reservation. The only phone is the public one in the lobby. ⊠ *San Martín 823, San Ignacio, 3322* ☎ *3752/470047* 🖷 *3752/470422* ⇆ *4 cabañas* ⌂ *Bar, recreation room* ▤ *No credit cards.*

Nuestra Señora de Loreto

9 km (6 mi) south of San Ignacio Miní, 50 km (31 mi) northeast of Posadas.

The history of this Jesuit mission is very much intertwined with that of San Ignacio Miní. They were founded near each other in the same year by the same Jesuits, and they migrated together in 1632 from what is now Brazil to the Río Paraná area. The mission moved around several more times before ultimately arriving at its final location in 1686. Because of its great economic productivity, Nuestra Señora de Loreto was one of the most important missions in the region. It was a major supplier of yerba mate and cloth to other parts of the Spanish colony and had extensive cattle-ranch land. When demand for yerba mate declined during the mid-18th century, the mission successfully turned much of its efforts toward rice farming. Nuestra Señora de Loreto also obtained widespread fame around 1700 for its printing press, one of the first in the New World: this enabled the mission to publish numerous books, especially the Bible, in the native Guaraní language.

In 1731 the mission reached its maximum number of inhabitants: close to 7,000 Guaranís. However, most left in the years following the Jesuits' expulsion in 1767. Those who remained were forced to move away in 1817 by the Paraguayans, who were trying to seize large parts of Misiones Province. After evacuating the inhabitants, the Paraguayans set fire to the entire mission, and for this reason little of it exists today. The jungle engulfed the remains, and only within the last decade or so have they been uncovered. No restoration or reconstruction has yet taken place. Nonetheless, a visit to the ruins gives you an idea of the Jesuit missions' original environment. There's also a visitor center with a small museum displaying ceramics and metal objects found during excavations. Spanish-speaking guides are available during high season (November, December, July, and Easter). ⊠ *3 km (2 mi) off R12, look for the sign* ☎ *3752/470190* ⊠ *1 peso* ☼ *Daily 7–7.*

Santa María la Mayor

108 km (67 mi) southeast of Posadas.

It's worth trying to get to Santa María la Mayor, the least visited of the missions due to its inaccessibility, because the walls of the artisan workshop, school, and church remain almost entirely intact. The mission was founded in 1636 near the site of the Mbororé War, during which the Jesuits and Guaranís defeated the Portuguese slave traders who had been raiding the missions and capturing the Guaranís to sell as slaves. In 1637 the mission moved to its present-day spot. Santa María has a distinct layout: instead of just one central plaza, it has a whole sequence of plazas throughout. It never reached the size or importance of many of the other missions, but construction of a new and grander church was just beginning when the Jesuits were expelled in 1767. There's an information center on the premises, and guided tours are available in Spanish only. ⊠ *Off R2 W* 🖃 *Free* ☉ *Daily 7–7.*

Cataratas de Iguazú

FodorśChoice
★
17 km (11 mi) east of Puerto Iguazú, 297 km (184 mi) northeast of Posadas, 1,357 km (841 mi) northeast of Buenos Aires.

The Cataratas del Iguazú (Iguazú Falls) are one of the wildest wonders of the world, with nature on the rampage in a unique show of sound and fury. The grandeur of this cinemascopic sheet of white water cascading in constant cymbal-banging cacophony makes Niagara Falls and Victoria Falls seem sedate. At a bend in the Río Iguazú, on the border with Brazil, the falls extend for almost 3 km (2 mi) in a 270-degree arch. Iguazú consists of some 275 separate waterfalls—in the rainy season there are as many as 350—that send their white cascades plunging more than 200 feet onto the rocks below. Dense, lush jungle surrounds the falls: here the tropical sun and the omnipresent moisture make the jungle grow at a pace that produces a towering pine tree in two decades instead of the seven it takes in, say, Scandinavia. By the falls and along the roadside, rainbows and butterflies are set off against vast walls of red earth, which is so ubiquitous that eventually even peso bills long in circulation in the area turn red from exposure to the stuff.

Allow at least two full days to take in this magnificent sight, and be sure to see it from both the Argentine and Brazilian sides. The Brazilians are blessed with the best panoramic view, an awesome vantage point that suffers only from the sound of the gnatlike helicopters that erupt out of the lawn of the Hotel das Cataratas right in front of the falls. (Unfortunately, most indigenous macaws and toucans have abandoned the area to escape the whine of the helicopters' engines.) The Argentine side offers the better close-up experience of the falls, with excellent hiking paths, catwalks that approach the falls, a sandy beach to relax on, and places to bathe in the froth of the Río Iguazú. Local travel agencies and tour operators offer trips that will take you to both sides. If you want to set your own pace, you can tour the Argentine side and then take a taxi or one of the regularly scheduled buses across the International Bridge, officially called the Ponte Presidente Tancredo Neves, to Brazil. Note that if you're a Canadian, British, or American citizen crossing into Brazil from Argentina or Paraguay, you don't need a visa for a short visit to the falls. You must, however, pay an entry fee and have your passport stamped. Always keep your passport handy, as immigration authorities keep the region under close watch.

The best way to immerse yourself in the falls is to wander the many access paths, which are a combination of bridges, ramps, stone staircases, and new metal catwalks set in a forest of ferns, begonias, orchids, and tropical trees. The catwalks over the water put you right in the middle of the action, so be ready to get doused by the rising spray. (Be sure to bring rain gear—or buy it from vendors along the trails on the Brazilian side.) If tropical heat and humidity hamper your style, plan to visit between April and October, though the falls are thrilling year-round. Five upstream Brazilian barrages (mini-dams) on the river Iguazú cast a man-made unreliability on the natural wonder: depending on the river flow and seasonal rains, barrages may affect the water volume in the falls anywhere from 1,500 cubic meters per second up to 8,000 or more (usually dam operators are careful not to shut down the falls on weekends or holidays).

The falls on the Argentine side are in the **Parque Nacional Iguazú** (Iguazú National Park), which was founded in 1934, declared a World Heritage Site in 1984, and refurbished by a private concession in 2001. There's a new **Visitor Center,** called Yvyra Reta ("country of the trees" in Guaraní tongue) with excellent facilities, including a good explanation of the region's ecology and human history. From here you can catch the gas-propelled **Tren de la Selva** (Jungle Train), which departs every 20 minutes. It makes a stop at **Estación Cataratas** and then proceeds to **Estación Garganta del Diablo** (Devil's Throat Station), where a new wheelchair-accessible, metal catwalk leads to a platform right beside one of the most dizzying spots in the world. Here the Iguazú river plummets, with an awesome roar, more than 230 feet into a horseshoe-shape gorge, amid a perennial cloud of mist.

If a more relaxed stroll is preferred, take the well-marked, ½ km (.3 mi) **Sendero Verde** (Green Path) past Estación Cataratas and connect with **Circuito Superior** (Upper Circuit), which stretches along the top of the falls for 1 km (½ mi). With six sightseeing balconies, this easy walk of about an hour and a half provides great upper views of the falls **Dos Hermanas, Ramírez, Bossetti, Méndez,** and the most impressive, named after the *Libertador* (Liberator) **San Martín.** Near the falls look for *vencejos,* swallows that nest behind the curtains of water. Note that the paths beyond the San Martín have more than a few stairways and, therefore, are not wheelchair-accessible.

The **Circuito Inferior** (Lower Circuit) starts by a water-and-watch tower and is a 1.7-km-long (1.1-mi-long) loop that consists of a metal catwalk, lots of stairways, and protected promontories at the best spots. At the beginning of this walk, you'll pass the small **Salto Alvar Núñez Cabeza** de Vaca falls, named after the Spanish conquistador who stumbled onto the spectacle in the 16th century; the **Peñón de Bella Vista** (Rock of the Beautiful View); and the **Salto Lanusse** (Lanusse Falls). These are just preliminaries to get you warmed up for the main event. Halfway along this circuit you get a panoramic peek at what's to come—through the foliage you can see the gigantic curtain of water in the distance. The trail leads along the lower side of **Brazo San Martín,** a branch of the Iguazú river that makes a wide loop to the south before following the same vertical fate as the main branch, along a mile-long series of falls. The last part of the trail offers the most exciting views of the main falls, including Garganta del Diablo in the background. Allow about an hour and a half to walk this circuit. There's no way to get lost on the catwalk, but English-speaking guides, found at the visitor center, can be hired to provide detailed explanations of the falls.

From Circuito Inferior you can reach the pier where a free boat service crosses the river to **Isla San Martín** (San Martín Island). This free boat service operates all day, except when the river is too high. On the island, after a steep climb up a rustic stairway, a circular trail opening presents three spectacular panoramas of Salto San Martín, Garganta del Diablo, and Salto Ventana (Window Falls). Few people make the effort to cross the river to Isla San Martín and do this climb, so you can often enjoy the show in solitary splendor.

The **Sendero Macuco** (Macuco Trail) extends 4 km (2½ mi) into the jungle, ending at the **Salto Arrechea** (Arrechea Falls) farther downriver from the main falls. The trail is very carefully marked, and descriptive signs in Spanish explain the jungle's flora and fauna. The closest you'll get to a wild animal is likely to be a paw print in the dirt, though you may be lucky enough to glimpse a monkey. The foliage is dense, so the most common surprises are the jungle sounds that seem to emerge out of nowhere. You can turn back at any point, or continue on to the refreshing view of the river and Salto Arrechea. The best time to hear animal calls and to avoid the heat is either early in the morning or just before sunset. The battalions of butterflies, also best seen in the early morning or late afternoon, can be marvelous, and the intricate glistening cobwebs crisscrossing the trail are a treat in the dawn light. Plan on spending about three hours for the whole trip. The **Centro de Investigaciones Ecológicas Subtropicales** (Center for Subtropical Ecological Investigation; ☎ 3757/421222) maintains the trail.

On the Brazilian side, the falls, known in Portuguese as the Foz do Iguaçu, can be seen from the **Parque Nacional Foz do Iguaçu,** Brazil's national park. The park runs for 25 km (16 mi) along a paved highway southwest of downtown Foz do Iguaçu, the nearest town. The **park entrance** (✉ Km 17, Rodovia das Cataratas ☎ 005545/529–8383) is the best place to get information; it's open daily 8–5, and the entrance fee is roughly 3 pesos. Much of the park's 457,000 acres is protected rain forest—off-limits to visitors and home to the last viable populations of panthers as well as rare flora such as bromeliads and orchids. The falls are 11 km (7 mi) from the park entrance. The luxurious, historic Hotel das Cataratas sits near the trailhead. Public parking is allowed on the highway shoulder and in a small lot near the hotel. The path to the falls is 2 km (1 mi) long, and its walkways, bridges, and stone staircases lead through the rain forest to concrete and wooden catwalks that take you to the falls. Highlights of the Brazilian side of the falls include first the **Salto Santa Maria,** from which catwalks branch off to the **Salto Deodoro** and **Salto Floriano,** where you'll be doused by the spray. The end of the catwalk puts you right in the heart of the spectacle at **Garganta do Diablo** ("Devil's Throat" in Portuguese), for a different perspective from the Argentine side. Back on the last section of the main trail is a building with facilities, including a panoramic elevator; it's open daily 8:30–6, and there's a small fee. A balcony brings you close to the far left of **Salto Deodoro.** The trail ends at the road some 35 feet above.

Where to Stay & Eat

$$ ✕ **Garganta del Diablo.** As the harpist plucks away, you can savor the expertly prepared dishes from the international menu at one of the area's finest restaurants. The trout in pastry and the surubí in banana leaves are exquisite. The restaurant, which is in the Sheraton Internacional Iguazú, only serves dinner (which starts after the last bus has left for Puerto Iguazú, which means an expensive taxi ride if you're not a guest at the hotel). ⊠ *Sheraton Internacional Iguazú, Parque Nacional Iguazú* ☎ *3757/491800* ▭ *AE, DC, MC, V* ☾ *No lunch.*

$$ ✕ **Zaragoza.** In a quiet neighborhood on a tree-lined street in Brazil's Foz do Iguaçu, this cozy restaurant is owned by Paquito, a Spanish immigrant. The Spanish fare includes a great paella, the house specialty, as well as several delicious fish options. The surubí definitely merits a try. ⊠ *Rua Quintino Bocaiúva 882, Foz do Iguaçu, Paraná, Brazil* ☎ *045/574–3084* ▭ *AE, V.*

★ **$$$$** ✕▥ **Tropical das Cataratas.** Not only is this stately hotel in the national park on the Brazilian side, but it also provides the more traditional comforts—large rooms, terraces, hammocks—of a colonial-style establishment. Galleries and gardens surround this pink building, and its main section has been declared a Brazilian national heritage sight. The restaurant serves traditional Brazilian food. ⊠ *Km 25, Rodovia das Cataratas, 85850–970, Brazil* ☎ *005545/521–7000* ⊕ *www.tropicalhotel.com.br* ⇗ *200 rooms* ♨ *2 restaurants, coffee shop, 2 tennis courts, pool, bar, shops, meeting room, business services* ▭ *AE, DC, MC, V.*

$$$$ ▥ **Sheraton Internacional Iguazú.** Half of the rooms in this luxury hotel have direct views of the falls, so be sure to reserve one well in advance (they are about 30% more expensive). Floor-to-ceiling windows reveal the inspiring scene to the lobby, restaurants, bars, and even the pool. The spacious balconies are ideal for breakfast or a drink. Rooms are large and comfortable and have been refurnished recently under Sheraton management. ⊠ *Parque Nacional Iguazú, 3372* ☎ *3757/491800* ▤ *3757/491810* ⊕ *www.sheraton.com* ⇗ *180 rooms, 4 suites* ♨ *2 restaurants, room service, minibars, 3 tennis courts, pool, sauna, bicycle, 2 bars, laundry service, meeting room, business services, Internet* ▭ *AE, DC, MC, V.*

FodorśChoice
★

Misiones and Cataratas del Iguazú A to Z

AIR TRAVEL

Aerolíneas Argentinas/Austral and LAPA each have two daily flights between Buenos Aires and Posadas; the trip takes about an hour and a half.

Aerolíneas Argentinas/Austral flies three times daily between Buenos Aires and the Argentine airport near Iguazú; the trip takes an hour and a half. LAPA also flies to and from Buenos Aires and is usually cheaper. Normal rates are about 200 pesos each way, but promotional rates, called *bandas negativas,* are sometimes available if you reserve ahead. The Brazilian airlines—Transbrasil, Varig, and Vasp—have offices in Foz do Iguaçu and offer connecting flights all over Brazil.

🛫 **Aerolíneas Argentinas/Austral** ✉ Av. Victoria Aguirre 295, Puerto Iguazú ☎ 3757/ 420849 or 3757/420168. **LAPA** ☎ 3757/420390. **Varig** ☎ 5545/523-2111 in Foz do Iguaçu, 11/4329-9211 in Buenos Aires. **Vasp** ☎ 5545/529-6216.

AIRPORTS

Posadas's airport, the Aeropuerto Libertador General San Martín, is 10 km (6 mi) southwest of the town center; flights only go to and from Buenos Aires. A taxi from the airport into Posadas costs 10–15 pesos and takes a half hour. You could also take the Becivega Bus 28 from the airport to Calle Junín in front of Plaza San Martín.

Argentina and Brazil each have an airport at Iguazú. The Argentine airport is 20 km (12 mi) southeast of Puerto Iguazú, Argentina; the Brazilian airport is 11 km (7 mi) from Foz do Iguaçu and 17 km (11 mi) from the national park. The Colectivo Aeropuerto shuttle has service to hotels in Puerto Iguazú for 3 pesos. To get from the hotel to the airport, call two hours before your departure, and the shuttle will pick you up. Taxis to Puerto Iguazú cost 18 pesos.

🛫 **Aeropuerto Internacional de Rosario** ✉ R9 ☎ 0341/451-2997. **Aeropuerto Libertador General San Martín** ✉ Off R12 ☎ 3752/451903.

BUS TRAVEL

Traveling to the Northeast from Buenos Aires is relatively easy, and buses are one of the best ways to travel from town to town within the Northeast.

POSADAS La Estrella and Crucero del Norte have several daily buses to Buenos Aires. Buses to Puerto Iguazú leave five times a day, and the trip takes five hours: Aguila Dorada runs the leading service. All of these buses pass by the three Jesuit ruins on R12, and some actually enter the town of San Ignacio, making an even more convenient trip. To get to Yacyretá Dam, you must take the bus to Ituzaingo; the trip is made nearly every hour, most frequently by Ciudad de Posadas. To Soberbio, take Aguila Dorada or Capital del Monte, each of which goes twice daily. The Posadas Terminal de Omnibus is 6 km (4 mi) southwest of the town center (a 4 peso taxi ride).

🚌 **Aguila Dorada** ☎ 3752/458888. **Crucero del Norte** ☎ 3752/455515. **La Estrella** ☎ 3752/453120. **Posadas Terminal de Omnibus** ✉ R12 and Av. Santa Catalina, ☎ 3752/ 456106.

PUERTO IGUAZÚ   Organized tours to Puerto Iguazú and the Cataratas del Iguazú by bus can be arranged through most Buenos Aires travel agencies. Via Bariloche has the quickest and most comfortable service between Puerto Iguazú and Buenos Aires; the trip takes 16 hours, costs about 75 pesos, and includes meals. Expreso Singer takes 18 hours and costs 82 pesos. The Puerto Iguazú Terminal de Omnibus is in the center of town.

From Puerto Iguazú to the falls, take El Práctico from the terminal; buses leave every 45 minutes 7–7 and cost 5.60 pesos round-trip. To get to the Minas de Wanda from Puerto Iguazú, you can take any bus going to Posadas. These buses leave nearly every hour and take about 45 minutes. For information call Agencia de Pasajes Noelia at the bus terminal.

🚌 Agencia de Pasajes Noelia ☎ 3757/422722. **Expreso Singer** ☎ 3757/422891. **El Práctico** ☎ 3757/422722. **Puerto Iguazú Terminal de Omnibus** ✉ Avs. Córdoba and Misiones ☎ 3757/423006. **Via Bariloche** ☎ 3757/420854.

CAR RENTAL
There aren't many places to rent cars in the region; you're better off renting a car in Buenos Aires and driving from there. Daniel Marrochi SRL has offices in Posadas, and Puerto Iguazú.

🚌 Daniel Marrochi SRL ✉ Almafuerte 1300, Paraná ☎ 343/423-3885.

CAR TRAVEL
To reach San Ignacio Miní, Santa Ana, and Nuestra Señora de Loreto (3 km [2 mi] off R12) from Posadas, take R12 northeast. Continue on R12 to reach Puerto Iguazú. To get to Santa María la Mayor from Posadas, take R12 northeast to R4 and then southeast to R2 west.

Puerto Iguazú is a two-day, 1,363-km (848-mi) drive from Buenos Aires on R12 and R14 (it's quickest to take R14 to Posadas, then R12 to the falls).

CONSULATE
In Puerto Iguazú, the Brazilian consulate is open weekdays 8–12:30. If you're not an American, British, or Canadian citizen, a tourist visa is necessary to enter Brazil from Argentina, and it may take a couple of days, so do it ahead of time.

🚌 Brazilian consulate ✉ Av. Córdoba 264 ☎ 3757/421348.

EMERGENCIES
For ambulances call the hospitals directly. Several of the pharmacies listed are open 24 hours or share rotating 24-hour shifts with other pharmacies.

🚌 Fire Posadas ☎ 100.

🚌 Hospitals Posadas ✉ Hospital Dr. Ramón Madariaga, Av. Lopez Tones and Cabral ☎ 3752/447000, 107 emergencies. **Puerto Iguazú** ✉ Hospital Samic, Av. Victoria Aguirre 131 ☎ 3757/420288.

🚌 Police Posadas ☎ 101. **Puerto Iguazú** ☎ 3757/421224.

MONEY MATTERS
ATMs linked to the Cirrus system are found throughout the region.

In Posadas, Cambio Mazza is open weekdays 8–noon and 3:30–6:30. For other banking needs in Posadas, go to Bank Boston; it has ATMs and is open weekdays 8–1. Dollars and pesos are used interchangeably in Puerto Iguazú; to exchange other currencies, but not traveler's checks, go to Argecam, open weekdays 8–7. For other banking needs in Puerto Iguazú, try Banco Macro, open weekdays 8–1; it has ATMs.

🏦 Bank Information **Argecam** ✉ Av. Victoria Aguirre 562, Puerto Iguazú ☎ 3757/420273. **Banco Macro** ✉ Av. Victoria Aguirre 330, Puerto Iguazú ☎ 3757/420212. **Bank Boston** ✉ Colón 1630, Posadas ☎ 3752/420113. **Cambio Mazza** ✉ Bolívar 1932, Posadas ☎ 3752/440505.

TAXIS

Taxis (*remises*) are generally inexpensive; the fare is based on the number of blocks traveled. Taxis can be hailed, but it's generally easier to call one. In San Ignacio, independently owned taxis can often be found on Avenida San Martín near the ruins. A good way to explore the other ruins is to have a taxi take you from San Ignacio to Nuestra Señora de Loreto, wait, and then drop you off at Santa Ana. From there you can return to Posadas by catching a bus on the highway, a short walk from the ruins. It should cost about 15 pesos and take about two hours. If you want the taxi driver to wait at Santa Ana with you and then drop you off on the highway, it will probably cost an additional 10 pesos. In Puerto Iguazú, one of the biggest taxi companies is Remis Unión; taxis are available for short rides and longer day trips. With a group of three or four, you may find this a more economical and certainly more convenient way to get around.

VISITOR INFORMATION

The Cataratas del Iguazú visitor center, at the park entrance, is open daily 7 AM–8 PM. Colón's visitor center is open daily 6 AM–8 PM in winter, 6 AM–11 PM in summer. Puerto Iguazú's visitor center is open daily 7–1 and 2–8. Secretaría de Turismo de la Provincia de Misiones in Posadas is the tourism authority for the province; it's open weekdays 7 AM–8 PM and weekends 8–noon and 4:30–8.

🏛 **Cataratas del Iguazú** ✉ Visitor center at park entrance ☎ 3757/420180. **Puerto Iguazú** ✉ Av. Victoria Aguirre 311 ☎ 3757/420800. **Secretaría de Turismo de la Provincia de Misiones** ✉ Colón 1985, Posadas ☎ 3752/447540, 0800/555-0297 toll-free for local calls.

THE CUYO

Updated by
Eddy Ancinas

In the center of Argentina, on the dry side of the Andes, this semi-arid region is blessed with water from mountain glaciers that flows via rivers and canals into the fields and vineyards that surround the parks, plazas, and tree-lined streets of Mendoza, San Juan, and San Rafael. Argentina is the fifth-largest wine producer in the world (grapevines were first planted by Jesuit missionaries in 1556), and 80% of the country's vineyards thrive in the hot sun and sandy soil of Mendoza and San Juan provinces.

Today the area is known not only for its wine but also for its outdoor activities. River-rafting, horseback riding, skiing at Las Leñas and Penitentes in Mendoza Province, and hiking on Aconcagua, the highest mountain in the Americas, attract outdoor enthusiasts year-round. Parque Provincial Ischigualasto, a World Heritage site in San Juan Province, is one of the richest paleontological areas in the world.

Mendoza, one of Argentina's prettiest cities, is a good base for exploring the Cuyo's lush vineyards and orchards, deep river gorges, and high mountain passes.

Mendoza

1,040 km (250 mi) west of Buenos Aires

Mendoza, the capital of the province of the same name and the main city in the Cuyo, prides itself on having more trees than people. The result is a town with cool canopies of poplars, elms, and sycamores over its streets, sidewalks, plazas, and low buildings. Water runs in canals along the streets, disappears at intersections, and then reappears in bursts of spray from the fountains in the city's 74 parks and plazas. Many of these canals were built by the Huarpes and improved upon by the Incas long before 1561, when García Hurtado de Mendoza, governor of Chile, commissioned Pedro del Castillo to lead an expedition over the Andes with the purpose of founding a city and opening the way so that "knowledge could be brought back of what lay beyond."

Argentina's beloved hero, José de San Martín, resided here while preparing his army of 40,000 soldiers to cross the Andes in 1817 on the campaign to liberate Argentina from Spain. In 1861 an earthquake destroyed the city, killing 11,000 people. The city of Mendoza and the Cuyo remained isolated from eastern Argentina until 1884, when the railroad to Buenos Aires was completed and the city was rebuilt. Immigrants from Italy, Spain, and France then moved here in search of good land to farm and grow grapes, introducing their skills and crafts to the region.

Avenida San Martín is the town's major thoroughfare. Between it and the Plaza Independencia, Mendoza's central square, are many shops and restaurants. Maipú, Luján de Cuyo, and Godoy Cruz, notable for their wineries, and Las Heras and Guaymallén are all suburbs of Mendoza with shopping centers, restaurants, and hotels. Take a taxi: they're cheap and more direct than local bus service.

★ Five minutes by car from the center of Mendoza, **Bodega Escorihuela** occupies several blocks of an urban area once covered with vineyards. This huge winery was founded in 1884 by Spaniard Miguel Escorihuela Gascón. Its 63,000-liter barrel, made in France, is the largest in the province. In the old house are art exhibits and a restaurant, 1884. ✉ *Belgrano 1188, Godoy Cruz* ☎ *261/424–2282* ⊕ *www.escorihuela. com.ar* ⊗ *Weekdays 9:30–12:30 and 2:30–3:30; tours on the hr.*

The **Bodega la Rural,** founded in 1883 by Felipe Rutini, is still family-owned and -operated. It produces San Felipe, Rutini, and Trumpeter wines. Not to be missed is the outstanding **Museo del Vino** (Wine Museum), where everything from 100-year-old leather, wood, and copper tools to an ingenious mousetrap is displayed in the original adobe barns. ⊠ *Montecaseros 2625, Maipú* ☎ *261/497–2013* ⊕ *www.bodegalarural.com. ar* ⊙ *Mon.–Sat. and holidays 9:30–5, Sun. 10–1.*

Dolium is the Latin word for the amphoras used by the Romans to store wine underground. Hand-picked grapes are delivered to this underground winery, where processing, fermenting, storing, bottling, and packaging all take place underground. You can sample wine in a glass-and-steel reception area while looking down into the wine works. ⊠ *R15, Km 30, Agrelo* ☎ *261/490–0200* ⊕ *www.dolium.com* ⊙ *Weekdays 9–5, weekends by appointment.*

The first vines were planted at **Finca Flichman** in 1873, in the stony soil near the Mendoza River. Caballero de la Cepa wines are exported to the United States, Japan, and Europe. Stainless-steel tanks and computerized temperature controls make this one of Argentina's most modern wineries. ⊠ *Munives 800, Barrancas/Maipú* ☎ *261/497–2039* ⊙ *Wed.–Sun. 10–1 and 2–5.*

On the site of the original civic center of Mendoza, the **Museo del Area Fundacional** (Foundation Museum) explains the social and historical development of the region, from the time of indigenous people through Spanish colonization to the present. Of special note is the display of a mummified child found on Aconcagua, with photos of his burial treasures—presumably an Inca or pre-Inca sacrifice. After the 1861 earthquake, the city center was moved from this location. Underground excavations, made visible by a glass-covered viewing area, reveal layers of pre-Hispanic and Spanish remains. ⊠ *Beltrán and Videla Castillo* ☎ *261/425–6927* ⊡ *$1.50* ⊙ *Tues.–Sat. 8 AM–10 PM, Sun. 3 PM–8 PM.*

Twice governor and later senator Emilio Civit's 1873 mansion had 26 bedrooms and 4 courtyards and was the gathering place of the elite in the belle epoque. It's now the **Museo del Pasado Cuyano** (Museum of Cuyo's Past), a gallery and archive with paintings, antiques, manuscripts, and a library on Argentine and Chilean history. ⊠ *Montevideo 544* ☎ *261/ 423–6031* ⊡ *Donation* ⊙ *Weekdays 9–12:30.*

The **Parque General San Martín**, about 10 blocks from the city center, is a grand public space with thousands of species of plants and trees, tropical flowers, and a rose garden. A racecourse, golf club, tennis courts, observatory, rowing club, and museums are some of the attractions in the park. Atop **Cerro de la Gloria** (Glory Hill), in the center of the park, a monument depicts scenes of San Martín's historic Andes passage.

Plaza Independencia is Mendoza's main square, filled daily with both visitors and Mendocinos alike. You may just sit on a bench in the shade of a sycamore tree and watch children playing in the fountains, browse the stands at a weekend fair, visit the **Museo de Arte Moderno** or perhaps cross the square after lunch at the historic **Plaza Hotel** (now a Hyatt) on your way to the shops and outdoor cafés on the pedestrian-only **Calle Sarmiento,** which bisects the square.

Where to Stay & Eat

$$–$$$
Fodor'sChoice
★ ✕ **1884 Restaurante Francis Mallman.** The soft glow of candles on the patio under the prune trees at the Godoy Cruz Winery's 100-year-old Bodega Escorihuela sets the tone for one of Argentina's premier chefs to show what Patagonian cuisine can be. Born in Bariloche and trained in France and Italy, Francis Mallman put Argentina on the map of international *alta cocina* (haute cuisine). Students from his culinary school keep wineglasses full and forks flying as they attend to guests with discreet enthusiasm. The 36-page wine list has detailed information on grapes and bodegas. ⊠ *Belgrano 1188* ☎ *261/424–2698* ▤ *AE, DC, MC, V.*

$ ✕ **El Meson Español.** Stained-glass windows, bullfighting posters, reproductions of works by famous Spanish artists, and a well-trodden tile floor take you right back to Spain when you enter this old colonial house. Start with a cup of garlic soup, followed by paella or tapas, as Lucho, the blind piano player, plays blues, tango, swing, and Sinatra. ⊠ *Montevideo 244* ☎ *261/429–6175* ▤ *AE, DC, MC, V* ☻ *No lunch.*

$ ✕ **La Florencia.** Sidewalk tables invite strollers to stop and peruse the menu: grilled, baked, and broiled meats and fish; pastas; pizzas; game; and a variety of salads, along with a lengthy wine list. Step inside and admire the eclectic displays of antique weapons, telephones, and gaucho artifacts. Fine silver and crystal is stored in antique chests. An upstairs dining room has a breezy street view. ⊠ *Sarmiento and Perú* ☎ *261/429–1564* ▤ *AE, DC, MC, V.*

$ ✕ **La Marchigiana.** Homemade pasta has been served since 1950 under the thatched roof and whirring fans of this cheerful Italo-Argentine eatery. Concoct your own salad and try a pitcher of sangria or clérico on hot summer afternoons. ⊠ *Patricias Mendocinas 1550* ☎ *261/423071* ⊠ *Palmares Shopping Mall, Godoy Cruz* ☎ *261/439–1961* ▤ *AE, DC, MC, V.*

★ **¢–$** ✕ **Azafrán.** In this wine bar (whose name means saffron), wooden stools surround an old wine press, which has been converted into a tasting table. Wines are displayed from floor to ceiling. Farther inside this 19th-century brick building, diners seated at small café tables enjoy cheeses, pâtés, and hot and cold tapas served on wooden platters. Shelves are stocked with Mendoza's finest: olive oils, smoked meats, dried herbs, mushrooms, olives, jams, and breads. Whether you view it as a gourmet grocery, wine shop, or restaurant, Azafrán is a pleasant diversion. ⊠ *Sarmiento 765* ☎ *261/429–4200* ⊠ *Park Hyatt Mendoza, Calle Chile 1124* ▤ *MC, V* ☻ *Closed Sun.*

$$ ▦ **Hotel Aconcagua.** Business travelers, tourists, and people in the wine trade appreciate the efficient service at this modern hotel on a quiet street near shops and restaurants. Serene tones of mauve and blue create a soothing atmosphere throughout the lobby and meeting and guest rooms. Although it doesn't have a bar for pre- or post-dinner schmoozing, friends and associates seem perfectly happy to gather in the lobby or in the restaurant, where a copious buffet is served, as well as regular entrées. ⊠ *San Lorenzo 545, 5500* ☎ *261/420–4499* 🖷 *261/420–2083* ⊕ *www.hotelaconcagua.com.ar* 🛏 *159 rooms, 9 suites* 🗘 *Restaurant, pool, massage, sauna, business services, meeting rooms, travel services, parking* ▤ *AE, DC, MC, V* ⃝◎ *CP.*

$$ ▦ **Park Hyatt Mendoza.** Hyatt has preserved the 19th-century Spanish colonial facade of the landmark Plaza Hotel's grand pillared entrance and wide veranda, which extends to either side of the street. Lunch, afternoon tea, and dinner are served on this gracious terrace overlooking Mendoza's main square. A two-story wine wall separates the restaurant from the lobby. Minimalist bedrooms are softened by plump white pillows and duvets covering the simple ebony beds. Bathrooms have plenty of mirrors to compliment chrome and marble accents. ⊠ *Calle Chile 1124, 5500* ☎ *261/441–1234* 🖷 *261/441–1235* ⊕ *mendoza.park. hyatt.com* ➪ *170 rooms, 15 suites* ♨ *Restaurant, café, dining room, pool, health club, spa, bar, casino, meeting rooms, business services, parking* ☰ *AE, DC, MC, V* ⵙⵔ *CP.*

$ ▦ **Hotel Cervantes.** The simple rooms in this small downtown hotel are cheerfully decorated in floral prints. The hotel is owner-operated, and the front desk is helpful and knowledgeable. A big-screen TV in the living room makes you feel at home. Sancho, the hotel's excellent restaurant and bar is a popular lunch spot for the local wine trade. ⊠ *Amigorena 65, 5500* ☎ *261/520–0400* 🖷 *261/520–0458* ⊕ *www.hotelcervantesmza.com.ar* ᯤ *261/520–0446* ➪ *60 rooms, 5 suites* ♨ *Restaurant, bar, business services, meeting rooms, travel services, free parking* ☰ *AE, DC, MC, V* ⵙⵔ *CP.*

$ ▦ **Hotel Crillón.** The loyal clientele of this small hotel returns for the tranquil neighborhood—within walking distance of plazas, restaurants, museums, and shops. Small suites with a separate work station are good for business travelers. The staff can help you plan excursions. ⊠ *Perú 1065, 5500* ☎ *261/429–8494* 🖷 *261/423–9658* ⊕ *www.hcrillon.com.ar* ➪ *70 rooms, 6 suites* ♨ *Café, pool, bar, meeting room* ☰ *AE, DC, MC, V* ⵙⵔ *CP.*

¢ ▦ **Damajuana.** The only property in Mendoza resembling a hostel has rooms for two, four, or six people, with lockers and shared bath. Guests feel at home inside or out: a bar, restaurant, and a fireplace and TV are in the living room, and the spacious backyard has a grill and hammocks. The neighborhood is the most popular among young Mendocinos, with bars, boutiques, and cafés just steps away. ⊠ *Aristedes Villanueva 282, 5500* ☎ *261/425–5858* 🖷 *261/425–5858* ⊕ *www.damajuanahostel.com. ar* ➪ *8 rooms* ♨ *Restaurant, pool, tennis court, bar, Internet; no a/c.*

Nightlife

The formerly sleepy **Avenida Arístedes Villanueva** is now a hot spot of inexpensive bars and cafés. The area wakes up around 6 PM, when the bars, boutiques, wine shops, and sidewalk cafés open their doors, and young Mendocinos, foreign tourists, and strolling couples converge on the area. As the evening progresses, crowds get bigger, and music—rock, tango, salsa—louder. The action peaks between 10 and midnight. Inexpensive, casual **El Bar del José** (⊠ Arístedes Villanueva 740 ☎ no phone) was the first gathering place in the trendy Villanueva neighborhood. **Por Acá** (⊠ Arístedes Villanueva 557 ☎ no phone) attracts a cosmopolitan crowd of locals and European travelers—many en route to hike or climb in the nearby Andes. Live rock music begins after 10 PM.

The **Regency Casino** at the **Park Hyatt Mendoza** has blackjack, stud poker, and roulette tables, slot machines, and an exclusive bar. (⊠ 25 de Mayo and Sarmiento ☎ 261/441–2844).

Cinemark (⊠ At the Palmeares shopping mall, Godoy Cruz ☎ 261/ 439–5555) has 10 screens. **Microcine Municipal "David Eisenchlass"** (⊠ 9 de Julio ☎ 261/449–5100) shows foreign films Thursday through Sunday. **Village** (⊠ Mendoza Plaza Shopping Center, Guaymallén ☎ 261/ 421–0700) has 10 movie screens.

Sports & the Outdoors

Along with local guides offering specific services, Mendoza also has several outfitters that seem to do it all. **Aymara Turismo** (⊠ 9 de Julio 1023 ☎☎ 261/420–5304 or 261/420–2064 ⊕ www.aymara.com.ar) organizes hikes, horseback riding trips, mountain climbing, white-water rafting, and mountain bike tours. They offer everything from day hikes to full mountaineering excursions to all the highest mountain peaks, including Mercederio and Aconcagua, plus volcano treks in Chile and Argentina. **Inka** (⊠ Av. Juan B. Busto 343 ☎ 261/425–0871) is an owner-operated company with ten years experience guiding hikers and mountaineers to the base camp at the foot of Aconcagua; an optional six-hour climb on Mt. Bonete, for an exceptional view of climbers making their way up Aconcagua, is also available. They also offer horseback riding trips.

HIKING Day-hikes or weeklong treks along rivers, canyons, on an Inca trail, through indigenous forests, or to the highest mountain peaks in the Andes can be arranged with local travel and tour offices. November through March is the best time to do these journeys. **Huentata** (⊠ Las Heras 680 ☎ 261/425–3108 ⊕ www.huentata.com.ar) offers day hikes out of Potrerillos in the pre-Cordillera.

HORSEBACK The beauty of the surrounding foothills, valleys, and mountains, com-
RIDING bined with Mendoza's tradition of fine horsemanship, makes *cabalgatas* (horseback riding) an enjoyable and natural way to explore the area. You can ride to the foot of Aconcagua, Tupungato, or experience the grand adventure of a nine-day trip over the Andes following the hoof prints of San Martín. **Juan Jardel** (☎ 264/48303) takes riders from his ranch at Las Carditas in Potrerillos high into the mountains, where guanacos roam and condors soar. **Raúl Labat** (☎☎ 261/429–7257) takes groups from his ranch, El Puesto, near Tupungato, into the high rugged country where San Martín returned from Chile with his army.

MOUNTAIN Many of Mendoza's back roads lead through the suburbs and vineyards
BIKING into the Andean foothills and upward to mountain villages—or all the way to Chile. The Valle de Uco slopes gently from the foothills down. **Betancourt Rafting** (⊠ Lavalle 36, Loc. No. 8 ☎☎ 261/429–9665 ⊕ www. betancourt.com.ar), has short trips into the mountains and valleys around Potrerillos, as well as an all-day trip to Vallecitos. **Huentata** (⊠ Las Heras 680 ☎ 261/425–3108 ⊕ www.huentata.com.ar) also offers day excursions from Potrerillos into the surrounding mountains. **Travesía** (⊠ Montecaseros 699, Godoy Cruz ☎ 261/448–0289) conducts tours and provides maps for the suburbs and foothills outside of Mendoza.

Every February, **La Vuelta Ciclista de Mendoza,** a bicycle race around Mendoza Province, attracts cycling enthusiasts.

MOUNTAIN
CLIMBING
Mendoza offers challenging mountaineering adventures. Climbing in the Cordón de Plata or on Tupungato as well as Aconcagua can be arranged. Permits for climbing Aconcagua can be obtained personally in Mendoza at **Centro de Visitantes** (✉ Av. de Los Robles and Rotondo de Rosedal), in Parque San Martín near the entrance. The center is open weekdays 8–6 and weekends 9–1.

Aymara Turísmo (✉ 9 de Julio 1023 ☎ 261/420–5304 or 261/420–2064 ⊕ www.aymara.com.ar) offers a 19-day guided ascent of Aconcagua, which includes airport pickup, hotels, pack mules, and assistance in securing permits. They also offer shorter climbs for acclimatization. **Fernando Grajales** (✉ 25 de Mayo 2985, Guaymallén ☎☎ 261/429–3830) is an experienced guide and veteran of many Aconcagua summits.

SKIING
Skiers, bound for **Las Leñas,** in Malargüe near San Rafafel arrive from July through September and use Mendoza as their base. Two resorts closer to Mendoza attract local clientele.

Los Penitentes is 153 km (95 mi) northwest of Mendoza on the Panamerican Highway. Day-trippers and weekenders from Mendoza and the surrounding provinces come for the 20 runs for all abilities and the cross-country skiing. Note that in spite of the elevation (10,479 feet), the snow is often thin and when it does snow a lot, the danger of avalanches is severe. At the base of the ski area are hotels, restaurants, ski rentals, day care, a first-aid clinic, and a disco. Between the Andes and the Cordon de Plata, a range that reaches 20,000 feet, **Vallecitos,** 80 km (49 mi) from Mendoza, attracts mostly families with nearby vacation homes, as well as summer hikers and mountaineers who come to train for an assault on Aconcagua.

WHITE-WATER
RAFTING
Many adventure tour companies organize rafting or kayaking trips on the Río Mendoza. They can be combined with horseback treks and often include an asado.

Argentina Rafting (✉ Ruta Nacional 7, Luján de Cuyo ☎ 2624/482037 ⊕ www.argentinarafting.com.ar), located in Potrerillos, offers rafting and kayack classes and day trips. **Betancourt Rafting** (✉ Lavalle 36, Loc. No. 8, Galería Independencia ☎☎ 261/429–9665 ⊕ www.betancourt. com.ar) has three small cabins and a lodge 25 km (15 mi) from Mendoza at the Cacheuta Hot Springs, which they use as a base for rafting trips on the Mendoza River. Their standard two-day trip, with medium to difficult rapids, includes an asado and accommodations in the cabins. Day trips vary from one to six hours. Transportation to and from Mendoza is included for all trips.

Parque Provincial Aconcagua

Fodor'sChoice
★
195 km (121 mi) northwest of Mendoza via R7, 86 km (54 mi) west of Uspallata on R7.

The Parque Provincial Aconcagua extends for 165,000 acres over wild, high country with few trails other than those used by climbing expeditions up the impressive Cerro Aconcagua (Aconcagua Mountain). Organized tours on horse or foot can be arranged in Mendoza or at the Hostería Puente del Inca.

The drive up the Uspallata Pass to the Parque Provincial Aconcagua is as spectacular as the mountain itself. Tours can be arranged, but renting a car is well worth it, as there are many sights to stop and photograph along the way. You can make the trip from Mendoza in one long, all-day drive or stay a night en route. Note that driving in winter on the icy roads can be treacherous and that you should be aware of the change in altitude from 2,500 feet in Mendoza to 10,446 feet at the top.

Leaving Mendoza early in the morning, head south on Avenida San Martín to the Panamerican Highway (R7) and turn right. Green vineyards soon give way to barren hills and scrub brush as you follow the river for 30 km (19 mi) to the **Termas Cacheuta.** If you're still engulfed in fog and drizzle, don't despair: it's likely that you'll break through into brilliant sunshine when you reach the **Potrerillos Valley** at 39 km (24 mi). The road follows the Río Mendoza and an abandoned railroad track that once crossed the Andes to Chile. In 1934 an ice dam broke and sent a flood of mud, rocks, and debris down the canyon, carrying off everything in its path. Evidence of this natural disaster is still visible all along the river.

After passing Uspallata, the last town before the Chilean frontier, the road goes through rolling hills and brooding black mountains. The Ríos Blanco and Tambillos rush down from the mountains into the Río Mendoza, and remnants of Inca tambos remind you that this was once an Inca route. At **Punta de Vacas,** the corrals that once held herds of cattle on their way to Chile lie abandoned alongside now defunct railway tracks. Two kilometers (1 mi) beyond the army barracks and customs office, three wide valleys converge. Looking south, you can see the second-highest mountain in the region, **Cerro Tupungato** (22,304 feet). The mountain is accessible from the town of the same name, 73 km (45 mi) southwest of Mendoza.

After passing the ski area at Los Penitentes (named for the rock formations on the southern horizon that resemble penitent monks), you arrive at **Puente del Inca** (9,000 feet), a natural bridge of red rocks encrusted with yellow sulphur that spans the river. The hot springs below are slippery to walk on but fine for soaking tired feet. A splendid hotel was once here, but it, too, was a victim of the 1934 flood. A few miles farther west, after you pass the customs check (for Chile), is the entrance to the park and a cabin where the park ranger lives. About 15 km (9 mi) beyond the park entrance, the highway passes Las Cuevas, a settlement where the road forks right, to a tunnel and the road to Chile, or left, to the statue of **Cristo Redentor** (Christ the Redeemer) on the Chilean border (13,800 feet), commemorating the 1902 peace pact between the two countries.

The main attraction of the Parque Provincial Aconcagua is **Cerro Aconcagua** itself. At 22,825 feet, it's the highest mountain in the Americas and it towers over the Andes, its five gigantic glaciers gleaming in the sun. Although it seems amazingly accessible from the roadside, Aconcagua has claimed 37 climbers from the more than 400 expeditions that have attempted the summit. Nevertheless, every year hundreds of mountaineers arrive, ready to conquer the "giant of America." A trail into the park begins at the ranger's cabin and follows the **Río Horcones** past a lagoon and continues upward to the **Plaza de Mulas** base camp at 14,190 feet, where there's a hotel (☎ 261/423–1571 in Mendoza for reservations).

Where to Stay & Eat

$$$ ✕⊡ **Hotel Termas Cacheuta.** Stop at this mountain spa for a sauna in a natural grotto, a volcanic mud bath, a hydromassage, and a soak in the large swimming pool filled with water from the hot springs that have been curing devotees since 1902. Rooms overlook the lawn and swimming pool. The restaurant serves healthful, natural cuisine using vegetables from its own garden. Rates include three meals, two thermal baths, and one massage per day; hiking, river rafting, and mountain biking can be arranged. ⊠ *R7, Km 38, Cacheuta, 5500* ☎ *2624/482082* ⊠ *Reservations: Rodríguez Peña 1412, Godoy Cruz, 5501* ☎ *261/431–6085* ☎ *261/431–6089* ⋐ *16 rooms* ⚹ *Restaurant, massage, sauna* ⊟ *No credit cards* ⊺⊙⏐ *FAP.*

¢ ⊡ **Hostería Puente del Inca.** Mountaineers gather here to assemble equipment before climbing Aconcagua and return here afterward to relate their adventures. The hostel's history as a mountaineering outpost is told in vintage photos on the dining room walls. Guides and mules can be arranged. ⊠ *R7, Puente del Inca* ⊠ *Turismo Aymara SRL, 9 de Julio 1023, Mendoza, 5500* ☎ *261/420–2064* ⊘ *info@aymara.com.ar* ⋐ *82 beds in doubles, 4- to 6-person dorms* ⚹ *Dining room* ⊟ *MC.*

Sports & the Outdoors

To climb Aconcagua, you must first get a permit in Mendoza. Horseback rides and hikes can be arranged with a guide or on your own. *See* Mountaineering *in* Mendoza. The best time to climb is in mid-January to mid-February.

Parque Provincial Ischigualasto

★ *494 km (307 mi) northeast of Mendoza.*

Popularly known as *Valle de la Luna* ("valley of the moon"), this 15,134-acre park is a World Heritage site. Two hundred twenty-five million years of wind and erosion have sculpted strange rock formations in the red sandstone and pale gray volcanic ash cliffs, laying bare a graveyard of extinct dinosaurs from the Triassic period of the Mesozoic era. When the 6-foot-long Dicinodonte roamed the valley, a large lake surrounded by trees and shrubs was the habitat for a variety of reptiles. Some of these fossils can be seen in the visitor center at the park entrance, where a diorama explains the paleontologic history of the area. You can take three routes through the park, one of which will lead you to a petrified forest. Early morning fog usually dissipates by mid-morning, and the varied colors of the rocks become more vivid in late afternoon. Roads inside the park are unpaved, unpatrolled, and difficult to follow, especially after rainstorms. A ranger must accompany all private cars. Tours can be arranged in Mendoza.

The Cuyo A to Z

AIR TRAVEL
Mendoza's Aeropuerto Internacional Francisco Gabrielli is 6 km (4 mi) from town on R40. Aerolíneas Argentinas has flights to Mendoza from Buenos Aires. AIRG (formerly LAPA) and Southern Winds fly from Buenos Aires and Santiago, Chile to Mendoza.

🛪 Airlines & Contacts **Aerolíneas Argentinas** ⊠ Sarmiento 82, Mendoza ☎ 261/420–4100. **Aeropuerto Internacional Francsico Gabarielli** ☎ 261/448–2603 in Mendoza. **AIRG** ⊠ España 1002, Mendoza ☎ 261/423–1000 ⊠ Av. J. I. de la Roza, San Juan ☎ 264/421–6039 ⊠ Pedernera 863, San Luís ☎ 2652/431753. **Southern Winds** ⊠ España 943, Mendoza ☎ 261/429–3200.

BUS TRAVEL
Mendoza's big and busy Terminal del Sol is in Guaymallén, a suburb east of downtown. Buses go from Mendoza to every major city in Argentina. Chevallier has daily service to Buenos Aires. La Estrella has service to Buenos Aires via San Luís. Jocoli has a sleeper via San Luís to Buenos Aires. El Rápido has daily buses to Buenos Aires and Santiago, Chile, and three trips weekly to Lima, Peru. T.A.C. has service to Buenos Aires.

Every town has local buses, and if you can express where you want to go and understand the reply, you can travel cheaply (but slowly). A number in brackets on the bus indicates the route. Almost every tour agency runs minivans to local sights.

🚌 **Chevallier** ☎ 261/431–0235. **El Rápido** ☎ 261/431–4094. **La Estrella** ☎ 261/431–1324. **Jocoli** ☎ 261/431–4409. **T.A.C.** ☎ 261/431–1039. **Terminal del Sol** ⊠ Av. Gobernador Videla and Av. Acceso Oeste ☎ 261/448–0057.

CAR RENTAL
Cars and 4x4s can be rented in all major cities. It's a good idea to make reservations in advance during peak season. Avis has a large fleet at the Mendoza airport.

🚗 Rental Agencies **Andina Rent A Car** ⊠ Sarmiento 129, Mendoza ☎ 261/461–0210 ⊕ www.andinarentacar.com.ar. **Avis** ⊠ Primitivo de la Reta 914, Mendoza ☎ 261/420–3178, 261/447–0150 airport ⊕ www.avis.com. **Dollar Rent A Car** ⊠ Primitivo de la Reta 936, Loc. No. 6, Mendoza ☎ 261/429–9939 ⊕ www.dollar.com. **Localiza** ⊠ San Juan 931, Mendoza ☎ 261-429–0876 ⊕ www.localiza.com.ar.

CAR TRAVEL
The trip from Buenos Aires to Mendoza is 1,060 km (664 mi) along lonely, paved R7. From Santiago, Chile, it's 250 km (155 mi) east (the road is sometimes closed in winter) on R7. Mendoza locals are known for their cavalier attitude toward traffic rules. Outside the major cities, however, there's very little traffic.

You can drive to most sights and wineries in the Cuyo, although finding wineries on your own requires a good map and some knowledge of Spanish.

Pay attention to weather and road information. In winter, snow and avalanches close some roads. Torrential rainstorms cause flash floods and can obliterate seldom-used dirt roads. Good maps can be found in bookstores and at Automóvil Club Argentino.

🚩 Auto Club **Automóvil Club Argentino (ACA)** ✉ Av. del Libertador 1850, Buenos Aires ☎ 11/4808-4460 🖷 11/4808-4601 ✉ Gdor. Videla and Reconquista, Mendoza ☎ 261/431-4100 ⊕ www.aca.org.ar. **Roadside Assistance** ☎ 0800/888-9888.

EMERGENCIES

🚩 **Ambulance-Medical Emergencies** ☎ 107. **Fire** ☎ 100. **Police** ☎ 101.

HOSPITALS &
PHARMACIES

🚩 In Mendoza **Hospital Central** ✉ José F. Moreno and Alem, near the bus station ☎ 261/420-0600. **Farmacia del Puente (open 24 hrs)** ✉ Av. Las Heras 201 ☎ 261/425-9209.

MONEY MATTERS

Banks in the region are generally open weekdays 10–4. ATMs are available everywhere (Banelco and LINK have ATMs in most cities). Hotels and sometimes travel agencies will change dollars to pesos. Traveler's checks are inconvenient; you have to go to the bank to change them and pay a fee.

🚩 Mendoza Bank Information **Banelco** ✉ Av. San Martín 831 ✉ Sarmiento 29. **Banco de la Nación** ✉ Av. San Martín and Gutiérrez ☎ 261/423-4500 ✉ At bus terminal. **Citibank** ✉ Av. San Martín 1098 ☎ 261/420-4113. **Exprinter** ✉ Espejo 74 ☎ 261/429-1200.

TAXIS

Taxis in the region are inexpensive, metered, and plentiful. There's usually a taxi stand near the central plaza, and you can always have one called at hotels and restaurants. For tips—give the fare rounded up. Although drivers are generally honest, it's a good idea for long trips to agree upon the fare before you go. Remises cost a little more than a taxi, but they are reliable, and a good value for groups sharing expenses. Arrangements can be made through your hotel or at the airport or bus station.

🚩 Remises **Class Remise** ☎ 261/431-8238 local guided tours, 261/431-8244 airport transfers, 261/431-5810 business trips 🖷 261/431-9264. **Imperio Remises** ✉ At the bus station, Loc. D23 ☎ 261/432-2222 or 0800/433368. **La Veloz del Este** ✉ Alem 439 ☎ 261/423-9090.

TELEPHONE & INTERNET

Most *locutorios* (long-distance telephone centers) are large, modern, and user-friendly, with Internet access and fax machines. Local calls can be made on public phones with tokens or phone cards available at kiosks. The cybercafé in San Rafael has few machines, but it does have good coffee and helpful, English-speaking attendants.

🚩 In Mendoza **Cyber Café** ✉ Av. San Martín and Garibaldi 7 ☎ 261/425-4020. **Internet Mendoza** ✉ Sarmiento 25 ☎ 261/429-0143. **Telefónica** ✉ Av. San Martín 650.

TOURS

For ski tours in Mendoza, contact Mendoza Viajes, Badino, or Feeling Turísmo.

Aymará Turismo and Mendoza Viajes organize wine tours, excursions to mountains and villages and outdoor adventures. Huentata and Inka offer local excursions and outdoor adventures. Argentine Rafting and Betancourt Rafting specialize in rafting, kayaking, and trekking.

🖪 **Argentina Rafting Expeditions** ☒ Ruta Nacionál 7, Km 53, Potrerillios-Luján de Cuyo 🕾 262/448-2037 ⊕ www.argentinarafting.com. **Aymará Turismo** ☒ 9 de Julio 1023, Mendoza 🕾🕾 261/420-2064 ⊕ www.aymara.com.ar. **Badino** ☒ Paraguay 930, Buenos Aires 🕾 11/4326-1351 ⊕ www.badino.com.ar/patagonia/. **Betancourt Rafting** ☒ Lavalle 36, Galería Independencia Loc. No. 8, Mendoza 🕾🕾 261/429-9665 ⊕ www. betancourt.com.ar. **Huentata** ☒ Av. Las Heras 680, Mendoza 🕾🕾 261/425-3108 ⊕ www.huentata.com.ar. **Inka** ☒ Av. Juan B. Busto, Mendoza 🕾 261/425-0871 ⊕ www. inka.com.ar. **Mendoza Viajes** ☒ Paseo Sarmiento 129, Mendoza 🕾🕾 261/461-0210 ⊕ www.mdzviajes.com.ar.

VISITOR INFORMATION
🖪 **Mendoza** ☒ Av. San Martín 1143 at Garibaldi 🕾 261/420-2800 🖷 261/420-2243 ⊕ www.turismo.mendoza.gov.ar.

PATAGONIA

Updated by Eddy Ancinas and Michael de Zayas

Patagonia, that fabled land of endless, empty, open space at the end of the world, has humbled the most fearless explorers. Many have described it as a cruel and lonely windswept place unfit for humans. Darwin called Patagonia "wretched and useless," yet he was deeply moved by its desolation and forever attracted to it. Today, the 800,000 square km (309,000 square mi) that make up Argentine Patagonia continue to challenge and fascinate explorers, mountaineers, nature lovers, sports enthusiasts, and curious visitors from around the world. Because the population in Patagonia is small relative to its land mass, a staggering variety of plants and wildlife exists in pristine habitats.

A new airport in Calafate, with direct flights from Buenos Aires and Bariloche has made the far reaches of Patagonia much more accessible to tourists. Covering the great distances between Bariloche, in the north; Ushuaia, in the south; and El Calafate, Río Gallegos, and Trelew, in the middle, requires careful planning—air travel is essential. Tours to popular sights along the Atlantic coast, to the glaciers, or in and around Bariloche, can be arranged in Buenos Aires or in each destination. If you want to see it all, packaged tours can make the whole trip easier.

Bariloche & the Parque Nacional Nahuel Huapi

1,615 km (1,001 mi) southwest of Buenos Aires (2 hrs by plane), 1,639 km (1,016 mi) north of Río Gallegos, 876 km (543 mi) northwest of Trelew, 357 km (221 mi) east of Puerto Montt, Chile, via lake crossing.

In 1620, the governor of Chile sent Captain Juan Fernández and his troops across the Andes in search of the "Enchanted City of the Caesars," a mythological city alleged to be somewhere in Patagonia. By 1670, the Jesuits had established a mission on the shores of the lake, near what is now Isla Huemúl. They attempted to convert the Tehuelches, who ultimately massacred the missionaries in 1717, including the missions' founder, Father Mascardi. No Europeans returned to the area until the next century, when Captain Cox arrived by boat from Chile in 1870.

Later, in 1876, *perito* (expert) Francisco Moreno led an expedition from the Atlantic, becoming the first explorer to arrive from the East.

Most of the indigenous people of the area were massacred during the infamous Campaña del Desierto (Desert Campaign, 1879–83). Settlers then felt safe to colonize, and a fort (called Chacabuco) was built at the mouth of the Río Limay in 1883. Many settlers were German farmers immigrating from Chile, followed by Swiss, Scandinavian, and northern Italian immigrants. They found a rugged and relatively unexplored land similar to their mountainous homelands and built chalets in the town that would become **Bariloche** and along the shore of Lago Nahuel Huapi.

Bariloche's first house, built by a German immigrant named Karl Wiederhold (1867–1935), also became the town's first hotel, called La Cuchara Sucia ("the dirty spoon"). By 1924 tourists could travel two days from Buenos Aires by train, then drive 560 km (350 mi) on dirt roads. The railway finally reached Bariloche in 1934, and by 1938 people from all over the world were coming to ski on the slopes at nearby Cerro Catedral.

These days, Bariloche is the gateway to all the recreational and scenic splendors of the northern lake district. Although planes, buses, trains, boats, and tour groups arrive daily, you can escape into the stunning wilderness of clear blue lakes, misty lagoons, rivers, waterfalls, mountain glaciers, forests, and flower-filled meadows on foot, mountain bike, or horseback or by boat. You can also fish peacefully in one of the 40 nearby lakes and countless streams. It's also possible to get around on your own with a rented car or go on a planned excursion with a local tour company.

The rustic gray-green stone-and-log buildings of the Centro Cívico (Civic Center) were designed by Alejandro Bustillo, the architect who also designed the Llao Llao Hotel and the National Park office in San Martín de los Andes. His Andean-Swiss style is recognizable in lodges and buildings throughout the lake district. The spacious square in front of the Civic Center, with an equestrian statue of General Roca (1843–1914) and a wide-angle view of the lake, is a good place to begin exploring Bariloche. Note that the Civic Center is Km 0 for measuring points from Bariloche.

For information on mountain climbing, trails, *refugios* (mountain cabins), and campgrounds, visit the **Intendencia de Parques Nacional Nahuel Huapi** (✉ Av. San Martín 24 ☎ 2944/423111 ⊕ www.parquesnacionales. gov.ar) at the Civic Center. Another source of information on local activities, excursions, lodging, and private and public campgrounds is the **Oficina Municipal de Turismo** (✉ Centro Cívico, across from clock tower ☎ 2944/429850), open daily 8:30 AM–9 PM.

The **Museo de la Patagonia** (Patagonia Museum) tells the social and geological history of northern Patagonia through displays of Indian and gaucho artifacts and exhibits on regional flora and fauna. The history of the Mapuche and the Conquista del Desierto (Conquest of the Desert) is also explained in detail. ✉ *Centro Cívico, next to arch over Bartolomé Mitre* ☎ *2944/422309* 🎟 *10 pesos* ⊙ *Mon. and Sat. 10–1, Tues.–Fri. 10–12:30 and 2–7.*

The **Parque Nacional Nahuel Huapi,** created in 1943, is Argentina's oldest national park, and **Lago Nahuel Huapi** is the sapphire in its crown. The park extends over 2 million acres along the eastern side of the Andes in the provinces of Neuquén and Río Negro, on the frontier with Chile. It contains the highest concentration of lakes in Argentina. The biggest is Lago Nahuel Huapi, a 897-square-km (557-square-mi) body of water, whose seven long arms (the longest is 96 km [60 mi] long, 12 km [7 mi] wide) reach deep into forests of *coihué* (a native beech tree), *cyprés* (cypress), and *lenga* (deciduous beech) trees. Intensely blue across its vast expanse and aqua green in its shallow bays, the lake meanders into distant lagoons and misty inlets where the mountains, covered with vegetation at their base, rise straight up out of the water. Every water sport invented and tours to islands and other extraordinarily beautiful spots can be arranged through local travel agencies, tour offices, and through hotels. Information offices throughout the park offer help in exploring the miles of mountain and woodland trails, lakes, rivers, and streams.

The most popular excursion on Lago Nahuel Huapi is the 30-minute boat ride to **Isla Victoria** (Victoria Island), the largest island in the lake. A grove of redwoods transplanted from California thrives in the middle of the island. After a walk on trails that lead to enchanting views of emerald bays and still lagoons, the boat crosses to the tip of the **Península Quetrihué** for a visit to the **Parque Nacional los Arrayanes,** a unique forest of cinnamon-color myrtle trees.

The renowned ski area at **Cerro Catedral** (Mt. Cathedral) is 46 km (28½ mi) west of town on Avenida Ezequiel Bustillo (R237); turn left at Km 8½ just past Playa Bonita. The mountain was named for the Gothic-looking spires that crown its peaks. Though skiing is the main activity here, the view from the top of the chairlift at 6,600 feet is spectacular any time of year. To the southwest, Monte Tronadór, a 12,000-foot extinct volcano, straddles the border with Chile, towering above lesser peaks that surround Lago Nahuel Huapi as it meanders around islands and disappears into invisible bays beneath mountains and volcanoes miles away. Lanín Volcano is visible on the horizon.

You can reach the summit of **Cerro Otto** (Mt. Otto; 4,608 feet), a small ski area, by hiking, mountain biking, or driving 8 km (5 mi) up a gravel road from Bariloche. Hiking to the top of the mountain takes you through a forest of lenga trees to Argentina's first ski area, at Piedras Blancas. Here Herbert Tutzauer, Bariloche's first ski instructor, won the first ski race by climbing the mountain, then skiing down it through the forest in 1½ hours. You can also take the **Teleférico Cerro Otto** (⊠ Av. de Los Pioneros), 5 km (3 mi) west of town; a free shuttle bus leaves from the corner of Mitre and Villegas, and Perito Moreno and Independencia. The ride to the top takes about 12 minutes. All proceeds go to local hospitals. At the top, a revolving cafeteria with a 360-degree panorama takes in Monte Tronadór, lakes in every direction, and Bariloche. In winter, skis and sleds are available for rent at the cafeteria. In summer, hiking and mountain biking are the main activities. For a real thrill, try soaring in a paraplane out over the lake with the condors. Call for **information** (☎ 2944/41031) on schedules and sled or ski rentals.

A visit to **Monte Tronadór** (Thunder Mountain) requires an all-day outing of 170 km (105 mi) round-trip from Bariloche. The 12,000-foot extinct volcano, the highest mountain in the northern lake district, sits astride the frontier with Chile, with one peak on either side. Take R258 south along the shore of **Lago Gutiérrez** and **Lago Mascardi**. Between the two lakes the road crosses from the Atlantic to the Pacific watershed. At Km 35, turn off onto a road marked TRONADÓR and PAMPA LINDA and continue along the shore of Lago Mascardi, passing a village of the same name. Just beyond the village, the road forks and you continue on a gravel road, R254. Near the bridge the road branches left to **Lago Hess** and **Cascada Los Alerces**—a detour you might want to take on your way out. As you bear right after crossing Los Rápidos Bridge, the road narrows to one direction only: it's important to remember this when you set out in the morning, as you can only go up the road before 2 PM and down it after 4 PM. The lake ends in a narrow arm (Brazo Tronadór) at the Hotel Tronadór, which has a dock for tours arriving by boat. The road then follows the **Río Manso** (Manso River) to **Pampa Linda,** which has a lodge, restaurant, park ranger's office, campsites, and the trailhead for the climb up to the **Refugio Otto Meiling** at the snow line. Guided horseback rides are organized at the lodge. The road ends 7 km (4 mi) beyond Pampa Linda in a parking lot that was once at the tip of the now receding **Glaciar Negro** (Black Glacier). As the glacier flows down from the mountain, the dirt and black sediment of its lateral moraines are ground up and cover the ice. At first glance, it's hard to imagine the tons of ice that lie beneath its black cap.

The detour to **Cascada Los Alerces** (Los Alerces Falls), 17 km (10 mi) from the turnoff at the bridge near Mascardi, follows the wild Río Manso, where it branches off to yet another lake, **Lago Hess**. At this junction are a campground, refugio, restaurant, and trailhead for the 1,000-foot climb to the falls. The path through dense vegetation over wooden bridges crosses a rushing river as it spills over steep, rocky cliffs in a grand finale to a day of viewing nature at its most powerful and beautiful.

A possible excursion from Bariloche is the **Circuito Chico** (Small Circuit), a half-day, 70-km (43½-mi) scenic trip along the west shore of Lago Nahuel Huapi. You can do it by car, tour bus, or mountain bike. First, head west on Avenida Bustillo (R237) toward Península Llao Llao. At Km 20, you can take a brief side trip on an 11-km-long (7-mi-long) dirt road to the **Península San Pedro**, then follow the coast road that passes some fine homes set back in the woods. At the **Ahumadero Familia Weiss** (Weiss Family Smokehouse), along the way, you can buy smoked fish and game. Back on R237, continue west to **Puerto Pañuelo** (Km 25½) in a little bay on the right; it's the embarkation point for lake excursions and for the boat crossing to Chile. Across from the port, a long driveway leads up a knoll to the Hotel Llao Llao, which is worth a visit even if you're not staying here. The Circuito Chico then follows R77 to Bahía Lopez, winding along the lake's edge through a forest of ghostly, leafless lenga trees. After crossing the bridge that links **Lago Moreno** (Lake Moreno) and Lago Nahuel Huapi at Bahía Lopez, the road crosses the Arroyo Lopez (Lopez Creek). Here you can stop for a hike up to a waterfall and then climb above Lago Moreno to **Punto Panoramico,** a scenic overlook well worth a photo stop. Just before you cross Lago Moreno, an unmarked dirt road off to the right leads to the rustic village of **Colonia Suiza,** a good spot to stop for tea or lunch. After passing **Laguna El Trebol** (a small lake on your left), R77 joins R237 from Bariloche.

The **Circuito Grande** (Large Circuit), a more ambitious excursion than the Circuito Chico that's particularly lovely in spring or fall, covers 250 km (155 mi). Along the way there are plenty of spots to stop and enjoy the view, have a picnic lunch, or even stay overnight. Leaving Bariloche on R237, follow the **Río Limay** into the **Valle Encantado** (Enchanted Valley), with its magical red-rock formations. Before crossing the bridge at **Confluéncia** (where the Río Traful joins the Limay), turn left onto R65 to Lago Traful. Five kilometers (3 mi) beyond the turnoff, on a dirt road heading toward Cuyín Manzano, are some astounding sandstone rock formations. As you follow the shore of Lago Traful, a sign indicates a *mirador* (lookout) on a high rock promontory, which you can climb up to on wooden stairs. The road from Villa Traful dives into a dense forest until it comes to the intersection with the Seven Lakes Circuit (R237). Turn right if you want to add the Seven Lakes Circuit. Otherwise, turn left and follow the shore of **Lago Correntoso** to the paved road down to the bay at **Villa La Angostura.**

The **Circuito de los Siete Lagos** (Seven Lakes Circuit) is an all-day trip of 360 km (223½ mi) round-trip, which could be extended to include an overnight in San Martín de los Andes or Villa La Angostura). Drive north on R237 for 21 km (13 mi), and turn left on R231 to **Villa La Angostura,** 65 km (40 mi) from Bariloche. About 11 km (7 mi) farther along the same road is the Seven Lakes Road (R234), which branches right and along the way passes **Lago Correntoso, Lago Espejo, Lago Villarino, Lago Falkner,** and **Lago Hermoso.** After lunch or tea or an overnight in San Martín de los Andes, head south to Bariloche on the dirt road over Paso Córdoba, passing **Lago Meliquina** on the way. At Confluéncia, the road joins R237, following the Río Limay through Valle Encantado to Bariloche.

A longer, less traveled, all-day boat excursion to **Puerto Blest** leaves from Puerto Pañuelo on the Península Llao Llao (accessible by bus, car, or tour). The boat heads west along the shore of Lago Nahuel Huapi to Brazo Blest, a 1-km-long (½-mi-long) fjordlike arm of the lake. Along the way, waterfalls plunge down the face of high rock walls. A Valdivian rain forest of coihués, cypress, lengas, and *arrayanes* (myrtle) covers the canyon walls. After the boat docks at Puerto Blest, a bus transports you over a short pass to Puerto Alegre on **Laguna Frías** (Cold Lagoon), where a launch waits to ferry you across the frosty green water to **Puerto Fríos** on the other side. Monte Tronadór towers like a great white sentinel. The launch returns to the dock at Puerto Alegre, where you can return by foot or by bus to Puerto Blest. From there, the trail to **Cascada Los Cántaros** (Singing Waterfalls) climbs 600 steps to a series of waterfalls cascading from rock to pool to rock. After lunch in **Puerto Blest** at its venerable old hotel, the boat returns to Bariloche. Note: this is the first leg of the Cruce a Chile por Los Lagos.

Fodor's Choice   The **Cruce a Chile por Los Lagos** (Chile Lake Crossing) is a unique ex-
★   cursion by land and lakes that began in the 1930s when oxcarts used
to haul people. These days you can do the tour in one or two days. Follow the itinerary above, stopping for lunch in **Puerto Blest** and then continuing on to **Puerto Fríos** on **Laguna Frías.** After docking at Puerto Fríos
and clearing Argentine customs, get on another bus that climbs through
lush rain forest over a pass, then descends to **Peulla,** where Chilean customs is cleared (bring your passport). A little farther on is a comfortable lodge by **Lago Todos los Santos.** Early the next morning a catamaran
sets out across the lake, providing views of the volcanoes **Putiagudo** (which
lost its *punto* [peak] in an earthquake) and **Osorno.** The boat trip ends
at the port of **Petrohué.** Another (and final) bus skirts **Lago Llanquihue,** stopping for a visit at the rockbound Petrohué waterfalls, passing
through the town of **Puerto Varas** (famous for its roses) and arriving,
at last, at the Chilean port town of Puerto Montt. Catedral Turismo specializes in this trip and can arrange a one-day return by bus to Bariloche.

Where to Stay & Eat

Accommodations range from family-run *residenciales* (bed-and-breakfasts) to resort hotels. If you don't have a car, it's better to stay in town.
If you're looking for serenity, consider a lake-view hotel, inn, or cabins
along the route to the Llao Llao Peninsula. Addresses for out-of-town
dining and lodging properties are measured in kilometers from the Bariloche Civic Center. The most crowded time of the year is during school
vacations (July and January). Of the many fine restaurants, most are
casual and open noon–3 for lunch and 8–midnight for dinner.

$$$$ ╳ **Kandahar.** A rustic wood building with a woodstove and cozy window seats in alcoves around the bar is the perfect setting for a pisco sour,
smoked meats, and guacamole. Former ski champion, Marta Peirano,
prepares and presents her tasty creations while greeting friends and guests.
Start with unusual appetizers such as *tarteleta de hongos* (mushroom
tart), followed by wild game and profiteroles with hot chocolate sauce.
✉ *20 de Febrero 698* ☎ *2944/424702* ▭ *AE, MC, V.*

★ $$–$$$ ╳ **El Patacón.** Constructed of local stone and wood, with large picture
windows looking out over the lake, this ranch-style restaurant displays
gaucho tools, local art, and weavings on its wood and stucco walls. Leather
and sheepskin furniture add to the country atmosphere. An organic garden with fresh herbs, berries, and vegetables enhances the menu of
meats, game, and fish. ✉ *Av. Bustillo, Km 7* ☎ *2944/442800* ▭ *AE,
DC, MC, V.*

$$–$$$ ╳ **Jauja.** Big, friendly, and casual, this spot is a favorite with locals and
families for its great variety of entrées: meats from the Pampas, fish from
both oceans, local game, and pasta dishes are enhanced by fresh vegetables and salads. Take-out food is available around the corner at the
Quaglia address. ✉ *Elflein 128* ☎ *2944/429986* ✉ *Quaglia 366*
☎ *2944/422952* ▭ *AE, DC, MC, V.*

★ $$–$$$ ╳ **La Marmite.** If there's a Euro-Argentine cuisine, this is it: wild boar in
wine with local mushrooms served with cabbage and elderberry jam,
and venison, trout, and lamb prepared equally imaginatively. Argentina's
famous malbecs and cabernets are the perfect companion for this in-

ternational fare. ✉ *Mitre 329* ☎ *2944/441008* ▭ *AE, DC, MC, V* ⊙ *No lunch Sun.*

$ ✕ **El Boliche de Alberto.** Just point at a slab of beef, chicken, lamb or sausages, and have it grilled to your liking. It'll arrive sizzling on a wooden platter, accompanied by empanadas, salad, fried potatoes, and chimichurri sauce (slather it on the bread). ✉ *Villegas 347* ☎ *2944/431433* ▭ *AE, DC, MC, V.*

★ $$$ **Hotel Edelweiss.** Fresh flowers from the owner's nursery are arranged throughout this excellent medium-size hotel, which is three blocks from the Civic Center and within walking distance of tour offices, restaurants, and shops. The modern, spacious rooms and suites have lake views from their bay windows. Breakfast includes eggs, bacon, sausages, fresh fruits, and juices—unusual in this country of *medias lunas* (croissants) and coffee. Both lunch and dinner consist of good salads, grilled fish, fowl, game, and beef prepared with fresh vegetables and tasty sauces. Most ski and tour buses, whether arranged through the hotel or other travel agencies, pick up passengers at this hotel. ✉ *Av. San Martín 202, 8400* ☎ *2944/426165* *2944/425655* *www.edelweiss.com.ar* *94 rooms, 6 suites* *Restaurant, in-room safes, indoor pool, gym, hair salon, massage, sauna, bar, meeting room, travel services, free parking* ▭ *AE, DC, MC, V* *CP.*

$$$$ Fodor'sChoice ★ **Llao Llao Hotel & Resort.** This masterpiece by architect Alejandro Bustillo sits on a grassy knoll surrounded by three lakes with a backdrop of rock cliffs and snow-covered mountains. Local wood—alerce, cypress, and hemlock—has been used for the walls along the 100-yard hallway, where paintings by local artists are displayed between fine boutiques. Every room has a view worth keeping the curtains open. A hospitality suite at Cerro Catedral allows hotel guests to buy tickets and store equipment while skiing. ✉ *Av. Ezequiel Bustillo, Km 25, 25 km (15½ mi) west of Bariloche, 8400* ☎ *2944/448530* *2944/445781* *www.llaollao.com* *162 rooms, 12 suites, 1 cabin* *Restaurant, café, in-room safes, minibars, cable TV, 18-hole golf course, tennis court, pool, fitness classes, gym, hair salon, hot tub, massage, sauna, spa, dock, windsurfing, boating, mountain bikes, archery, paddle tennis, bar, piano bar, recreation room, baby sitting, children's programs (ages 2–12), business services, convention center, meeting rooms, travel services, no-smoking rooms* ▭ *AE, DC, MC, V* *CP.*

$$$–$$$$ **La Cascada.** Named for its lovely waterfall plunging into an idyllic pool a few steps from the entrance, this lake-view hotel 6 km (4 mi) from Bariloche on the road to Llao Llao brings the outdoors inside through its floor-to-ceiling windows in the living room, dining room, and bar. Views through the trees of blue Nahuel Huapi Lake and distant peaks are enhanced by bay windows in most of the bedrooms. ✉ *Av. E. Bustillo, Km 6, CC 279, 8400* ☎ *2944/441088* *2944/441076* *www.lacascada.com* *22 rooms* *Restaurant, indoor pool, gym, sauna, bar* ▭ *DC, MC, V* *CP.*

$$$–$$$$ **Villa Huinid.** The two-story log and stucco cabins (one, two, or three bedrooms), with their stone chimneys and wooden decks, look like private homes surrounded by lawns and well-tended gardens. Well-equipped kitchens with large family dining tables invite week-long stays with family and friends. Cypress plank floors with radiant heat, carved wooden

counters, slate floors in the bathroom, and cozy plaids and prints in the bedrooms add to the total comfort—all this and a view of Nahuel Huapi Lake. ⊠ *Av. Bustillo, Km 2.5, R8402* 🏠🏠 *2944/523523* ⊕ *www. villahuinid.com.ar* ⤳ *11 cabins* ⬧ *IDD phones, kitchens, cable TV, library, playground* ⊟ *AE, MC, V.*

$ 🏨 **Hotel Tunquelen.** Surrounded by 20 acres of woods and gardens, this châteaulike hotel outside Bariloche is visible from the lake but not from the busy road to Llao Llao. An uninterrupted view across the water to distant peaks—even from the indoor pool—has a calming effect. Rooms are small, but adequate, with whitewashed stucco and native wood, and open onto the garden or overlook the lake. A downstairs dining room serves breakfast and dinner, and cocktails are served in the garden, weather permitting. ⊠ *Av. Bustillo, Km 24½, 24½ km (13 mi) west of Bariloche on the road to Llao Llao, 8400* 🏠🏠 *2944/448400* ⊕ *www. maresur.com* ⤳ *31 rooms, 1 suite, 8 apartments* ⬧ *Restaurant, cable TV, indoor pool, dock, bicycles, piano bar, meeting rooms, travel services, free parking* ⊟ *AE, DC, MC, V* ⧀⧁ *CP.*

¢–$ 🏨 **Casita Suiza.** Swiss-owned and -operated since 1961, this charming downtown chalet exudes old-world hospitality. The owners have lovingly painted flowers on the walls. Rooms are well maintained, and rates include a hearty breakfast with homemade wheat bread, jams, and juices. In summer and spring the street-side terrace explodes with blossoming pansies and violets. ⊠ *Quaglia 342, 8400* 🏠🏠 *2944/23775 or 2944/426111* ✉ *cassuiza@bariloche.com.ar* ⤳ *13 rooms* ⬧ *Restaurant, cable TV, bar, laundry service* ⊟ *AE, DC, MC, V* ⧀⧁ *CP.*

¢–$ 🏨 **Patagonia Sur.** This tall, slender seven-story structure sits high on a hill overlooking the town and the lake. The view of the church spire, rooftops, and blue lake make the five-block walk from town worth the effort. Inside and out it's clean and modern, from the softly upholstered benches in the lobby to the sparsely furnished rooms. The fifth floor is accessible by elevator from Aguas del Sur Hotel on the street below (Moreno). ⊠ *Elfleín 340, 8400* ☎ *2944/422995* 🖷 *2944/424329* ⤳ *55 rooms* ⬧ *Café, cable TV, business services, meeting room, free parking* ⊟ *DC, MC, V* ⧀⧁ *CP.*

¢ 🏨 **Albergue La Bolsa.** Cyclists, mountaineers, skiers, and friends from around the world have been staying at this popular family home for years. This lively hostal provides beds and lockers in rooms for two, four, or five—each room has its own bathroom. Walls are decorated with photos of guests and friends enjoying every sport invented, and information on outings and excursions with sign-up sheets invite an active clientele to participate. Meals are prepared by guests in a large kitchen and eaten on bicycle seats at the counter, outdoors in the enclosed front yard or around the living room. ⊠ *Palacios 405, 8400* ☎ *2944/423520* ⊕ *www.labolsadeldeporte.com* ⤳ *4 rooms* ⬧ *Kitchen, Internet* ⊟ *No credit cards.*

Nightlife & the Arts

Three of the town's most popular *discotecas* (discos) are all on the same street, Avenida J. M. de Rosas. Whole families—from children to grandparents—go to discos, though on Saturday night only people 25 years and older are admitted. The clubs are especially busy during school holidays and ski season. You can dance the night away at **Cerebro** (⊠ 405 Av. J. M. de Rosas ☎ 2944/424965). Bariloche's oldest disco is **El Grisu** (⊠ 574 Av. J. M. de Rosas ☎ 2944/422269). **Roket** (⊠ 424 Av. J. M. de Rosas ☎ 2944/420549 day, 2944/431940 night) has blue-and-purple lights and a cutting-edge sound system. Around the corner from the Avenida J. M. de Rosas strip of clubs is the **Casino Worest** (⊠ España 476 ☎ 2944/424421), which is open daily 10 PM–4 AM.

Sports & the Outdoors

FISHING Fishing season runs November 15–May 1. In some areas, catch-and-release is allowed year-around; in some places it's compulsory, and in some, catches may be kept. Guides are available by the day or the week. Nahuel Huapi, Gutiérrez, Mascardi, Correntoso, and Traful are just a few of the many lakes in the northern lake district that attract fishing fanatics from all over the world. If you're seeking the perfect pool or secret stream for fly-fishing, you may have to do some hiking, particularly along the banks of the Chimehuín, Limay, Traful, and Correntoso rivers. Near Junín de los Andes, the Río Malleo (Malleo River) and the Currihué, Huechulafquen, Paimún, and Lácar lakes are also good fishing grounds. Near El Bolsón and Esquel in the Parque Nacional los Alerces, many remote lakes and streams are accessible only by boat or seldom-traveled dirt roads. Fishing lodges offer rustic comfort in beautiful settings; boats, guides, and plenty of fishing tales are usually included. Make reservations early, as they're booked well in advance by an international clientele of repeat visitors.

Fishing licenses allowing you to catch brown, rainbow, and brook trout as well as perch and *salar sebago* (landlocked salmon) are available in Bariloche at the **Direcciones Provinciales de Pesca** (⊠ Elfleín 10 ☎ 2944/425160). You can also get licenses at the Nahuel Huapi National Park office and at most tackle shops. Boats can be rented at **Charlie Lake Rent-A-Boat** (⊠ Av. Ezequiel Bustillo, Km 16.6 ☎🖷 2944/448562).

Oscar Baruzzi at **Baruzzi Deportes** (⊠ Urquiza 250 ☎ 2944/424922 🖷2944/428374) is a good local fishing guide. **Martín Pescador** (⊠ Rolando 257 ☎ 2944/422275 🖷 2944/421637) has a shop with fishing and hunting equipment. Ricardo Almeijeiras, also a guide, owns the **Patagonia Fly Shop** (⊠ Quinchahuala 200, Av. Bustillo, Km 6.7 ☎🖷 2944/441944).

Arturo Domínguez is a professional English-speaking guide (☎ 2944/15552237 cell ☎🖷 2944/461937).

For trolling or spinning contact **Jorge Lazzarini** (☎ 2944/294411). **Luís Navarro** (☎ 2944/0668–55044) also knows good spots on Nahuel Huapi Lake for spinning and trolling.

HIKING Nahuel Huapi National Park has many forest trails that lead to hidden lakes, tumbling streams, waterfalls, glaciers, and mountaintop vistas. For maps and information in English on trails, distances, and degree of difficulty, visit the **Parques Nacionales** (⊠ Av. San Martín 24 ☎ 2944/423111) office at the Civic Center. For ambitious treks, mountaineering, or use of mountain huts and climbing permits, contact **Club Andino Bariloche** (⊠ 20 de Febrero 30 ☎ 2944/422266).

HORSEBACK RIDING   *Cabalgatas* (horseback outings) can be arranged by the day or the week. Argentine horses are sturdy and well trained, much like American Quarter Horses, and saddles are typically covered with a thick sheepskin. *Tábanas* (horseflies) attack humans and animals in summer months, so bring repellent. **El Manso** (☎ 2944/523641 or 2944/441378) combines riding and rafting over the border to Chile. Tom Wesley at the **Club Hípico Bariloche** (⊠ Av. Bustillo, Km 15.5 ☎☎ 2944/448193 ⊕ www.bariloche.org/twesley.html) does rides lasting from one hour to a week. **Cumbres Patagonia** (⊠ Villegas 222 ☎ 2944/423283 ☎ 2944/431835) arranges day trips to Monte Tronadór and other sights.

MOUNTAIN BIKING   The entire Nahuel Huapi National Park is ripe for mountain biking. Whether you're a beginner or an expert, you can find a trail to suit your ability. Popular rides are from the parking lot at the Cerro Catedral ski area to Lago Gutiérrez and down from Cerro Otto. Local tour agencies can arrange guided tours by the hour or day and even international excursions to Chile. Rental agencies provide maps and suggestions and sometimes recommend guides.

Adventure World (⊠ Base of Cerro Catedral ☎ 2944/460164 or 2944/422637) rents bikes at the ski area. From there you can ride off on your own or follow a guide down to Lago Guitérrez. **Alunco** (⊠ Moreno 187 ☎ 2944/422283) is a full service travel agency that arranges bike tours with local companies. **Cumbres Patagonia** (⊠ Villegas 222 ☎ 2944/423283) offers guided bike tours for a day or a week. **Dirty Bikes** (⊠ Vice Almirante O'Conner 681 ☎ 2944/425616) rents, repairs, and sells bikes and arranges local tours. **La Bolsa del Deporte** (⊠ Diagonal Capraro 1081 ☎ 944/433111) rents and sells new and used bikes.

SKIING   **Cerro Catedral** is the largest and oldest ski area in South America, with 29 lifts, mostly intermediate terrain, and a comfortable altitude of 6,725 feet. The runs are long, varied, and very scenic. Two ski areas share 4,500 acres of skiable terrain, making it necessary to purchase two separate tickets. **Lado Bueno** (The Good Side) has a vertical drop of 3,000 feet, mostly in the fall line. **Robles** goes about 300 feet higher, offering open bowls and better snow for beginners and intermediates at higher elevation. From the top of the second Robles chair, a Poma Lift transports skiers to a weather station at 7,385 feet, where a small restaurant, **Refugio Lynch,** is tucked into a wind-sculpted snow pocket on the edge of an abyss with a stupendous 360-degree view of Nahuel Huapi Lake, Monte Tronadór, and the Andes. **Villa Catedral,** at the base of the mountain, has ski retail and rental shops, information and ticket sales, ski school offices, restaurants, private ski clubs, an ice rink, and even a disco. Frequent buses transport skiers from Bariloche to the ski area. For information and trail maps, contact **La Secretaría de Turismo de Río Negro** (⊠ 12 de Octubre 605 ☎ 2944/423188). **Club Andino Bariloche** (⊠ 20 de Febrero 30 ☎ 2944/422266) also has information and trail maps.

WHITE-WATER RAFTING   With all the interconnected lakes and rivers in the national park, there's something for everyone—from your basic family float down the swift-flowing, scenic Río Limay to a wild and exciting ride down Río Manso (Class II), which takes you 16 km (10 mi) in three hours. If you're really adventurous, you can take the Manso all the way to Chile (Class IV) through spectacular scenery. Some tour companies organize a trip down the Manso with return by horseback and a cookout at a ranch. **Adventure World** (⊠ At the Base of Cerro Catedral ☎ 2944/460164) does one-day and three-day raft trips on the Río Manso, with a combination horseback trip to the Chilean border available. **Alunco** (⊠ Moreno 187 ☎ 2944/422283 🖷 2944/422782) arranges rafting trips throughout the area. **Bariloche Rafting** (⊠ Mitre 86, Room 5 ☎ 2944/435708) offers trips along the Limay. **Cumbres Patagonia** (⊠ Villegas 222 ☎ 2944/423283 🖷 2944/431835) arranges trips on the Ríos Limay and Manso. **El Manso** (☎ 2944/523641 or 2944/1558–3114 cell) specializes in white-water rafting trips on the Manso River.

Trelew

876 km (543 mi) southeast of Bariloche; 1,800 km (1,116 mi) north of Ushuaia.

Trelew (pronounced Tre-LEH-ew) is a commercial, industrial, and service hub with hotels, restaurants, gas stations, mechanics, and anything else you might need as you travel from point to point. Its biggest attractions are its paleontology museum and its proximity to the Punta Tombo Reserve and Península Valdés. Like Gaiman, Trelew has a strong Welsh tradition. If you come in the second half of October, you can participate in the Eisteddfod, a Welsh literary and musical festival, first held in Patagonia in 1875. Trelew itself was founded in 1886 as a result of the construction of the Chubut railway line, which joined the Chubut River valley with the Atlantic coast. It's named after its Welsh founder, Lewis Jones (Tre means "town" in Welsh, and Lew stands for Lewis), who fought to establish the rail line. Trelew gained another kind of infamy in 1974 for the massacre of political prisoners who had escaped from the local jail. For more information about the town, contact the **tourist office** (⊠ Mitre 387 ☎🖷 2965/420139 ⊕ www.trelewpatagonia.gov.ar).

The tourist office is in front of the town's main square, **Plaza Independencia,** which features a central gazebo with intricate woodwork and a steeple. In 1910 the plaza and gazebo were inaugurated in a spot formerly used for grazing by horses of the train station's employees.

The **Museo de Arte Visuales de Trelew** (Museum of Visual Arts) is east of the plaza and hosts good monthly contemporary art exhibitions. It's in a Flemish- and German-influenced building designed by a French architect in 1900. From 1913 to 1932, this was city hall. ⊠ *Mitre 389* ☎ *No phone* ⊕ *http://ar.geocities.com/museotw* ⊙ *Daily 8–8.*

FodorśChoice ★ ☾ At Trelew's most prominent attraction, **Museo Paleontológico Egidio Feruglio (MEF),** the most modern display is 2 million years old. This state-of-the-art educational extravaganza features exhibits on extinct dinosaurs from Patagonia. There's a fossil of a 290-million-year-old spider with a 3-foot leg span and the 70-million-year-old petrified dinosaur eggs of a carnotaurus. The museum's tour de force is the bones of a 100-ton, 120-foot-long dinosaur. You can also glimpse into a workshop where archaeologists study newly unearthed fossils. Tours in English are available. ⊠ *Av. Fontana 140* ☏ *2965/432100 or 2964/420012* 🎫 *8 pesos* ☉ *Oct.–Feb. daily 10–8; Mar.–Sept. daily 10–6.*

Across the street from MEF is Trelew's old train station, which operated from 1889 to 1961, when the government shut down the country's rail service. The national historic landmark now holds a small museum of town history, the **Museo Regional Pueblo de Luís** (Lewistown Regional Museum). It has a mishmash of displays on the European influence in the region, the indigenous populations of the area, and wildlife. ⊠ *Avs. 9 de Julio and Fontana* ☏ *2965/424062* 🎫 *2 pesos* ☉ *Weekdays 8–8, Sun. 5–8.*

Where to Stay & Eat

$ ✕ **El Viejo Molino.** It's fun to find a restaurant that outclasses its city. The
Fodor'sChoice thoughtful design and renovation of this 1886 mill have set a new
★ benchmark for dining on the Patagonian coast. Beneath the Alexander Calder–inspired mobiles that hang from the two-story-high ceilings, elegant hostesses and courteous waiters deliver cosmopolitan service. The interior's coup de grace is a glassed-in parrilla, where you can watch an attendant pour wine over the roast and attend to it lovingly. Old blackand-white photos on the wall document this location's history from a brick cube into an ivy-hung gem of a steak house. ⊠ *Mitre and Av. Galés* ☏ *2965/428019* 🍴 *AE, MC, V.*

¢–$ ✕ **Touring Club.** This classic old *confitería* was founded in 1907 by the Chubut Railway Company as a restaurant and became Chubut's first hotel in 1926. In its heyday it was one of Patagonia's most luxurious options. It was the choice of Argentine presidents Juan Perón and Arturo Frondizi, both of whose photos grace the restaurant walls. Now, the hotel's rooms are too shabby to recommend. But the café staff is proud of its past; after a coffee, ask to see the old ballroom, which hasn't been used in 12 years: it's a spectacle of grace in ruins. ⊠ *Av. Fontana 240, 9100* ☏ *2965/433997 or 2965/433998* 🍴 *AE, DC, MC, V.*

$ 🛏 **Hotel Libertador.** This big hotel has seen better days, but because it caters to tour groups, the friendly, English-speaking staff is very reliable. Rooms are clean and light and reasonably modern. Fourteen "superior" rooms are more recently renovated and are worth the modest increase in price. ⊠ *Av. Rivadavia 31, 9100* ☏ *2965/420220 or 2965/426026* ⊕ *www.hotellibertadortw.com* 🛏 *90 rooms* ♨ *Restaurant, snack bar, in-room data ports, cable TV, laundry service, business services, car rental, free parking* 🍴 *AE, DC, MC, V* 🍽 *CP.*

$ 🛏 **Rayentray.** The nicest, and most expensive, hotel in Trelew is this 22-year-old building, part of an Argentine chain. Rayentray, which means "stream of flowers" in Mapuche, has more amenities than any other local hotel. It's a block from Plaza Independencia. ⊠ *San Martín 101, 9100* ☏ *2965/434702* ⊕ *www.cadenarayentray.com.ar* 🛏 *110 rooms* ♨ *Restaurant, minibars, cable TV, pool, massage, sauna, laundry service, business services* 🍴 *AE, DC, MC, V* 🍽 *CP.*

Nightlife & the Arts

Trelew's biggest discoteca is **La Recova** (⊠ Av. Yrigoyen and Av. Los Mártires). For people 25 years and older, the pub turns into a big dance floor after midnight. You can give gaming a try at **Casino Club Trelew** (⊠ Belgrano 477 ☎ 2965/425236), which has eight roulette and two black-jack tables along with 100 slot machines.

Punta Tombo

120 km (74 mi) south of Trelew.

FodorśChoice The **Reserva Faunística Punta Tombo** (Punta Tombo Wildlife Reserve) has
★ the largest colony of Magellanic penguins in the world and one of the most varied seabird rookeries. Roughly 325,000 penguins live here from the middle of September to March. You can walk among them (along a designated path) as they come and go along well-defined "penguin highways" that link their nests with the sea, and you can see them fishing near the coast. Other wildlife found here in abundance includes cormorants, guanacos, seals, and Patagonian hares. Although December is the best month to come—that's when the adult penguins are actively going back and forth from the sea to feed their newborns—anytime is good, except from April through August when the penguins feed at sea. Other than driving, the easiest way to get to Punta Tombo is with a tour guide from Trelew, Rawson, Gaiman, or even Puerto Madryn, the stopover points for the reserve.

Península Valdés

FodorśChoice *Puerto Pirámides is 171 km (106 mi) northwest of Trelew.*
★

The Península Valdés is one of Argentina's most important wildlife reserves. Its biggest attractions are the 1,200 southern right whales that feed, mate, give birth, and nurse their offspring here. One unique characteristic of these whales is that they have two external blowholes on top of their heads, and when they emerge from the water, they blow a V-shape water blast that can be seen for miles away. The protected mammals attract some 100,000 visitors every year from September through December, when people crowd into boats small and large to observe at close range the 30- to 35-ton whales leap out of the water and blow water from their spouts. Once 100,000-strong, the worldwide population of these giant mammals has declined to only 4,000, a result of being hunted for their blubber.

Off-season the peninsula is still worth visiting: sea lions, elephant seals, Magellanic penguins, egrets, and cormorants as well as land mammals like guanacos, gray fox, and Patagonian *mara,* a harelike animal, all make their home here. Discovered by Spanish explorer Hernando de Magallanes in 1520 and named after Don Antonio Valdés, minister of the Spanish navy in the late 18th century, Península Valdés is a protected zone. So valued is the peninsula's animal population that UNESCO is considering declaring it a site of universal patrimony. It's also the lowest point on the South American continent, at 132 feet below sea level.

To get to the peninsula, you must drive along desolate, unpaved roads surrounded by vast estancias dotted with sheep and a handful of cows. The biggest landholder since the late 19th century, the Ferro family owns one-quarter of Península Valdés—3,625 square km (5,850 square mi), with five airstrips from which they can visit their property. You also pass abandoned salt mines, an important industry in the early 1900s. But the salt is a reminder of the at least 260,000 sea lions killed in the peninsula between 1917 and 1953, at which point hunting was prohibited: salt was used to preserve the sea lions' blubber. Today only about 20,000 sea lions remain.

Puerto Pirámides, the only village on Península Valdés, is a more tranquil, isolated base than Puerto Madryn from which to explore the area's natural attractions. For ecological reasons, only 200 people are allowed to live here, but there are a handful of campsites, hotels, and restaurants. Aside from lounging around with a beer in hand and looking out on the pyramid-shape cliffs of Valdés Bay, the only activities in town are scuba diving and surfing.

Where to Stay & Eat

$$ ✕🖼 **The Paradise.** This hotel and restaurant is overpriced, but lacks competition. If you're seeking reliability, look no further. Rooms are clean and spare; those on the second floor have cable TVs. The restaurant is the most fun in town, with postcards and photographs left behind by visitors, and a fireplace in the back. Two bars create atmosphere enough to cover for seafood dishes like squid or prawns in garlic sauce that lack flair. The hotel can organize scuba-diving tours and activities like sand surfing. ⊠ *Av. Julio A. Roca, 9121* 🖼🖼 *2965/495030 or 2965/495003* ⊕ *www.puerto-piramides.com.ar* 🛏 *12 rooms* ᗷ *Restaurant, some room TVs, some in-room hot tubs, fishing, bar, laundry service* ☰ *AE, MC, V* ❙⊙❙ *CP.*

$ 🖼 **Cabañas en el Mar.** Families would do well to stay in one of these wooden cabañas that have small private balconies that look toward the sea. They come with small kitchens and can accommodate up to six people. Since the food options in town are limited, the cabañas are popular with biologists on extended stays. A recent group was a team from *National Geographic* working on a documentary on orcas. ⊠ *Av. de las Ballenas s/n, 9121* 🖼 *2965/495049* ✐ *cabanas@piramides.net* 🛏 *6 cabañas* ᗷ *Cafeteria, laundry service; no room TVs* ☰ *No credit cards.*

$ 🖼 **Posada Aguamarina.** The three rooms at this friendly and accommodating inn are converted classrooms from Puerto Principe's first school, built in 1914. Instead of school desks, you'll find now the town's most comfortable beds. Owners and environmentalists Gabriela and Fabian couldn't be more hospitable or knowledgeable about the area; they speak English. ⊠ *Av. de las Ballenas s/n, 9121* 🖼 *02965/495008* ✐ *fauna@wef. org.ar* 🛏 *3 rooms* ᗷ *Cafeteria, laundry service* ☰ *No credit cards.*

Sports & the Outdoors

Scuba-diving equipment is easy to find in Puerto Pirámides. **Jorge Schmid** (🖼🖼 2965/295012 or 2965/295112) rents scuba-diving equipment and organizes whale-watching tours. **Mar Patag** (🖼 2965/1545–798963 ⊕www.crucerosmarpatag.com) offers multiday luxury boat tours of Valdés Bay and the Atlantic Ocean. Its brand-new ship has seven well-equipped rooms and can accommodate up to 50 people. The all-inclusive cruises run two to three days and cost about $150 per person per day.

Sarmiento & the Bosque Petrificado José Ormaechea

Fodor's Choice ★ *660 km (410 mi) southwest of Trelew; 1,095 km (680 mi) northwest of Río Gallegos.*

Sarmiento is a one-horse town of dirt and paved roads, with small, low structures—primarily houses, a couple of churches, a gas station, a few small restaurants, and some no-frills hotels. It's also the jumping-off point for the Bosque Petrificado José Ormaechea (José Ormaechea Petrified Forest), about 30 km (19 mi) from Sarmiento on R26. There, you can see trunks of petrified wood 65 million years old, with their colorful stratifications, and feel the overpowering wind. Let the park's resident attendant and self-professed "Patagonia fanatic," Juan José Balera, give you a whirl through the eerily lonely landscape in his Mercedes-Benz bus (just show up; he's usually there). If you rent a car, make it a four-wheel-drive vehicle because you'll have to drive a half hour on a rough, unpaved road once you leave Sarmiento. For more information about the park, contact the **tourist office** (☎0297/489–8220) in Sarmiento. While you're in the area, stop at **Lago Musters** (Musters Lake), 7 km (4 mi) from Sarmiento, and **Lago Olhue Huapi** (Olhue Huapi Lake), a little farther on. At Lago Musters you can take an isolated swim or go fishing.

Where to Stay & Eat

¢ ✕ **Restaurant Heidy's.** About a mile off the main highway in Sarmiento is this restaurant owned by Luís Kraan, of Dutch heritage, and his German-descended wife, Kathy Mueller. Enjoy delicious vegetable broth, called *puchero*, homemade pasta, and steak. And don't skip their delicious chimichurri sauce. ⊠ *Perito Moreno and Patagonia* ☎ *2965/489–3308* ▤ *No credit cards.*

¢ ▦ **Hotel Ismar.** This is the best lodging in Sarmiento. Rooms are clean and have simple wood furnishings and cable TV. ⊠ *Patagonia 248, 9020* ☎ *0297/489–3293* ⚒ *Cable TV, free parking* ▤ *MC, V* ⭘ *CP.*

El Calafate & the Parque Nacional los Glaciares

320 km (225 mi) north of Río Gallegos via R5, 253 km (157 mi) east of Río Turbio on Chilean border via R40, 213 km (123 mi) south of El Chaltén via R40.

Founded in 1927 as a frontier town, El Calafate is the base for all excursions to the Parque Nacional los Glaciares (Glaciers National Park), which was created in 1937. Because of its location on the southern shore of Lago Argentino, the town enjoys a microclimate much milder than the rest of southern Patagonia. During the long summer days between December and February (when the sun sets around 10 PM), and during Easter vacation, thousands of visitors come to see the glaciers and fill the hotels and restaurants. This is the area's high season, so be sure to make reservations well in advance. October, November, March, and April are less crowded and less expensive periods to visit. March through May can be rainy and cool and sometimes quite pleasant. Winter lasts through September.

Daily flights from Buenos Aires, Ushuaia, and Río Gallegos, as well as direct flights from Bariloche, transport tourists in a few hours to

Calafate's modern glass and steel airport—an island of modernity surrounded by the lonely expanse of Patagonia—with the promise of adventure and discovery in distant mountains and unseen glaciers.

Driving from Río Gallegos takes about four hours across desolate plains, enlivened occasionally by the sight of a gaucho, his dogs, and a herd of sheep, as well as *ñandú* (rheas), shy llamalike guanacos, silver-gray foxes, and fleet-footed hares the size of small deer. **Esperanza** (Hope) is the only gas, food, and bathroom stop halfway between the two towns.

Avenida del Libertador San Martín (known as Libertador or San Martín) is the main street, with tour offices, restaurants, and shops selling regional specialties, sportswear, camping and fishing equipment, souvenirs, and food. A staircase in the middle of San Martín ascends to Avenida Julio Roca, where you'll find the bus terminal and a very busy **Oficina de Turismo** (✉ Av. Julio Roca 1004 ☎ 2902/491090 ⊕ www. elcalafate.gov.ar) with a board listing available accommodations and campgrounds; you can also get brochures and maps, and there's a multilingual staff to help plan excursions. It's open daily 7 AM–10 PM. The **Parques Nacionales** (✉ Av. Libertador 1302 ☎ 2902/491545), open weekdays 7–2, has information on the entire park, the glaciers, area history, hiking trails, and flora and fauna.

The Hielo Continental (Continental ice cap) spreads its icy mantle from the Pacific Ocean across Chile and the Andes into Argentina, covering an area of 21,700 square km (8,400 square mi). Approximately 1.5 million acres of it are contained within the **Parque Nacional los Glaciares**, a UNESCO World Heritage site. Extending along the Chilean border for 350 km (217 mi), the park is 40% covered with ice fields that branch off into 47 major glaciers that feed two lakes—the 15,000-year-old **Lago Argentino** (Argentine Lake, the largest body of water in Argentina) in the southern end of the park and **Lago Viedma** (Lake Viedma) at the northern end near **Cerro Fitzroy**, which rises 11,138 feet. Visits to the park are usually by tour, though you could rent a car and go on your own. Travel agents in El Calafate, Río Gallegos, or Buenos Aires can book tours if you haven't made arrangements from home. Plan on a minimum of three days to see the glaciers and enjoy the town—more if you plan to visit El Chaltén or any of the other lakes.

Fodor'sChoice One of the few glaciers in the world still growing after 3,000 years, the
★ **Glaciar Moreno** lies 80 km (50 mi) away on R11, which is paved from El Calafate to the national park entrance. From there, a dirt road winds through hills and forests of lengas and ñires, until suddenly, the startling sight of the glacier comes into full view. Descending like a long white tongue through distant mountains, it ends abruptly in a translucent blue wall 3 km (2 mi) wide and 165 feet high at the edge of frosty green Lago Argentino. A viewing area, wrapped around the point of the **Península de Magallanes,** allows you to wander back and forth, looking across the **Canal de los Tempanos** (Iceberg Channel). Here you listen and wait for nature's number one ice show—first, a cracking sound, followed by tons of ice breaking away and falling with a thunderous crash into the lake. Sometimes the icy water splashes onlookers across the channel!

As the glacier creeps across this narrow channel and meets the land on the other side, an ice dam builds up between the inlet of **Brazo Rico** on the left and the rest of the lake on the right. As the pressure on the dam increases, everyone waits for the day it will rupture again. The last time was in 1986, when the whole thing collapsed in a series of explosions that lasted hours and could be heard in El Calafate. Videos of this event are sold locally.

Glaciar Upsala (Upsala Glacier), the largest glacier in South America, is 60 km (37 mi) long and 10 km (6 mi) wide, and accessible only by boat. Daily cruises depart from **Puerto Banderas** (40 km [25 mi] west of El Calafate via R11) for the 2½-hour trip. While dodging floating icebergs (*tempanos*), some as large as a small island, the boats maneuver as close as they dare to the wall of ice rising from the aqua-green water of Lago Argentino. The seven glaciers that feed the lake deposit their debris into the runoff, causing the water to cloud with minerals ground to fine powder by the glacier's moraine (the accumulation of earth and stones left by the glacier). Condors and black-chested buzzard eagles build their nests in the rocky cliffs above the lake. When the boat stops for lunch at **Onelli Bay**, don't miss the walk behind the restaurant into a wild landscape of small glaciers and milky rivers carrying chunks of ice from four glaciers into Lago Onelli.

Where to Stay & Eat

$$ ✕ **Barricas de Enopio.** The emphasis in this restaurant-bar is on the extensive wine list and great cheeses to accompany each glass. A variety of brochettes and dinner entrées are big enough to split or share. The space is chic, casual, and cozy, with natural cotton curtains and table cloths, handmade lamps, and Tehuelche influences. ✉ *Av. Libertador 1610* ☎ *2902/493414* ▭ *AE, MC, V.*

$$ ✕ **La Tablita.** This typical parrilla lets you watch your food as it's prepared: Patagonian lamb and beef ribs cook gaucho-style on an asador; steaks, chorizos, and chicken sizzle on the grill. Grilled fish and homemade pastas are alternatives to the Patagonian fare. ✉ *Coronel Rosales 28* ☎ *2902/491065* ▭ *AE, DC, MC, V.*

$ ✕ **La Cocina.** This casual café on the main shopping street serves homemade pasta, quiches, crepes, and hamburgers. Homemade ice cream and delicious cakes make good snacks any time of the day. "*Postre Chancho*" (Pig's Dessert) is ice cream with hot dulce de leche sauce. Note that there is a long siesta daily from 2 to 7:30. ✉ *Av. Libertador 1245* ☎ *2902/491758* ▭ *MC, V.*

$$$$ ▦ **Kosten Aike.** The stone-and-brick accents and wood balconies outside, and the slate floors, wood-beamed ceilings, and unfailing attention to detail inside, will please aficionados of Andean Patagonian architecture. Tehuelche symbols and designs are used in everything from the curtains to the room plaques. A lobby bar and living room with fireplace, card tables, magazines, and a large TV is conducive to lounging about indoors anytime of day. ✉ *G. Moyano y 25 de Mayo, 9405* ☎ *2902/492424, 11/ 4811–1314 in Buenos Aires* ⊟ *2902/491538* ⊕ *www.kostenaike.com.ar* ⇥ *58 rooms, 2 suites* ⚬ *Restaurant, gym, bar, shop, Internet, business services, meeting room, car rental* ▭ *AE, DC, MC, V.*

$$$$ 🖼 **Posada los Alamos.** Surrounded by tall, leafy alamo trees and constructed of brick and dark *quebracho* (ironwood), this attractive country manor house uses rich woods, leather, and handwoven fabrics to produce conversation-friendly furniture groupings in the large lobby. Plush comforters and fresh flowers in the rooms, and a staff ready with helpful suggestions make this a top-notch hotel. Lovingly tended gardens surround the building and line a walkway through the woods to the restaurant and the shore of Lago Argentino. ⊠ *Moyano 1355, 9405* ☎ *2902/491144* 🖷 *2902/491186* ⊕ *www.posadalosalamos.com* ⤴ *140 rooms, 4 suites* ᠔ *Restaurant, 3-hole golf course, tennis court, 2 bars, travel services* 🖃 *AE, MC, V* � *CP.*

$$$–$$$$ 🖼 **El Mirador del Lago.** The best thing about this hotel is not the zigzag brick facade offering all the front rooms a corner view of Lago Argentino, nor the cozy bar and sitting room, nor the collection of games, books, videos, and magazines to enjoy on stormy days. The best thing is the unfailingly friendly staff. They're all related and take great pride in helping their guests enjoy everything the region has to offer. They know the roads, the restaurants, and the best way to get to all the attractions. ⊠ *Av. Libertador 2047, 9405* ☎ *2902/491045* 🖷 *2902/493176* ⊕ *www. miradordellago.com.ar* ⤴ *20 rooms* ᠔ *Dining room, sauna, bar, recreation room, travel services* 🖃 *AE, DC, MC, V* ⱦ *CP.*

$$$ 🖼 **El Quijote.** Sun shining through picture windows onto polished slate floors and high beams gives this modern hotel, on a quiet side street in town, a light and airy feel. The carpeted rooms with plain white walls and wood furniture provide peaceful comfort. It's right next to Sancho restaurant and a few blocks from the main street. ⊠ *Gregores 1155, 9405* ☎ *2902/491017* 🖷 *2902/491103* ✑ *elquijote@cotecal.com.ar* ⤴ *80 rooms* ᠔ *Café, bar, travel services* 🖃 *AE, DC, MC, V* ⱦ *CP.*

$$ 🖼 **Michelangelo.** Bright red and yellow native flowers line the front of the low log-and-stucco building with its distinctive A-frames over rooms, restaurant, and lobby. A fine collection of local photographs is displayed on the walls next to a sunken lobby, where easy-chairs and a banquette surround the fireplace. Motel-style rooms have individual heaters, and there's an excellent restaurant next door. ⊠ *Moyano 1020, 9405* ☎ *2902/491045* 🖷 *2902/491058* ✑ *michelangelo@cotecal.com.ar* ⤴ *20 rooms* ᠔ *Restaurant, café, cable TV* 🖃 *AE, MC, V* ⊘ *Closed June* ⱦ *CP.*

$ 🖼 **Ariel.** This small hotel on a hill at the edge of town is surrounded by a carefully tended garden. The small, wall-papered bedrooms open onto a wide indoor passageway that is more like a solarium, protecting guests from Patagonian winds and chill. Breakfast and afternoon tea with homemade cakes are served in a homey dining room conducive to sharing conversation with other guests. ⊠ *Casimiro Biguá 35, 9405* ☎ *2902/ 493131* 🖷 *2902/493131* ✑ *hoyelariel@cotecal.com.ar* ⤴ *5 rooms* ᠔ *Cable TV* 🖃 *No credit cards.*

Sports & the Outdoors

HIKING   You can hike anywhere in the Parque Nacional los Glaciares. Close to El Calafate are trails along the shore of Lago Argentino and in the hills south and west of town. El Chaltén is usually a better base than El Calafate for hikes up mountain peaks like Cerro Torre.

HORSEBACK
RIDING
Anything from a short day-ride along Lago Argentino to a weeklong camping excursion in and around the glaciers can be arranged in El Calafate by **Gustavo Holzmann** (✉ Av. Libertador 3600 ☎ 2902/493203, 2966/1562–0935 cell) or through the tourist office. *Estancias Turísticas* (tourist ranches) are ideal for a combination of horseback riding, ranch activities, and local excursions. Information on **Estancias de Santa Cruz** is available in Buenos Aires at the **Provincial tourist office** (✉ Suipacha 1120 ☎ 11/4325–3098 ⊕ www.estanciasdesantacruz.com). **Estancia Alice** (✉ Ruta 11, Km 22 ☎☎ 2902/491793 Calafate; 11/4312–7206 Buenos Aires) welcomes guests overnight or for the day—for a horseback ride, bird-watching, or an afternoon program that includes a demonstration of sheep dogs working, a walk to the lake with a naturalist, sheep-shearing, and dinner in the former sheep-shearing barn, served right off the grill and the asador by knife-wielding gauchos. Other estancias close to Calafate are **Nibepo Aike** (⚓ 60 km/37 mi from Calafate ☎ 2966/422626), **Alta Vista** (⚓ 33 km/20 mi from Calafate ☎ 2966/491247), and **Huyliche** (⚓ 3 km/2 mi from Calafate ☎ 2902/491025).

ICE TREKKING
A two-hour minitrek on the Moreno Glacier involves transfer from El Calafate to Brazo Rico by bus and a short lake crossing to a dock and refugio, where you set off into the woods, with a guide, through the treacherous terrain. Crampons (provided) are attached over hiking boots and the climb commences. The entire outing lasts about five hours, culminating with cocktails over 1,000-year-old ice cubes. Most hotels arrange minitreks, as does **Hielo y Aventura** (✉ Av. Libertador 935 ☎ 2902/492205 📠 2902/491053), which also organizes much longer, more difficult trips of eight hours to a week to other glaciers.

MOUNTAIN
BIKING
Mountain biking is popular along the dirt roads and mountain paths that lead to the lakes, glaciers, and ranches. Rent bikes and get information at **Alquiler de Bicicletas** (✉ Av. Libertador 689 and Comandante Espora ☎ 2902/491398).

Río Gallegos

2,640 km (1,639 mi) south of Buenos Aires, 319 km (197 mi) south of El Calafate, 596 km (370 mi) north of Ushuaia, and 251 km (157 mi) east of Puerto Natales, Chile, via R40.

The administrative and commercial capital of Santa Cruz Province and perhaps the windiest town in the world (from September to November), Río Gallegos was founded in 1885 and served as a port for coal shipments from Río Túrbio (Túrbio River), on the Chilean border. Wool and sheepskins were its only other economic factors. As the gateway city to southern Patagonia, travelers en route south to Ushuaia, north to the Parque Nacional los Glaciares, or west to Chile, are often obliged to spend a night here. A desk at the airport has information on all the tourist attractions in the area, and helpful attendants will also make hotel reservations. More information is available at the **Subsecretaría de Turismo** (✉ Av. Roca 863 ☎ 2966/438725 📠 2966/422702 ⊕ www.scruz.gov.ar) in town.

If you're into dinosaurs, visit the **Museo Regional Provincial Padre Manuel Jesus Molina** (Provincial Museum), which exhibits reconstructed skeletons excavated at sites in Patagonia. Exhibits on biology, geology, history, paleontology, and Tehuelche ethnology are displayed in different sections of the museum. ⊠ *Ramón y Cajal 51* ☎ *2966/423290* ☑ *Free* ⊙ *Weekdays 10–5, weekends 11–7.*

off the beaten path

CABO VIRGENES – *From September through April, this provincial nature preserve plays host to 150,000 mating Magellanic penguins—the second largest penguin colony in Patagonia. A lighthouse guarding the entrance to the Strait of Magellan has a tea house inside. You can go on an organized tour or on your own by following the signed interpretive trail. ⊹ 128 km (79 mi) south on RN3. At 17 km, branch left on to RP1, a dirt road, and continue past the ranches to the Reserva Faunística Provincial (Provincial Nature Preserve).*

Where to Stay & Eat

$$–$$$ ✕ **El Horreo.** A well-heeled clientele begins to fill this rather classy Spanish-looking restaurant around 10:30 PM. Complimentary pisco sours begin your repast. It's hard to beat the local spring lamb, the steaks, or the mountain trout, crab, and seafood—grilled or in homemade sauces. ⊠ *Av. Roca 862* ☎ *2966/426462* ☐ *MC, V.*

$ ✕ **Trattoría Diaz.** This big, open family-style café in the center of town has been serving grilled lamb and beef, homemade pastas, seafood, and fish since 1932. ⊠ *Av. Roca 1157* ☎ *2966/420203* ☐ *DC, MC, V.*

$$$$ ▦ **Costa Río.** Flags flutter above the entrance to this modern white-brick apart-hotel on a quiet side street. For business travelers and families in town for an extended stay, having a room with chairs, sofas, and tables makes the hotel worth the extra money. A kitchenette and eating area provide an alternative to going out for every meal. All rooms are carpeted and have comfortable, contemporary furnishings. ⊠ *Av. San Martín 673, 9400* ☎☎ *2966/423412* ✎ *costario@infivia.com.ar* ⧖ *54 apartments* ⅄ *Café, kitchenettes, minibars, baby-sitting, dry cleaning, laundry service, free parking* ☐ *AE, DC, MC, V.*

¢ ▦ **Hotel Santa Cruz.** Although the hotel looks old, rooms are comfortable, if a little utilitarian. Intimate seating areas, plants, and a friendly staff make the lobby bar a pleasant retreat on a windy day. Avoid rooms on the Avenida Roca side, as they can be noisy. ⊠ *Av. Roca 701, 9400* ☎ *2966/420601* ☒ *2966/420603* ⧖ *53 rooms, 1 suite* ⅄ *Restaurant, sauna, free parking* ☐ *AE, DC, MC, V* ⓧ *CP.*

Shopping

Monte Aymond (⊠ *Maipú 1320* ☎ *2966/438012*) is a factory outlet for sheepskin and leather coats; the children's jackets, hats, and little sheepskin booties make great gifts. There's also a branch at the airport.

Ushuaia & the Tierra del Fuego

Southeast of Bariloche; 914 km (567 mi) south of El Calafate, 3,580 km (2,212 mi) south of Buenos Aires.

Ushuaia—which at 55 degrees latitude south is closer to the South Pole (2,480 mi) than to Argentina's northern border with Bolivia (2,540 mi)—is the capital and tourism base for Tierra del Fuego, an island at the southernmost tip of Argentina. Although its physical beauty is tough to match, Tierra del Fuego's historical allure is based more on its mythical past than on reality. The island was inhabited for 6,000 years by Yamana, Haush, Selk'nam, and Alakaluf Indians. But in the late 19th century, after vanquishing the Indians in northern Patagonia, the Argentine Republic was eager to populate Patagonia to bolster its territorial claims in the face of European and Chilean territorial ambitions. An Anglican mission had already been established in Ushuaia in 1871, and Argentina had seen Great Britain claim the Falklands, a natural Argentine territory. Thus, in 1902 Argentina moved to initiate an Ushuaian penal colony, establishing the permanent settlement of its most southern territories and, by implication, everything in between.

At first, only political prisoners were sent to Ushuaia. Later, however, fearful of losing Tierra del Fuego to its rivals, the Argentine state sent increased numbers of more dangerous criminals. When the prison closed in 1947, Ushuaia had a population of about 3,000, made up mainly of former inmates and prison staff. Another population boom occurred after Argentina's 1978 industrial incentives law, which attracted electronics manufacturers like Philco and Grundig to Ushuaia. Many of these television and home-appliance factories have shut down because they weren't able to compete in the global marketplace, but the children those boom times produced now populate Ushuaia's streets.

Today the Indians of Darwin's "missing link" theory are long gone—wiped out by disease and indifference brought by settlers—and the 50,000 residents of Ushuaia are hitching their star to tourism. The city rightly promotes itself as the southernmost city in the world (Puerto Williams, a few miles south on the Chilean side of the Beagle Channel, is but a tiny town). Ushuaia feels a bit like a frontier boomtown, with the heart of a rugged, weather-beaten fishing village and the frayed edges of a city that quadrupled in size in the '70s and '80s. In the late '90s the local government completed an airport that has the capacity to handle direct flights from abroad and finished a deep-water pier that welcomes cruise ships stopping for provisions in Ushuaia on their way to the Antarctic. Unpaved portions of R3, the last stretch of the Panamerican Highway, which connects Alaska to Tierra del Fuego, are finally, albeit slowly, being paved. The summer months—December to March—draw 120,000 visitors, and the city is trying to extend those visits with events like March's Marathon at the End of the World.

Tierra del Fuego could be called picturesque, at a stretch. A chaotic and contradictory urban landscape includes a handful of luxury hotels amid the concrete of public housing projects. Scores of "sled houses" (wooden shacks) sit precariously on upright piers, ready for speedy displacement to a different site. Many of the newer homes are built in a Swiss-chalet style, reinforcing the idea that this is a town that tourism has breathed new life into. At the same time, the weather-worn pastel colors that dominate the town's landscape remind you that Ushuaia was once just a tiny fishing village, populated by criminals, snuggled at the end of the Earth.

As you stand on the banks of the Canal Beagle (Beagle Channel) near Ushuaia, as Captain Robert Fitzroy—the captain who was sent by the English government in 1832 to survey Patagonia, including Tierra del Fuego—must have done, the spirit of the farthest corner of the world takes hold. What stands out is the light: at sundown the landscape is cast in a subdued, sensual tone; everything feels closer, softer, more human in dimension despite the vastness of the setting. The snowcapped mountains of Chile reflect the setting sun back onto a stream rolling into the channel, as nearby peaks echo their image—on a windless day—in the still waters.

Above the city, the last mountains of the Andean Cordillera rise, and just south and west of Ushuaia they finally vanish into the often stormy sea. Snow dots the peaks with white well into summer. Nature is the principal attraction here, with trekking, fishing, horseback riding, and sailing among the most rewarding activities, especially in the Parque Nacional Tierra del Fuego (Tierra del Fuego National Park).

As Ushuaia converts to a tourism-based economy, the city seeks ways to utilize its 3,000 hotel rooms in the lonely winter season. Though most international tourists stay home to enjoy their own summer, the adventurous have the place to themselves for snowmobiling, dogsledding, and cross-country and downhill skiing at new ski resorts just outside town.

The **tourist office** (⊠ Av. San Martín 674 ☎ 2901/424550 ⊕ www.tierradelfuego.org.ar/ushuaia or www.e-ushuaia.com) is a great resource for information on the town's and Tierra del Fuego's attractions. It's open weekdays 8 AM–10 PM, weekends 9–8. Several people on the cheerful staff speak English. While the office also has a stand at the airport that greets all flights, it's worth a stop into the main office to plan a stay in the area.

The **Antigua Casa Beben** (Old Beben House) is one of Ushuaia's original houses, and long served as the city's social center. Built between 1911 and 1913, Fortunato Beben is said to have ordered the house through a Swiss catalog. In the 1980s the Beban family donated the house to the city to avoid demolition. It was moved to its current location along the coast and restored, and is now a cultural center with art exhibits. ⊠ *Maipú and Pluschow* ☎ *No phone* ✆ *Free* ☉ *Tues.–Fri. 10–8, weekends 4–8.*

Rainy days are a reality in Ushuaia, but two museums give you an avenue for urban exploration and a glimpse into Tierra del Fuego's fascinating past. Part of the original penal colony, the Presidio building was built to hold political prisoners, street orphans, and a variety of other social undesirables from the north. Today it holds the **Museo Marítimo** (Maritime Museum), within Ushuaia's naval base, which has exhibits on the town's extinct indigenous population, Tierra del Fuego's navigational past, Antarctic explorations, and life and times in an Argentine penitentiary. You can enter cell blocks and read the stories of the prisoners who lived in them while gazing upon their eerie effigies. Well-presented tours (in Spanish only) are conducted at 3:30 daily. ⊠ *Gobernador Paz and Yaganes* ☎ *2901/437481* ✆ *13 pesos* ☉ *Daily 9–8.*

At the **Museo del Fin del Mundo** (End of the World Museum), you can see a large stuffed condor, as well as other native birds, indigenous artifacts, maritime instruments, and such seafaring-related objects as an impressive mermaid figurehead taken from the bowsprit of a galleon. There are also photographs and histories of El Presidio's original inmates, such as Simon Radowitzky, a Russian immigrant anarchist who received a life sentence for killing an Argentine police colonel. The museum is in the 1905 residence of a Fuegonian governor. The home was later converted into a bank, and some of the exhibits are showcased in the former vault. ⊠ *Maipú 173 and Rivadavía* ☎ *2901/421863* ▦ *5 pesos* ⊘ *Daily 10–1 and 3–7:30.*

Tierra del Fuego was the last land mass in the world to be inhabited—until 9000 BC, when the ancestors of those native coastal inhabitants, the Yamana, arrived. The **Museo Yamana** chronicles their lifestyle and history. The group was decimated in the late 19th century, mostly by European disease. (There is said to be, at this writing, one remaining Yamana descendant, who lives a few miles away in Puerto Williams.) Photographs and good English placards depict the unusual, hunched posture of the Yamana; their unusual, wobbly walk; and their hunting of cormorants, which were killed with a bite through the neck. ⊠ *Rivadavía 56* ☎ *2901/422874* ⊕ *www.tierradelfuego.org.ar/mundoyamana* ▦ *5 pesos* ⊘ *Daily 10–8.*

The **Tren del Fin del Mundo** (End of the World Train) takes you to the Parque Nacional Tierra del Fuego, 12 km (7½ mi) away. The two-hour train ride is a simulation of the trip on which El Presidio prisoners were taken into the forest to chop wood; but unlike them, you'll also get a good presentation of Ushuaia's history (in Spanish and English). The train departs daily at 10, noon, 3, and 7 in summer, and just once a day, at 10 AM, in winter, from a stop near the national park entrance. ⊠ *Ruta 3, Km 3042* ☎ *2901/431600* 🖷 *2901/437696* ⊕ *www.trendelfindelmundo.com.ar* ▦ *72 pesos first-class ticket, 58 pesos tourist-class ticket, 12 pesos national park entrance fee.*

Tour operators run trips along the **Canal Beagle,** on which you can get a startling close-up view of all kinds of sea mammals and birds on **Sea Lion's Island** and near **Les Eclaireurs Lighthouse.**

One good excursion in the area is to **Lago Escondido** (Hidden Lake) and **Lago Fagnano** (Fagnano Lake). The Panamerican Highway out of Ushuaia goes through deciduous beechwood forest and past beavers' dams, peat bogs, and glaciers. The lakes have campsites and fishing and are good spots for a picnic or a hike. A rougher, more unconventional tour of the lake area goes to **Monte Olivia** (Mt. Olivia), the tallest mountain along the Canal Beagle, rising 4,455 feet above sea level. You also pass the **Five Brothers Mountains** and go through the **Garibaldi Pass,** which begins at the Rancho Hambre, climbs into the mountain range, and ends with a spectacular view of Lago Escondido. From here you continue on to Lago Fagnano through the countryside past sawmills and lumberyards. To do this lake tour in a four-wheel-drive truck with an excellent bilingual guide, contact **Canal Fun** (⊠ Rivadavía 82 ☎ 2901/437395); you'll drive *through*

Lago Fagnano (about 3 feet of water at this point) to a secluded cabin on the shore and have the best asado of your life, complete with wine and dessert. For a more conventional tour in a comfortable bus with a bilingual guide and lunch at Las Cotorras, try **All Patagonia** (⊠ Juana Fadul 26 ☎ 2901/433622 or 2901/430725 🖷 2901/430707).

Estancia Harberton (Harberton Ranch; ☎ 2901/422742) consists of 50,000 acres of coastal marshland and wooded hillsides. The property was a late-19th-century gift from the Argentine government to Reverend Thomas Bridges, officially considered the Father of Tierra del Fuego. Today the ranch is managed by Bridges's great-grandson, Thomas Goodall, and his American wife, Natalie, a scientist and author who has cooperated with the National Geographic Society on conservation projects. Most people visit as part of organized tours, but you'll be welcome if you arrive alone. They serve up a solid and tasty tea in their home, the oldest building on the island. For safety reasons, exploration of the ranch can only be done with a guide. Lodging is not available, but you can arrange to dine at the ranch by calling ahead for a reservation. Most tours reach the estancia by boat, offering a rare opportunity to explore the **Isla Martillo** penguin colony, in addition to a sea lion refuge on **Isla de los Lobos** (Island of the Wolves) along the way.

If you've never butted heads with a glacier, check out **Glaciar Martial,** in the mountain range just above Ushuaia. Named after Frenchman Luís F. Martial, a 19th-century scientist who wandered this way aboard the warship *Romanche* to observe the passing of planet Venus, the glacier is reached via a panoramic ski lift. Take the Camino al Glaciar (Glacier Road) 7 km (4 mi) out of town until it ends. Even if you don't plan to hike to see the glacier, it's a great pleasure to ride the 15-minute lift (locally called Aerosilla), which is open daily 10–6:30 and costs 7 pesos round-trip. If you're afraid of heights, you can instead enjoy a small nature trail here, and a teahouse. You can return on the lift, or continue on to the beginning of a 1-km (½-mi) trail that winds its way over lichen and shale straight up the mountain. After a strenuous 90-minute hike, you can cool your heels in one of the many gurgling, icy rivulets that cascade down water-worn shale shoots or enjoy a picnic while you wait for an early sunset. When the sun drops behind the glacier's jagged crown of peaks, brilliant rays beam over the mountain's crest, spilling a halo of gold-flecked light on the glacier, valley, and channel below. Moments like these are why this land is so magical. Note that temperatures drop dramatically after sunset, so come prepared with warm clothing.

★ The pristine **Parque Nacional Tierra del Fuego,** 21 km (33½ mi) west of Ushuaia, offers a chance to wander through peat bogs; stumble upon hidden lakes; trek through native *canelo,* lenga, and wild cherry forests; and experience the wonders of Tierra del Fuego's rich flora and fauna. Visits to the park, which is tucked up against the Chilean border, are commonly arranged through tour companies. Trips range from bus tours to horseback riding to more adventurous excursions, such as canoe trips across Lapataia Bay. Another way to get to the park is to take the Tren del Fin del Mundo. **Transporte Kaupen** (☎ 2901/434015), one of several private bus companies, has buses that travel through the park, making several stops within it; you can get off the bus, explore the park, and then wait for the next bus to come by or trek to the next stop. Yet one more option is to drive to the park on R3 (take it until it ends and you see the last sign on the Panamerican Highway, which starts at Alaska and ends here). Trail and camping information is available at the park-entrance ranger station or at the Ushuaia tourist office. A nice excursion in the park is by boat from lovely **Ensenada Bay** to **Isla Redonda,** a wildlife refuge where you can follow a footpath to the western side and see a wonderful view of the Canal Beagle. While on Isla Redonda you can send a postcard and get your passport stamped at the world's southernmost post office. Tours to the park are run by **All Patagonia** (⊠ Juana Fadul 26 ☎ 2901/433622 or 2901/430725 🖶 2901/430707).

Where to Stay & Eat

Dotting the perimeter of the park are five free campgrounds, none of which has much more than a spot to pitch a tent and a fire pit. Call the **park office** (☎ 2901/421315) or consult the ranger station at the park entrance for more information. **Camping Lago Roca** (⊠ South on R3 for 20 km [12 mi] ☎ No phone), also within the park, charges 8 pesos per person per day and has bathrooms, hot showers, and a small market. Of all the campgrounds, **La Pista del Andino** (⊠ Av. Alem 2873 ☎ 2901/435890) is the only one within the city limits. Outside of town, **Camping Río Pipo** (☎ 2901/435796) is the closest to Ushuaia (it's 18 km [11 mi] away).

Choosing a place to stay depends in part on whether you want to spend the night in town or 3 mi uphill. Las Hayas Resort, Hotel Glaciar, and Cumbres de Martial have stunning views, but require a taxi ride to reach Ushuaia.

$$–$$$ ✕ **Chez Manu.** Provence herbs in the greeting room tip French owner chef Manu Herbin's hand: he uses local seafood with a French touch to create some of Ushuaia's most memorable meals. Perched a couple of miles above town, across the street from the Hotel Glaciar, the all-glass restaurant has grand views of the Beagle Canal. The rest of the restaurant is understated, with an aquarium in the center of the dining room, a kind of throne to the king crab. The menu's highlights include *centolla* (king crab) au gratin and a seafood and fish bouillabaisse. ⊠ *Camino Luís Martial 2135* ☎ *2901/432253* ⊕ *www.chezmanu-ushuaia.ifrance.com* 🖃 *AE, MC, V* ☾ *Closed Mon. and May–Sept.*

$–$$$ ✕ **La Cabaña Casa de Té.** This cottage, in a verdant wood of lenga trees beside the surge of a powerful river, overlooks the Beagle Channel and provides a warm, cozy spot for tea or snacks before or after a hike to the Martial glacier—it's at the end of the Martial road that leads up from Ushuaia. Fondues are a specialty at lunch time; at 8 PM the menu shifts to pricier dinner fare with dishes like salmon in wine sauce. ⊠ *Camino Luís Martial 3560* ☎ *2901/434699* 🖃 *AE, DC, MC, V* ☾ *Closed Mon.*

★ **$–$$$** ✕ **Volver.** A giant plastic king crab sign beckons you into this red tin restaurant, which provides some major relief from Avenida San Martin's row of all-you-can-eat parrillas. The name means "return" and it's the kind of place that calls for repeat visits. Newspapers from the 1930s line the walls in this century-old home; informal table settings have placemats depicting old London landmarks; and fishing nets hang from the ceiling, along with hams, a disco ball, tricycles, and antique lamps. The culinary highlight is, of course, king crab (*centolla*), which comes served with a choice of five different sauces. ⊠ *Maipú 37* ☎ *2901/423977* ▤ *AE, DC, MC, V.*

$ ✕ **La Estancia.** This restaurant in the center of town has mouth-watering lamb and other typical Patagonian meats. Sit by the glass wall to see the chef artfully coordinate the flames, the cooking, and the cutting of tender pieces of lamb and parrilla-style meats. Don't be bashful about requesting more lamb if you're still hungry—all-you-can-eat is implied for all entrées. ⊠ *Av. San Martín 253* ☎ *2901/432700* ▤ *AE, DC, MC, V.*

$$$$ ▦ **Cumbres de Martial.** This charming wood complex, painted fire-engine red, is high above Ushuaia at the foot of the ski lift that leads to the Martial glacier. Depending on your take, the hotel can seem desolate and removed from town, or a peaceful sanctuary close to glacier hiking. Each spacious room has a small wooden deck with terrific views down to the Beagle Channel. There are also a teahouse and a small nature trail beside the Martial River. There is, however, no complimentary shuttle service to town, so you'll need to take a (cheap) taxi to access Ushuaia. ⊠ *Camino Luís Martial 3560, 9410* ☎☎ *2901/434699* ⤴ *14 rooms* ⌂ *Restaurant, tea shop, in-room safes, bar, lounge, laundry service, airport shuttle* ▤ *AE, DC, MC, V* ⊚ *BP.*

$$$$ ▦ **Hotel y Resort Las Hayas.** Las Hayas is in the wooded foothills of the
Fodor'sChoice   Andes, overlooking the town and channel below. Every single one of its
★   rooms is decorated differently; you're bound to run into such luxurious details as Portuguese linen, solid oak furnishings, and fabric-padded walls. A suspended glass bridge connects the hotel to a complete health spa. Frequent shuttle buses take you into town. ⊠ *1650 Camino Luís Martial, Km 3, 9410* ☎ *2901/430710, 11/4393–4750 in Buenos Aires* ☎ *2901/430710 or 2901/430719* ⊕ *www.lashayas.com* ⤴ *102 rooms, 8 suites* ⌂ *Restaurant, coffee shop, in-room safes, golf privileges, indoor pool, health club, hot tub, massage, sauna, spa, squash, bar, laundry service, convention center, meeting rooms, airport shuttle, travel services* ▤ *AE, DC, MC, V* ⊚ *CP.*

★ $$ ▦ **Hostería Patagonia Jarké.** Jarké means "spark" in a local native language, and indeed this B&B is a vibrant addition to Ushuaia proper. This two-story lodge, on a dead-end street in the heart of town, is an amalgam of alpine and Victorian styles on the outside; inside, a spacious contemporary design incorporates a glass-roofed lobby, lounge, and breakfast room. Rooms have polished wood floors, peaked-roof ceilings, artisanal soaps, woven floor mats, and lovely views. ⊠ *Sarmiento 310, 9410* ☎☎ *2901/437245* ✉ *hpatagoniaj@speedy.com.ar* ⤴ *10 rooms* ⌂ *Café, in-room safes, cable TV, bar, laundry service, Internet* ▤ *AE, DC, MC, V* ⊚ *BP.*

$$ ▦ **Hotel Cabo de Hornos.** Cabo de Hornos is a cut above other downtown hotels in the same price category. The rooms are clean and simple, and all have cable TV and telephones. The lobby-lounge is tacky and tasteful at the same time, decorated with currency and postcards from all over the world. Its old ski-lodge feel makes it a nice place to relax and watch *fútbol* with a cup of coffee or a beer. ⊠ *San Martín and Rosas, 9410* ☎ *2901/422187* ☎ *2901/422313* ⤴ *30 rooms* ⌂ *Restaurant, bar* ▤ *AE, MC, V* ⊚ *CP.*

$$ ▦ **La Posada.** This family-run hotel in the middle of town is a decent, lower-cost alternative to the bigger, more costly hotels, but don't expect much in the way of amenities. Rooms on one side face the mountains; on the other side they face the bay and more mountains. ⊠ *Av. San Martín 1299, 9410* ☏ *2901/433222 or 2901/433330* ✇ *17 rooms* ⌂ *Some room TVs, travel services* ▤ *AE, MC, V* ⦿❙ *CP.*

Nightlife & the Arts

Ushuaia has a lively nightlife scene in summer, with its casino, discos, and cozy cafés all within close proximity of each other. The biggest and most popular disco is **El Nautico** (⊠ Maipú 1210 ☏ 2901/430415), which plays all kinds of music, from Latin to techno. It's pumping Thursday through Saturday nights from midnight to 6 AM.

Another popular nightspot is **Lenon Pub** (⊠ Maipú 263 ☏ 2901/435255), which serves drinks and food to those 21 and older. It's open 11 AM–6 AM. Try your luck at the only full-fledged casino, **Casino Club S.A.** (⊠ Av. San Martín 638 ☏ 2901/430415), which features roulette and black-jack tables. There's a 5 peso entrance fee in the evening. The casino is open Sunday–Thursday 11 AM–4 AM and weekends 11 AM–5 AM. For more traditional Argentine entertainment, **Hotel del Glaciar** (⊠ 2355 Camino Glaciar Martial, Km 3½) has tango shows Saturday at 11 PM.

Sports & the Outdoors

FISHING The rivers of Tierra del Fuego are home to trophy-size freshwater trout—including browns, rainbows, and brooks. Both fly- and spin-casting are available. The fishing season runs November–March; fees range from 10 pesos a day to 40 pesos for a month. Fishing expeditions are organized by the following companies. Founded in 1959, the **Asociación de Caza y Pesca** (⊠ Av. Maipú 822 ☏ 2901/423168) is the principal hunting and fishing organization in the city. **Rumbo Sur** (⊠ Av. San Martín 342 ☏ 2901/422441 or 2901/421139) is the city's oldest travel agency and can assist in setting up fishing trips. **Wind Fly** (⊠ Av. San Martín 54 ☏ 2901/431713 or 2901/1556-1573 ⊕ www.windflyushuaia.com.ar) is dedicated exclusively to fishing, and offers classes, arranges trips, and rents equipment.

FLIGHT-SEEING The gorgeous scenery and island topography is readily appreciated on a Cessna tour of the area. A half-hour flight (US$50 for two) with a local pilot takes you over Ushuaia and the Beagle Channel with views of area glaciers and snow-capped islands south to Cape Horn. A 60-minute flight crosses the Andes to the Escondida and Fagnano lakes. **Aero Club Ushuaia** (⊠ Antiguo Aerpuerto ☏ 2901/421717 ⊕ www.aeroclubushuaia.org.ar) offers half-hour and hour-long trips.

MOUNTAIN BIKING A mountain bike is an excellent mode of transport in Ushuaia, giving you the freedom to roam without the rental car price tag. Good mountain bikes normally cost about 5 pesos an hour or 15–20 pesos for a full day. They can be rented at **D. T. T. Ushuaia** (⊠ Av. San Martín 1258 ☏ 2901/434939). Guided bicycle tours (including rides through the national park), for about 50 pesos a day, are organized by **All Patagonia** (⊠ Fadul 26 ☏ 2901/430725 🖷 2901/430707). **Rumbo Sur** (⊠ Av. San Martín 342 ☏ 2901/422441 or 2901/421139) is the city's biggest travel agency and can arrange trips. **Tolkeyén Patagonia** (⊠ Av. Maipú 237 ☏ 2901/437073) rents bikes and arranges trips.

SKIING Ushuaia is the cross-country skiing (*esquí de fondo* in Spanish) center of South America, thanks to enthusiastic **Club Andino** (☎ 2901/422335) members who took to the sport in the 1980s and made the forested hills of a high valley about 20 minutes from town a favorite destination for skiers. **Hostería Tierra Mayor** (☎ 2901/423240), **Hostería Los Cotorras** (☎ 2901/499300), and **Haruwen** (☎ 2901/424058) are three places where you can ride in dog-pulled sleds, rent skis, go cross-country skiing, get lessons, and eat; contact the Ushuaia tourist office for more information. **Glaciar Martial Ski Lodge** (☎ 2901/2433712), open year-round, Tuesday–Sunday 10–7, functions as a cross-country ski center from June to October. Skis can also be rented in town, as can snowmobiles.

For downhill (or *alpino*) skiers, Club Andino has bulldozed a couple of short, flat runs directly above Ushuaia. The area's newest downhill ski area, **Cerro Castor** (☎ 2901/422335 ⊕ www.cerrocastor.com), is 26 km (16 mi) northeast of Ushuaia on R3, and has 15 trails and four high-speed ski lifts. More than half the trails are at beginner level, three are for intermediate skiers, and the rest are for experts. You can rent skis and snowboards and take ski lessons here.

Patagonia A to Z

AIR TRAVEL
The best way to get to Patagonia is to fly from Buenos Aires. Aerolíneas Argentinas flies daily from Buenos Aires to Bariloche, with service from Bariloche to Calafate, Trelew, Río Gallegos, and Ushuaia. Its "Visit Argentina" pass allows you to fly to multiple destinations at a discount; it must be purchased outside of Argentina.

LADE flies from Buenos Aires to Trelew, El Calafate, and Río Gallegos. Airg (formerly LAPA) flies between Buenos Aires and Trelew, El Calafate, Río Gallegos, and Ushuaia.

🛈 **Aerolíneas Argentinas** ☎ 0810/2228-6527 24-hr reservations and sales in Argentina, 11/4317-3000 in Buenos Aires, 2944/423161 in Bariloche, 2966/422020 in Río Gallegos. **Airg (formerly LAPA)** ☎ 11/4114-5272 24-hr reservations and sales in Argentina, 11/4819-5272 in Buenos Aires, 2944/425032 in Bariloche, 2902/491171 in El Calafate, 2966/430446 in Río Gallegos. **LADE** ☎ 11/4361-7071 in Buenos Aires, 2944/423562 in Bariloche, 2966/422326 in Río Gallegos, 2902/491262 in Calafate, 2901/421123 in Ushuaia.

BOAT & FERRY TRAVEL
Traveling between Bariloche and Puerto Montt, Chile, by boat is one of the most popular excursions in Argentina. It requires three lake crossings and various buses and can be done in a day or overnight. Travel agents and tour operators in Bariloche and Buenos Aires can arrange this trip and many foreign tour companies include it in their itineraries. Cruises to Antarctica and the Malvinas (Falkland Islands) rarely stop at Ushuaia nowadays; they call instead at Punta Arenas, Chile.

BUS TRAVEL
Every Patagonian town, no matter how small or insignificant, has a bus station; and it's not uncommon for buses to stop and pick up a passenger

standing by the road where there's nothing in sight for hundreds of miles. Andesmar Autotransportes and La Puntual are two of the main regional bus companies. They stop at almost every major and minor city along the coast and also cross Patagonia between Bahía Blanca and Neuquén. To the west, buses reach Chile's cities of Los Andes and Santiago, among others, and they go as far south as Río Gallegos. You can pick up schedules at bus stations.

Buses arrive in Bariloche from every corner of Argentina. Several companies have daily service to Buenos Aires. Bariloche's Terminal de Omnibus is in the Estación de Ferrocarril General Roca (Railroad Station) east of town, where all bus companies have offices. Most have downtown offices, too, but your best bet is to go directly to the terminal. The following bus companies run comfortable and reliable overnight buses between Buenos Aires and Bariloche (the trip takes 22 hours): Chevallier, El Valle, and Via Bariloche. Buses also run daily between Bariloche and Chile (Osorno, Puerto Montt, Valdivia, and Santiago) via the Puyehue Pass; contact Tas–Choapa.

The following bus companies connect Buenos Aires to Río Gallegos and El Calafate: Don Otto, Interlagos, El Pingüino, and TAC. In summer, Bus Sur and Turismo Zaahj make the five-hour run from Puerto Natales, Chile, to El Calafate. El Pingüino also has service to Trelew and to Bariloche with a change in Comodoro Rivadavía.

You'll probably want to fly to Ushuaia to make the most of your time in the Tierra del Fuego (besides being much faster, it's also cheaper to fly), but direct bus service between Buenos Aires and Ushuaia exists. Trans los Carlos and Turismo Ghisoni make the 12-hour run between Punta Arenas, Chile, and Ushuaia.

▐ Bus Companies **Andesmar** ⊠ Mitre 385, Bariloche ☎ 2944/422140, 2944/430211 at bus terminal. **Bus Sur** ⊠ At the bus station, Av. Julio A. Roca 1004, Río Gallegos ☎ 2966/442687, 2902/491631 in Calafate. **Chevallier** ⊠ Moreno 105, Bariloche ☎ 2944/423090 or 11/4314–0111, 11/4314–5555 in Buenos Aires. **Don Otto** ⊠ At the bus terminal in Bariloche, B. Mitre 321 ☎ 2944/437699. **El Pingüino** ☎ 11/4315–4438 in Buenos Aires, 2966/442169 in Río Gallegos. **Interlagos** at the bus terminals: ☎ 2902/491179 in El Calafate, 2966/442080 in Río Gallegos. **La Puntual** ☎ 11/4313–2441 in Buenos Aires, 297/429176 in Comodoro Rivadavía. **TAC** ⊠ Moreno 138, Bariloche ☎ 2944/434727, 2972/428878 in San Martín de los Andes, 2966/29805 in Río Gallegos, 11/4313–3627 in Buenos Aires. **Tas-Choapa** ⊠ Moreno 138, Bariloche ☎ 0944/26663, 562/697–0062 in Santiago. **Trans los Carlos** ⊠ Av. San Martín 880, Ushuaia ☎ 0901/22337. **Turismo Ghisoni** ⊠ Lautaro Navarro 975, Punta Arenas ☎ 5661/223205. **Turismo Zaahj** ☎ 5661/412260 in El Calafate. **El Valle** ⊠ 12 de Octubre 1884, Bariloche ☎ 2944/431444, 11/4313–3749 in Buenos Aires. **Via Bariloche** ⊠ Mitre 321, Bariloche ☎ 2944/432444, 2972/422800 in San Martín de Los Andes, 11/4663–8899 in Buenos Aires.

▐ Bus Terminals **Bariloche Terminal de Omnibus** ⊠ Av. 12 de Octubre ☎ 2944/432860. **Río Gallegos** ⊠ Av. Eva Perón.

CAR RENTAL

For short excursions, renting a car gives you the freedom to stop when and where you want. Gas is 30% less south of El Bolsón. Almost all hotels have off-street parking, some in locked yards—a good idea at night.

A number of U.S. car rental agencies can be found in Patagonia's major cities and tourist centers, as well as locally owned agencies with knowledgable staff that can help you plan excursions, suggest hotels, and even make reservations. For winter travel, it's a good idea to rent a 4x4, especially if you're traveling on dirt roads.

Hiring a *remis* (car with driver) is another option; it costs a little more, but you get a bigger vehicle and the rate is set before you depart on your trip.

🚗 Major Agencies **Avis** ☎ 11/4326-5542 in Buenos Aires ✉ At the airport, Bariloche ☎ 2944/431648 ✉ Paraguay 105, Trelew ☎ 2965/434634. **Budget** ☎ 11/4313-9870 in Buenos Aires ✉ Mitre 106, Bariloche ☎ 2944/422482, 2944/15551168 cell ⊕ www. budgetbariloche.com.ar. **Dollar** ☎ 11/4315-8800 in Buenos Aires ✉ Villegas 282, Location 6, Bariloche ☎📠 2944/430333 ⊕ www.patagoniarentacar.com. **Hertz** ☎ 11/4312-1317 in Buenos Aires, 2944/434543 in Bariloche. **Localiza** ☎ 11/4327-5288 in Buenos Aires, 0800/999-2999 toll free ✉ Av. San Martín 531, Bariloche ☎ 2944/424767 ✉ Av. del Libertador 687, El Calafate ☎ 2902/491398 ✉ Sarmiento 237, Río Gallegos ☎ 2966/424417 ✉ Urquiza 310, Trelew ☎ 2965/435344 ✉ Av. San Martín 1222, Ushuaia ☎ 2901/430739 or 2901/432136.

🚗 Local Agencies **Ai Rent A Car International** ✉ Av. San Martín 235, across from Edelweiss Hotel, Bariloche ☎ 2944/427494 ⊕ www.rentacarbariloche.com. **Bariloche Rent a Car** ✉ Moreno 115, fl. 1, No. 15, Bariloche ☎ 2944/427638 ☎📠 2944/427638. **Cristina** ✉ Av. del Libertador 695, El Calafate ☎ 2902/491674 ✉ Libertad 123, Río Gallegos ☎ 2960/425709. **Freelander** ✉ Av. del Libertador 1329, El Calafate ☎ 2902/491437. **Rastro** ✉ Maipú 13, Ushuaia ☎ 2901/422021. **Rent-A-Car** ✉ Av. San Martín 125, Trelew ☎ 2965/420898. **Visita Rent-a-Car** ✉ Maipú, Ushuaia ☎ 2901/235181.

🚗 Remis **Calafate** ✉ Av. Julio A. Roca ☎ 2902/492005. **Centenario** ✉ Maipú 285, Río Gallegos ☎ 2966/422320. **De La Ciudad** ✉ Quaglia 268 Bariloche ☎ 2944/428000. **Patagonia Remises** ✉ Av. Pioneros 4400, Bariloche ☎ 2944/443700.

CAR TRAVEL

Driving to any of the towns in Patagonia from Buenos Aires is a long haul (1,593 km [990 mi]; two–three days) of interminable stretches without motels, gas stations, or restaurants. Fuel in Argentina is expensive and if you break down in the hinterlands, it's unlikely that you'll find anyone who speaks much English. Note, too, that what seem like towns marked on the map may just be private estancias not open to the public. On the other hand, driving exposes you to the heart of the country (and roads are paved all the way to Bariloche). Planning is essential, and Automóvil Club Argentino can provide maps and advice. To get to Bariloche from Buenos Aires: take R5 to Santa Rosa (615 km [382 mi]), then R35 to General Acha (107 km [66 mi]), then R20 to Colonia 25 de Mayo, then R151 to Neuquén (438 km [272 mi]), and then R237 to Bariloche (449 km [279 mi]).

Driving to Río Gallegos (2,504 km [1,555 mi] from Buenos Aires) is even more daunting, more isolated, and more monotonous. The most sensible solution is to fly and rent a car at your destination. Roads between towns and sights in both the northern and southern lake districts are mostly paved, and if not, generally kept in good condition, except in rainy seasons, when it's a good idea to seek local advice about road conditions.

🚗 Auto Club**Automóvil Club Argentino (ACA)** ✉ Av. del Libertador 1850, Buenos Aires 📞 11/4802-6061 🌐 www.aca.org.ar.

EMERGENCIES
🛟**Coast Guard** 📞 106. **Fire** 📞 100. **Forest Fire** 📞 103. **Hospital** 📞 107. **Police** 📞 101.

HOSPITALS &
PHARMACIES
🏥 In Bariloche**Farmacia Suizo Andino** ✉ Rolando 699, Bariloche 📞 2944/524040. **Farmacia Zona Vital** ✉ Moreno 301 and Rolando, Bariloche 📞 2944/420752. **Hospital Ramón Carillo** ✉ Moreno 601 📞 2944/426117 or 2944/426119. **Hospital Sanatorio del Sol** ✉ 20 de Febrero 640 📞 2944/525000 or 2944/524800.

🏥 In El Calafate**Farmacia El Calafate** ✉ Av. Libertador 1190 📞 9405/491407. **Hospital Municipal** ✉ Av. Roca 1487 📞 2902/492101 or 2902/491173.

🏥 In Río Gallegos**Hospital Regional** ✉ José Ingeniero 98 📞 2966/420025 📠 2966/420641.

HEALTH
The water in Bariloche and throughout Patagonia is generally safe. But if you're susceptible to intestinal disturbances, it's best to stick to bottled water, which is available in stores, restaurants, and at some kiosks. *Tabanas* (horseflies) are pests around horses and in the woods in summer. Horsefly repellent is more effective than general bug spray; bring enough for yourself and the horse.

MONEY MATTERS
Banks are open weekdays 10–4 in most towns and most have ATMs.

BANKS
🏦 In Bariloche **Citibank** ✉ Mitre 694 📞 2944/436301. **Frances BBV** ✉ Av. San Martín 336 📞 2944/430325. **Scottiabank Quilmes** ✉ Mitre 433 📞 2944/422792.

🏦 In El Calafate**Provincia de Santa Cruz** ✉ Av. Libertador 1285 📞 2902/491168.

🏦 In Río Gallegos**Bancos de Galicia** ✉ Av. Roca 802. **Banco de Santa Cruz** ✉ Roca 802. **Hipotecario Nacional** ✉ Zapiola 49. **Nazionale de Lavoro** ✉ Fagnano off Av. Roca.

🏦 In Trelew**Banco Nación** ✉ Fontana and 25 de Mayo 📞 2965/449114 or 2965/449101. **Lloyds Bank** ✉ 9 de Julio 102 📞 2965/434264 or 2965/434058.

SAFETY
Argentina is safer than almost any country in South America, and Patagonia even more so. Reasonable precautions, such as locking your car and leaving nothing inside, leaving large amounts of cash and travel documents in hotel safes, and carrying money in a money belt are advised. In bus stations and airports, keep an eye on your luggage and wear backpacks in front. To avoid car break-ins, park in hotel garages off the street.

TAXIS
Since taking a taxi doesn't cost much and drivers know their way around, arranging tours or quick trips by taxi to sights near Bariloche, El Calafate, or other locales makes sense. If you're in El Calafate and have a sudden urge to see the Moreno Glacier, for example, or if you

missed the bus to a boat departure on Lago Nahuel Huapi, taking a taxi is a good solution. In Bariloche, there are taxi stands at the Civic Center and at Calles Mitre and Villegas. In other towns, taxis line up at the airport, the bus terminal, and at main intersections. Your hotel can also call a taxi for you.

TELEPHONES & INTERNET ACCESS

When you call from outside a particular area code within Argentina, a 0 precedes the area code. Local calls can be made from *telecabinas* (phone booths) with a phone card purchased at kiosks. There are numerous *locutorios* (telephone offices) in all towns. They're easy to use: an attendant sends you to a booth where you can call all over the country or the world, and then pay one bill when you leave. Since hotels charge exorbitant rates for long-distance calls, it's best to go to one of the closest locutorios, which are centrally located and open late into the night. Most locutorios now have fax machines and Internet access. The lowest price for Internet use is 1 peso an hour; you're liable to find the best rates at small, privately run Internet cafés.

▪ In Bariloche **AAT Communicaciones** ✉ Moreno 107 ☎ 2944/437883. **Locutorio Quaglia** ✉ Quaglia 220 ☎📠 2944/426128. **Mas** ✉ Moreno 724, in front of the hospital ☎ 2944/428414. **Telecentro Melipal** ✉ Pioneros 4400 ☎ 2944/520111.

▪ In Trelew **Arnet** ✉ San Martín and Mitre. **Locutorio del Centro** ✉ Av. 25 de Mayo 219.

▪ In Ushuaia **Nido de Condores** ✉ Gobernador Campos and 9 de Julio ☎ 2920/437753.

TOURS

If you want a comprehensive tour of Patagonia, including the Parque Nacional los Glaciares, Lago Argentino, Trelew, and Bariloche, contact Gador Viajes in Buenos Aires, Causana Viajes in Puerto Madryn (67 km [41½ mi north of Trelew), or any of the tour operators listed below. Carlos and Carol de Passera of Causana Viajes have 17 years of experience leading custom and special-interest trips—focusing, for example, on archaeology, birding, botany, natural history, or whale-watching—for American and Canadian adventure travel companies. Gador Viajes has ecovolunteer trips, wildlife and horseback adventures, and general tours. Provincial tourist offices in Buenos Aires and local tourist offices throughout Patagonia are well-stocked with brochures, and staff are knowledgeable and helpful.

▪ Tour Information **Causana Viajes** ✉ Moreno 390, Puerto Madryn ☎ 2965/455044 📠 2965/452769 ⊕ www.causana.com.ar. **Gador Viajes** ✉ Av. Santa Fe 1339, Buenos Aires ☎ 11/4811-8498 or 4813-8696 📠 11/4815-6888 ⊕ www.gadorviajes.com.ar ✉ Gob. Moyano 1082, El Calafate ☎ 2902/491143.

EL CALAFATE, EL CHALTÉN & RÍO GALLEGOS
In El Calafate, most hotels arrange excursions to Moreno and Upsala glaciers. Hielo y Aventura specializes in glacier tours with "minitrekking" (walking on the glacier with crampons). Upsala Explorer combines a day at an estancia and a boat trip to Upsala Glacier. Horseback riding can be arranged by Gustavo Holzman or through the tourist office. Alberto del Castillo, owner of El Calafate's E.V.T. Fitzroy Expeditions, has English-speaking guides and organizes both glacier and mountain treks.

Interlagos Turismo arranges tours between Río Gallegos and El Calafate and to the glaciers. Tur Aiké Turismo organizes tours in and around Río

Gallagos. In El Calafate, Cal Tur, Hielo y Aventura, and Upsala Explorer run local tours.

🖪 **Fitzroy Expeditions** ✉ Av. San Martín, El Chaltén ☎ 2962/493017 🖨 2962/49136. **Gador Viajes** ✉ Gob. Moyano 1082, El Calafate ☎ 2962/491143. **Gustavo Holzman** ✉]. A. Roca 2035, El Calafate ☎ 2902/491203. **Hielo y Aventura** ✉ Av. Libertador 935, El Calafate ☎ 2902/492205. **Interlagos Turismo** ✉ Fagnano 35, Río Gallegos ☎ 2966/422614 🖂 Av. Libertador 1175, El Calafate ☎ 2902/491175 🖨 2902/491241. **Tur Aiké Turismo** ✉ Zapiola 63, Río Gallegos ☎ 2902/422436. **Upsala Explorer** ✉ 9 de Julio 69, El Calafate ☎ 2902/491034 🖨 2902/491292 ⊕ www.upsalaexplorer.ccom.ar.

PENÍNSULA
VALDÉS &
SARMIENTO
Aiké Tour, Cuyun Co Turismo, and Factor Patagonia arrange all-day tours of the Península Valdés; reserve ahead, especially if you want an English-speaking guide. These companies also organize tours to Punta Tombo, Gaiman, the Dique Ameghino, and Camarones. Jorge Schmid specializes in whale-watching tours; his boat has ample covered space in case it rains. Zonotrikia leads treks through paleontological sites in the area.

Aonik'Enk de Patagonia gives tours of Sarmiento, the Bosque Petrificado, and other nearby destinations; it also rents four-wheel-drive vehicles.

🖪 **Aiké Tour** ✉ Av. Julio Roca 353, Puerto Madryn ☎ 2965/450720. **Aonik'Enk de Patagonia** ✉ Av. Rawson 1190, Comodoro Rivadavía 🖨🖨 0297/446-6768 or 0297/446-1363. **Cuyun Co Turismo** ✉ Julio A. Roca 165, Puerto Madryn ☎ 2965/454950 or 2965/451845 🖨 2965/452065 ⊕ www.cuyunco.com.ar. **Factor Patagonia** ✉ 25 de Mayo, Puerto Madryn, ☎ 2965/454990 or 2965/454991. **Jorge Schmid** ✉ Av. Julio A. Roca, Puerto Pirámides ☎ 2965/495112 or 2965/495029. **Zonotrikia** ✉ Av. Roca 536, Puerto Madryn ☎ 2965/451427 or 2965/455888 🖨 2965/451108.

TIERRA DEL
FUEGO
In Ushuaia and the Tierra del Fuego, All Patagonia, Canal Fun and Nature, Tiempo Libre, and Tolkar all offer a wide variety of adventurous treks through the Parque Nacional Tierra del Fuego and around the Canal Beagle. Tolkeyén Patagonia and Rumbo Sur organize tours of the Canal Beagle and bus trips that give an overview of the national park. All Patagonia organizes bus trips to Lago Escondido and other spots in the area. Sailing out to sea usually means contact with wide-eyed seals, sea elephants, and sea lions sunning on the rocks. All Patagonia and Rumbo Sur do sea excursions as well as trips to Antarctica. To charter a sailboat, head to Club Naútico, where locals gather to talk about fishing.

🖪 **All Patagonia** ✉ Juana Fadul 26, Ushuaia ☎ 2901/433622 or 2901/430725 🖨 2901/430707 ⊕ www.allpatagonia.net. **Canal Fun and Nature** ✉ Rivadavía 82, Ushuaia ☎ 2901/437395 ⊕ www.canalfun.com. **Club Naútico** ✉ Maipú 1210, Ushuaia ☎ No phone. **Rumbo Sur** ✉ Av. San Martín 342, Ushuaia ☎ 2901/422441 or 2901/421139 🖨 2901/430699. **Tiempo Libre** ✉ 25 de Mayo 260, Ushuaia ☎ 2901/431374 🖨 2901/421017. **Tolkar** ✉ Roca 157, Ushuaia ☎ 2901/431408 or 2901/431412. **Tolkeyén Patagonia** ✉ Maipú 237, Ushuaia ☎ 2901/437073 or 2901/434341 🖨 2901/430532.

VISITOR INFORMATION

Chubut (Trelew, Punta Tomba, Sarmiento, Río Gallegos), Río Negro (Bariloche), Santa Cruz (El Calafate), and Tierra del Fuego (Ushuaia) all have provincial tourism offices in their capital cities and in Buenos Aires. Local tourist offices (Direcciónes de Turismo) are very helpful, easy to find, and usually open every day and into the evening.

✈ Provincial Tourist Offices Casa de La Provincia de Chubut ⊠ Sarmiento 1172, Buenos Aires ☎ 11/4432-8815. **Casa de la Provincia de Río Negro** ⊠ Tucumán 1916, Buenos Aires ☎ 11/4371-7066. **Subsecretaría de Turismo Santa Cruz** ⊠ Av. Roca 863, Río Gallegos ☎☎ 2966/422702 ✆ tur@spse.com.ar ⊠ Suipacha 1120, Buenos Aires ☎☎ 11/4325-3098. **Tierra del Fuego Tourism Institute** ⊠ Av. Maipú 505, Ushuaia ☎ 2901/421423.

✈ Local Tourist Offices Bariloche ⊠ Civic Center ☎ 2944/423022 or 2944/43122 ☎ 2944/426784. **El Calafate** ⊠ Terminal de Omnibus, Julio A. Roca 1004 ☎☎ 2902/491090. **Río Gallegos** ⊠ Av. Roca 863 ☎ 2966/438725 ☎ 2966/422702 ⊕ www.scru.gov.ar. **Sarmiento** ⊠ Av. Reg. de Infantería 25 ☎ 0297/489-8220. **Trelew** ⊠ Mitre 387 ☎☎ 2965/420139. **Ushuaia** ⊠ Av. San Martín 674 ☎ 2901/432000 or 0800/333-1476.

ARGENTINA A TO Z

AIR TRAVEL

If your national airline does not fly directly into Buenos Aires, it's often possible to fly into Brazil and take a two- to three-hour flight on Aerolíneas Argentinas into Ezeiza. Miami and New York are the primary departure points for flights to Argentina from the United States. Regular flights also depart from Los Angeles, but these usually have at least one stopover.

Major sights within Argentina are often far apart, and although transportation over land can be more economical, it is slower, so it's best to save time and travel the country by plane.

CARRIERS **✈ To & from the U.S. Aerolíneas Argentinas** ☎ 800/333–0276 in U.S., 0/810–2228–6527 in Buenos Aires ⊕ www.aerolineas.com.ar. **Air Canada** ☎ 888/247–2262 in U.S. and Canada, 11/4327–3640 in Buenos Aires ⊕ www.aircanada.com. **American Airlines** ☎ 800/433–7300 in U.S., 11/4318–1111 in Buenos Aires ⊕ www.aa.com. **LanChile** ☎ 800/735–5526 in U.S., 11/4378–2200 in Buenos Aires ⊕ www.lanchile.com to Buenos Aires via Santiago. **Lloyd Aéro Boliviano** ☎ 800/327–7407 in U.S., 11/4323–1900 in Buenos Aires ⊕ www.labairlines.com to Buenos Aires via Santa Cruz. **Southern Winds** ☎ 800/379–9179 in U.S., 0/810–777–7979 in Argentina ⊕ www.sw.com.ar. **United Airlines** ☎ 800/538–2929 in U.S., 11/4316–0777 in Buenos Aires ⊕ www.united.com. **Varig Brasil** ☎ 800/468–2744 in U.S. and Canada, 11/4329–9211 in Buenos Aires ⊕ www.varig.com to Buenos Aires via Rio de Janeiro and São Paulo.

✈ To & from the U.K. American Airlines ☎ 0345/789789 ⊕ www.aa.com from London Heathrow via Miami or New York. **British Airways** ☎ 0345/222111 in the U.K., 11/4320-6600 in Buenos Aires ⊕ www.britishairways.com from London Gatwick. **Iberia** ☎ 0171/830-0011 in the U.K., 11/4327-2739 or 11/4131-1000 in Buenos Aires ⊕ www.iberia.com via Madrid.

✈ Within Argentina Aerolíneas Argentinas ☎ 800/333-0276 in U.S., 0/810-2228-6527 in Buenos Aires ⊕ www.aerolineas.com.ar. **Austral** ☎ 11/4340-7800 in Buenos Aires. **Dinar** ☎ 11/5371-1111 in Buenos Aires ⊕ www.dinar.com.ar. **LADE** ☎ 11/5129-9000 ⊕ www.lade.com.ar. **Laer** ☎ 343/436-2177 in Argentina. **LAPA** ☎ 0810/777-5272 in Buenos Aires ⊕ www.lapa.com.ar. **Southern Winds** ☎ 800/379-9179 in U.S., 0810/777-7979 in Argentina ⊕ www.sw.com.ar.

AIRPORTS & TRANSFERS

The major gateway to Argentina is Buenos Aires's Ezeiza International Airport, 47 km (29 mi) and a 45-minute drive from the city center. Ezeiza, also known as Aeropuerto Internacional Ministro Pistarini, is served by a variety of foreign airlines, along with domestic airlines running international routes. Though Argentina has other international airports, they generally only serve flights from other South American countries.

Flights from Buenos Aires to other points within Argentina depart from the Aeroparque Jorge Newbery, a 15-minute cab ride from downtown. ✈ **Aeroparque Jorge Newbery** ☎ 11/5480-6111. **Ezeiza Airport** ☎ 11/5480-6111 ⊕ www.aa2000.com.ar.

AIRPORT TRANSFERS Bus, van, taxi, and *remis* (car service charging a fixed, prearranged price) service is available at Buenos Aires's Ezeiza International Airport. There are several round-the-clock private bus and remis services run by licensed companies; buses depart from the airport at scheduled intervals while taxis and remises are readily available.

Transportation tickets can be purchased from the well-marked service counters right outside the customs area. Taxis and remises from the airport to downtown cost around 35 pesos; vans 11–16 pesos, per person. Taxis and remises can transport up to four people; if your party does not exceed this limit, a remis is the cheaper option. Prices do not include tolls. City buses (2 pesos) operate on a regular schedule, but it's a two-hour ride and there's a limit of two bags. Beware of unsolicited chauffeurs who accost you with offers to drive you to your destination; they may not be a licensed service.

APTA provides licensed, metered taxi service to and from Ezeiza International Airport. Manuel Tienda León vans run from 4 AM to 8:30 PM between the airport and Buenos Aires. If you speak Spanish, call Remis Le Coq upon your arrival. They offer the best rate, around 20 pesos, plus tolls. They pick up passengers in front of the Banco Nacion outside Terminal A on the outdoor walkway.
🚖 Taxis & Shuttles **APTA** ☎ 11/4480-9383 ⊕ www.taxiaeropuerto.com.ar. **Manuel Tienda León** ☎ 11/4383-4454 or 0810/888-5366 ⊕ www.tiendaleon.com.ar. **Remis Le Coq** ☎ 11/4964-2000.

BOAT & FERRY TRAVEL

Buquebus provides frequent ferry service between Argentina and Uruguay and has several packages and promotions. Round-trip rates for economy travel range 100–300 pesos from Buenos Aires to the cities of Colonia, La Paloma, Montevideo, Piriápolis, and Punta del Este, all in Uruguay. All destinations, except Colonia, include bus transfers; the duration of the trip varies from 45 minutes to around 3 hours. You can order tickets by phone or on the Web site.

The more modest Ferry Lineas Argentina also serves the Buenos Aires–Uruguay route on a smaller scale with fewer boats per day; they sometimes work in conjunction with Buquebus.
⛴ **Buquebus** ✉ Antártida Argentina 821, at Av. Córdoba, Buenos Aires ✉ Patio Bullrich in Unicenter [Martínez] shopping mall, Buenos Aires ☎ 11/4316-6550 ⊕ www.

buquebus.com. **Ferry Lineas** ✉ Maipú 866, Buenos Aires ☎ 11/4311-2300 ⊕ www. ferrylineas.com.uy.

BUSINESS HOURS

BANKS & OFFICES Official business hours are weekdays 9–noon and 2–7 for offices and 9–3 for banks; some currency exchange offices remain open until 7 PM. Offices in larger cities remain open all day.

GAS STATIONS Most gas stations in cities are open 24 hours.

MUSEUMS & SIGHTS Museums are usually closed on Tuesday. Many close for one month during the summer. In small towns and more rural areas, museums may close for lunch.

POST OFFICES & PHONE CENTERS Post offices are open weekdays from around 9 to 8 and Saturday 9–1. Telephone centers generally stay open daily 8–8.

SHOPS In Buenos Aires street shops are open weekdays 10–8 to compete with the malls, which remain open until 10 daily. On Saturday, street shops remain open until 1 PM, and almost all are closed Sunday. In the provinces, store hours are weekdays 9–noon and 2–7. The larger, more modern supermarket chains are open daily until 9.

CAR RENTAL

Renting a car in Argentina is expensive (around 150 pesos per day plus tax for a midsize car). Extras such as car seats and air-conditioning drive the fee even higher. Ask about special rates; generally a better price can be negotiated. Keep in mind that almost all cars have manual transmission rather than automatic.

All cities and most areas that attract tourists have car-rental agencies. You can also rent cars from airports and some hotels. If the rental agency has a branch in another town, arrangements can usually be made for a one-way drop off. Offices in Buenos Aires can make reservations in other locations; provincial government tourist offices also have information on car-rental agencies.

An alternative to renting a car is to hire a *remis,* a car with a driver, especially for day outings. Hotels can arrange this service for you. Remises are more comfortable and cheaper than taxis for long rides. They're also usually less expensive for rides within cities, especially on round-trip journeys because there's no return fare. You have to pay cash— but you'll often spend less than you would for a rental car. In cities, remises cost about 25–30 pesos per hour; sometimes there's a three-hour minimum and an additional charge per kilometer when you go outside city limits. In smaller towns, the rate is often much less (perhaps 20–25 pesos for the entire day). Some local car agencies offer chauffeur-driven rentals as well. Refer to individual chapters for more information on hiring remises.

🚗 Major Agencies **Avis** ☎ 800/331-1084, 800/879-2847 in Canada, 0870/606-0100 in the U.K., 02/9353-9000 in Australia, 09/526-2847 in New Zealand, 11/4130-0130 in Buenos Aires ⊕ www.avis.com. **Dollar** ☎ 800/800-6000, 0124/622-0111 in the U.K., where it's affiliated with Sixt, 02/9223-1444 in Australia, 11/4315-8800 in Buenos Aires ⊕ www.dollar.com. **Hertz** ☎ 800/654-3001, 800/263-0600 in Canada, 0870/844-

8844 in the U.K., 02/9669-2444 in Australia, 09/256-8690 in New Zealand, 11/4129-7777 in Buenos Aires ⊕ www.hertz.com. **National Car Rental** ☎ 800/227-7368, 0870/600-6666 in the U.K. ⊕ www.nationalcar.com.

🔢 Local Agencies **ABC Rent a Car** ⊠ Embassy Gallery, Marcelo T. de Alvear 628, Buenos Aires 🖼🖼 11/4315-0313 ⊕ www.abc-car.com.ar. **AI International** ⊠ Marcelo T. de Alvear 678 ☎ 11/4311-1000 or 11/4313-1515 ⊕ www.airentacar.com.ar.

INSURANCE   When driving a rented car you are generally responsible for any damage to or loss of the vehicle. You also may be liable for any property damage or personal injury that you may cause while driving. Before you rent, see what coverage you already have under the terms of your personal auto-insurance policy and credit cards. Argentine rental-car insurance is often higher than in the United States.

REQUIREMENTS &   Your own driver's license may be valid in Argentina, though you may
RESTRICTIONS   want to take out an International Driver's Permit; contact your local automobile association (⇨ Auto Clubs *in* Car Travel). The minimum driving age is 18. You'll need to present a major credit card at the agency counter in order to rent a car.

CAR TRAVEL

AUTO CLUBS   The Automóvil Club Argentino (ACA) provides complete mechanical assistance, including towing, detailed maps and driver's manuals, and expert advice (often in English). The ACA can help chart your itinerary, give you gas coupons, and even set you up with discounted accommodations in affiliated hotels and campgrounds. Present your own auto-club membership card to enjoy these benefits.

Note that ACA service is also available at many of the YPF service stations throughout Argentina.
🔢 In Argentina **Automóvil Club Argentino (ACA)** ⊠ Av. del Libertador 1850 ☎ 11/4802-6061 ⊕ www.aca.org.ar.

EMERGENCY   The ACA will provide emergency mechanical assistance, as will your
SERVICES   rental-car agency (included in the rate).

You can get your tires filled at gas stations, but if you have a flat you'll have to find a *gomería* (tire repair), many of which are open 24 hours.

GASOLINE   You'll find Esso, Shell, and national YPF service stations throughout Buenos Aires, in the provinces, and along major highways. The stations usually include full service, convenience stores, snack bars, and ATMs. In rural areas, gas stations are few and far between and have reduced hours; when traveling in the countryside, it's a good idea to **start looking for a station when your tank is half empty.**

Gas is expensive (around 1.50 pesos per liter, or about 6 pesos per gallon) and may run you 80 pesos to fill a midsize car. There are several grades of unleaded fuels, as well as diesel and gas oil.

INTERNATIONAL   Paved highways run from Argentina to the Chilean, Bolivian, Paraguayan,
TRAVEL   and Brazilian borders. If you do cross the border by land you'll be required to present your passport, visa, and documentation of car ownership at immigration and customs checkpoints. It's also common for cars and bags to be searched for contraband, such as food, livestock, and drugs.

ROAD
CONDITIONS
Ultramodern multilane highways exist in Argentina, usually connecting the major cities. Gradually these highways become narrower routes, and then county roads. Many of these rural roads are not divided and are not in particularly good condition.

You must pay tolls on many highways, and even on some unpaved roads. Tolls come frequently and can be steep.

Night driving can be hazardous: some highways and routes are poorly lit, routes sometimes cut through the center of towns, cattle often get onto the roads, and in rural areas *rastreros* (old farm trucks) seldom have all their lights working.

City streets throughout Argentina are notorious for potholes, and lanes are generally poorly marked.

For highway-condition reports, updated daily, and basic routes in Spanish, contact La Dirección Nacional de Vialidad.

▪ **La Dirección Nacional de Vialidad** ☎ 0800/333-0073 ⊕ www.vialidad.gov.ar.

RULES OF
THE ROAD
Don't drive after dark. Obey speed limits (marked in kilometers per hour) and traffic regulations. If you do get a traffic ticket, don't argue. Although you'll see Argentines offering cash on the spot to avoid getting a written ticket, this isn't a good idea.

Seat belts are required by law, as are car lights at daytime on highways. The use of cellular phones while driving is forbidden, and turning left on two-way avenues is prohibited unless there's a left-turn signal; likewise, there are no right turns on red. Traffic lights turn yellow before they turn red, but also before turning green, which is interpreted by drivers as an extra margin to get through the intersection, so take precautions.

In Buenos Aires, drivers in general, and buses and taxis (which cruise slowly on the right-hand side), often drive as though they have priority, so it's a good idea to defer to them for safety. If you experience a small accident, jot down the other driver's information and supply your own. A police officer will not assist you; you must go down to the police station in the area to file a report. Contact your rental agency immediately.

In towns and cities, a 40-kph (25-mph) speed limit applies on streets, and a 60-kph (37-mph) limit is in effect on avenues. On expressways the limit is 100 kph (62 mph), and on other roads and highways out of town it's 80 kph (50 mph). These limits are enforced by strategically placed cameras triggered by excessive speed.

CUSTOMS & DUTIES

IN ARGENTINA
Upon arriving to Buenos Aires by air or ship, you'll find that customs officials usually wave you through without close inspection. International airports have introduced a customs system for those with "nothing to declare," which has streamlined the arrival process.

If you enter the country by bus, take the time to have the border officials do a proper inspection of your belongings and documents. This could prevent problems later when you are trying to leave the country.

Personal clothing and effects are admitted free of duty, provided they have been used, as are personal jewelry and professional equipment. Fishing gear presents no problems. Up to 2 liters of alcoholic beverages, 400 cigarettes, and 50 cigars are admitted duty-free.

Note that you must pay $30.50 dollars in departure tax upon leaving through Ezeiza International Airport.

ELECTRICITY
The electrical current in Argentina is 220 volts, 50 cycles alternating current (AC); wall outlets usually take Continental-type plugs, with two round prongs or three flat, angled prongs.

To use electric-powered equipment purchased in the United States or Canada, **bring a converter and adapter;** some high-end accommodations provide these, but you're better off bringing them if you're unsure.

EMBASSIES
In addition to providing assistance, many embassies also host cocktail parties, where both foreigners and locals mingle. There's usually a small entrance fee; call any embassy to find out the location of the next event. 🚩 **Australia** ✉ Villanueva 1400, Belgrano, Buenos Aires 🕾 11/4779-3500 ⊕ www. argentina.embassy.gov.au. **Canada** ✉ Tagle 2828, Palermo, Buenos Aires 🕾 11/ 4808-1000 ⊕ www.dfait-maeci.gc.ca/argentina. **Ireland** ✉ Suipacha 1280, fl. 2, El Centro, Buenos Aires 🕾 11/4325-8588. **New Zealand** ✉ Carlos Pelligrini 1427, 5th fl., El Centro, Buenos Aires 🕾 11/4328-0747, 15/4148-7633 emergencies. **South Africa** ✉ M. T. de Alvear 590, fl. 8, El Centro, Buenos Aires 🕾 11/4317-2900. **United Kingdom** ✉ Luis Agote 2412, La Recoleta, Buenos Aires 🕾 11/4803-7799 or 11/4576-2222, 15/ 5331-7129 emergencies ⊕ www.britain.org.ar. **United States** ✉ Av. Colombia 4300, Palermo, Buenos Aires 🕾 11/5777-4533 ⊕ www.usembassy.state.gov.

ETIQUETTE & BEHAVIOR
Argentines are very warm and affectionate people, and they greet each other as such. The customary greeting between both friends and strangers is one kiss on the right cheek. This is done by both men and women. If you don't feel comfortable kissing a stranger, a simple hand shake will suffice, but don't be surprised when you see men kissing men and women kissing women.

When arriving at parties, Argentines will often have something in hand to offer the hosts: a bottle of wine, a cake or other goodies, but there is certainly no rule about giving gifts.

When you leave a party or restaurant it's normal to say good-bye to everyone in the room or in your party, which means kissing everyone once again. Argentines are never in a hurry to get anywhere, so a formal good-bye can certainly take awhile.

Smoking is very common in Argentina, so be prepared for some smoke with your steak. Most restaurants offer nonsmoking sections, but make sure to ask before you are seated. If you are at a dinner party, don't be surprised if the room fills up with smoke right after the main course; if it bothers you, you should excuse yourself—don't ask others to smoke outside.

HEALTH

ALTITUDE
SICKNESS

Soroche, or altitude sickness, which results in shortness of breath and headaches, may be a problem when you visit the Andes. To remedy any discomfort, walk slowly, eat lightly, and drink plenty of fluids (avoid alcohol). If you have high blood pressure and a history of heart trouble, **check with your doctor before traveling to high Andean elevations.** If you experience an extended period of nausea, dehydration, dizziness, severe headache or weakness while in a high-altitude area, seek medical attention.

FOOD & DRINK

Buenos Aires residents drink tap water and eat uncooked fruits and vegetables. However, if you've got just two weeks, you don't want to waste a minute of it in your hotel room; exercise caution when choosing what you eat and drink—on as well as off the beaten path. It's best to drink bottled water, which can be found throughout Argentina for about 1.50 pesos for a half liter.

Each year there are cases of cholera in the northern part of Argentina, mostly in the indigenous communities near the Bolivian border; your best protection is to avoid eating raw seafood.

SHOTS &
MEDICATIONS

No specific vaccinations are required for travel to Argentina. According to the Centers for Disease Control (CDC), however, there's a limited risk of cholera, hepatitis B, and dengue. The local malady of Chagas' disease is present in remote areas. If you plan to visit remote regions or stay for more than six weeks, **check with the CDC's International Travelers Hot Line.** In areas with malaria (in Argentina, you are at risk for malaria only in northern rural areas bordering Bolivia and Paraguay) and dengue, which are both carried by mosquitoes, take mosquito nets, wear clothing that covers the body, apply repellent containing DEET, and use a spray against flying insects in living and sleeping areas. The hot line recommends chloroquine (analen) as an antimalarial agent; no vaccine exists against dengue or Chagas.

Children traveling to Argentina should have current inoculations against measles, mumps, rubella, and polio.

A major health risk is traveler's diarrhea, caused by eating unfamiliar foods or contaminated fruit or vegetables or drinking contaminated water. Mild cases may respond to Imodium (known generically as loperamide) or Pepto-Bismol (not as strong), both of which can be purchased over the counter; paregoric, another antidiarrheal agent, does not require a doctor's prescription in Argentina. Drink plenty of purified water or tea—chamomile is a good folk remedy. In severe cases, rehydrate yourself with a salt-sugar solution (½ teaspoon salt and 4 tablespoons sugar per quart of water).

Note that many medications that require a prescription in the United States and elsewhere, including some antibiotics, are available over the counter in Argentina.

LANGUAGE

Argentines speak *Castellano,* Castilian Spanish, which differs slightly from the Spanish of most other Latin American countries. For example, the informal *vos* (you) is used instead of *tu,* in conjunction with the verb *sos* (are) instead of *eres.* The double "L" found in words like *pollo* phonetically translates to the ZH-sound, rather than a Y-sound. English is considered the second most widely used language. Services geared toward tourism generally employ an English-speaking staff. It's also common to find English-speaking staff at commercial and entertainment centers.

MAIL & SHIPPING

Mail delivery is quite dependable and should take around 6–15 days from Buenos Aires to the United States and 10–15 days to the United Kingdom, but like many things in Argentina, this is not guaranteed. Put postcards in envelopes and they will arrive more quickly.

There are mail drops located around the city, and you can usually buy stamps from your hotel.

EXPRESS MAIL   Express mail takes three–five days for all international destinations, and the cost can be steep (for instance, a letter to the United States via FedEx costs $27).
▪ Major Services **Correo Argentino** ⊠ Sarmiento 151, Buenos Aires ☎ 11/4316–3000 ⊕ www.correoargentino.com.ar. **DHL** ⊠ Moreno 927, Buenos Aires ☎ 0800/2222–345 ⊕ www.dhl.com.ar. **Federal Express** ⊠ Maipú 753, Buenos Aires ☎ 11/4630–0300 ⊕ www.fedex.com. **UPS** ⊠ Bernardo de Yrigoyen 974, Buenos Aires ☎ 11/4307–2174 or 0800/2222–877 ⊕ www.ups.com.

POSTAL RATES   An international airmail letter costs 3 pesos (up to 20 grams).

RECEIVING MAIL   You can receive mail in Buenos Aires at the Correo Central (Central Post Office). Letters should be addressed to your name, A/C Lista/Poste Restante, Correo Central, 1000 Capital Federal, Argentina. You will be asked to present ID and pay 1.50 pesos for handling when recovering your mail. American Express cardholders can have mail sent to American Express. Some embassies allow your mail to be delivered to their consulate address; inquire beforehand.
▪ Locations **American Express** ⊠ c/o American Express, Arenales 707, 1061 Buenos Aires ☎ 11/4310–3000. **Buenos Aires Correo Central** ⊠ Sarmiento 151, fl. 1, Buenos Aires ☎ 11/4316–3000.

MONEY MATTERS

If you're traveling from a country with a strong currency like the U.S. dollar or the euro, Argentina is very inexpensive. Bargains are everywhere to be found. Sumptuous dinners, particularly in finer restaurants, can run as high as 100 pesos per person with wine, dessert, and tip—the equivalent of around $35. A large wood-grilled sirloin with salad, potatoes, a house wine, and an espresso will run around 30 pesos at steak houses in Buenos Aires and much less in the hinterlands.

In Buenos Aires you're likely to pay 1.50–2 pesos for a *cafecito* (small cup of coffee) in a café. A soda costs 1.50 pesos. A taxi ride will run you 4–8 pesos in the larger cities. A tango show dinner with a couple of drinks costs about 100 pesos. A double room in a moderately priced, well-situated hotel costs $100–$130 dollars, including taxes.

Many hotels are now in the habit of charging all their prices in dollars. **Make sure that the rate you are paying is valid for both tourists and Argentines;** some hotels have been known to take advantage of foreigners who are unaware of the favorable exchange rate by charging them an increased price.

When ordering alcoholic drinks, ask for Argentine liquors or suffer the import fees. A bottle of Chivas Regal costs 80 pesos in shops, for instance. When ordering drinks, specify your preference for whiskey or vodka *nacional,* for example. Happy hours, with half-price drinks and a party ambience, have become standard in the trendier city areas.

Prices throughout this guide are given for adults. Substantially reduced fees are almost always available for children, students, and senior citizens. For information on taxes, *see* Taxes.

ATMS ATMs are easy to find, especially in major cities and resort towns; you'll find them in banks, services stations, and shopping malls, and all airports have at least one. The Banelco ATM system is the most widely used, indicated by a burgundy-color sign with white lettering. During the height of Argentina's recent economic crisis, banks were allowing only limited withdraws from ATMs. This problem is effectively over; you should have no trouble withdrawing large amounts.

Before leaving home, **make sure that your credit cards have been programmed for ATM use in Argentina.** Your local bank card may not work overseas; ask your bank about a MasterCard–Cirrus or Visa–Plus debit card, which works like a bank card but can be used at any of the ATMs displaying their logo.

Although fees charged for ATM transactions may be higher, Cirrus and Plus exchange rates are excellent because they are based on wholesale rates offered only by major banks.

🔲 ATM Locations **Banelco** ✉ Mexico 444, Buenos Aires ☎ 11/4334-5466. **Cirrus** ☎ 800/424-7787 ⊕ www.mastercard.com. **Plus** ⊕ www.visa.com/pd/atm.

CREDIT CARDS If you choose to bring just one card, Visa is recommended, as it is the most readily accepted. American Express, Diners Club, and MasterCard are the most commonly accepted after Visa. It may be easiest to use your credit card whenever possible—the exchange rate only varies by a fraction of a cent, so you won't need to worry whether your purchase is charged on the day of purchase or at some point in the future. Note, however that you may get a better deal if you pay with cash. Because of the recent economic instability in Argentina, some restaurants have temporarily suspended the use of credit cards. It's best to **inquire before you dine whether credit cards are accepted.**

Throughout this guide, the following abbreviations are used: **AE,** American Express; **DC,** Diners Club; **MC,** MasterCard; and **V,** Visa.

🔲 Reporting Lost Cards **American Express** ☎ 11/4310-3000 ⊕ www. americanexpress.com. **Diners Club** ☎ 0810/444-2484 toll free ⊕ www.dinersclub. com.ar. **MasterCard** ☎ 0800/555-0507 toll free ⊕ www.mastercard.com. **Visa** ☎ 114379-3333 ⊕ www.visa.com.

CURRENCY Throughout its history, Argentina has had one of the most volatile economies in the world, and that tradition continues today. After a decade of relative calm, the Argentine economy crashed in 2001, when the country defaulted on billions of dollars in foreign debt. The economic uncertainty sent citizens scurrying to the banks to withdraw their savings, only to be denied access because of government-imposed banking restrictions known as *el corralito*. Angry, and sometimes bloody, protests followed, as many middle-class Argentines joined the lower-class in a revolt against the government and the banks. The banking sanctions have since been lifted and most Argentines once again have access to their money, but the value of their savings has been slashed by two-thirds.

One peso equals 100 centavos. Peso notes are in denominations of 100, 50, 20, 10, 5, and 2. Coins are in denominations of 1 peso, and 50, 25, 10, 5, and 1 centavos. When giving change, the cashier may round your purchase to the nearest 5 or even 10 centavos. Always check your change.

CURRENCY EXCHANGE During the 1990s the Argentine peso was pegged to the U.S. dollar. This policy provided Argentina with a decade of unparalleled prosperity, when foreign products were available and affordable for the first time. This 1:1 peg eventually proved fatal for Argentina, and in 2002 the peso was unhinged on the open market. It has since lost around 60 percent of its value. This currency meltdown wiped out many Argentines' life savings, but has proved to be advantageous for tourists. Once one of the most expensive countries on the planet, Argentina is now a bargain for travelers.

If possible, exchange your local currency for pesos before you travel, but check to make sure you are getting a good rate. Once you arrive in Buenos Aires, there are many places where you can get pesos. Ask in your hotel or visit a *casa de cambio* (money changers) in El Centro, where you should be prepared to show your passport to complete the transaction.

There are two exchange desks at Buenos Aires's Ezeiza Airport, on the upper level in Terminal A, and a desk at the city's domestic Jorge Newbery Airport. Keep in mind that banks charge exchange fees, as do some hotels. Plan ahead, since it's often hard to change large amounts of money at hotels on weekends, even in cities.

For the most favorable rates, change money through banks. Although ATM transaction fees may be higher abroad than at home, ATM rates are excellent because they are based on wholesale rates offered only by major banks. To avoid lines at airport exchange booths, get a bit of local currency before you leave home.

You may not be able to change currency in rural areas at all, so **don't leave major cities without adequate amounts of pesos** in small denominations.

At this writing, the rate of exchange was 2.8 pesos to the U.S. dollar, 2 pesos to the Canadian dollar, 1.59 pesos to the pound sterling, 3.15 pesos to the euro, 1.81 pesos to the Australian dollar, 1.60 to the New Zealand dollar, and 0.36 pesos to the South African rand.

🛪 Exchange Services **International Currency Express** ✉ 427 N. Camden Dr., Suite F, Beverly Hills, CA 90210 ☎ 888/278-6628 orders 🖷 310/278-6410 ⊕ www.foreignmoney. com. **Thomas Cook International Money Services** ☎ 800/287-7362 orders and retail locations ⊕ www.us.thomascook.com.

TRAVELER'S CHECKS Most larger stores in Buenos Aires accept traveler's checks, but smaller shops and restaurants are leery of them. When using traveler's checks, remember to carry a valid ID with you for any purchases or when changing them at a bank or the American Express office. You'll have trouble changing traveler's checks outside of Buenos Aires, so if you want to bring them plan on changing them before you leave the city.

PASSPORTS & VISAS

ENTERING ARGENTINA U.S., Canadian, and British citizens do not need a visa for visits of up to 90 days, though they must carry a passport. Upon entering Argentina, you'll receive a tourist visa stamp on your passport valid for 90 days. If you need to stay longer, exit the country for one night; upon reentering Argentina, your passport will be stamped allowing an additional 90 days. The fine for overstaying your tourist visa is $50 dollars, payable upon departure at the airport. If you do overstay your visa, plan to arrive at the airport several hours in advance of your flight so that you have ample time to take care of the fine.

SAFETY

Buenos Aires is one of the safer cities in the world; however, recent political and economic stability has produced an increase in crime. Most of these crimes are limited to robberies and petty theft, but you should be aware of your surroundings at all times and don't take any unnecessary chances. Do your best to blend in with the locals and you will not attract attention. Police constantly patrol any areas where tourists are likely to be, and violent crime is rare. Smaller towns and villages in Argentina are even safer.

If you're hailing a taxi, make sure it says "radio taxi"; this means that the driver works for a licensed company and is required to call in every new fare over the radio. Also look for the driver's photo ID, which should be well displayed inside the car. Better yet, call a licensed *remis,* which is always safer and usually cheaper, as you agree on a fixed-price beforehand.

Argentines like to speak their minds, and there has been a huge increase in street protests in recent years. Most of these have to do with government policies, but there has been an increase in anti-U.S. and anti-British sentiment, stemming primarily from Argentina's strained relationship with the International Monetary Fund (IMF) and the war in Iraq. If you do see a demonstration, don't panic—as the overwhelming majority of them are peaceful—just be aware of the atmosphere.

Don't wear any jewelry you're not willing to lose—there have been incidents of chains and even earrings being yanked off of unsuspecting tourists. Keep cameras in a secure camera bag, preferably one with a chain or wire embedded in the strap.

Generally you'll find that people are friendly and helpful and that the biggest crime you're likely to encounter is the exorbitant price of a gaucho poncho.

WOMEN IN
ARGENTINA
If you carry a purse, choose one with a zipper and a thick strap that you can drape across your body; adjust the length so that the purse sits in front of you at or above hip level. (Don't wear a money belt or a waist pack.) Store only enough money in the purse to cover casual spending. Distribute the rest of your cash and any valuables between deep front pockets, inside jacket or vest pockets, and a concealed money pouch.

Women are safer in Buenos Aires than in many other major cities in the world, but crimes still occur. It's best not to over- or underdress, or wear flashy jewelry on the street.

Women can expect pointed looks, the occasional catcall, and some advances. Act confident, and ignore the men.

TAXES

Sales tax (IVA) in Argentina is 21%. The tax is usually included in the price on your receipt. Keep your receipts: the IVA tax is entirely refundable for purchases exceeding $200 dollars at stores displaying a duty-free sign. When you depart, plan enough time to visit the return desk at the airport to obtain your refund.

TELEPHONES

With the deregulation in telecommunications, new phone numbers and additional prefixes have been added, and telephoning can be confusing. Your hotel operator can assist you, or call for information.

Telecom's *telecentros* and Telefónica's *locutorios* offer a variety of services, including metered phone calls, faxes, telegrams, and access to the Internet; some even provide wire transfers. They are convenient to use and abound throughout all cities; some are specially equipped for people with hearing impairments.

📲 Telecom ☎ 0800/555-0112 ⊕ www.telecom.com.ar. **Telefónica** ☎ 0800/222-4262 ⊕ www.telefonica.com.ar.

AREA &
COUNTRY CODES
The country code for Argentina is 54. To call Argentina from overseas, dial 00 + country code (54) + area code (omitting the first 0, which is for long-distance calls within Argentina). The area code for Buenos Aires is 11.

OPERATOR
ASSISTANCE
For information, dial 110. For the time, dial 113. For information about international calls, dial 19 or 000.

INTERNATIONAL
CALLS
Hotels have *DDI*, international direct dialing, but may charge up to 3 pesos for a long-distance call. You're best off calling from telecentros or locutorios, where your call is metered and will run around 95 centavos for the first minute, and 68 centavos each additional minute, during peak hours to the United States. Rates are much higher for England (starting at 1.40 pesos for the first minute and 1.25 pesos for each additional minute) and Australia (2.85 pesos for the first minute and 2.30 pesos for each additional minute).

The country code is 1 for the United States and Canada, 61 for Australia, 64 for New Zealand, and 44 for the United Kingdom. To call out from Argentina, dial 00 + country code + area code + number.

LOCAL CALLS Hotels charge steep rates for local calls; before dialing, ask at the front desk about phone charges.

Local calls can be made from public phones booths and telephone centers with coins or phone cards sold at kiosks. A local call will cost you 23 centavos for two minutes during peak hours (weekdays 8 AM–8 PM, Saturday 8 AM–1 PM).

LONG-DISTANCE CALLS When calling from one area code to another in Argentina, add a 0 before the area code, then 1 for Capital Federal and Greater Buenos Aires, 2 for the Southern region, and 3 for provinces in the North. Charges increase with distances, beginning at 30 km (18½ mi) outside of the city.

Many hotels charge up to 4 pesos per call on top of the regular rate. It's best to call from a public phone or telephone center.

MOBILE PHONES To call the cell phone number of a Buenos Aires resident, dial 15 before the number (unless you're also calling from a cell phone with a Buenos Aires number). Local cell phone charges vary depending on certain factors, such as the company and time of day, and can cost up to 2 pesos per call; the fee is charged to the caller, not the recipient, unless on a pay phone.

Cellular phone rentals are available, though pricey. Some hotels even rent phones.
🚹 Mobile Phone Rental **Unifon** ✉ Av. Corrientes 645, Buenos Aires ☎ 0800/333-6868 ⊕ www.unifon.com.ar.

PHONE CARDS Phone cards, called *tarjetas chip,* are available at kiosks, pharmacies, and telephone centers. Prices range 4–10 pesos, at 23¢ for every two minutes during peak hours (weekdays and Sunday 8–8, Saturday 8 AM–1 PM), and half rate off-peak. You can use them for local, long-distance, and international calls.

PUBLIC PHONES Public phones in Argentina are reliable and can be found on nearly every block. You can make your call using coins or a phone card. Simply slide the card in, wait for the reading of how many minutes you have remaining, then dial.

To make a long-distance call from a public phone, you're better off finding a telephone center.

TIME
New York is one time zone behind Buenos Aires from April to October (it's two hours behind the rest of the year, as Argentina does not observe daylight savings time). There's a four-hour difference between Los Angeles and Buenos Aires.

TIPPING
Propinas (tips) range 10%–15% in bars and restaurants (10% is enough in a casual café or if the bill runs high). Note that some restaurants charge

a *cubierto,* covering table service, not waiter's tip. Argentines round off a taxi fare, though some cabbies who frequent hotels popular with tourists seem to expect more. Hotel porters should be tipped at least 1 peso. Also give doormen and ushers about 1 peso. Beauty- and barbershop personnel generally get around 10%.

TRAIN TRAVEL

Argentina's rail system, which was built by the British, no longer plays an important role in the national transportation system. Most lines lead out of Buenos Aires to various destinations and are often not as comfortable as luxury buses. The most popular routes are from Buenos Aires to Mar del Plata and Bariloche. There are also two special tourist-oriented trains: the Tren a las Nubes (Train of the Clouds), which goes through the Andes, and the Tren de la Costa (Coast Train), which runs from Buenos Aires to the river delta area of Tigre.

FARES & SCHEDULES Train tickets are inexpensive. Usually there are two classes. Plan to **buy your train tickets a few days ahead of your trip** (two weeks in summer months), and arrive at the station well before departure time. Reservations must be made in person at the local train station. Refer to individual chapters for more information about train service.

VISITOR INFORMATION

The city of Buenos Aires has a tourist office representing each province of Argentina. These offices can provide you with maps and regional information. Ask at your hotel for their locations throughout the city. Check out the Argentine Government Tourist Offices.

Argentina Government Tourist Offices **Miami** ✉ 2655 Le Jeune Rd., Miami, FL 33134 ☎ 305/442–1366. **New York** ✉ 12 W. 56th St., New York, NY 10019 ☎ 212/603–0443.

WEB SITES

Don't rule out foreign-language sites; some have links to sites that present information in more than one language, including English.

Web Sites **Argentina phone book** 🌐 www.guiatelefonica.com. **Argentina Secretary of Tourism** 🌐 www.turismo.gov.ar. **Buenos Aires Herald** 🌐 www.buenosairesherald.com. **Embassy of Argentina** 🌐 www.embajadaargentinaeeuu.org. **Tango** 🌐 www.abctango.com.

WHEN TO GO

CLIMATE Because of the great variety of latitudes, altitudes, and climatic zones in Argentina, you're likely to encounter many different climates during any given month. The most important thing to remember is the most obvious—when it's summer in the northern hemisphere, it's winter in Argentina, and vice versa. Winter in Argentina stretches from July to October, and summer settles in from December to March.

The sea moderates temperatures in the coastal region of Argentina, while the mountains do so for the hinterland. Winter can be chilly and rainy, although average winter temperatures are usually above freezing in the coastal cities (it hasn't snowed in Buenos Aires in more than 100 years).

If you can handle the heat (January–February temperatures usually range in the high 90s to low 100s [35°C–40°C]), Buenos Aires can be wonderful in summer, which peaks in January. At this time, the traditional vacation period, Argentines are crowding inland resorts and Atlantic beaches, but Buenos Aires has no traffic, and a host of city-sponsored events and concerts takes place, bringing city dwellers out into the sun and moonlight.

In January a few businesses shut down and others may have reduced hours in the provinces, though this does not apply for major cities. Government offices close for January, but this should not affect your vacation.

If you have an aversion to large crowds, avoid visiting popular resort areas in January and February and in July, when they become overcrowded again due to school holidays.

Spring and fall—the most temperate seasons—are excellent times to visit Argentina. It's usually warm enough (over 50°F) for just a light jacket, and it's right before or after the peak (and expensive) tourist season.

The best time to visit the Iguazú Falls is August–October, when temperatures are lower and the spring coloring is at its brightest. Rain falls all year, dropping about 80 inches annually. **Bring a lightweight waterproof jacket** for this reason.

Resort towns such as Bariloche and San Martín de los Andes are packed during the peak winter season. Summer temperatures can get up into the high 70s (about 25°C), but most of the year, the range is from the 30s to the 60s (0°C–20°C).

The Patagonia coast is on the infamous latitude that sailors call the "Roaring Forties," with southern seas that batter Patagonia throughout the year. Thirty-mile-per-hour winds are common, and 100-mile-per-hour gales are not unusual. Summer daytime temperatures reach the low 80s (about 28°C) but can drop suddenly to the 50s (10°C–15°C). Winters hover near the freezing mark.

Most travelers visit Tierra del Fuego in summer, when temperatures range from the 40s to the 60s (5°C–20°C). Fragments of glaciers cave into southern lakes with a rumble throughout the thaw from October to the end of April, which is the best time to enjoy the show.

🛈 Forecasts **Servicio Meteorológico Nacional** (National Weather Service for Argentina) ☎ 11/4514–4248 automated information ⊕ www.meteofa.mil.ar has information in Spanish.

BUENOS AIRES	Jan.	85F	29C	May	64F	18C	Sept.	64F	18C
		63	17		47	8		46	8
	Feb.	83F	28C	June	57F	14C	Oct.	69F	21C
		63	17		41	5		50	10
	Mar.	79F	26C	July	57F	14C	Nov.	76F	24C
		60	16		42	6		56	13
	Apr.	72F	22C	Aug.	60F	16C	Dec.	82F	28C
		53	12		43	6		61	16

BARILOCHE	**Jan.**	70F	21C	**May**	50F	10C	**Sept.**	50F	10C
		46	6		36	2		34	1
	Feb.	70F	21C	**June**	45F	7C	**Oct.**	52F	11C
		46	8		34	1		37	3
	Mar.	64F	18C	**July**	43F	6C	**Nov.**	61F	16C
		43	6		32	0		41	5
	Apr.	57F	14C	**Aug.**	46F	8C	**Dec.**	64F	18C
		39	4		32	0		45	7

BOLIVIA

2

GET YOUR LICKS AND YOUR KICKS
at Potosí's bizarre San Marcos eatery ⇨ *p.169*

KEEP YOURSELF QUENCHED
while roaming Salar de Uyuni, the
world's highest salt desert ⇨ *p.170*

SIFT THROUGH THE REMNANTS
of ancient excavation in Cerro
Rico's 5,000 tunnels and mines ⇨ *p.169*

ASCEND THE STAIRWAY TO HEAVEN
at Isla del Sol's sacred Inca ruins ⇨ *p.156*

RUB ELBOWS WITH OLD MONEY
at the Royal Mint in Potosí ⇨ *p.168*

LIVE LIKE ROYALS (ON CIVILIAN FUNDS)
at Gran Hotel Paris in La Paz ⇨ *p.144*

DIVE INTO THE RAIN FOREST
at Parque Nacional Madidi ⇨ *p.149*

Updated by
Joan Gonzalez

PEOPLE DESCRIBE BOLIVIA AS THE "ROOFTOP OF THE WORLD." The dizzying altitude of this mountainous country in the center of South America is almost always mentioned. Bolivia's largest city, La Paz, is the world's highest capital, at 11,942 feet. The city's Aeropuerto Internacional El Alto, at 13,310 feet, is the world's highest commercial airport. And glimmering Lake Titicaca is the highest navigable lake in the world.

But these high-flying statistics don't reveal much about the country itself. For *Bolivianos,* the ancient and the modern are conjoined here. On city streets you'll see business executives in the latest designer fashions shouting into mobile phones alongside indigenous women with bowler hats perched precariously on their heads and voluminous petticoats under pleated satin skirts. Colonial mansions stand cheek-by-jowl with modern office buildings.

Bolivia is larger than Texas and California combined, but has only as many inhabitants as New York City. Most of its 8 million people are concentrated in a handful of urban centers, including La Paz, Santa Cruz, Cochabamba, and Sucre. Bolivia contains every type of geologically classified land, from tropical lowlands to parched desert to rugged mountain peaks. Although generally considered an Andean nation, nearly two-thirds of the country sweats it out in the steamy Amazon Basin—remote, overlooked, and as inhospitable as it is soul-stirring. On Bolivia's wildest frontier, indigenous tribes live as they have for centuries, unimpressed, it seems, by the displays of the modern world. In the provinces of Beni and Santa Cruz, near the border of Brazil, tribes still hunt with bows and arrows.

To the west of these tropical lowlands, just beyond Cochabamba and Santa Cruz, the Andes rise sharply to form the backbone of South America's Pacific coast. This two-prong mountain range shelters between its eastern and western peaks a long, rambling plain. Known as the altiplano, this bleak, treeless plateau, averaging 136 km (85 mi) wide and 832 km (520 mi) long, comprises 30% of Bolivia's landmass and supports more than half of its population. For centuries the Aymara people have clung to the hostile place, harvesting small crops of potatoes and beans or fishing the deep-blue waters of Lake Titicaca, which straddles Bolivia's western border with Peru.

From its earliest days, Bolivia's fortunes have risen and fallen with its mineral wealth. Centuries ago it was the Inca and Aymara who dug deep for precious silver. In the 17th century, Spain's colonization of South America was fueled largely by the vast amounts of silver hidden deep in Cerro Rico, the "Rich Hill" that towers over the city Potosí in southern Bolivia. Cerro Rico's seemingly inexhaustible lode, first discovered in 1545, quickly brought thousands of prospectors to what was at the time the greatest mining operation in the New World. During the 17th and 18th centuries, Potosí was the most populous city in the Americas. Silver transformed it with grand colonial mansions, stately baroque churches, and thick-walled fortresses. For the Spanish, the phrase *"vale un Potosí"* ("worth a Potosí") became a favorite description for untold wealth. But there's a darker side to the story. Some 8 million of the in-

If you have 5 days

If you have a limited amount of time to visit Bolivia, divide it between **La Paz** and **Lake Titicaca.** When you arrive in La Paz—unless you're coming from another high-altitude destination—make sure you take it easy for a day or so to adjust to the thin air. On the second day, visit the outdoor markets in the morning and then head out to see the Valley of the Moon in the afternoon. Visit the fascinating ruins of **Tiwanaku** on the third day, then head to the Inca Utama Hotel & Spa with its Andean Roots Eco Village on **Lake Titicaca** and spend the night. On the fourth day, catch the hydrofoil to **Isla del Sol** to see its sparkling beaches and Inca ruins, and spend the night. On the fifth day, head back to La Paz, stopping to visit **Copacabana** en route.

2

If you have 10 days

Follow the above itinerary, then on day six, fly to the colonial town of **Sucre,** where the altitude is lower and the weather warmer. Spend the next day touring its well-ordered colonial streets and museums. Make sure to visit the market in nearby **Tarabuco** if you're there on a Sunday. On your eighth day, travel southwest to the colonial mining town of **Potosí.** Take a walking tour of the city and visit its churches and museums. Overnight here. On day nine, take a bus back to Sucre and spend the night before flying back to La Paz or Santa Cruz the following day. (All international flights out of La Paz also go through Santa Cruz, so both are convenient.)

If you have 15 days

Follow the 10-day itinerary above and continue to **Santa Cruz** or **La Paz**—you can arrange a short visit to the Amazon from either place. From Santa Cruz try a three- or four-day birding trip, an overnight four-wheel-drive trip to a lodge in nearby Amboro National Park (especially if you're a birder), or fly northeast to the jungle town of Trinidad for a three-day float trip on the Río Mamoré aboard the flotel Reina Enin. The flotel is essentially a large barge with cabins on it; during the day, as you drift, you stop at little villages along the river. If, instead, you prefer to fly back to La Paz, you can head to the thick of the rain forest by visiting Chalalan Ecolodge, a short flight north, in the **Parque Nacional Madidi.** First you must fly to the town of Rurrenabaque and spend the night there, then you can head to the Chalalan Ecolodge the next day— via a five-hour canoe trip on the Beni river followed by a 30-minute walk through the rain forest. Spend the next two days in the Madidi park, then return to Rurrenabaque for your flight back to La Paz.

digenous Quechua people died in the mines after being forced to stay inside the airless tunnels for as long as six months. While these barbaric practices no longer exist, men who work in the mines today still have far shorter life spans than average.

Bolivia was named in honor of its liberator, Simón Bolívar, who proclaimed the country's independence from Spain in 1825; until then, it had been simply called Alto Peru. The country was once much larger than it is today. It originally extended to the Pacific, but after rich deposits of nitrates were discovered in the Atacama Desert, Chile began to eye the region. During the War of the Pacific that broke out in 1879, Chile captured Bolivia's short stretch of coastline. Bolivia stubbornly believes that someday, with the support of other countries, it will once again have a seaport. Bolivia lost about 100,000 square km (38,000 square mi) when Brazil annexed a large part of the Amazon basin in 1903, then about twice as much after a dispute with Paraguay in 1938.

Centuries of Spanish conquest have left their mark here, particularly on the cities of Sucre and Potosí, where ornate cathedrals crowd the narrow streets. But Bolivia remains a land of indigenous farmers, ranchers, and artisans. On the windswept Andean plateaus you will still see local weavers toting their crafts and red-cheek children to weekly markets. By the time the sun has risen, the brightly dressed Aymara are in place, ready to sell textiles and ponchos, not to mention vegetables, fruits, and medicinal herbs.

About the Restaurants

Bolivian cuisine is healthful, wholesome, and satisfying. Soups make a complete meal in themselves, as they are loaded with meat, potatoes, vegetables, and a ricelike grain called *quinua*. Fresh trout from Lake Titicaca is fried, stuffed, steamed, grilled, spiced, or covered in a rich sauce. Another excellent, delicate fish from the lake is the *pejerrey*, which is especially good in *ceviche*, a marinated fish dish.

In the highlands, where carbohydrates are the dietary mainstay, look for *chuño* and *tunta*, two kinds of freeze-dried potatoes that are soaked overnight and boiled, then used to accompany main dishes. Other traditional highland fare includes *asado de llama* (llama steak) and *pique macho*, beef grilled with hot peppers, chopped tomatoes, and onions, often served with fried potatoes and gravy. Also popular is *sajta de pollo* (chicken stew with peppers and onions).

Each major city still has its own brewery, generally founded by Germans who emigrated here at the same time as they came to the United States. Try Paceña in La Paz or Sureña in Sucre. Taríja, in the Andean foothills near the Argentine border, is Bolivia's wine growing area. Wines have been produced here since the early 17th century. The major producers are La Concepcion and Kolhberg. Their Malbec and Cabernet Sauvignon have won international medals. For something a little different try *singani*, the local liquor. It's best in the potent pisco sour made from singani and lime juice or the slightly smoother *chuflay* made from singani and lemonade. *Chicha* is a grain alcohol locals concoct by chewing maize, spitting out the resulting mash, adding water, and allowing the mixture to ferment. The sweet, rather cloudy result is drunk mainly in the lowland valleys in and around Cochabamba.

WHAT IT COSTS In Bolivianos					
	$$$$	**$$$**	**$$**	**$**	**¢**
AT DINNER	over 100	70–100	50–70	30–50	under 30

Prices are for per person for a main course at dinner.

2

History

Bolivians are proud of their history, and you'll find them willing to share what they know with anyone eager to learn. Almost everywhere in Bolivia you'll stumble across reminders of the country's long and eventful history. A civilization said to be more advanced than the Incas thrived in Bolivia sometime between 600 BC and AD 1200 in an area 90 km (50 mi) west of La Paz called Tiwanaku. It is considered by many to be the "cradle of the American civilizations." When the Incas arrived, the city was already in ruins, possibly destroyed by an earthquake. Spanish conquistadors conquered the Incan civilization in the 1500s. Sucre and Potosí are the best-preserved examples of the legacy of Spanish architecture.

Shopping

Bolivia's rich selection of crafts includes silver jewelry, hand-woven rugs, intricate embroidery, and traditional musical instruments, such as the *quena* (flute) and *charango* (mandolin). You'll also find sweaters, gloves, scarves, and ponchos made from alpaca or llama wool. Crafts shops are usually grouped together—in La Paz, for instance, most can be found on Calle Sagárnaga. It is always worth looking for cooperatives outside the capital, however. These sell traditional textiles made in rural areas, especially in the provinces of Chuquisaca and Potosí. The shawls, hats, and skirts worn by highland women are sold in most of the local markets and in some stores in La Paz, but shopkeepers sometimes refuse to sell some types of traditional garments to foreigners. However, the felt bowler hats are for sale everywhere and make an interesting fashion statement back home. Due to the low level of tourism, souvenirs tend to be realistically priced. Although bargaining is expected, many sellers will drop their prices only by small amounts, typically 5% to 10%.

About the Hotels

With growing competition for tourist dollars, there has been a push within the past several years to upgrade older hotels, and, where possible, to build new ones. You now have a wider range, from cozy guest houses to luxury resorts. Some hotels have two pricing systems—one for Bolivians and one for foreigners. Even if you fall into the latter category, nice accommodations can be found for $35 or less, particularly away from the cities. Do not be afraid to ask to see the room in advance—it's common practice in Bolivia.

WHAT IT COSTS In Bolivianos				
$$$$	$$$	$$	$	¢
FOR 2 PEOPLE over 1,000	700–1,000	500–700	300–500	under 300

Prices are for two people in a standard double room in high season, excluding tax.

Exploring Bolivia

Bolivia is most famous for the Andes, which take up a large chunk of the west. Also well-known are the vast jungle regions of Amazonia that extend all the way east into Brazil. But Bolivia has a surprisingly varied series of ecosystems within those two major regions. Mountain areas vary from cool and dry (as in the high-altitude cities of La Paz and Potosí), to temperate (the cities of Cochabamba and Sucre), to warm and pleasant almost year-round (in the fertile, grape-growing lands near the southern city of Tarija). Jungle areas also vary: from humid and warm, as in Santa Cruz, to the more temperate climates in the northwest province of Pando. In the northeast province of Beni, encompassing the city of Trinidad, the hot, wet climate is occasionally broken by cold spells called *surazos*.

LA PAZ

Perched on the edge of the altiplano, La Paz overlooks a landscape of great—if stark—beauty. If you fly into Aeropuerto Internacional El Alto, the plateau breaks without warning and reveals the deep, jagged valley that cradles the town. At dusk, as the sun sets on the bare flatlands that surround La Paz, a reddish glow envelops the city's greatest landmark: the towering, snow-capped peaks of Illimani.

La Paz is nestled in a bowl-shape valley that ranges in altitude from 9,951 feet to 11,930 feet, an elevation so high that even the locals walk slowly. If you find yourself a little light-headed, take a nap or sip a rejuvenating potion made from the coca leaf called *mate de coca*. The altitude might make things difficult at first, but it also ensures that La Paz is free of the heat and humidity and devoid of mosquitoes and other pesky insects.

Nearly half of the city's 1.5 million residents live in poorly constructed adobe and brick homes on a barren plateau in El Alto neighborhood, as well as in the valleys that encircle the settlement. In downtown La Paz the feeling is more cosmopolitan, as buses, taxis, business executives, and Aymara Indians share the city's cobblestone streets.

Exploring La Paz

Heading into La Paz from the airport, the city's main thoroughfare changes names several times: Avenida Ismael Montes, Avenida Mariscal Santa Cruz, El Prado, Avenida 16 de Julio, and Avenida Villazón. The street, a colorful blur of trees, flowers, and monuments, is often clogged with pedestrians and vendors, especially on weekends. Many of La Paz's luxury hotels are found here, rising high above the old colonial-style homes with their elaborate latticework and balustrades. The street then splits into two one-way streets, Avenida 6 de Agosto and Avenida Arce, which lead to the residential areas of San Jorge and Sopocachi, which hold most of La Paz's most exclusive bars and restaurants.

Numbers in the text correspond to numbers in the margins and on the La Paz map.

Plaza Murillo area

In the center of colonial La Paz, (Zona Central–Downtown), Plaza Murillo and the cobblestone streets that surround it are steeped in history. The square dates from 1549, the year after the city was founded.

Bolivia

R. Purus

R. Ituxi

Pôrto Relho

AMAZONIA

Rio Branco

PANDO

Guaporé

BRAZIL

Vilhena

R. Jiparaná

Puerto
Maldonado

San José de
Uehupiamonas

PARQUE
NACIONAL
MADIDI

Rurrenabaque

Laguna
Rogaguado

BENI

Trinidad

PERU

Beni

Laguna
Rogagua

CORDILLERA

San Borja

San Javier
(Jesuit missions)

LA PAZ

Lake
Titicaca

Sorata

Huatajata

Copacabana

Coroico

BOLIVIA

San Ignacio

Suriqui

Tiwanaku

Chulumani

La
Paz

COCHABAMBA

Cochabamba

Villa Tunari

Lake
Concepcion

ALTIPLANO

Tarata

CHAPARE

Santa Cruz

Samaipata

El Pantanal

Oruro

DE

ORURO

Lago de
Poopó

Sucre

Tarabuco

Corumbá

Arrea

Potosí

Salar de
Uyuni

POTOSÍ

CHUQUISACA

Villa Montes

Tocopilla

ANDES

Villazón

TARIJA

Pilcomayo

PARAGUAY

CHILE

ARGENTINA

R. Verde

R.

0 ——— 100 miles

0 ——— 150 km

Nearby you'll find the city's grand governmental buildings and some of its most beautiful churches.

a good walk

Starting in Plaza Murillo (originally Plaza de Armas), head south on Ayacucho past the **Palacio Legislativo** ❶ ⌐. As you turn right at Comercio, the Italian Renaissance–style **Palacio de Gobierno** ❷ is the first structure on your left. Just beyond is the neoclassical **Catedral Metropolitana** ❸ and the **Museo Nacional de Arte** ❹. Two blocks beyond the museum, head north on Genaro Sanjinés. On your right is a restored colonial mansion housing the **Museo Nacional de Etnografía y Folklore** ❺ and the imposing facade of the **Iglesia de Santo Domingo** ❻. A block farther on the left is the **Teatro Municipal** ❼. Walk west on Indaburo and then head north on Calle Jaén, a lovely colonial street. Here you'll find four interesting smaller museums: **Museo Costumbrista Juan de Vargas** ❽ recounts the political and cultural history of La Paz, **Museo de Metales Preciosos** ❾ exhibits precious metals, **Museo del Litoral Boliviano** ❿, collects memorabilia from the War of the Pacific, and **Museo Casa Murillo** ⓫ collects memorabilia from past presidents.

TIMING Because La Paz is so compact, visiting the city's main sights would seem easy; however, add time for climbing the hills and taking frequent breaks to assuage the effects of the altitude. You'll need a full day for a thorough exploration. Museums are generally open Tuesday to Friday 9:30–12:30 and 3–7, and Saturday and Sunday 10–12:30, and are closed Monday.

SIGHTS TO SEE **Catedral Metropolitana.** The cathedral was built in 1835 in a severe neoclassical style, with a sober facade and imposing bronze doors. It faces
❸ the lovely gardens of Plaza Murillo. ☒ *Zona Central (Downtown), Plaza Murillo* ☎ *Free* ☉ *Mon.–Sat. 7–9 AM and 6–8, Sun. 7–noon and 6–8.*

❻ **Iglesia de Santo Domingo.** This church, constructed in the 17th century, served as the cathedral before the Catedral Metropolitana was built. It is known for its distinctive baroque-style facade. ☒ *Calles Yanacocha and Ingavi, Zona Central (Downtown).*

⓫ **Museo Casa Murillo.** Housed in a restored colonial mansion that has been declared a national landmark, this museum exhibits the personal effects of past presidents. It was once the home of Pedro Domingo Murillo, one of the heroes of the independence movement. ☒ *Calle Jaén 79, Zona Central (Downtown)* ☎ *02/237–5273* ☒ *(B)6 for group ticket to Museo Casa Murillo, Museo de Metales Preciosos, Museo Costumbrista Juan de Vargas, Museo del Litoral Boliviano (purchase at Costumbrista)* ☉ *Tues.–Fri. 9:30–12:30 and 3–7, weekends 10–12:30.*

❽ **Museo Costumbrista Juan de Vargas.** Dedicated to the political and cultural history of Bolivia, this museum hosts exhibits about life in La Paz from the 16th century to the present. Especially interesting are the miniature scenes of old La Paz. ☒ *Calle Jaén at Calle Sucre, Zona Central (Downtown)* ☎ *02/237–8478* ☒ *(B)6 for group ticket to Museo Casa Murillo, Museo de Metales Preciosos, Museo Costumbrista Juan de Vargas, Museo del Litoral Boliviano (purchase at Costumbrista)* ☉ *Tues.–Fri. 9:30–12:30 and 3–7, weekends 10–12:30.*

⑩ Museo del Litoral Boliviano. This museum is a repository for artifacts from the 1879 War of the Pacific, when Bolivia lost its sliver of coastline to Chile. Bolivia continues to make international appeals to regain its lost territory. The museum has photographs, documents, flags, and armaments from that battle. ✉ *Calle Jaén 789, Zona Central (Downtown)* ☎ *02/237–1222* 🎫 *(B)6 for group ticket to Museo Casa Murillo, Museo de Metales Preciosos, Museo Costumbrista Juan de Vargas, Museo del Litoral Boliviano (purchase at Costumbrista)* ⊙ *Tues.–Fri. 9:30–12:30 and 3–7, weekends 10–12:30.*

⑨ Museo de Metales Preciosos. An extensive collection of pre-Columbian gold and silver artifacts, as well as Inca and pre-Inca ceramics, can be found in this museum, which also houses archaeological exhibits. ✉ *Calle Jaén 777, Zona Central (Downtown)* ☎ *02/237–1470* 🎫 *(B)6 for group ticket to Museo Casa Murillo, Museo de Metales Preciosos, Museo Costumbrista Juan de Vargas, Museo del Litoral Boliviano (purchase at Costumbrista)* ⊙ *Tues.–Fri. 9:30–12:30 and 3–7, weekends 10–12:30.*

④ Museo Nacional de Arte. Housed in the pink marble Palacio de los Condes de Arana, commissioned by a Spanish noble in 1775, the National Art Museum holds three stories of paintings and sculpture. The first floor is devoted to contemporary foreign artists; the second to works by Melchor Pérez Holguín, considered to be the master of Andean colonial art; and the third to a permanent collection of Bolivian artists. Relax in the central courtyard beside the lovely alabaster fountain. ✉ *Plaza Murillo at Calle Comercio, Zona Central (Downtown)* ☎ *02/237–1177* 🎫 *(B)7* ⊙ *Tues.–Fri. 9–12:30 and 3–7, weekends 10–1.*

⑤ Museo Nacional de Etnografía y Folklore. Housed in an ornate 18th-century building, the National Museum of Ethnography and Folklore exhibits feathers, masks, and weavings from indigenous peoples. It also has permanent displays on the Ayoreos, who live in the Amazon region, and the Chipayas, who come from the surrounding altiplano. ✉ *Calle Ingavi 916, Zona Central (Downtown)* ☎ *02/235–8559* 🎫 *Free* ⊙ *Tues.–Fri. 9–12:30 and 3–7, weekends 9–1.*

② Palacio de Gobierno. The imposing Presidential Palace was guarded by tanks and machine gun–toting soldiers until 1982, when the constitutional government was restored following a 1979 coup and three years of military rule. In front of the palace is a statue of former president Gualberto Villarroel. In 1946 a mob stormed the building and dragged Villarroel to the square, where he was hanged from a lamppost. The structure, which is closed to the public, is also known as Palacio Quemado (Burned Palace) because it has twice been gutted by fire. ✉ *Plaza Murillo, Zona Central (Downtown).*

▶ **① Palacio Legislativo.** The meeting place for Bolivia's Congress, the Legislative Palace was built in 1905. This imposing classical structure has a visitor's gallery where you can observe the legislators in session. ✉ *Plaza Murillo, Zona Central (Downtown)* 🎫 *Free* ⊙ *Weekdays 9–noon and 2:30–5.*

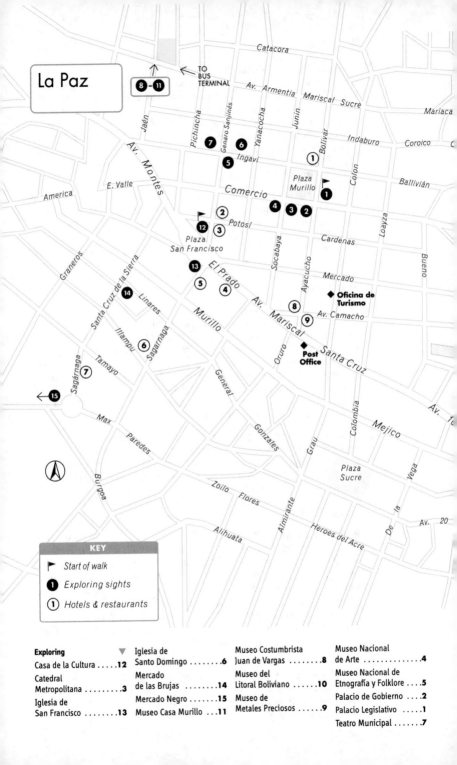

La Paz

KEY

▶ *Start of walk*

● *Exploring sights*

① *Hotels & restaurants*

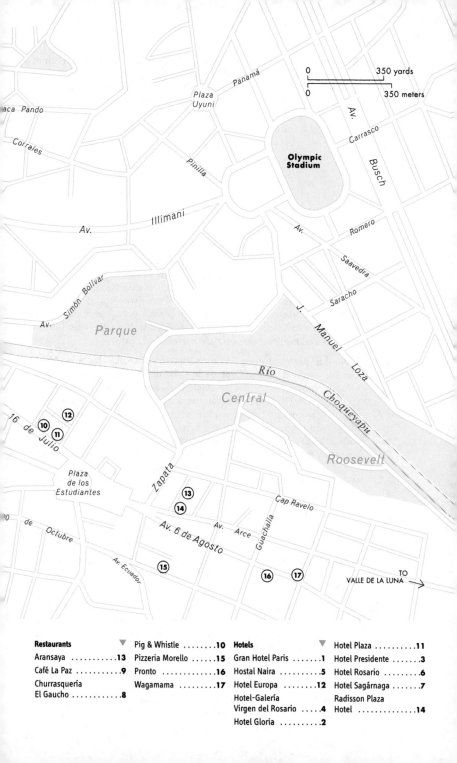

Restaurants ▼

Aransaya **13**

Café La Paz **9**

Churrasquería
El Gaucho **8**

Pig & Whistle **10**

Pizzeria Morello **15**

Pronto **16**

Wagamama **17**

Hotels ▼

Gran Hotel Paris **1**

Hostal Naira **5**

Hotel Europa **12**

Hotel-Galería
Virgen del Rosario **4**

Hotel Gloria **2**

Hotel Plaza **11**

Hotel Presidente **3**

Hotel Rosario **6**

Hotel Sagárnaga **7**

Radisson Plaza
Hotel **14**

❼ Teatro Municipal. A handsome building both inside and out as a result of an extensive restoration, the Municipal Theater regularly stages traditional dance and music, as well as classical music performances and opera. ⊠ *Calle Genaro Sanjinés 629, Zona Central (Downtown)* ☎ *02/237–5275.*

off the beaten path

VALLE DE LA LUNA – Erosion has shaped the Valley of the Moon into jagged peaks and canyons, forming an eerie, surrealistic landscape. From the bridge at Barrio Aranjuez it's a 10-minute walk to the cactus garden, the only patch of green in the area, and about 15 minutes more to the maze of pinnacles and crevasses that gives this unusual landscape its name. The valley (actually a hillside) is about 10 km (6 mi) from La Paz. To get here, take a tour, hire a taxi, or hop aboard Microbus 11 to Barrio Aranjuez.

Plaza San Francisco Area

This broad plaza just south of Avenida Mariscal Santa Cruz is the city's cultural heart. Indigenous people come here to hawk all sorts of handicrafts, as well as more prosaic goods, such as cassette tapes, watches, and electrical items. If you're lucky you'll see a wedding at the beautiful Iglesia de San Francisco. Behind this plaza are a network of narrow cobblestone streets climbing up the steep hillside. Here you'll find shops and stalls where you can purchase native handicrafts.

a good walk

From the sprawling Plaza San Francisco, head north a block on Calle Genaro Sanjinéz to the **Casa de la Cultura** ⑫ ▶. Backtrack on Calle Genaro Sanjinéz to the beautiful **Iglesia de San Francisco** ⑬, one of the country's most famous colonial structures. Heading uphill on Calle Sagárnaga you'll find street vendors selling just about everything imaginable. Turn right on Linares, the first street after Murillo, to the **Mercado de las Brujas** ⑭, the "Witches Market" where you can buy the items necessary to ward off evil spirits. A few blocks farther up Calle Sagárnaga turn right on Calle Max Paredes. At Calle Graneros you'll find the **Mercado Negro** ⑮. The "Black Market" is a maze of stalls selling shawls, skirts, and hats.

TIMING   The timing for this walk depends entirely on how much time you spend in the stalls along Calle Sagárnaga and Calle Max Paredes. If you enjoy shopping it's easy to spend half a day on this relatively short walk.

WHAT TO SEE   **Casa de la Cultura.** Rotating art exhibits, movies, and concerts are held
▶ ⑫   at this cultural center across from the Iglesia de San Francisco. ⊠ *Plaza Perez Velasco.*

⑬ Iglesia de San Francisco. Considered one of the finest examples of Spanish colonial architecture in South America, the carved facade of the 1549 Church of San Francisco is adorned with birds of prey, ghoulish masks, pine cones, and parrots—a combination of Spanish and Indian motifs created by local artisans who borrowed heavily from the style then popular in Spain. Weddings sometimes spill out onto the plaza on Saturdays. Crafts stalls line the church wall; most days you'll find colorful weavings and handmade musical instruments. ⊠ *El Prado at Calle Sagárnaga.*

⑭ **Mercado de las Brujas** On Calle Linares, just off bustling Calle Sagárnaga, you'll find the Witches Market, where indigenous women in tall derby hats sell lucky charms and ingredients for powerful potions. If you are building a new house, you can buy a dried llama fetus to bury in the yard for good luck.

⑮ **Mercado Negro.** Near the intersection of Calle Max Parede and Calle Graneros, the streets are filled with peddlers hawking clothing and household goods, as well as traditional medicines. Tucked into alleys and courtyards are *tambos* (thatch-roof structures) where you can purchase oranges, bananas, and coca leaves. The last are officially illegal but are chewed by farmers and miners (and tourists) to ward off hunger and the effects of the altitude.

Where to Eat

La Paz restaurants are becoming increasingly cosmopolitan, with cuisines that range from Chinese and Japanese to French and Swiss, in addition to traditional Bolivian fare. The area around Plaza de los Estudiantes and the residential neighborhood of Sopocachi have the widest selection of restaurants in La Paz, while the area around Calle Sagárnaga (Zona Central–Downtown) generally harbors the least expensive.

Argentine

★ $$-$$$ ✕ **Churrasquería El Gaucho.** This Argentine-style steak house serves slabs of tender, grilled steak and kabobs on a wood plank, with delicious sauces on the side. ⊠ *Av. 20 de Octubre 2041* ☎ *02/235-9125* ▤ *AE, MC, V.*

Bolivian

$$-$$$ ✕ **Aransaya.** From its location on the penthouse floor of the Radisson
Fodor'sChoice Plaza Hotel, this restaurant gives diners spectacular views of the city.
★ The presentation of the food is exquisite, and the menu includes both international dishes and regional specialties. ⊠ *Av. Arce 2177* ☎ *02/ 231-6161* ▤ *AE, MC, V.*

¢-$ ✕ **Café La Paz.** This old café, opposite the main post office, is a popular hangout for many La Paz politicians, journalists, and expatriates. Try the potent espresso, cappuccino, and *café helado* (coffee with ice cream). Don't miss the elaborate pastries, including *empanada de manzana* (apple tart). ⊠ *Calle Ayacucho at Av. Camacho* ☎ *02/235-0292* ▤ *No credit cards.*

Italian

$ ✕ **Pizzeria Morello.** This is possibly the best pizzeria in La Paz. You can order something piping hot from the oven or design your own pizza from the voluminous list of toppings. Many Paceños use Morello's prompt takeout and delivery services. ⊠ *Av. Arce 2132* ☎ *02/237-2973* ▤ *AE, MC, V.*

¢-$ ✕ **Pronto.** Delicious pastas make this inexpensive Italian restaurant pop-
Fodor'sChoice ular with locals and tourists alike. The service is top-notch. ⊠ *Calle Gen-*
★ *eral Gonzalo Jaúregui 2248* ☎ *02/235-5869* ▤ *No credit cards.*

Pan-Asian

★ $-$$ ✕ **Pig & Whistle.** A short walk south from the Universidad Mayor de San Andrés is this replica of a cozy British pub. Don't ask for fish-and-chips—

authentic Southeast Asian dishes are what's on the menu. Low-key music, performed live on weekends, ranges from light classical to bossa nova to jazz. ⊠ *Calle Goitia 155, off Av. Arce* ☏ *No phone* ☱ *No credit cards* ⊘ *Closed Sun.*

$-$$ ✕ **Wagamama.** The specialty is fresh trout from Lake Titicaca cooked
Fodor'sChoice Japanese style. It's often referred to as the "noodle restaurant"; you can
★ even get trout sushi rolls here. It's near the American and British embassies. ⊠ *Pasaje Pinilla 2557 (Off Av. Arce, one block downhill from Plaza Isabel la Católica)* ☏ *02/224–4911* ☱ *MC, V* ⊘ *Closed Mon.*

Where to Stay

Although the number of rooms in La Paz increases every year, hotels are often booked solid during holidays and festivals. Make reservations at least a month in advance when possible. Inexpensive hotels tend to be located near Calle Sagárnaga.

$$$$ ☷ **Hotel Europa.** The view of snowcapped Mt. Illimani from the rooftop
Fodor'sChoice garden sets this downtown hotel apart. There's original artwork on dis-
★ play in the lobby, and the generously proportioned rooms, decorated with an understated elegance, have extras that business travelers will appreciate. On the premises is a fitness center with a Turkish bath. ⊠ *Calle Tiahuanacu 64,* ☏ *02/231–5656* ⊕ *www.hotel-europa-bolivia.com* ↝ *110 rooms* ☖ *Restaurant, room service, in-room data ports, minibars, pool, health club, 2 bars, laundry service* ☱ *AE, MC, V.*

$$$–$$$$ ☷ **Hotel Plaza.** The rooftop restaurant and bar of this luxurious business hotel have excellent views of La Paz and the Andes. Ask for a room facing Mt. Illimani; besides good views you'll have less noise from the street. ⊠ *Av. 16 de Julio 1789* ☏ *02/378–311* ⎙ *02/237–8318* ↝ *175 rooms, 10 suites* ☖ *2 restaurants, indoor pool, health club, hot tub, sauna, 2 bars, laundry service* ☱ *AE, MC, V.*

$$$ ☷ **Hotel Presidente.** This modern hotel has an excellent downtown location and plain but comfortable rooms. Most face the street; those on the upper floors are quietest. The restaurant, which has stunning views of the city, serves inexpensive buffet lunches. ⊠ *Calle Potosí 920* ☏ *02/236–7193* ⎙ *02/235–4013* ↝ *101 rooms, 18 suites* ☖ *2 restaurants, indoor pool, gym, sauna, 2 bars* ☱ *AE, MC, V.*

$$$ ☷ **Radisson Plaza Hotel.** The focus at this high-rise business hotel not far from Plaza de los Estudiantes is on luxury and service. Upper-floor rooms have excellent views of the city and the surrounding mountains, as does the rooftop restaurant. ⊠ *Av. Arce 2177* ☏ *02/231–6161, 800/ 777–7800 in the U.S.* ⎙ *02/231–6302* ⊕ *www.radisson.com* ↝ *239 rooms, 7 suites* ☖ *2 restaurants, café, in-room safes, minibars, indoor pool, health club, hair salon, hot tub, massage, sauna, bar, lounge, shops, laundry service, meeting rooms* ☱ *AE, MC, V.*

$$ ☷ **Gran Hotel Paris.** Built in 1911 on historic Plaza Murillo, this hotel
Fodor'sChoice is one of Bolivia's most charming lodgings. The standard rooms are well
★ appointed, but the suites have furnishings that would make Louis XVI feel at home. Many have balconies overlooking the square. Although you might feel you've stepped back in time two centuries or so—traditional afternoon tea is accompanied by a live orchestra—you'll find the

hotel is also well-suited to business travelers. Rates include a breakfast buffet. ✉ *Plaza Murillo* ☎ *02/231–9170* 🖷 *02/236–2547* 🛏 *41 rooms, 6 suites* ♨ *Restaurant, café, bar* ⊟ *AE, MC, V.*

$ ⊞ **Hotel Gloria.** This clean, friendly hotel a block from Plaza San Francisco has an inexpensive rooftop restaurant that specializes in international and vegetarian dishes. It also has a tour desk in the lobby. ✉ *Calle Potosí 909* ☎ *02/237–0010* 🖷 *02/239–1489* 🛏 *90 rooms, 2 suites* ♨ *Restaurant, café, bar* ⊟ *AE, MC, V.*

¢ ⊞ **Hostal Naira.** This charming hostel, whose bright, cheerful rooms surround a central courtyard, sits above the famous Peña Naira, where groups perform traditional folk music. There's always hot water—a luxury in this price range. ✉ *Sagárnaga 161* ☎ *02/235–5645* ⊕ *www.hostalnaira. com* 🛏 *22 rooms* ♨ *Cafeteria* ⊟ *No credit cards.*

★ ¢ ⊞ **Hotel-Galería Virgen del Rosario.** A gem in the middle of the bustling Mercado de Hechicería, this hotel has an amiable restaurant. The rooms are small, but each room has nice murals on the walls. ✉ *Calle Santa Cruz 583* ☎ *02/237–1565* 🖷 *02/231–6857* 🛏 *75 rooms* ♨ *Restaurant, Internet, shops, bar* ⊟ *AE, MC, V.*

¢ ⊞ **Hotel Rosario.** This charming, Spanish-style hotel has changed its name

Fodor'sChoice   from Residential Rosario to Hotel Rosario, after a complete makeover

★   and expansion. The sunny courtyard with a fountain surrounded by clay pots overflows with flowers. Rooms are on the small side, but most have private baths and all are clean and bright; many have spectacular views of Mt. Chacaltaya. The restaurant has live music from 8 to 9 Friday and Saturday. The travel agency, Turisbus, has an office in the lobby. ✉ *Calle Illampu 704* ☎ *02/231–6156* 🖷 *02/237–5532* 🛏 *41 rooms, 1 suite* ♨ *Restaurant, travel services* ⊟ *AE, MC, V.*

¢ ⊞ **Hotel Sagárnaga.** This quiet hotel on a steep cobblestone street near the Mercado de las Brujas has an unbeatable location. It also offers reasonable prices and an on-site travel agency. Peñas (folk music and dance groups) perform here every Wednesday and Sunday from 8 to 10 PM. ✉ *Calle Sagárnaga 326* ☎ *02/235–0252* 🖷 *02/236–0831* 🛏 *56 rooms* ♨ *Restaurant, travel services* ⊟ *AE, MC, V.*

Nightlife & the Arts

The Arts

For concert and cinema listings pick up a copy of the Spanish-language *Última Hora, La Razón,* or *El Diario,* or the English-language *Bolivian Times,* which hits the streets on Fridays. The **Oficina de Turismo** (✉ Edificio Mariscal Ballivián, 18th floor, Calle Mercado ☎ 02/236–7463 or 02/236–7464) can fill you in on local festivals and special events.

FILM   The art theater **Cinemateca Boliviana** (✉ Calle Pichincha at Calle Indaburo ☎ 02/232–5346) regularly shows foreign and even a few Bolivian films.

GALLERIES   The **Galería Emusa** (✉ Av. 16 de Julio 1607 ☎ 02/375–042), in El Prado, hosts rotating exhibits of Bolivian sculpture and art. **Arte Unico** (✉ Av. Arce 2895 ☎ 02/232–9238) mounts varied exhibits.

THEATER   The **Teatro Municipal** (✉ Calle Genaro Sanjinés 629 ☎ 02/237–5275) stages folk events and traditional music and dance concerts.

Nightlife

BARS Sopocachi, southeast of the Plaza de los Estudiantes, has the largest concentration of bars. Most start to fill up around 10:30 PM. **Cabrinus** (⊠ Av. 20 de Octubre 2453 ☏ 02/243–0913) is an old-fashioned piano bar. Drop in late in the evening to hear some good tunes. You might think you're in France when you step in the door of **Café Montmartre** (⊠ Calle Fernando Guachalla 399 ☏ 02/232–0801), a popular singles hangout with live music on weekends. If you get hungry, it also serves delicious crepes. The intimate **Matheus** (⊠ Calle Guachalla at Av. 6 de Agosto ☏ 02/232–4376) has a well-stocked bar and the occasional live band.

DANCE CLUBS **Forum** (⊠ Calle Víctor Sanjinés 2908 ☏ 02/232–5762) is a cavernous club two blocks from Plaza España. It's frequented mainly by the under-30 set. **Mongo's** (⊠ Hermanos Manchego 2444 ☏ 02/235–3914) is a popular hamburger joint, but it turns into a lively disco in the evenings Thursday through Saturday. Get there early or expect a long wait. Trendy **Socavón** (⊠ Av. 20 de Octubre near Calle Guachalla ☏ 02/235–3998) draws younger Paceños with live music most nights.

PEÑAS Peñas are nightclubs that showcase traditional Bolivian music and dance. The energetic live performances—as popular with Paceños as they are with tourists—cost from $8 to $20 per person. Dinner is usually included. The most famous is **Peña Naira** (⊠ Sagárnaga 161 ☏ 02/235–0530), located near Plaza San Francisco. Shows are a bargain at $4–$5. **Casa del Corregidor** (⊠ Murillo 1040 ☏ 02/236–3633) has performances most evenings.

Sports & the Outdoors

Soccer

Bolivians would be lost without their weekly soccer fix. Even the poorest, most remote villages have a playing field. Games are usually played on the only flat piece of land in town, so sheep and cows often graze on the field when there's not a match. La Paz itself has two teams: Bolívar and the Strongest. Both compete in the **Estadio Hernando Siles** (⊠ Plaza de los Monolitos ☏ 02/235–7342), in the Miraflores district.

Skiing

Chacaltaya, a primitive ski resort, is 35 km (22 mi) from La Paz. At a height of 17,150 feet it's recommended only for expert skiers who have had at least a week to adjust to the altitude. The season runs from December to April. For information call the local ski organization **Club Andino** (⊠ Calle México 1638 ☏ 02/232–4682 ☐ 02/235–2279).

Volleyball

Three major teams—San Antonio, Litoral, and Universidad—compete regularly in the **Coliseo Julio Borelli** (⊠ Calle México ☏ 02/232–0224), in the San Pedro district.

Shopping

In La Paz you'll find everything from rough-hewn silver plates to intricate jewelry, from woven-rope sandals to sweaters made of the softest alpaca and angora wools. Prices are reasonable by North American standards, although good quality does not come cheaply.

Calle Sagárnaga, near Plaza San Francisco, is a good place to look for local handicrafts. Along the tiny streets that lead off to the right and left are numerous crafts shops. On Calle Linares, just off Calle Sagárnaga, you'll find the **Mercado de las Brujas.** The Witches Market is where you'll find folk remedies and herbal treatments. For Aymara embroidered shawls, try the **Mercado Negro** on Calle Max Paredes. Prices start at $15 and peak at more than $200 for those made of buttery soft vicuña wool. Colorful *polleras,* the traditional skirts worn by indigenous women, are priced between $50 and $100; bowler hats start at around $20. In the heart of the Sopocachi district—where Avenida Ecuador intersects Calle Fernando Guachalla in the southeastern part of the city— is the site of the vast indoor **Mercado Sopocachi,** worth seeing for its colorful displays of fresh produce and flowers. Do not take photos of women tending their stalls unless you ask permission first—if you don't, you may have a bottle thrown at you.

Shopping Centers

Two of the biggest malls in the city center are on Calle Potosí near Calle Ayacucho. The best shopping center in La Paz is the glass-pyramid–capped **Shopping Norte,** which has small restaurants that serve good-value *almuerzos* (set lunches) on the top floor. **Handal Center** is on Avenida Mariscal Santa Cruz, just down from Plaza San Francisco. It carries a wide selection of jeans, T-shirts, shoes, and sports equipment.

Specialty Shops

Before you begin bargain hunting for alpaca sweaters, visit one or two stores to get an idea of what to look for. High-quality hand-knit designs that sell for around $100 here fetch three times that amount in the United States. The shops along Calle Sagárnaga, near Plaza San Francisco, are a good place to compare quality and price.

Artesanías Sorata (⊠ Calle Linares 862 ☎ 02/231–7701) carries traditional alpaca knitwear with ethnic designs. **Casa Fisher** (⊠ Av. Mariscal, Handal Center ☎ 02/239–2946) is known for high-quality knits. One of the best places in town to buy reasonably priced *chompas,* colorful jackets made with traditional textiles, is **Coral** (⊠ Calle Linares 836 ☎ 02/ 234–2599).

Side Trips from La Paz

Tiwanaku

★ On a treeless plain an hour's drive west of La Paz, Tiwanaku (also spelled Tiahuanacu) is Bolivia's most important archaeological site. Partial excavations have revealed the remains of five different cities, one built on top of the other. The site's most impressive monument is the 10-ton La Puerta del Sol (Gate of the Sun), an imposing stone fixture believed to be a solar calendar built by a civilization that surfaced around 600 BC and mysteriously disappeared around AD 1200. The gate is part of an elaborate observatory and courtyard that contain monoliths and a subterranean temple. Although the site lacks the sweep and splendor of Peru's Machu Picchu, it does provide a glimpse into the ancestry of the Aymara, the last indigenous people to be conquered by the Inca before the Spanish arrived. The descendants of the Aymara still farm the ingeniously constructed terraces built by their ancestors.

Start your visit with the Tiwanaku Museum next to the ruins. It displays artifacts found at the sight, the most spectacular of which is a 20-ton, 7.3-meter (24-foot) tall monolithic statue sculpted out of red sandstone. The monolith was discovered by an American, Wendell C. Bennett during excavations in 1934 and has been on display in an open–air garden museum in La Paz, where it was being seriously eroded by weather. It was returned to Tiwanaku when the new indoor museum opened in 2002. Admission to the ruins and the museum is around 19 Bolivianos.

Since it's not always possible to find a guide at Tiwanaku, it's best to book a full-day tour in La Paz. If you decide to come on your own, take a local bus, which takes 90 minutes, and costs about (B)8. Be sure to ask about the return schedule so you won't get stuck here, and bring a warm sweater or poncho—the area is frequently windy and cold, as there are no trees to break the wind. There's a small café where you can have a light lunch.

Oruro

Come to this former mining town 225 km (140 mi) southeast of La Paz to witness an annual pre-lenten Carnaval tradition, started more than 200 years ago, when workers, dressed as devils, danced to honor the Virgin in a festival called La Diablada. The parade of the elaborately costumed dancing devils takes place during Carnaval. Although the Saturday before Ash Wednesday is the biggest day, festivities last for a week. Public buses make the three-hour trip from La Paz for less than 22 Bolivianos. A one-day tour can be booked with a travel agency in La Paz.

Coroico

Your first glimpse of the small resort town of Coroico will be unforgettable, particularly after three hours of tortuous hairpin bends. People come here to see Los Yungas, an astounding region where the snow-covered Andes suddenly drop off into lush valleys. The mostly single-lane highway that brings you here, which drops in altitude by some 9,840 feet in just under 80 km (50 mi), is one of the most hair-raising in South America. It's best not to drive, if possible. The government has been experimenting with not allowing two-way traffic by designating hours when traffic can go in each direction, so be sure to check in advance in case the experiment is still on. Under any circumstances, it is a very dangerous, cliff-hugging road.

Work continues on a 2½-km (1½-mi) tunnel on the Yungas road that will not only reduce travel time from La Paz to Coroico to an hour, but will make it much safer. In the meantime, taking a small bus, that can maneuver better on the dangerous road, is the safest way to go, or hitch onto a bicycle tour, which is the safest of all.

off the beaten path	**PARQUE NACIONAL MADIDI –** The Chalalan Ecolodge in Madidi National Park offers a chance to experience Bolivia's rain forest. The lodge, owned and operated by the Quechua-Tacana community of San José de Uchupiamonas, immerses you into a culture that has lived in the tropical rain forest for 300 years. The project is supported by Conservation International, a U.S. organization that helps indigenous communities become self-sustaining while at the same time conserving their culture and environment. While you're here, be on the lookout for hundreds of species of birds, troops of monkeys, herds of wild peccary, and the elusive jaguar. You reach the park by taking a one-hour flight from La Paz to the jungle town of Rurrenabaque, where you overnight—and on the next day you take a five-hour canoe trip and a 30-minute walk through the rain forest to your thatch-roof cabin facing Lago Chalalan. A 5-day/4-night package, with three nights at Chalalan, is $399 per person plus $130 for air fare. For information, contact **America Tours SRL** (⊠ Av. 16 de Julio 1490, La Paz ☎ 02/231–0023 🖨 02/231–0023 ⊕ www.america-ecotours.com).

WHERE TO STAY & EAT

$ 🔲 **El Viejo Molino.** This beautiful Spanish-style resort hotel is perched high above the valley, among clusters of sugarcane and banana trees heavy with fruit. Relax by the pool or play a few games of tennis. At the tour office you can make arrangements for a rafting trip on a nearby river. The grilled steak in the restaurant is one of the excellent entrées. ⊠ *On the highway into Caroico, Camino Santa Barbara, Km 1* ☎ *02/220–1499* 🛏 *28 rooms* ⬧ *Restaurant, room service, cable TV, in-room safes, pool, bar, laundry service, Internet, meeting room* 🖃 *MC, V.*

¢ 🔲 **Hotel Esmeralda.** From the sunny patio at this hotel, up the hill from Coroico's central plaza, you'll get astounding views of the valley below. The hotel is also surrounded by gardens. The restaurant, with a charcoal pizza oven, is excellent. From the hotel you can arrange hiking tours of nearby Parque Nacional Madidi. ⊠ *On the highway into Coroico, 5 minutes uphill from the plaza* ☎ *02/213–6017* ⊕ *www.hotelesmeralda. com* ⬧ *Restaurant, pool, sauna, Internet* 🖃 *MC, V.*

La Paz A to Z

AIR TRAVEL TO & FROM LA PAZ

All international and domestic flights to La Paz arrive at El Alto airport, which is on the altiplano in the town of El Alto, 12 km (7 mi) from downtown. American Airlines and Lloyd Aéreo Boliviano, Bolivia's international airline, have daily flights between Miami and La Paz. Lloyd Aéreo Boliviano and AeroSur, Bolivia's domestic airline, fly to most major cities in Bolivia.

Taxis are the quickest alternative for getting to and from the airport. The current going rate for the 30- to 45-minute journey is around $7.50, but settle on a price with the driver before you get in. Minibuses also service the airport. The cost is approximately $1.

🛪 Airlines **AeroSur** ✉ Av. 16 de Julio 1616 ☎ 02/236-9292. **American** ✉ Av. 16 de Julio 1440 ☎ 02/237-2009, 800/433-7300 in the U.S. **Lloyd Aéreo Boliviano** ✉ Av. Camacho 1456 ☎ 02/236-7710, 800/337-0918 in the U.S.

🛪 Airports **Aeropuerto Internacional El Alto** ☎ 02/281-0122.

BUS TRAVEL TO & FROM LA PAZ

Buses to major cities in Bolivia and neighboring countries arrive and depart from the Terminal de Buses, which is west of the city center on Avenida Perú. Securing a seat is usually no problem, though you should reserve at least a day in advance for the long and tedious rides to Sucre, Potosí, and Santa Cruz. Reliable bus companies include Expreso Mopar, Trans Copacabana, and Trans El Dorado. Consult a travel agency in La Paz before setting out on a longer trip, as you may decide to save time by flying.

Until the new La Paz–Coroico tunnel is finished (sometime in 2004), the trip by bus to most towns in Los Yungas will take three to four hours and will cost approximately $8. Private bus companies traveling between La Paz and Los Yungas include Transporte 20 de Octubre and Veloz del Norte.

🚌 Bus Companies **Expreso Mopar** ✉ Terminal de Buses ☎ 02/237-7443. **Trans Copacabana** ✉ Terminal de Buses ☎ 02/237-7894. **Trans El Dorado** ✉ Terminal de Buses ☎ 02/235-9153. **Transporte 20 de Octubre** ✉ Calle Yanacachi 1434 ☎ 02/231-7391. **Veloz del Norte** ✉ Av. de las Américas 283 ☎ 02/231-1753.

🚌 Bus Terminals **Terminal de Buses** ✉ Av. Perú ☎ 02/236-7275.

BUS TRAVEL WITHIN LA PAZ

La Paz is served by a comprehensive network of buses called *colectivos* that run daily from 6:30 AM to 10 PM. There is a flat fare of roughly 17¢, payable to the driver upon entry. Slightly more expensive are *micros*, 12-seat minivans that travel roughly the same bus routes. They're more comfortable and quicker. Colectivos and micros are often very crowded but are generally safe. Listen carefully before you board, as destinations are shouted out the window as the vehicles roll through the city. Better yet, ask a local to help you locate the right one.

CAR RENTAL

Renting a car in La Paz is not cheap. Depending on the size of the vehicle, prices run from $30 to $75 per day. If you're driving outside major cities, four-wheel-drive vehicles are essential. Dollar, Economy, and Imbex all have reasonable rates. If you want to hire a car and driver, EBA Transtur is a good choice.

🚗 Rental Agencies **EBA Transtur** ✉ Calle Carlos Medinacelly 1120 ☎ 02/236-1423. **Dollar** ✉ Plaza Isabel ☎ 02/243-0043 🖷 02/244-2887. **Economy** ✉ Canónigo Ayllón 510 ☎ 02/236-1848. **Kolla Motors Ltda.** ✉ Calle Rosendo Gutierrez 502 ☎ 02/241-9141 🖷 02/241-1344. **Localiza Rent-a-Car** ✉ Av. Arce 2177 ☎ 02/244-1011 ⊕ www.localiza.com.br. **Imbex** ✉ Av. Montes 522 ☎ 02/231-6895.

CAR TRAVEL

Don't even think about driving in La Paz. The streets are a maze running along the steep hills, and the traffic is horrific. Before driving outside the city, inquire about the conditions around your proposed destination. Most roads are unpaved and poorly maintained. During the rainy season many roads are subject to flash floods and landslides. If you can, hire a driver familiar with the area so that you can enjoy the scenery without frazzling your nerves.

EMBASSIES

⌘ Embassies Australia Honorary Consul ✉ Edificio Montevideo Mezzanine, Av. Arce 2081, Casilla 7186 La Paz ☎ 02/244-0459 🖷 02/244-0801. **Canada** ✉ Av. 20 de Octubre 2475, Plaza Abaroa, La Paz ☎ 02/243-1215 🖷 02/243-2330. **United Kingdom** ✉ Av. Acre 2732, Casilla 694 La Paz ☎ 02/243-3424 🖷 02/243-1073. **United States** ✉ Av. Arce 2780, Casilla 425, La Paz ☎ 02/243-0251 or 02/243-0120 🖷 02/243-3900.

ENGLISH-LANGUAGE PUBLICATIONS

The weekly *Bolivian Times* is the only English-language newspaper in La Paz. You will find international newspapers at most newsstands and hotels.

MAIL & SHIPPING

The main post office in La Paz is on Avenida Mariscal Santa Cruz, a few blocks south of Plaza Murillo. Both DHL and Federal Express have offices in La Paz.

⌘ Overnight Services DHL ✉ Av. 14 de Septiembre 5351 ☎ 02/278-5522. **Federal Express** ✉ Calle Capitán Ravelo 2401 ☎ 02/231-3355.

⌘ Post Offices La Paz Post Office ✉ Av. Mariscal Santa Cruz at Calle Oruro.

MONEY MATTERS

Banks in La Paz will exchange cash and traveler's checks. Reliable banks include Banco La Paz, Banco Mercantil, Banco Nacional, and Provincia de San Cruz. Most have 24-hour ATMs marked ENLACE that dispense local currency.

You'll find *casas de cambio* throughout the city, particularly on the major streets. Most are open the same hours as regular shops: 9–noon and 3–6. They usually offer better rates than at the banks. You may be approached on the streets by money changers offering similar rates—although most are honest, it's best not to take a chance. Your hotel will probably change cash and traveler's checks as well, albeit for a higher fee.

Wherever you exchange money, make sure you receive new bills, as most vendors won't accept currency that is marked or torn. Also ask for some small change to use in the markets.

⌘ Banks Banco La Paz ✉ Calle Mercado, Edificio Electra 1190. **Banco Mercantil** ✉ Av. Ballivián and Calle 9. **Banco Nacional** ✉ Av. Camacho and Colon ✉ Av. Garcia Lanza and Calle 14. **Provincia de San Cruz** ✉ Av. Arce 2177.

SAFETY

While violent crime has never been a problem in Bolivia, you should use the same precautions you would in any large city: avoid flashy jewelry and expensive watches, keep an eye on your bags at all times, and be aware of your surroundings.

TAXIS & TRUFIS

Taxis and *trufis* (shared taxis), easily identifiable from the taxi sign lodged in the windshield, are cheap and plentiful. Expect to pay less than 50¢ for most trips within the city center. Newer Radio Taxis, identified by the illuminated sign perched on the roof, are the safest option for tourists. Rates are fixed at $1 to $2, depending on the length of your journey.

🛈 Taxi Companies **Radio Taxis** ☎ 02/241-3838.

TELEPHONES

You can make local and international calls from offices run by Entel, Bolivia's telephone company. The main office on Calle Ayacucho is open daily from 7:30 AM to 10:30 PM. There is also an office in the airport. Connections aren't always reliable, so making a call often requires some patience. Public phones are operated by using coins or phone cards (*tarjetas telefónicas*) that you can purchase in many shops and newsstands. After you insert a coin or card, the phone displays how much credit you have.

🛈 Entel Office **Entel** ✉ Calle Ayacucho 267.

TOUR OPERATORS

Crillón Tours, one of the oldest tour companies in La Paz, offers interesting trips throughout Bolivia. Crillón is also the owner and operator of the hydrofoils on Lake Titicaca, the Inca Utama Resort & Spa, Andean Roots Eco Village on Lake Titicaca, and the Posada del Inca on Isla del Sol. Fremen Tours, Magri Turismo, and America Tours SRL offer numerous tours in and around La Paz.

🛈 Tour Information **America Tours SRL** ✉ Av. 16 de Julio 1490 ☎ 02/232-8584 ⊕ www.america-ecotours.com. **Crillón Tours** ✉ Av. Camacho 1223 ☎ 02/213-6612 🖷 02/213-6614 ⊕ www.titicaca.com. **Fremen Tours** ✉ Calle Pedro Salazar 537 ☎ 02/241-7062 🖷 02/241-7327 ⊕ www.andes-amazonia.com. **Magri Turismo** ✉ Calle Capitán Ravelo 2101 ☎ 02/244-2727 🖷 02/244-3060 ⊕ www.bolivianet.com/magri.

VISITOR INFORMATION

🛈 **Oficina de Turismo** ✉ Edificio Mariscal Ballivián, Calle Mercado ☎ 02/36-7463 or 02/236-7464.

LAKE TITICACA

Considered sacred by the Aymara people who used to live on its shores, Lake Titicaca was also revered by the Tiwanaku and Inca civilizations who inhabited the area more than 2,000 years ago. Here you'll find islands with mysterious names like Isla del Sol (Sun Island) and Isla de la Luna (Moon Island), each with ruins in varying states of decay. According to legend, Isla del Sol is where the Inca Empire was founded when Manco Kapac and Mama Ojillo, son and daughter of the Sun God Inti, came down to Earth to improve the life of the altiplano people.

At an altitude of 12,506 feet, Titicaca is the world's highest navigable lake. Actually, it's two bodies of water joined by the narrow Estrecho de Tiquina (Strait of Tiquina). The smaller section, shimmering Lago Huiñaymarca, is the easiest to reach from La Paz. To see the much larger part, brackish Lago Chucuito, you should include Copacabana on

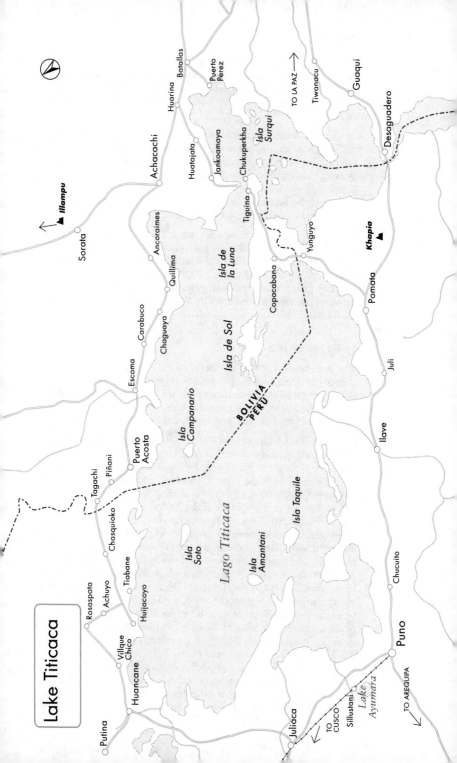

your itinerary. Titicaca covers an area of 7,988 square km (3,474 square mi) in the antiplano, with some of the highest peaks in the Andes rising along the northeastern shore. Its still waters reflect an equal measure of the cloudless blue sky and the sunbaked brown hills that encircle it.

Evidence of settlements more than 3,000 years old can be seen on Isla del Sol. There are also unrestored archaeological sites on several islands on the lake, as well as hundreds of terraces used by ancient people for farming. Many are still used today by the Aymara people, who plant potatoes, quinua, fava beans, and corn. Those Aymara who live on the islands on the Bolivian side of the lake are descendants of the aboriginal inhabitants of the altiplano, not of the Quechua-speaking Incas.

All of the archaeological sites are not so easy to reach. Below the surface of the lake, archaeologists have discovered what is believed to be a pre-Columbian temple that's at least 1,000 years old. So far they have found a pre-Incan road and a 2,601-foot-long wall. An international scientific group, Akakor Geographical Exploring, came across the underwater site after making more than 200 dives into water 98 feet deep.

Huatajata

85 km (53 mi) from La Paz.

This popular weekend escape for Paceños is a regular stop on the guided tour circuit. Huatajata is a practical base for exploring the area. For picnics, try the tree-lined waterfront park at Chúa, the village beyond Huatajata. The real reason people come here, however, is to experience the Inca Utama Hotel & Spa–Andrean Roots Eco Village.

Part of the Inca Utama Hotel & Spa is the **Andean Roots Eco Village,** a sight in itself, even if you don't stay at the hotel. It contains several museums depicting the history and culture of the region, from pre-Columbian times to the present. Headsets with taped guided tours in several languages are available. One exhibit details the lives of the Kallawaya, known as the doctors of the Andes, who still travel from village to village carrying natural medicines on their shoulders, and who developed and used penicillin, streptomycin, and quinine long before modern doctors. Replicas of mud houses that many of the Chipaya people of the surrounding antiplano still live in are outside the museum. A cooperative weaving project in an adobe workshop shows the different systems used by local weavers. Here you can also meet the Limachi brothers, who live at the complex. (They built the reed rafts used by explorer Thor Heyerdahl for his expeditions across the Pacific and Atlantic oceans.) A replica of the *Kon-Tiki* Heyerdahl sailed from Lima to the Polynesia islands in 1947 is on exhibit; the brothers can show you how to make your own reed boats. There's also the Alajpacha native observatory, which is equipped with powerful telescopes donated by NASA. You can study the stars and watch eclipses, and listen to legends handed down from past generations. After the lecture and slide presentation, the roof rolls back for an incredible view of the crystal clear southern skies above Lake Titicaca.

Where to Stay & Eat

$$–$$$ ✕🏠 **Inca Utama Hotel & Spa–Andean Roots Eco Village.** This hotel in-
Fodor'sChoice cludes the Andrean Roots Eco Village, with museums, an observatory,
★ a spa, and a children's park. The Kallawaya Natural Spa uses the natural medicine of the Andes: hydrotherapy, mud and salt baths, and
other treatments. The children's park is also popular: local children
are invited to come and play with your own. The Eco Village includes
museums depicting the history and culture of the region, from pre-
Columbian times to the present. Also at the Eco Village is the Alajpacha native observatory, to which NASA has donated telescopes.
Hydrofoils depart daily from the dock alongside the hotel to the Sun
and Moon Islands, Copacabana, and Puno (on the Peruvian side of
the lake). You can make reservations at the hotel or with Crillon
Tours' office in La Paz. Two restaurants serve fine international cuisine; fresh trout from the lake is a specialty. Folk music performances
take place every evening at the Sumaj Untavi restaurant. A boardwalk
extends out onto the lake to the Choza Nautica thatch-roof restaurant, where you can watch a spectacular sunset over Lake Titicaca.
⊠ *Off hwy from La Paz to Cocacabana (km 45, look for sign), Huatajata* 🕾 *02/213–6612, or 800/488–5353 in the U.S.* 🕾🕾 *02/213–
6614* ⊕ *www.titicaca.com* 🛏 *70 rooms* ⬟ *2 restaurants, cable TV,
health club, massage, spa, bar, meeting room, Internet, travel services*
🖃 *AE, MC, V.*

$–$$ 🏠 **Hotel Lake Titicaca.** Coming from La Paz, you'll see this well-equipped
complex on the lakeshore a few minutes before you reach Huatajata.
The furnishings are slightly dated, but the sweeping views of the lake
make up for it. ⊠ *Midway between Huarina and Huatajata* 🕾 *02/
235–6931* 🖨 *02/235–1792* 🛏 *24 rooms* ⬟ *Restaurant, sauna, boating, racquetball, bar, recreation room* 🖃 *AE, MC, V.*

Isla de Suriqui

Offshore from Huatajata.

In 1970, when Norwegian explorer Thor Heyerdahl wanted to sail
from Morocco to South America to prove that Europeans could have
made contact with South Americans long before the age of Columbus,
he commissioned the Limachi brothers on Isla de Suriqui to construct
his vessel, the *Ra II.* Sailing a tiny reed boat across an ocean was nothing
new to Heyerdahl: two decades before he had sailed from Peru to Polynesia in the reed boat, *Kon-Tiki,* to test his theory that the people of
Easter Island came from South America.

Copacabana

79 km (49 mi) from Huatajata.

After Huatajata the road continues to Tiquina, where you can see the
handful of patrol boats that make up what is left of Bolivia's navy (Bolivia was left landlocked after Chile annexed its coastline in 1879).
Your bus or car is loaded onto a raft and taken across the Strait of Tiquina.
From here it's a 90-minute drive to Copacabana, a pleasant, if touristy,

town on Lago Chucuito. Copacabana, the main stopping point for those headed to Peru, provides easy access to the lake (Crillón Tours now bases a hydrofoil there) and the surrounding countryside.

Copacabana's breathtaking Moorish-style **Catedral,** built between 1610 and 1619, is where you'll find the striking sculpture of the Black Virgin. There was no choice but to build the church because the statue, carved by Francisco Yupanqui in 1592, was already drawing pilgrims in search of miracles. If you see decorated cars lined up in front of the cathedral, the owners are waiting to have them blessed. Throngs of young Paceños walk to Copacabana from La Paz to pay homage to the statue with a candlelight procession on Good Friday.

Where to Stay & Eat

¢–$ ✕ **Snack 6 de Agosto.** Although it serves various entrées, this place is best known for its trout, fresh from Lake Titicaca. There's also a selection of vegetarian dishes. ⊠ *Av. 6 de Agosto* ☎ *08/622–040* ▭ *No credit cards.*

¢–$ ✕ **Sujna Wasi.** This Spanish-owned restaurant is tiny, with seating for fewer than two dozen people. It's the place to come in Copacabana for vegetarian food. The restaurant has a small library with books, maps, and travel information. ⊠ *Calle General Gonzalo Jaúregui 127* ☎ *No phone* ▭ *No credit cards.*

$ ✕▭ **Hotel Rosario Del Lago.** One of the nicest accommodations in Copacabana, this colonial-style hotel is a few blocks from the main plaza. Its clean, homey rooms, including a spacious suite that sleeps six, have excellent views of the shore. Restaurant Kota Kahuana ("View of the Lake") specializes in expertly prepared trout caught in Lake Titicaca, as well as international fare. ⊠ *Calle Rigoberto Paredes and Av. Costanera* ☎ *0813/622–140, 02/245–1341 in La Paz* 🖷 *02/245–1991 in La Paz* ⇘ *31 rooms, 1 suite* ⚒ *Restaurant* ▭ *AE, MC, V.*

¢ ▭ **Ambassador Hotel.** This hotel near the lake is aligned with a youth hostel, which means it offers special rates for students. Although the rooms are somewhat small, it's hard to beat the view from the rooftop restaurant. ⊠ *Calle General Gonzalo Jaúregui* ☎ *0862/2216* ⇘ *42 rooms* ⚒ *Restaurant* ▭ *No credit cards.*

¢ ▭ **Hotel Playa Azul.** Many of the comfortable rooms at this hotel overlook a small courtyard. The most charming thing about this well-located hotel is its cozy dining room lit with gas lamps. Groups frequently stop here for the filling and tasty lunches. ⊠ *Av. 6 de Agosto* ☎ *0862/2228* 🖷 *0862/2227* ⇘ *39 rooms* ⚒ *Restaurant, room service, bar, laundry service* ▭ *MC, V.*

Isla del Sol & Isla de la Luna

12 km (7½ mi) north of Copacabana.

FodorśChoice The largest of Lake Titicaca's islands, **Isla del Sol** has beautiful coves sheltering white sandy beaches. It's popular to make brief stops at the small port of Yumani, where steep Inca steps and a sacred fountain are located. Most people don't, unfortunately, actually spend time on the island. If you do, you'll be well rewarded—there are ruins of the Inca palace of Pilkokaina and a strange rock formation said to be the birthplace of the sun and moon. In the late afternoon, climb to the top of the ridge to watch the sun set among the snowcapped Andes.

En route to Isla del Sol, hydrofoils usually stop at **Isla de la Luna,** where the ruins of Iñacuy date back to the Inca conquest. You'll find an ancient convent called Ajlla Wasi (House of the Chosen Women). Stone steps lead up to the unrestored ruins of the convent.

Where to Stay

$$–$$$ 🏨 **La Posada del Inca.** This beautifully restored colonial-style hacienda on Isla del Sol is covered with flowering bougainvillea. Rooms are small but attractively furnished and all have private baths. Electric heaters and electric blankets powered with solar energy cut the night chill. The hillside location offers sweeping views of the lake. Golf carts provide transportation to the Posada if you find the 30-minute walk up the cobblestone path a challenge in the nearly 3,965-meter (13,000-foot) altitude. The restaurant serves meals family-style at a long table in the dining room. Rooms must be booked as part of a hydrofoil tour with Crillón Tours in La Paz. ☎ *02/213–6612 in La Paz* 📠 *02/213–6614 in La Paz* 🛏 *20 rooms* ⚒ *Restaurant* ☰ *AE, MC, V.*

¢ 🏨 **Inca Sama Albergue.** Follow a stone path up from the ruins of Palacio de Pilkokaina and you'll see this lodge, where three large rooms have mattresses on the floor that sleep up to 20. Baths are outside the lodge, and simple meals are served outdoors. What the hotel lacks in privacy, though, it makes up for in splendid views. Reservations are made through Hotel Playa Azul in Copacabana. ⊠ *Near Palacio de Pilkokaina* ☎ *0862/2228* 📠 *0862/2227* 🛏 *3 rooms* ☰ *No credit cards.*

Sorata

45 km (28 mi) north of Huatajata.

Sorata lies nearly 8,200 feet above sea level in a tropical valley at the foot of Mt. Illampu. This is a starting point for experienced hikers to climb the snowcapped mountain or to make the arduous, weeklong trek along the Camino del Oro (Trail of Gold) to the gold-mining cooperatives.

Where to Stay & Eat

¢–$ ✕🏨 **Hotel Ex-Prefectural Sorata.** A sparkling renovation makes the most of this hotel's charming outdoor garden and lovely views across the valley. The restaurant specializes in the traditional dishes of the region. If you are coming from La Paz, the hotel is on the main highway 1 km (½ mi) from Sorata's central square. ⊠ *Carretera Principal Sorata* ☎ *02/722–846* 📠 *08/115–201* ⚒ *Restaurant* ☰ *AE, MC, V.*

Lake Titicaca A to Z

BOAT & FERRY TRAVEL

Crillón Tours operates hydrofoils on Lake Titicaca between Copacabana and Huatajata in Bolivia and Puno in Peru. The boats visit the floating

Urus Islands, Isla del Sol, and Isla de la Luna. Arrangements can be made through travel agencies in La Paz or Puno.

🔝 Boat & Ferry Information **Crillón Tours** ✉ Av. Camacho 1223, La Paz ☎ 02/213-6612 🖷 02/213-6614 ⊕ www.titicaca.com.

BUS TRAVEL

Minibuses run regularly from the gates of El Viejo Cementerio in La Paz to destinations along Lake Titicaca, including Batallas, Huatajata, and Tiquina. One-way tickets are about $1. Private bus companies that collect passengers at their hotel charge roughly $10 round-trip to Copacabana (four hours) and $15 to Sorata (six hours). Diana Tours and Turibus are two well-known companies operating this route.

🔝 Bus Information **Diana Tours** ✉ Calle Sagárnaga 328 ☎ 02/235-0252. **Turibus** ✉ Calle Illampu ☎ 02/232-5348 or 02/236-9542 🖷 02/237-5532.

CAR TRAVEL

To reach Lake Titicaca from La Paz, take El Alto Highway northwest. The road is paved between La Paz and Tiquina, and barring heavy traffic, takes less than two hours. Be very careful about leaving your car unattended, particularly in Copacabana.

MAIL & SHIPPING

The post office in Copacabana is open Monday–Saturday 9–noon and 2–6.

🔝 Post Offices **Copacabana** ✉ Av. 6 de Agosto.

MONEY MATTERS

In Copacabana, most hotels will change U.S. dollars, as will many shops along Avenida 6 de Agosto. Some will also change traveler's checks, but don't count on it. Banco Union on Avenida 6 de Agosto in Copacabana exchanges foreign currency and gives cash advances on Visa cards. There are a few casas de cambio at Copacabana's main plaza.

TOUR OPERATORS

The best company offering tours of Lake Titicaca is Crillón Tours, in business since 1958. Crillón Tours runs daily hydrofoil trips from Huatajata and Copacabana to many of the islands, as well as to Puno on Peru's side of the lake.

🔝 Tour Companies **Crillón Tours** ✉ Av. Camacho 1223 ☎ 02/213-6612 🖷 02/215-6614 ⊕ www.titicaca.com.

VISITOR INFORMATION

In the center of Copacabana's main plaza, the tourist information booth is the place to find information about the area. The opening hours are erratic (no one knows what they are), but if they're closed, hotels are more than happy to answer your questions and to help with booking tours.

🔝 **Information Booth** ✉ Av. Abaroa and Av. José Mejía.

CENTRAL BOLIVIA

The two major cities in central Bolivia, Cochabamba and Santa Cruz, are both southeast of La Paz—but here ends all similarity. Cochabamba, the country's third-largest city, is in a fertile valley in the foothills of the

Andes. Often referred to as the "breadbasket of Bolivia," Cochabamba produces a large share of the country's fruit and vegetables, as well as much of its meat and dairy products. Nestled in the eastern foothills of the Andes, it is known for its mild, sunny weather. No wonder tourist brochures call this the "city of eternal spring."

Hot and humid Santa Cruz, Bolivia's second-largest city, is on the edge of the Amazon basin. In addition to agriculture, its economy is fueled by lumber, gas, and oil. The downtown area, with its covered sidewalks, looks a little like a movie set of an old frontier town.

Cochabamba

400 km (250 mi) southeast of La Paz.

This bustling metropolis is one of the oldest cities in Bolivia, and many buildings from the 16th century still stand along its narrow streets. Built on the traditional grid pattern, the central part of Cochabamba is divided into quadrants beginning at the intersection of Avenida de las Heroínas and Avenida Ayacucho. Streets are labeled *norte* (north), *sur* (south), *este* (east), and *oeste* (west). The quadrant is included as an abbreviation in the address; for example, Hotel Aranjuez is located at Avenida Buenos Aires E-0563.

A gleaming white statue of Christ with his arms outstretched, called **El Cristo de la Concordia,** stands watch on a hilltop overlooking Cochabamba—at 108 feet it's slightly taller than a similar monument in Rio de Janeiro. This is where many people come to get a feeling for this city with a population of more than half a million. There are also astounding views of Cochabamba from La Coronilla, a hill on the outskirts of the city. At the top is a monument called **La Heroínas de la Coronilla,** honoring women who died during Bolivia's protracted War of Independence.

Many of the sights in Cochabamba, a colonial town founded in 1571, are scattered around the palm-lined **Plaza 14 de Septiembre,** where bougainvillea, magnolias, and jacarandas bloom. Facing the main square is the **Catedral de Cochabamba,** which was started in 1571 but took more than 150 years to complete. One block southeast from the main square is a church called the **Templo de San Francisco,** a colonial masterpiece built in 1581 but thoroughly renovated in 1782 and again in 1926. Inside the Temple of St. Francis are elaborately carved wooden galleries and a striking gold-leaf altar.

Cochabamba's excellent **Museo Arqueológico** is one of the more comprehensive and interesting collections of artifacts outside of La Paz. On display in the Museum of Archaeology are pre-Columbian pottery, silver and gold work, and strikingly patterned handwoven Indian textiles. ⊠ *Jordán and Aguirre* ☎ *No phone* 🎫 *(B)20* ⊙ *Weekdays 9–noon and 3–7, Sat. 9–1.*

Across the Río Rocha is the **Palacio Portales,** which was built but never occupied by Simón Patiño, a local tin baron who amassed one of the world's largest fortunes. The mansion and 10-acre gardens reflect his predilection for French Renaissance style. Chambers on the upper floor mimics Italy's Sistine Chapel. The mansion, a five-minute taxi ride from the center of town, is now a cultural and educational center. ⊠ *Av. Potosí 1450* ☎ *04/424–3137* 🖾 *(B)15* ☉ *Weekdays 5–6 PM, Sat. 10–11 AM, Sun. 11–noon.*

Where to Stay & Eat

★ **$$–$$$** ✕ **Bufalo Rodizio.** At this Argentine-style eatery, all the meat you can eat is carved at your table by waiters dressed as gauchos. There's also an excellent salad bar. Reserve a table on Sundays, which are usually packed with diners enjoying the great views of the city. ⊠ *Edificio Torres Sofer, Av. Oquendo N-0654* ☎ *04/425–1597* 🖃 *AE, MC, V.*

$–$$ ✕ **Casa de Campo.** This informal and lively restaurant serves traditional Bolivian specialties—mostly grilled meats and a perfectly fiery *picante mixto* (grilled chicken and beef tongue). You dine outdoors on a shaded patio. ⊠ *Av. Aniceto Padilla and Av. Bolivar* ☎ *04/424–3937* 🖃 *No credit cards.*

¢–$ ✕ **Chifa Lai Lai.** This *chifa*, or Chinese restaurant, has the excellent service usually found only in much more expensive places. The food is tasty, and the wines are cheap. Try the Ecuadoran shrimp dishes. ⊠ *Av. Aniceto Padilla* ☎ *04/424–0469* 🖃 *MC, V.*

¢–$ ✕ **Quinta Guadalquivir.** Parrots in cages set around a small but beautifully landscaped garden lend a tropical feeling to this popular outdoor eatery. Its shady trees mean it's a pleasant place to stop for lunch. Dishes are a mix of traditional Bolivian and international food. ⊠ *Calle J. Bautista 370* ☎ *04/424–3491* 🖃 *AE, MC, V.*

$ 🏨 **Gran Hotel Cochabamba.** Most of the simple but comfortable rooms at this two-story hotel overlook the gazebo in the center of the plant-filled courtyard. The adjoining Restaurante Carillón serves a tasty pique macho. ⊠ *Plaza Ubaldo Anze* ☎ *04/428–2551* 🖷 *04/248–2558* 🛏 *43 rooms, 5 suites* ♨ *Restaurant, tennis court, pool, bar* 🖃 *AE, MC, V.*

$ 🏨 **Hotel Aranjuez.** This elegant hotel is noted for its lovely gardens overflowing with bougainvillea. The well-appointed rooms are spacious and comfortable; most have baths attached. A live jazz band plays in the lobby bar most weekends. ⊠ *Av. Buenos Aires E-0563* ☎ *04/428–0076 or 04/424–1935* 🖷 *04/424–0158* ⊕ *www.aranjuezhotel.com* 🛏 *30 rooms, 3 suites* ♨ *Restaurant, cable TV, pool, hair salon, bar, meeting rooms, travel services* 🖃 *AE, MC, V.*

$ 🏨 **Hotel Portales.** In a quiet residential area in the northern part of the city, this Spanish-colonial-style hotel surrounded by lush gardens is Cochabamba's most luxurious accommodations. It has numerous recreation facilities, from a racquetball court to two heated pools. The well-equipped rooms have everything you'll require if you're traveling on business. It's a short taxi ride from the center of town and local swing bands play in the bar. ⊠ *Av. Pando 1271* ☎ *04/428–5444* 🖷 *04/424–2071* ⊕ *www.portaleshotel.com* 🛏 *98 rooms, 8 suites* ♨ *2 restaurants, 2 pools, health club, hair salon, hot tub, racquetball, piano bar, laundry service, meeting rooms* 🖃 *AE, MC, V.*

¢ 🏨 **Hotel Uni.** You'll appreciate this hotel's location—just a block from the main square. The rooms are simple and clean. Ask for an upper-floor room away from noisy Avenida de las Heroínas. ⊠ *Calle Baptista S-*

0111 📠 *04/423–5065* 🛏 *43 rooms, 5 suites* ⚴ *Restaurant, bar, travel services* 🖃 *AE, MC, V.*

Shopping

Cochabamba is well known for its alpaca sweaters and leather goods, but don't expect prices much lower than in La Paz. Plaza Colón marks the start of **El Prado** (sometimes called Avenida Ballivián), a shop-lined avenue that stretches north to the Río Rocha. The local market, **La Cancha,** is open daily on Avenida Aroma. It's a good place to browse for less expensive crafts.

Asarti (⊠ Calle México and Av. Ballivián ☎ 04425–0455) sells high-quality knits. **Casa Fisher** (⊠ Calle Ramorán Rivero 0204 ☎ 04/428–4549) sells beautiful alpaca sweaters. **Tipay** (⊠ Calle Jordán E-0732 ☎ 04/425–1303) is a clothing cooperative of local women who sell handmade knits in alpaca and cotton.

Tarata

25 km (15 mi) southeast of Cochabamba.

A well-preserved colonial village, Tarata is known for its busy outdoor market on Thursday. For the best view of Tarata, take the 15-minute walk uphill to the **Iglesia de San Pedro.** The Convento de San Francisco is currently being restored, as are many of the fine old buildings around town. Also interesting is the nearby village of Hayculi, famous for its pottery and ceramics.

In Cochabamba, buses for Tarata depart from Avenida Barrientos at the corner of Avenida 6 de Agosto. Many tour companies, such as the La Paz–based Fremen Tours, offer trips here.

Santa Cruz

900 km (560 mi) southeast of La Paz.

Just 20 years ago, oxen pulled carts through the muddy streets of Santa Cruz. Today, by contrast, you'll see well-dressed business executives dodging taxis and darting in and out of office buildings. Nonetheless, Santa Cruz, with more than 700,000 inhabitants, hasn't been completely transformed—you can still find traces of its colonial past.

The **Basílica Menor de San Lorenzo** was built between 1845 and 1915 on the ruins of a 17th-century cathedral. The imposing church, on Plaza 24 de Septiembre, holds a small museum displaying colonial-era religious icons, paintings, and sculptures. ⊠ *Plaza 24 de Septiembre* ☎ *03/332–7381* 🖾 *(B)6* ☉ *Tues. and Thurs. 10–noon and 4–6, Sun. 10–noon and 6–8.*

Facing Plaza 24 de Septiembre, the **Casa de la Cultura** hosts cultural exhibits, recitals, and concerts, in addition to a permanent exhibit of crafts made by indigenous people. ⊠ *Plaza 24 de Septiembre* ☎ *03/334–0270* 🖾 *Free* ☉ *Daily 9–noon and 3–6.*

Considered one of the finest zoos in South America, the **Zoológico Municipal** houses a collection of species from the Amazon, including jaguars, tapirs, and toucans. You'll also see such Andean creatures as llamas, alpacas, and flamingos. Taxis will take you from the main square to the zoo for approximately $1.50. ⊠ *Anillo Interno at Radial 26* ☎ *03/342–9939* 🖅 *(B)8* ⊘ *Daily 9–6.*

Where to Stay & Eat

¢–$ ✕ **Victory.** This bar and restaurant serves tasty pastas and pizzas, but most diners gather on the balcony to sip cold beer, play cards or chess, and watch the action on the street below. ⊠ *Junín at 21 de Mayo* ☎ *03/332–2935* ▤ *MC, V.*

$$$$ 🏨 **Hotel Camino Real.** A free-form pool meanders through the tropical gardens at this low-rise hotel in a residential neighborhood on the outskirts of Santa Cruz. The La Tranquera restaurant serves international fare. ⊠ *Calle K 279, Equipetrol Norte* ☎ *03/423–535* 🖷 *03/343–1515* 🌐 *www.caminoreal.com.bo* ⇌ *102 room, 8 suites* ⚒ *Restaurant, cafeteria, pool, gym, sauna, spa, soccer, volleyball, shops, business services, meeting room, travel services* ▤ *AE, MC, V.*

$$$$ 🏨 **Hotel Los Tajibos.** This sprawling resort hotel on the edge of the city includes a series of low-slung buildings surrounded by lush gardens. El Papagayo restaurant serves excellent seafood. ⊠ *Av. San Martín 455* ☎ *03/421–000* 🖷 *03/342–6994* 🌐 *www.lostajiboshotel.com* ⇌ *185 rooms, 6 suites* ⚒ *Restaurant, café, pool, gym, shops, convention center* ▤ *AE, MC, V.*

$$$$ 🏨 **Yotaú.** The spacious accommodations in this all-suite hotel are more like apartments, complete with kitchens and washing machines. Just outside of Santa Cruz in the suburb of Barrio Equipetrol, this strikingly modern hotel has a landscaped garden. Breakfast is included. ⊠ *Av. San Martín 7* ☎ *03/336–7799* 🖷 *03/336–3952* 🌐 *www.yotau.com.bo* ⇌ *100 suites* ⚒ *2 restaurants, pool, bar, business services* ▤ *AE, MC, V.*

$–$$ 🏨 **Gran Hotel Santa Cruz.** This family-owned hotel dating from the 1930s is a few blocks south of Plaza 24 de Septiembre. Rooms are like a comfortable den; those that overlook the pool have small private balconies. The restaurant serves very good international cuisine. ⊠ *Calle Pari 59* ☎ *03/334–8811* 🖷 *03/332–4194* ⇌ *40 rooms, 12 suites* ⚒ *Restaurant, cafeteria, pool, gym, 2 bars* ▤ *AE, MC, V.*

$ 🏨 **Hotel Viru Viru.** These downtown lodgings offer clean, modern rooms that overlook the swimming pool in the courtyard. Breakfast is included in the rate. ⊠ *Calle Junín 338* ☎ *03/333–5298* 🖷 *03/336–7500* ⇌ *44 rooms* ⚒ *Café, pool* ▤ *No credit cards.*

Shopping

Crafts shops and street vendors are scattered around Plaza 24 de Septiembre. Don't expect any real bargains. **Artecampo** (⊠ Calle Monseñor Salvatierra 407 ☎03/334–1843) is a cooperative with a colorful selection of handmade hammocks made from locally grown cotton. There are also mobiles and intricate hand-painted woodwork.

Central Bolivia A to Z

AIR TRAVEL

International flights on Lloyd Aéreo Boliviano stop at Aeropuerto Internacional Viru-Viru in Santa Cruz before continuing to La Paz. American flights from La Paz stop in Santa Cruz on the way to Miami. The airport is about 15 km (9 mi) north of the city. Buses to the center of town depart every 20 minutes and cost about $1. Taxis should run about $6.50.

Lloyd Aéreo Boliviano and AeroSur fly daily from La Paz and Sucre to Aeropuerto Jorge Wilsterman in Cochabamba. The airport is 10 km (6 mi) from downtown. A taxi into town is about $4.

✈ Airlines **AeroSur** ✉ Av. Villarroel 1105, Cochabamba ☎ 04/440-0909 ✉ Calle Arenales 31, Santa Cruz ☎ 03/336-7400. **American** ✉ Beni 171, Santa Cruz ☎ 03/334-1314. **Lloyd Aéreo Boliviano** ✉ Av. de las Heroínas, Cochabamba ☎ 04/423-0320 ✉ Calle Warnes, Santa Cruz ☎ 03/334-4596.

✈ Airports **Aeropuerto Internacional Viru-Viru** ✉ Santa Cruz ☎ 03/334-4411. **Aeropuerto Jorge Wilsterman** ✉ Cochabamba ☎ 04/422-6548.

BUS TRAVEL

Depending on the state of the road, it takes about seven hours to travel by bus between La Paz and Cochabamba. If you're headed from La Paz to Santa Cruz, figure on a 20-hour trip. One-way tickets for either journey cost between $10 and $15. To avoid standing in the aisle for the entire journey, book tickets at least a day in advance. Trans Copacabana and Expreso Mopar have buses that leave several times a day.

🚌 Bus Companies **Expreso Mopar** ☎ 02/237-7443. **Trans Copacabana** ☎ 02/237-7894.

🚌 Bus Terminals **Terminal de Cochabamba** ✉ Av. Ayacucho at Av. Aroma. **Terminal de Santa Cruz** ✉ Av. Cañoto at Av. Irala.

CAR RENTAL

Car rentals in Cochabamba or in Santa Cruz will cost a minimum of $50 per day. A. Barron's rents cars in both Cochabamba and Santa Cruz. Toyota is a reputable company in Cochabamba, while Imbex is well known in Santa Cruz.

🚗 Rental Agencies **A. Barron's** ✉ Calle Sucre E-0727, Cochabamba ☎ 04/422-2774 ✉ Av. Alemana 50, Santa Cruz ☎ 03/342-0160. **Imbex** ✉ Calle Monseñor Peña 320, Santa Cruz ☎ 03/353-3603. **Toyota** ✉ Av. Libertador Bolívar 1567, Cochabamba ☎ 04/428-5703.

CAR TRAVEL

Driving yourself is not a particularly good idea in most parts of Bolivia—and certainly not anywhere near the Chapare area, in north-central Bolivia (east of Cochabamba), with an ongoing disagreement about whether coca farmers should be allowed to raise their crops. It takes nearly five hours to drive southeast from La Paz to Cochabamba. From La Paz, drive 190 km (118 mi) south to Caracollo, one of the few villages along the way with a gas station, and then head east toward Cochabamba. The drive between Cochabamba and Santa Cruz takes 10 hours on the Nuevo Camino (New Road). Don't try this route without a four-wheel-drive vehicle. You can break the trip into almost equal parts by staying overnight at Villa Tunari.

HEALTH

Take the normal health precautions when traveling in this area—drink only bottled water and don't eat from street stands where food is sitting around. Make sure to bring along plenty of mosquito repellent.

INTERNET

Internet cafés, such as Center Internet in Cochabamba and Café Internet in Santa Cruz, charge $2–$5 an hour. Many Entel offices in these and other towns offer Internet services. Make sure to inquire at your hotel—even the smallest ones often have Internet access for $2–$4 an hour.

🔧 Internet Cafés **Café Internet** ✉ Calle Sucre 673, Santa Cruz ☎ 03/335-2161. **Center Internet** ✉ Av. de las Heroínas E-0267, Cochabamba ☎ 04/423-3423.

MAIL & SHIPPING

In Cochabamba, the post office is located near Plaza 24 de Septiembre. In Santa Cruz, it is found near Plaza 14 de Septiembre. Both are open Monday–Saturday 8–7 and Sunday 8–noon.

🔧 Post Offices **Santa Cruz** ✉ between Junín and Florida. **Cochabamba** ✉ Av. de las Heroínas and Av. Ayacucho.

MONEY MATTERS

In Cochabamba, you'll find casas de cambio around Plaza 14 de Septiembre. Independent money changers are often found along Avenida de las Heroínas. In Santa Cruz, there are several casas de cambio around the Plaza 24 de Septiembre that will exchange cash and traveler's checks. Freelancers stroll through the main square and the bus terminal, but you'll probably feel more comfortable using an official change house.

Most banks in Cochabamba and Santa Cruz, including Banco Mercantil and Banco Nacional, have 24-hour ATMs.

🔧 Banks **Banco Mercantil** ✉ Calle Calama E-0201, Cochabamba ☎ 04/425-1865 ✉ René Moreno at Suárez de Figueroa, Santa Cruz ☎ 03/334-5000. **Banco Nacional** ✉ Calle Nataniel Aguirre S-0198, Cochabamba ☎ 04/425-1860 ✉ René Moreno 258, Santa Cruz ☎ 03/336-4777.

TAXIS

Taxis are readily available on the streets in Cochabamba and Santa Cruz. If you want to call a taxi, try Radio Taxi in Cochabamba and Radio Taxi Equipetrol in Santa Cruz.

🔧 Taxi Companies **Radio Taxi** ✉ Lanza N-579, Cochabamba ☎ 04/422-8856. **Radio Taxi Equipetrol** ✉ Av. General Martínez 338, Santa Cruz ☎ 03/335-2100.

TELEPHONES

Public phones can be found on the streets of both Santa Cruz and Cochabamba and even along some highways. You can purchase a phone card from any Entel office, as well as from many shops and newsstands.

🔧 Telephone Companies **Entel** ✉ Av. de las Heroínas and Av. Ayacucho, Cochabamba ⊙ Mon.-Fri. 7:30 AM-11 PM; Sat.-Sun. and holidays 8 AM-9 PM. **Entel** ✉ Av. Warnes 83, between Moreno and Chuquisaca, Santa Cruz ☎ 03/432-5526 ⊙ Mon.-Fri. 7:30 AM-11 PM; Sat.-Sun. and holidays 8-9 AM-9 PM.

TOUR OPERATORS

Fremen Tours in La Paz offers tours of the central Bolivian market towns of Tarata and Hayculi, famous for pottery and ceramics. Flota Chiquitano and Magri Turismo in Santa Cruz also organize tours in the area.

🔧 Tour Operators **Flota Chiquitano** ✉ Irala at Cañoto, Santa Cruz ☎ 03/336-0320. **Fremen Tours** ✉ Calle Pedro Salazar 537, Plaza Abaroa, La Paz ☎ 02/241-7062 ⊕ www.

andes-amazonia.com. **Magri Turismo** ⊠ Ingavi 14, Santa Cruz ☏ 03/334-4559 ⊕ www.bolivianet.com/magri.

VISITOR INFORMATION

🚹 **Cochabamba** ⊠ Calle General Achá ☏ 04/422-3364 ⊙ Weekdays 9-noon and 2:30-5. **Santa Cruz** ⊠ Casa de la Cultura (first floor)-on the Plaza ☏ 03/333-2770 ⊙ Weekdays 8:30-noon and 2:30-6.

SOUTHERN BOLIVIA

Sucre

740 km (460 mi) southeast of La Paz.

Sucre has had many names since it was founded by the Spanish in 1538. The town's first official name was La Plata, but it was just as often called Charcas. In 1776, after splitting the region from Peru, the Spanish changed the name to Chuquisaca. Locals now refer to Sucre as *la ciudad blanca* (the white city)—no wonder, since by government edict all buildings in the center of the city must be whitewashed each year.

It was in Sucre that the region declared its independence from Spain in 1825. The country was named for its liberator, Simón Bolívar. Sucre was the country's original capital, but the main government functions were transferred to La Paz in the late 1800s, leaving the Corte Suprema de Justicia (Supreme Court) as Sucre's main governmental function.

Although its population now tops 120,000, Sucre—with its ornate churches, cobblestone streets, and broad plazas—retains the feel of a colonial town. Its moderate year-round climate and friendly people make it a pleasant place to stay while taking side trips to Tarabuco or Potosí.

Exploring Sucre

a good walk

Start at the **Corte Suprema de Justicia,** the last remnant of Sucre's proud past as capital of Bolivia. Here you'll find the Parque Bolívar, which extends several blocks to the northwest. Four blocks to the southeast is the heart of the old city, the Plaza 25 de Mayo. Ice cream vendors and shoe-shine boys leisurely ply their wares throughout the tree-lined square. Waiting taxis can take you on city tours for less than $5 per hour, but there's little in Sucre that's not within walking distance. On the western corner sits the **Casa de la Libertad,** where Bolivia signed the document severing the country's ties to Spain. To the south is the **Catedral Metropolitana.** Walk a block southwest on España and then another southeast on Delence to reach the **Museo Charcas.** Another block southeast on Delence and then two blocks northeast on Potosí you'll come to **Museo de Santa Clara,** which holds a hand-painted organ from the 17th century. Across the street is **Museo Textil Etnográfico.** Return to Delence and head southeast several blocks to the **Museo de la Recoleta.**

TIMING Depending on how much time you spend in the museums, the walk could be done in two to three hours. Budget some extra time to sit and watch the crowds in the Plaza 25 de Mayo.

Casa de la Libertad. Bolivia's formal declaration of independence was signed in the House of Liberty, a former Jesuit chapel, where it's now on display. A small museum displays historical documents and artifacts related to Bolivia's turbulent struggle for independence, as well as Argentina's first flag. ✉ *Plaza 25 de Mayo* ☎ *064/442–4200* ✆ *(B)15* ☉ *Weekdays 9–noon and 2:30–5, Sat. 9:30–11:40.*

Catedral Metropolitana. Started in 1559, this neoclassical cathedral is famous for its statue of the Virgin of Guadalupe, which is adorned with diamonds, gold, emeralds, and pearls donated during the 17th century by mining barons. ✉ *Plaza 25 de Mayo* ✆ *Free* ☉ *Weekdays 10–noon and 3–5, Sat. 10–noon.*

Corte Suprema de Justicia. The imposing Supreme Court building is a reminder that Sucre was once the sole capital of Bolivia. The beautiful Parque Bolívar, which covers several city blocks northwest of the court, is a favorite place for students from the Universidad de San Francisco Xavier to study. ✉ *Ravelo and Pilinco.*

Museo Charcas. The most popular exhibits at the Charcas Museum are mummified bodies discovered outside of Sucre in the 1960s. Curators believe the centuries-old mummies were entombed as human sacrifices. Also featured at this university-run museum are galleries of colonial paintings and textiles. ✉ *Calle Bolívar 698* ☎ *064/423–285* ✆ *(B)15* ☉ *Weekdays 8:30–noon and 3–6, Sat. 8:30–noon.*

Museo de la Recoleta. Founded in 1601 by Franciscan monks, the Museum of the Retreat displays colonial religious works in a setting of serene courtyards and gardens. Equally noteworthy is the restored chapel with its intricately carved choir seats. ✉ *Plaza Pedro Anzures* ☎ *064/421–860* ✆ *(B)10* ☉ *Weekdays 9–11:30 and 3–5:30.*

Museo de Santa Clara. Founded in 1639, the Museum of Santa Clara houses a magnificent hand-painted organ built in 1664. Also on display are works by colonial painter Melchor Pérez Holguín and his Italian mentor, Bernardo Bitti. Visit the chapel, where the nuns who died here were buried under a special floor. ✉ *Calle Calvo 212* ☎ *No phone* ✆ *(B)10* ☉ *Weekdays 9–noon and 3–6, Sat. 9–noon.*

Fodor's Choice **Museo Textil Etnográfico.** This museum is housed in the colonial Caserón
★ de la Capellanía. The Textile and Ethnographic Museum preserves the 4,000-year-old weavings and tapestry art of the Andean world, especially communities around Tarabuco. A display of costumes showcases regional fiesta garb; there are also loom demonstrations. ✉ *Calle San Alberto 413* ☎ *064/453–841* ✆ *(B)15* ☉ *Sept.–June, weekdays 8:30–noon and 2:30–6, Sat. 9:30–noon; July and Aug., Mon.–Sat. 8:30–noon and 2:30–6.*

Plaza Pedro de Anzures. From this beautiful residential square at the foot of Cerro Churuquella you'll get a panorama of Sucre's red-tile roofs and whitewashed homes.

Where to Stay & Eat

Sucre's large student population keeps its many inexpensive restaurants in business. Around the Plaza 25 de Mayo, many offer a *menú del día* (meal of the day) for $2 or $3. If you're not a fan of spicy food, avoid dishes prefaced with the words *ají* (pepper) or *picante* (spicy). Rather than large chain hotels, Sucre has many small hotels and hostels, almost all of which are comfortable, clean, and friendly. Most include breakfast.

¢–$ ✕ **Alliance Française la Taverna.** The traditional French menu includes coq au vin, ratatouille, and sweet crepes. Seating is available in the dining room or outside in the courtyard. The location, near the Plaza 25 de Mayo and the Universidad San Francisco, makes it a popular spot. ⊠ *Calle Aniceto Arce 35* ☎ *064/445–3599* ▱ *No credit cards* ☺ *Closed Sun.*

¢–$ ✕ **El Huerto.** At this restaurant near the municipal park, adventurous carnivores should try a traditional Bolivian entrée, such as *picante de lengua* (spicy tongue). There's plenty on the menu for vegetarians, too. The outdoor patio has a beautiful garden, and is a pleasant place to linger over a long meal. Bring a sweater at night, as it gets a bit chilly. ⊠ *Ladislao Cabrera 86* ☎ *064/451–538* ▱ *No credit cards.*

¢–$ ✕ **New Kactus.** In addition to good food, especially heaping plates of pasta, this restaurant has a nice bar with live music on weekends. ⊠ *Dalence 39* ☎ *064/452–783* ▱ *No credit cards.*

¢ ✕ **Penco Penquitos.** For pocket change you can have a sandwich or nibble on an impressive selection of fresh pastries, from eclairs to empanadas, at this café near the university. ⊠ *Calle Estudiantes 66* ☎ *064/443–946* ▱ *No credit cards.*

$ ▥ **Hotel Mendez Roca.** A short walk from the Plaza 25 de Mayo, this pleasant hotel has colonial furnishings and modern amenities. Discounts are often available, so feel free to ask. ⊠ *Calle Francisco Argandoña 24* ☎ *064/454–282* 📠 *064/455–472* ⇆ *20 rooms* ☖ *Restaurant* ▱ *MC, V.*

¢ ▥ **Hostal de Su Merced.** When you notice the colorful wood ceiling in the reception room—a reproduction of the original painted by a Jesuit priest—you know instantly that this family-owned hotel is a gem. Built as a private home in the late 17th century, the gleaming white colonial structure with a handsome tin roof has large, airy rooms with sunlight streaming in through the tall windows. From the intimate central courtyard, a stairway with wrought-iron railings leads to the upper floors. From the rooftop sundeck you get excellent views of the entire city. ⊠ *Calle Azurduy 16* ☎📠 *064/442–706* ⇆ *14 rooms, 2 suites* ☖ *Restaurant* ▱ *MC, V.*

¢ ▥ **Hostal Sucre.** This colonial-style place, just two blocks from the Plaza 25 de Mayo, is built around two inner courtyards—which means the rooms are all quiet. A restaurant serves light meals and snacks. ⊠ *Calle Bustillos 113* ☎ *064/451–411* 📠 *064/452–677* ⇆ *30 rooms* ☖ *Restaurant, travel services* ▱ *AE, MC, V.*

Shopping

For a touch of local flavor, check out the market at Calle Ravelo and Calle Junín, which sells locally grown fruits and vegetables. The gift shop at the **Museo Textil Etnográfico** (⊠ Calle San Alberto 413 ☎ 064/453–841) has an excellent selection of local weavings. The cooperative ensures that the majority of profits go directly to the weavers.

Tarabuco

64 km (40 mi) east of Sucre.

If you are in Sucre over a weekend, take a full-day excursion to the village of Tarabuco to experience its famous Sunday market. Here you will still see indigenous women wearing tri-cornered hats fringed with coins and men with brightly colored ponchos and leather helmets that resemble those worn centuries ago by the Spanish conquistadors. As is many towns in the region, Tarabuco is filled with vendors from end to end selling finely woven belts and *charangos,* a stringed instrument made from armadillo shells. In mid-March, Tarabuco is the location of one of South America's liveliest traditional festivals, called Pujilay. It celebrates the victory of the local people over the Spanish in 1816.

Potosí

169 km (105 mi) southwest of Sucre.

Potosí has a split personality. Its soaring churches and opulent mansions call to mind a time when this was the wealthiest city in South America. The sagging roofs and crumbling facades, however, make it difficult to put the town's painful past and difficult present out of your mind.

Silver, tin, and zinc from nearby Cerro Rico made fortunes for the mineral barons who built their grand homes along Potosí's winding cobblestone streets. Tens of thousands of people flocked here hoping to make a little money of their own. In 1650, with a population topping 160,000, Potosí was the largest and most prosperous city on the continent. But that wealth came from the labor of more than 8 million indigenous people forced to work in the mines.

There's another old saying that puts all this wealth into perspective: "Bolivia had the cow, but the other countries got the milk." In a strange twist of fate, Potosí is now one of Bolivia's poorest cities. Depleted mines, outdated machinery, and an inhospitable terrain—Potosí sits on a windy plain at 13,452 feet above sea level—are not leading to prosperity. But as more and more buildings are restored (some as an act of contrition by the Spanish), more people are being drawn to one of Bolivia's most interesting cities.

Exploring Potosí

The only way to get around Potosí is to walk. The steep, winding streets and sidewalks are narrow, so pedestrian traffic can often be more of a problem than cars. To visit the museums and historic buildings, you'll need a guide. English-speaking guides aren't always available, so consider arranging a tour through a travel agency.

WHAT TO SEE **Casa Real de Moneda.** The showpiece of Potosí is the Royal Mint, built
FodorsChoice in 1773 at a cost of $10 million. This massive stone structure, where
★ coins were once forged with silver from nearby Cerro Rico, takes up an entire city block. It now holds Bolivia's largest museum. On display are huge wooden presses that fashioned the strips of silver from which the coins were pressed, as well as an extensive collection of the coins minted

here until 1953. There's also an exhibit of paintings, including works by Bolivia's celebrated 20th-century artist, Cecilio Guzmán de Rojas. A guard accompanies all tours to unlock each room as it's visited. The building is cool, so bring along a sweater. To see everything will take about three hours. ⊠ *Ayacucho at Lanza* 🖼 *062/222-777* ☞ *(B)20* ☉ *Tues.–Sat. 9–noon and 2–6:30, weekends 9–1.*

Fodor'sChoice **Cerro Rico.** Five thousand tunnels crisscross Cerro Rico, the "Rich Hill,"
★ which filled Spain's coffers until the silver reserves were exhausted in the early 19th century. Today tin is the primary extract, though on the barren mountainside you still see miners sifting through the remnants of ancient excavations. If you don't mind tight spaces, take a tour through one of the mines that are still active. You'll descend into the dark, humid tunnels where the hundreds of workers usually strip down to next to nothing because of the intense heat. Keep in mind that these mines are muddy—wear clothes you don't mind getting dirty. Hard hats, raincoats, boots, and carbide lamps are provided, but take along a flashlight to get a better look at things. The extremely narrow entrance to the mine may scare you off, but go in far enough to give *El Tío* (a statue of a small, grinning devil) a cigarette and add more coca leaves to the pile around his feet. The miners say he brings safety and prosperity.

Convento y Museo de Santa Teresa. The Convent and Museum of St. Theresa displays a strange mix of religious artifacts. In one room are sharp iron instruments once used to inflict pain on penitent nuns, as well as a blouse embroidered with wire mesh and prongs meant to prick the flesh. Other rooms contain works by renowned colonial painters, including Melchor Pérez Holguín. ⊠ *Calle Chicas* 🕾 *064/223-847* ☞ *(B)25* ☉ *Weekdays 9–noon and 2–5:30.*

Iglesia de San Lorenzo. Potosí's most spectacular church, built between 1728 and 1744, has some of the finest examples of Baroque carvings in South America. Elaborate combinations of mythical figures and indigenous designs are carved in high relief on the stone facade. If the front doors are locked, try to get in through the courtyard. ⊠ *Calle Bustillos* 🖼 *No phone.*

Iglesia y Convento de San Francisco. Built of granite during the colonial period, this was Potosí's first church. It has a brick dome and beautiful arches. On the main altar is the statue of the "Lord of the Veracrúz," the patron of Potosí. It also has many beautiful paintings. A panoramic view of the city can be enjoyed from a viewing platform. ⊠ *On the corner of Nagales and Tarija* 🕾 *062/222-539* ☞ *(B)10* ☉ *Weekdays 2:30–4:30.*

Where to Stay & Eat

¢–$ ✕ **El Mesón.** Potosí's most exclusive restaurant has a quiet dining room where you can get both traditional Bolivian and international food. ⊠ *Calle Tarija at Calle Linares* 🕾 *062/223-087* 🖃 *MC, V.*

¢–$ ✕ **San Marcos.** Potosí's most unusual restaurant occupies a former sil-
Fodor'sChoice ver processing plant. Each piece of ancient machinery has been put to
★ use—the bar, for example, is a platform where stones were once washed. Both local and international dishes are served, including *trucha al gusto* (trout broiled with lemon, garlic, and pesto sauce) and

filete flambé San Marcos (steak doused with cognac and set aflame). Be sure to have ice cream made from *chirimoya* (custard apple). There's live music every Friday night. ⊠ *La Paz and Betanzos* ☎ *062/ 222–781* ▤ *MC, V.*

¢–$ ✕ **Sky Room.** You'll be treated to fine views of the sunset from this aptly named rooftop restaurant. The restaurant serves traditional dishes, such as *pichanga* (various types of meats served with salad) and grilled chicken. ⊠ *Edificio Matilde, Calle Bolívar 701* ☎ *062/ 226–345* ▤ *MC, V.*

¢ ✕ **Cherry's.** At this delightful coffee shop you can sip mugs of refreshing mate de coca while you ponder the delicious selection of cakes and strudels. ⊠ *Calle Padilla 8* ☎ *062/222–969* ▤ *No credit cards.*

$ ▦ **Hotel Libertador.** Original artwork by local Potosi painters brighten hallways and rooms in this centrally located hotel. There's a small patio on the top floor where you can catch a little sun. The staff is friendly. The big plus here is central heating. ⊠ *Millares 58* ☎ *062/223–470 or 062/227–877* 🖷 *062/224–629* ⊕ *hostal-libertador-potosi.com* ⇆ *20 rooms, 3 suites* ⸝ *Restaurant, bar, cable TV, Internet* ▤ *MC, V.*

★ ¢ ▦ **Hotel Cima Argentum.** Near the Santa Teresa Convent and six blocks from the Casa de Moneda, this is one of Potosí's most modern hotels. The large rooms with marble baths and the suites are spread over three floors with balconies overlooking a courtyard under a glass dome. Each room has its own radiator for heat. There's a coffee pot in your room and the chef cooks up tasty local and international dishes. The restaurant is open from 7 AM to 11 PM. ⊠ *Av. Villazon 239,* ☎ *062/229–538* ⊕ *www.hca-potosi.com* ⇆ *20 rooms, 9 suites* ⸝ *Restaurant, room service, cable TV, Internet* ▤ *MC, V.*

¢ ▦ **Hotel Claudia.** A little far from the center of town, this place has well-equipped rooms and a terrace perfect for relaxing after a day exploring the city. It has features rarely found in Potosí's budget lodgings, including a restaurant and bar. Many tour groups stop here. ⊠ *Av. El Maestro 322* ☎ *062/222–242* 🖷 *062/224–005* ⇆ *22 rooms* ⸝ *Restaurant, bar* ▤ *MC, V.*

¢ ▦ **Hotel Colonial.** This whitewashed colonial hotel is just two blocks from the colorful Plaza 10 de Noviembre. Many rooms overlook the hotel's two airy courtyards. Ask to see one of the modern rooms in the back, which are more spacious. ⊠ *Calle Hoyos 8* ☎ *062/224–809* 🖷 *062/ 227–164* ⇆ *20 rooms* ⸝ *Dining room* ▤ *MC, V.*

Shopping

Despite Potosí's rich mineral wealth, don't expect bargains on handcrafted silver jewelry. Brass and low-grade silver items can be found at the **Mercado Central** at Bustillos and Bolívar. The **Mercado Artesenal**, on the corner of Sucre and Omiste, has locally produced crafts.

Salar de Uyuni

FodorśChoice *219 km (136 mi) southwest of Potosí.*
★

One of Bolivia's most spectacular sites, the vast Salar de Uyuni is the world's highest desert of salt. Its cracked white surface is at 11,976 feet.

Once part of a prehistoric salt lake covering most of southwestern Bolivia, it still extends for about 12,000 square km (4,600 square mi). Here you'll find a series of eerie, translucent lagoons tinted green and red due to high copper and sulfur contents. On the salt flat live flamingos, rheas, vicuñas, and foxes.

It takes four to five hours of travel on rough roads to reach Uyuni from Potosi and most people choose to make arrangements with a travel agency. The site is remote and cold, with nightly temperatures falling to -25°C (-13°F). While the area is accessible year-round, the most popular time is from March to December. Whenever you go, take plenty of sunblock, sunglasses, and warm clothing.

Where to Stay

$ ▨ **Palacio de Sal.** Built entirely of blocks of salt—including the beds—this hotel is right on the Salar de Uyuni. Relax in the sauna, take a dip in a small pool, or even play a round of golf on a nine-hole course. While far from luxurious, it's certainly unique. It may not be around long, however, because Bolivia has plans to remove all accommodations on the Salar de Uyuni due to the danger of contamination to the lake. Book reservations through Hidalgo Tours or Crillon Tours. ⊠ *Salar de Uyuni* ☎ *062/222–5186 for Hidalgo in Potosí, 02/213–6612 for Crillón in La Paz* ⫶ *10 rooms* ⚭ *Restaurant, bar* ▤ *MC, V.*

Southern Bolivia A to Z

AIR TRAVEL

Sucre's Aeropuerto Juana Azurduy de Padilla—about 5 km (3 mi) north of Sucre—has regular flights to La Paz on AeroSur and Lloyd Aéreo Boliviano. A taxi ride into town should cost about $1.50. Potosí has a small airstrip just outside of town but has no regularly scheduled flights.

🛈 Airlines **AeroSur** ⊠ Calle Arenales 31, Sucre ☎ 064/454–895 or 0800/3030. **Lloyd Aéreo Boliviano** ⊠ Bustillos 121 y 143, Sucre ☎ 0800/3001 in Bolivia.
🛈 Airports **Aeropuerto Juana Azurduy de Padilla** ☎ 064/454–445.

BUS TRAVEL

Buses bound for Potosí and Sucre leave La Paz daily. The 19-hour trip to Sucre costs less than $15. Buses between Sucre and Potosí depart approximately every hour. The trip takes about five hours and costs $4.
🛈 Bus Terminals **Potosí** ⊠ Av. Universitaria ☎ 062/227–354. **Sucre** ⊠ Calle Ostria Gutiérrez ☎ 06/442–2029.

CAR TRAVEL

Although the highways aren't in the best condition, driving can be a nice way to see some areas of southern Bolivia. When visiting Potosí, it is best to fly to Sucre and drive from there. You should also consider hiring a car and driver or take a tour through a travel agency. The highway is good between Sucre and Potosí but plan to overnight, as it passes through mountains and is not lighted.
🛈 Car Rentals **Imbex** ⊠ Potosí 499, Sucre ☎ 06/461–222.

MAIL & SHIPPING

You can receive letters at Sucre's main post office, a block northwest of Plaza 25 de Mayo, and at Potosí's post office, a block south of Plaza 10 de Noviembre.

▣ Post Offices **Potosí** ⊠ Av. Lanza 13. **Sucre** ⊠ Av. Argentina 50.

MONEY MATTERS

In Sucre, you'll find casas de cambio along Avenida Hernando Siles near the main market. Your best bet in Potosí is along Calle Bolívar and Calle Sucre. In both places, cash fetches a better rate than traveler's checks. If you need an ATM, one of the most convenient is Banco La Paz in Sucre. You won't find ATMs in the countryside.

▣ Banks **Banco La Paz** ⊠ Calle San Alberto and España.

TAXIS

In Sucre and Potosí, taxis are readily available. There are several reliable radio taxi companies in both cities. In Sucre, call Exclusivo or Sucre. In Potosí, contact I.N.N. or Potosí.

▣ Taxi Companies **Exclusivo** ⊠ Jaime Mendoza 960, Sucre ☎ 064/451-414. **I.N.N.** ⊠ Calle Frias 58 ☎ 062/222-606. **Potosí** ⊠ Zona San Clemente 125 ☎ 062/225-257. **Sucre** ⊠ Playa 25 de Mayo, Sucre ☎ 064/451-333.

TELEPHONES

Sucre's Entel office, three blocks northeast of Plaza 25 de Mayo, is one of the more reliable places to make local or long-distance calls. Potosí has an Entel office on Plaza Aniceto Arce. There are also public phones along the streets and some highways. Purchase a phone card at an Entel offices or from shops and newsstands.

▣ Telephone Companies **Entel** ⊠ España and Urcullo, Sucre ☎ 064/423-830 ⊠ Plaza Aniceto Arce, Potosí ☎ 062/222-023.

TOUR OPERATORS

Candelaria Tours in Sucre organizes trips to Potosí and to nearby Tarabuco for the Sunday market. In Potosí, Sin Fronteras and Hidalgo Tours organize excursion around the city as well as to the Cerro Rico mines. Fremen Tours in La Paz arranges wine tours of the Tarija area.

Toñito Tours, run by American expatriate Chris Sarage, specializes in tours in southwestern Bolivia. Trips to the Salar de Uyuni are usually for four days and cost about $30 a day, including accommodations, a car and driver, and a cook who prepares three meals a day.

▣ Tour Companies **Candelaria Tours** ⊠ Calle Audiencia 1, Sucre ☎ 064/461-661. **Fremen Tours** ⊠ Plaza Abaroa, La Paz ☎ 02/232-7073. **Hidalgo Tours** ⊠ Av. Bolívar at Av. Junín, Potosí ☎ 062/222-5186. **Magri Turismo** ⊠ Calle Capitán Ravelo 2101, La Paz ☎ 02/244-2727 ☐ 02/244-3060 ⊕ www.bolivianet.com/magri. **Sin Fronteras** ⊠ Calle Bustillos 1092, Potosí ☎ 062/224-058. **Toñito Tours** ⊠ Sagárnaga 189, La Paz ☎ 02/233-6250 ⊠ Av. Ferroviaria 152, Uyuni ☎☐ 0693/2094 ⊕ www.bolivianexpeditions.com.

VISITOR INFORMATION

▣ **Potosí Oficina de Turismo** ⊠ Cámara de Minería, Calle Quijarro ☎ 062/225-288 ◷ Weekdays 9-noon and 3-6. **Sucre Oficina de Turismo** ⊠ Nicolás Ortiz 182 ☎ 064/455-9836 ◷ Weekdays 8-noon and 2-6.

BOLIVIA A TO Z

To research prices, get advice from other travelers, and book travel arrangements, visit www.fodors.com.

AIR TRAVEL

American and Lloyd Aéreo Boliviano (LAB) operate daily flights from Miami. Flights on both airlines stop in Santa Cruz. Lloyd Aéreo Boliviano also flies to La Paz from other South American cities, including Buenos Aires, Rio de Janeiro, Santiago, Lima, and Asunción.

LAB flies between most Bolivian cities, as does domestic carrier Aero-Sur. One-way tickets range from $60 to $150. Both LAB and AeroSur offer 30-day passes for approximately $160 that allow travel to four cities. Destinations include Trinidad, Santa Cruz, Tarija, Sucre, Cochabamba, and La Paz. Domestic flights can be heavily booked, so always reconfirm your reservation a day or so in advance. If you do not, your reservation may be canceled.

🛪 Airlines **AeroSur** ✉ Edificio Petrolero, Av. 16 de Julio ☎ 02/23-5152. **American** ✉ Plaza Venezuela 1440, La Paz ☎ 02/235-1360. **Lloyd Aéreo Boliviano** ✉ Av. Camacho 1460, La Paz ☎ 800-10-3001 or 800-4321 in Bolivia.

BUS TRAVEL

Private bus companies connect Bolivia's major cities—two of the best are Expreso Mopar and Trans Copacabana. Because of the often poor roads, bus journeys can be a very slow way to travel—a trip from La Paz to Santa Cruz, for example, can take more than 24 hours. Some routes are crowded, so reserve a seat a day or two ahead.

🛪 Bus Companies **Expreso Mopar** ☎ 02/237-7443. **Trans Copacabana** ☎ 02/237-7894.

BUSINESS HOURS

Long lunch closings for government offices have been eliminated. This has changed the way cities—particularly La Paz—conduct business. New office hours are weekdays 8–4.

BANKS Banks are open weekdays 9–11:30 and 2:30–5. A few are open for a limited time on Saturdays.

MUSEUMS Museums are usually open weekdays 9–noon and 2:30–5 and Sat. 8:30–noon.

SHOPS Shops are open Monday–Saturday 9–noon and 3–8. Many in La Paz and other larger cities are also open on Sunday.

CAR TRAVEL

Car travel in Bolivia is difficult, as few of the major highways are well maintained. Conditions have been so bad that drivers have held brief strikes in protest. During the rainy season (Nov.–Mar.), roads are often impassable. There's no national roadside automobile service, though Bolivians will often stop and offer help in the case of a breakdown. It's unwise to drive, but if you're compelled to do so, make sure you rent a vehicle with four-wheel-drive.

GASOLINE The national oil company, YPFB, maintains service stations on most major roads. Many are open 24 hours a day. Away from the main roads, GASOLINA signs alert you to private homes where fuel is sold. (Make sure they filter the gasoline for impurities when they fill your tank.) Unleaded gasoline is still a novelty in Bolivia. The price of gasoline is approximately $1.70 per gallon.

RENTAL Renting a car can be expensive in Bolivia, particularly because you need
AGENCIES a four-wheel-drive vehicle to reach many destinations. The rate for a four-wheel-drive vehicle is $300–$700 per week. Compact cars suitable for short trips cost $150–$250 per week. The minimum age for most car rentals in Bolivia is 25. You need a passport, driver's license (some rental companies require an International Driver's License), and a credit card.

CUSTOMS & DUTIES
Bags are usually checked on arrival at La Paz's El Alto Airport. You're allowed to import 400 cigarettes and three bottles of wine or two liters of spirits. There is no limit on the amount of foreign currency you can bring into the country. For certain electronic goods—video cameras and personal computers, for example—you should carry your receipts unless they show obvious signs of wear. Do not attempt to import or export contraband drugs of any kind—penalties are severe.

ELECTRICITY
Bolivia's electric current is 110/220 volts AC in La Paz and 220 volts AC in the rest of the country. You'll need adapters for two-pronged outlets, which are used for both types of current.

FESTIVALS & SEASONAL EVENTS
The two-week Feria de Alicitas takes place in La Paz beginning January 24. The Fiesta de la Virgen de Candelaria is held in Copacabana on Lake Titicaca in February. February also brings Carnaval, a weeklong celebration that includes music and dancing in the streets. The biggest bash is held in the mining town of Oruro, where wildly costumed performers parade through the streets. Pujilay, a colorful festival commemorating the 1816 victory by the Tarabucan people over the Spanish, is celebrated the following week in the village of Tarabuco. Good Friday celebrations—which are characterized by candlelit religious processions by masked supplicants—are particularly lively in La Paz and Copacabana.

On June 24, at the Fiesta de San Juan in La Paz, you'll see bonfires and fireworks. On August 5–8, the Fiesta de la Virgen Negra takes place in Copacabana. Tarija holds the Fiesta de San Rogue on the first Sunday of September. El Día de Todos los Santos (All Saints' Day) and El Día de los Muertos (All Souls' Day) take place all around Lake Titicaca on November 1 and 2.

HEALTH & SAFETY
FOOD & DRINK To play it safe, do not drink tap water and order beverages without ice. Never eat food from street vendors. Take the U.S. government's Centers for Disease Control and Prevention's advice: "Boil it, cook it, peel it, or forget it."

OTHER PRECAUTIONS At present, no shots or vaccination certificates are required for entering Bolivia. If you'll be spending time in remote areas, ask your doctor about typhoid, hepatitis A and B, yellow fever, and tetanus vaccinations. If you're headed for the Amazon, consider antimalarial prophylactics.

Due to the high altitude in La Paz, you may suffer from *soroche,* or altitude sickness. Symptoms include dizziness, fatigue, and shortness of breath. Avoid alcohol, drink lots of water, and rest for at least a half day. Symptoms will usually disappear by the second day. If not, consult a doctor, especially if you have a history of high blood pressure. Locals recommend several cups of mate de coca, an herbal (and completely legal) tea made from coca leaves.

Bring plenty of sunblock—the high altitudes feel cool, but the sun can burn, particularly when reflected off snow or water. Don't pet the cute llamas or alpacas, as they can hurl spit wads that burn the eyes. Don't stand too close behind these animals, as they can throw a sharp kick.

HOLIDAYS
New Year's Day; Good Friday (April); Labor Day (May 1); Corpus Christi (June); Independence Day (August 6); All Saints' Day (November 1); Christmas.

LANGUAGE
Spanish is the predominant language in the cities, and travelers often find Bolivian Spanish to be one of the easiest on the continent to understand. Quechua and Aymara are spoken by highlanders who may or may not also speak Spanish. Hotel staff usually have some knowledge of English, French, or German.

MAIL & SHIPPING
Most cities and towns have at least one post office, which is generally open weekdays 8–7:30, Saturday 9–6, and Sunday 9–noon.

POSTAL RATES International airmail letters and postcards cost 67¢ to the United States and 76¢ to Europe, and arrive in 5–10 days. International packages to the United States and Europe cost $26 and $37 per 2 kilos (4½ pounds).

RECEIVING MAIL In major cities, mail can be sent to you in care of Poste Restante, Correo Central (General Delivery, Central Post Office). You will need your passport to retrieve mail.

MONEY MATTERS
You can change U.S. dollars in banks and casas de cambio. Make sure the bills are in perfect condition, with no smudges or torn edges. Traveler's checks are often difficult to cash outside the larger cities. Most banks in Bolivia's larger cities have ATMs. Those labeled ENLACE dispense local currency 24 hours a day.

CREDIT CARDS Visa is welcomed throughout Bolivia, MasterCard less so. American Express is often not accepted. Credit cards are accepted in most cities and towns but never in small villages. If you will be traveling in a rural area, make sure to bring along enough cash.

CURRENCY The unit of currency is the boliviano, which can be divided into 100 centavos. Bolivianos come in bills of 5, 10, 20, 50, 100, and 200. Coins come in denominations of 10, 20, and 50 centavos and 1 and 2 bolivianos. At press time, the exchange rate was (B)7.60 to the U.S. dollar. Bolivians frequently refer to their currency as *pesos*.

WHAT IT WILL COST Because the boliviano is a relatively stable currency, Bolivia remains one of the least expensive countries in South America for travelers. A basic meal at a basic restaurant should cost no more than $5, and even at the most elegant restaurants you can eat well for less than $10. Moderate hotels cost $30–$50 for a double room, which often includes breakfast. The most expensive luxury hotels are more pricey, at $120–$150 per night for a double.

Sample costs: cup of coffee, (B)4; bottle of beer, (B)8; soft drink, (B)4; bottle of house wine, (B)38; sandwich, (B)15; 2-km (1-mi) taxi ride, (B)15; city bus ride, (B)2; museum entrance, (B)8–(B)16.

PASSPORTS & VISAS
Australia, Canada, United Kingdom, New Zealand, and United States citizens need only a valid passport and receive a free visa upon arrival in Bolivia. Visas for the United Kingdom and the United States are valid for 90 days and for Australia, Canada, and New Zealand for 30 days (however, it doesn't hurt to ask if they will extend it to 90). If you want to stay longer than your free days, you have the option of overstaying your visa and being fined (B)10 for each day you overstay or purchase a 30-day extension for (B)150.

SAFETY
Crime is not a major problem in Bolivia. In larger cities such as La Paz, Cochabamba, Sucre, and Santa Cruz, petty theft—from pickpocketing to purse-snatching—is on the rise. Avoid wearing flashy jewelry and watches and be aware of your surroundings at all times, especially in busy plazas and on jam-packed buses. Carry only as much cash as necessary when in the city, especially in crowded market areas.

TAXES
DEPARTURE TAX All passengers must pay a departure tax—$25 for international flights, $2 for domestic flights—at an easily identifiable booth marked IMPUESTOS. You can pay in dollars or bolivianos.

VALUE ADDED TAX Throughout Bolivia, a 13% value-added tax (IVA) is added to hotel and restaurant prices and to most items purchased in stores.

TELEPHONES
The international code for Bolivia is 591. Dial the country code, then the area code, then the five- or six-digit number. If you are calling from abroad, drop the "0" from the area code.

INTERNATIONAL CALLS Long-distance and international calls can be made from local offices of Entel, Bolivia's phone company. Collect and direct-dial calls can be made from Entel offices or by calling 356–700, which connects you with an international operator. A connection can take up to 20 minutes to secure. The least expensive way to make international calls is through your own long-distance carrier.

🛈 Long-distance Carriers **AT&T** ☎ 0800–1111. **MCI** ☎ 0800–2222. **Sprint** ☎ 0800–3333. **British Telecom** ☎ 0800–0044.

LOCAL CALLS Pay phones are operated by using either coins or phone cards (*tarjetas telefónicas*), which can be purchased at Entel offices and at many shops. After you insert a coin or card and enter the number, the phone will indicate how much credit you have.

TIPPING

In restaurants, a tip of 5%–10% is in order unless the service is really dismal. Taxi drivers do not expect tips unless you hire them for the day, in which case 10% is appropriate. Airport porters expect (B)8 per baggage cart they handle.

VISITOR INFORMATION

At the present time there are no tourist information offices outside of Bolivia. The most reliable way to get accurate information is either by contacting a travel agent knowledgeable about Bolivia or checking out Web sites, such as ⊕ www.bolivianet.com.

WHEN TO GO

With its extremes of terrain, altitude, and climate, Bolivia has something to appeal to nearly every traveler. During the rainy season from November to March, heavy downpours make many roads in the lowlands virtually impassable. In the highlands the season brings dark, cloudy skies but little rain. If you plan to travel by bus or car—though this isn't recommended—it's best to go between April and October.

CLIMATE In high-altitude cities like La Paz and Potosí, the weather can get very chilly, particularly at night. Lowland cities like Santa Cruz, sitting in the Amazon basin, are hot and humid the entire year; it's only in the lowlands that rain can be a real impediment. Cochabamba, dubbed the "city of eternal spring," enjoys a mild Mediterranean climate year-round.

The following are the average monthly maximum and minimum temperatures for La Paz.

Jan.	64F	18C	May	66F	19C	Sept.	62F	17C
	43	6		35	2		38	3
Feb.	64F	18C	June	60F	16C	Oct.	65F	18C
	43	6		36	2		40	4
Mar.	64F	18C	July	61F	16C	Nov.	67F	20C
	43	6		34	1		42	6
Apr.	66F	19C	Aug.	62F	17C	Dec.	64F	18C
	40	4		35	2		43	6

BRAZIL

3

BARE IT ALL
on Copacabana Beach ⇨*p.197*

CELEBRATE CARNIVAL EVERY DAY
with samba shows at Plataforma ⇨*p.214*

PIG OUT
on *churrasco* at Porcão ⇨*p.204*

FOLLOW FRED AND GINGER
at Copacabana Palace, the set of
1933's *Flying Down to Rio* ⇨*p.208*

WAKE TO THE CALL OF THE WILD
at Ariaú Amazon Towers ⇨*p.311*

FALL FOR THE VIEW
from the Brazilian side of the
Foz do Iguaçu ⇨*p.259*

GET FRIED
noshing *acarajé* (bean fritters) on
Estrada do Coco beaches ⇨*p.283*

EXPERIENCE ANIMAL MAGNETISM
in the Pantanal Wetlands ⇨*p.264*

MANY CONSIDER BRAZIL A CONTINENT IN ITS OWN RIGHT. It's larger than the continental United States, four times the size of Mexico, and more than twice as large as India. Occupying most of the eastern half of South America, it borders on all of the other nations of the continent, with the exception of Chile and Ecuador. Its population of 163 million is almost equal to that of the continent's other nations combined, making it South America's true colossus.

Brazil is also a land well versed in extremes. Its continuous, 7,700-km (4,800-mi) coast offers a seemingly infinite variety of beaches. Styles range from the urban setting of Rio's Copacabana and Ipanema to isolated, unspoiled treasures along the northeastern coast. Brazil's Portuguese colonizers concentrated on the coastal regions, avoiding the inland areas with rare exceptions—a preference that has dictated national life to this day. In the 1960s, the government moved the capital from Rio to inland Brasília in an effort to overcome the "beach complex," but three decades later, the majority of the population remains concentrated along a narrow coastal strip.

By contrast, the Amazon jungle, which covers 40% of the nation's land mass, has a population of only about 16 million—less than the city of São Paulo alone. Twenty percent of the world's freshwater reserves are found here, and the area is responsible for more than 30% of the earth's oxygen and is home to two-thirds of the world's existing species. Brazil's other hinterland regions are as sparsely populated as they are diverse. The northeast contains the rugged *sertão,* a region that frequently suffers droughts; the central-west is the site of the immense *cerrado* (savanna) area; still farther west are the Pantanal Wetlands—an enormous swamp.

The country is also a melting pot of races and cultures. Beginning with its Portuguese colonizers, Brazil has drawn waves of immigrants from around the globe, including more than 15 million Africans who were transported here as slaves. The result is the ethnic mix of modern-day Brazil—Italian and German communities in the south, prosperous Japanese and Korean colonies in the state of São Paulo, a thriving Afro-Brazilian culture in Bahia, and remnants of Indian cultures in the north. Brazilians are white, tan, gold, black, brown, red, and seemingly all shades in between. Yet the various groups are united by a common language and a cultural heritage distinct from that of the remainder of South America. Brazilians speak Portuguese, not Spanish, and unlike all their neighbors, they were never a Spanish colony.

The variety of cultures, beliefs, and topographies makes this warm nation a showcase of diversity. An array of nature's bounty—from passion fruit and papaya to giant river fish and coastal crabs—has inspired chefs from all over the world to try their hands in Brazilian restaurants, adding lightness and zest to the country's already exquisite cuisine. Whether you travel to the Amazon rain forest or the urban jungle of São Paulo, you'll plunge into an exotic mix of colors, rhythms, and pastimes.

About the Restaurants

Eating is a national passion in Brazil, and portions are huge. In many restaurants plates are prepared for two people; when you order, ask if one plate will suffice. Some restaurants automatically bring a *couvert* (an appetizer course of such items as bread, cheese or pâté, olives, quail eggs, and the like). You'll be charged extra for this, and you're perfectly within your rights to send it back if you don't want it.

Mealtimes vary according to locale. In Rio and São Paulo, lunch and dinner are served later than in the United States. In restaurants lunch usually starts around 1 and can last until 3. Dinner is always eaten after 8 and in many cases not until 10. In smaller towns, dinner and lunch are taken at roughly the same time as in the States. It's hard to find breakfast outside a hotel restaurant. Unless otherwise noted, the restaurants listed in this guide are open daily for lunch and dinner.

Credit cards are widely accepted at restaurants in the major cities. In the countryside all but the smallest establishments generally accept credit cards as well. Gratuity is 10% of the total sum, and it is sometimes included in the bill; when it is not, it is optional to give the waiter a tip.

We mention reservations only when they're essential or not accepted; they're always a good idea. We mention dress only when men are required to wear a jacket and/or a tie.

The restaurants we list are the cream of the crop in each price category. Properties indicated by an ✕🏨 are lodging establishments whose restaurant warrants a special trip.

About the Hotels

When you consider your lodgings in Brazil, add these three terms to your vocabulary: *pousada* (inn), *fazenda* (farm), and "flat" or "block" hotel (apartment-hotel). Flat hotels are popular with Brazilians. These have kitchen facilities and room for a group. If you ask for a double room, you'll get a room for two people, but you're not guaranteed a double mattress. If you'd like to avoid twin beds, ask for a *cama de casal* ("couple's bed").

Carnaval (Carnival), the year's principal festival, occurs during the four days preceding Ash Wednesday. For top hotels in Rio, Salvador, and Recife—the three leading Carnaval cities—you must make reservations a year in advance. Hotel rates rise 20% on average for Carnaval. Not as well known outside Brazil but equally impressive is Rio's New Year's Eve celebration. More than a million people gather along Copacabana Beach for a massive fireworks display and to honor the sea goddess Iemanjá. To ensure a room, book at least six months in advance.

Hotels accept credit cards for payment, but first ask if there's a discount for cash. Try to bargain hard for a cash-on-the-barrel discount, then pay in local currency.

The lodgings we list are the cream of the crop in each price category. We always list the facilities that are available, but we don't specify whether they cost extra; when pricing accommodations, always ask what's included and what costs extra. Properties are assigned price categories based on the range between their least and most expensive standard double rooms at high season (excluding holidays). Properties marked ✕🏨 are lodging establishments whose restaurants warrant a special trip.

If you have 5 to 7 days
Choose one destination and fully explore it. Let your interests guide you. **São Paulo** offers lots of fine arts, fine dining, and fine nightlife. **Salvador** is perfect for beach lovers and Afro-Brazilian culture aficionados. **Rio** has its famous beaches as well as chic shops and many colonial sights.

If you have 10 to 14 days
If you have 10 days, you could fly to **Rio,** and spend a few days shopping as well as exploring Centro and the inland sights. Spend a few more days on the beaches, perhaps visiting Copacabana and Ipanema on one day, São Conrado on another, and Barra da Tijuca or Prainha and Grumari on still another. Another option is to spend some time in **São Paulo** and then catch a plane west to visit the phenomenal **Iguaçu Falls,** on the border of Argentina and Paraguay. With 14 days, you can visit the Amazon. Fly into **Manaus,** spend a few nights in a jungle lodge and take a boat trip on the river, then continue to **Belém** for a couple days of in-town sightseeing. For the best wildlife viewing in Brazil, consider spending at least four days in the **Pantanal.**

If you have 21 days
With 21 days you can easily combine more than one city and take in some bucolic sights as well. Consider visiting **Rio, São Paulo,** and **Iguacú.** Another option would be to explore **Salvador, Belém,** and/or **Manaus.** A five-day tour of the **Pantanal** could easily be added to your vacation. Or you could spend your entire vacation exploring the rainforest and its colonial cities on an Amazonian cruise, traveling from Manaus or Belém and stopping in **Santarém.**

Assume that hotels operate on the European Plan (EP, with no meals) unless we specify that they use either the Continental Plan (CP, with a Continental breakfast), Breakfast Plan (BP, with a full breakfast), Modified American Plan (MAP, with breakfast and dinner), Full American Plan (FAP, with all meals), or are all-inclusive (AI, including all meals and most activities).

WHAT IT COSTS In Reais				
	$$$$	**$$$**	**$$**	**$**	**¢**
RESTAURANTS	over $60	$45–$60	$30–$45	$15–$30	under $15
HOTELS	over $500	$375–$500	$250–$375	$125–$250	under $125

Restaurant prices are for a main course at dinner. Hotel prices are for two people in a standard double room in high season, excluding taxes.

Exploring Brazil

When planning your trip, don't underestimate the country's size or the travel times. Determine your interests up front, and pick your destinations accordingly. Beaches, fun, and sun are the calling cards of Rio and Salvador. São Paulo is a huge, bustling city, full of activity day and night. Use Manaus and Belém as hubs for trips into the Amazon.

RIO DE JANEIRO

Updated by
Denise Garcia
and Ana Lúcia
do Vale

Rio is a pulsating city, synonymous with the girl from Ipanema, the dramatic Pão de Açúcar Mountain, and the wild and outrageous Carnaval (Carnival) celebrations. But Rio is also a city of stunning architecture, good museums, and marvelous food; it's a teeming metropolis where the very rich and the very poor live in uneasy proximity and where enthusiasm is boundless—and contagious.

Rio was named—or misnamed—by the crew of a Portuguese ship that arrived here on January 1, 1502. Thinking they had found the mouth of a river, instead of the bay that became known as the Baía de Guanabara (Guanabara Bay), they dubbed the spot Rio de Janeiro (January River). Sixty-five years later, on the feast of St. Sebastian, the city was founded with the official name of São Sebastião do Rio de Janeiro.

In 1736 Brazil's colonial capital was moved to Rio from Salvador, and in 1889, when the country became independent, Rio was declared the capital of the Republic of Brazil. It held this title until 1960, when the federal government was moved to Brasília.

Prepare to have your senses engaged and your inhibitions untied. You'll be seduced by a host of images: the joyous bustle of vendors at Sunday's Feira Hippie (Hippie Fair); the tipsy babble at sidewalk cafés as patrons sip their last glass of icy beer under the stars; the blanket of lights beneath Pão de Açúcar; the bikers, joggers, strollers, and power walkers who parade along the beach each morning. Borrow the *carioca* (as residents of Rio are known) spirit for your stay; you may find yourself reluctant to give it back.

Exploring Rio de Janeiro

Cariocas divide their city into three sections: Zona Norte (North Zone), Zona Sul (South Zone), and Centro, the downtown area that separates them. Most of the tourist activity is in beach- and hotel-laden Zona Sul. From Copacabana you can walk the Avenida Atlântica to Ipanema. The western extension of Ipanema, Leblon, is an affluent, intimate community flush with good, small restaurants and bars (sadly, the water is polluted). The more distant southern beaches, beginning with São Conrado and extending past Barra da Tijuca to Grumari, become richer in natural beauty and increasingly isolated.

Most of historic structures are far-flung, though a few churches and villas are still tucked in and around Centro. Consider seeing them on an organized walking or bus tour. You can use the *metrô* (subway) and comfortable walking shoes to explore, or the bus is another option. Just be sure you know where you're going, and memorize some key phrases in Portuguese, as bus drivers don't speak English.

Centro & Environs

What locals generally refer to as Centro is a sprawling collection of several districts that contain the city's oldest neighborhoods, churches, and most enchanting cafés. Rio's beaches, broad boulevards, and mod-

Beaches

Brazil's Atlantic coast runs more than 7,300 km (4,600 mi), edging the country with sandy, palm-lined shores as well as some dramatic, rugged stretches. Many northeastern *praias* (beaches) offer sweeping, isolated expanses of gloriously high dunes; warm aquamarine waters; and constant breezes. Of course, Rio's famous beaches seem to embody the Brazilians themselves: vibrant, social, joyful, and beautiful. São Paulo's cleanest and best sands are along the north shore, where mountains and bits of Atlantic forest hug small sandy coves. Not all the best beaches are on the ocean. The banks of the Amazon and its tributaries also have splendid sandy stretches.

3

Carnaval

Carnaval (Carnival) is the biggest festivity of the year. In some areas events begin right after Reveillon (New Year's) and continue beyond the four main days of the celebration (just before the start of Lent) with smaller feasts and parties. At Carnaval's peak, businesses close throughout the country as Brazilians don costumes—from the elaborate to the barely there—and take to the streets singing and dancing. These four explosive days of color include formal parades as well as spontaneous street parties fueled by flatbed trucks that carry bands from neighborhood to neighborhood.

Eating Out

Between the extremes of sophistication and austere simplicity, each region has its own cuisine. You find exotic fish dishes in the Amazon, African-spiced dishes in Bahia, and in major cities, the variety of eateries is staggering: restaurants of all sizes and categories, snack bars, and fast-food outlets line downtown streets and fight for space in shopping malls. Pricing systems vary from open menus to buffets where you weigh your plate.

Outside the cities you find primarily typical, low-cost Brazilian meals that consist simply of *feijão preto* (black beans) and *arroz* (rice) served with beef, chicken, or fish. Manioc, a root vegetable that's used in a variety of ways, and beef are ubiquitous. Note that Brazilians eat few vegetables, and these often must be ordered separately.

Many Brazilian dishes are adaptations of Portuguese specialties. Fish stews called *caldeiradas* and beef stews called *cozidos* (a wide variety of vegetables boiled with different cuts of beef and pork) are popular, as is *bacalhau*, salt cod cooked in sauce or grilled. *Salgados* (literally, "salteds") are appetizers or snacks served in sit-down restaurants as well as at stand-up *lanchonetes* (luncheonettes). Dried salted meats form the basis of many dishes from the interior and northeast of Brazil. Brazil's national dish is *feijoada* (a stew of black beans, sausage, pork, and beef), which is often served with rice, shredded kale, orange slices, and manioc flour or meal—called *farofa* if it's coarsely ground, *farinha* if finely ground—that has been fried with onions, oil, and egg.

One of the most avid national passions is the *churrascaria*, where meats are roasted on spits over an open fire, usually *rodízio* style. Rodízio means "going around," and waiters circulate nonstop carrying skewers laden with charbroiled hunks of beef, pork, and chicken, which are sliced onto your plate with ritualistic ardor. For a set price you get all the meat and side dishes you can eat.

Brazilian *doces* (desserts), particularly those of Bahia, are very sweet, and many are descendants of the egg-based custards and puddings of Portugal and France. *Cocada* is shredded coconut caked with sugar; *quindim* is a small tart made from egg yolks and coconut; *doce de banana* (or any other fruit) is banana cooked in sugar; *ambrosia* is a lumpy milk-and-sugar pudding.

Coffee is served black and strong with sugar in demitasse cups and is called *cafezinho*. (Requests for *descafeinado* [decaf] are met with a firm shake of the head "no," a blank stare, or outright amusement.) Coffee is taken with milk—called *café com leite*—only at breakfast. Bottled mineral water is sold in two forms: carbonated or plain (*com gas* and *sem gas*, respectively).

The national drink is *caipirinha*, crushed lime, ice, sugar, and *cachaça*, a liquor distilled from sugarcane. Whipped with fruit juices and condensed milk, cachaça becomes *batida*. Bottled beer is sold in most restaurants, but many Brazilians prefer the tap beer, called *chopp*, sold in most bars and some restaurants. Be sure to try the carbonated soft drink *guaraná*, made with the Amazonian fruit of the same name.

Music A great variety of rhythms and dances, tunes and lyrics—*axé*, bossa nova, *forró*, *frevo*, *lundu*, *maxixe*, samba, *tropicalismo* weave a seamless and enchanting blend of European, African, and regional sounds into the popular musical arts. If the famed samba has the Bantu hip-swiveling lundu dance in its vein, it also has maxixe, a polkalike Afro-Portuguese shuffle. The more mournful samba (from the Bantu word *semba*, meaning "gyrating movement") originated in Rio de Janeiro in the early 20th century but wasn't refined until the 1940s, when Rio's Carnaval competitions began. Today its many forms include the pure samba *de morro* (literally, "of the hill"; figuratively, "of the poor neighborhood"), which is performed using only percussion instruments, and the samba *cançao* (the more familiar "samba song").

During the late 1950s the new-wave bossa nova—with Rio composers such as Tom Jobim, Vinícius de Morais, João Gilberto—began to blend mellow Brazilian samba, cool American jazz, and French impressionistic chanson. During the politically turbulent '60s and '70s, musicians inspired by the traditions of the Northeast combined contemporary instruments (including the electric guitar and keyboard) and avant-garde experimentation with samba and other traditional rhythms to produce a new style: tropicalismo. Tunes such as those by Caetano Veloso, Chico Buarque, and Gilberto Gil were upbeat even though the lyrics were highly critical of social injustice and political tyranny. In addition to being linked with tropicalismo, Brazil's Northeast is known for several other musical styles. Many of these have gained popularity throughout the country. Among them are forró (which uses the accordion at its best, and most rhythmic, advantage), and axé (a Bahian blend of samba and reggae).

ern architecture may be impressive; but its colonial structures, old narrow streets, and alleyways in leafy inland neighborhoods are no less so.

Numbers in the text correspond to numbers in the margin and on the Rio de Janeiro maps.

A GOOD TOUR (OR TWO) Start at the **Mosteiro de São Bento** ① ⛨ for your first taste of Brazilian baroque architecture. From here move south into the heart of Centro. At the beginning of Avenida Presidente Vargas is the **Igreja de Nossa Senhora da Candelária** ②. From this church walk south along Avenida 1° de Março, crossing it and heading west to a network of narrow lanes and alleys highlighted by the **Beco do Comércio** ③, a pedestrian street. After wandering this area, return to Avenida 1° de Março and walk southeast to the Praça 15 de Novembro, a square that's dominated by the **Paço Imperial** ④. A few blocks away is the large **Museu Histórico Nacional** ⑤.

From the Museu Histórico Nacional, follow Rua Santa Luzia southeast to Avenida Rio Branco, Centro's main thoroughfare. North one block is the Victorian **Biblioteca Nacional** ⑥, and one block up from it is the French neoclassical **Museu Nacional de Belas Artes** ⑦. In the middle of the next block up and across Rio Branco is the **Teatro Municipal** ⑧. Continue north on Rio Branco and turn left on Avenida Almirante Barroso. A short walk northwest brings you to the Largo da Carioca, a large square near the Carioca metrô stop. Atop a low hill overlooking it are the **Igreja de São Francisco da Penitência** ⑨ and the **Convento do Santo Antônio** ⑩. The **Catedral de São Sebastião do Rio de Janeiro** ⑪ is just south, off Avenida República do Chile, as is the station where you can take a *bonde* (trolley) over the **Aqueduto da Carioca** ⑫ and along Rua Joaquim Murtinho into Santa Teresa. This neighborhood is famed for its cobblestone streets and **Museu Chácara do Céu** ⑬.

TIMING & PRECAUTIONS Although you can follow this tour in a day if you set out early, you might want to break it up into two days or be selective about which museums you fully explore. You can also mix some of the southernmost sights in with those in the Flamengo, Botafogo, and Pão de Açúcar tours. However you organize your tour, you'll need plenty of energy to get everything in. Leave your camera at your hotel if you're planning to use public transportation. Wear no jewelry, and keep your cash in a money belt or safe pocket.

WHAT TO SEE ⑫ **Aqueduto da Carioca.** The imposing Carioca Aqueduct, with its 42 massive stone arches, was built between 1744 and 1750 to carry water from the Rio Carioca in the hillside neighborhood of Santa Teresa to Centro. In 1896 the city transportation company converted the then-abandoned aqueduct to a viaduct, laying trolley tracks along it. Since then Rio's distinctive trolley cars (called "bondes" because they were financed by foreign bonds) have carried people between Santa Teresa and Centro. Guard your belongings when you ride the bondes. Every Saturday at 10 the bondes make a 90-minute tour through Santa Teresa. ✉ *Estação Carioca, Rua Professor Lélio Gama, Centro,* ☎ *021/ 2240–5709 or 021/2240–5709* 🎟 *Aqueduct R$4, bonde trips R$1* ☉ *Bondes leave every 15 mins 6 AM–10 PM* Ⓜ *Carioca or Cinelândia.*

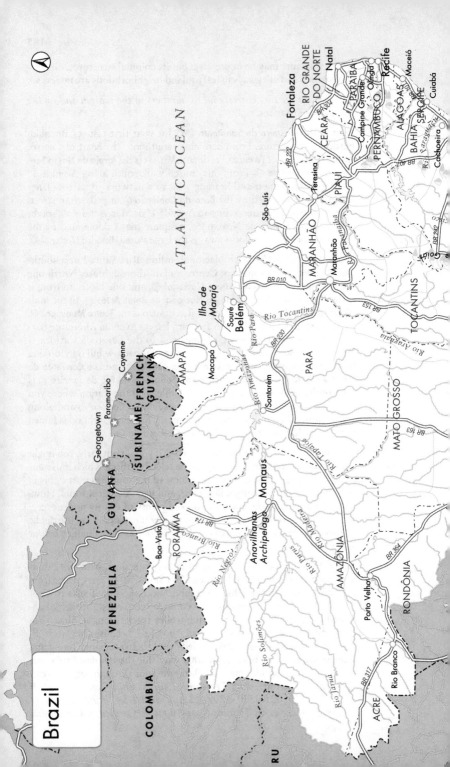

Brazil

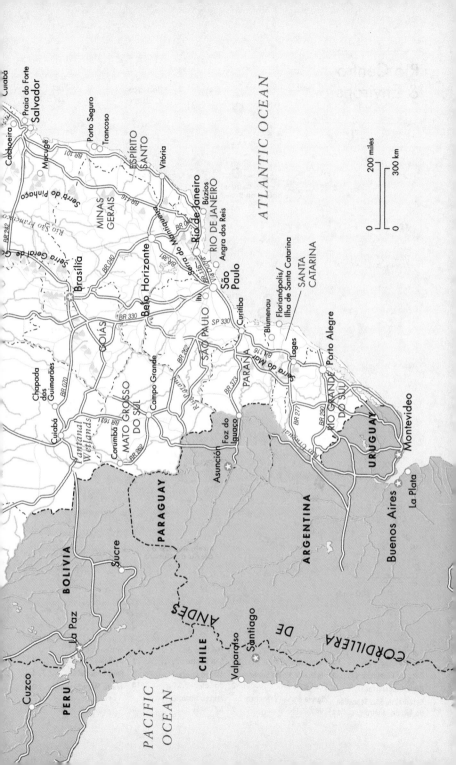

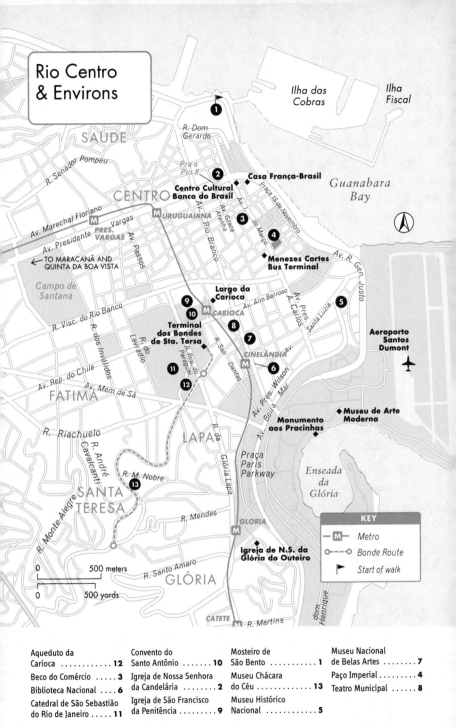

Rio Centro & Environs

SAUDE

R. Dom Gerardo

Praça Pio X

CENTRO

1

Ilha das Cobras

Ilha Fiscal

2 **Casa França-Brasil**

Centro Cultural Banco do Brasil

Guanabara Bay

Av. Marechal Floriano

M URUGUAIANA

Av. Presidente Vargas

PRES. VARGAS

Av. Graça Aranha

3

Praça 15 de Novembro

Av. Rio Branco

4

Av. 1º de Março

← TO MARACANÃ AND QUINTA DA BOA VISTA

Campo de Santana

R. Visc. do Rio Banco

R. dos Inválidos

Menezes Cortes Bus Terminal

Largo da Carioca

9

10

M CARIOCA

8

Terminal dos Bondes de Sta. Tersa

11

12

Av. Rep. do Chile

Av. Mem de Sá

FATIMA

Av. Alm Barroso

Av. A. Carlos

Av. Pres. Santa Luzia

5

Av. R. Gen. Justo

Aeroporto Santos Dumont

7

CINELÂNDIA

6

Av. Pres. Wilson

Av. Beira Mar

R. São. Dantas

R. Teófilo Ottoni

R. Rep. do Paraguai

LAPA

R. Riachuelo

R. André Cavalcanti

R. M. Nobre

13

R. Monte-Alegre

SANTA TERESA

R. Mendes

Monumento aos Pracinhas

♦ Museu de Arte Moderna

Praça Paris Parkway

Enseada da Glória

GLORIA

M

0   500 meters

0   500 yards

GLÓRIA

Igreja de N.S. da Glória do Outeiro

R. Santo Amaro

CATETE **M** R. Martins

dom Henrique

KEY

— **M** — *Metro*

○---○ *Bonde Route*

▶ *Start of walk*

❸ **Beco do Comércio.** A network of narrow streets and alleys centers on this pedestrian thoroughfare. The area is flanked by restored 18th-century homes, now converted to offices. The best known is the Edifício Telles de Menezes. A famous arch, the Arco do Teles, links this area with Praça 15 de Novembro. ⊠ *Praça 15 de Novembro 34, Centro* Ⓜ *Uruguaiana.*

❻ **Biblioteca Nacional.** Corinthian columns adorn the neoclassical National Library (built between 1905 and 1908), the first such establishment in Latin America. Its original archives were brought to Brazil by King João VI in 1808. Today it contains roughly 13 million books, including two 15th-century printed Bibles, and manuscript New Testaments from the 11th and 12th centuries; first-edition Mozart scores as well as scores by Carlos Gomes (who adapted the José de Alencar novel about Brazil's Indians, *O Guarani,* into an opera of the same name); books that belonged to Empress Teresa Christina; and many other manuscripts, prints, and drawings. Tours are available in English, but groups with more than 20 people must book the visit in advance. ⊠ *Av. Rio Branco 219, Centro* ☎ *021/2262–8255, 021/2220–9484 for guided tours for groups* ⊕ *www.bn.br* 🎟 *Tours R\$2* ☉ *Weekdays 9–8, Sat. 9–3; tours weekdays at 11, 1, and 4* Ⓜ *Cinelândia.*

⓫ **Catedral de São Sebastião do Rio de Janeiro.** The exterior of this circa-1960 metropolitan cathedral, which looks like a concrete beehive, can be off-putting. The daring modern design stands in sharp contrast to the baroque style of other churches. But don't judge until you've stepped inside. Outstanding stained-glass windows transform the interior— which is 80 meters (263 feet) high and 96 meters (315 feet) in diameter—into a warm yet serious place of worship that accommodates up to 20,000 people. An 8½-ton granite rock lends considerable weight to the concept of an altar. ⊠ *Av. República do Chile 245, Centro* ☎ *021/2240–2869* 🎟 *Free* ☉ *Daily 7–5:30* Ⓜ *Carioca or Cinelândia.*

❿ **Convento do Santo Antônio.** The Convent of St. Anthony was completed in 1780, but some parts date from 1615, making it one of Rio's oldest structures. Its baroque interior contains priceless colonial art—including wood carvings and wall paintings. The sacristy is covered with azulejos (Portuguese tiles). Note that the church has no bell tower: its bells hang from a double arch on the monastery ceiling. An exterior mausoleum contains the tombs of the offspring of Dom Pedro I and Dom Pedro II. ⊠ *Largo da Carioca 5, Centro* ☎ *021/2262–0129* 🎟 *Free* ☉ *By appointment only* Ⓜ *Carioca.*

❷ **Igreja de Nossa Senhora da Candelária.** The classic symmetry of Candelária's white dome and bell towers casts an unexpected air of sanity over the chaos of downtown traffic. The church was built on the site of a chapel founded in 1610 by Antônio de Palma after he survived a shipwreck; paintings in the present dome tell his tale. Construction on the present church began in 1775, and although it was formally dedicated by the emperor in 1811, work on the dome wasn't completed until 1877. The sculpted bronze doors were exhibited at the 1889 world's fair in Paris. ⊠ *Praça Pio X, Centro* ☎ *021/2233–2324* 🎟 *Free* ☉ *Weekdays 8–4, weekends 8–noon* Ⓜ *Uruguaiana.*

⑨ Igreja de São Francisco da Penitência. The church was completed in 1737, nearly four decades after it was started. Today it's famed for its wooden sculptures and rich gold-leaf interior. The nave contains a painting of St. Francis, the patron of the church—reportedly the first painting in Brazil done in perspective. ⊠ *Largo da Carioca 5, Centro* ☎ *021/ 2262–0197* ➂ *Free* ☉ *Wed–Fri. 8–noon and 2–4* Ⓜ *Carioca.*

❶ Mosteiro de São Bento. Just a glimpse of this church's main altar can fill you with awe. Layer upon layer of curvaceous wood carvings coated in gold create a sense of movement. Spiral columns whirl upward to capitals topped by cherubs so chubby and angels so purposeful they seem almost animated. Although the Benedictines arrived in 1586, they didn't begin work on this church and monastery until 1617. It was completed in 1641, but such artisans as Mestre Valentim (who designed the silver chandeliers) continued to add details almost through to the 19th century. Every Sunday at 10, mass is accompanied by Gregorian chants. ⊠ *Rua Dom Gerardo 32, Centro* ☎ *021/2291–7122* ➂ *Free* ☉ *Weekdays 7–11 and 2–5:30.*

★ ⑬ Museu Chácara do Céu. With its cobblestone streets and bohemian atmosphere, Santa Teresa is a delightfully eccentric neighborhood. Gabled Victorian mansions sit beside alpine-style chalets as well as more prosaic dwellings—many hanging at unbelievable angles from the flower-encrusted hills. Here, too, is the Museum of the Small Farm of the Sky. The outstanding collection of mostly modern works was left—along with the hilltop house that contains it—by one of Rio's greatest arts patrons, Raymundo de Castro Maya. Included are originals by 20th-century masters Picasso, Braque, Dalí, Degas, Matisse, Modigliani, and Monet. The Brazilian holdings include priceless 17th- and 18th-century maps and works by leading modernists. The grounds afford fine views of the aqueduct, Centro, and the bay. ⊠ *Rua Murtinho Nobre 93, Centro* ☎ *021/2507–1932* ➂ *R$2* ☉ *Wed.–Mon. noon–5.*

❺ Museu Histórico Nacional. The building that houses the National History Museum dates from 1762, though some sections—such as the battlements—were erected as early as 1603. It seems appropriate that this colonial structure should exhibit relics that document Brazil's history. Among its treasures are rare papers, Latin American coins, carriages, cannons, and religious art. ⊠ *Praça Marechal Ancora, Centro* ☎ *021/2550–9224 or 021/2220–2328* ➂ *Tues.–Sat. R$5, free Sun.* ☉ *Tues.–Fri. 10–5, weekends 2–6* Ⓜ *Carioca or Cinelândia.*

❼ Museu Nacional de Belas Artes. Works by Brazil's leading 19th- and 20th-century artists fill the space at the National Museum of Fine Arts. The most notable canvases are those by the country's best-known modernist, Cândido Portinari, but be on the lookout for such gems as Leandro Joaquim's heartwarming 18th-century painting of Rio (a window to a time when fishermen still cast nets in the waters below the landmark Igreja de Nossa Senhora da Glória do Outeiro). After wandering the picture galleries, tour the extensive collections of folk and African art. ⊠ *Av. Rio Branco 199, Centro* ☎ *021/2240–0068* ⊕ *www.iphan.gov.br* ➂ *R$4, free Sun.* ☉ *Tues.–Fri. 10–6, weekends 2–6* Ⓜ *Carioca or Cinelândia.*

❹ Paço Imperial. This two-story colonial building with thick stone walls and ornate entrance was built in 1743 and for the next 60 years was the headquarters for Brazil's captains (viceroys), appointed by the Portuguese court in Lisbon. When King João VI arrived, he made it his royal palace. After Brazil's declaration of independence, emperors Dom Pedro I and II called the palace home. When the monarchy was overthrown, the building became Rio's central post office. Restoration work in the 1980s transformed it into a cultural center and concert hall. The building houses a restaurant, a coffee shop, a stationery-and-CD shop, and a movie theater. The square on which the palace sits, Praça 15 de Novembro, known in colonial days as Largo do Paço, has witnessed some of Brazil's most significant historic moments: it is where two emperors were crowned, slavery was abolished, and Emperor Pedro II was deposed. The square's modern name is a reference to the date of the declaration of the Republic of Brazil: November 15, 1889. ⊠ *Praça 15 de Novembro 48, Centro* ☎ *021/2533–4407* ⊕ *www.pacoimperial.com.br* ⊠ *Free* ☉ *Tues.–Sun. noon–6:30.*

❽ Teatro Municipal. Carrara marble, stunning mosaics, glittering chandeliers, bronze and onyx statues, gilded mirrors, German stained-glass windows, brazilwood inlay floors, and murals by Brazilian artists Eliseu Visconti and Rodolfo Amoedo make the Municipal Theater opulent, indeed. Opened in 1909, it's a scaled-down version of the Paris Opera House. The main entrance and first two galleries are particularly ornate. As you climb to the upper floors, the decor becomes more ascetic, a reflection of a time when different classes entered through different doors and sat in separate sections. The theater seats 2,357—with outstanding sight lines—for its dance performances and classical music concerts. ⊠ *Praça Floriano 210, Centro* ☎ *021/2299–1717, 021/2299–1695 for guided tour* ⊠ *Tours R$4* ☉ *Tours by appointment weekdays 10–5* ⊕ *www.theatromunicipal.rj.gov.br* Ⓜ *Cinelândia or Carioca.*

Flamengo, Botafogo & Pão de Açúcar

These neighborhoods and their most famous peak—Pão de Açúcar—are like a bridge between the southern beach districts and Centro. Several highways intersect here, making it a hub for drives to Corcovado, Copacabana, Barra, or Centro. The metrô also travels through the area. Although the districts are largely residential, Rio Sul—one of the city's most popular shopping centers—is here, as are some of the city's best museums and public spaces.

The eponymous beach at Flamengo no longer draws swimmers (its gentle waters look appealing but are polluted; the people you see are sunning, not swimming). A marina sits on a bay at one end of the beach, which is connected via a busy boulevard to the smaller beach (also polluted), at Botafogo. This neighborhood is home to the city's yacht club, and when Rio was Brazil's capital, it was also the site of the city's glittering embassy row. The embassies were long ago transferred to Brasília, but the mansions that housed them remain. Among Botafogo's more interesting mansion- and tree-lined streets are Mariana, Sorocaba, Matriz, and Visconde e Silva.

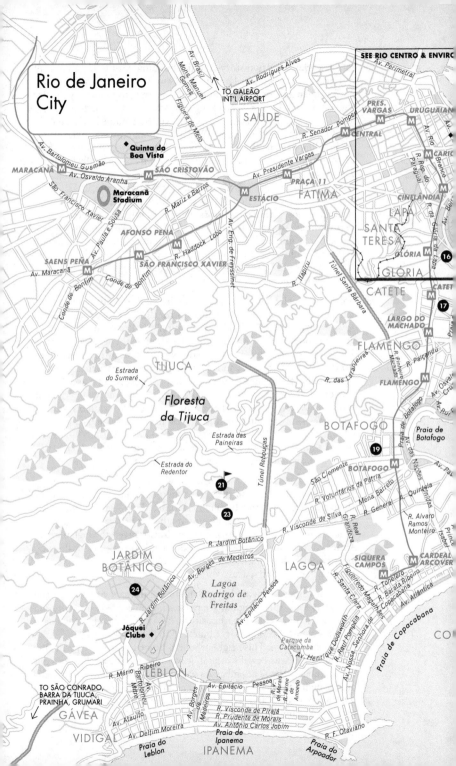

KEY

🚩 *Start of walk*

Ⓜ *Metro*

⊦⊦⊦⊦⊦ *Street Car*

••••• *Cable Car*

Botafogo faces tiny sheltered Urca, which is separated by Pão de Açúcar from a small patch of yellow sand called Vermelha. This beach is, in turn, blocked by the Urubu and Leme mountains from the 1-km (½-mi) Leme Beach at the start of the Zona Sul.

A GOOD TOUR   Start at the northern end of the lovely, landscaped Atêrro do Flamengo (Flamengo Landfill) at the **Museu de Arte Moderna (MAM)** ⑭ ▶. Nearby is the **Monumento aos Pracinhas** ⑮, which honors the dead of World War II. Wander south along the Atêrro before hopping into a cab and heading inland to the hilltop **Igreja de Nossa Senhora da Glória do Outeiro** ⑯. Get on the subway—called the *metrô*—at the Glória station and take it one stop to the Catete terminal, or walk south along Rua da Glória da Lapa to Rua da Catete and the **Palácio do Catete** ⑰. From here, either head to the Parque do Flamengo by cab and walk south to the **Museu Carmen Miranda** ⑱, or take the metrô to the Botafogo stop and the nearby **Casa Rui Barbosa** ⑲. Finish the tour by riding the cable car up the **Pão de Açúcar** ⑳ for panoramic views of the bay and the neighborhoods you've just explored.

TIMING &   This tour takes a full day and involves a lot of walking and time out-
PRECAUTIONS   doors. You can shorten the itinerary by taking a cab to sights off the Atêrro do Flamengo and/or from one end of the Atêrro to the other. As always, keep your money and other valuables out of sight while strolling.

WHAT TO SEE   **Casa Rui Barbosa.** Slightly inland from the Atêrro is a museum in what
⑲   was once the house of 19th-century Brazilian statesmen and scholar Rui Barbosa (a liberal from Bahia State who drafted one of Brazil's early constitutions). The pink mansion dates from 1849 and contains memorabilia of Barbosa's life, including his 1913 car and an extensive library that's often consulted by scholars from around the world. ⊠ *Rua São Clemente 134, Botafogo* ☎ *021/2537–0036* ⊠ *Free* ☉ *Tues.–Fri. 9–4, weekends 2–5* Ⓜ *Botafogo.*

⑯   **Igreja de Nossa Senhora da Glória do Outeiro.** Set atop a hill, this baroque church is visible from many spots in the city, making it a landmark that's truly cherished by the cariocas. Its location was a strategic point in the city's early days. Estácio da Sá took this hill from the French in the 1560s and then went on to expand the first settlement and found a city for the Portuguese. The church, which wasn't built until 1739, is notable for its octagonal floor plan, large dome, ornamental stonework, and vivid tile work. The church has a small museum inside with baroque art. Tours are given by appointment only. ⊠ *Praça Nossa Senhora da Glória 135, Glória* ☎ *021/2557–4600* ⊠ *Church free, museum R$2* ☉ *Tues.–Fri. 9–noon and 1–5, weekends 9–noon* Ⓜ *Glória.*

⑮   **Monumento aos Pracinhas.** The Monument to the Brazilian Dead of World War II (the nation sided with the Allies during the conflict) is actually a museum and monument combined. It houses military uniforms, medals, stamps, and documents belonging to soldiers. Two soaring columns flank the tomb of an unknown soldier. The first Sunday of each month Brazil's armed forces perform a colorful changing of the guard. ⊠ *Parque Brigadeiro Eduardo Gomes, Flamengo* ☎ *021/2240–1283* ⊠ *Free* ☉ *Tues.–Sun. 10–4* Ⓜ *Cinelândia.*

⓭ **Museu de Arte Moderna (MAM).** In a striking concrete-and-glass building, the Modern Art Museum has a collection of some 1,700 works by artists from Brazil and elsewhere. It also hosts significant special exhibitions and has a movie theater that plays art films. ⊠ *Av. Infante Dom Henrique 85, Flamengo* ☎ *021/2240–4944* ⊕ *www.mamrio.org.br* 🖼 *Thurs.–Tues. R$8, Wed. R$4* ⊘ *Tues.–Fri. noon–6, weekends noon–7* Ⓜ *Cinelândia.*

⓲ **Museu Carmen Miranda.** This tribute to the Brazilian bombshell is in a circular building that resembles a concrete spaceship (its door even opens up rather than out). On display are some of the elaborate costumes and incredibly high platform shoes worn by the actress, who was viewed as a national icon by some and as a traitor to true Brazilian culture by others. Hollywood photos of Miranda, who was only 46 when she died of a heart attack in 1955, show her in her trademark turban and jewelry. Also here are her records and movie posters and such memorabilia as the silver hand mirror she was clutching when she died. Guided tours are given by appointment, but guides do not speak English. ⊠ *Atêrro do Flamengo park, Av. Rui Barbosa s/n, across from Av. Rui Barbosa 560, Flamengo* ☎ *021/2551–2597* ⊕ *www.sec.rj.gov.br* 🖼 *R$2* ⊘ *Weekdays 11–5, weekends 1–5* Ⓜ *Flamengo.*

⓱ **Palácio do Catete.** Once the villa of a German baron, the elegant, 19th-century granite-and-marble palace became the presidential residence after the 1889 coup overthrew the monarchy and established the Republic of Brazil. Eighteen presidents lived here. Gaze at the palace's gleaming parquet floors and intricate bas relief ceilings as you wander through its **Museu da República** (Museum of the Republic). The permanent exhibits include a shroud-draped view of the bedroom where President Getúlio Vargas committed suicide in 1954 after the military threatened to overthrow his government. Presidential memorabilia, furniture, and paintings that date from the proclamation of the republic to the end of Brazil's military regime in 1985 are also displayed. A small contemporary art gallery, a movie theater, a restaurant, and a theater operate within the museum. ⊠ *Rua do Catete 153, Catete* ☎ *021/2558–6350* 🖼 *Tues. and Thurs.–Sun. R$5, free Wed.* ⊘ *Tues.–Fri. noon–5:30, weekends 2–5:30* Ⓜ *Catete.*

FodorśChoice
★

★ ⓴ **Pão de Açúcar.** This soaring 1,300-meter (390-foot) granite block at the mouth of Baía de Guanabara was originally called *pau-nh-acugua* (high, pointed peak) by the indigenous Tupi people. To the Portuguese the phrase seemed similar to *pão de açúcar,* or "sugarloaf"; the rock's shape reminded them of the conical loaves in which refined sugar was sold. Italian-made bubble cars holding 75 passengers each move up the mountain in two stages. The first stop is at Morro da Urca, a smaller, 212-meter (705-foot) mountain; the second is at the summit of Pão de Açúcar itself. The trip to each level takes three minutes. In high season long lines form for the cable car; the rest of the year the wait is seldom more than 30 minutes. ⊠ *Av. Pasteur 520, Praia Vermelha, Urca* ☎ *021/2546–8400* ⊕ *www.bondinho.com.br* 🖼 *R$30* ⊘ *Daily 8 AM–10 PM.*

Parque do Flamengo. Flanking the Baía de Guanabara from the Glória neighborhood to Flamengo is this waterfront park designed by landscape architect Roberto Burle Marx. Paths used for jogging, walking, and biking wind through it. On weekends the freeway beside the park is closed to traffic, and the entire area becomes one enormous public space. ⊠ *Inland of the beach, from Glória to Botafogo* 🎫 *Free* 🕙 *Daily 24 hours* Ⓜ *Glória or Flamengo.*

Zona Sul

Rio is home to 23 *praias* (beaches), an almost continuous 73-km (45-mi) ribbon of sand. All are public and are served by buses and taxis. At intervals along the beaches at Copacabana and Ipanema are small *postos* (bathhouses) with washrooms, showers, and dressing rooms that can be used for about R$2. Kiosks manned by police also pepper the avenues running parallel to the beach, and crime has dropped dramatically as a result.

A GOOD BEACH STRATEGY
Although the circuit starts to the northeast at the beaches of Flamengo, Botafogo, Urca, and Vermelha, the waters off their shores are often polluted. The best sands are farther south. **Praia do Leme,** which is popular with senior citizens, runs into the city's grande dame, **Praia de Copacabana.** Its 3-km (2-mi) stretch is lined by a sidewalk whose swirling pattern was designed by Roberto Burle Marx. Copacabana has outdoor cafés, high-rise hotels, and juice kiosks. At its end cut around on the small **Praia Arpoador** or take Avenida Francisco Otaviano to **Praia de Ipanema.**

Beyond Ipanema and Leblon, mountains again form a natural wall separating you from the next beach, little Vidigal. Still more mountains block it from **São Conrado,** a beach where hang gliders land after leaping from a nearby peak. A highway through a mountain tunnel forms the link between São Conrado and the long, spectacular **Praia Barra da Tijuca.** Its waters are clean and cool, and its far end, known as Recreio dos Bandeirantes, was home to a small fishing village until the late 1960s. Beyond are **Prainha,** whose rough seas make it popular with surfers, and the lovely **Praia de Grumari.** It's worth continuing down the hill beyond Grumari to the **Sítio Roberto Burle Marx** for an in-depth look at one of Brazil's greatest artists.

City buses and small green minivans pick you up and drop you off wherever you request along the shore. If you're brave enough to drive, the city has established small, affordable parking lots (look for attendants in green-and-yellow vests) along waterfront avenues. There are several organized tours that take in the beaches, and agents at Turismo Clássico can arrange for drivers and guides.

TIMING & PRECAUTIONS
Although you can tour the shoreline in several hours, consider spending a full day just wandering from Copacabana to Ipanema or sunbathing on Barra da Tijuca. Remember that Rio's beaches aren't just about sunning and swimming; they're also about volleyball games, strolling, biking, and people-watching.

Don't shun the beaches because of reports of crime, but *do* take precautions. Leave jewelry, passports, and large sums of cash at your hotel; avoid wandering alone and at night; and be alert when groups of friendly youths engage you in conversation (sometimes they're trying to distract you while one of their cohorts snatches your belongings). The biggest danger is the sun. From 10 to 3 the rays are merciless, making heavy-duty sunscreen, hats, cover-ups, and plenty of liquids essential; you can also rent a beach umbrella from a vendor or your hotel. Hawkers stroll the beaches with beverages—take advantage of their services. Lifeguard stations are found every kilometer. (Note: beach vendors aren't supposed to charge more than R$5.50 for a bottle of beer or other alcoholic beverage and R$3 for a coconut water.)

WHAT TO SEE **Praia Barra da Tijuca.** Cariocas consider the beach at Barra da Tijuca to
★ be Rio's best, and the 18-km-long (11-mi-long) sweep of sand and jostling waves certainly is dramatic. Pollution isn't a problem, and in many places neither are crowds. Barra's water is cooler and its breezes more refreshing than those at other beaches. Strong waves in spots attract surfers, windsurfers, and jet skiers, but you should swim with caution. The beach is set slightly below a sidewalk, where cafés and restaurants beckon. Condos have also sprung up here, and the city's largest shopping centers and supermarkets have made inland Barra their home.

At the far end of Barra's beachfront avenue, Sernambetiba, is Recreio dos Bandeirantes, a 1-km (½-mi) stretch of sand anchored by a huge rock, which creates a small protected cove. Its quiet seclusion makes it popular with families. The calm, pollution-free water, with no waves or currents, is good for bathing, but don't try to swim around the rock—it's bigger than it looks. At this writing, hotels, restaurants, and other tourist attractions are opening in the Barra da Tijuca neighborhood in preparation for the 2007 Pan-American Games, which are to be held here.

Praia de Copacabana. Maddening traffic, noise, packed apartment blocks, and a world-famous beach—this is Copacabana, Manhattan with bikinis. A walk along the neighborhood's classic crescent is a must to see the essence of beach culture, a cradle-to-grave lifestyle that begins with toddlers accompanying their parents to the water and ends with graying seniors walking hand in hand along the sidewalk. It's here that athletic men play volleyball using only their feet and heads, not their hands. Brazilians call it *futevôlei*. As you can tell by all the goal nets, soccer is also popular (Copacabana hosts the world beach soccer championships every January and February). You can swim here, although pollution levels and a strong undertow can sometimes be discouraging.

Copacabana's privileged live on beachfront Avenida Atlântica, famed for its wide mosaic sidewalks, hotels, and cafés. On Sunday two of the avenue's lanes are closed to traffic and are taken over by joggers, rollerbladers, cyclists, and pedestrians. Two blocks inland from and parallel to the beach is Avenida Nossa Senhora de Copacabana, the main commercial street, with shops, restaurants, and sidewalks crowded with the colorful characters that give Copacabana its flavor. ⊠ *Av. Princesa Isabel to Rua Francisco Otaviano, Copacabana.*

★ **Praia de Grumari.** About five minutes beyond Prainha, off Estrada de Guaratiba, is Grumari, a beach that seems an incarnation of paradise. What it lacks in amenities—it has only a couple of groupings of thatch-roof huts selling drinks and snacks—it makes up for in natural beauty: the glorious red sands of its quiet cove are backed by low, lush hills.

Weekends are extremely crowded. Take a lunch break at Restaurante Pointe de Grumari, which serves excellent fish dishes. ⊠ *Grumari.*

Praia de Ipanema. As you stroll along this beach, you catch a cross section of the city's residents, each favoring a particular stretch. One area is dominated by families, another is favored by the gay community. A spot near Copacabana, **Praia do Arpoador** (⊠ Rua Joaquim Nabubo to Rua Francisco Otaviano, Arpoador), tantalizes surfers. Ipanema, nearby Praia do Leblon (whose waters are too polluted for swimming), and the blocks surrounding Lagoa Rodrigo de Freitas are part of Rio's money belt. Sophisticated boutiques line Rua Garcia D'Ávila and Praça Nossa Senhora da Paz has wonderful restaurants and bars. ⊠ *Rua Joaquim Nabuco to Av. Epitácio Pessoa, Ipanema.*

Praia do Leme. A natural extension of Copacabana Beach to the northeast, toward the Pão de Açúcar, is Leme Beach. A rock formation juts into the water here, forming a quiet cove that's less crowded than the rest of the beach. Along a sidewalk, at the side of the mountain overlooking Leme, anglers stand elbow to elbow with their lines dangling into the sea. ⊠ *Av. Princesa Isabel to Morro do Leme, Leme.*

★ **Prainha.** The length of two football fields, Prainha is a vest-pocket beach favored by surfers, who take charge of it on weekends. The swimming is good, but watch out for surfboards. On weekdays, especially in the off-season, the beach is almost empty; on weekends, particularly in peak season, the road to and from Prainha and nearby Grumari is so crowded it almost becomes a parking lot. ⊠ *35 km (22 mi) west of Ipanema on the coast road; accessible only by car from Av. Sernambetiba.*

São Conrado. Blocked by the imposing Dois Irmãos Mountain, Avenida Niemeyer snakes along rugged cliffs that offer spectacular sea views on the left. The road returns to sea level again in São Conrado, a natural amphitheater surrounded by forested mountains and the ocean. A short stretch along its beach includes the condominiums of a former president, the ex-wife of another former president, an ex-governor of Rio de Janeiro State, and a one-time Central Bank president. The far end of São Conrado is marked by the towering Pedra da Gávea, a huge flat-top granite block. Next to it is Pedra Bonita, the mountain from which gliders depart. (Although this beach was the city's most popular a few years ago, contaminated water has discouraged swimmers.) Ironically, the neighborhood is surrounded by favelas (shantytowns). Much of the high ground has been taken over by Rio's largest favela, Rocinha, where an estimated 200,000 people live. ⊠ *Just west of Leblon.*

★ **Sítio Roberto Burle Marx** (Roberto Burle Marx Farm). Beyond Grumari, the road winds through mangrove swamps and tropical forest. It's an apt setting for the plantation-turned-museum where Brazil's famous landscape designer Roberto Burle Marx is memorialized. Marx, the mind behind Rio's mosaic beachfront walkways and the Atêrro do Flamengo, was said to have "painted with plants" and was the first designer to use Brazilian flora in his projects. More than 3,500 species—including some discovered by and named for Marx as well as many on the endangered list—flourish at this 100-acre estate. Plant groupings mix the modern with the traditional. The results are both whimsical and elegant. The house is now a cultural center full of Marx's belongings, including collections of folk art. ✉ *Estrada Barra de Guaratiba 2019, Pedra de Guaratiba* ☎ *021/2410–1412* 💲 *R$5* ◷ *By appointment only.*

The Lush Inland

Beyond the sand and sea in the Zona Sul are lush parks and gardens as well as marvelous museums, seductive architecture, and tantalizing restaurants. You can't say you've seen Rio until you've taken in the view from Corcovado and then strolled through its forested areas or beside its inland lagoon—hanging out just like a true carioca.

Numbers in the text correspond to numbers in the margin and on the Rio de Janeiro City map.

A GOOD TOUR Head first to the imposing **Corcovado** ㉑ ▶ and its hallmark Cristo Redentor statue. As you slide up the side of the steep mountain in the train, you pass through the lush forested area known as **Floresta da Tijuca** ㉒. (To explore the forest more, hire a cab or join a tour that offers both Corcovado and Floresta da Tijuca.) Back down the hill and at the train station again, stroll downhill a short distance to the **Museu de Arte Naïf do Brasil** ㉓. The same street leads uphill to the delightful colonial square called Largo do Boticário—a good place to rest your feet. From here grab a taxi and journey west to the inviting **Jardim Botânico** ㉔, across from which is the Jóckey Clube. The botanical gardens are within walking distance from the Lagoa Rodrigo de Freitas, the giant saltwater lagoon that serves as one of the city's playgrounds—for children and adults alike.

TIMING & PRECAUTIONS You can see these sights in a day if you start early. Try to visit Corcovado on a clear day; clouds often obscure the Christ statue on its summit. You can join an organized tour or hire a cabbie to take you out for the day (public transportation doesn't conveniently reach these sights). The security is good at Corcovado and Floresta da Tijuca, so you can usually carry your camera without worry. At the Jardim Botânico and the Lagoa Rodrigo de Freitas, however, be alert. Throughout this tour, keep valuables in a money belt or somewhere else out of sight.

WHAT TO SEE ▶ ㉑ Fodor'sChoice ★ **Corcovado.** There's an eternal argument about which view is better, from Pão de Açúcar or from here. Corcovado has two advantages: at 690 meters (2,300 feet), it's nearly twice as high and offers an excellent view of Pão de Açúcar itself. The sheer 300-meter (1,000-foot) granite face of Corcovado (the name means "hunchback" and refers to the mountain's shape) has always been a difficult undertaking for climbers.

It wasn't until 1921, the centennial of Brazil's independence from Portugal, that someone had the idea of placing a statue atop Corcovado. A team of French artisans headed by sculptor Paul Landowski was assigned the task of erecting a statue of Christ with his arms apart as if embracing the city. (Nowadays, mischievous cariocas say Christ is getting ready to clap for his favorite escola de samba.) It took 10 years, but on October 12, 1931, the *Cristo Redentor* (Christ the Redeemer) was inaugurated. The sleek, modern figure rises more than 30 meters

(100 feet) from a 6-meter (20-foot) pedestal and weighs 700 tons. In the evening a powerful lighting system transforms it into a dramatic icon.

There are two ways to reach the top from the entrance to Corcovado: by cogwheel train (R$30, which includes R$5 entrance fee) or by taxi (R$10 per person, plus R$5 entrance fee). The train, built in 1885, provides delightful views of Ipanema and Leblon from an absurd angle of ascent, as well as a close look at thick vegetation and butterflies. (You may wonder what those oblong medicine balls hanging from the trees are, the ones that look like spiked watermelons tied to ropes—they're *jaca,* or jackfruit.) Trains leave the **Cosme Velho station** (⊠ Rua Cosme Velho 513, Cosme Velho ☎ 021/2558–1329 ⊕ www.corcovado.com. br) for the steep, 5-km (3-mi), 17-minute ascent. Late-afternoon trains are the most popular; on weekends be prepared for a long wait. To get to the summit, you can climb up 220 steep, zigzagging staircases (which was the only option available prior to 2003), or take an escalator or a panoramic elevator. If you choose the stairs, you pass little cafés and shops selling film and souvenirs along the way. Once at the top, all of Rio stretches out before you. ⊠ *Floresta da Tijuca* ☎ *021/2558–1329* ▧ *R$5* ⊘ *Daily 8:30–6:30; trains depart every 30 mins.*

㉒ **Floresta da Tijuca** (Quagmire Forest). Surrounding Corcovado is the dense, tropical Tijuca Forest. Once part of a Brazilian nobleman's estate, it's studded with exotic trees and thick jungle vines and has a delightful waterfall, the Cascatinha de Taunay. About 180 meters (200 yards) beyond the waterfall is the small pink-and-purple Capela Mayrink (Mayrink Chapel), with painted panels by the 20th-century Brazilian artist Cândido Portinari.

From several points along this national park's 96 km (60 mi) of narrow winding roads the views are breathtaking. Some of the most spectacular are from Dona Marta, on the way up Corcovado; the Emperor's Table, supposedly where Brazil's last emperor, Pedro II, took his court for picnics; and, farther down the road, the Chinese View, the area where Portuguese king João VI allegedly settled the first Chinese immigrants to Brazil, who came in the early 19th century to develop tea plantations. A great way to see the forest is by Jeep; you can arrange tours through a number of agencies, such as **Jeep Tour** (⊠ Praça Seve 22, Galpão, São Cristovão ☎ 021/3890–9336, 021/3878–0325, 021/3878–0324, or 021/9977–9610), which is open daily 7 AM–10 PM. Jeep tours are about four hours and cost around R$80. ⊠ *Entrance at Praça Afonso Viseu 561, Tijuca* ☎ *021/2492–2253* ▧ *Free* ⊘ *Daily 8–6.*

㉔ **Jardim Botânico.** The 340-acre Botanical Garden contains more than 5,000 species of tropical and subtropical plants and trees, including 900 varieties of palms (some more than a century old) and more than 140 species of birds. The temperature is usually a good 12°C (22°F) cooler in the shady garden that was created in 1808 by Portuguese king João VI during his exile in Brazil. In 1842 the garden gained its most impressive adornment, the Avenue of the Royal Palms, 720-meter (800-yard) double row of 134 soaring royal palms. Elsewhere in the gardens, the Casa dos Pilões, an old gunpowder factory, has been restored and displays objects that pertained to both the nobility and to their slaves. ✉ *Rua Jardim Botânico 1008* ☎ *021/2294–6012* ⊕ *www.jbrj.gov.br* ✑ *R$4* ⊙ *Daily 8–5.*

㉓ Museu de Arte Naif do Brasil. More than 8,000 art naïf works by Brazil's
FodorśChoice best (as well as works by other self-taught painters from around the world)
★ grace the walls of this lovely colonial mansion that was once the studio of painter Eliseu Visconti. The pieces in what is reputedly the world's largest and most complete collection of primitive paintings date from the 15th century through contemporary times. Don't miss the colorful, colossal 7×4–meter (22×13–foot) canvas that depicts the city of Rio; it reportedly took five years to complete. This museum sprang from a collection started decades ago by a jewelry designer who later created a foundation to oversee the art. ✉ *Rua Cosme Velho 561, Cosme Velho* ☎ *021/2205–8612 or 021/2205–8547* ✑ *R$8* ⊙ *Tues.–Fri. 10–6, weekends noon–6.*

Where to Eat

With more than 900 restaurants, Rio's dining choices are broad, from low-key Middle Eastern cafés to elegant contemporary eateries with award-winning kitchens and first-class service. The succulent offerings in the *churrascarias* (restaurants specializing in grilled meats) can be mesmerizing for meat lovers—especially the places that serve *rodízio* style (grilled meat on skewers is continuously brought to your table—until you can eat no more). Hotel restaurants often serve the national dish, feijoada (a hearty stew of black beans and pork), on Saturday—sometimes Friday, too.

For vegetarians there is an abundance of salad bars, where you pay for your greens by the kilo. And seafood restaurants are everywhere. Note that it's perfectly safe to eat fresh produce in clean, upscale places; avoid shellfish in all but the best restaurants.

Cariocas have scaled back on *almoço* (lunch), which used to be a full meal, and now tend to eat only a *lanche* (sandwich). Dinner is a late affair; if you arrive at 7, you may be the only one in the restaurant. Popular places seat customers until well after midnight on weekends, when the normal closing hour is 2 AM. Cariocas love to linger in *botecos,* plain but pleasant bars that may also serve food, and such establishments abound. Most serve dishes in the $–$$ range, and portions are large enough for two people to share.

Brazilian

$$$–$$$$ ✕ **Esplanada Grill.** This churrascaria serves high-quality meat like T-bone steak or *picanha,* a tasty Brazilian cut of beef marbled with some fat. All the grilled dishes come with fried palm hearts, baked potatoes, and rice. An average meal is R$80. ✉ *Rua Barão da Torre 600, Ipanema* ☎ *021/2512–2970* ▤ *DC, MC, V* Ⓜ *Siquera Campos, then shuttle bus to Praça General Osório.*

$$$ ✕ **Marius Crustáceos.** This well-regarded churrascaria serves more than a dozen types of sizzling meats rodízio style. Marius is famed for taking the usual meat cuts to a higher level of sophistication. There is a great

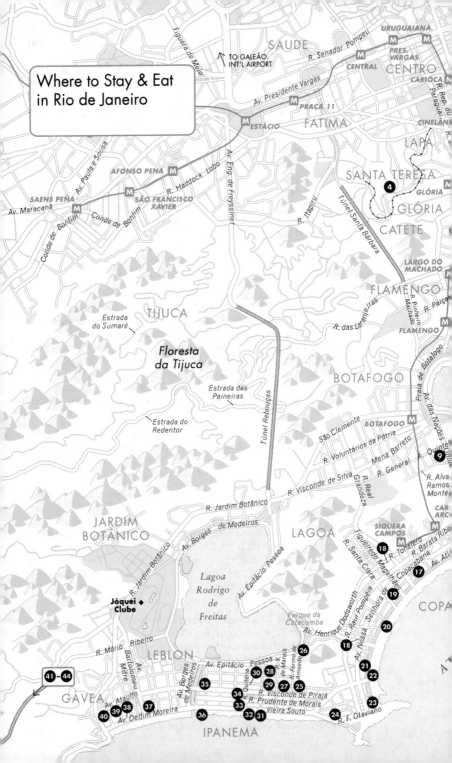

Where to Stay & Eat
in Rio de Janeiro

TO GALEÃO
INT'L AIRPORT

Menezes Cortes
Bus Terminal

Baía de
Guanabara

Aeroporto
Santos
Dumont

Av. Gal. Justo

Av. Gen. Carlos

Av. Beira Mar

M

Av. Pres. A. Carlos

Av. Rio Branco

Parque do
Flamengo

CATETE

Praia do Flamengo

Av. Oswaldo
Cruz

Av. Rui Barbosa

URCA

Av. João
Luis Alves

Av. São Sebastião

Av. Portugal

Av. Pasteur

Av. Princesa Isabel

VERDE

VERMELHA

R. Gustavo
Sampaio

LEME

ATLANTIC OCEAN

COPABANA

0 ___ 1 mile
0 ___ 1 km

KEY

Ⓜ Metro

Street Car

Cable Car

variety of side dishes, including Japanese food and fish. ⊠ *Av. Atlântica 290, loja A, Leme* ☏ *021/2542–2393* ▤ *DC, MC, V.*

$$ ✕**Porcão.** Waiters at these rodízio-style churrascarias fly up and down
FodorśChoice between rows of linen-draped tables wielding giant skewers laden with
★   sizzling barbecued beef, pork, and chicken. Save room if you can: the
papaya cream pudding topped by a bit of cassis shouldn't be missed.
⊠ *Rua Barão da Torre 218, Ipanema* ☏ *021/2522–0999* ⏣ *Reservations not accepted* ▤ *AE, DC, MC, V* Ⓜ *Siquera Campos, then shuttle bus to Praça General Osório* ⊠ *Av. Armando Lombardi 591, Barra da Tijuca* ☏ *021/2492–2001* ⊠ *Av. Infante Dom Henrique, Parque do Flamengo* ☏ *021/2554–8862* Ⓜ *Flamengo.*

★ **$$**   ✕**Casa da Feijoada.** Brazil's savory national dish is the specialty here,
where huge pots of the stew simmer every day. The restaurant's desserts
include a selection of traditional sweets with flavors like banana, guava,
or pumpkin. *Quindim,* a coconut, yolk, and sugar cake, and Romeo and
Juliet (guava compote with fresh cheese) are two favorite desserts. The
caipirinhas are made not only with lime but also with tangerine, passion fruit, pineapple, strawberry, or kiwi. Be careful—they're strong.
⊠ *Rua Prudente de Morais 10, Ipanema* ☏ *021/2523–4994 or 021/2247–2776* ⊕ *www.cozinhatipica.com.br* ▤ *AE, DC, MC, V* Ⓜ *Siquera Campos, then shuttle bus to Praça General Osório.*

$–$$ ✕**Bar do Arnaudo.** For more than 30 years residents of beautiful Santa
Teresa have flocked to this informal eatery that serves generous portions
of Brazilian food. It's a bit far from the city center, but the restaurant
has nice views of the city and Guanabara Bay. The goat and broccoli
with *pirão* (cassava, or *mandioca,* mush) and rice is one of the traditional dishes served. Portions are large enough to serve two or even three.
For dessert, sweetened condensed milk is cooked to a creamy caramel-like paste and served atop slices of *coalho* (a semihard Brazilian cow
cheese). ⊠ *Rua Almirante Alexandrino 316-B, Santa Teresa* ☏ *021/2252–7246* ▤ *No credit cards.*

★ **$–$$**   ✕**Yorubá.** Exotic and delicious dishes are served at this restaurant, one
of the few places that goes beyond traditional African–Brazilian cuisine.
Try the Afro menu, a selection of contemporary West African cuisine.
Service can be slow, but you are well rewarded for the wait. The *piripiri*
(a spicy rice with ginger, coconut milk, and shrimp) is worth the price
of R$65 for two. ⊠ *Rua Arnaldo Quintela 94, Botafogo* ☏ *021/2541–9387* ▤ *No credit cards.*

¢–$ ✕**Yemanjá.** Typical food from Bahia is served in portions big enough for
two here. Try the *bobó de camarão,* made of shrimp and *aipim* (mashed
cassava). For dessert opt for the white or black *cocada,* a sugar-and-coconut confection cooked either a short time (white), or a longer time (black).
⊠ *Rua Visconde de Pirajá 128, Ipanema* ☏ *021/2247–7004* ▤ *AE, DC, MC, V* Ⓜ *Siquera Campos, then shuttle bus to Praça General Osório.*

Cafés

★ **¢–$**   ✕**Garcia & Rodrigues.** Cariocas breakfast at this cozy combination café,
delicatessen, liquor shop, and trendy restaurant. At lunchtime choose
from a selection of sandwiches, such as marinated salmon, pastrami, or
buffalo milk cheese. Dinner, based on French cuisine, is served until 12:30
AM Monday–Thursday and Sunday and until 1 AM Friday and Satur-

day. ⊠ *Av. Ataulfo de Paiva 1251, Leblon* ☎ *021/2512–8188* ▭ *AE, DC, MC, V.*

★ ¢ ✕ **Colombo.** At the turn of the century this belle epoque structure was Rio's preeminent café, the site of afternoon teas for upper-class *senhoras* and a center of political intrigue and gossip. Jacaranda-framed mirrors from Belgium and stained glass from France add to the art nouveau decor. Portions are generous, but you can also just stop by for a pastry and coffee while you absorb the opulence. ⊠ *Rua Gonçalves Dias 32, Centro* ☎ *021/2232–2300* ▭ *AE, MC, DC, V* ☉ *Closed Sun. No dinner* Ⓜ *Carioca.*

Eclectic

$$–$$$$ ✕ **Alho & Óleo.** Pasta is the hallmark of this place of vivid European inspiration. There are many options, including *picatina alcapone* (spaghetti in cream sauce), beef fillet with lime sauce, and sage-and-ricotta tortellini. Finish with a pear dessert cooked in white wine with vanilla ice cream and chocolate topping. The restaurant is near the Cosme Velho area and the *Cristo Redentor.* ⊠ *Rua Buarque de Macedo 13, Flamengo* ☎ *021/ 2225–3418* ▭ *AE* Ⓜ *Largo do Machado.*

¢–$ ✕ **Doce Delícia.** Make your own dish by choosing from 5 to 15 of the 42 combinations of vegetables, side dishes, hot dishes, and fruit. Quiche, salmon, grilled tenderloin, chicken, and cold pasta are some of the choices. Dressings range from the light and yogurt based to innovative creations combining mustard and lemon. There are plenty of vegetarian options. The slick decor and fresh ingredients make this popular a choice for a regular clientele in the trendy area of Ipanema. For a reasonable price you can also pick main dishes from the menu—for example, the chicken breast with honey and rosemary sauce for R$17. ⊠ *Rua Aníbal de Mendonça 55, Ipanema* ☎ *021/2259–0239* ▭ *V.*

French

★ $$$$ ✕ **Le Pré-Catalan.** Considered the best French cuisine in Rio, this is the *carioca* version of the charming Parisian restaurant of the same name in the Bois du Boulogne. This highly reputed establishment has a prix-fixe menu (R$95) with three choices for appetizers, main dish, and dessert that changes every two weeks. ⊠ *Sofitel Rio Palace, Av. Atlântica 4240, Level E, Copacabana* ☎ *021/2525–1160* ⌕ *Reservations essential* ▭ *AE, DC, MC, V* ☉ *No lunch* Ⓜ *Cardeal Arcoverde.*

★ $$$$ ✕ **Le Saint Honoré.** An extraordinary view of Copacabana Beach from atop Le Meridien hotel accompanies fine French cuisine at Le Saint Honoré. Brazilian fruits and herbs are tucked into dishes such as *les pièces du boucher marquées sauces gamay et béarnaise* (beef fillet with béarnaise and red-wine sauces). ⊠ *Av. Atlântica 1020, 37th floor, Copacabana* ☎ *021/3873–8880* ⌕ *Reservations essential* 🏛 *Jacket and tie* ▭ *AE, DC, MC, V.*

$$$$ ✕ **Olympe.** The menu's all-Brazilian ingredients are a unique trait of this
Fodor'sChoice innovative restaurant that blends native flavors with nouvelle techniques.
★ Every dish—from the crab or lobster flan to chicken, fish, and duck prepared with exotic herbs and sauces—is exceptionally light. The passion-fruit mousse is a favorite dessert. ⊠ *Rua Custódio Serrão 62, Jardim Botânico* ☎ *021/2537–8582* ⌕ *Reservations essential* ▭ *AE, DC.*

★ $$ ╳ **Le Champs Elysées.** Try the salmon with spinach cream and onion confit or puff pastry with parfait glacé and apple at this restaurant in the Maison de France cultural institute. Dinner includes an appetizer, main dish, and dessert. ⊠ *Maison de France, Av. Presidente Antônio Carlos 58, 12th floor, Centro* ☎ *021/2220–4713* ⚄ *Reservations essential* ⊟ *AE, DC, MC, V* ⊗ *Closed Sun. No dinner Mon.–Wed.; no lunch Sat.* Ⓜ *Carioca.*

Italian

★ $$$$ ╳ **Cipriani.** For a superb dining experience, start with a Cipriani, champagne with fresh peach juice (really a Bellini), and move on to an appetizer of snook carpaccio with apple and fennel or a salad of endive marinated in red wine. The pasta dishes are prepared with great care, and the meat and fish entrées are appropriate to their lavish surroundings—with a view to the hotel's beautiful pool. The degustation menu is R$150, or R$220 with wine. ⊠ *Copacabana Palace hotel, Av. Atlântica 1702, Copacabana* ☎ *021/2545–8747* ⚄ *Reservations essential* ⊟ *AE, DC, MC, V* Ⓜ *Cardeal Arcoverde.*

★ $$$–$$$$ ╳ **D'Amici.** This place has the largest wine list in Rio, with 300 labels, ranging from R$26 to R$10,000—for the Romanée Conti—and also serves 30 types of wine by the glass (R$7–R$26). The lamb with arugula risotto is a specialty. ⊠ *Rua Antônio Vieira 18, Leme* ☎ *021/2541–4477* ⊟ *AE, DC, MC, V.*

$$–$$$ ╳ **Alfredo.** The pasta here is excellent, especially the fettuccine Alfredo. Start your meal with something from the cold buffet of antipasti, which may include traditional pastas served with a variety of sauces. The restaurant has a view of the hotel pool. ⊠ *Inter-Continental Rio hotel, Av. Prefeito Mendes de Morais 222, São Conrado* ☎ *021/3323–2200* ⊟ *AE, DC, MC, V* ⊗ *No lunch.*

Japanese

$$–$$$$ ╳ **Madame Butterfly.** At this fine Japanese restaurant, start with pumpkin *gyoza* (dumplings) with shrimp, a platter with six servings, or the Beijing duck salad, a mix of greens and shredded duck with tangerine sauce. Main dishes include grilled salmon with honey and miso, and the best sukiyaki in Rio. ⊠ *Rua Barão da Torre 472, Ipanema* ☎ *021/2267–4347* ⊟ *AE, D, DC, MC.*

$–$$$$ ╳ **Tanaka San.** The cult following of VIPs and demanding palates at Tanaka San is well-deserved. The roasted salmon sashimi with teriyaki sauce, a platter with eight servings, is excellent. For an unusual treat, order the *yosenabe,* a vegetable-and-seafood fondue, which serves three. ⊠ *Rua Bartolomeu Mitre 112, Leblon* ☎ *021/2239–0198* ⊟ *AE, D, MC.*

Portuguese

★ $$$–$$$$ ╳ **Antiquarius.** This much-loved establishment is famous for its flawless rendering of Portuguese classics. Wander through the antiques shop at the restaurant before settling in at a table. A recommended dish is the *cozido,* a stew with onions, yams, carrots, pumpkin, cabbage, bananas, and more. The *cataplana,* a seafood stew with rice, is also marvelous, and the *perna de cordeiro* (leg of lamb) is the most requested dish on the menu. The wine list impresses even Portuguese gourmands. ⊠ *Rua Aristides Espínola 19, Leblon* ☎ *021/2294–1049* ⚄ *Reservations essential* ⊟ *DC.*

Seafood

★ **$$–$$$$** ✕ **Satyricon.** Some of the best seafood in town is served at this eclectic Italian seafood restaurant, which also has a branch in Búzios. The *pargo* (fish baked in a thick layer of rock salt) is a specialty, and the sushi and sashimi are well loved. ⊠ *Rua Barão da Torre 192, Ipanema* ☎ *021/ 2521–0627* ▭ *DC, MC, V* Ⓜ *Siquera Campos, then shuttle bus to Praça General Osório.*

★ **$–$$$** ✕ **Quatro Sete Meia.** This restaurant is 30 km (19 mi) west of Copacabana, at the end of a road with stunning coastal views. Simplicity is the soul of the restaurant—whose name is its street number—and the village in which it's set. There are only 11 tables: five indoors and six in a garden at water's edge. The menu lists seven delicious options, including *moquecas* (seafood stews), grilled seafood, and curries. ⊠ *Rua Barros de Alarcão 476, Pedra de Guaratiba* ☎ *021/2417–1716* ⚐ *Reservations essential* ▭ *No credit cards* ✆ *Closed Mon.–Tues. No dinner Wed.–Thurs.*

$–$$$ ✕ **Restaurante Pointe de Grumari.** From Grumari, Estrada de Guaratiba climbs up through dense forest, emerging atop a hill above the vast Guaratiba flatlands. Here you find this eatery famed for grilling fish to perfection. With its shady setting, glorious vistas, and live music performances (samba, bossa nova, jazz), it's the perfect spot for lunch (open daily 11:30–7) after a morning on the beach and before an afternoon at the Sítio Roberto Burle Marx or the Museu Casa do Pontal. ⊠ *Estrada do Grumari 710, Grumari* ☎ *021/2410–1434* ✆ *No dinner.* ▭ *AE, V.*

★ **¢–$$** ✕ **Don Camillo.** There's always something new on the menu at this Copacabana beachfront restaurant. Try the baked mix of lobster, shrimp, squid, mussels, tomato, potato, and fresh fish of the day. The Italian atmosphere is completed by a musical group that sings traditional songs. ⊠ *Av. Atlântica 3056, Copacabana* ☎ *021/2549–9958* ⊕ *www.tempero.com. br* ▭ *AE, D, DC, MC, V* Ⓜ *Cardeal Arcoverde.*

Vegetarian

$–$$ ✕ **Vegetariano Social Clube.** Vegan restaurants are rare in Rio, and this is by far the most sophisticated. The small eatery has carefully prepared dishes free of any animal products that go much beyond brown rice or burdock. ⊠ *Rua Conde de Bernadotte 26, Lj L, Leblon* ☎ *021/ 2540–6499* ▭ *D, MC, V.*

Where to Stay

Most hotels are in Copacabana and Ipanema. Copacabana hotels are close to the action (and the metrô), but the neighborhood is noisier than Ipanema (which is itself noisier than São Conrado and Barra da Tijuca). If you plan to spend time at the beach, your best bet is a hotel along Copacabana, Ipanema, or Barra da Tijuca (Copacabana has the advantage of being on the *metrô,* or subway, line). Note that Rio's "motels" aren't aimed at tourists. They attract couples looking for privacy and usually rent by the hour.

★ **$$$$** 🏨 **Caesar Park.** In the heart of Ipanema, close to high-class shops and gourmet restaurants, this beachfront hotel has established itself as a favorite of business travelers, celebrities, and heads of state, who appreciate its impeccable service. The hotel provides secretarial services, fax machines, and laptops for in-room use. On the top floor it has a pool with a breathtaking view and an excellent Italian restaurant, Galani, which serves a Sunday brunch, feijoada every Saturday, and an impeccable executive lunch. ⊠ *Av. Vieira Souto 460, Ipanema 22420-000* ☏ *021/ 2525–2525 or 0800/210789, 800/2223–6800 in the U.S.* ⊕ *www. caesarpark-rio.com* ⤴ *186 rooms, 32 suites* ⌂ *Restaurant, room service, in-room safes, in-room data ports, cable TV, pool, gym, hair salon, massage, sauna, bar, baby-sitting, dry cleaning, laundry service, business services, meeting room, concierge, free parking* ⊟ *AE, DC, MC, V.*

$$$$ ⊞ **Copacabana Palace.** Built in 1923 for the visiting king of Belgium and
Fodor'sChoice inspired by Nice's Negresco and Cannes's Carlton, the Copacabana was
★ the first luxury hotel in South America, but it still retains more soul and elegance than any other. Marlene Dietrich, Robert De Niro, and Princess Di have stayed here. It has a neoclassical facade and one of the city's largest and most attractive swimming pools. One of its two restaurants, the Cipriani, is rated among the city's best for its northern Italian cuisine. The Saturday feijoada is extraordinary. ⊠ *Av. Atlântica 1702, Copacabana 22021-001* ☏ *021/2548–7070 or 0800/211533, 800/237– 1236 in the U.S.* ⊟ *021/2235–7330* ⊕ *www.copacabanapalace.orient- express.com* ⤴ *122 rooms, 102 suites* ⌂ *2 restaurants, room service, in-room data ports, in-room safes, cable TV, in-room VCRs, tennis court, pool, health club, sauna, 2 bars, cinema, laundry service, dry cleaning, business services, meeting room, concierge, parking (fee), no-smoking rooms* ⊟ *AE, DC, MC, V* Ⓜ *Cardeal Arcoverde.*

$$$$ ⊞ **Everest Rio.** With standard service but one of Rio's finest rooftop views— a postcard shot of Corcovado and the lagoon—this hotel is in the heart of Ipanema's shopping and dining district, a block from the beach. Back rooms offer sea views. It lacks decor but it has many amenities for business travelers. The restaurant 360°, on the top floor close to the swimming pool, has seafood and some specialties from the south of Brazil. There's a sushi bar on the ground floor. ⊠ *Rua Prudente de Morais 1117, Ipanema 22420-041* ☏ *021/2525–2200 or 0800/244485* ⊟ *021/ 2521-3198* ⊕ *www.everest.com.br* ⤴ *156 rooms, 11 suites* ⌂ *Restaurant, room service, in-room data ports, in-room safes, cable TV, pool, sauna, bar, laundry service, dry cleaning, concierge, business services, parking (fee), no-smoking floors* ⊟ *AE, DC, MC, V.*

$$$$ ⊞ **Inter-Continental Rio.** One of the city's only resorts is in São Conrado, on its own slice of beachfront next to the Gávea Golf and Country Club. Attractions include a cocktail lounge, an Italian restaurant (the Alfredo), and a buffet with feijoada every Saturday. Every room has an original tapestry done by a Brazilian artist and a balcony overlooking the ocean. The nearby mall is much less crowded than those with more central locations. The club floor, on the higher levels, has extra facilities like massage, daily newspapers, and a tearoom. ⊠ *Av. Prefeito Mendes de Morais 222, São Conrado 22610-090* ☏ *021/3323–2200, 800/327–0200 in the U.S.* ⊟ *021/3323–5500* ⊕ *www.interconti.com* ⤴ *391 rooms, 53 suites, 20 cabanas* ⌂ *4 restaurants, room service, in-room data ports, in-room safes, cable TV, golf privileges, 3 tennis courts, 3 pools, health club, hair salon, sauna, 2 bars, piano bar, dance club, shops, dry cleaning, laundry service, concierge, business services, con-*

vention center, car rental, travel services, free parking, no-smoking rooms ⊟ *AE, DC, MC, V.*

$$$$ ✕⊡ **Le Meridien.** Of the leading Copacabana hotels, the 37-story French-owned Meridien is the closest to Centro, making it a favorite of business travelers. Rooms are soundproof and have dark-wood furniture. Some rooms are wheelchair accessible. If you have work to do, the hotel has a complete executive center. Afterward, relax over a meal in Le Saint Honoré restaurant (⇨ *above*) and then head for the jazz bar, which books some of the best acts in town. ⊠ *Av. Atlântica 1020, Copacabana 22010-000* ☎ *021/3873–8888 or 0800/257171* 🖷 *021/3873–8788* ⊕ *www.meridien-br.com/rio* ⇱ *443 rooms, 53 suites* ⚷ *2 restaurants, room service, in-room data ports, in-room safes, cable TV, pool, hair salon, sauna, bar, dry cleaning, laundry service, concierge, business services, free parking, no-smoking floors* ⊟ *AE, DC, MC, V.*

$$$$ ⊡ **Praia Ipanema.** This hotel isn't deluxe, but it has a great location across from the beach and between Ipanema and Leblon. You can see the sea from all its rooms. Choose the higher floors to enjoy the view and avoid the traffic noise. Take in the dramatic beach view from the pool area on the roof of the 15-story building. You can also catch a breeze from your private balcony (every room has one). ⊠ *Av. Vieira Souto 706, Ipanema 22440-000* ☎ *021/2540–4949* 🖷 *021/2239–6889* ⊕ *www.praiaipanema. com* ⇱ *105 rooms* ⚷ *Pool, room service, in-room data ports, in-room safes, cable TV, sauna, bar, health club, dry cleaning, laundry service, concierge, business services, parking (fee)* ⊟ *AE, DC, MC, V* ⟡ *BP.*

$$$$ ⊡ **Sofitel Rio Palace.** Anchoring one end of Copacabana Beach, this hotel is one of the best on the strip. The building's H shape gives views of the sea, the mountains, or both from the balconies of many rooms. The most reasonably priced rooms face one of the pools opposite the beach. All other units have an ocean view. The first floors are home to Shopping Casino Atlântico, an upscale mall. One pool gets the morning sun; the other, afternoon rays. The bar areas are always lively. The restaurant Le Pré-Catalan is as good as its Parisian original. Chef Roland Villard, from the French Culinary Academy, is welcoming and creates new dishes every two weeks. ⊠ *Av. Atlântica 4240, Copacabana 22070-002* ☎ *021/ 2525–1232 or 0800/703–7003, 800/7763–4835 in the U.S.* ⊕ *www. accorhotels.com.br* ⇱ *388 rooms, 32 suites* ⚷ *2 restaurants, in-room data ports, in-room safes, cable TV, 2 pools, health club, sauna, 2 bars, shops, dry cleaning, laundry service, concierge, business services, convention center, free parking, no-smoking rooms* ⊟ *AE, DC, MC, V.*

$$$–$$$$ ⊡ **Excelsior.** This hotel, part of the Windsor chain, may have been built in the 1950s, but its look is sleek and contemporary—from the sparkling marble lobby to the guest-room closets paneled in gleaming jacaranda (Brazilian redwood). Service is top rate. The expansive breakfast buffet is served in the hotel's window-banked restaurant facing the avenue and beach. The equally elaborate lunch and dinner buffets cost roughly R$30. The rooftop bar–pool area offers an escape from the hustle and bustle. Ask for a room with a water view. ⊠ *Av. Atlântica 1800, Copacabana 22021-001* ☎ *021/2545–6000 or 0800/704–2827, 800/444– 885 in the U.S.* 🖷 *021/2257–1850* ⊕ *www.windsorhoteis.com.br* ⇱ *233 rooms* ⚷ *Restaurant, room service, in-room data ports, in-room safes,* *minibars, cable TV, pool, health club, 2 bars, dry cleaning, laundry service, concierge, meeting room, free parking, no-smoking rooms* ▭ *AE, DC, MC, V* ⑂ *BP* Ⓜ *Cardeal Arcoverde.*

$$$–$$$$ 🏨 **Sol Ipanema.** Another of Rio's crop of tall, slender hotels, this one has a great location (between Rua Vinícius de Moraes and Farme de Amoedo, where there are several bars), anchoring the eastern end of Ipanema Beach. All rooms have motel-style beige carpets and drapes and light-color furniture; deluxe front rooms have panoramic beach views, while back rooms from the eighth floor up, which are the same size, have views of the lagoon and Corcovado. Marble bathrooms are large and clean. ✉ *Av. Vieira Souto 320, Ipanema 22420-000* ☎ *021/2525–2020* 🖷 *021/2247–8484* ⊕ *www.solipanema.com.br* ⤴ *90 rooms* ♿ *Restaurant, pool, bar* ▭ *AE, DC, MC, V* ⑂ *BP.*

$$$ 🏨 **Atlântico Copacabana.** Just three blocks from Copacabana Beach and close to the Siqueira Campos metrô station, this hotel has a great location for the price. Rooms are simple and slightly larger than average. Choose a room on one of the top floors to avoid the street noise of this residential area. ✉ *Rua Siqueira Campos 90, Copacabana 22031-070* ☎ *021/2548–0011* 🖷 *021/2235–7941* ⊕ *www.atlanticocopacabana.com. br* ⤴ *97 rooms, 18 suites* ♿ *Restaurant, room service, in-room data ports, in-room safes, cable TV, pool, hair salon, sauna, bar, health club, dry cleaning, laundry service, concierge, business services, parking (fee), no-smoking floors* ▭ *AE, DC, MC, V* ⑂ *BP* Ⓜ *Siqueira Campos.*

$$$ 🏨 **Sheraton Barra Hotel e Suites.** Opened in 2003, this mammoth gleaming-white hotel has balconies in each room that overlook Barra Beach. The decor is futuristic, with white walls, brushed nickel and mahogany accents, skillful lighting, and clean lines. Rooms have high-speed Internet access. Be prepared to rent a car or spend a good deal on taxis when staying in this neighborhood, as there's no metrô station and unreliable bus service. ✉ *Av. Lúcio Costa 3150, Barra da Tijuca 22630-010* ☎ *021/ 3139–8000* 🖷 *021/3139–8025* ⊕ *www.sheraton.com/barra* ⤴ *263 rooms, 30 suites* ♿ *Restaurant, room service, in-room data ports, cable TV, pool, wading pool, gym, 2 hot tubs, sauna, spa, squash, bar, concierge, business services, meeting rooms, parking (fee)* ▭ *AE, DC, MC, V.*

$$–$$$ 🏨 **Glória.** A grande dame of Rio's hotels, this classic was built in 1922 and is full of French antiques. What makes it a draw for business travelers—it's a five-minute cab ride from Centro—may discourage sun worshipers since it's a slightly longer cab ride to the beaches. ✉ *Rua do Russel 632, Glória 22210-010* ☎ *021/2205–7272 or 0800/213077* 🖷 *021/2555–7282* ⊕ *www.hotelgloriario.com.br* ⤴ *596 rooms, 20 suites* ♿ *4 restaurants, room service, in-room data ports, some in-room safes, cable TV, 2 pools, gym, sauna, 3 bars, dry cleaning, laundry service, concierge, meeting room, parking (fee), no-smoking rooms* ▭ *AE, DC, MC, V* ⑂ *BP* Ⓜ *Glória.*

$$–$$$ 🏨 **Luxor Regente Hotel.** The best of the Luxor hotels in Rio, the Regente has drab furnishings but solid service. The restaurant Forno e Fogão has a good feijoada, though it's not as well known as that of the Copacabana Palace. The suites have whirlpool baths. The gym area is small, but the hotel is committed to continually updating its equipment. If you choose a standard room, be sure that it's not one that faces south, without any view at all. Other rooms have beach views onto Avenida Atlântica. ✉ *Av. Atlântica 3716, Copacabana 22070-001* ☏ *021/2525–2070 or 0800/165322* 🖷 *021/2267–7693* ⊕ *www.luxor-hotels.com/regente* 🛏 *233 rooms; 7 suites* 🔥 *Restaurant, room service, some in-room data ports, in-room safes, cable TV, pool, sauna, health club, dry cleaning, laundry service, concierge, business services, parking (fee), no-smoking rooms* ▤ *AE, DC, MC, V* ⏚ *BP.*

$$–$$$ 🏨 **Rio Internacional.** The red frame of this beachfront hotel has become a Copacabana landmark. Swiss owned and aimed at business travelers, the hotel offers a rarity for Avenida Atlântica: all rooms have balconies with sea views. All guests are welcomed with a glass of champagne. ✉ *Av. Atlântica 1500, Copacabana 22021-000* ☏ *021/2543–1555 or 0800/ 211559* 🖷 *021/2542–5443* ⊕ *www.riointernacional.com.br* 🛏 *117 rooms, 13 suites* 🔥 *Restaurant, room service, in-room data ports, in-room safes, cable TV, pool, sauna, 2 bars, health club, dry cleaning, laundry service, concierge, business services, parking (fee), no-smoking floors* ▤ *AE, DC, MC, V* Ⓜ *Cardeal Arco Verde.*

$$–$$$ 🏨 **Windsor Palace Hotel.** Close to the shopping area of Copacabana, the Windsor Palace has a modern but simple style. From the fifth floor up, rooms have balconies, but only those from the 12th floor up have ocean views. Overall, this is a low-budget option with solid services. The rooftop pool has a view of Copacabana beach, and it's just two blocks from the Siqueira Campos metrô station. ✉ *Rua Domingos Ferreira 6, Copacabana 22050-010* ☏ *021/2545–9000* 🖷 *021/2549–9373* ⊕ *www. windsorhoteis.com/windsor* 🛏 *73 rooms; 1 suite* 🔥 *Restaurant, room service, in-room safes, cable TV, bar, pool, sauna, dry cleaning, laundry service, concierge, meeting room, free parking, no-smoking floors* ▤ *AE, DC, MC, V* ⏚ *BP* Ⓜ *Siqueira Campos.*

$–$$ 🏨 **Arpoador Inn.** This simple pocket-size hotel occupies the stretch of sand known as Arpoador. Surfers ride the waves, and pedestrians rule the roadway—a traffic-free street allows direct beach access. At sunset the view from the rocks that mark the end of the beach is considered one of Rio's most beautiful. The spectacle is visible from the hotel's back rooms (deluxe rooms) that face Arpoador Beach; avoid the front rooms, which are on the noisy side. Built in the '70s, the hotel has since been renovated and has a restaurant on the ground floor overlooking the beach. ✉ *Rua Francisco Otaviano 177, Ipanema 22080-040* ☏ *021/2523–0060* 🖷 *021/2511–5094* 🛏 *50 rooms* 🔥 *Restaurant, room service, in-room safes, cable TV, bar, dry cleaning, laundry service* ▤ *AE, DC, MC, V* ⏚ *BP.*

$–$$ 🏨 **Grandville Ouro Verde.** For three decades folks have favored this hotel for its efficient, personalized service. The tasteful Brazilian colonial decor and dark-wood furniture are in step with the emphasis on quality and graciousness. All front rooms face the beach; those in the back on the 6th–12th floors have a view of Corcovado. ✉ *Av. Atlântica 1456, Copacabana 22021–000* ☏ *021/2543–4123* 🖷 *021/2542–4597* ⊕ *www.grandarrell.com.br/ouroverde/gouro.htm* 🛏 *60 rooms, 1 suite* 🔥 *Restaurant, room service, in-room data ports, in-room safes, cable TV, bar, library, dry cleaning, laundry service, no-smoking rooms* ▤ *AE, DC, MC, V* Ⓜ *Cardeal Arco Verde.*

$–$$ ⌶ **Guanabara Palace Hotel.** A member of the Windsor chain that was remodeled in 2001, the Guanabara is one of the only solid hotel choices right in Centro. Rooms are reasonably sized and tastefully done in brown and beige. Like the one in its sister hotel, the Excelsior, the restaurant serves elaborate buffet meals. The contemporary rooftop pool area, with its stunning views of Guanabara Bay, absolutely gleams thanks to its pristine white tiles, white trellises, and white patio furnishings. The hotel has 30 meeting rooms. ⊠ *Av. Presidente Vargas 392, Centro 20071-000* ☎*021/2216–1313* 🖷*021/2516–1582* ⊕*www.windsorhoteis. com.br* 🛏*467 rooms, 3 suites* ♨ *Restaurant, room service, in-room data ports, in-room safes, cable TV, minibars, pool, health club, sauna, dry cleaning, laundry service, bar, business services, meeting rooms, parking (fee), no-smoking rooms* ⊟ *AE, DC, MC, V* ⏆*BP* Ⓜ *Uruguaiana.*

$ ⌶ **Copacabana Rio Hotel.** Colorful room decor—such as yellow walls paired with blue beds—greets you at this hotel a block for the beach. Rooms have wonderful views of Pedra da Gávea. From the heated rooftop pool you can see Copacabana Beach and Sugarloaf. The Siqueira Campos metrô station is 10 blocks away. ⊠ *Av. Nossa Senhora de Co-pacabana 1256, Copacabana 22070-010* ☎ *021/2267–9900* 🖷 *021/ 2267–2271* ⊕ *www.copacabanariohotel.com.br* 🛏 *77 rooms, 6 suites* ♨ *Restaurant, in-room safes, cable TV, pool, sauna, baby-sitting, concierge, laundry service, meeting room, parking (fee)* ⊟ *AE, MC, V* ⏆*BP* Ⓜ *Siqueira Campos.*

$ ⌶ **Ipanema Inn.** If you want to stay in Ipanema and avoid the high prices of beachfront accommodations, this no-frills hotel with great service fits the bill. Just a half block from the beach, close to Praça Nossa Senhora da Paz, it's convenient not only for sun worshipers but also for those seeking to explore Ipanema's varied nightlife. ⊠ *Rua Maria Quitéria 27, Ipanema 22410-040* ☎ *021/2523–6092 or 021/2274–6995* 🛏 *54 rooms* ♨ *Dining room, in-room safes, cable TV, bar, dry cleaning, laundry service* ⊟ *AE, DC, MC, V* ⏆*BP.*

$ ⌶ **Novo Mundo.** A short walk from the Catete metrô station and just five minutes by car from Santos Dumont Airport, this traditional hotel is on Guanabara Bay in Flamengo, near Glória. Convention rooms are popular with the business crowd. Deluxe rooms have a view of the bay and also of the Pão de Açúcar. The traditional restaurant, Flamboyant, has buffet service during the week and feijoada every Saturday. ⊠ *Praia do Flamengo 20, Flamengo 22210-030* ☎ *021/2557–6226 or 0800/ 253355* ⊕ *www.hotelnovomundo-rio.com.br* 🛏 *208 rooms, 23 suites* ♨ *Restaurant, in-room data ports, in-room safes, refrigerators, cable TV, hair salon, bar, dry cleaning, laundry service, meeting room, parking (fee), no-smoking floor* ⊟ *AE, D, MC, V* ⏆*BP* Ⓜ *Catete.*

$ ⌶ **Toledo.** Although it has few amenities, the Toledo goes the extra mile to make the best of what it does have. The staff is friendly, the service is efficient, and the location—on a quiet backstreet of Copacabana, a block from the beach—isn't bad either. Back rooms from the 9th to the 14th floors have sea views and sliding floor-to-ceiling windows. ⊠ *Rua Domin-gos Ferreira 71, Copacabana 22050-010* ☎ *021/2257–1990* 🖷 *021/ 2257–1931* ⊕ *www.hoteisgandara.com.br* 🛏 *92 rooms* ♨ *Coffee shop, in-room safes, cable TV* ⊟ *AE, DC, MC, V* ⏆*BP* Ⓜ *Siqueira Campos.*

Nightlife & the Arts

Rio's nightlife is as hard to resist as its beaches. Note that establishments in this carefree city often have carefree hours; call ahead to confirm opening times. For opera, theater, music, dance, film, and other performing arts listings, pick up the Portuguese-language *Rio Prá Você*, published by Riotur, the city's tourist board, at Riotur booths (⇨ Visitor Information *in* Rio de Janeiro A to Z). *Este Mês no Rio* (This Month in Rio) and similar publications are available at most hotels, and your hotel concierge is also a good source of information. The Portuguese-language newspapers *Jornal do Brasil* and *O Globo* both publish schedules of events in the entertainment sections of their Friday editions, which may also be found online at www.jb.com.br and www.oglobo.com.br.

Nightlife

BARS Back in the '60s, regulars Tom Jobim and Vinícius de Moraes, who wrote the song "The Girl from Ipanema," sat at tables at **Bar Garota de Ipanema** (⊠ Rua Vinícius de Moraes 39, Ipanema ☎ 021/2267–5757 Ⓜ Siquera Campos, then shuttle bus to Praça General Osório), then called Bar Veloso, and longingly watched the song's heroine head for the beach. See if you can guess where they usually sat (hint: it's a table for two near a door). The unpretentious beachfront choperia **Barril 1800** (⊠ Av. Vieira Souto 110, Ipanema ☎ 021/2287–0085 Ⓜ Siquera Campos, then shuttle bus to Praça General Osório) is an Ipanema landmark and is usually jammed with people grabbing an icy beer or cocktail and a snack.

Don't expect anything fancy at **Bracarense** (⊠ Rua José Linhares 85B, Leblon ☎ 021/2294–3549), a small informal place where cariocas linger with their beers on the sidewalk in front of the bar. It's perfect for after a soccer game in Maracanã; many come just to talk about sports. Near the Jóquei Clube, **Hipódromo** (⊠ Praça Santos Dumont, Gávea ☎ 021/2294–0095) has good chopp, honest food, and crowds of young people living it up.

★ **Nova Capela** (⊠ Av. Mem de Sá 96, Lapa ☎ 021/2252–6228 Ⓜ Cinelândia) is a 100-year-old restaurant-bar in Rio's traditional downtown nightlife area. Beer, cachaça, and Brazilian meals and appetizers are served in generous portions. At **Seu Martin** (⊠ Av. General San Martin 1196, Leblon ☎ 021/2274–0800 ⊘ Closed for lunch on Mon.) cocktails, cheesecake, light food, sandwiches, and salad are served to the sound of jazz.

DANCE CLUBS If you prefer to be where the trends are, try **00** (⊠ Av. Padre Leonel Franca 240, Gávea ☎ 021/2540–8041), a restaurant–café–sushi bar with a variety of DJs playing sets of house music, drum and bass, and trance, depending on the DJ. Call to get the program. It's open Tuesday through Sunday; arrive after 10 PM. Dance to samba rhythms at the compact club **Carioca da Gema** (⊠ Rua Mem de Sá 79, Lapa ☎ 021/2221–0043). At the large nightclub **Asa Branca** (⊠ Av. Mem de Sá 17, Lapa ☎ 021/ 2232–5704 ⊟ AE, D, DC, V ⊘ Closed Mon.–Tues.), modern geometric designs are combined with old-fashioned fixtures. Big bands and popular Brazilian musicians keep the crowd busy from 10 PM until dawn. National and international bands play nearly every night at **Ballroom**

(⊠ Rua Humaitá 110, Humaitá ☎ 021/2537–7600 ⊕ www.ballroom. com.br), a concert hall and dance club. Call to check the program. Arrive after midnight.

Estudantina (⊠ Praça Tiradentes 79, Centro ☎ 021/2232–1149 Ⓜ Presidente Vargas) is an extremely popular nightclub that packs in as many as 1,500 people on weekends to dance to the sound of samba. Brazilian rhythms, drum and bass, rock, and trip-hop are played different nights of the week at **Sítio Lounge** (⊠ Rua Marquês de São Vicente 10, Gávea ☎ 021/2274–2226). The decor is sophisticated and cozy. It used to be an antiques shop, and most of the furniture remains part of the space. It's open from Tuesday to Sunday; arrive after 11 PM.

GAY & LESBIAN BARS & CLUBS

The young energetic crowd at **Bar Bofetada** (⊠ Rua Farme de Amoedo 87–87A, Ipanema ☎ 021/2227–1675) downs chopp and caipirinhas and delicious seafood (the owners are Portuguese) or meat platters large enough to share. Downstairs the tables flow out onto the street; upstairs large windows open to the sky and afford a good view of the action below. The **Galeria Café** (⊠ Rua Teixeira de Mello 31E–F, Ipanema ☎ 021/ 2523–8250 ⊕ www.galeriacafe.com.br) is a bar with house–techno music for a sophisticated crowd. From Thursday to Saturday it's packed not only inside but has patrons overflowing out onto the sidewalk. The drink minimum is R$10. **Le Boy** (⊠ Rua Paul Pompéia 94, Copacabana ☎ 021/2521–0367 ⊕ www.leboy.com.br) is a gay disco that draws an upscale clientele.

MUSIC CLUBS

At **Mistura Fina** (⊠ Av. Borges de Medeiros 3207, Lagoa Rodrigo de Freitas, Lagoa ☎ 021/2537–2844)fine jazz combines with excellent food. It's open midnight–3 AM. **Plataforma** (⊠Rua Adalberto Ferreira 32, Leblon ☎ 021/2274–4022), the most spectacular of Rio's samba shows, has elaborate costumes and a variety of musical numbers including samba and rumba. A two-hour show costs about R$100, drinks not included. Downstairs is a hangout for many local luminaries and entertainers. Upstairs you can eat at Plataforma's famed barbecue restaurant. **Rio Scenarium** (⊠ Rua do Lavradio 20, Lapa ☎ 021/2233–3239) occupies three floors of an old townhouse that doubles as an antiques emporium. Dance to some of the best samba and *choro* (instrumental music with improvisational classical guitar) bands around on the spacious dance floor. **Semente** (⊠ Rua Joaquim Silva 138, Lapa ☎ 021/242–5165) is a small but popular samba club. You may rightly associate sultry bossa nova with Brazil, but it's increasingly hard to find venues that offer it. **Vinicius** (⊠Rua Vinícius de Moraes 39, Ipanema ☎021/2287–1497 Ⓜ Siquera Campos, then shuttle bus to Praça General Osório) is one of the few that does. Along with nightly live samba, jazz, popular music, or bossa nova music, it has a good kitchen.

The Arts

The 4,500-seat **ATL Hall** (⊠Av. Ayrton Senna 3000, Barra da Tijuca ☎021/ 2430–0790 or 021/2285–0773) hosts music concerts, theater, and dance events. Many pop stars have performed here. Check the daily newspapers for programs. **Canecão** (⊠Av. Venceslau Brás 215, Botafogo ☎021/ 2543–1241) is the most traditional venue for the biggest names on the national music scene. It seats up to 5,000 people; reserve a table up front. **Centro Cultural Banco do Brasil** (⊠ Rua 1° de Março 66, Centro ☎ 021/2216–0237 or 021/2216–0626 Ⓜ Uruguaiana), constructed in 1880, was once the headquarters of the Banco do Brasil. In the late 1980s the six-story domed building with marble floors was transformed into a cultural center for plays, art exhibitions, and music recitals. It's open Tuesday–Sunday 10–8 for guided tours.

Opened in 1922, the **Escola de Música da UFRJ** (⊠ Rua do Passeio 98, Lapa ☎ 021/2240–1391 ⊕ www.musica.ufrj.br Ⓜ Cinelândia), the Music School auditorium, inspired by the Gauveau Hall in Paris, has 1,100 seats where you can listen to chamber music, symphony orchestras, and opera, all free of charge. **Instituto Moreira Salles** (⊠ Rua Marquês de São Vicente 476, Gávea ☎ 021/3284–7400 ⊕ www.ims.com.br), surrounded by beautiful gardens, has just the right atmosphere for listening to classical music. *Projeto Villa-Lobinhos,* whose performances are dedicated to children, is one of their projects. Listen to musicians performing pieces from Bach, Chopin, Debussy, and other classical composers.

★ The traditional **Teatro João Caetano** (⊠ Praça Tiradentes, Centro ☎ 021/2221–0305 Ⓜ Presidente Vargas) holds 1,200 seats and offers a large choice of programs, from drama to dance, inexpensively. **Teatro Municipal** (⊠ Praça Floriano, Centro ☎ 021/2262–3501 or 021/2299–1717 ⊕ www.theatromunicipal.rj.gov.br) is the city's main performing arts venue, hosting dance, opera (often with international divas as guest artists), symphony concerts, and theater events year-round—although the season officially runs from April to December. The theater also has its own ballet company.

Sports & the Outdoors

Auto Racing
Brazilian race-car drivers rank among the world's best and frequently compete in international events. At the **Autódromo Internacional Nelson Piquet** (Nelson Piquet International Racetrack; ⊠ Av. Embaixador Abelardo Bueno, Jacarepaguá ☎ 021/2421–4949), you get a taste of the speed as you watch the checkered flag drop on competitions in the Formula I Grand Prix circuit named after one of the country's most famous racers, Emerson Fittipaldi.

Bicycling & Running
Bikers and runners share the boulevards along the beach and, for cooler and quieter outings, the path around Lagoa Rodrigo de Freitas. On weekends a stretch of Floresta da Tijuca Road is closed to traffic and many cariocas bike or run there. Although hotels can arrange bike rentals, it's just as easy to rent from stands along beachfront avenues or the road ringing the lagoon. Rates are about R$10 per hour. You're usually asked to show identification and give your hotel name and room number, but deposits are seldom required. (Note that helmets aren't usually available.)

THE BEAUTIFUL GAME

BRAZILIANS ARE MAD ABOUT *FUTEBOL* (soccer), and players here are fast and skillful. The best possess ginga (literally, "sway"), a quality that translates roughly as a feline, almost swaggering grace. Some of their ball-handling moves are so fluid they seem more akin to ballet—or at least to the samba—than to sport.

Futebol is believed to have been introduced in the late 19th century by employees of British-owned firms. By the early 20th century upper-class Brazilians had formed their own leagues, as had the nation's European immigrants. Because it requires little equipment, the sport also found a following in Brazil's poor communities.

You can see young brasileiros everywhere practicing—any of these boys could be a future futebol hero. Brazil has turned out many international stars: the most famous, Pelé, retired more than 20 years ago and

is still revered as a national hero. The country's team is consistently included in World Cup competitions and is a repeat titleholder. Nothing inspires more pride in Brazilians than their fifth World Cup win, in Korea and Japan in 2002.

Fans come to games with musical instruments, flags, banners, streamers, talcum powder, and firecrackers. There's no better spot for the brave to witness the spectacle than at the world's largest soccer stadium, Rio's Estádio Maracanã. Here you and 91,999 other people can make merry. Even if you don't have a great view of the field, you'll certainly be a part of the event. The main carioca teams are Flamengo, Vasco da Gama, Fluminense, and Botafogo. A match between any of these teams is a great spectacle.

Boating & Sailing

Saveiro's Tour (✉ Rua Conde de Lages 44, Glória ☎ 021/2224–0313 Ⓜ Glória) charters all types of crewed vessels for any length of time. You can arrange an afternoon of waterskiing with a speedboat or a weekend aboard a yacht.

Golf

Golden Green Golf Club (✉ Av. Canal de Marapendi 2901, Barra da Tijuca ☎ 021/2434–0429 ⊕ www.fgerj.com.br/conheca_golfe/clubes/golden.asp) was the first public golf club in Brazil. You can rent equipment for the six-hole course. The greens fee is R$30 Tuesday–Friday and R$40 weekends and holidays. The club is open 7 AM–10 PM.

Hang Gliding

A 30-minute hang-glider flight at **Just Fly** (☎ 021/2268–0565 or 021/9985–7540), during which you jump from Pedra Bonita in the Parque Nacional da Tijuca and land at Praia do Pepino in São Conrado, costs R$250 including transportation to and from your hotel. For a little more you can have 12 pictures taken. **Superfly** (✉ Estrada das Canoas 1476, Casa 2, São Conrado ☎ 021/3332–2286) has hang-gliding classes and tandem flights with instructors. A package including pickup at your hotel and 12 photos taken in-flight costs about R$220.

Soccer

You can watch a game at the **Estádio Maracanã** (⊠ Rua Prof. Eurico Rabelo, Maracanã ☎ 021/2568–9962 ⊕ www.suderj.rj.gov.br/maracana/main.asp Ⓜ Maracana), where the fans are part of the spectacle. During the season the top game is played each Sunday at around 5. The four most popular teams are Botafogo, Flamengo, Fluminense, and Vasco da Gama. A game between any of them is soccer at its finest. Tickets are available at the door. Arrive 30 minutes early to get the best seats.

Shopping

Stroll down streets lined with fashionable boutiques, barter with vendors at street fairs, or wander through one of more than two-dozen air-conditioned malls. Good bets are leather, suede, jewelry, and cool summer clothing in natural fibers. Also look for coffee, art, and samba and bossa nova CDs.

Ipanema is Rio's most fashionable shopping district. Its many exclusive boutiques are in arcades, with the majority along Rua Visconde de Pirajá. Copacabana has souvenir shops, bookstores, and branches of some of Rio's better shops along Avenida Nossa Senhora de Copacabana and connecting streets. For upscale jewelry, head to Avenida Atlântica. Brazil is one of the world's largest producers of gold and the largest supplier of colored gemstones, with deposits of aquamarines, amethysts, diamonds, emeralds, rubellites, topazes, and tourmalines. If you're planning to go to Minas Gerais, do your jewelry shopping there; otherwise, stick with shops that have certificates of authenticity and quality.

Centers & Malls

Although **Barra Shopping** (⊠ Av. das Américas 4666, Barra da Tijuca ☎ 021/3089–1100 ⊕ www.barrashopping.com.br) is about 30 km (19 mi) from the city center, shoppers from all over town head to this mall, one of South America's largest. It has a medical center and a bowling alley as well as shops. The view of the Pão de Açúcar from **Botafogo Praia Shopping** (⊠ Praia de Botafogo 400, Botafogo ☎ 021/2559–9559 ⊕ botafogo-praia-shopping.globo.com Ⓜ Botafogo) is more appealing than the 170 shops and six movie screens at this mall on Botafogo Beach. Some of the restaurants have seats with a panoramic view. With more than 400 sophisticated shops selling jewelry, fine quality clothing, and more. **Rio Sul** (⊠ Av. Lauro Müller 116, Botafogo ☎ 021/2545–7200 ⊕ www.riosul.com.br) is one of the city's most popular retail complexes. There are also four movie screens and a giant food court.

Domestic and international fashions are sold at **São Conrado Fashion Mall** (⊠ Estrada da Gávea 899, São Conrado ☎ 021/3083–0000), which may be Rio's most appealing mall—it's the least crowded and has an abundance of natural light. A newer section, opened in 2002, has giant shops of Emporio Armani, Ermenegildo Zegna, Kenzo, and Petit Lippe. There's a four-screen movie theater. At **Shopping Center da Gávea** (⊠ Rua Marquês de São Vicente 52, Gávea ☎ 021/2274–9896) several top art galleries—of which the best are Ana Maria Niemeyer, Beco da Arte, Borghese, Bronze, Paulo Klabin, Saramenha, and Toulouse—join a small but select mix of fashionable clothing and leather-goods stores. Four theaters here show the best plays in town.

Markets

In the evenings and on weekends along the median of Avenida Atlântica, **artisans** spread out their wares. You can find paintings, carvings, handicrafts, sequined dresses, and hammocks from the northeast. **Babilônia Feira Hype** (⊠ Jockey Club Brasileiro, Rua Jardim Botânico, Jardim Botânico ☎ 021/2253–9800 or 021/2263–7667 ⊕ www.babiloniahype. com.br) takes place every other weekend from 2 PM to 10 PM. This fair combines fashion, design, art, and gastronomy. Admission is R$5.

The **Feira Hippie** (⊠ Praça General Osório, Ipanema) is a colorful handicrafts street fair held every Sunday 9–6. Shop for jewelry, hand-painted dresses, T-shirts, paintings, wood carvings, leather bags and sandals, rag dolls, knickknacks, furniture, and samba percussion instruments. Saturday (9–6) an open-air fair, **Feira de Antiquários da Praça 15 de Novembro,** near the Praça 15 de Novembro has china and silver sets, watches, Asian rugs, and chandeliers. On Sunday (9–5) the same fair goes to Praça Santos Dumont, in Jardim Botânico. Vendors at **Feira do Rio Antigo** (Rio Antique Fair; ⊠ Rua do Lavradio, Centro ☎ 021/2252–2669) sell antiques, rare books, records, and all types of objets d'art on every first Saturday afternoon of the month. They move to the Casa Shopping Center in Barra da Tijuca on Sunday. A street fair, **Feirarte** (⊠ Praça do Lido, Copacabana), similar to the Feira Hippie, takes place weekends 8–6. Cardeal Arcoverde is the closest metrô station to the Feirarte.

Specialty Shops

ART **Contorno** (⊠ Shopping Center da Gávea, Rua Marquês de São Vicente 52, loja 261, Gávea ☎ 021/2274–3832) shows eclectic selection of Brazilian art. Several shops and some art galleries at **Rio Design Center** (⊠ Av. Ataulfo de Paiva 270, Leblon ☎ 021/3206–9100 ⊕ www. riodesign.com.br), like Anita Schwartz Galeria, have contemporary art.

BEACHWEAR A bikini shop with many mall locations in addition to the Rio Sul branch, **Blueman** (⊠ Rio Sul, Av. Lauro Müller 116, loja B01, Botafogo ☎ 021/ 2541–6896 ⊕ www.bluemanbrazil.com.br) carries *tangas* (string bikinis) that virtually define Brazil in much of North America's imagination. Tangas are said to have been invented in Ipanema—and they don't take up much room in your luggage. The market leader in beachwear, **Bum Bum** (⊠ Rua Visconde de Pirajá 351, loja B, Ipanema ☎ 021/2521–3859 ⊕ www.bumbum.com.br ⊠ Shopping Rio Sul, Rua Lauro Muller 116, loja 401, Botafogo ☎ 021/2542–9614 ⊠ Barra Shopping, Av. das Américas 4666, loja 134B, Barra da Tijuca ☎ 021/2431–8323) opened in 1979, when the stylist Alcindo Silva Filho, known as Cidinho, decided to create the smallest—and by some accounts the sexiest—bikinis in town.

At pricey **Lenny** (⊠ Fórum Ipanema, Rua Visconde de Pirajá 351, loja 114, Ipanema ☎ 021/2523–3796 ⊕ www.lenny.com.br), expect sophistication, comfortable sizes, lots of fashionable beach accessories, and particularly creative bikinis. A *très* chic bikini designer, **Salinas** (⊠ Rio

Sul, Rua Lauro Müller 116, loja C, Botafogo ☎ 021/2275–0793) is the label de rigueur with the fashionable set in Búzios and other resort areas. For bikinis larger than a postage stamp, try **Track & Field** (✉ Rio Sul, Rua Lauro Müller 116, loja 401 B09, Botafogo ☎ 021/2295–5996 ⊕ www.tf.com.br), a sportswear shop.

CLOTHING **Complexo B** (✉ Rua Francisco Otaviano 67, loja 42—Galeria River, Copacabana ☎ 021/2521–7126 ⊕ www.complexob.com.br) is a men's sportswear shop created by the stylist Beto Neves. The collection focuses on T-shirts with a touch of humor, with prints of saints and superheroes. At **Krishna** (✉ Rio Sul, Av. Lauro Müller 116, loja B30, Botafogo ☎ 021/ 2542–2443 ✉ São Conrado Fashion Mall, Estrada da Gávea 899, São Conrado ☎ 021/3322–0437) the specialty is classic feminine dresses and separates—many in fine linens, cottons, and silks. **Osklen** (✉ Rua Maria Quitéria 85, Ipanema ☎ 021/2227-2911 ✉ São Conrado Fashion Mall, Estrada da Gávea 899, São Conrado ☎ 021/3083–0000 ✉ Barra Shopping, Av. das Américas 4666, Barra da Tijuca ☎ 021/3089–1100 ⊕ www.barrashopping.com.br) is a synonym for sporty casual clothing with a fashionable flair. The clothes—from trousers to coats to tennis shoes—are designed for outdoor use. Two additional branches of the shop are at São Conrado Fashion Mall and Barra Shopping (⇨ Centers & Malls, *above*).

HANDICRAFTS Inside the Museu do Índio (Museum of the Indian), **Artíndia** (✉ Rua das Palmeiras 55, Botafogo ☎ 021/2286–8899 Ⓜ Botafogo) has handcrafted items made by several Brazilian tribes: toys, necklaces made of seeds and feathers, musical instruments, and traditional Brazilian cooking pans made of iron. The shop is open Tuesday–Friday 10–5:30 and weekends 1–5. Handcrafted items made of everything from porcelain to wood and papier-mâché to clay are available at **Casa do Pequeno Empresário** (✉ Rua Real Grandeza 293, Botafogo ☎ 021/2286–9991 Ⓜ Botafogo), an exhibition center. The metrô station is a 10-block walk.

Curio L Folclore (✉ Rua Visconde de Pirajá 490, Ipanema ☎ 021/ 2259–7442), owned by H. Stern jewelry, bursts with primitive paintings, costume jewelry, leather and ceramic crafts, and birds and flowers carved from stone. Quality is high, but take note: some items have been imported from other South American nations. Close to the train station to Corcovado, **Jeito Brasileiro** (✉ Rua Erre 11 A, Cosme Velho ☎ 021/2205–7636) has a great variety of paintings; handcrafted wood, leather, and ceramic items; and also some pieces from the Camurim tribe. The shop is open weekdays 10–7, Saturday 10–1, and Sunday 9–1.

JEWELRY **Amsterdam Sauer** (✉ Rua Visconde de Pirajá 484, Ipanema ☎ 021/ 2512–9878, 021/2239–8045 for the museum), one of Rio's top names in jewelry, has top prices and is known for its emeralds. The on-site gemstone museum is open weekdays 10–5 and Saturday 9:30–1 (reserve ahead). For nearly 30 years **Antônio Bernardo** (✉ Fórum Ipanema, Rua Visconde de Pirajá 351, loja 114, Ipanema ☎ 021/2523–3192 ⊕ www. antoniobernardo.com.br ✉ São Conrado Fashion Mall, Estrada da Gávea 899, São Conrado ☎ 021/3083–0000 ✉ Shopping Center da Gávea, Rua Marquês de São Vicente 52, Gávea ☎ 021/2274–9896) has been making gorgeous jewelry with contemporary designs. Designers create truly distinctive contemporary pieces for the world headquarters of **H. Stern** (✉ Rua Visconde de Pirajá 490, Ipanema ☎ 021/2259–7442). Here you can see exhibits of rare stones and watch craftspeople transform rough stones into sparkling jewels. There's also a museum with tours by appointment. The shops downstairs sell more affordable pieces and folkloric items.

LEATHER GOODS   **Frankie Amaury** (✉ Fórum de Ipanema, Rua Visconde de Pirajá 351, loja 106, Ipanema ☎ 021/2522–0633) is *the* name in leather clothing. All kinds of modern yet refined leather jackets, skirts, and trousers are available. Traditional carioca boutique **Mariazinha** (✉ Rio Sul, Av. Lauro Müller 116 loja C34A, Botafogo ☎ 021/2541–6695 ✉ Rio Visconde de Pirajá 365 Ipanema ☎ 021/2523–2340), almost 40 years old, carries fashionable and modern footwear for women and is one of the city's finest clothing brands that follows international trends. **Mr. Cat** (✉ Botafogo Praia Shopping, Praia de Botafogo 400 ☎ 021/2237–9087 ⊕ www.mrcat.com.br Ⓜ Botafogo) carries some of Rio's best handbags and leather shoes for men and women. **Victor Hugo** (✉ Rio Sul, Av. Lauro Müller 116, loja B19, Botafogo ☎ 021/2543–9290) is nationally famous nationally for quality leather handbags that are similar in quality to more expensive brands like Louis Vuitton, Gucci, and Prada.

MUSIC   Samba, jazz, bossa nova, and more are sold at **Gramophone** (✉ Rua 7 de Setembro 92, loja 105, Centro ☎ 021/2221–2032 Ⓜ Uruguaiana ✉ Shopping Center da Gávea, Rua Marquês de São Vicente 52, Gávea ☎ 021/2274–9896). Look for difficult-to-find titles. **Modern Sound** (✉ Rua Barata Ribeiro 502 D, Copacabana ☎ 021/2548–5005 ⊕ www. modernsound.com.br Ⓜ Siqueira Campos) was a traditional shop that turned into a self-designated megamusic store. Aside from the 50,000 CD titles—which include lots of rarities—the store carries music equipment and accessories and has a charming bistro, where live music, from jazz to bossa nova, is played by the finest carioca musicians. **Toca do Vinicius** (✉ Rua Vinícius de Moraes 129, loja C, Ipanema ☎ 021/2247–5227), though tiny, seems like a gathering place for bossa nova aficionados from around the world. Amid the friendly atmosphere, you can find books (a few in English), sheet music, and T-shirts as well as CDs.

Rio de Janeiro A to Z

AIR TRAVEL

CARRIERS   Nearly three-dozen airlines regularly serve Rio. Several of the international carriers also offer Rio–São Paulo flights. International carriers include Aerolíneas Argentinas, American Airlines, British Airways, Air Canada, Continental, Delta, and United. Varig and VASP are domestic carriers that serve international destinations. Varig, TAM, and Gol cover domestic routes. Non-Brazilian citizens must purchase tickets for Gol flights in person and with cash; the advantage is that Gol flights tend to be cheaper. ⇨ For airline information, *see* Air Travel *in* Brazil A to Z.

All international flights and most domestic flights arrive and depart from the Aeroporto Internacional Antônio Carlos Jobim, also known as

Galeão. The airport is about 45 minutes northwest of the beach area and most of Rio's hotels. Aeroporto Santos Dumont, 20 minutes from the beaches and within walking distance of Centro, serves the Rio–São Paulo air shuttle and a few air-taxi firms.

🗐 Airport Information **Aeroporto Internacional Antônio Carlos Jobim (Galeão)** 🕾 021/3398-4526. **Aeroporto Santos Dumont** 🕾 021/3814-7070 or 021/3814-7646.

AIRPORT TRANSFERS Special airport taxis have booths in the arrival areas of both airports. Fares to all parts of Rio are posted at the booths, and you pay in advance (about R$41–R$56). Also trustworthy are the white radio taxis parked in the same areas; these charge an average of 20% less. Three reliable special taxi firms are Transcoopass, Cootramo, and Coopertramo. Buses run by Empresa Real park curbside outside customs at Galeão and outside the main door at Santos Dumont; for R$13.50 they make the hour-long trip from Galeão into the city, following the beachfront drives and stopping at all hotels along the way. Buses leave from the airport every half hour from 5:20 AM to 11 PM. There are also air-conditioned buses—called *frescão* (literally, "fresh")—that leave the Galeão to Barra da Tijuca, passing through Zona Sul (R$5). Cootramo has a van (with 11 seats) to downtown for R$57 and to Copacabana for R$78. Coopertramo does the same for R$70 and R$80, but the van has a capacity to transport 15.

🗐 Taxis & Shuttles **Cootramo** 🕾 021/2560-5442 or 021/3976-9944 or 021/3976-9945. **Coopertramo** 🕾 021/2560-2022. **Empresa Real** 🕾 021/2560-7041 or 0800/240-850. **Transcoopass** 🕾 021/2560-4888.

BUS TRAVEL TO & FROM RIO

Regular service is available to and from Rio. Long-distance and international buses leave from the Rodoviária Novo Rio. Any local bus marked RODOVIÁRIA will take you to the station. You can buy tickets at the depot or, for some destinations, from travel agents. Buses also leave from the more conveniently located Menezes Cortes Terminal, near Praça 15 de Novembro. These buses travel to different neighborhoods of Rio (Barra da Tijuca, Santa Cruz, Campo Grande, and Recreio) and to nearby cities Nieterói, Petrópolis, and Nova Friburgo, among others.

🗐 Bus Information **Rodoviária Novo Rio** ✉ Av. Francisco Bicalho 1, São Cristóvão 🕾 021/3213-1800. **Menezes Cortes Terminal** ✉ Rua São José 35, Centro 🕾 021/ 2533-8819.

BUS TRAVEL WITHIN RIO

Much has been made of the threat of being robbed on Rio's buses. However, crime has dropped significantly in the last few years; if you're discreet, you shouldn't have any problems. Just don't wear expensive watches or jewelry, carry a camera or a map in hand, or talk boisterously in English. It's also wise to avoid buses during rush hour.

Local buses are inexpensive and can take you anywhere you want to go. You enter buses at the rear, where you pay the attendant and pass through a turnstile, then exit at the front. Have your fare in hand when you board to avoid flashing bills or wallets. Most bus drivers speak no English, and they drive like maniacs. The upscale, privately run, and air-conditioned frescão buses run between the beaches, downtown, and Rio's two airports. These vehicles, which look like highway buses, stop at regular bus stops but also may be flagged down wherever you see them. Green minivans run back and forth along beachfront avenues. Fares start at about R$1.40.

CAR RENTAL
Car rentals can be arranged through hotels or agencies and at this writing cost about R$110–R$250 a day for standard models. Major agencies include Avis, Hertz and Unidas. Localiza is a local agency. Hertz and Unidas have desks at the international and domestic airports. ⇨ For information on major car rental agencies, *see* Car Rental *in* Brazil A to Z.

CAR TRAVEL
The carioca style of driving is passionate to the point of abandon: traffic jams are common, the streets aren't well marked, and red lights are often more decorative than functional. Although there are parking areas along the beachfront boulevards, finding a spot can still be a problem. If you do choose to drive, exercise extreme caution, wear seat belts at all times, and keep the doors locked.

Arriving from São Paulo (429 km [266 mi] on BR 116) or Brasília (1,150 km [714 mi] on BR 040), you enter Rio via Avenida Brasil, which runs into Centro's beachside drive, the Avenida Infante Dom Henrique. This runs along Rio's Baía de Guanabara and passes through the Copacabana Tunnel to Copacabana Beach. The beachside Avenida Atlântica continues into Ipanema and Leblon along Avenidas Antônio Carlos Jobim (Ipanema) and Delfim Moreira (Leblon). From Galeão take the Airport Expressway (known as the Linha Vermelha, or Red Line) to the beach area. This expressway takes you through two tunnels and into Lagoa. Exit on Avenida Epitácio Pessoa, the winding street encircling the lagoon. To reach Copacabana, exit at Avenida Henrique Dodsworth (known as the Corte do Cantagalo). For Ipanema and Leblon there are several exits, beginning with Rua Maria Quitéria.

Turismo Clássico Travel, one of the country's most reliable travel and transport agencies, can arrange for a driver, with or without an English-speaking guide (US$30 per hour). Classico's owners, Liliana and Vera, speak English, and each has 20 years of experience in organizing transportation. They also lead sightseeing tours.
🚗 **Turismo Clássico Travel** ✉ Av. Nossa Senhora de Copacabana 1059, Sala 805, Copacabana ☎ 021/2523-3390.

GASOLINE There's a gas station on every main street in Rio. International companies, such as Shell and Esso, are represented. The gas stations run by Brazilian oil company Petrobras are called BR. Ipiranga is another local option. Half the gas stations are open from 6 AM until 10 PM, and half are open 24 hours and have convenience stores. Gas stations don't have emergency service, so ask when you rent whether your car-rental insurance includes it.

EMERGENCIES
The Tourism Police station is open 24 hours.
🚨 Emergency Services **Ambulance and Fire** ☎ 193. **Police** ☎ 190 ⊕ www.novapolicia. rj.gov.br. **Tourism Police** ✉ Rua Humberto de Campos 315, Leblon ☎ 021/3399-7170.

🏥 Medical Clinics **Cardio Plus** ✉ Rua Visconde de Pirajá 330, Ipanema ☎ 021/
2521-4899. **Galdino Campos Cardio Copa Medical Clinic** ✉ Av. Nossa Senhora de Copacabana 492, Copacabana ☎ 021/2548-9966. **Medtur** ✉ Av. Nossa Senhora de Copacabana 647, Copacabana ☎ 021/2235-3339. **Copa D'Or** ✉ Rua Figueiredo Magalhães
875, Copacabana ☎ 021/2545-3600.

🏥 24-Hour Pharmacies **Drogaria Pacheco** ✉ Av. Nossa Senhora de Copacabana 534,
Copacabana ☎ 021/2548-1525. **Farmácia do Leme** ✉ Av. Prado Júnior 237, Leme
☎ 021/2275-3847.

HEALTH & SAFETY

Avoid tap water, though ice in restaurants and bars is safe, as it's usually made from bottled water. Take care not to soak up too much sun.
Despite Rio's reputation, crime is no more likely than in any large city.
Be particularly wary of children who thrust themselves in front of you
and ask for money or offer to shine your shoes. Another member of the
gang may strike from behind, grabbing your valuables and disappearing into the crowd. Another tactic is for criminals to approach your car
at intersections. Always keep doors locked and windows partially closed.
Leave valuables in your hotel safe, don't wear expensive jewelry or
watches, and keep cameras out of sight. Walking alone at night on the
beach isn't a good idea; neither is getting involved with drugs—penalties for possession are severe, and dealers are the worst of the worst.

MAIL, INTERNET & SHIPPING

The main post office is in Centro, but there are branches all over the
city, including one at Galeão, several on Avenida Nossa Senhora de Copacabana in Copacabana, and one on Rua Visconde de Pirajá in Ipanema.
Most are open weekdays 8–5 and Saturday 8–noon. Federal Express and
DHL have offices open weekdays, but shipping usually takes longer than
just overnight. You can call a day ahead to schedule pickup.

The staff at many hotels can arrange Internet access for guests. In addition, you can head to several cybercafés around town for coffee while
you check your e-mail. At Café do Ubaldo (Sunday–Thursday 8 AM–midnight and Friday–Saturday 8 AM–2 AM), Web access is R$5 for 30 min-
utes. At Cyber Coffee (Monday–Saturday 10–10; Sunday 3–9) Web access
is R$9.50 for an hour and R$3.50 for each additional 15 minutes.

🖥 Internet Centers **Café do Ubaldo** ✉ Rua Visconde de Pirajá 276, Ipanema ☎ 021/
2521-6110 Ⓜ Siquera Campos, then shuttle bus to Praça General Osório. **Cyber Coffee**
✉ Rio Sul Shopping Center, Rua Lauro Muller 16, 3rd floor, Botafogo ☎ 021/2543-6886.
🖥 Post Office **Agência Central** (Main Branch) ✉ Av. Presidente Vargas 3077 ☎ 021/
2503-8467 or 021/2273-5998.

🖥 Overnight Services **DHL** ✉ Rua Teófilo Otoni 15 A, Centro ☎ 021/2516-0828 or
0800/701-0833. **Federal Express** ✉ Av. Calógeras 23, Centro ☎ 021/2262-8405 or 0800/
903-333.

METRÔ TRAVEL

Rio's subway system, the metrô, is clean, relatively safe, and efficient,
but it's not comprehensive. Trains run daily from 6 AM to 11 PM along
two lines: Linha 1 runs north from the Siqueira Campos stop in Copacabana, three blocks from the beach and into downtown, then west
to its terminus at the Saens Pena station; Linha 2 starts four stops be-

fore Saens Pena at Estácio and heads northwest to Rio's edge at the Pavuna station. A single metrô ticket at this writing costs R$1.47. Combination metrô-bus tickets allow you to take special buses to and from the Botafogo station: the M-21 runs to Leblon via Jardim Botânico and Jóckey; the M-22 goes to Leblon by way of Túnel Velho, Copacabana, and Ipanema. Some metrô stations have maps. To get to Praça General Osório, you can take the metrô to Siquera Campos, then catch the free shuttle bus; you must buy a ticket for Praça General Osório (not for Siquera Campos) when entering the metrô.

🚲 Metrô Information **Metrô Rio Information Line** ☎ 021/3982-3600 or 021/3211-6300.

MONEY MATTERS

Generally, exchange rates are better in the city than at the airport, and cash gets better rates than traveler's checks. Most Brazilian banks don't exchange money. One that does is Banco do Brasil. The branch at Galeão offers good exchange rates, but it won't provide credit-card advances.

Casas de câmbio (exchange houses) are found all over the city, especially along the beaches and on Avenida Nossa Senhora de Copacabana and Rua Visconde de Pirajá in Ipanema. Many change money without charging a service fee. Sometimes, depending on the amount of money you wish to exchange, exchange houses have a better rate than the banks. American Express is another option. Some hotels, such as the Caesar Park and the Copacabana Palace, offer competitive rates but charge a commission if you're not a guest. On weekends hotels may be your best bet because few other places are open. Or try the Banco 24 Horas automatic teller machines (ATMs) throughout town, which dispense reais.

🚲 Banks & Exchange Services **American Express** ✉ Av. Atlântica 1702 B, Copacabana ☎ 021/2548-2148 or 0800/702-0777. **Banco do Brasil** ✉ Rua Bartolomeu Mitre 438 A, Leblon ☎ 021/2512-9992 or 021/2274-4664 ✉ Av. Nossa Senhora de Copacabana 594 ☎ 021/3808-2689 ✉ Aeroporto Internacional Antônio Carlos Jobim, 3rd floor ☎ 021/3398-3652. **Banco 24 Horas ATM** ✉ Av. Nossa Senhora de Copacabana 202 ✉ Av. Nossa Senhora de Copacabana 599 ✉ Av. Nossa Senhora de Copacabana 1366 ✉ Visconde de Pirajá 174, Ipanema. **Casa Universal** ✉ Av. Nossa Senhora de Copacabana 371 E, Copacabana ☎ 021/2548-6696.

TAXIS

Yellow taxis have meters that start at a set price and have two rates. The "1" rate applies to fares before 8 PM, and the "2" rate applies to fares after 8 PM, on Sunday, on holidays, throughout December, in the neighborhoods of São Conrado and Barra da Tijuca, and when climbing steep hills. Drivers are required to post a chart noting the current fares on the inside of the left rear window. Most carioca cabbies are pleasant, but there are exceptions. Remain alert and trust your instincts. Few cab drivers speak English. Pay attention to the meter, as some cab drivers might neglect to turn on the meter and then try to overcharge.

Radio taxis and several companies that routinely serve hotels (and whose drivers often speak English) are also options. They charge 30% more than other taxis but are reliable and usually air-conditioned. Other cabs working with the hotels also charge more, normally a fixed fee that you should agree on before you leave. Reliable radio cab companies include Centro de Taxis, Coopacarioca, and Coopatur.

🚖 Taxi Companies **Centro de Taxis** ☎ 021/2593-2598 or 021/3899-1010. **Coopacarioca** ☎ 021/2518-1818. **Coopatur** ☎ 021/2573-1009.

TELEPHONES

Rio's area code is 021. There are public phones on corners throughout the city. They work with cards that you can buy in a variety of denominations at newsstands, banks, and some shops (some phones also work with credit cards). For long-distance calls there are phone offices at the main bus terminal, Galeão, downtown at Praça Tiradentes 41, and in Copacabana at Avenida Nossa Senhora de Copacabana 540. To make international calls through the operator, dial 000111. For operator-assisted long-distance within Brazil, dial 101; information is 102. You can also make international calls through the long-distance providers Embratel (dial 21 before the number you're calling), Telefonica (dial 15), and Intelig (dial 23). You can make international calls from any public phone that reads D.D.I (*discagen direta internacional,* or "international calls"). Numbers in Rio have eight digits.

TOURS

You can ride around the Floresta da Tijuca and Corcovado, Angra dos Reis, and Teresópolis in renovated World War II jeeps (1942 Dodge Commanders, Willys F-75s, and others) with the well-organized Atlantic Forest Jeep Tours. Guides speak English. The company also has a range of ecological tours, including some on horseback. English-speaking guides at Gray Line are superb. In addition to a variety of city tours, the company also offers trips outside town, whether you'd like to go white-water rafting on the Rio Paraíbuna, tour a coffee plantation, or spend time in Petrópolis. Helicopter tours are also an option.

Carlos Roquette is a history teacher who runs Cultural Rio, an agency that hosts trips to 8,000 destinations. Most are historic sites. A guided visit costs around US$110 for four hours, depending on the size of the group. Ecology and Culture Tours offers hiking and jeep tours of Tijuca, Sugar Loaf, Santa Teresa, and various beaches. Guides speak English: morning and afternoon excursions are available. Favela Tour offers a fascinating half-day tour of two favelas. For anyone with an interest in Brazil beyond the beaches, such tours are highly recommended. The company's English-speaking guides can also be contracted for other outings.

Private Tours take you around old Rio, the favelas, Corcovado, Floresta da Tijuca, Prainha, and Grumari in a jeep. Guides are available who speak English, Hungarian, French, and German. Hang glide or paraglide over Pedra da Gávea and Pedra Bonita under the supervision of São Conrado Eco-Aventura.

Helisight gives a number of helicopter tours whose flights may pass over the Cristo Redentor, Copacabana, Ipanema, and/or Maracanã stadium. There are night flights as well; reserve ahead for these daily 9–6. Rio Hiking tours combine the city sightseeing with nature hikes to the Floresta da Tijuca and other areas. The company also runs nightlife tours in the city and overnight trips to Parati and Ilha Grande.

🚩**Atlantic Forest Jeep Tours** ☎ 021/2495-9827 🖷 021/2494-4761. **Cultural Rio** ☎ 021/9911-3829 or 021/3322-4872 ⊕www.culturalrio.com.br. **Ecology and Culture Tours** ☎021/2522-1620. **Favela Tour** ☎ 021/3322-2727. **Gray Line** ☎ 021/2512-9919. **Helisight** ✉ Rua Visconde de Pirajá 580, loja 107 ☎ 021/2511-2141, 021/2542-7895, or 021/2259-6995 ⊕ www.helisight.com.br. **Private Tours** ☎🖷 021/2232-9710 ⊕ www.privatetours.com.br. **São Conrado Eco-Aventura** ☎ 021/2522-5586, 021/3902-8558, or 021/9966-7010 ⊕www.4ventos.com.br. **Rio Hiking** ☎021/9721-0594 ⊕www.riohiking.com.br.

TRAIN TRAVEL

Intercity trains leave from *the* central station that starred in the Oscar-nominated movie of the same name, Estação Dom Pedro II Central do Brasil. Trains, including a daily overnight train to São Paulo, also leave from the Estação Leopoldina Barao de Maria, near Praça 15 de Novembro.

🚩 Train Information **Estação Dom Pedro II Central do Brasil** ✉ Praça Cristiano Otoni on Av. President Vargas, Centro ☎ 021/2588-9494.

VISITOR INFORMATION

The Rio de Janeiro city tourism department, Riotur, has an information booth, which is open 8–5 daily. There are also city tourism desks at the airports and the Novo Rio bus terminal. The Rio de Janeiro state tourism board, Turisrio, is open weekdays 9–6. You can also try contacting Brazil's national tourism board, Embratur. Disque-Turismo runs an English-language tourist-information hot line weekdays 8–8 and Saturday 8–1:30.

🚩 Tourist Information **Disque-Turismo** ☎0800/282-2007. **Embratur** ✉ Rua Uruguaiana 174, Centro ☎ 021/2509-6017 ⊕ www.embratur.gov.br. **Riotur** ✉ Rua da Assembléia 10, near Praça 15 de Novembro, Centro ☎ 021/2217-7575 or 0800/7071808 ⊕ www.rio.rj.gov.br/riotur. **Riotur information booth** ✉ Av. Princesa Isabel 183, Copacabana ☎ 021/2542-8080. **Turisrio** ✉ Rua da Ajuda 5, Centro ☎ 021/2215-0011 ⊕ www.turisrio.rj.gov.br.

SÃO PAULO

Updated by Karla Brunet

Crowded buses grind down streets spouting black smoke, endless stands of skyscrapers block the horizon, and the din of traffic deafens the ear. But native *paulistanos* (inhabitants of São Paulo city; inhabitants of São Paulo State are called *paulistas*) love this megalopolis of 17 million. São Paulo sprawls across 7,951 square km (3,070 square mi), 1,502 square km (580 square mi) of which make up the city proper. The largest city in South America makes New York City, with its population of 8 million, seem small.

In 1554 Jesuit priests, including José de Anchieta and Manoel da Nóbrega, founded the village of São Paulo de Piratininga and began converting Indians to Catholicism. The mission town remained unimportant to the Portuguese Crown until it became the departure point for expeditions whose members set out to look for gemstones and gold and to enslave Indians. São Paulo saw Emperor Dom Pedro I declare independence from Portugal by the Rio Ipiranga (Ipiranga River), near the city.

In the late 19th century São Paulo became a major coffee producer, attracting both workers and investors from many countries. Italians, Portuguese, Spanish, Germans, and Japanese put their talents and energies to work. By 1895, 70,000 of the 130,000 residents were immigrants. Their efforts transformed the place from a sleepy mission post into a dynamic financial and cultural hub. In the 1950s the auto industry began to develop and contributed greatly to São Paulo's contemporary cityscape. Over the next 30 years, people from throughout Brazil came seeking jobs, many in the Cubatão Industrial Park—one of the largest in the developing world—just outside the city limits. Today, like many major European or American hubs, São Paulo struggles to meet its citizens' transportation and housing needs, and goods and services are expensive. Yet, even as the smog reddens your eyes, you'll see that there's much to explore. As a city committed to making dreams come true, São Paulo offers top-rate nightlife and dining as well as thriving cultural and arts scenes.

Exploring São Paulo

Each neighborhood seems a testament to a different period of the city's history. São Paulo's first inhabitants, Jesuit missionaries and treasure-hunting pioneers, lived in the largely pedestrians-only hilltop and valley areas, particularly Vale do Anhangabaú. Later these areas became Centro (downtown district), a financial and cultural center that's still home to the stock exchange and many banks. It's now the focus of revitalization efforts.

The Bela Vista and Bixiga (the city's little Italy) neighborhoods, near Centro, are home to many theaters and bars. In the 19th century many families who made fortunes from coffee built whimsical mansions in the ridge-top Avenida Paulista neighborhood. Beginning with the post–World War II industrial boom, these homes gave way to skyscrapers. Many of the best hotels are also on or near this avenue.

During the economic growth of the 1970s, many businesses moved west, and downhill to a former swamp. You'll find the tall buildings of Avenida Brigadeiro Faria Lima, the stylish homes of the Jardins neighborhood, and the Shopping Center Iguatemi (Brazil's first mall) just off the banks of the Rio Pinheiros. Large-scale construction of corporate headquarters continues south, between the Marginal Pinheiros Beltway and the Avenida Engenheiro Luís Carlos Berrini, not far from the luxurious Shopping Center Morumbi.

Centro

Even though the downtown district has its share of petty crime, it's one of the few places with a historical flavor. Explore the areas where the city began and see examples of architecture, some of it beautifully restored, from the 19th century.

Numbers in the text correspond to numbers in the margin and on the São Paulo City map.

A GOOD TOUR   Begin at the **Edifício Copan** ❶ ▶, designed by Brazilian architect Oscar Niemeyer. Farther up Avenida Ipiranga is the city's tallest building, the **Edifício Itália** ❷ (you might want to return at the end of the day for a terrific view of the city from the bar or the restaurant on the 41st floor). Continue north along the avenue to the **Praça da República** ❸. Cross Ipiranga and walk down the pedestrians-only Rua Barão de Itapetininga, with its many shops and street vendors. Follow it to the neobaroque **Teatro Municipal** ❹, in the Praça Ramos de Azevedo. Head east across the square to the Viaduto do Chá, a monumental overpass above the Vale do Anhangabaú—the heart of São Paulo. At the end of this viaduct, turn right onto Rua Líbero Badaró and follow it to the baroque **Igreja de São Francisco de Assis** ❺. A short walk along Rua Benjamin Constant will bring you to the **Praça da Sé** ❻, the city's true center and the site of the Catedral Metropolitana da Sé.

You can take the *metrô* (subway) from the station at the cathedral west to the Barra Funda station and the **Memorial da América Latina.** Or you can head north out of Praça da Sé and follow Rua Roberto Simonsen to the **Solar da Marquesa de Santos** ❼. Nearby is the **Pátio do Colégio** ❽. Walk north along Rua Boa Vista and Rua do Tesouro. Turn right onto Rua Álvares Penteado. On the next corner is **Centro Cultural Banco do Brasil** ❾. Continue on Rua Álvares Penteado and turn right onto Rua Miguel Couto. Walk a block onto Rua 15 de Novembro. Number 275, on the left, houses **BOVESPA** ❿, the São Paulo Stock Exchange. Near the end of Rua 15 de Novembro, at Rua João Brícola 24, stands the 36-floor **Edifício BANESPA** ⓫. To the northwest is the **Edifício Martinelli** ⓬. Walk two blocks up on Rua São Bento to the **Basílica de São Bento** ⓭. Near it is Café Girondino, a good spot for a break. From the basilica, you can take a train north from the São Bento station to the Luz stop and the **Pinacoteca do Estado** ⓮, the state gallery. On Avenida Tiradentes walk north to the **Museu de Arte Sacra** ⓯.

TIMING & PRECAUTIONS   This route requires at least five hours on foot and use of the metrô. An early start will allow you to be more leisurely should one sight pique your interest more than another. If you're planning to take taxis or hire a driver, bear in mind that traffic jams are common. Being a tourist in Centro is a bit hazardous. If you keep a low profile and speak at least some Portuguese or Spanish, you'll most likely avoid being the target of thieves. Otherwise, you might feel more comfortable touring with a guide. Whatever you do, leave your Rolex back at the hotel.

WHAT TO SEE   **Basílica de São Bento.** This church, constructed between 1910 and 1922, ⓭ was designed by German architect Richard Berndl. Its enormous organ has some 6,000 pipes. ⊠ *Largo de São Bento* ☎ *011/228–3633* ▨ *Free* ☉ *Mon.–Sat. 6–1 and 3–7:30, Sun. 5–1 and 3–6* Ⓜ *São Bento.*

⓾   **BOVESPA.** If you leave an ID with the guard at the front desk, you can go up to the mezzanine and watch the hurly-burly of the busy São Paulo Stock Exchange—a hub for the foreign investment Brazil has attracted in its efforts to privatize state-owned companies. Computer terminals in the observation gallery carry the latest stock quotes as well as general information in various languages. ⊠ *Rua 15 de Novembro*

275, Centro ☎ *011/3233–2000 Ext. 2456, 011/2333–2110 tours* ✉ *Free* ⊙ *Weekdays 10–1 and 2–4:45* Ⓜ *São Bento.*

❾ Centro Cultural Banco do Brasil. Opened in 2001, this has become a popular space in town for modern and contemporary art. The center has three floors of exhibitions rooms, a theater, an auditorium, a movie theater, and a video room. ⊠ *Rua Álvares Penteado 112, Centro* ☎ *011/ 3113–3600* ✉ *Free* ⊙ *Tues.–Sun. 12–6:30* Ⓜ *Sé.*

⓫ Edifício BANESPA. If you can't fit tea or drinks at the top of the Edifício Itália into your Centro tour, get your panoramic view of the city atop the 36-floor BANESPA Building. It was constructed in 1947 and modeled after New York's Empire State Building. A radio traffic reporter squints through the smog every morning from here. ⊠ *Praça Antônio Prado, Centro* ☎ *no phone* ✉ *Free* ⊙ *Weekdays 9–6* Ⓜ *São Bento.*

▶ **❶ Edifício Copan.** The architect of this serpentine apartment and office block, Oscar Niemeyer, went on to design much of Brasília. The building has the clean, white, undulating curves characteristic of his work. Although many Brazilians prefer colonial architecture, all take pride in Niemeyer's international reputation. The Copan was constructed in 1950, and its 1,850 apartments house about 4,500 people. If you want to shop in the first-floor stores, be sure to do so before dark, after which the area is overrun by prostitutes and transvestites. ⊠ *Av. Ipiranga at Av. Consolação, Centro* ☎ *No phone* Ⓜ *Anhangabaú.*

❷ Edifício Itália. To see the astounding view from atop the Itália Building, you'll have to patronize the bar or dining room of the Terraço Itália restaurant, on the 41st floor. As the restaurant is expensive (and isn't one of the city's best), afternoon tea or a drink is the quickest, least expensive option. Tea is served 3–5:30, and the bar opens at 6. ⊠ *Av. Ipiranga 336, Centro* ☎ *011/3257–6566 for restaurant* Ⓜ *Anhangabaú.*

FodorśChoice
★

⓬ Edifício Martinelli. Amid São Paulo's modern 1950s-era skyscrapers, the Gothic Martinelli Building is a welcome anomaly. The city's first skyscraper, it was built in 1929 by Italian immigrant-turned-count Giuseppe Martinelli. The whimsical penthouse is worth checking out. The rooftop, which has a great view, is open weekdays 10:30–4. To go there, you need permission from the building manager on the ground floor, take the elevator to the 34th floor and walk up two more flights. ⊠ *Av. São João 35, Centro* ☎ *No phone* ✉ *Free* Ⓜ *São Bento.*

❺ Igreja de São Francisco de Assis. The baroque St. Francis of Assisi Church is actually two churches with a common name, one run by Catholic clergy and the other by lay brothers. One of the city's best-preserved Portuguese colonial buildings, it was built from 1647 to 1790. ⊠ *Largo São Francisco 133, Centro* ☎ *011/606–0081* ✉ *Free* ⊙ *Daily 7 AM–8 PM; lay brothers' church weekdays 7–11:30 and 1–8, weekends 7–10* Ⓜ *Sé or Anhangabaú.*

⓯ Museu de Arte Sacra. If you can't get to Bahia during your stay in Brazil, the Museum of Sacred Art is a must-see. It houses an extremely interesting collection of wooden and terra-cotta masks, jewelry, and liturgical objects that date from the 17th century to the present. Don't miss the on-site convent, founded in 1774. ⊠ *Av. Tiradentes 676, Centro* ☎ *011/3326–1373* 🖃 *R$4* ⊙ *Tues.–Fri. 11–6, Sat.–Sun. 10–7* Ⓜ *Luz.*

❽ Pátio do Colégio/Museu Padre Anchieta. São Paulo was founded by the Jesuits José de Anchieta and Manoel da Nóbrega in the College Courtyard in 1554. The church was constructed in 1896 in the same style as the chapel built by the Jesuits. In the small museum you can see some paintings from the colonization period and an exhibition of early sacred art. ⊠ *Pátio do Colégio 84, Centro* ☎ *011/3105–6899* ⊙ *Museum Tues.–Sun. 9–5; church Mon.–Sat. 8:15–7, Sun. mass at 10 AM* Ⓜ *Sé.*

⓮ Pinacoteca do Estado. The building that houses the State Art Gallery was constructed in 1905. In the permanent collection you can see the work of such famous Brazilian artists as Tarsila do Amaral, whose work consists of colorful, somewhat abstract portraits; Anita Malfatti, a painter influenced by fauvism and German expressionism; Cândido Portinari, whose oil paintings have social and historical themes; and Emiliano Di Cavalcanti, a multimedia artist whose illustrations, oil paintings, and engravings are influenced by cubism and contain Afro-Brazilian and urban themes. ⊠ *Praça da Luz 2, Centro* ☎ *011/229–9844* ⊕ *www.uol.com.br/pinasp* 🖃 *R$5* ⊙ *Tues.–Sun. 10–6* Ⓜ *Luz.*

❸ Praça da República. Republic Square is the site of a huge Sunday street fair where you'll find arts and crafts, semiprecious stones, food, and often live music. Some artisans display their work all week long, so it's worth a peek anytime. ⊠ *Centro* Ⓜ *República.*

❻ Praça da Sé. Two major metrô lines cross under the large, busy Cathedral Square. Migrants from Brazil's poor northeast often gather to enjoy their music and to sell and buy regional items such as medicinal herbs. It's also the central hangout for street children and the focus of periodic (and controversial) police sweeps to get them off the street. The square and most of the historic area and financial district to its north have been set aside for pedestrians, official vehicles, and public transportation only. ⊠ *Bounded by Rua Quinze de Novembro, Rua Anita Garibaldi, and Av. Rangel Pestana.*

❼ Solar da Marquesa de Santos. This manor house is the city's only surviving late-18th-century residence. It was bought by Marquesa de Santos in 1843. It now contains a museum that hosts temporary art exhibits that usually center on a metropolitan São Paulo theme. ⊠ *Rua Roberto Simonsen 136, Centro* ☎ *011/3106–2218* 🖃 *Free* ⊙ *Tues.–Sun. 9–5* Ⓜ *Sé.*

❹ Teatro Municipal. Inspired by the Paris Opéra, the Municipal Theater was built between 1903 and 1911 with art nouveau elements. The house has hosted such luminaries as Isadora Duncan in 1916 and Anna Pavlova in 1919. Plays and operas are still staged here. Buy tickets at the theater; local newspapers have schedules. The fully restored auditorium, resplendent with gold leaf, moss-green velvet, marble, and mirrors, is open only to those attending cultural events, but sometimes you can walk in for a quick look at the vestibule. ⊠ *Praça Ramos de Azevedo, Centro* ☎ *011/223–3022* Ⓜ *Anhangabaú.*

Liberdade

At the beginning of the 20th century, a group of Japanese arrived to work as contract farm laborers in São Paulo State. During the next five decades, roughly a quarter of a million of their countrymen followed, forming what is now the largest Japanese colony outside Japan. Distinguished today by a large number of college graduates and successful businesspeople, professionals, and politicians, the colony has made important contributions to Brazilian agriculture and the seafood industry. Liberdade, which is south of Praça da Sé behind the cathedral, and whose entrance is marked by a series of red porticoes, is home to many first-, second-, and third-generation Nippo-Brazilians. Clustered around Avenida Liberdade are shops with everything from imported bubble gum to miniature robots to Kabuki face paint. The Sunday street fair holds many surprises.

A GOOD TOUR From the **Praça Liberdade** ⑯, by the Liberdade metrô station, walk south along Rua Galvão Bueno. About six blocks from the square is the intriguing **Museu da Imigração Japonesa** ⑰.

TIMING & The best time to visit Liberdade is on Sunday during the street fair, where
PRECAUTIONS Asian food, crafts, and souvenirs are sold. This tour takes about two hours—a little longer if you linger in the museum. Don't follow the tour at night.

WHAT TO SEE **Museu da Imigração Japonesa.** The Museum of Japanese Immigration has
⑰ two floors of exhibits about Nippo-Brazilian culture and farm life and Japanese contributions to Brazilian horticulture. The Japanese are credited with introducing the persimmon, the azalea, the tangerine, and the kiwi to Brazil, among other things. Call ahead to arrange for an English-language tour. ⊠ *Rua São Joaquim 381, Liberdade* ☎ *011/3209–5465* ⌨ *R$3* ⊙ *Tues.–Sun. 1:30–5:30* Ⓜ *São Joaquim.*

⑯ **Praça Liberdade.** On Sunday morning and afternoon Liberdade hosts a sprawling Asian food and crafts fair where the Brazilian ethnic mix is in plain view; you may see, for example, Afro-Brazilians dressed in colorful kimonos hawking grilled shrimp on a stick. Liberdade also hosts several ethnic celebrations, such as April's Hanamatsuri, commemorating the birth of the Buddha. Apart from the fair and special events, the only other reason to visit this square is to stop by at the nearby Japanese shops and restaurants. ⊠ *Av. da Liberdade and Rua dos Estudantes Liberdade* Ⓜ *Liberdade.*

Avenida Paulista & Bixiga

Money once poured into and out of the coffee barons' mansions that lined Avenida Paulista, making it, in a sense, the financial hub. And so it is today, though instead of mansions there are major banks. Like the barons before them, many of these financial institutions generously support the arts. Numerous places have changing exhibitions—often free—in the Paulista neighborhood. Nearby Bixiga, São Paulo's Little Italy, is full of restaurants.

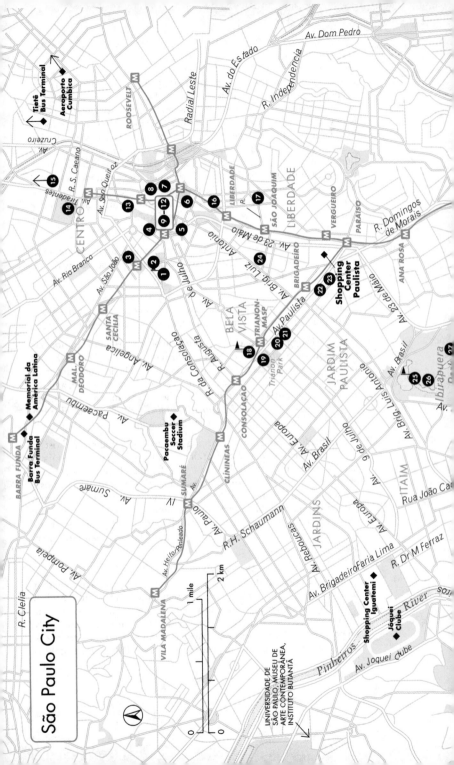

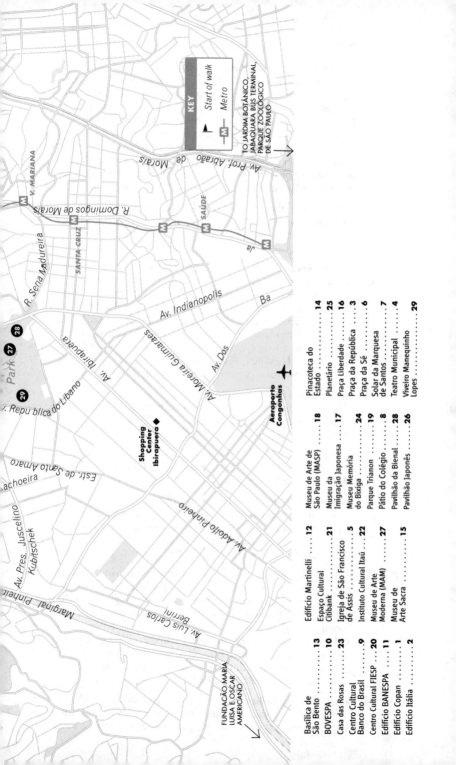

KEY

▲ Start of walk

Ⓜ Metro

TO JARDIM BOTÂNICO, JABAQUARA BUS TERMINAL, PARQUE ZOOLÓGICO DE SÃO PAULO

Aeroporto Congonhas ✈

Shopping Center Ibirapuera ◆

A GOOD TOUR Begin your tour at the **Museu de Arte de São Paulo (MASP)** ⑱ ☞. Across the street is **Parque Trianon** ⑲, where many businesspeople eat lunch. Leaving the park, veer right onto Avenida Paulista and head for the **Centro Cultural FIESP** ⑳, which frequently has art and theatrical presentations. Farther down Avenida Paulista is the **Espaço Cultural Citibank** ㉑, a gallery with temporary exhibitions. Continue a few more blocks along Avenida Paulista to the **Instituto Cultural Itaú** ㉒, a great place to see contemporary Brazilian art. In the next block is the **Casa das Rosas** ㉓, with yet another noteworthy gallery. From here you can hop a bus or a taxi to the **Museu Memória do Bixiga** ㉔, with its displays on Italian immigration.

TIMING & PRECAUTIONS This tour takes about five hours, including a visit to MASP and the Museu do Bixiga. Busy, well-lighted Avenida Paulista may well be the safest place in city. Even so, stay alert and hold onto your bags, particularly in Parque Trianon.

WHAT TO SEE

㉓ Casa das Rosas. The House of the Roses, a French-style mansion, seems out of place next to the skyscrapers of Paulista. It was built in 1935 by famous paulistano architect Ramos de Azevedo for one of his daughters. The building was home to the same family until 1986, when it was made an official municipal landmark. It was later opened as a cultural center—with changing fine-arts exhibitions and multimedia displays by up-and-coming artists, and it's one of the avenue's few remaining early-20th-century buildings. ⊠ *Av. Paulista 37, Paraíso* ☏ *011/251–5271* ⊕ *www.casadasrosas.sp.gov.br* ☞ *Free* ⊙ *Tues.–Sun. 1–7* Ⓜ *Brigadeiro.*

⑳ Centro Cultural FIESP. The cultural center of São Paulo State's Federation of Industry has a theater, a library of art books, and temporary art exhibits. ⊠ *Av. Paulista 1313, Jardim Paulista* ☏ *011/3253–5877* ☞ *Free* ⊙ *Tues.–Sun. 9–7* Ⓜ *Trianon.*

㉑ Espaço Cultural Citibank. Citibank's cultural space hosts temporary exhibitions of Brazilian art. ⊠ *Av. Paulista 1111, Jardim Paulista* ☏ *011/5576–2744* ☞ *Free* ⊙ *Weekdays 9–7, weekends 10–5* Ⓜ *Trianon.*

㉒ Instituto Cultural Itaú. Maintained by Itaú, one of Brazil's largest private banks, this cultural institute has art shows as well as lectures, workshops, and films. Its library specializes in works on Brazilian art and culture. ⊠ *Av. Paulista 149, Paraíso* ☏ *011/3238–1777* ⊕ *www.itaucultural. org.br* ☞ *Free* ⊙ *Tues.–Sun. 10–7* Ⓜ *Brigadeiro.*

☞ ★ **⑱ Museu de Arte de São Paulo (MASP).** A striking low-rise elevated on two massive concrete pillars 256 feet apart, the São Paulo Museum of Art contains the city's premier collection of fine arts. Highlights include dazzling works by Hieronymous Bosch, Vincent van Gogh, Pierre-Auguste Renoir, and Edgar Degas. Lasar Segall and Cândido Portinari are two of the many Brazilian artists represented in the collection. The huge open area beneath the museum is often used for cultural events and is the site of a Sunday antiques fair. ⊠ *Av. Paulista 1578, Bela Vista* ☏ *011/251–5644* ⊕ *www.masp.art.br* ☞ *R$10* ⊙ *Tues.–Sun. 11–6.*

㉔ Museu Memória do Bixiga. This museum, established in 1980, contains objects that belonged to Italian immigrants who lived in the Bixiga neighborhood. On weekends you can extend your tour to include the

Feira do Bixiga, at Praça Dom Orione, where handicrafts, antiques, and furniture are sold. ⊠ *Rua dos Ingleses 118, Bixiga* ☎ *011/3285–5009* ▣ *Free* ⊗ *Wed.–Sun. 2–5.*

⓳ **Parque Trianon.** The park was originally created in 1892 as a showcase for local vegetation. In 1968 Roberto Burle Marx (the Brazilian landscaper famed for Rio's mosaic-tile beachfront sidewalks) renovated it and incorporated new trees. You can escape the noise of the street and admire the flora while seated on one of the benches sculpted to look like chairs. ⊠ *Rua Peixoto Gomide 949, Jardim Paulista* ☎ *011/289–2160* ▣ *Free* ⊗ *Daily 6–6* Ⓜ *Trianon.*

Parque Ibirapuera

Only 15 minutes by taxi from downtown, Ibirapuera is São Paulo's answer to New York's Central Park, though it is slightly less than half the size and gets infinitely more crowded on sunny weekends. In the 1950s the land, which originally contained the municipal nurseries, was chosen as the site of a public park to commemorate the city's 400th anniversary. Oscar Niemeyer was called in to head the team of architects assigned to the project. The park was inaugurated in 1954, and some pavilions used for the opening festivities still sit amid its 160 hectares (395 acres). The park has jogging and biking paths, a lake, and rolling lawns.

A GOOD WALK   Enter at Gate 9 and walk around the lake to the starry sights at the **Planetário** ㉕ ▶. As you exit the planetarium, veer left to the **Pavilhão Japonês** ㉖. Then turn left and follow the path to the Marquise do Ibirapuera, a structure that connects several buildings, including the **Museu de Arte Moderna (MAM)** ㉗ and the **Pavilhão da Bienal** ㉘, which houses the park branch of the Museu de Arte Contemporânea. When you exit the compound, walk toward Gate 7 and the **Viveiro Manequinho Lopes** ㉙, with its many species of Brazilian trees.

TIMING &   The park deserves a whole day, though you can probably do this tour
PRECAUTIONS   in one afternoon. Avoid the park on Sunday, when it gets really crowded, and after sundown.

WHAT TO SEE   **Museu de Arte Moderna (MAM).** The permanent collection of the Museum
㉗   of Modern Art includes more than 2,600 paintings, sculptures, and drawings from the Brazilian modernist movement, which began in the 1920s, when artists were developing a new form of expression influenced by the city's rapid industrial growth. The museum also hosts temporary exhibits that feature works by new local artists. Brazilian architect Lina Bo Bardi gave the building a wall of glass, creating a giant window that beckons you to peek at what's inside. ⊠ *Gate 10, Parque Ibirapuera* ☎ *011/5549–9688* ⊕ *www.man.org.br* ▣ *R$5 (free Tues.)* ⊗ *Tues., Wed., Fri. noon–6, Thurs. noon–10, weekends and holidays 10–6.*

㉘ **Pavilhão da Bienal.** From October through November in every even-numbered year, this pavilion hosts the Bienal (Biennial) art exhibition, which draws more than 250 artists from more than 60 countries. The first such event was held in 1951 in Parque Trianon and drew artists from 21 countries. It was moved to this Oscar Niemeyer–designed building after Ibirapuera Park's 1954 inauguration. The pavilion also houses a branch of the **Museu de Arte Contemporânea** (MAC; ☎ 011/5573–9932 ⊕ www.mac.usp.br). There's much more to see at the main branch of the museum, at the University of São Paulo, but this park branch has some temporary exhibits. The museum is open Tuesday–Sunday noon–6; admission is free. ✉ *Gate 10, Parque Ibirapuera.*

㉖ Pavilhão Japonês. An exact replica of the Katsura Imperial Palace in Kyoto, Japan, the Japanese Pavilion was designed by University of Tokyo professor Sutemi Horiguti and built in Japan. It took four months to reassemble beside the man-made lake in the midst of the Japanese-style garden. The main building has displays of samurai clothes, 11th-century sculptures, and pottery and sculpture from several dynasties. Rooms used for traditional tea ceremonies are upstairs. ✉ *Gate 10, Parque Ibirapuera* ☎ *011/5573–6453* 🖾 *R$3* ☉ *Weekends and holidays 10–5.*

👆 ▶ **㉕ Planetário.** Paulistanos love the planetarium and frequently fill the 350 seats under its 48-ft-high dome. You can see a projection of the 8,900 stars and five planets (Mercury, Venus, Mars, Jupiter, and Saturn) clearly visible in the southern hemisphere. Shows last 50 minutes and always depict the night sky just as it is on the evening of your visit. Be sure to buy tickets at least 15 minutes before the session begins. ✉ *Gate 10, Av. Pedro Álvares Cabral, Parque Ibirapuera* ☎ *011/5575–5206* 🖾 *R$5* ☉ *Weekends and holidays, projections at 3:30 and 5:30.*

㉙ Viveiro Manequinho Lopes. The Manequinho Lopes Nursery is where most plants and trees used by the city are grown. The original was built in the 1920s; the current version was designed by Roberto Burle Marx. Specimens are of such Brazilian trees as *ipê*, *pau-jacaré*, and *pau-brasil*, the tree for which the country was named (the red dye it produced was greatly valued by the Europeans). The Bosque da Leitura (Reading Forest) has a stand that provides books and magazines (all in Portuguese) as well as chairs so people can read among the trees. ✉ *Enter park from Av. República do Líbano, Parque Ibirapuera* ☎ *No phone* ☉ *Daily 5–5.*

Beaches

São Paulo rests on a plateau 72 km (46 mi) inland. If you can avoid traffic, getaways are fairly quick on the parallel Imigrantes (BR 160) or Anchieta (BR 150) highways, each of which becomes one-way on weekends and holidays. Although the port of Santos (near the Cubatão Industrial Park) has beaches in and around it, the cleanest and best beaches are along what is known as the North Shore. Mountains and bits of Atlantic rain forest hug numerous small, sandy coves. On weekdays when school is in session, the beaches are gloriously deserted.

Buses run along the coast from São Paulo's Jabaquara terminal, near the Congonhas Airport, and there are once-daily trains from the Estação da Luz to Santos and the sands along the North Shore. Beaches often don't have bathrooms or phones right on the sands, nor do they have beach umbrellas or chairs for rent. They generally do have restaurants nearby, however, or at least vendors selling sandwiches, soft drinks, and beer. All beaches are free and open at all hours.

★ **Praia da Barra do Sahy.** Families with young children favor this small, quiet beach. Its narrow strip of sand (with a bay and a river on one side and rocks on the other) is steep but smooth, and the water is clean and very calm. Kayakers paddle about, and divers are drawn to the nearby Ilha das Couves. Area restaurants serve only basic fish dishes with rice and salad. Note that Barra do Sahy's entrance is atop a slope and appears suddenly. ⊠ *Rio-Santos Hwy. (SP 055), 165 km (102 mi) southeast of São Paulo.*

Praia do Camburi. The young and the restless flock here to sunbathe, surf, and party. At the center of the beach is a cluster of cafés, ice-cream shops, and bars and the Tiê restaurant. The service may be slow, but Tiê's menu is extensive, and the open-air setup is divine. Another good bet is Bom Dia Vietnã, with its delicious pizzas, sandwiches, sushi, and salads. Camburi is just north of Barra do Sahy. If you're coming from the south, use the second entrance; although it's unpaved, it's in better shape than the first entrance. ⊠ *Rio-Santos Hwy. (SP 055), 167 km (104 mi) southeast of São Paulo.*

Praia de Maresias. The beach itself is also nice, with its 4-km (2-mi) stretch of white sand and its clean, green waters that are good for swimming and surfing. Maresias is popular with a young crowd. ⊠ *Rio-Santos Hwy. (SP 055), 180 km (111 mi) southeast of São Paulo.*

Ubatuba. Many of the more than 30 beaches around Ubatuba are truly beautiful enough to merit the long drive. For isolation and peace, try **Prumirim Beach,** which can only be reached by boat; for a little more action try the centrally located **Praia Grande,** with its many kiosks. Ubatuba itself has a very active nightlife. Nearby Itaguá has several gift shops, a branch of the Projeto Tartarugas Marinhas (Marine Turtles Project), and a large aquarium. ⊠ *229 km (148 mi) southeast of São Paulo along Carvalho Pinto and Oswaldo Cruz Hwys.*

Where to Eat

São Paulo's social scene centers on dining out, and there are many establishments from which to choose (new ones seem to open as often as the sun rises), particularly in the Jardins district. You can find German, Japanese, Spanish, Italian, and Portuguese restaurants as well as top-quality French and Indian spots. The innumerable *churrascarias* (places that serve a seemingly endless stream of barbecued meat) are beloved by paulistanos. As in other Brazilian cities, many restaurants serve feijoada on Wednesday and Saturday; top restaurants do it up in fancy buffets. São Paulo restaurants frequently change their credit-card policies, sometimes adding a surcharge for their use or not accepting them at all.

Brazilian

$$$-$$$$ ✕ **Baby Beef Rubaiyat.** The family that owns and runs this restaurant serves meat from their ranch in Mato Grosso do Sul State. Charcoal-grilled fare—from baby boar (on request at least two hours in advance) and steak to chicken and salmon—is served at the buffet. A salad bar has all sorts of options. Wednesday and Saturday are feijoada nights, and on Friday the emphasis is on seafood. ⊠ *Alameda Santos 86, Paraíso* ☎ *011/289–6366* ▭ *V* Ⓜ *Paraíso.*

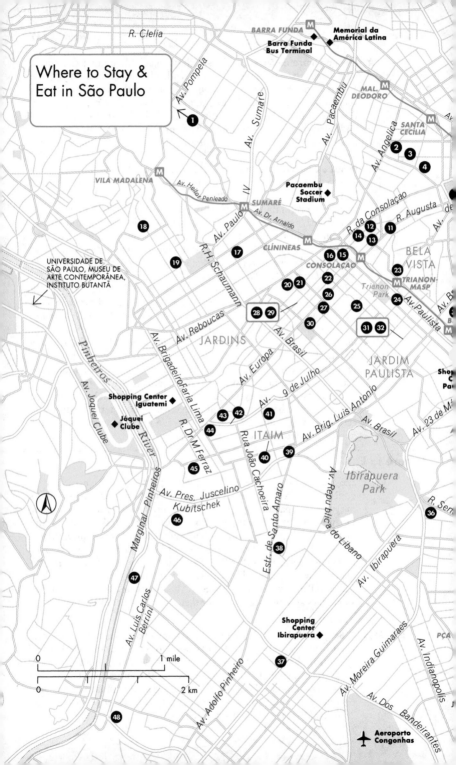

★ **$-$$$** ✕ **Esplanada Grill.** The beautiful people hang out in the bar of this highly regarded churrascaria. The thinly sliced *picanha* steak (similar to rump steak) is excellent; it goes well with a house salad (hearts of palm and shredded, fried potatoes), onion rings, and creamed spinach. The restaurant's version of the traditional *pão de queijo* (cheese bread) is widely viewed as one of the best. ⊠ *Rua Haddock Lobo 1682, Jardins* ☎ *011/3081–3199* ▤ *AE, DC, MC, V.*

$$ ✕ **Bargaço.** The original Bargaço has long been considered the best Bahian restaurant in Salvador. If you can't make it to the northeast, be sure to have a meal in the São Paulo branch. Seafood is the calling card. ⊠ *Rua Oscar Freire 1189, Cerqueira César* ☎ *011/3085–5058* ▤ *DC, MC* Ⓜ *Consolação.*

$-$$ ✕ **Consulado Mineiro.** During and after the Saturday crafts and antiques fair in Praça Benedito Calixto, it may take an hour to get a table at this homey restaurant set in a house. Among the traditional mineiro dishes are the *mandioca com carne de sol* (cassava with salted meat) appetizer and the *tutu* (pork loin with beans, pasta, cabbage, and rice) entrée. ⊠ *Rua Praça Benedito Calixto 74, Pinheiros* ☎ *011/3064–3882* ▤ *AE, DC, MC, V* ۩ *Closed Mon.*

¢-$$ ✕ **Sujinho–Bisteca d'Ouro.** The modest Sujinho serves churrasco without any frills. It's the perfect place for those who simply want to eat an honest, gorgeous piece of meat. The portions are so large here that one dish can usually feed two. A few options on the menu creep into the $$$ price range. ⊠ *Rua da Consolação 2078, Cerqueira César* ☎ *011/3231–5207* ▤ *No credit cards* Ⓜ *Consolação.*

¢-$ ✕ **Frevo.** Paulistanos of all types and ages flock to this Jardins luncheonette for its *beirute* sandwiches, filled with ham and cheese, tuna, or chicken, and for its draft beer and fruit juices in flavors such as *acerola* (Antilles cherry), passion fruit, and papaya. ⊠ *Rua Oscar Freire 603, Jardins* ☎ *011/3082–3434* ▤ *AE, DC, MC, V.*

Continental

$-$$$ ✕ **Cantaloup.** That paulistanos take food seriously has not been lost on the folks at Cantaloup. The converted warehouse houses two dining areas: Oversize photos decorate the walls of the slightly formal room, and a fountain and plants make the second area feel more casual. Try the filet mignon with risotto or the St. Peter's beef tenderloin fillet with almonds and spinach. Save room for the papaya ice cream with mango soup or the mango ice cream with papaya soup. ⊠ *Rua Manoel Guedes 474, Itaim Bibi* ☎ *011/3846–6445* ▤ *AE, DC, MC, V.*

Eclectic

$$-$$$$ ✕ **La Tambouille.** This Italo-French restaurant with a partially enclosed garden isn't just a place to be seen; it also has some of the best food in town. Among chef André Fernandes's recommended dishes are the linguini with fresh mussels and prawn sauce and the filet mignon *rosini* (served with foie gras and saffron risotto). ⊠ *Av. Nove de Julho 5925, Jardim Europa* ☎ *011/3079–6276* ▤ *AE, DC, MC, V.*

★ **$-$$** ✕ **Mestiço.** Tribal masks peer down from the walls of the large, modern dining room. Consider the Thai *huan-hin* (chicken with shiitake mushrooms in ginger sauce and rice) followed by a dessert of lemon ice cream with *baba de moça* (a syrup made with egg whites and sugar). An eclectic menu also includes Italian, Brazilian, and Bahian dishes. ⊠ *Rua Fernando de Albuquerque 277, Consolação* ☎ *011/3256–3165* ⊟ *AE, DC, MC, V* Ⓜ *Consolação.*

French

$$–$$$$ ✕ **Freddy.** Leave the grunge and noise of the streets behind in this eatery with the feel of an upscale Parisian bistro. Try the duck with Madeira sauce and apple purée, the pheasant with herb sauce, or the hearty cassoulet with white beans, lamb, duck, and garlic sausage. ⊠ *Praça Dom Gastão Liberal Pinto 111, Itaim Bibi* ☎ *011/3167–0977* ⊟ *AE, DC, MC, V* ☉ *No dinner Sun., no lunch Sat.*

$–$$$ ✕ **La Casserole.** Facing a little Centro flower market, this charming bistro has been around for generations. Surrounded by wood-paneled walls decorated with eclectic posters, you can dine on such delights as *gigot d'agneau aux soissons* (roast leg of lamb in its own juices, served with white beans) and cherry strudel. ⊠ *Largo do Arouche 346, Centro* ☎ *011/3331–6283* ⊟ *AE, DC, MC, V* ☉ *Closed Mon. No lunch Sat.* Ⓜ *República.*

★ $ ✕ **La Tartine.** An ideal place for a cozy romantic dinner, this small bistro has a good wine selection, movie posters on its walls, and simple but comfortable furniture. The menu changes daily; a favorite is the classic coq au vin, or you can fill up on entrées from beef tenderloin to soups and quiches. It is usually crowded with São Paulo's trendy people, and you might have to wait to get a table on weekends. ⊠ *Rua Fernando de Albuquerque 267, Consolação* ☎ *011/3259–2090* ⊟ *V* ☉ *Closed Sun.–Mon.* Ⓜ *Consolação.*

Indian

$–$$$ ✕ **Ganesh.** Many consider this the best Indian restaurant in town. The traditional menu includes curries and *tandoori* dishes from many regions of India. Indian artwork and tapestries fill the interior. ⊠ *Morumbi Shopping Center, Av. Roque Petroni Jr. 1089, Morumbi* ☎ *011/5181–4748* ⊟ *AE, DC, MC, V.*

Italian

$$–$$$$ ✕ **Ca' D'Oro.** This is a longtime northern Italian favorite among Brazilian bigwigs, many of whom have their own tables in the old-world-style dining room. Quail, osso buco, and veal-and-raisin ravioli are winners, but the specialty is the Piedmontese *gran bollito misto*, steamed meats and vegetables accompanied by three sauces. ⊠ *Grande Hotel Ca' D'Oro, Rua Augusta 129, Bela Vista* ☎ *011/3236–4300* ⊟ *AE, DC, MC, V* Ⓜ *Anhangabaú.*

$$–$$$$ **Fodor'sChoice ★** ✕ **Famiglia Mancini.** A huge wheel of provolone cheese is the first thing you see at this warm, cheerful restaurant. An incredible buffet with cheeses, olives, sausages, and much more is the perfect place to find a tasty appetizer. The menu has many terrific pasta options, such as the cannelloni with palm hearts and a four-cheese sauce. ⊠ *Rua Avanhandava 81, Centro* ☎ *011/3256–4320* ⊟ *AE, DC, MC, V* Ⓜ *Anhangabaú.*

$–$$$ ✕ **La Vecchia Cucina.** Chef Sergio Arno changed the face of the city's Italian restaurants with his *nuova cucina*, exemplified by dishes like frogs' legs risotto and duck ravioli with watercress sauce. Well-to-do patrons dine in the glass-walled garden gazebo or the ocher-color dining room decorated with Italian engravings and fresh flowers. ⊠ *Rua Pedroso Alvarenga 1088, Itaim Bibi* ☏ *011/3167–2822* ⊟ *AE, DC, MC, V* ☺ *No dinner Sun., no lunch Sat.*

$–$$$ ✕ **Lellis Trattoria.** Photos of famous patrons (mostly Brazilian actors) hang on the walls, and the doors and bar are made of metal, giving this typical Italian cantina a sophisticated twist. Salmon fillet *marinatta* (in white sauce with potatoes, raisins, and rice) is one of the best choices on the menu. ⊠ *Rua Bela Cintra 1849, Jardim Paulista* ☏ *011/3064–2727* ⊟ *AE, DC, MC, V.*

$–$$ ✕ **Jardim di Napoli.** The white, green, and red of the Italian flag is just about everywhere you look in this restaurant. People come for the unmatchable *polpettone alla parmigiana,* a huge meatball with mozzarella and tomato sauce. There are many other meat dishes, pasta selections, and pizza. ⊠ *Rua Doutor Martinico Prado 463, Higienópolis* ☏ *011/3666–3022* ⊟ *V.*

Japanese

$$–$$$$ ✕ **Nagayama.** Low-key, trustworthy, and well loved, Nagayama consistently serves excellent sushi and sashimi at both its locations. The chefs like to experiment: the California *uramaki* Philadelphia has rice, cream cheese, grilled salmon, roe, cucumber, and spring onions rolled together. ⊠ *Rua Bandeira Paulista 369, Itaim Bibi* ☏ *011/3079–7553* ⊟ *AE, DC, MC* ⊠ *Rua da Consolação 3397, Cerqueira César* ☏ *011/3064–0110* ⊟ *AE, DC, MC.*

$–$$ ✕ **Nakombi.** Chefs prepare sushi from a *kombi* (Volkswagen van) in the middle of the dining room. In this eclectic environment, tables are surrounded by a small artificial river crowded with fish. The menu includes a good variety of sushi and nonsushi dishes. Try the salmon fillet with *shimeji* mushrooms. ⊠ *Rua Pequetita 170, Vila Olímpia* ☏ *011/3845–9911* ⊟ *AE, DC, MC, V.*

Lebanese

$–$$ ✕ **Arábia.** For more than 10 years, Arábia has served traditional Lebanese cuisine at this beautiful high-ceilinged restaurant. Simple dishes such as hummus and stuffed grape leaves are executed with aplomb. The lamb melts in your mouth. The reasonably priced "executive" lunch includes one cold dish, one meat dish, a drink, and dessert. Don't miss the pistachio marzipan covered in rose syrup for dessert. ⊠ *Rua Haddock Lobo 1397, Jardins* ☏ *011/3061–2203* ⊕ *www.arabia.com.br* ⊟ *AE, DC, MC.*

★ ¢–$ ✕ **Almanara.** Part of a chain of Lebanese semi-fast-food outlets, Almanara is perfect for a quick lunch of hummus, tabbouleh, grilled chicken, and rice. There's also a full-blown restaurant on the premises that serves Lebanese specialties *rodízio* style, where you get a taste of everything until you can ingest no more. ⊠ *Rua Oscar Freire 523, Jardins* ☏ *011/3085–6916* ⊟ *AE, DC, MC, V.*

Pan-Asian

$–$$ ✕ **Sutra.** A coconut tree grows in the middle of this cozy bar–restaurant with sofas and pillows and a huge map of Thailand covering one wall. Vietnamese, Thai, and Japanese cuisines are prepared creatively. *Kaeng kung* (prawns with broccoli and vegetables in a curry–coconut milk sauce) is recommended. Aphrodisiac drinks have names inspired by the Kama Sutra (tabletop cards even have illustrations). The "bamboo splitting," is Absolut, tequila, Cointreau, lemon juice, and Coca-Cola. ⊠ *Rua Salvador Cardoso 20, Itaim Bibi* ☏ *011/3849–4758* ▭ *DC, MC, V* ☉ *Closed Sun.–Mon. No lunch.*

$–$$ ✕ **Oriental Café.** High ceilings and tile floors convey a sense of space, while flickering candles keep things intimate. Sophisticated dishes like shark's fin soup are the reason this is considered the best pan-Asian restaurant in São Paulo. There are less exotic dishes, such as marinated chicken thighs. ⊠ *Rua José Maria Lisboa 1000, Jardim Paulista* ☏ *011/3060–9495* ▭ *AE, DC, MC, V* ☉ *Closed Mon. No lunch Tues.–Sat.*

Pizza

★ $ ✕ **Galpão.** Lights that shine from behind bottle bottoms embedded in exposed brick walls is one of the interesting design elements in this restaurant owned by an architect. Fast service is also a hallmark. The arugula, sun-dried tomatoes, and mozzarella pizza is one of the best choices. ⊠ *Rua Doutor Augusto de Miranda 1156, Pompéia* ☏ *011/3672–4767* ▭ *DC, MC, V* ☉ *Closed Mon.*

$ ✕ **Speranza.** One of the most traditional pizzerias, this restaurant is famous for its margherita pie. The crunchy *pão de linguiça* (sausage bread) appetizers have a fine reputation as well. ⊠ *Rua 13 de Maio 1004, Bela Vista* ☏ *011/288–8502* ▭ *DC, MC, V.*

¢–$ ✕ **Braz.** Its name comes from one of the most traditional Italian neighborhood in São Paulo. There's a wide selection of crisp-crusted pizzas here; all are delicious, from the traditional margherita to the house specialty, pizza *braz,* with tomato sauce, zucchini, and mozzarella and Parmesan cheeses. The pizzeria is also known for its great *chopp* (draft beer). ⊠ *Rua Grauna 125, Moema* ☏ *011/5561–0905* ▭ *MC, D.*

FodorsChoice ★

Seafood

$–$$$ ✕ **Truta Rosa.** Fresh trout prepared in endless ways makes this small restaurant with a huge fish-shape window a hit. You cross a metal bridge over a small lagoon to reach the dining room, where sashimi and quenelles reel in the customers. ⊠ *Av. Vereador José Diniz 318, Santo Amaro* ☏ *011/5523–7021* ▭ *AE, DC, MC, V* ☉ *Closed Mon. No dinner Sun.*

$–$$ ✕ **Amadeus.** The quality and preparation of the fish is famous among the business lunch crowd. Appetizers such as fresh oysters and salmon and endive with mustard and entrées like shrimp in a cognac sauce make it a challenge to find better fruits of the sea elsewhere in town. ⊠ *Rua Haddock Lobo 807, Jardins* ☏ *011/3061–2859* ▭ *AE, DC* ☉ *No dinner weekends* Ⓜ *Consolação.*

Where to Stay

São Paulo's hotels are almost exclusively geared to business travelers, both homegrown and foreign. For this reason, most hotels—many of them world-class—are near Avenida Paulista, with a few in the Marginal Pinheiros and charming Jardins neighborhoods. Many hotels offer discounts of 20%–40% for cash payment or weekend stays. Few include breakfast in the room rate. São Paulo hosts many international conventions, so it's wise to make reservations well ahead of your arrival.

For information about youth hostels, contact the **Associaçaõ Paulista de Albergues da Juventude** (⊠ Rua 7 de Abril 386, República, 01320-040 ☎ 011/258–0388). The association sells a book ($2.50) that lists hostels throughout Brazil.

$$$$ 🏨 **Hotel Sofitel São Paulo.** Near the Congonhas Airport and Ibirapuera Park, this modern, luxury hotel is noted for its French style. The restaurant serves French cuisine. Dark-wood furniture fills the rooms, many of which have views of park. It's a privilege in São Paulo to be able to see trees from your window. ⊠ *Rua Sena Madureira 1355, Bloco 1, Ibirapuera 04021-051* ☎ *011/5574–1100 or 0800/11–1790* 🖷 *011/5575–4544* ⊕ *www. accorhotels.com.br* ➩ *219 rooms* ⟡ *Restaurant, room service, cable TV, tennis court, pool, gym, sauna, bar, laundry facilities, business services, meeting rooms, helipad, parking (fee)* ▤ *AE, DC, MC, V.*

★ $$$$ 🏨 **Inter-Continental São Paulo.** This exquisite hotel is by far the most attractive of the city's top-tier establishments. Service is attentive, and both the private and public areas are well appointed. Creams, pastels, and marble come together with seamless sophistication and elegance. ⊠ *Av. Santos 1123, Jardins 01419-001* ☎ *011/3179–2600* 🖷 *011/3179–2666* ⊕ *www.interconti.com* ➩ *160 rooms, 33 suites* ⟡ *Restaurant, room service, cable TV, pool, health club, massage, sauna, bar, business services, helipad, parking (fee)* ▤ *AE, DC, MC, V* Ⓜ *Trianon.*

$$$$ 🏨 **Renaissance São Paulo.** A stay at this Jardins hotel, a block from Avenida Paulista, puts you close to both shops and businesses. From the street, it has the appeal of a roll of tinfoil, but its interior is graceful and elegant. There are six Renaissance Club floors with 57 suites that include a buffet breakfast, evening hors d'oeuvres, butler service, express check-in and check-out, and fax machines. If you want to arrive in style, the hotel's helipad is key. ⊠ *Alameda Santos 2247, Jardins 01419-002* ☎ *011/3069–2233, 800/468–3571 in the U.S.* 🖷 *011/3064–3344* ⊕ *www.renaissancehotels.com* ➩ *452 rooms, 100 suites* ⟡ *3 restaurants, room service, cable TV, pool, health club, massage, squash, 3 bars, shops, laundry facilities, business services, helipad, travel services, parking (fee)* ▤ *AE, DC, MC, V* Ⓜ *Consolação.*

$$$–$$$$ 🏨 **Gran Meliá São Paulo.** This all-suites luxury hotel is in the same building as São Paulo's world trade center and the D&D Decoração & Design Center. Suites have king-size beds, two phone lines, living rooms with sofas, and small tables that are the perfect places to set up your laptop. Stay on one of the apartment floors and get special amenities like pass-key access and bathroom faucets that can be programmed to maintain your preferred water temperature. Off the large marble lobby is a bar whose comfortable leather chairs are perfect for unwinding after a day of meetings or shopping. ⊠ *Av. das Nações Unidas 12559, Brooklin 04578-905* ☎ *011/3043–8000 or 0800/15–5555* 🖷 *011/3043–8001* ⊕ *www.solmelia.es* ➩ *300 suites* ⟡ *Restaurant, room service, in-room data ports, in-room safes, cable TV, tennis court, indoor pool, gym, hair salon, massage, sauna, paddle tennis, bar, laundry facilities, business services, meeting room, parking (fee)* ▤ *AE, DC, MC, V.*

FodorśChoice
★

★ $$$–$$$$ 🏨 **Sheraton Mofarrej Hotel & Towers.** Just behind Avenida Paulista and next to Parque Trianon, the Mofarrej is part of Sheraton's A-class Luxury Collection hotels. Rooms are a mix of modern and classic styles, and the four floors that have butler service offer other amenities that make you feel all the more pampered. Rooms on the west side overlook the park. ⊠ *Alameda Santos 1437, Jardins 01419-905* ☎ *011/3253–5544 or 0800/11–6000* 🖷 *011/283–0160* ⊕ *www.sheraton-sp.com* ♿ *2 restaurants, room service, cable TV, indoor pool, gym, massage, sauna, 2 bars, laundry facilities, business services, convention center, parking (fee)* 🖃 *AE, DC, MC, V* Ⓜ *Trianon.*

$$–$$$$ 🏨 **L'Hotel.** Close to the major business hubs, this European-style hotel has rooms and suites decorated in somewhat sterile floral patterns. The place was modeled after the famous L'Hotel in Paris, and the small number of rooms allows it to focus on providing superior service. Though at its inception L'Hotel wanted to retain an air of exclusivity, reports have been mixed as to its success. ⊠ *Alameda Campinas 266, Jardins 01404-000* ☎🖷 *011/283–0500* ⊕ *www.lhotel.com.br* ⇔ *82 rooms, 5 suites* ♿ *2 restaurants, room service, cable TV, pool, health club, sauna, pub, laundry facilities, business services, meeting room, parking (fee)* 🖃 *AE, DC, MC, V* Ⓜ *Trianon.*

$$–$$$$ 🏨 **Maksoud Plaza.** Once *the* place for luxury accommodations in São Paulo, Maksoud must now share the bill with a bevy of high-end hotels. Still, its decor, comfort, and good location make it one of the top hotels in the city. The staff provides professional service, the restaurants are excellent, and the in-house theater and the Maksoud 150 nightclub offer entertainment. ⊠ *Alameda Campinas 1250, Jardins 01404-900* ☎ *011/3145–8000* 🖷 *011/3145–8001* ⊕ *www.maksoud.com.br* ⇔ *416 rooms, 99 suites* ♿ *6 restaurants, room service, cable TV, indoor pool, health club, 3 bars, nightclub, theater, laundry facilities, business services, parking (fee)* 🖃 *AE, DC, MC, V* Ⓜ *Trianon.*

$–$$$$ 🏨 **Grande Hotel Ca' D'Oro.** Owned and run by a northern Italian family for more than 40 years, this old-world-style hotel near Centro has bar-side fireplaces, lots of wood and Persian carpeting, a great variety of classic European design styles, ultrapersonalized service, and the beloved Ca' D'Oro restaurant. All these amenities attract many repeat customers, including quite a few Brazilian bigwigs. ⊠ *Rua Augusta 129, Cerqueira César 01303-001* ☎ *011/3236–4300* 🖷 *011/3236–4311* ⊕ *www.cadoro.com.br* ⇔ *240 rooms, 50 suites* ♿ *Restaurant, room service, cable TV, indoor pool, gym, sauna, 2 bars, laundry facilities, parking (fee)* 🖃 *AE, DC, MC, V* Ⓜ *Consolação.*

★ $ 🏨 **Eldorado Higienópolis.** In one of the city's oldest and most attractive residential neighborhoods, only a five-minute taxi ride from Centro, this hotel has a large pool and a lobby dressed in travertine marble with a pink-granite floor. The on-site café is lovely, and the rooms are all pleasant; the noise level is lowest in those at the front above the fifth floor or those in back. ⊠ *Rua Marquês de Itu 836, Higienópolis 01223-000* ☎ *011/3361–6888* 🖷 *011/222–7194* ⊕ *www.hoteiseldorado.com.br* ⇔ *152 rooms* ♿ *Restaurant, room service, cable TV, laundry facilities, pool, bar, parking (fee)* 🖃 *AE, DC, MC, V.*

$ 🏨 **Bourbon.** Both guests and furnishings are well cared for in this small hotel near the Largo do Arouche, a charming downtown district. A brass-accented basement bar features live piano music. The lobby has upholstered print sofas, an abstract handcrafted black-and-white wall hanging, and granite flooring. Rooms are done in beige and blue and have marvelously large, sunlighted bathrooms. ✉ *Av. Vieira de Carvalho 99, Centro 01210-010* ☎ *011/3337–2000* 🖷 *011/3331–8187* 📞 *123 rooms* ⚘ *Restaurant, sauna, bar, parking (fee)* ☰ *AE, DC, MC, V* Ⓜ *República.*

$ 🏨 **Parthenon Golden Tower.** A full-service establishment with apartment-like amenities, this hotel is popular with business travelers and families alike. The rooms are nicely decorated, and each has a private balcony. ✉ *Av. Cidade Jardim 411, Pinheiros 01453-000* ☎ *011/3081–6333 or 011/3079–9445* 🖷 *011/3088–3531* ⊕ *www.accorhotels.com.br* 📞 *73 suites* ⚘ *Restaurant, room service, cable TV, pool, gym, sauna, bar, laundry facilities, meeting room, parking (fee)* ☰ *AE, DC, MC, V.*

¢ 🏨 **Carillon Plaza.** Walk out of the heated hustle and bustle of the Jardins neighborhood and into this hotel's cool lobby, full of mirrors and marble. You can retreat still farther by heading to the rooftop pool for an afternoon of sunbathing or by sinking into a leather chair for a meal in the restaurant. The multilingual staff is very helpful. ✉ *Rua Bela Cintra 652, Jardins 01415-000* ☎ *011/3257–9233* 🖷 *011/3255–3346* ⊕ *www.redepandehoteis.com.br* 📞 *39 rooms, 10 suites* ⚘ *Restaurant, room service, in-room safes, pool, bar, parking (fee)* ☰ *AE, DC, MC, V* Ⓜ *Consolação.*

¢ 🏨 **La Guardia.** If you don't need to be surrounded by luxury, consider this simple, affordable hotel. Rooms are small but comfortable and have thick carpets and marble-top tables. Its a friendly place, and the service is good. ✉ *Rua Peixoto Gomide 154, Cerqueira César 01409-000* ☎ *011/3255–0600* 🖷 *011/3258–7398* 📞 *28 rooms, 14 suites* ⚘ *Restaurant, free parking* ☰ *AE, DC, MC, V* Ⓜ *Consolação.*

¢ 🏨 **Ville Hotel.** This hotel is in the lively Higienópolis neighborhood of apartment buildings, bars, and bookstores abutting Mackenzie University. The small lobby features a black-and-pink-granite floor, recessed lighting, and leather sofas; rooms are done in pastels and have brown carpeting. ✉ *Rua Dona Veridiana 643, Higienópolis 01238-010* ☎ *011/3257–5288* 🖷 *011/3241–1871* ⊕ *www.hotelville.com.br* 📞 *54 rooms* ⚘ *Restaurant, meeting room, parking (fee)* ☰ *AE, DC, MC, V.*

★ ¢ 🏨 **Hotel Formule 1.** One of the first hotels in São Paulo to offer quality and cheap prices, this budget hotel has a simple and practical style. Rooms are small, but each has a queen-size bed with a twin bunk above, a table, and a closet. You pay the same price for 1–3 people in a room. The service and location are good. ✉ *Rua Vergueiro 1571, Paraiso* ☎ *011/5085–5699* 🖷 *011/5575–8122* ⊕ *www.accorhotels.com.br* 📞 *300* ⚘ *Business services, cable TV, parking (fee)* ☰ *AE* Ⓜ *Paraíso.*

¢ 🏨 **Hotel Joamar.** Popular with backpackers, this small hotel in downtown São Paulo was renovated in 2002. It has a clean neat look, with small simple rooms. You can choose from one to three twin beds or a queen-size bed. The hotel is three blocks from the metrô station. ✉ *Rua Dom José de Barros 187, Centro 01208-010* ☎ *011/221–3611* 🖷 *011/222–1087* 📞 *60 rooms* ⚘ *Room service, laundry facilities* ☰ *AE, MC, V* Ⓜ *República.*

Nightlife & the Arts

São Paulo is a city beset by trends, so clubs and bars come and go at a dizzying pace. Though the places listed here were all thriving spots at press time, the nightlife scene is always changing, and it's best to check with hotel concierges and paulistanos you meet to confirm that a place is still open before heading out on the town.

The world's top orchestras, opera and dance companies, and other troupes always include São Paulo in their South American tours. Most free concerts—with performances by either Brazilian or international artists—are presented on Sunday in Parque Ibirapuera. City-sponsored events are held in Centro's Vale do Anhangabaú area. State-sponsored concerts take place at the Memorial da América Latina, northwest of Centro.

Listings of events appear in the "Veja São Paulo" insert of the newsweekly *Veja*. The arts sections of the dailies *Folha de São Paulo* and *O Estado de São Paulo* also have listings and reviews. In addition, *Folha* publishes a weekly guide on Friday called "Guia da Folha." Tickets for many events are available at booths throughout the city and at theater box offices. Many of these venues offer ticket delivery to your hotel for a surcharge. **Fun by Phone** (☎ 011/3097–8687 ⊕ www.funbynet.com.br) sells tickets to music concerts, theater, and theme parks. **Ticketmaster** (☎ 011/6846–6000 ⊕ www.ticketmaster.com.br) also sells tickets by phone and Internet. **Show Ticket at Shopping Center Iguatemi** (⊠ Av. Brigadeiro Faria Lima 1191, 3rd floor ☎ 011/3031–2098) sells tickets to the main concerts and performances in town. It's open Monday–Saturday 10 AM–10 PM and Sunday 2–8. **Serviço Social do Comércio** (SESC, Commerce Social Service; ☎ 0800/118–220 ⊕ www.sescsp.org.br) is very active in cultural programming, and many of its events are free.

Nightlife

BARS First opened in 1949, **Bar Brahma** (⊠ Av. São João 677, Centro ☎ 011/3333–0855) used to be the meeting place of artists, intellectuals and politicians. The decor is a time-warp to the mid–20th-century, with furniture, lamps, and a piano true to the period. This is one of the best places in São Paulo for live music. **Barnaldo Lucrécia** (⊠ Rua Abílio Soares 207, Paraíso ☎ 011/3885–3425 Ⓜ Paraíso) draws crowds with live *música popular brasileira* (MPB; popular Brazilian music). The crowd is intense but jovial. **Elias** (⊠ Rua Cayowaá 70, Perdizes ☎ 011/3864–4722) place is a hangout for fans of the Palmeiras soccer team, whose stadium is just a few blocks away. If you want something to eat, the carpaccio is undoubtedly the best choice on the menu.

Most patrons stop at **Empanadas** (⊠ Rua Wisard 489, Vila Madalena ☎ 011/3032–2116) for a beer en route to another Vila Madalena bar. It's a good place to "warm up" for an evening out with a quick drink and a bite to eat. Appropriately, the empanadas are particularly appealing. A stop at **Frangó** (⊠ Largo da Matriz de Nossa Senhora do Ó 168, Freguesia do Ó ☎ 011/3932–4818 or 011/3931–4281) makes you feel as if you've been transported to a small town. The bar has 90 varieties of beer, including the Brazilian export beer Xingu. Its rich, molasseslike flavor nicely complements the bar's unforgettable *bolinhos de frango com queijo* (chicken balls with cheese). The fashionable patrons at **Grazie a Dio** (⊠ Rua Girassol 67, Vila Madalena ☎ 011/3031–6568 ⊕ www.grazieadio.com.br) may vary in age, but they always appreciate good music. The best time to go is at happy hour for daily live performances. On Saturday it's jazz, and on Friday, bossa nova. The natural decorations, including trees and constellations, complement the Mediterranean food served in the back.

Canto da Ema (✉ Av. Brigadeiro Faria Lima 364, Pinheiros ☎ 011/3813–4708 ⊕ www.cantodaema.com.br) is considered the best place to dance forró in town. Here you'll find people of different ages and ★ styles coming together on the dance floor. The tiny round tables at **Piratininga** (✉ Rua Wizard 149, Vila Madalena ☎ 011/3032–9775), a small bar-restaurant, are perfect for a quiet rendezvous. The live MPB and jazz music add to the romance. The decor at **Sem Eira Nem Beira** (✉ Rua Fiandeiras 966, Itaim Bibi ☎ 011/3845–3444 ⊕ www.semeiranembeira.com.br) was inspired by Brazilian bars circa 1940. The club is famous for its live MPB performances on Friday and Saturday.

At **Avenida Club** (✉ Av. Pedroso de Morais 1036, Pinheiros ☎ 011/3814–7383) some nights are dedicated to Caribbean rhythms, others to MPB. The large wooden dance floor—one of the finest in town—attracts a crowd of thirtysomethings. **Buena Vista Club** (✉ Rua Atílio Innocenti 780, Vila Olímpia ☎ 011/3045–5245 ⊕ www.buenavistaclub.com.br) is a good place to take dance classes. On Sunday you can learn to dance *Gafieira* and *Zouk*. Live music and DJs heat up the dance floor for hours. The club also has good appetizers and drinks. At **Dolores Bar** (✉ Rua Fradique Coutinho 1007, Vila Madalena ☎ 011/3031–3604) DJs spin funk, soul, and hip-hop tunes for a crowd in its twenties and thirties. Wednesday and Friday nights are the most popular, and people really do fill up the floor only after the witching hour.

★ At **Lov.e Club & Lounge** (✉ Rua Pequetita 189, Vila Olímpia ☎ 011/3044–1613) you might feel that you're on the set of an *Austin Powers* movie. Before 2 AM the music isn't too loud, and you can sit and talk on the '50s-style sofas. Then the techno effects keep people on the small dance floor until sunrise. **Mood Club** (✉ Rua Teodoro Sampaio 1109, Pinheiros ☎ 011/3060–9010) has a bar, a lounge with lots of sofas, and two dancing areas called *The Home* and *The Hole*. DJs keep things going until 7 AM with electronic music.

Alegro (✉ Rua da Consolação 3055, Cerqueira César ☎ 011/3086–0538 Ⓜ Consolação), in the gay nightlife hub of the city, is popular even on weekdays. It has good food and cocktails, and is popular with the pre–dance-club crowd. On Saturdays the crowd can reach up to 2,500 people at **Level** (✉ Av. Marques de São Vicente 319, Barra Funda ☎ 011/3612–4151 Ⓜ Barra Funda). It has an arcade game room, a cyber café, and lots of house music. **A Lôca** (✉ Rua Frei Caneca 916, Cerqueira César ☎ 011/3120–2055 Ⓜ Consolação) has an large dance floor, a video room, and two bars. A mixed gay and lesbian crowd often dances until dawn and then has breakfast in the club.

People come to tiny **All of Jazz** (✉ Rua João Cachoeira 1366, Vila Olímpia ☎ 011/3849–1345) to actually *listen* to very good jazz and bossa nova. Local musicians jam here weekly. Call ahead to book a table on weekends. With a name right out of New Orleans, it's no wonder that **Bour-**

bon Street (✉ Rua Dos Chanés 127, Moema ☎ 011/5561–1643) is where the best jazz and blues bands play. **Café Piu Piu** (✉ Rua 13 de Maio 134, Bixiga ☎ 011/258–8066 ⊕ www.cafepiupiu.com.br) is best-known for jazz, but it also hosts groups that play rock, bossa nova, and even tango.

The Arts

CLASSICAL MUSIC, DANCE & THEATER VENUES
Credicard Hall (✉ Av. das Nações Unidas 17995, Santo Amaro ☎ 011/5643–2500 ⊕ www.credicardhall.com.br) is one of the biggest theaters in São Paulo and can accommodate up to 7,000 people. It housed concerts by famous Brazilian and International artists. Tickets can be bought by phone or Internet using the services by Ticketmaster. Opera, ballet, music, and symphony performances are held at **Teatro Alfa** (✉ Rua Bento Branco de Andrade Filho 722, Santo Amaro ☎ 011/5693–4000 or 0800/55–8191 ⊕ www.teatroalfa.com.br). It's one of the newest theaters in the country, with all the latest sound and lighting technology—and the biggest foreign stars grace the stage.

Most serious music, ballet, and opera is performed at **Teatro Municipal** (✉ Praça Ramos de Azevedo, Centro ☎ 011/222–8698 ⊕ www.prodam. sp.gov.br/theatro Ⓜ Anhangabaú), a classic theater with an intimate gilt and moss-green-velvet interior. There are lyrical performances on Monday at 8:30 and concerts on Wednesday at 12:30. A local cultural organization, the Mozarteum Brasileira Associação Cultural, holds classical music concerts, which include performances by visiting artists, April–October. **Via Funchal** (✉ Rua Funchal 65, Vila Olímpia ☎ 011/3846–2300 or 011/3842–6855 ⊕ www.viafunchal.com.br) is capable of seating more than 3,000 people, and is the site of many large international music, theater, and dance shows.

Sports & the Outdoors

Brazilians have a reputation for being obsessed with soccer, but in truth, stadiums are normally only full during the finals. Many paulistas prefer to watch soccer on TV at home or in a bar. During the Formula 1 auto race, the city is crowded with foreigners and Brazilians from other states. Ibirapuera Park is a popular spot for jogging. Check the air quality before you practice outdoor sports.

Auto Racing

São Paulo hosts a **Formula 1** race every March, bringing this city of 4.5 million cars to heights of spontaneous combustion, especially when a Brazilian driver wins. The race is held at **Autódromo de Interlagos** (✉ Av. Senador Teotônio Vilela 315, Interlagos ☎ 011/5666–8822 ⊕ www.ainterlagos.com), which also hosts other kinds of races on weekends. For ticket information contact the **Confederação Brasileira de Automobilismo** (✉ Rua da Glória 290, 8th fl., Rio de Janeiro, RJ 20241-180 ☎ 021/2221–4895 ⊕ www.cba.org.br).

Bicycling

Night Biker's Club (✉ Rua Pacheco de Miranda 141, Moema ☎ 011/3871–2100 ⊕ www.nightbikers.com) offers bike tours of the city at night. In **Parque Ibirapuera,** which has a bike path, you can rent bicycles at a number of places near park entrances for about R$5 an hour. There are also bike lanes on Avenida Sumaré and Avenida Pedroso de Morais. **Sampa Bikers** (✉ Rua São Sebastião 454, Chácara Santo Antônio ☎ 011/5183–9477 ⊕ www.sampabikers.com.br) offers tours in the city and excursions outside town. A day tour starts at a R$50 fee, including transport and lunch.

Golf

The greens fee at the 18-hole **Clube de Campo** (✉ Praça Rockford 28, Vila Represa ☎ 011/5529–3111) is R$50. It's open Monday–Tuesday and Thursday–Friday 7–7. **Golf School** (✉ Av. Guido Caloi 2160, Santo Amaro ☎ 011/5515–3372) is a driving range that has 30-minute classes. For R$18 you get 100 balls.

Scuba Diving

Most dive schools take you to Ilhabela and other places outside town on weekends and offer NAUI and PADI certification courses. **Claumar** (✉ Av. Brigadeiro Faria Lima 4440, Itaim Bibi ☎ 011/3846–3034 ⊕ www.claumar.com.br) has a 15-m (49-ft) diving tower used during classes in São Paulo. **Deep Sea** (✉ Rua Manoel da Nóbrega 781, Paraíso ☎ 011/3889–7721 ⊕ www.deepsea.com.br) leads small groups on dive trips to Lage de Santos. **Diving College** (✉ Rua Doutor Mello Alves 700, Jardins ☎ 011/3061–1453 ⊕ www.divingcollege.com.br) is one of the oldest diving schools in Brazil and offers all the PADI courses.

Soccer

São Paulo has several well-funded soccer teams with some of the country's best players. The five main teams—São Paulo, Palmeiras, Portuguesa, Corinthians, and Juventus—even attract fans from other states. The two biggest stadiums are Morumbi and the municipally run Pacaembu. Covered seats offer the best protection, not only from the elements but also from rowdy spectators. Buy tickets at the stadiums or online at **www.igressofacil.com.br**. Regular games usually don't sell out, but finals do; you can buy tickets up to five days in advance for finals.

Morumbi (✉ Praça Roberto Gomes Pedrosa, Morumbi ☎ 011/3749–8000), the home stadium of São Paulo Futebol Clube, has a capacity of 85,000. The first games of the 1950 World Cup were played at the **Pacaembú** (✉ Praça Charles Miller, Pacaembú ☎ 011/3661–9111) stadium, home of the Corinthians team.

Shopping

People come from all over South America to shop in São Paulo, and shopping is considered an attraction in its own right by many paulistanos. In the Jardins neighborhood, stores that carry well-known brands from around the world alternate with the best Brazilian shops. Stores are open weekdays 9–6:30, Saturday 9–1, and are closed Sunday. Mall hours are generally weekdays 10–10 and Saturday 9 AM–10 PM; malls are open on Sunday during the Christmas season.

Areas

In **Centro**, Rua do Arouche is noted for leather goods. In **Itaim** the area around Rua João Cachoeira has evolved from a neighborhood of small clothing factories into a wholesale- and retail-clothing sales district. Several shops on Rua Tabapuã sell small antiques. Also, Rua Dr. Mário Ferraz is stuffed with elegant clothing, gift, and home-decoration stores. In **Jardins**, centering on Rua Augusta (which crosses Avenida Paulista) and Rua Oscar Freire, double-parked Mercedes-Benzes and BMWs point the way to the city's fanciest stores, which sell leather items, jewelry, gifts, antiques, and art. Jardins also has many restaurants and beauty salons. Shops that specialize in high-price European antiques are on or around Rua da Consolação. A slew of lower-price antiques stores line Rua Cardeal Arcoverde in **Pinheiros**.

Centers & Malls

Shopping Center Ibirapuera (⊠ Av. Ibirapuera 3103, Moema ☎ 011/5095–2300 ⊕ www.ibirapuera.com.br), once the largest shopping mall in Brazil, has more than 500 stores and three movie theaters. One of
★ the newest shopping malls in São Paulo, **Shopping Pátio Higienópolis** (⊠ Av. Higienópolis 618, Higienópolis ☎ 0800/159–777) is a mixture of old and new architecture styles. Its design is not as cold as the other malls constructed in the '60s. It has plenty of shops and restaurants. **Shopping Center Iguatemi** (⊠ Av. Brigadeiro Faria Lima 2232, Jardim Paulista ☎ 011/3038–6000 ⊕ www.iguatemisaopaulo.com.br) is the city's oldest and most sophisticated mall and has the latest in fashion and fast food. The Gero Café, built in the middle of the main hall, has a fine menu. **Shopping Center Morumbi** (⊠ Av. Roque Petroni Jr. 1089, Morumbi ☎ 0800/17–7600 ⊕ www.morumbishopping.com.br), in the city's fastest-growing area, is giving Iguatemi a run for its money. That said, it houses about the same boutiques, record stores, bookstores, and restaurants as Iguatemi.

Markets

On Sunday there are **antiques fairs** near the Museu de Arte de São Paulo and (in the afternoon) at the Shopping Center Iguatemi's parking lot. Many stall owners have shops and hand out business cards so you can browse throughout the week at your leisure. An **arts and crafts fair** (⊠ Praça da República, Centro)—selling jewelry, embroidery, leather goods, toys, clothing, paintings, and musical instruments—takes place Sunday morning. Many booths move over to the nearby Praça da Liberdade in the afternoon, joining vendors there selling Japanese-style ceramics, wooden sandals, cooking utensils, food, and bonsai trees.

Specialty Shops

ANTIQUES   **Antiquário Paulo Vasconcelos** (⊠ Alameda Gabriel Monteiro da Silva 1881, Jardins ☎ 011/3062–2444) has folk art and 18th- and 19th-century Brazilian furniture, among other treasures. **Edwin Leonard** (⊠ Rua Oscar Freire 146, Jardins ☎ 011/3088–1394) is a collective of three dealers that sell Latin American and European antiques.

Head to **Patrimônio** (⊠ Alameda Ministro Rocha Azevedo 1068, Jardins ☎ 011/3064–1750) for Brazilian antiques at reasonable prices. It also sells some Indian artifacts as well as modern furnishings crafted from iron. **Renato Magalhães Gouvêa Escritório de Arte** (⊠ Rua Pelotas 475, Vila Mariana ☎ 011/5084–7272) sells a potpourri of European and Brazilian antiques, modern furnishings, and art. **Renée Behar Antiques** (✉ Rua Peixoto Gomide 2088, Jardins ☎ 011/3085–3622 ⊕ www.reneebehar. com.br) has 18th- and 19th-century antiques. It also has temporary exhibitions of antique pieces.

ART **Arte Aplicada** (✉ Rua Haddock Lobo 1406, Jardins ☎ 011/3062–5128) is the place for Brazilian paintings, sculptures, and prints. The staff at **Camargo Vilaça** (✉ Rua Fradique Coutinho 1500, Vila Madalena ☎ 011/ 3032–7066) has an eye for the works of up-and-coming Brazilian artists. At **Espaço Cultural Ena Beçak** (✉ Rua Oscar Freire 440, Jardins ☎ 011/ 3088–7322 ⊕ www.enabecak.com.br) you can shop for Brazilian prints, sculptures, and paintings and then stop in at the café.

If art *naïf* (literally, "naive" art) is your thing, **Galeria Jacques Ardies** (✉ Rua do Livramento 221, Vila Mariana ☎ 011/3884–2916 ⊕ www.ardies. com Ⓜ Paraíso) is a must. As the name suggests, art naïf is simple, with a primitive and handcrafted look. At **Galeria Renot** (✉ Alameda Ministro Rocha Azevedo 1327, Jardins ☎ 011/3083–5933 ⊕ www.renot. com.br) you find oil paintings by such Brazilian artists as Vicente Rego Monteiro, Di Cavalcanti, Cícero Dias, and Anita Malfatti.

Galeria São Paulo (✉ Rua Estados Unidos 1456, Jardins ☎ 011/ 3062–8855) is a leader in contemporary, mainstream art. Many a trend has been set at **Mônica Filgueiras Galeria** (✉ Alameda Ministro Rocha Azevedo 927, Jardins ☎ 011/3082–5292), which has all types of art, but mostly paintings and sculpture.

BEACHWEAR **Beira Mar Beachwear** (✉ Rua José Paulino 592 Bom Retiro ☎ 011/ 222–7999 ⊕ www.maiosbeiramar.com.br Ⓜ Tiradentes) was founded in 1948. Since then it has been known for innovative and good-quality products. The Brazilian brand has its own factory and produces a great variety of bikinis and swimming suits. **Track & Field** (✉ Rua Oscar Freire 959 Jardins ☎ 01/3062–4457 ⊕ www.tf.com.br) is a very good place to buy beachwear and sports clothing. The store sells bikinis and swimsuits from **Cia. Marítima** (⊕ www.ciamaritima.com.br), a famous Brazilian beachwear brand. The shops are in almost every mall in São Paulo.

CLOTHING **Alexandre Herchcovitch** (✉ Rua Haddock Lobo 1151, Jardins ☎ 011/ 3063–2888) is a famous Brazilian designer, and his store has pret-a-porter and tailor-made clothes. At designer-label boutique **Daslu** (✉ Rua Domingos Leme 284, Vila Nova Conceição ☎ 011/3842–3785), mingle with elite ladies who enjoy personalized attention. There's no storefront. **Le Lis Blanc** (✉ Rua Oscar Freire 809, Jardins ☎ 011/3083–2549) is Brazil's exclusive purveyor of the French brand Vertigo. Look for party dresses in velvet and sheer fabrics. If you have a little money in your pocket, shop at **Maria Bonita** (✉ Rua Oscar Freire 702, Jardins ☎ 011/3082–6649 ⊕ www.mariabonitaextra.com.br), which has elegant women's clothes with terrific lines. At Maria Bonita Extra the prices are a little lower.

At **Petistil** (✉ Rua Teodoro Sampaio 2271, Pinheiros ☎ 011/3816–2865 ⊕ www.petistil.com.br) younger family members aren't forgotten. It sells clothes for infants and children up to 11 years old. **Richard's** (✉ Rua Oscar Freire 1129, Jardins ☎ 011/3088–8761 Ⓜ Consolação) is one of Brazil's best lines of sportswear. The collection includes outfits suitable for the beach or the mountains. At **Uma** (✉ Rua Girassol 273, Vila Madalena 🕾 011/ 3813–5559 ⊕ www.uma.com.br) young women are intrigued by the unique designs of the swimsuits, dresses, shorts, shirts, and pants.

The prices at **Vila Romana Factory Store** (✉ Via Anhanguera, Km 17.5, Osasco 🕾 011/3604–5293 ✉ Av. Ibirapuera 3103—Shoppig Ibirapuera, Moema 🕾 011/5535–1808 ⊕ www.vilaromana.com.br) for suits, jackets, jeans, and some women's wear (silk blouses, for example) are unbeatable. The store is a 40-minute drive from Centro. The in-town branch is more convenient, but its prices are higher. At **Viva Vida** (✉ Rua Oscar Freire 969, Jardins 🕾 011/3088–0421 ⊕ www.vivavida. com.br) long evening dresses—many done in shiny, sexy, exotic fabrics— steal the show. **Zoomp** (✉ Rua Oscar Freire 995, Jardins 🕾 011/ 3064–1556 ⊕ www.zoomp.com.br) is famous for its jeans and high-quality street wear. Customers from 13 to 35 mix and match the clothes, creating some unusual combinations.

HANDICRAFTS **Art Índia** (✉ Rua Augusta 1371, Loja 117, Cerqueira César 🕾 011/283– 2102 Ⓜ Consolação) is a government-run shop that sells Indian arts and crafts made by tribes throughout Brazil. As its name suggests, **Casa do Amazonas** (✉ Galeria Metropôle, Av. Jurupis 460, Moema 🕾 011/5051–3098 Ⓜ São Luís) has a wide selection of products from the Amazon.

Galeria de Arte Brasileira (✉ Alameda Lorena 2163, Jardins 🕾 011/ 3062–9452) specializes in Brazilian handicrafts. Look for objects made of pau-brasil wood, hammocks, jewelry, T-shirts, *marajoara* pottery (from the Amazon), and lace. **Marcenaria Trancoso** (✉ Rua Harmonia 233 Vila Madalena 🕾 011/3032–3505 ⊕ www.marcenariatrancoso.com. br) sells wooden products that are an elegant mixture of interior design and handicraft. At **Mundareu** (✉ Rua Mourato Coelho 988, Vila Madalena 🕾 011/3032–4649 ⊕ www.mundareu.org.br), browse through quality products made by different types of artisans from all over Brazil.

JEWELRY An internationally known Brazilian brand for jewelry, **H. Stern** (✉ Rua
★ Oscar Freire 652 Jardins 🕾 011/3068–8082 ⊕ www.hstern.com.br) has shops in more than 30 countries. This one has designs made especially for the Brazilian stores.

São Paulo A to Z

AIR TRAVEL

CARRIERS American Airlines offers three flights a day from Miami and one a day from New York and Dallas. Continental Airlines flies from New York daily; United Airlines flies daily from Miami, New York, and Chicago. British Airways flies from London every day but Tuesday and Wednesday. From London you can also connect through Paris on Air France and through Madrid on Aerolínas Argentinas. Air Canada flies from Toronto every day but Monday. Aerolíneas Argentinas has twice-a-week service from Auckland and Sydney.

Rio-Sul and Nordeste connect São Paulo with most major Brazilian cities daily. TAM flies daily to Miami, Paris, and most major Brazilian cities.

Transbrasil has daily flights to major Brazilian cities. Varig has daily service to many U.S. and Brazilian cities; it also offers regular service to more than 18 countries in Latin America, Europe, Asia, and Australia. GOL, the youngest Brazilian airline, offers budget tickets to major national capitals. ⇨ For airline information, *see* Air Travel *in* Brazil A to Z.

São Paulo's international airport, Aeroporto Cumbica, is in the suburb of Guarulhos, 30 km (19 mi) and a 45-minute drive northeast of Centro. Aeroporto Congonhas, 14 km (9 mi) south of Centro (a 15- to 30-minute drive, depending on traffic), serves regional airlines, including the Rio–São Paulo shuttle. From June to September both airports are sometimes fogged in during the early morning, and flights are rerouted to the Aeroporto Viracopos in Campinas; passengers are transported by bus (an hour's ride) to São Paulo.

🚇 Airport Information **Aeroporto Congonhas** 🕿 011/5090-9000. **Aeroporto Cumbica** 🕿 011/6445-2945. **Aeroporto Viracopos** 🕿 019/725-5000.

AIRPORT TRANSFERS EMTU *executivo* buses—fancy, green-stripe "executive" vehicles—shuttle between Cumbica and Congonhas (5:30 AM–11 PM, every 30 minutes) as well as between Cumbica and the Tietê bus terminal (5:40 AM–10:10 PM, every 45 minutes); the downtown Praça da República (5:30 AM–11 PM, every 30 minutes); and the Hotel Maksoud Plaza (6:45 AM–11:05 PM every 35 minutes), stopping at most major hotels on Avenida Paulista. The cost is R$16.50. Municipal buses, with CMTC painted on the side, stop at the airport and go downtown by various routes, such as via Avenida Paulista, to the Praça da Sé and the Tietê bus station.

The sleek, blue-and-white, air-conditioned Guarucoop radio taxis take you from Cumbica to downtown for around R$53. *Comum* (regular) taxis charge R$45 from Cumbica and around R$18 from Congonhas. Fleet Car Shuttle (counter at Cumbica Airport's arrivals Terminal 1) is open daily 6 AM–midnight and serves groups of up to 10 people in a van, stopping at one destination of choice. The fee (for the vanload) is about R$90.

🚇 Taxis & Shuttles **EMTU** *executivo* **buses** 🕿 0800/19-0088 011/6445-2505. **Fleet Car Shuttle** 🕿 011/945-3030. **Guarucoop radio taxis** 🕿 011/6440-7070.

BUS TRAVEL TO & FROM SÃO PAULO

The four bus stations in São Paulo serve 1,105 destinations combined. The huge main station—serving all major Brazilian cities (with trips to Rio every hour on the half hour) as well as Argentina, Uruguay, Chile, and Paraguay—is the Terminal Tietê in the north, on the Marginal Tietê Beltway. Terminal Bresser, in the eastern district of Brás, serves southern Minas Gerais State and Belo Horizonte. Terminal Jabaquara, near Congonhas Airport, serves coastal towns. Terminal Barra Funda, in the west, near the Memorial da América Latina, has buses to and from western Brazil. All stations have or are close to metrô stops. You can buy tickets at the stations; although those for Rio de Janeiro can be bought a few minutes before departure, it's best to buy tickets in advance for other destinations and during holiday seasons.

🚇 Bus Information **Terminal Barra Funda** ✉ Rua Mário de Andrade 664, Barra Funda 🕿 011/3235-0322. **Terminal Bresser** ✉ Rua do Hipódromo, Brás 🕿 011/

3235-0322. **Terminal Jabaquara** ✉ Rua Jequitibas, Jabaquara ☎ 011/3235-0322. **Terminal Tietê** ✉ Av. Cruzeiro do Sul, Santana ☎ 011/3235-0322.

BUS TRAVEL WITHIN SÃO PAULO

There's ample municipal bus service, but regular buses (white with a red horizontal stripe) are overcrowded at rush hour and when it rains. Stops are clearly marked, but routes are spelled out only on the buses themselves. Buses do not stop at every bus stop, so if you are waiting, put out your arm horizontally to flag one down. The fare is R$1.70. You enter at the front of the bus, pay the *cobrador* (fare collector) in the middle, and exit from the rear of the bus. The cobrador gives out *vale transporte* slips, or fare vouchers (with no expiration time), and often has no change.

The green-and-gray SPTrans executivo buses, whose numerical designations all end with the letter *E*, are more spacious and cost around R$2.80 (you pay the driver upon entry). Many *clandestino* buses (unlicensed, privately run) traverse the city. Although not very pleasing to the eye—most are battered white vehicles that have no signs—it's perfectly fine to take them; they charge the same as SPTrans buses.

For bus numbers and names, routes, and schedules for SPTrans buses, purchase the *Guia São Paulo Ruas,* published by Quatro Rodas and sold at newsstands and bookstores for about R$30.

🚌 Bus Information **Municipal bus service** ☎ 0800/12-3133. **SPTrans executivo** ☎ 158.

CAR RENTAL

Car-rental rates range from R$60 to R$200 a day. Major international rental companies include Avis and Hertz. Localiza is a major local company. ⇨ For information on major car rental agencies, *see* Car Rental *in* Brazil A to Z.

CAR TRAVEL

The main São Paulo–Rio de Janeiro highway is the Via Dutra (BR 116 North), which has been repaved and enlarged in places. The speed limit is 120 kph (74 mph) along most of it, and although it has many tolls, there are many call boxes you can use if your car breaks down. The modern Rodovia Ayrton Senna (SP 70) charges reasonable tolls, runs parallel to the Dutra for about a quarter of the way, and is an excellent alternative route. The 429-km (279-mi) trip takes five hours. If you have time, consider the longer, spectacular coastal Rio-Santos Highway (SP 55 and BR 101). It's an easy two-day drive, and you can stop midway at the colonial city of Parati, in Rio de Janeiro State.

Other main highways are the Castelo Branco (SP 280), which links the southwestern part of the state to the city; the Via Anhanguera (SP 330), which originates in the state's rich northern agricultural region, passing through the university town of Campinas; SP 310, which also runs from the farming heartland; BR 116 south, which comes up from Curitiba (a 408-km [265-mi] trip); plus the Via Anchieta (SP 150) and the Rodovia Imigrantes (SP 160), parallel roads that run to the coast, each operating one-way on weekends and holidays.

Driving isn't recommended because of the heavy traffic (nothing moves at rush hour, especially when it rains), daredevil drivers, and inadequate parking. If, however, you do opt to drive, there are a few things to keep in mind. Most of São Paulo is between the Rio Tietê and the Rio Pinheiros, which converge in the western part of town. The high-speed routes along these rivers are Marginal Tietê and Marginal Pinheiros. There are also *marginais* (beltways) around the city. Avenida 23 de Maio runs south from Centro and beneath the Parque do Ibirapuera via the Ayrton Senna Tunnel. You can take avenidas Paulista, Brasil, and Faria Lima southwest to the Morumbi, Brooklin, Itaim, and Santo Amaro neighborhoods, respectively. The Elevado Costa e Silva, also called Minhocão, is an elevated road that connects Centro with Avenida Francisco Matarazzo in the west.

In most commercial neighborhoods you must buy hourly tickets (called Cartão Zona Azul) to park on the street during business hours. Buy them at newsstands, not from people on the street. Booklets of 20 tickets cost R$18. Fill out each ticket—you'll need one for every hour you plan to park—with the car's license plate and the time you initially parked. Leave the tickets in the car's window so they're visible to officials from outside. After business hours or at any time near major sights, people may offer to watch your car. Although paying these "caretakers" about R$3 is enough to keep your car's paint job intact, to truly ensure its safety opt for a parking lot. Rates are R$5–R$7 for the first hour and R$1–R$2 each hour thereafter.

EMERGENCIES

The three main pharmacies have more than 20 stores, each open 24 hours—Droga Raia, Drogaria São Paulo, and Drogasil. The police department in charge of tourist affairs, Delegacia de Turismo, is open weekdays 8–8.

🚩 Emergency Services **Ambulance** ☎ 192. **Delegacia de Turismo** ✉ Av. São Luís 91, Centro ☎ 011/3107-8712. **Fire** ☎ 193. **Police (military)** ☎ 190.

🚩 Hospitals **Albert Einstein** ✉ Av. Albert Einstein 627, Morumbi ☎ 011/3745-1233. **Beneficência Portuguesa** ✉ Rua Maestro Cardim 769, Paraíso ☎ 011/3253-5022 Ⓜ Vergueiro. **Sírio Libanês** ✉ Rua. D. Adma Jafet 91, Bela Vista ☎ 011/3155-0200.

🚩 24-Hour Pharmacies **Droga Raia** ✉ Rua José Maria Lisboa 645, Jardim Paulistano ☎ 011/3884-8235. **Drogaria São Paulo** ✉ Av. Angélica 1465, Higienópolis ☎ 011/3667-6291. **Drogasil** ✉ Av. Brigadeiro Faria Lima 2726, Cidade Jardim ☎ 011/3812-6276.

HEALTH & SAFETY

Don't drink tap water. Ask for juice and ice made with bottled water in restaurants and bars. Don't eat barbecued meats sold by street vendors; even those served in some bars are suspect. The air pollution might irritate your eyes, especially in July and August (dirty air is held in the city by thermal inversions), so pack eye drops.

Stay alert and guard your belongings at all times, especially at major sights. Avoid wearing shorts, expensive running shoes, or flashy jewelry—all of which attract attention. Also beware of the local scam in which one person throws a dark liquid on you and another offers to help you clean up while the first *really* cleans up!

MAIL, INTERNET & SHIPPING

There's a branch of the *correio* (post office) in Centro. International couriers include DHL and FedEx. At Saraiva Megastore, Internet access is available Monday–Saturday 10–10 and Sunday 2–8; the cost is about R$8 per hour. The Fnac Internet café is open daily 10–10 and access is about R$7 per hour. Monkey, which specializes in gaming, has 10 shops around the city, with Web access for about R$4 per hour. Play Net charges R$4 per hour for access and has games rooms. Smartbiz charges about R$5 per hour and has electronic music events Fridays and Saturdays.

🖪 Internet Centers **Coffee & Book at Saraiva Megastore** ⊠ Shopping Eldorado, Av. Rebouças 3970, Pinheiros ☎ 011/3819-1770. **Frans Café at Fnac** ⊠ Av. Pedroso de Morais 858, Pinheiros ☎ 011/3814-2404. **Monkey** ⊠ Rua da Consolação 2961, Jardins ☎ 011/3085-4646 ⊕ www.monkey.com.br. **Play Net** ⊠ Rua Três Rios 90, Bom Retiro ☎ 011/3326-9720 ⊕ www.playnetgame.com.br Ⓜ Tiradentes. **Smartbiz** ⊠ Rua Augusta 2690, Loja 17 Jardins ☎ 011/3082-6937 ⊕ www.smartbiz.com.br

🖪 Post Office **Correio** ⊠ Alameda Santos 2224, Jardins ☎ 011/3085-2394 Ⓜ Consolação.

🖪 Overnight Services **DHL** ⊠ Rua da Consolação 2721, Jardins ☎ 0800/773-0552. **FedEx** ⊠ Av. São Luís 187, Loja 43, Centro ☎ 011/5641-7788 Ⓜ República.

METRÔ TRAVEL

The metrô is safe, quick, comfortable, and clean, but unfortunately it doesn't serve many of the city's southern districts. The blue line runs north–south, the orange line runs east–west, and the green line runs under Avenida Paulista from Vila Mariana to the stations at Sumaré and Vila Madalena, near Avenida Pompéia. The metrô operates daily 5 AM–midnight. Tickets are sold in stations and cost R$1.60 one-way. (You can get discounts on round-trip fares and when you buy 10 tickets at once; note that ticket sellers aren't required to change large bills.) You insert the ticket into the turnstile at the platform entrance, and it's returned to you only if there's unused fare on it. Transfers within the metrô system are free, as are bus-to-metrô (or vice-versa) transfers. You can buy a *bilhete integração* (integration ticket) on buses or at metrô stations for R$2.65. Maps of the metrô system are available from the Departamento de Marketing Institucional, or you can pick up the *Guia São Paulo* at newsstands and bookstores. Call the Metrô for ticket prices, schedules, and locations of metrô stations.

🖪 Metrô Information **Departamento de Marketing Institucional** ⊠ Av. Paulista 1842, 19th fl., Jardins ☎ 011/3371-4933 Ⓜ Consolação. **Metrô** ☎ 011/3286-0111.

MONEY MATTERS

Avenida Paulista is the home of many banks (generally open 10–4), including Citibank. For currency exchange services without any extra fees, try Action. In Centro you can exchange money at Banco do Brasil and at Banespa. Several banks have automatic-teller machines (ATMs) that accept international bank cards and dispense reais.

🖪 Banks & Exchange Services **Action** ⊠ Aeroporto Cumbica, TPS2 arrival fl., Guarulhos ☎ 011/6445-4458 ⊠ Rua Melo Alves 357, Jardins ☎ 011/3064-2910 ⊠ Shopping Paulista, Rua 13 de Maio 1947, Paraíso ☎ 011/288-4222 Ⓜ Brigadeiro. **Banco do Brasil** ⊠ Av. São João 32, Centro ☎ 011/234-1646 Ⓜ República. **Banespa** ⊠ Av. Paulista 1842-Torre Norte, Jardins ☎ 011/3016-9955 Ⓜ Consolação. **Citibank** ⊠ Av. Paulista 1111, Jardins ☎ 011/5576-1190 Ⓜ Trianon-Masp.

TAXIS

Taxis in São Paulo are white. Owner-driven taxis are generally well maintained and reliable, as are radio taxis. Fares start at R$3.20 and run R$1.30 for each kilometer (½ mi) or R$.40 for every minute sitting in traffic. After 8 PM and on weekends fares rise by 20%. You'll also pay a tax if the taxi leaves the city, as is the case with trips to Cumbica Airport. Good radio-taxi companies include Chame Taxi, Ligue-Taxi, and Paulista.

🚖 Taxi Companies **Chame Taxi** ☎ 011/3865-3033. **Ligue-Taxi** ☎ 011/3873-2000. **Paulista** ☎ 011/3746-6555.

TELEPHONES

Phone booths are bright green and yellow. Most operate using prepaid cards, but some still use tokens. Both cards and tokens are sold at newsstands. Cards with 30 credits are sold for R$3. Each credit allows you to talk for 3 minutes on local calls and 17 seconds on long-distance calls.

International calls can be made at special phone booths found in Telesp offices around the city. You can choose your own long-distance company. After dialing 0, dial a two-digit company code, followed by the country code and/or area code and number. To call Rio, for example, dial 0, then 21 (for Embratel, a major long-distance and international provider), then 21 (Rio's area code), and then the number. To call the United States, dial 00 (for international calls), 23 (for Intelig, another long-distance company or 21 for Embratel), 1 (country code), and the area code and phone number. For operator-assisted (in English) international calls, dial 000111. To make a collect long-distance call (which will cost 40% more than normal calls), dial 9 + the area code and the number. São Paulo's area code is 11. Phone numbers in the city and state have six, seven, or eight digits. Most cellular phone numbers have eight digits (a few have seven) and start with the numeral 9.

TOURS

You can hire a bilingual guide through a travel agency or hotel concierge (about R$15 an hour with a four-hour minimum), or you can design your own walking tour with the aid of information provided at Anhembi booths around the city. Anhembi also offers Sunday tours of museums, parks, and Centro that are less expensive than those offered in hotels. The tourist board offers three half-day Sunday bus tours, one covering the parks, one centered on the museums, and one focused on the historical downtown area. Officially, none of the board's guides speaks English; however, it may be able to arrange something on request.

Gol Tour Viagens e Turismo and Opcional Tour and Guide Viagens e Turismo offer custom tours as well as car tours for small groups. A half-day city tour costs about R$40 a person (group rate); a night tour—including a samba show, dinner, and drinks—costs around R$100; and day trips to the beach or the colonial city of Embu cost R$80–R$90. The English-speaking staff at Savoy specializes in personalized tours.

Canoar is one of the best rafting tour operators in São Paulo State. Trilha Brazil arranges treks in forests around São Paulo. Reputable operators that offer rain-forest, beach, and island excursions include Biotrip, Pisa Trekking, and Venturas e Aventuras.

🏢 Tour-Operator Recommendations **Biotrip** ✉ Rua Gama Cerqueira 187, Cambuci ☎ 011/ 3253-7111. **Canoar** ✉ Rua Caetés 410, Sumaré ☎ 011/3871-2282. **Gol Tour Viagens e Turismo** ✉ Av. São Luís 187, Basement, Loja 12, Centro ☎ 011/3256-2388 Ⓜ República. **Opcional Tour and Guide Viagens e Turismo** ✉ Av. Ipiranga 345, 14th fl., Suite 1401, Centro ☎ 011/3259-1007 Ⓜ República. **Pisa Trekking** ✉ Alameda dos Tupiniquins 202, Moema ☎ 011/5571-2525. **Savoy** ✉ Rua James Watt 142, Suite 92, Itaim Bibi ☎ 011/ 5507-2064 or 011/5507-2065. **Tourist board** ☎ 011/6971-5000. **Trilha Brazil** ✉ Rua Professor Rubião Meira 86, Jardim América ☎ 011/3082-7089. **Venturas e Aventuras** ✉ Rua Minerva 268, Perdizes ☎ 011/3872-0362.

VISITOR INFORMATION

The most helpful contact is the São Paulo Convention and Visitors Bureau, open 9–6. The sharp, business-minded director, Roberto Gheler, speaks English flawlessly and is extremely knowledgeable. Branches of the city-operated Anhembi Turismo e Eventos da Cidade de São Paulo are open daily 9–6. The bureaucracy-laden Secretaria de Esportes e Turismo do Estado de São Paulo, open weekdays 9–6, has maps and information about the city and state of São Paulo. SEST also has a booth at the arrivals terminal in Cumbica airport; it's open daily 9 AM–10 PM.

🏢 Tourist Information **Anhembi Turismo e Eventos da Cidade de São Paulo** ✉ Anhembi Convention Center, Av. Olavo Fontoura 1209, Santana ☎ 011/6224-0400 ⊕ www. cidadedesaopaulo.com ✉ Praça da República at Rua 7 de Abril, Centro Ⓜ República ✉ Av. Paulista, across from MASP, Cerqueira César Ⓜ Trianon-Masp ✉ Av. Brigadeiro Faria Lima, in front of Shopping Center Iguatemi, Jardim Paulista ✉ Av. Ribeiro de Lima 99, Luz Ⓜ Luz ✉ bus station, Tietê, Tietê Ⓜ Tietê ✉ Cumbica Airport Terminals 1 and 2, Aeroporto de Guarulhos. **São Paulo Convention and Visitors Bureau** ✉ Rua Dom José de Barros 17, Centro ☎ 011/289-7588 Ⓜ República. **Secretaria de Esportes e Turismo do Estado de São Paulo** (SEST) ✉ Praça Antônio Prado 9, Centro ☎ 011/ 3241-5822 Ⓜ São Bento.

FOZ DO IGUAÇU

The Foz do Iguaçu cascades in a deafening roar at a bend in the Rio Iguaçu where southwestern Paraná State meets the borders of both Argentina and Paraguay. This Brazilian town and the Argentine town of Puerto Iguazú are the hubs for exploring the falls (the Paraguayan town of Ciudad del Este is also nearby).

The avalanche of water actually consists of some 275 separate falls (in the rainy season they can number as many as 350) that plunge 80 meters (250 feet) onto the rocks below. The backdrop is one of dense, lush jungle, pitch-black basalt, and rainbows, ferns, and butterflies. The falls and the lands around them are protected by Brazil's Parque Nacional do Iguaçu and Argentina's Parque Nacional Iguazú (where the falls are referred to by their Spanish name, the Cataratas de Iguazú).

The Brazilians are blessed with the best panoramic view of the falls (allow half a day to traverse the catwalks and stop at the lookouts); the Argentine side—where most of the falls are actually situated—offers better up-close experiences. Allow another half day for this tour. Local tour operators run trips that take you to both. To set your own pace, take one of the regularly scheduled buses to the Brazilian park and then take a taxi across the international bridge, Ponte Presidente Tancredo Neves, to Argentina. Note that immigration authorities keep the region under close watch, and you will have to go through immigrations and customs. To avoid delays, make sure you have a valid visa before attempting to cross the Argentina–Brazil border either way.

The summer months (November–March) are hot and humid, so if you're bothered by the heat, plan to visit between April and October. Be aware, however, that high waters from heavy rainfall on the upper Iguaçu River basin occasionally restrict access to some walkways. Whatever time of year you visit, bring raingear: some paths take you extremely close to the falling water, where the spray can leave you drenched.

As of 2006, phone numbers in Brazil will change from seven to eight digits. All seven-digit numbers will be preceded by a 3. For example, 555–5555 will become 3555–5555.

WHAT TO SEE
Fodor'sChoice
★
The **Parque Nacional do Iguaçu** extends 25 km (16 mi) along a paved highway southwest of downtown Foz do Iguaçu. Park administration is handled by a private operator, which runs the visitor center and all tourist service and facilities. ATMs, a snack bar, a souvenir shop, and currency exchange are available at the center. You cannot drive into the park—park at the entrance by the visitor center and take an 11-km (7-mi) double-decker shuttle trip from there. The shuttle departs every 10 minutes and drops you by the trailhead, where the luxurious Tropical Cataratas EcoResort stands. The path to the falls is about 2 km (1 mi) long, and its walkways and staircases lead through the rain forest to concrete and wooden catwalks. (Much of the park's 457,000 acres are protected rain forest that is off-limits to visitors and home to the last viable populations of jaguars as well as of rare bromeliads and orchids.)

At the Salto Macuco (Macuco Falls) in the park, the crystal-clear waters of the Rio Macuco, a small tributary of the Iguaçu River, fall 18 meters (60 feet) into a natural pool. The only way to visit the falls is on a tour that takes about two hours and costs roughly R$120 per person. The trip requires a 7-km (5-mi) ride in a four-wheel-drive vehicle, followed by a short hike through the forest and a breathtaking 30-minute Zodiac ride on the Iguaçu to the falls.

Highlights of the Brazilian side of the falls include the Salto Santa Maria, from which catwalks branch off to Salto Deodoro and Salto Floriano, where you'll be doused by the spray. The end of the catwalk puts you right at the tallest and most popular falls, Garganta do Diabo (Devil's Throat), which extend for 3 km (1½ mi) in a 270-degree arch; the water thunders down 54 meters (180 feet). ⊠ *Km 17, Rodovia das Cataratas* ☎ *045/572–2261* ✉ *Park R$18, parking R$6.50* ◷ *Mon. 1–6, Tues.–Sun. 8–6.*

There are other notable sights near the national park, including the privately run **Parque das Aves** (Bird Park). Here, on 36 acres of mostly untouched tropical forest right outside the national park, are 8-meter-high (25-foot-high) aviaries with 160 species of birds, as well as reptiles and a butterfly collection. A gift shop and a restaurant round out the facilities. ⊠ *Km 17, Rodovia das Cataratas* ☎ *045/529–8282* 🎫 *R$18* 🕑 *Daily 9–6.*

About 21 km (13 mi) up the Rio Paraná (which flows into the Rio Iguaçu just below the falls) is a great achievement of Brazilian civil engineering: the mighty **Hidrelétrica de Itaipú** (Itaipú Hydroelectric Power Plant) and the Itaipú Dam. It is the world's largest hydroelectric power plant, at 8 km (5 mi) long; its powerhouse alone is 2 km (1 mi) long. Twenty-five percent of Brazil's electricity is produced here. Watch a 15-minute video about the construction of the dam at the visitor center and join the hour-long guided bus tour of the complex—visits to the power plant have to be booked in advance. ⊠ *Km 11, Av. Tancredo Neves* ☎ *045/ 520–5252* 🎫 *Free* 🕑 *Mon.–Sat. 8–6.*

Where to Stay & Eat

Near the borders of two other countries, the town of Foz do Iguaçu has a cosmopolitan atmosphere that's reflected in the cuisine. For a city of its size, the options are great. There's also one noteworthy hotel on the Argentine side—the Internacional Cataratas de Iguazú. For convenience, most visitors stay in the establishments that line BR 469 (Rodovia das Cataratas), the highway that runs from the city of Foz do Iguaçu to the national park and the falls. All major hotels can make arrangements for tours.

★ **$–$$$** ✕ **Zaragoza.** In a quiet neighborhood on a tree-lined street, this cozy restaurant, owned by a Spanish immigrant, is very popular with the international crowd as well as the locals. The fare includes the seafood paella, the house specialty, as well as several delicious fish options. The *surubi*, a regional fish, definitely merits a try. ⊠ *Rua Quintino Bocaiúva 882* ☎ *045/574–3084* ☰ *AE, V.*

$ ✕ **Cataratas Iate Clube.** One of the draws here is that this is the only restaurant where you can dine with the Paraná River as the backdrop. The fish rodízio includes the best *moqueca de surubi* (stew made with surubi, a local fish) and *piapara ao vinagrete* (fried *piapara* fish marinated in vinegar sauce) in Foz do Iguaçu. ⊠ *Km 0.5, Av. Gen. Meira* ☎ *045/ 523–2335* ☰ *No credit cards.*

¢ ✕ **Bufalo Branco.** This is the city's finest and largest churrascaria. The picanha stands out from the 20-plus grilled meat choices. The salad bar is well stocked, a boon for vegetarians. ⊠ *Av. Rebouças 530* ☎ *045/ 523–9744* ☰ *AE, DC, MC, V.*

$$$ ✕🏨 **Tropical Cataratas EcoResort.** Not only is this stately hotel *in* the na-
Fodor'sChoice tional park, with wonderful views of the falls from the front-side apart-
★ ments, but it also provides the traditional comforts of a colonial-style establishment: large rooms, terraces, vintage furniture, and hammocks. The main building, declared a National Heritage Site, is surrounded by verandas and gardens. The Itaipú restaurant ($$–$$$$) serves a traditional Brazilian dinner, with feijoada and a variety of side dishes. Any entrées featuring fish from the Paraná basin are also recommended. ⊠ *Km 25, Rodovia das Cataratas, 85850-970* ☎ *045/521–7000 or 0800/701– 2670* 🖷 *045/522–1717* ⊕ *www.tropicalhotel.com.br* ⤺ *200 rooms* ♨ *2 restaurants, cable TV, coffee shop, 2 tennis courts, gym, bar, pool, playground, volleyball, shops, airport shuttle* ☰ *AE, DC, MC, V* 🍴 *CP.*

★ **$$–$$$** ✕⊡ **Sheraton Internacional Iguazú.** Half the rooms in this top-notch hotel over the Argentine border have direct views of the falls, so be sure to ask for a view when you make a reservation. Floor-to-ceiling windows let the inspiring scene into the lobby, restaurants, and bars; even the pool has a vista. The handsomely decorated Garganta del Diablo restaurant ($$–$$$$) serves a memorable trout wrapped in pastry and the Argentine version of the *surubí* follows suit. ⊠ *Parque Nacional Iguazú, Km 4, Ruta 12, Puerto Iguazú, Argentina* ☎ *0757/21100* 🖷 *0757/21090* ◁ *180 rooms, 4 suites* ⟨ *2 restaurants, cable TV, 3 tennis courts, biking, pool, 2 bars, meeting room, airport shuttle* ⊟ *AE, DC, MC, V* ⦿⏐ *CP.*

★ **$$** ⊡ **Iguaçu Golf Club and Resort.** Even the most demanding visitors find the Iguaçu Golf Club unforgettable. The resort hosts a national pro golf tournament annually. Accommodations are in small eight-room buildings surrounded by spacious and plush gardens with tropical vegetation—a preview of what lies beyond in the national park. If you're traveling with family or a group of friends, ask for one of the separate guest houses. ⊠ *Km 7, Rodovia das Cataratas, 85863-000* ☎ *045/529–9999* 🖷 *045/529–8888* ⊕ *www.iguassugolf.com.br* ◁ *67 rooms, 4 guest houses* ⟨ *Restaurant, cable TV, driving range, 18-hole golf course, putting green, pool, health club, hot tub, bar, lounge, shops, airport shuttle* ⊟ *AE, DC, MC, V* ⦿⏐ *CP.*

¢ ⊡ **Florença Iguaçu.** In a sprawling wooded lot on the road to the national park, Florença combines budget rates with excellent service. Rooms are large and have walk-in closets and views of the gardens. ⊠ *Km 13, Rodovia das Cataratas, 85863-000* ☎ *045/529–7755* 🖷 *045/529–8877* ⊕ *www.hotelflorenca.com* ◁ *63 rooms* ⟨ *Restaurant, cable TV, pool, volleyball, tennis court, bar, meeting room, playground* ⊟ *AE, DC, MC, V* ⦿⏐ *CP.*

¢ ⊡ **Foz Presidente.** The main draw of this budget hotel is the downtown location, with easy access to all attractions and the business district. Rooms are nondescript but comfortable, with queen-size beds, and look out onto downtown Foz. ⊠ *Av. Marechal Floriano 1851, 85851-030* ☎ *045/523–2318* 🖷 *045/523–2318* ⊕ *www.fozpresidentehoteis.com* ◁ *115 rooms* ⟨ *Cable TV, bar, lounge, pool* ⊟ *AE, DC, MC, V* ⦿⏐ *CP.*

Foz do Iguaçu A to Z

AIR TRAVEL
CARRIERS Foz do Iguaçu is served by TAM, Varig, and VASP. TAM also serves Ciudad del Este, in Paraguay, across the border from the falls. ⇨ For airline information, *see* Air Travel *in* Brazil A to Z.

AIRPORTS & TRANSFERS
The Aeroporto Internacional Foz do Iguaçu (IGU) is 13 km (8 mi) southeast of downtown. The 20-minute taxi ride should cost R$35, the 45-minute regular bus ride about R$1.75. Note that several major hotels are on the highway to downtown, so a cab ride from the airport may be less than R$25. A cab ride directly to the Parque Nacional in Brazil costs R$60, and a full tour including both the Brazilian and Argentine sides of the falls costs R$160 (tickets not included).

�; Airport Information **Aeroporto Internacional Foz do Iguaçu** ⊠ Km 13, Rodovia das Cataratas ☎ 045/521–4200.

BUS TRAVEL

For the most part, each city is served by a different bus company. For long-distance trips it's best to opt for special services, often called *executivo* or *leito* (pullman) buses, which have air-conditioning, wide reclining seats, and rest rooms. Regular buses are 20%–30% less but aren't nearly as comfortable. Sulamericana buses make the 10-hour trip to Foz do Iguaçu from São Paulo. The Terminal Rodoviário in Foz do Iguaçu is 5 km (3 mi) northeast of downtown.

✈ Bus Information Sulamericana ☎ 041/373-1000 in Curitiba, 045/522-2050 in Foz do Iguaçu. **Terminal Rodoviário** ✉ Av. Costa e Silva s/n, Foz do Iguaçu ☎ 045/522-3633.

CAR RENTAL

Don't expect to find vehicles in the luxury range of the car spectrum. Automatic transmission is not normally available, and there's a surcharge for air-conditioning. ⇨ For information on major car rental agencies, *see* Car Rental *in* Brazil A to Z.

CAR TRAVEL

The southern states have extensive highway systems connecting major cities and tourist destinations. Be prepared for stretches that aren't in top condition; some are being renovated, and there may be delays. When planning a road trip, ask at the nearest Polícia Rodoviária (Highway Patrol) station for guidance. These are by the main roads, usually a few miles from major cities. Privatized toll roads in Paraná are generally in good shape, but you'll have to pay R$3–R$7. You can drive from Curitiba to Foz do Iguaçu on BR 277, which traverses Paraná State. It's a long drive, but this toll highway is kept in good shape.

EMERGENCIES

✈ Emergency Contacts Ambulance ☎ 192. **Fire** ☎ 193. **Police** ☎ 190.
✈ Hospitals Hospital Internacional ✉ Av. Brasil 1637, Foz do Iguaçu, Paraná ☎ 045/523-1404.
✈ 24-Hour Pharmacies FarmaRede ✉ Av. Brasil 46, Foz do Iguaçu, Paraná ☎ 045/523-1929.

HEALTH

Here, in Brazil's most developed region, tap water is safe to drink in most areas. It's usually highly chlorinated, so you may prefer the taste of bottled water. As in the rest of Brazil, avoid eating unpeeled fruit.

MAIL & INTERNET

Fax and Internet services are available at hotels and major post offices.
✈ Internet Center Digital Land ✉ Av. das Cataratas 1118, Foz do Iguaçu ☎ 045/523-4245.
✈ Post Offices Correios ✉ Praça Getúlio Vargas 72, Foz do Iguaçu ☎ 045/523-0327.

MONEY MATTERS

In general, banks are open weekdays 10–4, though major airport branches have extended hours for currency exchange (daily 8 AM–9 PM); some also have weekend hours. ATMs dispense only reais; for security reasons most ATMs shut down after 8 PM and restart after 6 AM; usually ATMs at airports and main branches will accept international bank or credit cards. Banco 24 Horas ATMs are linked with Cirrus/Maestro network; Banco do Brasil and HSBC ATMs are connected with Plus/Pulse.

🖪 Banks & Exchange Services **Banco do Brasil** ⊠ Av. Brasil 1377, Foz do Iguaçu ☎ 045/521-2500. **STTC** ⊠ Av. das Cataratas 1419, Foz do Iguaçu ☎ 045/574-2527.

SAFETY

Crime is low compared with the northern parts of the country. However, you should guard your belongings on city buses and in crowded public spaces—especially bus terminals, which are havens for pickpockets. Be extra cautious at night, especially when leaving a nightclub or bar.

TAXIS

In Foz do Iguaçu independent tour operators (certified by the city government) offer their services outside hotel lobbies. These special cabs are usually large sedans with air-conditioning. The driver doubles as a tour guide, and you can tailor the route and pace according to your interests. A half-day trip to the Argentinean Foz side of the falls from downtown costs about R$160.

🖪 Taxi Companies **Foz do Iguaçu radio-taxi service** ☎ 045/523-4800.

TELEPHONES

The area code for Foz do Iguaçu is 45.

TOURS

STTC Turismo in Foz do Iguaçu is reliable. Macuco Safari arranges Zodiac trips to Salto Macuco and on to the main falls. Helisul Táxi Aéreo offers helicopter tours of the falls between 9 and 6 and, if you like, of Itaipú Dam. The shortest flight (10 minutes) costs US$60 per person (with a minimum of three passengers).

🖪 **Helisul Táxi Aéreo** ⊠ Km 16.5, Rodovia das Cataratas, Foz do Iguaçu ☎ 045/529-7474 ⊕ www.helisul.com. **Macuco Safari** ⊠ Km 21, Rodovia das Cataratas, Foz do Iguaçu ☎ 045/574-4244. **STTC Turismo** ⊠ Av. Morenitas 2250, Padre Monti, Foz do Iguaçu ☎ 045/523-1115 🖷 045/523-3137 ⊕ www.sttcturismo.com.br.

VISITOR INFORMATION

🖪 Tourist Information **FozTur** ⊠ Rua Alm. Barroso 1300, 2nd floor, Foz do Iguaçu ☎ 0800/45-1516 ⊠ Aeroporto Internacional Foz do Iguaçu, Km 13, ☎ 045/521-4276.

THE PANTANAL WETLANDS

Right in the middle of South America, the gigantic flood plain of the Rio Paraguay and its tributaries cover about 225,000 square km (140,000 square mi), two-thirds of which are in Brazil. Much of the land is still owned by ranching families that have been here for generations. The Portuguese had begun colonizing the area by the late 18th century; today it's home to more than 21 million head of cattle and some 4 million people (most of them living in the capital cities). Yet there's still abundant wildlife in this mosaic of swamp, forest, and savanna. From your base at a *fazenda* (ranch) or lodge—with air-conditioning, swimming pools, and well-cooked meals—you can experience the *pantaneiro* lifestyle, yet another manifestation of the cowboy culture. Folklore has it that pantaneiros can communicate with the Pantanal animals.

It's widely held that the Pantanal is the best place in all of South America to view wildlife, and it is slated to become a UNESCO Biosphere Reserve. More than 600 species of birds live in the Pantanal during different migratory seasons, including *araras* (hyacinth macaws), fabulous blue-and-yellow birds that can be as long as 3 feet from head to tail; larger-than-life rheas, which look and walk like aging modern ballerinas; the *tuiuiú,* known as the "lords of the Pantanal" and one of the largest birds known (their wingspan is 5–6 feet); as well as cormorants, ibis, herons, kingfishers, hawks, falcons, and egrets, to name a few. You're also sure to spot *capivaras* (capybaras; large South American rodents), tapirs, anteaters, marsh and jungle deer, maned wolves, otters, and one of the area's six species of monkey.

The amphibian family is well represented by *jacarés* (caiman alligators), whose population of 200 per square mile is a large increase from the 1970s, when poaching had left them nearly extinct. (The skin of four animals made just one pair of shoes.) Jacarés are much more tranquil than their North American and African relatives—they don't attack unless threatened. It's hard to spot jaguars and pumas during the day; a night photographic safari is the best way to try your luck. Native guides (some are actually converted hunters) take you safely to the animals' roaming areas. Sightings are not uncommon in the fazendas that go the extra mile to protect their fauna. Though all commercial hunting and the pelt trade in wild species has been illegal since 1967, some ranchers still kill jaguars that prey on livestock. Don't let scary tales about *sucuri* (anacondas), which can grow to 30 feet in length, worry you. Sightings of the snakes are extremely rare and instances of them preying on humans are even rarer.

October is the beginning of the Pantanal's rainy season, which peaks in March but lasts through May. The land is much greener than at other times of the year, but the wildlife is harder to spot. In the dry season (July–October), when some trees shed their leaves and grasses die, land animal sightings are more frequent. As the waters continue to disappear, fish get caught in the remaining pools and attract a great variety of animals, especially birds. The best fishing season is May through October, and considering the more than 240 varieties of fish in the area, anglers won't be disappointed. *Piraputanga* and *dourado* are the most prized catches, but the abundant *pacú, pintado,* and *traíra* are also popular. Piranhas are endemic to the area, but much like caimans, seldom cause trouble—they only attack animals or humans with open wounds. Nevertheless, always check with locals before venturing into unknown waters.

As of 2006, phone numbers in Brazil will change from seven to eight digits. All seven-digit numbers will be preceded by a 3. For example, 555–5555 will become 3555–5555.

Cuiabá

1,130 km (700 mi) west of Brasília, 1,615 km (1,000 mi) northwest of São Paulo.

The capital of Mato Grosso is well known for being the hottest city in Brazil: mean annual temperature is a sizzling 27°C (81°F). Daily highs surpass 45°C (113°F) several times during the year. The city name comes from the Bororo native people, who lived in the area—it means "place where we fish with spears." Originally settled in the 18th century, when gold was found in the nearby rivers, Cuiabá is at a crossroad: it is the southernmost gateway to the Cerrado and the Amazon beyond and the northern gateway to the Pantanal. You can visit one of several museums while you're waiting for a tour into the wetlands or to Chapada dos Guimarães, a mountain range with impressive gorges, waterfalls, and vistas.

The **Museu História Natural e Antropologia,** close to the center of town, is really a complex of museums with everything from ancient Indian artifacts to contemporary art. ☒ *Palácio da Instrução, Praça da República* ☎ *065/321–3391* ☒ *R$5* ⊙ *Weekdays 12:30–5:30.*

Northeast of the town's main square is the **Museu de Pedras Ramis Bucair,** with a stunning collection of area fossils and stones, including what's purportedly a meteorite. ☒ *Rua Galdino Pimentel 195* ☒ *R$5* ⊙ *Weekdays 7–11 and 1–4.*

Slightly outside town is the **Museu Rondon,** known informally as the Museu do Índio (Indian Museum). Displays include photos of and objects from the indigenous peoples—the Bororo, Pareci, Xavante, and Txukarramãe—of Mato Grosso. The museum is on the UFMT (Universidade Federal do Mato Grosso) campus, whose grounds also contain a zoo populated by Pantanal wildlife. ☒ *Av. Fernando Correia da Costa, 4 km (2 mi) east of town* ☎ *065/615–8489* ☒ *R$2* ⊙ *Weekdays 8–11 and 2–5.*

Where to Stay & Eat

$–$$ ✕ **Getúlio Grill.** For those who have had their share of fish from the Pantanal, this is a good choice. The menu is full of churrasco fare, but other options such as fillet *a Parmegianna* are highly recommended. There is a dance club on the second floor. ☒ *Av. Getulio Vargas 1147, Goiabeiras* ☎ *065/624–9992* ⊙ *Closed Mon.* ⊟ *AE, DC, MC, V.*

¢–$ ✕ **Morro de St. Antônio.** This surf-and-turf place has a Polynesian vibe and caters to a yuppie crowd. Many entrées are enough for two people. Dinner is served nightly until 1 AM; on weekends this is a good place to drink and be merry into the wee hours. ☒ *Av. Isaac Póvoas 1167, Centro* ☎ *065/622–0502* ⊟ *AE, DC, MC, V.*

★ ¢–$ ✕ **Peixaria Popular.** This is the place in town for Pantanal fish; don't miss the delicious *piraputanga,* either prepared in a stew or fried. Other options are the *pintado* (a large freshwater fish) and *pacu* (a smaller fish that resembles a piranha). All orders include a side serving of pirão and *banana frita* (fried bananas). ☒ *Av. São Sebastião 2324, Goiabeiras* ☎ *065/322–5471* ⊟ *MC, V* ⊙ *No dinner Sun.*

¢–$ ✕ **Regionalíssimo.** In the same building as the Casa do Artesão, a shop filled with indigenous artifacts, this self-service eatery has regional cuisine as well as Brazilian staples such as rice and beans. After a hearty meal you can browse for ceramics, baskets, and wood handicrafts. ⊠ *13 de Junho 314, Porto* ☎ *065/623–6881* ⊟ *DC, MC, V* ☉ *Closed Mon. No dinner.*

$ ✕⊡ **Paiaguás Palace.** Rooms are simple and rather small but charming. The top-floor restaurant, which has a buffet of international fare, is highly regarded by local businesspeople and has good views—on clear nights you can see the plains. Location is one of the main draws of this hotel; it's right in the business district with easy access to the airport. ⊠ *Av. Rubens de Mendonça 1718, Bosque da Saúde* ☎ *065/642–5353* ⊟ *065/642–2910* ⊕ *www.hotelpaiaguas.com.br* ⬎ *121 rooms* ♨ *Restaurant, gym, bar, business services, travel services, Internet* ⊟ *AE, DC, MC, V* ⦿*I CP.*

$–$$ ⊡ **Eldorado Cuiabá.** A vision of glass and brass (no gold, as the name would suggest), this hotel has some of the best rooms in town. The pleasant decor, air-conditioning, and cable TV are a welcome break from the surrounding sparse Pantanal fazendas. ⊠ *Av. Isaac Póvoas 1000, Centro 78045-640* ☎ *065/624–4000 or 0800/17–1888* ⊟ *065/624–1480* ⊕ *www.hoteiseldorado.com.br/hcuiaba.htm* ⬎ *141 rooms, 6 suites* ♨ *Restaurant, cable TV, pool, bar, shops, business services, convention center, Internet, meeting rooms* ⊟ *AE, DC, MC, V* ⦿*I CP.*

¢ ⊡ **Áurea Palace.** The amenities are few, but this hotel is clean, and the staff is reliable. Each room has two single beds. Make this your choice if you have a tight budget. ⊠ *Rua Gen Mello 63, Bandeirantes* ☎ *065/623–5008* ⊟ *065/3027–5728* ⬎ *75 rooms* ♨ *Restaurant, refrigerators, pool, bar, Internet; no room TVs* ⊟ *AE, V* ⦿*I CP.*

Chapada dos Guimarães

74 km (40 mi) north of Cuiabá.

This quasi-mystical mesa is the area's most popular attraction after the Pantanal, and much of it is protected by a national park. Traveling northeast of Cuiabá, you see the massive sandstone formations from miles away, rising 3,000 feet above the flat cerrado landscape. After navigating the steep and winding MT 251 through breathtaking canyons to reach the top of the mesa, you discover the pretty town of Chapada dos Guimarães, which still retains some of its colonial charm.

In 1972 satellite images proved that the continent's true center was not in Cuiabá, where a monument had been built, but right here at **Mirante do Centro Geodésico,** on the mesa's edge. If the geodesic center doesn't hold spiritual meaning for you, come for the fantastic vista; on a clear day you can see as far as the Pantanal. ⊠ *8 km (5 mi) southwest of town.*

Along the road to Chapada dos Guimarães from Cuiabá, you pass the **Portão do Inferno** (Hell's Gate), a scenic viewpoint over the chasm that was created by the Rio Cuiabá's waters eroded the mesa. ⊠ *48 km (30 mi) northeast of Cuiabá.*

Parque Nacional da Chapada dos Guimarães. Beyond the Portão do Inferno you come to the park's **visitor center** (⊠ Km 51, MT 251 ☎ 065/

301–1133), which is open daily 8–5. One step from the visitor center, the **Cachoeira Véu de Noiva** (Bridal Veil Falls), with a 250-foot freefall, is the most impressive of the five falls in the park. You can enjoy lunch at the nearby open-air restaurant. Beyond this point there are hills, caves, more falls, and archeological sites. ⊠ *13 km (8 mi) west of town* ☎ *065/301–1113* ▢ *R$3* ⊗ *Daily 8–5.*

Where to Eat

$–$$ ✕ **Nivo's Fogão Regional.** The restaurant is true to its motto, QUALIDADE: INGREDIENTE FUNDAMENTAL DE BOA COZINHA, which translates as "quality: the basic ingredient of good cooking." The fish entrées such as pacu and *dourado* are delicious and are always served with pirão and *farofa de banana* (cassava flour with bananas). ⊠ *Praça Dom Wunibaldo 63* ☎ *065/791–1284* ▢ V ⊗ *Closed Mon. No dinner.*

$ ✕ **Morro dos Ventos.** This restaurant is right on the edge of the cliff. Enjoy the scenery as you enjoy one of the regional dishes such as *vaca atolada* (cow stuck-in-the-mud), beef ribs served in cooked cassava chunks. The restaurant is in a condominium complex, and you have to pay a R$5 entrance fee. ⊠ *Road to Campo Verde, 1 km (½ mi) east of town* ☎ *065/301–1030* ⌕ *Reservations essential* ▢ V ⊗ *No dinner.*

Transpantaneira Highway

From Poconé, 103 km (64 mi) south of Cuiabá, the highway runs 149 km (93 mi) southward to Poconé to Porto Jofre.

The Rodovia Transpantaneira (MT 080) was originally planned to cut a north–south line through the Pantanal. Lack of funds and opposition from environmentalists resulted in a stalemate. Today the road dead-ends at the banks of the Cuiabá River, in a village called Porto Jofre, about 150 km (93 mi) south of the town of Cuiabá. Still, the Transpantaneira makes it possible to observe the abundant fauna and plush vegetation of the northern part of the wetlands. A large number of fazendas and pousadas organize popular activities such as fishing and photo safaris.

This "highway" is actually a dirt road with some 125 log bridges that allow the annual floods to flow in the natural system without major interference. Even during dry season traversing the Transpantaneira is time consuming and relatively dangerous. The bridges on the last section, from the Pixaim village to Porto Jofre, are the most precarious. Sections of some bridges have caved in while cars were passing over them. It's best to join an organized tour; leave the driving to experienced guides in four-wheel-drive vehicles and concentrate on the region's fascinating landscapes.

Where to Stay

$ ✕▣ **Pousada Araras EcoLodge.** Rooms are cozy and impeccably clean at
Fodor'sChoice this ecolodge, and the restaurant serves great Pantanal fish. Environ-
★ mental education and awareness is the motto here: this pousada goes the extra mile to keep the environmental impact of tourism to a minimum and explains why and how they do it. One highlight is the 3,000-foot wooden walkway over the wetlands that ends on a 75-foot-high lookout, well above the treetops. From there you have a bird's-eye view of the surroundings. There's a two-day minimum stay, which leaves you

time to join the trekking, canoe, horseback, or other tours of the area. ✉ *Km 33, Rodovia Transpantaneira, Pixaim* ☎ *065/682–2800* 🖷 *065/ 682–1260* ⊕ *www.araraslodge.com.br* 📞 *15 rooms* ⚒ *Restaurant, pool, boating, marina, fishing, hiking, horseback riding, bar, airport shut- tle; no room TVs, no room phones* 🖃 *V* 🍽 *FAP.*

$ 🏨 **Pantanal Mato Grosso Hotel.** This member of the Best Western chain is one of the northern Pantanal's more upscale choices. Its rooms may be sparsely decorated but are comfortable enough to make your stay pleasant. The hotel arranges fishing expeditions, guided treks on horse- back or on foot, and visits to the Campo Largo ranch, an adjoining work- ing ranch owned by the hotel. Two- to four-night packages are available, but you can take advantage of some activities on a day-use basis. Book several weeks ahead, particularly in high season (June–October). ✉ *Km 65, Rodovia Transpantaneira, Pixaim* ☎ *065/391–1324 or 065/628– 1500* ⊕ *www.hotelmatogrosso.com.br* 📞 *35 rooms* ⚒ *Restaurant, pool, boating, marina, fishing, hiking, horseback riding, bicycles, air- port shuttle, airstrip; no room TVs* 🖃 *AE, DC, MC, V* 🍽 *FAP.*

Campo Grande

1025 km (638 mi) west of São Paulo, 694 km (430 mi) south of Cuiabá.

Nicknamed the Cidade Morena (Brunette City) because of the reddish- brown earth on which it sits, this relatively young city (founded in 1899) was made the capital of Mato Grosso do Sul in 1978, when the state separated from Mato Grosso. Campo Grande's economy tradi- tionally relied on ranching, but in the 1970s farmers from the south set- tled in the region, plowed the flat lands, and permanently changed the landscape. Now ecotourism is booming in the region. The number of foreign and Brazilian visitors to Campo Grande, the gateway to the south- ern Pantanal and the town of Bonito, is increasing each year.

To get acquainted with Mato Grosso's indigenous population, which includes more than 50,000 Terenas, Kaiowas, Guaranis, and Kadiweu, visit the **Memorial da Cultura Indígena**, a 25-foot-high bamboo *maloca* (Indian hut) built in the middle of an urban Indian reservation (Aldeia Marçal de Souza), the first urban reservation in Brazil. You can shop for pottery and tapestries. The reservation is in the Tiradentes neigh- borhood. ✉ *BR 262, exit to Tres Lagoas* ☎ *067/725–4822.*

Founded by Salesian missionaries, the **Museo Dom Bosco**, known as the Museu do Índio, has more than 5,000 indigenous artifacts of the Bororo, Kadiweu, and Carajás native peoples. Noteworthy are the taxidermy exhibits of the Pantanal fauna and the formidable seashell collection. Don't miss the bug room, whose walls are covered from floor to ceil- ing with insects of every type. ✉ *Rua Barão do Rio Branco 1843* ☎ *067/312–6491* 💲 *R$3* 🕐 *Tues.–Sat. 8–6, Sun. 8–noon and 2–6.*

Where to Stay & Eat

$–$$ ✕ **Casa Colonial.** In a colonial-style house is one of Campo Grande's best restaurants, which serves eclectic fare with a strong leaning toward Italian cuisine. ✉ *Rua Afonso Pena 3997* ☎ *067/383–3207* 🖃 *AE, DC, MC, V* 🕐 *No lunch Mon.*

¢–$$ ✕ **Fogo Caipira.** This is the place for regional cuisine. Call ahead for stuffed
Fodor'sChoice pintado or piraputanga. The standout here is the *picanha grelhada na*
★ *pedra* (grilled picanha steak). The *carreteiro* (rice with sun-dried meat)
is also recommended. ⊠ *Rua José Antônio Pereira 145, Centro* ☎ *067/*
324–1641 ▤ *AE, DC, MC, V.*

¢–$$ ✕ **Radio Clube.** One of the fanciest places in town, this restaurant–nightclub adds some energy to the somewhat lifeless Praça da República. You
can stop by for a drink or a meal of Continental fare. ⊠ *Rua Padre João*
Cripa 1280 ☎ *067/321–0131* ▤ *AE, DC, MC, V* ☉ *Closed Mon.*

$ ▥ **Jandaia.** The Jandaia is so thoroughly modern that it almost seems
out of place in this wild-west town. Though it has little character—it's
geared toward businesspeople, so convenience wins over aesthetics—it
does have all the facilities and amenities you'd expect at a deluxe hotel.
The upscale Imperium restaurant, on the second floor, serves international fare with Brazilian options. ⊠ *Rua Barão do Rio Branco 1271,*
79002-174 ☎ *067/721–7000* 🖷 *067/721–1401* ⊕ *www.jandaia.com.*
br ⇌ *130 rooms, 10 suites* ⚭ *2 restaurants, pool, gym, bar, meeting*
room ▤ *AE, DC, MC, V.*

¢ ▥ **Hotel Internacional.** Though modest, this budget option is clean and
well maintained; what's more, management doesn't feel compelled to jack
up the rates just because there's a pool. The dormitorylike rooms have
firm single beds and private bathrooms. The only problem here is the location near the bus station—a part of town that can be dangerous at night.
⊠*Rua Allan Kardac 223, 79008-330* ☎*067/784–4677* 🖷*067/721–2729*
⇌ *100 rooms* ⚭ *Restaurant, pool, bar* ▤ *AE, DC, MC, V.*

¢ ▥ **Metropolitan.** Well located near Avenida Afonso Pena, this hotel is popular with business travelers. Rooms are nicely decorated. The tile floors
make the rooms feel extra cool—you might even forget to turn on the
air-conditioning. ⊠ *Av Pres. Ernesto Geisel 5100, 79006-000* ☎ *067/*
389–4600 🖷 *067/389–4601* ⊕ *www.hotelintermetro.com.br* ⇌ *80*
rooms ⚭ *Cable TV, pool, bar, meeting room* ▤ *AE, DC, MC, V.*

Corumbá

435 km (272 mi) west of Campo Grande.

This port city on the Rio Paraguai's banks is a couple of miles from the
Bolivian border. Often called the "capital of the Pantanal," the 100,000-
inhabitant city itself is not particularly pretty, with the exception of the
riverfront area where you can see some 19th-century buildings (which
are National Historic Landmarks) and the wetlands well into Bolivia.
Corumbá means "faraway place" in the Tupi language, and the main
lures of this far-flung region are the chartered fishing trips in fully outfitted riverboats and the yachts that travel up the Paraguay river into
the heart of the Pantanal. Waters are clearest and fish are most concentrated during the dry season (May–September).

Where to Stay & Eat

$ ✕ **Peixaria do Lulu.** This family-run business adds personal flavor to the
regional cuisine. The fare is essentially Pantanal fish, which can be fried,
grilled, or stewed and is served with several side dishes such as *pirão* (black

beans with cassava flour). ⊠ *Rua Don Aquino Correia 700* ☎ *067/232–2142* ⚲ *Reservations essential* ⊟ *No credit cards* ⊘ *Closed weekends.*

¢ 🏨 **Nacional Palace.** This hotel is the best in the region, with comfortable rooms and reliable air-conditioning—an absolute requirement in the tropical heat. Amenities are few, but service is good, and the staff is helpful in recommending local attractions and tours. ⊠ *Rua América 936, 79301-060* ☎ *67/231–6868* 🖶 *067/231–6202* ⬎ *100 rooms* ⚄ *Cable TV, pool, bar, playground, business center, Internet, meeting rooms* ⊟ *AE, DC, MC, V.*

Sports & the Outdoors

Corumbá is known across the country as port of call for comfortable riverboats and yachts with weeklong fishing trips—called locally *barcos-hotel* (hotel boats). Daily sightseeing trips are also available. A great travel agency and tour operator is **Pérola do Pantanal** (☎ 067/231–1470 ⊕ www.peroladopantanal.com.br), which has several boats and yachts of different sizes, including the largest on the Paraguay river, the *Kalypso*. This luxury riverboat has 28 cabins with air-conditioning, plus a pool, a restaurant, a satellite phone link, and freezers for the fish you catch.

Miranda

205 km (128 mi) west of Campo Grande.

This tiny settlement on the Miranda River grew into a city after the construction of the railway linking São Paulo to Corumbá and on to Bolivia. In its heyday the railway was called *Ferrovia da Morte* (Death Railway) because of the many cattle thieves, train robbers, and smugglers that rode the rails. Since the 1980s the railway has been closed to passengers. At this writing, there is a project, pending government funding, to open a portion of the railway for a tourist *trem do Pantanal* (Pantanal Train) between Campo Grande and Corumbá. Ecotourism is Miranda's main source of revenue. Comfortable pousadas and farms allow you to get acquainted with the *pantaneiro* lifestyle. The Rio Miranda area has abundant fauna, including a sizable population of jaguars. Here is a great opportunity to practice *focagem*, a local version of a photographic safari: as night falls, guides take you into the Pantanal in 4x4 pickup trucks with powerful searchlights that mesmerize the animals for some time, so you can get a really close look.

Where to Stay & Eat

¢–$ ✕ **Cantina Dell'Amore.** Make this small restaurant your choice for pasta—with the owner's original tomato sauce recipe—and fish. You can also try caiman meat here. Owner Angelo Dell'Amore, an Italian expatriate who came to the Pantanal as a professional hunter and later became a caiman breeder, entertains you with his tales. ⊠ *Rua Barão do Rio Branco 515* ☎ *067/242–2826* ⊟ *No credit cards.*

$$$–$$$$ 🏨 **Caiman Ecological Refuge.** This 100,000-plus-acre ranch pioneered
Fodor's Choice the idea of ecotourism in the Pantanal. The service is excellent—from
★ the professional manner of the kitchen and bar staffs to the knowledgeable guides, all of whom hold a degree in biology or a related science and most of whom speak English. Lodges are spread out over the

ranch. The main lodge has the nicest common areas. The Baiazinha (Small Bay) lodge, which is surrounded almost entirely by water, is another great choice. Activities include horseback rides through the wetlands, boat trips to islands on the refuge's vast holdings, and *focagem* of the fauna. Rates include transfers from Campo Grande's airport. ⊠ *37 km (23 mi) north of Miranda, 235 km (146 mi) west of Campo Grande* ☎ *067/687–2102, 011/3079–6622 for reservations in São Paulo* 🖷 *067/ 687–2103* ⓓ *Rua Campos Bicudo, 98-112 São Paulo 04536-010* ☎ *011/3079–6622* 🖷 *011/3079–6037* ⊕ *www.caiman.com.br* ☜ *29 rooms* ⚫ *Restaurant, pool, bicycles, boating, hiking, horseback riding, volleyball, bar, airstrip; no room TVs, no room phones* 🖃 *AE, DC, MC, V* ⍩ *FAP.*

$–$$$ ⊡ **Fazenda Rio Negro.** This 25,000-acre farm gained notoriety and helped further the cause of wildlife conservation when a popular Brazilian soap opera (incidentally called *Pantanal*) was shot here. The farm now belongs to the Brazilian chapter of Conservation International, which preserves its wildlife and habitat. The good regional food is one lure of this rustic but charming farm built in 1920. Although facilities aren't up to international hotel standards, rooms are comfortable and kept spotless by the attentive staff. The only way to reach this property is by plane (roughly R$650) from either Campo Grande or Aquidauana. ⊠ *About 200 km (125 mi) northwest of Campo Grande* ☎🖷 *067/751–5191; 067/751–5248 for reservations in Campo Grande* ⊕ *www.fazendarionegro.com.br* ☜ *10 rooms* ⚫ *Dining room, boating, hiking, horseback riding, airstrip; no room TVs, no room phones* 🖃 *No credit cards* ⍩ *FAP.*

¢ ⊡ **Pousada Águas do Pantanal.** In an old house with period furniture, this inn is a recommended budget choice in the city. You receive a warm welcome by the friendly staff and the owner, Fátima, who also runs a travel agency next to the inn. The hearty breakfast, with several kinds of bread, jelly, and pastries, is a rarity in a region where buttered bread and coffee are the norm. ⊠ *Av. Afonso Pena 367, Centro 79380-000* ☎ *067/242–1314* 🖷 *067/242–1242* ⊕ *www.aguasdopantanal.com.br* ☜ *17 rooms* ⚫ *Pool, travel services; no a/c in some rooms, no room phones, no room TVs* 🖃 *No credit cards* ⍩ *CP.*

Sports & the Outdoors

As more and more tourists are coming to the Pantanal, the last reluctant ranchers are beginning to see tourism as a viable economic alternative, which means you can visit a working ranch or farm for a day without having to stay as guest. **Fazenda San Francisco** (⊠ BR 262, 36 km/22 mi west of Miranda on BR 262 ☎ 067/242–1088 ⊕ www. fazendasanfrancisco.tur.br/turism/turism.html) is a 15,000-hectare (37,065-acre) working ranch where you can go on a photo safari in the morning and a boat tour on Rio Miranda in the afternoon for R$80. The fee includes a *pantaneiro* lunch—rice and beans with beef and vegetables. **Reserva das Figueiras** (⊠ BR 262, 20 km/12 mi west of Miranda ☎ 067/9988–4082 Miranda, 067/326–9070 Campo Grande ⊕ www. reservadasfigueiras.com.br) offers guided wildlife sighting trips via canoe on Rio Salobra for R$60.

The Pantanal A to Z

AIR TRAVEL

CARRIERS Airlines that serve the Pantanal are Gol, Varig, and TAM. Airlines that serve Brasília, where the nearest international airport is located, include American Airlines, British Airways, Air Canada, Gol, Varig, and TAM. ⇨ For airline information, *see* Air Travel *in* Brazil A to Z.

AIRPORTS & TRANSFERS

Major airports near the Pantanal are Aeroporto Marechal Rondon (CGB), in Cuiabá and Aeroporto International de Campo Grande (CGR). 🔳 Airport Information **Aeroporto Internacional de Brasília** ☎ 61/365-1224. **Aeroporto International de Campo Grande** ⊠ 7 km (4 mi) west of downtown Campo Grande ☎ 67/368-6093. **Aeroporto Marechal Rondon** ⊠ 7 km (4 mi) south of Cuiabá ☎ 65/614-2500.

BUS TRAVEL

Buses remain the primary mode of transportation in the states of Mato Grosso and Mato Grosso do Sul because of high airfares and limited air service. A dazzling array of companies have regular bus service connecting Brasília and Goiânia (three hours, R$23); Goiânia and Cuiabá (13 hours, R$110); Cuiabá and Campo Grande (10 hours, R$70); Cuiabá and Chapada dos Guimarães (two hours, R$15); and Campo Grande and Corumbá (seven hours, R$65). Andorinha has frequent service between Campo Grande, Cuiabá, and Corumbá.

🔳 Bus Information **Andorinha** ⊠ Corner of Dom Aquino and Joaquim Nabuco, upstairs inside Rodoviária, Campo Grande ☎ 67/383-5314. **Campo Grande bus terminal** ⊠ Dom Aquino and Joaquim Nabuco, east of downtown ☎ 67/783-1678. **Cuiabá bus terminal** ⊠ Av. Marechal Deodoro, Alvorada, north of city center ☎ 65/621-2429.

CAR RENTAL

Expect to pay at least R$175 a day for a compact car with air-conditioning, including insurance and taxes. Because the roads are in such bad shape, a 15% surcharge is added to car rentals in Campo Grande and Cuiabá. ⇨ For information on major car rental agencies, *see* Car Rental *in* Brazil A to Z.

CAR TRAVEL

Driving isn't recommended around the Pantanal, as in some stretches highways are in bad shape and there is heavy truck traffic. Also consider that Brazilian truck drivers are frightening in their disregard for basic rules of the road. Further, getting around on your own by car is difficult without a very good working knowledge of Portuguese. Outside the cities, few people speak English, making it hard to get directions if you get lost.

EMERGENCIES

There's a late-night pharmacy in Cuiabá near the corner of Avenida Getúlio Vargas and Rua Joaquim Murtinho. In Campo Grande try the late-night pharmacy at the corner of Avenida Afonso Pena and Rua 14 de Julho. Elsewhere in the region, use the 24-Hour Pharmacy Hotline.

🏥 **Hospital Santa Casa** ⊠ Rua Eduardo Santos Pereira 88, Campo Grande ☎ 67/321-5151. **Hospital Santa Casa** ⊠ Praça Seminário 141, Cuiabá ☎ 65/624-4222.
🏥 **General Numbers Ambulance** ☎ 192. **Fire** ☎ 193. **Police** ☎ 190. **Tropical Disease Control Hotline** ☎ 61/225-8906. **24-Hour Pharmacy Hotline** ☎ 132.

HEALTH

Stick to bottled water (and check that restaurants use it to make juice and ice). Malaria is quite rare in tourist areas. Yellow fever is of greater concern. It's best to get a yellow fever shot before arriving, but if you decide to travel at the last minute, it is possible to get shots at the airport; all airports have a Ministry of Health booth (open 8–5). Dengue fever, for which there is no vaccination or preventive medication, has also appeared around the Pantanal. The best way to prevent it is to avoid being bitten by mosquitoes. Pousadas and hotels in the Pantanal have insect-tight screened windows, doors, and verandas. Use insect repellent with DEET at all times.

MAIL, INTERNET & SHIPPING

Fax services are available at major *correio* (post office) branches and hotels. Most city hotels have full-fledged business centers. Smaller establishments and pousadas offer only the slowest Internet dial-up connections; Internet cafés are practically nonexistent.
📮 **Post Offices Campo Grande post office** ⊠ Av. Calógeras 2309, at corner of Rua Dom Aquino, Campo Grande ⊠ Rua Barão do Rio Branco, across from bus depot, Campo Grande. **Cuiabá post office** ⊠ Praça da República, center of town, just south of tourist office, Cuiabá ⊠ Aeroporto Marechal Rondon, 2nd floor.

MONEY MATTERS

Banking hours are weekdays 10–4 in major cities; 10–3 in the interior. Major banks are equipped with ATMs (dispensing reais), but only a few are available 24 hours—usually only those at airports and shopping malls. Outside state capitals, most ATMs operate from 8 AM–10 PM. Most ATMs run on the Plus network; if your card is only affiliated with Cirrus, plan accordingly. Banco do Brasil is the best establishments for cashing traveler's checks, with relatively low fees and decent exchange rates. Throughout the region, the better hotels will either exchange money for you (though rates aren't great) or tip you off to the area's best *casas de câmbio* (exchange houses).

Banco do Brasil's main Cuiabá branch is in the middle of town and is open weekdays 10–4, with ATMs that operate from 6 AM to 10 PM; there are also ATMs at the airport. Several little câmbios line Rua Cândido Mariano, including Guimel He Tour, which is open weekdays 8:30–6 and offers good rates. All the major banks have offices in the center of Campo Grande, along Avenida Afonso Pena. Try Banco do Brasil, which is open weekdays 10–5; there are also a branch and several ATMs at the airport.
🏦 **Banco do Brasil** ⊠ Av. Afonso Pena at Rua 13 de Maio, Campo Grande ⊠ Av. Getúlio Vargas and Rua Barão de Melgaço, Cuiabá. **Guimel He Tour** ⊠ Rua Cândido Mariano 402, Cuiabá ☎ 65/624-1667.

TAXIS

As most of the tourist areas are compact, you rarely need a cab except for trips to the airport, the bus depot, or to and from your hotel at night.

But they're all metered, so you shouldn't have to haggle. They're safe and comfortable, and you can hail them on the street. Tips aren't expected. ⚽ Taxi Companies **CooperTáxi** ⊠ Campo Grande ☎ 61/3361-1111. **Rádio Táxi Cuiabana** ⊠ Cuiabá ☎ 65/322-6664

TELEPHONES

The area code for Cuiabá is 65 and for Campo Grande is 67. You can call long distance from all pay phones—they work with prepaid magnetic cards. Before making a long-distance call from a pay phone, you must choose a long-distance carrier and dial its designated access code prior to dialing the area code and number. Rates vary depending on time of day and promotions; check with the operator before dialing. You can choose from several companies: the most popular are Embratel (access code 021), Intelig (access code 023), and Telebrasília/Brasil Telecom (access code 014). Embratel and Intelig are the only ones that work throughout the country. The others are regional, and whether they work depends on if you're in the city or regional area to which they pertain. To sum up, to make a phone call, dial 0 + (21 or 23) + the city code + the phone number.

TOURS

Arriving in one of the Pantanal's gateway cities without having a tour already booked isn't a problem. Just be careful when choosing a guide upon arrival—some budget travelers have had bad experiences. To avoid being overcharged, compare prices. Also be sure your guide has adequate equipment, sufficient knowledge about area wildlife, and good English-language skills.

In southern Pantanal you may choose to book tours out of Bonito, where more than a dozen establishments vie for your business—you will need to contact local agents because all local attractions require booking. Pant-Tour is a reliable operator with good knowledge of the best spots in the region.

Pantanal Adventure in Cuiabá, Pérola do Pantanal in Corumbá, and Impacto Turismo in Campo Grande run large tours into the north and south of the Pantanal—including longer river trips in luxurious riverboats (locally known as "hotel-boats") that are equipped with many amenities and comfortable air-conditioned cabins. These boat tours usually stop in fazendas for treks into the wetlands by horseback, 4x4 vehicle, by zodiac, and by foot—whatever it takes to get the best animal sightings. The cost is about R$150 per person, per day, with everything included; most tours last 4–7 days. ⚽ Tour Operators **Ecotur** ⊠ Rua Emílio 21, Pirenópolis ☎ 62/331-1392. **Impacto Turismo** ⊠ Rua Padre João Crippa 496, Campo Grande ☎ 67/325-1333 🖷 67/384-8179 ⊕www.impactotour.com.br. **Pantanal Adventura** ⊠Rua Commandante Costa 649, Cuiabá ☎ 65/333-6352 ⊕ www.pantanaladventure.com.br. **Pérola do Pantanal** ⊠ Rua Manoel Cavassa 255, Corumbá ☎ 067/231-1460 ⊕ www.peroladopantanal.com.br. **Pant-Tour** ⊠ Rua Senador Felinto Müller 578, Bonito ☎ 67/255-1000 🖷 67/255-1707.

VISITOR INFORMATION

The staff members in Campo Grande's Morada dos Baís can give you information about everything under the sun in Campo Grande and environs. SEDTUR, in Cuiabá, doesn't have much information; your hotel is probably a better option.

🚹 **The West Tourist Info** **Atendimento Turismo** ✉ Praça Central, Bonito ☎ 67/251-1799. **Morada dos Baís: Centro de Informação Turística e Cultura** ✉ Av. Noroeste at Av. Afonso Pena, Campo Grande ☎ 67/324-5830. **SEDTUR** ✉ Praça da República 131, Cuiabá ☎ 65/624-9060.

SALVADOR

Updated by
Joan Gonzalez

Though the city of Salvador, founded in 1549, lost its status as capital of Brazil in 1763 when that honor was given to Rio (and later to Brasília), it remains the capital of Bahia. At least 70% of its 2,250,000 population is classified as Afro-Brazilian. African rhythms roll forth everywhere—from buses and construction sites to the rehearsals of percussion groups. The scents of coriander, coconut, and palm oil waft around corners, where turbaned women in voluminous lace-trim white dresses cook and sell local delicacies.

Churches whose interiors are covered with gold leaf were financed by the riches of the Portuguese colonial era, when slaves masked their religious beliefs under a thin Catholic veneer. And partly thanks to modern-day acceptance of those beliefs, Salvador has become the fount of Candomblé, a religion based on personal dialogue with the *orixás*, a family of African deities closely linked to both nature and the Catholic saints. The influence of Salvador's African heritage on Brazilian music has also turned this city into one of the most stirring places to spend Carnaval, the bacchanalian fling that precedes Lent and only one of more than 20 festivals punctuating the local calendar.

Exploring Salvador

Salvador sprawls across a peninsula surrounded by the Baía de Todos os Santos on one side and the Atlantic Ocean on the other. The original city, referred to as the Cidade Histórica (Historic City), is divided into the *Cidade Alta* (Upper City) and *Cidade Baixa* (Lower City). The Cidade Baixa is a commercial area—known as Comércio—that runs along the port and is the site of Salvador's largest market, Mercado Modelo. You can move between the Upper and Lower cities on foot, by *comum* taxis, or via the Elevador Lacerda, behind the market.

From the Cidade Histórica you can travel north along the bay to the hilltop Igreja de Nosso Senhor do Bonfim. Salvador's southern tip is home to the trendy neighborhoods of Vitória, Barra, Ondina, and Rio Vermelho, which are full of museums, theaters, shops, and restaurants. The beaches that run north from the tip and along the Atlantic coast are among the city's cleanest. Many are illuminated at night and have bars and restaurants that stay open late.

As of 2006, phone numbers in Brazil will change from seven to eight digits. All seven-digit numbers will be preceded by a 3. For example, 555–5555 will become 3555–5555.

Numbers in the text correspond to numbers in the margin and on the Salvador Cidade Histórica map.

Cidade Alta

The Cidade Alta neighborhood of Pelourinho, or Pelô, is on UNESCO's list of World Heritage sites and is a captivating blend of European and African cultures. It contains some of the most significant examples of colonial and baroque architecture in the Americas. Along its winding and sometimes steep streets, whose cobbles were laid by slaves, restored 17th- and 18th-century buildings, now house museums, galleries, shops, and cafés. The buildings, all freshly painted in bright pastel colors, add to the festive atmosphere of Cidade Alta, along with the sounds of street musicians and their *axé* music, a blend of local, African, and Jamaican rhythms.

A GOOD WALK Early morning is a good time for a walk in Cidade Alta, Salvador's historic Pelourinho neighborhood. Whether coming by taxi or bus (there's a bus terminal nearby on Rua Chile) start at the **Elevador Lacerda** ►. If arriving at the lower level, take the elevator to the Upper City, exiting onto the Municipal Square (mainly a parking lot), where you have a spectacular view of the Todos os Santos Bay and, unfortunately, also of the "temporary" mayor's office (erected around 1987, it was supposed to have been replaced in two years), an oblong cement building on columns with large, round, yellow pipes around the sides. Also on the square is the **Palacio Rio Branco** ❶. Turn left onto Rua da Misericórdia, heading northeast past the Igreja da Misericórdia and through the Praça da Sé (named after a colonial church, the Igreja da Sé, which was demolished in 1933) to the large square, **Terreiro de Jesus** ❷. On your left, at the northwest end of the square, is the 17th-century **Catedral Basílica** ❸. Next to the cathedral is the **Museu Afro-Brasileiro** ❹. From here walk along the south side of the Terreiro de Jesus Square and through the Praça Anchieta, with its statue of the patron saint of Salvador, São Francisco de Xavier, on a cross—to the 18th-century baroque **Igreja de São Francisco** ❺ and the Igreja da Ordem Terceira de São Francisco. Walk back to the Terreiro de Jesus Square, turn right when you reach the square to the **Igreja São Domingos de Gusmaño da Ordem Terceira** ❻. Continue to **Fundação Casa de Jorge Amada/Museu da Cidade** ❼, where you can see memorabilia of the author of such famous titles as *Dona Flor e Seus dos Maridos* (*Dona Flor and Her Two Husbands*), as well as exhibits on Candomblé. The Rua Alfredo de Brito leads into the famed plaza called **Largo do Pelourinho** ❽. To the north stands the baroque **Igreja de Nossa Senhora do Rosário dos Pretos** ❾. If you're hungry, a good place for a restful lunch is Casa de Gamboa, south of the Largo de Pelourinho.

TIMING Simply walking this route will take about three hours. Pelourinho, with its music, cafés, restaurants, and shops, is a place that can be explored several times over a period of days and yet always seem new.

WHAT TO SEE **Catedral Basílica.** Hints of Asia permeate this 17th-century masterpiece,
❸ though it is a rather simple structure. Note the Asian facial features and clothing of the figures in the transept altars; the 16th-century tiles from Macao in the sacristy; and the intricate ivory-and-tortoise-shell inlay from

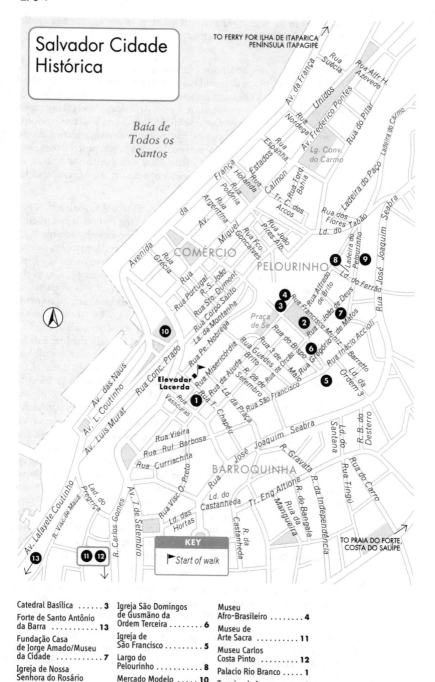

Salvador Cidade Histórica

Baía de Todos os Santos

TO FERRY FOR ILHA DE ITAPARICA
PENÍNSULA ITAPAGIPE

COMÉRCIO

PELOURINHO

Praça de Sé

Elevador Lacerda

BARROQUINHA

TO PRAIA DO FORTE,
COSTA DO SAUÍPE

KEY

▶ Start of walk

Goa on the Japiassu family altar, third on the right as you enter. A Jesuit who lived in China painted the ceiling over the cathedral entrance. ⊠ *Terreiro de Jesus, Pelourinho* ☎ *071/321–4573* ✆ *Free* ⊙ *Tues.–Sat. 8–11 and 3–6, Sun. 5–6:30.*

❼ Fundação Casa de Jorge Amado/Museu da Cidade. The Jorge Amado House contains Bahia's most beloved writer's photos and book covers, as well as a lecture room. Amado lived in the Hotel Pelourinho when it was a student house, and he set the locale of many of his books in this part of the city. Next door is the Museu da Cidade, with exhibitions on Candomblé orixás. ⊠ *Rua Alfredo Brito and Largo do Pelourinho, Pelourinho* ☎ *071/321–0122* ✆ *R$3* ⊙ *Fundação weekdays 9:30 AM–10 PM. Museum Tues.–Fri. 10–5, weekends 1–5.*

❾ Igreja de Nossa Senhora do Rosário dos Pretos. Guides tend to skip over the Church of Our Lady of the Rosary of the Blacks, which was built in a baroque style by and for slaves between 1704 and 1796. It's worth a look at the side altars to see statues of the Catholic church's few black saints. Each has a fascinating story. ⊠ *Ladeira do Pelourinho s/n, Pelourinho* ☎ *No phone* ✆ *Free* ⊙ *Weekdays 8–5, weekends 8–2.*

❻ Igreja São Domingos de Gusmão da Ordem Terceira. The baroque Church of the Third Order of St. Dominic (1723) houses a collection of carved processional saints and other sacred objects. Such sculptures often had hollow interiors and were used to smuggle gold into Portugal to avoid taxes. Asian details in the church decoration are evidence of long-ago connections with Portugal's colonies of Goa and Macau. Upstairs are two impressive rooms with carved wooden furniture used for lay brothers' meetings and receptions. ⊠ *Terreiro de Jesus, Pelourinho* ☎ *071/242–4185* ✆ *Free* ⊙ *Mon.–Sat. 8–noon and 2–5.*

★ ❺ Igreja de São Francisco. The famous 18th-century baroque Church of St. Francis has an active monastery. Listen for the sound of African drums in the square outside as you take in the ceiling, painted in 1774 by José Joaquim da Rocha, a mulatto who founded Brazil's first art school. The ornate cedar-and-rosewood interior writhes with images of mermaids, acanthus leaves, and caryatids—all bathed in gold leaf. Guides say that there's as much as a ton of gold here, but restoration experts maintain there's much less, as the leaf used is just a step up from a powder. A Sunday-morning alternative to crowded beaches is to attend a mass here (9–11 and 11–11:45). Stay until the end, when the lights go off, to catch the wondrous subtlety of gold leaf under natural light. The **Ordem Terceira de São Francisco** (☎ *071/321–6968*), part of the complex, has an 18th-century Spanish plateresque sandstone facade—the only of its kind in Brazil—that is carved to resemble Spanish silver altars that are made by beating the metal into wooden molds. ⊠ *Praça Padre Anchieta, Pelourinho* ☎ *071/322–6430* ✆ *Free* ⊙ *Mon.–Sat. 8–noon and 2–5, Sun. 8–noon.*

★ ❽ Largo do Pelourinho (Pelourinho Square). This small plaza commemorates the day in 1888 when Dom Pedro II freed the slaves. It was at this spot where slaves were sold and tied to a pillory and publicly beaten, which was legal in Brazil until 1835 (the word *pelourinho* means "whipping post"). The plaza is now the setting for one of the largest and most charming groupings of Brazilian colonial architecture and a thriving cultural renaissance. There are four public stages in Pelourinho, at least two of which have music nightly. The **Dia & Noite** (☎ 071/322–2525) association organizes Largo do Pelourinho's music shows. It publishes a monthly schedule that's available in tourist offices and hotels. ⊠ *Rua Alfredo de Brito at Ladeira do Taboão.*

❹ **Museu Afro-Brasileiro** (Afro-Brazilian Museum). The most interesting of
FodorśChoice the three museums in the Antiga Facilidade de Medicinos (Old Faculty
★ of Medicine) building and former Jesuit school is the Afro-Brazilian Museum, next to the Catedral Basílica. The Afro-Brazilian Museum has a collection of more than 1,200 pieces of a religious or spiritual nature, including pottery, sculpture, tapestry, weavings, paintings, crafts, carvings, and photographs. There's an interesting display on the meanings of Candomblé orixás, with huge carved wood panels portraying each one. The other two museums are the Memorial de Medicina (Memorial to the Old Faculty of Medicine) and the Museu Arqueologia e Etnologia (Archaeology and Ethnology Museum). ⊠ *Terreiro de Jesus, Pelourinho* ☎ *071/321-0983* ⊠ *R$3* ⊙ *Weekdays 9–5.*

❶ **Palácio Rio Branco.** Salvador's Chamber of Commerce and Bahíatursa, the state tourist office, now occupy the beautiful Palácio Rio Branco, erected on the Municipal Square in 1919 for the governor of Bahia. This was the site of the original headquarters of the colonial government of Brazil. The large square is near the entrance to the Elevador Lacerda, which connects upper and lower Salvador. ⊠ *Rua Chile 2, Pelourinho* ☎ *071/241–4333* ⊙ *Tues.–Sat. 10–6.*

❷ **Terreiro de Jesus.** A large square with three churches and a small crafts fair, Terreiro de Jesus opens the way to historic Salvador. Where nobles once strolled under imperial palm trees, men today practice capoeira—a stylized dancelike fight with African origins—to the *thwang* of the *berimbau,* a rudimentary bow-shape musical instrument. If you stop to watch and take photographs of the capoeira fighters, you are expected to leave a financial contribution.

Cidade Baixa & Beyond

The Lower City is Bahia's commercial and financial center. In the port large cruise ships and small boats jockey for space. Ferryboats and catamarans leave from here for Ilha de Itaparica (Itaparica Island). It is busy during the day but is practically deserted at night, especially near the base of the Lacerda Elevator. Take a taxi between restaurants or hotels at night.

A GOOD WALK You can travel between the Cidade Alta and the Cidade Baixa aboard the popular **Elevador Lacerda** ▶. Exiting the elevator in the Lower City, cross the Praça Visconde de Cairú to the **Mercado Modelo** ⑩ for some shopping and people-watching. From here you have several options. If you head north along the bay and past the port, you come to the terminal where you can catch a ferry or hop a schooner for **Ilha de Itaparica.** Or you can head due south by cab to one of several museums: the **Museu de Arte Sacra** ⑪, with its religious paintings, or the **Museu Carlos Costa Pinto** ⑫, with art and artifacts gathered by private collectors. Another option is to visit the tip of the peninsula, which is marked by the **Forte de Santo Antônio da Barra** ⑬, with its lighthouse, a nautical museum, and a popular beach.

TIMING   No need to arise at dawn, but the earlier you get started the better for a full yet relaxing day. If you're starting from the Upper City, take the elevator down to the Mercado Modelo. The market can easily be done in an hour unless you're really in a browsing mood and want to visit all 300-plus stalls. The trip to either the nearby Ilha de Itaparica or to one or more of the museums will fill up a leisurely afternoon, with time for lunch.

WHAT TO SEE   **Elevador Lacerda.** For just a few centavos, ascend 236 feet in a minute ☞   in this elevator that runs between the Praça Municipal, in the Upper City, and Praça Visconde de Cairú and the Mercado Modelo. Built in 1872, the elevator ran on hydraulics until its 1930 restoration, when it was electrified. Bahians joke that the elevator is the only way to "go up" in life. A word of caution—when the elevator is crowded, watch out for pickpockets.

⑬ **Forte de Santo Antônio da Barra.** Fort St. Anthony has guarded Salvador since 1583. The lighthouse, Farol da Barra, wasn't built until 1696, after many a ship wrecked on the coral reefs and sandbanks. The fort now houses the **Museu Nautico** (☎ 071/264–3296), with exhibitions of old maps, navigational equipment, artillery, model vessels, and remnants of shipwrecks found by Brazil's first underwater archaeological research team. The museum is open Tuesday–Sunday 9–7. An eatery, Café do Farol, is open Tuesday through Sunday, from 9 AM to 11 PM. The Praia (beach) do Farol da Barra, which starts at the fort and runs east along Avenida Oceánica, is calm, with small waves, and is popular with locals, especially on weekends. ⊠ *Av. 7 de Setembro s/n, Barra* ☎ *No phone* 🖃 *R$2* ☉ *Thurs.–Tues. 9–7.*

★ **Ilha de Itaparica.** The largest of 56 islands in the Baía de Todos os Santos, Itaparica, was originally settled because its ample supply of fresh mineral water was believed to have rejuvenating qualities. Its beaches are calm and shallow, thanks to the surrounding reefs. The ferry ride takes 45 minutes. Another option is a slightly longer but very pleasant schooner cruise and tour that can include lunch and music. You can always take a schooner to the island, opt out of the tour group lunch, and take a taxi to the restaurant of your choice. Then you can enjoy an afternoon stroll before catching the ferry back to Salvador. Fares range from US$2 to US$10, depending on services. Catamarans, ferries, and *pequena lanchas* (small boats) leave for the island every hour. **Bahiatursa** (⊠ On right, just before exit to Mercado Modelo, Praça Visconde de Cayru 250 ☎ 071/241–0242) can provide information. The office is open Monday–Saturday 9–6 and Sunday 9–2. Volkswagen vans (*kombis*) provide transportation around the island. ⊠ *Ferries and catamarans leave from Terminal São Joaquim at other end of Porto de Salvador, Av. da França. Small boats leave from Terminal Turítico Maritimo in front of Mercado Modelo.*

⑩ **Mercado Modelo.** This enclosed market may not be the cheapest place to buy handicrafts—and you do have to bargain—but it must be experienced. Some of the many items you find here are *cachaça* (a strong

Brazilian liquor made from sugarcane), cashew nuts, pepper sauces, cigars, manioc flour, dried shrimp (an integral part of Bahian cooking), leather goods, hammocks, lace, musical instruments, African sculptures, and gems. Outside, you can hear the nasal-voiced *repentistas,* folksingers who make up songs on the spot. Notice the blue *azulejos* on the building with Gothic-style windows. If you are entering the market from the back (having come down the Elevador Lacerda from the Upper City, just inside the door along the back wall are a post office and a tourist office where you can pick up maps and brochures. ⊠ *Praça Visconde de Cayru 250, Comércio* 🖼 *Free* ⊙ *Mon.–Sat. 9–6, Sun. 9–2.*

⓫ Museu de Arte Sacra. Housed in a former Carmelite monastery, the museum and the adjoining Igreja de Santa Teresa (St. Theresa Church) are two of Salvador's best-cared-for repositories of religious objects. An in-house restoration team has worked miracles that bring alive Bahia's 1549–1763 golden age as Brazil's capital and main port. See the silver altar in the church, moved here from the demolished Sé (Church), and the blue-and-yellow-tile sacristy replete with a bay view. ⊠ *Rua do Sodré 276, Centro* 🕾 *071/243–6511* 🖼 *R$5* ⊙ *Weekdays 11:30–5:30.*

⓬ Museu Carlos Costa Pinto. A collection of more than 3,000 objects, including furniture, crystal, silver pieces and paintings collected from around the world by a wealthy couple, is on display at this museum. Among the collection are examples of gold and silver *balangandãs* (or *pencas*), chains with large silver charms in the shapes of tropical fruits and fish, which were worn by slave women around the waist. A prized slave was given a chain by her master, who continued to reward loyalty and service with gifts of charms, sometimes freeing the slave after her chain was full. The balangandã usually included a *figa*—a closed fist with a thumb sticking out through the fingers—which, according to African legend, could increase warriors' fertility. In Brazil it's simply considered a good-luck charm. For it to work, though, it must always be a gift. ⊠ *Av. 7 de Setembro 2490, Vitória* 🕾 *071/336–6081* 🖼 *R$11* ⊙ *Mon. and Wed.–Fri. 2:30–7, weekends 3–6.*

Urban beaches. In general, the farther east and northeast from the lighthouse point, the better are the city beaches. Some Salvadorans, especially singles, swear by the Cidade Baixa beaches **Praia Porto da Barra** and **Praia Farol da Barra,** which are frequented by a colorful mix of people who live nearby and tourists staying at neighboring hotels. To avoid large crowds, don't go on weekends. Regardless of when you go, keep an eye on your belongings; petty thievery has been reported. There are no bathrooms, but you can rent a beach chair for about R$2. The corner of Porto da Barra closest to the Grande Hotel da Barra is a gay hangout. Porto da Barra is north from the lighthouse, while the Farol da Barra starts at the lighthouse and goes around the corner east along Avenida Oceánica to the hotel districts of Ondina and Rio Vermelho, where the beaches intermittently suffer pollution problems. One of the nicest beaches along Avenida Oceánica is **Praia Corsário** (Third Bridge Beach), a wide stretch popular with surfers and the young crowd. There are beach huts where you can sit in the shade and enjoy seafood and an ice-cold beer or soft drink from the kiosks. The beach follows Avenida Oceánica and Avenida Otávio Mangabeira northeast past the convention center and is near the Parque Metropolitan de Pituaçu. Another nice beach is the **Praia Itapuã**, near the Sofitel hotel and the Farol de Itapuã. The next good beach is **Praia Stella Maris**, also popular with surfers and the young crowd. It is 18 km (11 mi) north of downtown.

Estrada do Coco Beaches

To reach some of Bahia's more pristine and less crowded beaches, head north of Salvador on the Estrada do Coco as far as the fishing village and turtle sanctuary of Praia do Forte, and then take Linha Verde (BA 099) up the coast. Bus transportation is readily available, but it's also a good area for a rental car. Beaches are all along the way, but if you have rented a Jeep, turn off the main road and drive between the sand dunes to Santo Antônio (just before the entrance to Costa do Sauípe) and walk through the village with only 30 houses, up a sand dune, and then down onto a nearly deserted beach. Drinks are available in the little village store, handicrafts are sold by villagers, and sometimes a stand is open on the beach for drinks and snacks.

Barra do Jacuípe. A river runs down to the ocean at this long, wide, pristine beach lined with coconut palms. There are beachfront snack bars, and the Santa Maria/Catuense bus company operates six buses here daily. ☒ *40 km (25 mi) north of Salvador.*

Guarajuba. With palm trees and calm waters banked by a reef, this is the nicest beach of them all, though it's lined with condos. The bus to Barra do Jacuípe continues on to Guarajuba, which has snack kiosks, fishing boats, surfing, dune buggies, and a playground. ☒ *60 km (38 mi) north of Salvador.*

Itapuã. Frequented by artists who live nearby, Itapuã is polluted in some places but has a terrific atmosphere. Around K and J streets there are food kiosks, music bars, and amusement park rides. It was once a whale cemetery, and bones are still an occasional find. A mystical freshwater lagoon, the Lagoa de Abaeté, lies inland from Itapuã. Its black depths provide a startling contrast with the fine white sand of its shores. No one knows the source of these waters. City buses going to the lagoon leave from Campo Grande or Estação da Lapa. Tour operators include the lagoon on their beach tours, which cost about R$55. ☒ *Take the Orla Marítima north to Itapuã, at Largo da Sereia (a square with a mermaid statue), follow signs for lagoon; 30-min drive from downtown.*

Piatã. Heading north and leaving the more built-up areas of the city behind, the first truly clean beach you'll come to is the wide Piatã. Its calm waters and golden sand attract families. ☒ *20 km (13 mi) northeast of downtown Salvador.*

Where to Eat

You can easily find restaurants serving Bahian specialties in Barra, a neighborhood full of bars and sidewalk cafés. There are also many good spots in bohemian Rio Vermelho and a slew of places along the beachfront drive beginning around Jardim de Alah and also in Pelourinho. It's wise to order meat only in *churrascarias* (barbecued-meat restaurants) and

CloseUp

AFRO-BRAZILIAN HERITAGE

OF ALL OF BRAZIL'S STATES, Bahia has the strongest links with its African heritage. There are few other countries with such a symphony of skin tones grouped under one nationality. This rich Brazilian identity began when the first Portuguese sailors were left to manage the new land. From the beginning Portuguese migration to Brazil was predominantly male, a fact that unfortunately led to unbridled sexual license—ranging from seduction to rape— with first Indian and then African women.

The first Africans arrived in 1532, along with the Portuguese colonizers, who continued to buy slaves from English, Spanish, and Portuguese traders until 1855. All records pertaining to slave trading were destroyed in 1890, making it impossible to know exactly how many people were brought to Brazil. It's estimated that from 3 to 4.5 million Africans were captured and transported from the Sudan, Gambia, Guinea, Sierra Leone, Senegal, Liberia, Nigeria, Benin, Angola, and Mozambique. Many were literate Muslims who were better educated than their white overseers and owners.

As was the case in the southern United States, it was common in the great houses of sugar plantations in Brazil, which relied on slave labor, for the master to have a white wife and slave mistresses. However, in Brazil cohabitation between white men and women of other races was openly accepted. It was also fairly common for the master to free the mother of his mixed-race offspring and allow a son of color to learn a trade or inherit a share of the plantation. The legendary Xica da Silva—a slave concubine elevated to mistress of the manor by her wealthy master (and then consigned to oblivion and abandonment when he was ordered back to Portugal)— vividly demonstrates the nexus of Brazilian sexual and racial politics.

When the sugar boom came to an end, it became too expensive for slave owners to support their "free" labor force. Abolition occurred gradually, however. It began around 1871, with the passage of the Law of the Free Womb, which liberated all Brazilians born of slave mothers. In 1885 another law was passed, freeing slaves over age 60. Finally, on May 13, 1888, Princess Isabel signed a law freeing all slaves.

The former slaves, often unskilled, became Brazil's unemployed and underprivileged. Although the country has long been praised for its lack of discrimination, this veneer of racial equality is deceptive. Afro-Brazilians still don't receive education on a par with that of whites, nor do they always receive equal pay for equal work. There are far fewer black or mulatto professionals, politicians, and ranking military officers than white ones.

Although a civil rights movement like that of the United States is unlikely, subtle activism to bring about racial equality and educate all races about the rich African legacy continues. For many people the most important holiday isn't September 7 (Brazilian Independence Day) but rather November 20 (National Black Consciousness Day). It honors the anniversary of the death of Zumbi, the leader of the famous quilombo (community of escaped slaves) of Palmares, which lasted more than 100 years and was destroyed by bandeirantes (adventurers who tracked runaway slaves) in one final great battle for freedom.

to avoid it in seafood places. You may discover that in Bahia one main course easily serves two; ask about portions when you order. Don't order the spicy dishes unless you are used to highly spiced food.

African

$–$$ ✕ **Casa do Benin.** Both a restaurant and a museum, Casa do Benin honors the West African country of Benin, home to many of the slaves brought to Bahia. The cuisine is strictly Bahian, a blend of the Old and New worlds. Fish and shrimp are the featured dishes. Reservations are essential September through February. ⊠ *Rua Padre Agostinho Gomes 17, Pelourinho* ☎ *071/326–3127* ▭ *AE, DC, MC* ☾ *Closed Mon.*

Brazilian

★ **$$–$$$** ✕ **Casa da Gamboa de Conceição Reis.** A longtime favorite of Bahian writer Jorge Amado, this is a Bahian cooking institution. *Casquinha de siri* (breaded crab in the shell) comes as a complimentary starter; then try the *peixe com risoto de ostras* (grilled fish with oyster risotto), followed by a traditional dessert. ⊠ *Rua João de Deus 32, Pelourinho* ☎ *071/ 321–3393* ▭ *AE, MC, V* ☾ *No dinner Sun.*

$$–$$$ ✕ **Solar do Unhão.** You get a lot for your money at this restaurant on the bay. There's a show every evening presenting different African traditions still alive today. In the 18th century the colonial estate housed a sugar mill that in the next century became a "snuff" factory. The Museu de Arte Moderna occupies a corner of the estate but is only open for special exhibitions. The restaurant is in former slave quarters and is said to be haunted. Dinner is buffet style, with regional and international dishes. ⊠ *Av. do Contorno, 08* ☎ *071/329–5551* ⌕ *Reservations essential* ▭ *AE, MC, V.*

$$–$$$ ✕ **Trapiche Adelaide.** Near the Mercado Modelo in downtown Salvador,
FodorsChoice this is one of the best restaurants in town. It's known for its blending of
★ Bahian and international dishes. Having drinks before dinner on the deck overlooking the Todos os Santos Bay is a pleasant way to wind down after a day of sightseeing. ⊠ *Praça dos Tupinambás, Av. Contorno 02, Contorno* ⌕ *Reservations essential* ☎ *071/326–2211* ▭ *MC, V.*

$$ ✕ **Maria Mata Mouro.** At this intimate restaurant you almost feel as if you're at a friend's house for dinner. Bahian food is cooked with a lighter touch than in most restaurants. Try the *badejo* (grouper) in ginger. ⊠ *Rua Inácio Acciole 8, Pelourinho* ☎ *071/321–3929* ▭ *AE, V* ☾ *Closed Sun.*

$ ✕ **Uauá.** The cuisine here is representative of many Brazilian regions. The clientele, which includes most of the city, is devoted. There are two locations, one in Pelourinho and one at Itapuã Beach. ⊠ *R. Gregório de Matos 36, Pelourinho* ☎ *071/321–3089* ⊠ *Av. Dorival Caymi 46, Itapuã* ☎ *071/249–9579* ▭ *AE, DC, MC, V* ☾ *Closed Mon.*

Eclectic

$$ ✕ **Boi Preto.** After the Jesuits were run out of Brazil, their herds of cattle roamed the country, and beef became a main source of food here. It is no longer roasted in a hole in the ground, but beef is still cooked to perfection at one of the best barbecue places in Salvador: Boi Preto (Black Bull). Seafood, including lobster, crab, and sushi, and more exotic fare, like alligator, are also on the menu. A piano bar keeps the atmosphere light. It is near the Convention Center. ⊠ *Av. Otávio Mangabeira s/n, Jardim Armação/Boca do Rio* ☎ *071/362–8844* 🖃 *AE, MC, V.*

French

$$$$ ✕ **Chez Bernard.** Discerning *soteropolitanos* (the pompous but nonetheless correct term for natives of the city) find this to be undoubtedly the best French restaurant in town, as well as one of the oldest. Everything is worth trying. ⊠ *Gamboa de Cima 11, Aflitos* ☎ *071/329–5403* 🖃 *AE, V* ☺ *Closed Sun.*

Seafood

$–$$ ✕ **Bargaço.** Good, typical Bahian seafood dishes are served at this old favorite. *Pata de caranguejo* (vinegared crab claw) is hearty and may do more than take the edge off your appetite for the requisite *moqueca de camarão* (shrimp stew) or *moqueca de siri mole* (soft-shell crab stew); try the *cocada baiana* (sugar-caked coconut) for dessert, if you have room. Reservations are essential September through February. ⊠ *Rua das Laranjeiras 28, Pelourinho* ☎ *071/231–3900* 🖃 *AE, DC, MC.*

★ **$$–$$$** ✕ **Yemanjá.** A bubbly underwater atmosphere—replete with aquariums and sea goddess murals—sets the tone for meals of traditionally prepared seafood dishes. The service is somewhat slow, and there's no air-conditioning, but most patrons don't seem to mind, concentrating instead on plowing through enormous portions of moqueca, a seafood mixture heavy with spices and *dendê* (palm oil) or *ensopado,* seafood cooked in a similar but lighter sauce. Reservations are essential on weekends and in the high season. ⊠ *Av. Otávio Mangabeira 4655, Jardim Armação/Boca do Rio* ☎ *071/231–3036* 🖃 *AE, DC, MC, V.*

Where to Stay

There are only a few hotels in the Cidade Histórico. Heading south into the Vitória neighborhood along Avenida 7 de Setembro, there are many inexpensive establishments convenient to beaches and sights. In the yuppie Barra neighborhood, many hotels are within walking distance of cafés, bars, restaurants, and clubs. The resorts in the beach areas of Ondina and Rio Vermelho are a 20-minute taxi ride from downtown. High seasons are from December 21 to March and the month of July. Low seasons are after Carnaval until June 30 and from August 1 to December 20, when you may be able to get better rates.

$$$ 🏨 **Bahia Othon Palace Hotel.** A short drive from most sights, nightspots, and restaurants, this busy, modern hotel sits on a cliff overlooking Ondina Beach. Top local entertainers often perform at the hotel's outdoor park, and in high season the friendly staff organizes poolside activities and trips to better beaches. ⊠ *Av. Presidente Vargas 2456, Ondina 40170-010* ☎ *071/247–1044* 🖷 *071/245–4877* 🌐 *www.hoteis-othon.com.br* 🛏 *300 rooms, 25 suites* ⚭ *Restaurant, coffee shop, in-room safes, minibars, cable TV, pool, health club, sauna, dance club, free parking* 🖃 *AE, DC, MC, V.*

★ **$$–$$$** 🏨 **Catussaba Hotel.** Amid a garden of flowers and palm trees, this hotel has large rooms with balconies and ocean views. All rooms open directly onto a beach that's good for swimming. The airport is nearby, and the hotel is 40 km (25 mi) from the city center. It is near the Stella Maris Beach, an ideal spot for surfing, jet skiing, and body boarding. Stands on the beach sell food, soda, and beer. If you tire of saltwater and sand, head for the large, attractive pool area. ⊠ *Alameda da Praia, Itapuã 41600-270* ☎ *071/374–8000* 🖷 *071/374–4749* ⊕ *www.catussaba. com.br* ⇘ *186 rooms, 4 suites* ⚭ *Restaurant, room service, minibars, cable TV, tennis court, pool, health club, sauna, bar, Internet, meeting rooms, travel services, convention center, free parking* ⊟ *AE, MC, V.*

$$ 🏨 **Hotel Sofitel Salvador.** The only hotel in Salvador with its own golf course, albeit a 9-hole one, the Sofitel is in a tropical park 27 km (4 mi) from the international airport between Itapuã Beach and the Abaeté Lagoon. It is also near the Carlos Costa Pinto Museum and the Itapuã Lighthouse. The hotel provides transportation to Salvador's Pelourinho historic district. Sofitel will open a second Salvador hotel in Pelourinho in mid-2005. That 70-room hotel is part of a 16th-century architectural complex that includes the Convento do Carmo and Museum and the Church of Ordem Terceiro. The convent, museum, and church are protected as a National Historical Heritage site and have been closed for several years. In opening a small hotel at the site, the hotel agreed to conserve and protect the convent, museum, and church. ⊠ *Rua da Passargada s/n, Itapuã 41620-430* ☎ *071/374–9611, 800/763–4835 in U.S.* 🖷 *071/374–6946* ⊕ *www.sofitel.com* ⇘ *197 rooms, 9 suites* ⚭ *2 restaurants, room service, in-room safes, cable TV, 3 tennis courts, 9-hole golf course, 2 outdoor pools, hair salon, health club, massage, boating, billiards, 3 bars, shops, baby-sitting, concierge, dry cleaning, Internet, business services, free parking, airport shuttle* ⊟ *AE, DC, MC, V.*

$$ 🏨 **Ondina Apart-Hotel Residência.** In the resort hotel district, a short drive from the sights, nightlife, and restaurants of Salvador, this outstanding beachside complex has simple modern furniture. Businesspeople and families opt for this hotel when they're staying in Salvador for extended periods. ⊠ *Av. Presidente Vargas 2400, Ondina 40170-010* ☎ *071/203–8000* 🖷 *071/203–8112* ⇘ *100 rooms* ⚭ *Restaurant, coffee shop, in-room safes, minibars, cable TV, tennis court, pool, gym, bar, baby-sitting, laundry service, parking (fee)* ⊟ *AE, DC, MC, V.*

$–$$ 🏨 **Tropical Hotel da Bahia.** Owned by Varig Airlines and often included in package deals, this centrally located hotel is a bit tattered, but it's practical for those whose priority is Salvador's history and culture. The hotel is away from the beaches, but there's a free beach shuttle. Some rooms overlook the square where Carnaval begins. The Concha Acústica do Teatro Castro Alves, site of many big musical shows, is within walking distance; performers in those shows often stay here. ⊠ *Av. 7 de Setembro 1537, Campo Grande 40080-121* ☎ *071/336–0102* 🖷 *071/336–9725* ⊕ *www.tropicalhotel.com.br* ⇘ *282 rooms, 10 suites* ⚭ *Restaurant, coffee shop, room service, cable TV, 2 pools, massage, sauna, bar, dance club, concierge, parking (fee)* ⊟ *AE, DC, MC, V.*

★ $ 🏨 **Caesar Towers.** Though it doesn't have sea views, Caesar Towers is in the Ondina district, with easy access to the historic center and the beaches. Rooms are comfortable and have wicker furniture and tile floors. From here it's only 8 km (5 mi) to downtown, 15 km (10 mi) to the best beaches, and a short distance to the many restaurants and bars of the Barra district. The breakfast buffet and the Alfredo di Roma Italian restaurant are both excellent. ⊠ *Av. Oceánica 1545, Ondina 41140-131* ☎ *071/331–8200* 🖷 *071/237–4668* 🖙 *133 rooms* ⌂ *Restaurant, coffee shop, room service, in-room safes, kitchenettes, minibars, cable TV, outdoor pool, health club, sauna, meeting room, business center, laundry service, parking (fee)* ⊟ *AE, DC, MC, V* ⊚ *BP.*

★ ¢ ⊞ **Hotel Bahia do Sol.** It may be simple, but this hotel has a prime location close to museums and historic sights. Front rooms have a partial ocean view, but those in the back are quieter. ⊠ *Av. 7 de Setembro 2009, Vitória 40080-002* ☎ *071/336–7211* 🖷 *071/336–7776* 🖙 *86 rooms, 4 suites* ⌂ *Restaurant, bar, cable TV, meeting room, free parking* ⊟ *AE, DC, MC, V.*

★ ¢ ⊞ **Hotel Catharina Paraguaçu.** The sleeping areas at this intimate hotel in a 19th-century mansion are small but comfortable and include six split-level suites. It's family run and in a neighborhood of good restaurants and bars. The kitchen serves snacks and meals, from fettuccine to salmon. It is wheelchair accessible, unusual for a pousada. ⊠ *Rua João Gomes 128, Rio Vermelho 40210-090* ☎🖷 *071/334–0089* ✍ *hotel-catharina@svn.com.br* 🖙 *23 rooms, 6 suites* ⌂ *Dining room, minibars, cable TV* ⊟ *MC, V* ⊚ *BP.*

★ ¢ ⊞ **Pousada Ambar** From this pousada, just cross a couple of streets to enjoy the beautiful Barra Beach. The inn is also near banks, shopping malls, restaurants, and nightlife; bus stops are nearby. If you're braving Salvador at Carnaval time, the parade passes noisily just two blocks away on Avenida Oceânica. There's a nice terrace and courtyard. The living room has a television. ⊠ *Rua Afonso Celso 485 Barra 40140-080* ☎ *071/264–6956* 🖷 *071/264–3791* ⊕ *www.ambarpousada.com.br* 🖙 *5 rooms* ⌂ *Fans, Internet no room TVs* ⊟ *AE, MC, V* ⊚ *BP.*

★ ¢ ⊞ **Pousada das Flores.** The Brazilian-French owners have made this inn, northeast of Pelourinho and within walking distance of the historical district, one of the city's best budget options. Rooms are large and have high ceilings and hardwood floors. For peace and quiet as well as an ocean view, opt for a room on an upper floor. If you feel like splurging, request the penthouse, which has a fantastic view of the harbor. Breakfast is served on the patio. ⊠ *Rua Direita de Santo Antônio 442, Santo Antônio, 40301-280* ☎🖷 *071/243–1836* 🖙 *6 rooms, 3 suites* ⌂ *Fans.* ⊟ *AE, DC, MC, V.*

Nightlife & the Arts

Pelourinho is filled with music every night and has more bars and clubs than you can count. Most bars serve food as well as drink. Activity also centers along the seashore, mainly at Rio Vermelho and between the Corsário and Piatã beaches, where many hotels have bars or discos.

Salvador is considered by many artists as a laboratory for the creation of new rhythms and dance steps. As such, this city has an electric performing arts scene. See the events calendar published by Bahiatursa (the tourist office), or see local newspapers for details on live music performances as well as the rehearsal schedules and locations of the Carnaval *blocos* (organized groups of dancers and musicians). In Pelourinho groups often give free concerts on Tuesday and Sunday nights.

Nightlife

BARS Enjoy live music and typical Bahian food at **Casquinha de Siri** (✉ Coqueiros de Piatã, s/n, Piata ☎ 071/367–1234). **Sancho Pança** (✉ Av. Otávio Mangabeira 112, Pituba ☎ 071/248–3571) is a great place for sangria and typical Spanish fare. Sooner or later you must have a *caipirinha* (lemon and sugar-cane brandy cocktail) at **Cantina da Lua** (✉ Praça Terreirro de Jesus 2, Pelourinho ☎ No phone).

DANCE SHOWS Shows at the **Moenda** (✉ Rua P, Quadra 28, Lote 21, Jardim Armação/Boca do Rio ☎ 071/231–7915 or 071/230–6786) begin daily at 8 PM. There are Afro-Brazilian dinner shows at the **Solar do Unhão** (✉ Av. do Contorno 08, Comércio, near Mercado Modelo ☎ 071/321–5551), which is open Monday through Saturday from 8 PM on. The entertainment is better than the food. The unforgettable Afro-Bahian show at the **Teatro Miguel Santana** (✉ Rua Gregório de Mattos 47, Pelourinho ☎ 071/321–0222) has the town's best folkloric dance troupes. This is an entertaining way to learn about African-Brazilian culture.

NIGHTCLUBS Have dinner or drinks and listen to quality jazz, blues, soul, and pop at the **French Quartier** (✉ Aeroclube Plaza complex, Av. Otávio Mangabeira s/n, Lote 1, Pituba ☎ 071/240–1491 ⊕ www.frenchquartier.com.br). Happy hour is between 6 PM and 8 PM. Dress isn't formal, but wear something nice. The view of the bay is fantastic, but ocean breezes are cool, so bring a coat or sweater. French Quartier opens at 5 PM every day. The **Queops disco** (✉ Hotel Sol Bahia Atlântico, Rua Manoel Antônio Galvão 100, Patamares ☎ 071/370–9000) has a large dance floor and weekly shows by local bands. **Rock in Rio Café** (✉ Av. Otávio Mangabeira 6000, Jardim Armação/Boca do Rio ☎ 071/371–0979) is in the shopping-and-entertainment complex Aeroclube Plaza. The atmosphere here is more like Miami than Salvador.

The Arts

CAPOEIRA You can see capoeira on Tuesday, Thursday, and Saturday evenings at 7 at the Forte de Santo Antônio. Two schools practice here. The more traditional is the Grupo de Capoeira Angola. Weekday nights are classes; the real show happens on Saturday. There are several capoeira schools in Salvador for anyone who wants to learn the art that trains both the mind and body for combat. Mestre Bamba (Rubens Costa Silva) teaches at **Bimba's Academy** (✉ Rua das Laranjeiras 01, Pelourinho ☎ 071/322–0639). A 10-day course costs around R$70.

CARNAVAL REHEARSALS Afro-Brazilian percussion groups begin Carnaval rehearsals—which are really more like creative jam sessions—around midyear. **Ilê Aiyê**, which started out as a Carnaval bloco, has turned itself into much more in its 25-year history. It now has its own school and promotes the study and practice of African heritage, religion, and history. Practices are held every Saturday night at Forte de Santo Antônio and should not be missed. Olodum, Salvador's most commercial percussion group, gained fame when it made a recording with Paul Simon. The group has its own venue, the **Casa do Olodum** (✉ Rua Gregório de Matos 22, Pelourinho ☎ 071/321–

5010). Pre-Carnaval rehearsals take place at Largo do Pelourinho Tuesday evenings and Sunday afternoons.

Casa do Comércio (⊠ Av. Tancredo Neves 1109, Ramal ☎ 071/341–8700) hosts music performances and some theatrical productions. All kinds of musicians play at the **Concha Acústica do Teatro Castro Alves** (⊠ Ladeira da Fonte s/n, Campo Grande ☎ 071/247–6414 or 071/339–8000), a band shell with great acoustics. Catch a free jam session with Salvador's best jazz and blues musicians between 7 PM and 10 PM some Saturdays at **Solar do Unhão** (⊠ Av. do Contorno 08, Comércio, near Mercado Modelo ☎ 071/321–5551), on the waterfront. The **Teatro ACBEU** (⊠ Av. 7 de Setembro 1883, Vitória ☎ 071/247–4395 or 071/336–4411) has contemporary and classic music, dance, and theater performances by Brazilian and international talent. See theatrical, ballet, and musical performances at the **Teatro Yemanjá** (⊠ Jardim Armacão s/n, Centro de Convenções da Bahia ☎ 071/370–8494).

Sports & the Outdoors

Bicycling & Running

The park **Dique do Tororó** (⊠ Entrances at Av. Presidente Costa e Silva and Av. Vasco da Gama, Tororó) has a jogging track and a lake with luminous fountains and statues of Candomblé orixás. You can bike here, too. At **Jardim dos Namorados** (⊠ Av. Otávio Mangabeira, Pituba) you can rent bikes, play volleyball, or perhaps join a soccer game. The **Parque Metropolitano de Pituaçu** (⊠ Av. Otávio Mangabeira s/n, Pituaçu), surrounding a lagoon, is the nicest public park in town. The park is an ecological reserve with a lake, bike rentals, and a track, plus bars and restaurants, as well as sculptures by artist Mário Cravo. Entrance to the park is free; hours are 8–5 Wednesday–Sunday.

Soccer

Bahia and Vitória are the two best local teams, and they play year-round Wednesday and Sunday at 5 in the **Estádio da Fonte Nova** (⊠ Av. Vale do Nazaré, Dique do Tororó Tororó ☎ 071/243–3322 Ext. 237). Tickets are sold at the stadium a day in advance. Avoid sitting behind the goals, where the roughhousing is worst. The best seats are in the *arquibancada superior* (high bleachers).

Shopping

Areas & Malls

For paintings, especially art naïf, visit the many galleries in the Cidade Alta and around the **Largo do Pelourinho** (⊠ Rua Alfredo de Brito at Ladeira do Taboão). The **Mercado Modelo** is your best bet for local handicrafts, such as lace, hammocks, wood carvings, and musical instruments. **Shopping Barra** (⊠ Av. Centenário 2992, Barra) is the best shopping mall in Salvador. It isn't far from the historic center and has cinemas, restaurants, and local boutiques, as well as branches of the major Rio, São Paulo, and Minas Gerais retailers. It is open from 10 to 10 weekdays and from 9 to 8 on Saturday. Many hotels provide transportation to the mall, but you can take the Rodoviário bus line.

Specialty Stores

ART Top local artists (many of whom use only first names or nicknames) include Totonho, Calixto, Raimundo Santos, Joailton, Nadinho, Nonato, Maria Adair, Carybé, Mário Cravo, and Jota Cunha. **Atelier Portal da Cor** (⊠ Ladeira do Carmo 31, Pelourinho ☎ 071/242–9466) is a gallery run by an artists' cooperative.

HANDICRAFTS The **Casa Santa Barbara** (⊠ Rua Alfredo de Brito s/n, Pelourinho ☎ 071/ 244–0458) sells Bahian clothing and lacework of top quality, and at high prices. It's closed Saturday afternoon and Sunday. Of Salvador's state-run handicrafts stores, the best is the **Instituto de Artesanato Visconde de Mauá** (⊠ Praça Azevedo Fernandes 2, Porto da Barra ☎ 071/264–5440 ⊠ R. Gregorio de Mattos 27, Pelourinho ☎ 071/321–5638). Look for exquisite lace, musical instruments of African origin, weavings, and wood carvings. **Kembo** (⊠ Rua João de Deus 21, Pelourinho ☎ 071/322–1379) carries native handicrafts. The owners travel to reservations all over the country and buy from the Pataxós, Kiriri, Tupí, Karajá, Xingú, Waiwai, Tikuna, Caipós, and Yanomami, among others.

JEWELRY & Stones found in Brazil include agate, amethyst, aquamarine, emerald, GEMSTONES and tourmaline. Prices are usually cheaper here than in comparable stores outside South America, but it's a good idea to have an idea of what stones are worth before you go. The well-known, reputable **H. Stern** (⊠ Largo do Pelourinho s/n, Pelourinho ☎ 071/322–7353) Salvador has several branches of the store, most of them in malls and major hotels. **Simon** (⊠ Rua Ignácio Accioli s/n, Pelourinho ☎ 071/242–5218), the city's most famous jewelers, allows you to peer through a window into the room where goldsmiths work.

Salvador A to Z

AIR TRAVEL

CARRIERS Flights from major cities in Brazil are easy, but with the exception of TAP from Portugal, flights from other countries usually require a change of plane and airline in Rio de Janeiro or São Paulo. Airlines that serve Salvador are Gol, Nordest LInhas Aéreas, TAM, Varig, and VASP. ⇨ For airline information, *see* Air Travel *in* Brazil A to Z.

The Aeroporto Deputado Luís Eduardo Magalhães, 37 km (23 mi) northeast of Salvador, accommodates international and domestic flights. 🛈 Airport Information **Aeroporto Deputado Luís Eduardo Magalhães** ⊠ Praça Gago Coutinho s/n, São Cristovão ☎ 071/204-1010.

AIRPORT Avoid taking *comum* (common) taxis from the airport; drivers often jack TRANSFERS up the fare by refusing or "forgetting" to turn on the meter. Opt for one of the prepaid *cooperativa* (co-op) taxis, which are white with a broad blue stripe; the cost is R$79–R$113 for the 20- to 30-minute drive downtown. The *ônibus executivo,* an air-conditioned bus, runs daily from 6 to 9 at no set intervals; it costs about R$9 and takes an hour to reach downtown, stopping at hotels along the way. Drivers don't speak English, so write your hotel's address on a piece of paper to show to them. Several companies operate these buses, of which the largest is Transportes Ondina. The municipal Circular buses, operated by both Transportes

Ondina and Transportes Rio Vermelho, cost mere centavos and run along the beaches to downtown, ending at São Joaquim, where ferries depart for Ilha de Itaparica.

🚍 Shuttles **Transportes Ondina** ⊠ Av. Vasco da Gama 347 ☎ 071/245-6366. **Transportes Rio Vermelho** ⊠ Av. Dorival Caymmi 18270 ☎ 071/377-2587.

BOAT & FERRY TRAVEL

Itaparica and the other harbor islands can be reached by taking a ferry or a launch from Salvador, by hiring a motorized schooner, or by joining a harbor schooner excursion—all departing from the docks behind the Mercado Modelo. Launches cost about R$2 and leave every 45 minutes from 7 to 6 from the Terminal Turístico Marítimo. The ferry takes passengers and cars and leaves every half hour between 6 AM and 10:30 PM from the Terminal Ferry-Boat. The fare is around R$2 for passengers and R$14–R$18 for cars, and it takes 45 minutes to cross the bay. You reach Cachoeira by a combination of boat and bus: boats depart weekdays at 2:30 from the Terminal Turístico Marítimo for the three-hour trip to Maragojipe; you then board a bus for the bumpy half-hour ride.

🚢 **Terminal Ferry-Boat** ⊠ Terminal Marítimo, Av. Oscar Ponte 1051, São Joaquim ☎ 071/321-7100 or 071/319-2890. **Terminal Turístico Marítimo** ⊠ Behind Mercado Modelo, Av. França s/n ☎ 071/243-0741.

BUS & METRÔ TRAVEL

Bus tickets are sold at the Terminal Rodoviário in Salvador, which is where all buses heading out of the city depart. Itapemirim has three buses a day to Recife (13 hours, R$90–R$125), Fortaleza (19 hours, R$150), and Rio (28 hours, R$200–R$375). Santa Maria/Catuense has hourly service to Praia do Forte starting at 7:30 AM, with the last bus returning to the city at 5:30 PM; tickets cost about R$11. Camurujipe has hourly service to Cachoeira between 5:30 AM and 7 PM. Comfortable Real Expresso buses make the seven-hour trip to Chapada Diamantina (Lençóis or Palmeiras) for about R$28, with departures at 11:30 PM daily and at 7 AM Tuesday, Thursday, and Saturday. Return is at 11:30 PM daily, with an additional departure at 7:30 AM Monday, Wednesday, and Friday.

Within Salvador, use the *executivo* (executive) buses. Although other buses serve most of the city and cost a pittance (R$1.40), they're often crowded and dirty and are favored by pickpockets. Fancier executivo buses (R$3.50) serve tourist areas more completely. The glass-sided green, yellow, and orange Jardineira bus (marked PRAÇA DA SÉ; R$6) runs every 40 minutes 7:30 to 7:30 daily from the Praça da Sé in Pelourinho to the Stella Maris Beach, traveling along the Orla Marítima series of avenues. The Santa Maria/Catuense company operates six buses (marked PRAIA DO FORTE) daily that stop at Barra do Jacuípe Beach.

🚌 Bus Information **Camurujipe** ☎ 071/358-4704. **Comfortable Real Expresso** ☎ 071/450-2991 or 071/246-8355. ⊕ www.realexpresso.com.br. **Itapemirim** ☎ 071/358-0037. **Santa Maria/Catuense** ☎ 071/359-3474. **Terminal Rodoviário** ⊠ Av. Antônio Carlos Magalhães, Iguatemi ☎ 071/358-6633.

CAR RENTAL

Rental companies in Salvador include Avis, Hertz, and Localiza. The dearth of places to park in Salvador makes rental cars impractical for sightseeing in the Cidade Alta. Further, many soteropolitanos are reckless drivers, making driving a dangerous proposition, especially if you don't know your way around. That said, cars are handy for visits to outlying beaches and far-flung attractions.

⚑ Agencies Avis ⊠ Aeroporto Deputado Luís Eduardo Magalhães, Salvador ☎ 071/237-0155 071/377-2276 at airport. **Hertz** ⊠ Aeroporto Deputado Luís Eduardo Magalhães, Salvador ☎ 071/377-3633. **Localiza** ⊠ Aeroporto Deputado Luís Eduardo Magalhães, Salvador ☎ 071/377-2272, 0800/99-2000 in Brazil ⊕ www.localiza.com.br.

CAR TRAVEL

Two highways—BR 101 and BR 116—run between Rio de Janeiro and Salvador. If you take the BR 101, get off at the city of Santo Antônio/Nazaré and follow the signs to Itaparica, 61 km (38 mi) away. At Itaparica you can either take the 45-minute ferry ride to Salvador or continue on BR 101 to its connection with BR 324. If you opt for the BR 116, exit at the city of Feira de Santana, 107 km (67 mi) from Salvador and take the BR 324, which approaches the city from the north. Follow the signs marked IGUATEMI/CENTRO for downtown and nearby destinations. To reach Praia do Forte by car, take the Estrada do Coco north and follow the signs. To reach Cachoeira, take BR 324 north for about 55 km (34 mi), then head west on BR 420 through the town of Santo Amaro. The trip takes 1½ hours. To drive to Lençóis for Chapada Diamantina, take BR 324 to Feira de Santana and BR 116 to connect with BR 242. If you are going to Andarai to stay at the Posada Sincora, turn left onto BA 142 just before Lençóis.

EMERGENCIES

In an emergency, dial ☎ 192 for Pronto Socorro (first aid). In Salvador the office of the Delegacia de Proteção do Turista (Tourist Police) is down the steps at the back of the Belvedere at the Praça da Sé in Pelourinho. It deals as best it can (on a shoestring budget) with tourist-related crime after the fact. Officers, some of whom have rudimentary second-language skills, wear armbands that say POLÍCIA TURÍSTICA. There are also military-police foot patrols. For the nearest 24-hour pharmacy, dial 136 or ask at your hotel's front desk.

⚑ Emergency Services Delegacia de Proteção do Turista ☎ 071/320-4103.

⚑ Hospitals Aliança Hospital ⊠ Av. Juracy Magalhães Jr. 2096 ☎ 071/350-5600. **Hospital Jorge Valente** ⊠ Av. Garibaldi 2135 ☎ 071/203-4333. **Hospital Português** ⊠ Av. Princesa Isabel 2, Santa Isabel ☎ 071/203-5555.

⚑ Hot Lines Police ☎ 190. **Pronto Socorro** (First Aid) ☎ 192.

MAIL, INTERNET & SHIPPING

Salvador's main post office is in the Cidade Baixa's Praça Inglaterra. Other branches are in Pelourinho on Rua Alfredo de Brito, on the Avenida Princesa Isabel in Barra, the Rua Marques de Caravelas in Ondina, at the Barra and Iguatemi shopping centers, just inside the back door of the Mercado Modelo, and at the airport. The airport branch is open 24 hours; all others are open weekdays 8–5. All branches offer express-mail service. Make sure your letter or package has been stamped.

Most hotels and even many small pousadas have Internet services for a small fee. There are also Internet cafés scattered around the city. In Pelourinho, the historic district, try Internet Café.com, open Monday–Saturday 9–9.

🖪 Internet Center **Internet Café.com** ⊠ Rua Joãa de Deus 02 ☎ 071/331-2147

🖪 Post Office **Correio Pelourinho** ⊠ Rua Alfredo de Brito 43 Pelourinho ☎ 071/243-9383.

MONEY MATTERS

Never change money on the streets, especially in the Cidade Alta. Major banks have exchange facilities, but only in some of their branches. Try Citibank, which has good rates, Banco Económico or Banco do Brasil, which also offers exchange services at its branches in the Shopping Center Iguatemi and at the airport. Credit cards and even dollars are welcome in most areas of tourist-friendly Brazil, but if you are traveling to villages or small towns, exchange at least what you think you will need for tips, taxis, restaurants, and purchases from street vendors or small shops while you are in Salvador.

🖪 Banks **Banco do Brasil** ⊠ Av. Estados Unidos 561, Comércio. **Banco Económico** ⊠ Rua Miguel Calmon 285. **Citibank** ⊠ Rua Miguel Calmon 555, Comércio.

SAFETY

The Centro Histórico area of Pelourinho has become one of the safest places in Salvador. There are friendly tourist police on almost every corner; however, that doesn't mean you shouldn't take normal precautions, especially at night. Stick to the main tourist areas and don't walk down streets that appear to be deserted. It's a good idea to stay away from any deserted area, even a beach. At night take a taxi (registered cabs only— they have identification stickers on the window) to wherever you want to go. The lower station of the Lacerda Elevator is renowned for crime, and pickpocketing is common on buses and in crowded places.

During Carnaval there are *huge* crowds in the streets. The recommendation is to join a bloco, which is surrounded by a rope with security guards. The tourist office, Bahiatursa (⇨ Visitor Information, *below*), can tell you how to join up with one, or contact a tour operator and join one of their groups, or watch it from one of the boxes installed along the route. If these options don't appeal to you, reread the safety instructions above.

TELEPHONES

Salvador's area code is 071. Public phones take cards that are sold in a variety of denominations at many shops.

TAXIS

Taxis in Salvador are metered, but you must convert the unit shown on the meter to reais using a chart posted on the window. Tipping isn't expected. You can hail a comum taxi (white with a red-and-blue stripe) on the street (they often line up in front of major hotels), or summon one by phone. If you bargain, you can hire a comum taxi for the day for as little as R$135. Try Ligue Taxi. The more expensive, though usually air-conditioned, *especial* (special) taxis also congregate outside major hotels, though you must generally call for them. Cometas is a reliable company.

🖪 Taxi Companies **Cometas** ☎ 071/244-4500. **Ligue Taxi** ☎ 071/357-7777.

TOURS

Salvador's large group tours are cursory, and their guides often speak minimal English; such tours are also targeted by hordes of street vendors. Private tours with an accredited Bahiatursa guide can be hired through your hotel or a travel agency or at a Bahiatursa office (⇨ Visitor Information). Prices vary depending on the size of the group but always includes a car that picks you up and drops you off at your hotel. Beware of guides who approach you at churches and other sights; they tell tall tales and overcharge you for the privilege.

Bahia Adventure Ecoturismo can help you arrange Jeep tours and other adventure treks to the Reserva de Sapiranga, in the Praia do Forte area. BBTUR has excellent buses and vans; request an English-speaking guide ahead of time. The company has a full line of tours not only of Salvador but also of surrounding areas; there's also a branch in the lobby of the Breezes Costa do Sauípe resort. Odara Turismo, in the arcade at the Praia do Forte Eco Resort Hotel, arranges four-wheel-drive tours of the area plus horseback and hiking trips.

Though Tatur Tours specializes in African-heritage tours of Bahia, it also gives personalized special-interest city tours and arranges top-notch excursions from Salvador. Top Hilton Turismo offers the usual city tours and interesting boat cruises, including a trip around Baía de Todos os Santos in a trimaran and a schooner cruise to the islands. It also has a tour to the nudist beach at Massarandupió, along the northern coast. For trips to Chapada Diamante, Trekking Tours is your best bet.

Several travel agencies offer half-day minibus tours with hotel pickup and drop-off for about R$60–R$80. Agencies also offer daylong harbor tours on motorized schooners (R$80–R$90) and night tours (R$100–R$115) that include dinner and an Afro-Brazilian music-and-dance show. A beach tour that includes the Lagoa de Abaeté can be arranged as well, about R$80 a head including a car and a guide (minimum two people).

🚩 Tour Operators **Bahia Adventure Ecoturismo** ☒ Rodovia BA099, Km 76, Costa do Sauípe, Mata de São João ☎ 71/464-2525 ⊕ www.bahiaadventure.com. **BBTUR** ☒ Vila Nova da Praia, Loja 22–23, Costa do Sauípe, Mata de São João ☎ 071/464-2121 71/341-8800 in Salvador. ☒ Av. Tancredo Neves 450, Edifício Suarez Trade Sala 1.702, Pituba, ☎ 071/341-8800 **Odara Turismo** ☒ Rua do Farol s/n, Praia do Forte, Mata de São João ☎071/876-1080. **Tatur Tours** ☒ Av. Antônio Carlos Magalhães 2573, Edifício Royal Trade, Pituba Salvador ☎ 071/358-7216. **Top Hilton Turismo** ☒ Rua Fonte do Boi 05, Rio Vermelho Salvador ☎ 071/334-5223. **Trekking Tours** ☒ Bahia Praia Hotel, Av. Oceániana 2483, Ondina Salvador ☎ 071/332-5557.

VISITOR INFORMATION

Emtursa, the municipal tourist board, is open weekdays 8–6. Through Emtursa, Salvador's city hall operates mobile tourist information units in the Central Histórico area (Pelourinho). Emtursa has bilingual receptionists and gives out leaflets with information on restaurants, tours, and prices.

🚩 Tourist Information **Emtursa** ☒ Largo do Pelourinho 12 ☎ 071/243-6555 ⊕ www.emtursa.salvador.ba.gov.br.

THE AMAZON

Updated by
Rhan Flatin

The world's largest tropical forest seems an endless carpet of green that's sliced only by the curving contours of rivers. Its statistics are as impressive: the region covers more than 10 million square km (4 million square mi) and extends into eight other countries (French Guiana, Suriname, Guyana, Venezuela, Ecuador, Peru, Bolivia, and Colombia). It takes up roughly 40% of Brazil in the states of Acre, Rondônia, Amazonas, Roraima, Pará, Amapá, and Tocantins. The Amazon forest is home to 500,000 cataloged species of plants and a river that annually transports 15% of the world's available freshwater to the sea, yet it's inhabited by only 16 million people. That's less than the population of metropolitan São Paulo.

Life centers on the rivers, the largest of which is the Amazon itself. From its source in southern Peru, it runs 6,300 km (3,900 mi) to its Atlantic outflow. Of its hundreds of tributaries, 17 are more than 1,600 km (1,000 mi) long. In places it is so wide you can't see the opposite shore, earning it the appellation Rio Mar (River Sea). Although there has been increasing urbanization in the Amazon region, between one-third and one-half of the Amazon's residents live in rural settlements, many of which are along the riverbanks, where transportation, water, fish, and good soil for planting are readily available.

Spaniard Vicente Pinzón is credited with being the first to sail the Amazon, in 1500. But the most famous voyage was undertaken by Spanish conquistador Francisco de Orellano, who set out from Ecuador on a short mission to search for food in 1541. Orellano was also familiar, no doubt, with the legend of El Dorado (the Golden One), a monarch whose kingdom was so rich in gold he covered his naked body in gold dust each day. Instead of gold or a lost kingdom, however, Orellano ran into natives, heat, and disease. When he emerged from the jungle a year later, his crew told a tale of women warriors they called the Amazons (a nod to classical mythology). This captivating story lent the region its name.

Documented accounts indicate that early Portuguese contacts with the Indians were relatively peaceful. But it wasn't long before the peace ended, and the indigenous populations were devastated. Diseases brought by the Europeans and against which the Indians had no resistance took their toll; Portuguese attempts to enslave them did the rest. When the Portuguese arrived in Brazil, there were roughly 4.5 million Indians, many of them in the Amazon; today there are just over 300,000 in the nation and fewer than 200,000 in the Amazon.

The late 19th century rubber boom transformed Belém and Manaus from outposts to cities. In 1928 Henry Ford began to pour millions of dollars into vast rubber plantations. After much struggle and few results, the project was scrapped 20 years later. Since the rubber era, huge reserves of gold and iron have been discovered. Land-settlement schemes and development projects, such as hydroelectric plants and major roadworks, have followed. Conservation has not always been a priority. Vast portions of tropical forest have been indiscriminately cut; tribal lands have again been encroached on; and industrial by-products, such as mercury used in gold mining, have poisoned wildlife and people.

And yet, 500 years after the first Europeans arrived, much of the Amazon has not been thoroughly explored by land. You can stand on a riverboat deck and be astounded by the vastness of the mighty Rio Amazonas or charmed by wooden huts along a narrow waterway; and hike through dense vegetation and gawk at trees that tower 35 meters (150 feet).

Exploring the Amazon

Although there are regular flights in the Amazon, many visitors opt for the area's primary mode of transportation—boat. Though much slower, boats offer a closer look at Amazon culture, nature, and the river system, and they go just about everywhere you'd want to go. A trip along the Amazon itself, especially the 1,602-km (993-mi) four- to five-day journey between Belém and Manaus, is a singular experience.

Neotropical environments can be hostile, so it's a good idea to hire a guide or go with a tour company specializing in backcountry adventures. To join a tour or to choose a destination, contact one of the tour companies we suggest, or consult with a state-run tour agency. Paratur in Belém and SEC in Manaus can also be helpful. The more remote your destination, the more seriously you should heed the travel advice and health precautions in this book.

As of 2006, phone numbers in Brazil will change from seven to eight digits. All seven-digit numbers will be preceded by a 3. For example, 555–5555 will become 3555–5555.

Boat Travel

Whatever the style, budget, or length of your Amazonian journey, there's a boat plying the river to suit your needs. Sleep in a hammock on the deck of a thatch-roof riverboat or in the air-conditioned suite of an upscale tour operator's private ship. Keep in mind that wildlife viewing is not good on boats far from shore. Near shore, however, the birding can be excellent. Binoculars and a bird guide can help, and shorebirds, raptors, and parrots can be abundant. Common in many parts of the river system are *boto* (pink dolphins) and *tucuxi* (gray dolphins). To see the most wildlife, plan your travels to allow time in the forest and streams.

ADVENTURE CRUISES
Adventure cruises combine the luxury of cruising with exploration. Their goal is to get you close to wildlife and local inhabitants without sacrificing comforts and amenities. Near daily excursions include wildlife viewing in smaller boats with naturalists, village visits with naturalists, and city tours. Abercrombie and Kent, Aurora Expeditions, and INTRAV/ Clipper Cruises make these trips. They run from 9 to 16 days.

MACAMAZON BOATS
Longer boat routes on the lower Amazon are covered by MACAMAZON. Regular departures run between Belém, Santarém, Macapá, Manaus, and several other destinations. The boats are not luxurious but are a step above regional boats. You can get a suite for two from Belém to

Manaus with air-conditioning and bath for about R$800. *Camarote* (cabin) class gets you a tiny room for two with air-conditioning and a shared bath. *Rede* (hammock) class is the cheapest and most intimate way to travel since you'll be hanging tight with the locals on the main decks. Hammocks are hung in two layers very close together, promoting neighborly chats. Arrive early for the best spots, away from the bar, engine, and bathrooms. Keep your valuables with you at all times and sleep with them. Conceal new sneakers in a plastic bag. In addition to a hammock (easy and cheap to buy in Belém or Manaus), bring two 4-foot lengths of ⅜-inch rope to tie it up. Also bring a sheet, since nights get chilly. MACAMAZON also runs a high-speed catamaran—with cushioned seats and air-conditioning—between Macapá and Belém (R$110). It takes 10 hours, about a third of the time that other boats take. It travels far from the riverbanks, so don't plan on seeing much.

OCEANGOING SHIPS Some cruise ships call at Manaus, Belém, and Santarém as part of their itineraries. Most trips take place October through May. They range in length from 10 to 29 days, and costs vary. Two major lines making such journeys are Princess Cruises and Royal Olympic Cruises.

REGIONAL BOATS To travel to towns and villages or to meander slowly between cities, go by *barco regional* (regional boat). A trip from Belém to Manaus takes about four days; Belém to Santarém is two days. The double- or triple-deck boats carry freight and passengers. They make frequent stops at small towns, allowing for interaction and observation. You might be able to get a cabin with two bunks (around R$400 for a two-day trip), but expect it to be claustrophobic. Most passengers sleep in hammocks with little or no space between them. Bring your own hammock, sheet, and two 4-foot sections of rope. Travel lightly and inconspicuously.

Booths sell tickets at the docks, and even if you don't speak Portuguese, there are often signs alongside the booths that list prices, destinations, and departure times. If you plan to sleep in a hammock, arrive at least one hour early to get a good spot away from the engine, toilets, and bar. Keep valuables with you in your hammock while you sleep, including any new-looking clothing items (like sneakers), which you should conceal in a plastic bag. Sanitary conditions in bathrooms vary from boat to boat. Bring your own toilet paper, sunscreen, and insect repellent. Food is sometimes served, but the quality ranges from so-so to deplorable. Consider bringing your own water and a *marmita* (carry-out meal) if you'll be on the boat overnight. Many boats have a small store at the stern where you can buy drinks, snacks, and grilled *mixto quente* (ham-and-cheese) sandwiches. Fresh fruit and snacks are available at stops along the way. Be sure to peel or wash fruit thoroughly with bottled water before eating it.

TOURIST BOATS Private groups can hire tourist boats that are more comfortable than standard riverboats. They generally travel close to the riverbank and have open upper decks from which you can observe the river and forest. The better tour operators have a regional English-speaking expert on board—usually an ecologist or botanist. You can either sleep out on the deck in a hammock or in a cabin, which usually has air-conditioning or a fan. Meals are generally provided.

SPEEDBOATS You can take a speedboat to just about anywhere the rivers flow. Faster than most options, speedboats can be ideal for traveling between smaller towns, a morning of wildlife viewing, or visiting a place that doesn't have regular transportation, such as a secluded beach or waterfall. You design the itinerary, including departure and return times. Prices and availability vary with distance and locale. Contact tour agencies, talk with locals, or head down to the docks to find a boat willing to take you where you want to go. Work out the price, destination, and travel time before leaving. You may have to pay for the gas up front, but don't pay the rest until you arrive. For trips longer than an hour, bring water, snacks, and sunscreen.

Belém

The capital of Pará State, Belém is a river port of around 1.3 million people on the south bank of the Rio Guamá, 120 km (74 mi) from the Atlantic, and 2,933 km (1,760 mi) north of Rio de Janeiro. The Portuguese settled here in 1616, using it as a gateway to the interior and an outpost to protect the area from invasion by sea. Because of its ocean access, Belém became a major trade center. Like the upriver city of Manaus, it rode the ups and downs of the Amazon booms and busts. The first taste of prosperity was during the rubber era. Architects from Europe were brought in to build churches, civic palaces, theaters, and mansions, often using fine, imported materials. When Malaysia's rubber supplanted that of Brazil in the 1920s, wood and, later, minerals provided the impetus for growth.

Belém has expanded rapidly since the 1980s, pushed by the Tucuruvi hydroelectric dam (Brazil's second largest), the development of the Carajás mining region, and the construction of the ALBRAS/Alunorte bauxite and aluminum production facilities. Wood exports have risen, making Pará the largest wood-producing state in Brazil. As the forests are cut, pastures and cattle replace them, resulting in an increase in beef production. In 2000 the state government began construction of a bridge network connecting Belém to outlying cities. The resulting increase in commerce has spurred economic growth in the region, though there is still considerable poverty and high unemployment. In the city highrise apartments are replacing colonial structures. Fortunately, local governments have launched massive campaigns to preserve the city's rich heritage while promoting tourist-friendly policies. This effort has earned state and federal government funds to restore historical sites in the Belém area. Tourism is on the rise in the city and is becoming increasingly important for Belém's economic well-being.

Cidade Velha

Cidade Velha (Old City) is the oldest residential part of Belém. Many of the houses are colonial with clay walls and tile roofs. Three stories is the tallest they get, though 15-floor apartment buildings are invading from the north. Much of Cidade Velha is middle-income with a variety of hardware, auto parts, and fishing supply stores. On its northwestern edge, the Forte Presépio lies along the banks of the Rio Guamá.

Casa das Onze Janelas. At the end of the 17th century, sugar baron Domingos da Costa Barcelar built the neoclassical House of Eleven Windows as his private mansion. Today Barcelar's mansion is a gallery for contemporary plastic art and other visual art, including photography. The view from the balcony is impressive. Take a walk through the courtyard and imagine scenes of the past. This is where the aristocracy took tea and watched over the docks as slaves unloaded ships from Europe and filled them with sugar and rum. ⊠ *Praça Frei Caetano Brandão, Cidade Velha* ▤ *R$2, free Tues.* ☉ *Tues.–Fri. 1–6, weekends 9–1.*

Catedral da Sé. In 1771 Bolognese architect Antônio José Landi, whose work can be seen throughout the city, completed the cathedral's construction on the foundations of an older church. Carrara marble adorns the rich interior, which is an interesting mix of baroque, colonial, and neoclassical styles. The high altar was a gift from Pope Pius IX. ⊠ *Praça Frei Caetano Brandão, Cidade Velha* ▤ *Free* ☉ *Tues.–Fri. 8–noon and 2–4, Sat. 5 PM–6:30 PM, Sun. 6 PM–7 PM.*

Estação das Docas. Next to Ver-o-Peso market on the river, three former warehouses have been artfully converted into a commercial/tourist area. All have one wall of floor-to-ceiling glass that provides a full river view when dining or shopping. The first warehouse is a convention center, the second is full of shops and kiosks selling crafts and snacks, and the third has a microbrewery and 14 upscale restaurants. The buildings are air-conditioned and connected by glass-covered walkways and contain photos and artifacts from the port's heyday. A stroll outside along the docks provides a grand view of the bay. Tourist boats arrive and depart at the dock—a good place to relax both day and night. ⊠ *Boulevard Castilhos França s/n, Comercio* ☏ *091/212-5525* ▤ *Free* ☉ *Weekdays noon–1 AM, weekends 10 AM–1 AM.*

Forte do Presépio (Fort of the Crèche). Founded January 12, 1616, this fort is considered Belém's birthplace. From here the Portuguese launched conquests of the Amazon and watched over the bay. The fort's role in the region's defense is evidenced by massive English- and Portuguese-made cannons pointing out over the water. They are poised atop fort walls that are 3 yards thick in places. Renovations completed in 2002 unearthed more than two dozen cannons, extensive military middens from the moat, and native Tupi artifacts. A small museum of prefort indigenous cultures is at the entrance. Just outside the fort, cobblestone walkways hug the breezy waterfront. ⊠ *Praça Frei Caetano Brandão, Cidade Velha* ☏ *No phone* ▤ *R$4, free Tues.* ☉ *Tues.–Fri. 1–6, weekends 9–1.*

Igreja Nossa Senhora das Mercês (Our Lady of Mercy Church). Another of Belém's baroque creations attributed to Antônio Landi, this church is notable for its pink color and convex facade. It's part of a complex that includes the Convento dos Mercedários, which has served both as a convent and a prison, though not simultaneously. ⊠ *Gaspar Viana e Frutuosa Guimarães Comercio* ▤ *Free* ☉ *Mon.–Sat. 8–1.*

Igreja de São João Batista (St. John the Baptist Church). Prodigious architect Antônio Landi finished this small octagonal church in 1777. It was completely restored in the late 1990s and is considered the city's purest example of baroque architecture. ⊠ *Rua João Diogo and Rodriguês Dos Santos, Cidade Velha* 🖙 *Free* ⊘ *Mon.–Sat. 6:30 AM–9 AM.*

Museu de Arte de Belém (MABE). Temporary exhibits on the bottom level of the Metropolitan Art Museum are free to view. On the second level staff members hand you brown furry slippers that you must wear over your shoes to protect the wooden floors. The permanent collection of furniture and paintings dates from the 18th century through the rubber boom. The museum is housed in the Palácio Antônio Lemos (circa 1883), a municipal palace built in the imperial Brazilian style with French influences. ⊠ *Praça Dom Pedro II s/n, Cidade Velha* 🕾 *091/ 219–8228* 🖙 *R$4, free Tues.* ⊘ *Tues.–Fri. 10–6, weekends 9–1.*

Museu de Arte Sacra. A guided tour (call 48 hours in advance to reserve an English-speaking docent) begins in the early-18th-century baroque Igreja de Santo Alexandre (St. Alexander's Church), which is distinguished by intricate woodwork on its altar and pews. On the second half of the tour you see the museum's collection of religious sculptures and paintings. Temporary exhibitions, a gift shop, and a café are on the first floor. ⊠ *Praça Frei Caetano Brandão, Cidade Velha* 🕾 *091/219–1166* 🖙 *R$4, free Tues.* ⊘ *Tues.–Fri. 1–6, weekends 9–1.*

Museu do Estado do Pará. Pará State Museum is in the sumptuous Palácio Lauro Sodré (circa 1771), an Antônio Landi creation with Venetian and Portuguese elements. Consistently outstanding visiting exhibits are on the first floor; the second floor contains the permanent collection of furniture and paintings. ⊠ *Praça Dom Pedro II, Cidade Velha* 🕾 *091/ 219–1138* 🖙 *R$4* ⊘ *Tues.–Fri. 1–6, weekends 9–1.*

★ **Ver-o-Peso.** Its name literally meaning "see the weight" (a throwback to the time when the Portuguese weighed everything entering or leaving the region), this market is a hypnotic confusion of colors and voices. Vendors hawk tropical fruits, regional wares, and an assortment of tourist kitsch. Most interesting are the *mandingueiras,* women who claim they can solve any problem with "miracle" jungle roots and charms for the body and soul. They sell jars filled with animal eyes, tails, and even heads, as well as herbs, each with its own legendary power. The sex organs of the pink river dolphin are a supposedly unrivaled cure for romantic problems. In the fish market you get an up-close look at pirarucu, the Amazon's most colorful fish and the world's second-largest freshwater species. Look for bizarre armored catfish species, such as the *tamuatã* and the huge *piraiba.* Across the street is a small arched entrance to the municipal meat market. Duck in and glance at the French-style pink-and-green-painted ironwork, imported from Britain. Be sure to visit Ver-o-Peso before noon, when most vendors leave. It opens around 6 AM. Leave your jewelry at home and beware of pickpockets. ⊠ *Av. Castilhos França s/n, Comércio.*

Nazaré

Just east of the Cidade Velha, Nazaré's mango tree–lined streets create the sensation of walking through tunnels. Among the historic buildings there's a tremendous variety of pastel colors and European styles. Many of the newer buildings house elegant shops.

★ **Basílica de Nossa Senhora de Nazaré.** It's hard to miss this opulent Roman-style basilica. Not only does it stand out visually, but there's an enormous *samauma* tree (kapok variety) filled with screeching white-winged parakeets in the plaza out front. Built in 1908 on the site where a *caboclo* (rural inhabitant) named Placido is said to have seen a vision of the Virgin in the early 1700s. The basilica's ornate interior is constructed entirely of European marble and contains elaborate mosaics, detailed stained-glass windows, and intricate bronze doors. In the small, basement-level Museu do Círio, displays explain the Círio de Nazaré festival, which is held each October to honor the city's patron saint. ⊠ *Av. Nazaré s/n at Av. Generalisimo Deodoro, Nazaré* ☎ *091/224–9614 museum* ⊠ *Free* ☉ *Basilica Mon. 6–11 and 3–5, Tues.–Sat. 6–11 and 3–7, Sun. 3–7; museum Tues.–Fri. 9–6.*

Bosque Rodrigues Alves. In 1883 this 40-acre plot of rain forest was designated an ecological reserve. Nowadays it has an aquarium and two amusement parks as well as natural caverns, a variety of animals (some in the wild), and mammoth trees. ⊠ *Av. Almirante Barroso, Marco* ☎ *091/226–2308* ⊠ *R$1* ☉ *Tues.–Sun. 8–5.*

★ **Museu Emílio Goeldi.** Founded by a naturalist and a group of intellectuals in 1866, this complex contains one of the Amazon's most important research facilities. Its museum has an extensive collection of Indian artifacts, including the distinctive and beautiful pottery of the Marajó Indians, known as *marajoara*. A small forest has reflecting pools with giant *vitória régia* water lilies. But the true highlight is the collection of Amazon wildlife, including manatees, anacondas, macaws, sloths, and monkeys. ⊠ *Av. Magalhães Barata 376, Nazaré* ☎ *091/249–1230* ⊠ *Park R$2, park and museum R$4* ☉ *Tues.–Thurs. and weekends 9–noon and 2–5:30, Fri. 9–noon.*

Parque da Residência. For decades this was the official residence of the governor of Pará. Now it provides office space for the Secretaria de Cultura (SECULT; Executive Secretary of Culture), as well as public space. Within the park are a 400-seat theater, an orchid conservatory, an ice cream parlor, a restaurant, and shaded spots to relax and soak in the atmosphere. ⊠ *Av. Magalhães Barata 830, São Brás* ☎ *091/219–1200* ⊠ *Free* ☉ *Tues.–Sun. 9 AM–10 PM.*

Praça da República. At this square you'll find a large statue that commemorates the proclamation of the Republic of Brazil, an amphitheater, and several French-style iron kiosks. On Sunday vendors, food booths, and musical groups create a festival-like atmosphere that attracts crowds of locals. ⊠ *Bounded by Av. Presidente Vargas, Trv. Osvaldo Cruz, and Av. Assis de Vasconcelos.*

Teatro da Paz. A complete renovation of this 1878 neoclassical theater was finished in 2001. Concert pianos were acquired to facilitate production of operas. Greek-style pillars line the front and sides; inside, note the imported details such as Italian marble pillars and French chandeliers. Classical music performances are also held in the theater, which seats more than 800 people. English-speaking guides are available to give 20-minute tours. ⊠ *Av. da Paz s/n, Praça da República, Campina*

☎ *091/224–7355* ✉ *Call for ticket prices* ⊙ *Tues.–Fri 9:30–11; tours Tues.–Fri. 12:30, 2:30, 4, and 5:30, Sat. 9:30, 11, and 12:30.*

Where to Eat

$–$$ ✕ **Dom Giuseppe.** From gnocchi to ravioli, flawless preparation of the basics distinguishes this Italian eatery from others. Everyone in town knows this, so reservations are a good idea—particularly on weekends. Don't leave without ordering a scrumptious *dolce* Paula (ice cream–and–brownie dessert). ⊠ *Av. Conselheiro Furtado 1420, Batista Campos* ☎ *091/241–1146* ▭ *AE, DC, MC, V.*

¢–$$ ✕ **Casa Portuguesa.** Although it's in the heart of the commercial district, this restaurant does its best to replicate the charm of a Portuguese country home. Specialties include dishes with chicken and, of course, salted cod. ⊠ *Rua Senador Manoel Barata 897, Campina* ☎ *091/242–4871* ▭ *AE, DC, MC, V.*

$ ✕ **Lá em Casa.** From inauspicious beginnings has emerged one of Belém's
Fodor'sChoice most popular restaurants. Regional cuisine, prepared to exacting spec-
★ ifications, has earned Lá em Casa its good reputation. Consider trying Belém's premier dish, *pato no tucupi,* duck in a yellow manioc–herb sauce served with the mildly intoxicating *jambu* leaf. Crabs on the half-shell covered with *farofa* (finely ground manioc fried in margarine) is another good choice, as is *açaí* sorbet for dessert. Sitting on the patio fringed by tropical vines and bromeliads, you feel like you're dining in the middle of the forest. ⊠ *Av. Governador José Malcher 247, Nazaré* ☎ *091/223–1212* ▭ *AE, DC, MC, V.*

$ ✕ **Rodeio.** Grilled and roasted meats are the focus of this *churrascaria.* A reasonable fixed-price menu includes not only as many servings as you can eat but also salads and dessert. The wood interior, warm lighting, and excellent service make for a relaxing atmosphere. ⊠ *Padre Eutíquio 1308, Batista Campos* ☎ *091/212–2112* ▭ *AE, DC, MC, V* ⊙ *No dinner Sun.–Mon.*

¢–$ ✕ **Miako.** Belém has a large Japanese community (second only to that of São Paulo), so there's no lack of Japanese restaurants. This one is a tried-and-true favorite for excellent service, attractive wooden decor, and consistently good food. The sushi is terrific. ⊠ *Rua 1 de Março 76, Campina* ☎ *091/242–2355* ▭ *AE, DC, MC, V.*

¢ ✕ **Bom Paladar.** A convenient location across from Telemar and the Praça da República make this pay-per-kilo restaurant a good choice for a quick lunch. The buffet table always has several main dishes, along with salads, beans, and rice. ⊠ *Riachuelo 357, Campina* ☎ *091/241–3723* ⊙ *Closed Sun. No dinner.*

¢ ✕ **Casa do Caldo.** Eight soups (out of 36) are featured every night for family dining in the "House of Soup." One price covers unlimited soup, toast, and dessert porridge. Try the crab soup with cilantro and the cow's-foot soup. It's air-conditioned and casual, with superb service. ⊠ *Rua Diogo Moia 266, Umarizal* ☎ *091/230–3110* ▭ *AE, V* ⊙ *Closed Mon.*

¢ ✕ **O Gato Comeu.** The best sandwiches in town are here. Try the Big Miau (fillet, vegetables, banana) or the Galinhão (chicken, vegetables, and banana). Sidewalk seating is best in the evening, so consider a stop here in conjunction with a stroll in adjacent Praça Batista Campos. ⊠ *Serzedelo Correa, Batisto Campos* ⊟ *No credit cards* ⊙ *Closed Mon.*

Where to Stay

$$ ⊞ **Hilton International Belém.** The Hilton's reliability and amenities are topped only by its location right on the Praça da República. Although rooms have few decorations, bland color schemes, and simple furniture, they are well equipped and comfortable. Executive rooms have the nicest views as well as access to a lounge with a VCR, a meeting area, and complimentary food and drink. ⊠ *Av. Presidente Vargas 882, Campina 66017-000* ☎ *091/217–7000, 800/445–8667 in U.S.* 🖷 *091/225–2942* ⊕ *www.hilton.com* 🛏 *361 rooms* ⋄ *Restaurant, pool, hair salon, health club, sauna, 2 bars, convention center* ⊟ *AE, DC, MC, V.*

$ ⊞ **Equatorial Palace.** Widely considered to be one of the nicest hotels in town, the Equatorial Palace has a spacious dining hall and several shops (including a tour agency). The pool and bar are on the roof, with a nearly 360-degree view. The Nazaré location is within walking distance of the port, Centro, and Cidade Velha. ⊠ *Av. Braz de Aguiar 612, Nazaré 66035-000* ☎ *091/241–2000* 🖷 *091/223–5222* 🛏 *204 rooms, 7 suites* ⋄ *2 restaurants, pool, bar, no-smoking rooms* ⊟ *AE, DC, MC, V.*

$ ⊞ **Hotel Regente.** This hotel has excellent service and a prime location for a reasonable price. Stained-glass windows and soft leather couches welcome you in an attractive lobby. Rooms on the 12th floor are nicer and more modern than those on other floors yet cost the same. ⊠ *Av. Governador José Malcher 485, Nazaré 66035-100* ☎ *091/3181–5000* 🖷 *091/242–0343* 🛏 *196 rooms, 6 suites* ⋄ *Restaurant, pool, bar* ⊟ *AE, DC, MC, V.*

¢–$ ⊞ **Itaoca Hotel.** It comes as no surprise that this small, reasonably priced hotel has the highest occupancy rate in town. Its rooms are extremely comfortable, well equipped, and modern, and most have a fantastic view of the dock area and river. ⊠ *Av. Presidente Vargas 132, Campina 66010-902* ☎🖷 *091/241–3434* 🛏 *32 rooms, 4 suites* ⋄ *Restaurant, in-room safes, cable TV, meeting room* ⊟ *AE, DC, MC, V.*

★ ¢ ⊞ **Manacá Hotel.** This small, bright-red hotel with a slanted brown-tile roof looks like a cross between a Monopoly™ hotel piece and a pagoda. Cozy, artfully decorated common areas with soft lighting have more charm than those at larger places—for about a quarter of the price. It's a clean, simple alternative if you can live without a pool or a bar. Make sure to call ahead, since it's often booked during the week. ⊠ *Trv. Quintino Bocaiuva 1645, Nazaré 66033-620* ☎ *091/223–3335* 🛏 *16 rooms* ⋄ *Cable TV; no room phones* ⊟ *AE, DC, MC, V.*

¢ ⊞ **Victoria Palace Hotel.** One of the quietest, friendliest, and safest hotels in town is a two-minute walk from the Basilica of Nazaré. It also provides some unique entertainment: Every morning at 5:45 in the enormous *samauma* tree in the square out front, hundreds of white-winged parakeets awaken, scream like crazy, and leave to feed for the day. At 5:30 PM they return to their roost and scream some more. If you're not sure where they are, exit the hotel and follow your ears. Don't be late. ⊠ *Praça Justo Chermont Alam. Maria de Jesus, 83, Nazaré* ☎ *091/212–0734* 🖷 *091/225–1973* 🛏 *21 rooms* ⋄ *Cable TV; no room phones* ⊟ *MC, V.*

Nightlife & the Arts

Doca Boulevard, about eight blocks east of Escadinha (the dock area used for boat trips), has many bars and dance clubs. The main nightlife strip is Avenida Visconde de Souza Franco, but there are several places a few blocks off it as well. The hot spots for dancing are open on Friday and Saturday nights (only) and are all downtown. Mixed-age crowds frequent them no matter what the music. Prices vary depending on the show. Drinks are available but no food. All clubs except Signos have live music on occasion. Clubs open around 10 PM, though they don't get lively before 11 or midnight.

Nightlife

BARS **Água Doce** (✉ Rua Diogo Móia 283, Umarizal ☎ 091/222–3383) specializes in *cachaça* (Brazilian sugarcane liquor. Listed on its menu are 182 kinds of cachaça and 605 different drinks, along with appetizers and entrées. Softly lighted with lots of tables, this place gets busy on weekends. It's open Tuesday–Sunday. If you prefer your music in a relaxed environment, head to **Cosanostra Caffé** (✉ Rua Benjamin Constant 1499, Nazaré ☎ 091/241–1068), which has live MPB(Música Popular Brasileira) and jazz. It serves food from an extensive menu until late in the night. **Roxy Bar** (✉ Av. Senador Lemos 231, Umarizal ☎ 091/224–4514) tops nearly everyone's list of hip spots at which to sip a drink and people-watch. **Strike 60** (✉ Rua Diogo Móia 123, Umarizal ☎ 091/212–1068) is a throwback to an American 1960s bowling-alley diner, Brazilian style. Sixties music is all that's played in this family-friendly place. Balls roll and pins crash on eight hardwood lanes. Beer and liquor are served.

DANCE CLUBS **African Bar** (✉ Marechal Hermes 2, Reduto ☎ 091/241–1085) has one area with rock or pop playing, another with techno, and a third with regional dance music such as *brega*—a mix of country and rock with a lot of rude lyrics. **Bora Bora** (✉ Rua Bernal do Couto 38, Umarizal ☎ 091/ 241–6364) attracts a dance crowd with country music on some nights and fast-paced *pagode* on others. **Signos** (✉ Governador José Malcher 247, Nazaré ☎ 091/242–7702), underneath the Lá em Casa restaurant, has the fanciest decor of the clubs, with lots of mirrors and red booths. A DJ runs video clips on a huge screen. At **Zeppelin Club** (✉ Av. Senador Lemos 108, Umarizal ☎ 091/241–1330) techno is mixed with American and Brazilian pop and rock.

The Arts

For information about cultural events, contact the state-run **Secretaria de Cultura** (SECULT; ✉ Av. Governador Magalhães Barata 830, São Brás ☎ 091/219–1207), which prints a monthly listing of cultural events throughout the city.

Live music is played nightly at the **Estação das Docas** (✉ Boulevard Castilhos França s/n, Comercio ☎ 091/219–1207). Weekdays shows usually consist of acoustic singers/guitarists. On weekends rock, jazz, and MPB bands play on a suspended stage that moves back and forth on tracks about 8 meters (25 feet) above patrons of the microbrewery and surrounding restaurants. Outstanding theatrical productions in Portuguese are presented at the **Teatro Experimental Waldemar Henrique** (✉ Av. Presidente Vargas s/n, Praça da República, Campina ☎ 091/222–4762). **Teatro da Paz** (✉ Av. da Paz s/n, Praça da República, Campina ☎ 091/224–7355) often hosts plays, philharmonic concerts, and dance recitals.

Sports & the Outdoors

Belém's two *futebol* (soccer) teams are Payssandú and Remo—neither of which is currently in the premier league. Still, attending a Brazilian match, regardless of the quality of the team, is a memorable experience. For Remo games head to **Estádio Evandro Almeida** (✉ Av. Almirante Barroso s/n, Marco ☎ 091/223–2847). Payssandú plays at **Estádio Leônidas de Castro** (✉ Av. Almirante Barroso s/n, Marco ☎ 091/241–1726).

Shopping

Indigenous-style arts and crafts are popular souvenir items in Belém. Note that import regulations of Australia, Canada, New Zealand, the United Kingdom, and the United States strictly prohibit bringing endangered species (dead or alive) into those countries, and the fines can be hefty. Nonendangered wildlife and plant parts are also illegal to import, though there are some exceptions. Wooden and woven items, for example, are usually not a problem. Avoid headdresses and necklaces of macaw feathers and caiman teeth, and go for the marajoara pottery and the tropical fruit preserves (pack them carefully).

Areas & Malls

Belém's main shopping street is **Avenida Presidente Vargas,** particularly along the Praça da República. **Icoaraci,** a riverside town 18 km (11 mi) northeast of Belém, is a good place to buy marajoara pottery. There are many boutiques and specialty shops in the neighborhood of **Nazaré.** To shop in air-conditioning, head for the upscale **Shopping Center Iguatemi** (✉ Trv. Padre Eutíquio 1078, Batista Campos), a mall in the truest sense of the word.

Markets

Ver-O-Peso (✉ Av. Castilhos França s/n, Comércio) is one of the most popular markets in town. It sells fresh fruits, vegetables, fish, and meats. The city's largest concentration of vendors of medicinal plants and various concoctions is clustered under a canvas roof in the outdoor section. There are lots of hammocks for sale. **Praça da República** (✉ Bounded by Av. Presidente Vargas, Trv. Osvaldo Cruz, and Av. Assis de Vasconcelos) is busy only on weekends when *barracas* (small shops) pop up to sell electronic objects, paintings, snacks, artisanal items, and regional foods. A popular shopping district is **Comércio** (✉ From Av. President Vargas take Senador Manoel Barata toward Cidade Velha). The streets are lined with shops selling hardware, fishing supplies, televisions, hammocks, and much more.

Specialty Shops

Artesanato Paruara (✉ Rua Sezedelo Correo 15, Nazaré ☎ 091/248–4555) specializes in oils, stones, and other "mystical" items. **Casa das Ervas Medicinais** (✉ Rua 28 de Setembro 130 ☎ 091/3087–3519) has dozens of kinds of medicinal plants, tinctures, syrups, oils, and soaps. A great souvenir shop, **Canto do Uirapurú** (⊠ Av. President Vargas 594, Campina) is well-stocked with medicinal plant concoctions, T-shirts, hats, pottery, and more. **Casa Amazonia Artesanatos** (⊠ Av. President Vargas 512, Campina ☎ 091/225–0150), though small, is packed with natural soaps, regional fruit preserves, pottery, and wood carvings. A short walk from Av. President Vargas, **Loja Jaguar** (⊠ Sen. Manoel Barata 298, Comércio ☎ 224–9771) sells hammocks and *mosquiteiros* (mosquito nets). **Pólo Joalheiro** (⊠ Rua 16 de Novembro s/n, Jurunas ☉ Tues–Sat. 10–8) is a combination museum and high-priced jewelry and craft shops with Amazonian wares of gold, amethyst, and wood; pottery; and seeds and plant fibers. Museum admission is R$4; free on Tuesday.

Manaus

Manaus, the capital of Amazonas State, is a hilly city of around 1.5 million people that lies 1,602 km (993 mi) southwest of Belém. It was built on the banks of the Rio Negro 10 km (6 mi) upstream from its confluence with the Amazon. Founded in 1669, it took its name, which means "mother of the Gods," from the Manaó tribe. The city has long flirted with prosperity. Of all the Amazon cities and towns, Manaus is most identified with the rubber boom. In the late 19th and early 20th centuries it supplied 90% of the world's rubber. The industry was monopolized by rubber barons, whose number never exceeded 100 and who lived in the city, and spent enormous sums on ostentatious lifestyles. They dominated the region like feudal lords and recruited *seringueiros* (rubber tappers) from indigenous tribes and from Brazil's crowded and depressed northeast.

The 25-year rubber era was brought to a close thanks to Englishman Henry A. Wickham, who took 70,000 rubber-tree seeds out of Brazil in 1876. The seeds were planted in Kew Gardens in England. The few that germinated were transplanted to Malaysia, where they flourished. Within 30 years Malaysian rubber ended the Brazilian monopoly. Manaus entered a depression that lasted until 1967, when the downtown area was made a free-trade zone. The economy was revitalized, and its population jumped from 200,000 to 900,000 in less than 20 years. Then in the 1970s the industrial district was given exclusive free-trade-zone status to produce certain light-industry items. Companies moved in and began making motorcycles and electronic items. In the mid-1990s the commercial district lost its free-trade-zone status. Hundreds lost their jobs and businesses crumbled, but the light-industrial sector held strong and even grew. Today it employs 80,000, has the largest motorcycle factory in South America, and makes 90% of the TVs made in Brazil.

Manaus is the Amazon's most popular destination, largely because of the 19 jungle lodges in the surrounding area. The city's principal attractions are its lavish, brightly colored houses and civic buildings—vestiges of an opulent time when the wealthy sent their laundry to be done in Europe and sent for old-world artisans and engineers to build their New World monuments.

Exploring Manaus

Manaus is a sprawling city with few true high-rises. Although many hotels and sights are in the city center (Centro), it's neither large nor attractive, and it's congested. It is also exotic and hilly and is on the edge of a river one and a half times larger than the Mississippi.

Centro

Although Manaus is more spread out than Belém or Santarém, its downtown area has a lot going on. The floating docks are here, with tourist shops nearby. Open markets sell fish, meats, and all sorts of produce, while general stores ply machetes, hoes, hardtack, cassava flour, and boat motor parts to those pursuing a livelihood outside the city. Centro is also the most important historical section of the city. The Teatro Amazonas, the Customs House (Alfândega), and the Adolfo Lisboa Market are here, along with old churches, government buildings, and mansions. The result is a mix of neoclassic, Renaissance, colonial, and modern architecture.

WHAT TO SEE **Alfândega.** The Customs House was built by the British in 1902 with bricks imported as ship ballast. It stands alongside the floating dock that was built at the same time to accommodate the annual 12-meter (40-foot) rise and fall of the river. It's now home to the regional office of the Brazilian tax department, and the interior is of little interest. ⊠ *Rua Marquês de Santa Cruz s/n, Centro* ☎ *092/234–5481.*

Catedral da Nossa Senhora da Conceição. Built originally in 1695 by Carmelite missionaries, the Cathedral of Our Lady of the Immaculate Conception (also called Igreja Matriz) burned down in 1850 and was reconstructed in 1878. It's a simple, predominantly neoclassical structure with a bright, colorful interior. ⊠ *Praça da Matriz, Centro* ☎ *No phone* ☒ *Free* ☉ *Usually Mon.–Sat. 9–5, but hours vary.*

Hidroviária. Everyone traveling by boat from the floating docks must go through the Water Transportation Terminal. There is one area for regional travelers and another for international travelers; both have food shops. The international area has high-end gift shops. ⊠ *Rua Marques de Santa Cruz 25, Centro* ☎ *092/621–4301.*

Igreja São Sebastião. This neoclassical church (circa 1888), with its charcoal-gray color and medieval characteristics, seems foreboding. Its interior, however, is luminous and uplifting, with white Italian marble, stained-glass windows, and beautiful ceiling paintings. The church has a tower on only one side. No one is sure why this is so, but if you ask, you may get one of several explanations: the second tower wasn't built because of lack of funds; it was omitted as a symbolic gesture to the poor; or the ship with materials for its construction sank. As you stroll through the church plaza and the one in front of the Teatro Amazonas, note the black-and-white Portuguese granite patterns at your feet. They are said to represent Manaus's meeting of the waters. ⊠ *Praça São Sebastião, Centro* ☎ *No phone* ☒ *Free* ☉ *Usually Mon.–Sat. 9–5, but hours vary; call ahead.*

Mercado Adolfo Lisboa. Vendors sell Amazon food products and handicrafts at this market. Built in 1882, it is a wrought-iron replica of the original Parisian Les Halles (now destroyed); the ironwork is said to have been designed by Gustave Eiffel himself. ⊠ *Rua dos Barés 6, Centro* ☎ *092/234–8441* ⊗ *Daily dawn–noon.*

Museu do Índio. The Indian Museum is maintained by Salesian Sisters, an order of nuns with eight missions in the upper Amazon. It displays handicrafts, weapons, ceramics, ritual masks, and clothing from the region's tribes. ⊠ *Rua Duque de Caxias 356, Centro* ☎ *092/635–1922* ⊠ *R$5* ⊗ *Weekdays 8:30–noon and 2–5, Sat. 8:30–noon.*

Palácio Rio Negro. The extravagant Rio Negro Palace was built at the end of the 19th century as the home of a German rubber baron. Later it was used as the official governor's residence. Today it houses some of the city's finest art exhibits and a cultural center. The Museu da Imagem e do Som, on the same property, has three daily screenings of art films and documentaries Tuesday through Friday and four screenings daily on weekends. ⊠ *Av. 7 de Setembro 1546, Centro* ☎ *092/633–2850* ⊠ *Free* ⊗ *Tues.–Sun. 3–9.*

Fodor'sChoice **Teatro Amazonas.** The city's lavish opera house was completed in 1896
★ after 15 years. Its Italian Renaissance–style interior provides a clear idea of the wealth that marked the Amazon rubber boom. It has marble doorways, crystal chandeliers, handblown glass sconces from Italy, English wrought-iron banisters, and panels of French tiles. Italian frescoes depict Amazon legends. Operas and other events are presented regularly. Monday-evening performances are free and usually feature local artists of various musical genres. The Amazonas Philharmonic Orchestra plays Friday night and can be seen and heard practicing in the theater weekdays 9–2. A variety of foreign entertainers, from José Carreras to the Spice Girls, have performed here. Half-hour tours are conducted daily 9–4. ⊠ *Praça São Sebastião s/n, Centro* ☎ *092/622–2420* ⊕ *www.teatroamazonas. com.br* ⊠ *R$5* ⊗ *Mon.–Sat. 9–4.*

Usina Chaminé. Transformed from a sewage treatment plant that never functioned, this art gallery displays exhibits and holds dance and theatre performances. Its neo-Renaissance style with hardwood floors and massive wood beams is another reason to visit. ⊠ *Av. Lourenço da Silva Braga, Centro* ☎ *092/633–3026* ⊠ *Free* ⊗ *Tues.–Fri. 10–5, weekends 4–8.*

Where to Eat

¢–$$$ ✕ **Suzuran.** For more than 20 years this festive restaurant has served the town's best Japanese food. If you can't decide between raw fish and fried favorites, don't. The *suzuran teishoku* platter has sushi, sashimi, shrimp and vegetable tempura, and grilled fish. ⊠ *Rua Teresina 155, Adrianópolis* ☎ *092/633–3570* ☐ *AE, DC, MC, V.*

$ ✕ **Canto da Peixada.** When Pope John Paul II came to Manaus in 1981,
Fodor'sChoice this restaurant was chosen to host him. The dining areas aren't elegant,
★ but the fish dishes are outstanding, and there are 43 types of salad. One platter feeds two. ⊠ *Rua Emilio Moreira 1677, Praça 14* ☎ *092/234– 1066* ☐ *V* ⊗ *No dinner Sun.*

★ $ ✕ **Churrascaria Búfalo.** Twelve waiters, each offering a different cut of chicken, beef, or goat, scurry around this large, crowded restaurant. As if the delectable meats weren't enough, the table is also set with side dishes, including manioc root, pickled vegetables, and caramelized bananas. ⊠ *Rua Joaquim Nabuco 628-A, Centro* ☎ *092/633–3773* ⊕ *www. churrascariabufalo.com.br* ☰ *AE, DC, MC, V.*

$ ✕ **Moronguêtá.** Why not dine on deliciously prepared river fish while looking out over the meeting of the waters? The *costela de tambaqui no molho de camaráo* (tambaqui ribs in tomato-shrimp sauce) is amazing. It's only 15 minutes by taxi from downtown. ⊠ *Rua Jaith Chaves 30, Vila da Felicidede* ☎ *092/615–3362* ☰ *V.*

¢–$ ✕ **Fiorentina.** The green awning and red-and-white-check tablecloths are hints that this restaurant serves authentic Italian cuisine. Pasta dishes are delicious, especially the lasagna *fiorentina* (with a marinara and ground-beef sauce). ⊠ *Praça da Polícia 44, Centro* ☎ *092/215–2233* ☰ *AE, DC, MC, V.*

Where to Stay

Although there are several decent in-town hotels, the jungle lodges outside town offer far more opportunity for adventure. Whether you choose a treetop lodge, a floating barge, or a cabana on a scenic lake, they usually have guides and exciting activities. Most offer swimming, nature walks, caiman "hunts" (the animals are blinded with flashlights, photographed, and released), piranha fishing, and canoe trips. Many lodges are near the Rio Negro, where mosquitoes are less of a problem because they can't breed in acidic black water. Unless otherwise noted, prices are for two-day, one-night packages, which generally include transport to and from the lodge, meals (not drinks), and a variety of activities that depend on the length of your stay.

Hotels

$$$ 🏨 **Hotel Tropical.** Nothing in the Amazon can match the majesty of this resort hotel. It's 20 km (12 mi) northwest of downtown and overlooks the Rio Negro, with a short path to the beach. In addition to the zoo, sports facilities, and two gorgeous pools, the Tropical has its own dock. The location is remote, far from Centro. The Tarumã restaurant is a reliable choice for dinners of regional and international fare. ⊠ *Av. Coronel Teixeira 1320, Ponta Negra 69029-120* ☎ *092/659–5000* 🖷 *092/658–5026* ↩ *588 rooms, 8 suites* ♦ *2 restaurants, coffee shop, in-room safes, 4 tennis courts, 2 pools, gym, sauna, beach, dock, boating, basketball, bar, dance club, recreation room, shops, helipad, travel services* ☰ *AE, DC, MC, V.*

$ 🏨 **Taj Mahal.** Much of the charming East Indian artwork of the original hotel disappeared in the last renovation, although you can still see some in the lobby. Although the Taj Mahal is now more standardized, it's still a pleasant option, with a rooftop pool, a revolving restaurant, and a convenient location. Request a room with a river view. ⊠ *Av. Getúlio Vargas 741, Centro 69020-020* ☎ *092/627–3737* ↩ *144 rooms, 26 suites* ♦ *Restaurant, pool, hair salon, massage, sauna, bar, meeting room* ☰ *AE, DC, MC, V.*

$ 🏨 **St. Paul.** If you're planning an extended stay, this apartment hotel in Centro is your best bet. Accommodations are immaculate and have living rooms and fully equipped modern kitchens. For stays of more than a week you may get a discount. ⊠ *Av. Ramos Ferreira 1115, Centro 69010-120* ☎ *092/622-2131* 🖷 *092/622-2137* 📞 *45 apartments* ♦ *Kitchenettes, pool, gym, sauna* ⊟ *AE, DC, MC, V.*

¢–$ 🎦 **Lider Hotel.** Although far from luxurious, this hotel is clean, comfortable, and conveniently located in Centro. It's a good base from which to branch out on city tours. ⊠ *Av. 7 de Setembro 827, Centro 69005-140* ☎ *092/621–9700* 📞 *60 rooms* ♦ *Restaurant, bar* ⊟ *AE, DC, MC, V.*

¢ 🎦 **Manaós.** Across from Teatro Amazonas and just up the street from the busy part of downtown, this hotel is in a great spot. Rooms are small but are clean and have nice woodwork. The hotel staff is warm and friendly. ⊠ *Av. Eduardo Ribeiro 881, Centro* ☎ *092/633–5744* 🖷 *092/232–4443* ✉ *manaos@argo.com.br* 📞 *39 rooms* ♦ *Restaurant, bar, Internet* ⊟ *AE, DC, MC, V.*

¢ 🎦 **Central.** In the free-trade zone, this hotel is a good option if you're on a tight budget. Rooms are simple and clean, with standard amenities. ⊠ *Rua Dr. Moreira 202, Centro 69005-250* ☎ *092/622-2600* 🖷 *092/622-2609* 📞 *50 rooms* ♦ *Minibars* ⊟ *AE, DC, MC, V.*

Jungle Lodges

$$$$ 🎦 **Acajatuba Jungle Lodge.** You forget that the city is a mere four hours away at this thatch-hut lodge on Acajatuba Lake. Twenty individual screened cabins are elevated 1 meter (3 feet) aboveground and connected to the rest of the lodge by walkways. Lighting is provided by 12-volt batteries and kerosene lamps (generators would keep wildlife away), and there is no hot water, but what it lacks in luxury, it more than makes up for by putting you in the middle of the tropical forest. The boat leaves from the CEASA port near the Meeting of the Waters. ⊠ *60 km (35 mi) west of Manaus, via boat along Rio Negro* ✪ *Contact: Anaconda Turismo, Rua Lima Bacuri 345, Manaus 69005-220* ☎ *092/233–7642* 📞 *40 rooms* ♦ *Bar; no a/c, no room TVs, no room phones* ⊟ *MC* ⊗ *FAP.*

$$$$ 🎦 **Amazon Lodge.** Nearly four hours by boat from Manaus, this lodge consists of rustic floating cabins with air-conditioning and baths. Because of its remote location, there is an excellent chance of spotting monkeys and birds. The English-speaking guides are knowledgeable and friendly. The minimum stay is two nights. Boats leave from the CEASA port near the Meeting of the Waters. ⊠ *Lago Juma, 74 km (50 mi) south of Manaus* ✪ *Heliconia Amazônia Turismo Ltda. Rua José Clemente 500, Room 214 Manaus 69010-070* ☎ *092/234–5915* 🖷 *092/633–7094* 📞 *14 rooms* ♦ *Restaurant, fishing, hiking* ⊟ *No credit cards* ⊗ *FAP.*

★ $$$$ 🎦 **Ariaú Amazon Towers.** Undoubtedly the most famous of the Amazon jungle lodges, Ariaú is composed of four-story wooden towers on stilts and linked by catwalks. The effect is more dramatic in the rainy season, when the river floods the ground below. Although the idea is to make you feel integrated with nature, the size of this complex generally prevents much of a sense of this, or much contact with wildlife for that matter. The exceptions are brightly colored macaws and adorable semiwild monkeys that visit and make mischief. The lodge serves excellent food, though of limited variety, and has small comfortable rooms. Its most popular accommodation, sought by honeymooners and celebrities, is the Tarzan House, 30 meters (100 feet) up in the treetops. It can be had for R$2,300 above the price of any package. The lodge is two hours from Manaus. Boats depart near the Hotel Tropical. ✉ *Rio Ariaú, 60 km (40 mi) northwest of Manaus,* ✆ *Rua Silva Ramos 41, Manaus 69010-180* ☎ *092/622–5000* 🖷 *092/233–5615* 🛏 *291 rooms, 19 suites* ⚓ *2 restaurants, 5 pools, dock, fishing, hiking, 4 bars, shops, helipad, auditorium, Internet; no room TVs* ⊟ *AE, DC, MC, V* ⚓¶ *FAP.*

$$ 🏨 **Jungle Palace.** It's quite a sight to cruise down the Rio Negro and see the neoclassical columns of this "flotel" looming on the horizon. Built on a steel barge, this lodge combines remote location and luxury. Explore the region by day, and at night return to your air-conditioned cabin for a hot shower or to take a stroll on the observation deck. Catch your boat at the Hotel Tropical. ✉ *35 km (20 mi) west of Manaus via boat along Rio Negro* ✆ *Rua Saldanha Marinho 700, Manaus* ☎ *092/633–6200* 🛏 *42 rooms* ⚓ *Restaurant, cable TV, pool, health club, bar, meeting room* ⊟ *AE, MC, V* ⚓¶ *FAP.*

$$ 🏨 **Lago Salvador.** Although it's only a 45-minute boat ride from Man-

Fodor'sChoice
★ aus and a 15-minute ride from the Hotel Tropical, this lodge feels secluded. Four cabanas with three apartments each are on the shore of the lake from which the lodge takes its name. During the high-water season the lake flows over its shores to join the Rio Negro. Rooms are simple and comfortable, with running water. All of the small cabins have trails leading to them, but your guide will probably use the most direct route—paddling a canoe across the lake—to get you there. Boats leave from the Hotel Tropical. ✉ *15 km (10 mi) northwest of Manaus* ✆ *Amazônia Expeditions, Hotel Tropical, Av. Coronel Teixeira 1320, Manaus 69029-120* ☎ *092/659–5119* 🖷 *092/658–4221* 🛏 *12 cabins* ⚓ *Restaurant, room service, fans, boating, hiking* ⊟ *V* ⚓¶ *FAP.*

Nightlife & the Arts

Pick up a copy of *Manaus Em Tempo* at any newsstand for event listings in Portuguese.

Nightlife

Boi bumbá (ox legend) music and dance—native to the central Amazon region—tells stories with tightly choreographed steps and strong rhythms. The amphitheater at Praia da Ponta Negra holds regular boi-bumbá performances. **Alegro** (✉ Av. Djalma B 483 ☎ 092/216–5099), open every night, is a nightclub and restaurant with a varied Italian-heavy menu. The club plays MPB, rock, and *sertanejo* (country music from Ceará). For a traditional boi-bumbá experience in a nightclub environment, head to **Boiart's** (✉ Rua José Clemente 500, Centro ☎ 092/637–6807), which is just across from the Teatro Amazonas. **Coração Blue** (✉ Estrada da Ponta Negra 3701, Km 6 ☎ 092/658–4057) is an outdoor bar that has techno, *axé* (a Bahian rhythm), boi-bumbá, and dance music. Weeknights it's often the busiest place in town. A popular but somewhat highbrow dance club is the Hotel Tropical's **Studio Tropical**

(✉ Av. Coronel Teixeira 1320, Ponta Negra ☎ 092/659–5000), which plays high-energy dance music for a well-dressed clientele. It's open Thursday–Saturday.

The Arts

Teatro Amazonas (✉ Praça São Sebastião s/n, Centro ☎ 092/622–2420) draws some of the biggest names in theater, opera, and classical music. Monday-evening performances are free. The Amazonas Philharmonic Orchestra plays every Friday night.

Sports & the Outdoors

Jet Skiing

Clube do Jet (✉ Rua Praiana 13, access through Av. do Turismo, Ponta Negra ☎ 092/657–5435) rents equipment for about R$100 an hour on the Rio Negro.

Jungle & River Excursions

Though Belém and other communities are great places for jungle and river excursions, they don't have nearly the selection or number of visitors that Manaus has. The most common excursion is a half- or full-day tourist-boat trip that travels 15 km (9 mi) east of Manaus to the point where the coffee-color water of the Rio Negro flows beside and gradually joins the coffee-with-cream-color water of the Rio Solimões. According to Brazilians, this is where the Amazon River begins. The waters flow alongside one another for 6 km (4 mi) before merging. Many of these meeting-of-the-waters treks include motorboat side trips along narrow streams or through bayous. Some also stop at the Parque Ecológico do Janauary, where you can see birds and a lake filled with the world's largest water lily, the *vitória régia*.

Nighttime boat trips into the forest explore flooded woodlands and narrow waterways. Some stop for trail hikes. Some companies take you by canoe on a caiman "hunt," where caimans are caught and released. Trips to the Rio Negro's upper reaches, where wildlife is a little wilder, are also offered. Such trips usually stop at river settlements to visit with local families. They may include jungle treks, fishing (they supply the gear and boat), and a trip to Anavilhanas, the world's largest freshwater archipelago. It contains some 400 islands with amazing Amazon flora, birds, and monkeys. To arrange any of these excursions, contact an area tour operator.

Soccer

Manaus's professional soccer teams, Rio Negro and Nacional, play at **Estádio Vivaldo Lima** (✉ Av. Constantino Nery, Flores ☎ 092/236–3219). A taxi ride to the stadium and a ticket should each cost about R$20.

Shopping

Here, as in other parts of the Amazon, you can find lovely indigenous artisanal items made from animal parts. Macaws, for example, are killed in the wild for feathers to make souvenir items for tourists. As a result, there are no longer many macaws in the forests close to Manaus. Traveling home with items made from animal parts, certain types of wood, or plant fibers can result in big fines and even jail time, so beware.

Areas & Malls

The largest, most upscale mall is **Amazonas Shopping** (⊠ Av. Djarma Batista 482, Parque 10 ☎ 092/642–3555), with 300 stores with 38 restaurants. **Studio 5 Festival Mall** (⊠ Av. Rodrigo Octavio 2555, Vila da Felicidade ☎ 092/3048–7048) is a large mall.

Specialty Stores

Ecoshop (⊠ Centro ☎ 092/232–0409), in the Hidroviária International Terminal, sells regional art and a variety of indigenous crafts. **Museu do Índio** (⊠ Rua Duque de Caxias 296, Centro ☎ 092/635–7922) has a gift shop that sells traditional crafts such as necklaces made from seeds and feathers and baskets.One of the best places to buy all kinds of things, from fresh fish to hammocks and souvenirs, is **Mercado Adolfo Lisboa** (⊠ Rua Dos Barés 46, Centro), down along the water.

The Amazon A to Z

AIR TRAVEL

BELÉM   All flights are served by Aeroporto Internacional Val-de-Cans, which is 11 km (7 mi) northwest of the city. Varig sometimes offers direct flights to Miami. Carriers that fly regularly to Rio, São Paulo, Brasília, and Manaus include TAM, Gol, VASP, Tavaj, and Varig. These carriers also have regular flights to Santarém, Macapá, and Marabá. Regional flights to smaller airports are offered by Penta and Meta.

The easiest route from the airport is south on Avenida Julio Cesár and then west on Avenida Almirante Barroso. The 20-minute taxi ride costs around R$25. There are also buses. Look for those labeled MAREX/PRES. VARGAS, for the Hilton and other hotels; MAREX/PRAÇA KENNEDY, for Paratur and the docks; or MAREX/VER-O-PESO, for Cidade Velha.

MANAUS   The international Aeroporto Brigadeiro Eduardo Gomes is 17 km (10 mi) south of downtown. Varig has a weekly direct flight to Miami. Most flights connect in São Paulo, where you can fly direct to Miami, New York, L.A., and Houston. VASP, Varig, TAM, and Tavaj have regular flights to and from Santarém, Belém, Brasília, Rio, and São Paulo. Tavaj and Rico also fly to smaller towns like Tabatinga, Parintins, and Tefé. The trip to Centro from the airport takes 20 minutes and costs R$30–R$45 by taxi. A trip on one of the city buses, which depart regularly during the day and early evening, costs R$1.50. ⇨ For airline information, *see* Air Travel *in* Brazil A to Z.

🛪 Airport Information **Aeroporto Brigadeiro Eduardo Gomes** ⊠ Av. Santos Dumont s/n, Manaus ☎ 092/652-1210. **Aeroporto Internacional Val-de-Cans** ⊠ Av. Julio Cesár s/n, Belém ☎ 091/210-6400.

BOAT & FERRY TRAVEL

BELÉM   Most ships arrive and depart in the general dock area on the edge of downtown called the Escadinha. MACAMAZON ships and standard riverboats head to Santarém and Manaus from nearby Cais do Porto.

The tourist-boat terminal, 20 minutes south of town on Avenida Alcindo Cacela (Praça Princesa Isabel), is where many excursions start.

MANAUS   If you're looking for a boat to another town, a lodge, or a beach, visit the Hidroviária Regional Terminal. At the ticket or tourist information booths you can get information about prices and departure times and days to all the locations. You can also walk down to Porto Flutuante via the bridge behind the terminal to take a look at the regional boats. Their destinations and departure times are listed on plaques. To reach most Manaus-area beaches, catch a boat from Porto Flutuante. Sunday is the only day with regularly scheduled trips; boats transport great crowds for about R$8 per person. You can hire small craft to the beaches and other attractions, such as the meeting of the waters. Look for people wearing the green vests of the Associação dos Canoeiros Motorizados de Manaus near the Porto Flutuante or in the Escadinha area closer to the market in Belém. They can set you up with local boat trips at reasonable prices. You can also make arrangements through tour operators.

7 Boat & Ferry Information **Macamazon** ☎ 091/222-5604.

BUS TRAVEL

BELÉM   The bus station in Belém, Rodoviário São Brás, is east of Nazaré. Reservations for buses are rarely needed. Boa Esperança makes the 209-km (125-mi) journey to Salinas Beach every couple of hours daily. Beira-Dão leaves every half hour on the 60-km (36-mi), two-hour, R$8 journey to Ilha Mosqueiro. Clearly marked buses to Outeiro Beach and the town of Icoaraci pass the bus station regularly and cost about R$1. Belém's local bus service is safe and comprehensive, but a little confusing. Ask a resident for guidance. You board buses at the rear, pay an attendant, and pass through a turnstile. Keep an eye on your belongings.

MANAUS   The bus station in Manaus, Terminal Rodoviário Huascar Angelim, is 7 km (4 mi) north of the city center. The city bus system is extensive and easy to use. The fare is about R$1.50. Most of the useful buses run along Avenida Floriano Peixoto, including Bus 120, which goes to Ponta Negra and stops near the Hotel Tropical. The Fontur bus, which costs about R$12, travels between Centro and the Tropical several times a day. To get to Presidente Figueiredo, take the bus labeled ARUANÃ, which runs regularly from the terminal and costs around R$15.

7 Bus Information **Beira-Dão** ☎ 091/226-1162. **Boa Esperança** ☎ 091/266-0033. **Rodoviário São Brás** ⊠ Av. Almirante Barroso s/n, São Brás, Belém. **Terminal Rodoviário Huascar Angelim** ⊠ Rua Recife 2784, Flores, Manaus ☎ 092/642-5805.

CAR RENTAL

In Belém rental cars cost between R$91 and R$162 a day. Several companies have offices at the airport and in town. You can rent a car at the Manaus airport through Unidas Rent a Car.

7 Local Agencies **Bill Car** ⊠ Av. Mendoço Furtado Santarém ☎ 093/522-1705 **Locvel** ⊠ Av. Fab 2093, Macapá ☎ 096/223-7999. **Norauto** ⊠ Av. Gentil Bittencourt 2086, Nazaré, Belém ☎ 091/249-4900. **Unidas Rent a Car** ⊠ Aeroporto Brigadeiro Eduardo Gomes, Av. Santos Dumont s/n, Manaus ☎ 092/621-1575.

CAR TRAVEL

The BR 316 begins on the outskirts of Belém and runs eastward toward the coast and then south, connecting the city with Brazil's major northeastern hubs. From Manaus BR 174 runs north to Boa Vista, and BR 319 travels south to Porto Velho, which is south of Manaus in Rondônia State. To get to BR 319, you have to take a ferry across the Amazon. You can go about 100 km (63 mi) on paved road. Then it turns to dirt or mud. Even if you're after adventure, don't think about driving to Porto Velho. A four-wheel-drive vehicle takes you farther than 100 km (62 mi) but won't get you across the rivers and lakes that take over the road farther south.

Although Belém has the most traffic of any Amazon city and what seems like more than its fair share of one-way streets, in-town driving is relatively easy. Parking is only tricky in a few areas, such as Avenida Presidente Vargas and the Escadinha. Traffic and parking problems don't exist in the region between Belém and Manaus. Manaus has its share but is calmer than Belém.

EMERGENCIES

🛈 Emergency Contacts **Ambulance** ☎ 192 in Belém, 192 in Manaus. **Fire** ☎ 193 in Belém, 092/611–5040 in Manaus. **Police** ☎ 190 in Belém, 190 in Manaus.

🛈 Hospitals **Hospital e Maternidade Dom Luiz I** ✉ Av. Generalíssimo Deodoro 868, Umarizal, Belém ☎ 091/241–4144. **Hospital e Pronto Socorro Municipal 28 de Agosto** ✉ Rua Recife s/n, Adrianópolis, Manaus ☎ 092/236–0326.

🛈 24-Hour Pharmacies **Big Ben** ✉ Av. Gentil Bittencourt 1548, Nazaré, Belém ☎ 091/241–3000. **Drogaria 24h** ✉ Boulevard Álvaro Maio 744, Centro, Manaus ☎ 092/633–6040.

HEALTH

Several months before you go to the Amazon, visit a tropical medicine specialist to find out what vaccinations you need. Describe your planned adventure, and get tips on how to prepare. Read about tropical diseases in the Amazon so you know the symptoms and how to treat them should you fall ill.

In a remote area the likeliest health issues are infection and dehydration. Infections are common from insect bites and cuts. Treat them quickly, so they don't worsen. Dehydration can result from gastrointestinal problems or inadequate water. Be sure to keep yourself hydrated with clean water, and learn what to do about gastrointestinal issues. Schistosomiasis, a water-borne parasite, is rarely a problem in the Amazon. However, rabies, Chagas' disease, malaria, and dengue fever are problematic.

Safety issues can quickly become health issues. Tropical forests are home to lots of ants, bees, spiders, scorpions, centipedes, and caterpillars, many of which bite or sting. Their unpleasant attacks largely can be avoided by wearing protective clothing and by not playing with them. If you are allergic to bites and stings, you should carry an adrenaline kit. Remember to check your shoes in the morning for small guests. Many plants have spines and thorns that may also result in wounds, so beware of where you place your hands and feet. Mosquitoes and gnats are abundant in some places. Only stronger versions of repellents with

DEET (N,N-diethyl-m-toluamide) keep them away. A *mosquiteiro* (netting for hammock or bed) helps tremendously at night. Most lodges and hotels in mosquito-heavy areas provide these for guests. Ticks live in forests, too. If you find one on you, remove it and treat the site with disinfectant. Chiggers inhabit grassy areas and are nearly invisible. Repellent sprayed on shoes, socks, and pants helps, as does powdered sulfur. Anti-itch cream helps you sleep at night.

Other safety issues include water and larger creatures. Though you can swim in many places, get local information beforehand. Is the water too shallow to jump or dive? Are there rocks or dead trees just under the surface? Piranhas are rarely a problem, except as supporting actors in B movies, but ask your neighbors first. Freshwater stingrays are another potential peril. They hide in shallow water, and they're difficult to see, but if you step on one, you'll feel it. A sting from its barbed tail can be excruciating and long in healing. This bad memory can usually be avoided by dragging your feet as you move slowly through shallow areas or by heading directly to deeper water, where the rays can avoid you. Another unlikely though possible encounter is with venomous snakes. Bushmasters, fer-de-lance relatives, and several others are present though rarely seen. Shoes or boots and long pants are excellent preventive measures. Also, watch closely where you step, especially if you venture off a trail.

Throughout the region, avoid drinking tap water and using ice made from it. In the cities most restaurants buy ice made from purified water. Bottled water is generally easy to find. Beware of where you eat. Many of the street-side stands are not very clean. Over-the-counter remedies can ease some discomfort. For loose bowels, Floratil can be purchased without a doctor's prescription. Estomazil and Sorrisal are two remedies for upset stomach. They may contain aspirin. For more information on health *see* Health *in* Smart Travel Tips A to Z.

MAIL, INTERNET & SHIPPING

In Belém, NetG@mes Cyber Café provides Internet service for R$3 an hour and is open Monday–Saturday 8 AM–11 PM. Telemar, the phone company, offers Internet access for R$6 per hour. The central branch of the Belém post office is open weekdays 8–noon and 2–5. You can send faxes, and, as in all Brazilian post offices, SEDEX international courier service is available. In Manaus, Internext has 14 computers and charges R$3 per hour for Internet access. The most central Manaus post office is open weekdays 9–5 and on Saturday 9–1. Cybercity charges R$6 per hour for Internet access.

🖪 Internet Centers **Cybercity** ⊠ Av. Getúlio Vargas 188, Centro, Manaus ☎ 092/234-8930. **Internext** ⊠ Av. Eduardo Ribeiro, Rio Negro Center 220, 2nd fl., Centro, Manaus ☎ 092/633-4409. **NetG@mes Cyber Café** ⊠ Av. Nazaré 947, Loja 7, Nazaré, Belém ☎ 091/224-3344.

🖪 Post Offices **Belém post office** ⊠ Av. Presidente Vargas 498, Campina ☎ 091/212-1155. **Manaus post office** ⊠ Rua Marechal Deodoro 117, Centro ☎ 092/622-2181.

MONEY MATTERS

In Belém the airport branch of the Banco do Brasil charges a hefty commission to cash traveler's checks. In town Banco Amazônia has the best rates; it's open weekdays 10–4. Casa Francesa Câmbio e Turismo is one of several exchange houses that offer comparable rates. ATMs are available at most bank branches in major cities. In smaller towns neither ATMs nor change are easy to come by: bring cash and lots of small bills. At the airport in Manaus you can exchange money at Banco do Brasil and Banco Real. In town Cortez Câmbio has the best rates.

🏦 Banks & Exchange Services **Banco Amazônia** ⊠ Av. Presidente Vargas 800, Comércio, Belém ☎ 091/216-3252. **Casa Francesa Câmbio e Turismo** ⊠ Trv. Padre Prudêncio 40, Batista Campos, Belém ☎ 091/241-2716. **Cortez Câmbio** ⊠ Av. 7 de Setembro 1199, Centro, Manaus ☎ 092/622-4222.

SAFETY
In Belém watch out for pickpockets everywhere, but especially at Ver-O-Peso, on Avenida President Vargas, and in Comércio. Avoid walking alone at night or on poorly lighted streets, and don't wear jewelry, especially gold. Manaus has similar crime problems; beware in Centro near the docks. Smaller towns tend to be safer, though not all are. Ask locals or tour office personnel for more information.

TELEPHONES
Throughout the region there are card-operated public phones. Cards are sold in newsstands and often in restaurants. The area code for Belém is 091 and in Manaus it's 092. You can make long-distance calls at Telemar. Hours vary depending on the city, but mostly they're open daily from 8 AM to 9 PM.

🏦 **Telamazon** ⊠ Av. Getúlio Vargas 950, Centro, Manaus ☎ 092/621-6339. **Telepará** ⊠ Av. Presidente Vargas 610, Campina, Belém;.

TAXIS
There are plenty of taxis in Amazon cities, and they're easy to flag down. All have meters, and tips aren't necessary. At odd hours call the taxi company. You can find them listed in the yellow pages, or call one of the companies below. Smaller towns also have mototaxis. They are much cheaper but only carry one passenger.

🏦 Taxi Companies **Coopertaxi** ☎ 091/257-1041 or 091/257-1720 in Belém. **Taxi Nazaré** ☎ 091/242-7867 in Belém. **Tucuxi** ☎ 092/800-5050 or 092/622-4040 in Manaus.

TOURS
Tours vary considerably in price and quality and are from one day to three weeks in length. The majority are ecotours, fishing tours, cultural tours, and city tours, or a mixture of these. Some companies have longer educational tours, and trekking and camping trips.

For excursions in Belém as well as help with plane and hotel reservations, contact Angel Turismo in the Hilton Hotel. Valeverde Turismo has a tour boat and office at the Estação das Docas. Amazon Star can do just about everything. In Manaus, Amazônia Expeditions can book stays at jungle lodges, tours to the meeting of the waters, and piranha fishing. They also have a floatplane, with half-hour flights starting at R$250. Fontur arranges boat and city tours. Another operator, Tarumã, can help with hotel arrangements and transportation in the city or on the river. For information about fishing trips in Pará State, contact the Secretaria de Estado de Ciência, Tecnologia e Meio Ambiente (SECTAM).

🖪 Tour Information **SECTAM** ⊠ Trv. Lomas Valentinas 2717, Marco ☎ 091/266-5000.
🖪 Tour-Operator Recommendations **Amapá Tours** ⊠ Hotel Macapá, Av. Azarias Neto 17, Macapá ☎ 096/223-2553. **Amazon Explorers** ⊠ Rua Nhamundá 21, Centro, Manaus ☎ 092/633-1978. **Amazon Star Tours** ⊠ Rua Henrique Gurjão 236, Campina, Belém ☎ 091/212-6244. **Amazônia Expeditions** ⊠ Hotel Tropical, Av. Coronel Teixeira 1320, Ponta Negra, Manaus ☎ 092/658-4221. **Angel Turismo** ⊠ Hilton International Belém, Av. Presidente Vargas 882, Praça da República, Campina, Belém ☎ 091/224-2111. **Fontenele** ⊠ Av. Assis de Vasconcelos 199, Reduto, Belém ☎ 091/241-3218. **Fontur** ⊠ Hotel Tropical, Av. Coronel Teixeira 1320, Ponta Negra, Manaus ☎ 092/658-3052. **Lusotur** ⊠ Av. Brás de Aguiar 471, Nazaré, Belém ☎ 091/241-1011. **Tarumã** ⊠ Av. Eduardo Ribeiro 620, Centro, Manaus ☎ 092/648-8347. **Valeverde Turismo** ⊠ Boulevard Castilhos França s/n, Campina, Belém ☎ 091/212-3388.

ECOTOURS Heliconia Amazônia Turismo Ltda., across the street from the Teatro Amazonas, can help any size group set up a tour of the Amazon region. Swallows and Amazons has an excellent reputation.

🖪 Ecotour Operator Recommendations **Heliconia Amazônia Turismo Ltda.** ⊠ Rua José Clemente 500, Room 214, Centro, Manaus ☎ 092/234-5915 🖷 092/633-7094 ⊕ www.heliconia-amazon.com. **Swallows and Amazons** ⊠ Rua Quintino Bocaiuva 189, Manaus ☎🖷 092/622-1246 ⊕ www.swallowsandamazonstours.com.

FISHING TOURS Santana in Manaus has well-run peacock bass (*tucunaré*) sportfishing tours that are popular with North Americans. Augusto Albuquerque runs a small operation setting up fishing tours for small groups to out-of-the-way places.

🖪 Fishing Tour Operator Recommendations **Augusto Albuquerque** ⊠ Rua Cândidi Mariano 61, Centro, Manaus ☎ 092/232-1346. **Santana** ⊠ Rua dos Andrades 106, Centro, Manaus ☎ 092/234-9814 🖷 092/233-7127 ⊕ www.santanaecologica.com.br.

VISITOR INFORMATION

Belemtur, the city tourist board, is open weekdays 8–noon and 2–6. Pará State's tourist board, Paratur, is open weekdays 8–6. Both agencies are well organized and extremely helpful. Amazonas State's tourism authority, the Secretaria de Estado da Cultura e Turismo, is open weekdays 8–6. The Manaus tourism authority, Manaustur, is open weekdays 8–2.

🖪 Tourist Information **Belemtur** ⊠ Av. Governador José Malcher 592, Nazaré, Belém ☎ 091/242-0900 or 091/242-0033. **Manaustur** ⊠ Av. 7 de Setembro 157, Centro, Manaus ☎ 092/622-4986 or 092/622-4886. **Paratur** ⊠ Praça Maestro Waldemar Henrique s/n, Reduto, Belém ☎ 091/223-6198 or 091/212-0669 ⊕ www.paratur.pa.gov.br. **Secretaria de Estado da Cultura e Turismo** ⊠ Av. 7 de Setembro 1546, Centro, Manaus ☎ 092/232-5550 ⊕ www.visitamazonas.com.br

BRAZIL A TO Z

To research prices, get advice from other travelers, and book travel arrangements, visit www.fodors.com.

AIR TRAVEL

Miami, Newark, New York, and Toronto are the major gateways for flights to Brazil from North America. Several airlines fly directly from

London, but there's no direct service from Australia or New Zealand. At this writing, all flights to Brazil from North America and the United Kingdom connect through São Paulo.

There's regular jet service within the country between all major cities and most medium-size cities. Remote areas are also accessible—as long as you don't mind small planes. Flights can be long, lasting several hours for trips to the Amazon, with stops en route. The most widely used service is the Varig Ponte Aérea (Air Bridge), the Rio–São Paulo shuttle, which departs every half hour from 6 AM to 10:30 PM (service switches to every 15 minutes during morning and evening rush hours). Plane tickets (one-way) for the Rio–São Paulo shuttle service cost R$50–R$190 ($18–$68); reservations aren't necessary.

CARRIERS Varig, Brazil's largest airline, flies nonstop from New York, Los Angeles, Miami, and London to São Paulo. Varig also has nonstop service to Manaus from Miami. TAM, another Brazil-based international carrier, flies nonstop from Miami to São Paulo, with continuing service to Rio and connections to other cities. TAM also offers nonstop service between Miami and Manaus.

American Airlines has an agreement with TAM that allows passengers to accumulate AA miles and awards on TAM flights. United Airlines has a similar agreement with Varig. Continental Airlines flies nonstop from Newark to São Paulo. Delta offers nonstop service from Atlanta to São Paulo. Air Canada, another Varig partner, has nonstop service between Toronto and São Paulo.

British Airways has nonstop service from London to Rio and São Paulo. Continental flies from London to Newark and Houston, with connecting flights to Rio and São Paulo.

From Sydney, Australia, you can fly to Los Angeles, then continue to Brazil on Varig. Another option is to fly Qantas to Buenos Aires, where you connect to Varig and fly on to São Paulo, Rio, Porto Alegre, Florianópolis, Salvador, or Brasília. Air New Zealand offers flights to major Brazilian cities through its partnership with Varig.

Gol is a low-cost airline whose tickets can only be purchased in person and in cash (unless you have a Brazilian credit card).

▇ To & From Brazil **Aerolíneas Argentinas** ☎ 021/3398-3520 or 021/2292-4131 in Rio, 011/6445-3806 in São Paulo ⊕ www.aeroargentinas.com. **Air Canada** ☎ 888/247-2262 in North America, 021/2220-5354 or 0800/127-590 in Rio, 011/3259-9066 in São Paulo. **Air France** ☎ 011/3049-0909 in São Paulo ⊕ www.airfrance.com. **Air New Zealand** ☎ 13-24-76 in Australia, 0800/737-000 in New Zealand. **American Airlines** ☎ 800/433-7300 in North America, 0845/778-9789 in the U.K., 021/3398-4053 or 021/2210-3126 in Rio, 011/3214-4000 in São Paulo ⊕ www.aa.com. **British Airways** ☎ 0845/773-3377 in the U.K., 021/3398-3888 or 021/2221-0922 in Rio ⊕ www.ba.com. **Continental Airlines** ☎ 800/231-0856 in North America, 0800/776-464 in the U.K., 0800/55-4777 in Rio and São Paulo ⊕ www.continental.com. **Delta Airlines** ☎ 800/241-4141 in North America, 021/2549-1010 in Rio. **Qantas** ☎ 13-13-13 in Australia, 357-8900 in Auckland, 0800/808-767 elsewhere in New Zealand. **United Airlines** ☎ 800/241-6522 in North America, 0845/844-4777 in the U.K., 0800/16-2323 in Rio or São Paulo ⊕ www.ual.

com. **Varig** ☎ 800/468-2744 in the U.S., 0207/478-2114 in the U.K., 0300/788-7000 in Rio or São Paulo, 071/204-1395 or 0800/997-000 in Salvador, 091/3083-4521 in Belém, 092/622-3161 in Manaus ⊕ www.varig.com.

🛦 Within Brazil **Gol** ☎ 021/3398-5132, 021/3398-5136, or 0300/789-2121 in Brazil ⊕ www. voegol.com.br. **Meta** ☎ 091/522-1697 in Belém. **Nordeste Linhas Aéreas** ☎ 071/377-0130 in Salvador ⊕ www.voenordeste.com.br. **Norte Jet** ☎ 091/212-6244 in Belém. **Penta** ☎ 091/222-7777 in Belém. **Rico** ☎ 092/652-1391 in Manaus. **Rio-Sul and Nordeste** ☎ 0300/788-7000 or 011/5091-7000 in São Paulo ⊕ www.varig.com. **TAM** ☎ 888/235-9826 in the U.S., 305/406-2826 in Miami, 0207/707-4586 in the U.K., 091/210-6400 in Belém, 67/763-4100 in Campo Grande, 65/682-3650 in Cuiabá, 045/523-8500 or 045/523-3533 in Foz do Iguaçu, 092/652-1382 in Manaus, 021/2524-1717 or 021/2524-8102 in Rio, 071/204-1167 in Salvador, 0300/123-1000 in São Paulo ⊕ www.tamairlines.com. **Tavaj** ☎ 091/210-6257 in Belém, 092/652-1486 in Manaus. **Varig** ☎ 800/468-2744 in the U.S., 0207/478-2114 in the U.K., 0800/99-7000 in Brazil, 091/3083-4521 in Belém, 67/763-0000 in Campo Grande, 65/682-1140 in Cuiabá, 045/523-2155 or 045/529-6601 in Foz do Iguaçu, 092/622-3161 in Manaus, 0300/788-7000 in Rio or São Paulo, 071/204-1395 or 0800/997-000 in Salvador, ⊕ www.varig.com. **VASP** ☎ 091/224-5588 in Belém, 045/523-7161 in Foz do Iguaçu, 092/622-3470 in Manaus, 021/3814-8079 or 0300/789-1010 in Rio, 071/204-1304 or 0800/998-277 in Salvador ⊕ www.vasp.com.br.

FLYING TIMES   The flying time from New York is 8½ hours to Rio, 9½ hours to São Paulo. From Miami it's seven hours to Rio, eight hours to São Paulo. Most flights from Los Angeles go through Miami, so add five hours to the Miami times given; direct flights to São Paulo from Los Angeles take about 13 hours. From London it's seven hours to São Paulo.

Within Brazil it's one hour from Rio to São Paulo or Belo Horizonte, 1½ hours from Rio to Brasília, two hours from Rio to Salvador, and 2½ hours from Rio to Belém or Curitiba. From São Paulo it's four hours to Manaus and 1½ hours to Iguaçu Falls.

BUSINESS HOURS

Banks are, with a few exceptions, open weekdays 10–4. Office hours are generally 9–6. Within cities and along major highways, many gas stations are open 24 hours a day, seven days a week. In smaller towns they may only be open during daylight hours Monday–Saturday. Many museums are open from 10 or 11 to 5 or 6 (they may stay open later one night a week). Some museums, however, are open only in the afternoon, and many are closed on Monday. Always check before you go. Generally, small shops are open weekdays from 9 to 7 and on Saturday from 9 to 1 or 2. Centers and malls are often open from 10 to 10. Some centers and malls are open on Sunday.

BUS TRAVEL

The nation's *ônibus* (bus) network is affordable, comprehensive, and efficient—compensating for the lack of trains and the high cost of air travel. Every major city can be reached by bus as can most small- to medium-size communities.

Lengthy bus trips anywhere will involve travel over some bad highways, an unfortunate fact of life in Brazil today. Trips to northern, northeastern, and central Brazil tend to be especially trying; the best paved highways are in the southeast, so trips to and within this region may go more smoothly. When traveling by bus, **bring water, toilet paper, and an additional top layer of clothing** (the latter will come in handy if it gets cold, or it can serve as a pillow). Travel light, dress comfortably, and **keep a close watch on your belongings**—especially in bus stations.

Tickets are sold at bus-company offices and at city bus terminals. Note that larger cities may have different terminals for buses to different destinations, and some small towns may not have a terminal at all (you're picked up and dropped off at the line's office, invariably in a central location). **Expect to pay with cash,** as credit cards aren't accepted everywhere. Reservations or advance-ticket purchases generally aren't necessary except for trips to resort areas during high season—particularly on weekends—or during major holidays (Christmas, Carnaval, etc.) and school-break periods. In general, **arrive at bus stations early, particularly for peak-season travel.**

CAR RENTAL

Driving in cities is chaotic at best, mortally dangerous at worst; in the countryside the usually rough roads, lack of clearly marked signs, and language difference are discouraging for driving. Further, the cost of renting can be steep. All that said, certain areas are most enjoyable when explored on your own in a car: the beach areas of Búzios and the Costa Verde (near Rio) and the Belo Horizonte region; the North Shore beaches outside São Paulo; and many of the inland and coastal towns of the south, a region with many good roads. Always **give the rental car a once-over** to make sure the headlights, jack, and tires (including the spare) are in working condition. The minimum driving age in Brazil is 18.

🚗 Rental Agencies **Avis** ☎ 0800/55-8066 nationwide, 67/325-0072 in Campo Grande, 65/682-7360 in Cuiabá, 045/523-1510 in Foz do Iguaçu, 021/2543-8579 in Rio, 071/237-0155 or 071/377-2276 in Salvador, 011/288-3733 in São Paulo ⊕ www.avis.com. **Hertz** ☎ 0800/14-7300 nationwide, 65/682-6767 in Cuiabá, 021/2275-7440, 021/2262-0612, 021/3398-4338, or 0800/701-7300 in Rio, 071/377-3633 in Salvador, 011/3258-8422 or 0800/701-7300 in São Paulo ⊕ www.hertz.com. **Localiza** ☎ 0800/99-2000 nationwide, 65/624-7979 in Cuiabá, 045/529-6300 or 045/522-1608 in Foz do Iguaçu, 021/2275-3340, 021/3398-5445, or 021/2533-2677 in Rio, 071/377-2272 or 071/676-0321 in Salvador ⊕ www.localiza.com.br. **Norauto** ✉ Av. Gentil Bittencourt 2086, Nazaré, Belém ☎ 091/249-4900. **Unidas** ☎ 0800/12-1211 nationwide, 67/363-2145 in Campo Grande, 092/621-1575 in Manaus, 021/4001-2222 in Rio.

CAR TRAVEL

Brazil has more than 1.65 million km (1.02 million mi) of highway, about 10% of it paved. Recent construction has improved the situation, but independent land travel in Brazil definitely has its liabilities. In addition, Brazilian drivers are, to say the least, daredevils. For these reasons, it is recommended that you rely on taxis and buses for short distances and on planes for longer journeys.

Your own driver's license is acceptable—sort of. Police (particularly highway police) have been known to claim that driving with a foreign license is a violation in order to shake down drivers for money. An international driver's license, available from automobile associations, is a *really* good idea. International driving permits (IDPs) are available from the American, Canadian, and New Zealand automobile associations; in the United Kingdom from the Automobile Association and Royal Automobile Club; and in Australia from the Royal Automobile Club or state-run automobile associations. These international permits, valid only in conjunction with your regular driver's license, are universally recognized; having one may save you a problem with local authorities. If you do get a ticket for some sort of violation—real or imagined—don't argue. And plan to spend longer than you want settling it.

Some common-sense rules of the road: before you set out, **establish an itinerary** and **ask about gas stations**. Be sure to **plan your daily driving distance conservatively** and **don't drive after dark**. Always **obey speed limits and traffic regulations.**

EMERGENCY SERVICES
: The Automóvel Clube do Brasil (Automobile Club of Brazil) provides emergency assistance to foreign motorists in cities and on highways but only if they're members of an automobile club in their own nation.
🚗 **Automóvel Clube do Brasil** ⊠ Rua do Passeio, 90, Rio de Janeiro 📞 021/2240-4191 weekdays 9-7, 021/2262-2141 at other times.

GASOLINE
: Gasoline in Brazil costs around R$2.15 (74¢) a liter, which is about $2.75 per gallon. Unleaded gas, called *especial,* costs about the same. Brazil also has an extensive fleet of ethanol-powered cars. Ethanol fuel is sold at all gas stations and is priced a little lower than gasoline. However, these cars get lower mileage, so they offer little advantage over gas-powered cars. Stations are plentiful both within cities and on major highways, and many are open 24 hours a day. In smaller towns few stations take credit cards, and their hours are more limited.

PARKING
: Finding a space in most cities is a major task. It's best to **head for a garage or a lot** and leave your car with the attendant. There are no meters; instead, there's a system involving coupons that you must post in your car's window, which allows you to park for a certain time period (usually two hours). You can buy them from uniformed street-parking attendants or at newsstands. Should you find a space on the street, you'll probably have to pay a fee for parking services. Or you might run into unauthorized street parking offered by the so-called *flanelinhas* (literally, "flannel wearers"), who may charge from R$2 (68¢) to R$5 ($1.71) in advance.

No-parking zones are marked by a crossed-out capital letter *E* (which means *estacionamento,* the Portuguese word for "parking"). These zones, more often than not, are filled cars that rarely are bothered by the police.

ROAD CONDITIONS
: Brazil's federal highways were built between 1964 and 1976, and maintenance was nearly nonexistent in the 1980s. The country's highway department estimates that 40% of the federal highways (those with either the designation *BR* or a state abbreviation such as *RJ* or *SP*), which constitute 70% of Brazil's total road system, are in a dangerous state of disrepair. Evidence of this is everywhere: potholes, lack of signage, inadequate shoulders. Landslides and flooding after heavy rains are frequent and at times shut down entire stretches of key highways. Increasing traffic adds

to the system's woes, as does the fact that neither speed limits nor basic rules of safety seem to figure in the national psyche. The worst offenders are bus and truck drivers. If you drive, do so with the utmost caution.

ROAD MAPS Quatro Rodas is *the* name for maps of Brazil. It has atlases, books, and maps of different sizes for states, regions, and cities. If you're a beach aficionado, look for this company's four-color book of topographical maps of all the nation's beaches.

RULES OF THE ROAD Brazilians drive on the right, and in general, traffic laws are the same as those in the United States. The use of seat belts is mandatory. The national speed limit is 80 kph (48 mph) but is seldom observed.

CUSTOMS & DUTIES

In addition to personal items, you're permitted to bring into Brazil, duty-free, up to R$1,700 ($500) worth of gifts purchased abroad, including up to 2 liters of liquor. If you plan to bring in plants, you may do so only with documentation authenticated by the consular service. When shopping abroad, keep receipts for all purchases. Upon reentering the country, **be ready to show customs officials what you've bought.** Pack purchases together in an easily accessible place. If you think a duty is incorrect, appeal the assessment. If you object to the way your clearance was handled, note the inspector's badge number. In either case, first ask to see a supervisor. If the problem isn't resolved, write to the appropriate authorities, beginning with the port director at your point of entry. Check with the customs service for your home country for allowances.

Australian Customs Service ⌂ Regional Director, Box 8, Sydney, NSW 2001 ☎ 02/9213-2000 or 1300/363263, 02/9364-7222 or 1800/803-006 quarantine-inquiry line 🖷 02/9213-4043 ⊕ www.customs.gov.au. **Canada Customs and Revenue Agency** ✉ 2265 St. Laurent Blvd., Ottawa, Ontario K1G 4K3 ☎ 800/461-9999, 204/983-3500, 506/636-5064 ⊕ www.ccra.gc.ca. **HM Customs and Excise** ✉ Portcullis House, 21 Cowbridge Rd. E, Cardiff CF11 9SS, England ☎ 0845/010-9000 or 0208/929-0152, 0208/929-6731 or 0208/910-3602 complaints ⊕ www.hmce.gov.uk.

New Zealand Customs ✉ Head office: The Customhouse, 17-21 Whitmore St., Box 2218, Wellington ☎ 09/300-5399 or 0800/428-786 ⊕ www.customs.govt.nz. **U.S. Bureau of Customs and Border Protection** ✉ 1300 Pennsylvania Ave. NW, Washington, DC 20229 ⊕ www.customs.gov ☎ 877/287-8667, 202/354-1000.

EMBASSIES

Embassy Information American Embassy ✉ Lote 3, Unit 3500, Av. das Nações, 70403-900, Brasília, DF ☎ 061/321-7272 ⊕ www.embaixada-americana.org.br. **Australian Embassy** ✉ SES, Quadra 9 Conjunto 16, Casa 1, 70469-900, Brasília, DF ☎ 061/248-5569 🖷 061/226-1112 ⊕ www.embaixada-australia.org.br. **Canadian Embassy** ✉ SES, Av. das Nações, Quadra 803, Lote 16, 70410-900, Brasília, DF ☎ 061/321-2171 ⊕ www.dfait-maeci.gc.ca/brazil. **New Zealand Embassy** ✉ SHIS QI-9, Conjunto 16, casa 01 Lago Sul 71625-160 Brasília DF ☎ 061/248-9900 🖷 061/248-9916. **British Embassy** ✉ SES, Av. das Nações, Quadra 801, Loto 8, Conjunto K, 70408-900, Brasília, DF ☎ 061/225-2710 🖷 061/225-1777.

HEALTH

DIVERS' ALERT **Do not fly within 24 hours of scuba diving.** Neophyte divers should have a complete physical exam before undertaking a dive. If you have travel insurance that covers evacuations, **make sure your policy applies to scuba-related injuries,** as not all companies provide this coverage.

FOOD & DRINK   The major health risk in Brazil is traveler's diarrhea, caused by eating contaminated fruit or vegetables or drinking contaminated water. So watch what you eat—on and off the beaten path. Avoid ice, uncooked food, and unpasteurized milk and milk products, and **drink only bottled water** or water that has been boiled for at least 20 minutes, even when brushing your teeth. Don't use ice unless you know it's made from purified water. (Ice in city restaurants is usually safe.) Peel or thoroughly wash fresh fruits and vegetables. Avoid eating food from street vendors.

INFECTIOUS   Most travelers to the Amazon return home unscathed apart from a bit
DISEASES   of traveler's diarrhea. However, you should visit a doctor at least six weeks prior to traveling to discuss recommended vaccinations, some of which require multiple shots over a period of weeks. If you get sick weeks, months, or in rare cases, years after your trip, make sure your doctor administers blood tests for tropical diseases.

Meningococcal meningitis and typhoid fever are common in certain areas of Brazil—and not only in remote areas like the Amazon. Meningitis has been a problem around São Paulo in recent years. Common ailments in Brazil are diarrhea and dengue fever. To avoid diarrhea, be careful about what you eat and drink. Avoid mosquito bites to protect yourself from dengue, which is a virus that is usually not too serious if it is treated. Less common ailments are malaria; hepatitis A and B (vaccines are recommended); leishmaniasis (from sandfly bites); rabies; and yellow fever (vaccination recommended for the Amazon). Extremely uncommon are Chagas' Disease (spread by insects in rural areas); cholera; and schistosomiasis (from a parasite). In the Amazon, intestinal worms are a problem; avoid undercooked meat.

OVER-THE-   Mild cases of diarrhea may respond to Imodium (known generically
COUNTER   as loperamide) or Pepto-Bismol (not as strong), both of which can be
REMEDIES   purchased over the counter at a pharmacy (*farmácia*). Rehydrating solutions are available at pharmacies, or you can concoct your own version by mixing one teaspoon of sugar and a quarter teaspoon of salt per liter of water. Drink plenty of purified water or *chá* (tea)—*camomila* (chamomile) is a good folk remedy. In severe cases rehydrate yourself with a salt–sugar solution: ½ teaspoon *sal* (salt) and 4 tablespoons *açúcar* (sugar) per quart of *agua* (water). Pharmacies also sell antidiarrheal medicines, but an effective home remedy is the same as the rehydrating concoction: a teaspoon of sugar plus a quarter teaspoon of salt in a liter of water.

The word for aspirin is *aspirina*; Tylenol is pronounced *tee*-luh-nawl.

PESTS & OTHER   In forested areas, especially in the Amazon, insects and other pests can
HAZARDS   cause plenty of annoyance but rarely serious problems. Still, it is advisable to err on the side of caution. In areas with malaria and dengue fever, which are both carried by mosquitoes, take *mosquiteiros* (mosquito nets for beds or hammocks), wear boots and clothing that covers the body, apply repellent containing DEET (non-DEET repellents don't work in

the Amazon) to shoes and clothing, and use a spray against flying insects in living and sleeping areas.

Carry an adrenaline kit if you are allergic to bites and stings. Repellent can also ward off ticks and chiggers. Check your clothing and skin when you return from hikes to be sure you haven't brought any stowaways home. Make sure your shoes are empty before putting them on each morning. And if all of these devices fail, anti-itch cream gives you some relief.

Bichos de pé, parasites found in areas where pigs, chickens, and dogs run free, embed themselves in humans feet. To avoid these parasites, never walk barefoot in areas where animals are loose.

Heatstroke and heat prostration are common though easily preventable maladies. The symptoms for either can vary but always start with headaches, nausea, and dizziness. If ignored, these symptoms can worsen until you require medical attention. In hot weather be sure to rehydrate regularly, wear loose lightweight clothing, and avoid overexerting yourself.

Aside from the obvious safe-sex precautions, keep in mind that Brazil's blood supply isn't subject to the same intense screening as it is in North America, western Europe, Australia, and New Zealand. If you need a transfusion and circumstances permit it, ask that the blood be screened. Insulin-dependent diabetics or those who require injections should pack enough of the appropriate supplies—syringes, needles, disinfectants—for the entire trip. It's best to resist the temptation to get a new tattoo or body piercing in Brazil, but if you're determined, be sure to carefully inspect the equipment.

SHOTS & MEDICATIONS For travel anywhere in Brazil, you must have updated vaccines for diphtheria, tetanus, and polio. Children must additionally have current inoculations against measles, mumps, and rubella. For travel to jungle areas and some other regions of the country, vaccinations against hepatitis A and B, meningitis, typhoid, and yellow fever are highly recommended. Consult your doctor about whether to get a rabies vaccination. If you plan to visit remote regions or stay for more than six weeks, **check with the CDC's International Travelers' Hotline.**

Discuss the option of taking antimalarial drugs with your doctor. Note that in parts of northern Brazil, a particularly aggressive strain of malaria has become resistant to one antimalarial drug—chloroquine (Aralen®). Some antimalarial drugs have rather unpleasant side effects—from headaches, nausea, and dizziness to psychosis, convulsions, and hallucinations.

🔝 Health Warnings **National Centers for Disease Control and Prevention (CDC)** ✉ National Center for Infectious Diseases, Division of Quarantine, Travelers' Health, 1600 Clifton Rd. NE, Atlanta, GA 30333 ☏ 877/394-8747 for International Travelers' Hotline, 404/498-1600 for Division of Quarantine, 800/311-3435 for other inquiries 🖶 888/232-3299 ⊕ www.cdc.gov/travel.

HOLIDAYS
Major national holidays include: New Year's Day; Epiphany (Jan. 6); Carnaval (the week preceding Ash Wednesday); Good Friday (the Friday be-

fore Easter Sunday); Easter Sunday; Tiradentes Day (Apr. 21); Labor Day (May 1); Corpus Christi (60 days after Easter Sunday); Independence Day (Sept. 7); Our Lady of Aparecida Day (Oct. 12); All Souls' Day (Nov. 1); Declaration of the Republic Day (Nov. 15); and Christmas.

LANGUAGE

The language in Brazil is Portuguese, not Spanish, and Brazilians will appreciate it if you know the difference. The two languages are distinct, but common origins mean many words are similar, and fluent speakers of Spanish will be able to make themselves understood. English is spoken among educated Brazilians and, in general, by at least some of the staff at hotels, tour operators, and travel agencies. Store clerks and waiters may speak a smattering of English; taxi and bus drivers won't. As in many places throughout the world, you're more likely to find English-speaking locals in major cities than in small towns or the countryside. In the northeast you may even have difficulty in the cities.

MONEY MATTERS

Top hotels in Rio and São Paulo go for more than R$430 ($125) a night, and meals can—but do not have to—cost as much. Outside Brazil's two largest cities and Brasília, prices for food and lodging tend to drop considerably. Self-service salad bars where you pay by weight (per kilo, about 2.2 pounds) are inexpensive alternatives everywhere, though be sure to choose carefully among them. Taxis can be pricey. City buses, subways, and long-distance buses are all inexpensive; plane fares aren't.

Prices throughout this guide are given for adults. Substantially reduced fees are almost always available for children, students, and senior citizens.

ATMS   Nearly all the nation's major banks have automated teller machines (*caixas automaticos*), for which you must use a card with a credit-card logo. MasterCard/Cirrus holders can withdraw at Banco Itau, Banco do Brasil, HSBC, and Banco24horas ATMs; Visa holders can use Bradesco ATMs and those at Banco do Brasil. American Express cardholders can make withdrawals at most Bradesco ATMs marked 24 HORAS. To be on the safe side, carry a variety of cards. Note also that if your PIN is more than four digits long and/or uses letters instead of numbers, it might not work. Get a four-digit numerical PIN before your trip. For your card to function in some ATMs, you may need to hit a screen command (perhaps, *estrangeiro*) if you are a foreign client.

CREDIT CARDS   Throughout this guide, the following abbreviations are used: **AE**, American Express; **DC**, Diners Club; **MC**, MasterCard; and **V**, Visa.

CURRENCY   Brazil's unit of currency is the real (R$; plural: *reais,* though it's sometimes seen as *reals*). One real is 100 centavos (cents). There are notes worth 1, 5, 10, 20, 50, and 100 reais, together with coins worth 1, 5, 10, 25, and 50 centavos and 1 real.

PASSPORTS & VISAS

U.S., Canadian, Australian, and New Zealand citizens must have both a passport and a tourist visa (valid for five years) to enter Brazil. Visas are $100 for U.S. citizens, C$72 for Canadians, NZ$50 for New Zealanders, and A$88 for Australians. Citizens of the U.K. don't need visas.

SAFETY

Although there has been a real effort to crack down on tourist-related crime, particularly in Rio, petty street thievery is still prevalent in urban areas. **Lock traveler's checks and cash in a hotel safe,** except for what you need to carry each day. Ask the manager to sign a list of what you put in a hotel safe.

Don't wear a waist pack or a money belt because thieves can cut the strap. Instead, distribute your cash and any valuables (including credit cards and passport) between a deep front pocket, an inside jacket or vest pocket, and a hidden money pouch. If carrying a backpack, put it in front or at least over your shoulder and hang on tight. Likewise, wallets go in your front pocket.

Wear the simplest of timepieces and **do not wear any jewelry you aren't willing to lose**—stories of thieves yanking chains or earrings off travelers aren't uncommon. If you're taking photos, unless you're with a tour group, take your photo and then put your camera away. **Keep cameras in a secure camera bag,** preferably one with a chain or wire embedded in the strap. If you're traveling by bus or boat, or just walking in crowded areas, carabiners come in handy for clipping your bag or other items to a luggage rack, your belt loops, or any other ingenious place to provide extra security. Always **remain alert for pickpockets,** particularly in market areas, and **follow local advice about where it's safe to walk.**

Never leave valuables visible in a car. Take them inside with you whenever possible, or lock them in the trunk. Talk with locals or your hotel's staff about crime whenever you arrive in a new location. They will be able to tell you if it's safe to walk around after dark and what areas to avoid. Most important, **don't bring anything you can't stand to lose.**

Note that Brazilian law requires everyone to have official identification with them at all times. Carry a copy of your passport's data page and of the Brazilian visa stamp (leave the actual passport in the hotel safe).

LOCAL SCAMS Most tourist-related crimes occur in busy public areas: beaches, sidewalks or plazas, bus stations (and on buses, too). In these settings pickpockets, usually young children, work in groups. One or more will try to distract you while another grabs a wallet, bag, or camera. **Beware of children who suddenly thrust themselves in front of you** to ask for money or who offer to shine your shoes. Another member of the gang may strike from behind, grab whatever valuable is available, and disappear in the crowd. It's best not to protest while being mugged. Those on the take are sometimes armed or will tell you that their backup is, and although they're often quite young, they can be dangerous.

WOMEN IN BRAZIL Although women are gradually assuming a more important role in the nation's job force, machismo is still a strong part of Brazilian culture. Stares and catcalls aren't uncommon. Although you should have no fear of traveling unaccompanied, you should still take a few precautions.

Ask your hotel staff to recommend a reliable cab company, and **call for a taxi instead of hailing one on the street,** especially at night. **Dress to avoid unwanted attention.** For example, always wear a cover-up when heading to or from the beach. Avoid eye contact with unsavory individuals. If such a person approaches you, discourage him by politely but firmly saying, "*Por favor, me dê licença*" (pohr fah-**vohr,** meh day lee-**sehn**-see-ah), which means "Excuse me, please," and then walk away with resolve.

TAXES

Sales tax is included in the prices shown on goods in stores. Hotel, meal, and car rental taxes are usually tacked on in addition to the costs shown on menus and brochures. At this writing, hotel taxes are roughly 5%, meal taxes 10%, and car rental taxes 12%.

Departure taxes on international flights from Brazil aren't always included in your ticket and can run as high as R$86 ($25); domestic flights may incur a R$22 ($7) tax. Although U.S. dollars are accepted in some airports, be prepared to **pay departure taxes in reais.**

TELEPHONES

As of 2006, phone numbers in Brazil will change from seven to eight digits. All seven-digit numbers will be preceded by a 3. For example, 555–5555 will become 3555–5555.

COUNTRY & AREA CODES   The country code for Brazil is 55. When dialing a Brazilian number from abroad, drop the initial zero from the local area code. The country code is 1 for the United States and Canada, 61 for Australia, 64 for New Zealand, and 44 for the United Kingdom. The area code for Rio is 021, for São Paulo 011. Other area codes are listed in the front of local phone directories and in chapter A to Z sections throughout this guide.

DIRECTORY INFORMATION   For local directory assistance, dial 102. For directory assistance in another Brazilian city, dial the area code of that city plus 121.

LOCAL CALLS   Local calls can be made most easily from pay phones, which take phone cards only. A bar or restaurant may allow you to use its private phone for a local call if you're a customer.

LONG-DISTANCE & INTERNATIONAL SERVICES   AT&T, MCI, and Sprint access codes are blocked in many hotel rooms. First ask the hotel operator to connect you. If the hotel operator balks, ask for an international operator, or dial the international operator yourself. One way to improve your odds of getting connected to your long-distance carrier is to travel with more than one company's calling card (a hotel may block Sprint, for example, but not MCI). If all else fails, call from a pay phone, but note that not all pay phones allow long-distance calls.

 Access Codes **AT&T Direct** ☎ 0800/890–0288 or 0800/8888–288. **MCI WorldPhone** ☎ 000–8012. **Sprint International Access** ☎ 0800/88–87800, 0800/890–8000, or 0800/88–88000.

PHONE CARDS   All pay phones in Brazil take phone cards only. Buy a phone card, a *cartão de telefone*, at a *posto telefônico* (phone office), newsstand, or post office. Cards come with a varying number of units (each unit is usually worth a couple of minutes), which will determine the price. Buy a couple of cards if you don't think you'll have the chance again soon.

TIME

Although Brazil covers several time zones, most Brazilian cities are three hours behind GMT (Greenwich mean time), which means that if it's 5 PM in London, it's 2 PM in Rio and noon in New York. Manaus is an hour behind Rio.

TIPPING

Wages can be paltry in Brazil, so a little generosity in tipping can go a long way. At hotels it can go even farther if you tip in U.S. dollars or pounds sterling (bills, not coins). At restaurants that add a 10% service charge onto the check, it's customary to give the waiter an additional 5% tip. If there's no service charge, leave 15%. In deluxe hotels tip porters R$2 per bag, chambermaids R$2 per day, and bellhops R$4–R$6 for room and valet service. Tips for doormen and concierges vary, depending on the services provided. A good tip would be at least R$22, with an average of R$11. For moderate and inexpensive hotels, tips tend to be minimal (salaries are so low that virtually anything is well received). If a taxi driver helps you with your luggage, a per-bag charge of about R$1 is levied in addition to the fare. In general, tip taxi drivers 10% of the fare.

Tipping in bars and cafés follows the rules of restaurants, although at outdoor bars Brazilians rarely leave a gratuity if they have had only a soft drink or a beer. At airports and at train and bus stations, tip the last porter who puts your bags into the cab (R$1 a bag at airports, 50 centavos a bag at bus and train stations). In large cities you'll often be accosted on the street by children looking for handouts; 50 centavos is an average "tip."

VISITOR INFORMATION

EMBRATUR, Brazil's national tourism organization, doesn't have offices overseas, though its Web site is helpful. For information in your home country, contact the Brazilian embassy or the closest consulate—some of which have Web sites and staff dedicated to promoting tourism. Cities and towns throughout Brazil have local tourist boards, and some state capitals also have state tourism offices.

🗐 Tourist Information **Brazilian Embassy** ⌂ Box 1540, Canberra, ACT 2601 ☎ 616/273-2372. **Brazilian Embassy** ✉ 450 Wilbrod St., Ottawa, Ontario K1N 6M8 ☎ 613/237-1090. **Brazilian Embassy** ✉ Box 5432, 10 Brandon St., level 9, Wellington ☎ 04/473-3516 🖷 04/473-3517 ⊕ www.brazil.org.nz. **Brazilian Embassy in London Tourism Office** ✉ 32 Green St., London W1K 7AT ☎ 020/7629-6909 ⊕ www.brazil.org.uk. **Tourism Office at the Brazilian Embassy** ✉ 3006 Massachusetts Ave. NW, Washington, DC 20008 ☎ 800/727-2945 ⊕ www.braziltourism.org.

WEB SITES

Do check out the World Wide Web when planning your trip. You'll find everything from weather forecasts to virtual tours of famous cities. Be sure to visit Fodors.com (⊕ www.fodors.com), a complete travel-planning site. You can research prices and book plane tickets, hotel rooms, rental cars, vacation packages, and more. In addition, you can post your pressing questions in the Travel Talk section. Other planning tools include a currency converter and weather reports, and there are loads of links to travel resources.

The following sites should get you started: ⊕ www.embratur.gov.br (the official Brazilian tourist board site, with information in English provided by the Brazilian embassy in London), ⊕ www.varig.com (Varig Airlines' site, with English information), ⊕ www.brazilny.org (the official consular Web site in New York, with details about other consulates and the embassy as well as travel information and links to other sites), ⊕ www.brazilinfocenter.org (a Washington, D.C.–based organization that promotes political and business issues rather than tourism, but whose Web site has an incredible number of helpful links), ⊕ www.vivabrazil. com (a site with background and travel info on Brazil's different regions as well as links that will help you arrange your trip). The online magazine *Brazzil,* ⊕ www.brazzil.com, has interesting English-language articles on culture and politics.

WHEN TO GO

Prices in beach resorts are invariably higher during the Brazilian summer (November–April). If you're looking for a bargain, stick to the off-season (May–June and August–October; July is school-break month). Rio and beach resorts along the coast suffer from oppressive summer heat November–April, but in Rio the temperature can drop to uncomfortable levels for swimming from June through August.

CLIMATE   Seasons below the equator are the reverse of the north—summer in Brazil runs from December to March and winter from June to September. The rainy season in Brazil occurs during the summer months, but this is rarely a nuisance. Showers can be torrential but usually last no more than an hour or two. The areas of the country with pronounced rainy seasons are the Amazon and the Pantanal. In these regions the rainy season runs roughly from November to May and is marked by heavy, twice-daily downpours.

Rio de Janeiro is on the tropic of Capricorn, and its climate is just that—tropical. Summers are hot and humid. The same pattern holds true for all of the Brazilian coastline north of Rio, although temperatures are slightly higher year-round in Salvador. In the Amazon, where the equator crosses the country, temperatures are in the high 80s to the 90s (30s C) all year. In the south and in São Paulo, winter temperatures can fall to the low 40s (5°C–8°C). In the southernmost states, snowfalls occur in winter, although they're seldom more than dustings.

🕅 Forecasts **Weather Channel Connection** ☎ 900/932–8437, 95¢ per minute from a Touch-Tone phone ⊕ www.weather.com.

RIO DE JANEIRO	**Jan.**	84F	29C	**May**	77F	25C	**Sept.**	75F	24C
		69	21		66	19		66	19
	Feb.	85F	29C	**June**	76F	24C	**Oct.**	77F	25C
		73	23		64	18		63	17
	Mar.	83F	28C	**July**	75F	24C	**Nov.**	79F	26C
		72	22		64	18		68	20
	Apr.	80F	27C	**Aug.**	76F	24C	**Dec.**	82F	28C
		69	21		64	18		71	22

CHILE

4

I LIVE NOW IN A COUNTRY AS SOFT as the autumnal flesh of grapes,"
begins "Country," a poem by Pablo Neruda. With his odes to the place
of his birth, the Nobel Prize winner sang Chile into being and taught
us to inhale the bouquet of its salty breezes and its soaring Andean peaks
before we hold them to our lips and drink them down.

Chile is as luminous and pungent, as rustic and romantic, as any of Neruda's
poems describing it. It encompasses a bone-dry desert that blooms in a
riot of color once or twice a decade, sprawling glaciers that bellow like
thunder, and snow-covered volcanoes that perpetually smolder—all in
one sliver of land squeezed between the Andes and the Pacific Ocean. In
some places the 320-km (200-mi) territorial limit is actually wider than
the country itself, making Chile as much water as earth.

As might be expected in a country with a coastline stretching 6,435 km
(3,999 mi), many parts of Chile are inaccessible by land. Because of the
unusual topography, highways simply end when they reach fjords or ice
fields. You'll need to take a ship to see the mammoth glacier in the heart
of Parque Nacional Laguna San Rafael. A ferry ride is necessary to visit
Chiloé, an archipelago where you'll find charming wooden churches built
by missionaries. Distant Easter Island, in the middle of the Pacific
Ocean, is reachable only by a five-hour flight from the mainland.

The first European to reach Chile barely gave it a glance: Spanish conquistador Hernando de Magallanes left his name and little else behind
when he journeyed up the southern coast in 1520. Diego de Almagro
was the first Spaniard actually to explore the region. Setting out from
Peru in 1535, Almagro and a ragged crew of 500 adventurers marched
south in search of fame and fortune. When the band reached the
Aconcagua Valley, they fled after an extended battle with the Mapuche
people. Pedro de Valdivia, who led another gang of adventurers south
along the roads constructed by the Incas, broke ground for Santiago
in 1541.

Spain had its hands full with the rest of its empire in South America, so
Chile was pretty much ignored. The residents, even those who had
profited under colonial rule, eventually grew tired of having others gov-
ern their land. After Chile won its independence in a war that lasted from
1810 to 1818, the new nation sought to establish firm control of its entire territory. In 1843, it sent a frigate carrying a ragtag contingent of
19 men to the Strait of Magellan. There the men built a wooden fort
called Fuerte Bulnes, thus establishing the country's first permanent settlement in the southernmost reaches of Patagonia. Chile also began to
dream about expansion northward. The 1879 War of the Pacific pitted
Chile against its two neighbors to the north, Bolivia and Peru. Chile gained
much of the nitrate-rich land of the Atacama Desert, and Bolivia lost
its only outlet to the sea.

From 1973 to 1990, Chile was virtually synonymous with the name General Augusto Pinochet. With support from the United States, the military leader led a bloody coup in September 1973. He dissolved the
legislature, banned political organizations, and exiled opponents. Tens
of thousands are said to have been murdered during his years in power.

In 2000 Pinochet returned to Chile to stand trial for alleged human rights abuses, but the trial has been repeatedly delayed.

Pinochet's regime discouraged many visitors, but in the decade since his fall from power tourism has steadily increased. Chile's beaches draw sun-worshipers from all over South America, and its towering volcanoes and roaring rivers draw adventure travelers from around the world. Fishing aficionados head south to the Lake District, while armchair archaeologists are attracted to the 5,000-year-old mummies of the Atacama. Today Chile is one of the most popular destinations in South America. It doesn't hurt that the country also has one of the continent's most stable economies.

Pleasures & Pastimes

About the Restaurants

Kissing her shores from tip to toe, the Pacific Ocean is the breadbasket of Chile's cuisine, proffering delicacies like the conger eel, sea bass, king crab, and *locos* (abalone the size of fat clams). Awaken your palate with a seafood appetizer, such as *choritos al vapor* (mussels steamed in white wine), *machas a la parmesana* (similar to razor clams but unique to Chile, grilled with tomatoes and Parmesan cheese), or *chupo de centolla* (king crab). Simply seasoned grilled fish is a Chilean favorite, usually garnished with steamed potatoes or an *ensalada a la chilena* (peeled tomatoes with onions marinated in brine to reduce their acidic flavor).

But the Pacific isn't Chile's only answer to fine dining—many simple country dishes are among the best offerings of Chilean cuisine. *Cazuela,* a superb soup that includes a piece of meat (beef, pork, chicken, or turkey, usually on the bone), potatoes, and corn on the cob in a thick broth, is a meal in itself. In summer, *porotos granados,* a thick bean, corn, and squash soup, is all the rage with Chileans, as are *humitas,* ground corn seasoned and steamed in its own husk. At markets all over the country you'll be wooed by women selling the ubiquitous *pastel de choclo,* a corn-meal pastry pie that usually contains ground beef, a piece of chicken, and seasonings.

WHAT IT COSTS In pesos (in thousands)				
	$$$$	**$$$**	**$$**	**$**	**¢**
AT DINNER	over 11	8–11	5–8	2.5–5	under 2.5

Prices are for a main course at dinner.

About the Hotels

Power and wealth have historically orbited around Chile's capital—Santiago—so it has a wide range of luxury lodging options. In sluggish response to increased tourism, however, new hotels have sprung up in the provinces. In the more heavily touristed areas you'll find cozy wooden cabins, hot-springs retreats, and elaborate hotels richly adorned in Patagonian hardwoods. The always homey and hospitable *residenciales* (bed-and-breakfasts) are found everywhere.

4

If you have
6 days

Take at least three days to explore and enjoy **Santiago,** Chile's capital and largest city. Skiers may opt for spending a day in one of the nearby ski resorts. On your fourth day, hop a bus to **Valparaíso** in the morning, meandering among this port city's picturesque hills and many funiculars. Spend the next day in neighboring **Viña del Mar,** exploring its chic cafés and restaurants and relaxing on its miles of beaches. On your last day head back to Santiago to catch your flight home.

If you have
10 days

beach resorts, fly north on your fifth day to **San Pedro de Atacama,** in the middle of the driest desert in the world. Spend two days exploring the bizarre moonscape of the Valle de la Luna and the desolate salt flats of the Salar de Atacama. On your eighth day drive up the coast to **Iquique,** where you can visit the Gigante de Atacama, the world's largest geoglyph. The next day head to **Arica,** the northernmost city in Chile. Visit the Museo Arqueológico de San Miguel de Azapa to see the Chinchorro mummies. On your last day fly back to Santiago.

If you have
14 days

Spend your first four days exploring **Santiago** and the beach towns along the Central Coast. Fly south to **Puerto Montt** and explore the lovely resort towns of the Lake District on your fifth and sixth days. Make sure to take time to relax in one of the region's many hot springs. From Puerto Montt, take a three-night cruise down the coast to the unforgettable glacier in **Parque Nacional Laguna San Rafael.** When you return to Puerto Montt, take a spectacular morning flight over the Andes to the Patagonian city of **Punta Arenas.** On your 12th day drive to **Puerto Natales,** gateway to the **Parque National Torres del Paine.** You'll need at least two days to wander through the wonders of the park's granite spires. On your final day head back to Punta Arenas, stopping en route at one of the penguin sanctuaries, and catch your flight back to Santiago.

Traditionally, *hotel* referred to upscale accommodations; *hostería* and *hostal* denoted something more basic. Those distinctions have blurred, and there are some pretty snazzy hosterías and hostales to be found. A lodging that calls itself a *hospedaje* means your room will be in a private home. A *cabaña* is any type of lodging with detached cabin units, while a *refugio*, often found in national parks, has bunks and little else.

WHAT IT COSTS In pesos (in thousands)				
	$$$$	**$$$**	**$$**	**$**	**¢**
FOR 2 PEOPLE	over 105	75–105	45–75	15–45	under 15

Prices are for a double room in high season, excluding tax.

Shopping

Chile is one of only three countries in the world that mine lapis lazuli, so it's worth checking out the workshops and stores in Santiago. The city's artisans are increasingly sophisticated, and you can find earrings,

rings, and necklaces to please virtually every taste. Handicrafts you'll find all over Chile include warm sweaters that are hand-dyed, -spun, and -knitted in the southern parts of the country (it's cheaper to purchase them there) and ponchos whose designs vary according to the region; the best are by the Mapuche artisans in and around Temuco and by the Chilote women on Chiloé. Thick wool blankets are woven in Chiloé but are heavy to carry, as are the figures of reddish clay from Pomaire and the famous black clay ceramics of Quinchamalí. Purchase them at the end of your trip. Several towns specialize in wicker, particularly Chimbarongo (about an hour's drive from Santiago) and Chiloé, where baskets and woven effigies of that island's mythical figures abound.

Wine

An oft-repeated fact about Chilean wine is that the best is exported. Although you can find some good quality vintages at upscale Chilean restaurants, most are still headed for the international market. To that end, the best wineries are modernizing the growing and fermenting methods (with help from French and Californian oenological experts) to produce wines that are better suited for the European and North American markets. These changes have paid off in recent years with improved overall quality of Chilean wines. In fact, a small number of Chilean vintners are already turning out truly first-rate wines.

Exploring Chile

When Chileans joke that the creator made their nation of the universe's leftovers, they are only partly in jest. Chile's narrow territory comprises some of nature's most spectacular anomalies: the looming Andes impose the country's eastern boundaries, stretching from the desolate Atacama Desert to the icy fjords of Patagonia. Here you'll find the granite peaks of Parque Nacional Torres del Paine, one of the continent's natural wonders.

SANTIAGO

Ancient and modern stand side-by-side in the heart of Santiago—one of the most common photographs on postcards is the neoclassical cathedral reflected in the windows of the glass office tower across the street. You may be amazed at the amount of green in a city so large. Downtown you're never far from the leafy Plaza de Armas or the paths that meander along the Río Mapocho. To take in the entire city, climb the maze of trails up Cerro Santa Lucía, or take the funicular to the top of Cerro San Cristóbal. Not that the views from the ground are so shabby—on a clear day you can see the majestic peaks of the Andes in the distance.

Exploring Santiago

Much of Santiago, especially communities such as Bellavista, Providencia, and the Centro, is best explored on foot. The subway is the quickest, cleanest, and most economical way to shuttle among neighborhoods. To travel to more distant neighborhoods, or to get anywhere in the evening after the subway closes, you'll probably want to hail a taxi.

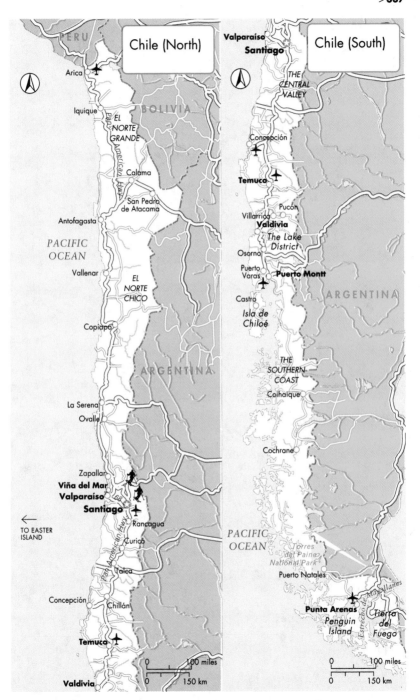

Chile (North)

PERU

Arica

Iquique

EL
NORTE
GRANDE

BOLIVIA

Calama

San Pedro
de Atacama

Antofagasta

PACIFIC
OCEAN

Vallenar

EL
NORTE
CHICO

Copiapó

ARGENTINA

La Serena

Ovalle

Zapallar

Viña del Mar
Valparaíso
Santiago

Rancagua

TO EASTER
ISLAND

Curicó

Talca

Concepción

Chillán

Temuco

Valdivia

Pan American Hwy

0   100 miles

0   150 km

Chile (South)

Valparaíso
Santiago

THE
CENTRAL
VALLEY

Concepción

Temuco

Villarrica   Pucón
Valdivia

The Lake
District

Osorno

Puerto
Varas   **Puerto Montt**

Castro

Isla de
Chiloé

ARGENTINA

THE
SOUTHERN
COAST

Coihaique

Cochrane

PACIFIC
OCEAN

Torres
del Paine
National Park

Puerto Natales

Punta Arenas

Penguin
Island

Tierra
del
Fuego

Estrecho de Magallanes

0   100 miles

0   150 km

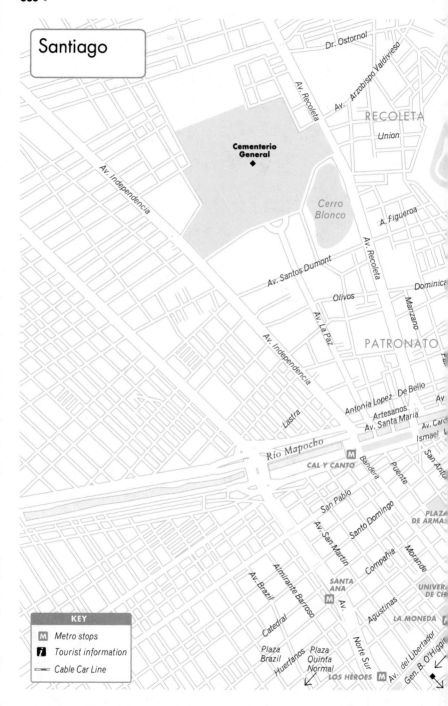

Santiago

Dr. Ostornol

Av. Arzobispo Valdivieso

Av. Recoleta

RECOLETA

Union

Cementerio General ◆

Cerro Blonco

Av. Independencia

A. Figueroa

Av. Recoleta

Av. Santos Dumont

Olivos

Dominica

Manzano

Av. La Paz

Av. Independencia

PATRONATO

Antonía Lopez   De Bello

Lastra

Artesanos

Av. Santa María

Av. Car

Av.

Ismael

San Anto

Río Mapocho

Ⓜ CAL Y CANTO

Bandera

Puente

San Pablo

San Antonio

Av. San Martín

Santo Domingo

PLAZA DE ARMAS

Almirante Barroso

Compañía

Morande

Av. Brazil

SANTA ANA

Ⓜ Av.

Agustinas

UNIVER DE CH

Catedral

Norte Sur

LA MONEDA

Plaza Brazil

Plaza Quinta Normal

Huerfanos

Av. del Libertador

Gen. B. O'Higgi

↙ LOS HÉROES Ⓜ Av. del ↙   Gen. B. ◆

KEY

Ⓜ Metro stops

🛈 Tourist information

▭ Cable Car Line

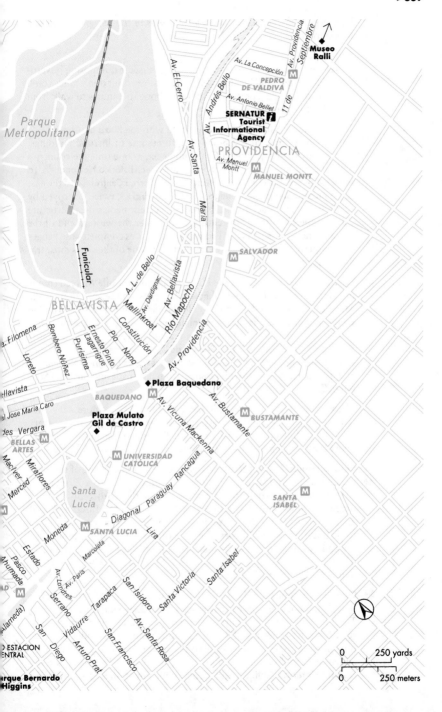

Parque
Metropolitano

Av. El Cerro

Av. La Concepción

Av. Andrés Bello

Av. Providencia

11 de Septiembre

◆ **Museo
Ralli**

**PEDRO
DE VALDIVA**

Av. Antonio Bellet

Av. Santa

**SERNATUR
Tourist
Informational
Agency**

PROVIDENCIA

Av. Manuel
Montt

MANUEL MONTT

María

SALVADOR

Funicular

A. L. de Bello

Av. Dardignac

Av. Bellavista

Río Mapocho

BELLAVISTA

a. Filomena

Mallinkroat

Constitución

Bombero Núñez

Ernesto Pinto
Lagarrigue

Pío
Nono

Purísima

Loreto

Av. Providencia

llavista

◆ **Plaza Baquedano**

al José María Caro

BAQUEDANO

Av. Vicuña Mackenna

Av. Bustamante

BUSTAMANTE

des Vergara

**Plaza Mulato
Gil de Castro**
◆

**BELLAS
ARTES**

Maciver

Miraflores

Merced

**UNIVERSIDAD
CATÓLICA**

Paraguay

Rancagua

Santa
Lucía

Moneda

Diagonal

**SANTA
ISABEL**

Estado

SANTA LUCÍA

Lira

Ahumada

Pasco

Av. París

Marcoleta

San Isidoro

Santa Victoria

Santa Isabel

AD

Av. Londres

Tarapacá

San Diego

Serrano

Vidaurre

Av. Santa Rosa

Alameda)

San

Arturo Prat

San Francisco

ESTACIÓN
ENTRAL

rque Bernardo
Higgins

0   250 yards

0   250 meters

Numbers in the text correspond to numbers in the margin and on the Santiago maps.

Santiago Centro

In Santiago Centro you'll find interesting museums, imposing governmental buildings, and bustling commercial streets. But don't think you'll be lost in a sprawling area—it takes only about 10 minutes to walk from one edge to the other.

a good walk

To really know Santiago, get acquainted with the **Plaza de Armas ❶** ▐ . Across Calle Catedral is a block-long threesome of historic buildings, centered by the Palacio de la Real Audiencia, at one time the country's highest court and currently home to the **Museo Histórico Nacional ❷**. To the west of the museum is the whitewashed **Correo Central ❸**; to the east is the **Municipalidad de Santiago ❹**. The **Catedral ❺**, twice destroyed by earthquakes and once by fire before the current neoclassical structure was completed in the 18th century, looms over the western end of the plaza. A motley assortment of commercial arcades completes the fringes of the square, adding a touch of modernity to one of the city's most traditional neighborhoods.

On the southeast corner of the Plaza de Armas on Calle Merced stands the attractive **Edificio Comercial Edwards ❻**; just to the east along Calle Merced is a beautifully restored colonial mansion called the **Casa Colorada ❼**. The **Museo de Arte Precolombino ❽** is two blocks west of Casa Colorada on the corner of Calle Compañía and Calle Bandera. Across the street stands Chile's lordly **Palacio de los Tribunales de Justicia ❾**. Encompassing an entire city block to the north is the **Ex Congreso Nacional ❿** and its gated gardens, providing refuge from the hustle and bustle of Santiago Centro.

TIMING   The walk itself should take less than an hour. If you explore a few museums, wander around the squares, and rest here and there, this itinerary could take a full morning. Each of the small museums on this route should take about 45 minutes to see thoroughly.

WHAT TO SEE   **Casa Colorada.** The appropriately named Red House is one of the best-
❼ preserved colonial structures in the city. Mateo de Toro y Zambrano, Santiago's most prosperous businessman of the 18th century, once made his home here. The building today houses the Museo de Santiago, a modest but informative museum that makes an excellent place to dive into the city's history. For an explanation of the exhibits, ask for an English guidebook. ⊠ *Merced 860, Santiago Centro* ☎ *2/633–0723* 🖳 *Tues.–Sat. 500 pesos, Sun. free* ☉ *Tues.–Fri. 10–6, Sat. 10–5, Sun. 11–2* Ⓜ *Plaza de Armas.*

❺ **Catedral.** Conquistador Pedro de Valdivia declared in 1541 that a house of worship would be constructed at this site bordering the Plaza de Armas. The first adobe building burned to the ground, and the structures that replaced it were destroyed by the earthquakes of 1647 and 1730. The finishing touches of the neoclassical cathedral standing today were added in 1789 by Italian architect Joaquín Toesca. Be sure to see the stunning interior—a line of gilt arches topped by stained-glass windows

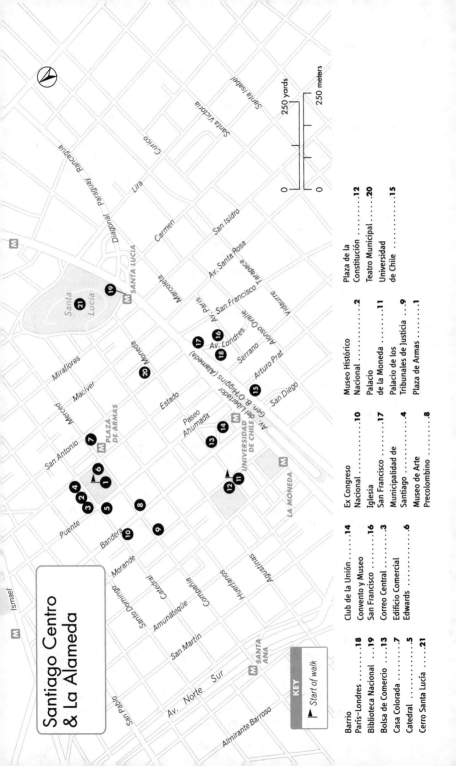

Santiago Centro & La Alameda

KEY

▶ *Start of walk*

0   250 yards
0   250 meters

parades down the long nave. ⊠ *Plaza de Armas, Santiago Centro* ☎ *2/ 696–2777* ⊙ *Daily 9–7* Ⓜ *Plaza de Armas.*

❸ **Correo Central.** Housed in what was once the ornate Palacio de los Gobernadores, this building dating from 1715 is one of the most beautiful post offices you are likely to see. It was reconstructed by Ricardo Brown in 1882 after being ravaged by fire and is a fine example of neoclassical architecture. The third story, which includes an attractive half dome, was added in the early 20th century. ⊠ *Plaza de Armas, Santiago Centro* ☎ *2/698–7274* ⊕ *www.correos.cl* ⊙ *Weekdays 8–7, Sat. 8–2* Ⓜ *Plaza de Armas.*

❻ **Edificio Comercial Edwards.** Architect Eugenio Joannon sent the plans for his prized shopping emporium to Paris, where it was prefabricated in cast iron before being shipped back to Santiago and constructed in 1893. Its distinctive glass and blue metallic facades form the corner building on Calle Merced and Calle Estado, overlooking the Plaza de Armas. It still fulfills a commercial role as a shop selling children's clothes. ⊠ *Merced at Estado, Santiago Centro* Ⓜ *Plaza de Armas.*

❿ **Ex Congreso Nacional.** Once the meeting place for the National Congress (the legislature moved to Valparaíso in 1990), this palatial neoclassical building now houses the offices of the Ministry of Foreign Affairs. The original structure on the site, the Iglesia de la Compañía de Jesús, was destroyed by a fire in 1863 in which 2,000 people perished. Inside the peaceful gated gardens is a monument commemorating the victims. ⊠ *Bandera 345, at Morandé, Santiago Centro* Ⓜ *Plaza de Armas.*

❹ **Municipalidad de Santiago.** Today's governmental center for Santiago can be found on the site of the colonial city hall and jail. The original structure, built in 1552, survived until a devastating earthquake in 1730. Joaquín Toesca, the architect who also designed the presidential palace and completed the cathedral, reconstructed the building in 1785, but it was destroyed by fire a century later. In 1891, Eugenio Joannon, who favored an Italian Renaissance style, erected the structure standing today. On the facade hangs an elaborate coat of arms presented by Spain. The interior is not open to the public. ⊠ *Plaza de Armas, Santiago Centro* Ⓜ *Plaza de Armas.*

> **need a break?**
>
> You can shut out the bustle of Santiago Centro in the cool, dim, dark-wood-paneled bar of the **City Hotel** (⊠ Compañía 1063, Santiago Centro ☎ 2/695–4526), close to the Plaza de Armas. Order a coffee, cold beer, or sandwich and look for the regulars—dapper old Santiaguinos who sit at the hotel's well-stocked bar.

❽ **Museo de Arte Precolombino.** If you plan to visit only one museum in Santiago, it should be the Museum of Pre-Columbian Art, a block from the
Fodor'sChoice Plaza de Armas. The well-endowed collection of artifacts of Central and
★ South America's indigenous peoples is displayed in a beautifully restored Royal Customs House dating to 1807. The permanent collection, on the upper floor, showcases textiles and ceramics from Mexico to Patagonia. Unlike many of the city's museums, the displays here are well la-

beled in Spanish and English. ✉ *Bandera 361, at Av. Compañía, Santiago Centro* ☎ *2/688–7348* ⊕ *www.museoprecolombino.cl* ✆ *Tues.–Sat. 2,000 pesos, Sun. free* ☉ *Tues.–Sat. 10–6, Sun. 10–2* Ⓜ *Plaza de Armas.*

❷ **Museo Histórico Nacional.** The colonial-era Palacio de la Real Audiencia served as the meeting place of Chile's first Congress in September 1810. The building then functioned as a telegraph office before the museum moved here in 1911. It's worth the small admission charge to see the interior of the 200-year-old structure, where exhibits tracing Chile's history are arranged chronologically in rooms centered around a courtyard. Among the exhibits are large collections of coins, stamps, and traditional handicrafts, including more than 3,000 examples of native textiles. ✉ *Plaza de Armas, Santiago Centro* ☎ *2/633–1815* ⊕ *www. museohistoriconacional.cl* ✆ *Tues.–Sat. 600 pesos, Sun. free* ☉ *Tues.–Sun. 10–5:30* Ⓜ *Plaza de Armas.*

❾ **Palacio de los Tribunales de Justicia.** During Augusto Pinochet's rule, countless human-rights demonstrations were held outside the Courts of Justice, which house the country's Supreme Court. Protests are still held near this stately neoclassical building a block from the Plaza de Armas, including some in support of the former dictator. In front of the building, perhaps ironically, is a monument celebrating justice and the promulgation of Chile's civil code. ✉ *Bandera 344, Santiago Centro* Ⓜ *Plaza de Armas.*

> off the beaten path

PARQUE BERNARDO O'HIGGINS – Named for Chile's national hero, whose troops were victorious against the Spanish, this park has plenty of open space for everything from ball games to military parades. Street vendors sell *volantines* (kites) outside the park year-round; high winds make September and early October the prime kite-flying season. ✉ *Av. Jorge Alessandri Rodríguez between Av. Blanca Encalada and Av. General Rondizzoni, Santiago Centro* ☎ *2/556–1927* ✆ *Free* ☉ *Daily 8–8* Ⓜ *Parque O'Higgins.*

★ ⮞❶ **Plaza de Armas.** This square has been the symbolic heart of Chile—as well as its political, social, religious, and commercial center—since Pedro de Valdivia established the city on this spot in 1541. The Palacio de los Gobernadores, the Palacio de la Real Audiencia, and the Municipalidad de Santiago front the square's northern edge. The dignified Catedral graces the western side of the square. Among the palm trees are distinctive fountains and gardens revealing the Chileans' pride about their history. Also here is a bronze well that once served as the city's main source of water. On any given day, the plaza teems with life—vendors selling religious icons, artists painting the activity around them, street performers juggling fire, and tourists clutching guidebooks. In the southern corner of the plaza you can watch people playing chess. ✉ *Calle Compañía and Calle Estado, Santiago Centro* Ⓜ *Plaza de Armas.*

La Alameda

Avenida Libertador Bernardo O'Higgins, more frequently called La Alameda, is the city's principal thoroughfare. Along with the Avenida Norte Sur and the Río Mapocho, it forms the wedge that defines the city's historic district.

a good walk

Unthinkable only a few years ago, today you can walk unescorted into the courtyard of the **Palacio de la Moneda** ⓫ ▶, the nerve center of the Chilean government. Across Calle Moneda you'll find **Plaza de la Constitución** ⓬, a formal square where you can watch the changing of the guard. Walk a block east along Calle Moneda to the cobblestone Calle La Bolsa. On this narrow diagonal street stands the ornate **Bolsa de Comercio** ⓭, the country's stock exchange. A block down, at a dainty fountain, the street turns into Calle Nueva York, where you'll find the **Club de la Unión** ⓮. Across the street is the main building, or casa central, of the **Universidad de Chile** ⓯. Reach it by crossing under the Universidad de Chile Metro stop, which contains monumental murals depicting Chilean history painted by Mario Toral, part of the fine MetroArte series in all subway stops. Two blocks east are the **Convento y Museo San Francisco** ⓰ and the **Iglesia San Francisco** ⓱. Turn left after exiting Iglesia San Francisco onto Calle Londres and into the **Barrio París-Londres** ⓲. Enjoy a pleasant stroll through this charming area otherwise known as Little Europe. On returning to the Alameda, avoid the crazy drivers by crossing back to the other (north) side via the Santa Lucia Metro station. Directly ahead of you is the **Biblioteca Nacional** ⓳. After leaving the library make a left and then another left. Cross Calle Maciver and then turn right down pedestrian-only German Tenderini to the **Teatro Municipal** ⓴. Head east through Plaza Vicuña Mackenna to survey the entire city from **Cerro Santa Lucía** ㉑.

TIMING & PRECAUTIONS

This walk itself is fairly short, but it's full of beautiful old buildings you'll want to explore. You could spend an hour at La Moneda—try to time your visit with the changing of the guard—every other day at 10 AM. Across the Alameda, give yourself another hour to explore the Iglesia San Francisco, the adjacent museum, and the Barrio París-Londres.

WHAT TO SEE

Barrio París-Londres. Many architects contributed to what is frequently
⓲ referred to as Santiago's Little Europe, among them Alamos, Larraín, and Mönckeberg. The string of small mansion houses lining the cobbled streets of Calles París and Londres sprang up in the mid-1920s on the vegetable patches and gardens that once belonged to the convent adjoining Iglesia San Francisco. The three- and four-story town houses are all unique; some have redbrick facades or terra-cotta-tile roofs, and others are done in Palladian style. ⊠ *Calles Londres and París, La Alameda.*

⓳ **Biblioteca Nacional.** Near the foot of Cerro Santa Lucía is the block-long classical facade of the National Library. With more than 3 million titles, this is one of the largest libraries in South America. The vast interior includes arcane collections. The attractive Sala Medina holds the most important collection of prints by native peoples in Latin America. ⊠ *Av. O'Higgins 651, La Alameda* ☏ *2/360–5259* ✆ *Free* ☉ *Weekdays 9–8, Sat. 9–3:30* Ⓜ *Santa Lucía.*

⓭ **Bolsa de Comercio.** Chile's stock exchange is housed in a 1917 French neoclassical structure with an elegant clock tower surmounted by an arched slate cupola. Weekdays you can watch the shouting of traders in the three buying and selling circles called *redondeles.* ⊠ *Calle La Bolsa 64, La Alameda* ☏ *2/399–3000* ⊕ *www.bolsadesantiago.com* ✆ *Free* ☉ *Weekdays noon–1:20 and 4–4:30* Ⓜ *Universidad de Chile.*

need a break? Alongside the Bolsa de Comercio runs the narrow cobbled street of La Bolsa. Here you'll find **Kebab, Kebab** (⊠ La Bolsa 67, La Alameda ☎ 2/569–0642), a hole-in-the-wall Mediterranean eatery consisting of two tiny rooms, one at street level, the other up a spiral staircase. Sit at the horseshoe-shape bar and order a refreshing carrot juice, followed by a bowl of fresh salad garnished with sizzling kebab meat.

㉑ Cerro Santa Lucía. The mazelike park of St. Lucía is a hangout for souvenir vendors, park-bench smoochers, and photo-snapping tourists. Walking uphill along the labyrinth of interconnected paths and plazas takes about 30 minutes. An elevator two blocks north of the park's main entrance is a little faster, but its schedule is erratic. The crow's nest, reached via a series of steep and slippery stone steps, affords an excellent 360-degree view of the entire city. Be careful near dusk, as the park also attracts the occasional mugger. ⊠ *Santa Lucía and Av. O'Higgins, La Alameda* ☎ *No phone* ☉ *Oct.–Mar., daily 9–6.30; Apr.–Sept., daily 7–8* Ⓜ *Santa Lucía.*

⑭ Club de la Unión. The facade of this neoclassical building, dating to 1925, is one of the city's finest. The interior of this private club, whose roster has included numerous Chilean presidents, is open only to members. ⊠ *Av. O'Higgins at Calle Bandera, La Alameda* Ⓜ *Universidad de Chile.*

⑯ Convento y Museo San Francisco. This former convent next to Iglesia San Francisco functions as a religious and colonial art museum: inside is the best collection of 17th-century colonial paintings on the continent, with 54 large-scale canvases portraying the life of St. Francis and a plethora of religious iconography. Most pieces are labeled in Spanish and English. Fans of literature shouldn't miss a small exhibit devoted to Gabriela Mistral, who won the Nobel Prize in 1945 for her poetry about Chile. ⊠ *Londres 4, La Alameda* ☎ *2/639–8737* 🎫 *1,000 pesos* ☉ *Tues.–Sat. 10–1 and 3–6, Sun. 10–2* Ⓜ *Santa Lucía, Universidad de Chile.*

★ ⑰ Iglesia San Francisco. Santiago's oldest structure, greatest symbol, and principal landmark, the Church of St. Francis is the last trace of 16th-century colonial architecture in the city. Construction began in 1586, and although the church survived successive earthquakes, early tremors took their toll and portions had to be rebuilt in 1698. Today's neoclassical tower, which forms the city's most recognizable silhouette, was added in 1857 by architect Fermín Vivaceta. Inside are rough stone-and-brick walls, marble columns, and ornate wood ceilings. Visible on the main altar is the image of the Virgen del Socorro (Virgin of Assistance) that conquistador Pedro de Valdivia carried for protection and guidance. ⊠ *Av. O'Higgins 834, La Alameda* ☎ *2/638–3238* ☉ *Daily 7 AM–8 PM* Ⓜ *Santa Lucía, Universidad de Chile.*

▶ ⑪ Palacio de la Moneda. Originally the royal mint, this sober neoclassical edifice built by Joaquín Toesca in 1805 became the presidential palace in 1846 and served that purpose for more than a century. It was bombarded by the military in the 1973 coup, when Salvador Allende defended his presidency against the assault of General Augusto Pinochet. Allende's death is still shrouded in mystery—some say he went down fighting, others claim he took his own life before the future dictator entered the palace in triumph. The two central courtyards are open to the public, and tours of the interior can be arranged at the reception desk. ✉ *Plaza de la Constitución, Moneda between Teatinos and Morandé, La Alameda* ☎ *No phone* ☉ *Daily 10–6* Ⓜ *La Moneda.*

★ ⑫ **Plaza de la Constitución.** Palacio de la Moneda and other government buildings line Constitution Square, the country's most formal plaza. The changing of the guard takes place every other day at 10 AM within the triangle defined by 12 Chilean flags. Adorning the plaza are three monuments, each dedicated to a notable national figure: Diego Portales, founder of the Chilean republic; Jorge Alessandri, the country's leader from 1958 to 1964; and Don Eduardo Frei, president from 1964 to 1970. The plaza also serves as the roof of the underground bunker Pinochet had installed when he "redecorated" La Moneda. Pillars in each of the four corners of the square serve as ventilation ducts for the bunker, which is now a parking lot. Locals joke that these monoliths represent the four founding members of the military junta—they're made of stone, full of hot air, and no one knows their real function. One pillar has been converted into a memorial honoring President Salvador Allende. ✉ *Moneda and Morande, La Alameda* Ⓜ *La Moneda.*

⑳ **Teatro Municipal.** The opulent Municipal Theater is the city's cultural center, with performances of opera, ballet, and classical music from April to November. Originally built in 1857, with major renovations in 1870 and 1906 following a fire and an earthquake, the Renaissance-style building is one of the city's most refined monuments. The lavish interior deserves a visit. Tours can be arranged with a week's notice. ✉ *Plaza Alcade Mekis, Av. Agustinas at Av. San Antonio, La Alameda* ☎ *2/463–8888* Ⓜ *Universidad de Chile, Santa Lucía.*

⑮ **Universidad de Chile.** The main branch of the University of Chile, the country's largest educational institution, is a symmetrical ocher edifice completed in 1872, when it was known as the University Palace. It's not officially open to the public, but you are free to stroll through the grounds. ✉ *Av. O'Higgins, La Alameda* Ⓜ *Universidad de Chile.*

Parque Forestal

After building a canal in 1891 to tame the unpredictable Río Mapocho, Santiago found itself with a thin strip of land that it didn't quite know what to do with. Under the watchful eye of Enrique Cousiño, it was transformed into the leafy Forest Park.

a good walk

Near the park's western edge you'll find the wrought-iron **Mercado Central** ㉒ ▶, the city's fish market. Stroll in the park along the Río Mapocho a block west to reach the former train terminal, the **Estación Mapocho** ㉓. Cross the river and follow your nose to the flower market **Pérgola de las Flores** ㉔. After leaving the flower market, head east on Artesanos and walk until you see the lime-green entrance to the gritty **Vega Chica and Vega Central** ㉕ (the peach-color Vega Central is a full block to the north of Vega Chica).

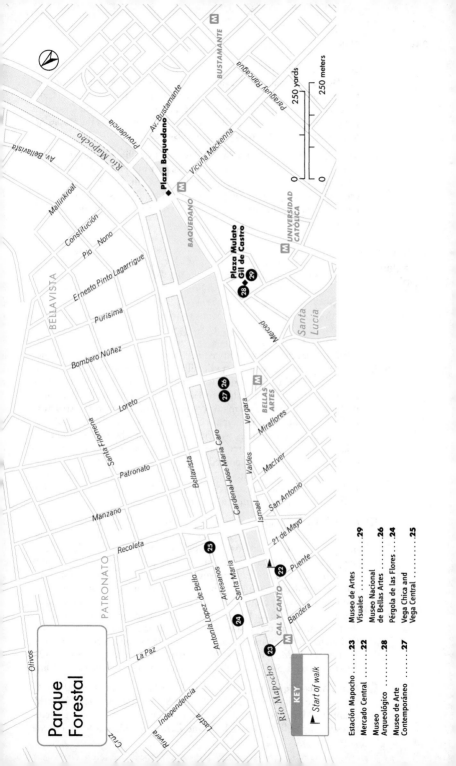

Parque Forestal

250 yards
250 meters

Strolling east through the Parque Forestal will bring you to the jewel-like **Museo Nacional de Bellas Artes** ㉖ and the adjacent **Museo de Arte Contemporáneo** ㉗. Just south of the park, near where Calle Merced and Calle José Victorino Lastarria meet, is the Plaza Mulato Gil de Castro, a pleasant little nook with bookshops and cafés, as well as the **Museo Arqueológico** ㉘ and the **Museo de Artes Visuales** ㉙.

TIMING &
PRECAUTIONS You can make a pleasant, relaxing day out of strolling through the city's most popular park, losing yourself in the art museums, and exploring Mercado Central. Vega Chica and Vega Central are usually very crowded, so keep an eye on your personal belongings. When the markets are closing, around sunset, it's best to return to neighborhoods south of the river.

off the
beaten
path

ANTIGUEDADES BALMACEDA – A taxi ride away or a good 20-minute walk from the Estación Mapocho on Balmaceda is a large warehouse-type building that houses the Antiguedades Balmaceda. If you like antiques then it's worth browsing among the corridors of stands for something that catches your fancy. On display is everything from furniture to books to jewelry. ✉ *Av. Brasil at Balmaceda, Santiago Centro* ☏ *No phone* ✆ *Daily 10:30–7.*

WHAT TO SEE
★ ㉓ **Estación Mapocho.** This mighty edifice, with its trio of two-story arches framed by intricate terra-cotta detailing, is as elegant as any train station in the world. The station was inaugurated in 1913 as a terminus for trains arriving from Valparaíso and points north, but steam engines no longer pull in here. A major conversion transformed the structure into one of the city's principal cultural centers. The Centro Cultural Estación Mapocho houses two restaurants, a fine bookstore and café, a large exhibition and arts space, and a handicrafts shop. The cavernous space that once sheltered steam engines now hosts musical performances and other events. ✉ *Plaza de la Cultura, Independencia and Balmaceda, Parque Forestal* ☏ *2/361–1761* ⊕ *www.estacionmapocho. cl* ✆ *Daily 9–6* Ⓜ *Puente Cal y Canto.*

► ㉒ **Mercado Central.** At the Central Market you'll find a matchless selection of creatures from the sea. Depending on the season, you might see the delicate beaks of *picorocos,* the world's only edible barnacles; *erizos,* the prickly shelled sea urchins; or shadowy pails full of succulent bullfrogs. If the fish don't capture your interest, the architecture may: the lofty wrought-iron ceiling of the structure, reminiscent of a Victorian train station, was prefabricated in England and erected in Santiago between 1868 and 1872. Diners are regaled by musicians in the middle of the market, where two restaurants compete for customers. You can also find a cheap, filling meal at a stand along the market's southern edge. ✉ *Ismael Valdés Vergara 900, Parque Forestal* ☏ *2/696–8327* ✆ *Mon.–Thurs. 5–5, Fri. 5–9, Sat. 5–7, Sun. 5–6* Ⓜ *Puente Cal y Canto.*

㉘ **Museo Arqueológico.** The little Archaeological Museum is devoted specifically to the indigenous peoples of Chile. Some 3,000 artifacts bring the country's Mapuche, Aymara, Fueguino, Huilliche, and Pehuenche cultures vividly to life. ✉ *José Victorino Lastarria 307, 2nd floor, Parque*

Forestal 📷 *2/664–9337* 🎟 *Free* ☉ *Weekdays and Sun. 10–2 and 3:30–6:30, Sat. 10–2* Ⓜ *Baquedano, Universidad Católica.*

The pleasant Plaza Mulato Gil de Castro, a cobblestone square off the colorful Calle José Victorino Lastarria, is an unexpected treat. In the midst of it is **R** (✉ Plaza Mulato Gil de Castro, Parque Forestal 📷 2/664–9844), a cozy café serving English teas and light fare. Weary travelers relax beneath the kettles and cups hanging from the ceiling.

㉗ **Museo de Arte Contemporáneo.** The Museum of Contemporary Art, on the opposite side of the building housing the Museo de Bellas Artes, showcases a collection of modern Latin American paintings, photography, and sculpture. The museum is run by the art school of the Universidad de Chile, so it isn't afraid to take risks; the rather dilapidated interior is a perfect setting for the edgier art. Look for Fernando Botero's pudgy *Caballo* sculpture gracing the square out front. ✉ *Bounded by Jose M. de la Barra and Ismael Valdés Vergara, Parque Forestal* 📷 *2/639–6488* ⊕ *www.mac.uchile.cl* 🎟 *400 pesos* ☉ *Tues.–Sat. 11–7, Sun. 11–5* Ⓜ *Bellas Artes.*

★ ㉙ **Museo de Artes Visuales.** You'll never confuse this dazzling museum of contemporary art with the crumbling Museo de Arte Contemporáneo. Displaying the combined private holdings of Chilean construction moguls Manuel Santa Cruz and Hugo Yaconi, this gallery has one of the finest collections of contemporary Chilean art. The building itself is a masterpiece: six gallery levels float into each other in surprising ways. The wood floors and Plexiglas-sided stairways create an open and airy space for paintings and sculptures by Roberto Matta, Arturo Duclos, Roser Bru, José Balmes, and Eugenio Dittborn, among others. ✉ *José Victorino Lastarria 307, Plaza Mulato Gil de Castro, Parque Forestal* 📷 *2/638–3502* 🎟 *1,000 pesos* ☉ *Tues.–Sun. 10:30–6:30* Ⓜ *Bellas Artes.*

㉖ **Museo Nacional de Bellas Artes.** Paintings, drawings, and sculpture by 16th- to 20th-century Chilean and European artists fill the grand National Museum of Fine Arts. The elegant, neoclassical building, which was originally intended to house the city's school of fine arts, has an impressive glass-domed ceiling that illuminates the main hall. A theater on the second floor screens short films about the featured artists. ✉ *Bounded by Jose M. de la Barra and Ismael Valdés Vergara, Parque Forestal* 📷 *2/633–0655* ⊕ *www.mnba.cl* 🎟 *Tues.–Sat. 600 pesos, Sun. free* ☉ *Tues.–Sun. 10–6:45* Ⓜ *Bellas Artes.*

PARQUE DE LAS ESCULTURAS – Providencia is mainly a business district, but it has one of the city's most captivating—and least publicized—public parks. Here, the gardens are filled with sculptures by Chile's top artists. Because of its pastoral atmosphere, the park is popular with joggers and cuddling couples. In the center is a wood pavilion that hosts sculpture exhibitions. To get here from the Pedro de Valdivia Metro stop, walk a block north to the Río Mapocho and cross the bridge to Avenida Santa María. The park is on your right.

㉔ **Pérgola de las Flores.** Santiaguinos come to the Trellis of Flowers to buy wreaths and flower arrangements to bring to the city's two cemeteries. *La Pérgola de las Flores,* a famous Chilean musical, is based on the conflict that arose in the 1930s when the mayor of Santiago wanted to shut down the market. Find a chatty florist here and you may learn all about it. ⊠ *Corner of Av. La Paz and Artesanos, Recoleta* 🕾 *No phone* 🕙 *Daily, sunrise–sunset* Ⓜ *Puente Cal y Canto.*

㉕ **Vega Chica and Vega Central.** From fruit to furniture, meat to machinery, these lively markets stock just about anything you can name. Alongside the ordinary items you can find delicacies like *piñones,* giant pine nuts found on monkey puzzle trees. If you're undaunted by crowds, try a typical Chilean meal in a closet-size eatery or picada. Chow down with the locals on *pastel de choclo,* a pie filled with ground beef, chicken, olives, boiled egg, and sultanas, and topped with mashed corn. ⊠ *Antonia López de Bello between Av. Salas and Av. Gandarillas, Recoleta* Ⓜ *Puente Cal y Canto.*

Bellavista & Parque Metropolitano

If you happen to be in Santiago on one of the rare days when the smog dissipates, head straight for Parque Metropolitano, where you'll be rewarded with spectacular views in all directions. In the shadow of Cerro San Cristóbal is Bellavista. The neighborhood has but one sight—Pablo Neruda's hillside home of La Chascona—but it's perhaps the city's best place to wander around antiques shops, bustling outdoor markets, and the city's most adventurous and colorful eateries.

a good walk

Starting from Plaza Baquedano, cross the bridge over the Río Mapocho to Bellavista. Acacia trees line the streets here, which are filled with quaint cafés, trendy restaurants, and one-story homes painted in pinks, aquamarines, and blues. Walk three blocks north on Calle Pío Nono and turn right onto Calle Antonia López de Bello. Make a left onto Constitución and head north—you'll soon enter Santiago's most lively restaurant district. On Fernando Márquez de la Plata sits the house Pablo Neruda designed, **La Chascona** ㉚ ⌐.

At the northern end of Calle Pío Nono is Plaza Caupolicán, the entrance to Parque Metropolitano. The funicular, housed in an old castlelike terminus, climbs up Santiago's highest hill, **Cerro San Cristóbal** ㉛. A quarter of the way up the hill, the funicular stops at the **Jardín Zoológico** ㉜, which you can also reach on foot by following the road. After reaching the summit, take in the expansive views, then follow the signs to the *teleférico* (cable car) and get out halfway at **Plaza Tupahue** ㉝. A short walk away is **Jardín Botánico Mapulemu** ㉞, an expansive botanical garden. A 15-minute walk east and slightly downhill will bring you to the authentic and well-kept **Jardín Japonés** ㉟.

TIMING & PRECAUTIONS Figure on an entire day to see Parque Metropolitano's major attractions. Give yourself at least an hour to wander through Bellavista, and another hour for a tour of La Chascona.

WHAT TO SEE **Cerro San Cristóbal.** St. Christopher's Hill, within Parque Metropolitano, ㉛ is one of the most popular tourist attractions in Santiago. From the west-

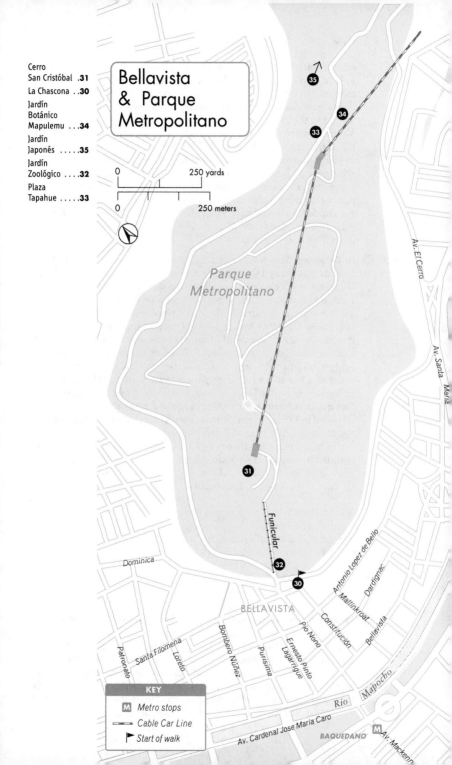

Cerro
San Cristóbal .**31**

La Chascona . .**30**

Jardín
Botánico
Mapulemu . . .**34**

Jardín
Japonés **35**

Jardín
Zoológico **32**

Plaza
Tapahue **33**

Bellavista & Parque Metropolitano

Parque
Metropolitano

Funicular

Dominica

BELLAVISTA

Patronato
Santa Filomena
Loreto
Bombero Núñez
Purísima
Ernesto Pinto Lagarrigue
Pío Nono
Constitución
Antonio López de Bello
Mallinkroat
Dardignac
Bellavista

Av. El Cerro
Av. Santa María

Río Mapocho

Av. Cardenal Jose Maria Caro

BAQUEDANO
Av. Mackenn

KEY

Ⓜ *Metro stops*

⊶⊶ *Cable Car Line*

▶ *Start of walk*

0   250 yards

0   250 meters

ern entrance at Plaza Caupolicán you can walk—it's a steep but enjoyable one-hour climb—or take the funicular. Either route leads you to the summit, which is crowned by a gleaming white statue of the Virgen de la Inmaculada. If you are coming from the eastern entrance, you can ascend in the cable car that leaves seven blocks north of the Pedro de Valdivia Metro stop. The ride, which seats two in a colored-glass bubble, can be terrifying for acrophobics. Tree branches whack at your lift as you glide over the park. ⊠ *Cerro San Cristóbal, Bellavista* ☎ *2/777–6666 for park administration, 2/735–2081 for lift information* ⊕ *www.parquemet.cl or www.funicular.cl* ☒ *Park free; round-trip funicular 1,500 pesos; round-trip cable car 1,500 pesos* ☉ *Park: Sun.–Thurs. 8 AM–10 PM, Fri.–Sat. 8 AM–midnight. Funicular: Mon. 1–8, Tues.–Fri. 10–8, weekends 10–8:30. Cable car: Mon. 1–8:30, Tues.–Sun. 10–8:30* Ⓜ *Baquedano, Pedro de Valdivia.*

★ ⮕ ㉚ **La Chascona.** This house designed by the Nobel-winning poet Pablo Neruda was dubbed the "Woman with the Tousled Hair" after Matilde Urratia, the poet's third wife. The two met while strolling in nearby Parque Forestal, and for years the house served as a romantic hideaway before they married. The pair's passionate relationship was recounted in the 1995 Italian film *Il Postino.* Tours allow you to step into the extraordinary mind of the poet whose eclectic designs earned him the label "organic architect." Winding garden paths, stairs, and bridges lead to the house and its library stuffed with books, a bedroom in a tower, and a secret passageway. Scattered throughout are collections of butterflies, seashells, wineglasses, and other odd objects that inspired Neruda's tumultuous life and romantic poetry. Neruda, who died in 1973, had two other houses on the coast—one in Valparaíso, the other in Isla Negra. All three are open as museums. Though it's not as magical as the other two, La Chascona can still set your imagination dancing. ⊠ *Fernando Márquez de la Plata 0192, Bellavista* ☎ *2/777–8741* ☒ *La Chascona 1,800 pesos, tour 3,000 pesos* ☉ *Tues.–Sun. 10–6* Ⓜ *Baquedano.*

---

need a break?

A short walk from La Chascona is Calle Antonia López de Bello, a street overflowing with bars and restaurants. Here, the café **Off the Record** (⊠ Antonia López de Bello 0155, Bellavista ☎ 2/777–7710) has a decidedly bohemian air. The wooden booths, for example, seem to have been designed with witty conversation and artistic bonhomie in mind. Black-and-white photographs recall visitors from Pablo Neruda to Uma Thurman.

㉞ **Jardín Botánico Mapulemu.** Gravel paths lead you to restful nooks among acres of well-labeled local flora at the Mapulemu Botanical Garden. Some 80 native-Chilean species grow here, including the araucaria, canelo, and macci trees. The botanical star is the squat *jubea chilena,* the ubiquitous Chilean palm. Every path and stairway seems to bring you to better views of Santiago and the Andes. Sunday mornings there are tai chi, yoga, and aerobics free of charge. ⊠ *Cerro San Cristóbal, Bellavista* ☎ *2/777–6666* ☒ *Free* ☉ *Daily 10–4* Ⓜ *Pedro de Valdivia, Baquedano.*

㉟ **Jardín Japonés.** The tranquil Japanese Garden affords a sumptuous view over the skyscrapers of Las Condes and Bellavista. Paths edged with bamboo and lit by Japanese lanterns lead past lily ponds and a gazebo beside a trickling fountain. ⊠ *Cerro San Cristóbal, Bellavista* ☎ *2/777–6666* ☑ *Free* ☉ *Daily 10–6* Ⓜ *Pedro de Valdivia, Baquedano.*

㉜ **Jardín Zoológico.** The Zoological Garden is a good place to see examples of many Chilean animals, some nearly extinct, that you might not otherwise encounter. As is often the case with many older zoos, the creatures aren't given a lot of room. Be careful with children, as some of the cages aren't properly protected, and the animals can bite. A larger, modern zoo is being built outside the city near the Universidad de Chile. ⊠ *Cerro San Cristóbal, Bellavista* ☎ *No phone* ☑ *1,700 pesos* ☉ *Tues.–Sun. 10–5* Ⓜ *Baquedano.*

🖐 ㉝ **Plaza Tupahue.** The middle stop on the teleférico deposits you in the center of Parque Metropolitano. The main attraction here in summer is the delightful **Piscina Tupahue,** a 46-m (150-ft) pool with a rocky crag running along one side. Beside the pool is the 1925 **Torreón Victoria,** a stone tower surrounded by a trellis of bougainvillea. If Piscina Tupahue is too crowded, try the nearby **Piscina Antilén.** From Plaza Tupahue you can follow a path below to **Plaza de Juegos Infantiles Gabriela Mistral,** a popular playground. ⊠ *Cerro San Cristóbal, Bellavista* ☎ *2/777–6666* ☑ *Park free, Piscina Tupahue 4,500 pesos, Piscina Antilén 5,000 pesos* ☉ *Piscina Tupahue: Nov.–Mar., Tues.–Sun. 10–7. Piscina Antilén: Nov.–Mar., Wed.–Mon. 10–7* Ⓜ *Pedro de Valdivia, Baquedano.*

Where to Eat

Santiago is overwhelming when it comes to dining, as hundreds of restaurants are strewn about the city. No matter your mood, there are likely to be half a dozen eateries within easy walking distance. Tempted to taste hearty Chilean fare? Pull up a stool at one of the counters at Vega Central and enjoy a traditional pastel de choclo. Craving seafood? Head to the Mercado Central, where you can choose from the fresh fish brought in that morning. Want a memorable meal? Trendy new restaurants are opening every day in neighborhoods like Bellavista, the most colorful of the city's dining districts.

Bellavista

CHILEAN ✕ **El Camino Real.** On a clear day, treat yourself to the stunning views
$$$–$$$$ of the city through the floor-to-ceiling windows at this restaurant atop Cerro San Cristóbal. The menu lists such dishes as pork tenderloin in mustard sauce with caramelized onions, and warm scallop salad with quail eggs and asparagus. Oenophiles appreciate the 168-bottle wine list with many Chilean vintages. Neophytes can head across a central courtyard to Bar Dalí, where the servers can organize an impromptu *degustación* of a half dozen varietals. Downstairs is a small wine museum. ⊠ *Parque Metropolitano, Bellavista* ☎ *2/232–3381 or 2/233–1238* ⚞ *Reservations essential* ▤ *AE, DC, MC, V* Ⓜ *Pedro de Valdivia, Baquedano.*

★ **$$–$$$$** ✕ **Como Agua Para Chocolate.** Inspired by Laura Esquivel's romantic 1989 novel *Like Water for Chocolate,* this Bellavista standout is part restau-

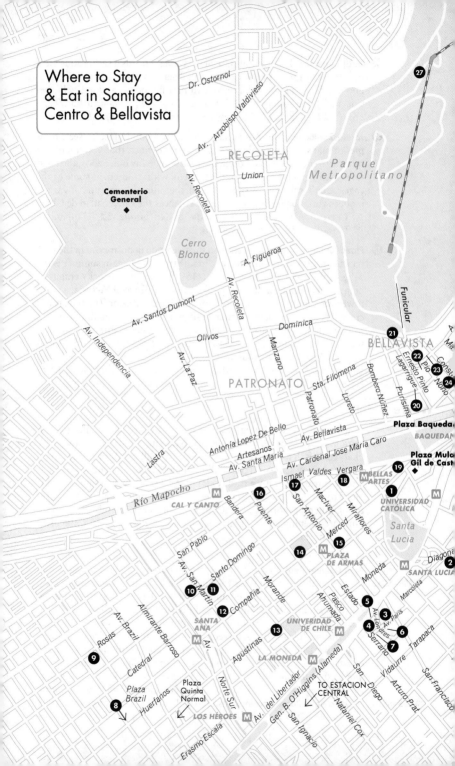

Where to Stay
& Eat in Santiago
Centro & Bellavista

Dr. Ostornol

Av. Arzobispo Valdivieso

RECOLETA

Union

Parque
Metropolitano

Cementerio
General

Cerro
Blonco

A. Figueroa

Av. Recoleta

Av. Santos Dumont

Av. Independencia

Av. La Paz

Olivos

Manzano

Dominica

Funicular

BELLAVISTA

PATRONATO

Sta. Filomena

Loreto

Purísima

Ernesto Pinto
Lagarrigue

Pío Nono

Constit

21

22

23

24

20

Plaza Baqueda

BAQUEDAN

Lastra

Antonia Lopez De Bello

Artesanos
Av. Santa Maria

Av. Bellavista

Bombero Núñez

Plaza Mula
Gil de Cast

Río Mapocho

CAL Y CANTO

Ismael Valdes Vergara

Av. Cardenal Jose María Caro

19

BELLAS
ARTES

1

Santa
Lucia

UNIVERSIDAD
CATOLICA

Bandera

Puente

16

17

San Antonio

Maclver

Miraflores

18

Merced

Diagona

SANTA LUCIA

2

San Pablo

Santo Domingo

Morande

14

15

PLAZA
DE ARMAS

Moneda

Marcoleta

Av. San Martin

10

11

12

Compañia

SANTA
ANA

Av.

UNIVERIDAD
DE CHILE

13

Estado

Paseo

Ahumada

5

3

4

6

7

Av. Londres

Av. Paris

Serrano

Vidaurre

Tarapaca

Almirante Barroso

Rosas

9

Av. Brazil

Catedral

Agustinas

LA MONEDA

Plaza
Brazil

Plaza
Quinta
Normal

Huerfanos

Norte Sur

Av. del Libertador

Gen. B. O'Higgins (Alameda)

TO ESTACION
CENTRAL

San Diego

Arturo Prat

San Francisco

8

LOS HÉROES

Av. B. O'Higgins

San Ignacio

Nataniel Cox

Erasmo Escala

KEY

Ⓜ Metro stops

🛈 Tourist information

▭ Cable Car Line

rant, part theme park. It focuses on the aphrodisiacal qualities of food, so it shouldn't be surprising that one long table is actually an iron bed, with place settings arranged on a crisp white sheet. The food compares to the decor like the film version compares to the book: it's good, but not nearly as imaginative. *Ave de la pasión,* for instance, means Bird of Passion. It may be just chicken with mushrooms, but it's served on a copper plate. ⊠ *Constitución 88, Bellavista* ☎ 2/777–8740 ▤ *AE, DC, MC, V* Ⓜ *Baquedano.*

$–$$ ╳ **Eladio.** At Eladio you can eat a succulent *bife de chorizo,* entrecôte steak, or any other cut cooked as you like; order a good bottle of Chilean wine; and even finish with a slice of *amapola* (poppy-seed) sponge cake—and you still wouldn't be much out of pocket. Come here any night but Friday, as the place fills up with office workers celebrating the arrival of the weekend. ⊠ *Pío Nono 251, Bellavista* ☎ 2/777–5083 Ⓜ *Baquedano* ⊠ *Avenida 11 de Septiembre 2250, 2nd floor, Providencia* ☎ 2/231–4224 Ⓜ *Los Leones* ⊠ *Avenida Ossa 2234, La Reina* ☎ 2/277–0661 ▤ *AE, DC, MC, V* ☉ *Bellavista branch closed Sun.*

★ ¢–$ ╳ **El Venezia.** Long before Bellavista became fashionable, this bare-bones picada was where movie stars and TV personalities rubbed elbows with the hoi polloi. While gourmands now head a block or two in either direction to the latest hot spots, tacky El Venezia still fills to capacity each day at lunch. And what's not to like? The beer is icy, the waiters are efficient, and the food is abundant. The *congrio frito* (fried conger eel) is delicious, as are the *costillar de chancho* (pork ribs). What they accomplish here is nothing short of a miracle—while you can't pinpoint exactly why, you leave tremendously satisfied. ⊠ *Pío Nono 200, Bellavista* ☎ 2/737–0900 ▤ *AE, DC, MC, V* Ⓜ *Baquedano.*

PERUVIAN ╳ **Sarita Colonia.** Easily the most outrageous restaurant in Santiago, Sarita
$–$$ Colonia is a collection of colorful dining rooms, one more vibrant than the last. The food is authentic Peruvian—try the *cau cau* (scallops stewed with vegetables) or the *pollo al maní* (chicken with a spicy peanut sauce)—and the presentation is fun and fanciful. You can also stop by for a late-night cocktail in the second-floor lounge, but don't come here if it's quiet you seek—the music is often blaring. ⊠ *Av. Dardignac 50, Bellavista* ☎ 2/737–0242 ▤ *AE, DC, MC, V* ☉ *No lunch weekends* Ⓜ *Baquedano.*

SEAFOOD ╳ **Azul Profundo.** Not so many years ago, this was the only restaurant
$$ you'd find on this street near Parque Metropolitano. Today it's one of
Fodor'sChoice dozens of restaurants in trendy Bellavista, but its two-level dining
★ room—with walls painted bright shades of blue and yellow, and racks of wine stretching to the ceiling—ensure that it stands out in the crowd. Choose your fish from the extensive menu—swordfish, sea bass, shark, flounder, salmon, trout, and haddock are among the choices—and enjoy it *a la plancha* (grilled) or *a la lata* (served on a sizzling plate with tomatoes and onions). ⊠ *Constitución 111, Bellavista* ☎ 2/738–0288 ⌕ *Reservations essential* ▤ *AE, DC, MC, V* Ⓜ *Baquedano.*

SPANISH ╳ **La Bodeguilla.** This authentic Spanish restaurant is a great place to
$–$$ stop for a glass of sangria after a tour of Cerro San Cristóbal. After all, it's right at the foot of the funicular. The dozen or so tables are set among wine barrels and between hanging strings of garlic bulbs. Nib-

ble on tasty tapas like Chorizo *riojano* (a piquant sausage), *pulpo a la gallega* (octopus with peppers and potatoes), and *queso manchego* (a mild white cheese) while perusing the long wine list. Then consider ordering the house specialty—*cabrito al horno* (oven-roasted goat). ⊠ *Av. Dominica 5, Bellavista* ☎ *2/732–5215* 🗐 *No credit cards* ⊘ *Closed Sun.* Ⓜ *Baquedano.*

★ **$–$$** ✕ **La Esquina al Jerez.** Iron lanterns and suits of armor decorate Bellavista's longtime favorite eatery, bringing to mind traditional Spanish restaurants, but the overall feeling here is contemporary, with billowing curtains and splashes of bright reds and yellows. Among the best dishes are *paella de mariscos* (seafood with rice) and tapas like *calamares fritos al alioli* (fried squid with garlic mayonnaise). There are zarzuela dance performances and live jazz weekends. ⊠ *Dardignac 0192, Bellavista* ☎ *2/777–4407* ⌒ *Reservations essential* 🗐 *AE, DC, MC, V* ⊘ *Closed Sun.* Ⓜ *Baquedano.*

Centro

CHILEAN ✕ **Bristol.** The indefatigable Guillermo Rodríguez, who has commandeered
$$–$$$ the kitchen here for more than a decade, has won just about all the country's culinary competitions. No wonder he also serves as a private chef
Fodor'sChoice to Chilean president Ricardo Lagos. Besides the innovative takes on tra-
★ ditional Chilean dishes, the buffet includes unlimited access to a wine cart stocked with a dozen quality vintages. The expertise offered by the city's most prized sommelier, Alejandro Farias, is reason enough to visit. The restaurant's prime location in Hotel Plaza San Francisco makes it a good meeting point for Santiago's movers and shakers in politics and business. ⊠ *Av. O'Higgins 816, Santiago Centro* ☎ *2/639–3832* 🗐 *AE, DC, MC, V* Ⓜ *Universidad de Chile.*

$$–$$$ ✕ **El Jardin Secreto.** Relax on a red-velvet-upholstered chaise lounge or sit back on an elegant dining-room chair in this stylish yet distinctly informal eatery. Large vases overflowing with hand-made ornamental foliage, Chinese cabinets, and small white-wood tables occupy a large section of the lobby restaurant in the Carrera Hotel. From here you can look through huge plate glass windows onto the Plaza de la Constitución as you tuck into a carefully prepared fresh fillet of *alfonsino* (an Easter Island fish) in a sauce of ginger and orange, or ravioli stuffed with *ostiones* (scallops). ⊠ *Teatinos 180, Santiago Centro* ☎ *2/698–2011* 🗐 *AE, DC, MC, V* Ⓜ *La Moneda.*

$–$$ ✕ **Atelier del Parque.** In this vast orange building the menus come on palette boards along with their own paintbrushes. On offer are creations named for artists, such as the Da Vinci—fettuccine with squid ink—and the Warhol—salmon with caramelized almonds. The restaurant's quietly satisfying interior has lots of separate seating areas, including one in a large glass atrium and another filled with comfy armchairs. A connected gallery showcases temporary exhibits of art and sculpture. ⊠ *Casa Naranja, Santo Domingo 528, Parque Forestal* ☎ *2/639–5843* 🗐 *AE, DC, MC, V* Ⓜ *Bellas Artes.*

FRENCH ✕ **Les Assassins.** Although this appears at first glance to be a rather somber
$–$$ bistro, nothing could be further from the truth. The service is friendly, and the Provence-influenced food is first-rate. The steak au poivre and

crepes suzette would make a Frenchman's eyes water. If you want to practice your Spanish, you're in luck: there's always a line of talkative locals in the cozy ground-floor bar. ⊠ *Merced 297, Santiago Centro* ☎ *2/ 638–4280* ⊟ *AE, DC, MC, V* ✆ *Closed Sun.* Ⓜ *Universidad Católica.*

INDIAN
★ **$–$$**

✕ **Majestic.** The dining area is a little cramped, but most people forgive this as soon as they taste what chef Haridas Chauhan, originally of the Sheraton in New Delhi, has to offer. Among his deliciously spicy dishes are *rogan josh* (hot lamb curry) and a pungent *murgh makhanwala* (chicken in a tangy butter sauce). The *kulfi de almendras,* made from evaporated milk, ice cream, walnuts, and almonds, is a sweet finish to a meal. Large copper base plates set on immaculate white tablecloths are a nice touch. ⊠ *Santo Domingo 1526, Santiago Centro* ☎ *2/695– 8366* ⌣ *Reservations essential* ⊟ *AE, DC, MC, V* Ⓜ *Santa Ana.*

JAPANESE
$–$$

✕ **Japón.** Take off your shoes, settle onto a cushion, and prepare yourself for authentic flavors from the floating kingdom. Frequented by Santiago's small but growing Japanese community, this restaurant off Plaza Baquedano has a first-rate sushi bar and three comfortable dining rooms. The most patient waiters in town help you make a selection, and the chef is happy to custom-prepare a dish at your request. The *unagi* (eel) is fantastic, and the noodle soup is a meal in itself. ⊠ *Barón Pierre de Coubertin 39, Santiago Centro* ☎ *2/222–4517* ⊟ *AE, DC, MC, V* Ⓜ *Baquedano.*

$–$$

✕ **Primado.** This self-service basement restaurant, accessible from Calle Agustinas or through the hotel lobby of the Carrera, is a new concept in fast food. A chalk board behind the long stainless-steel counter lists the day's choices, everything from sushi to baked *congrio* (conger eel). Serve yourself, pay at the end of the counter, and take your tray to a table in any one of several dining areas. Primado's light wood floors, soft illumination, and burlap screens have an instantly relaxing effect. ⊠ *Teatinos 180, Santiago Centro* ☎ *2/680–3600* ⊟ *AE, DC, MC, V* ✆ *No dinner* Ⓜ *La Moneda.*

SEAFOOD
★ **$–$$**

✕ **Donde Augusto.** For the best value on seafood in town, head to this eatery within the bustling Mercado Central. If you don't mind the unhurried service and the odd tear in the tablecloth, you may have the time of your life dining on everything from sea urchins to ceviche. Placido Domingo eats here on every visit to Chile, attended to by the white-bearded Segovian Augusto Vasquez, who has run Donde Augusto for more than four decades. ⊠ *Mercado Central, Santiago Centro* ☎ *2/672–2829* ⌣ *Reservations not accepted* ⊟ *AE, DC, MC, V* ✆ *No dinner* Ⓜ *Puente Cal y Canto.*

VEGETARIAN
¢–$

✕ **Govinda's.** Cheap but hearty vegetarian lunches are prepared here by Hari Krishnas. Card tables and lawn chairs are the extent of the decor, but the fresh juices and homemade bread are delicious. Try the yogurt with mixed fruit and honey for dessert. ⊠ *Av. Compañía 1489, Santiago Centro* ☎ *2/673–0892* ⊟ *No credit cards* ✆ *Closed weekends. No dinner* Ⓜ *Santa Ana.*

Las Condes

CAFÉS
¢–$

✕ **Cafe Melba.** Almost unheard of in Santiago, this small café-restaurant serves breakfast for as long as it's open, starting at 7:30 AM on weekdays and 8 AM on weekends. If you're particularly hungry, order The Works—baked beans, mushrooms, sausage, bacon, and more. Drink it down with a caffe latte, served in a large white bowl. The owner of Cafe Melba is hands-on, which may explain why this popular eatery continues to thrive. The interior is airy, with simple wood tables, black-metal chairs, light-wood floors, and whitewashed walls. ☒ *Don Carlos 2898, off El Bosque Norte, Las Condes* ☎ *2/232–4546* 🖃 *AE, DC, MC, V* ☯ *No dinner* Ⓜ *Tobalaba.*

ITALIAN ⨯ **Bice.** Bice has revolutionized Santiago's notion of elegant dining. The
★ **$$$–$$$$** small, two-tiered dining room has soaring ceilings that lend a dramatic flair, while gleaming floors of alternating stripes of dark and light wood add a touch of contemporary glamour. The service is a breed apart—white-jacketed waiters zip around, attending to your every need. The menu leans toward imaginatively prepared pastas, such as linguine with scallops, razor clams, shrimp, and mussels. Be sure to leave room for desserts such as the *cioccolatíssimo,* a hot, chocolate soufflé with melted chocolate inside, served with an exquisite *dulce de leche* ice cream. ☒ *Hotel Inter-Continental, Av. Luz 2920, Las Condes* ☎ *2/381–5500* ⌂ *Reservations essential* 🖃 *AE, DC, MC, V* Ⓜ *Tobalaba.*

$$–$$$$ ⨯ **Le Due Torri.** For excellent homemade pastas, head to this longtime favorite. If you think the *agnolotti,* stuffed with ricotta cheese and spinach, resembles a feathered hat, you're right. The owner, who lived in Italy during World War II, intentionally shaped it like a Red Cross nurse's cap. The rear of the dining room, with its small cypress trees and a corner pergola, is traditional; seating in the front is more contemporary. The name of the restaurant, by the way, refers to the two towers erected by the dueling Garisenda and Asinelli families in the owner's native Bologna. ☒ *Av. Isidora Goyenechea 2908, Las Condes* ☎ *2/231–3427* ⌂ *Reservations essential* 🖃 *AE, DC, MC, V* Ⓜ *Tobalaba.*

JAPANESE ⨯ **Matsuri.** With a sleek design that calls to mind Los Angeles as much
$–$$ as Tokyo, this restaurant in the Hyatt Regency is one of Santiago's most stylish eateries. The dining room's eclectic mix of materials includes porous stone from China and wood from Madagascar. Downstairs are a sushi bar and two tatami rooms (no shoes allowed, but slippers are provided) with sliding screens for privacy, while upstairs are two grill tables. Try the eight-piece dragon roll—cucumber and eel covered with avocado and smelt roe. ☒ *Av. Kennedy 4601, Las Condes* ☎ *2/363–3051* 🖃 *AE, DC, MC, V* Ⓜ *Escuela Militar.*

MEXICAN ⨯ **Café Santa Fe.** Santiago's twentysomething crowd flocks to this Tex-
$ Mex restaurant for its authentic guacamole, sizzling fajitas (with seafood or meat fillings), and frozen margaritas. Don't come here if you want a quiet meal, as the place is always noisy. Bright shades of blue, pink, and ocher decorate the restaurant. ☒ *Vitacura 9435, Las Condes* ☎ *2/325–5293* 🖃 *AE, DC, MC, V* Ⓜ *Escuela Militar.*

SEAFOOD ⨯ **Isla Negra.** The sails flying from the roof let you know that Isla Negra
$–$$ means business when it comes to seafood. The restaurant takes its name from a coastal town south of Santiago that was Nobel laureate Pablo Neruda's last home. The poet's favorite dish was conger eel soup, and

you'll find it served here as a starter. Don't miss the empanadas stuffed with everything from cheese to razor clams. The *chupe de marisco*, a delicious seafood chowder, comes in a quaint earthenware bowl. ⊠ *Av. El Bosque Norte 0325, Las Condes* ☎ *2/231–3118* 🖷 *2/233–0339* ⚑ *Reservations essential* 🖃 *AE, DC, MC, V* Ⓜ *Tobalaba.*

SPANISH   ✕ **Gernika.** The Basque owners of this wood-and-stone restaurant have
$$$–$$$$ created a little slice of their homeland with black-and-white photographs of traditional scenes, tapestries bearing an ancient coat of arms, and even jai alai equipment. Head upstairs to the more intimate upper level, which has three well-decorated private dining salons. Chilean seafood is cooked with Spanish flair, as in the *congrio donostiarra* (conger eel coated in chili sauce and fried in olive oil). Fresh *centolla* (king crab) is brought in from Punta Arenas at the foot of Chile. Several selections from Spain's Rioja region appear on the wine list. ⊠ *Av. El Bosque Norte 0227, Las Condes* ☎ *2/232–9954* ⚑ *Reservations essential* 🖃 *AE, DC, MC, V* ☽ *No lunch Sat.* Ⓜ *Tobalaba.*

THAI   ✕ **Anakena.** This spacious Thai eatery in the Hyatt Regency serves some
★ **$–$$** of the finest spicy food in Santiago. You can tuck into the tastiest *pad thai* (rice noodles, peanuts, egg, sprouts, and shrimp) or the spiciest green-curry chicken while admiring the beautifully kept gardens and attractive pool. There's also a buffet with a terrific choice of dishes, including pork with walnuts and celery in a tangy sauce, and tiger prawns with lemongrass and cashews. ⊠ *Av. Kennedy 4601, Las Condes* ☎ *2/363–3177* 🖃 *AE, DC, MC, V* Ⓜ *Escuela Militar.*

VEGETARIAN   ✕ **El Naturista.** A green-and-white-checkered floor is the most prominent
¢–$ feature of this large, airy restaurant, which has sidled away from run-of-the-mill vegetarian fare. It conjures up such dishes as *fricasé de cochayuyo* (seaweed stew)—a distinctly slimy but good dish that's typically Chilean in that seaweed is widely eaten throughout the country. The scrumptious lasagne is made from home-grown eggplants. ⊠ *Vitacura 2751, Las Condes* ☎ *2/236–5140* 🖃 *AE, DC, MC, V* ☽ *Closed Sun.* Ⓜ *Tobalaba.*

Nuñoa

CHILEAN   ✕ **Restorán Don Peyo.** For first-rate Chilean food, join the families that
★ **$** flock to Don Peyo. The ceilings are low and the walls patched stucco, but what this place lacks in aesthetics it more than makes up for in flavor. The hot sauce and the garlic spread are tasty, but meat dishes—especially a Chilean roast beef called *plateada del horno*—are what put this restaurant on the map. ⊠ *Av. Grecia 448, Nuñoa* 🖃 *AE, DC, MC, V* ☽ *Closed Sun.* Ⓜ *Irrazaval.*

Providencia

CHILEAN   ✕ **El Cid.** Considered by critics to be among the city's top restaurants,
$$–$$$$ El Cid is the culinary centerpiece of the classic Sheraton Santiago. The dining room, which overlooks the pool, is simple. All the excitement here is provided by the food, which is served with a flourish. Don't miss the famous *parrillada* of grilled seafood—king crab, prawns, squid, and scallops with a sweet, spicy sauce. If you're new to Chilean cuisine, you can't go wrong with the excellent lunch buffet, which includes ap-

petizers, entrées, desserts, and unlimited wine. ⊠ *Av. Santa María 1742, Providencia* ☏ *2/233–5000* ▤ *AE, DC, MC, V* Ⓜ *Pedro de Valdivia.*

$$ ✕ **El Parrón.** One of the city's oldest restaurants, dating from 1914, specializes in parrilladas, or meat platters, and serves just about every cut you can imagine. The dining areas are large and slightly impersonal, but the extensive wine list and menu make up for them. The congenial, wood-paneled bar is the perfect place to sample the refreshing national aperitif—the pisco sour. For dessert try a popular Chilean street-trolley offering, *mote con huesillos* (peeled wheat kernels and dried peaches). ⊠ *Providencia 1184, Providencia* ☏ *2/251–8911* ▤ *AE, DC, MC, V* ☾ *No dinner Sun.* Ⓜ *Manuel Montt.*

★ $–$$ ✕ **Lomit's.** There's nothing particularly smart about Lomit's, a traditional Chilean sandwich bar, but it unfailingly serves up some of the city's best *barro lucos,* steak sandwiches with melted cheese. You can eat at the long, central, diner-style bar and watch the sandwich maker at work, or find a small table to the side. Black-trimmed red jackets are the everyday attire of the mature and slightly stern-faced waiters here. ⊠ *Providencia 1980, Providencia* ☏ *2/233–1897* ▤ *AE, DC, MC, V* Ⓜ *Pedro de Valdivia.*

¢–$ ✕ **Liguria.** This extremely popular picada has four branches in the city where you can get reliable, typical Chilean food cheaply. A large selection of Chilean wine accompanies such favorites as *jardín de mariscos* (shellfish stew) and the filling *cazuela* (a stew of beef or chicken and potatoes). ⊠ *Av. Providencia 1373, Providencia* ☏ *2/235–7914* Ⓜ *Manuel Montt* ⊠ *Pedro de Valdivia 047, Providencia* ☏ *2/334–4346* Ⓜ *Pedro de Valdivia* ⊠ *Av. Providencia 2682, Providencia* ☏ *2/232–4918* Ⓜ *Los Leones* ⊠ *Av. Las Condes 12265, Las Condes* ☏ *2/243–6121* Ⓜ *Escuela Militar* ▤ *No credit cards* ☾ *Closed Sun.*

FRENCH ✕ **Le Flaubert.** You could be dining at home in this French tea room–restau-
$–$$ rant with picture-filled walls, table lamps, magazine racks, and classical music. The menu of the day, written on a blackboard, might tempt you with such dishes as a traditional coq au vin or a *pastel de jaiba* (crab pie) cooked to perfection. Homesick Brits come here to reminisce over freshly baked scones and refreshing cups of tea. There's also a large, shady patio garden. ⊠ *Orrego Luco 125, Providencia* ☏ *2/231–9424* ▤ *AE, DC, MC, V* Ⓜ *Pedro de Valdivia.*

MEDITERRANEAN ✕ **De Cangrejo a Conejo.** Don't bother looking for a sign because there
$–$$ isn't one—which seems to be the fashion for the hippest Santiago restaurants. From the outside this restaurant could be the house next door, an attractive beige period residence. You enter through tall, heavy wooden double doors into a large, high-ceilinged interior. Here, tables and chairs of light wood and steel have been thoughtfully arranged around a long curving bar, and flourishing greenery extends out into the patio garden. The menu is all encompassing, reflecting its name, with everything from crab pie to stewed rabbit. Try the lamb shanks on a bed of creamy mashed potatoes, or the sole with sautéed vegetables. ⊠ *Avenida Italia 805, Providencia* ☏ *2/634–4041 or 2/634–4064* ▤ *No credit cards* ☾ *Closed Sun.*

MEXICAN ✕ **Los Geranios.** Maize, chile, and *refrijoles* (kidney beans) form the
$ base of nearly all the dishes at this authentic Mexican restaurant in an

attractive, dark red house with bright blue window frames. Stuffed peppers, enchiladas, and burritos are served with spicy rice and black beans. Dine at heavy wooden tables and chairs to the sounds of Mexican music. ⊠ *Santa Beatríz 93, Providencia* ☎ *2/236–6487* ▭ *No credit cards* ⊘ *Closed Sun.* Ⓜ *Pedro de Valdivia, Manuel Montt.*

SEAFOOD
$$–$$$
Fodor'sChoice
★

✕ **Aquí Está Coco.** The best seafood in Santiago is served in a dining room where the walls are covered with flotsam and jetsam found on Chilean beaches. Ask your waiter—or friendly owner "Coco" Pacheco—which fish was caught that day. This is a good place to try Chile's famous *machas* (clams), served with tomatoes and Parmesan cheese, or *corvina* (sea bass) grilled with plenty of butter. Don't miss the cellar, where you can sample wines from the extensive collection of Chilean vintages. ⊠ *La Concepción 236 Providencia* ☎ *2/235–8649* ⊕ *www.aquiestacoco.cl* ⌂ *Reservations essential* ▭ *AE, DC, MC, V* ⊘ *Closed Sun.* Ⓜ *Pedro de Valdivia.*

VEGETARIAN
$

✕ **Café del Patio.** The chef uses all organic produce, half of which is grown in the owner's garden, at this vegetarian eatery hidden in the back of quaint Galería del Patio. The chef's salad—with lettuce, tomato, hearts of palm, and Gruyère cheese—is exquisite, as is the vegetarian ravioli. The menu also includes a handful of dishes with an Asian flair. At night, Café del Patio turns into a bar. ⊠ *Providencia 1670, Providencia* ☎ *2/236–1251* ▭ *AE, DC, MC, V* ⊘ *Closed Sun. No lunch Sat.* Ⓜ *Pedro de Valdivia.*

$

✕ **El Huerto.** In the heart of Providencia, this vegetarian eatery is a hangout for hip young Santiaguinos. Even the wood paneling and high windows here feel healthy. Simple dishes like stir-fried veggies (made with organic produce) and pancakes stuffed with asparagus and mushrooms are full of flavor, but it's the hearty soups and freshly squeezed juices that register the highest praise. Try the tasty *jugo de zanahoria* (carrot juice). Besides lunch and dinner, those in the know also drop by for afternoon tea. ⊠ *Orrego Luco 054, Providencia* ☎ *2/233–2690* ▭ *AE, DC, MC, V* ⊘ *No lunch Sun.* Ⓜ *Pedro de Valdivia.*

Vitacura

FRENCH
$–$$

✕ **Le Fournil.** Rumor has it that the French owners import even their flour from France at this café-boulangerie. The croissants and baguettes are excellent, but the *tarte tatin* steals the show—large, thick chunks of perfectly baked apple atop a thin layer of pastry, served with a scoop of creamy vanilla ice cream. The *plato del dia* (dish of the day) is always a tasty concoction, but equally good bets are the mixed green salad with grilled goat's cheese and the succulent entrecôte steak with chips. Wicker chairs, wooden tables, whitewashed walls, and large shady terraces make for comfortable dining. ⊠ *Vitacura 3841, Vitacura* ☎ *2/228–0219* ⊠ *Las Condes 7542, Las Condes* ☎ *2/212–5272* ⊠ *Don Carlos 2879, Las Condes* ☎ *2/231–3583* ▭ *AE, DC, MC, V* Ⓜ *Tobalaba.*

MOROCCAN
$–$$

✕ **Zanzibar.** Although you can order a tabouleh salad or lamb *tagine* (stew), this ostensibly Moroccan restaurant is more about conjuring up an exotic atmosphere than re-creating the cuisine of the region. (The first clue would be that Zanzibar isn't anywhere near Morocco.) The food is tasty, but the real reason to come is to glide across the multi-colored mosaic floors and settle into a chair placed beneath dozens of silver lanterns. Tables are just as fanciful, with designs made from pistachio nuts, red peppers, and beans. It's all a bit over-the-top, but fun nonetheless. ⊠ *Borde Río, Av. Monseñor Escrivá de Balaguer 6400, Vitacura* ☎ *2/218–0119* ⚖ *Reservations essential* ▤ *AE, DC, MC, V.*

SEAFOOD ✕ **Europeo.** Whether you dine on the crisp white-linen tablecloths in the
$$–$$$ elegant dining room or under an umbrella in the open-air brasserie, you're in for a fine meal at this trendy yet relaxed eatery on Santiago's most prestigious shopping avenue. The menu leans toward fish: try the succulent parrillada *de pescado,* with scallops, squid, salmon, and crispy fried noodles; a lightly grilled smoked salmon steak on a bed of watercress; or the catch of the day. Juicy steaks, venison, and lamb are good choices for landlubbers. Save room for a dessert of crème brûlée *de lucuma* (lucuma is a fruit native to Peru) or chocolate mousse with almonds. ⊠ *Av. Alonso de Cordova, Vitacura* ☎ *2/208–3603* ⚖ *Reservations essential* ▤ *AE, DC, MC, V.*

$$–$$$ ✕ **Ibis de Puerto Varas.** Nattily nautical sails stretch taut across the ceiling, pierced here and there by mastlike wood columns, and the walls are a splashy blue at this seafood restaurant. Choose from appetizers such as baby eels with hot pepper and garlic or shrimp and squid with an orange sauce. *Panqueque Ibis* is a pancake stuffed with shrimp, calamari, and scallops; the whole thing is sautéed in butter, flambéed in cognac, and served with a spinach and cream sauce. ⊠ *Borde Río, Av. Monseñor Escrivá de Balaguer 6400, Vitacura* ☎ *2/218–0111* ⚖ *Reservations essential* ▤ *AE, DC, MC, V.*

Where to Stay

Santiago's accommodations range from luxurious *hoteles* to comfortable *residenciales,* the Chilean equivalent of bed-and-breakfasts. The city also has more than a dozen five-star properties. Most newer hotels are in Providencia and Las Condes, a short taxi ride from Santiago Centro. Although the official room rates are pricey, you'll undoubtedly find discounts. Call and ask for the best possible rate. It's a good idea to reserve in advance during the peak seasons (January–February and July–August). Note that the 18% hotel tax is removed from your bill if you pay in U.S. dollars or with a credit card.

Centro

$$$$ ▦ **Hotel Plaza San Francisco.** This central hotel facing the historic Iglesia
Fodor'sChoice San Francisco has everything corporate travelers need, from business ser-
★ vices to a convention center. Between meetings there's plenty to do—take a dip in the lovely pool, stroll through the art gallery, or select a bottle from the well-stocked wineshop. Bristol, the restaurant, serves Chilean food and has perhaps Chile's most talented chef. Large beds, lovely antique furniture, and marble-trim baths fill the hotel's cozy rooms. And while all these amenities are tremendous draws, one of the best reasons to choose this hotel is for its helpful, professional staff. ⊠ *Av. O'Higgins 816, Santiago Centro* ☎ *2/639–3832, 800/223–5652 toll free in the U.S.* ☎ *2/639–7826* ⊕ *www.plazasanfrancisco.cl* ➦ *155 rooms, 8 suites* ♨ *Restaurant, room service, in-room data ports, in-room safes, minibars,*

indoor pool, gym, hot tub, massage, sauna, lobby lounge, piano bar, laundry service, Internet, business services, convention center, meeting rooms, free parking ▤ *AE, DC, MC, V* ⅥⓄⅼ *BP* Ⓜ *Universidad de Chile.*

★ **$$$** ⊞ **Carrera.** Santiago's oldest luxury hotel occupies a prominent corner of Plaza de la Constitución, and the rooftop restaurant here provides a matchless view of the country's most important square. Because it has been around for more than 60 years, the Carrera has the prestige that newer hotels lack. The opulent two-story lobby preserves its original art deco murals, and chintz draperies, prints of hunting scenes, and comfortable armchairs lend the suites overlooking the plaza an air of distinction. Live jazz performances are held in the dark-paneled bar, popular among business executives and politicians. ✉ *Teatinos 180, Santiago Centro* ☎ *2/698–2011* 🖷 *2/672–1083* ⊕ *www.hotelcarrera.com* 🖙 *305 rooms, 22 suites* ⅋ *4 restaurants, room service, in-room data ports, in-room safes, minibars, cable TV, in-room VCRs, golf privileges, pool, gym, hair salon, racquetball, piano bar, baby-sitting, laundry service, concierge, Internet, business services, meeting room, airport shuttle, car rental, travel services, free parking, no-smoking floor* ▤ *AE, DC, MC, V* Ⓜ *La Moneda, Plaza de Armas.*

$$ ⊞ **Hotel Majestic.** Towering white pillars, peaked archways, and glittery brass ornaments welcome you to this Indian-inspired hotel, which also houses an excellent Indian restaurant. A welcoming staff and a location several blocks from the Plaza de Armas make the Majestic a good choice. Even though the bright, airy rooms have "soundproof" windows, ask for one facing away from the street. ✉ *Santo Domingo 1526, Santiago Centro* ☎ *2/695–8366* 🖷 *2/697–4051* ⊕ *www.hotelmajestic.cl* 🖙 *50 rooms* ⅋ *2 restaurants, café, fans, in-room safes, minibars, cable TV, pool, bar, laundry service, free parking, no smoking rooms; no a/c in some rooms* ▤ *AE, DC, MC, V* ⅥⓄⅼ *BP* Ⓜ *Santa Ana.*

★ **$** ⊞ **City Hotel.** Suitably bedecked porters open the heavy front doors of this 70-year-old establishment, a former rival in its heyday of the upscale Carrera hotel. The City seems stuck in a time warp, but this is what gives the hotel its old-fashioned charm. The slightly dated rooms are spacious with high ceilings, and bathrooms still have the original large white tubs. Request one of the quieter rooms not facing the street. This place is a real bargain right in the heart of downtown, less than a minute from the Plaza de Armas. ✉ *Compañía 1063, Santiago Centro* ☎🖷 *2/695–4526* 🖙 *72 rooms* ⅋ *Restaurant, room service, minibars, cable TV, bar, laundry service, meeting room, free parking; no a/c* ▤ *AE, DC, MC, V* ⅥⓄⅼ *CP* Ⓜ *Plaza de Armas.*

$ ⊞ **Foresta.** Staying in this seven-story hotel across the street from Cerro Santa Lucía is like visiting an elegant old home. Cheery floral wallpaper, lovely antique furnishings, and bronze and marble accents decorate the guest rooms. The best ones are those on the upper floors overlooking the hill. A rooftop restaurant-bar is a great place to enjoy the view. The quaint cafés and shops of Plaza Mulato Gil de Castro are just around the corner. ✉ *Victoria Subercaseaux 353, Santiago Centro* ☎🖷 *2/639–6261* 🖙 *35 rooms, 8 suites* ⅋ *Restaurant, room service, minibars, cable TV, piano bar, laundry service, Internet, meeting room, free parking; no a/c* ▤ *AE, DC, MC, V* Ⓜ *Bellas Artes.*

$ 🏨 **Hostal Río Amazonas.** The narrow lobby of this small hostelry, overflowing with foliage, is painted a warm, welcoming orange. All the rooms have high ceilings and double doors, many of which open onto the table-filled lobby, where you can breakfast and sit around reading. Each evening, the friendly owner Fabian serves cocktails and cold beers to his crowd of foreign guests. ✉ *Rosas 2234, Barrio Brasil* ☎ *2/671–9013 or 2/698–4092* 🖷 *2/671–9013* ⊕ *www.hostalrioamazonas.cl* 🛏 *10 rooms* ⚫ *Bar, laundry service, Internet, parking (fee); no a/c, no room phones, no room TVs* ▤ *AE, DC, MC, V* ⵔ *CP* Ⓜ *Santa Ana.*

$ 🏨 **Hotel Los Arcos.** Young foreigners on a budget flock to this modest hotel off Plaza Brasil. Rooms are simple but clean, and some have windows overlooking an interior courtyard and café. ✉ *Agustinas 2173, Santiago Centro* ☎ *2/699–0998 or 2/696–5602* 🛏 *20 rooms* ⚫ *Café, room service, fans, laundry service; no a/c* ▤ *AE, DC, MC, V* Ⓜ *República.*

$ 🏨 **Hotel Santa Lucia.** The rooms are on the small side and are a little tired looking—the hotel has been operating for more than 40 years—but they're spotlessly clean, and the hotel is central. The lobby is bright, airy, and spacious. The large terrace restaurant, unusually quiet given its location, serves nothing but typical Chilean fare. Each weekday, without fail, it plays host to the father of Marcelo Rios, who for a short time topped the world tennis rankings. ✉ *San Antonio 327, Paseo Huérfanos 779, Santiago Centro* ☎ *2/639–8201* 🖷 *2/633–1844* 🛏 *70 rooms* ⚫ *Fans, in-room safes, minibars, cable TV, laundry service, Internet, meeting rooms, parking (fee); no a/c* ▤ *AE, DC, MC, V* ⵔ *CP* Ⓜ *Plaza de Armas.*

$ 🏨 **Hotel Vegas.** This colonial-style building, adorned with a bullet-shape turret on the corner, is in the heart of the charming Barrio París-Londres. Minutes away is the stunning Iglesia San Francisco. Rooms here have plenty of windows—ask for one with a view of gently curving Calle Londres. ✉ *Londres 49, Santiago Centro* ☎ *2/632–2498 or 2/632–2514* 🖷 *2/632–5084* ⊕ *www.hotelvegas.net* 🛏 *20 rooms* ⚫ *Café, room service, in-room safes, cable TV, bar, laundry service, Internet, free parking, no-smoking rooms; no a/c in some rooms* ▤ *AE, DC, MC, V* Ⓜ *Universidad de Chile.*

$ 🏨 **El Marqués del Forestal.** A good budget choice for families, these small apartments sleep up to four people. The simply furnished rooms also have kitchenettes. The hotel overlooks Parque Forestal, not far from Mercado Central. ✉ *Ismael Valdés Vergara 740, Santiago Centro* ☎ *2/633–3462* 🖷 *2/639–4157* 🛏 *15 apartments* ⚫ *Kitchenettes, laundry service, free parking; no a/c* ▤ *AE, DC, MC, V* ⵔ *CP* Ⓜ *Puente Cal y Canto, Plaza de Armas.*

★ $ 🏨 **Residencial Londres.** This inexpensive, 1920s-era hotel in the picturesque Barrio París-Londres is just a stone's throw from most of the city's major sights. Rooms are spacious, with high ceilings ringed by detailed moldings and expansive wood floors. The best rooms have stone balconies overlooking this charmingly atypical neighborhood. The hosts are friendly and helpful. ✉ *Londres 54, Santiago Centro* ☎ *2/638–2215* 🛏 *27 rooms* ⚫ *Laundry service; no a/c, no room phones, no room TVs* ▤ *No credit cards* Ⓜ *Universidad de Chile.*

¢–$ 🏨 **Hotel París.** In the heart of Barrio París-Londres stands this mansion-turned-hotel with a large lobby and a quaint courtyard garden. Rooms are old-fashioned and well furnished. Those in the more comfortable half, which you reach by a winding, marble staircase, are more spacious, come with cable TV, and are just a few thousand pesos extra. ⊠ *París 813, La Alameda* ☎ *2/664–0921* 🖷 *2/639–4037* 📠 *40 rooms* ⚬ *Dining room; no a/c* ⊟ *AE, DC, MC, V* Ⓜ *Universidad de Chile, Santa Lucía.*

Las Condes

★ **$$$$** 🏨 **Hyatt Regency.** The soaring spire of the Hyatt Regency leaves a lasting impression, especially if you're shooting up a glass elevator through a 24-story atrium. An architectural eye-catcher, the hotel has rooms that wrap around the cylindrical lobby, providing a panoramic view of the Andes. Executive suites in the upper-floor Regency Club include express check-in, a billiards room, and a private dining area. Duke's, the spitting image of an English pub, fills to standing capacity each day after work hours. The hotel's three restaurants—Tuscan, Thai, and Japanese—are all worth a visit. ⊠ *Av. Kennedy 4601, Las Condes* ☎ *2/218–1234* 🖷 *2/218–2513* ⊕ *www.santiago.hyatt.com* 📠 *287 rooms, 23 suites* ⚬ *3 restaurants, room service, in-room data ports, some in-room faxes, in-room safes, minibars, cable TV, in-room VCRs, golf privileges, 2 tennis courts, pool, hair salon, health club, massage, sauna, bar, lobby lounge, shops, baby-sitting, laundry service, concierge, Internet, business services, convention center, meeting rooms, airport shuttle, free parking, no-smoking floor* ⊟ *AE, DC, MC, V.*

$$$$ 🏨 **Radisson Royal.** Santiago's most dynamic office building, the World Trade Center, is also home to the Radisson Royal, a combination that will make sense to many corporate travelers. The windows here are huge, with three wide glass panels for triptych perspectives of the city and the Andes beyond. The upholstered leather chairs and wood paneling in meeting rooms make it clear the hotel is serious in its attitude toward luxury. ⊠ *Av. Vitacura 2610, Las Condes* ☎ *2/203–6000, 800/333–3333 toll free in the U.S.* 🖷 *2/203–6001* ⊕ *www.radisson.com/santiagocl* 📠 *159 rooms, 26 suites* ⚬ *Restaurant, room service, in-room data ports, in-room safes, minibars, cable TV, indoor pool, gym, bar, lounge, library, baby-sitting, laundry service, concierge, Internet, business services, meeting rooms, helipad, free parking, no-smoking floors* ⊟ *AE, DC, MC, V* Ⓜ *Tobalaba.*

$$$$ 🏨 **Santiago Marriott Hotel.** The first 25 floors of the tallest building in Santiago—40 stories in all—house the Marriott hotel. An impressive two-story, cream-marble lobby sprouts full-grown palm trees in and around comfortable seating areas. The hotel caters to those on business, and if you opt for an executive room you can breakfast in a private lounge while you scan the newspaper and marvel at the snowcapped Andes. You needn't venture out for entertainment either: there are tango evenings in the Latin Grill restaurant along with weekly wine tasting sessions. ⊠ *Av. Kennedy 5741, Las Condes* ☎ *2/426–2000, 800/228–9290 toll free in the U.S. and Canada* 🖷 *2/426–2001* ⊕ *www.santiagomarriott.com* 📠 *280 rooms, 60 suites* ⚬ *2 restaurants, in-room data ports, minibars, cable TV, indoor pool, health club, hot tub, sauna, bar, lobby lounge, shops, baby-sitting, laundry service, concierge, Internet, business services, convention center, meeting rooms, airport shuttle, travel services, free parking, no-smoking floor* ⊟ *AE, DC, MC, V.*

$$$–$$$$ Ⓗ **Hotel Inter-Continental.** A two-story marble lobby announces that you have entered one of the city's top hotels; beyond the welcome desk there are comfortable lounges, including one next to an indoor waterfall. In the back is Bice, one of the city's most memorable restaurants. The rooms are sumptuous, with doors made from handsome panels of the native blond wood called *mañio* and a menu card listing five types of pillows, from "very soft" to "stiff." Five executive floors have express check-in, a sleek private dining area with open bar, and an elegant meeting room. ⊠ *Av. Vitacura 2885, Las Condes* ☎ *2/394–2000* 🖷 *2/394–2078* ⊕ *www.interconti.com* ⬎ *297 rooms, 9 suites* ⚭ *2 restaurants, room service, in-room data ports, in-room safes, minibars, cable TV with movies and video games, indoor pool, gym, massage, sauna, 2 bars, lobby lounge, shops, baby-sitting, laundry service, concierge, Internet, business services, convention center, meeting rooms, travel services, free parking, no-smoking floors* ⊟ *AE, DC, MC, V* ⍾⦿⍾ *BP* Ⓜ *Tobalaba.*

$$–$$$ Ⓗ **Hotel Montebianco.** The four-floor Montebianco manages to combine a professional attitude that many larger places lack with an informal setting and a friendly, helpful staff. The rooms, which wind around a central staircase, are on the small side; the king-size beds take up most of the space. A few dollars extra secures a room with more elbow room. The hotel is right on a popular dining thoroughfare. ⊠ *Av. Isidora Goyenechea 2911, Las Condes* ☎ *2/232–5034* 🖷 *2/233–0420* ⊕ *www. hotelmontebianco.cl* ⬎ *33 rooms* ⚭ *Cafeteria, dining room, in-room safes, some minibars, cable TV, bar, laundry service, Internet, business services, airport shuttle, travel services* ⊟ *AE, DC, MC, V* ⍾⦿⍾ *BP* Ⓜ *El Golf, Tobalaba.*

$$ Ⓗ **Hotel Tarapacá.** This smaller hotel may have a smudge here and there, but its location in fashionable Las Condes makes up for it. Rooms facing the commercial hub of Avenida Apoquindo are susceptible to traffic noise, so ask for one in the back. Better yet, pay a few extra dollars for one of two spacious suites on the 11th floor. The dormer windows make you feel that you're in a garret. ⊠ *Vecinal 40, at Av. Apoquindo, Las Condes* ☎ *2/245–1300* 🖷 *2/245–1440* ⊕ *www.hoteltarapaca.cl* ⬎ *52 rooms* ⚭ *Restaurant, room service, in-room safes, minibars, cable TV, sauna, bar, laundry service, Internet, business services, meeting rooms, free parking* ⊟ *AE, DC, MC, V* ⍾⦿⍾ *BP* Ⓜ *El Golf, Tobalaba.*

Providencia

$$$$ Ⓗ **Four Points Sheraton.** Río Mapocho and the heart of Providencia's shopping district are just steps away from this small luxury hotel. The cool rooftop terrace is a real pleasure in summer, when you can relax with a pisco sour and take in the city views. If you prefer a more active nightlife scene, you're in luck. The hotel is adjacent to one of the city's main party thoroughfares: Suecia, lined with pubs, restaurants, and discos. Rooms facing these streets can be noisy, even through double-paned windows. ⊠ *Av. Santa Magdalena 111, Providencia* ☎ *2/750–0300* 🖷 *2/750–0350* ⊕ *www.fourpoints.com* ⬎ *112 rooms, 16 suites* ⚭ *Restaurant, room service, in-room data ports, in-room safes, minibars, cable TV, golf privileges, pool, gym, sauna, bar, laundry service, Internet, business services, convention center, meeting rooms, airport shuttle, travel services, free parking, no-smoking rooms* ⊟ *AE, DC, MC, V* Ⓜ *Los Leones.*

$$$$ ⊞ **Park Plaza.** It bills itself as a "classic European-style" hotel, and the receptionists that greet you from behind individual mahogany desks certainly call to mind the Continent. The refined decor, with rich burgundy and cream accents, extends to the adjoining Park Lane restaurant, whose chef masterfully combines international and Chilean cuisine. Although the glass-covered pool on the top floor is tiny, it has a great view. ⊠ *Av. Ricardo Lyon 207, Providencia* ☎ *2/233–6363* 🖷 *2/233–6668* ⊕ *www.parkplaza.cl* ⊲ *104 rooms, 6 suites* ⟁ *Restaurant, in-room data ports, in-room safes, minibars, cable TV, golf privileges, indoor pool, health club, sauna, bar, lobby lounge, shop, baby-sitting, laundry service, Internet, business services, convention center, meeting rooms, airport shuttle, travel services, free parking, no-smoking floor* ▤ *AE, DC, MC, V* ⑩ *BP* Ⓜ *Los Leones.*

★ $$$$ ⊞ **Sheraton Santiago and San Cristóbal Tower.** Two distinct hotels stand side-by-side at this unrivaled resort. The Sheraton Santiago is certainly a luxury hotel, but the adjoining San Cristóbal Tower is in a class by itself, popular with business executives and foreign dignitaries who value its efficiency, elegance, and impeccable service. A lavish, labyrinthine marble lobby links the two hotels, three fine restaurants, and the city's largest hotel convention center. Pampering is not all that goes on at the San Cristóbal Tower—attentive staff members at the business center can provide you with everything from secretarial services to Internet access. ⊠ *Av. Santa María 1742, Providencia* ☎ *2/233–5000* 🖷 *2/234–1732* ⊕ *www.sheraton.cl* ⊲ *Sheraton Santiago: 379 rooms, 14 suites. San Cristóbal Tower: 139 rooms, 3 suites* ⟁ *3 restaurants, picnic area, in-room data ports, in-room faxes, in-room safes, minibars, tennis court, 2 pools, gym, hair salon, sauna, 2 bars, lobby lounge, shops, baby-sitting, laundry service, concierge, Internet, business services, convention center, meeting rooms, airport shuttle, car rental, helipad, travel services, no-smoking floors* ▤ *AE, DC, MC, V* Ⓜ *Pedro de Valdivia.*

$$–$$$ ⊞ **Hotel Bonaparte.** Resembling a small château, this charming hotel on a corner of tree-lined Avenida Ricardo Lyon is often overshadowed by its flashier neighbors. The rooms with the most light are on the top floor, but all are tastefully decorated and have large baths. ⊠ *Mar del Plata 2171, at Av Ricardo Lyon, Providencia* ☎ *2/274–0621* 🖷 *2/204–8907* ⊕ *www.hotelbonaparte.com* ⊲ *25 rooms, 2 suites* ⟁ *Restaurant, room service, in-room data ports, minibars, cable TV, pool, gym, sauna, lobby lounge, baby-sitting, laundry service, Internet, business services, meeting rooms, free parking, no-smoking rooms* ▤ *AE, DC, MC, V* ⑩ *BP* Ⓜ *Los Leones.*

★ $$–$$$ ⊞ **Hotel Orly.** This is a rare find—a moderately priced hotel with many of the comforts of those costing twice as much. That you can find a treasure like this in the middle of Providencia is nothing short of a miracle. The shiny wood floors, country-manor furnishings, and glass-domed breakfast room make this hotel as sweet as it is economical. Most of the credit can go to the owner, who decorated it herself. Rooms come in all shapes and sizes, so ask to see a few before you decide. Cafetto, the downstairs café, serves some of the finest coffee drinks in town. ⊠ *Av. Pedro de Valdivia 027, Providencia* ☎ *2/231–8947* 🖷 *2/252–0051* ⊕ *www.orlyhotel.com* ⊲ *25 rooms, 3 suites* ⟁ *Restaurant, café, room* *service, in-room safes, minibars, cable TV, laundry service, Internet, free parking* ⊟ *AE, DC, MC, V* ⫮⊙⫮ *BP* Ⓜ *Pedro de Valdivia.*

Vitacura

$$ ⊡ **Acacias de Vitacura.** The extraordinary location of this hotel—in the midst of towering eucalyptus and acacia trees thought to be more than a century old—is unforgettable. It's a pleasure to drink your morning coffee in the lush garden under one of the oversize umbrellas. The rooms here are simple but bright, and the owner's collection of old carriages gives the hotel a quirky personality. ⊠ *El Manantial 1781, Vitacura* ☎ *2/211–8601* 🖶 *2/212–7858* ⊕ *www.hotelacacias.cl* ⫶ *33 rooms, 2 suites* ⟁ *Restaurant, minibars, cable TV, pool, gym, baby-sitting, Internet, meeting room, travel services, free parking* ⊟ *AE, DC, MC, V* ⫮⊙⫮ *BP.*

$$ ⊡ **Hotel Kennedy.** This glass tower may seem impersonal, but the small details—such as beautiful vases of flowers atop the wardrobes—show the staff cares about keeping guests happy. Bilingual secretarial services and an elegant boardroom are among the pluses for visiting executives. The Aquarium restaurant serves international cuisine and has a cellar full of excellent Chilean wines. ⊠ *Av. Kennedy 4570, Vitacura* ☎ *2/219–4000* 🖶 *2/218–2188* ⊕ *www.hotelkennedy.cl* ⫶ *123 rooms, 10 suites* ⟁ *Restaurant, room service, in-room data ports, minibars, cable TV, pool, gym, massage, sauna, bar, laundry service, Internet, business services, meeting rooms, travel services, free parking, no-smoking floor* ⊟ *AE, DC, MC, V* ⫮⊙⫮ *BP.*

Nightlife & the Arts

Nightlife

Bars and clubs are scattered all over Santiago, but a handful of streets have such a concentration of establishments that they resemble block parties on Friday and Saturday nights. Try pub crawling with all the well-heeled young locals on Avenida Suecia in the chic neighborhood of Providencia. To the east in Las Condes, Paseo San Damián is an outdoor complex of bars and clubs. If you're looking for something a little more bohemian, head for Avenida Pío Nono, the main drag through the colorful neighborhood of Bellavista.

BARS & CLUBS **Boomerang** (⊠ General Holley 2285, Providencia ☎ 2/334–5081) is a raucous pub with a few pool tables. From the doorway, **Casa de Cena** (⊠ Almirante Simpson 20, Providencia ☎ 2/635–4418) looks like your average hole-in-the-wall, but it's actually a gem. Most nights a band wanders through the maze of wood-paneled rooms singing folk songs. **Entre Negros** (⊠ Suecia 0188, Providencia ☎ 2/334–2094) might be the most popular of Avenida Suecia's discos. This longtime favorite also hosts live music on weekends. **Flannery's Geo Pub** (⊠ Encomenderos 83, Las Condes ☎ 2/233–6675), a few blocks up from Suecia and close to El Bosque Norte, is Chile's first real Irish drinking hole, a long-running establishment serving Irish food, beer, and occasionally Guinness on tap. The **Green Bull** (⊠ Av. Suecia 0150, Providencia ☎ 2/334–5619), next door to Mister Ed, competes for pretty much the same crowd with live performances nightly. The **Libro Café** (⊠ Purísima 165, Bellavista ☎ 2/735–3901) is a late-night haunt for starving artists and those who wish they were. Most of the neighborhood's nightspots are found along the pedestrian street of Avenida Suecia. One of the most popular is **Mister Ed** (⊠ Av. Suecia 0152, Providencia ☎ 2/231–2624), the best place to hear up-and-coming local bands. The **Phone Box** (⊠ Galería del Patio, Av. Providencia 1652, Providencia ☎ 2/235–9972) is a fairly convincing re-creation of a British pub that serves steak-and-kidney pie to homesick Brits. **Publicity** (⊠ El Bosque Norte 0155, Las Condes ☎ 2/333–1214) is a large, popular, glass-fronted building permanently teeming with people in their 20s and early 30s. **Remix Restobar** (⊠ Antonía Lopez de Bello 94, Bellavista ☎ 2/777–8067) mixes food and music—sushi and tapas with deep house, down tempo, and bossa nova. Reservations are advisable. Stop by for a drink in the evening at the sleek and stylish **Tantra** (⊠ Ernesto Pinto Lagarrigue 154, Bellavista ☎ 2/732–3287) and watch the restaurant transform itself into a disco at midnight.

GAY & LESBIAN CLUBS On Bellavista's main drag, **Bokhara** (⊠ Pío Nono 430, Bellavista ☎ 2/732–1050 or 2/735–1271) is one of the city's largest and most popular gay discos. It has two dance floors playing house and techno. **Bunker** (⊠ Bombero Nuñez 159, Bellavista ☎ 2/737–1716 or 2/777–3760), a mainstay of the gay scene, is in a cavernous space with numerous platforms overlooking the dance floor. Don't get here too early—people don't arrive until well after midnight. Note that it's only open Fridays and Saturdays. The venerable **Fausto** (⊠ Av. Santa María 0832, Providencia ☎ 2/777–1041), in business for more than 20 years, has polished wood paneling that calls to mind a gentlemen's club. The disco pumps until the wee hours. The friendly and unpretentious dance club **Naxos** (⊠ Av. O'Higgins 776, Santiago Centro ☎ 2/639–9629), in a high-ceilinged basement, plays everything from techno to Latin rock. If you're looking for a place to kick back with a beer, try **Pub Friend's** (⊠ Bombero Nuñez 365, Bellavista ☎ 2/777–3979). Live music performances and karaoke take place on Thursdays, Fridays, and Saturdays. **Quasar** (⊠ Coquimbo 1458, Santiago Centro ☎ 2/671–1267), frequented by men and women, has been around for more than 20 years and stages drag shows.

SALSA CLUBS **Arriba de la Bola** (⊠ General Holley 171, Providencia ☎ 2/232–7965) shakes things up with a live Cuban band. It gets packed, so reservations are necessary. On Fridays and Saturdays **Cimarrón** (⊠ Av. Irarrázabal 1730, Nuñoa ☎ 2/225–1627) comes alive with sensuous salsa, merengue, and milonga. For salsa and merengue, try **Ilé Habana** (⊠ Bucarest 95, Providencia ☎ 2/231–5711), where you can boogie to the beat of a live band.

The Arts

With dozens of museums scattered around the city, it's clear Santiaguinos also have a strong love of culture. Music, theater, and other artistic endeavors supplement weekends spent dancing the night away.

MUSIC **Parque de las Esculturas** (⊠ Av. Santa María between Av. Pedro de Valdivia Norte and Padre Letelier, Providencia ☎ no phone) hosts open-air concerts in the early evenings in summer. The **Teatro Municipal** (⊠ Plaza Alcade Mekis, Av. Agustinas at Av. San Antonio, Santiago Centro ☎ 2/463–8888 ⊕ www.municipal.cl), Santiago's 19th-century theater, presents classical concerts, opera, and ballet. **Teatro Oriente** (⊠ Av. Pedro de Valdivia, between the Costanera and Providencia, Providencia ☎ 2/ 335–0023) is a popular venue for classical concerts. The Coro Sinfónico and the Orquestra Sinfónica, the city's highly regarded chorus and orchestra, perform near Plaza Baquedano at the **Teatro Universidad de Chile** (✉ Providencia 043, Providencia ☎ 2/634–5295).

THEATER Provided that you understand Spanish, you can enjoy Chilean theater, which is among the best in Latin America. Performances take place all year, mainly from Thursday to Sunday at around 8 PM. **El Conventillo** (✉ Bellavista 173, Bellavista ☎ 2/777–4164). **Teatro Bellavista** (✉ Dardignac 0110, Bellavista ☎ 2/735–2395). The well respected ICTUS theater company performs in the **Teatro la Comedia** (✉ Merced 349, Santiago Centro ☎ 2/639–1523). **Teatro Lo Castillo** (✉ Candelaria Goyenechea 3820, Vitacura ☎ 2/244–5856). **Teatro San Ginés** (✉ Mallinkrodt 76, Bellavista ☎ 2/738–2159).

Sports & the Outdoors

Horse Racing

Races take place Mondays and alternating Thursdays at **Club Hípico** (✉ Blanco Encalada 2540, Santiago Centro ☎ 2/693–9600), south of downtown. El Ensayo, an annual race that's a century-old tradition, is held here in early November. **Hipódromo Chile** (✉ Hipódromo Chile 1715, Independencia ☎ 2/270–9270) is the home of the prestigious Gran Premio Internacional, which draws competitors from around South America. Regular races are held Saturdays and alternating Thursdays.

Soccer

First-division soccer matches, featuring the city's handful of local teams, are held in the **Estadio Nacional** (✉ Av. Grecia 2001, Nuñoa ☎ 2/238–8102), south of the city center. Soccer is played year-round, with most matches taking place on weekends. It was here in the Estadio that Pinochet's henchmen killed thousands of political opponents in 1973, including Chilean folk singer Victor Jara. To assure that he would never again provoke Chileans to action with his music, Jara's hands were mutilated before he was put to death.

Shopping

Providencia, the city's most popular shopping district, has exclusive boutiques, two department stores, and a small mall. In Las Condes you'll find shopping malls filled with hundreds of specialty shops. Bohemian Bellavista attracts those in search of the perfect woolen sweater or the right piece of lapis lazuli jewelry. Shops in Santiago are generally open weekdays 10–7 and Saturdays 10–2. Malls are usually open daily 10–10.

Markets

Aldea de Vitacura (✉ Av. Vitacura 6838, Vitacura ☎ 2/219–3161) is a pleasant outdoor market where you can browse among the various stands selling local and national craftwork. It's open Tuesday–Sunday 11–9. **Centro Artesanal Santa Lucía,** an art fair at the base of Cerro Santa Lucía, is an excellent place to find Aymara and Mapuche crafts. It's open daily 10–7. Bellavista's colorful **Feria Artesanal Pío Nono,** held in the park along Avenida Pío Nono, comes alive every night of the week. It's even busier on weekends, when more vendors gather in Parque Domingo Gómez to display their handicrafts. **Los Graneros de Alba** (⊠ Av. Apoquindo 9085, Las Condes ☎ 2/248–2295), more commonly known as Pueblito Los Dominicos, is a "village" of more than 200 shops where you can find everything from fine leather to semiprecious stones and antiques. It's open Tuesday–Saturday 10:30–9:30 and Sunday 10:30–8.

Specialty Shops

HANDICRAFTS   You'll find replica Diaguita pottery, Mapuche rugs, and many other typical Chilean crafts in the **Centro de Artesanía** (⊠ Mall, Estación Central, Estación Central ☎ no phone). Shops of all sorts, selling local and national crafts, line the winding passageways of the **Centro de Artesanía Manquehue** (⊠ Av. Manquehue Sur at Apoquindo, Las Condes ☎ no phone), alongside the Apumanque Mall. **Cooperativa Almacén Campesino** (⊠ Torreón Victoria, Bellavista ☎ 2/335–4443), in the middle of Parque Metropolitano, is a cooperative of artisans from various indigenous cultures. This shop sells the best handicrafts from all over Chile.

JEWELRY   Chile is one of the few places in the world where lapis lazuli, a brilliant blue mineral, is found in abundance. In Bellavista, a cluster of shops deals solely in lapiz lazuli, selling a range of products made from this semiprecious stone: paperweights, jewelry, and chess sets. Several larger shops selling lapis lazuli are dotted around the rest of the city. **Blue Stone** (⊠ Av. Costanera Norte 3863, Vitacura ☎ 2/207–4180). **Faba-Fina** (⊠ Av. Alonso de Cordova 4227, Vitacura ☎ 2/208–9526). **Rocco** (⊠ José Victorino Lastarria 53, Santiago Centro ☎ 2/633–4036).

WINE   In Las Condes, **El Mundo del Vino** (⊠ Isidora Goyenechea 2931, Las Condes ☎ 2/244–8888) is a world-class store with an international selection, in-store tastings, wine classes, and books for oenophiles. **La Vinoteca** (⊠ Av. Isidora Goynechea 2966, Las Condes ☎ 2/334–1987), Santiago's first fine wine shop, offers an excellent selection. **Vinopolis** (⊠ Av. El Bosque Norte 380, Las Condes ☎ 2/333–0080 ⊠ Av. Pedro de Valdivia 36, Providencia ☎ 2/333–0816) has a top-notch selection.

Side Trips from Santiago

Ski Resorts

No wonder skiing aficionados from around the world head to Chile—the snow-capped mountains to the east of Santiago have the largest number of runs not just in Chile or South America, but the entire southern hemisphere. The other attraction is that the season here lasts from June to September, so savvy skiers can take to the slopes when everyone else is hitting the beach.

The closest ski area to Santiago is **Farellones,** at the foot of Cerro Colorado. This area, consisting of a couple of ski runs for beginners, is used mainly by locals out for a day trip. Facilities are scant—just a couple of unremarkable restaurants and a few drink stands. Farther up the road is El Colorado, which has 568 acres of groomed runs—the most in Chile. There are 18 runs here: seven beginner, four intermediate, three advanced, and four expert. Ski season here runs from mid-June to mid-October.

About 3 km (2 mi) up the road is **La Parva,** a colorful conglomeration of private homes set along a handful of mountain roads. At the resort itself there are 14 ski runs, most for intermediate level skiers. La Parva is positioned perfectly to give you a stunning view of Santiago, especially at night. The slopes open in May, meaning the season can sometimes last six months.

Just 13 km (8 mi) beyond La Parva is Chile's largest ski area, **Valle Nevado.** This luxury resort area has 11 ski lifts that take you up to 27 runs on more than 300 acres of groomed trails. Three of the extremely difficult runs from the top of Cerro Tres Puntas are labeled "Shake," "Rattle," and "Roll." That doesn't intimidate you? Then you might be ready for some heliskiing. A Bell 407 helicopter whisks you to otherwise inaccessible peaks where you can ride a vertical drop of up to 8,200 ft.

WHERE TO STAY & EAT

$$$$ 🏨 **Puerta del Sol.** The largest of the Valle Nevado hotels, Puerta del Sol can be identified by its signature sloped roof. Rooms here are larger than those at Tres Puntas, but still rather small. One good option are the "altillo rooms," which have a loft bed that gives you more space. North-facing rooms cost more but have unobstructed views of the slopes. Since all three hotels share facilities, Puerta del Sol is your best value. ⊠ *Valle Nevado* 🕿 *2/206–0027, 800/669–0554 toll free in the U.S.* 📠 *2/208–0697* ⊕ *www.vallenevado.com* 🛏 *124 rooms* ⌂ *2 restaurants, room service, in-room data ports, in-room safes, minibars, cable TV, gym, massage, sauna, Ping-Pong, downhill skiing, cinema, dance club, recreation room, baby-sitting, laundry service, airport shuttle* ▱ *AE, DC, MC, V* ⊘ *Closed Oct.–June 14* ⒶⒺ *MAP.*

★ **$$$$** ✕🏨 **La Cornisa.** This year-round hotel on the road to Farellones is great if you want to get to the slopes early, as there's free shuttle service to and from the nearby ski areas. The quaint old inn, run by the same family for years, has 10 rooms with wood floors and heaters to keep out the chill. The best are the two corner rooms, which are a bit larger and have wide windows with excellent views. The rate includes breakfast and dinner in the small restaurant, warmed by a fireplace and looking directly down the mountain to Santiago. ⊠ *Av. Los Cóndores 636, Farellones* 🕿 *2/321–1173* 📠 *2/220–7581* ⊕ *www.lacornisa.cl* 🛏 *10 rooms* ⌂ *Restaurant, baby-sitting, laundry service* ▱ *AE, DC, MC, V* ⒶⒺ *MAP.*

Wineries

The wineries in the Valle de Maipo are some of the oldest in Chile. Here you'll find most of the biggest and best-known vineyards in the country. For years tourists were virtually ignored by these wineries, but they are finally getting attention. Now you'll find many wineries are throwing their doors open to visitors for the first time, often letting them see behind-the-scenes activities like harvesting and pressing.

Chile's largest wine maker, **Viña Concha y Toro** produces 11 million cases annually. Some of its table wines—identifiable by the short, stout bottles—are sold domestically for about $2. The best bottles, however, fetch sky-high prices abroad. This is one of the oldest wineries in the region. Melchor de Concha y Toro, who once served as Chile's minister of finance, built the *casona,* or main house, in 1875. He imported vines from Europe, significantly improving the quality of the wines he was able to produce. Hour-long tours begin with an introductory video, a stroll through the vineyards and the century-old gardens, a look at the modern facilities, and a tasting. Reserve a week ahead for Saturday tours. ✉ *Virginia Subercaseaux 210, Pirque* ☎ *2/821-7069* ⊕ *www. conchaytoro.cl* 🖃 *Tour: 3,000 pesos* ⊙ *Weekdays 10:30–6, Sat. 10–12. English tours weekdays 11:30–3, Sat. 11 AM.*

Residential development keeps creeping closer to **Viña Cousiño-Macul,** a 625-acre estate where grapes have been grown since the mid-16th century. For the moment the venerable vineyard has managed to hang on. The Cousiño family home, set next to a beautiful 110-acre park, isn't open to the public, but you can visit the rest of the facilities. Especially interesting is the vaulted brick cellar, built in 1872, which can store more than 1 million bottles. ✉ *Av. Quilín 7100, Peñalolén Santiago* ☎ *2/284-1011* ⊕ *www.cousinomacul.cl* 🖃 *Free* ⊙ *Tours: Mon.–Sat. at 11 AM.*

Chile's third-largest winery, **Viña Santa Rita,** played an important historical role in Chile's battle for independence. In 1814, 120 soldiers led by revolutionary hero Bernardo O'Higgins hid here in the cellars. Paula Jaraquemada, who ran the estate, refused to let the Spanish enter, saving the soldiers. (Santa Rita's 120 label commemorates the event.) At the center of Santa Rita's Maipo Valley estate half an hour south of Santiago, the lovely colonial hacienda now serves as the winery's headquarters. Its restaurant, La Casa de Doña Paula, is a delightful place to have a bite after the tour.

Tours take you down into the winery's musty cellars, which are worthy of Edgar Allen Poe. Built by French engineers in 1875 using a lime-and-stone technique called *cal y canto,* the fan-vault cellars have been named a national monument. The wine was once aged in the barrels you'll see, which are more than 120 years old and are made of *raulí* wood; today the wine is aged in stainless-steel towers. Unfortunately, the wonderful gardens and the original proprietor's house, with its chapel steeple peeking out from behind a thick canopy of trees, are not part of the tour. Note that you must reserve ahead for these tours. ✉ *Camino Padre Hurtado 695, Alto Jahuel-Buín* ☎ *2/362-2594 or 2/362-2000* ⊕ *www. santarita.com* 🖃 *Tours: 3,000 pesos; tastings cost extra* ⊙ *Bilingual tours (English and Spanish): Tues.–Fri. at 10:30, 11:30, 12:15, 3, 4; weekends at 12:30 and 3:30.*

Don Francisco Undurraga Vicuña founded **Viña Undurraga** in 1885 in the town of Talagante, 34 km (21 mi) southwest of Santiago. The opulent mansion he built here has hosted various visiting dignitaries, from the queen of Denmark to the king of Norway. Today you can tour the house and the gardens—designed by Pierre Dubois, who planned Santiago's Parque Forestal—take a look at the facilities, and enjoy a tasting. Reserve ahead for a spot on the tour. ✉ *Camino a Melipilla Km 34, Talagante* ☎ *2/817-2346* ⊕ *www.undurraga.cl* 🖃 *Free* ⊙ *Tours: weekdays 9:30–4, Sat. 10–3.*

WHERE TO EAT ✕ **La Casa de Doña Paula.** A two-century-old colonial hacienda with thick
★ **$–$$** adobe walls houses Viña Santa Rita's restaurant. Under a peaked wood
ceiling, the restaurant is decorated with old religious sculptures and portraits, including one of Paula Jaraquemada, who once ran the estate. If
you plan to lunch here, it's a good idea to arrange to take the winery's
12:15 tour. Locally raised meats are the draw here; try the delicious *cos-
tillar de cerdo* (pork ribs). For dessert, the house specialty is *pon-
deración,* a crisp swirl of fried dough atop vanilla ice cream and caramel
syrup. ⊠ *Viña Santa Rita, Camino Padre Hurtado 695, Alto Jahuel-
Buín* ☎ *2/821–4211* ⌂ *Reservations essential* ☉ *Closed Mon. No dinner* ⊟ *AE, DC, MC, V.*

Santiago A to Z

AIR TRAVEL TO & FROM SANTIAGO

Among the U.S. carriers, American serves Santiago's Arturo Merino
Benítez International Airport (SCL) from Dallas and Miami, while Delta
connects from Atlanta. LanChile flies nonstop to Santiago from both
Miami and Los Angeles and with a layover in Lima from New York.
British Airways flies from London with a stop in Buenos Aires; LanChile
connects London to Santiago with a stop in Frankfurt or Madrid. Most
of the major Central and South American airlines also fly to Santiago,
including Aerocontinente, Aerolíneas Argentinas, Aeromexico, Avianca,
Lacsa, Lloyd Aéreo Boliviano, and Varig.

Lan Express, LanChile's domestic subsidiary, has daily flights from Santiago to most cities throughout Chile. Sky airline also flies to most large
cities within Chile.

🛪 Carriers **Aerocontinente** ☎ 2/690–9399 in Chile. **Aerolíneas Argentinas** ☎ 2/690–
1030 in Chile. **Aeromexico** ☎ 2/690–1028 in Chile. **American Airlines** ☎ 2/690–1090
in Santiago. **Avianca** ☎ 2/690–1051 in Chile. **British Airways** ☎ 0845/222–111. **Delta
Airlines** ☎ 2/690–1551 in Santiago. **Lacsa** ☎ 2/690–1276 in Chile. **LanChile** ☎ 2/
565–2525 or 600/526–2000 in Chile. **Lan Express** ☎ 2/565–2525. **Lloyd Aéreo Boliviano** ☎ 2/671–2334 in Chile. **Sky** ☎ 600/600–2828. **Varig** ☎ 2/690–1930 in Chile.
🛪 Airports **Comodoro Arturo Merino Benítez International Airport** ☎ 2/690–1900.

AIRPORTS & TRANSFERS

You have several options for getting to and from the airport. The most
expensive is a taxi, which should cost you around 11,000 pesos for a
trip downtown. Less expensive, especially if you are traveling alone, are
the comfortable minibuses operated by Transfer. They whisk you from
the airport to any location downtown for about 4,000 pesos.

Centropuerto, which runs buses every 10 minutes between the airport
and Terminal Los Héroes, charges about 1,500 pesos. Tur-Bus has service between the airport and its own terminal near the Los Héroes Metro
station; it departs every half hour and costs 1,200 pesos. Alpha Service,
Casual, and Transvip operate minibus service between the airport and
various locations in the city. The cost is usually anywhere from 3,500
pesos to 4,500 pesos. Note that there is no Metro service to the airport.
🛪 **Alpha Service** ☎ 2/555–8855. **Casual** ☎ 2/777–7707. **Centropuerto** ☎ 2/695–
5958. **Transfer** ☎ 2/677–3000. **Transvip** ☎ 2/677–3000. **Tur-Bus** ☎ 2/270–7500.

BUS TRAVEL TO & FROM SANTIAGO

All the country's major highways pass through Santiago, which means you won't have a problem catching a bus to almost any destination. Finding that bus, however, can be a problem. The city has several terminals, each with buses heading in different directions. Terminal Los Héroes is on the edge of Santiago Centro near the Los Héroes Metro station. Several companies have buses to points north and south from this station. The other three stations are clustered around the Universidad de Santiago Metro station. The modern Terminal San Borja has buses headed north and west. Terminal Santiago is the busiest, with dozens of small companies going west to the coast and to the south. Terminal Alameda, which handles only Tur-Bus and Pullman Bus, is for coastal and southern traffic. Terminal Los Héroes and Terminal Santiago also handle a few international routes, heading to far-flung destinations such as Buenos Aires, Rio de Janeiro, and Lima.

Several bus companies run regularly scheduled service to the Andes in winter. Skitotal buses depart from the office on Avenida Apoquindo and head to all of the ski resorts except Portillo. Buses depart at 8:45 AM; a round-trip ticket costs 10,000 pesos. Also available for hire here are taxis—(65,000 pesos, including driver) and 12-person minibuses (90,000 pesos). Manzur Expediciones runs buses to Portillo on Wednesday, Saturday, and Sunday for about the same price. Buses leaves at 8:30 AM from the Plaza Italia in front of the Teatro Universidad de Chile.

Bus service to the Cajón del Maipo is frequent and inexpensive—Manzur offers a round-trip ticket to Lo Valdés Mountain Center for less than 8,000 pesos. Only the 8 AM bus makes the two-hour trek to Baños de Colina, however. Sit on the right side of the bus for a good view of the river.

🚌 Bus Companies **Manzur Expediciones** ⊠ Sótero del Río 475, Santiago Centro 🕾 2/777-4284. **Pullman Bus** ⊠ Terminal Alameda, Estación Central 🕾 2/779-2026. **Skitotal** ⊠ Av. Apoquindo 4900, Las Condes 🕾 2/246-0156. **Tur-Bus** ⊠ Terminal Alameda, Estación Central 🕾 2/270-7500.

🚌 Bus Depots **Terminal Alameda** ⊠ Av. O'Higgins 3750, Estación Central 🕾 2/270-7500. **Terminal Los Héroes** ⊠ Tucapel Jiménez 21, Estación Central 🕾 2/420-9900. **Terminal San Borja** ⊠ San Borja 184, Estación Central 🕾 2/776-0645. **Terminal Santiago** ⊠ Av. O'Higgins 3850, La Alameda 🕾 2/376-1755.

BUS TRAVEL WITHIN SANTIAGO

Bus service has improved, but it is still too confusing for most newcomers. (It's confusing for most residents, too.) For one thing, there are dozens of private companies operating on hundreds of routes around the city. For another, drivers almost invariably say they go where you want to go, whether they do or not. Bus fare is usually less than 300 pesos, paid upon boarding. Drivers are good about providing change for small bills.

CAR RENTAL

Renting a car is convenient in Santiago, as most companies have offices at the airport and downtown. The international agencies such as Avis, Budget, and Hertz generally rent compact cars with unlimited mileage and insurance coverage for about 38,000 pesos a day. They can provide ski-equipped vehicles for climbs to the Andes. Two reputable local agencies are Chilean Rent A Car and Diamond, whose rates can be as low as 26,000 pesos a day.

🚗 Agencies **Avis** ✉ airport, ☎ 2/690-1382 ✉ Av. Santa María 1742, Providencia ☎ 2/274-7621 ✉ Av. San Pablo 9900, Pudahuel ☎ 2/601-9747. **Budget** ✉ airport ☎ 2/690-1386 ✉ Av. Francisco Bilbao 1439, Providencia ☎ 2/690-1489. **Chilean Rent A Car** ✉ Bellavista 0183, Bellavista ☎ 2/737-9650. **Diamond** ✉ Av. Manquehue Sur 795, Las Condes ☎ 2/212-1523. **Hertz** ✉ airport, ☎ 2/690-1029 ✉ Av. Costanera 1469, Providencia ☎ 2/420-5210.

CAR TRAVEL

You don't need a car if you're not going to venture outside the city limits, as most of the downtown sights are within walking distance of each other. A car is the best way to see the surrounding countryside, however. Although the highways around Santiago are generally well maintained, weather conditions can make them dangerous. Between May and August, rain can cause roads in low-lying areas to flood. Avoid driving if it has been raining for several hours. If you're headed north or south, you'll probably use the Pan-American Highway, also called Ruta 5. To reach Valparaíso, Viña del Mar, or the northernmost beach resorts on the Central Coast, take Highway 68; for the southern beaches, take Ruta 78.

It can take up to two hours to reach the region's three major ski resorts, which lie 48–56 km (30–35 mi) from Santiago. The road is narrow, winding, and full of Chileans racing to get to the top. If you decide to drive, make sure you have either a four-wheel-drive vehicle or snow chains, which you can rent along the way. The chains are installed for about 8,000 pesos. Don't think you need them? There's a police checkpoint just before the road starts to climb into the Andes, and if the weather is rough they'll make you turn back.

HEALTH

In terms of food, Santiago is one of the safest cities in South America. Because of strict health codes, you shouldn't worry too much about the food in most restaurants. If you decide to sample something from a street vendor, make sure it has been thoroughly cooked. The tap water in Santiago and most of Chile is quite safe, but if you have any concerns you can always drink the bottled water available everywhere.

Altitude sickness—which is marked by difficulty breathing, dizziness, headaches, and nausea—is a danger when heading to the Andes. The best way to ward off altitude sickness is to take it slowly. Try to spend a day or two acclimatizing before any physical exertion. When skiing, rest often and drink as much water as possible. If symptoms continue, return to a lower altitude.

MAIL & SHIPPING

Correo Central, housed in the ornate Palacio de los Gobernadores, is in Santiago Centro on the north side of the Plaza de Armas. There is a second downtown branch near the Palacio de la Moneda, as well as one in Providencia near the Manuel Montt Metro stop.

📮 Post Office **Correo Central** ☎ 800/362-236 ⊕ www.correos.cl.

MONEY MATTERS

Unlike other South American countries, Chile rarely accepts U.S. dollars. (The exception is larger hotels, where prices are often quoted only in dollars.) Credit cards and travelers checks are accepted everywhere in Santiago's most touristy areas.

You can exchange money in many places in Santiago Centro, such as Citibank. Banks in Santiago are usually open weekdays 9–2, while *casas de cambio* (currency-exchange offices) are open weekdays 9–2 and 3–6. They normally cluster together; in Providencia, for example, along Pedro de Valdivia, just before La Costanera, there are three or four.

Automatic teller machines only dispense Chilean pesos. To use an ATM issued by a foreign bank, select the "foreign client" option from the menu. Citibank, with the most ATMs in town, has instructions in English, as do most other ATMS, and is linked to both the Plus and Cirrus systems. ATMs belonging to Chilean banks are often only linked to Cirrus. There are two ATMs on the second floor of the airport.

🏦 Banks **American Express** ⊠ Av. Andrés Bello 2711, Las Condes ☎ 2/350-6955 ⊠ Isidora Goyenechea 3621, Las Condes ☎ 2/350-6700. **Citibank** ⊠ Teatinos 180, Santiago Centro ☎ 2/338-8000 ⊠ Av. Andrés Bello 2681, Providencia ☎ 2/338-8000 ⊠ Av. Apoquindo 5470, Las Condes ☎ 2/338-8000.

SAFETY

Santiago Centro, Providencia, Las Condes, and other areas frequented by tourists are generally very safe. Use the same precautions you would anywhere—don't wear flashy jewelry and watches, keep your camera in a secure bag, and don't handle money in public. Remain alert for pickpockets, especially in crowded markets and parks.

SUBWAY TRAVEL

Santiago's excellent subway system is the best way to get around town. The Metro is comfortable, inexpensive, and safe. The system operates Monday–Saturday 6:30 AM–10:30 PM and Sunday 8–10:30 PM. Línea 1 runs east–west along the axis of the Río Mapocho. This is the most popular line, and perhaps the most useful, because it runs past most of the heavily touristed areas. Línea 2 runs north–south; it's rarely used by nonresidents because it heads to residential areas. Línea 5 also runs north–south except at its northern tip, where it bends to the west to connect with the Bellas Artes and Plaza de Armas stations. Every station has an easy-to-read map of all the stations and the adjoining streets. Buy tickets in any station at the glass booths or at the nearby machines. Individual tickets cost 300 to 350 pesos, depending on the time of day. A *boleto inteligente* (smart ticket) or *boleto valor* (value ticket) costs around 3,000 pesos and is good for up to 10 trips; these tickets save you time, if not money. After depositing your ticket in the turnstile, pass through and retrieve it to use again later. Single-ride tickets are not returned.

TAXIS

With some 50,000 taxis in Santiago, you can easily flag one down on most streets. The average ride costs around 2,000 to 3,000 pesos. The driver will turn the taxi meter on when you start your journey; it should read 150 pesos, the minimum charge. Taxi drivers don't always know where they are going and frequently ask directions; it's a good idea to carry a map. Radio-dispatched cabs are slightly more expensive but will pick you up at your door.

Taxi Companies **Alborada** ☎ 2/246-4900. **Alto Oriente** ☎ 2/226-2116. **Andes Pacífico** ☎ 2/225-3064 or 2/204-0104. **Apoquindo** ☎ 2/211-6073.

TELEPHONES

When calling Santiago from other parts of the country, use the area code 02; if you are using a carrier, then dial just 2. Within the city, skip the area code and just dial the seven-digit local number.

TOUR OPERATORS

Sernatur, the national tourism agency, maintains a listing of experienced individual tour guides who will take you on a half-day tour of Santiago and the surrounding area for about 25,000 pesos. Altué Expediciones arranges adventure trips such as white-water rafting on nearby rivers and hiking at the mouths of volcanoes. Chilean Travel Services and Sportstour handle tours of both Santiago and other parts of Chile. With more than a dozen locations, Turismo Cocha, founded in 1951, is one of the city's biggest private tour operators. It arranges tours of the wineries of the Cajón del Maipo and the beach resorts of Valparaíso and Viña del Mar, in addition to the usual city tours. It also has offices in the domestic and international terminals of the airport as well as in some of the larger hotels.

Tour Companies **Altué Expediciones** ✉ Encomenderos 83, Las Condes ☎ 2/232-1103 ☎ 2/233-6799. **Chilean Travel Services** ✉ Antonio Bellet 77, Office 101, Providencia ☎ 2/251-0400 ☎ 2/251-0426 ⊕ www.ia.cl/cts. **Sernatur** ✉ Av. Providencia 1550, Providencia ☎ 2/731-8336 or 2/731-8337 ⊕ www.sernatur.cl. **Sportstour** ✉ Moneda 970, Santiago Centro ☎ 2/549-5200 ☎ 2/698-2981 ⊕ www.sportstour.cl. **Turismo Cocha** ✉ Av. El Bosque Norte 0430, Las Condes ☎ 2/464-1000 ☎ 2/464-1010 ✉ Pedro de Valdivia 0169, Providencia ☎ 2/464-1600 ☎ 2/464-1699 ✉ Huérfanos 653, Santiago Centro ☎ 2/464-1950 ⊕ www.cocha.com.

TRAIN TRAVEL

Chileans once boasted about the country's excellent rail service, but there's little left today aside from the limited service from Santiago to points south. Santiago's Estación Central, in Santiago Centro at the Metro station of the same name, is where you catch trains headed to the Central Valley. Note that you can also purchase tickets for the trains at the Estación Metro Universidad de Chile.

Metrotrens run from Santiago to Nos, Rancagua, and San Fernando. Terrasur operates a service between Santiago and Chillán four times daily. Trains run from Santiago through the larger cities of Rancagua, Curicó, Talca, Chillán, Concepción, and Temuco.

Train Information **Estación Central** ✉ Av. O'Higgins 3170, Santiago Centro ☎ 2/376-8500 ⊕ www.efe.cl. **Estación Metro Universidad de Chile** ✉ Local 10, La Alameda ☎ 2/688-3284.

VISITOR INFORMATION
Sernatur, the national tourist service, stocks maps and brochures and has a large and friendly staff that speaks English. The Providencia office, located between the Manuel Montt and Pedro de Valdivia Metro stops, is open daily 9 AM–10 PM.

🖪 Tourist Information **Sernatur** ⊠ Av. Providencia 1550, Providencia ☎ 2/731-8336 or 2/731-8337 ⊕ www.sernatur.cl.

THE CENTRAL COAST

Most people head to the Central Coast for a single reason: the beaches. Yet this stretch of coastline west of Santiago offers much more than sun and surf. Valparaíso is a bustling port town with a jumble of colorful cottages nestled in the folds of its many hills. Ride any of the *acensores* (funiculars) for a great view. Viña del Mar has polished parks and modern high-rises.

Valparaíso

120 km (75 mi) northwest of Santiago.

Valparaíso has served as Santiago's port for hundreds of years. The *porteños* (the name for locals, referring to the port) live in hills around the port in an undulating array of colorful wooden homes. Glance up any of the dozens of stairways and you're likely to see an unobstructed vista of blue sky. Valparaíso's dramatic topography—45 hills overlooking the ocean—requires the use of winding pathways and wooden *ascensores* (funiculars) to get up many of the grades. At the tops you'll find *paseos,* or promenades; many are named after prominent Yugoslavian, Basque, and German immigrants.

Numbers in the text correspond to numbers in the margin and on the Valparaíso map.

a good walk

Take a taxi, or any bus that has ADUANA written on its windshield, to the Plaza Aduana, at the northwestern end of El Plano. Here is the scarlet Dirección Nacional de Aduana, the 19th-century customs house still in use today. Next door is the Ascensor Artillería, a funicular that carries you up to the **Paseo 21 de Mayo❶** ▶. Behind this promenade with a sweeping view of the bay is the **Museo Naval y Marítimo de Valparaíso❷**. Take the funicular back to the plaza, or walk down the stairway that ends near the base of the customs house. Walk southeast along Calle Cochrane, the first block of which has some tawdry bars—note the WELCOME SAILOR signs (avoid this area at night). Follow Cochrane to **Plaza Sotomayor❸**, dominated by the stately Comandancia building and the Monumento de los Héroes de Iquique.

North of the monument is **Muelle Prat❹**, with the tourist office, the Estación Puerto for trains bound for Viña del Mar, and boats leaving for short tours of the bay. Return to Plaza Sotomayor and cross it, heading to the left of the Comandancia building, where a smaller square lies before the courthouse called the Tribunales de Justicia. On your left is the Ascensor El Peral; take it up to the art nouveau **Museo de Bellas Artes❺** and the lovely neighborhood of Cerro Alegre. Afterwards, return to the base of the hill, turn right on Calle Prat and walk two blocks southeast to the Ascensor Concepción, at the end of a narrow passage on your right. Ride this up to the neighborhood of **Cerro Concepción** ⑥, with its views of Paseo Gervason.

If you return to Calle Prat and continue right, it becomes Calle Esmeralda; follow this and you'll pass the neoclassical structure that houses the world's oldest Spanish-language newspaper, *El Mercurio de Valparaíso.* Esmeralda then curves south to Plaza Anibal Pinto. Head east on Calle Condell to Calle Ecuador, where you can find some of the city's most popular nightspots. Here are taxis that can take you to **La Sebastiana** ⑦. From there you can walk down the narrow streets of Cerro Bellavista and get a look at a series of murals known as the **Museo a Cielo Abierto** ⑧, near the top of the Ascensor Espíritu Santo. Then ride down to Calle Huito, which in turn leads back to Calle Condell. Turn left, and go to the old Palacio Lyon, which houses the **Museo de Historia Natural de Valparaíso** ⑨ and the **Galería Municipal de Arte** ⑩. A block east of the Palacio on Calle Condell is **Plaza Victoria** ⑪, across from which stands the city's cathedral. Take a taxi or bus east from here to Plaza O'Higgins, which lies between the neoclassical Teatro Municipal and the modern **Congreso Nacional** ⑫.

TIMING You need a good pair of shoes to fully appreciate Valparaíso. Walking past all the sights, exploring the museums, and enjoying a meal and drinks makes for a long, full day. You might visit La Sebastiana the next day to break up the walk. Definitely bring sunblock or a hat. Even if it's cloudy when you start, the sun often comes out by afternoon.

What to See

⑥ **Cerro Concepción.** Ride the Ascensor Concepción to this hilltop neighborhood covered with houses and cobblestone streets. The greatest attraction is the view, which is best appreciated from Paseo Gervasoni, a wide promenade to the right when you exit the ascensor, and Paseo Atkinson, one block to the east. Over the balustrades that line those paseos lie amazing vistas of the city and bay. Nearly as fascinating are the narrow streets above them, some of which are quite steep. The stairway descent below Calle Concepción, however, should be avoided, since tourists have been robbed there. ⊠ *Ascensor Concepción, Calle Pratt.*

⑫ **Congreso Nacional.** The first three weeks of each month you can watch the 120 *diputados* (representatives) meet Tuesday–Thursday noon–2:30 and 4–6. Meetings of the Senate, which consists of 40 elected members and two *senadores vitalicios* (former presidents who were granted senator-for-life status), are closed to the public. Tours in English explain the bicameral workings of Chile's government. Dictator Augusto Pinochet had this building constructed on the site of one of his boyhood homes. ⊠ *Plaza O'Higgins* 🕾 *No phone* 🎟 *Free* 🕓 *Weekdays 10–6.*

⑩ **Galería Municipal de Arte.** This crypt in the basement of the Palacio Lyon is the finest art space in the city. Temporary exhibits by top-caliber Chilean artists are displayed on stone walls under a series of brick arches. It's easy to miss the entrance, which is on Calle Condell beyond the Museo

Valparaíso

Bahía de Valparaíso

Antonio Varas

Ascensor Artilleria

Plaza Advana

Artilleria

Av. Carampangue

Av. Errázuriz

Marquez

Valdivia

San Martín

Clave

Grohl

Serrano

Estación Puerto

Blanco

Cochrane

Pral

Ascensor El Peral

Museo a Cielo Abierto

Castillo

Av. Tomás Ramos

Monte Alegre

Morrison

Av. Pedro Montt

Esmeralda

Ascensor Concepción

Papudo

Concepción

Urriola

Templeman

Cumming

Cumming

Munich Hospital

Plaza Bismarck

Estación Bellavista

Melgarejo

Bella Vista

Pudeto

O'Higgins

E. Ramírez

Av. Brasil

Salvador Dono

Condell

Cementerio Cat lico

Cementerio de Disidentes

Av. Yer

Av. Ecuador

KEY

▶ *Start of walk*

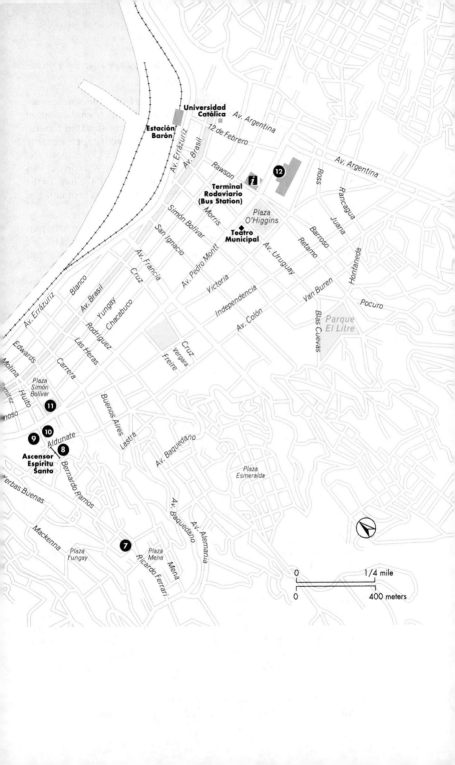

de Historia Natural de Valparaíso. ✉ *Calle Condell 1550* ☎ *32/939–562* 🖰 *Free* ⊗ *Weekdays 10–7, Sat. 10–5.*

❹ Muelle Prat. Though its name translates as Prat Dock, the Muelle is actually a wharf with steps leading to the water. Sailors from the ships in the harbor arrive in *lanchas* (small boats), or board them for the trip back to their vessels. It's a great place to watch the activity at the nearby port, and the ships anchored in the harbor. To get a closer look, you can board one of the lanchas—it costs 2,000 pesos for the trip out to a ship and back, or 10,000 pesos for a 40-minute tour of the bay. To the east of the Muelle is the tourist information office, and behind it is a row of souvenir shops. ✉ *Av. Errázuriz s/n.*

❽ Museo a Cielo Abierto. The Open Sky Museum is a winding walk past 20 official murals (and a handful of unofficial ones) by some of Chile's best painters. There's even one by the country's most famous artist, Roberto Matta. The path is not marked—there's no real fixed route— as the point is to get lost in the city's history and culture. ✉ *Ascensor Espíritu Santo up to Cerro Buenavista.*

need a break?   While exploring Cerro Bellavista, be sure to stop by **Gato Tuerto** (✉ Calle Hector Calvo Jofré 20 ☎ 32/220–867), the One-Eye Cat. This meticulously restored 1910 Victorian house affords lovely views. It's an Internet café, a book shop, a handicrafts boutique, and a popular night spot.

★ ❺ Museo de Bellas Artes. The art nouveau Palacio Baburizza houses the city's fine arts museum. Former owner Pascual Baburizza donated his large collection of European paintings to the city. The fanciful decorative exterior is reminiscent of the style of Spanish architect Antoni Gaudí. The museum was closed for renovation at press time, but even if it hasn't reopened by the time you visit it's still worth a look at the exterior. ✉ *Ascensor El Peral to Paseo Yugoslavo* ☎ *32/915–1028* ⊕ *www. museobaburizza.cl.*

❾ Museo de Historia Natural de Valparaíso. Within the Palacio Lyon, one of the few buildings to survive the devastating 1906 earthquake, is this rather outdated natural history museum. Among the more unusual exhibits are a pre-Columbian mummy, newborn conjoined twins in formaldehyde, and stuffed penguins. ✉ *Calle Condell 1546* ☎ *32/257–441* 🖰 *600 pesos* ⊗ *Tues.–Sat. 10–1 and 2–6, Sun. 10–2.*

❷ Museo Naval y Marítimo de Valparaíso. Atop Cerro Artillería is the large neoclassical mansion that once housed the country's naval academy. It now contains a maritime museum, with displays that document the history of the port and the ships that once defended it. Cannons positioned on the front lawn frame the excellent view of the ocean. ✉ *Ascensor Artillería up to Paseo 21 de Mayo* ☎ *32/437–651* 🖰 *500 pesos* ⊗ *Tues.–Sun. 10–5.*

▶ ❶ Paseo 21 de Mayo. Ascensor Artillería pulls you uphill to Paseo 21 de Mayo, a wide promenade surrounded by well-tended gardens and stately trees from which you can survey the port and a goodly portion of Valparaíso. It's in the middle of Cerro Playa Ancha, one of the city's more colorful neighborhoods. ⊠ *Ascensor Artillería at Plaza Advana.*

need a break?

If you can't get enough of the views from Paseo 21 de Mayo, stroll down the stairs that run parallel to the ascensor to the small restaurant, **Poseidon** (⊠ Subida Artillería 99 ☎ 32/346–713). With a terrace superbly perched on a high corner overlooking the city, this makes a great spot for a cool drink, or coffee and a slice of homemade pie.

❸ **Plaza Sotomayor.** Valparaíso's most impressive square, Plaza Sotomayor, serves as a gateway to the bustling port. **Comandancia en Jefe de la Armada,** headquarters of the Chilean navy, is a grand, gray building that rises to a turreted pinnacle over a mansard roof. At the north end of the plaza stands the **Monumento de los Héroes de Iquique,** which honors Arturo Prat and other heroes of the War of the Pacific. In the middle of the square (beware of traffic—cars and buses come suddenly from all directions) is the **Museo del Sitio.** Artifacts from the city's mid-19th century port, including parts of a dock that once stood on this spot, are displayed in the open under Plexiglas. ⊠ *Av. Errázuriz s/n.*

⓫ **Plaza Victoria.** The heart of the lower part of the city is this green plaza with a lovely fountain bordered by four female statues representing the seasons. Two black lions at the edge of the park look across the street to the neo-Gothic **Catedral,** the city's cathedral, and its unusual freestanding bell tower. Directly to the north is **Plaza Simon Bolívar,** which delights children with swings, slides, and simple carnival rides. ⊠ *Calle Condell s/n.*

★ ❼ **La Sebastiana.** Some say the views from the windows of Pablo Neruda's hillside house are the best in all of Valparaíso. People come to La Sebastiana to marvel at the same ocean that inspired so much poetry. The house is named for Sebastián Collado, a Spanish architect who began it as a home for himself but died before it was finished. The incomplete building stood abandoned for 10 years before Neruda finished it, revising the design (Neruda had no need for the third-floor aviary or the helicopter landing pad) and adding curvaceous walls, narrow stairways, a tower, and a polymorphous character.

A maze of twisting stairwells leads to an upper room where a video shows Neruda enunciating the five syllables of the city's name over and again as he rides the city's ascensores. His upper berth contains his desk, books, and some original manuscripts. What makes the visit to La Sebastiana memorable, however, is Neruda's nearly obsessive delight in physical objects. The house is a shrine to his many cherished things, such as the beautiful orange-pink bird he brought back embalmed from Venezuela. His lighter spirit is here also, in the carousel horse and the pink and yellow bar room stuffed with kitsch. ⊠ *Calle Ferrari 692* ☎ *32/256–606* 🖼 *1,800 pesos* 🕓 *Jan.–Feb., Tues.–Sun. 10:30–6:50; Mar.–Dec., Tues.–Sun. 10:30–2:30 and 3:30–6.*

Where to Stay & Eat

$$–$$$$ × **Bote Salvavidas.** This restaurant next to Muelle Prat has great views of the harbor and, naturally, specializes in seafood. Dishes such as congrio *margarita* (conger eel with shellfish sauce), *salmón salsa espinaca y nueces* (salmon smothered in a spinach and walnut sauce), and *pastel de jaiba* (crab pie) are among the popular specialties. A three-course *menu ejecutivo* (set lunch), available on weekdays, is quite the deal. ⊠ *Muelle Prat* ☎ *32/251–477* ⊟ *AE, DC, MC, V* ☺ *No dinner Sun.–Mon.*

$$–$$$ × **Café Turri.** Near the top of Ascensor Concepción, this 19th-century
FodorsChoice   mansion commands one of the best views of Valparaíso. It also has some
★   of the finest seafood. House specialties such as sea bass or shrimp in almond sauce or ostiones Cleopatra (scallops in a mushroom cream sauce) are alone worth the effort of driving to the coast from Santiago. Outside there's a terrace and inside are two floors of dining rooms. The service is excellent. ⊠ *Templeman 147, at Paseo Gervasoni* ☎ *32/252–091* 🖷 *32/259–198* ⊟ *AE, DC, MC, V.*

$$–$$$ × **La Colombina.** This restaurant is in an old home on Cerro Alegre, one of the city's most beautiful hilltop neighborhoods. Dining rooms on two floors are notable for their elegance, stained-glass windows, and impressive views of the city and sea. Seafood dominates the menu, with such inventive dishes as *albacora del bufón* (swordfish in a caper and mushroom cream sauce) and *trilogía del mar* (salmon, sea bass, and conger eel in a white wine, mushroom, and vegetable sauce). Choose from a list of 80 national wines. ⊠ *Paseo Yugoslavo 15* ☎ *32/236–254* ⊟ *AE, DC, MC, V* ☺ *No dinner Mon.*

$–$$$ × **Coco Loco.** It takes a little more than an hour to turn 360 degrees in this impressive *giratorio* (revolving restaurant), meaning you can savor all the smashing views of the city. The vast menu ranges from *filete de ciervo salsa hongos* (venison in a mushroom sauce) to fettuccine with a squid and mussels sauce. ⊠ *Blanco 1781* ☎ *32/227–614* ⚐ *Reservations essential* ⊟ *AE, DC, MC, V* ☺ *No dinner Sun.*

¢–$ × **Brighton.** Nestled below the eponymous bed-and-breakfast on the edge of Cerro Concepción, this popular restaurant has an amazing view from its black-and-white-tiled balcony. Vintage advertisements hang on the walls of the intimate dining room. A limited menu includes such Chilean standards as machas *a la parmesana* (razor clams Parmesan) and ceviche, as well as several kinds of crepes and a Spanish *tortilla* (egg and potato pie). An extensive wine list and cocktail selection make it a popular night spot, especially on weekends, when there's Latin music. ⊠ *Paseo Atkinson 151* ☎ *32/223–513* ⊟ *AE, DC, MC, V.*

¢–$ × **Casino Social J. Cruz M.** This eccentric restaurant is a Valparaíso institution, thanks to its legendary status for inventing the *chorillana* (minced beef with onions, cheese, and an egg atop french fries), which is now served by most local restaurants. There is no menu—choose either a chorillana for two or three, or *carne mechada* (stewed beef), with a side of french fries, rice, or tomato salad. Glass cases choked with dusty trinkets surround tables covered with plastic cloths in the cramped dining room. You may have to share a table. The restaurant is at the end of a bleak corridor off Calle Condell. ⊠ *Calle Condell 1466* ☎ *32/211–225* ⊟ *No credit cards.*

$ **Brighton B&B.** This bright yellow Victorian house enjoys an enviable
Fodor'sChoice location at the edge of tranquil Cerro Concepción, within blocks of sev-
★ eral restaurants and an ascensor. The house is furnished with antiques
chosen by owner Nelson Morgado, who taught architecture for two
decades at the University of Barcelona. The terrace of its restaurant and
three of its six rooms have vertiginous views of El Plano and the bay
beyond it. Only one room has a private balcony. Room size varies considerably—only the so-called suite (just a larger room) is spacious—and
those with the best views can be noisy on weekends. Some rooms have
cable TV. ⊠ *Paseo Atkinson 151* ☎ *32/223–513* 🖷 *32/598–802* 📞 *6
rooms* ♿ *Restaurant, bar, laundry service; no a/c, no room phones*
▤ *AE, DC, MC, V* ⦿⧽ *CP.*

$ **Hostal Colombina.** The location here is excellent: on a quiet street just
up the hill from the Ascensor Concepción, near Paseo 21 de Mayo in
the heart of Cerro Concepción. Rooms in this old house may be sparsely
furnished, but they are ample, with high ceilings and wooden floors. Most
have big windows, though none of them have much of a view. ⊠ *Calle
Abtao 575* ☎ *32/236–254 or 32/234–980* 📞 *8 rooms with shared
bath* ♿ *Dining room, wine bar; no a/c, no room phones, no room TVs*
▤ *AE, DC, MC, V* ⦿⧽ *CP.*

★ $ **Porto Principal.** Though small and fairly basic, this hotel on a side street
near Plaza Victoria has comfortable, secure accommodations at a reasonable price. Clean, carpeted rooms with large windows are on the second floor of a two-story building—those in back are slightly quieter. The
ground floor has a tiny bar and restaurant, where breakfast is served.
⊠ *Calle Huito 361* ☎ *32/745–629* 🖷 *32/226–738* 📞 *6 rooms* ♿ *Restaurant, room service, cable TV, bar, laundry service; no a/c* ▤ *AE, DC,
MC, V* ⦿⧽ *CP.*

$ **Puerta de Alcalá.** The rooms surround a five-story atrium flooded with
light at this central hotel. They have little personality, but are clean and
well equipped, with little extras like hair dryers. Those facing the street
are bright, but can be noisy on weekends. If you're a light sleeper, take a
room in the back, but try to get on the fourth floor—the lower floors get
less sunlight because they are blocked by the building next door. There's
a decent restaurant and bar on the ground level. ⊠ *Pirámide 524* ☎ *32/
227–478* 🖷 *32/745–642* ⊕ *www.chileinfo.cl/puertadealcalahotel* 📞 *21
rooms* ♿ *Restaurant, room service, in-room data ports, minibars, cable
TV, bar, laundry service, meeting room; no a/c* ▤ *AE, DC, MC, V* ⦿⧽ *CP.*

Nightlife

Since Valparaíso is a university town, the nightlife is reliably rowdy. On
Thursday, Friday, and Saturday nights young people are out on the streets
until daybreak. Subida Ecuador near Plazuela Ecuador crawls with
pubs, and Avenida Errázuriz, facing the port, has the best discos.

BARS & DANCE **Bar Inglés** (⊠ Cochrane 851 ☎ 32/214–625) is dingy but authentic, a
CLUBS short walk east of Plaza Sotomayor. It serves decent food and has the
longest bar in town. The huge antique mirrors of **Bar La Playa** (⊠ Serrano 567), just west of Plaza Sotomayor, make it seem historic. Poetry
readings are held Wednesday at 11 PM, and it becomes packed with party
animals after midnight on weekends January–February. **Valparaíso Eterno**

(⊠ 150 Almirante Señoret ☎ 32/228–374), one block from Plaza Sotomayor, is filled with paintings of Valparaíso and floor-to-ceiling graffiti lovingly supplied by patrons. It only opens on weekends.

Among the top dance clubs is **Aché Havana** (⊠ Av. Errázuriz 1042 ☎ 9/521–9872), which plays mostly salsa and other Latin rhythms. Near several other large dance clubs, **Bulevar** (⊠ Av. Errázuriz 1154 ☎ no phone) has eclectic music on weekend nights. The basement **Eterno** (⊠ Calle Blanco 698 ☎ 32/219–024), one block east of Plaza Sotomayor, plays only Latin dance music, and opens weekends only. The four-story **Mr. Egg** (⊠ Calle Ecuador 50 ☎ no phone) has a bar on the ground floor and a dance club above it.

Sports & the Outdoors

BEACHES   If it's beaches you're after, head to Viña del Mar. Valparaíso has only one notable beach, **Playa Las Torpederas,** a sheltered crescent of sand east of the port. Though less attractive than the beaches up the coast, it does have very calm water.

BOATING   Informal boat operators at **Muelle Prat** take groups on a 40-minute circuit of the bay for 2,000 pesos per person. If you have several people, consider hiring your own boat for 10,000 pesos.

Shopping

Cooperativa Artesanal de Valparaíso (⊠ Pedro Montt and Calle Las Heras ☎ no phone) is a daily market where you can buy local crafts. The weekend flea market, **Feria de Antigüedades** (⊠ Av. Argentina at Plaza O'Higgins ☎ no phone), has an excellent selection of antiques. **Paulina Acuña** (⊠ Almirante Montt 64 ☎ 9/871–8388), a small boutique up the hill from Plaza Anibal Pinto, sells an unusual collection of handicrafts.

Viña del Mar

10 km (6 mi) north of Valparaíso.

In contrast to Valparaíso's hodgepodge of hillside houses, Viña de Mar has stylish high-rise apartment buildings that tower above its excellent shoreline. Here you'll find wide boulevards lined with palms, lush parks with sharply edged landscaping, and manicured beaches that stretch for miles.

A GOOD WALK

Downtown Viña del Mar is completely flat and organized on a grid. To make things even easier, almost all of the street names are numbers in sequential order. For the streets running north–south, the numbers start on either side of Avenida Libertad. So you have 1 Poniente (west) and 1 Oriente (east).

Plaza José Francisco Vergara is the heart of the city. Just to the south is a smaller square called Plaza Sucre. Grandly filling the east end of the square is the **Club Viña del Mar.** Walking south past Plaza Sucre you reach the **Palacio Vergara,** with the Museo de Bellas Artes and the magnificently landscaped gardens of the Quinta Vergara. Return to Plaza Vergara and head north across the Estero Marga Marga via the Puente Libertad. Walk north along Avenida Libertad then turn east on 4 Norte. An early-20th-century mansion houses the **Museo de Arqueológico e Historia Francisco Fonck,** renowned for its Easter Island artifacts. Continue east two more blocks until the street ends at a lush park, in the heart of which stands the lovely **Palacio Rioja.**

TIMING The terrain in Viña del Mar is flat, so walking is easy. You can take in all the sights on this tour in a few hours. Save yourself for the beach— it's the main attraction.

What to See

Club Viña del Mar. It would be a shame to pass up a chance to see this private club's magnificent interior. The neoclassical building, constructed in 1901 of materials imported from England, is where wealthy locals come to play snooker. Nonmembers are usually only allowed to enter the grand central hall, but the club hosts occasional art shows, during which you may be able to circumambulate the second-floor interior balcony. ⊠ *Plaza Sucre at Av. Valparaíso* ☎ *32/680–016* 🖾 *Free* 🕓 *Mon.–Sat. 9–9.*

> **need a break?**
>
> Even die-hard shoppers may be overwhelmed by the myriad shops along Avenida Valparaíso. Take a load off at **286 Rue Valparaíso** (⊠ Av. Valparaíso 286 ☎ 32/710–140), an Internet café with tables on the sidewalk. Enjoy a cappuccino, a milk shake, or perhaps a crepe.

Museo de Arqueológico e Historia Francisco Fonck. A 500-year-old stone *moai* (a carved stone head) brought from Easter Island guards the entrance to this archaeological museum. The most interesting exhibits are the finds from Easter Island, which indigenous people call Rapa Nui, such as wood tablets displaying ancient hieroglyphics. The museum, named for ground-breaking archaeologist Francisco Fonck—a native of Viña del Mar—also has an extensive library of documents relating to the island. ⊠ *4 Norte 784* ☎ *32/686–753* 🖾 *1,000 pesos* 🕓 *Tues.–Fri. 9:30–6, weekends 9:30–2.*

Palacio Rioja. This grand palace was built by Spanish banker Francisco Rioja immediately after the earthquake that leveled much of the city in 1906. It contains a decorative arts museum showcasing a large portion of Rioja's belongings and a conservatory, so there's often music in the air. Performances are held in the main ballroom. The beautifully landscaped grounds are great for shady lounging or a picnic. ⊠ *Quillota 214* ☎ *32/689–665* 🖾 *300 pesos* 🕓 *Tues.–Sun. 10–1:30 and 3–5:30.*

Plaza José Francisco Vergara. Viña del Mar's central square, Plaza Vergara is lined with majestic palms. Presiding over the east end of the plaza is the patriarch of coastal accommodations, the venerable Hotel O'Higgins, which has seen better days. Opposite the hotel is the neoclassical Teatro Municipal, where you can watch a ballet, theater, or music performance. To the west on Avenida Valparaíso is the city's main shopping strip, a one-lane, seven-block stretch with extra-wide sidewalks and numerous stores and sidewalk cafés. You can hire a horse-drawn carriage to take you from the square past some of the city's stately mansions.

★ **Palacio Vergara.** Lose yourself on the paths that wind amid soaring eucalyptus trees on the grounds that contain one of Chile's best botanical gardens, **Quinta Vergara.** An amphitheater here holds an international music festival, *Festival Internacional de la Canción de Viña del Mar,* in February. The neo-Gothic Palacio Vergara, erected after the 1906 earthquake as the residence of the wealthy Vergara family, houses the **Museo de Bellas Artes.** Inside is a collection of classical paintings dating from the 15th to the 19th centuries, including works by Rubens and Tintoretto. ✉ *Av. Errázuriz 563* ☎ *32/680–618* ✉ *Gardens free, museum 500 pesos* ☉ *Gardens daily 7:30–7; museum Tues.–Sun. 10–2 and 3–6.*

Where to Stay & Eat

$–$$$ ✕ **Armandita.** Meat-eaters need not despair in this city of seafood saturation. A seemingly small restaurant half a block west of Avenida San Martín serves almost nothing but grilled meat, including various organs. The menu ranges from the popular *lomo a lo pobre* (flank steak, french fries, and a fried egg) to chateaubriand. The *parrillada especial,* a mixed grill of steak, chicken, ribs, pork, and sausage, serves two or three people. ✉ *6 Norte 119* ☎ *32/671–607* 🖃 *AE, DC, MC, V.*

$–$$$ ✕ **San Marcos.** More than five decades after Edoardo Melotti emigrated to Chile from northern Italy to open San Marcos, the restaurant maintains a reputation for first-class food and service. A modern dining room with abundant foliage and large windows overlooks busy Avenida San Martín. Farther inside, the two dining rooms in the house the restaurant originally occupied are elegant and more refined. The menu includes the traditional gnocchi and cannelloni, as well as *lasagna di granchio* (crab lasagna) and *pato arrosto* (roast duck). Complement your meal with a bottle from the extensive wine list. ✉ *Av. San Martín 597* ☎ *32/975–304* 🖃 *AE, DC, MC, V.*

$–$$ ✕ **Delicias del Mar.** Nationally renowned chef Raúl Madinagoitía, who
FodorśChoice has his own television program, runs the show here. The menu lists such
★ seafood delicacies as Peruvian-style ceviche, stuffed sea bass, machas *curadas* (steamed clams with dill and melted cheese), and the house's own version of paella. Oenophiles are impressed by the extensive, almost exclusively Chilean wine list. Save room for one of the excellent desserts, maybe crème brûlée, or cheesecake with a raspberry sauce. ✉ *San Martín 459* ☎ *32/901–837* 🖃 *AE, DC, MC, V.*

¢–$ ✕ **Fogón Criollo.** Hearty food at low prices: this unassuming restaurant in a residential neighborhood specializes in authentic Chilean cuisine. Try the *brasero al estilo Fogón Criollo,* a stew of beef, chicken, sausages, and potatoes. Old photos of Viña del Mar line the walls of this former home. Weekday lunch specials are a bargain. ✉ *5 Norte 476* ☎ *32/973–312* 🖃 *AE, DC, MC, V.*

★ **$$–$$$** ✕▦ **Hotel Oceanic.** Built on the rocky coast between Viña and Reñaca, this boutique hotel has luxurious rooms with gorgeous ocean views. The nicest ones have terraces, ideal for watching waves crash against the coast. The pool area, perched on the rocks below, is occasionally drenched by big swells. While there's no beach access, the sands of Salinas are a short walk away. The restaurant is one of the area's best, serving French-inspired dishes such as shrimp crepes, *filete café de Paris* (tenderloin with herb butter), and congrio *oceanic* (conger eel in an artichoke mushroom sauce). ✉ *Av. Borgoño 12925, north of town* ☎ *32/830–006* 🖶 *32/830–390* 🌐 *www.hoteloceanic.cl* ⇆ *22 rooms, 6 suites* ⚒ *Restaurant, room service, in-room data ports, in-room safes, minibars, cable TV, pool, hot tub, massage, sauna, bar, business services, meeting rooms; no a/c* ☰ *AE, DC, MC, V* ⊺⊙⊦ *BP.*

\$\$ ✕⊡ **Cap Ducal.** This ship-shaped building on the waterfront is a bit of an eyesore, but the views from its spacious restaurant and guest rooms are excellent. Like the building, rooms are oddly shaped, but they are nicely decorated with plush carpets and pastel wallpaper. Those on the third floor have narrow balconies. Be sure to ask for a view of Reñaca, or you may see, and hear, the road. The restaurant serves European cuisine to top the view. Try the congrio *a la griega* (conger eel with a mushroom, ham, and cream sauce) or *pollo a la Catalana* (chicken with an olive, mushroom, and tomato sauce). ✉ *Av. Marina 51* ☎ *32/828–655* 🖶 *32/665–478* 🌐 *www.capducal.cl* ⇆ *17 rooms, 3 suites* ⚒ *Restaurant, in-room safes, minibars, cable TV, bar, laundry service; no a/c* ☰ *AE, DC, MC, V* ⊺⊙⊦ *BP.*

\$\$\$\$ ⊡ **Hotel Del Mar.** Marble floors, fountains, abundant gardens, and im-
Fodor'sChoice peccable service make Hotel Del Mar one of Chile's most luxurious. It
★ occupies a recent annex to the 1930 Casino Viña del Mar. The hotel's exterior is true to the casino's neoclassical design, but spacious guest rooms are pure 21st century, with sleek furnishings, original art, and sliding glass doors that open onto sea-view balconies. An eighth-floor spa and infinity pool share the view. A stay here includes free access to the upscale casino, which evokes Monaco rather than Las Vegas. ✉ *Av. San Martín 199* ☎ *32/500–600* 🖶 *32/500–701* 🌐 *www.casino.cl* ⇆ *50 rooms, 10 suites* ⚒ *3 restaurants, café, in-room date ports, in-room safes, minibars, cable TV, indoor pool, exercise equipment, spa, bar, cabaret, shop, baby-sitting, laundry service, concierge, Internet, business services, convention center* ☰ *AE, DC, MC, V* ⊺⊙⊦ *BP.*

\$\$ ⊡ **Hotel Alcazar.** Ground-floor rooms (called cabanas here) with giant windows overlooking a tiny lawn and garden are the best deal. Though slightly neglected and on the small side, they have a pinch more personality than the more expensive rooms in the main building. Those have more amenities and large bathrooms with tubs—rooms in front are brighter, but suffer a bit from street noise. The hotel is south of the train tracks. ✉ *Alvarez 646* ☎ *32/685–112* 🖶 *32/884–245* ⇆ *52 rooms, 22 cabanas* ⚒ *Restaurant, in-room safes, minibars, cable TV, bar, laundry service, meeting rooms; no a/c* ☰ *AE, DC, MC, V* ⊺⊙⊦ *BP.*

\$\$ ⊡ **Hotel Gala.** Modern rooms in this upscale 14-story hotel have panoramic views of the city. The rooms are spacious, and large windows let in lots of light. The bathrooms are crisp and clean and outfitted in white tile. There's a small heated pool next to the bar. One block from the Avenida Valparaíso shopping strip, Gala is near most of the city's attractions. Be sure to pay with pesos, since the dollar rate is considerably higher. ✉ *Arlegui 273* ☎ *32/686–688* 🖶 *32/689–568* ⇆ *64 rooms, 13 suites* ⚒ *Restaurant, in-room data ports, minibars, cable TV, pool, massage, sauna, bar, laundry service, business services, convention center* ☰ *AE, DC, MC, V* ⊺⊙⊦ *BP.*

★ \$ ⊡ **Hotel Tres Poniente.** Come for the personalized service and for many of the same amenities as larger hotels at a fraction of their rates. Rooms are carpeted, nicely furnished, and impeccably clean. Two "apartments," larger rooms in back, are ideal for small families. Complimentary breakfast, and light meals are served at the bright café in front, behind which is a small lounge with armchairs and a sofa. The small hotel is half a block from busy 1 Norte. ⊠ *3 Poniente between 1 and 2 Norte* ☎ *32/ 977–833* 🖷 *32/478–576* 🖢 *12 rooms* ⚭ *Café, room service, in-room safe, minibars, cable TV, bar, baby-sitting, laundry service, Internet, nosmoking rooms; no a/c* ▤ *AE, DC, MC, V* ⑩ *BP.*

$ 🖭 **Residencia 555.** A stay in this old wood-frame house, built in 1912, may just make you feel like a local. Antiques fill the high-ceilinged living room, and a wide, curvaceous staircase leads to rooms on the second floor, several with balconies overlooking the garden. Considering the inn's charm, cleanliness, and central location, it's no surprise that Residencia 555 has twice been named the city's top guest house. ⊠ *5 Norte 555* 🕾🕾 *32/739–035* ⊕ *www.gratisweb.com/residencial555* 🖢 *12 rooms* ▤ *AE, DC, MC, V* ⑩ *BP.*

Nightlife & the Arts

Viña's nightlife varies considerably according to the season, with the most glittering events concentrated in the summer months of January and February.

BARS Though it's surrounded by the dance clubs and loud bars of Paseo Cousiño, **Kappi Kua** (⊠ Paseo Cousiño 11-A ☎ 32/977–331) is a good place for a quiet drink. The Mexican restaurant **Margarita** (⊠ Av. San Martín 348 ☎ 32/972–110) becomes a popular watering hole late at night. **Rituskuan** (⊠ Av. Valparaíso at Von Schroeders ☎ 9/305–0340) is colorful and has excellent beer and electronic music.

CASINO With a neoclassical style that wouldn't be out of place in a classic James Bond movie, **Casino Viña del Mar** (⊠ Av. San Martín 199 ☎ 32/500– 600) has a restaurant, bar, and cabaret, as well as roulette, blackjack, and 1,500 slot machines. It's open nightly until the wee hours of the morning most of the year. There's a 3,000-peso cover charge.

DANCE CLUBS The cabaret on the second floor of the **Casino Viña del Mar** (⊠ Av. San Martín 199 ☎ 32/500–600) becomes a chic discotheque after midnight. The popular **El Burro** (⊠ Paseo Cousiño 12-D ☎ no phone) only opens Friday and Saturday. **El Mezón con Zeta** (⊠ Paseo Cousiño 9 ☎ no phone) has a small dance floor. Viña's most sought-out dance club is **Scratch** (⊠ Calle Bohn 970 ☎ 32/978–219), a long block east of Plaza Sucre.

Sports & the Outdoors

BEACHES Just north of the rock wall along Avenida Peru is a stretch of sand that draws throngs of people December–March. Viña del Mar really has just one **main beach,** bisected near its southern end by an old pier, though its parts have been given separate names: Playa El Sol and Playa Blanca. South of town, on the far side of Cerro Castillo, the small **Playa Caleta Abarca** receives fewer sun worshippers than the main beach. A short drive north of town is the tiny **Las Salinas,** a crescent of sand that has the calmest water in the area.

HORSE RACING **Valparaíso Sporting Club** (⊠ Av. Los Castaños 404 ☎ 32/689–393) hosts horse racing every Friday. The Clásico del Derby, Chile's version of the Kentucky Derby, takes place the first Sunday in February. Rugby, polo, cricket, and other sports are also played here.

Shopping

Outside of Santiago, there are more shops in Viña del Mar than anywhere else in Chile. Viña's main shopping strip is **Avenida Valparaíso** between Cerro Castillo and Plaza Vergara, where wide sidewalks accommodate throngs of shoppers. Stores here sell everything from shoes to cameras, and there are also sidewalk cafés, bars, and restaurants. South of Plaza Vergara is the city's largest department store, **Ripley** (⊠ Sucre 290 ☎ 32/384–480). **Falabella** (⊠ Sucre 250 ☎ 32/264–740) is a popular small department store south of Plaza Vergara. For one-stop shopping, locals head to the mall, **Shopping Viña** (⊠ Av. 15 Norte 961 ☎ no phone), on the north end of town.

There are collections of **handicraft stands** on the road to Reñaca, across from the Hotel Oceanic, and in Paseo Cousiño, off the Avenida Valparaíso shopping strip's eastern end. Local crafts are sold at the **Cooperativa de Artesanía de Viña del Mar** (⊠ Quinta between Viana and Av. Valparaíso ☎ no phone). On the beach, just off Vergara dock, the **Feria Artesanal Muelle Vergara** is a crafts fair open daily in summer and on weekends the rest of the year.

The Central Coast A to Z

AIR TRAVEL

The Central Coast is served by LanChile via Santiago's Aeropuerto Comodoro Arturo Merino Benítez, an hour and a half from Viña del Mar and Valparaíso.

▪ Carriers **LanChile** ⊠ Esmerelda 1048, Valparaíso ☎ 32/251–441 ⊠ Ecuador 76, Viña del Mar ☎ 600/526–2000.

BUS TRAVEL

There is hourly bus service between Santiago and both Valparaíso and Viña del Mar. The two-hour trip costs about 2,100 pesos. Regular buses between Viña del Mar and Valparaíso cruise the main north-south routes of those cities. Buses to more distant towns along the Central Coast depart from Valparaíso's Terminal Rodoviario, across from the Congreso Nacional, and Viña's Terminal Rodoviario, two blocks east of Plaza Vergara.

▪ Bus Depots **Terminal Rodoviario** ⊠ Av. Pedro Montt 2800, Valparaíso ☎ 32/213–246. **Terminal Rodoviario** ⊠ Av. Valparaíso and Quilpué, Viña del Mar ☎ 32/882–661.

CAR RENTAL

Since it's so easy to get around in Valparaíso and Viña del Mar, there's no need to rent a car to explore these cities. But if you want to travel to other towns on the coast, renting a car is advisable. Hertz is the only international chain with an office in the region (Viña del Mar). The Chilean company Rosselot is well represented, as are the smaller local companies Bert and Kovac's.

⊟ Agencies Bert ✉ Victoria 2681, Valparaíso ☎ 32/352-365. **Hertz** ✉ Quillota 766, Viña del Mar ☎ 32/381-025 or 32/689-918. **Kovac's** ✉ Colón 2537, Valparaíso ☎ 32/255-505 ✉ 5 Norte 650, Viña del Mar ☎ 32/686-820. **Rosselot** ✉ Victoria 2675, Valparaíso ☎ 32/352-365 ✉ Av. Libertad 892, Viña del Mar ☎ 32/382-373.

MAIL & SHIPPING

Perhaps because it is so close to Santiago, the postal system along the Central Coast is fairly efficient. On average, letters take five to seven days to reach the United States or Europe.

⊟ Post Offices Valparaíso ✉ Southeast corner of Plaza Sotomayor. **Viña del Mar** ✉ North side of Plaza Vergara.

MONEY MATTERS

All but the smallest Central Coast towns have at least one ATM, and both Valparaíso and Viña del Mar have dozens of them, but it's wise to take a fair amount of U.S. dollars, since some hotels require payment in them to discount the 18% tax from your bill. ATMs at well distributed Banco de Chile branches also give cash advances on international credit cards. All but the least expensive restaurants and hotels accept major credit cards.

⊟ ATMs Banco de Chile ✉ Cochrane 785, Valparaíso ☎ 32/356-500 ✉ Av. Valparaíso 667, Viña del Mar ☎ 32/648-760 ✉ Av. Borgoño 14675, Reñaca ☎ 32/836-938 ✉ Olegario O'Valle 336, Zapallar ☎ 33/741-613 ✉ Carlos Alessandri 1666, Algarrobo ☎ 35/482-857. **Citibank** ✉ 1 Norte 633, Viña del Mar ☎ 32/338-500.

SAFETY

Like most port cities, Valparaíso has its share of street crime. Avoid deserted areas and be on the lookout for suspicious characters. It's best not to walk alone and to avoid side streets after dark. In both Valparaíso and Viña del Mar you should always be alert to the possibility of pickpockets in tourist areas. Keep an eye on cameras and other valuables, or keep them in your hotel safe.

Look out for red warning flags on popular beaches, which indicate the sea is unsafe for swimming. If the waves are big and you aren't an experienced ocean swimmer, don't go in any deeper than your waist. Rip currents can be deadly.

TAXIS

In Valparaíso and Viña del Mar you can hail a taxi on busy streets and at plazas. Most smaller towns have a taxi stand on the main road. If you prefer to phone a cab, have your hotel receptionist call a reputable company, such as Radio Taxis Turismo in Valparaíso, and Radio Taxi in Viña del Mar.

⊟ Taxi Companies Radio Taxi ☎ 32/690-227. **Radio Taxis Turismo** ☎ 32/212-885.

TELEPHONES

There are several different telephone companies in the Central Coast, and each has its own public telephones. Calling cards can be purchased in many shops and newsstands. The card you buy must match the company that owns the individual phone for it to work. You can also place local and international calls, or send faxes, from one of the central Entel or Telefónica offices located throughout the region.

TOUR OPERATORS

You need a tour guide to really get to know the twisting streets of Valparaíso. Claudia Acevedo of Claudia Tours helps you see the city through the eyes of a local. If she's unavailable, contact Enlace Turístico, which has several city tours and trips to the Central Coast's smaller towns. In Viña del Mar, Aguitur and Chile Guías have bilingual guides for city tours, and trips to beaches north and south.

🖪 Tours **Aguitur** ✉ Av. Valparaíso, Viña del Mar ☎ 32/711-052. **Chile Guías** ✉ Errázuriz 670, Viña del Mar ☎ 32/692-580. **Claudia Tours** ✉ Valparaíso ☎ 32/256-854 or 9/665-6333. **Enlace Turístico** ✉ Cerro Bellavista, Valparaíso ☎ 32/232-313, or 9/896-4887.

TRAIN TRAVEL

Merval, a commuter train linking Viña de Mar and Valparaíso, is a fun way to shuttle between the two cities, though service isn't as frequent as abundant city buses. Trains depart about every half hour 6 AM–10 PM; note, however, that there are no trains to Viña for about 90 minutes during the morning rush, and no trains to Valparaíso during the evening rush. The ride costs about 200 pesos. In Valparaíso the main station is at the Muelle Prat. In Viña del Mar, it's south of Plaza Vergara.

🖪 Train Stations **Estación Puerto** ✉ Plaza Sotomayor ☎ 32/217-108. **Estación Viña del Mar** ✉ Plaza Sucre ☎ no phone.

VISITOR INFORMATION

Viña del Mar has the best tourist office on the coast, north of Plaza Vergara. It's open Monday–Saturday 9–2 and 3–7. Valparaíso has two information booths: one at Muelle Prat that is open daily 10–2 and 3–6, and one at the Rodoviario bus terminal, with the same hours except it closes Mondays.

🖪 Tourist Information **Muelle Prat Information Booth** ✉ Muelle Prat, Valparaíso ☎ 32/939-489. **Rodoviario Information Booth** ✉ Av. Pedro Montt 2800, Valparaíso ☎ 32/939-669. **Viña del Mar Central de Turismo** ✉ Av. Libertad and Av. Arlegui, Viña del Mar ☎ 800/800-830.

EL NORTE GRANDE

A land of rock and earth, El Norte Grande is one of the world's most desolate regions. Here you will find the Atacama Desert, so dry that in many parts no rain has ever been recorded. Twice a decade it explodes in a riot of color known as *el desierto florido,* or "the flowering desert." Also here is the *altiplano,* or high plains, where you'll find such natural marvels as crystalline salt flats, geysers, and volcanoes. You'll also spot flocks of flamingos and odd mammals like the vicuña, a cousin to the llama.

Antofagasta

565 km (350 mi) north of Copiapó.

Antofagasta is the most important—and the richest—city in El Norte Grande. It was part of Bolivia until 1879, when it was annexed by Chile in the War of the Pacific. The port town became an economic powerhouse during the nitrate boom. With the rapid decline of nitrate production, copper mining stepped in to keep the city's coffers filled.

The historic customs house, the town's oldest building, dates from 1866. Housed inside is the **Museo Regional de Antofagasta,** which displays clothing and other bric-a-brac from the nitrate era. ⊠ *Bolívar 1888* ☎ *55/227–016* 🖾 *600 pesos* ☉ *Tues.–Sat. 10–1 and 3:30–6:30, Sun. 11–2.*

Where to Stay & Eat

$$–$$$ ✕ **Club de Yates.** This seafood restaurant with nice views of the port caters to yachting types, which may explain why the prices are a bit higher than at other restaurants in the area. The food is quite good, especially the *ostiones a la parmesana* (oysters with Parmesan cheese). The maritime theme is taken to the extreme—the plates, curtains, tablecloths, and every decoration imaginable come in the mandatory navy blue. The service is excellent. ⊠ *Balmaceda 2705* ☎ *55/263–942* ☒ *Reservations essential* ⊟ *AE, DC, MC, V.*

★ **$–$$** ✕ **Restaurant Arriero.** Serving up traditional dishes from Spain's Basque country, Arriero is the place to go for good barbecued meats. The restaurant is in a pleasant Pyrenees-style inn decorated with traditional cured hams hanging from the walls. The restaurant's owners play jazz on the piano almost every evening. ⊠ *Condell 2644* ☎ *55/264–371* ⊟ *AE, DC, MC, V.*

$ ✕ **Don Pollo.** This rotisserie restaurant prepares some of the best chicken in Chile—a good thing, because it's the only item on the menu. The thatched-roof terrace is a great place to kick back after a long day of sightseeing. ⊠ *Ossa 2594* ☎ *No phone* ⊟ *No credit cards.*

★ **$$** 🏨 **Hotel Antofagasta.** Part of the deluxe Panamericana Hoteles chain, this high-rise on the ocean comes with all the first-class luxuries, from an elegant bar with a grand piano to a lovely kidney-shape pool. The rooms are comfortably furnished, and some have ocean views. A semiprivate beach is just steps from the hotel's back door. ⊠ *Balmaceda 2575* ☎ *55/228–811* 🖨 *55/268–415* ⊕ *www.hotelantofagasta.cl* 📞 *145 rooms, 18 suites* ঊ *Restaurant, room service, minibars, cable TV, pool,*

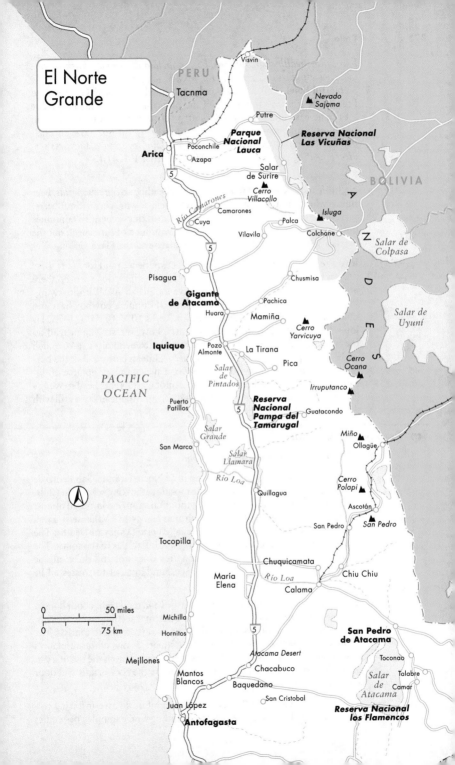

El Norte Grande

PERU

Visvin

Tacnma

Nevado
Sajama ▲

Putre

Arica

Poconchile

Azapa

**Parque
Nacional
Lauca**

**Reserva Nacional
Las Vicuñas**

BOLIVIA

Salar
de Surire

*Cerro
Villacollo* ▲

Isluga ▲

Río Camarones

Cuya

Camarones

Palca

Vilavila

Colchane

*Salar de
Colpasa*

Pisagua

Chusmisa

**Gigante
de Atacama**

Pachica

Huara

Mamiña

*Cerro
Yarvicuya* ▲

*Salar de
Uyuni*

Iquique

Pozo
Almonte

La Tirana

Pica

*Salar
de
Pintados*

*Cerro
Ocana* ▲

Irruptanco ▲

**PACIFIC
OCEAN**

Puerto
Patillos

**Reserva
Nacional
Pampa del
Tamarugal**

Guatacondo

Miño ○ ▲

Ollagüe

San Marco

*Salar
Grande*

*Salar
Llamara*

Río Loa

Quillagua

*Cerro
Polapi* ▲

Ascotán

San Pedro

San Pedro ▲

Tocopilla

Chuquicamata

Río Loa

Chiu Chiu

María
Elena

Calama

| 0 | | 50 miles |
| 0 | | 75 km |

Michilla

Hornitos

**San Pedro
de Atacama**

Toconao

Mejillones

Atacama Desert

Chacabuco

Talabre

*Salar
de
Atacama*

Camar

Mantos
Blancos

Baquedano

San Cristobal

Juan López

Antofagasta

**Reserva Nacional
los Flamencos**

hair salon, health club, billiards, bar, shop, laundry service, business services, meeting rooms ⊟ *AE, DC, MC, V* ⚹❘ *BP.*

$ ⊡ **Marsal Hotel.** This modern and clean hotel faces busy Calle Arturo Prat, so be sure to ask for one of the pleasant rooms in the back. The service here is quite friendly—the staff goes out of its way to recommend restaurants and arrange excursions. ⊠ *Arturo Prat 867* 🕾🕾 *55/268–063* ✎ *18 rooms* ⚲ *Minibars, cable TV, laundry service, business services, meeting rooms; no a/c* ⊟ *AE, DC, MC, V* ⚹❘ *CP.*

Nightlife

Nightlife in El Norte Grande often means heading to the *schoperias*, beer stands where the almost entirely male clientele downs *schops* (draft beers) served by scantily clad waitresses. The drinking generally continues until everyone is reeling drunk. If this is your idea of fun, check out the myriad schoperias in the center of town around the Plaza Colón.

If you're not quite ready for the schoperia experience (and for many these are not the most pleasant places to spend an evening), don't worry: there are also a few bars where you can have a quiet drink. With its swinging saloon-style doors and a great waitstaff donning cowboy hats and blue jeans, the **Country Pub** (⊠ Salvador Reyes 1025 🕾 55/371–751) is lots of fun. The music doesn't go country, however, staying instead on the modern side of pop. The friendly, funky **Nueva Raices** (⊠ Condell 3033 🕾 no phone) is steeped in northern Chilean culture. Ask the bartender to show you how to play *cacho*, a dice game popular with locals. Weekends the bar hosts live music. Antofagasta's elite head to **Wally's Pub** (⊠ Antonino Toro 982 🕾 55/223–697), an American-style grill with American-style prices.

San Pedro de Atacama

★ *320 km (199 mi) northeast of Calama.*

The most popular tourist destination in El Norte Grande, San Pedro de Atacama is in the midst of some of the most breathtaking scenery in Chile. To the west is La Cordillera de Sal, a mountain range composed almost entirely of salt. Here you'll find such marvels as the Valle de la Luna (Valley of the Moon) and the Valle de la Muerte (Valley of Death). The desolate Salar de Atacama, Chile's largest salt flat, lies to the south. The number of attractions in the Atacama area does not end there: alpine lakes, steaming geysers, colonial villages, and ancient fortresses all lie within easy reach.

With its narrow streets lined with whitewashed and mud-color adobe houses, San Pedro centers around a small Plaza de Armas teeming with artisans, tour operators, and others who make their living catering to tourists. The 1744 **Iglesia San Pedro,** to the west of the square, is one of the altiplano's largest churches. It was miraculously constructed without the use of a single nail—the builders used cactus sinews to tie the roof beams and door hinges. ⊠ *Padre Le Paige s/n* 🕾 *No phone* ☉ *Daily 8–8.*

FodorśChoice The **Museo Arqueológico Gustavo Le Paige** exhibits an awe-inspiring col-
★ lection of artifacts from the region, including fine examples of textiles

and ceramics. The museum traces the history of the area from pre-Columbian times through the Spanish colonization. The most impressive exhibit is the well-preserved, fetal-positioned Atacameño mummy with her swatch of twisted black hair. Most of the items on display were gathered by the founder, Jesuit missionary Gustavo Le Paige. ⊠ *Calle Padre Le Paige and Paseo Artesenal* ☎ *55/851–002* ☏ *2,000 pesos* ⊙ *Weekdays 9–noon and 2–6, weekends 10–noon and 2–6.*

The world's highest geothermal field, **Geysers del Tatio** are a breathtaking natural phenomenon. The sight of dozens of *fumaroles,* or geysers, throwing columns of steam into the air is unforgettable. The geysers are 95 km (59 mi) north of San Pedro, and most tours arrive here at daybreak. The jets of steam are already shooting into the air as the sun slowly peaks over the adjacent cordillera. The rays of light illuminate the steam in a kaleidoscope of chartreuses, violets, reds, oranges, and blues. Be careful—the crust is thin in places and people have been badly burned falling into the boiling-hot water.

| need a break? | Stop at **Café del Viaje** (⊠ Tocopilla 359 ☎ 09/822–4787) for sweet, fresh juices and an excellent vegetarian fixed-menu lunch or dinner. The dining area is in a huge courtyard splashed with chañar trees. |

Just 3 km (2 mi) north of San Pedro lies the ancient fortress of **Pukara de Quitor.** This group of stone structures at the entrance to the Valle de Catarpe was built in the 12th century to protect the Atacameños from invading Incas. It wasn't the Incas but the Spanish who were the real threat, however. Spanish conquistador Pedro de Valdivia took the fortress by force in 1540. The crumbling buildings were carefully reconstructed in 1981 by the University of Antofagasta. ⊠ *On the road to Valle Catarpe* ☎ *No phone* ☏ *1,200 pesos* ⊙ *Daily 8–8.*

The archaeological site of **Tulor,** 9 km (6 mi) southwest of San Pedro, marks the remains of the oldest known civilization in the region. Built around 800 BC, the village of Tulor was home to the Linka Arti people, who lived in small mud huts resembling igloos. The site was only uncovered in the middle of the 20th century, when Jesuit missionary Gustavo Le Paige excavated it from a sand dune. Archaeologists hypothesize that the inhabitants left because of climatic changes and a possible sand storm. Little more about the village's history is known, and only one of the huts has been completely excavated. As one of the well-informed guides will tell you, even this hut is sinking back into the obscurity of the Atacama sand. ⊕ *9 km (6 mi) southwest of San Pedro, then 3 km (2 mi) down the road leading to the Valle de la Luna* ☎ *No phone* ☏ *1,500 pesos* ⊙ *Daily 8–8.*

Where to Stay & Eat

★ **$–$$** ✕ **Café Adobe.** With an earthy, lattice-covered dining area surrounding an open terrace and a blazing fire at night, Adobe is San Pedro's definitive hangout and its finest eatery. The Chilean and international cuisine is excellent, and the animated (at times downright frenetic) waitstaff makes for a unique dining experience. At night, a white-capped chef grills meat in the center courtyard. Try the grilled steaks, quesadillas, or pasta. There's an Internet café here, too. ⊠ *Carcoles 211* ☎ *55/851–132* ▭ *AE, DC, MC, V.*

$–$$ ✕ **Casa Piedra.** This rustic stone house affords views of the world-famous Atacama skies from its central courtyard. As at most San Pedro eateries, a blazing fire keeps you company. The food here, including the seafood, is simple and good, mixing international and local dishes. Specialty sauces spice up any dinner. ⊠ *Caracoles 225* ☎ *55/851–271* ▭ *AE, DC, MC, V.*

★ **$$$$** ▦ **Hotel Explora.** Is it a modern monstrosity or an expressionist showpiece? Hotel Explora, built by the same company that constructed the much-lauded Hotel Explora in Parque Nacional Torres del Paine, attracted much criticism for not fitting in with the local architecture. On the other hand, it has also won architectural prizes for its skewed lines and sleek courtyard. The hotel, which has three-, four-, and seven-day all-inclusive stays—with tours, meals, and drinks included—delivers the best service and amenities of any lodging in northern Chile. ⊠ *Domingo Atienza s/n* ☎ *55/851–110* 🖷 *55/851–115* ⊕ *www.explora.com* 🛏 *52 rooms* ♨ *Restaurant, fans, in-room safes, 4 pools, massage, sauna, mountain bikes, horseback riding, bar, shop, baby-sitting, laundry service, Internet, meeting rooms, airport shuttle, free parking, no-smoking rooms; no a/c, no room phones, no room TVs* ▭ *AE, DC, MC, V* ❙❍❙ *All-inclusive.*

$$$ ▦ **Lodge Andino Terrantai.** An architectural beauty with river-stone walls, the Terrantai has high-ceilinged rooms highlighted by beautiful tile floors and big beds piled with down comforters. Throw open the huge windows to let in the morning breeze. The candlelit restaurant, perfect for a romantic dinner, serves international fare. There's also a tiny, natural-rock plunge pool in the center. The hotel is just a block away from the Plaza de Armas. ⊠ *Tocopilla 411* ☎ *55/851–140* 🖷 *55/851–037* ⊕ *www.adex.cl* 🛏 *16 rooms* ♨ *Restaurant, room service, pool, laundry service; no a/c, no room TVs* ▭ *AE, DC, MC, V* ❙❍❙ *BP.*

Fodor'sChoice
★

$$ ▦ **Hotel Altiplanico.** This boutique hotel just outside the center of San Pedro has the look and feel of an altiplano pueblo. A river-stone walkway leads you from room to room, each with its own private terrace. Muted whites decorate the guest chambers, making them quite welcoming. Some rooms have private watchtowers for stargazing. ⊠ *Domingo Atienza 282* ☎ *55/851–212* ⊕ *www.altiplanico.cl* 🛏 *14 rooms, 2 with shared bath* ♨ *Restaurant, pool, massage, laundry service, Internet, travel services; no a/c, no room phones, no room TVs* ▭ *AE, DC, MC, V* ❙❍❙ *BP.*

$$ ▦ **Hotel Kimal.** The adobe-walled Hotel Kimal has comfortable rooms and a cheery central courtyard dotted with islands of desert shrubbery. The rooms are pleasantly airy, with skylights and reed ceilings. The excellent, small restaurant serves Chilean fare. The pool is ideal for cooling off after your desert exploration. ⊠ *Domingo Atienza 452* ☎ *55/851–030* 🖷 *55/851–152* ⊕ *www.kimal.cl* 🛏 *11 rooms* ♨ *Restaurant, minibars, pool, shop, laundry service; no a/c, no room TVs* ▭ *AE, DC, MC, V* ❙❍❙ *BP.*

$ ▦ **Hotel Tambillo.** A good budget alternative, Hotel Tambillo has simple, rather drab rooms along a long, outdoor walkway. There's also a restaurant. ⊠ *Gustavo Le Paige 159* ☎☎ *55/851–078* ✉ *tambillo@sanpedrodeatacama.com* 🛏 *15 rooms* ♨ *Restaurant; no a/c, no room phones, no room TVs* ▭ *No credit cards.*

Nightlife

The bohemian side of San Pedro gets going after dinner and generally ends around 1 AM. Most of the bars are on Caracoles. At night there's seating around a bonfire in the courtyard of **Café Adobe** (⊠ Caracoles 211 ☎ 55/851–132), which occasionally hosts live music. During the day the latticed roof around the edges protects you from the sun's rays. **Café Export** (⊠ Caracoles and Toconao ☎ 55/851–547) is smaller and more intimate than the other bars in town. There's a small terrace out back. **La Estaka** (⊠ Caracoles 259B ☎ 55/851–201) is a hippie bar with funky decor, including a sculpted dragon hanging on one of the walls. Reggae music rules, and the international food isn't half bad either.

Shopping

Just about the entire village of San Pedro is an open-air market. The **Feria Artesenal,** just off the Plaza de Armas, is bursting at the seams with artisan goods. Here, you can buy high-quality knits from the altiplano, such as sweaters and other woolen items. **Galeria Cultural de Pueblos Andinos** (⊠ Caracoles s/n, east of town ☎ no phone) is an open-air market selling woolens and crafts. **Mallku** (⊠ Caracoles s/n ☎ no phone) is a pleasant store carrying traditional altiplano textiles, some up to 20 years old. **Taller de Artesania Rayo de La Luna** (⊠ Caracoles 378 ☎ 09/473–9018) sells jewelry made by local artisans.

Reserva Nacional los Flamencos

10 km (6 mi) south and east of San Pedro.

Many of the most astounding sights in El Norte Grande lie within the boundaries of the protected Reserva Nacional los Flamencos. This sprawling national reserve to the south and east of San Pedro encompasses a wide variety of geographical features, including alpine lakes, salt flats, and volcanoes. You can get information about the park at the station run by CONAF, the Chilean forestry service. ⊠ *CONAF station near Laguna Chaxa* ☎ *No phone* 🎫 *2,000 pesos* ☉ *Daily 8:30–1 and 2:30–6:30.*

★ About 10 km (6 mi) south of San Pedro you arrive at the edge of the **Salar de Atacama,** Chile's largest salt flat. The rugged crust measuring 3,000 square km (1,158 square mi) formed when salty water flowing down from the Andes evaporated in the stifling heat of the desert. Unlike other salt flats, which are chalkboard-flat surfaces of crystalline salt, the Salar de Atacama is a jumble of jagged rocks. **Laguna Chaxa,** in the middle of Salar de Atacama, is a very salty lagoon that is home to three of the world's four species of flamingos. The elegant pink and white birds are mirrored by the lake's glassy surface. Near Laguna Chaxa, beautiful plates of salt float on the calm surface of **Laguna Salada.**

★ One of the most impressive sights in Reserva Nacional los Flamencos is the 4,350-m-high (14,270-ft-high) **Laguna Miscanti,** an awe-inspiring blue lake that merits a few hours of rest and repose. **Laguna Miñeques,** a smaller lake adjacent to Laguna Miscanti, is spectacular. Here you will find vicuña and huge flocks of flamingos.

★ Very few places in the world can compare to the **Valle de la Luna** (⊠ 14 km [9 mi] west of San Pedro). This surreal landscape of barren ridges, soaring cliffs, and pale valleys could be from a canvas by Salvador Dalí. Originally a small corner of a vast inland sea, the valley rose up with the Andes. The water slowly drained away, leaving deposits of salt and gypsum that were folded by shifting of the earth's crust and then worn away by wind and rain. It's best to visit Valle de la Luna in the late afternoon to take advantage of the incredible sunsets visible from atop the immense sand dune. Not far from the Valle de la Luna are the reddish rocks of the **Valle de la Muerte.** Jesuit missionary Gustavo Le Paige, the first archaeologist to explore this desolate area, found many human bones. He hypothesized that people may have come here to die.

Iquique

390 km (242 mi) northwest of San Pedro de Atacama.

Iquique is the capital of Chile's northernmost region, but it wasn't always so important. For hundreds of years it was a tiny fishing community. It was not until the great nitrate boom of the 19th century that Iquique became the major port. Many of those who grew rich on nitrate moved to the city and built opulent mansions, almost all of which still stand today.

Unlike most cities, Iquique does not have a cathedral on the main plaza. Here instead you'll find the sumptuous **Teatro Municipal,** built in 1890 as an opera house. The lovely statues on the Corinthian-columned facade represent the four seasons. If you're lucky you can catch a play or musical performance here. ⊠ *Plaza Prat* ☎ *57/411–292* 💺 *Tickets 1,500–5,000 pesos* ☽ *Daily 8–7.*

For a tantalizing view into the opulence of the nitrate era, visit the Geor-
★ gian-style **Palacio Astoreca.** This palace, built in 1903, include such highlights as the likeness of Dionysus, the Greek god of revelry; a giant billiards table; and a beautiful skylight over the central hall. An art and natural history museum on the upper level houses modern works by Chilean artists and such artifacts as pottery and textiles. ⊠ *O'Higgins 350* ☎ *57/425–600* 💺 *Free* ☽ *Tues.–Fri. 10–1 and 4–7:30, Sat. 10–1:30, Sun. 11–2.*

Along the historic Calle Baquedano is the **Museo Regional,** a natural history museum of the region. It showcases pre-Columbian artifacts such as deformed skulls and arrowheads, as well as an eclectic collection from the region's nitrate heyday. ⊠ *Baquedano 951* ☎ *57/411–214* 💺 *Free* ☽ *Mon.–Sat. 9:30–1 and 3–6:30.*

Where to Stay & Eat

$$–$$$ ✕ **Casino Español.** This venerable gentleman's club on Plaza Prat has been
FodorśChoice transformed into a palatial Spanish restaurant, with beautiful Moorish
★ architecture that calls to mind the Alhambra in Granada. The service is good, though rather fussy, and the food is extravagant in the traditional Andalucian style. The paella *Valenciana* is quite good. ⊠ *Plaza Prat 584* ☎ *57/423–284* ♨ *Reservations essential* 🞔 *AE, DC, MC, V.*

$$–$$$ ✕ **Restaurant Nautico Cavancha.** Located away from the center of the city, this seafood restaurant treats you to views of Playa Cavancha. It's very stylish, right down to the cloth napkins (a rarity in El Norte Grande). Try the paella for two, served by friendly bow-tied waiters. ⊠ *Los Rieles 110* ☎ *57/432–896* ⌕ *Reservations essential* ▤ *DC, MC, V.*

★ $$ ✕ **Taberna Barracuda.** An immensely popular bar and grill, Taberna Barracuda serves everything from Spanish tapas to rib-eye steak. The wine list is good, making this an ideal place to sample some of Chile's labels. A general sense of joviality and merriment here harken to the decadent days of the nitrate boom. Antiques ranging from brass instruments to time-stained photos decorate the labyrinthine, salitrera-era house. ⊠ *Gorostiaga 601* ☎ *57/427–969* ⌕ *Reservations essential* ▤ *AE, DC, MC, V* ⊗ *Closed Sun. mid-June–early Sept.*

$–$$ ✕ **Boulevard.** Excellent seafood is served in a variety of ways at this intimate, candlelit restaurant. The cuisine is an interesting mélange of French and international recipes—try hake served in a creamy sauce or the *tagine,* a savory Moroccan stew. There's live music on weekends. ⊠ *Baquedano 790* ☎ *57/413–695* ⌕ *Reservations essential* ▤ *MC, V.*

$ ✕ **Restaurant Protectora.** A soaring molded ceiling and a huge chandelier overlook this elegant contemporary restaurant next to the Teatro Municipal. The international menu includes such succulent items as lamb cooked in mint sauce and merluza con salsa margarita. The service, though a bit dotting, is top-notch. ⊠ *Thompson 207* ☎ *57/421–923* ▤ *AE, DC, MC, V.*

$$ ▦ **Terrado Suites.** A skyscraper at the southern end of Playa Cavancha, the Terrado is Iquique's most upscale hotel. A marble entryway chaperones you down to the comfortable lounge and restaurant area. Overstuffed sofas, Andean prints, and hardwood accents decorate the large suites, which have private balconies. The pool and underground sauna are a delight after a day in the desert. ⊠ *Los Rieles 126,* ☎ *57/437–878* 🖶 *57/437–755* ⊕ *www.terrado.cl* ⤳ *91 suites* ⌕ *2 restaurants, room service, in-room data ports, in-room safes, minibars, cable TV, 2 pools, gym, hot tub, massage, sauna, bar, baby-sitting, laundry service, business services, meeting rooms, airport shuttle, car rental; no a/c in some rooms* ▤ *AE, DC, MC, V* ⅠⅠ *BP.*

$–$$ ▦ **Hotel Arturo Prat.** The only thing this luxury hotel in the heart of Iquique's historic district lacks is access to the ocean. To make up for this, it has a very pleasant roof-top pool area decorated with white umbrellas and navy-blue sails. The rooms are all comfortable and modern, though some look out onto the parking lot. Ask for one of the newer rooms, which are several steps above the rooms in the older section of the hotel. The Arturo faces the central square, and the restaurant, which serves good but somewhat uninspired fare, sits right on Plaza Prat. ⊠ *Anibal Pinto 695* ☎ *57/427–000* 🖶 *57/429–088* ⊕ *www. hotelarturoprat.cl* ⤳ *83 rooms, 9 suites* ⌕ *Restaurant, room service, in-room safes, minibars, cable TV, pool, exercise equipment, sauna, billiards, bar, laundry service, business services, meeting rooms; no a/c in some rooms* ▤ *AE, DC, MC, V* ⅠⅠ *BP.*

★ $ ▦ **Hotel Atenas.** Housed in a venerable nitrate-era mansion on the beach, Hotel Atenas is truly a taste of the city's history. Antiques and wood furnishings fill most of the rooms. There are more modern rooms in the back, but these are not nearly as charming. The honeymoon suite has a giant tub where you can imagine the nitrate barons bathing in champagne.

There's also a pleasant pool in the garden. ⊠ *Los Rieles 738* ☏ *57/431–100* 🖨 *57/431–100* ⊕ *www.iquiqueonline.cl/atenas* 🛏 *40 rooms* ☖ *Restaurant, room service, fans, in-room safes, minibars, cable TV, pool, hot tub, laundry service, Internet; no a/c* ☰ *AE, DC, MC, V* ⦿⦿ *CP.*

Nightlife

Bars, most of which feature folk and jazz performances, get crowded around midnight. At about 2 AM the beachfront discos start filling with a young, energetic crowd. Check out the dance clubs along Playa Brava and just south of town. **Bar Sovia** (⊠ Tarapaca 173 ☏ 57/517–015), perhaps the North's only microbrewery, is a relaxed place for a frothy brew. For sunset drinks and excellent empanadas head to **Choza Bambu** (⊠ Arturo Prat s/n, Playa Cavancha ☏ 57/519–002). One of the city's most popular bars is **Circus Pub** (⊠ Thompson 123 ☏ 57/316–827), with live music, a very friendly staff, and—in keeping with its name—occasional trapeze shows. **Kamikaze** (⊠ Bajo Molle, Km 7 ☏ no phone), part of a popular chain of discos, is jam-packed on weekends with young people dancing to salsa music. **Timber House** (⊠ Bolívar 553 ☏ 57/422–538) has a disco upstairs and an Old West–style saloon downstairs.

Beaches

Just south of the city center on Avenida Balmaceda is **Playa Cavancha,** a long stretch of white, sandy beach that's great for families. You can stroll along the boardwalk and pet the llamas and alpacas at the small zoo. Because it's so close to town, the beach is often crowded. If you crave solitude, follow the coast south of Playa Cavancha for about 3 km (2 mi) on Avenida Balmaceda to reach **Playa Brava,** a pretty beach that's often deserted. The currents here are quite strong, so swimming is not recommended. **Playa Blanca,** 13 km (8 mi) south of the city center on Avenida Balmaceda, is a sandy spot that you can often have all to yourself.

Shopping

Many Chileans come to Iquique with one thing on their minds—shopping. About 3 km (2 mi) north of the city center is the **Zona Franca**—known to locals as the Zofri—the only duty-free zone in the country's northern tip. This big, unattractive mall is stocked with cheap cigarettes, alcohol, and electronic goods. Remember that large purchases, such as personal computers, are taxable upon leaving the country. ⊠ *Av. Salitrera Victoria* ☏ *57/515–100* ⊙ *Mon. 4–9, Tues.–Fri. 10–9, Sat. 10–2 and 5–9.*

Reserva Nacional Pampa del Tamarugal

96 km (60 mi) southeast of Iquique.

The tamarugo tree is an anomaly in the almost lifeless desert. These bush-like plants survive where most would wither because they are especially adapted to the saline soil of the Atacama. Reserva Nacional Pampa del Tamarugal has dense groves of tamarugos, which were almost wiped out during the nitrate era when they were felled for firewood. At the entrance is a CONAF station. ⊠ *24 km (15 mi) south of Pozo Almonte on the Pan-American Hwy.* ☏ *57/751–055* 🎟 *Free.*

The amazing **Cerros Pintados** (Painted Hills), within the Reserva Nacional Pampa del Tamarugal, are well worth a detour. Here you'll find the largest group of geoglyphs in the world. These figures, which scientists believe ancient peoples used to help them navigate the desert, date from AD 500 to 1400. They are also enormous—some of the figures are decipherable only from the air. Drawings of men wearing ponchos were probably intended to point out the route to the coast to the llama caravans coming from the Andes. More than 400 figures of birds, animals, and geometric patterns adorn this 4-km (2½-mi) stretch of desert. There is a CONAF kiosk on a dirt road 2 km (1 mi) west of the Pan-American Highway. ⊠ *45 km (28 mi) south of Pozo Almonte* ☎ *57/751–055* 🖻 *1,000 pesos* 🕙 *Daily 9:30–6.*

Gigante de Atacama

84 km (52 mi) northeast of Iquique.

The world's largest geoglyph, the Gigante de Atacama, measures an incredible 86 m (282 ft). The Atacama Giant, thought to represent a chief of an indigenous people or perhaps created in honor of Pachamama (Mother Earth), looks a bit like a space alien. It is adorned with a walking staff, a cat mask, and a feathered headdress that resembles rays of light bursting from his head. The exact age of the figure is not known, but it certainly hails from before the arrival of the Spanish, perhaps around AD 900. The geoglyph, which is on a hill, is best viewed just before dusk, when the long shadows make the outline clearer. ⊠ *Cerro Unita, 13 km (8 mi) west of the turnoff to Chusmiza* ☎ *No phone* 🖻 *Free.*

Arica

301 km (186 mi) north of Iquique.

Arica boasts that it is "the land of the eternal spring," but its temperate climate is not the only reason to visit this small city. On Plaza Colón is the **Iglesia de San Marcos,** constructed entirely from iron. Gustave Eiffel, designer of that famed eponymous Parisian tower, had the individual pieces cast in France before erecting them in Arica in 1876. Across from Parque General Baquedano, the **Aduana de Arica,** the city's former customs house, is one of Eiffel's creations. It currently contains the town's cultural center, where you can find exhibits about northern Chile, old photographs of Arica, and works by local painters and sculptors. ☎ *No phone* 🖻 *Free* 🕙 *Daily 10–6.*

North of Parque General Baquedano is the defunct **Estación Ferrocarril,** the train station for the Arica-La Paz railroad. Though trains no longer run across the mountains to the Bolivian capital, this 1913 building houses a small museum with a locomotive and other remnants of the railroad. ☎ *No phone* 🖻 *Free* 🕙 *Daily 10–6.*

Hanging over the town, the fortress of **El Morro de Arica** is impossible to ignore. This former Peruvian stronghold was the site of one of the key battles in the War of the Pacific. The fortress now houses the **Museo de las Armas,** which commemorates that battle. As you listen to the proud drumroll of military marches you can wander among the uniforms and weapons of past wars. ⊠ *Reached by footpath from Calle Colón* ☎ *58/ 254–091* ⚏ *500 pesos* ☉ *Daily 8–8.*

The **Museo Arqueológico de San Miguel de Azapa,** a short drive from Arica, is a must for any visitor to El Norte Grande. In an 18th-century olive-oil refinery, this museum houses an impressive collection of artifacts from the cultures of the Chinchorros (a coastal people) and Tijuanacotas (a group that lived in the antiplano). Of particular interest are the Chinchorro mummies, the oldest in the world, dating to 6000 BC. The incredibly well-preserved mummies are arranged in the fetal position, which was traditional in this area. To look into their wrinkled, expressive faces is to get a glimpse at a history that spans more than 8,000 years. ⊠ *12 km (7 mi) south of town on the route to Putre* ☎ *58/205– 555* ⚏ *1,000 pesos* ☉ *Daily 10–6.*

Where to Stay & Eat

$–$$ ✕ **Maracuyá.** Wicker furniture enhances the cool South Pacific atmosphere of this pleasant, open-air restaurant that literally sits above the water on stilts. The international menu focuses on seafood. The food, lauded by locals, is always fresh; ask the waiter what fish was caught that day. ⊠ *Av. Comandante San Martin 0321* ☎ *58/227–600* ▤ *AE, DC, MC, V.*

¢–$ ✕ **Casino La Bomba.** In the old fire station, Casino La Bomba is more of a cultural curiosity than a culinary one. That said, the traditional food isn't bad, and the service is friendly. You'll have to maneuver around the parked fire trucks to get inside, where you are greeted by wagon-wheel furnishings and a menu heavy on grilled fish. ⊠ *Colon 357* ☎ *58/231–312* ▤ *No credit cards.*

¢–$ ✕ **Club de Deportes Náuticos.** This old yacht club with views of the port serves succulent seafood dishes in a relaxed terrace setting. One of the friendliest restaurants in town, this former men's club is a great place to meet the old salts of the area. Bring your fish stories. ⊠ *Thompson 1* ☎ *58/234–396* ▤ *MC, V.*

¢–$ ✕ **El Rey de Mariscos.** Locals call this the best seafood restaurant in town, for good reason. The merluza con salsa margarita is a winner. The dreary fluorescent lights and tacky furnishings give this restaurant on the second story of a cement-block building an undeserved down-at-the-heel air. ⊠ *Colon 565* ☎ *58/229–232* ▤ *AE, MC, V.*

★ $$–$$$ ✕▥ **Hotel Arica.** The finest hotel in Arica, this first-class establishment sits on the ocean between Playa El Laucho and Playa Las Liseras. The rooms, which are elegant if a bit dated, have views of the ocean and great showers with plenty of hot water. The courteous and attentive staff can help set up sightseeing tours or book a table at a local eatery. The hotel's tony restaurant ($–$$), which looks onto the ocean, serves fresh seafood cooked to order. ⊠ *Av. Comandante San Martin 599* ☎ *58/ 254–540* 🖷 *58/231–133* ⊕ *www.panamericanahoteles.cl* ⬎ *108 rooms, 13 suites, 20 cabanas* ⚘ *Restaurant, room service, in-room safes, mini-bars, cable TV, tennis court, pool, gym, bar, shop, children's programs (ages 2–10), laundry service, business services, convention center, meeting rooms, car rental* ▤ *AE, DC, MC, V* ❰❂❱ *BP.*

$ ▥ **Hotel El Paso.** This modern lodging in the center of Arica surrounds a landscaped courtyard and a pool with a swim-up bar. Though not on the ocean, it's a short walk from any of the city's beaches. There are plenty of diversions here, including a petting zoo that kids love. The superior rooms, with newer furnishings and larger televisions, are a far better value than the standard ones. ⊠ *Av. General Velasquez* ☎ *58/230–808* 🖷 *58/231–965* ⊕ *www.hotelelpaso.cl* ⟿ *71 rooms, 10 suites* 🖒 *Restaurant, in-room safes, minibars, cable TV, tennis court, pool, bar, laundry service, Internet, free parking* ⊟ *AE, DC, MC, V* ⑩ *BP.*

$ 🏨 **Hotel Plaza Colon.** The central Plaza Colon is a good budget option if you don't mind being so far from the beach. The pink-walled rooms are small but clean. ⊠ *San Marcos 261* ☎ *58/254–424* 🖷 *58/231–244* ✎ *hotel_plaza_colon@entelchile.net* ⟿ *39 rooms* 🖒 *Restaurant, room service, minibars, cable TV, baby-sitting, laundry service, free parking; no a/c* ⊟ *AE, DC, MC, V* ⑩ *CP.*

$ 🏨 **Hotel Sainte Georgette.** Although it's quite a hike from Arica's city center, this pleasant ocean-front hotel is great for weary travelers who simply want to relax on the beach. Some of the rooms and common areas feel a bit run-down, but the hotel is still a good value. Many rooms have their own hot tubs. ⊠ *Av. Comandante San Martin 1020* ☎ *58/257–697* 🖷 *58/229–187* ⊕ *www.hotelsaintegeorgette.cl* ⟿ *28 rooms, 8 suites* 🖒 *Restaurant, some kitchenettes, cable TV, indoor-outdoor pool, exercise equipment, massage, billiards, bar, dance club, Internet, airport shuttle, free parking* ⊟ *AE, DC, MC, V* ⑩ *CP.*

Nightlife

You can join the locals for a beer at one of the cafés lining the pedestrian mall of 21 de Mayo. These low-key establishments, many with outdoor seating, are a great place to spend an afternoon watching the passing crowds. An oddity in Arica is the attire of the servers in various tranquil cafés and tea salons: women serve coffee and tea dressed in lingerie.

For a refined setting, try the lively, funky **Barrabas** (⊠ 18 de Septiembre 520 ☎ 58/230–928), a bar and adjoining disco that attracts Arica's younger set. **Discoteca SoHo** (⊠ Buenos Aires 209 ☎ 58/215–892), near Playa Chinchorro, livens things up weekends with the sounds of pop and cumbia. The beachfront **Puesta del Sol** (⊠ Raul Pey 2492 ☎ 58/216–150) plays '80s tunes and appeals to a slightly older crowd. Weekends you can enjoy live music on the terrace.

Beaches

Part of the reason people flock to Arica is the beaches. South of El Morro, **Playa El Laucho** is the closest to the city, and thus the most crowded. South of Playa El Laucho you'll find **Playa Brava,** with a pontoon that keeps the kids occupied. At the somewhat secluded white-sand **Playa Chinchorro,** 2 km (1 mi) north of the city, you can rent Jet Skis in high season.

Shopping

Calle 21 de Mayo is a good place for window-shopping. **Calle Bolognesi,** just off Calle 21 de Mayo, is crowded with artisan stalls. The **Feria Internacional** on Calle Máximo Lira sells everything from bowler hats (worn by Aymara women) to blankets to batteries. Outside of the city, in the Azapa Valley, the **Poblado Artesenal** (⊠ Calle Hualles ☎ 58/222–683) is an artisan cooperative designed to resemble an altiplano community. This is a good place to pick up traditionally styled ceramics and leather.

Parque Nacional Lauca

★ *192 km (119 mi) east of Arica.*

On a plateau more than 13,000 ft above sea level, the magnificent Parque Nacional Lauca offers flora and fauna found in few other places in the world. Cacti, grasses, and a brilliant emerald-green moss called *llareta* dot the landscape. Playful vizcacha—rabbitlike rodents with long tails—laze in the sun, and llamas, graceful vicuñas, and alpacas make their home here as well. About 10 km (6 mi) into the park you come upon a CONAF station with informative brochures. ⊠ *Off Ruta 11* ☎ *No phone* ✆ *Free.*

Lago Chungará sits on the Bolivian border at an amazing altitude of 4,600 m (15,100 ft) above sea level. Volcán Parinacota, at 6,330 m (20,889 ft), casts its shadow onto the lake's glassy surface. Hundreds of flamingos make their home here. There is a CONAF-run office at Lago Chungará on the highway just before the lake. ✛ *From Ruta 11, turn north on Ruta A-123* ☎ *No phone* ✆ *Free* ☉ *CONAF office daily 8–8.*

Reserva Nacional Las Vicuñas

★ *266 km (165 mi) east of Arica.*

Although it attracts far fewer visitors than neighboring Parque Nacional Lauca, Reserva Nacional Las Vicuñas contains some incredible sights—salt flats, high plains, and alpine lakes. And you can enjoy the vistas without running into buses full of tourists. The reserve, which stretches some 100 km (62 mi), has a huge herd of graceful vicuñas. Although quite similar to their larger cousins, llamas and alpacas, vicuñas have not been domesticated. Their incredibly soft wool, among the most prized in the world, led to so much hunting that these creatures were threatened with extinction. Today it is illegal to kill vicuña. Getting to this reserve, unfortunately, is quite a challenge. There is no public transportation, and the roads are only passable in four-wheel-drive vehicles. Many people choose to take a tour out of Arica. ⊠ *From Ruta 11, take Ruta A-21 south to park headquarters* ☎ *58/250–570 in Arica.*

After passing through the high plains, where you'll spot vicuña, alpaca, and the occasional desert fox, you'll catch your first glimpse of the sparkling **Salar de Surire.** Seen from a distance, the salt flat appears to be a giant white lake. Three of the world's four species of flamingos live here. ⊠ *South of Reserva Nacional Las Vicuñas on Ruta A-235* ☎ *58/250–570* ✆ *Free.*

El Norte Grande A to Z

AIR TRAVEL TO & FROM EL NORTE GRANDE
Since there are no international airports in El Norte Grande, you can't fly here directly from the United States, Canada, Europe, or Australia. You must fly into Santiago and transfer to a flight headed to Antofa-

gasta, Iquique, or Arica. Avant and LanChile fly from Santiago to El Norte Grande. Round-trip flights can run up to 210,000 pesos.

You can also get here from other South American countries. LanChile runs direct flights between El Norte Grande and neighboring Bolivia and Peru.

Since the cities in El Norte Grande are far apart, taking planes between them can save you both time and a lot of hassle. Both Avant and Lan-Chile offer service between the major cities. Prices range from 28,000 to 105,000 pesos.

Antofagasta's Aeropuerto Cerro Moreno lies 25 km (16 mi) north of the city. Iquique's Aeropuerto Diego Aracena is a little far from the center of the city, about 40 km (25 mi) to the south. Arica's Aeropuerto Internacional Chacalluta lies 18 km (11 mi) north of the center.

🛪 Airlines **Avant** ☎ 55/452-050 in Antofagasta. **LanChile** ☎ 55/265-151 in Antofagasta, 55/313-927 in Calama, 57/427-600 in Iquique, 58/251-641 in Arica.

🛪 Airports **Aeropuerto Cerro Moreno** ☎ 55/269-077 in Antofagasta. **Aeropuerto Diego Aracena** ☎ 57/424-547 in Iquique. **Aeropuerto Internacional Chacalluta** ☎ 58/211-116 in Arica.

BUS TRAVEL

Getting around by bus in El Norte Grande is easy. There is a terminal in every major city with frequent departures to the other cities as well as smaller towns in the area. Keep in mind that there may be no bus service to the smaller villages or the more remote national parks.

No bus company has a monopoly, so there are often several bus stations in each city. Because many companies may be running buses along the same route, shop around for the best price. The fare for a 300-km (186-mi) trip usually runs around 7,000 pesos. For longer trips find a bus that has a *salon semi-cama,* with comfortable seats that make all the difference.

CAR TRAVEL

A car is definitely the best way to see El Norte Grande. If you want to get far off the beaten path, there is no other way to travel. You can rent cars in Antofagasta, Iquique, and Arica at both the airport and downtown. Most hotels will also help you arrange a rental. Avis, Budget, and Hertz have offices in most major cities in northern Chile. The best deals are probably in Iquique. However, cars rented here cannot be taken out of the Iquique area.

🚗 Agencies **Avis** ✉ Balmaceda 2556, Antofagasta ☎ 55/319-797 ✉ Manuel Rodriguez 734, Iquique ☎ 57/472-392. **Budget** ✉ Baquedano 300, Antofagasta ☎ 55/283-667 ✉ Bolívar 615, Iquique ☎ 57/416-332. **Hertz** ✉ Balmaceda 2566, Antofagasta ☎ 55/269-043 ✉ Anibal Pinto 1303, Iquique ☎ 57/510-136 ✉ Hotel El Paso, Baquedano 999, Arica ☎ 58/231-487.

HEALTH

Because of El Norte Grande's extremely varied topography, you should be prepared for many different weather conditions. If you're heading up into the Andes, remember to bring along warm clothes, even during the warmer months. A weather phenomenon called Bolivian winter, which actually takes place in the summer, brings rains and even snow to the Andes. The Atacama Desert, where some areas have never recorded any rainfall, can take its toll on unsuspecting tourists. Bring sunblock, a wide-brimmed hat, and plenty of water.

Altitude sickness—which is marked by difficulty breathing, dizziness, headaches, and nausea—is a danger for visitors to the high elevations of the antiplano. The best way to ward off altitude sickness is to take things slowly. Spend a day or two acclimatizing before any physical exertion. When hiking or climbing, rest often and drink as much water as possible. If symptoms continue, return to a lower altitude.

The tap water in the major cities and even most smaller communities is drinkable. In general, the water is safer on the coast than in some towns farther inland. To be on the safe side, stick to bottled water.

MAIL & SHIPPING

Mailing letters and packages from El Norte Grande is a formidable task. Although most cities have a post office, you often are faced with long lines that move at a snail's pace. Your best bet is to ask your hotel to post a letter for you. But don't expect your letter to reach its destination quickly. Mail headed out of the country can often take weeks.

🛈 Post Offices **Antofagasta** ✉ Washington 2613. **Arica** ✉ Arturo Prat 305. **Iquique** ✉ Bolívar 485.

SAFETY

El Norte Grande experiences very little crime. Nevertheless, you should use the same precautions as anywhere else. Women traveling alone should be careful, especially at night. It's best to travel in pairs or groups.

TAXIS

Taxis are the most efficient way to get around any city in El Norte Chico. They're easy to hail on the streets, but late at night you might want to ask someone at a hotel or restaurant to call one for you. Taxis often function as *colectivos*, meaning they will pick up anybody going in the same direction. The driver will adjust the price accordingly. Almost no taxis have meters, but many have the price posted on the windshield. Make sure you establish the price before getting inside. Prices range from 700–2,800 pesos, depending on the distance traveled and whether the taxi is a colectivo. Prices rise an average of 20% at night. Taxi drivers often will rent out their services for the day for a flat fee.

TELEPHONES

There are several different telephone companies in El Norte Grande, and each has its own public telephones. Calling cards for each company can be purchased in many shops and newsstands. Much easier than calling from the street is to call from one of the many Entel or CTC offices in every city. Here you can dial direct or collect to anywhere in the world.

TOUR OPERATORS

Tours can be arranged in the major cities and a number of the smaller towns. It's a good idea to shop around to make sure that you're getting the best itinerary and the best price. In Antofagasta, Desertica Expediciones arranges trips into the interior, including excursions to Parque Nacional Pan de Azucar. There are myriad tour agencies in San Pedro de Atacama. Cosmo Andino Expediciones offers excellent tours with well-informed guides. Herradura runs horseback tours. In Arica and Iquique, a well-respected agency called Geotour arranges trips to Parque Nacional Lauca, the Salar de Surire, and the Reserva Nacional las Vicuñas.

🖪 Tour Operators **Cosmo Andino Expediciones** ⊠ Calle Caracoles s/n, San Pedro de Atacama ☎ 55/851–069. **Desertica Expediciones** ⊠ La Torre 2732, Antofagasta ☎ 55/386–877. **Geotour** ⊠ Bolognesi 421, Arica ☎ 58/253–927 ⊠ Baquedano 982, Iquique ☎ 57/428–984. **Herradura** ⊠ Tocopilla s/n, San Pedro de Atacama ☎ 55/851–087.

VISITOR INFORMATION

Most major cities in El Norte Grande have an office of Sernatur, Chile's tourism agency. Here you'll find helpful information about the region, including maps and brochures. Some staff members speak English.

🖪 Sernatur Offices **Antofagasta** ⊠ Maipú 240 ☎ 55/264–044. **Arica** ⊠ San Marcos 101 ☎ 58/252–054. **Iquique** ⊠ Anibal Pinto 436 ☎ 57/312–238. **San Pedro de Atacama** ⊠ Toconao and Gustavo Le Paige ☎ 55/851–420.

THE LAKE DISTRICT

As you travel the winding roads of the Lake District, the snowcapped shoulders of volcanoes emerge, mysteriously disappear, then materialize again, peeping through trees or towering above broad valleys. The sometimes difficult journey through breathtaking mountain passes is almost inevitably rewarded by views of a glistening lake, vibrant and blue. Often, there are hot springs in which you can soak stiff muscles.

Temuco

675 km (405 mi) south of Santiago.

The south's largest city, and Chile's fastest-growing metropolis, Temuco has a more Latin flavor than the communities farther south. (It could be the warm weather and the palm trees swaying in Plaza Aníbal Pinto.) This northern gateway to the Lake District is an odd juxtaposition of modern architecture and indigenous markets, of traditionally clad Mapuche women darting across the street and business executives talking on cell phones.

Housed in a 1924 mansion, the **Museo Regional de la Araucanía** covers the history of the area. It has an eclectic collection of artifacts and relics, including musical instruments, utensils, and the country's best collection of indigenous jewelry. Upstairs, exhibits document the Mapuche people's three-century struggle to keep control of their land. The presentation could be more evenhanded: the rhetoric glorifies the Central European colonization of this area as the *pacificación de la Araucanía* (taming of the Araucanía territories). But the museum gives you a reasonably good Spanish-language introduction to Mapuche history, art, and culture. ⊠ Av. Alemania 84 ☎ 45/211–108 ⌨ 500 pesos ☉ Weekdays 9–5, Sat. 11–5, Sun. 11–1.

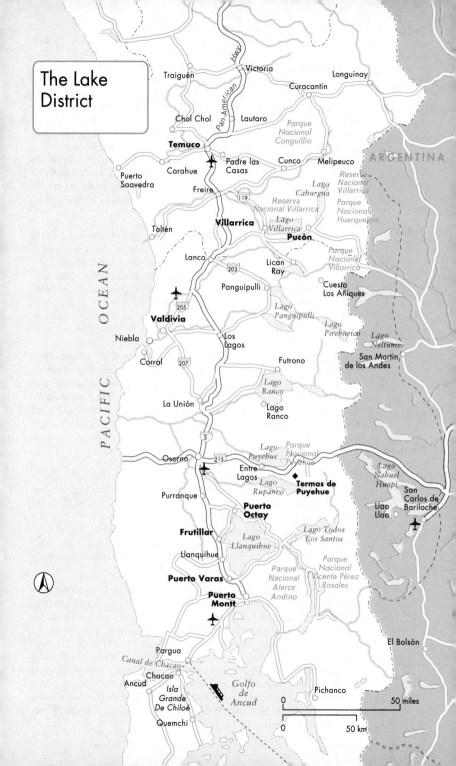

The imposing **Monumento Natural Cerro Ñielol** is the hillside site where the 1881 treaty between the Mapuche and the Chilean army was signed, allowing for the city of Temuco to be established. Trails bloom with bright red *copihues* (a bell-like flower with lush green foliage), Chile's national flower, in autumn (March–May). The monument, not far from downtown, is part of Chile's national park system. ⊠ *Av. Prat, 5 blocks north of Plaza Teodoro Schmidt* 🕾 *700 pesos* ⊗ *Jan.–Mar., daily 8 AM–11 PM; Apr.–Nov., daily 8:30–12:30 and 2:30–6.*

Where to Stay & Eat

$$–$$$ ✕ **El Fogón.** The Chilean-style *parrillada*, or grilled beef, is the specialty of the house. Barbecue here has subtler spices than its better-known Argentine counterpart. Even though this is close to downtown, you should splurge on a cab if you're coming to this dark street at night. ⊠ *Aldunate 288* 🕾 *45/952–163* 🗐 *AE, DC, MC, V.*

$$–$$$ ✕ **La Estancia.** The Ranch restaurant occupies a rustic wooden house with reindeer heads on the walls and cured hams hanging from the ceiling. You can dine out in the garden during the summer. It serves good southern beef in the form of steaks, roasts, and barbecues. ⊠ *Rudecindo Ortega 02340-A Interior* 🕾 *45/220–287* 🗐 *AE, DC, MC, V* ⊗ *No dinner Sun.*

$$–$$$ ✕ **La Pampa.** The wealthy professionals of this bustling city frequent this upscale modern steak house for its huge, delicious cuts of beef and the best *papas fritas* (french fries) in Temuco. Although most Chilean restaurants douse any kind of meat with a creamy sauce, this is one of the few exceptions: the entrées are served without anything but the simplest of seasonings. ⊠ *Caupolicán 0155* 🕾 *45/329–999* 🖄 *Reservations essential* 🗐 *AE, DC, MC, V* ⊗ *No dinner Sun.*

$–$$ ✕ **Centro Español.** The basement dining room of Centro Español, an association that promotes Spanish culture in Temuco, is open to all for lunch and dinner. You have your choice of four or five rotating prix-fixe menus. ⊠ *Brunes 483* 🕾 *45/217–700* 🗐 *AE, DC, MC, V.*

$–$$ ✕ **Confitería Central.** Coffee and homemade pastries are the specialties of this café, but sandwiches and other simple dishes are also available. Piping-hot empanadas are served on Sundays and holidays. ⊠ *Bulnes 442* 🕾 *45/210–083* 🗐 *DC, MC, V.*

$–$$ ✕ **Mercado Municipal.** In the central market around the produce stalls are small stands offering such typical Chilean meals as cazuela and pastel de choclo. Many have actually taken on the trappings of sit-down restaurants, and a few even have air-conditioning. The complex closes at 8 in the summer and 6 the rest of the year. ⊠ *Manuel Rodríguez 960* 🕾 *No phone.*

★ **$** ✕🖾 **Hotel Continental.** If you adore faded elegance, the 1890 Continental is for you. Checkered in black-and-white tiles, the lobby has leather furniture, antique bronze lamps, and handsome *alerce* and *raulí* (native wood) trims. Rooms have hardwood floors and lofty ceilings. The hotel has hosted Nobel laureates Pablo Neruda and Gabriela Mistral, and former president Salvador Allende. The restaurant serves delicious French cuisine. ⊠ *Antonio Varas 708* 🕾 *45/238–973* 🖹 *45/233–830* ⊕ *www.turismochile.cl/continental/* 🛏 *40 rooms, 18 with bath* ⚴ *Restaurant, bar, meeting room; no a/c, no room TVs* 🗐 *AE, DC, MC, V* ⦿ *CP.*

$ ✕▦ **Hotel Frontera.** This lovely old hotel is really two in one, with *nuevo* (new) and *clásico* (classic) wings facing each other across Avenida Bulnes. Tastefully decorated rooms have double-paned windows to keep out the street noise. Opt for the less expensive rooms in the newer wing—they're nicer anyway. La Taberna restaurant has excellent steak and seafood. ✉ *Bulnes 733–726* ☎ *45/200–400* 🖷 *45/200–401* ⊕ *www. hotelfrontera.cl* ⇴ *60 rooms, 2 suites* ⚘ *Restaurant, minibars, bar, convention center, meeting room; no a/c* ⊟ *AE, DC, MC, V* ¡❂¡ *BP.*

$$–$$$ ▦ **Hotel Terraverde.** Temuco's most luxurious lodging combines all the comforts of a modern hotel with the style of a hunting lodge. The dramatic, glass-enclosed spiral staircase has a view of Cerro Ñielol. Cheerful rooms have lovely wood furnishings. Rates include a huge breakfast buffet. The hotel is part of Chile's Panamericana Hoteles chain. ✉ *Av. Prat 220* ☎ *45/239–999, 2/234–9610 in Santiago* 🖷 *45/239–455, 2/234– 9608 in Santiago* ⊕ *www.panamericanahoteles.cl* ⇴ *64 rooms, 9 suites* ⚘ *Restaurant, in-room safe, minibars, pool, piano bar, convention center, meeting rooms, no-smoking rooms* ⊟ *AE, DC, MC, V* ¡❂¡ *BP.*

$$ ▦ **Holiday Inn Express.** This hotel is one of four of the chain's outlets in Chile. It comes complete with U.S.-style amenities, including the do-it-yourself breakfast for which the chain is known. It's adjacent to a shopping mall on the northern outskirts of town. ✉ *Av. Rudecindo Ortega 1800* ☎ *45/223–300* 🖷 *45/224–100* ⊕ *www.hiexpress.com* ⇴ *62 rooms* ⚘ *Dining room, pool, hot tub, gym, laundry facilities, business services, no-smoking rooms* ⊟ *AE, MC, V* ¡❂¡ *CP.*

$ ▦ **Don Eduardo Hotel.** Orange inside and out, this pleasant nine-story hotel is made up entirely of cozy furnished apartments. All have two or three bedrooms and kitchenettes. The many business travelers who frequent the place appreciate the work area. An eager-to-please staff tends to your needs. ✉ *Bello 755* ☎ *45/214–133* 🖷 *45/215–554* ⇴ *33 apartments* ⚘ *Business services; no a/c* ⊟ *AE, DC, MC, V.*

$ ▦ **Hotel Aitué.** The exterior is unimposing, but this small, pleasant business-class hotel has bright, airy rooms with a tan and lavender color scheme. ✉ *Antonio Varas 1048* ☎ *45/212–512* 🖷 *45/212–608* ⊕ *www. hotelaitue.cl* ⇴ *34 rooms* ⚘ *Coffee shop, minibars, bar, business services, meeting rooms, laundry service; no a/c* ⊟ *AE, DC, MC, V.*

Shopping

A little more rough-and-tumble than the Mercado Municipal is the **Feria Libre** (✉ Barros Arana and Miraflores). You can bargain hard with the Mapuche vendors who sell their crafts and produce in the blocks surrounding the railroad station and bus terminal. Leave the camera behind, as the vendors aren't happy about being photographed. It's open until 2 Monday–Saturday.

The **Mercado Municipal** (✉ Manuel Rodríguez 960 ☎ no phone) is one of the best places in the country to find Mapuche woolen ponchos, pullovers, and blankets. The interior of the 1930 structure has been extensively remodeled, opening it up. The low-key artisan vendors share the complex with butchers, fishmongers and fruit sellers. There is no bargaining, but the prices are fair. It's open daily, but closes around 3 on Sundays

Villarrica

87 km (52 mi) southeast of Temuco.

Villarrica was founded in 1552, but the Mapuche wars prevented extensive settlement of the area until the early 20th century. Today, the pleasant town on the lake of the same name is the first community you'll encounter in one of the loveliest, least spoiled areas of the southern Andes.

The municipal museum, **Museo Histórico y Arqueológico de Villarrica**, displays an impressive collection of Mapuche ceramics, masks, leather, and jewelry. A replica of a ruca graces the front yard. It's made of thatch so tightly entwined that it's impermeable to rain. ☒ *Pedro de Valdivia 1050* ☎ *45/413–445* ☜ *100 pesos* ☽ *Jan.–Feb., Mon.–Sat. 9–1 and 4–10; Mar.–Dec., Mon.–Sat. 9–1 and 3–7:30.*

Where to Stay & Eat

$–$$$ ✕ **The Travellers.** This restaurant's owners met by happenstance and decided to open a place serving food from their far-flung homelands. The result is a place that serves one or two dishes from Thailand, Italy, Mexico, and many countries in between. Dining on the front lawn under umbrella-covered tables is the best option on a summer evening. ☒ *Valentín Letelier 753* ☎ *45/412–830* ☰ *AE, DC, MC, V.*

$–$$ ✕ **Café 2001.** For a filling sandwich, a homemade küchen, and an espresso or cappuccino brewed from freshly ground beans, this is the place to stop in Villarrica. Pull up around a table in front or slip into one of the quieter booths by the fireplace in the back. The *lomito completo* sandwich—with a slice of pork, avocado, sauerkraut, tomato, and mayonnaise—is one of the best in the south. ☒ *Camillo Henríquez 379* ☎ *45/411–470* ☰ *AE, DC, MC, V.*

$$$$ ▦ **Villarrica Park Lake Hotel.** Expect the perfect mix of plushness and clean, uncluttered design—a sumptuous old European spa with thoroughly modern touches. There's ample use of hardwood in the bright, spacious common area and the rooms—each with its own balcony—that descend down a hill toward Lago Villarrica. ☒ *13 km (8 mi) east of Villarrica* ☎ *45/45–0000, 2/207–7070 in Santiago* ☎ *45/45–0202, 2/207–7020 in Santiago* ⊕ *www.villarrica.com/parklake/* ⇔ *61 rooms, 10 suites* ⚬ *Restaurant, in-room data ports, in-room safes, minibars, 2 pools, indoor pool, gym, hair salon, hot tub, sauna, spa, 3 bars, babysitting, dry cleaning, laundry service, business services, meeting rooms* ☰ *AE, DC, MC, V.*

★ $$–$$$ ▦ **Hostería de la Colina.** The friendly American owners of this hostería, Glen and Beverly Aldrich, provide attentive service as well as special little touches like homemade ice cream. Rooms in the main house are a mix of large and small, all tastefully decorated with wood furnishings. Two bright, airy hillside cottages are carpeted and wood-paneled and have private patios. There's a hot tub heated by a wood-burning stove and a serene *vivero* (greenhouse) and garden that attracts birds. The terrace has stupendous views of Lago Villarrica. ☒ *Las Colinas 115* ☎ *45/411–503* ⊕ *www.hosteriadelacolina.com* ⇔ *8 rooms, 2 cabins* ⚬ *Dining room, hot tub, Ping-Pong, bar; no a/c, no room phones, no room TVs* ☰ *AE, DC, MC, V* ⭘ *BP.*

$$ ⬚ **El Parque.** You can take in the commanding views of Lago Villarrica from just about anywhere at this 70-year-old rustic, quaint retreat—from the plush lobby, the sitting area, the restaurant, and the rooms. Warm earth tones color the guest rooms. Eleven modern cabins amble down the hill to a private beach and dock. Each cabin, which accommodates 2–10 people, comes with a kitchen, fireplace, and terrace. ⊠ *Camino Villarrica–Pucón, Km 2.5* ☎ *45/411–120* 🖷 *45/411–090* ⊕ *www. hotelelparque.cl* 🛏 *8 rooms, 11 cabins* ⌂ *Restaurant, tennis court, pool, meeting room* ⊟ *AE, MC, V* ⫯⦿⫯ *BP.*

$$ ⬚ **Hotel El Ciervo.** Villarrica's oldest hotel is an unimposing house on a quiet street, but inside are elegant details such as wrought-iron fixtures and wood-burning fireplaces. Spacious rooms, some with their own fireplaces, have huge beds and sparkling bathrooms. Just outside is a lovely pool and a secluded patio. Rates include an enormous German breakfast with loads of fruit, muesli, and fresh milk. El Ciervo also has all-inclusive seven-day tour packages. ⊠ *General Körner 241* ☎ *45/411–215* 🖷 *45/410–925* ⊕ *www.hotelelciervo.cl* 🛏 *12 rooms* ⌂ *Restaurant, pool, laundry service, meeting rooms; no a/c* ⊟ *AE, DC, MC, V* ⫯⦿⫯ *BP.*

Pucón

25 km (15 mi) east of Villarrica.

The trendy resort town of Pucón, on the southern shore of Lago Villarrica, attracts wealthy, fashionable Chileans. Like their counterparts in the Colorado ski resort of Vail, they come to enjoy their luxurious vacation homes, stroll along the main strip, and flock to the major night spots.

One of Chile's most popular national parks, **Parque Nacional Villarrica** offers skiing, hiking, and many other outdoor activities. The main draw, however, is the volcano that gives the 610-square-km (235-square-mi) national park its name. You don't need to have any climbing experience to reach the 9,350-ft summit of Volcán Villarrica, but a guide is a good idea. The volcano sits in the park's Sector Rucapillán, a Mapuche word meaning "house of the devil." That name is apt, as the perpetually smoldering volcano is one of South America's most active. ⊠ *15 km (9 mi) south of Pucón* ☎ *45/298–221 in Temuco* 🚳 *Admission* 🕙 *Daily 8–6.*

Where to Stay & Eat

$$–$$$$ ✕ **La Maga.** Argentina claims to prepare the perfect parrillada, or grilled beef, but here's evidence that Uruguayans just might do it best. Watch the beef cuts or salmon turn slowly over the wood fire at the entrance. The end product is a wonderfully smoked, natural taste, accented with a hint of spice in the mild *chimichurri* (a tangy steak sauce) ⊠ *Fresia 125* ☎ *45/444–277* ⊟ *No credit cards.*

$$–$$$$ ✕ **¡Viva Perú!** As befits the name, Peruvian cuisine reigns supreme at this restaurant in a thatch-roof house with rustic wooden tables. Try the *ají de gallina* (hen stew with cheese, milk, and peppers) or the ceviche, thoroughly cooked but served cold. ⊠ *O'Higgins 761* ☎ *45/444–285* ⊟ *AE, DC, MC, V.*

$$-$$$ ✕ **En Alta Mar.** The best seafood in Pucón is served here, so don't be frightened off by the nondescript dining room: basic wooden tables and the ubiquitous nautical theme. You'll receive a free welcoming pisco sour when you arrive. ⊠ *Fresia and Urrutia* ☎ *45/442–294* 🖃 *AE, DC, MC, V.*

¢–$ ✕ **Arabian Restaurant.** The dishes served here reflect the friendly owner's Palestinian roots. Try the tasty falafel or *shawarma* (a pita-bread sandwich filled with spicy beef or lamb). Most everyone opts for the outdoor tables over the tiny indoor dining area. ⊠ *Fresia 354* ☎ *45/443–469* 🖃 *No credit cards.*

¢   ✕⊡ **¡école!** It's part hostel and part beach house—and it takes its name from a Chilean expression meaning "Great!" Cozy two-, three-, and four-person rooms can be shared or private. The vegetarian restaurant ($-$$), a rarity in the Lake District, merits a trip in itself. The environmentally conscious staff can organize hiking and horseback-riding trips and expeditions to volcanoes and hot springs. ⊠ *General Urrutia 592* ☎☎ *45/441–675* ⊕ *www.ecole.cl* ↘ *23 rooms, 9 with bath* ⚭ *Restaurant, bar, travel services; no a/c, no room phones, no room TVs* 🖃 *AE, DC, MC, V.*

$$$$ ⊡ **Gran Hotel Pucón.** This imposing hotel, Pucón's largest, has wonderful views of Lago Villarrica. Its location right on the shore provides direct access to the beach. The rooms, however, are somewhat plain. ⊠ *Clemente Holzapfel 190* ☎ *45/441–001, 2/353–0000 in Santiago* 🖷 *2/207–4586 in Santiago* ⊕ *www.granhotelpucon.cl* ↘ *145 rooms* ⚭ *2 restaurants, 2 pools, massage, sauna, squash, bar, travel services; no a/c* 🖃 *AE, DC, MC, V* ⦿ *BP, MAP.*

$$$$ ⊡ **Hotel Antumalal.** Perched atop a cliff overlooking Lago Villarrica,
Fodor'sChoice   this Frank Lloyd Wright–inspired masterpiece is easily one of the best
★   hotels in Chile. Queen Elizabeth, Neil Armstrong, and Jimmy Stewart are just a few who thought so. This family-run hotel, just outside of Pucón, has the feel of a country inn. The cozy rooms have fireplaces and huge windows overlooking the spectacularly landscaped grounds. If you tire of relaxing on the wisteria-shaded deck, just ask owner Rony Pollak to arrange an adventure for you. Favorites include fly-fishing, white-water rafting, and volcano cave tours. ⊠ *Casilla 84* ☎ *45/441–011* 🖷 *45/441–013* ⊕ *www.antumalal.com* ↘ *16 rooms, 2 suites* ⚭ *Restaurant, pool, 2 tennis courts, bar, travel services* 🖃 *AE, DC, MC, V* ⦿ *BP.*

$$$$ ⊡ **Hotel del Lago.** Short on charm, this glitzy hotel has everything else you could hope for—even a movie theater. Enter through the five-story atrium lobby, then let one of the glass elevators whisk you upstairs. The rooms are simple and elegant, with blond wood and crisp white linens. The hotel is known as "the Casino" for its Las Vegas–style ground floor, complete with rows of one-arm bandits and tables for roulette and poker. ⊠ *Miguel Ansorena 23* ☎ *45/291–000, 2/462–1900 in Santiago* 🖷 *45/291–200, 2/370–5942 in Santiago* ⊕ *www.hoteldellago.cl* ↘ *81 rooms, 2 suites* ⚭ *Restaurant, snack bar, minibars, 2 pools, gym, hair salon, massage, sauna, bar, casino, business services, meeting room; no a/c* 🖃 *AE, DC, MC, V* ⦿ *BP, MAP.*

$$-$$$$ ⊡ **Termas de San Luis.** The famous San Luis hot springs are the main attraction of this hideaway east of Pucón. Here you can rent a rustic cabin that sleeps up to six people. Rates include all meals and free use of the baths. If you're not staying, 6,000 pesos gets you a day of soaking in the thermal springs. ⊠ *Carretera Internacional, Km 27, Catripulli* 🏨 *45/412–880* ⊕ *www.termasdesanluis.cl* 🛏 *6 cabins* ⚥ *2 restaurants, 2 pools, massage, sauna; no a/c* ⊟ *No credit cards* ¶◎¶ *FAP.*

$$$ ◫ **Hotel Huincahue.** The elegant Huincahue is close to the center of town and has the attentive service that only a small hotel can offer. Lots of windows brighten the lobby of the German-style building, which is warmed by a roaring fire. Rates for the airy rooms include a hearty American breakfast. ⊠ *Pedro de Valdivia 375* 🏨 *45/443–540* ⊕ *www. hotelhuincahue.cl* 🛏 *20 rooms* ⚥ *Coffee shop, pool, bar, laundry service; no a/c* ⊟ *AE, DC, MC, V* ¶◎¶ *BP.*

$$ ◫ **Del Volcán.** In keeping with the region's immigrant heritage, the furnishings of this chalet-style hotel look like they come straight from Germany. Checked fabrics cover carefully fluffed duvets in the guest apartments. Many of the generously proportioned apartments also have balconies. Each unit in this central hotel sleeps up to six people. ⊠ *Fresia 420* ☎ *45/442–055* 🖨 *45/442–053* ⊕ *www.aparthoteldelvolcan.cl* 🛏 *18 apartments* ⚥ *Dining room, in-room safes, kitchenettes, gym, free parking; no a/c* ⊟ *AE, DC, MC, V* ¶◎¶ *BP.*

$$ ◫ **Hotel Munich.** The Bavarian-style Hotel Munich stands out because the owner is a stickler for good service. Each of the rooms, furnished in native woods and decorated in soft pastels, is unique. The buffet breakfast is enormous. ⊠ *Gerónimo de Alderete 275* 🏨 *45/444–595* ⊕ *www.pucon.com/munich* 🛏 *14 rooms* ⚥ *Café, bar, laundry service; no a/c* ⊟ *No credit cards* ¶◎¶ *BP.*

¢ ◫ **Kila Leufu.** Part of a growing agro-tourism trend in Chile, a Mapuche family has opened its red farmhouse, 15 minutes from Pucón, to temporary urban refugees anxious to partake of rural life. You can bake bread and milk the cows if you like, or just relax and read. Horseback-riding excursions cost an extra 14,000 pesos. ⊠ *Camino a Curarrehe, Puente Cabedane* ☎ *09/711–8064* ⊕ *www.kilaleufu.homestead.com* 🛏 *5 rooms, 2 with bath* ⚥ *Dining room, horseback riding; no a/c, no room phones, no room TVs* ⊟ *No credit cards* ¶◎¶ *FAP.*

Sports & the Outdoors

Pucón is the center for rafting expeditions in the Lake District. Friendly **Aguaventura** (⊠ Palguín 336 ☎ 45/444–246 ⊕ www.aguaventura. com) outfits for rafting, as well as canoeing, kayaking, snowshoeing, and snowboarding. **Politur** (⊠ O'Higgins 635 ☎ 445/441–373 ⊕ www. politur.com) can take you rafting on the Río Trancura, trekking in nearby Parque Nacional Huerquehue, on ascents of the Volcán Villarrica, and skydiving. William Hatcher of **Sol Y Nieve** (⊠ O'Higgins and Lincoyan 🏨 45/441–070 ⊕ www.chile-travel.com/solnieve.htm) runs rafting trips and hiking and skiing expeditions. **Trawen** (⊠ O'Higgins 311 ☎ 45/442–024 ⊕ www.trawenchile.com) specializes in kayaking—with standard and inflatable kayaks, otherwise known as duckies—on the Río San Pedro. It also leads snow trekking or canyoning excursions in the nearby Cañi mountains.

Valdivia

120 km (72 mi) southwest of Villarrica.

One of the Lake District's oldest and most beautiful cities, Valdivia gracefully combines Chilean wood-shingle construction with the architectural style of the well-to-do German settlers who colonized the area in the late 1800s. Enjoy evening strolls through Valdivia's quaint streets and along its two rivers, the Valdivia and the Calle Calle.

For a historic overview of the region, visit the **Museo Histórico y Antropológico Maurice van de Maele,** on neighboring Isla Teja. The collection focuses on the city's colonial period, during which it was settled by the Spanish, burned by the Mapuche, and invaded by Dutch corsairs. Downstairs, rooms re-create the interior of the late-19th-century Anwandter mansion that belonged to one of Valdivia's first immigrant families; the upper floor delves into Mapuche art and culture. ⊠ *Los Laureles, Isla Teja* ☎ *63/212–872* 🎫 *1,200 pesos* ☉ *Dec.–Feb., Tues.–Sun. 10–1 and 2–6; Mar.–Nov., Tues.–Sun. 10–1 and 2–8.*

Fondly known around town as the "MAC," the **Museo de Arte Contemporáneo** is one of Chile's foremost modern art museums. This Isla Teja complex was built on the site of the old Anwandter brewery destroyed in the 1960 earthquake. The minimalist interior, formerly the brewery's warehouses, contrasts sharply with ongoing construction of a modern glass wall fronting the Río Valdivia, a project slated for completion by 2010. ⊠ *Los Laureles, Isla Teja* ☎ *63/221–968* ⊕ *www.macvaldivia. uach.cl* 🎫 *Free* ☉ *Tues.–Sun. 10–1 and 3–7.*

The **Jardín Botánico,** north and west of the Universidad Austral campus, is awash with 1,000 species of flowers and plants native to Chile. It's a lovely place to walk whatever the season, but it's particularly enjoyable in spring and summer. ⊠ *Isla Teja* ☎ *63/216–964* 🎫 *Free* ☉ *Dec.–Feb., daily 8–8; Mar.–Nov., daily 8–4.*

Where to Stay & Eat

$$–$$$$ ✕ **Camino de Luna.** The Way of the Moon floats on the Río Valdivia just north of the Pedro de Valdivia bridge. As the city is only a few miles from the ocean, it's no surprise that seafood is a specialty here. The *congrío calle calle* (conger eel in a cheese-and-tomato sauce) is particularly good. Tables by the windows offer views of Isla Teja. ⊠ *Av. Prat Costanera s/n* ☎ *63/213–788* ▭ *AE, DC, MC, V.*

$$–$$$$ ✕ **Salón de Té Entrelagos.** This swanky café caters to Valdivian business executives. The specialties are sandwiches such as the Isla Teja—a grilled chicken sandwich with tomato, artichoke hearts, asparagus, olives, and red peppers—decadent crepes, and sweet-tooth goodies. ⊠ *Vicente Pérez Rosales 640* ☎ *63/218–333* ▭ *AE, DC, MC, V.*

$–$$$ ✕ **Café Haussmann.** Take advantage of the fact that Valdivia was a center of German immigration by sampling the excellent *crudos* (steak tartare) and German-style sandwiches here. Don't forget delicious küchen for dessert. The place is small—a mere four tables and a bar, but worth a stop. ⊠ *O'Higgins 394* ☎ *63/213–878* ▭ *AE, DC, MC, V* ☉ *Closed Sun.*

$$$ 🏨 **Hotel Pedro de Valdivia.** This pink palace near Valdivia's central

FodorśChoice   square is, in a word, magnificent. With pleasant views of the Río Calle

★   Calle, the historic hotel is most notable for its elegant appointments and excellent service. All the tasteful rooms have lovely wood furniture, and some have small terraces. ✉ *Carampague 190* ☎ *63/212–931* 🖷 *63/203–888* ⊕ *www.hotelpedrodevaldivia.telsur.cl* ⊷ *77 rooms, 17 suites, 8 apartments* ⚇ *Restaurant, in-room data ports, pool, bar, laundry service, concierge, business services, meeting rooms, airport shuttle; no a/c* ▭ *AE, DC, MC, V* ¶⊙¶ *CP.*

$$$ 🏨 **Hotel Puerta del Sur.** Expect lavish pampering at a highly regarded lodging if you stay here. Spacious rooms, all with views of the river, are decorated in soft lavender tones. Play a few games of tennis, then hit the pool or relax in the hot tub. ✉ *Los Lingues 950, Isla Teja* ☎ *63/224–500, 2/633–5101 in Santiago* 🖷 *63/211–046, 2/633–6541 in Santiago* ⊕ *www.hotelpuertadelsur.com* ⊷ *40 rooms, 2 suites* ⚇ *Restaurant, in-room safes, tennis court, pool, outdoor hot tub, sauna, dock, volleyball, 2 bars, meeting room, travel services* ▭ *AE, DC, MC, V* ¶⊙¶ *BP.*

$$ 🏨 **Hotel Naguilán.** Here, you can relax in the garden by a pool while watching the boats pass by on the Río Valdivia. Ask for one of the rooms in the newer building of this charming hotel seven blocks south of the city center; they are bigger, with balconies and more modern furnishings. The older rooms are a bit dated, but cheaper. All are great value. ✉ *General Lagos 1927* ☎ *63/212–851* 🖷 *63/219–130* ⊕ *www.hotelnaguilan.com* ⊷ *33 rooms, 3 suites* ⚇ *Restaurant, pool, dock, bar, baby-sitting, laundry service, meeting room* ▭ *AE, DC, MC, V.*

$ 🏨 **Hostal Prat.** The friendly, eager-to-please owner and the reasonable rates make this one of those terrific finds that you want to keep to yourself. Rooms in this lodging near the bus station are mostly tan, but a few splashes of color liven things up. ✉ *Prat 595* ☎ *63/222–020* ⊷ *10 rooms* ⚇ *Dining room; no a/c, no room phones* ▭ *No credit cards* ¶⊙¶ *CP.*

Sports & the Outdoors

Valdivia-based tour operator **Jumping Chile** (✉ Pasaje 11 No. 50 ☎ 63/217–810) organizes marvelous fly-fishing trips for two to six people on the nearby rivers. An astonishing variety of wetland birds inhabits this part of the country. **Hualamo** (☎ 63/215–135 ⊕ www.hualamo.com) lets you get a close look if you join its bird-watching and natural-history tours based out of a lodge 20 km (12 mi) upriver from Valdivia.

Puerto Octay

50 km (30 mi) southeast of Osorno.

With spectacular views of the Osorno and Calbuco volcanoes, Puerto Octay was the birthplace of Lake District tourism: a wealthy Santiago businessman constructed a mansion outside of town in 1912, using it as a vacation home to host his friends. Puerto Octay doesn't have the frenetic energy of neighboring Frutillar and Puerto Varas, but its many fans enjoy its less frenzied, more authentic atmosphere.

The small **Museo El Colono** displays great old photographs and maps documenting the town's turn-of-the-last-century German settlers. An annex in a barn outside of town at the turnoff to Centinela exhibits farm machinery. ⊠ *Independencia 591* ☎ *64/391–523* 💲*500 pesos* 🕐 *Dec.–Mar., daily 9:30–1 and 3–7; Apr.–Nov., Tues.–Sun. 9:30–1 and 3–7.*

Where to Stay & Eat

$–$$ ✕ **Restaurant Baviera.** Because it's on the Plaza de Armas, this is a popular lunch stop for tour groups. Baviera serves solid German fare—schnitzel, sauerkraut, sausage, and küchen are among the favorites. Beer steins and other Bavarian paraphernalia on the walls evoke the Old Country. ⊠ *German Wulf 582* ☎ *64/391–460* 🚫 *No credit cards.*

★ **$–$$$** 🏨 **Hotel Centinela.** Simple and elegant, the venerable 1912 Hotel Centinela remains one of Chile's best-known accommodations. This imposing wood-shingled lodge with a dramatic turret sits amid 20 forested acres at the tip of Península Centinela jutting into Lago Llanquihue. Imposing beds and armoires fill the huge rooms in the main building. The cabins, whose rates include three meals a day delivered to the door, are more modern than the rooms in the lodge. ⊠ *Península de Centinela* ☎ *64/391–326* ⊕ *www.hotelcentinela.cl* ⬧ *11 rooms, 1 suite, 18 cabins* 🍴 *Restaurant, sauna, bar; no a/c, no TV in some rooms* 🚪 *AE, DC, MC, V* 🍽️ *BP, FAP.*

★ **$** 🏨 **Zapato Amarillo.** Backpackers make up the majority of the clientele here, but this is no scruffy youth hostel. This modern alerce-shingled house with wood-panel rooms affords a drop-dead gorgeous view of Volcán Osorno outside of town. The eager-to-please Chilean-Swiss couple that owns it will arrange guided horseback-riding, hiking, and cycling tours, as well as a cheese-fondue evening. Rates include a Continental breakfast that's a cut above the rest, tossing in fruit and local dairy products. You also have access to the kitchen. ⊠ *2 km (1 mi) north of Puerto Octay on road to Osorno* ☎ *64/391–575* ⊕ *zapatoamarillo.8k.com* ⬧ *4 rooms with shared bath* 🍴 *Dining room, horseback riding, library, laundry facilities, Internet, travel services; no a/c, no room phones, no room TVs* 🚫 *No credit cards* 🍽️ *BP.*

Frutillar

30 km (18 mi) southwest of Puerto Octay.

Halfway down the western edge of Lago Llanquihue lies the small town of Frutillar, one of the main destinations of European immigrants in the late 19th century. The town—actually two adjacent hamlets, Frutillar Alto and Frutillar Bajo—is known for its perfectly preserved German architecture.

You step into the past when you step into one of southern Chile's best ★ museums, the **Museo Colonial Alemán.** Besides displays of the 19th-century agricultural and household implements, this open-air museum has full-scale reconstructions of buildings—a smithy and barn, among others—used by the original German settlers. Exhibits at this complex administered by Chile's Universidad Austral are labeled in Spanish and, *natürlich,* German, but there are also a few signs in English. A short walk from the lake up Avenida Arturo Prat, the museum also has beautifully landscaped grounds and great views of Volcán Osorno. ⊠ *Vicente Pérez*

Rosales at Arturo Prat ☎ *65/421–142* ☏ *1,600 pesos* ☉ *Dec.–Feb.,*
daily 10–8; Mar.–Nov., Tues.–Sun. 10–2 and 3–6.

Where to Stay & Eat

$$ ✕ **Club Alemán.** One of the German clubs that dot the Lake District, this
restaurant in the center of town has a selection of four or five rotating
prix-fixe menus. ☒ *Philippi 747* ☎ *65/421–249* ☰ *AE, DC, MC, V.*

$–$$ ✕ **Selva Negra.** Friendly, attentive service and good, solid German food
are the hallmark of the casual semicircular restaurant just up the hill
from the beach road. A special summer-only treat is a mixed seafood
platter served in a pineapple half. ☒ *Antonio Varas 24* ☎ *65/421–164*
☰ *No credit cards.*

$$ ✕▥ **Hotel Salzburg.** Rooms at this Tyrolean-style lodge command ex-
cellent views of the lake. Cozy cabins and slightly larger bungalows, all
made of native woods, are fully equipped with kitchens and private ter-
races. The staff will gladly organize fishing trips. The restaurant serves
some of the best smoked salmon in the area. ☒ *Costanera Norte* ☎ *65/
421–569* 🖷 *65/421–599* ⊕ *www.salzburg.cl* ⇆ *31 rooms, 9 cabins, 5
bungalows* ♿ *Restaurant, pool, sauna, billiards, Ping-Pong, volleyball,
bar, laundry service, meeting rooms, travel services; no a/c, no room TVs*
☰ *AE, DC, MC, V.*

★ $$ ▥ **Hotel Elun.** From just about every vantage point—the lobby, the library,
and, of course, the guest rooms—you have a spectacular view of Lago
Llanquihue. Each room has huge bay windows framing Volcán Osorno.
Rooms have polished wood furniture. Add the exceptionally attentive
owners to the mix, and you have a real find just south of town. ☒ *Costanera Sur* ☎ *65/420–055* 🖷 *65/420–170* ⊕ *www.hotelelun.cl* ⇆ *14 rooms*
♿ *Restaurant, in-room safes, sauna, bar, meeting rooms, no-smoking
rooms; no a/c, no TV in some rooms* ☰ *AE, DC, MC, V* ⦿ *BP.*

$$ ▥ **Hotel Volcán Puntiagudo.** This redwood lodge sits on a hillside a mile
north of town. Decorated in soft earth tones, the rooms have views of
Lago Llanquihue and Volcán Osorno. Rates, which drop for stays over
three days, include a large breakfast. ☒ *Camino Fundo las Piedras*
☎ *65/421–646* 🖷 *65/421–640* ⊕ *www.hotelvolcanpuntiagudo.com*
⇆ *10 rooms* ♿ *Restaurant, tennis court, pool, bar, meeting room; no
a/c, no room phones* ☰ *DC, MC, V* ☉ *Closed May–Nov.* ⦿ *BP.*

$ ▥ **Hotel Frau Holle.** The friendly owner of the 1930s German-style house
is not exactly Frau Holle, a character out of the Grimm brothers' fairy
tales, but she will provide you with attentive service and serve fruit for
breakfast from the orchard on the property. Rooms are bright and cheery
with hardwood floors and period furnishings. A few have views of Lago
Llanquihue and both volcanoes. ☒ *Antonio Varas 54* ☎🖷 *65/421–345*
✉ *frauholle@frutillarsur.cl* ⇆ *8 rooms* ♿ *Dining room, laundry service;
no a/c, no room phones, no room TVs* ☰ *AE, DC, MC, V* ⦿ *CP.*

$ ▥ **Hotel Klein Salzburg.** Gingerbread cutouts and swirls adorn a cozy 1911
home-turned-inn. Flowered bedspreads and curtains decorate the taste-
ful wood-panel rooms. The German breakfast is quite filling. And you
couldn't ask for a much better location—the property is right on the
lake. ☒ *Av. Philippi 663* ☎ *65/421–201* 🖷 *65/421–750* ⊕ *www.
salzburg.cl* ⇆ *8 rooms* ♿ *Restaurant, coffee shop; no a/c, no TV in some
rooms* ☰ *AE, DC, MC, V* ⦿ *BP.*

$ ⊡ **Hotel Serenade.** Names of the rooms here reflect musical compositions—*Fantasia* or the *Wedding March,* for example—and the doors display the first few measures of the work. Inside are plush quilts and comforters, hardwood floors, and throw rugs. Enjoy the fireplace in the cozy sitting room of this 1940 house on a quiet side street. ⊠ *Pedro Aguirre Cerda 50* ☎ *65/ 420–332* 🖙 *6 rooms ⚐ Meeting room; no a/c, no room TVs* ⊙ *CP.*

Beaches

Packed with summer crowds, the gray-sand **Playa Frutillar** stretches for 15 blocks along Avenida Philippi. From this point along Lago Llanquihue you have a spectacular view due east of the conical Volcán Osorno, as well as the lopsided Volcán Puntiagudo.

Puerto Varas

27 km (16 mi) south of Frutillar.

A small resort town on the edge of Lago Llanquihue, Puerto Varas is known for the stunning rose arbors that bloom from December to March and is often described as the "Lucerne of Chile." The view of the Osorno and Calbuco volcanoes graces dozens of postcards and travel brochures for the Lake District.

Chile's oldest national park, **Parque Nacional Vicente Pérez Rosales** was established in 1926. The 2,538-square-km (980-square-mi) preserve includes the Osorno and lesser-known Puntiagudo volcanoes, as well as the deep blue Lago Todos los Santos. ☎ *65/290–711* 🖻 *1,000 pesos* ⊙ *Dec.–Feb., daily 9–8; Mar.–Nov., daily 9–6.*

Where to Stay & Eat

$$–$$$$ ✕ **Merlin.** Often called the best restaurant in southern Chile, this charming establishment combines fish and vegetables in unusual ways. Specialties include razor clams with vegetable strips in a curry vinaigrette and beef tenderloin in a morel-mushroom sauce. ⊠ *Imperial 605* ☎ *65/ 233–105* ⊟ *AE, DC, MC, V* ⊙ *No lunch.*

$$–$$$ ✕ **Kika.** These folks get going early in the morning, cranking out rich German pastries for breakfast, and don't quit until well into the evening when they serve seafood for dinner. ⊠ *Walker Martínez 584* ☎ *65/234– 703* ⊟ *AE, DC, MC, V.*

$–$$ ✕ **Restaurant Aníbal.** Although the dining room in this Italian restaurant is plain, the food is anything but. The friendly staff dishes up pasta with a tangy Argentine flavor. Instead of tomato or marinara on your spaghetti, you might get a tangy Argentine chimichurri sauce. ⊠ *Del Salvador at Santa Rosa* ☎ *65/235–222* ⊟ *MC, V.*

$$$ ⊡ **Hotel Cabañas del Lago.** It's the pine-panel cabins that make this spot special. Hidden in carefully tended gardens, each A-frame unit is decorated with lace curtains and floral-pattern bedding. The cabins, which can accommodate five people, have wood stoves and full kitchens. Most rooms in the main hotel are cozy and have lovely views of Volcán Osorno. ⊠ *Klenner 195* ☎ *65/232–291* 🖷 *65/232–707* ⊕ *www. cabanasdellago.cl* 🖙 *63 rooms, 13 cabins, 2 suites ⚐ Restaurant, indoor pool, massage, sauna, billiards, bar, baby-sitting, meeting rooms; no a/c* ⊟ *AE, DC, MC, V.*

$$ ☒ **Hotel Bellavista.** This hotel, an eclectic mix of traditional Bavarian and modern architectural styles, sits right on the lake. Most of the bright rooms have views of the nearby volcanoes, and some have their own balconies. Stylish contemporary furnishings are upholstered in tailored stripes. ☒ *Vicente Pérez Rosales 60* ☎ *65/232–011* ☒ *65/232–013* ⊕ *www.hotelbellavistachile.com* ⌲ *51 rooms* ♢ *Restaurant, sauna, bar, laundry service; no a/c* ☰ *AE, DC, MC, V* ⦿*⧽ BP.*

$$ ☒ **Hotel Colonos del Sur.** This five-story building, with peaked gables that give it a Germanic look, dominates the waterfront in Puerto Varas. The views from the upper floors are magnificent. Warm alerce and pine dominate the interior, including the paneled guest rooms. ☒ *Del Salvador 24* ☎ *65/233–369* ☒ *65/233–394* ⊕ *www.colonosdelsur.cl* ⌲ *64 rooms* ♢ *Restaurant, coffee shop, minibars, indoor pool, sauna, bar, meeting room; no a/c* ☰ *AE, DC, MC, V* ⦿*⧽ BP.*

$$ ☒ **Hotel Licarayén.** Ask for a room with a balcony overlooking Lago Llanquihue at this rambling Bavarian-style chalet. Those rooms without views of the lake overlook the garden. There's a fireplace in the common sitting room. ☒ *San José 114* ☎ *65/232–305* ☒ *65/232–955* ⌲ *23 rooms* ♢ *Dining room, gym, sauna; no a/c* ☰ *AE, DC, MC, V* ⦿*⧽ CP.*

★ $ ☒ **The Guest House.** The aroma of fresh coffee greets you all day long, and little homemade chocolates await on your pillow at this central B&B, a restored 1926 mansion. Period furnishings and antiques fill the rooms, which are bright and cheery. The exuberant American owner, a longtime resident of Chile and a fount of information, truly treats you like a valued guest. ☒ *O'Higgins 608* ☎ *65/231–521* ☒ *65/232–240* ⊕ *www.vicki-johnson.com* ⌲ *10 rooms* ♢ *No a/c, no rooms TVs, no-smoking* ☰ *No credit cards* ⦿*⧽ BP.*

Sports & the Outdoors

Al Sur Expediciones (☒ Del Salvador 100 ☎ 65/232–300 ⊕ www.alsurexpeditions.com) is known for rafting and kayaking trips on the Class III Río Petrohué. It also runs horseback-riding and fly-fishing trips. **Aqua Motion** (☒ San Francisco 328 ☎ 65/232–747 ⊕ www.aqua-motion.com) leads rafting and kayaking excursions on the nearby Río Petrohué, as well as trekking, horseback riding, helicopter rides, bird-watching, and fly-fishing tours. Based in nearby Cochamó, **Campo Aventura** (☒ Valle Cochamó ☎ 65/232–910) leads one- to ten-day horseback and trekking expeditions to its base camp in Parque Nacional Vicente Pérez Rosales.

Tranco Expediciones (☒ San Pedro 422 ☎ 65/311–311 ⊕ www.trancoexpediciones.cl) leads photo hikes up Volcánes Osorno and Calbuco, in addition to rafting trips on the Río Petrohué, and bike excursions. **Pachamagua** (☒ San Pedo 418 ☎ 65/346–100) specializes in half- and full-day canyoning and rappelling trips near Volcán Calbuco, in addition to kayaking and horseback-riding excursions.

Puerto Montt

20 km (12 mi) south of Puerto Varas.

For most of its history, windy Puerto Montt was the end of the line for just about everyone traveling in the Lake District. Now the Carretera

Austral carries on southward, but for all intents and purposes Puerto Montt remains the region's last significant outpost, a small provincial city that is the hub of local fishing, textile, and tourist activity. Today the town consists of low clapboard houses perched above its bay, the Seno de Reloncaví.

The **Museo Juan Pablo II,** east of the city's bus terminal, has a collection of crafts and relics from the nearby archipelago of Chiloé. Historical photos of Puerto Montt itself give a sense of the area's slow and often difficult growth and the impact of the 1960 earthquake, which virtually destroyed the port. Pope John Paul II, for whom the museum was renamed, celebrated mass on the grounds during his 1987 visit. One exhibit documents the event. ⊠ *Av. Diego Portales 991* 🕾 *65/344–457* 💷 *250 pesos* ☼ *Daily 9–7.*

About 3 km (2 mi) west of downtown along the coastal road lies the **Caleta Angelmó,** Puerto Montt's fishing cove. This busy port serves small fishing boats, large ferries, and cruisers carrying travelers and cargo southward through the straits and fjords that form much of Chile's shoreline. On weekdays small launches from Isla Tenglo and other outlying islands arrive early in the morning and leave late in the afternoon. The fish market here has one of the most varied selections of seafood in all of Chile.

Barely a stone's throw from Puerto Montt, the mountainous 398-square-km (154-square-mi) **Parque Nacional Alerce Andino,** with more than 40 small lakes, was established to protect some 20,000 endangered alerce trees. Comparable to California's hardy sequoia, alerce grow to average heights of 40 m (130 ft), and can reach 4 m (13 ft) in diameter. Immensely popular for construction of houses in southern Chile, they are quickly disappearing from the landscape. Many of these are 3,000–4,000 years old. ⊠ *Carretera Austral, 35 km (21 mi) east of Puerto Montt* 🕾 *65/212–036* 💷 *1,000 pesos* ☼ *Daily 9–6.*

Where to Stay & Eat

★ $–$$$ ✕ **Balzac.** One of Puerto Montt's finest restaurants specializes in seafood prepared with a French flair. Try the *jaiba de chardonnay* (a stew of king crab, Parmesan cheese, and white wine). ⊠ *Urmeneta 305* 🕾 *65/313–251* 💳 *No credit cards* ☼ *Closed Sun. Apr.–Oct.*

$–$$$ ✕ **Club Alemán.** As befitting an old German association, Club Alemán serves delicious küchen and other pastries, but the rest of the menu doesn't recall Deutschland. Seafood—delicious clams, oysters, and lobster—as well as freshwater trout are the specialties here. ⊠ *Antonio Varas 264* 🕾 *65/252–551* 💳 *AE, DC, MC, V* ☼ *No dinner Sun.*

$–$$$ ✕ **Club de Yates.** There are no yachts here, despite the tony-sounding name, and prices are reasonable—you can feast on lobster for just a few dollars. You can't miss this place, as it sits on a high pier jutting out into the bay. ⊠ *Av. Juan Soler Manfredini 1* 🕾 *65/276–888* 💳 *AE, DC, MC, V* ☼ *No dinner Sun.*

$–$$$ ✕ **Feria Artesanal Angelmó.** Several kitchens here prepare *mariscal* (shellfish soup) and *caldillo* (seafood chowder), as well as *almejas* (clams), *machas* (razor clams), and *ostiones* (scallops) with Parmesan cheese. Separate tables and counters are at each kitchen in this enclosed market, which is 3 km (2 mi) west of Puerto Montt along the coast road. ⊠ *Caleta Angelmó* ☎ *No phone* ▭ *No credit cards.*

$–$$$ ✗ **New Harbor Café.** When you step into this café decorated with pale woods and chrome, you might think it's a bit too trendy. In reality it's a fun, friendly place serving sandwiches and other light meals—a great destination for late-night noshing. ⊠ *San Martín 85* ☎ *65/293–980* ▭ *AE, DC, MC, V.*

$–$$ ✗ **Restaurant Kiel.** Hospitable German-born proprietor Helga Birkir stands guard at this Chilean-Teutonic seafood restaurant on the coast west of Puerto Montt. Fresh produce from her well-kept garden makes lunch here a delight. ⊠ *Camino Chinquihue, Km 8, Chinquihue* ☎ *65/255–010* ▭ *AE.*

$$–$$$ ▥ **Hotel Don Luis.** This modern lodging next to the cathedral, a favorite among upscale business travelers, has panoramic views of the Seno de Reloncaví. There's a small salon for the big American-style breakfast included in the rate. ⊠ *Urmeneta and Quillota* ☎ *65/259–001* 🖷 *65/259–005* ⊕ *www.hoteldonluis.com* ⇆ *60 rooms, 1 suite* ⚐ *Restaurant, coffee shop, snack bar, gym, sauna, bar, laundry service, meeting rooms; no a/c* ▭ *AE, DC, MC, V.*

$$ ▥ **Gran Hotel Don Vicente.** The grandest of Puerto Montt's hotels underwent a much needed remodeling and face-lift in 2002–2003. Its Bavarian-style facade resembles that of countless other Lake District lodgings, but the lobby's huge picture window overlooking the Seno de Reloncaví lets you know this place is something special. ⊠ *Diego Portales and Guillermo Gallardo* ☎ *65/432–900, 2/953–5037 in Santiago* 🖷 *65/437–699, 2/953–5900 in Santiago* ⊕ *www.granhoteldonvicente. cl* ⇆ *71 rooms* ⚐ *Restaurant, coffee shop, minibars, bars, laundry service, concierge, business services, travel services, meeting rooms, airport shuttle; no a/c* ▭ *AE, DC, MC, V* ❘O❘ *BP.*

$$ ▥ **O'Grimm.** This four-story lodging is in the heart of Puerto Montt, but O'Grimm's warmth and charm would make it equally appropriate to a small town in Germany. The helpful staff makes you feel right at home. Muted shades of gray, rose, and green decorate the simple rooms. ⊠ *Guillermo Gallardo 211* ☎ *65/252–845* 🖷 *65/258–600* ⊕ *www. ogrimm.com* ⇆ *27 rooms, 1 suite* ⚐ *Restaurant, minibars, bar, laundry service, meeting rooms; no a/c* ▭ *AE, DC, MC, V* ❘O❘ *BP.*

$$ ▥ **Viento Sur.** An old Victorian house sits proudly on a hill, offering a majestic view of both the city and the sea. Rooms are comfortably furnished with generous use of native Chilean woods. The restaurant serves excellent Chilean seafood. ⊠ *Ejército 200* ☎ *65/258–701* 🖷 *65/314–732* ⇆ *27 rooms, 2 suites* ⚐ *Restaurant, sauna, bar, laundry service, business services; no a/c* ▭ *AE, DC, MC, V* ❘O❘ *BP.*

$ ▥ **Hostal Pacífico.** European travelers favor this solid budget option up the hill from the bus station. The rooms are small, but they have comfy beds with lots of pillows. Look at a few before you pick one, as some of the interior rooms have skylights rather than windows. The staff is exceptionally friendly and helpful. ⊠ *Juan J. Mira 1088* ☎ *65/256–229* ⇆ *22 rooms* ⚐ *Dining room, travel services; no a/c* ▭ *No credit cards* ❘O❘ *CP.*

$ ▥**Hotel Gamboa.** The floors creak, the rooms are very plain, and the bright yellow exterior looks strangely out of place in staid downtown Puerto Montt. But the sweetly fussy owner makes this second-story lodging a good budget choice. ⊠*Pedro Montt 157* ☎*65/252–741* ✆*8 rooms, 4 with bath* ♿ *No a/c, no room phones, no room TVs* ▤ *No credit cards.*

Shopping

An excellent selection of handicrafts is sold at the best prices in the country in the **Feria Artesanal Angelmó,** on the coastal road near Caleta Angelmó. Baskets, ponchos, figures woven from different kinds of grasses and straws, and warm sweaters of raw, hand-spun and hand-dyed wool are all offered. Much of the merchandise is geared toward tourists, so look carefully for more authentic offerings. Haggling is expected. It's open daily 9–dusk.

The Lake District A to Z

AIR TRAVEL TO & FROM THE LAKE DISTRICT

LanChile and its domestic partner LanExpress have flights from Santiago to Temuco, Valdivia, and Puerto Montt. Sky Airline connects Temuco and Puerto Montt to Santiago.

Puerto Montt's Aeropuerto El Tepual is 16 km (10 mi) west of the city center. Temuco's Aeropuerto Maquehue is 6 km (4 mi) south of the city. Valdivia's Aeropuerto Pichoy lies 29 km (18 mi) north of the city.

🛪 Airlines **LanChile/LanExpress** ⊠ San Martin 200, Puerto Montt ☎ 65/253–315 ⊠ Bulnes 687, Temuco ☎ 45/211–339 ⊠ Maipú 271, Valdivia ☎ 63/213–042. **Sky Airline** ⊠ Bulnes 655, Temuco ☎ 45/747–300 ⊠ San Martín 189, Puerto Montt ☎ 65/ 437–555.

🛪 Airports **Aeropuerto El Tepual** ⊠ Puerto Montt ☎ 65/294–159. **Aeropuerto Maquehue** ⊠ Temuco ☎ 45/337–703. **Aeropuerto Pichoy** ⊠ Valdivia ☎ 63/272–224.

BUS TRAVEL

There's no shortage of bus companies traveling the Pan-American Highway (Ruta 5) from Santiago south to the Lake District. The buses aren't overcrowded on these long routes, and seats are assigned. Tickets may be purchased in advance, always a good idea if you're traveling during summer. Cruz del Sur and Tur-Bus connect the major cities. Buses JAC connects the resort towns of Pucón and Villarrica with Temuco and Valdivia.

In Temuco, there's no central bus terminal, but several companies are close together along Vicuña Mackenna and Lagos. Osorno, Puerto Montt, and Valdivia have their own central terminal.

🚌 Bus Depots **Puerto Montt** ⊠ Av. Diego Portales ☎ no phone. **Valdivia** ⊠ Anfión Muñoz 360 ☎ 63/212–212.

🚌 Bus Lines **Buses JAC** ⊠ Vicuña Mackenna 798, Temuco ☎ 45/210–313 ⊠ Bilbao 610, Villarrica ☎ 45/411–447 ⊠ Anfión Muñoz 360, Valdivia ☎ 63/212–925. **Cruz del Sur** ⊠ Vicuña Mackenna 671, Temuco ☎ 45/210–701 ⊠ Anfión Muñoz 360, Valdivia ☎ 63/213–840 ⊠ Av. Diego Portales, Puerto Montt ☎ 65/254–731. **Tur Bus** ⊠ Lagos 538, Temuco ☎ 45/239–190.

CAR TRAVEL

You'll see a lot more of the Lake District if you have your own vehicle. A few rental-car companies, including Hertz, will allow you to rent a car in one city and return it at another, so you can avoid the inconvenience of retracing your steps.

The Pan-American Highway through the region is a well-maintained four-lane toll highway. Once you're this far south, driving is easy because there's little traffic, even on the major highways. Roads to most of the important tourist centers are paved, but many of the routes through the mountains are gravel or dirt, so a four-wheel-drive vehicle is ideal.

🚩 Agencies **Autovald** ✉ Portales 1330, Puerto Montt ☎ 65/256-355 ✉ Vicente Pérez Rosales 660, Valdivia ☎ 63/212-786. **Avis** ✉ Urmeneta 783, Puerto Montt ☎ 65/253-307 ✉ Aeropuerto El Tepual, Puerto Montt ☎ 65/255-155 ✉ Vicuña Mackenna 448, Temuco ☎ 45/238-013 ✉ Aeropuerto Maquehue, Temuco ☎ 45/337-715. **Hertz** ✉ Antonio Varas 126, Puerto Montt ☎ 65/259-585 ✉ Aeropuerto El Tepual, Puerto Montt ☎ 65/268-944 ✉ Las Heras 999, Temuco ☎ 45/318-585 ✉ Aeropuerto Maquehue, Temuco ☎ 45/337-019 ✉ Picarte 640, Valdivia ☎ 63/218-316 ✉ Aeropuerto Pichoy, Valdivia ☎ 63/272-273.

HEALTH

The tap water is fine to drink in most places, although many people opt for bottled water. As far as food goes, the standards of hygiene are generally high. The Ministry of Health has beefed up its warnings about eating raw shellfish, citing the risk of contracting intestinal parasites.

MAIL & SHIPPING

Reasonably efficient, Correos de Chile has post offices in most towns. They are generally open weekdays 9–7 and Saturday 9–1. Mail posted from the Lake District's four hub cities takes up to two weeks to reach North America and three to reach Europe. Anything of value (or valuable looking) should be sent via courier. DHL has offices in Temuco and Puerto Montt.

🚩 Post Offices **Correos de Chile** ✉ Av. O'Higgins 645, Osorno ✉ Av. Rancagua 126, Puerto Montt ✉ Av. Diego Portales at Av. Prat, Temuco ✉ Av. O'Higgins 575, Valdivia.

MONEY MATTERS

All of the major cities in the Lake District have several banks that will exchange U.S. dollars. Most banks will not touch traveler's checks, which are best cashed at a *casa de cambio* (exchange office). Many larger hotels will also exchange currency and a few will exchange traveler's checks. ATMs at Banco Santander and Banco de Chile, part of the omnipresent Redbanc network, accept both Cirrus- and Plus-affiliated cards. The district's four main airports have ATMs and casas de cambio.

SAFETY

Volcano climbing is a popular pastime here, with Volcán Villarrica the most popular because of its easy ascent and proximity to Pucón. But Villarrica is also one of South America's most active. CONAF cuts off access to any volcano at the slightest hint of out-of-normal activity. Check with CONAF before heading out on any hike in this region.

TAXIS

As elsewhere in Chile, solid black or solid yellow cabs operate as *colectivos,* or collective taxis, following fixed routes and picking up up to four people along the way. A sign on the roof shows the general destination. The cost is little more than that of a city bus. A black cab with a yellow roof will take you directly to your requested destination for a metered fare. Hail these in the street.

TELEPHONES

Entel, CTC, and Telefónica del Sur have call centers throughout the region. All allow you to place calls and send faxes. Each company also has its own network of public telephones. Phone booths use calling cards, which you can purchase at many shops and newsstands. Each works only in that company's telephones, so make sure you have the right one.

TOURS

The Lake District is the jumping-off point for luxury cruises. Many companies that offer trips to the fjords of Chilean Patagonia are based in Puerto Montt. Skorpios, with a trio of luxurious ships, has first-class cruises from Puerto Montt to the Laguna San Rafael. The ships carry between 70 and 130 passengers.

A number of companies offer cruises on the region's lakes. Andina del Sud operates between Puerto Varas and San Carlos de Bariloche, and traverses the Lago Todos los Santos.

🚢 Boat Tours **Andina del Sud** ✉ Del Salvador 72, Puerto Varas ☎ 65/232-811. **Skorpios** ✉ Augosto Leguia Norte 118, Santiago ☎ 2/231-1030 ⊕ www.skorpios.cl.

TRAIN TRAVEL

Chile's State Railway Company, the Empresa de los Ferrocarriles del Estado, has daily service southward from Santiago as far as Temuco. It's a far cry from the journey Paul Theroux recounted in *The Old Patagonian Express.* Trains run daily all year; the overnight trip takes about 12 hours. Prices range from 14,000 pesos for an economy-class seat to 70,000 pesos for a sleeper with all the trimmings. If you prefer to rent a vehicle in Santiago, you can use the auto-train service from there to Temuco. The price is an extra 70,000 pesos each way, with surcharges assessed for vehicles longer than 5 m (16 ft).

🚆 Train Information **Empresa de los Ferrocarriles del Estado** ☎ 2/376-8500 in Santiago, 45/233-522 or 45/233-416 in Temuco ⊕ www.efe.cl.

🚆 Train Stations **Estación de Ferrocarriles** ✉ Av. Barros Arana, Temuco ☎ 45/233-416.

VISITOR INFORMATION

The Lake District's four major cities have offices of Sernatur, Chile's national tourist office, which can help you book travel arrangements. City tourist offices, run by the government or a chamber of commerce, are in most communities catering to tourists. They are valuable resources but cannot book rooms or tours.

ℹ️ Tourist Information **Frutillar Tourist Office** ✉ Philippi at San Martín ☎ 65/420-198. **Pucón Tourist Office** ✉ O'Higgins 483 ☎ 45/293-002. **Puerto Montt Tourist Office** ✉ San Martín at Diego Portales ☎ 65/261-700. **Puerto Octay Tourist Office**

✉ La Esperanza 55 ☎ 64/391–491. **Puerto Varas Tourist Office** ✉ Costanera at San José ☎ 65/233–315. **Sernatur** ✉ Av. de la Décima Región 480, Puerto Montt ☎ 65/254–850 ✉ Claro Solar and Bulnes, Temuco ☎ 45/211–969 ✉ Arturo Prat 555, Valdivia ☎ 63/342–300. **Temuco Tourist Office** ✉ Mercado Municipal ☎ 45/216–360. **Valdivia Tourist Office** ✉ Terminal de Buses, Anfión Muñoz 360 ☎ 63/212–212. **Villarrica Tourist Office** ✉ Pedro de Valdivia 1070 ☎ 45/206–618.

CHILOÉ

Steeped in magic, shrouded in mist, the 41-island archipelago of Chiloé is that proverbial world apart, isolated not so much by distance from the mainland—it's barely more than 2 km (1 mi) at its nearest point—but by the quirks of history. Some 130,000 people populate 35 of these rainy islands, with most of them living on the 8,394-square-km (3,241-square-mi) Isla Grande. Its residents will regale you with the same myths and legends their ancestors told about these foggy green islands. Much of what is identified as Chilean folklore originated here, though the rest of the country happily embraces it as its own.

Nothing symbolizes Chiloé like the more than 150 wooden churches that dot the eastern half of the main island. Built by Jesuit missionaries who came to the archipelago after the 1598 Mapuche rebellion on the mainland, the chapels were an integral part of the effort to convert the indigenous peoples. Pairs of missionaries traveled the region by boat, making sure to celebrate mass in each community at least once a year.

Ancud

90 km (54 mi) southwest of Puerto Montt.

Unless you're one of those rare visitors who approaches the archipelago from the south, Ancud is the first encounter you'll have with Chiloé. Founded in 1769 as a fortress city on the northern end of Isla Grande, Ancud was repeatedly attacked during Chile's war for independence. It remained the last stronghold of the Spaniards, and the seat of their government-in-exile after fleeing from Santiago, a distinction it retained until Chiloé was finally annexed by Chile in 1826.

Statues of mythical Chilote figures, such as the Pincoya and Trauco, greet you on the terrace of the fortresslike **Museo Regional de Ancud,** just uphill from the Plaza de Armas. The ship *La Goleta Ancud,* the museum's centerpiece, carried Chilean settlers to the Strait of Magellan in 1843. Inside is a collection of island handicrafts. ✉ *Libertad 370* ☎ *65/622–413* 🖅 *600 pesos* ◷ *Jan.–Feb., daily 10:30–7:30; Mar.–Dec., weekdays 9:30–5:30, weekends 10–2.*

Northwest of downtown Ancud, the 16 cannon emplacements of the **Fuerte de San Antonio** are nearly all that remain of Spain's last outpost in the New World. The fort, constructed in 1786, was a key component in the defense of the Canal de Chacao, especially after the Spanish colonial government fled to Chiloé during Chile's war for independence. ✉ *Lord Cochrane at San Antonio* ☎ *No phone* 🖅 *Free.*

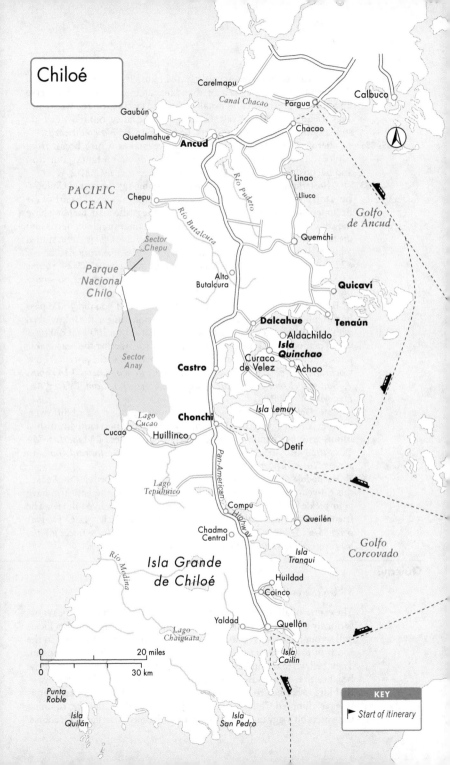

Chiloé

PACIFIC
OCEAN

Carelmapu

Canal Chacao

Pargua

Calbuco

Gaubún

Quetalmahue

Ancud

Chacao

Linao

Lliuco

Chepu

Río Pudeto

Río Butalcura

Sector
Chepu

Quemchi

Golfo
de Ancud

Parque
Nacional
Chilo

Alto
Butalcura

Quicaví

Sector
Anay

Dalcahue

Tenaún

Aldachildo

*Isla
Quinchao*

Castro

Curaco
de Velez

Achao

Isla Lemuy

Chonchi

Lago
Cucao

Cucao

Huillinco

Detif

Lago
Tepuhuico

Compu

Queilén

Chadmo
Central

Río Medina

*Isla Grande
de Chiloé*

*Isla
Tranqui*

Golfo
Corcovado

Huildad

Coinco

Lago
Chaiguata

Yaldad

Quellón

0   20 miles
0   30 km

*Isla
Cailín*

Punta
Roble

*Isla
Quilán*

*Isla
San Pedro*

KEY
⚑ *Start of itinerary*

Where to Stay & Eat

$$–$$$ ✕ **Restaurant La Pincoya.** According to Chilote legend, the presence of the spirit La Pincoya signals an abundant catch. La Pincoya does serve up abundant fresh fish and usually whips up curanto on the weekends. This friendly waterfront restaurant is nothing fancy, but the views are stupendous. ✉ *Arturo Prat 61* ☎ *65/622–613* ▭ *No credit cards.*

$$–$$$ ✕ **Retro's Pub.** This cozy, intimate place makes a nice break from Chiloé's ubiquitous seafood. Instead, chow down on fajitas, burritos, and nachos. ✉ *Maipú 615* ☎ *65/626–410* ▭ *AE, DC, MC, V.*

$$ ✕▭ **Hostería Ancud.** Ancud's finest hotel—some say the best in Chiloé—
Fodor'sChoice sits atop a bluff overlooking the Fuerte de San Antonio. It's part of the
★ Panamericana Hoteles chain. The rooms in the rustic main building have log-cabin walls. The wood-panel lobby, with a huge fireplace, opens into the town's loveliest restaurant. Try the *salmón del caicavilú* (salmon stuffed with chicken, ham, cheese, and mushrooms). ✉ *San Antonio 30* ☎ *65/ 622–340* ▤ *65/622–350* ⊕ *www.hosteriancud.com* ⬦ *24 rooms* ⌂ *Restaurant, coffee shop, bar, meeting room, travel services, no-smoking rooms; no a/c* ▭ *AE, DC, MC, V.*

$ ▭ **Hostal Lluhay.** Don't judge a book by its cover: if you did you'd pass by this hillside hostal because of its drab exterior, missing the lobby filled with knickknacks and the dining room dominated by a 200-year-old rosewood piano. Rooms are plain, but pleasant considering the reasonable rates. The amiable owners include a buffet breakfast in the price. ✉ *Lord Cochrane 458* ☎▤ *65/622–656* ✉ *lluhay@entelchile.net* ⬦ *14 rooms* ⌂ *Bar, travel services; no a/c, no room phones, no room TVs* ▭ *AE, DC, MC, V* ⦿ *BP.*

$ ▭ **Hotel Galeón Azul.** Perched like a ship run aground on a bluff overlooking Ancud's waterfront, this modern hotel has pleasantly furnished rooms with big windows and great views of the sea. ✉ *Libertad 751* ☎ *65/622–567* ▤ *65/622–543* ⬦ *16 rooms* ⌂ *Restaurant, bar; no a/c* ▭ *No credit cards* ⦿ *CP.*

¢ ▭ **Hospedaje O'Higgins.** The nicest of the many hospedajes in Ancud, this 60-year-old home sits on a hillside overlooking the bay. You have your pick of eight bright rooms. The place has a cozy, lived-in feel. The friendly service will make you overlook any inadequacies. ✉ *O'Higgins 6* ☎ *65/622–266* ⬦ *8 rooms, 2 with bath* ⌂ *Laundry service; no a/c, no room phones, no room TVs* ▭ *No credit cards.*

Quicaví

87 km (52 mi) southeast of Ancud.

The center of all that is magical and mystical about Chiloé, Quicaví sits forlornly on the eastern coast of Isla Grande. More superstitious locals will strongly advise you against going anywhere near the coast to the south of town, where miles of caves extend to the village of Tenaún. They believe that witches, and evil ones at that, inhabit them. On the beaches are mermaids—not the beautiful and benevolent Pincoya—that lure fishermen to their deaths. And many a Quicaví denizen claims to have glimpsed Chiloé's notorious ghost ship, the *Caleuche,* roaming the waters on foggy nights, searching for its doomed passengers. Of course, a brief glimpse of the ship is all anyone dares admit, as legend holds that a longer gaze could spell death.

In an effort to win converts, the Jesuits constructed the enormous **Iglesia de San Pedro,** on the Plaza de Armas. The original structure survives from colonial times, though it underwent extensive remodeling in the early 20th century. It's open for services the first Sunday of every month at 11 AM, which is the only time you can get a look inside.

Tenaún

12 km (7 mi) south of Quicaví.

A small fishing village, Tenaún is notable for its 1861 neoclassical **Iglesia de Tenaún,** on the Plaza de Armas, which replaced the original 1734 structure built by the Jesuits. The style differs markedly from that of other Chilote churches, as the two towers flanking the usual hexagonal central bell tower are painted a striking deep blue. You can see the interior during services on Sundays at 9:30 AM and the rest of the week at 5 PM.

Dalcahue

74 km (44 mi) southeast of Ancud.

Most days travelers in Dalcahue stop only long enough to board the ferry that deposits them 15 minutes later on Isla Quinchao. But everyone lingers in Dalcahue if it's a Sunday morning, when they can visit the weekly artisan market. Dalcahue is a pleasant coastal town—one that deserves a longer visit.

The 1850 **Iglesia de Nuestra Señora de los Dolores,** modeled on the churches constructed during the Jesuit era, sits on the main square. A portico with nine arches, an unusually high number for a Chilote church, fronts the structure. The church, which is on Plaza de Armas, holds a small museum and is open daily 9–6.

A *fogón*—a traditional indigenous cooking pit—sits in the center of the small palafito housing the **Museo Histórico de Dalcahue,** which displays historical exhibits from this part of the island. ⊠ *Pedro Montt 105* ☎ 6 5/642–375 ⊠ *Free* ۞ *Daily 8–6.*

Where to Stay
$ 🏨 **Hotel La Isla.** One of Chiloé's nicest lodgings, the wood-shingled Hotel La Isla greets you with a cozy sitting room and big fireplace off the lobby. Huge windows and vaulted ceilings make the wood-panel rooms bright and airy. Comfortable mattresses with plush pillows and warm comforters invite you to sleep tight. ⊠ *Mocopulli 113* ☎☎ *65/641–241* ➾ *16 rooms* ♻ *Bar, laundry service; no a/c* ▤ *No credit cards* ⏋◎⏉ *BP.*

Shopping
Dalcahue's Sunday-morning art market, **Feria Artesanal,** on Avenida Pedro Montt near the waterfront municipal building, draws crowds who

come to shop for Chilote woolens, baskets, and woven mythical figures. Things get underway at about 8 AM and begin to wind down about noon. Bargaining is expected, though the prices are already quite reasonable. There's fun to be had and bargains to be found, but the market is more touristy than the ramshackle daily market in nearby Castro.

Isla Quinchao

1 km (½ mi) southeast of Dalcahue.

For many visitors, the elongated Isla Quinchao, the easiest to reach of the islands in the eastern archipelago, defines Chiloé. Populated by hardworking farmers and fishermen, Isla Quinchao provides a glimpse into the region's past. Most visitors head to Achao, Quinchao's largest community, to see the alerce-shingle houses, busy fishing pier, and colonial church.

Fodor'sChoice On Achao's Plaza de Armas, the town's centerpiece is its 1706 **Iglesia Santa María de Loreto**, the oldest remaining house of worship on the archipelago. In addition to the alerce so commonly used to construct buildings in the region, the church also uses wood from cypress and *mañío* trees. Its typically unadorned exterior contrasts with the deep-blue ceiling embellished with gold stars inside. Rich baroque carvings grace the altar. Mass is celebrated Sunday at 11 AM and Tuesday at 7 PM, but docents give guided tours in Spanish while the church is open. An informative Spanish-language museum behind the altar is dedicated to the period of Chiloé's Jesuit missions. All proceeds go to much-needed church restoration—termites have taken their toll. ⊠ *Delicias at Amunategui* ☎ *65/661–881* ✉ *500 pesos* ☉ *Daily 10:30–1 and 2:30–7.*

About 10 km (6 mi) south of Achao is the archipelago's largest church, the 1869 **Iglesia de Nuestra Señora de Gracia.** As with many other Chilote churches, the 200-ft structure sits in solitude near the coast. The church has no tours, but may be visited during Sunday mass at 11 AM.

Where to Stay & Eat

$–$$ ✕ **Mar y Velas.** Scrumptious oysters and a panoply of other gifts from the sea are served in this big wooden house at the foot of Achao's dock. It has the friendliest service in town. ⊠ *Serrano 2, Achao* ☎ *65/661–375* ▭ *No credit cards.*

$–$$ ✕ **Restaurant La Nave.** This place on the beach serves seafood in a rambling building. The matter-of-fact staff dishes up curanto most days during the January–March high season, but usually only weekends the rest of the year. ⊠ *Arturo Prat at Sargento Aldea, Achao* ☎ *65/661–219* ▭ *No credit cards.*

¢ ▥ **Hostal La Plaza.** This cozy private home is close to the hubbub of the Plaza de Armas, but being down an alley and behind a chocolate shop affords it a degree of privacy and quiet. Simply furnished rooms have private baths, which is surprising considering the very reasonable rates. The owners are warm and friendly. ⊠ *Amunategui 20, Achao* ☎▭ *65/661–283* ➥ *8 rooms* ♨ *Dining room; no a/c, no room phones* ▭ *No credit cards* ❏ *CP.*

Castro

88 km (53 mi) south of Ancud.

Next to its wooden churches, *palafitos* are the best-known architectural symbol of Chiloé. These shingled houses—built on stilts and hanging over the water—are found all along the island's coast. The Pedro Montt coastal highway is the best place to see palafitos in Castro, Chile's third-oldest city. Many of these ramshackle structures have been turned into restaurants and artisan markets.

Any tour of Castro begins with the much-photographed 1906 **Iglesia de San Francisco,** constructed in the style of the archipelago's wooden churches, only bigger and grander. The dark-wood interior's centerpiece is the monumental carved crucifix hanging from the ceiling. A Spanish firm installed a soft, energy-efficient external illumination system in 2002; by evening, the church is one of Chiloé's most impressive sights. ☒ *Plaza de Armas* ☎ *No phone* ☉ *Dec.–Feb., daily 9–12:30 and 3–11:30; Mar.–Nov., daily 9–12:30 and 3–9:30.*

Fodor'sChoice
★
The **Museo Regional de Castro,** just off the Plaza de Armas, gives a good Spanish-language introduction to the region's history and culture. Packed into a fairly small space are artifacts from the Huilliche era (primarily rudimentary farming and fishing implements) through the 19th century (looms, spinning wheels, and plows). One exhibit displays the history of the archipelago's wooden churches; another shows black-and-white photographs of the damage caused by the 1960 earthquake that rocked southern Chile. ☒ *Esmeralda 205* ☎ *65/ 635–967* ☒ *Free* ☉ *Jan.–Feb., daily 9:30–8; Mar.–Dec., daily 9:30–1 and 3–6:30.*

All that remains of Chiloé's once thriving Castro–Ancud rail service is the locomotive and a few old photographs displayed on the outdoor **Plazuela del Tren** down on the waterfront road. Nobel laureate Pablo Neruda called the narrow-gauge rail service "a slow, rainy train, a slim, damp mushroom." Service ended with the 1960 earthquake. ☒ *Pedro Montt s/n.*

Northwest of downtown, the **Museo de Arte Moderno de Chiloé** is housed in five refurbished barns. Referred to locally as the MAM, the complex in a city park exhibits works by Chilote artists. ☒ *Pasaje Díaz 181* ☎ *65/ 635–454* ☒ *Free* ☉ *Jan.–Mar., daily 10–7; closed Apr.–Dec.*

Conozca Castro Caminando, or "Get to Know Castro Walking," runs two-hour historical walking tours in English, Spanish, or German, at least four times weekly December–February and at other times by request. The folks here are quite flexible about accommodating your schedule. ☒ *Plaza de Armas* ☎ *09/411–6198* ☒ *7,000 pesos.*

Where to Stay & Eat

$–$$$ ✕ **Octavio.** A devoted tourist clientele flocks to this waterside establishment for its well-known curanto, seafood stews, and some of the most attentive service around. And unlike at other restaurants in town, you can also chow down on steak and pork chops here. Enjoy the great views from this alerce-shingled palafito-style building. ⊠ *Pedro Montt 261* ☎ *65/632–855* ⊟ *No credit cards.*

$–$$ ✕**Café la Brújula del Cuerpo.** Next to the fire station on the Plaza de Armas, this little place bustles with all the commotion of a big-city diner. Sandwiches are standard fare—burgers and clubs are favorites. Don't leave without trying one of the mouthwatering ice-cream sundaes or banana splits. ⊠ *O'Higgins 308* ☎ *65/633–229* ⊟ *No credit cards.*

$–$$ ✕ **1 Palafito Restaurant.** This is the first of five palafitos on Castro's downtown waterfront that have been converted into seafood restaurants. You really can't go wrong with the other four, but locals swear this one is the best. This is no place to escape the crowds: the cavernous restaurant can easily seat a few hundred on a bright summer night. ⊠ *Eusebio Lillo 30* ☎ *65/635–476* ⊟ *No credit cards.*

★ $$ ▦ **Hotel Unicornio Azul.** Taking its name from a popular song by Cuban singer Silvio Rodríguez, the Blue Unicorn is actually pink, though its roof is bright blue. The rambling hotel dates from 1910. There are lots of stairs, and many twists and turns as it makes its ascent, but you'll find a sitting room and reading alcove at every landing and big windows to catch the view across the waterfront. Furnishings in the bright rooms echo the facade's pastel hues. ⊠ *Pedro Montt 228* ☎ *65/632–359* ☐ *65/632–808* ✑ *hotelunicornioazul@hotmail.com* ➴ *18 rooms* ⚷ *Restaurant, bar; no a/c* ⊟ *No credit cards* ⍓ *CP.*

$ ▦ **Hostal Kolping.** Great inexpensive lodging is yours in an alerce-shingled building with a big porch in the center of town. Paneled rooms are bright, sunny, spacious, and sparkling clean, with comfortable beds and lots of pillows. ⊠ *Chacabuco 217* ☎☎ *65/633–273* ➴ *11 rooms* ⚷ *Dining room; no a/c, no room phones* ⊟ *No credit cards* ⍓ *CP.*

$ ▦ **Hostería de Castro.** Looming over downtown Castro, this place near the estuary has a sloped, chalet-style roof with a long skylight. Nice modern rooms have simple furnishings and cheery flowered bedspreads. The downstairs seafood restaurant has huge windows with great views of the Golfo de Corcovado. ⊠ *Chacabuco 202* ☎ *65/632–301* ☐ *65/635–688* ⊕ *www.hosteriadecastro.cl* ➴ *29 rooms* ⚷ *Restaurant, bar, laundry service; no a/c* ⊟ *AE, DC, MC, V* ⍓ *BP.*

$ ▦ **Hotel Esmeralda.** This hot-pink storefront hotel sits just off the bustling Plaza de Armas. The compact four-story building has lots of windows and all the amenities that you would expect from such a modern place. It's popular among corporate travelers. ⊠ *Esmeralda 266* ☎ *65/637–900* ☐ *65/637–910* ⊕ *www.bosquemodelochiloe.cl/chwb/ hotelesmeralda/* ➴ *32 rooms, 2 suites* ⚷ *Restaurant, pool, bar, recreation room, laundry service, business services, meeting rooms; no a/c* ⊟ *AE, DC, MC, V* ⍓ *BP.*

Shopping

The city's **Feria Artesanal,** a lively, often chaotic artisan market on Eusebio Lillo, is regarded by most as the best place on the island to pick up the woolen sweaters, woven baskets, and the straw figures for which Chiloé is known. Prices are already quite reasonable, but vendors expect a bit of bargaining. The stalls are open daily 9–dusk.

Chonchi

23 km (14 mi) south of Castro.

The colorful wooden houses of Chonchi are situated on a hillside so steep that it is known as the *Ciudad de los Tres Pisos,* meaning the "City of Three Stories." The town's name means "slippery earth" in the Huilliche language, and if you tromp up the town's steep streets on a rainy day you'll understand why.

The town's centerpiece is the **Iglesia de San Carlos,** on the Plaza de Armas. Started by the Jesuits in 1754, it was left unfinished until 1859. Rebuilt in the neoclassical style, the church is now a national monument. An unusually ornate arcade with five arches fronts the church, and inside are an intricately carved altar and wooden columns. The church contains Chonchi's most prized relic, a statue of the Virgen de la Candelaria. According to tradition, this image of the Virgin Mary protected the town from the Dutch pirates who destroyed neighboring Castro in 1600. Townspeople celebrate the event every February 2 with fireworks and gunpowder symbolizing the pirate attack. A March 2002 storm felled the church's tower; fund-raising for reconstruction has been painfully slow, but the building remains open for mass on Sunday at 11 AM.

Where to Eat

$ ✕ **El Trébol.** This seafood restaurant is on the second floor inside Chonchi's waterfront market. The decorations are basic, and there's no view—this is the market, after all. But the food is good, and the prices are very reasonable. You have a better chance of getting curanto or salmón ahumado if you're here in high season. ⊠ *Irarrázaval s/n* ☎ *65/671–203* ▭ *No credit cards.*

Chiloé A to Z

AIR TRAVEL

Chiloé has a small military airstrip, but there's no airport for either national or international flights. Most people flying to the region head to Aeropuerto El Tepual, 90 km (54 mi) northeast of Ancud in Puerto Montt. LanChile and its domestic partner LanExpress maintain an office in Castro.

🛪 Airlines **LanChile/LanExpress** ⊠ Blanco 299, Castro ☎ 65/632–866.

BOAT & FERRY TRAVEL

Since Chiloé is an archipelago, the only way to drive here is by taking one of the frequent ferries across the Golfo de Ancud. Most people arrive by crossing from the mainland to the tiny town of Chacao in the north. Cruz del Sur operates the frequent ferry service connecting mainland Pargua with Chacao on the northern tip of Isla Grande. Boats leave twice an hour from early morning until late at night, and trips take about 30 minutes (8,000 pesos for a car, no passenger fee).

Catamaranes del Sur provides twice-weekly catamaran service during January and February between Castro and mainland Chaitén at a relatively quick three hours, with continuing service to Puerto Montt. Pehuén Expediciones is the sales agent in Castro.

🛈 Boat & Ferry Information **Catamaranes del Sur** ⊠ Pehuén Expediciones, 299 Blanco, Castro 🕾 65/632–361 ✉ Diego Portales and Guillermo Gallardo, Puerto Montt 🕾 65/267–533 ⊕ www.catamaranesdelsur.cl. **Cruz del Sur** ⊠ Chacabuco 672, Ancud 🕾 65/622–265.

BUS TRAVEL

Cruz del Sur and its subsidiary Transchiloé operate some 30 buses per day between Ancud and the mainland, usually terminating in Puerto Montt. Many of the routes continue north to Temuco, and a few travel all the way to Santiago. Bus service is timed to coincide with the company's frequent ferries between Pargua and Chacao. Buses arriving from the mainland provide *very* local service once they reach the island, making frequent stops.

Cruz del Sur and Transchiloé also operate hourly service along the Pan-American Highway between Ancud, Castro, Chonchi, and Quellón. Queilén Bus has service between Chiloé's major cities about 10 times daily. It also makes twice daily runs between Castro and Quemchi.

Many other companies operate small buses or comfortable minivans. Dalcahue Expreso connects Castro with Dalcahue every half hour during the week, less often on weekends. Buses Gallardo runs buses between Castro and Isla Lemuy three times a day during the week, less often on weekends. Buses Arroyo has twice-a-day service between Castro and Cucao, the gateway to Parque Nacional Chiloé.

🛈 Bus Information **Buses Arroyo** ⊠ San Martín s/n, Castro 🕾 65/635–604. **Buses Gallardo** ⊠ San Martín 667, Castro 🕾 65/634–521. **Cruz del Sur** ⊠ Chacabuco 672, Ancud 🕾 65/622–265 ✉ San Martín 486, Castro 🕾 65/632–389 ✉ Av. Portales at Lota, Puerto Montt 🕾 64/254–731. **Dalcahue Expreso** ⊠ Ramírez 233, Castro 🕾 65/ 635–164. **Queilén Bus** ⊠ San Martín 667, Castro 🕾 65/632–173.

CAR TRAVEL

Rather than terminating in Puerto Montt, the Pan-American Highway skips over the Golfo de Ancud and continues through Ancud, Castro, and Chonchi before stopping in Quellón. The Carretera Austral continues on down the mainland Southern Coast. Paved roads also lead to Quemchi, Dalcahue, and Achao on Isla Quinchao. You can reach a few other communities by *ripios*, rough gravel roads. Plan ahead, as it's often slow going during the long rainy season. Most of the western half of the island is inaccessible by car.

Most visitors who rent a vehicle do so on the mainland, but if you decide you need wheels after your arrival, try the local firm of ADS Rent-a-Car in Castro.

🛈 Rental Agency **ADS Rent-a-Car** ⊠ Esmeralda 260, Castro 🕾 65/637–373.

HEALTH

Chiloé shares Chile's generally high standard of hygiene, so eating and drinking shouldn't cause you too much concern. The government continues to warn against eating raw or steamed shellfish, citing the risk of intestinal parasites. Though some visitors drink tap water here, most stick to bottled water, especially outside Castro.

WHERE TO STAY

Following a trend seen elsewhere in Chile, Chiloé has developed a system of so-called agro-tourism lodgings called the Red Agroturismo Chiloé, head-quartered in the northern community of Ancud. The network of 19 farms, most of them on Isla Grande, gives the adventurous Spanish-speaking traveler a chance to partake of rural life, helping to milk the cows, churn the butter, or just relax. Rates run 10,000–12,000 pesos per person including breakfast. Accommodations are in no-frills farmhouses, but plenty of smog- and traffic-weary Santiago residents are lapping up the experience.
🚩 **Red Agroturismo Chiloé** ✉ Eleuterio Ramírez 207, Ancud 🕾 65/628–333 ⊕ www.portalsur.cl/rural/INDEX.HTM.

MAIL & SHIPPING

Mail sent from Chiloé can take a few weeks to reach North America or Europe. Posting from mainland Puerto Montt is a quicker option. You can find a Correos de Chile office in most larger cities. They are generally open weekdays 9–6 and Saturdays 9–noon.
🚩 Post Offices **Correos de Chile** ✉ O'Higgins 388, Castro ✉ Pudeto and Blanco Encalada, Ancud ✉ 22 de Mayo and Ladrilleros, Quellón.

MONEY MATTERS

With few businesses equipped to handle credit cards, Chiloé is primarily a cash-and-carry economy. Banks will gladly change U.S. dollars for Chilean pesos, but most will not touch traveler's checks. The situation is not as frustrating as it sounds; ATMs are popping up everywhere in larger cities like Castro and Ancud. You can use your Plus- or Cirrus-affiliated card to get cash at the going rate at any of the ATMs on the Redbanc network.

SAFETY

Crimes against travelers are almost unheard of in pastoral Chiloé, but the standard precautions about watching your possessions apply.

TAXIS

As is true elsewhere in the region, solid black or solid yellow cabs operate as *colectivos,* or collective taxis. They follow fixed routes with fixed stops, picking up up to four people along the way. A sign on the roof shows the general destination. The cost (less than 700 pesos within town) is little more than that of a city bus. Black cabs with yellow roofs take you directly to your requested destination for a metered fare. You can hail them on the street.

Colectivos also operate between many of Isla Grande's communities. They may look like a regular cabs, or they may be minivans. They have fixed stops, often near a town's central bus station.

TELEPHONES

Chiloé shares Puerto Montt's area code of 65. Anywhere in the archipelago or the southern Lake District you can drop the area code and dial the six-digit number. CTC, Entel, and Telefónica del Sur are the three most prominent telephone companies. Their *centros de llamados* (call centers) are the place to make calls and send faxes. Each company also has its own network of public telephones. Make sure you have the right company's calling card to match the phone booth. Calling cards can be purchased in many shops and newsstands.

TOURS

Highly regarded Dalcahue sea kayaking expert Francisco Valle is the local contact for Santiago tour operator Altue. He leads kayakers on two- to nine-day tours through the region. Austral Adventures, the region's best tour operator, runs intimate guided tours of Chiloé and neighboring Patagonia. Austral Adventures can custom-design tours of Chiloé itself, whether your tastes run to sea kayaking, church visits, farmstays, or hikes in Chiloé National Park. Pehuén Expediciones has guided tours of the archipelago, in particular land tours to Dalcahue and Isla Achao and the island churches, as well as horseback riding and hiking in Parque Nacional Chiloé. A few of Skorpios' luxury cruises from Puerto Montt to the Laguna San Rafael call at Castro on their return trip.

🚩 Tour Operators **Altue** ⊠ Encomenderos 83 Santiago 🕾🕾 2/232-1103 ⊕ www. seakayakchile.com. **Austral Adventures** ⊠ Lord Cochrane 432, Ancud 🕾🕾 65/625–977 ⊕ www.austral-adventures.com. **Pehuén Expediciones** ⊠ Blanco 299, Castro 🕾 65/632–361. **Skorpios** ⊠ Augosto Leguia Norte 118, Santiago 🕾 2/231-1030 ⊕ www.skorpios.cl.

VISITOR INFORMATION

Sernatur, Chile's national tourist office, operates a friendly, well-staffed information office on the Plaza de Armas in Ancud. It's open January–February, daily 9–8; March–December, Monday–Saturday 9–noon and 2–6.

For more information about the islands' churches, contact the Fundación de Amigos de las Iglesias de Chiloé, a nonprofit organization that raises funds for their restoration.

🚩 Tourist Information **Fundación de Amigos de las Iglesias de Chiloé** ⊠Victoria Subercaseaux 69, Santiago 🕾 2/632-1141. **Sernatur** ⊠ Libertad 665, Ancud 🕾 65/622-800.

PATAGONIA

Traditional boundaries cannot define Patagonia. This vast stretch of land east of the Andes is mostly a part of Argentina, but Chile shares its southern extremity. Geographically and culturally it has little in common with either country. Patagonia, isolated by impenetrable mountains and endless fields of ice, is really a region unto itself.

Because of the region's remote location, much of what Darwin described is still relatively undisturbed. Drive north until the road peters out and you'll reach Parque Nacional Torres del Paine, perhaps the region's most awe-inspiring natural wonder. The snow-covered pillars of granite seem to rise vertically from the plains below.

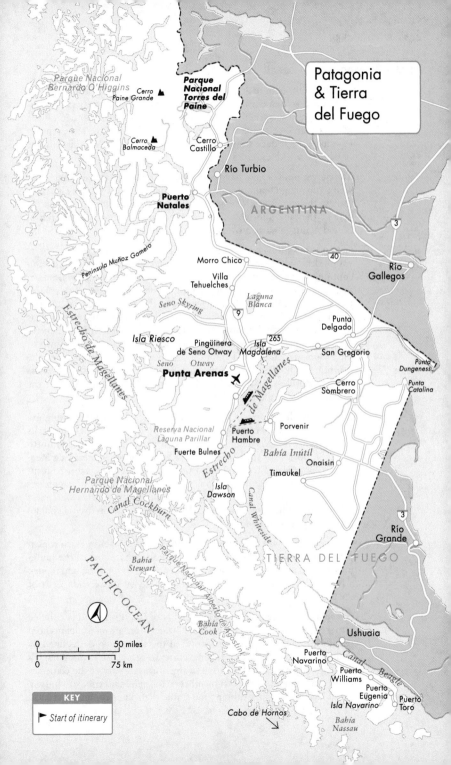

Patagonia & Tierra del Fuego

Parque Nacional Bernardo O'Higgins

Cerro Paine Grande

Parque Nacional Torres del Paine

Cerro Balmaceda

Cerro Castillo

Río Turbio

Puerto Natales

ARGENTINA

Península Muñoz Gamero

Morro Chico

Villa Tehuelches

Laguna Blanca

Seno Skyring

9

Isla Riesco

Pingüinera de Seno Otway

Seno Otway

Punta Arenas

Isla Magdalena

265

Punta Delgado

San Gregorio

Punta Dungeness

Punta Catalina

40

Río Gallegos

3

Estrecho de Magallanes

Reserva Nacional Laguna Parillar

Fuerte Bulnes

Puerto Hambre

Porvenir

Cerro Sombrero

Estrecho de Magallanes

Bahía Inútil

Parque Nacional Hernando de Magallanes

Isla Dawson

Canal Whiteside

Onaisin

Timaukel

Canal Cockburn

TIERRA DEL FUEGO

3

Río Grande

PACIFIC OCEAN

Bahía Stewart

Parque Nacional Alberto de Agostini

Bahía Cook

Ushuaia

Puerto Navarino

Puerto Williams

Canal Beagle

Puerto Eugenia

Isla Navarino

Puerto Toro

Cabo de Hornos

Bahía Nassau

0   50 miles

0   75 km

KEY

▶ *Start of itinerary*

Punta Arenas

Founded a little more than 150 years old, Punta Arenas was Chile's first permanent settlement in Patagonia. This port town, no longer an important stop on trade routes, exudes an aura of faded grandeur. Plaza Muñoz Gamero, the central square, is surrounded by 19th-century structures, their dark stone exteriors recalling a time when this was one of Chile's wealthiest cities.

The newer houses here have colorful tin roofs, best appreciated when seen from a high vantage point such as the Mirador Cerro la Cruz. Although the city as a whole may not be particularly attractive, look for details: the pink-and-white house on a corner, the bay window full of potted plants, a garden overflowing with flowers.

a good walk

Get an idea of the layout of the city at **Mirador Cerro la Cruz,** an observation deck with a stunning view of the city. Head down the stairs and continue for three blocks to reach the cedar-lined **Plaza Muñoz Gamero,** the center of the city. Here you'll find a monument honoring explorer Hernando de Magallanes. In deference to the many historical and political figures they honor, streets change their names as they pass by this square. The venerable **Palacio Sara Braun** overlooks Plaza Muñoz Gamero. A block east is the **Museo Regional de Magallanes,** commonly known as the Braun-Menéndez Palace for the family that built and occupied the mansion that houses the museum. Farther along Pedro Montt is the **Museo Naval y Marítimo,** with its overview of the all-important role of the Chilean Navy in the region's history.

A block north you reach Avenida Colón, one of four intersecting avenues designed to accommodate large flocks of sheep. Today the parks that run down the centers make pleasant places to stroll. Head north on Calle Bories for four blocks to reach the **Museo Salesiano de Maggiorino Borgatello.** Three blocks north on Avenida Bulnes is the main entrance to the **Cementerio Municipal.** Here among the manicured gardens and tall cypress trees are the grand mausoleums the town's wealthiest citizens erected in memory of themselves. Farther north on Avenida Bulnes is the **Museo de Recuerdo.**

TIMING   The walk itself will take at least 1½ hours, but budget in extra time if you wish to explore the museums. Remember that most of the museums, as well as many businesses, close for lunch about noon and reopen a few hours later. You might want to save a visit to Cerro la Cruz or the Cementerio Municipal for these times.

WHAT TO SEE   **Cementerio Municipal.** The fascinating history of this region is chiseled into stone at the Municipal Cemetery. Bizarrely ornate mausoleums honoring the original families are crowded together along paths lined by sculpted cypress trees. In a strange effort to recognize Punta Arenas's indigenous past, there's a shrine in the northern part of the cemetery where the remains of the last member of the Selk'nam tribe are buried. Local legend says that rubbing the statue's left knee brings good luck. ⊠ *Av. Bulnes 949* ☎ *No phone* ☞ *Free* ☉ *Daily dawn–dusk.*

PATAGONIA'S PENGUINS

A S THE FERRY SLOWLY APPROACHES Isla Magdalena, you begin to make out thousands of black dots along the shore. You catch your breath, knowing that this is your first look at the 120,000 residents of Monumento Natural Los Pingüinos, one of the continent's largest penguin sanctuaries.

But the squat little birds are much closer than you think. You soon realize that on either side of the ferry are large groups of penguins catching their breakfast. They are amazingly agile swimmers, leaping almost entirely out of the water before diving down below the surface once again. A few swim alongside the boat, but most simply ignore the intrusion.

Several different types of penguins, including the Magellanic penguins found on the gentle hills of Isla Magdalena, make their homes along the Chilean coast. Although most favor cooler climates, small colonies can be found in the warmer waters north of Santiago. But for the thrill of seeing tens of thousands in one place, nothing beats Monumento Natural Los Pingüinos. At this reserve, a two-hour trip by boat from Punta Arenas, the birds can safely reproduce and raise their young.

Found only along the coast of Chile and Argentina, Magellanic penguins are named for Spanish explorer Hernando de Magallanes, who spotted them when he arrived on these shores in 1520. They are often called jackass penguins because of the braying sound they make when excited. Adults, with the characteristic black-and-white markings, are easy to distinguish from the adolescents, which are a mottled gray. Also gray are the chicks, which hide inside their burrows when their parents are searching for food. A good time to get a look at the fluffy little fellows is when their parents return to feed them regurgitated fish.

A single trail runs across Isla Magdalena, starting at the dock and ending on a hilltop at a red-and-white lighthouse. Ropes on either side keep humans from wandering too far afield. The penguins, however, have the run of the place. They waddle across the path, alone or in small groups, to get to the rocky beach. Familiar with the boatloads of people arriving two or three times a week, the penguins usually don't pay much attention to the camera-clutching crowds. A few of the more curious ones will walk up to people and inspect a shoelace or pants leg. If someone gets too close to a nest, however, they cock their heads sharply from side to side as a warning.

An easier way to see penguins in their natural habitat is to drive to Pingüinera de Seno Otway, on the mainland about an hour northwest of Punta Arenas. Founded in 1990, the reserve occupies 2 km (1 mi) of coastline. There are far fewer penguins here—only about 7,500—but the number is still astounding. The sanctuary is run by a nonprofit group, which can provide English-language guides. Travel companies from Punta Arenas arrange frequent tours to the reserve.

–Pete Nelson

Isla Magdalena. Punta Arenas is the launching point for a boat trip to see the more than 100,000 Magellanic penguins at the **Monumento Natural Los Pingüinos** on this island. A single trail, marked off by rope, is accessible to humans. The trip to the island, in the middle of the Estrecho de Magallanes, takes about two hours. To get here, you must take a tour boat: Comapa and Cruceros Australis have service. However you get here, make sure to bring along warm clothing, even in summer; the island can be chilly, particularly if a breeze is blowing across the water.

Mirador Cerro la Cruz. From a platform beside the white cross that gives this hill lookout its name, you have a panoramic view of the city's colorful corrugated rooftops leading to the Strait of Magellan. Stand with the amorous local couples gazing out toward the flat expanse of Tierra del Fuego in the distance. ⊠ *Fagnano and Señoret* ☎ *No phone* ☜ *Free* ⊙ *Daily.*

Museo de Recuerdo. In the gardens of the Instituto de la Patagonia, part of the Universidad de Magallanes, the Museum of Memory is an enviable collection of machinery and heavy equipment used during the late-19th- and early-20th-century pioneering era. There are exhibits of rural employment, such as a carpenter's workshop, and displays of typical home life. ⊠ *Av. Bulnes* ☎ *61/207–056* ☜ *Free* ⊙ *Weekdays 8:30–12:30 and 2:30–6, Sat. 8:30–12:30.*

Museo Naval y Marítimo. The Naval and Maritime Museum extols Chile's high seas prowess, particularly concerning Antarctica. Its exhibits are worth a visit by anyone with an interest in ships and sailing, merchant and military alike. The second floor is designed in part like the interior of a ship, including a map and radio room. Aging exhibits include an account of the 1908 visit to Punta Arenas by an American naval fleet. Ask for a tour or an explanatory brochure in English. ⊠ *Pedro Montt 989* ☎ *61/205–558* ☜ *700 pesos* ⊙ *Oct.–May, weekdays 9:30–5, Sat. 10–1, Sun. 3–6; June–Sept., wee kdays 9:30–12:30 and 2–5, Sat. 10–1, Sun. 3–6.*

Fodor'sChoice ★ **Museo Regional de Magallanes.** Housed in what was once the mansion of the powerful Braun-Menéndez family, the Regional Museum of the Magallanes is an intriguing glimpse into the daily life of a wealthy provincial family at the beginning of the 20th century. Lavish Carrara marble hearths, English bath fixtures, and cordovan leather walls are among the original accoutrements. The museum also has an excellent group of displays depicting Punta Arenas's past, from the moment of European contact to its decline with the opening of the Panama Canal. The museum is half a block north of the main square. ⊠ *Magallanes 949* ☎ *61/244–216* ☜ *1,000 pesos* ⊙ *Oct.–Apr., Mon.–Sat. 10:30–5, Sun. 10:30–2; May–Sept., daily 10:30–2.*

Museo Salesiano de Maggiorino Borgatello. Commonly referred to simply as "El Salesiano," the museum is operated by Italian missionaries whose order arrived in Punta Arenas in the 19th century. The Salesians, most of whom spoke no Spanish, proved to be daring explorers. Traveling throughout the region, they collected the artifacts made by indigenous tribes that are currently on display. They also relocated many of the indigenous people to nearby Dawson Island, where they died by the hundreds. The museum contains an extraordinary collection of everything from skulls and native crafts to stuffed animals. ☒ *Av. Bulnes 398* 🕾 *61/241–096* 📧 *1,500 pesos* ◷ *Tues.–Sun., 10–12:30 and 3–5.*

★ **Palacio Sara Braun.** This resplendent 1895 mansion, a national landmark and architectural showpiece of southern Patagonia, was designed by French architect Numa Meyer at the behest of Sara Braun. Materials and craftsmen were imported from Europe during the home's four years of construction. The city's central plaza and surrounding buildings soon followed, ushering in the region's golden era. The Club de la Unión, a social organization that now owns the building, opens its doors to non-members for tours of some of the rooms and salons that remain in their original state (a good portion of the mansion is leased to a hotel). Noteworthy are the lavish bedrooms, magnificent parquet floors, marble fireplaces, and hand-painted ceilings. Don't miss portraits of Braun and her husband José Nogueira in the music room. Afterwards head to the cellar for a drink or snack in the warm public tavern. ☒ *Plaza Muñoz Gamero 716* 🕾 *61/241–489* 📧 *1,000 pesos* ◷ *Tues.–Fri. 10:30–1 and 6:30–8:30, Sat. 10:30–1 and 8–10, Sun. 11–2.*

Plaza Muñoz Gamero. A canopy of conifers shades this square, which is surrounded by splendid baroque-style mansions from the 19th century. A bronze sculpture commemorating the voyage of Hernando de Magallanes dominates the center of the plaza. Local lore has it that a kiss on the shiny toe of Calafate, one of the Fuegian people at the base of the monument, will one day bring you back to Punta Arenas. ☒ *José Nogueira and 21 de Mayo.*

Where to Stay & Eat

$–$$$ ✕ **La Pergola.** In what was once the sun room and patio garden of Sara Braun's turn-of-the-20th-century mansion, this restaurant has one of the city's most refined settings. A 100-year-old vine festoons the glass windows and ceiling. Choose from mainly Chilean seafood and meat specialties on the photo-illustrated menu: you might start with fried calamari and then have white fish in garlic sauce. The service is formal and attentive, as in the rest of the Hotel José Nogueira. ☒ *Bories 959* 🕾 *61/248–840* 🖃 *AE, DC, MC, V.*

$–$$ ✕ **El Remezón.** Even among the many fine restaurants in Punta Arenas, this cheerful little place stands out because of its deliciously seasoned grilled fish and meats. The dining room is unpretentious and homey. The restaurant is near the port, but the terrific food and potent pisco sours—brandy mixed with lemon, egg whites, and sugar—make it worth the walk. ☒ *21 de Mayo 1469* 🕾 *61/241–029* 🖃 *AE.*

$–$$ ✕ **Restaurant Asturias.** Rough-hewn wood beams and white stucco walls conjure up the Asturias region of Spain. The *salmón papillote* (salmon poached in white wine with cured ham, cream cheese, and tomatoes) combines smoky aromas with flavors from the sea. The *paella castellana* varies from the traditional dish because it includes meats, and the *congrio a la vasca* (with pepper and garlic) is an imaginative rendition of Chile's ubiquitous white fish. ☒ *Lautaro Navarro 967* 🕾 *61/243–763* 🖃 *AE, DC, MC, V.*

★ $–$$ ✕ **Sotito's.** This longtime favorite among locals is a virtual institution in Punta Arenas. The dining room is warm and cozy, with exposed-brick walls and wood-beam ceilings. More importantly, it serves some of the best king crab in the area. It's prepared a half dozen ways, including in an appetizer called *centolla con palta* (king crab with avocado). The restaurant is near the water a few blocks east of Plaza Muñoz Gamero. ✉ *O'Higgins 1138* ☎ *61/243–565* ▭ *AE, DC, MC, V.*

¢–$$ ✕ **Los Ganaderos.** Feel at home on the range in this restaurant resembling a rural *estancia* (ranch). The manager and waiters, dressed in authentic gaucho costumes, serve up tasty *corderos al ruedo* (spit-roasted lamb) cooked to perfection in the *salón de parilla* (grill room). Wash down your meal with something from the long list of Chilean wines. Interesting black-and-white photographs of past and contemporary ranch life are displayed along the walls. The restaurant is several blocks north of the center of town, but it's worth the long walk or very short taxi ride. ✉ *Bulnes 0977* ☎ *61/214–597* ▭ *AE, MC, V* ⊙ *Closed Sun.*

Fodor's Choice ★

$ ✕ **El Estribo.** Centered around a large fireplace used to grill the meats, this narrow restaurant is filled with intimate little tables covered with white tablecloths. The name means The Stirrup, and the walls are adorned with tastefully arranged bridles, bits, lariats, and—of course—all manner of stirrups. The success of this longtime favorite, however, is due to its excellent regional food, including lamb, salmon, and king crab. For dessert try rhubarb pie—uncommon in these parts. ✉ *Ignacio Carrera Pinto 762* ☎ *61/244–714* ▭ *No credit cards.*

$ ✕ **El Quijote.** Red neon inside and out boldly announces this restaurant. The kitchen dishes out delicious soups and sandwiches, as well as meat and seafood dishes, making it a reliable local hangout. Stop by for the espresso drinks as well as the *liquados* (fruit and milk shakes). ✉ *Lautaro Navarro 1087* ☎ *61/241–225* ▭ *AE, DC, MC, V.*

★ $ ✕ **La Taberna.** A jovial, publike atmosphere prevails in this labyrinthine cellar redoubt down the side stairway of Sara Braun's old mansion. A series of nearly hidden rooms are walled in cozy stone and brick, and black-and-white photos of historical Punta Arenas adorn the walls. You're likely to hear ragtime and jazz on the stereo while enjoying beers served cold in frosted mugs, tapas-style meat and cheese appetizers, sandwiches, tacos, pizza, fajitas, and even carpaccio. The owners belong to the elite Club de la Union headquartered upstairs, and many members relax down here. ✉ *Plaza Muñoz Gamero 716* ☎ *61/241–317* ▭ *AE, DC, MC, V* ⊙ *Closed Sun.*

¢–$ ✕ **Calipso.** The strong espresso and fresh pastries served here are certain to revive you after a day of strolling the broad avenues of Punta Arenas. More substantial fare includes moderately priced hamburgers with all the trimmings, as well as more expensive salmon and crab dinners. ✉ *Bories 817* ☎ *61/241–782* ▭ *DC, MC, V.*

¢–$ ✕ **Lomit's.** A fast-moving but friendly staff serves Chilean-style blue-plate specials at this bustling deli. In addition to traditional hamburgers you can eat the ubiquitous *completos*—hot dogs buried under mounds of toppings, from spicy mayonnaise to guacamole. Locals come here from morning to midnight. ✉ *José Menéndez between Bories and Magallanes* ☎ *61/243–399* ▭ *No credit cards.*

¢–$ ✕ **La Mamá.** Massive plates of lovingly prepared pasta, such as gnocchi and lasagna, have made this restaurant very popular with budget travelers. The hosts' warmth makes up for the unsightly red plastic furniture and low stucco ceiling. A bulletin board in the corner is plastered with raves from every corner of the globe. ✉ *Armando Sanhueza 720* 🕾 *61/225–127* ▤ *No credit cards.*

$$ ✕▨ **Hotel Los Navegantes.** This unpretentious, older hotel a block from the Plaza de Armas has spacious burgundy and green rooms. The nautical-theme restaurant, in a simple but comfortable dining room with a bright garden at one end, serves delicious grilled salmon and roast lamb. Don't pass up the shellfish appetizers. ✉ *José Menéndez 647* 🕾 *61/244–677* 🖷 *61/247–545* ⊕ *www.hotel-losnavegantes.com* ➴ *50 rooms, 2 suites* ♨ *Restaurant, in-room safes, minibars, bar, airport shuttle, travel services* ▤ *AE, DC, MC, V.*

$$$$ ▨ **Hotel Finis Terrae.** A Best Western affiliate, this modern interpretation of an alpine-style hotel has a very professional staff. Rooms are comfortable, with traditional floral-print bedcovers and overstuffed chairs, and the baths are spacious and modern. Head up to the sixth floor for panoramic views from the restaurant and bar. ✉ *Av. Colón 766* 🕾 *61/228–200* 🖷 *61/248–124* ⊕ *www.hotelfinisterrae.com* ➴ *60 rooms, 4 suites* ♨ *Restaurant, in-room safes, minibars, cable TV, 2 bars, Internet, business center, airport shuttle* ▤ *AE, DC, MC, V.*

$$$$ ▨ **Hotel José Nogueira.** Originally the home of Sara Braun, wealthy
Fodor's Choice widow of wool baron José Nogueira, this opulent 19th-century man-
★ sion also contains a museum. Carefully restored over many years, the building retains the original crystal chandeliers, marble floors, and polished bronze accents that were imported from France. Rooms are rather small, but compensate with high ceilings, thick carpets, English wallpaper, period furniture, and marble sinks. Suites have hot tubs and in-room faxes. ✉ *Bories 959* 🕾 *61/248–840* 🖷 *61/248–832* ⊕ *www. hotelnogueira.com* ➴ *25 rooms, 3 suites* ♨ *Restaurant, in-room data ports, in-room safes, minibars, cable TV, salon, pub, laundry service, business services* ▤ *AE, DC, MC, V.*

$$$ ▨ **Hotel Cabo de Hornos.** You can look out from this imposing eight-story hotel over the adjacent Plaza Muñoz Gamero park on one side and to the Estrecho de Magallanes on the other. Rooms and suites have contemporary beds and multicolor-striped drapes that match the flowers on the bedspread—think slightly bland, European conservative in style. Botanical prints line the halls. The fine restaurant, Navarino, serves international cuisine. ✉ *Plaza Muñoz Gamero 1025* 🕾🖷 *61/242–134* ⊕ *www.hch.co.cl* ➴ *90 rooms, 1 suite* ♨ *Restaurant, room service, in-room safes, minibars, cable TV, sauna, bar, baby-sitting, Internet, business services, convention center, airport shuttle, travel services, no-smoking floors* ▤ *AE, DC, MC, V.*

$$$ ▨ **Hotel Isla Rey Jorge.** Lofty wood windows let lots of light into the intimate rooms, decorated in mint and deep rose, at this English-style hotel with impeccable service. The hotel's richly toned *linga* and *coigüe* woodwork in the lobby continues down into the popular basement pub, El Galeón. The hotel is just one block from Plaza Muñoz Gamero. ✉ *21 de Mayo 1243* 🕾🖷 *61/248–220* ⊕ *www.islareyjorge.com* ➴ *25 rooms,*

4 suites ☼ Restaurant, cable TV, bar, Internet, airport shuttle, travel services ▤ AE, DC, MC, V.

$ ▦ **Hostal de la Avenida.** The rooms of this pea-green guest house all overlook the garden, lovingly tended by its owner, a local of Yugoslav origin. Flowers spill out from a wheelbarrow and a bathtub, birdhouses hang from trees, and a statue of Mary rests in a shrine with a grotto. The rooms offer modest comforts for those on a budget. The ones beyond the garden are the newest. Beside them is a funky bar (Chilean poet Pablo Neruda would have approved) that seems hunkered down for blustery winters. *⊠ Av. Colón 534 ☎ 61/247–532 ⤳ 10 rooms, 6 with bath ☼ Dining room, in-room safes, minibars, cable TV, bar, laundry service ▤ AE, DC, MC, V ⑪ CP.*

★ $ ▦ **Hostal Oro Fueguino.** On a slightly sloping cobblestone street near the observation deck at Cerro la Cruz, this funky little hostelry—tall, narrow, and rambling—welcomes you with lots of color. The first thing you notice is the facade, painted bright orange and blue. Inside are wall hangings and lamp shades made of eye-catching fabrics from as far off as India that create a hominess. The dining and living rooms are cheerful, and there's a wealth of tourist information. The warmth is enhanced by the personal zeal of the proprietor, Dinka Ocampo. *⊠ Fagnano 365 ☎☎ 61/249–401 ⊕ www.orofueguino.cl ⤳ 12 rooms ☼ Dining room, cable TV, laundry service, Internet ▤ AE, DC, MC, V ⑪ BP.*

$ ▦ **Hotel Condor de Plata.** The idiosyncratic decor at the Silver Condor includes scale models of ships and photographs of old-fashioned airplanes that once traversed the region. Like a handful of other small hotels on this busy, tree-lined avenue, it offers basic amenities for those on a budget—simple, clean rooms that have a bed and a TV. *⊠ Av. Colón 556 ☎ 61/247–987 ☎ 61/241–149 ⤳ 14 rooms ☼ Cafeteria, in-room safes, minibars, bar, laundry service ▤ AE, DC, MC, V.*

Nightlife & the Arts

Because Punta Arenas is so far south, the sun doesn't set until well into the evening. That means that locals don't think about hitting the bars until midnight. If you can't stay up late, try the hotel bars, such as Hotel Tierra del Fuego's **Pub 1900** (⊠ Av. Colón 716 ☎ 61/242–759), which attract an early crowd. If you're in the mood for dancing, try **Abracadabra** (⊠ Bories 546 ☎ 61/224–144), where the younger set goes to party until dawn.

Shopping

About 3 km (2 mi) north of town is the **Zona Franca** (⊠ Av. Bulnes s/n ☎ no phone). This duty-free zone is where people from all around the region come for low-priced electronics and other consumer items. It's open Monday–Saturday 9–8.

Almacén de Antaño (⊠ Colón 1000 ☎ 61/227–283) offers a fascinatingly eclectic selection of pewter, ceramics, mirrors, and graphics frames. **Dagorret** (⊠ Bories 587 ☎ 61/228–692), a Chilean chain with other outlets in Puerto Montt and Puerto Natales, carries top-quality leather clothing, including *gamuza* (suede) and *gamulán* (buckskin), some with wool trim. **Quilpue** (⊠ José Nogueira 1256 ☎ 61/220–960) is a shoe-repair shop that also markets *huaso* (cowboy) supplies such as bridles, bits, and spurs. Pick up some boots for folk dancing.

en route About 3,000 Magellanic penguins return to the **Pingüinera de Seno Otway** between October and March to breed. From behind a rope you'll see scores of the ungainly little guys waddling to the ocean. If you're lucky you'll catch sight of one of the downy gray chicks that stick their heads out of the burrows only when their parents return to feed them. The sanctuary is a 2-km (1-mi) walk from the parking lot. It gets chilly, so bring a windbreaker. ☒ *50 km (31 mi) northwest of Punta Arenas* ☜ *1,200 pesos* ☉ *Sept.–Apr., daily 8:30–8:30.*

Puerto Natales

242 km (150 mi) northwest of Punta Arenas.

The land around Puerto Natales held very little interest for Spanish explorers in search of riches. A not-so-warm welcome from the indigenous peoples encouraged them to continue up the coast, leaving only a name for the channel running through it: Seno Última Esperanza (Last Hope Sound). Today this town of fading fishing and meat-packing enterprises is rapidly emerging as the staging center for visits to Parque Nacional Torres del Paine and other remote sites. The town, with 15,000 friendly and hospitable residents, is still unspoiled by the spoils of tourism.

On a clear day, take an early morning walk along Avenida Pedro Montt, which follows the shoreline of the Seno Última Esperanza. A few blocks east of the shore is the not-quite-central **Plaza de Armas.** An incongruous railway engine sits prominently in the middle of the square. ☒ *Arturo Prat and Eberhard.* Across from the Plaza de Armas is the squat little **Iglesia Parroquial.** The ornate altarpiece in this church depicts the town's founders, indigenous peoples, and the Virgin Mary all in front of the Torres del Paine. A highlight in the small but interesting **Museo Historico Municipal** is a room of photos of indigenous peoples. Another room is devoted to the exploits of German-born Hermann Eberhard, considered the region's first settler. ☒ *Bulnes 285* ☎ *61/411–263* ☜ *Free* ☉ *Weekdays 8:30–12:30 and 2:30–6, weekends 2:30–6.*

In 1896, Hermann Eberhard stumbled upon a gaping cave that extended 200 m (650 ft) into the earth. Venturing inside, he discovered the bones and dried pieces of hide of an animal he could not identify. It was later determined that what Eberhard had discovered were the extraordinarily well-preserved remains of a prehistoric herbivorous mammal, about twice the height of a man, which they called a *milodón.* The cave and a somewhat kitschy life-size fiberglass rendering of the creature are at the **Monumento Natural Cueva de Milodón.** ☒ *Off Ruta 9, 28 km (17 mi) northwest of Puerto Natales* ☎ *No phone* ☜ *1,000 pesos* ☉ *Daily 8:30–6.*

Where to Stay & Eat

★ $$–$$$ ✕**Restaurant Edén.** Grilled lamb sizzles prominently near the entrance while Chilean folk music plays softly in the background. This expansive venue, with tables generously spaced on the white terrazzo floor, has floor-to-ceiling windows on two sides that give you the feeling of dining alfresco. ⊠ *Blanco Encalada 345* 🕾 *61/414–120* 🚍 *AE, MC, V.*

$–$$ ✕ **Centro Español.** Tables swathed in bright red, and hardwood floors that would be perfect for flamenco dancing create this restaurant's subtly Spanish style. It's a bit formal, but never stuffy. There's a wide selection of simply prepared meat and fish entrées, including succulent squid, served in ample portions. ⊠ *Magallanes 247* 🕾 *61/411–181* 🚍 *AE, MC, V.*

$–$$ ✕ **Don Pepe.** Creative seafood preparations draw a large crowd here, especially in summer. Try the salmon with a crab and cream sauce, a house specialty, and you likely won't mind that the place isn't much to look at. ⊠ *Ladrilleros 172* 🕾 *61/412–189* 🚍 *DC, MC, V.*

★ $–$$ ✕ **Indigo.** Eco-friendly vibes waft from this bright café, setting it apart from nearly every other eatery in Patagonia. Fossils collected from the nearby fjord, piles of *National Geographic*s and informational brochures about area attractions, Internet access, and an English-speaking staff make Indigo a de facto tourist office, museum, and library. The homemade pizzas are good—ask which toppings are fresh and which are canned— as are the sandwiches served on homemade wheat bread. The corner spot, overlooking the water and a backdrop of snowy peaks, makes this a pleasant place to visit, even if you come just for a cup of coffee. ⊠ *Ladrilleros 105* 🕾 *61/413–609* 🚍 *MC, V.*

$–$$ ✕ **Restaurant Última Esperanza.** Named for the strait on which Puerto Natales is located, Last Hope Restaurant sounds as if it might be a bleak place. It's known, however, for its attentive service and top-quality entrées that include meats and fish. *Salmón a la plancha* (grilled salmon) is a specialty. ⊠ *Av. Eberhard 354* 🕾 *61/411–391* 🚍 *No credit cards.*

★ $ ✕ **El Rincón del Tata.** In the evenings a strolling guitarist entertains with Chilean folk songs, encouraging diners to join in at this funky little spot. Artifacts, mainly household items, from the town's early days fill the dining room, including a working wood-burning stove to keep you warm. More expensive restaurants can't match the *salmón à la mantequilla* (salmon baked in butter and black pepper), and the grilled lamb with garlic sauce is a Patagonian highlight. ⊠ *Arturo Prat 236* 🕾 *61/413–845* 🚍 *AE, DC, MC, V.*

¢–$ ✕ **Café Melissa.** The best espresso in town is found at Café Melissa, which also serves pastries and cakes baked on the premises. In the heart of downtown, this is a popular meeting place for residents and visitors alike. ⊠ *Blanco Encalada 258* 🕾 *61/411–944* 🚍 *No credit cards.*

$$$–$$$$ 🏠 **Hotel CostAustralis.** The peaked green roof of this venerable three-story hotel—complete with turret—dominates the waterfront. Designed by a local architect, it's considered one of the finest hotels in Peurto Natales. Rooms have wood-paneled entryways and Venetian and Czech furnishings. Some have a majestic view of the Seno Última Esperanza and the snowcapped mountain peaks beyond, while others look out over the city. ⊠ *Pedro Montt and Bulnes* 🕾 *61/412–000* 🖷 *61/411–881* ⊕ *www.australis.com* 🛏 *50 rooms, 2 suites* ⚬ *Restaurant, café, room service, in-room safes, minibars, cable TV, bar, laundry service, Internet, travel services* 🚍 *AE, DC, MC, V.*

$$$ 🏠 **Hotel Martín Gusinde.** Part of Chile's modern AustroHoteles chain, this intimate inn possesses an aura of sophistication that contrasts with the laid-back atmosphere of Puerto Natales. The hotel is named after the Austrian ethnologist who studied the natives inhabitants of Tierra del Fuego. Rooms are decorated with wood furniture and colorfully patterned wallpaper. It's across from the casino, a block south of the Plaza de Armas. ⊠ *Carlos Bories 278* ☎ *61/412–770, reservations 61/229–512* 🖷 *61/412–820* ⊕ *www.austrohoteles.cl* 🛏 *20 rooms* 🖙 *Restaurant, room service, in-room safes, cable TV, bar* ⊟ *AE, MC, V.*

$$ 🖼 **Hostal Lady Florence Dixie.** Named after an aristocratic English immigrant and tireless traveler, this modern hostel with an alpine-inspired facade is on the town's main street. Its bright, spacious lounge is a great people-watching perch. Guest rooms are a bit spartan—mostly just a bed. ⊠ *Bulnes 659* ☎ *61/411–158* 🖷 *61/411–943* ⊕ *www. chileanpatagonia.com/florence* 🛏 *18 rooms* 🖙 *In-room safes* ⊟ *AE, MC, V* ❚◎❘ *CP.*

$$ 🖼 **Hotel Alberto de Agostini.** This is one of the modern hotels that have cropped up in Puerto Natales in the past few years. Small rooms—some with hot tubs—are unremarkable in style. A comfortably furnished lounge on the second floor looks out over the Seno Última Esperanza. ⊠ *Calle O'Higgins 632* ☎ *61/410–060* 🖷 *61/410–070* 🛏 *21 rooms* 🖙 *Restaurant, room service, minibars, sauna, bar* ⊟ *AE, MC, V.*

$$ 🖼 **Hotel Glaciares.** An enduring choice in Puerto Natales, this cheery place is half a block from the Seno Última Esperanza. Rooms have lots of windows letting in the sun. The hotel also offers tours of Parque Nacional Torres del Paine in its own fleet of minivans. ⊠ *Eberhard 104* ☎🖷 *61/411–452* ⊕ *www.hotelglaciares.co.cl* 🛏 *15 rooms* 🖙 *Restaurant, laundry service, travel services* ⊟ *DC, MC, V.*

$ 🖼 **Hostal Francis Drake.** Toss a coin in the wishing well out front before you enter this half-timbered house near the center of town. The proprietor is a delightful European lady who dotes on her guests and carefully maintains cleanliness. Rooms are small and basic. The beds are not the world's most comfortable. ⊠ *Philippi 383* ☎🖷 *61/411–553* ⊕ *www.chileaustral.com/francisdrake* 🛏 *12 rooms* 🖙 *Cable TV, lounge* ⊟ *DC, MC, V.*

★ **$** 🖼 **Indigo.** Rooms in this restored old home have amazing views down the Canal Señoret stretching as far as the Mt. Balmaceda glacier and the Paine Grande. Ask for one of the corner rooms, which have windows along two walls. The walls are sponge-painted in bright reds, yellows, and blues, and hung with local art. The funky and friendly café downstairs has an eclectic collection of artifacts. English is spoken well, as exhibited in the nightly slide shows about Torres del Paine park. ⊠ *Ladrilleros 105* ☎🖷 *61/413–609* ⊕ *www.conceptoindigo.com* 🛏 *7 rooms* 🖙 *Restaurant, laundry service, Internet, travel services; no room phones, no room TVs* ⊟ *MC, V.*

Parque Nacional Torres del Paine

FodorsChoice   *125 km (75 mi) northwest of Puerto Natales.*

★ Some 12 million years ago, lava flows pushed up through the thick sedimentary crust that covered the southwestern coast of South America, cooling to form a granite mass. Glaciers then swept through the region, grinding away all but the ash-gray spires that rise over the landscape of one of the world's most beautiful natural phenomena, now the Parque Nacional Torres del Paine (established in 1959). Snow formations dazzle along every turn of road, and the sunset views are spectacular.

Among the 2,420-square-km (934-square-mi) park's most beautiful attractions are its lakes of turquoise, aquamarine, and emerald green waters. Another draw is its unusual wildlife. Creatures like the guanaco (a woollier version of the llama) and the *ñandú* (resembling a small ostrich) abound. They are used to visitors, and don't seem to be bothered by the proximity of automobile traffic and the snapping of cameras. Predators like the gray fox make less frequent appearances. You may also spot the dramatic aerobatics of a falcon and the graceful soaring of the endangered condor. The beautiful puma is especially elusive, but sightings have grown more and more common. Pumas follow the guanaco herds and eat an estimated 40% of their young.

Although considerable walking is necessary to take full advantage of Parque Nacional Torres del Paine, you need not be a hard-core backpacker. Many people take five or six days to hike El Circuito, a route that leads around the entire park, spending the nights in tents or the dozen or so *refugios* (shelters) found along the trails. Others prefer to stay in one of the comfortable lodges and hit the trails for the morning or afternoon. Glaciar Grey, with its fragmented icebergs, makes a rewarding and easy hike. Driving is another way to enjoy the park: most of the more than 100 km (62 mi) of roads leading to the most popular sites are safe and well maintained, though unpaved.

The vast majority of visitors come during the summer months, which means the trails can get congested. Early spring, when wildflowers add flashes of color to the meadows, is an ideal time to visit because the crowds have not yet arrived. The park is open all year, and trails are almost always accessible. Storms can hit without warning, however, so be prepared for sudden rain or snow. The sight of the Paine peaks in clear weather is stunning; if you have any flexibility in your itinerary, be sure to visit the park on the first clear day.

There are three entrances: Laguna Amarga, Lago Sarmiento, and Laguna Azul. You are required to sign in when you arrive at the park. *Guardaparques* (park rangers) staff six stations around the reserve. They request that you inform them when setting out on a hike. CONAF, the national forestry service, has an office at the northern end of Lago del Toro with a scale model of the park, and numerous exhibits (some in English) about the flora and fauna. ✛ *CONAF station in southern section of the park past Hotel Explora* ☎ *61/691–931* 🖃 *8,000 pesos* ☉ *Ranger station: Nov.–Feb., daily 8–8; March–Oct., daily 8–12:30 and 2–6:30.*

Where to Stay & Eat

$$ ✕🖃 **Posada Río Serrano.** A welcoming staff will show you a selection of rooms, including those with bunk beds and those with regular beds. Rooms are small, but clean, and have colorful bedspreads. A few actually have lake views. A surprisingly warm salon with a fireplace makes a nice place to relax. Don't expect pampering—besides camping this is the cheapest dining and lodging in the park. The restaurant serves filling fish dishes *a lo pobre* (with fried eggs and french fries), as well as lamb. The inn also has a general store where you can find basic necessities such as batteries and cookies. ⊠ *Lago Toro* ☎ *61/411–129 for reservations (Puerto Natales)* ⛱ *20 rooms, 4 with bath* ⚌ *Restaurant, grocery; no a/c, no room phones, no room TVs* ⊟ *No credit cards* ⊠| *CP.*

$$$$ ⌸ **Hostería Lago Grey** The panoramic view past the lake to the glacier beyond is worth the journey here, which doesn't change the fact that this older hotel is overpriced and not very attractive. Rooms are comfortable, but the materials are inexpensive, and baths small. There's a TV with a VCR in the lounge. The view—and it's one you're not likely to forget—can also be enjoyed at dinner (a 16,800 pesos per person prix fixe with wine) or at the hotel's large breakfast. The hotel operates its own sightseeing vessel, the *Grey II,* for close-up tours to Glaciar Grey. ⊠ *Lago Grey* ☎ *61/229–512 or 61/225–986* ⊕ *www.lagogrey.com* ⛱ *20 rooms* ⚌ *Restaurant, boating, fishing, hiking, horseback riding, bar, lounge, laundry service; no room TVs* ⊟ *AE, DC, MC, V* ⊠| *BP.*

$$$$ ⌸ **Hosteria Tyndall.** A boat ferries you from the end of the road the few minutes along the Serrano River to this wooden lodge. The simple rooms in the main building are small but cute, with attractive wood paneling. The lodge can be noisy, a problem solved by renting a log cottage (a great value for groups). Owner Christian is a wildlife enthusiast and bird-watcher; ask him for a tour of the grassy plain looking out toward the central cluster of snowy peaks. Or fish for a river salmon—they'll cook it for you for free. The prix-fixe dinner costs 11,900 pesos. ⊠ *Lago Toro (Reservations: Av. Croacia 731, Punta Arenas)* ☎ *61/235–457 in Punta Arenas* ⊕ *www.hosteriatyndall.com* ⛱ *24 rooms, 6 cottages* ⚌ *Restaurant, boating, fishing, hiking, horseback riding, lounge, laundry service; no room phones, no room TVs* ⊟ *AE, DC, MC, V.*

$$$$ ⌸ **Hosteria Pehoé.** Cross a 30-m (100-ft) footbridge to get to this hotel on its own island in the middle of glistening Lake Pehoé, across from the beautiful Torres del Paine mountain peaks. Upon seeing the setting, nonguests are often tempted to cancel other reservations. Unfortunately, rooms at Pehoé—built in 1970 as the first hotel in the park—are dark, poorly furnished, and windowless, and they face an interior lawn. Management built a new wing (completed in early 2003) with newly obstructed views. However, it is a delight to walk over the footbridge and have a drink at the ski lodge–like bar, where the views are jaw-dropping. ⊠ *Lago Pehoé* ☎ *61/411–390* ⛱ *20 rooms* ⚌ *Restaurant, bar, laundry service; no room TVs, no room phones* ⊟ *AE, DC, MC, V* ⊠| *CP.*

$$$$ ⌸ **Hotel Explora.** On the southeast corner of Lago Pehoé, this lodge is
Fodor'sChoice   one of the most luxurious—and one of the most expensive—in Chile.
★   While there may be some debate about the aesthetics of the hotel's low-slung minimalist exterior, the interior is impeccable: it's Scandinavian in style, with local woods used for ceilings, floors, and furniture. No expense has been spared—even the bed linens were imported from Spain. A dozen full-time guides (for a maximum of 60 guests) tailor all-inclusive park outings to guests' interests. A three-night minimum stay is required. Nonguests may also enjoy the 42,000-peso prix-fixe dinner, with wine. ⊠ *Lago Pehoé* ☎ *2/206–6060 in Santiago* ☎ *2/228–*

4655 in Santiago ⊕ www.explora.com ≈ 26 rooms, 4 suites ⌂ Restaurant, indoor pool, gym, outdoor hot tub, massage, sauna, boating, hiking, horseback riding, piano bar, library, gift shop, baby-sitting, laundry service, Internet, business services, meeting rooms, airport shuttle; no room TVs ⊟ AE, DC, MC, V ⦿ All-inclusive.

Patagonia A to Z

AIR TRAVEL

LanChile and its subsidiary Ladeco operate a number of flights daily between Punta Arenas and Santiago, Coihaique, and Puerto Montt. It's a good idea to make air-travel arrangements through a reliable tour company, if possible. That way you can rely on the company if you need to make last-minute changes in your itinerary. Punta Arenas's Aeropuerto President Ibañez is 20 km (13 mi) north of town. Porvenir's airport is 5 km (3 mi) north of town.

✈ Airlines **LanChile/Ladeco** ✉ Lautaro Navarro 999, Punta Arenas ☎ 61/241-232 ⊕ www.lanchile.com.

BOAT & FERRY TRAVEL

Comapa runs a ferry three times a week between Punta Arenas and Porvenir. Navimag operates an inelegant, but highly serviceable, cargo and passenger ferry fleet between Puerto Montt and Puerto Natales. These are boats designed for transportation, not touring, but they are comfortable enough for all but the most finicky travelers.

⛴ Boat & Ferry Lines **Comapa** ✉ Independencia 803, Punta Arenas ☎ 61/224-256. **Navimag** ✉ Av. El Bosque Norte 0440, Santiago ☎ 2/442-3120 🖷 2/203-5025 ⊕ www.navimag.cl.

BUSINESS HOURS

Most shops in the region close for a few hours in the afternoon, usually noon–3. Grocery stores are the exception. Most restaurants close between lunch and dinner, which means most don't serve meals from 3–8 or even later.

BUS TRAVEL

The four-hour trip between Punta Arenas and Puerto Natales is serviced by small, private companies. One of the best is Buses Fernández, which has a fleet of first-class coaches and its own terminals in both towns.

🚌 Bus Information **Buses Fernández** ✉ Armando Sanhueza 745, Punta Arenas ☎ 61/221-429 ✉ Eberhard 555, Puerto Natales ☎ 61/411-111 ⊕ www.busesfernandez.com.

CAR RENTAL

Renting a car in Patagonia is not cheap—most companies charge about 70,000 pesos per day. Compare rental rates to the cost of tours; you may find a tour is far cheaper than driving yourself. Make sure you don't rent a more expensive car than you need. Four-wheel-drive vehicles are popular and readily available, but they often aren't necessary if you're not leaving the major roads. Make certain to understand the extent of your liability for any damage to the vehicle, including routine accidents such as a chipped or cracked windshield.

Of the international chains, Budget, Avis, and Hertz have offices in Punta Arenas. At the Punta Arenas airport, there are four rental agencies, Avis, Budget, Hertz, and Int'l Rent A Car. Check prices with each, as any one may be considerably lower than the other three. Avis also has a branch in Puerto Natales. Additional drivers are free. Reputable local companies in Punta Arenas include RUS and Payne.

🏢 Agencies **Avis** ✉ Roca 1044, Punta Arenas ☎ 61/241-182 ✉ Aeropuerto President Ibañez, Punta Arenas ☎ 61/210-861 ✉ Bulnes 632, Puerto Natales ☎ 61/410-775. **Budget** ✉ O'Higgins 964, Punta Arenas ☎ 61/241-696 ✉ Aeropuerto President Ibañez, Punta Arenas ☎ 61/241-696. **Hertz** ✉ O'Higgins 987, Punta Arenas ☎ 61/248-742 ✉ Aeropuerto President Ibañez, Punta Arenas ☎ 61/210-096. **Int'l Rent A Car** ✉ Aeropuerto President Ibañez, Punta Arenas ☎ 61/212-401. **Payne** ✉ José Menéndez 631, Punta Arenas ☎ 61/240-852. **RUS** ✉ Colón 614, Punta Arenas ☎ 61/221-529.

CAR TRAVEL

Driving in Patagonia isn't as difficult as you might think. Highways are paved. Secondary roads, including those in the more popular parks, are well maintained. Be careful of gravel roads—broken windshields are common.

HEALTH

As with other parts of the country, the tap water is safe to drink. If you want to be on the extra-safe side, stick to bottled water. Because of the thin ozone layer, the sun is particularly strong here. Make sure to slather yourself with sunscreen before going outdoors.

MONEY MATTERS

There are a number of banks in Punta Arenas and Puerto Natales where you can exchange cash, and withdraw money from ATMs that accept cards on the Cirrus or Plus systems. Do not count on banking services outside of these two cities. In Puerto Natales, ChileExpress on the main square has Western Union services.

When you're anticipating smaller purchases, try to have coins and small bills on hand at all times. Many vendors do not always have appropriate change for large bills.

🏢 Currency Exchange **ChileExpress** ✉ Av. Tomas Rogers, Puerto Natales ☎ 61/411-3000.

TAXIS

Taxis are readily available in Punta Arenas and Puerto Natales. Ordinary taxis, with yellow roofs, are the easiest. *Colectivos,* with black roofs, run on fixed routes. They cost less, but figuring them out can be tricky if you're not a fluent Spanish speaker.

TELEPHONES

Public telephones, plentiful in larger towns, are becoming more common in smaller villages. Some accept phone cards that can be purchased at nearby shops. Entel and CTC have offices throughout the region where you can send faxes and make international calls.

TOURS

A region-knowledgeable tour operator or travel agent is a must for travel to Patagonia and Tierra del Fuego. In the United States, a number of companies have experience. Among them is the Georgia-based Lost World Adventures, whose staff specializes in tailoring itineraries around your specific interests. There are many good companies in Chile as well.

Air tours are often a little more expensive than cruises, but they provide an entirely different perspective, and may take you farther than you could otherwise go. Aerovís DAP operates charter flights over Cape Horn for about 12,600 pesos per person. DAP was the first airline to have regular commercial flights to the Antarctic, beginning in 1987. In the austral summer (December–February) they fly small groups to comfortable refuges in the Chilean Antarctic, where you can stay in a lodge for up to three nights. DAP staffs a resident guide in Antarctica, and visits include trips to the air force bases of Russia, China, and Chile. Single-day visits begin at U.S.$2,500. The flight is 3½ hours. DAP also has helicopter service across Patagonia.

Boat tours are a popular way to see otherwise inaccessible parts of Patagonia and Tierra del Fuego. The *Barcaza Melinka,* run by Comapa, makes thrice-weekly trips to Isla Magdalena. Cruceros Australis operates the elegant *Terra Australis,* a 55-cabin ship that sails round-trip between Punta Arenas and Ushuaia. On the way, the ship stops at a number of sights, including the Garibaldi Glacier, a breathtaking mass of blue ice. You also ride smaller motorboats ashore to visit Isla Magdalena's colony of 120,000 penguins, and Ainsworth Bay's family of elephant seals. The cruises include lectures in English, German, and Spanish on the region's geography and history, flora and fauna.

Turismo 21 de Mayo operates two ships, the *21 de Mayo* and the *Alberto de Agostini,* to the Balmaceda and Serrano glaciers in Parque Nacional Bernardo O'Higgins. Passengers on these luxurious boats are treated to lectures about the region as the boat moves up the Seno Última Esperanza.

With offices in both cities, Comapa offers numerous tours all over Patagonia and Tierra del Fuego. In Santiago, SportsTour puts together individual itineraries. It also offers half- and full-day city tours and multiday excursions throughout the region. Most staff members speak excellent English. In Puerto Natales, TourExpress operates a fleet of small vans for comfortable tours into Parque Nacional Torres del Paine. The bilingual guides are well versed not only on the area's culture and history but on its geology, fauna, and flora. In Punta Arenas, one of the best companies is Ventistur. Operated by Gonzalo Tejeda, who studied in the United States, Ventistur offers expert advice on travel throughout the region.

🖪 Air Tours **Aerovís DAP** ✉ O'Higgins 891, Punta Arenas ☎ 61/223–340 ⊕ www. aeroviasdap.cl.

🖪 Boat Tours **Comapa** ✉ Independencia 803, Punta Arenas ☎ 61/224–256. **Cruceros Australis** ✉ Av. El Bosque Norte 0440, Santiago ☎ 2/442–3110 🖷 2/203–5173 ⊕ www. australis.com. **Turismo 21 de Mayo** ✉ Ladrilleros 171, Puerto Natales ☎ 61/411–176.

🖪 Regional Tours **Comapa** ✉ Independencia 803, Punta Arenas ☎ 61/200–202 ✉ Pedro Montt 262 ☎ 61/414–300 ⊕ www.comapa.com. **SportsTour** ✉ Moneda 790, 14th floor, Santiago ☎ 2/549–5200 🖷 2/698–2981 ⊕ www.chilnet.cl/sportstour. **Tour-**

Express ✉ Bulnes 769, Puerto Natales ☎ 61/410-734. **Ventistur** ✉ José Menéndez 647, Punta Arenas ☎ 61/241-463 🖷 61/229-081 ⊕ www.chileaustral.com/ventistur. 🖪U.S.-based Tours **Lost World Adventures** ✉112 Church St., Decatur, GA 30030 ☎404/ 373-5820 or 800/999-0558 🖷 404/377-1902 ⊕ www.lostworldadventures.com.

VISITOR INFORMATION

Sernatur, the national tourism agency, has offices in Punta Arenas and in Puerto Natales. The Punta Arenas office is open daily 8–5, and the small Puerto Natales office is open Monday–Thursday 8:15–6 and Friday 8:15–5. The Punta Arenas City Tourism Office, in an attractive kiosk in the main square, is quite helpful. It's open December–March, Monday–Saturday 8–8 and Sunday 9–3; April–November, Monday–Thursday 8–5 and Friday 8–4. They offer a free Internet connection.
🖪 **Punta Arenas City Tourism** ✉ Plaza Muñoz Gamero, Punta Arenas ☎ 61/200-610 ⊕ www.puntaarenas.cl. **Sernatur** ✉ Magallanes 960, Punta Arenas ☎ 61/241-330 ✉ Puerto Montt s/n, Puerto Natales ☎ 61/412-125.

CHILE A TO Z

To research prices, get advice from other travelers, and book travel arrangements, visit www.fodors.com.

AIR TRAVEL

Most international flights head to Santiago's Comodoro Arturo Merino Benítez International Airport (SCL), also known as Pudahuel, about 30 minutes west of the city. Domestic flights leave from the same terminal. The largest North American carrier is American Airlines, which has direct service from Dallas and Miami; Delta flies from Atlanta. No Canadian airlines fly directly to South American destinations, though Canadian Airlines has a partnership with American.

The major Chilean airline is LanChile, which flies directly to Santiago from New York and Miami. Many South American airlines have connecting flights to Santiago: Aerocontinente connects through Lima, Peru; Aerolíneas Argentinas has connections in Buenos Aires, Argentina; Avianca flies through Bogota, Colombia; Lloyd Aéreo Boliviano (LAB) flies through La Paz and other Bolivian cities; Tam flies through Asunción, Paraguay; TAME connects through the Ecuadoran cities of Guayaquil and Quito; and Varig stops in the Brazilian cities of Fortaleza, Manaus, Rio de Janeiro, and São Paulo.

Arriving from abroad, American, Canadian, and Australian citizens must pay a "reciprocity" fee (to balance out fees Chileans pay upon entering foreign countries) of $61, $55, and $30, respectively. Only cash, normally paid in the currency of your country, is accepted. A departure tax of $18 is included in the cost of your ticket.
🖪 To & From North America **American Airlines** ☎ 2/690-1090 in Chile, 800/433-7300 in North America. **Delta Airlines** ☎ 2/690-1551 in Chile, 800/221-1212 in North America. **LanChile** ☎ 2/565-2525 or 600/526-2000 in Chile, 800/735-5526 in North America. 🖪 Within Chile **Aerocontinente** ☎ 2/690-9399 in Chile, 888/586-9400 in North America. **Aerolíneas Argentinas** ☎ 2/690-1030 in Chile, 800/333-0276 in North America. **Aeromexico** ☎ 2/690-1028 in Chile, 800/237-6639 in North America. **Avianca** ☎ 2/

690–1051 in Chile, 800/284–2622 in North America. **Lacsa** ☎ 2/690–1276 in Chile, 800/225–2272 in North America. **LanChile** ☎ 2/565–2525 or 600/526–2000 in Chile, 800/735–5526 in North America. **Lloyd Aéreo Boliviano** ☎ 2/671–2334 in Chile. **Tam** ☎ 2/690–1156 in Chile, 888/235–9826 in North America. **TAME** ☎ 2/630–1681 in Chile. **Varig** ☎ 2/690–1930 in Chile, 800/468–2744 in North America.

🚩 Airport Information **Comodoro Arturo Merino Benítez International Airport** ☎ 2/690–1900.

BUS TRAVEL

Bus travel in Chile is relatively cheap and safe, provided you use one of the better lines. Intercity bus service is a comfortable, safe, and reasonably priced alternative for getting around. Luxury bus travel between cities costs about one-third that of plane travel and is more comfortable, with wide reclining seats, movies, drinks, and snacks. The most luxurious and expensive service offered by most bus companies is called *salon cama* or *semi-cama*.

BUSINESS HOURS

Most retail businesses are open weekdays 10–7 and Saturday until 2; most are closed Sunday. Many businesses close for lunch between about 1 and 3 or 4, though this is becoming less common, especially in larger cities.

BANKS & OFFICES   Most banks are open weekdays 9–2. Casas de cambio are open weekdays 9–2 and 3–6 for currency exchange.

GAS STATIONS   Gas stations in major cities and along the Pan-American Highway tend to stay open 24 hours. Others follow regular business hours.

MUSEUMS & SIGHTS   Most tourist attractions are open during normal business hours during the week and for at least the morning on Saturday and Sunday. Most museums are closed on Monday.

SHOPS   Shops generally are open weekdays 10–7 and Saturdays 10–2. Large malls often stay open daily 10–10. In small towns, shops often close for lunch between 1 and 3 or 4.

CAR RENTAL

On average it costs approximately 30,000 pesos (about $40) a day to rent the cheapest type of car, which usually includes unlimited mileage and insurance. To access some of Chile's more remote regions, it may be necessary to rent a four-wheel-drive vehicle, which can cost up to 70,000 pesos (about $90) a day. You can often get a discounted weekly rate.

It is by far easier to rent a car in Santiago, where all the international agencies have branches at the airport and in town. You'll find mostly local rental agencies in the rest of the country, except at airports, where many international companies often have small kiosks.

INSURANCE   When driving a rented car you are generally responsible for any damage to or loss of the vehicle. You also may be liable for any property damage or personal injury that you may cause while driving. Before you rent, see what coverage you already have under the terms of your personal auto-insurance policy and credit cards.

REQUIREMENTS & RESTRICTIONS Your own driver's license and an International Driving Permit make it legal for you to drive. The minimum age for driving in Chile is 18. To rent a car you usually have to be 25, but a few companies let you rent at 22.

CAR TRAVEL

Certain areas of Chile are most enjoyable when explored on your own in a car, such as the wineries of the Central Valley, the ski areas east of Santiago (for which you'll need snow chains), and the Lake District in the south. Some regions, such as parts of the Atacama Desert and the Carretera Austral highway, are impossible to explore without your own wheels.

Between May and August, roads, underpasses, and parks can flood when it rains. It's very dangerous, especially for drivers who don't know their way around. Avoid driving if it has been raining for several hours.

The Pan-American Highway runs from Arica in the far north down to Puerto Montt, in the Lake District. Much of it is now double lane, or in the process of being widened, and bypasses most large cities. The Carretera Austral, an unpaved road that runs for more than 1,000 km (620 mi) as far as Villa O'Higgins in Patagonia, starts just south of Puerto Montt. A few stretches of the road are broken by water and are linked only by car ferries. Some parts of the Carretera can be washed away in heavy rain; it is wise to consult local police for details. In order to drive to Punta Arenas in Patagonia you will need to cross into Argentina at Chile Chico or at one of the international border crossings beforehand. If you plan to do this you must tell your car-rental company, which will provide notarized authorization—otherwise you will be refused permission to cross.

Keep in mind that the speed limit is 60 kmh (37mph) in cities and 120 kmh (75 mph) on highways unless otherwise posted. Seat belts are mandatory in the front and back of the car, and police give on-the-spot fines for not wearing them. If the police find you with more than 0.5 milligrams of alcohol in your blood, you will be considered to be driving under the influence and arrested.

AUTO CLUBS El Automóvil Club de Chile offers low-cost road service and towing in and around the main cities to members of the Automobile Association of America (AAA).

🚩 In Chile **El Automóvil Club de Chile** ✉ Av. Andrés Bello 1863, Providencia, Santiago ☎ 2/431-1000.

CUSTOMS & DUTIES

You may bring into Chile up to 400 cigarettes, 500 grams of tobacco, 50 cigars, two open bottles of perfume, 2.5 liters of alcoholic beverages, and gifts. Prohibited items include plants, fruit, seeds, meat, and honey. Spot checks take place at airports and border crossings. Visitors, although seldom questioned, are prohibited from leaving with handicrafts and souvenirs worth more than $500. You are generally prohibited from taking antiques out of the country without special permission.

ELECTRICITY

Unlike the United States and Canada—which have a 110- to 120-volt standard—the current in Chile is 220 volts, 50 cycles alternating current (AC). To use an appliance from home, bring a converter.

If your appliances are dual-voltage—as many laptops are these days—you'll need only an adapter. Don't use 110-volt outlets, marked FOR SHAVERS ONLY, for high-wattage appliances such as hair dryers.

EMERGENCIES

The numbers to call in case of emergency are the same all over Chile.
🚑 **Ambulance** ☎ 131. **Fire** ☎ 132. **Police** ☎ 133.

FESTIVALS & SEASONAL EVENTS

The Festival Foclórico (Folklore Festival) is held in Santiago during the fourth week of January. From the end of the month through early February, Semanas Musicales (Music Weeks) in the Lake District town of de Frutillar bring virtuoso performances of classical music. The Lake District town of Villarrica hosts the Muestra Cultural Mapuche (Mapuche Cultural Show) from January 3 to February 28. Fiestas Costumbristas, a celebration of Chilote customs and folklore, take place over several weekends during January and February in the Chiloé towns of Ancud and Castro.

The annual Festival Internacional de la Canción (International Song Festival) takes place over a week in mid-February in Viña del Mar. February 9 is the beginning of the two-month-long Verano en Valdivia, a favorite celebration for those living in the Lake District. It culminates with a spectacular fireworks display. The four-day Fiesta de la Vendimia, the annual grape harvest festival, takes place in the Central Valley town of Curico the first weekend in March.

Semana Santa, or Holy Week, is popular all over Chile. Different events are held each day between Palm Sunday and Easter Sunday. In Valparaíso, colorful processions mark the Día de San Pedro (St. Peter's Day) on June 29. A statue of the patron saint of fishermen is paraded through town. On September 18, Fiestas Patrias (patriotic festivals) take place all over the country to mark National Independence Day. The most fun is around Rancagua, in the Central Valley, where you'll find hard-fought rodeo competitions. November 1 is Todos los Santos (All Saints' Day), when Chileans traditionally tend to the graves of relatives. It's followed November 2 by Día de los Muertos (All Souls' Day). In November, the Chilean wine industry shows off the fruits of its hard labor at the annual Feria International de Vino del Hemisferio Sur in Santiago.

HEALTH

From a health standpoint, Chile is one of the safer countries in which to travel. To be on the safe side, take the normal precautions you would traveling anywhere in South America.

In Santiago there are several large private *clinicas* (clinics), and many doctors can speak at least a bit of English. In most other large cities there are one or two private clinics where you can be seen quickly. Generally, *hospitales* (hospitals) are for those receiving free or heavily subsidized treatment, and they are often crowded with long lines of patients waiting to be seen.

ALTITUDE SICKNESS
Altitude sickness—which causes shortness of breath, nausea, and splitting headaches—may be a problem when you visit Andean countries. The best way to prevent *soroche* is to **ascend slowly.** Spend a few nights at 6,000–9,000 ft before you head higher. If you must fly straight in, plan on doing next to nothing for your first few days. The traditional remedy is herbal tea made from coca leaves. Over-the-counter analgesics and napping also help. If symptoms persist, return to lower elevations. Note that if you have high blood pressure and/or a history of heart trouble, check with your doctor before traveling to the mountains.

FOOD & DRINK
Visitors seldom encounter problems with drinking the water in Chile. Almost all drinking water receives proper treatment and is unlikely to produce health problems. If you have any doubts, stick to bottled water. Mineral water is good and comes carbonated (*con gas*) and noncarbonated (*sin gas*).

Food preparation is strictly regulated by the government, so outbreaks of food-borne diseases are very rare. But it's still a good idea to use the same common-sense rules you would in any other part of South America. Don't risk restaurants where the hygiene is suspect or street vendors where the food is allowed to sit around unrefrigerated. Always **avoid raw shellfish,** such as ceviche. Remember to steer clear of raw fruits and vegetables unless you know they've been thoroughly washed and disinfected.

SHOTS & MEDICATIONS
All travelers to Chile should get up-to-date tetanus, diphtheria, and measles boosters, and a hepatitis A inoculation is recommended. Children traveling to Chile should have current inoculations against mumps, rubella, and polio. Always check with your doctor about which shots to get.

According to the Centers for Disease Control and Prevention, there's no risk of contracting malaria, but a limited risk of cholera, typhoid, hepatitis B, dengue, and Chagas. While a few of these you could catch anywhere, most are restricted to jungle areas. The best way to avoid these diseases is to prevent insect bites by wearing long pants and long-sleeve shirts and by using insect repellents with DEET. If you plan to visit remote regions or stay for more than six weeks, **check with the CDC's International Travelers Hot Line.**

 Health Warnings **National Centers for Disease Control and Prevention (CDC)** ✉ National Center for Infectious Diseases, Division of Quarantine, Travelers' Health, 1600 Clifton Rd. NE, Atlanta, GA 30333 ☎ 877/394-8747 international travelers' health line, 800/311-3435 other inquiries 🖷 888/232-3299 ⊕ www.cdc.gov/travel.

HOLIDAYS
New Year's Day (Jan. 1), Labor Day (May 1), Day of Naval Glories (May 21), Corpus Christi (in June), Feast of St. Peter and St. Paul (June 29), Independence Celebrations (Sept. 18), Discovery of the Americas (Oct. 12), Day of the Dead (Nov. 1), Immaculate Conception (Dec. 8), Christmas (Dec. 25).

Many shops and services are open on most of these days, but transportation is always heavily booked up on and around the holidays. The two most important dates in the Chilean calendar are September 18 and New Year's Day. On these days shops close and public transportation is reduced to the bare minimum or is nonexistent. Trying to book a ticket around these dates will be impossible unless you do it well in advance.

LANGUAGE

Chile's official language is Spanish, so it's best to learn at least a few words and carry a good phrase book. Chilean Spanish is fast, clipped, and chock-full of colloquialisms. For example, the word for police officer isn't *policía,* but *carabinero.* Even foreigners with a good deal of experience in Spanish-speaking countries may feel like they are encountering a completely new language. However, receptionists at most upscale hotels speak English.

MAIL & SHIPPING

Postage on regular letters and postcards to Canada and the United States costs 250 pesos and 230 pesos, respectively. The postage to Australia, the United Kingdom, and New Zealand is 290 pesos for letters and postcards. The postal system is efficient and, on average, letters take five to seven days to reach the United States or Europe. Vendors often sell stamps at the entrances to larger post offices. If you want to save a potentially long wait in line, the stamps are valid, and selling them this way is legal.

MONEY MATTERS

The peso ($) is the unit of currency in Chile. Chilean bills are issued in 1,000, 2,000, 5,000, 10,000, and 20,000 pesos (some 500-peso bills are still in circulation); coins come in units of 1, 5, 10, 50, 100, and 500 pesos. Note that acquiring change for larger bills, especially from small shopkeepers, can be difficult. Make sure to get smaller bills when you exchange money. Note that some banks will not convert traveler's checks in U.S. dollars into pesos (though this is usually not a problem at casas de cambio), so you may want to order your traveler's checks in pesos.

At press time the exchange rate was approximately 445 pesos to the Australian dollar, 490 pesos to the Canadian dollar, 720 pesos to the U.S. dollar, 1,125 pesos to the British pound, and 394 pesos to the New Zealand dollar.

Credit cards are widely accepted in hotels, restaurants, and shops in most cities and tourist destinations. You should always carry some local currency, however, for minor expenses like taxis and tipping. Once you stray from the beaten path, you can often only pay with pesos.

ATMS   ATMs are widely available, and you can get cash with a Cirrus- or Plus-linked debit card or with a major credit card. Most ATMs in Chile have a special screen—accessed after entering your PIN code—for foreign-account withdrawals. In this case, merely selecting a "cash withdrawal" won't work—you need to access your account first via the "foreign client" option. Although ATM fees may be higher than back home, Cirrus and Plus offer excellent exchange rates because they are based on wholesale rates offered only by major banks.

Before leaving home, **make sure that your credit cards have been programmed for ATM use in Chile.** You may want to ask your bank about getting a debit card, which works like a bank card but can be used at any ATM displaying a MasterCard or Visa logo.

CREDIT CARDS   It may be easier to use your credit card whenever possible. The exchange rate only varies by a fraction of a cent, so you won't need to worry whether your purchase is charged on the day of purchase or at some point in the future. Note, however, that you may get a slightly better deal if you pay with cash.

TRAVELER'S   Do you need traveler's checks? It depends on where you're headed. If CHECKS   you're going to rural areas and small towns, go with cash; traveler's checks are best used in cities. Lost or stolen checks can usually be replaced within 24 hours. To ensure a speedy refund, buy your own traveler's checks—don't let someone else pay for them: irregularities like this can cause delays. The person who bought the checks should make the call to request a refund.

Note that some banks will not convert traveler's checks in U.S. dollars into pesos (though this is usually not a problem at casas de cambio), so you may want to order your traveler's checks in pesos.

PASSPORTS & VISAS
Citizens of the United States, Canada, Australia, New Zealand, and the United Kingdom need only a passport to enter Chile for up to three months. Upon arrival in Chile, you will be given a flimsy piece of paper that is your three-month tourist visa. This has to be handed in when you leave; because getting a new one involves waiting in many lines and a lot of bureaucracy, put it somewhere safe.

Before traveling, make two photocopies of your passport's data page (one for someone at home and another for you to carry separately from your passport). While sightseeing in Chile it's best to carry the copy of your passport and leave the original in your hotel's safe. If you lose your passport promptly call the nearest embassy or consulate and the local police.

SAFETY
Areas frequented by tourists are generally safe, provided you use common sense. Wherever you go, don't wear expensive clothing, don't wear flashy jewelry, and don't handle money in public. It's a good idea to keep your money in a pocket rather than a wallet, which is easier to steal. On buses and in crowded areas, hold purses or handbags close to the body; thieves use knives to slice the bottom of a bag and catch the contents as they fall out. Keep cameras in a secure bag. Always remain alert for pickpockets, and don't walk alone at night, especially in the larger cities.

TAXES
An 18% value-added tax (VAT, called IVA here) is added to the cost of most goods and services in Chile; often you won't notice because it's included in the price. When it's not, the seller gives you the price plus IVA. At many hotels you may receive an exemption from the IVA if you

pay in American dollars or traveler's checks; some also offer this discount if you use an American Express card.

TELEPHONES

To dial a local or international number from any phone, you first dial the three-digit number of the carrier you want to use. Then dial 0, followed by the country code, the area or city code, and the phone number.

AREA &
COUNTRY CODES
The country code for Chile is 56. When dialing a Chilean number from abroad, drop the initial 0 from the local area code.

INTERNATIONAL
CALLS
From Chile the country code is 01 for the United States and Canada, 061 for Australia, 064 for New Zealand, and 044 for the United Kingdom.

You can reach directory assistance in Chile by calling 103. English-speaking operators are not available.

An international call at a public phone requires anywhere from a 400- or 500-peso deposit (depending on the phone box), which will give you anywhere between 47 and 66 seconds of talking time. You can call the United States for between 39 and 76 seconds (depending on the carrier you use) for 200 pesos.

If you plan to call abroad while in Chile, it's in your best interest to buy a local phone card (sold in varying amounts at kiosks and calling centers) or use a calling center (*centro de llamadas*). For calls to the United States, EntelTicket phone cards, available in denominations of 1,000, 3,000, and 5,000 pesos, are the best deal. Regular phone cards cost about a dollar a minute; the EntelTicket costs about 25¢ a minute.

LOCAL CALLS
A 100-peso piece is required to make a local call in a public phone booth, allowing 110 seconds of conversation between the hours of 9 AM and 8 PM, and 160 seconds of talk from 8 PM to 9 AM. Prefix codes are not needed for local dialing. To call a cell phone within Chile you will need to insert 200 pesos in a phone box. If you will only be making a few local calls, it's not necessary to purchase a phone card.

Most public phones allow you to make several calls in succession, provided you don't hang up in between: there's a special button to push—marked with an R—that cuts off one call and starts another. Some phones also include English-language instructions, accessed by pressing a button marked with a flag icon.

Instead of using a public phone, you can pay a little more and use a *centro de llamadas,* small phone shops divided into booths. The number is dialed for you. For this service you pay an additional charge.

LONG-DISTANCE
SERVICES
AT&T, MCI, and Sprint access codes make calling long-distance relatively convenient, but you may find the local access number blocked in many hotel rooms. First ask the hotel operator to connect you. If the hotel operator balks, ask for an international operator, or dial the international operator yourself. One way to improve your odds of getting connected to your long-distance carrier is to travel with more than one company's calling card (a hotel may block Sprint, for example, but not MCI). If all else fails, call from a pay phone.

TIPPING
The usual tip, or *propina*, in restaurants is 10%. Leave more if you really enjoyed the service. City taxi drivers don't usually expect a tip because most own their cabs. However, if you hire a taxi to take you around a city, you should consider giving a good tip. Hotel porters should be tipped at least 800 pesos. Also give doormen and ushers about 800 pesos. Beauty- and barber-shop personnel generally get around 5%.

VISITOR INFORMATION
The national tourist office Sernatur (Servicio Nacional de Turismo) has branches in Santiago and in major tourist destinations around the country. Sernatur offices, often the best source for general information about a region, are generally open daily from 9 to 6, with lunch generally from 2 to 3. Municipal tourist offices, often located near a central square, usually have better information about their town's sights, restaurants, and lodging. Many have shorter hours or close altogether during low season, however.

🔢 Tourist Information **Sernatur main office** ⊠ Providencia 1550, Providencia, Santiago ☎ 2/731-8336 or 2/731-8337 ⊕ www.sernatur.cl.

WHEN TO GO
Chile's seasons are the reverse of North America's—that is, June–August is Chile's winter. Tourism peaks during the hot summer months of January and February, except in Santiago, which tends to empty as most Santiaguinos take their summer holiday. Though prices are at their highest, it's worth braving the summer heat if you're interested in lying on the beach or enjoying the many concerts, folklore festivals, and out- door theater performances offered during this period.

CLIMATE If you're heading to the Lake District or Patagonia and want good weather without the crowds, the shoulder seasons of December and March are the months to visit. The best time to see the Atacama Desert is late spring, preferably in November, when temperatures are bearable and air clarity is at its peak. In spring Santiago blooms, and the fragrance of the flowers distracts even the most avid workaholic. A second tourist season occurs in the winter, as skiers flock to Chile's mountaintops for some of the world's best skiing, available at the height of northern sum- mers. Winter smog is a good reason to stay away from Santiago during July and August, unless you're coming for a ski holiday and won't be spending much time in the city.

The following are the average daily maximum and minimum tempera- tures for Santiago.

Jan.	85F	29C	May	65F	18C	Sept.	66F	19C
	53	12		41	5		42	6
Feb.	84F	29C	June	58F	14C	Oct.	72F	22C
	52	11		37	3		45	7
Mar.	80F	27C	July	59F	15C	Nov.	78F	26C
	49	9		37	3		48	9
Apr.	74F	23C	Aug.	62F	17C	Dec.	83F	28C
	54	7		39	4		51	11

The following are the average daily maximum and minimum temperatures for Punta Arenas.

Jan.	58F	14C	May	45F	7C	Sept.	46F	8C
	45	7		35	2		35	2
Feb.	58F	14C	June	41F	5C	Oct.	51F	11C
	44	7		33	1		38	3
Mar.	54F	12C	July	40F	4C	Nov.	54F	12C
	41	5		31	0		40	4
Apr.	50F	10C	Aug.	42F	6C	Dec.	57F	14C
	39	4		33	1		43	6

COLOMBIA

5

GET YOUR MIDAS TOUCH ON
at Bogotá's Museo de Oro ⇨*p.474*

BOOK AN UNCONVENTIONAL CONVENT
Cartagena's Santa Clara hotel ⇨*p.494*

BE DAZZLED BY THE WORK OF NUNS
at Bogotá's Iglesia Museo Santa Clara ⇨*p.474*

SEE REAL THUMBSCREWS
at Cartegena's Palacio de la Inquisición ⇨*p.493*

SUP AT A NATIONAL MONUMENT
Bogotá's Casa Medina ⇨*p.480*

Updated by
Erik Riesenberg

COLOMBIA IS BLESSED IN MANY WAYS. Its regal location on the continent's northern tip makes it the only South American country that fringes both the Atlantic and Pacific. It's rich in emeralds, coffee, and oil. And, because it straddles the equator, it's one of the lushest countries in terms of tropical flora and wildlife—there are more species of birds in Colombia than anywhere else in the world. You can jump on a plane and in less than an hour find yourself in a different dramatic setting—be it the cobblestone streets of a weathered colonial port, the stalls of a crowded market where Guambiano merchants still speak the tongues of their ancestors, or at the base of snow-covered peaks rising sharply from a steamy coastal plain.

Bogotá, Colombia's sprawling capital of more than 7 million people, stands at the end of a vast plateau in the eastern Andes. The poverty and drug violence make the headlines, but rarely covered by the media are the elegant shopping streets, grand high-rises, lovely colonial neighborhoods, and chic nightclubs where stylish young *Bogotanos* (as inhabitants of Bogotá are called) party well into the night.

Most of the country's 39 million people live in Colombia's western half, where the Andes splits into three *cordilleras,* or ridges: Oriental, Central, and Occidental. As you ascend the mighty mountains, subtropical valleys give way to rigid, fern-carpeted peaks where the ever-present mists are brightened only by votive candles placed by truck drivers at roadside shrines. West of Bogotá, quiet villages hug the hillsides en route to Medellín, former base of the eponymous drug cartel of Pablo Escobar. Despite its notorious reputation, Medellín is a pleasant, relatively safe, modern city surrounded by velvety green hills and miles of lush farmland.

Cartagena, widely revered as the most striking colonial city in South America, is an excellent destination if you want to be on the Caribbean coast. If you equate vacationing with lounging in the sun, the beaches of San Andrés and Providencia islands are Colombia's most compelling. Undeterred by the 640-km (400-mi) trip from the mainland, Colombians escape to the resort islands for weekends of swimming, sunbathing, shopping, and sipping rum at thatch-roof waterfront bars.

Before the arrival of the Spanish, Colombia was sparsely inhabited by indigenous peoples. High in the Andes, the Muisca were master goldsmiths who may have sparked the myth of El Dorado with their tradition of anointing a new chief by rolling him in gold dust. The legend of El Dorado was an irresistible attraction for a host of European adventurers in search of gilded cities.

The Spanish settled in the region as early as 1510, but it wasn't until conquistador Rodrigo de Bastidas founded the port town of Santa Marta in 1525 that a permanent settlement was established in what is now known as Colombia. He banned the exploitation of the indigenous peoples, but those who followed him had other plans. Explorers like Gonzalo Jiménez de Quesada plundered and pillaged their way inland. After quickly dispatching the local Muisca tribes, he established a Spanish settlement in what is now Bogotá.

Despite their near decimation at the hands of brutal Europeans, Colombia's native peoples have left a lasting mark on the country. The extraordinary carved stones in the southwestern settlement of San Agustín speak of empires once rich in gold, emeralds, and the technological skills necessary to erect statues honoring long-forgotten gods. In the Andes and on the coastal plains you'll find modern descendants of these lost tribes living a life unchanged since Cristóbal Colón (better known as Christopher Columbus) presumptuously claimed Colombia in the name of King Ferdinand of Spain.

Colombians express with some pride that they live in the oldest democracy in Latin America. Colombia has enjoyed a constitutionally elected government for nearly all of its history. This has not, however, brought stability to the country, and guerrilla activity has echoed in the countryside since the 1940s. The rise of drug trafficking in the last 25 years has exacerbated the ongoing civil conflict that now involves the government, left-wing guerrillas, and right-wing paramilitary groups. Although the large-scale car bombings and other acts of terrorism that plagued Bogotá and Medellín a decade ago seem like a thing of the past, occasional political assassinations are grim reminders of the violence that is all too common in many parts of the country. Plans to create jobs and expand Colombian tourism are in the works, and while neither can remedy the country's safety issues, they may help to alleviate some conditions that contribute to crime. In 2002 President Alvaro Uribe met with guerrilla leaders to discuss a plan for peace. Although it hasn't brought about immediate progress, this attempt seems to indicate an active desire for reconciliation.

About the Restaurants

From the hearty stews served in the highlands to the seafood soups ladled out along the Caribbean coast, you'll find distinctive regional cuisine everywhere. Beef is popular everywhere—as steaks or in shish kebabs or stews—as is chicken. Bogotá's most traditional dish is *ajiaco,* a thick chicken and potato soup garnished with capers, sour cream, and avocado. On the Caribbean coast, you're more likely to dip your spoon into a *cazuela de mariscos,* a seafood soup with cassava. On the islands of San Andrés and Providencia, the local favorite is *rendón,* a soup made of fish and snails slowly simmered in coconut milk with yucca, plantains, breadfruit, and dumplings.

Restaurants in many cities often close for a few hours between lunch and dinner (roughly 3 to 6). Plan your mealtimes in advance. Appropriate attire in restaurants is comparable to U.S. or European standards—dressy for the more formal places, casual everywhere else.

WHAT IT COSTS In Pesos				
	$$$$	**$$$**	**$$**	**$**	**¢**
AT DINNER	over 40,000	25,000– 40,000	15,000– 25,000	10,000– 15,000	under 10,000

Prices are per person for a main course at dinner.

About the Hotels

Prices and standards at high-end hotels in Bogotá are usually comparable to those in North America. Outside of the capital, even in such tourist towns as Cartagena and San Andrés, rates for hotel rooms are surprisingly low. Consider staying at small, locally owned hotels where you're more likely to experience Colombian hospitality.

	WHAT IT COSTS In Pesos				
	$$$$	**$$$**	**$$**	**$**	**¢**
FOR 2 PEOPLE	over 360,000	280,000–360,000	200,000–280,000	100,000–200,000	under 100,000

Prices are for two people in a standard double room in high season, excluding tax.

Exploring Colombia

The extremes of Colombia's varied topography are epitomized by the cool temperatures of the highlands around Bogotá and the warm weather of the coast near Cartagena. Medellín lies somewhere between those two contrasting areas.

TIMING &
PRECAUTIONS
Recent developments in both the drug trade and the decades-old civil conflict have made travel outside of most major cities more risky than before. We consider travel to Cali and Popayán too dangerous, and so in this edition we are not covering those cities. Medellín, too, can be sketchy, so check with the local police or with your embassy before making overland excursions there or anywhere else. If you must travel by car in these regions, do so in the daytime, and rent a car with a driver, rather than trying to drive yourself.

BOGOTÁ

Bogotá, as it's officially named, is a city of contrasts. Here you find modern shopping malls and open-air markets, high-rise apartments and makeshift shanties, futuristic glass towers and colonial churches. Simultaneous displays of ostentatious wealth and shocking poverty have existed here for centuries. In the neighborhood of La Candelaria, a rich assemblage of colonial mansions grandly conceived by the Spanish were built by native peoples and financed by plundered gold.

Bogotá, a city of more than 7 million people, has grown twentyfold in the past 50 years. It suffers the growing pains typical of any major metropolis on the continent (insufficient public transportation, chronic air pollution, petty crime) and a few of its own (a scurrilous drug trade and occasional acts of political violence). However, recent mayors have made some progress in cleaning up parks, resurfacing roads, and implementing a new transportation system. In fact, a recent survey indicates that while a majority of Bogotanos feel that the political situation is worsening in Colombia, conditions are improving in Bogotá.

Spanish conquistadors built their South American cities in magnificent locations, and Bogotá, which stands on a high plain in the eastern

If you have
5 days

Start in **Bogotá** and spend two days exploring the museums and monuments, and the historic Candelaria district. On your third day visit **Sopó**, a scenic one-hour drive north of Bogotá, to appreciate the rural Andean region. Don't miss the chance to fly to the walled city of **Cartagena** for several days before returning to Bogotá.

If you have
7 days

Follow the five-day itinerary above, then take a two-day excursion to the **Islas del Rosario** before flying back to Bogotá. Alternately, if you're here in March, fly to Medellín for its annual flower festival, during the second week of March.

5

If you have
10 days

Follow the seven-day itinerary above, then head to a Caribbean resort on the islands of **San Andrés** or **Providencia** for a few nights before returning to Bogotá.

Andes, is no exception. During his disastrous search for the legendary El Dorado, Gonzalo Jiménez de Quesada, the Spanish explorer on whom Miguel de Cervantes reputedly modeled Don Quixote, was struck by the area's natural splendor and its potential for colonization. Though it's a mere 1,288 km (800 mi) from the equator, Bogotá's 8,700-foot altitude lends it a refreshing climate. Jiménez de Quesada discovered one of South America's most advanced pre-Columbian peoples, the Muisca. But they were no match for the Spaniards. On August 6, 1538, Jiménez de Quesada christened his new conquest Santa Fé de Bogotá, on the site where the Muisca village of Bacatá once stood.

Bogotá rapidly became an important administrative center and in 1740 was made the capital of the Viceroyalty of New Granada, an area comprising what is now Colombia, Venezuela, Ecuador, and Panama. With its new status, grand civic and religious buildings began to spring up, often with the hand-carved ceilings and sculpted doorways that were the hallmark of New Granada architecture. But by 1900 Bogotá was still a relatively small city of 100,000. It was not until the 1940s that rapid industrialization and the consequent peasant migration to urban centers spurred Bogotá's exponential growth.

Exploring Bogotá

Numbers in the text correspond to numbers in the margins and on the Bogotá map.

As you tour the city, take a taxi whenever possible—don't be carefree about strolling around, even during the day, or about lingering in places at night—it's simply not safe to do so. Keep in mind that *carreras* (roads) run north–south and *calles* (streets) run east–west. You'll probably spend much of your time in the charming neighborhood of La Candelaria. To the north of La Candelaria is the downtown area, which is seedy but holds a handful of bars and restaurants, mostly in La Macarena.

Farther uptown and marked by towering office buildings is the Centro Internacional, the city's financial center. To the north is the leafy Zona Rosa, a popular shopping district anchored by an upscale shopping mall called Centro Andino. Farther north along the Carrera 7, at Calle 116, is Hacienda Santa Barbara, another high-end shopping mall built as an extension of an old mansion. A few blocks north of Hacienda Santa Barbara is the plaza of Usaquén, an Andean village that became a neighborhood as Bogotá grew but still maintains its small-town manner.

La Candelaria

At the foot of Guadalupe Peak is Bogotá's oldest neighborhood, La Candelaria, a historic neighborhood of narrow streets lined with astounding colonial structures. It's packed with lovely mansions and exquisite churches. Most of the city's finest museums are found here.

WHAT TO SEE **Biblioteca Luis Angel Arango.** The modern Luis Angel Arango Library sponsors frequently changing international art exhibits. It is also known for its occasional chamber music concerts, which are listed in the local newspapers. ⊠ *Calle 11 No. 4–14, La Candelaria* ☎ *091/343–1212* ⊕ *www.banrep.gov.co/blaa/home.htm* ☑ *Free* ☉ *Library Mon.–Sat. 8–8, Sun. 10–4.*

Casa de la Moneda. The former national mint displays coins whose gold content was secretly reduced by the king of Spain, slugs made by revolutionaries from empty cartridges, and currency minted for use exclusively in Colombia's former leper colonies. This museum is part of the complex that houses the Donación Botero and the Colección Permanente de Artes Plásticas. ⊠ *Calle 11 No. 4–93, La Candelaria* ☎ *091/286–3570, 091/342–1111 Ext. 1358 and 1369* ⊕ *www.banrep.gov.co* ☑ *Free* ☉ *Mon. and Wed.–Fri. 10–8, Sat. 10–7, Sun. 10–4.*

Cerro de Monserrate. Although dense smog often obscures the skyline, the view of chaotic Bogotá from Monserrate Hill is still breathtaking. The panorama extends from the Río Bogotá to La Candelaria, whose red Spanish tiles make it easy to spot, especially in the early morning. On exceptionally clear days it is possible to see the snow-covered mountains of the Cordillera Central, some 300 km (188 mi) away. The church on top of Monserrate houses an image of the Fallen Christ that is a popular destination for pilgrims. The *teleférico* (cable car) or the tram leaves every half hour from Monserrate Station near Quinta de Bolívar for the 15-minute journey to the peak. Avoid the hour-long trek up a winding footpath except on Sunday, when it is crowded with pilgrims. Robberies have become all too common. ⊠ *Carrera 2E No. 21–48, La Candelaria* ☎ *091/284–5700* ☑ *8,000 pesos for cable car or tram* ☉ *Mon.–Sat. 10–midnight, Sun. 10–4.*

Colección Permanente de Artes Plásticas. This large collection, in the same complex as the Donación Botero, is an overview of Colombian art from the colonial period to the present, including works by such noted artists as Alejandro Obregón, Luis Caballero, and Débora Arango. ⊠ *Calle 11 No. 4–41, La Candelaria* ☎ *091/343–1340* ⊕ *www.banrep.gov.co* ☑ *Free* ☉ *Mon. and Wed.–Fri. 10–8, Sat. 10–7, Sun. 10–4.*

5

Archaeological Treasures
Several archaeological sites and many priceless artifacts testify to the cultural richness that thrived in the country before European domination. For a sojourn into Colombia's past, duck into Bogotá's Museo de Oro to see the world's largest collection of pre-Columbian gold, and a comprehensive collection of pre-Columbian artifacts from indigenous cultures, including the Muisca, Nariño, Calima, and Sinú. Here you'll also see the largest uncut emerald in the world. Also in Bogotá is the Museum of Archaeology, which houses splendid pre-Columbian ceramics.

Beaches
The country's favorite beaches are found along the northern coast and on the Caribbean islands of San Andrés and Providencia. These resort islands have gorgeous white-sand beaches that stretch along the coast for miles, and the water is crystal clear. Cartagena's beach is popular with locals, and gets to be quite a scene, especially during holidays.

Colonial Charm
The magnificent walled city of Cartagena, the crown jewel of Colombia's colonial heritage, is one of the most historically important and beautiful cities of the Americas. People say that the Ciudad Amurallada, as the old city is called, looks more Spanish than Spain. Cartagena was founded in 1533 by the Spanish conquistador Pedro de Heredia. At the time, Cartagena was the only port on the South American mainland, and much gold and silver looted from indigenous peoples passed through here en route to Spain. Bogotá's Candelaria neighborhood is another haven of colonial architecture, with massive churches and sprawling mansions that now house hotels, museums, and restaurants.

---

⑧ **Donación Botero.** In 2000, world-famous artist Fernando Botero made
FodorśChoice headlines when he donated dozens of works from his private collection
★ to Colombia. Botero's artwork interprets his subjects from a distinctly Latin-American standpoint—Colombians affectionately refer to him as "the man who paints fat people." Many of his subjects are well known in Colombia, especially in his native Medellín. The collection includes 123 of his own paintings, sculptures, and drawings. Equally impressive, however, are his donation of 85 original works of renowned European and North American artists. This part of the collection, practically a review of art history since the late 19th century, includes original pieces by Corot, Monet, Matisse, Picasso, Dalí, Chagall, Bacon, and de Kooning. ✉ *Calle 11 No. 4–41, La Candelaria* ☎ *091/343–1340* ⊕ *www. banrep.gov.co* ✆ *Free* ☉ *Mon. and Wed.–Fri. 10–8, Sat. 10–7, Sun. 10–4.*

⑪ **Iglesia de San Francisco.** The 16th-century Church of St. Francis is famous for its fabulous Mudéjar interior, carved with geometric designs borrowed from Islamic tradition. Its huge gilded altar is shaped like an amphitheater and has shell-top niches. ✉ *Av. Jiménez at Carrera 7, La Candelaria* ☉ *Daily 8–6.*

⑫ Iglesia de la Tercera Orden. The intricate carvings on the mahogany altar at the Church of the Third Order are the most beautiful in Bogotá. A local myth claims that the completion of the altar so exhausted sculptor Pablo Caballero that he died a madman. ⊠ *Carrera 7 at Calle 16, La Candelaria* ☉ *Daily 8–6.*

② Iglesia Museo Santa Clara. The simple, unadorned facade of the 17th-century Church of St. Clara gives no hint of the dazzling frescoes—the work of nuns once cloistered here—that bathe the interior walls. The small museum has paintings and sculpture by various 17th-century artists. ⊠ *Carrera 8 No. 8–91, La Candelaria* ☎ *091/341–1009* ☒ *2,000 pesos* ☉ *Tues.–Fri. 9–5, weekends 10–4.*

Fodor'sChoice
★

⑤ Museo Arqueológico. This magnificent mansion, which houses the Museum of Archaeology, once belonged to the Marquís de San Jorge, a colonial viceroy infamous for his cruelty. Today it displays a large collection of pre-Columbian ceramics. ⊠ *Carrera 6 No. 7–43, La Candelaria* ☎ *091/282–0940* ☒ *1,000 pesos* ☉ *Mon.–Sat. 8:30–noon and 1–5.*

⑥ Museo de Arte Colonial. Renovations in 1999 helped preserve this 17th-century Andalusian-style mansion, home of the Museum of Colonial Art. In its substantial collection are paintings by Vasquez and Figueroa, 17th- and 18th-century furniture, and precious metalwork. ⊠ *Carrera 6 No. 9–77, La Candelaria* ☎ *091/286–6768 or 091/341–6017* ☒ *1,000 pesos* ☉ *Weekdays 9–5, weekends 10–4.*

④ Museo de Artes y Tradiciones Populares. A former Augustinian cloister dating from 1583, the Museum of Folk Art and Traditions is one of Bogotá's oldest surviving buildings. Displays include contemporary crafts made by Indian artisans from across the country. There's also a gift shop and a restaurant specializing in traditional Andean cooking. ⊠ *Carrera 8 No. 7–21, La Candelaria* ☎ *091/342–1266* ☒ *1,000 pesos* ☉ *Weekdays 9–5, Sat. 9:30–1 and 2–5.*

⑬ Museo de Oro. Bogotá's phenomenal Gold Museum contains a comprehensive collection of pre-Columbian artifacts. The museum's more than 34,000 pieces (in weight alone worth $200 million) were gathered—often by force—from indigenous cultures, including the Muisca, Nariño, Calima, and Sinú. Don't dismiss them as merely primitive; these works represent virtually all the techniques of modern goldsmithing. Most of the gold, and the largest uncut emerald in the world, is in the guarded top-floor gallery. English audio tours are available. ⊠ *Carrera 6 at Calle 16 (Parque Santander), La Candelaria* ☎ *091/343–1424* ⊕ *www.banrep.gov.co* ☒ *Tues.–Sat. 3,000 pesos; Sun. and holidays 1,500 pesos* ☉ *Tues.–Sat. 9–4:30, Sun. 10–4:30.*

Fodor'sChoice
★

③ Palacio de Nariño. The Presidential Palace had to be rebuilt in 1949 following its destruction during *El Bogotazo,* an uprising sparked by the assassination of Liberal leader Jorge Eliécer Gaitán. Although it's not open to the public, the guard outside is changed ceremoniously each day at 5 PM. ⊠ *Carrera 7 between Calles 7 and 8, La Candelaria.*

① Plaza de Bolívar. Surrounded by stately structures, this square marks the spot where Bogotá was declared the seat of New Granada's colonial gov-

Colombia

← SAN ANDRÉS AND PROVIDENCIA ISLANDS

Caribbean Sea

GUAJIRA

Riohacha

Sta. Marta

Barranquilla
PARQUE TAYRONA

Cartagena
La Ciudad Perdida

El Rodadero

Islas del Rosario

CESAR

Caracas

PANAMA

Lago de Maracaibo

VENEZUELA

MAGDALENA

SUCRE

Mompós

Gulf of Panama

Magangué

CORDOBA

NORTE DE SANTANDER

Orinoco R.

ANTIOQUIA

BOLIVAR

Cauca R.

Bucaramanga

ARAUCA

Medellín

SANTANADER

Pan-American Hwy.

Villa de Leyua

Paipa

PACIFIC OCEAN

RISARALDA

CALDAS

BOYACA

Tunja

CASANARE

CHOCO

QUINDIO

CUNDINAMARCA

Bogotá

Magdalena R.

Meta R.

VICHADA

Buenaventura

Buga

TOLIMA

Palmira

Neiva

COLOMBIA

Guaviare R.

VALLE

Cali

CAUCA

HUILA

GUANINIA

Popayán

Tierradentro

META

Silvia

GUAVIARE

San Agustín

NARIÑO

VAUPES

Ipiales

CORDILLERA CENTRAL

PUTUMAYO

CAQUETA

Caquetá R.

Quito

ECUADOR

Napo R.

AMAZONAS

Amazon R.

PERU

BRAZIL

0   200 miles

0   300 km

Bogotá

0   1 mile

0   1 km

Carrera 2

Carrera 3

Carrera 4

Carrera 5

Carrera 6

Carrera 7

Pasaje Rivas

Calle 13
Calle 12
Calle 11

Av. 10

LA CANDELARIA

Av. Caracas

Av. 84

Calle 3

Carrera 18

KEY

❶ *Exploring sights*

① *Hotels & restaurants*

ernment. Today it's popular with photographers snapping pictures, unemployed men intermittently snoozing and chatting, street theater groups performing for a few hundred pesos, and children who never seem to grow bored with chasing pigeons. The Capitolio Nacional, Alcaldía Municipal, and the Palacio de Justicia are not open to the public.

On the plaza's east side, the **Catedral Primada de Colombia** was completed three centuries after construction began in 1565 due to a series of misfortunes—including the disastrous earthquake of 1785. Its French Baroque facade is made from locally mined sandstone. The expansive windows give the immense interior a light, airy feel, even on one of Bogotá's many gray rainy-season days. The ornate altar with gold leaf over heavily carved wood sharply contrasts with the lack of ornamentation elsewhere. In one of the side chapels lies conquistador Gonzalo Jiménez de Quesada's tomb. The church is open Monday through Saturday. Next door in the **Capilla del Sagrario** is an exquisite *baldacchino*, a smaller version of the ornate covered altar found at St. Peter's in Rome. The Sanctuary Chapel, open daily, also has a splendid collection of paintings, including works by the Taller de Figueroa and Gregorio Vasquez. ⊠ *Between Carreras 7 and 8 at Calle 10, La Candelaria.*

🄬 **Quinta de Bolívar.** Simón Bolívar, the revolutionary hero who drove the Spanish from the northern half of the continent, passed the last years of his life in this rustic house with his mistress, Manuela Saenz. Built in 1800, it was donated to Bolívar in 1820 for his services to the fledgling republic. The house has a distinct Spanish flavor and a lovely garden. Gabriel García Márquez's 1989 novel, *The General in His Labyrinth,* portrays Bolívar's final years. ⊠ *Calle 20 No. 2–91, La Candelaria* ☎ *091/284–6819* 🎫 *3,000 pesos* ☉ *Tues.–Fri. 9–5, weekends 10–4.*

Centro Internacional

The city's financial center, Centro Internacional, lies to the north of La Candelaria. This district, built largely in the 1970s, is fringed by Parque de la Independencia and Parque Bavaria, welcome areas of green in a concrete jungle. Among the modern office buildings you'll find a few interesting museums and the city's Spanish-style bullring.

WHAT TO SEE **Iglesia San Diego.** This simple two-aisle church built by Franciscan
🄭 monks in the early 17th century once stood on a quiet hacienda on the outskirts of colonial Bogotá. Trees and pastures have been replaced by the towering offices of Bogotá's "Little Manhattan." Both the church and its beautiful statue of the Virgin of the Fields, with her crown of intricate gold and silver filigree work, are a homage to the city's bucolic past. You can visit only during services. ⊠ *Carrera 7 No. 26–37, Centro Internacional* ☎ *091/341–2476* 🎫 *Free* ☉ *Sun.–Fri. at 8, noon, 6, 6:30, 7, 7:30.*

🄯 **Museo de Arte Moderno.** The huge windows in the beautifully designed Museum of Modern Art create a marvelous sense of spaciousness. Peruse the changing exhibits of works by national and international artists. The bookstore stocks (rather pricey) English-language titles on Colombian and international painters. ⊠ *Calle 24 No. 6–00, Centro Internacional* ☎ *091/283–3109* 🎫 *5,000 pesos* ☉ *Tues.–Sun. 10–6.*

⑰ Museo Nacional. The striking building that houses the National Museum was a prison until 1946; some parts, particularly the narrow top-floor galleries, maintain a sinister air. Designed by English architect Thomas Reed, the museum is arranged to give you a history of Colombia. Everything from ancient artifacts to contemporary art is on display, including works by Fernando Botero and Alejandro Obregón. The first-floor gallery is devoted to changing national and international exhibitions. A café and bookstore were added in 1999. ⊠ *Carrera 7 No. 28–66, between Calles 28 and 29, Centro Internacional* ☎ *091/334–8366* ⊠ *3,000* ◷ *Tues. 10–8, Wed.–Sat. 10–6.*

⑯ Plaza de Toros Santamaría. Bogotá's bullring was designed by Rogelio Salmona in a traditional Andalusian style. For a free peek, the best time to visit is in the morning when you may see young *toreros* (bullfighters) polishing their skills. Bullfighting season is January through February, but small displays are held throughout the year. ⊠ *Carrera 7 at Calle 26, Centro Internacional* ◷ *Practice Mon.–Sat. mornings. Bullfights Jan.–Feb., Sun. at 3 PM.*

Where to Eat

Bogotá's phone book lists more than 1,000 restaurants, and the best offer first-class service and outstanding Colombian cuisine. The most traditional recipes aim to fill the belly and ward off the cold. Soups, such as ajiaco and *puchero* (with chicken, pork, beef, potato, yucca, cabbage, corn, and plantain and accompanied by rice and avocado) are common on local menus. Bogotanos like to start the day off with *santafereño*, a steaming cup of chocolate accompanied by a slab of cheese—you melt the cheese in the chocolate. Lunch is generally served between noon and 2. Restaurants open for dinner around 7, and the more upscale ones stay open until after midnight.

Colombian

$$–$$$ ✕ **Carbón de Palo.** Bogotá's premier grilled-meat restaurant is a favorite north-end meeting place of senior politicians and plutocrats. The menu is dominated by grilled steak, chicken, and pork, but excellent salads are served with great aplomb. Choose a seat in the delightful indoor patio full of hanging plants. On weekends, musicians serenade you with traditional Colombian music. ⊠ *Av. 19 No. 106–12* ☎ *091/214–0450* ⊟ *AE, DC, MC, V.*

$–$$ ✕ **Casa Vieja.** Offering typical Colombian dishes, Casa Vieja is known for the quality of its ajiaco. Dinner in this Belle Epoque–style restaurant is accompanied by antiques and artwork from Colombia's colonial past. Three locations serve the Candelaria, Centro Internacional, and the northern part of town. ⊠ *Av. Jiménez No. 3–63* ☎ *091/334–8908* ⊠ *Carrera 10 No. 26–60* ☎ *091/336–7818* ⊠ *Carrera 11 No. 89–08* ☎ *091/236–3421* ◷ *Closed Sun.* ⊟ *AE, MC, V.*

Eclectic

$$–$$$ ✕ **Pajares Salinas.** International dishes are the stars at one of Bogota's most highly rated restaurants. *Callos a la madrileña* (tripe stew in slightly spicy sauce) and other Spanish dishes are among the top choices.

The classically elegant dining room is decorated with works of art from around the world. ⊠ *Carrera 10 No. 96–08* ☎ *091/616–1524* ▭ *AE, DC, MC, V* ⊘ *Closed Sun.*

$–$$ ✕ **Romana Cafetería.** Reminiscent of a 1960s-era diner, this unpretentious eatery in La Candelaria serves an appropriate selection of sandwiches. Breakfast here is typically Colombian—hot chocolate with cheese and bread. ⊠ *Av. Jiménez No. 6–65* ☎ *091/334–8135* ▭ *DC, MC, V* ⊘ *Closed Sun.*

¢–$ ✕ **Café y Crêpes.** The alpine style of this place celebrates hiking and climbing in the great outdoors, but the mood inside is surprisingly intimate. You can sit on pillows in front of a fire and sip mulled wine. Both sweet and savory crepes are served. ⊠ *Carrera 16 No. 82–17* ☎ *091/236–2688* ⊠ *Diagonal 108 No. 9A–11* ☎ *091/214–5312* ▭ *AE, DC, MC, V* ⊘ *No lunch Sun.*

¢–$ ✕ **Crêpes and Waffles.** This is a unique chain of restaurants serving, of course, crepes and waffles, as well as a delicious selection of ice-cream desserts. Posters of Colombian artist Fernando Botero's works cover the walls. ⊠ *Centro Internacional Bavaria (Carrera 10 at Calle 28), Interior 2–33* ☎ *091/243–1620* ⊠ *Carrera 9 No. 73-33* ☎ *091/211–2530* ⊠ *Carrera 11 No. 85–79* ☎ *091/610–5298* ▭ *No credit cards.*

French

$$$–$$$$ ✕ **Casa Medina.** Chef Francisco Rodriguez prepares French dishes, such
Fodor'sChoice as medallions of trout smothered in fennel and onion, with aplomb. The
★ stately restaurant, built in 1945 as a private mansion, has been declared a national monument. The elegant dining rooms, strewn with antiques imported by aristocratic Bogotano families, each evoke a different European country. ⊠ *Carrera 7 No. 69A–22* ☎ *091/312–0299* 🖷 *091/312–3769* ⊕ *www.hoteles-charleston.com* ▭ *AE, DC, MC, V.*

Italian

$–$$ ✕ **El Patio.** None of the cutlery matches, the plates are a hodgepodge of styles, and the small dining room is crammed with tables, but all this simply adds to the restaurant's eccentric charm. Its great location a couple blocks from the Plaza de Toros Santamaría in the bohemian neighborhood of La Macarena doesn't hurt. Try one of the masterful salads or the delicious veal parmigiana. ⊠ *Carrera 4A No. 27–86* ☎ *091/282–6141* ▭ *DC, V* ⊘ *Closed Sun.*

$–$$ ✕ **Sol de Napoles.** Family recipes and fresh bread make this reasonably priced eatery a longtime favorite among Bogotanos. Try pasta topped with one of the sauces—the meaty Bolognesa and the spicy arrabiata are favorites, but even the "plain" is enormously satisfying. ⊠ *Calle 69 No. 11–58* ☎ *091/249–2186* ▭ *DC, MC, V* ⊘ *Closed Mon.*

Seafood

★ **$$$–$$$$** ✕ **Casa San Isidro.** Specializing in masterfully prepared seafood and white-glove service, Casa San Isidro would be worth the trip for the location alone. Perched 2,000 feet over Bogotá on top of the Cerro de Monserrate, you'll dine fireside as a pianist tickles the ivories on the baby grand. Sample the San Isidro lobster with squid and shrimp, and then wash it down with your choice of wine from a dozen different countries. But be sure to leave by midnight, Cinderella, before the last cable car returns to the streets below. ⊠ *Cerro de Monserrate* ☎ *091/281–9270 or 091/281–9309* ⊟ *AE, DC, MC, V* ☺ *Closed Sun.*

$$$–$$$$ ✕ **La Fragata.** With its slowly revolving dining room, this is one of the capital's more unusual restaurants. Somehow the dimly lit, dark-oak interior successfully conveys the sensibility of a 19th-century frigate. The lobster, crab, red snapper, and locally caught rainbow trout are satisfying but slightly overshadowed by the presentation. ⊠ *Calle 100 No. 8A–55, 12th fl.* ☎ *091/616–7461* ⊟ *AE, MC, V* ☺ *Closed Sun.*

Where to Stay

Many of Bogotá's better hotels are in the wealthy northern districts—the most alluring parts of the city, and also the safest (there are security guards on nearly every corner). If you want to soak up the color of the colonial buildings, or are on a tight budget, book a room in La Candelaria. No matter where you stay, avoid wandering the streets at night.

$$ ⊞ **Bogotá Royal.** In addition to modern rooms with good views, this hotel has everything corporate travelers need. The hotel is in Bogotá's World Trade Center in the north end of town, a short taxi ride from many office buildings but far from museums and other attractions. ⊠ *Av. 100 No. 8A–01* ☎ *091/634–1777* ☏ *091/218–3261* ⊕ *www.bogotaroyal. com* ⇆ *143 rooms* ⚐ *2 restaurants, in-room data ports, health club, sauna, 2 bars, meeting rooms* ⊟ *AE, DC, MC, V.*

$$ ⊞ **Hotel Tequendama.** One of Bogotá's oldest and most refined hotels is now part of the Inter-Continental chain. Its rooms lack character, but they have impressive city views. The hotel is in the Centro International, conveniently close to La Candelaria and most downtown offices. ⊠ *Carrera 10 No. 26–21* ☎ *091/382–0300* ☏ *091/282–2860* ⊕ *www.interconti. com* ⇆ *643 rooms* ⚐ *3 restaurants, room service, health club, hair salon, sauna, 2 bars, casino, parking, shops* ⊟ *AE, DC, MC, V.*

★ $–$$ ⊞ **Hotel de la Opera.** This pair of colonial buildings adjacent to the Teatro Colón in La Candelaria found new life as an elegant hotel. The sleek tile and polished hardwood floors throughout are remarkable, as is the chic furniture imported from Italy. The generously proportioned rooms have high ceilings and huge windows, and some have balconies that open out onto a quiet side street. The Mediterranean cuisine at the hotel's restaurant, La Scala, is wonderful. The Automatico bar is a great place to relax with a brandy. ⊠ *Calle 10 No. 5–72* ☎ *091/336–2066* ☏ *091/337–4617* ⊕ *www.hotelopera.com.co* ⇆ *29 rooms* ⚐ *2 restaurants, room service, minibars, bar, baby-sitting, laundry service, business services, car rental* ⊟ *AE, DC, MC, V.*

$ ⊞ **Casa Dann Carlton Bogotá.** In a residential neighborhood in northern Bogotá, this hotel has modern rooms and plenty of recreational facilities, including a heated pool (necessary in the cool Bogotá climate). Ask about the golf package, and you'll get to play a round of golf at the Club Pueblo Viejo in the suburb of Chia. Golfers swear they can drive the ball farther at this altitude. ⊠ *Calle 94 No. 19–71* ☎ *091/633–8777* ☏ *091/633–8810* ⇆ *203 rooms* ⚐ *Restaurant, room service, health club, sauna, concierge, bar* ⊟ *AE, DC, MC, V.*

★ $ ⊞ **Los Urapanes.** This intimate boutique hotel in the heart of the leafy Zona Rosa has understated but luxurious rooms. Business travelers will appreciate the three phone lines in each room. The adjoining Los Samanes restaurant is popular for its exquisitely presented Colombian cuisine. ⊠ *Carrera 13 No. 83–19* ☎ *091/218–1188 or 091/218–5065* 🖷 *091/218–1242* ⊕ *www.hotellosurapanes.com.co* 🛏 *32 rooms, 16 suites* ⚘ *Restaurant, cable TV, room service, in-room data ports, in-room safes, minibars, bar, baby-sitting, Internet, business services, meeting rooms, free parking* ⊟ *AE, DC, MC, V.*

¢ ⊞ **Hotel Ambala.** Rooms in this small inn are a bit cramped, but they're clean and comfortable. They also have plenty of creature comforts for a lodging in this price range: firm beds and baths with lots of hot water. Rooms on the street are brighter but can be noisy. ⊠ *Carrera 5 No. 13–46* ☎ *091/341–2376 or 091/281–7124* 🖷 *091/286–3693* 🛏 *24 rooms* ⚘ *Cable TV* ⊟ *V.*

Nightlife & the Arts

Nightlife

Bogotá's reputation for street crime hasn't put a damper on its ebullient nightlife. The two main partying areas are the Zona Rosa, between Calles 81 and 84 and Carreras 11 and 15, and the nearby Parque 93. There are also a handful of popular salsa bars in La Candelaria. The Zona Rosa and Parque 93 are safer than downtown, but you should travel there by taxi.

BARS & DANCE CLUBS **San Angel** (⊠ Carrera 11A No. 93B-12 ☎ 091/336–3139 or 091/622–6437) plays rumba at the chic Parque 93 on Thursday, Friday, and Saturday. Dance on the outdoor patio or in the spacious indoor atrium. **Charlotte's** (⊠ Calle 82 No. 12–51 ☎ 091/257–3508) is a busy Zona Rosa nightclub with an outdoor dance floor and blazing fireplaces to keep you warm. **Salomé Pagana** (⊠ Carrera 14A No. 82–16 ☎ 091/218–4076) has live music in an intimate environment. Dance to boleros on Tuesday, folk music on Wednesday, and Cuban salsa on Thursday.

The Arts

THEATERS Bogotá has a lively theater scene, though you'll miss a lot if you don't understand Spanish. Bogotá is justly proud of its enormous biannual **Ibero-American Theater Festival,** which fills the two weeks before Easter with performing arts. Theater troupes arrive from all over the world to perform in Bogotá's numerous theaters and public parks. Recent festivals have included everything from Australian acrobats to African dance troupes.

Teatro La Candelaria (⊠ Calle 12 No. 2–59 ☎ 091/281–4814) has produced experimental theater for more than a decade. **Teatro Nacional** (⊠ Calle 71 No. 10–25 ☎ 091/217–4577 or 091/235–8069) presents musicals and popular comedies. Tickets can be purchased in advance at the box office.

Sports & the Outdoors

Bullfighting

The bullfighting season is January and February, with occasional special events held during the rest of year. All are held at the Plaza de Toros

Santamaría near the Parque de la Independencia. Spanish toreros delight the crowds, but Colombia's homegrown bullfighters are also quite exceptional: Bogotá native Cesar Rincón was once the most popular torero in Spain (he has since retired to raise bulls on his own ranch). Tickets can be purchased at the bullring weekdays from 9 AM to 5 PM. You can also get tickets on Sunday before the festivities begin at 3 PM, but you may not be able to secure seats for the more popular fights. Prices range from 10,000 pesos to 400,000 pesos depending on where you are seated, since *sol* (sun) is cheaper than *sombra* (shade).

Hiking

Although there are very real security issues in Colombia, hiking clubs have thrived in Bogotá over the last decade. Do not attempt to hike anywhere on your own—you should only go on a guided hike. In the region of Boyacá, in which Bogotá is located, are many safe hikes following *caminos reales,* stone-paved paths often dating from colonial times. **Sal Si Puedes** (⊠ Carrera 7 No. 17–01 ☎ 091/283–3765) is the venerable dean of Bogotá's hiking clubs. Established in 1979, it offers day hikes every weekend, with longer two- and three-day excursions at least once a month. Hikes are rated according to difficulty and guides are certified by the government.

Soccer

Fútbol games are held on most Sunday at 3:45 PM and Wednesday at 8 PM at **El Campín** (⊠ Carrera 30, between Calles 53 and 63). There's no need to book ahead except when there's a match between the two most popular local teams—Santa Fé and Millionarios. Tickets are from 5,000 pesos to 30,000 pesos and can be purchased at the stadium.

Shopping

Bogotá's shops and markets stock all types of leather and wool goods designed for life on the high plains. Handwoven *ruanas* (ponchos) are popular; the natural oils in the wool make them almost impervious to rain. Colombian artisans also have a way with straw: *toquilla,* a tough native fiber, is used to make hats, shoes, handbags, and even umbrellas.

Markets

In the warren of stalls at the daily **Pasaje Rivas indoor market** (⊠ Carrera 10 at Calle 10) look for bargain-price ponchos, blankets, leather goods, and crafts. The **flea market** (⊠ Calle 24, ½ block east of Carrera 7) in the Centro Internacional takes over a parking lot alongside the Museo de Arte Moderno, on Sunday. It is a good place to hunt for antiques, handicrafts, and just plain junk. An upscale Sunday **flea market** (⊠ Carrera 7 No. 119B–33) in Usaquén has a good selection of high-quality local crafts.

Shopping Centers

Stylish boutiques dominate the chic **Centro Andino** (⊠ Carrera 11 No. 82–71 ☎ 091/636–0012), an anchor of the Zona Rosa since 1993. Tower Records, the only major chain store, is a good place to buy English-language magazines and newspapers. There's a U.S.-style food court and a movie theater on the fourth floor. Farther north is the upscale **Hacienda Santa Barbara** (⊠ Carrera 7 No. 115–60 ☎ 091/612–0388), constructed as an extension of a colonial-era plantation home. The massive **Unicentro Shopping Center** (⊠ Av. 15 No. 123–30 ☎ 091/213–8800) in Bogotá's affluent north is one of South America's largest air-conditioned malls and has a huge selection of stores.

Specialty Shops

ANTIQUES Antiques shops are found mainly in the northern districts of Chapinero, Chicó, and Usaquén. One of the best is **Anticuarios Gilberto F. Hernández** (⊠ Calle 79B No. 7–48 ☎ 091/249–0041 or 091/248–7572). The two branches of **Maria Cancino** (⊠ Calle 63 No. 9–54 ☎ 091/212–6353 ⊠ Calle 70A No. 4–78 ☎ 091/249–5454) stock both Colombian antiques and European pieces. A good bet for quality antiques in the Candelaria is **Almacen de Antiguedades Leonardo F.** (⊠ Carrera 4 No. 12–34 ☎ 091/334–8312).

EMERALDS Seventy percent of the world's emerald supply is mined in Colombia. Value depends on weight, color, clarity, brilliance, and cut, with octagonal cuts being the most valuable. Emerald dealers gather to make deals among themselves on the southwest corner of Carrera 7 and Avenida Jiménez during business hours Monday through Saturday. It's interesting to watch the haggling, but don't even think about joining in. Unless you know how to spot a fake you should buy only from a reputable dealer. There are countless jewelry shops in the Centro Internacional along Carreras 6 between Calles 10 and 13. **H. Stern** (⊠ Tequendama Hotel, Carrera 10 No. 26–21 ☎ 091/283–2819) sells all kinds of precious gems. In both the Centro Internacional and the Centro Comercial Andino is **Galeria Cano** (⊠ Edificio Bavaria, Carrera 13 No. 27–98 ☎ 091/336–3255 ⊠ Edificio Banco Mercantil, Carrera 12 No. 84–07 ☎ 091/635–0529). It sells emeralds as well as gold jewelry using striking pre-Columbian designs taken from the Museo de Oro.

HANDICRAFTS In the cloister of Las Aquas, a neighborhood just off La Candelaria, **Artesanías de Colombia** (⊠ Carrera 3 No. 18–60 ☎ 091/286–1766 or 091/277–9010) stocks everything from straw umbrellas to handwoven ponchos. The shop at the **Museo de Artes y Tradiciones Populares** (⊠ Carrera 8 No. 7–21 ☎ 091/342–1266) carries handmade items. **Artesanías El Zaque** (⊠ Centro Internacional, Carrera 10 No. 26–71 ☎ 091/342–7883 ⊠ Zona Rosa, Carrera 15 No. 74–73 ☎ 091/217–2108) offers especially good buys on hammocks. **El Balay** (⊠ Carrera 15 No. 75–63 ☎ 091/248–5833) stocks the city's widest selection of souvenirs from around Colombia.

Bogotá A to Z

AIR TRAVEL TO & FROM BOGOTÁ

Aeropuerto El Dorado, a 20-minute taxi ride northwest of downtown, has flights to national and international destinations. Avianca, Colombia's national airline, flies from Miami and New York. American and Copa fly here from Miami. Continental has flights through Houston, and Delta has flights through Atlanta. Domestic routes are covered by Aces, Aerorepública, Aires, Intercontinental de Aviación, and Satena.

🛪 Airports **Aeropuerto El Dorado** ☎ 091/413–9500.

🛪 Domestic Airlines **Aces** ⊠ Aeropuerto El Dorado ☎ 091/401-2237. **Aerorepública** ⊠ Calle 10 No. 27-51, Oficina 303 ☎ 091/342-7766. **Aires** ⊠ Aeropuerto El Dorado ☎ 091/413-8500. **Satena** ⊠ Carrera 10A No. 27-51, Suite 211 ☎ 091/423-8500.

🛪 International Airlines **American** ⊠ Carrera 7 No. 26-20 ☎ 091/343-2424. **Avianca** ⊠ Calle 16 No. 6-66 ☎ 091/410-1011. **Continental** ⊠ Carrera 7 No. 71-52, Torre B, Oficina 1101 ☎ 091/312-2565. **Copa** ⊠ Calle 100 No. 8A-49 ☎ 091/623-1566. **Delta** ⊠ Carrera 13A No. 89-53, Oficina 301 ☎ 091/257-5997, 091/610-2295, or 091/610-9626.

INTERNET

There are several Internet cafés in Bogotá. In the north part of the city, @de café.com is open weekdays 7:30–9:30, Saturday 10–8, and Sunday noon–7. Café Internet has similar hours but is closed Sunday. In the Centro Internacional, Bar Interactivo offers Internet access weekdays 7:30–9:30, Saturday 8–8, and Sunday noon–7.

🛈 Internet Cafés **@de café.com** ⊠ Carrera 15 No. 74-18 ☎ 091/211-6397. **Bar Interactivo** ⊠ Carrera 7 No. 26-72, Apt. 901 ☎ 091/562-6252. **Café Internet** ⊠ Calle 72 No. 10-03 Pasaje Comercial, Local 1-10 ☎ 091/248-5411 or 091/249-0309.

MAIL & SHIPPING

Bogotá's Avianca Post Office, on Carrera 7 across from the Iglesia La Tercera, is open weekdays 9:30–7 and Saturday 8–3.

🛈 Post Office **Avianca Post Office** ⊠ Carrera 7 No. 16-36.

MONEY MATTERS

Banco de la República, on Carrera 7, exchanges cash at good rates. It is open weekdays 9–3. Several banks on Carrera 10 around the Hotel Tequendama also handle foreign currency. Your hotel is probably the most convenient place to exchange money, although it will charge a higher fee. ATMs are located around the city, clustering around the Centro Internacional and inside the shopping centers in north Bogotá. They are on both the Cirrus and Plus networks; you don't need a 4-digit PIN number here—a PIN of any length should work.

🛈 Banks **Banco de la República** ⊠ Carrera 7 No. 14-78.

SAFETY

Despite the city's reputation, most crimes against tourists are of the purse-snatching and pickpocketing variety that can be avoided with a little common sense. Avoid displays of wealth, such as expensive jewelry or watches. Never accept any food or cigarettes from a stranger and be wary of any unknown person approaching you on the street, especially if they are well dressed and overly friendly. Don't be duped by people claiming to be plainclothes police officers who demand to "register" your money—they are almost certainly thieves. In case of such confrontations, you may want to hand over a $20 bill to quickly extricate yourself from the situation.

TAXIS

Taxis are required by law to have a meter—make sure your driver turns it on. The minimum charge is 3,000 pesos, plus 50 pesos per 80 meters (260 feet). Fares increase by about a third after dark. It is always safer to call a taxi, especially in the northern parts of Bogotá, where thieves masquerading as taxi drivers have robbed passengers they picked up on the street. The taxi companies will tell you the number of the taxi, and when you are picked up the taxi driver will ask you for the last two digits of the phone number from which you called.

TELEPHONES

There are coin-operated public phones on street corners and inside shopping malls, but they are not always reliable. Many shops have small public phones; with these, dial first and deposit a coin when the other party answers.

TIPPING

As in most of Colombia, you should leave a tip of about 10% in restaurants. Gratuity is often included; if it is not, the bill will say *servicio no incluido*. Tip doormen and people guarding your car at least 2,000 pesos for their services. Taxi drivers do not expect a tip.

TOUR OPERATORS

Aviatur is one of the country's largest and oldest travel agencies and organizes tours in and around Bogotá.

🚩 Tour Operators **Aviatur** ⊠ Calle 19 No. 4-62 ☎ 091/282-7111 or 091/286-5555.

VISITOR INFORMATION

The Vice Ministerio de Turismo has information on hotels, restaurants, and sights. It's open weekdays 9–5.

🚩**Vice Ministerio de Turismo** ⊠ Calle 28 No. 13A-15, 18th fl. ☎ 091/283-9927 📠 091/ 284-8618.

MEDELLÍN

Nestled in the narrow Aburrá Valley, this northwestern city of 2 million people is the capital of Antioquia. The industrious *paisas,* as natives of the province are called, built the successful coffee and textile industries that have enabled Medellín to prosper; today it's the second-largest city in Colombia. Modern and affluent, Medellín has the country's only elevated train system. The city also has several interesting museums, three respected universities, and wide, tree-lined boulevards. But Medellín also has thousands of impoverished citizens whose shanties appear on the city's edges.

Although local and international intervention has lessened the drug trade, the city remains violent and unpredictable. Exercise caution when touring Medellín day or night, and always stick to central areas.

Exploring Medellín

Medellín is the country's main industrial hub, but don't expect a city full of smoking chimneys: the factories are well outside of town. Deep-green mountains that rise sharply around the city provide a bold backdrop to the glass-and-concrete towers of its elegant financial district. Well-developed tourist facilities in the city proper testify to the region's relative economic strength. When visiting sights, remember that calles run east–west and carreras run north–south. Also be careful not to walk around after sunset, as the city can be quite dangerous.

What to See

Catedral Basílica Metropolitana. The Metropolitan Cathedral, whose ornate coffee-color facade soars above the Parque de Bolívar, is among Medellín's most striking buildings. Designed by the French architect Charles Carré and built in 1875, it's South America's largest cathedral and the third-largest brick building in the world. ⊠ *Carrera 48 No. 56–81* ☎ *094/513–2269* ☒ *Free* ☉ *Weekdays 7 AM–10 AM, Sat. 7 AM–12:30 PM, Sun. 7–noon and 2–5.*

Ermita de la Veracruz. Distinguishing the interior of the Veracruz Hermitage are its white walls and columns with gilded capitals. Just off a picturesque plaza, it's a quiet escape from Medellín's noisy streets. ⊠ *Calle 51 No. 52–58* ☎ *094/512–5095* ☒ *Free* ☉ *Daily 7–6.*

Jardín Botánico Joaquín Antonio Uribe. The botanical gardens have more than 500 plant species, an aviary with strikingly colored birds, and a huge greenhouse teeming with orchids. ⊠ *Carrera 52 No. 73–298* ☎ *094/211–5607 or 094/263–4059* ☒ *4,000 pesos* ☉ *Daily 9–5.*

Museo de Antioquia. The Antioquia Museum contains a large collection of paintings and sculptures by native son Fernando Botero and other well-known Colombian artists. Botero, known for depicting people and objects with a distinctive "thickness," donated part of his personal collection to the museum (the bulk of his gift went to Bogotá). ⊠ *Carrera 52A No. 51A–29* ☎ *094/251–3636* ☒ *3,000 pesos* ☉ *Tues.–Fri. 9:30–5:30, Sat. 9–2.*

Museo El Castillo. The 1930s gothic-inspired Castle Museum, whose beautiful French-style gardens consist of sweeping lawns and exuberant flower beds, was once the home of a powerful Medellín family. On display is their furniture and art collected from around the world. ⊠ *Calle 9 Sur No. 32–269* ☎ *094/266–0900* ☒ *3,000 pesos* ☉ *Weekdays 9–7, Sat. 9–5:30.*

Parque Berrío. This small cement plaza is overwhelmed by the city's elevated train, the only one of its kind in Colombia. Nearby is the colonial church of **Nuestra Señora de la Candelaria.** To the south, the Banco de la República building stands next to a huge female torso sculpted by native son Fernando Botero. On the bank's other side, a bronze fountain and marble monument honor Atanasio Girardot, an 18th-century champion for Colombian independence. ⊠ *Carrera 50, between Calles 50 and 51.*

Parque de Bolívar. Despite its location in the middle of crowded Medellín, this shady park has a generous amount of open space. In the evenings it's popular with young people who congregate on the steps of the nearby cathedral. ⊠ *Carrera 49 and Calle 54.*

Parque de las Esculturas. This small sculpture park near the peak of Cerro Nutibara is a maze of paths dotted with modern and traditional sculptures by Latin American artists. ⊠ *Cerro Nutibara.*

Pueblito Paisa. As you enter this reproduction of an old-time Antioquian village, you'll see a traditional town square with a small church, town hall, barbershop, school, and village store. For your present-day needs, it also has a small restaurant and several souvenir shops. ⊠ *Cerro Nutibara.*

Where to Eat

Traditional Antioquian cooking means hearty peasant fare—plenty of meat, beans, rice, and potatoes. But Medellín is full of high-quality restaurants where you'll find many cuisines. On the first Saturday of every month, the **Parque de las Delicias** (⊠ Carrera 73 and Av. 39D) is packed with food stalls selling everything from *obleas* (thin jam-filled waffles) to *lechona* (roast stuffed pork).

Colombian

$–$$ ✕ **El Hato Viejo.** Generous portions draw locals to this second-story restaurant just a block from the Parque de Bolívar. Waiters in Panama hats serve
Fodor'sChoice you on a balcony overflowing with plants or in the large dining room with
★ terra-cotta floors. Try the *sopa de guineo* (plantain soup) before sinking your teeth into *lomito* (tenderloin) or *langostinos* (lobsters). Finish your feast with *brevas con queso* (figs with white cheese). ⊠ *Pasaje Junín No. 52–17* ☎ *094/251–2196 or 094/231–1108* ▤ *AE, DC, MC, V.*

¢–$ ✕ **Aguas Claras.** Experience many Colombian dishes in one meal—the hearty *plato típico* is a sampling of 10 different items. The lighter *plato del cura* (priest's plate) is a complete meal of soup, beef, rice, and bread for about $5. The nicest tables are on the balcony, which overlooks a popular pedestrian mall. ⊠ *Pasaje Junín No. 52–141* ☎ *094/231–6642* ▤ *AE, DC, MC, V.*

International

$$$–$$$$ ✕ **Las Cuatro Estaciones.** Medellín's most popular restaurant combines delicious food and first-rate service with an interior that borders on tacky. Choose one of four thematic dining rooms—decorated in gaudy Colombian, European, Asian, and Spanish styles. The house specialty is paella. ⊠ *Calle 16 No. 43–79, El Poblado* ☎ *094/266–7120* ▤ *094/311–5991* ▤ *AE, DC, MC, V.*

Where to Stay

$ ▥ **Inter-Continental Medellín.** This sprawling modern hotel in the hills outside Medellín has spectacular views of the city. The lobby is all marble, service is friendly, and rooms are well-appointed. The Poblado neighborhood is about 20 minutes by taxi from the city center and 40 minutes from the airport. ⊠ *Calle 16 No. 28–51* ☎ *094/266–0680, 800/327–0200 in the U.S.* ▤ *094/266–1548* ⊕ *medellin.colombia.intercontinental.com* ⇒ *249 rooms, 45 suites* ◇ *2 restaurants, tennis court, pool, beauty salon, gym, massage, sauna, bar, concierge, casino, dance club, meeting rooms* ▤ *AE, DC, MC, V.*

¢–$ ▥ **Hotel Nutibara.** This stylish hotel from the 1940s recalls a glamorous era. Rooms in the newer building across the street have less personality but cost half of those in the main building. From the hotel's downtown location it's a short taxi ride to restaurants and bars. ⊠ *Calle 52A No.*

50–46 ☎ 094/511–5111 📠 094/231–3713 💤 90 rooms ♨ Restaurant, café, indoor pool, hot tub, bar, casino, dance club ☰ AE, DC, MC, V.
¢ ⬚ **La Bella Villa.** Just a few blocks from Parque de Bolívar, this hotel has five floors of modern rooms surrounding a covered courtyard. ⊠ Calle 53 No. 50–28 ☎ 094/511–0144 📠 094/512–9477 💤 50 rooms ♨ Restaurant, sauna ☰ DC, MC, V.

Shopping

Medellín's **Centro Commercial San Diego** (⊠ Calle 34 No. 43–66 ☎ 094/232–0624) has crafts, jewelry, and clothing shops. You'll find souvenir shops at **Pueblito Paisa** atop Cerro Nutibara. Check the outdoor stalls along **Pasaje Junín** just south of Parque de Bolívar. For Antioquian crafts, visit the **open-air crafts market** held on the first Saturday of every month at the Parque de Bolívar.

Medellín A to Z

AIR TRAVEL
Medellín's Aeropuerto Jose Maria Córdoba is on top of a plateau 38 km (24 mi) southeast of the city. Aces, Aerorepública, Intercontinental, Sam, and Satena fly here from Bogotá and other Colombian cities.
🛈 Airlines **Aces** ☎ 094/513-1672. **Aerorepública** ☎ 094/351-1266. **Sam** ☎ 094/511-5100. **Satena** ☎ 094/255-1180.
🛈 Airports **Aeropuerto José María Córdoba** ☎ 094/562-2885.

INTERNET
More and more Internet cafés are opening in Medellín. Two of the best known are Café Internet Oriental and Café Internet Conavi.
🛈 Internet Cafés **Café Internet Conavi** ⊠ Centro Comercial Oviedo Local 3167 ☎ 094/321-3644 or 094/321-3986. **Café Internet Oriental** ⊠ Av. Oriental con La Playa Carrera 46 No. 52-35 ☎ 094/251-2051 or 094/512-5162.

MAIL & SHIPPING
The city's two Avianca post offices are open weekdays 8–11:30 and 2–6.
🛈 Post Offices **Avianca** ⊠ Calle 10 No. 56-06 ⊠ Carrera 50 No. 57-45.

METRO TRAVEL
Medellín has an excellent train system that opened in 1995. Because most of the track is elevated, it's a good way to see the city. There are two lines, one running north–south, the other east–west. One-way fares are 850 pesos and round-trip fares are 1,700 pesos.

MONEY MATTERS
Money can be exchanged at the Banco de la República, on Parque Berrío. It is open weekdays 9–3.
🛈 Banks **Banco de la República** ⊠ Calle 50 No. 50-21.

SAFETY
With the death of notorious drug trafficker Pablo Escobar in 1993, car bombings and other random acts of violence seem to be a thing of the past. Politically motivated assassinations and bombings still occur. Exer-

cise the usual caution you would in big cities, especially at night, and take taxis to get around. Travel to the area outside of Medellín is dangerous.

TELEPHONES
Local calls can be made from the coin-operated public phones found around Medellín. Newer phones that accept phone cards can be used to make long-distance calls.

TOUR OPERATORS
Aviatur, the travel agency with offices all over the country, offers tours of the region. At Abanico Tours, Ana Olavia puts together personalized tours of the city.

🏧 Tour Operators **Abanico Tours** ⊠ Calle 48D No. 65A–46 ☎ 094/230-3222. **Aviatur** ⊠ Carrera 49 No. 55-25 ☎ 094/576-5000.

VISITOR INFORMATION
The Oficina de Turismo, east of Parque de Bolívar, has a good city map, but little else. It's open Monday–Friday 7:30–12:30 and Saturday 1:30–5:30.

🏧 **Oficina de Turismo** ⊠ Calle 57 No. 45-129 ☎ 094/254-0800.

THE CARIBBEAN COAST

Colombia's sultry Caribbean Coast is linked to Bogotá only by the national flag, the milky Río Magdalena, and a couple of snaking highways. The *costeño* people, driven by salsa and the accordion-heavy *vallenato* music, possess an exuberant spirit not seen in the capital. Despite the strength-sapping heat and carnival-like sensibility, the Caribbean coast has nurtured some of Colombia's best-known writers and artists, including novelist Gabriel García Márquez and painter Alejandro Obregón.

Toward the western end of the 1,600-km (992-mi) shoreline is Cartagena, Colombia's greatest colonial city. With its barrel-tile roofs and wooden balconies, Cartagena's Ciudad Amurallada resembles many cities in Spain, but the feeling is definitely tropical. The Islas del Rosario, just off the coast, provide plenty of exploring options for snorkelers and divers.

Northeast of Cartagena is Barranquilla, a quiet city that bursts to life during Carnival in February, when it has pre-Lenten festivities. (If you go, fly—do not take a bus or car.)

Cartagena

When it was founded in 1533 by Spanish conquistador Pedro de Heredia, Cartagena was the only port on the South American mainland. Gold and silver looted from indigenous peoples passed through here en route to Spain, making Cartagena an obvious target for pirates. The most destructive of these was Sir Francis Drake, who in 1586 torched 200 buildings, including the cathedral, and made off for England with more than 100,000 gold ducats. Cartagena's magnificent city walls and countless fortresses were erected to protect its riches, as well as to safeguard the most important African slave market in the New World. The Ciudad Amurallada attracts many to Cartagena, but it actually comprises a small section of this city of half a million. Most of Cartagena's hotels and restaurants are in the Bocagrande district, an elongated peninsula where high-rise hotels overlook a long, gray-sand beach.

Numbers in the text correspond to numbers in the margin and on the Cartagena map.

a good walk

Begin in the Ciudad Amurallada at the ocher-color **Casa de Marqués Valdehoyos** ①▶. Walk one block south to the **Plaza Santo Domingo** ②. Continue one block south, past pricey antiques stores, and turn left onto Calle Inquisición. Follow it to the end and you'll reach the Plaza de Bolívar, dominated by the huge **Catedral** ③. On the west side stands the whitewashed **Palacio de la Inquisición** ④; directly opposite is the **Museo del Oro y Arqueología** ⑤. Two blocks south is **San Pedro Claver** ⑥, a convent. From here, walk northeast (across the Plaza de la Aduana and the Plaza de los Coches) and turn left onto Calle de las Carretas, which you should follow north three long blocks to the Plaza Fernández de Madrid. This garden square marks the beginning of the old city's **Barrio San Diego** ⑦, where you can shop for crafts. From here, hail a taxi for a five-minute ride to the impregnable **Castillo de San Felipe de Barajas** ⑧. When you've explored the fort, take a taxi up **Cerro de la Popa** ⑨, a 500-foot hill crowned by a 17th-century monastery.

TIMING & PRECAUTIONS

Spend the morning in the walled city, lunching in one of the nearby eateries, and take the afternoon to visit San Felipe and Cerro de la Popa. Because many sights are closed by 6 PM, you'll want to do the tour early in the day. Be sure to visit the Ciudad Amurallada at night by horse-drawn carriage in order to admire its monuments by moonlight.

What to See

⑦ **Barrio San Diego.** The seldom-visited streets of this enchanting north-end district are lined with squat colonial mansions painted white, ocher, and deep blue. Geraniums cascade over balconies, and open doorways reveal lush hidden courtyards. At the northern corner of the city walls you'll find **Las Bóvedas** (The Vaults), a row of storerooms built in the 18th century to hold gunpowder and other military essentials. Today they are occupied by the city's best crafts shops. After you've loaded up on hats, hammocks, and leather goods, take a stroll along the city walls and watch as the setting sun reddens the Caribbean. ⊠ *North of Plaza Fernández de Madrid.*

① **Casa de Marqués Valdehoyos.** Although scantily furnished, this elegant house exudes a powerful aroma of well-to-do colonial life. The sturdy mansion and its shady courtyard, low arches, and elaborate wooden balconies are the product of the marqués's slave-trade fortune. The tourist office inside provides useful maps. ⊠ *Calle Factoría No. 36–57* ☎ *095/664–6567* ✆ *Free* ⊙ *Daily 8–noon and 2–6.*

⑧ **Castillo de San Felipe de Barajas.** Designed by Antonio de Arévalo in 1639, the Fort of St. Philip's steep-angled brick and concrete battlements were arranged so that if part of the castle were conquered the rest could still

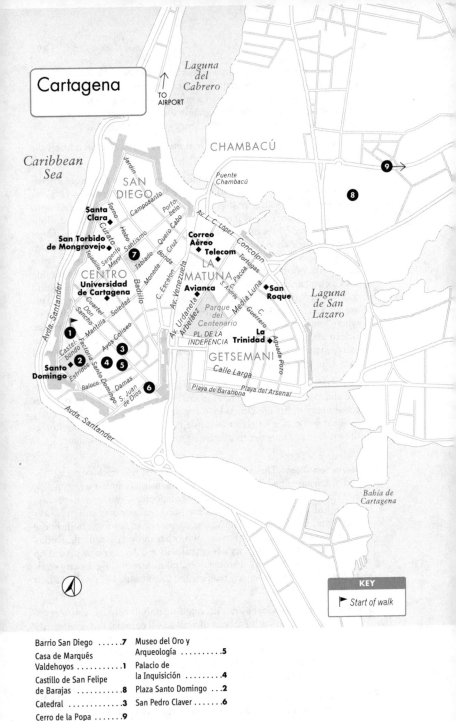

Cartagena

Laguna del Cabrero

↑ TO AIRPORT

Caribbean Sea

CHAMBACÚ

9 →

Puente Chambacú

8

SAN DIEGO

Av. L. C. López

Concolón

Santa Clara ◆

Jardín
Jorno
Curato
Frejelillo
Sargento
Mayol
Santísimo
Camposanto
Porto belo
Cruz
Santísmo

San Torbido de Mongrovejo ◆

Correo Aéreo ◆
Telecom ◆

LA MATUNA

CENTRO

Universidad de Cartagena

7

Tablado
Moneda
Bonda
Quero Cabo

C. Escalón
Av. Venezuela
Av. Urdaneta
Av. Arbeláez

C. S. Andres
Tortugas
Pacoa

Badillo
Soledad

Avianca ◆

Parque del Centenario

Media Luna
C. Guerrero

San Roque ◆

Laguna de San Lázaro

Avda. Santander

1

Castel-bondo
Don Sancho
Quartel
Factoria
Mantilla
Ayos Coliseo

PL. DE LA INDEPENDICIA

La Trinidad ◆

Aguada Pozo

Santo Domingo ◆
2

3

4 **5**

Santo Domingo
Estribos
Baloco
Damas
S. Juan de Dios

6

GETSEMANÍ

Calle Larga

Playa de Barahona

Playa del Arsenal

Avda. Santander

Bahía de Cartagena

KEY

► *Start of walk*

Ⓝ

be defended. A maze of tunnels, minimally lit today to allow for spooky exploration, still connects vital points of the fort. ⊠ *Avenida Pedro de Heredia at Carrera 17* ☎ *095/666–4790* 💲 *10,000 pesos* ⊙ *Daily 8–5:30.*

❸ **Catedral.** Plaza de Bolívar is a shady place from which to admire Cartagena's 16th-century cathedral, with its colorful bell tower and 20th-century dome. Inside is a massive gilded altar. ⊠ *Plaza de Bolívar.*

❾ **Cerro de la Popa.** For spectacular views of Cartagena, ascend this hill
Fodor'sChoice around sunset. Because of its strategic location, the 17th-century
★ monastery here intermittently served as a fortress during the colonial era. It now houses a museum and a chapel dedicated to the Virgin de la Candelaria, Cartagena's patron saint. ✚ *3 km (2 mi) southeast of Ciudad Amurallada* ☎ *095/666–2321* 💲 *5,000 pesos* ⊙ *Daily 8–5.*

❺ **Museo del Oro y Arqueología.** The Gold and Archaeological Museum displays an assortment of artifacts culled from the Sinús, an indigenous group that lived in the region 2,000 years ago. ⊠ *Carrera 4 No. 33–26* ☎ *095/ 660–0778* 💲 *Free* ⊙ *Tues.–Fri. 8–noon and 2–6, Sat. 9–5.*

❹ **Palacio de la Inquisición.** A baroque limestone doorway marks the en-
Fodor'sChoice trance to the Palace of the Inquisition, the headquarters of the repres-
★ sive arbiters of political and spiritual orthodoxy who once exercised jurisdiction over Colombia, Ecuador, and Venezuela. The ground floor contains implements of torture—racks and thumbscrews, to name but two—and architectural models of bygone Cartagena. ⊠ *Carrera 4 No. 33–26* ☎ *095/660–0778* 💲 *3,000 pesos* ⊙ *Daily 9–5.*

❷ **Plaza Santo Domingo.** The eponymous church looming over the plaza is the oldest in the city. Built in 1539, it has a simple whitewashed interior, bare limestone pillars, a raised choir, and an adjacent cloistered seminary. Local lore says the bell tower's twisted profile is the work of the Devil, who, dispirited at having failed to destroy it, threw himself into the plaza's well. At night the area fills up with tables from surrounding bars and restaurants. ⊠ *Calle Santo Domingo and Carrera Santo Domingo.*

❻ **San Pedro Claver.** San Pedro was a Spanish monk who ministered to slaves until his death in 1654 (in 1888 he was named South America's first saint). You can visit his dim, cell-like bedroom and the infirmary where he died from Parkinson's disease. His body rests in a glass coffin beneath the altar of the adjoining church. ⊠ *Plaza San Pedro Claver Carrera 4 No. 30–01* ☎ *095/664–7256* 💲 *3,000 pesos* ⊙ *Daily 9–5.*

Where to Eat

Seafood is the regional specialty, as are *arroz con coco* (rice cooked in coconut milk) and *sancocho de sábalo* (fish prepared in coconut milk with strips of plantains, bananas, and yucca). Tropical *jugos* (juices) are an excellent companion to *carimañolas* (stuffed yucca), *arepas de huevo* (egg-filled pancakes), and *butifarras* (small meatballs).

COLOMBIAN ✕ **Club de Pesca.** Time slips gently by at this 18th-century fortress in the
$$$–$$$$ nearby town of Manga. It's easy to linger on the waterfront terrace in the shade of a giant fig tree, especially when you're savoring one of the delicate specialties, such as snapper with lemon, soy, tahini, and mint.

✉ *Fuerte de San Sebastián del Pastelillo, Manga* ☎ *095/660–4594*
🍴 *AE, DC, MC, V.*

★ **$$$–$$$$** ✕ **La Vitrola.** This friendly restaurant on a quiet Ciudad Amurallada cor-
ner is the result of a New Yorker's love affair with the Caribbean. You can
begin with *ceviche catalina* (fish and octopus marinated in lime juice); then
try a *zarzuela de mariscos* (seafood casserole) or perhaps *corvina con salsa
de cebollin y jenibre* (sea bass with scallion-ginger sauce). Ceiling fans, his-
toric photos, and live Cuban music complete the mood. ✉ *Calle Baloco,
near Carrera Santo Domingo* ☎ *095/664–8243* 🍴 *AE, DC, MC, V.*

$$–$$$ ✕ **Paco's.** Heavy beams, rough terra-cotta walls, chunky wooden benches,
and tunes from an aging Cuban band are the hallmarks of this down-
town eatery. Drop by for a drink and some tapas, or try the more sub-
stantial *langostinos a la sifú* (lobsters fried in batter). You can sit in the
dining room or outside on the Plaza Santo Domingo. ✉ *Plaza Santo
Domingo* ☎ *095/664–4294* 🍴 *V.*

CAFÉS ✕ **Café de la Plaza.** One of seven cafés spilling out onto the Plaza Santo
$–$$ Domingo, this popular eatery serves tasty food in generous portions.
The menu is predominantly Italian, with a good selection of pastas, sal-
ads, and sandwiches. It's a good place to stop for breakfast. ✉ *Plaza
Santo Domingo* ☎ *095/664–0920* 🍴 *DC, MC, V* ☉ *Closed Sun.*

$–$$ ✕ **Café San Pedro.** Although it serves Colombian fare, this restaurant's
eclectic menu includes dishes from Thailand, Italy, and Japan. You can
also drop by to have a drink and to watch the activity on the plaza from
one of the outdoor tables. ✉ *Plaza San Pedro* ☎ *095/664–5121 or 095/
664–1433* 🍴 *DC, MC, V* ☉ *Closed Sun.*

Where to Stay

$$$$ 🏨 **Hilton.** Every spacious room at this modern hotel on the tip of the Bocagrande peninsula has a balcony facing the sea. They also have a great view
of the terrace with its leafy gardens and three pools. A path from the hotel
leads to a private beach lined with palms, magnolias, and thatched oyster bars. ✉ *Av. Almirante Brión, Carrera 1 No. 4–00, El Laguito* ☎ *095/
665–0666, 800/445–8667 in the U.S.* 📠 *095/665–2211* 🌐 *www.hilton.
com* 🛏 *289 rooms, 5 suites* ♨ *2 restaurants, cable TV, tennis court, 3
pools, hair salon, gym, massage, sauna, basketball, waterskiing, jet skiing, 2 bars, casino, children's programs (all ages), Internet, business services, convention center, meeting rooms* 🍴 *AE, DC, MC, V.*

$$$$ 🏨 **Santa Clara.** This elegant hotel in Ciudad Amurallada is housed in
Fodor'sChoice the 17th-century convent that was the setting for Gabriel García
★ Márquez's novel *Of Love and Other Demons*. Beyond the arched porticos and lush courtyard is a newer wing that holds the pool and the
comfortably furnished guest rooms. The former dining room for the
convent holds El Refectorio, which serves the city's best French cuisine. ✉ *Plaza San Diego* ☎ *095/664–6070, 800/221–4542 in the U.S.*
📠 *095/664–7010* 🌐 *www.hotelsantaclara.com* 🛏 *144 rooms, 18
suites* ♨ *3 restaurants, in-room safes, pool, gym, massage, sauna,
steam room, concierge, bar, business services, convention center, meeting rooms* 🍴 *AE, DC, MC, V.*

★ **$$** 🏨 **Charleston Hotel.** Housed in the historic Convento de Santa Teresa,
this 16th-century showplace in the Ciudad Amurallada has a studied

elegance combining colonial and republican architectural styles. Rooms and suites, sumptuously appointed with rich fabrics and antique furnishings, look out onto the ocean or the old city. The best views, however, are from the rooftop pool and restaurant. ⊠ *Plaza Santa Teresa* ☎ *095/664–9494* 🖷 *095/664–9447* ⊕ *www.hoteles-charleston.com* ↪ *70 rooms, 21 suites ♿ 2 restaurants, pool, bar, laundry service, business services, Internet, convention center, meeting rooms* ▤ *AE, DC, MC, V.*

$$ 🖾 **Hotel Caribe.** The oldest lodging on Bocagrande, this elegant hotel resembles a huge sand castle. Bedrooms in the refurbished older building have more charm than those in the modern wings, though they can be a bit noisy on weekends. Behind the hotel, giant ficus trees shade a large pool. A narrow lane separates the hotel from the beach. ⊠ *Carrera 1A No. 2–87, Bocagrande* ☎ *095/665–0155* 🖷 *095/665–4970* ⊕ *www.hotelcaribe.com* ↪ *346 rooms, 17 suites ♿ 2 restaurants, tennis court, pool, gym, hair salon, massage, sauna, bar, casino, meeting rooms, convention center, parking* ▤ *AE, DC, MC, V.*

¢ 🖾 **Casa Grande.** Built as a beach house, Casa Grande is a pleasant, quiet lodging in Bocagrande. Rooms vary quite a bit, so ask to see a few before you choose. The nicest are those in the old house, but those off the garden are a better value. ⊠ *Carrera 1 No. 9–128* ☎ *095/665–3943* 🖷 *095/665–6806* ↪ *30 rooms ♿ Restaurant, bar* ▤ *AE, DC, MC, V.*

★ ¢ 🖾 **Las Tres Banderas.** In the historic San Diego neighborhood, this attractive little 19th-century hotel is an inexpensive option. The rooms, all of which border a narrow courtyard, combine colonial style with modern amenities. ⊠ *Calle Cochera del Hobo No. 38–66* ☎ *095/660–0160* ↪ *8 rooms* ▤ *No credit cards.*

Nightlife

A great way to see the Ciudad Amurallada is to take a romantic ride in a horse-drawn *coche* (carriage), which you can hire in front of the Hotel Caribe or the Charleston Hotel. If you just want to watch the locals, the most popular destination in the Ciudad Amurallada is Plaza Santo Domingo, where several restaurants and cafés have outdoor seating.

A rowdier option is the popular *rumba en chiva*, a bar-hopping bus with a live band on the roof. You'll notice that many Colombians party on the beaches of Bocagrande. Vendors rent plastic chairs and sell cold beer, and roving trios play vallenato, the typical regional music.

BARS & DANCE CLUBS   The largest of the Bocagrande dance clubs is **La Escollera** (⊠ Carrera 1 at Calle 5 ☎ 095/665–3030), a two-story wooden building that vaguely resembles a ship. If all the dancing makes you hungry, order some seafood in the adjoining restaurant. **Mr. Babilla** (⊠ Av. del Arsenal No. 893 ☎ 095/664–7005) is a busy bar with good food and a live salsa band on weekends.

Sports & the Outdoors

BEACHES   For white sand and palm trees, your best bet is **Playa Blanca**, about 15 minutes away by boat. Many people opt for a visit to the **Islas del Rosario,** a verdant archipelago surrounded by aquamarine waters and coral reefs. Tour boats leave from the Muelle de los Pegasos, the pier flanked by statues of two flying horses that is just outside the city walls. Plenty of men with boats will also offer to take you on the one-hour journey. Most larger hotels offer a trip to Playa Blanca and Islas de Rosario as part of a package.

FISHING   The **Club de Pesca** (✉ Calle 24 at Carrera 17 ☎ 095/660–4593) in Manga can arrange fishing charters.

SCUBA DIVING   The **Caribe Dive Shop** (☎ 095/665–0813) at the Hotel Caribe organizes snorkeling trips to the Islas del Rosario and scuba diving at underwater wrecks.

Shopping

Las Bóvedas, a series of arched storerooms in the Ciudad Amurallada's northern corner, now houses about two dozen shops with the best selection of local and national crafts. If you're looking for emeralds, visit the jewelry shops on or near Calle Pantaleón, beside the cathedral.

The Caribbean Coast A to Z

AIR TRAVEL

Cartagena's Aeropuerto Rafael Nuñez lies 3 km (2 mi) east of downtown. There are daily flights from Bogotá and Medellín on domestic carriers Aces, Aerorepública, Intercontinental, and Sam. There are direct international flights from Panama with Copa, from Canada with Air Transat, and from Italy with Lauda Air.

🛈 Airlines **Aces** ☎ 095/664–6858 in Cartagena, 095/421–4251 in Santa Marta. **Aerorepública** ☎ 095/665–8495 in Cartagena, 095/421–3151 in Santa Marta. **Sam** ☎ 095/666–0239 in Cartagena, 0954/214–018 in Santa Marta.

🛈 Airports **Aeropuerto Rafael Nuñez** ☎ 095/666–6610.

BUS TRAVEL

It's not advisable to take buses from town to town along the coast, or from major cities, such as Bogotá, to the coast.

CAR TRAVEL

Traveling by car to the Caribbean Coast—or between cities on the coast—is not advisable because of the worsening civil conflict. (It's also a long haul—the drive between Bogotá and Cartagena takes 20 hours.)

MAIL & SHIPPING

In Cartagena, the post office is open from 9 to 3. You can also mail letters from any office of Avianca Airlines.

🛈 Post Offices **Cartagena** ✉ Plaza de los Coches, off Av. Venezuela.

MONEY MATTERS

You can exchange money at the Banco de la Republica, which has branches in Cartagena. It's open weekdays 9–3. ATMs, many accepting foreign cards, are easy to find in the tourist areas of Cartagena.

🛈 Banks **Banco de la Republica** ✉ Calle 33 No. 3-123, Cartagena.

SAFETY
Colombia's Caribbean Coast, especially the towns most popular among tourists, is relatively safe. In Cartagena beware of pickpockets in the tourist areas.

TELEPHONES
Coin-operated public phones are located throughout Cartagena. Newer phones that accept phone cards can be used to make long-distance calls.

TOUR OPERATORS
Although traveling around the Caribbean coast either by bus or car isn't safe, it's fine to go with an organized tour group. In Cartagena, Tesoro Tours arranges everything from city tours to boat trips to the Islas del Rosario. Caliente Tours offers a day trip to the town of Santa Marta (northeast of Cartagena, at the foot of the Sierra Nevada coastal range) and the beaches at El Rodadero. Media Naranja puts together trips to Isla Media Naranja and the Islas del Rosario. In Manga, Raphael Pérez has a unique trip to the Volcán Totumo, where you can enjoy a mud bath (25,000 pesos).

City tours of Santa Marta can be arranged through Aviatur. The company also offers a boat tour to Acuario Playa Blanca, an aquarium off the coast of Santa Marta. Turcol offers trips to Parque Nacional Tayrona, a reserve with forest-clad slopes, ancient ruins, and palm-fringed beaches.

🚩 Tour Agencies **Aviatur** ⊠ Calle 29 No. 27–05 ☎ 095/423-3159 or 095/421-3848. **Caliente Tours** ⊠ Carrera 2 No. 10–21 ☎ 095/665-5346, 095/665-5347, or 095/660-1516. **Media Naranja** ⊠ Calle Román No. 5–36 ☎ 095/666-4606. **Raphael Pérez** ⊠ Calle Real Callejón Ferrer No. 25-108, Manga ☎ 095/660-4214. **Tesoro Tours** ⊠ Av. San Martín No. 6-129, Bocagrande ☎ 095/665-4713, 095/665-4713, or 095/665-8838. **Turcol** ⊠ Carrera 1C No. 20-15, Santa Marta ☎ 095/421-2256.

VISITOR INFORMATION
Cartagena's Promotora de Turismo provides maps and other helpful materials for the city and the region. It is open daily 9–noon and 2–5.
🚩 **Promotora de Turismo** ⊠ Carrera 3 No. 36–57, Cartagena ☎ 095/664-7015.

SAN ANDRÉS & PROVIDENCIA

The resort islands of San Andrés and Providencia lie 645 km (400 mi) northwest of the Caribbean coast—closer to Nicaragua than to Colombia. Christopher Columbus was the first European to set foot on the islands during his fourth voyage to the New World. They were later settled by English pilgrims (who landed in their vessel, the *Seaflower,* at about the same time their counterparts came ashore at Plymouth Rock) and then by Jamaican cotton growers. Today the islands' roughly 60,000 residents speak an English patois and Spanish. Frequent air service and San Andrés's duty-free status mean both islands now receive a steady stream of visitors, mostly well-to-do Colombians who dive and snorkel when they aren't sunbathing and shopping.

San Andrés

645 km (400 mi) off Colombia's Caribbean Coast.

As it's only 13 km (8 mi) long, cigar-shape San Andrés is easy to explore by bicycle or motor scooter. Rent one from any of the shops along Avenida Colombia in El Centro. Along the coastal road is **Cueva Morgan,** a small beachfront settlement where the pirate Henry Morgan reputedly stashed his loot after pillaging coastal Cuba and Panama in the 1670s. Beach bums should head for **Johnny Cay,** a tiny islet just off the coast. Boats leave all day from San Andrés's beaches.

The island's duty-free status is responsible for the bland boutiques in the concrete jungle of **El Centro,** San Andrés's commercial center.

Where to Stay & Eat

$ ✕🏠 **Hotel Aquarium Super Decamerón.** Large rooms with stucco walls and terra-cotta floors occupy 15 towers overlooking the sea. You can enjoy live music shows at night in the Altamar bar. ⊠ *Av. Colombia 1–19, Punta Hansa* 🕾 *095/655–0123 reservations office in Cartagena* 🖷 *098/512–6938* 🛌 *250 rooms* ♧ *2 restaurants, pool, 2 bars* 🚇 *AE, DC, MC, V.*

$ ✕🏠 **Lord Pierre Hotel.** This beachfront hotel has a wide, private pier for sunbathing. Rooms have big beds and bamboo furniture. ⊠ *Av. Colombia No. 1B–106* 🕾 *098/512–7541* 🖷 *098/512–5666* 🛌 *58 rooms, 2 suites* ♧ *Restaurant, café, pool, beach, windsurfing, jet skiing, bar* 🚇 *AE, DC, MC, V.*

¢ 🏠 **Tiuna.** Right on the beach, this hotel has clean, comfortable rooms with great views of the ocean. Rates include two meals, making this hotel a good option for the budget traveler. ⊠ *Av. Colombia No. 4–31* 🕾 *098/512–3235* 🖷 *098/512–3478* 🛌 *160 rooms* ♧ *Restaurant, pool, beach, bar* 🚇 *AE, DC, MC, V.*

Sports & the Outdoors

Diving is one of the island's biggest attractions. You can join a diving trip or rent snorkeling gear from **Aquamarina** (⊠ *Av. Colombia* 🕾 *098/512–6649.*).

Providencia

90 km (56 mi) northwest of San Andrés.

Tiny Providencia, a mere 7 km (5 mi) long, has rugged hills forged from volcanic rock. There's much less development than on San Andrés, which makes it a quiet, easygoing Caribbean retreat. On the west coast is Aquadulce, the island's largest town, where you can rent bicycles and motor scooters or join a boat tour of the surrounding islets. Smaller Santa Isabel, on the island's northern tip, is the governmental center and therefore attracts fewer visitors. Choose a clear day to hike up the 1,000-foot summit of **El Pico,** which has superb views of the island's necklace of coral cays; it's a 90-minute trek each way from Casa Baja, the village at the bottom.

Where to Stay

¢–$ 🏠 **Sol Caribe.** These wooden cabins on Aquadulce's beach have clean and simple rooms with ocean views. Adjoining the complex is a no-frills but dependable restaurant. ⊠ *Aquadulce* ☎ *098/514–8036 or 098/512– 8810* ➪ *15 rooms* ⚲ *Restaurant, cable TV, fans* ▤ *No credit cards.*

San Andrés & Providencia A to Z

AIR TRAVEL
Aeropuerto Sesquicentenario in San Andrés is regularly served by Aces, Aerorepública, Avianca, Intercontinental, and Satena.

🛪 Airlines **Aces** ☎ 098/512-1427. **Aerorepública** ☎ 098/512-7325. **Avianca** ☎ 098/512-3307. **Satena** ☎ 098/512-3015.

🛪 Airports **Aeropuerto Sesquicentenario Gustavo Rojas Pinilla** ☎ 098/512-5389.

BOAT & FERRY TRAVEL
There is no passenger boat service from the Colombian mainland or between the islands.

BUS TRAVEL
There is a public bus service on San Andrés that circles the island, but the buses are rather old and beat up.

CAR RENTAL
There are no rental cars available on either island.

MAIL & SHIPPING
In San Andrés, the post office is open 9 to 3. In Providencia, mail can be sent through Servientrega.

🛈 Post Office **San Andrés** ⊠ Av. Duarte Blum, between Av. 20 de Julio and Av. Colombia. **Providencia** ⊠ Sucursal Santa Isabel ☎ 098/514-8871.

MONEY MATTERS
You have more options for payment in San Andrés, where banks and even some hotels will exchange foreign currency, cash traveler's checks, and even give cash advances on credit cards. Banco de la República, on Avenida Colón, is open weekdays 9–3. No pesos? That'll pose no problem, as some businesses even accept U.S. currency. Bring pesos to Providencia, where you'll have a hard time cashing traveler's checks or exchanging foreign currency.

🛈 Banks **Banco de la República** ⊠ Av. Colón, between Costa Rica and Av. Providencia, San Andrés Town.

SAFETY
Providencia and San Andrés have far less crime than most other tourist spots in Colombia. Regardless, keep an eye out for pickpockets.

TELEPHONES
There are fewer coin-operated public phones on the islands than elsewhere in the country. You can make long-distance calls at any hotel, but service can be erratic.

TOUR OPERATORS
Carnaval Tours in Bogotá specializes in package tours to San Andrés and Providencia. These four-night trips include tours to Johnny Cay.

🛈 Tour Agencies **Carnaval Tours** ⊠ Carrera 5 No. 14-55 ☎ 091/286-1129.

VISITOR INFORMATION

On San Andrés, the Oficina de Turismo has maps and information about the islands.

🏢 **Oficina de Turismo** ⊠ Aeropuerto Sesquicentenario ☎ 098/516-110 ⊠ Av. Colombia ☎ 098/512-4230.

COLOMBIA A TO Z

To research prices, get advice from other travelers, and book travel arrangements, visit www.fodors.com.

AIR TRAVEL

International airports in Barranquilla, Bogotá, Cartagena, Medellín, and San Andrés regularly serve destinations in the United States and Europe. As a safety precaution, you may be asked to arrive at the airport as much as three hours before your departure time. Flights from Houston to Bogotá take five hours; flights from Miami are less than three hours.

Regular flights connect all major Colombian cities. Since the country is fairly large—almost twice the size of Texas—it's usually more practical to fly to far-flung destinations, especially between the Caribbean coast and Medellín and Bogotá.

🏢 **Domestic Airlines Aces** ⊠ Aeropuerto El Dorado ☎ 091/401-2237. **Aerorepública** ⊠ Calle 10 No. 27-51, Oficina 303 ☎ 091/342-7766. **Aires** ⊠ Aeropuerto El Dorado ☎ 091/413-8500. **Sam** ⊠ Calle 16 No. 6-66 ☎ 091/410-1011. **Satena** ⊠ Carrera 10A No. 27-51, Suite 211 ☎ 091/423-8500.

🏢 **International Airlines Alitalia** ⊠ Calle 73 No. 9-42, 2nd fl. ☎ 091/317-2805. **American** ⊠ Carrera 7 No. 26-20 ☎ 091/343-2424. **Avianca** ⊠ Calle 16 No. 6-66 ☎ 091/410-1011. **British Airways** ⊠ Calle 98 No. 9-03, Oficina 904 ☎ 900/331-2777. **Continental** ⊠ Carrera 7 No. 71-52, Torre B, Oficina 1101 ☎ 091/312-2565. **Copa** ⊠ Calle 100 No. 8A-49 ☎ 091/623-1566. **Delta** ⊠ Carrera 13A No. 89-53, Oficina 301 ☎ 091/257-5997, 091/610-2295, or 091/610-9626. **Mexicana** ☎ 094/413-9500 or 094/610-7258.

BUSINESS HOURS

BANKS   Banks are generally open weekdays 9–3. In Bogotá many close an hour earlier. On the last working day of the month banks are only open in the early morning, although in Bogotá they're open until noon. Avoid the lunch hours, as these are the busiest times.

MUSEUMS   Museums are generally open roughly from 9 to 1 and 2 to 5. Most are closed on Monday.

SHOPS   Shops and stores are open 9 to 5, although a majority close daily for lunch between 12:30 and 2 PM. Most are also closed on Sunday.

BUS TRAVEL

The U.S. Department of State strongly warns against traveling by bus in Colombia due to the risk of theft, druggings, and political violence. If you must take the bus, be on your guard. Keep all jewelry, cameras, and other valuables out of sight. Avoid the basic *corriente* service; opt for a first-class bus (variously called *pullman, metropolitano,* or *directo*) or a deluxe bus with air-conditioning (called *thermo* or *climatizado*), which run between major cities and the Caribbean Coast. These buses have toilets, screen movies, and stop for meals.

CAR RENTAL

For safety reasons do not rent a car, but consider hiring a car and driver or using a taxi for excursions.

CAR TRAVEL

Do not drive in Colombia, and avoid excursions out of the cities. When you are traveling from one city to another, it's best to fly, take a tour, or hire a driver as a last resort. If you absolutely have to drive, avoid nighttime journeys because of the risk of ambush by guerrillas or thugs impersonating them. It is best to arrive at all destinations by 4 PM, since most illegal roadblocks are set up just before dark. Steer clear of north–south routes to the Caribbean Coast and travel around Popayán and Cali. Keep your car doors locked and windows rolled up at all times.

EMERGENCY ASSISTANCE
In an emergency contact the Policia Vial, which has a mobile workshop for fixing breakdowns. If you rent a car, it's a good idea to join the Automóvil Club de Colombia, which will tow your car to a garage if its mechanics can't fix it themselves.

🖪 Emergency Numbers **Automóvil Club de Colombia** ⊠ Av. Vitacura 8620, Bogotá ☎ 091/677–5966. **Policia Vial** ⊠ Calle 22 No. 132–06, Bogotá ☎ 091/247–1151.

GASOLINE
Gasoline comes in two grades: *extra* (95 octane), available only in large cities for 4,600 pesos per U.S. gallon; and *corriente* (84 octane), sometimes called *regular,* which costs 3,600 pesos per U.S. gallon and is available throughout the country. For safety reasons, and to avoid getting fined for running out of gas, consider bringing an extra gallon along with you.

ROAD CONDITIONS
Driving in Colombia is a bad idea, and not just because of the crime. Beware the crumbling, narrow, and winding roads. During rainy season they can turn to mud or wash out completely. Always bring a good map, as signs are irregularly posted. Tolls (up to 5,100 pesos) are common.

RULES OF THE ROAD
If you plan to drive here, get an international license before you leave home. National driver's licenses are accepted but must be accompanied by an official translation, which is a bureaucratic time waster. Police checkpoints are common, so make sure your documents are always close at hand. Highway speed limits are typically 100 kph (62 mph). There's an automatic fine for running out of gasoline on the road.

CUSTOMS & DUTIES

ON ARRIVAL
The duty-free allowance per person is 200 cigarettes, 50 cigars, 250 grams of tobacco, and two bottles of either wine or spirits. You can bring electronic equipment, such as video cameras and laptops, as long as they bear clear signs of use. Remember that such valuables can make you a target for robberies.

ON DEPARTURE
If you have purchased any gold, platinum, or emerald articles, you must present a proof of purchase. There is a limit of $10,000 U.S. you can bring in or out of the country. Colonial objects can be taken out of the

country without hindrance, but exporting pre-Columbian artifacts is against the law. Expect to pay an airport tax of $43.

ELECTRICITY

The electrical current in Colombia is 120 volts AC, just like in North America. Sockets take two-prong plugs.

EMBASSIES

Upon arrival in Colombia, U.S. citizens should register with the embassy. There's no embassy for citizens of Australia, but in an emergency Australians can call a representative in Caracas, Venezuela.

🏫 Embassies **Canada** ⊠ Carrera 7 No. 115–33, 14th fl., Bogotá ☎ 091/657–9800. **United Kingdom** ⊠ Calle 9 No. 76–49, 9th fl., Bogotá ☎ 091/317–6690. **United States** ⊠ Calle 22D Bis No. 47–51, Bogotá ☎ 091/315–0811.

FESTIVALS & SEASONAL EVENTS

Carnaval season (February–March) is particularly festive in Barranquilla. In March or April, Semana Santa (Palm Sunday through Easter Sunday) processions fill the town of Chia, a half hour north of Bogotá. During the two weeks before Easter, Bogotá hosts the Ibero-American Theatre Festival, with international theater and dance troupes performing.

The Flower Festival is held in Medellín in late May or early June. The Folklore Festival takes place in Ibagué, usually during the last week in June. In early November, Cartagena's Reinado Nacional de la Belleza has beauty contests and a full week of merrymaking celebrating the city's independence. Between Christmas and New Year's, Bogotá holds a Festival of Lights—in front of every house you'll find candles in colorful bags—and on New Year's Eve there's a fireworks celebration in the Presidential Plaza.

HEALTH

FOOD & DRINK   Don't drink the water, and ask for your beverages *sin hielo* (without ice). The water in Bogotá and Medellín is heavily chlorinated and may be safe enough to drink, but it's best to simply rely on bottled, purified water everywhere. Also avoid eating unpeeled fruit, uncooked vegetables, and salads.

SHOTS &   Colombia's pharmacies are well stocked, although you should bring some
MEDICATIONS   basic supplies to combat diarrhea, just in case. Some people experience dizziness and headaches upon arrival in Bogotá because of the thin mountain air. Until you acclimatize you should avoid alcohol and caffeine, get plenty of sleep, and drink a lot of water and juice to keep hydrated. Descend to a lower elevation if you experience vomiting, breathlessness, or disorientation. See a doctor if symptoms persist. Immunizations against the following diseases are recommended at least three months in advance of your trip: hepatitis A and B, tetanus-diphtheria, measles, typhoid, and yellow fever. The decision whether or not to take malaria pills should be made with your doctor.

HOLIDAYS

The Presentation of Our Lord (January 1); Epiphany (January 6 in 2004); St. Joseph's Day (March 19 in 2004); Holy Week (Palm Sunday through Easter—April 1–11 in 2004); Labor Day (May 1); Ascension Day (May 24 in 2004); Corpus Christi (June 14 in 2004); Sts. Peter and Paul's Day (June 30 in 2004); Independence Day (July 20); Battle of Boyacá (August 7); Assumption Day (August 15 in 2004); Discovery of America (October 12 in 2004); All Saints' Day (November 1); Independence of Cartagena (November 11 in 2004); Immaculate Conception (December 8); Christmas.

INTERNET
The Internet is becoming increasingly popular in Colombia. All of the larger cities have Internet cafés, and many hotels provide Internet access to their guests for a small fee.

LANGUAGE
Spanish is the official language, although you may overhear some of the roughly 90 indigenous languages that are also spoken. English is widely understood on the islands of San Andrés and Providencia and is commonly spoken in hotels and restaurants.

MAIL & SHIPPING
All international airmail is handled by Avianca, Colombia's largest airline. Airmail post offices are normally next to the airline's offices and are open weekdays 7:30–6, Saturday 8–noon. You can also use Colombia's postal service, although mail will generally take longer to arrive. Their hours of operation are shorter, usually weekdays 9 to 3.

POSTAL RATES An airmail letter to the United States costs 7,500 pesos; to Europe, 8,000 pesos. Postcards cost 2,000 pesos to anywhere outside of Colombia. Airmail service is relatively reliable, taking between 7 and 14 days.

RECEIVING MAIL Avianca holds letters for up to 30 days, and you'll need your passport to claim them from the *poste restante* desk.

WRITING TO COLOMBIA Letters should be sent to Poste Restante, Correo Aéreo Avianca, followed by the city and province name. If you have American Express traveler's checks or credit cards, you can have mail sent to its offices.

MONEY MATTERS
U.S. currency and traveler's checks can be exchanged for a small fee in larger hotels, travel agencies, and money exchange offices. British, Canadian, Australian, and New Zealand currencies or traveler's checks are harder to exchange. You'll get a better rate at banks, although this is not always convenient because of their limited hours. Credit cards give the best exchange rate, so you should use them for cash advances when possible. Either way, keep your exchange receipts to protect yourself against fraud. When departing, you can convert unused pesos into U.S. dollars (up to $100) at the airport's casa de cambio.

ATMS Automatic teller machines are widely available in the major cities. Most are connected internationally, so that it is often possible to withdraw directly from your account back home.

CREDIT CARDS You can use credit cards in larger hotels and in the shops and restaurants of major cities, though you should always carry some pesos with you. MasterCard and Visa are more commonly accepted than American Express or Diners Club. Elsewhere credit cards are only occasionally accepted, and you'll be expected to pay with cash.

CURRENCY   Colombia's monetary unit is the peso, which has lost so much value it's no longer divided into centavos. Peso bills are circulated in the following denominations: 2,000, 5,000, 10,000, and 20,000. Peso coins come in denominations of 100, 200, 500 and 1,000. At press time the official exchange rate was about 2,905 pesos to the U.S. dollar, 4,116 pesos to the pound sterling, and 1,720 to the Canadian dollar.

WHAT IT WILL COST   Bogotá, Cartagena, and San Andrés are the most expensive destinations; but, even then, you'll find first-class accommodations for around $50 per night. The least-expensive areas are coastal and mountain villages, where you'll part with $2 for a meal and $5 for lodging.

Sample prices: cup of coffee, 1,000 pesos; bottle of beer, 2,200 pesos; bottle of wine in a restaurant, 35,000 pesos–40,000 pesos; bottle of wine in store, 15,000 pesos–30,000 pesos; 2-km (1-mi) taxi ride, 5,000 pesos; city bus ride, 1,500 pesos; theater or cinema ticket, 5,000 pesos–15,000 pesos.

PASSPORTS & VISAS

Citizens from Australia, Canada, the United States, the United Kingdom, and New Zealand need only a valid passport to enter Colombia for up to 30 days; tourist visas aren't required.

SAFETY

Violence perpetrated by the drug cartels, the various armed groups involved in the civil conflict, and gangs of delinquents are a fact of life in Colombia, but if you're on your guard you'll be less likely to run into problems. Take the usual precautions you would when traveling anywhere—leave jewelry in your hotel safe, conceal your camera, and carry your money in more than one place. Watch your possessions in airports, bus terminals, and other public places where thieves work in teams to distract you and swipe a momentarily unattended bag.

Avoid black-market money changers or any dubious transaction offering a better rate of exchange—counterfeit bills are a very real problem. Have nothing to do with drug dealers, because many of them freelance as police informers. Possession of cocaine or marijuana can lead to a long sentence in an unpleasant Colombian jail. Don't accept gifts of food, drink, cigarettes, or chewing gum from strangers; there have been reports of travelers being drugged and relieved of their valuables.

🔒 U.S. Government Advisories **U.S. Department of State Travel Advisory** ☎ 202/647-4000 ⊕ www.travel.state.gov/colombia.html.

TAXES

DEPARTURE TAX   Colombia charges a departure tax of $20, or $30 for stays over 30 days. The tax is payable in U.S. dollars or the equivalent in pesos.

SALES TAX   Colombia charges a sales tax of 16% on most consumer items. Food, except that purchased in restaurants, is not taxed.

VALUE ADDED
TAX (VAT)
Throughout Colombia hotels add 16% to your bill. A charge of 2,000 pesos is added for hotel insurance.

TAXIS
Taxis are readily available in Colombia's larger cities. Calling a taxi is safer than hailing one on the street because thieves masquerade as taxi drivers, especially at night in heavily touristed areas.

TELEPHONES
Colombia's country code is 57. When dialing Colombia from abroad, drop the 0 from the in-country area code. Within Colombia, drop the 3-digit city code prefix when making local calls.

LOCAL CALLS
Direct dialing is available almost everywhere (exceptions include some isolated places along the Caribbean Coast, where you'll do best to visit a Telecom office). Public telephones are common in large cities but are scarce everywhere else; they accept 200- and 500-peso coins. If you don't have access to a phone, there's a Telecom office in nearly every town. For long-distance service at a Telecom office, you tell a clerk the number that you are calling, and enter a phone booth while the number is being dialed. You pay after making the call.

For directory assistance within Colombia, dial 113.

LONG-DISTANCE &
INTERNATIONAL
CALLS
When dialing long distance from within Colombia, dial 009 for Telecom, the area code, and then the number. Direct-dial international calls are best made from a Telecom office, where you must leave a deposit of $5–$10 before dialing, or from your hotel, where the rate will be substantially more. The average rate per minute to the United States is about $6 at a Telecom office; from a hotel it's closer to $10. For calls to other Colombian cities, use the blue-and-yellow or red long-distance booths marked *larga distancia*. They only accept 500-peso coins.

To make credit card and collect calls through an AT&T operator, dial 980–11–0011. For MCI, dial 980–16–0001. For Sprint, dial 980–13–0010.

TIPPING
Porters at airports and bellhops at hotels are usually given 1,000 pesos for each piece of luggage. In many restaurants, bars, and cafés, a 10% service charge is automatically added to the bill; if not, a 10% tip is expected. Taxi drivers don't expect tips.

VISITOR INFORMATION
🖪 Colombian Tourism Information **Colombian Embassy** ✉ 2118 Leroy Pl. NW, Washington, DC, 20008 ☎ 202/387-8338 🖷 202/232-8643 or 202/387-0176.

WHEN TO GO
December through February are the best months to visit Colombia, as they are the driest. Colombians also travel during these sometimes hot and humid months, so hotel rooms are harder to come by. While visiting during a festival will add an exciting cultural edge to your trip, you'll experience inflated prices and often overwhelming crowds.

CLIMATE   Colombia is often perceived as being a steamy tropical country, but its climate varies greatly with altitude. Along the Caribbean Coast temperatures are an average of 82°F (28°C); in frequently overcast Bogotá, the average is a chilly 54°F (12°C). The valley cities of Medellín and Cali have pleasant weather, with temperatures in between.

Seasons don't really exist in Colombia, but rainfall and brisk weather is common October to November and April to June. Rainfall is rarely excessive and is only a problem if you plan to travel off the beaten track on Colombia's rough-paved mountain roads. The dry season usually runs December to March in mountainous areas, mid-December to April and July to September in low-lying coastal regions.

The following are the average monthly maximum and minimum temperatures for Bogotá.

Jan.	67F	19C	May	66F	19C	Sept.	66F	19C
	48	9		51	10		49	9
Feb.	68F	20C	June	65F	18C	Oct.	66F	19C
	49	9		51	10		50	10
Mar.	67F	19C	July	64F	18C	Nov.	66F	19C
	50	10		50	10		50	10
Apr.	67F	19C	Aug.	65F	18C	Dec.	66F	19C
	51	10		50	10		49	9

ECUADOR

6

Updated by
Joan Gonzalez

IF YOU THINK ECUADOR IS JUST A JUMPING-OFF POINT for the Galápagos Islands, you're missing a great deal. From its Inca treasures and vibrant cities to the variety of its terrain—coastal, rain forest, and mountains—and its many species of birds and wildlife, Ecuador has much to get excited about.

The equator runs right through Ecuador, which means the night sky brings out the stars in both hemispheres. The mainland has three distinct regions: the Andes mountains that run north to south, the Pacific coast, and the Amazon basin in the east. You can indulge in a soft or more extreme adventures, from trekking, horseback riding, biking, and white-water rafting to scaling mountains and volcanoes. Interested in hooking a world-record marlin? That is possible, too, along the Pacific coast off Salinas.

You may also find, if you're an animal and bird lover, that Ecuador is hard to resist. More than 1,600 bird species, including crested quetzals, toucans, tanagers, macaws, parrots, cock-of-the-rock, and 35% of the world's species of hummingbirds have been counted in the country's cloud forests, dry forests, and rain forests. (Come in October for the best birding.) Rare and endangered tapirs, spectacled bears, llamas, and pigmy Silk Anteaters live in the Andes.

If you're like most travelers, you'll begin or end your journey in the highlands with a visit to Quito, which, at 9,206 feet above sea level, is the continent's second-highest capital (only La Paz, Bolivia, is higher). Quito is a pleasant mixture of modern and colonial, with stylish galleries and trendy cafés in the New City standing beside the historic Old City's striking colonial architecture. To the west towers the Volcán Pichincha (active since 1998 after 339 years of being dormant), and beyond that swells the Pacific.

The section of the Pan-American Highway south of Quito is called the "Avenue of the Volcanoes" because it winds past the country's tallest volcanoes, passing through at the tranquil and lovely city of Cuenca. Besides its well-preserved colonial architecture, cobblestone streets, and tradition of artisanal crafts, Cuenca also benefits from its location—south of the country's most important Inca treasure, Ingapirca. Not far from Cuenca you'll find Guayaquil—once South America's busiest port and still a major commercial center. An ambitious reconstruction project—"Malecon 2000"—transformed the rather dilapidated Río Guayas waterfront into one of the city's safest and most popular spots. The wide, fenced-in promenade that flanks the river is now alive with museums, restaurants, shops, children's playgrounds, street musicians, and live concerts.

Ecuador's piece of the Amazon, El Oriente, spans one-third of the country's landmass but includes only about 4% of its population. There are endless waterways to explore, wildlife to discover, and little-known indigenous cultures to encounter deep within this section of the country. A border dispute with Peru over a portion of the Amazon that led to fighting between the two nations in 1941, 1985, and 1995 was settled by a peace agreement in 1998. The agreement, brokered by the United States, Brazil, Argentina, and Chile, resulted in a reduction of Ecuador's portion of the rain forest but gave Ecuadorean boats access to the Amazon River and its tributaries. In March 2003, Ecuador's president, Lucio Gutierrez, and Peru's president, Alejandro Toledo, inaugurated a $1.8-million bridge over the Canchis River near the Peruvian town of Namballe, connecting the two countries, and may, eventually, lead to more tourism opportunities.

The most popular tourist area is, of course, the Galápagos, separated from the mainland by 960 km (600 mi) of ocean. This barren, volcanic archipelago is inhabited by giant turtles, spiny marine iguanas, lava lizards, sea lions, and countless other species. Tour the islands by boat—swim with sea lions and snorkel in waters rich with marine life—and you may understand why locals willingly accept a lack of modernization in exchange for life in what's known as Darwin's "living laboratory of evolution."

Ecuador still feels somewhat isolated from the rest of the world. Across the country's majestic, varied landscapes you'll find indigenous peoples who have lived off the earth for generations with comparatively little contact with the West. If you venture into the rural parts of Ecuador, in particular, you'll be pleasantly surprised at how generous a reception you'll receive. With the participation of indigenous communities, ecolodges have opened in the country's national parks and many owners of haciendas welcome those who want to experience living on a ranch. Ecuador, after all, is that kind of place.

About the Restaurants

In the major cities you can enjoy international or traditional Ecuadorian dishes at wonderfully low prices—but watch out, because wines and most liquors are imported and can double the tab. If you're on a tight budget, ask for a *set plate* meal for $1 to $2. The main meal of the day is *almuerzo,* a lunch that typically consists of meat or fish accompanied by rice and fried potatoes and a small salad. Time to relax after such a large meal is essential.

Most restaurants in Quito, Otavalo, and Baños offer vegetarian dishes. If you don't see any on the menu, just ask.

A word of caution: don't eat from vendors on the street, drink only bottled water, and to be on the safe side, ask for your drinks "sin hielo" (without ice).

Cafeterias and inexpensive restaurants are often open throughout the day. More expensive restaurants open for lunch between noon and 4, then reopen for dinner at 7 and serve until 10 or later. Many restaurants close on Sunday, a quiet day in most communities. While most upscale restaurants do not require a coat and tie, Ecuadorians *do* dress up for dinner. You may feel a bit shabby, or even be spurned by your waiter, if you do not follow suit.

WHAT IT COSTS In U.S. Dollars				
$$$$	**$$$**	**$$**	**$**	**¢**
AT DINNER	over $18	$15–$18	$12–$15	$10–$12	under $10

Prices are per person for a main course at dinner.

About the Hotels

Accommodations range from modern luxury hotels to centuries-old haciendas that have been converted to *hosterías* (country inns). While the highland hotels (such as those in Cuenca) offer exposure to local history and culture, those in El Oriente and the Galápagos Islands provide close contact with nature. Unless you stay in the most expensive hotels, you'll find the rates refreshing; most middle- and lower-range hotels offer remarkable service for the price. Check-out time is 1 PM at most hotels and breakfast is not usually included in the rate, except in *pousadas* or country Inns, where either an American or Continental breakfast is often included.

WHAT IT COSTS In U.S. Dollars				
$$$$	**$$$**	**$$**	**$**	**¢**
FOR 2 PEOPLE	over $150	$120–$150	$70–$120	$50–$70	under $50

Prices are for two people in a standard double room in high season, excluding tax.

Exploring Ecuador

The Pan-American Highway runs north–south through the heart of the Ecuadorian highlands in the middle of the country, passing near most of the country's important towns and cities and through some of its most spectacular scenery, including a section of what was once part of the Inca Trail. To the east is jungle—the Amazon—and to the west is the Pacific coast. Most attractions are easy to reach by land, although inexpensive flights connecting Quito, Cuenca, and Guayaquil make air travel a convenient option. Flying is essential for visiting the Galápagos Islands and most of El Oriente.

QUITO

Built on the ashes of the northern Inca capital following the Spanish conquest in 1533, Ecuador's capital city is a treasure trove of colonial riches. Not only is it a launching point for trips to the Galápagos Islands, it's also an excellent base for excursions into the Central Highlands, the Imbabura Province, and El Oriente—the Amazon.

Scenic Quito is ensconced in a long, narrow valley at the foot of the restless Volcán Pichincha. The city of Quito is 30 km (19 mi) from north to south and 4 km (2 mi) east to west. Rugged mountains surround the city, providing a striking deep-green backdrop to this sprawling metropolis of 1.2 million people. Quito lies only 24 km (15 mi) south of the equator, but because of its altitude it has a mild climate all year. Quiteños

You'll need at least 10 days to sample the country's varied attractions unless you decide to concentrate on just one or two regions. To visit even one of the areas, such as the Galápagos Islands, requires a minimum of four days. Visits to the coastal plains and other areas off the beaten track will require even more time. On any of the itineraries below, you can easily substitute a three- to five-day boat cruise to the Galápagos, or combine it with a visit to either Guayaquil or Quito (from which you can fly to the islands).

6

If you have
7 days

Most trips to Ecuador begin and end in **Quito,** which has a well-preserved colonial center, a good selection of museums, and many nearby attractions. Your best bet is to stay here at night and take day trips. On your first full day in Quito, take a walking tour of the Old City in the morning. After lunch, visit some of the museums in the New City. On day two, travel north to **Otavalo** (Saturday is the best market day), also visiting **Calderon,** home of the "bread dolls (a shop where everything is made of bread dough)"; **Cotacachi,** famous for leather goods; and **San Antonio de Ibarra,** known for its wood carvings. On day three, leave Quito and take a tour south on the Pan American highway along the Avenue of Volcanoes to **Riobamba,** overnight. Get to the train station early on day four, and board the train to **Alausi,** where you'll begin a thrilling 900-meter (3,000-foot) descent called the "Devil's Nose" to the Chanchan station. Continue by road to **Guayaquil** for two days and nights. Guayaquil is easy to get around; you can visit churches, museums, and parks, or head out to the Pacific coast for deep-sea fishing, whale-watching, or beachgoing. On day seven, fly home from Guayaquil or return to Quito.

If you have
10 days

On your first full day visit Quito's churches and museums, and the Middle of the World monument, which houses the Ethnographic Museum. Rent a car on the second day (or take a bus or arrange for transfers) and go to the **Arasha Rainforest Resort** northwest of Quito. Spend three nights at the resort, hiking through the rain forest, river-rafting, or exploring nearby villages. On day five return to Quito in time to catch a flight to **Guayaquil,** and spend the next two nights here exploring the town. On day seven, head north along the Pacific coast, overnighting at one of the lodges near **Machalilla National Park.** On day eight, visit the park then continue north to the eco-city of **Bahia de Caraquez,** and stay overnight. The following morning, take a boat trip over to **Isla Corazon** (Heart Island), and in the afternoon continue to the **Chirije** lodge on the ocean and spend the night there. The next day, fly out of Manta or drive back to Quito.

If you have
14 days or more

After exploring **Quito** for three or four days, head north to **Imbabura Province,** where the market towns are complemented by verdant volcanoes and mountain lakes. Spend two days here, and then head south overland into the **Central Highlands.** Take three days to explore the region by horseback or mountain bike, and then head to **El Oriente,** the eastern Amazon basin. Take two days here; then hop a quick flight to the colonial city of **Cuenca,** which has enough attractions nearby to keep you busy for several days. Finish up with a short flight from Cuenca to **Guayaquil,** where you'll have access to the ocean. Hop a plane to the **Galápagos Islands** for an unforgettable finale or, instead, drive up the Pacific coast to **Bahía de Carráquez** before heading back to Quito.

---

are fond of saying that their city gives you four seasons in one day—a statement supported by the springlike mornings, summery afternoons, autumnal evenings, and wintery nights.

After the weather, Quito's other surprise is its Old City, a maze of colonial mansions, stately cathedrals, and crowded cobblestone streets. UNESCO has declared the Old City a World Heritage Site, banning the destruction of colonial buildings and limiting new construction—which is why Quito's colonial sector is one of the best preserved in South America. Wandering the Old City's narrow lanes lined with blue-and-white houses (which, the law states, must be whitewashed each year) is the highlight of any stay in Quito. Nonetheless, after a morning in the crowded Old City, an afternoon in the relatively tranquil New City—with its outdoor cafés, sleek galleries, and chic shops—is a welcome change of pace.

Exploring Quito

The Old City

The oldest part of Quito was founded in 1534 by Spanish explorer Sebastián de Benalcázar on the site of the ancient town of Shyris. The original colonial town was bordered by its four most important monasteries: San Francisco, La Merced, San Agustín, and Santo Domingo. Today, informal markets and street vendors still crowd the cobbled routes that run between those ancient monuments, while the interiors of the churches and monasteries are quiet, timeless refuges.

Numbers in the text correspond to numbers in the margin and on the Quito map.

a good walk

Begin your walk at the regal **Plaza de la Independencia** ❶ ⌐, also known as the Plaza Grande. The **Catedral** ❷ flanks the square's southern edge. Adjoining the Catedral is the elegant **Iglesia Parroquial del Sagrario** ❸. Walk one block east from the plaza's northeast corner to **Iglesia de San Agustín** ❹. Return to Plaza de la Independencia, and then continue west two more blocks to the crowded plaza and sober Baroque facade of **Iglesia de la Merced** ❺, one block north of which is the **Museo de Arte Colonial** ❻. Head three blocks south to the rather barren Plaza San Francisco, which is dominated by **Iglesia de San Francisco** ❼, Quito's largest colonial building and the first church built in the Americas. There's a museum in the adjacent monastery. One block east of the plaza's northeast corner is **La Compañía de Jesús** ❽, whose magnificently sculpted stone facade has won it a reputation as one of the most beautiful religious structures in the Americas. Just south, on the corner of García Moreno and Sucre, is **Museo Casa de María Augusta Urrutia** ❾. On the other corner of the block to the southeast is **La Casa de Sucre** ❿, a lovely colonial mansion housing a small museum. One block to the east and south is **Iglesia de Santo Domingo** ⑪. From here you can walk three blocks north and three blocks west back to Plaza de la Independencia. Alternately, you could grab a taxi to the top of **El Panecillo** ⑫, a hill that offers a great view of Quito.

TIMING This walk should take no more than half a day unless you spend a long time exploring the churches. Most are open for limited hours, so you'll have a better chance to see the interiors if you take this walk during the morning or late afternoon. Once evening approaches, however, it's best to leave the Old City, which has a chronic crime problem. Be careful in crowds, where pickpockets make a good living. Leave your valuables in your hotel and keep close tabs on your belongings.

WHAT TO SEE **La Casa de Sucre.** The restored La Sucre House, once the residence of
⑩ Field Marshal Antonio José de Sucre, displays 19th-century furniture and clothing as well as photographs, historical documents, and letters. ⊠ *Calle Venezuela 573, at Calle Sucre, Old City* ☎ *02/251–2860* ☜ *$1.50* ⊗ *Tues.–Sat. 8:30–12:30 and 1:30–4.*

② **Catedral.** The city's cathedral houses the tomb of Quito's liberator, Antonio José de Sucre. The exceptional sculpting abilities of Manuel Chili Caspicara can be appreciated in the 18th-century tableau, *The Holy Shroud,* which hangs behind the choir, and in the intricate designs of the rococo Chapel of St. Ann in the right aisle. ⊠ *Plaza de la Independencia, Old City* ☜ *Free* ⊗ *Mon.–Sat. 8–10 and 2–4.*

⑧ **La Compañía de Jesús.** The most impressive of Quito's 86 churches and
Fodor'sChoice the wealthiest Jesuit church in South America, La Compañía has 10 side
★ altars and a high altar plated with gold. The high central nave and the delicacy of its Arab-inspired plasterwork give the church a sumptuous, almost sinfully rich appearance. Indeed, almost 1½ tons of gold were poured into the ceilings, walls, pulpits, and altars during its 170 years of construction (1605–1775). At the center of the main altar is a statue of the Quiteña saint Mariana de Jesús; her remains are entombed at the foot of the altar. ⊠ *Calle García Moreno at Calle Sucre, Old City* ☜ *Free* ⊗ *Daily 9:30–11 and 1–6.*

⑤ **Iglesia de la Merced.** The Church of Mercy's beautiful, light-filled interior contains a brilliant statue of the Virgin of Mercy above the main altar. It was sculpted to honor Mary, who supposedly intervened to save Quito from a series of 18th-century earthquakes and volcanic eruptions. The church's 153-foot tower houses the city's largest bell. The adjoining convent, shown by appointment only, features a rich collection of colonial paintings and sculptures. ⊠ *Calle Chile at Calle Cuenca, Old City* ☜ *Free* ⊗ *Mon.–Sat. 3–8.*

③ **Iglesia Parroquial del Sagrario.** The Church of the Shrine is noted for its beautiful facade in carefully sculpted stone, large gilded altar, and colorful interior, which includes an 18th-century mural of eight archangels covering the cupola. ⊠ *Calle García Moreno and Calle Espejo, Old City* ☜ *Free* ⊗ *Mon.–Sat. 8–11 and 1–6.*

④ **Iglesia de San Agustín.** In 1809, Ecuador's declaration of independence was signed in the Church of St. Augustine, and many of the soldiers who fought the Spanish crown are buried here. The gilded crucifix on the main altar offers an impressive example of a style of art called the School of Quito, which combines themes of Spanish and indigenous cultures. The altar displays paintings by Miguel de Santiago about the life of St. Augustine, while more paintings of the saint crowd the side aisles. ⊠ *Calle Chile at Calle Guayaquil, Old City* 🖅 *Free* ⊘ *Daily 9–1 and 3–6.*

★ **❼ Iglesia de San Francisco.** Established by Franciscan monks in 1536 and said to be the first church built in the Americas, the Church of San Francisco was named for the patron saint of the city. The twin towers, destroyed by an eruption of Volcán Pichincha in 1582, were rebuilt at half their original size, contributing to the facade's uninspiring appearance. Inside, however, you will find the first New World example of an interior entirely covered with gilded and painted wood. Stationed at the main altar is Bernardo de Legarda's famed 18th-century sculpture *Virgin of the Apocalypse of the Immaculate Conception*. The monastery at the north end of the complex now houses a museum of religious colonial art. ⊠ *Plaza San Francisco, Old City* 🕾 *02/221–1124* 🖅 *Free* ⊘ *Mon.–Sat. 9–11 and 3–6.*

⓫ Iglesia de Santo Domingo. The interior of the colonial Church of Santo Domingo may not be as impressive as the Old City's other temples, but it does feature an eye-catching clock and some interesting statues, including the Virgen del Rosario. The adjacent Dominican monastery also holds a small museum of religious art. South of the Plaza Santo Domingo, narrow cobblestone streets lead down to Calle Ronda, one of Quito's first streets. ⊠ *Calle Flores at Calle Rocafuerte, Old City* 🖅 *Free* ⊘ *Weekdays 3–5.*

❻ Museo de Arte Colonial. The Museum of Colonial Art, housed in a restored 17th-century colonial mansion, includes colonial furniture and 16th- to 18th-century sculpture and paintings by Miguel de Santiago and various other members of the School of Quito. The amusing *Vices and Virtues of the European Countries* is a series of 12 allegorical 18th-century paintings by colonial masters Samaniego and Rodríguez. ⊠ *Cuenca 415, at Calle Mejía, Old City* 🕾 *02/228–2297* 🖅 *$1.50* ⊘ *Tues.–Fri. 10–6, Sat. 10–2.*

❾ Museo Casa de Maria Augusta Urrutia. In the colonial section of Quito is the Museum of Maria Augusta Urrutia, which a grieving widow kept exactly as it had been when her husband was alive. Don't miss the collection of fine French porcelain, beautiful silver dinnerware, and Ecuadorian art from colonial times to the present. Especially interesting are the works of the Ecuadorian painter Victor Mideros. ⊠ *Calle Garcia Moreno 760, at Av. Mariscal Antonio José de Sucre, Old City* 🕾 *02/258–0107* 🖅 *Donation* ⊘ *Tues.–Sun. 9–5.*

⓬ El Panecillo. "The bread roll" is a rounded hill that affords a stunning view of the city and surrounding countryside. At the top stands the monumental cast-aluminum statue of the city's protectress, the Virgin of Quito—a copy of Bernardo de Legarda's famous 18th-century sculpture *Virgin of the Apocalypse of the Immaculate Conception* on display in the Iglesia de San Francisco. Muggers target tourists climbing the long

6

Ecuadorian Cuisine

Seafood is a mainstay on the coast, though even Quito menus routinely feature fresh fish and seafood. Lobster is a staple on the Pacific coast and along the north coast, seafood is prepared *encocados* (in coconut milk). If you're a very adventurous carnivore, you may want to try the succulent suckling pigs and guinea pigs (called *cuyes*), often roasted—teeth, paws, and all—over a charcoal fire. *Seco de chivo* is a fully garnished lamb stew. *Humitas* are sweet corn tamales eaten by tradition-minded Ecuadorians only in the late afternoon, generally with black coffee. Other Andean favorites include *llapingachos* (mashed cheese and potato pancakes) and *locro de queso* (a milk-based soup that contains corn, potatoes, and a garnish of fresh avocado). An Ecuadorian specialty, *ceviche*, is fish or seafood marinated in lime juice and seasoned with onion, tomato, chili peppers, and cilantro and often served with *cangil* (popcorn), as are most soups. *Churrasco* is a steak fillet with a fried egg, usually accompanied by rice and salad. Typical coastal cuisine includes, as a staple, *arroz con menestra,* huge portions of white rice served with either black beans or lentils and *patacones,* green bananas fried in oil, smashed, and refried. Many dishes are served with *ahí,* a hot sauce, on the side. In the chill of the Andes, you might be offered a *canelazo,* which is cane-sugar liquor heated and mixed with cinnamon and sometimes with fruit juice.

Markets

Market day, which begins early Saturday morning in villages across Ecuador, is when indigenous people head to the villages to sell fruits, vegetables, meats, textiles, and anything else they grow or make. Popular wares include colorful sweaters and jackets, wood carvings, handwoven bags, wool ponchos, Panama hats (quality is better in stores, but hats are cheaper at markets), and handmade jewelry; you can choose from among hundreds of Panama hats (which are produced in Ecuadorian villages, such as Sigsig, or in hat factories in Montecristi and Cuenca). Weekly markets, too, are a tradition in the Andes, where indigenous people in colorful regional dress arrive from the countryside on foot, astride burros (pack horses), or in the backs of pickup trucks. Bargaining is an indispensable yet polite ritual. An offer of half the asking price is typical; the norm is to agree on about 75% of the original price.

While the Otavalo Indian market north of Quito is a prime shopping destination, there are also three small towns—all near each other—worth stopping at: Cotacachi for leather; Calderon for jewelry boxes, picture frames, dolls, and Christmas tree ornaments made from bread dough; and San Antonio de Ibarra for expert woodcarvings.

Wildlife

There are few places on the planet that offer the same kind of close contact with nature as the Galápagos Islands, but there are other spots in Ecuador where the animal-watching and birding is no less spectacular. The isolated national parks of El Oriente protect important expanses of the tropical rain forest inhabited by anacondas, anteaters, howler monkeys, river dolphins, and 1,600 species of birds. In the highland forests are avian species ranging from delicate hummingbirds to mighty condors, while the plains that surround those forests offer close encounters with llamas, alpacas, and other Andean ungulates.

---

flight of stairs, so hire a taxi to take you to the top, wait for you as you enjoy the view, and carry you safely back down (about $8 round-trip).

⊩ ❶ **Plaza de la Independencia.** Also known as La Plaza Grande, the city's main square is shaded by palms and pines. The white, neoclassical **Palacio de Gobierno** (Government Palace), built in the 19th century, occupies the west side of the plaza. The portico gracing the plaza's northern end, once the archbishop's palace, now holds a variety of stores and businesses, including several souvenir and sweets shops. If you are here between 9 and 1, look for smiling people in blue uniforms who offer free English-speaking tours.

The New City

a good walk

Start your tour in the triangular **Parque La Alameda** ⓭ ⊩, at the southern extreme of the New City. Walk several blocks north to the larger **Parque El Ejido** ⓮. Across the street stands La Casa de la Cultura, a round, mirrored building that houses both the **Museo del Banco Central** ⓯ and the **Museo de Arte Moderno** ⓰. Just to the east is a large colonial building, on the third floor of which is the **Museo Arqueológico Weilbauer** ⓱. From here walk north along Avenida 12 de Octubre until you enter the campus of the Universidad Católica; ask to be pointed to the **Museo de Jijón Caamaño** ⓲ on the third floor of the *biblioteca* (library). Leaving the campus, continue north about five blocks along Avenida 12 de Octubre to the Centro Cultural Abya Yala, which holds the **Museo Amazónico** ⓳. From here, take a 15-minute taxi-ride to the residential neighborhood of Bellavista and the **Museo Guayasamín** ⓴, which is dedicated to Ecuador's most famous living artist.

TIMING   Because the New City holds more museums, it tends to take longer to explore than the Old City. You could easily complete this walk in the course of a morning or afternoon, but you'd have to move pretty quickly through the museums. A better plan is spreading the walk over two days and combine it with a walk in the Old City.

WHAT TO SEE   **Museo Amazónico.** The Amazon Museum houses an impressive collec-
⓳   tion of artifacts and utilitarian items from different Amazonian cultures, including cooking pots, bowls, jewelry, hunting implements, stuffed animals, and shrunken heads. The bookstore on the first floor has a superb collection of (mostly Spanish-language) volumes on Latin American culture and indigenous peoples. ⊠ *Av. 12 de Octubre 1430, at Wilson, New City* ☎ *02/250–6247* ☞ *$1* ☉ *Daily 10–4.*

⓱   **Museo Arqueológico Weilbauer.** The Weilbauer Archaeology Museum offers free English-language tours of its impressive collection of pre-Columbian ceramics and other artifacts. The building that houses the

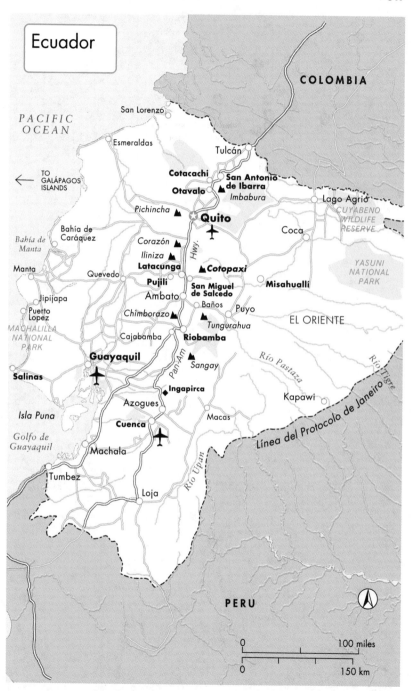

Ecuador

COLOMBIA

PACIFIC OCEAN

San Lorenzo

Esmeraldas

Tulcán

Cotacachi

San Antonio de Ibarra

Otavalo   *Imbabura*

Pichincha   ⊗ **Quito**

← TO GALÁPAGOS ISLANDS

Lago Agrio

CUYABENO WILDLIFE RESERVE

Coca

Bahía de Manta

Bahía de Caráquez

Corazón

Iliniza

Latacunga   **Cotopaxi**

YASUNI NATIONAL PARK

Manta

Quevedo

Pujilí

Ambato

San Miguel de Salcedo

Misahuallí

Baños   Puyo

Jipijapa

Puerto Lopez

Chimborazo

Tungurahua

EL ORIENTE

MACHALILLA NATIONAL PARK

Cajabamba

Riobamba

Pan-Am

Hwy.

Río Pastaza

Río Tigre

Guayaquil

Sangay

Salinas

Ingapirca

Kapawi

Isla Puna

Azogues

Macas

Golfo de Guayaquil

Cuenca

Río Upan

Machala

Línea del Protocolo de Janeiro

Tumbez

Loja

PERU

0 — 100 miles

0 — 150 km

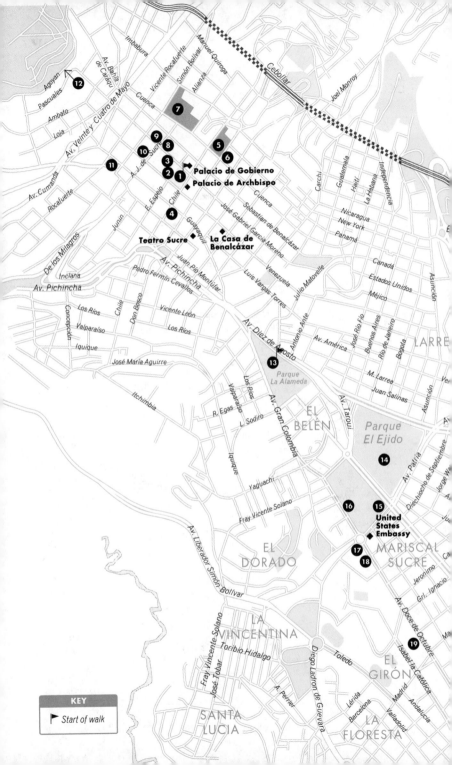

Palacio de Gobierno

Palacio de Archbispo

Teatro Sucre

La Casa de Benalcázar

United States Embassy

Parque La Alameda

EL BELÉN

Parque El Ejido

MARISCAL SUCRE

EL DORADO

LA VINCENTINA

SANTA LUCIA

EL GIRÓN

LA FLORESTA

LARRE

KEY

▶ *Start of walk*

Quito

collection dates from the colonial era and once served as the U.S. embassy. ⊠ *Av. Patria at Av. 12 de Octubre, New City* ☎ *02/223–0577* ✉ *Free* ⊙ *Weekdays 9–4.*

🔟 **Museo de Arte Moderno.** Exhibits at the Museum of Modern Art include two stories of contemporary Ecuadorian works, such as paintings by Eduardo Kingman and Oswaldo Guayasamín. There's an excellent collection of pre-Columbian and colonial musical instruments. ⊠ *Southern entrance of La Casa de la Cultura, New City* ☎ *02/222–3392* ✉ *$1* ⊙ *Tues.–Fri. 10–6, Sat. 10–2.*

★ 🔟 **Museo del Banco Central.** The Central Bank Museum, Quito's most modern museum, features an astonishing collection of pre-Columbian archaeology and Inca artifacts. Brightly lit cases containing sculptures from different Ecuadorian regions stand next to large-scale dioramas detailing the minutiae of pre-Columbian life. The first floor includes an unparalleled collection of gold artifacts; journey upstairs to an excellent exhibit of colonial paintings and sculptures. Up one flight more you'll find an impressive collection of modern Ecuadorian paintings. ⊠ *Northern entrance of La Casa de la Cultura, New City* ☎ *02/222–3258* ✉ *$2* ⊙ *Tues.–Fri. 9–5, weekends 10–3.*

🔟 **Museo Guayasamín.** One of Ecuador's most famous living artists, Guayasamín has a workshop and beautiful museum in the residential neighborhood of Bellavista. On display are pre-Columbian ceramics, colonial sculptures and paintings, and a permanent exhibit of his paintings. Original works by Guayasamín, as well as prints, posters, and T-shirts, are sold in the gift shop. ⊠ *Calle José Bosmediano 543, at José Carbo, New City* ☎ *02/244–6455* ✉ *Free* ⊙ *Weekdays 9:30–1 and 3–6:30, Sat. 9:30–1.*

🔟 **Museo de Jijón Caamaño.** On the third floor of the Universidad Católica, the Jijón Caamaño Museum contains a large collection of colonial art, with paintings and sculptures from some of the masters of the School of Quito. There is also a small collection of Ecuadorian and Peruvian archaeological finds. Well-informed docents lead free English-language tours. ⊠ *Av. 12 de Octubre at Calle Roca, New City* ☎ *02/252–9250* ✉ *Free* ⊙ *Weekdays 9–4.*

🔟 **Parque La Alameda.** The elongated triangle of La Alameda Park lies between the Old and New cities, near the **Asamblea Legislativa,** a large, modern building that houses the nation's congress. At the center of the park stands **El Observatorio,** the oldest astronomical observatory in South America, rendered useless by the bright city lights. A monument to Simón Bolívar dominates the southern apex of the triangle.

🔟 **Parque El Ejido.** One of the larger parks in Quito, El Ejido is popular for its extensive playgrounds and *ecuavoli* (three-person volleyball) courts. Theater groups regularly hold impromptu performances here, and there are often open-air art exhibitions on Saturday. You can also usually find a handicraft market in progress on weekends. But as pleasant as it is by day, Parque El Ejido should be avoided once the sun goes down.

off the
beaten
path

GUÁPULO – Nestled in a secluded valley below the Hotel Quito, the village of Guápulo is a preserved pocket of colonial architecture only 2 km (1 mi) from Quito's New City. The settlement, with narrow cobblestone lanes lined with two-story white houses trimmed in blue, grew up around its impressive 17th-century church, **El Santuario de Guápulo.** The Guápulo Sanctuary contains pieces by some of Quito's most exceptional sculptors and painters; the paintings in the central nave are the work of Miguel de Santiago, and the side altar and pulpit—completed in 1716 and considered masterpieces of colonial art—were carved by Juan Bautista Menacho. ⌨ *Free* ☉ *Mon.–Sat. 8–11 and 3–6.*

Early September brings Guápulo's annual festival, which features food, drink, and marching bands. To reach Guápulo, walk downhill via the steep staircase directly behind the Hotel Quito, located east of the city at Avenida Gonzáles Suarez 2500. To return, make the uphill trek or take a taxi for about $2.

Where to Stay & Eat

Quito's better restaurants are found in the New City. Even at the most glittering establishments, formal attire is never a requirement. Many restaurants close for a break between 3 and 7 PM, and some remain shuttered all day Sunday or close early. Some useful phrases: a la brasa (grilled), al vapor (steamed), apanada (batter-fried/breaded), brosterizada (deep fried), encocado (cooked in coconut oil), hornado (roasted), reventado (skillet fried), seco (stewed meat).

Accommodations range from modern high-rises with a range of services, from health clubs to baby-sitting, to family-run inns, where you'll get more personal attention. Almost all the luxury hotels are in the New City, but the best deals are in the pleasant Mariscal neighborhood. Less expensive hotels often lack air-conditioning and heating, although Quito's moderate climate means this usually isn't a worry.

★ **$$–$$$** ✕ **Il Risotto.** Fresh roses adorn candlelit tables and prints of northern Italy and opera programs from Milan's La Scala decorate the walls, providing a romantic mood at this excellent Italian restaurant. Begin your meal with *insalata del pescatore* (shellfish salad) followed by lobster on a bed of *pasta pomodoro* or a chicken roll with spinach and ricotta cheese. For dessert, order crêpe Suzette with Grand Marnier or the tiramisu with decadent chocolate and cognac. ⊠ *Pinto 209, at Almagro, Mariscal* ☎ *02/222–0400* ▭ *DC, MC, V* ☉ *Closed Mon.*

$–$$ ✕ **La Choza.** The mood, music, and menu are strictly Ecuadorian in this restaurant, which opened its doors in 1966. It's across the street from the World Trade Center, and there's a garden you can sit in if you prefer it to sitting indoors. Pastry stuffed with lobster, ricotta, and spinach—baked and topped with fresh mussels, clams, and prawns, and covered with a tomato cream sauce—is one of the mouth-watering specialties here. ⊠ *Av. 12 de Octubre N24–551, New City* ☎ *02/223–0839* ▭ *AE, D, DC, MC, V* ☉ *Weekdays noon–4 and 5–10, weekends noon–4.*

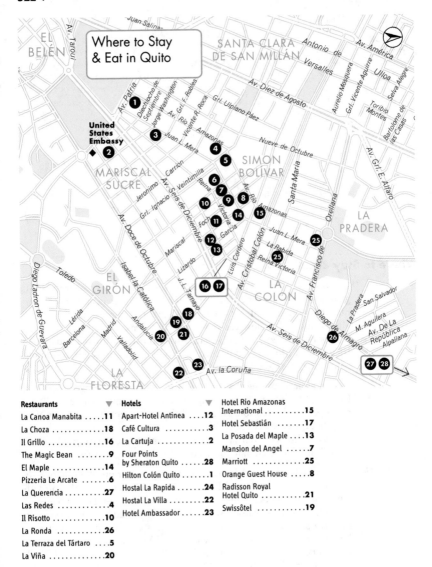

Where to Stay & Eat in Quito

Restaurants

La Canoa Manabita **11**
La Choza **18**
Il Grillo **16**
The Magic Bean **9**
El Maple **14**
Pizzeria Le Arcate **6**
La Querencia **27**
Las Redes **4**
Il Risotto **10**
La Ronda **26**
La Terraza del Tártaro **5**
La Viña **20**

Hotels

Apart-Hotel Antinea **12**
Café Cultura **3**
La Cartuja **2**
Four Points
by Sheraton Quito **28**
Hilton Colón Quito **1**
Hostal La Rapida **24**
Hostal La Villa **22**
Hotel Ambassador **23**

Hotel Rio Amazonas
International **15**
Hotel Sebastián **17**
La Posada del Maple **13**
Mansion del Angel **7**
Marriott **25**
Orange Guest House **8**
Radisson Royal
Hotel Quito **21**
Swissôtel **19**

$-$$ ✕ **La Viña.** Everyone raves about this upscale restaurant, which draws its share of businesspersons and government officials. If you order a complete meal from soup to nuts, plus wine, it will cost you around $50, but if you curb your appetite, you could get by for around $15 to $20 total. It is rumored that you could choose, blindfolded, from the menu, and consistently receive a masterpiece of taste and presentation. ⊠ *Corner of Isabel la Católica and Cordero New Town* ☎ *02/256–6033* ▤ *AE, MC, V.*

¢-$ ✕ **La Querencia.** Best known for its superb Ecuadorian dishes—try the
Fodor'sChoice *seco de chivo* (lamb stewed with fruit), or langostinos flambéed in
★ cognac—this restaurant has excellent views of Quito from its rustic fireside dining room. You can also eat in the serene outdoor garden. Some nights, the friendly waiters can be heard singing along to soft Ecuadorian music as they roam the restaurant. ⊠ *Av. Eloy Alfaro 2530, at Calle Catalina Aldaz, New City* ☎ *02/246–1664 or 02/244–6654* ▤ *AE, DC, MC, V* ☼ *Mon.–Sat. 11–11, Sun. 11–5.*

¢-$ ✕ **La Ronda.** During the day businesspeople gather here, in what looks like a Bavarian lodge, for traditional meals. Among the best dishes are *cazuela de mariscos* (a seafood casserole soup) and *pernil* (roast pork) with llapingachos, peanut sauce, and avocado. During the week, dinners are accompanied by guitar music, and folk dancing follows dinner on Sunday. ⊠ *Calle Bello Horizonte 400, at Calle Almagro, New City* ☎ *02/254–0459 or 02/254–5176* ▤ *AE, DC, MC, V* ☼ *Weekdays noon–11, weekends 1–10.*

¢-$ ✕ **La Terraza del Tártaro.** In the heart of the New City, this longtime favorite is known for its reliable service and delicious, if simply prepared, meats. The penthouse restaurant atop the Edificio Amazonas is cheered by a blazing fire at night; you'll enjoy views of the brilliantly lit city below. ⊠ *Calle Veintimilla 1106, at Av. Amazonas, New City* ☎ *02/252–7987* ▤ *AE, DC, MC, V* ☼ *Closed Sun.*

¢ ✕ **El Maple.** You'll find a good selection of vegetarian dishes at this busy little corner restaurant. One of the best choices is pasta with oyster mushrooms. Take a table and watch the crowds go by. ⊠ *Calle Calama 369, at Calle Juan León Mera* ☎ *No phone* ▤ *No credit cards.*

¢ ✕ **La Canoa Manabita.** Virtually unknown to tourists despite its location in the Mariscal district, this no-frills eatery serves exquisite Ecuadorian seafood lunches. Try the *viche* (a hearty fish and peanut soup with corn on the cob and plantain dumplings) or *corbina menestra* (fish served with rice, lentils, and patacones). ⊠ *Calle Calama 231, at Calle Almagro, Mariscal* ☎ *02/252–5353* ▤ *DC* ☼ *Closed Mon.*

¢ ✕ **Il Grillo.** Occupying a house across the street from the Parque Gabriela Mistral is one of the city's most popular eateries. The interior is elegant, and the fresh pasta, pizza, and salads keep the place packed during dinner. If the homemade gnocchi, ravioli, or tortellini don't strike your fancy, try the langostino bisque or a good steak. ⊠ *Calle Baquerizo 533 at Calle Diego de Almagro* ☎ *02/222–5531* ▤ *AE, DC, MC, V* ☼ *Closed Sun.*

¢ ✕ **Las Redes.** Fishing nets hanging from the wall clue you in to the fact that the specialty here is seafood—cooked Ecuadorian style, naturally. Small and informal, the restaurant opened in 1969 when Av. Amazonas was the most popular shopping street in Quito. If you haven't tried Corvina yet (a Pacific sea bass), have it here, drowned in shrimp sauce. ⊠ *Av. Amazonas 845 y Veintmilla, Pichincha* ☎ *02/252–5691* ⊟ *AE, DC, MC, V* ⊙ *11–11 Mon.–Sat., 11–4 Sun.*

¢ ✕ **The Magic Bean.** The powerful spell cast by high-quality food draws travelers, expatriates, and locals to "the Bean" to socialize over crisp salads and do business over cappuccinos. Blackberry pancakes and bagels are served for breakfast, while the lunch and dinner menu emphasizes soups, sandwiches, and shish kebabs. The atmosphere is casual and the service friendly; if you're solo you'll feel very comfortable here. The Magic Bean also has live music some nights. ⊠ *Calle Foch 681, at Calle J. L. Mera, New City* ☎ *02/256–6181* ⊟ *AE, DC, MC, V.*

¢ ✕ **Pizzeria Le Arcate.** This trendy pizzeria attracts well-heeled patrons who come to choose from 59 types of individual thin-crust pizzas. The emerald-color dining room, with inlaid wood floors, Romanesque columns, and an arched foyer buzzes with conversations in a dozen languages. Crowds reach their peak around 10 PM. The menu also offers a variety of pasta, fish, and meat dishes. ⊠ *Baquedano 358, at Juan León Mera* ☎ *02/223–7659* ⊟ *DC, MC, V* ⊙ *Closed Mon.*

$$$–$$$$ ▢ **Swissôtel.** The hotel has a spacious atrium lobby. Outside there's a pool and lovely gardens. Rooms have dark-wood furnishings. The hotel's four restaurants—French, Italian, international, and Japanese—have excellent reputations. The hotel is within walking distance of museums and restaurants. ⊠ *Av. 12 de Octubre 1820, at Calle Cordero, New City* ☎ *02/256–7600, 800/223–6800 in the U.S.* 🖷 *02/256–8080* ⤴ *193 rooms, 48 suites* ⟁ *4 restaurants, indoor-outdoor pool, gym, sauna, steam room, racquetball, squash, bar, casino, business services* ⊟ *AE, MC, V.*

$$$ ▢ **Four Points by Sheraton Quito.** This 13-story hotel is right across from a large shopping center and two blocks away from the exposition center. While it attracts mostly business travelers, it offers enough to do if you just want to relax. The City Pub in the lobby has live music. ⊠ *Av. Naciones Unidas y Av. Republica, New City* ☎ *02/297–0002* 🖷 *02/243–3906* ⊕ *www.sheraton.com* ⤴ *100 rooms, 40 suites* ⟁ *Restaurant, pool, health club, bar, nightclub, business services, travel services, free parking* ⊟ *AE, DC, MC, V.*

$$$ ▢ **Hilton Colón Quito.** If you love to shop, you'll also love this sleek hotel across from Parque El Ejido. If the shops on the first floor don't strike your fancy, just outside is one of the best shopping strips in Quito. The marble lobby is a bit sterile, and the rooms are functional but nondescript; those on the lower floors can be noisy. ⊠ *Av. Amazonas 110 at Av. Patria, Mariscal Sucre* ☎ *02/256–0666, 800/445–8667 in the U.S.* 🖷 *02/256–3903* ⊕ *www.hilton.com* ⤴ *333 rooms, 12 suites* ⟁ *2 restaurants, pool, health club, sauna, Turkish bath, shops, bar, business services, travel services* ⊟ *AE, DC, MC, V.*

$$$ ▢ **Marriott.** This futuristic pyramid has floor-to-ceiling windows offering expansive views of Volcán Pichincha or the city from every room. A large, glass-enclosed lobby adds elegance. Within walking distance are a business district and several shopping malls. The business crowd comes here for the executive floors and the largest meeting space in Quito, but it's also a good choice if you're just a tourist. ⊠ *Av. Francisco de*

Orellana 1172, at Av. Rio Amazonas, New City ☎ 02/297–2000 🖷 02/ 297–2050 ⊕ www.marriott.com ➷ 241 rooms, 16 suites ♧ 2 restaurants, some in-room hot tubs, in-room data ports, in-room safes, minibars, cable TV, pool, health club, bar, business services, meeting rooms, helipad, no-smoking rooms ☰ AE, DC, MC, V.

★ $$$ ⬚ **Radisson Royal Hotel Quito.** Part of the World Trade Center, this hotel is ideally located in the center of the city's financial district. The generously proportioned rooms exude understated elegance. Dine at the popular sushi bar, lively café, or grill. Live bands perform nightly in the Trader's Bar. ⊠ Av. 12 de Octubre, at Calle Luis Cordero 444, New City ☎ 02/223–3333 🖷 02/223–5777 ⊕ www.radisson.com/ quitoec ➷ 98 rooms, 14 suites ♧ 3 restaurants, health club, bar, business services ☰ AE, DC, MC, V.

$$ ⬚ **Mansion del Angel.** One of Quito's most luxurious accommodations,
Fodor's Choice this hotel is housed in a lavish fin-de-siècle mansion in the Mariscal Sucre
★ neighborhood. A chandelier-lit stairway leads you upstairs to beautifully decorated rooms with antique four-poster beds. A full American breakfast is included, served in the elegant parlor or on the tile terrace. Museums, restaurants, and shops are steps away. ⊠ Wilson E5-29, at Juan León Mera, Mariscal Sucre ☎ 02/255–7721, 800/327–3573 in the U.S. 🖷 02/223–7819 ⊕ www.mansionalcazar.com ➷ 10 rooms ♧ Cable TV, direct dial telephone ☰ MC, V.

$ ⬚ **Café Cultura.** The brilliant bougainvillea over the front gate lets you
Fodor's Choice know this colonial-style hotel—formerly the Center for Arts and Cul-
★ ture of the French Embassy—is something special. The wood-beamed lobby glows when there's a fire in the stone-trim hearth. A mezzanine above leads to the inn's comfortable guest rooms (some warmed by fireplaces). A popular café off the lobby serves breakfast and lunch. ⊠ Calle Robles at Calle Reina Victoria, Mariscal Sucre ☎ 02/250–4078 or 02/ 256–4956 🖷 02/222–4271 ➷ 21 rooms, 3 suites ♧ Café, business services ☰ AE, DC, MC, V.

$ ⬚ **Hostal La Rápida.** This beautifully restored colonial house is decorated with old mahogany furniture and antiques. All rooms have large private baths. Italian and international cuisine is on the dinner menu; after dinner you can relax and sip a glass of wine in front of the fireplace. Museums, shops, and restaurants are all within walking distance. ⊠ La Rápida 227 y Santa María, Mariscal, ☎ 02/222–1720 ➷ 11 rooms ♧ Restaurant, cable TV, bar, laundry service ☰ AE, MC, DC, V.

$ ⬚ **Hotel Rio Amazonas Internacional.** You might feel as if you're in the Amazon when you enjoy a cocktail at the Terraza Tropical bar, where wicker tables and chairs are set amid lush greenery. The rest of this gleaming glass high-rise, located within walking distance of most of the city's museums, is more austere. The restaurant serves up tasty local dishes with a friendly flourish. ⊠ Av. Luis Cordero 1342, at Av. Amazonas, Mariscal Sucre ☎ 02/255–6666 🖷 02/255–6670 ⊕ www. hotelrioamazonas.com ➷ 74 rooms, 1 suite ♧ Restaurant, café, bar, business services ☰ AE, DC, MC, V.

$ ⬚ **Hotel Sebastián.** This small, 4-star hotel is in the center of the restaurant and bank district. The large rooms are cheerfully decorated and the restaurant, Café Mistral, is open daily from 6 AM to 10:30 PM, serving international dishes and specials from Cuenca. The Café and Bar de Antaño is open from 3–11 daily for coffee, snacks, and cocktails. ⊠ *Calle Almagro 822, at Calle Cordero, Mariscal Sucre* ☎ *02/222–2400 or 02/222–2300* 🖷 *02/222–2500* ⊕ *www.hotelsebastian.com* 🛏 *49 rooms, 7 suites* ☖ *Restaurant, cable TV, bar, laundry service, Internet, business services, convention center* ▤ *AE, DC, MC, V.*

¢ ▥ **Apart-Hotel Antinea.** Once you check into this charming inn you may never want to check out. Two homes on a shady side street offer a variety of simple but elegant rooms, half of which are spacious apartments with well-stocked kitchenettes. Some open onto flower-filled courtyards, others have private balconies. For a special treat, ask for the room with a fireplace. ⊠ *Calle Juan Rodríguez 175, at Calle Almagro, Marisco Sucre* ☎ *02/250–6839 or 02/250–6838* 🖷 *02/250–4404* ⊕ *www. hotelantinea.com* 🛏 *7 rooms, 8 suites* ☖ *Restaurant, kitchenettes, minibars, laundry service* ▤ *AE, DC, MC, V.*

¢ ▥ **Hostal La Villa.** This small bed-and-breakfast, which occupies a darling half-timbered house, has a comfortable, casual style, and it's a convenient base for exploring the city. Internet and fax services are free. ⊠ *Calle Toledo 1455, at Av. Coruña, New City* ☎ *02/222–2755* 🖷 *02/ 222–6082* 🛏 *8 rooms, 3 suites, 1 apartment* ☖ *Restaurant, Internet, bar, travel services* ▤ *AE, DC, MC, V.*

¢ ▥ **Hotel Ambassador.** After a day of exploring the city, relax in front of the fireplace in one of this older hotel's sitting rooms. It's a bit threadbare, but the reasonable rate makes it one of the city's best bargains. ⊠ *Av. 9 de Octubre at Av. Colón, New City* ☎ *02/256–1777* 🖷 *02/ 250–3712* 🛏 *60 rooms* ☖ *Restaurant, bar* ▤ *AE, DC, MC, V.*

¢ ▥ **La Cartuja.** The present owner, Edurne Ayestarán, came to Ecuador from Spain on holiday and decided to turn this lovely colonial building—once the embassy of Great Britain—into a small hotel. Along with her partner, Iñigo Sagarna, she also has a jungle lodge ("Jaguar Lodge") on the Napo River. The hotel's front desk is open 24 hours; the library is stocked with books and magazines. Spanish and international meals are served in the restaurant. The hotel is near Parque El Ejido. ⊠ *Leonidas Plaza 170 y 18 de Septiembre, Mariscal Sucre* ☎ *02/252– 3721* 🖷 *02/222–8391* ⊕ *www.hotelacartuja.com* 🛏 *11 rooms* ☖ *Restaurant, massage, bar, library, tour agency* ▤ *AE, MC, DC, V.*

¢ ▥ **La Posada del Maple.** The friendly mood here (certainly not the small, plain rooms) lures everyone from seasoned travelers to Peace Corps volunteers. It's a friendly, inexpensive B&B, and the price includes a hearty American-style breakfast. ⊠ *Calle Juan Rodríguez 148, near Av. 6 de Diciembre, Mariscal Sucre* ☎ *02/254–4507* ⊕ *www.posadadelmaple. com* 🛏 *13 rooms* ☖ *Restaurant* ▤ *AE, MC, V.*

¢ ▥ **Orange Guest House.** This tangerine-color inn amid lush gardens has a small terrace where you can relax with your morning coffee. The rooms are nice—comfortable and decent. On top of all that, it's a good bargain. ⊠ *Mariscal Foch 726, at Av. Amazonas, Mariscal Sucre* ☎ *02/ 222–1305, 800/327–3573 in the U.S.* 🖷 *02/256–9960* 🛏 *8 rooms* ▤ *No credit cards.*

Nightlife & the Arts

Nightlife

The number of bars and dance clubs in Quito has multiplied in the past few years, so now there are plenty of *discotecas* and *salsatecas*. At the *peñas* (clubs where Andean musicians perform), you can listen to traditional Ecuadorian music and drink with locals until the wee hours. Bars usually open in the late afternoon, while dance clubs don't get going until 10 PM. Everything shuts down around 2 AM. Cover charges can be as much as $10.

BARS & CAFÉS The lively **Bangalo Salon de Te** (⊠ Foch 451, between Almagro and 6 de Diciembre ☎02/250–1332) features a blazing fireplace and nonstop Brazilian music. At **Ghoz** (⊠ Calle La Niña 425, at Calle Reina Victoria), you can munch on Swiss food, play a game of pool, and listen to high-decibel rock and salsa. **Papillón** (⊠ Calle Santa María at Calle Almagro ☎ 02/222–8251) blasts pop and techno, which draws a young crowd.

El Pobre Diablo (⊠ Calle Santa María 338, at Calle J. L. Mera ☎ 02/222–4982) is a gathering place for artists and intellectuals. A young crowd is found at **Tijuana** (⊠ Reina Victoria and Santa María ☎ 02/223–8324). **Varadero** (⊠ Calle Reina Victoria at Calle La Pinta) has live music on Wednesday, Friday, and Saturday. It fills up with locals early on weekends.

DANCE CLUBS Enjoy Latin rhythms at **Cali Salsateca** (⊠ Calle Almagro 1268, at Av. Orellana), a popular weekend spot that admits only couples. Locals head to **Salsateca Seseribó** (⊠ Calle Veintimilla 325, at Av. 12 de Octubre) to dance to cumbia, salsa, and merengue.

PEÑAS If you're looking for a peña in the Old City, one of the best is **La Taberna Quito Colonial** (⊠ Calle Marabí at Calle Vargas ☎ 02/228–3102). One of the New City's most established peñas is the **Nuncanchi Peña** (⊠ Av. Universitaria 496, at Calle Armero ☎ 02/254–0967). **Peña Pacha Camac** (⊠ Calle Jorge Washington 530, at Calle J. L. Mera ☎ 02/223–4855) is a small place in the Mariscal Sucre neighborhood.

The Arts

Quito's arts scene has grown significantly in the last few years. Check the national paper *El Universo,* local newspapers *El Comercio* and *Hoy,* and English-language newspapers *Inside Ecuador* and *Q* for information about theater, concerts, and art expositions.

CONCERTS Classical and folk concerts are sometimes held at the **Corporación Financiera Nacional** (⊠ Calle J. L. Mera, behind Hotel Colón ☎ 02/256–1026).

DANCE Jacchigua, the national folk ballet, performs Wednesday and Friday at 7:30 PM in the **San Gabriel Theater** (⊠ Av. América at Calle Mariana de Jesús ☎ 02/250–6650). Tickets cost $14–$20.

FILM Cinemas in Quito often screen American films in English with Spanish subtitles. Check with the **British Council** (⊠ Av. Amazonas at La Niña ☎ 02/222–5421) to find out what is on the schedule. **La Casa de la Cultura** (⊠ Av. Patria at Av. 12 de Octubre ☎ 02/256–5808) is a good bet for recent releases. Movies in Spanish and English are screened at **Multicines** (⊠ Av. Amazonas at Av. Naciones Unidas ☎ 02/225–9677).

Sports & the Outdoors

Bullfighting

The only regularly scheduled bullfights are held at the **Plaza de Toro** (⊠ Av. Amazonas and Calle Ascaray) during the weeklong Fiestas de Quito in early December. Hotels sometimes purchase tickets that they distribute to guests.

Soccer

Matches are held from March through December at noon on Sunday in the **Estadio Olímpico Atahualpa** (⊠ Av. 6 de Diciembre and Av. Naciones Unidas ☎ 02/224–7510). Tickets, which cost $3–$10, can be purchased at the stadium.

Shopping

Quito's best shopping area is the New City's Mariscal Sucre district. Bounded by Avenida Amazonas, Avenida 6 de Diciembre, Avenida Patria, and Avenida Cristóbal Colón, the neighborhood is a tightly packed collection of shops and boutiques. Items are reasonably priced, though they don't rival the outlying markets for bargains. The quality, however, is often superior. Look for brightly painted balsa-wood birds made in El Oriente and cedar carvings from highland villages. Wool and cotton sweaters, shawls, and tapestries vary in quality and price, as do leather goods. Many stores throughout Quito are closed Saturday afternoon and Sunday, but most shopping malls are open all week.

Handicrafts

The most extensive collection of handicraft shops is found at Quito's modern shopping mall, **El Jardín** (⊠ Av. Amazonas and Av. La República ☎ 02/246–6570). **Casa Indo Andina** (⊠ Calle Roca 606, at Calle J. L. Mera) sells top-of-the-line items, including original and reproduction pre-Columbian ceramics and colonial religious art, as well as bronze-plated frames and silver jewelry. **El Centro Artesanal** (⊠ Calle J. L. Mera 804 ☎ 02/254–8235) specializes in hand-knit sweaters and other items.

Galería Latina (⊠ Calle J. L. Mera 833 ☎ 02/222–1098) offers an enormous selection of sterling silver jewelry, ceramic figures, and antiques. In addition to regional crafts, **La Bodega** (⊠ Calle J. L. Mera 614 ☎ 02/222–5844) has an extensive collection of sweaters in wool and Fodor'sChoice cotton. **Folklore Olga Fisch** (⊠ Av. Colón 260 ☎ 02/254–1315 ⊕ www.
★ olgafisch.com) is one of Quito's more expensive, and curious, shopping experiences. The shop is in the colonial home of the late Olga Fisch (1901–1990) who worked with craftspeople to turn folk art into modern works of art. The store specializes in handwoven rugs, tapestries, clothing, and pottery, inspired by indigenous motifs. While you're here, visit the splendid museum upstairs and have lunch or afternoon tea in the small, informal restaurant in the garden, or dinner at the intimate indoor restaurant.

Markets

You can lose yourself among the stalls at the **Mercado de Santa Clara,** in the New City at the corner of Calle Versalles and Calle Marchena. At this traditional market you'll find fruits and vegetables piled in geometrical patterns, bundles of dried and fresh herbs, barrels of grains, and huge bunches of freshly cut flowers. You can listen to a musician play soulful tunes on the accordion or light a candle to the Virgin Mary at the shrine tucked between the vendors' stalls.

off the beaten path

ARASHÁ RAIN FOREST RESORT & SPA – Drive two hours along the main highway—an excellent road you take from the Middle of the World monument in Quito to the coast—northwest of Quito to this $476 all-inclusive (four days and three nights) hotel with colorfully painted two-bedroom thatch–roof cottages scattered over the hillsides. On the cusp of a cloud forest, Arasha is 598 meters (1,962 feet) above sea level, with an average temperature of 76 degrees, and it takes on an ethereal appearance in the early morning as clouds cut the visibility to zero. You can walk along trails and rivers and see waterfalls, wildlife, giant trees, and orchids; or swim in a free-form pool or in a lagoon. More than 300 species of birds have been counted here. The Spa has aromatherapy, and moisturizer, facial, and stress-relief treatments. There's also a chocolate factory on-site, so you can see how chocolate is made from cocoa beans (kids love this). Rates include all meals, some drinks (not imported liquor), entertainment (including karaoke and movies), and tours. Rafting, kayaking, and spa treatments are extra. ⊠ *Pedro Vicente Maldonado* ☎ *02/276–5348 in Quito, 09/924–0009 Arasha* ⊕ *www.arasharesortspa.homestead.com* ⊃ *27 bungalows* △ *2 restaurants, pool, hot tub, spa, theater* ⊟ *AE, DC, MC, V.*

Quito A to Z

AIR TRAVEL TO & FROM QUITO

From the United States flights to Quito and Guayaquil are through Miami, Houston, and New York. American Airlines and LanEcuador have daily flights between Miami and Quito. Continental flies nonstop between Houston and Quito and between Newark and Quito with a stop in Bogota, Columbia. The Peruvian carrier Aero Continente flies nonstop between Miami and Quito. If you're coming from the United Kingdom you can connect in Miami with American or LanEcuador. From Australia or New Zealand, connect in Los Angeles to flights on American or Continental.

Tame and ICARO are Ecuador's major domestic carriers; one or the other offers daily flights between Quito and Guayaquil and Cuenca. Tame also flies between Quito and San Cristóbal and Baltra in the Galápagos Islands, and between Quito and the mainland towns of Esmeraldas, Manta, and Loja. Aerogal–Galapagos Airlines flies between Quito and Guayaquil plus other smaller towns in Ecuador. Austro Aéreo is a privately owned airline based in Cuenca and flies daily between Cuenca, Guayaquil, and Quito.

🛫 Airlines & Contacts **American** ☎ 02/226-0900 in Quito, 04/256-4111 in Guayaquil, 800/433-7300 in the U.S. **Aerogal-Galapagos** ☎ 02/225-7202 in Quito. **Austro Aéreo** ☎ 07/848-659 in Cuenca, 04/229-6685 in Guayaquil. **Continental** ☎ 02/255-7170 in Quito, 04/256-7241 in Guayaquil, 800/523-3273 in the U.S. **ICARO** ☎ 02/225-4891 in Quito, 04/229-4265 in Guayaquil, 07/802-700 in Cuenca. **LanEcuador** ☎ 02/256-3003 in Quito, 800/735-5526 in the U.S. **Tame** ☎ 02/250-9382 in Quito, 800/555-999 toll free in Ecuador, 800/666-9687 in the U.S.

AIRPORTS & TRANSFERS

Quito's international gateway is Aeropuerto Mariscal Sucre, 10 km (6 mi) north of the city center. Most taxis in Quito use meters, but those leaving the airport are exempt. Agree on a price before you get into a cab. You should pay about $5 to the New City and $7 to the Old City.

🛫 Airport Information **Aeropuerto Mariscal Sucre** ☎ 02/243-0555 or 02/224-1580.

BUS TRAVEL WITHIN QUITO

Quito's buses are inexpensive (about 10¢) and run frequently during the day. Heavy crowds during the morning and afternoon rush, however, make them less appealing options. Clearly marked EJECUTIVO buses cost 20¢ and guarantee you a seat, making them a more comfortable option. Slightly more expensive, but much faster, are the *troles* (trolley buses) that run through the center of town along Avenida 10 de Agosto in the New City and Calle Guayaquil in the Old City.

CAR RENTAL

Three of the major international rental agencies—Avis, Budget, and Hertz—have offices in downtown Quito and at Aeropuerto Mariscal Sucre. You can also rent a car from Localiza, an Ecuadorean company, at the airport.

🚗 Major Agencies **Avis** ⊠ Av. Amazonas 3-22 ☎ 02/255-0243, 02/244-0270 at the airport. **Budget** ⊠ Av. Amazonas 1408, at Av. Colón ☎ 02/254-5761 or 02/245-9052. **Hertz** ⊠ Av. Amazonas at Río Arajuno ☎ 02/225-4257. **Localiza** ⊠ Aeropuerto Mariscal Sucre ☎ 800/562-254 ⊕ www.localiza.com.ec.

CAR TRAVEL

The Pan-American Highway runs right through Quito, which makes driving to most places in the country fairly easy. Short trips are possible to some of the nearby tourist areas, but should be carefully planned because road conditions are not always good once you leave the main highway. Do not drive into the Amazon or anywhere near the Colombian border. A better idea is to rent a car and driver.

EMERGENCIES

Quito has initiated a general telephone number of 111, similar to 911 in the United States, to handle most emergencies. Hospital Voz Andes has an English-speaking staff, as does Hospital Metropolitano, west of the city. The Farmacia Americana No. 1 is close to many of the city's hotels.

🚨 Emergency Numbers **General emergencies** ☎ 111. **Ambulance** ☎ 131. **Fire** ☎ 102. **Police** ☎ 101.

🏥 Hospitals **Hospital Metropolitano** ⊠ Av. Mariana de Jesús at Av. Occidental ☎ 02/243-1457. **Hospital Voz Andes** ⊠ Calle Juan Villalengue 267, at Av. 10 de Agosto ☎ 02/224-1540.

🖩 Pharmacies **Farmacia Americana No. 1** ✉ Av. Colón 112 ☎ 02/223-7677. **Farmacia Fybeca No. 1** ✉ Av. 6 de Diciembre 2077 ☎ 02/223-1263.

ENGLISH-LANGUAGE MEDIA

For English-language books, browse around Libri Mundi in the Mariscal Sucre neighborhood.

🖩 Bookstores **Libri Mundi** ✉ Calle J. L. Mera 851 ☎ 02/223-4971.

MAIL & SHIPPING

Quito's main post office is located in La Pradera neighborhood. It is open weekdays 7:30–5:45 and Saturday 8–11:45. To send a package overnight, contact DHL International.

🖩 Post Offices **Post Office** ✉ Av. General Eloy Alfaro 354, at Av. 9 de Octubre.

🖩 Shipping Services **DHL International** ✉ Av. República Dominicana 433, at Av. Diego de Almagro ☎ 02/248-5100.

MONEY MATTERS

Since Ecuador now uses U.S. currency, there is no need for Americans to exchange money. Even U.S. coins are accepted, although Ecuador also has some of their own. Most banks in downtown Quito have ATMs that dispense U.S. dollars.

TAXIS

Taxis are inexpensive, which makes them an ideal way to get around. Agree on a price beforehand if the driver says the meter isn't working. The fare to most destinations downtown should be less than $5. Expect a $2 surcharge after dark. Tele Taxi and City-Taxi are reliable companies that will send a driver to pick you up. They will also arrange city tours for less than $10 per hour.

🖩 Taxi Companies **City-Taxi** ☎ 02/263-3333. **Tele Taxi** ☎ 02/241-1119 or 02/241-1120.

TELEPHONES

Emetel is the national phone system that handles all calls. Although you can wait in line, seemingly forever, to make a call at Emetel offices, it's far easier to use the phone in your hotel, if more expensive. You can, of course, also use pay phones.

TOUR OPERATORS

There are many reliable tour companies in Quito. English-language tours cost $12–$25 per person and cover Quito's principal sights in less than four hours. Metropolitan Touring, around for nearly a half-century, offers quality tours on the mainland and has one of the largest ships in the Galápagos Islands, along with Kleintours. Angermeyer's Enchanted Excursions organizes tours of Quito, as well as biking, hiking, horseback riding, and canoeing trips. TOPPSA is a last-minute Internet booking service that represents a number of hotels, and which also has a separate company offering protective services to businesspersons.

🖩 Tour Agencies **Angermeyer's Enchanted Excursions** ✉ Av. Foch 769, at Av. Amazonas ☎ 02/256-9960, 800/327-3573 in the U.S. 🖶 02/256-9956 ⊕ www.angermeyer. com.ec. **Kleintours** ✉ Av. de los Shyris 1000, at Calle Holanda ☎ 02/243-0345 ⊕ www. kleintours.com. **Metropolitan Touring** ✉ Av. República de El Salvador 970 ☎ 02/246-4780, 800/527-2500 in the U.S. 🖶 02/246-4702, 214/783-1286 in the U.S. ⊕ www.

metropolitan-touring.com. **TOPPSA** ⊠ General Roca N33-73 y Bosmediano ☎ 02/226-0651, 866/809-3145 toll free from the U.S. 🖶 02/226-5727 ⊕ www.toppsa.com **Turisvision** ☎ 02/224-6756, 800/327-3573 toll free in the U.S. 🖶 02/224-5741 ⊕ www.turisvision.com.

TRAIN TRAVEL

Except for one small section of track between Riobamba and Alausí, storms and mudslides have put train travel to and from Quito out of business for good. Fortunately, the section still intact includes the exhilarating "Devil's Nose," operated by Metropolitan Touring, as a combination bus and train trip. The train—which usually runs Tuesday, Thursday, and Saturday—has a coach and an open-sided car that's often crowded with farmers, their crops, and small farm animals.

🚩 Train Information **Metropolitan Touring** ⊠ Av. República de El Salvador 970 ☎ 02/246-4780, 800/527-2500 in the U.S. 🖶 02/246-4702, 214/783-1286 in the U.S. ⊕ www.metropolitan-touring.com.

VISITOR INFORMATION

Cetur, the country's ministry of tourism, dispenses maps and brochures. It's open weekdays 8:30–5. The nonprofit South American Explorers Club, with offices in Ecuador as well as the United States, has an information board and travel library. It can also put members in touch with reliable guides for a variety of activities. Membership is $50. There is also a U.S. headquarters.

🚩 Tourist Information **Cetur** ⊠ Av. Eloy Alfaro 1214, at Calle Carlos Tobar ☎ 02/222-8304 or 02/250-7560. **South American Explorers Club** ⊠ Calle Jorge Washington 311 ☎ 02/222-5228 ⊠ 123 Indian Creek Rd., Ithaca, NY 14850 ☎ 607/277-0488 🖶 607/277-6122 ⊕ www.saexplorers.org/ithaca.htm.

IMBABURA PROVINCE

When the Spanish conquered the territory north of Quito—called Imbabura after the 15,190-foot volcano of the same name—they introduced sheep to the region. Over time the mountain-dwelling Otavaleños became expert wool weavers and dyers; even today you may find craftspeople who painstakingly collect and prepare their own natural dyes, despite the increasing popularity of modern synthetic colors. Traditional dyeing methods may be on the decline, but Otavaleños themselves proudly retain many of the old customs, including their manner of dress. The women wear embroidered white blouses, blue wraparound skirts, black or blue head-cloths, and row upon row of beaded gold necklaces. Though many younger men now sport modern attire, in the villages some still wear the traditional calf-length white pants, white shirt, and dark blue poncho, with a beige felt hat over long braided hair.

Many small weaving villages dot the green and gold valleys of Imbabura, and every weekend artisans make the trek to the colorful market in Otavalo, the largest and most prosperous of these crafts towns. Otavalo's Plaza de Ponchos and adjacent streets are brimming each Saturday with merchants selling weavings, rugs, sweaters, jewelry, and antiques. At a nearby street market, locals shop for *alpargatas* (rope-sole sandals) and medicinal herbs; just outside town, livestock dealers do a brisk business in squealing pigs, cackling hens, and colossal guinea pigs. Smaller villages—such as Cotacachi (famous for its leather) and San Antonio de Ibarra (known for its woodwork)—host their own markets, though none on such a grand scale as the Saturday market in Otavalo.

La Mitad del Mundo

FodorsChoice *26 km (16 mi) north of Quito.*
★

La Mitad del Mundo marks the spot that in 1736 the French Geodesic Mission—and an Ecuadorian scientist, Pedro Vicente Maldonado—determined to be the exact latitudinal center of the earth. A wide pathway leading to the monument is lined with the busts of these men. Also at the site is a French museum explaining the history of the measurements, museums about Ecuador and Spain, and a Planetarium. Visitors today seem to enjoy leaping back and forth between the hemispheres and having their photograph taken as they straddle the equator.

The Middle of the World monument is a 98-foot-tall stone obelisk topped by a 2½-ton metal globe. Take the elevator inside to the top of the monument, then start a winding walk down through the Ethnographic Museum, which has exhibits of the people, clothing, and dwellings of Ecuador's diverse ethnic groups. Each Sunday there's a program with music, dancing, and mimes. A good time to visit is during the equinoxes in March and September when the monument doesn't cast a shadow.

Taking an organized tour to the monument is a good idea, but if you prefer to go on your own, catch a pink and white bus with a MITAD DEL MUNDO sign from the corner of Av. América and Colon, or anywhere along the avenue. They run all day.

⊠ *1 km (½ mi) from San Antonio de Pichincha* ☎ *02/252-7077* 💸 *$2* ☉ *Mon.–Thurs. 7:30–6, Fri.–Sun. 9–7.*

Otavalo

113 km (70 mi) north of Quito.

Days are warm and sunny in Otavalo, nestled in the rugged valley nearly 8,530 feet above sea level. Nearby are the craggy peaks of three extinct volcanoes: Imbabura, Cotacachi, and Cayambe, Ecuador's third-tallest mountain. Villagers trudge along the road carrying huge loads or prodding their overburdened burros to do the same. If it's Thursday or Friday, chances are they're headed for Otavalo's famous Saturday market.

This gathering of stalls at the **Plaza de Ponchos** was once called "The Silent Market" because there was no loud bargaining or shouting to entice you to buy. Though it's still quiet compared to other markets, times have changed. Today you have to negotiate your way through a noisy and overwhelming conglomeration of stands crowded with tourists on the market's periphery before you get to the market proper at the core. Once inside the hurly burly, you deal with the dignified and astute

Otavalos, who speak slowly and softly as they negotiate. For sale are handknitted sweaters made from sheep or alpaca wool, colorful ponchos, patterned scarves, and Panama hats. You'll also find strings of gold-washed glass beads, worn in multiple strands by Otavalo women, lots of silver, and jewelry imbedded with Andean jade. You can usually get discounts of 20 to 30 percent by bargaining.

A produce market is held simultaneously at the Plaza 24 de Mayo; there's also an animal market at the Plaza San Juan. People from the surrounding countryside—many dressed in traditional clothing—come here to bargain for cows, pigs, and other livestock. The animal market begins at 5:30 AM, and most sellers are packing up by 11 AM. The Plaza de Ponchos market doesn't really begin until 7 or 8 AM and lasts until about 2 or 3 PM. A smaller market is held on Wednesday, and a few vendors appear every day of the week.

Where to Stay & Eat

Hotel reservations are essential on Friday nights, when many tourists arrive so they can be up early for the markets.

¢ ✕ **Mi Otavalito.** One block from the Plaza de Ponchos, this small restaurant has a simple menu that includes fresh trout and pepper steak. Seating is available on a covered patio or in the narrow dining room. The daily lunch specials are a great deal. ⊠ *Calle Sucre at Calle Morales* ☎ *06/ 922–105* ⊟ *No credit cards.*

¢ ✕ **Sisa.** This two-story cultural complex consists of an intimate restaurant on the second floor that serves excellent Ecuadorian cuisine, a ground-floor coffee bar, and a bookstore. The restaurant presents live folk music Friday evenings and all day on the weekends. ⊠ *Calle Abdón Calderón 409* ☎ *06/920–154* ⊟ *AE, DC, MC, V.*

¢ ✕🏠 **Ali Shungu.** In Quichua, the name of this colorful hotel means "good heart," and indeed the American owners go out of their way to make you feel at home. The spacious bedrooms with terra-cotta floors and local weavings surround a flower-filled courtyard, beyond which is Volcán Imbabura, in the distance. Two expansive suites are ideal for families. The bright restaurant has wholesome dishes, including vegetarian lasagna and deep-dish chicken pie served with organically grown vegetables. There's live folk music on Friday nights. ⊠ *Calle Quito at Calle Miguel Egas* ☎ *06/920–750* 🛏 *16 rooms, 2 suites* ⚒ *Restaurant, bicycles, shop, laundry service, travel services* ⊟ *MC, V.*

$$ 🏠 **Hostería Hacienda Pinsaquí.** Built in 1790, this colonial building 5 km north of Otavalo and 75 mi north of Quito is surrounded by palm trees. French and Spanish antiques fill the house, and the huge light-filled suites have canopy beds, fireplaces, and spacious sitting areas. Some rooms have views of Imbabura Volcano. Horseback riding trips are the hacienda's specialty. ⊠ *Pan-American Hwy.* ☎ *06/946–116 or 06/946–117* ⊕ *www.haciendapinsaqui.com* 🛏 *20 suites* ⚒ *Restaurant, mountain bikes, horseback riding* ⊟ *MC, V.*

Nightlife & the Arts

During the week things are very quiet in Otavalo (some would say downright dull), but the town has a reasonable selection of peñas (small local clubs) that open on weekends. You can't go wrong with either location of **Amauta** (✉ Jaramillo and Salinas ✉ Jaramillo and Morales ☎ 06/920–967). Both open around 8 PM.

San Pablo

8 km (5 mi) southeast of Otavalo.

Easily accessible from Otavalo, the highland town of San Pablo is a collection of adobe buildings along the shore of deep-blue Lago San Pablo. The lake sits at the base of the massive 15,190-foot Volcán Imbabura. Lodges on or near the lake are much nicer than those in town. Buses run between Otavalo and San Pablo about every 15 minutes, or you can take a taxi for around $3.

Where to Stay & Eat

$$$ ✕🖭 **Hostería Cusín.** This restored colonial hacienda on the edge of San Pablo is one of the country's most delightful inns. Rooms are filled with period furnishings, and many are warmed by fireplaces. The main buildings, which date from the 17th century, hold the restaurant, bar, and sitting rooms where you can enjoy the views of the colorful gardens. ✉ *San Pablo* ☎ *06/918–013, 800/683–8148 in the U.S.* 🖨 *06/918–003, 617/924–2158 in the U.S.* ☟ *40 rooms* ⚲ *Restaurant, mountain bikes, horseback riding, bar* ▭ *DC, MC, V.*

$$ ✕🖭 **Hostería Puerto Lago.** Volcanic peaks form a dramatic backdrop for this lakeside country inn, just a few miles southeast of Otavalo. The view from the restaurant, built out over the lake, is enough to warrant a stay here. Don't miss the panfried trout, served head and all. Bungalow-style rooms are spacious, with brick walls, wood-beam ceilings, and cozy fireplaces. You can rent a rowboat or kayak, or take an excursion on a festive pontoon boat with live music. Breakfast and dinner are included in the rate. ✉ *Pan-American Hwy. Km 5½* ☎ *06/920–920* 🖨 *06/920–900* ☟ *23 rooms, 3 suites* ⚲ *Restaurant, boating, waterskiing, bar* ▭ *AE, MC, V.*

Sports & the Outdoors

HORSEBACK   **IntiExpress** (✉ Otavalo ☎🖨 06/920–737) arranges horseback riding
RIDING   excursions to local villages and to natural mineral springs.

Cotacachi

15 km (9 mi) north of Otavalo.

Although most people just pass through here on the way to the lake of the same name, the quiet little town of Cotacachi is well worth a visit. The small central plaza is charming, with young children racing around while their grandparents settle back for a little gossip with friends. A few blocks away, Calle 10 de Agosto is lined with shops selling the quality leather goods for which the town is famous. The prices are amazingly low.

About 18 km (11 mi) west of Cotacachi, mile-wide **Laguna de Cuicocha** is an oblong lake cradled in the lower flanks of Volcán Cotacachi. A well-marked hiking trail heads up the crater's rim into an ecological reserve that affords fantastic views of the distant Imbabura and Cayambe volcanoes. Within the lake are islands that can be visited on inexpensive boat tours.

Where to Stay & Eat

$$$ ✕🖽 **La Mirage Hotel &Spa.** You'll pass trickling fountains and shady courtyards as you wind through flower-filled gardens on the way to your casita on this 200-year-old property. Suites are chock full of decorative touches, from handcrafted furnishings to crystal chandeliers, antique canopy beds, gilded mirrors, ornate trim, and lavish baths. International cuisine is served in the wood-beamed dining room. While you're at dinner, staff members slip in to build a fire and place hot water bottles at the foot of your bed, an example of the sort of pampering you can expect throughout a stay here. International cuisine is served in the wood-beamed dining room, part of which looks out onto the lawn, where peacocks roam. Much of the produce is organic and grown in the hotel's own garden. Aside from the standard massages, the spa has volcanic mud treatments, aromatherapy, massage instruction for couples, and unique shaman treatments. ⊠ *Av. 10 de Agosto* ☏ *06/915–237, 800/ 327–3573 in the U.S.* 🖷 *06/915–065* ⊕ *www.larc1.com* 🛏 *23 suites* ⚏ *Restaurant, tennis court, pool, spa, steam room, horseback riding, bar, no-smoking rooms* ▭ *DC, MC, V.*

¢ ✕🖽 **Hostería Mesón de las Flores.** This inexpensive lodging beside the town church provides an authentic Ecuadorian experience. Most rooms are on the second floor surrounding a courtyard restaurant and have small balconies and soft beds. A spacious suite on the third floor is a great deal for a couple. ⊠ *Calle García Moreno at Calle Sucre* ☏ *06/916–009* 🖷 *06/ 915–828* 🛏 *18 rooms, 1 suite* ⚏ *Restaurant, bar* ▭ *AE, DC, MC, V.*

San Antonio de Ibarra

10 km (6 mi) north of Cotacachi.

Renowned for its wood carvings, San Antonio de Ibarra, the capital of the province, is where you'll find skillful artisans who show off their wares in the shops surrounding the central plaza. Check out the chess sets, which use llamas in place of the horses usually used to signify the knights. Prices range from a few dollars to a few hundred. At the Galería de Arte Gabriel Cevallos you can drop off a photo or design for a wood carving and have it shipped home. The owners accept credit cards, ship the piece to you when it is finished, and you pay the shipping charges when it arrives. Carved wooden chess sets are another good purchase.

Where to Stay & Eat

$ ✕🖽 **Hostería Chorlaví.** Shaded verandas, whitewashed walls, and antique-filled rooms make this inn a favorite weekend retreat for Ecuadorians. The restaurant emphasizes fresh fish and typical Andean dishes, all served on a flower-strewn patio where live folk musicians play on weekends. Rooms in the old building are lovely, though they can be loud when the place is full; more private rooms in another building in back all have fireplaces. ⊠ *4 km (2½ mi) south of Ibarra* ☏ *06/955–777 or 06/955–775* 🖷 *06/ 932–224* 🛏 *51 rooms* ⚏ *Restaurant, tennis court, pool, hot tub, sauna, steam room, basketball, squash, volleyball* ▭ *AE, DC, MC, V.*

Imbabura Province A to Z

BUS TRAVEL

To reach the La Mitad del Mundo, buses marked MITAD DEL MUNDO depart every 20 minutes from the New City at the intersection of Avenida de las Américas and Avenida P. Guerrera. The 75-minute ride costs less than $1. Most Quito-based tour operators offer half-day tours for $10–$20 per person. From Quito's Terminal Terrestre, buses depart every 30 minutes for Otavalo (2 hours) and Ibarra (2½ hours). Round-trip fare should be less than $5. Transportes Otavalo deposits passengers in Otavalo's center. Flota Imbabura has direct service to Ibarra, but for Otavalo buses drop you a few blocks outside of town.

Buses run between Imbabura's major towns about every 15 minutes.
🚍 Bus Information **Flota Imbabura** ☎ 02/223-6940. **Transportes Otavalo** ☎ 02/257-0271.

CAR TRAVEL

Otavalo, located just off the Pan-American Highway, is 113 km (70 mi) north of Quito. Driving here can be a challenge because of poorly maintained roads and a lack of signs. If you decide to drive yourself, make sure to get very specific directions.

MONEY MATTERS

Bring all the cash you'll need when traveling to the Imbabura Province—banks are few and far between. When you find one, you often can withdraw only small amounts of cash. Most hotels are able to cash traveler's checks. If you'll be staying at country inns, check to see whether credit cards are accepted.

TAXIS

For around $50, taxis can be hired in Quito for a daylong trip to Otavalo and the surrounding countryside. A trip between Otavalo and Ibarra costs about $6.

TOUR OPERATORS

Diceny Viajes, owned and operated by indigenous people, offers a variety of trekking and horseback excursions to the area surrounding Otavalo. IntiExpress has a good selection of day trips to highland lakes and villages. Metropolitan Touring and most other operators in Quito have one- and two-day tours to the area, typically visiting several villages.
🚩 Tour Companies **Diceny Viajes** ✉ Sucre 1014, Otavalo ☎ 06/921-217. **IntiExpress** ✉ Calle Sucre and Calle Morales, Otavalo ☎ 06/920-737. **Metropolitan Touring** ✉ Av. República de El Salvador 970 ☎ 02/246-4780, 800/527-2500 in the U.S. ⊕ www.metropolitan-touring.com.

VISITOR INFORMATION

The Ibarra Tourist Office is open weekdays 8:30–5.
🚩 Tourist Information **Ibarra Tourist Office** ✉ Av. Olmedo 956, at Calle Velasco ☎ 06/958-547.

THE CENTRAL HIGHLANDS

South of Quito the Andes rise sharply on either side of the Pan-American Highway, creating a narrow corridor of fertile valleys that are home to nearly half of Ecuador's population. Along this 175-km (109-mi) stretch between Quito and Riobamba are most of Ecuador's tallest volcanoes, including the tallest active volcano in the world, Cotopaxi. Alexander von Humboldt, the German scientist who explored the area in 1802, was so impressed by the landscape that he coined a sobriquet still used today: the Avenue of the Volcanoes.

Latacunga, a few hours south of Quito, is an excellent base for visiting the area's colorful market villages, including Saquisilí, Pujilí, and San Miguel de Salcedo. Among the Central Highlands' most popular destinations is Baños, a sleepy tourist town surrounded by a wealth of natural attractions. Die-hard cyclists should contemplate the 65-km (40-mi) downhill ride from Baños to Puyo. Riobamba, the capital of Chimborazo Province, is the point of departure for the famous train trip past the Nariz del Diablo (Devil's Nose), a 1,000-foot drop that the narrow-gauge train negotiates via an ingenious system of hairpin turns, span bridges, and tunnels.

Termas de Papallacta

65 km (40 mi) east of Quito.

A stunning drive over the eastern range of the Andes brings you to the village of Papallacta. A mile beyond you'll find the Termas de Papallacta, natural hot springs with eight thermal baths and two cold crystalline pools. It's a beautiful setting, and on a clear day you can see the snowcapped peak of Volcán Antisana. ☉ *Daily 6 AM–10 PM.*

Where to Stay & Eat

$ ×⊞ **Canyon Ranch of Papallacta.** This ranch, set 9,000 feet above sea level, is surrounded by natural hot springs. The springs line the Cinnamon Trail, the route taken by Francisco de Orellana in 1542 when he crossed the Andes in search of spices and wound up discovering the Amazon. All rooms have private baths and breathtaking mountain views. Walk or ride horses through the rain forest, and bring binoculars to observe the varied species of birds. ⊠ *65 km (40 mi) southeast of Quito* ☎ *02/243–5292, 800/327–3573 in the U.S.* ☞ *24 rooms* ⌂ *Restaurant, pool* ⊟ *AE, MC, V.*

Parque Pasochoa

38 km (24 mi) southeast of Quito.

Parque Pasochoa, a protected area administered by the Quito-based Fundación Natura, covers 988 acres of high Andean forest. More than 100 species of birds and a variety of butterflies have been identified in the area. Walking trails include short loops and all-day hikes, with the trek to the 13,800-foot summit of Volcán Pasochoa being the most strenuous. Camping is permitted in designated areas with water spigots and latrines. Tour operators in Quito offer one-day tours for $40–$85, depending on the group size. If you want to go on your own, buses from Quito stop a couple of miles from the park entrance. ☎ *02/244–7341 or 02/224–6072* ⊠ *$1.50* ☉ *Daily.*

Parque Nacional Cotopaxi

67 km (42 mi) southeast of Quito.

Massive, snowcapped Volcán Cotopaxi is one of Ecuador's most impressive sights. At 5,897 meters (19,347 feet) above sea level, Cotopaxi is the highest active volcano in the world. Although mountaineers risk their lives to reach Cotopaxi's icy summit, you need risk little more than a slight case of altitude sickness to wander around its lower slopes, which are protected within Parque Nacional Cotopaxi.

The drive to Cotopaxi is unforgettable. As you make your way past the stands of red pine and into the higher altitudes, you are likely to spot llamas, white tail deer, and wild horses, as well as Andean condors and sparrow hawks. Fewer animals roam the semi-arid plains called the *páramo,* extending from 10,496 to 15,744 feet. There are no trees here, only small plants that have adapted to the harsh environment. Above the páramo lies the permafrost zone, where giant glaciers extend across the volcano's summit. Cotopaxi is most impressive at dawn, when sunlight sprinkles rays across the surface of the glaciers and casts shadows on the surrounding mountains.

A tour operator with a four-wheel-drive vehicle can take you to the base of the volcano, located at 15,744 feet. If you're not suffering from the altitude, it is possible to climb about 1,000 feet to the refugio, where simple dormitory accommodations serve as a base for eager climbers. From here, you'll need at least six hours and mountain climbing equipment—including ice picks—to climb to the glacier-covered summit. The crater has a circumference of 2,624 feet and is covered by snow. In case you're considering the sanity of a climb, the last major eruption was in 1877, with lava currents reaching the Pacific Ocean some 200 km (124 mi) away. ⊠ *$1* ☉ *Daily 7–3.*

Where to Stay

¢–$ ⌂ **El Porvenir at Tierra del Volcán.** Ecotourism is the focus at this rustic lodge in the foothills of Rumiñahui Volcano that acquaints you with the *chagra* (Andean cowboy) lifestyle. Most of the rooms are tiny nooks with straw ceilings and burlap walls and are big enough to hold only two cotlike single beds. Suites have fireplaces and double beds. The hacienda has horses and conducts riding, biking, hiking, trekking, and climbing trips that last from a few hours to seven days. Cotopaxi National Park is 3 miles away. ⊠ *San Ignacio 1015, at Gonzáles Suarez Machachi, 45 mi southeast of Quito* ☎ *02/223–1806* ⊕ *www.volcanoland.com* ⮑ *12 rooms, 2 suites, all with shared bath* ⌂ *Dining room, hiking, horseback riding* ⊟ *AE, MC, V* ⧙⊙⧘ *BP.*

¢ ⌂ **Hostería La Estación.** Owned by the same family for four generations, this log house B&B has a panoramic view of the mountains. Fresh flowers brighten the rooms, which are decorated with antiques. All rooms have private baths. The gracious owners will prepare meals and arrange day hikes for you to Volcán Cotopaxi. The hostería is a half hour from the entrance to Parque Nacional Cotopaxi, near the small village of Machachi. ⊠ *Machachi* ☎ *02/230–9246* ◗ *10 rooms* ⚭ *Restaurant, hiking* ▭ *No credit cards.*

¢ ▦ **Hostería Rumipamba de las Rosas.** In an Andean valley 100 km (61 mi) south of Quito, right at the stone gate to the colorful town of Salcedo, is this unexpectedly elegant hostel. Comfortable rooms filled with antiques, a shady pool, and three restaurants—one with seating in a garden—are the perfect antidote for the stresses of modern life. While you're here, explore Salcedo's market. ⊠ *Salcedo* ☎ *02/280–1863 or 02/223–3715* 🖷 *02/256–2743* ◗ *30 rooms* ⚭ *3 restaurants, tennis court, pool, fishing, horseback riding, bar* ▭ *AE, DC, MC, V.*

Latacunga

96 km (58 mi) south of Quito.

The capital of Cotopaxi Province, Latacunga has been rebuilt three times in the wake of massive eruptions of Volcán Cotopaxi, whose perfect, snow-covered cone dominates the city. Latacunga's main plaza, **Parque Vicente León**, is graced by juniper trees trimmed in an assortment of geometric shapes. At the Saturday market held on **Plaza San Sebastián** you'll find that most of the goods for sale are geared for locals—fruits, vegetables, and medicinal herbs. Pick up one of the *shigras*, the colorful, handwoven hemp bags used by indigenous people.

In the tiny mountain village of **Pujilí**, 10 km (6 mi) west of Latacunga, colorful markets are held on Sunday and, with much less ado, on Wednesday. Few tourists find their way here, so instead of gringos in T-shirts you'll see locals in bright turquoise or carmine ponchos and miniature fedoras buying and selling produce, pottery, and costume jewelry.

In **Saquisilí**, 13 km (8 mi) northwest of Latacunga, indigenous people in regional dress fill all eight of the village's dusty plazas during the Thursday market, where you can pick through piles of traditional wares—including painted wooden masks of animals and devils.

The market town of **San Miguel de Salcedo**, 14 km (9 mi) south of Latacunga, has pleasant streets and plazas that make it appealing on any day. However, it's most interesting to plan your visit around the Sunday market or the smaller one held on Thursday.

Where to Stay & Eat

The region has several hosterías with comfortable rooms. These former haciendas are found outside the towns and villages, so count on country solitude.

★ $$$–$$$$ ✕▦ **Hacienda San Agustín de Callo.** This place has been inhabited for more than five centuries—it began as an Inca fortress and was transformed into an Augustinian monastery after the Spanish conquest. It now belongs to an Ecuadorian family. Two original Inca structures are used as a chapel and a dining room. The hotel is a few miles from Parque Nacional Cotopaxi, where you have access to horseback riding, trout fishing, mountain biking, and trekking. ⊠ *San Agustín* ☎ *02/224–2508, 02/226–9884 in Quito* 🖶🖶 *03/719–160* ⊕ *www.incahacienda.com* ⟲ *4 rooms, 2 suites* ⟨ *Restaurant, dining room, horseback riding* ▤ *MC, V.*

★ ¢ 🖼 **The Black Sheep Inn.** It's not easy to get here, but you'll find this place— an eco-hostel—is one of the nicest in Ecuador. Prices include vegetarian dinners, farm fresh breakfasts, tea and coffee all day, purified drinking water, hiking maps, and hot showers. Most rooms have a woodstove fireplace. Dinner is family-style. Also available are lunches, home-baked desserts, Chilean Wines, cold beer, a full bar, and European-style cheeses. Perched on a hillside outside the village of Chugchilan in the Cotopaxi province, this hostel is five hours southwest of Quito. You can get here by bus, jeep, or taxi. The American owners, Andres Hammerman and Michelle Kirby, will help you make arrangements. ⊠ *Box 05–01–240, Chugchilan, Cotopaxi* ☎ *03/814–587* ⊕ *www.blacksheepinn. com* ⟲ *9 rooms and 1 bunkhouse* ⟨ *Dining room, sauna, hiking, mountain bikes* ▤ *No credit cards.*

Baños

84 km (53 mi) southeast of Latacunga.

At the base of Volcán Tungurahua and surrounded by heavily forested mountains, tumbling waterfalls, and natural hot springs, Baños is one of Ecuador's top tourist spots. Quiteños have been soaking in the thermal springs for decades. The town's real appeal—as tour operators will attest—are the abundant hiking trails, white-water rafting trips, and horseback excursions in the surrounding highlands.

In the heart of town, the twin spires of **La Iglesia de la Virgen del Agua Santa** rise above the tree-lined plaza. The Church of the Virgin of the Holy Water, whose black-and-white facade is slightly startling, was built to honor Baños's miracle-working patron saint. The huge paintings inside are testimonials from her many exultant beneficiaries.

A few blocks away from the church is the small but interesting **Museo Huillancuna** (⊠ Pasaje Velasco Ibarra and Av. Montalvo ☎ 03/740–973), a museum that has exhibits about pre-Columbian ceramics, Andean musical instruments, and local history.

Baños means "baths" in Spanish, and there are several thermal springs in town. The best of the bunch is a series of pools called **El Salado** (the Salty One). Its six rough-hewn pools, next to a fast-moving stream, overflow with mineral water of various temperatures. The pools are refilled each morning at dawn. ⊠ *2 km (1 mi) outside Baños on Vía al Salado* ▦ *$2* ⊘ *Daily dawn–dusk.*

Where to Stay & Eat

¢ ✕ **El Higuerón.** Hidden behind bougainvillea and flowering vines, this small restaurant serves tasty salads, sandwiches, and pastas. Dine at wood tables beside sunny windows or head outside to one of the inviting tables on the patio. The owner, William Navarette, is among the region's most knowledgeable mountaineers. ⊠ *Calle 12 de Noviembre 270* ☎ *03/740–910* ▤ *MC, V* ⊘ *Closed Wed.*

$$$ ✕⌧ **Luna Runtún.** Perched high over Baños on the slopes of Volcán Tungurahua, Swiss-run Luna Runtún combines colonial-style architecture with the attention to detail you would expect from a European resort. On your pillow will be fresh flowers carefully selected from the gardens outside. Hike along a route used by rum smugglers in the 1920s, ride horses through the nearby countryside, or join a trip to the hot springs. ⊠ *6 km (4 mi) from Baños* ☎ *03/740–882 or 03/740–883* 🖷 *03/740–376* ⊕ *www.lunaruntun.com* ⇆ *33 rooms, 2 suites* ♨ *Restaurant, horseback riding, bar* 🖃 *AE, DC, MC, V.*

¢–$ ⌧ **Hotel Sangay.** This family-oriented hotel across the street from the municipal baths has large cabañas behind the pool and spacious rooms with balconies overlooking the nearby Waterfall of the Virgin. From the second-floor restaurant you'll also get nice views. ⊠ *Plazoleta Ayora 101* ☎ *03/740–490* 🖷 *03/740–056* ⇆ *70 rooms* ♨ *Restaurant, tennis court, pool, 2 hot tubs, sauna, steam room, squash, bar* 🖃 *AE, DC, MC, V.*

¢–$ ✕⌧ **Le Petit Auberge and Restaurant.** After establishing a reputation as one of this town's best restaurants, this place expanded to include inexpensive rooms. All have hardwood floors, white stucco walls, and balconies. Many are warmed by wood-burning fireplaces. The restaurant serves French cuisine, with a menu that includes crêpes, ratatouille, and delicious fondues. ⊠ *Av. 16 de Diciembre at Calle Montalvo* ☎ *03/740–936* ⇆ *12 rooms* 🖃 *V* ⊙ *Restaurant closed Mon.*

¢ ⌧ **Hostería Monte Selva.** This quartet of three-room bungalows is nestled on a lush hillside at the edge of town. Each room has several beds and a small bath. Many have views of the town. At the foot of the hill is a swimming pool, a sauna, and a lovely little restaurant. ⊠ *Calle Halflants, near Calle Montalvo* ☎☎ *03/740–244* ⇆ *12 rooms* ♨ *Restaurant, pool, hot tub, sauna, steam room, bar* 🖃 *DC, MC, V.*

Sports & the Outdoors

BICYCLING   Cycling fans won't be able to resist the five-hour, 65-km (40-mi) downhill ride from Baños to Puyo. At the bottom you can board a bus, bike and all, for the return trip to Baños. **Auca** (⊠ Calle Maldonado and Calle Oriente ☎ 03/740–637) organizes bicycle tours through the highlands and canoeing expeditions through the jungle. Mountain bikes can be rented at affordable rates at **Bill Mountain** (⊠ Calle Ambato at Calle Maldonado ☎ 03/740–221), which also offers cycling tours that wind through subtropical jungle and past thundering waterfalls.

HORSEBACK   At least a dozen tour operators offer excellent day trips and overnight
RIDING   excursions around Baños. **Caballos con José** (⊠ Calle Maldonado, near Calle Martínez ☎☎ 03/740–929) is a reliable company that offers tours lasting from two hours to several nights. **Huillacuna Tours** (⊠ Calle Santa Clara 206 ☎ 03/740–187) schedules half- and full-day tours to Runtún. **Rio Loco** (⊠ Calle Maldonado and Calle Martínez ☎ 03/740–929) offers a variety of excursions outside Baños.

RAFTING   White-water rafting trips on the Patate and Pastaza rivers are the reason many people head to Baños. The Class III Patate is a good trip for beginners, while the Class III and IV Pastaza is a more challenging four-hour trip through some spectacular jungle. Trips can be booked through **Geotours** (✉ Calle Maldonado at Calle Espejo ☎ 03/740–332). **Remote Odysseys Worldwide** (✉ Calle Foch 721, at Calle Juan León Mera, Quito ☎ 02/270–3535 ⊕ www.rowinc.com) organizes Class III and IV whitewater trips on the Rió Upano, including side trips to Shuar villages in the Amazon and camping out in the Morona-Santiago Province.

Shopping

In Baños you'll find plenty of shopping. Most of the items you'll find come from other parts of Ecuador, but there are a few interesting local crafts that can be purchased from the people who produce them. Look for hand-carved toucans, turtles, and other tropical creatures. **Recuerdos** (✉ Calle Maldonado, near Calle Montalvo) sells balsa-wood carvings of parrots and other birds made in a workshop behind the store. **El Cade** (✉ Calle Maldonado 681) sells items carved from the seed of the tagua palm, a hard substance also known as vegetal ivory.

Riobamba

105 km (63 mi) south of Latacunga.

Three of Ecuador's most formidable peaks—Chimborazo, Altar, and Tungurahua—are visible from Riobamba, a pleasant town with wide, tree-lined streets and some well-preserved colonial architecture. Most travelers head to Riobamba because it's the starting point for the famous "Devil's Nose" train trip. Mudslides destroyed large sections of the Trans-Andean railroad, which once ran all the way from Quito to Duran.

There are good buys at the tourist-oriented Saturday market held in the **Parque de la Concepción** (✉ Calle Orozco at Calle Colón). Look for embroidered belts, hand-knit sweaters, and locally produced jewelry. Across the street from Parque de la Concepción, the **Museo de Arte Religioso** (✉ Calle Argentina ☎ 03/952–212) is housed in the beautifully restored Iglesia de la Concepción. The Religious Art Museum has an impressive collection of artifacts from the colonial period.

The hill in the center of the **Parque 21 de Abril** (✉ Calle Argentina) affords an excellent view of the city. On clear days you'll have eye-popping views of several snowcapped volcanoes. The mural here depicts the city's history.

Where to Stay & Eat

$ ✕🏨 **Hostería El Troje.** This place just outside Riobamba welcomes you back to your spacious room with a crackling fire in the hearth. When there are enough guests, the hotel puts on a show with folk music and dancing before dinner. The owner is one of the most famous mountain climbers in Ecuador. ✉ *4½ km (3 mi) southeast of Riobamba* ☎ *03/ 960–826 or 03/964–572* ⊕ *www.eltroje.com* ➘ *48 rooms* ⚭ *Restaurant, pool, basketball, bar, playground* ⊟ *AE, DC, MC, V.*

¢ ✕🏨 **Hostel Montecarlo.** This century-old house, with its fern-filled central courtyard, is conveniently located in the middle of town. Its elegant yet homey restaurant, around the corner from the hotel, is first-rate. ✉ *Av.*

10 de Agosto 2541 ☎ *03/960–557* ⤶ *18 rooms* ⚲ *Restaurant, cafeteria* ▭ *MC, V.*

$ 🏨 **Hostería Abraspungu.** Reminiscent of a mountain lodge, this place is among the most practical accommodations in the Central Highlands. Each of the clean, comfortable rooms is named after a different mountain peak; several rooms overlook the surrounding hills. Horses, stabled on-site, are available for day treks. The owner, mountaineer Marco Cruz, knows the best hikes in the region. ⊠ *5½ km (3½ mi) from Riobamba* ☎ *03/940–820* 🖷 *03/940–819* ⤶ *20 rooms* ⚲ *Restaurant, hiking, horseback riding, bar, laundry service* ▭ *AE, DC, MC, V.*

The Central Highlands A to Z

BUS TRAVEL

To reach Parque Nacional Cotopaxi, take any of the buses to Ambato that leave from Quito's Terminal Terrestre every 30 minutes. They will drop you off in Lasso, about 10 km (6 mi) from the park entrance. The 30-km (18-mi) ride takes just under an hour and costs $2. Most Quito tour operators offer day trips to the park for around $40. Buses headed to Tena travel every hour past the Termas de Papallacta. You may have to pay the full fare to Tena, which is under $3. There are no direct buses to Parque Pasochoa. Your best bet is taking a bus from Quito's La Marin square to Amaguaña and asking the bus driver to drop you off when you're about 7 km (4½ mi) away. From there you can either walk or hire someone to take you the rest of the way. From Quito, buses leave frequently for Latacunga (2 hours), Baños (3½ hours), and Riobamba (4 hours). All cost less than $5 each way. Local buses connect Latacunga with Pujilí, Saquisilí, and San Miguel de Salcedo.

CAR TRAVEL

Latacunga lies just off the Pan-American Highway, 89 km (55 mi) south of Quito. The nearby villages of Pujilí, San Miguel de Salcedo, and Saquisilí are accessed via gravel roads. Baños is 40 km (25 mi) east of Ambato on the road to Puyo. Riobamba is nestled along the Pan-American Highway 188 km (117 mi) south of Quito. Think twice about driving yourself, as poor roads will impede your progress.

MONEY MATTERS

Although most hotels in the Central Highlands accept traveler's checks and credit cards, inquire before you set out. Because banks are few and far between, bring all of the cash that you think you'll need. You'll find very few ATMs in the countryside.

TAXIS

You can hire a taxi to take you from Quito to the Central Highlands. The fare to Baños, for example, would cost around $100. Remember that you must also pay for the return fare back to the city. You can also hire the driver to accompany you on your travels, but you must pay for his food and lodging as well.

Taxis between Latacunga and the nearby villages of Pujilí, Saquisilí, and Salcedo cost less than $10 each way.

VISITOR INFORMATION

The local hotel association in Baños has an information office in front of Hostal Banana. There is also an information booth at the bus station. The Riobamba tourist office is open Monday–Saturday 8:30–5.

🖪 Tourist Information **Baños Hotel Association** ⊠ Calle 12 de Noviembre 500 ☎ 03/740-309. **Riobamba Tourist Office** ⊠ Av. 15 de Junio 2072, at Av. 10 de Agosto ☎ 03/941-213.

CUENCA & THE SOUTHERN HIGHLANDS

In 1557 after Spanish troops defeated Inca troops, the Viceroy of Lima gave Cuenca the official name of "Santa Ana de los Rios de Cuenca" (Saint Ann of the Rivers of Cuenca). This prosperous and beautiful highland city—in the Pucarabama Valley between the eastern and western Andes mountain range—has retained much of its colonial splendor. No building, for example, is allowed to be higher than the highest church steeple, and along its cobblestone streets you'll find colonial mansions with wrought-iron balconies overflowing with potted plants. Here you'll still find old men gossiping in the shady squares and women drying laundry on the grass along the river banks, but despite all that Cuenca is one of the most advanced cities in Ecuador—it's one of the few cities in Latin America with a controlled water and sewer system, and all electrical wiring downtown is underground.

On market days—Thursday and Sunday—hundreds of people from surrounding villages crowd into Cuenca's open-air plazas to buy and sell crafts and household items. It's not surprising that the *Cuencanos* have developed a stubborn pride in their skills. Cuenca produces fine ceramics and textiles but is best known for its handsome Panama hats. The *Cholas Cuencanas*—female descendants of mixed Spanish and Cañari couples—are striking in their colorful *polleras* (gathered wool skirts in violet, emerald, rose, or marigold), satiny white blouses, and fine straw hats.

Numbers in the text correspond to numbers in the margin and on the Cuenca map.

Exploring Cuenca

a good walk

In the heart of Cuenca's compact Old City stretches the shady **Parque Abdón Calderón** ❶ ⌐. The grand facade and periwinkle-blue domes of Cuenca's **Catedral de la Inmaculada** ❷, also known as the New Cathedral, tower over the park's western edge. Beside it you'll find a colorful flower market and the chapel called **Carmen de la Asunción** ❸. On the opposite side of the square sits delicate **El Sagrario** ❹, the Old Cathedral. Walk two blocks east of El Sagrario, then walk 1½ blocks south on Calle Hermano Miguel to the entrance of the **Museo de las Conceptas** ❺. Head west on Calle Presidente Córdova until you reach the vendor stalls that occupy **Plaza de San Francisco** ❻. The tan-and-white church that dominates the square is the **Iglesia de San Francisco** ❼. Four blocks west along Calle Mariscal Sucre is the **Museo de Arte Moderno** ❽ overlooking the plaza (which used to be a bull-fighting arena) and church of San Sebastián. If you still have energy, head south to the Río Tomebamba, which flows along the southern edge of the Old City. Cross the bridge for some fine views of the steeples of the town's churches soaring above the rooftops.

TIMING This walk will take two or three hours, a bit more if you spend a lot of time in the museums; note that these are closed on Sundays. It's worth-while to stop somewhere for lunch, since the nicest restaurants tend to be in the center of town.

What to See

❸ Carmen de la Asunción. The ornate carvings surrounding the doorway of this diminutive chapel are a good example of Spanish baroque de-sign. The interior is typically ostentatious—especially noteworthy is the gilded pulpit encrusted with tiny mirrors. The flower market held out-side on the Plazoleta El Carmen is in full bloom every day from sunrise to sunset. ⊠ *Calle Mariscal Sucre at Calle Padre Aguirre* 🕮 *Free* ☉ *Daily 6 AM–8 PM.*

★ **❷ Catedral de la Inmaculada.** Started in 1886 and finished more than 80 years later, the immense cathedral can hold more than 9,000 worshipers. The interior arches tower more than 100 feet high, and light that en-ters through the stained-glass windows casts a golden glow over the thick brick walls and Italian marble floors. The impressive pillars are Ecuado-rian marble and the choir chairs are hand-carved from native wood. ⊠ *Parque Abdón Calderón* 🕾 *07/842–097* ☉ *Daily 6:30–4:30.*

❹ El Sagrario. Also called the Old Cathedral, the lovely little church was begun in 1557, the year the city was founded. It is gleaming after a com-plete restoration. ⊠ *Parque Calderón.*

❼ Iglesia de San Francisco. Built in the 1920s, the Church of Saint Francis is famous for its soaring steeple and intricately carved, gold-drenched main altar, which contrasts nicely with its unassuming interior. ⊠ *Av. Gran Colombia at Calle Padre Aguirre* ☉ *Mon.–Wed. 7:30–8:15 AM, Thurs.–Sat. 6:30–7:15 AM, Sun. 7:30–9:30 AM and 4–5 PM.*

❽ Museo de Arte Moderno. The Museum of Modern Art, housed in a re-stored convent, features interesting exhibitions of works by local artists. Its permanent collection consists mainly of dark, bleak paintings by un-known colonial masters. ⊠ *Calle Mariscal Sucre at Calle Coronel Tal-bot* 🕾 *07/831–027* 🕮 *Free* ☉ *Weekdays 9–1 and 3–7, weekends 10–1.*

off the
beaten
path

MUSEO DEL BANCO CENTRAL – This museum in the concrete-and-glass Central Bank building houses a collection of archaeological treasures in addition to exhibits of colonial and postcolonial art. On the river behind the museum is a small archaeological site where some Inca ruins are being excavated. ⊠ *Calle Larga at Av. Huayna-Capac* 🕾 *07/831–255 Ext. 234* 🕮 *$1* ☉ *Weekdays 9–6, Sat. 9–1.*

❺ Museo de las Conceptas. One of Cuenca's leading citizens in the colonial era, Doña Ordóñez, donated her spacious home to the Catholic Church, whereupon it became the cloistered convent of the Order of the Immaculate Conception. Four centuries later, part of this well-preserved edifice houses the Museum of the Conception, which contains an impressive collection of religious art from the 16th to 19th century. Most of the collection was contributed by families whose daughters became cloistered nuns. ⊠ *Calle Hermano Miguel 6–33, between Calles Juan Jaramillo and Presidente Córdova* ☎ *07/830–625* ⊡ *$1.50* ☉ *Mon. 2:30–5:30, Tues.–Fri. 9–7:30, Sat. 10–1.*

▶ **①** **Parque Abdón Calderón.** Surrounded by beautiful colonial buildings, Cuenca's central square is one of the loveliest in South America. Manicured trees tower over men discussing politics, grandmothers walking arm-in-arm, and children running to and fro. The park is dominated by the pale rose Catedral de la Inmaculada towering over its western edge.

❻ **Plaza de San Francisco.** The noisy plaza is filled with vendors hawking a variety of bric-a-brac. Under the northern colonnade, merchants sell more enticing wares—colorful skirts, hand-knit sweaters, and intricate hangings.

off the beaten path	TURI – For a fantastic view of Cuenca by night or day, head up the mountain to the tiny village of Turi. Stroll along Turi's main street past the mural-covered church and you'll soon find yourself in rolling hills where stucco farmhouses punctuate cornfields and potato patches. Up here there's also a workshop of a well-known artist, where you'll see his ceramics and paintings. A cab is the best way to get here, but make sure to ask the driver to wait for you.

Where to Stay & Eat

¢ ✕ **El Jardín.** Hand-painted menus list a variety of steak and seafood dishes. Start with the tangy conch ceviche served in a crystal goblet, and then move on to the succulent grilled lobster. Consider a fine Chilean wine with your meal. The relaxed, friendly service here ensures many repeat visitors. ⊠ *Presidente Córdova 7–23* ☎ *07/831–120* ⊟ *AE, DC, MC, V.*

¢ ✕ **El Pedregal Azteca.** If you're tired of the local cuisine you couldn't do better than stopping in this Mexican eatery. Try the *chile rellenos* (deep-fried chili peppers stuffed with cheese) or the specialty of the house, *carne asada a la tampiqueña* (beef grilled with salt and lemon). On weekends there's live music and two-for-one margaritas. ⊠ *Av. Gran Colombia 1029, at Calle Padre Aguirre* ☎ *07/823–652* ⊟ *DC, MC, V* ☉ *Closed Sun.*

★ ¢ ✕ **Los Capulíes.** This restaurant in a 200-year-old mansion has greenery and fountains. Start with a delicately sweetened empanada, followed by the *plato típico cuencano*, a sampler dish of llapingachos, grilled pork, sweet sausages, and *mote pillo* (boiled corn mixed with onions and eggs). End your meal with a warm glass of *canelazo* (a concoction combining sugar cane, cinnamon, and bitter orange with the rumlike *zhumir*). The music of Andean flutes echoes in the air on weekends, and a bar in an attached building is a favorite hangout. ⊠ *Calle Borrero at Calle Córdova* ☎ *07/832–339* ⊟ *AE, DC, MC, V.*

¢ ✕ **Montebello.** This Mediterranean-style restaurant in nearby Turi affords panoramic views of Cuenca, so be sure to request a table by the window.

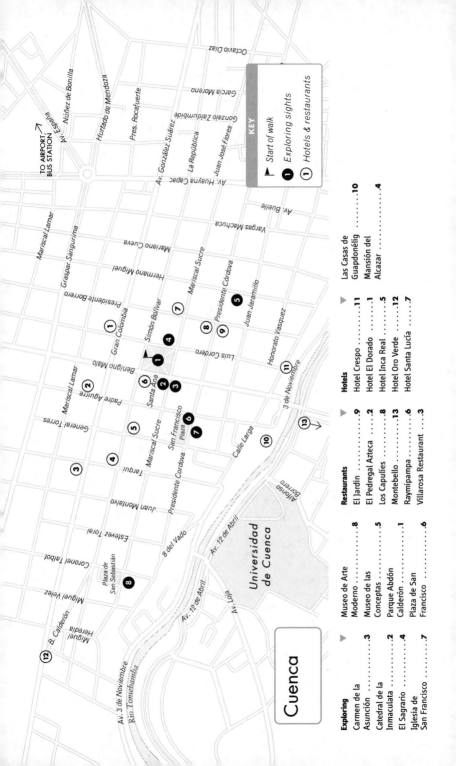

Cuenca

KEY

▲ Start of walk

● Exploring sights

① Hotels & restaurants

Exploring

▶

Carmen de la
Asunción **3**

Catedral de la
Inmaculada **2**

El Sagrario **4**

Iglesia de
San Francisco **7**

Museo de Arte
Moderno **8**

Museo de las
Conceptas **5**

Parque Abdón
Calderón **1**

Plaza de San
Francisco **6**

Restaurants

▶

El Jardín **9**

El Pedregal Azteca **2**

Los Capulíes **8**

Montebello **13**

Raymipampa **6**

Villarosa Restaurant ... **3**

Hotels

▶

Hotel Crespo **11**

Hotel El Dorado **1**

Hotel Inca Real **5**

Hotel Oro Verde **12**

Hotel Santa Lucía **7**

Las Casas de
Guapdonélig **10**

Mansión del
Alcazar **4**

TO AIRPORT;
BUS STATION

Universidad
de Cuenca

Tables and chairs are white and purple. Meat dishes are featured, including the excellent *parillada Montebello,* a casserole of pork, beef, chicken, sausage, and rice. Any taxi driver will know the way to the restaurant. ⊠ *Turi* ☎ *07/ 883–403 or 07/843–079* ▤ *AE, V* ۝ *Closed Mon.–Wed.*

¢ ✕ **Raymipampa.** An unbeatable location adjacent to the Catedral de la Inmaculada doesn't hurt, but it's the reasonably priced food and amiable mood that makes this restaurant a hit. The extensive menu includes crêpes and ceviches, and such Ecuadorian favorites as *locro de queso* (a milk-based potato soup garnished with avocado and cheese). ⊠ *Calle Benigno Malo 859* ☎ *07/834–159* ▤ *AE, DC, MC, V.*

¢ ✕ **Villarosa Restaurant.** One of the city's best restaurants and a favorite
Fodor'sChoice with locals is in a colonial house near the central Plaza. Soft music floats
★ through several tastefully decorated salons to the upper balcony, where an open fireplace chases out the evening chill. Try the grilled trout with almonds, then finish with the fruit-and-chocolate fondue. The same family owns the Hotel Santa Lucía. ⊠ *Av. Gran Colombia 1222* ☎ *07/837– 944* ▤ *AE, DC, MC, V* ۝ *Closed weekends.*

$$$ 🏨 **Hotel Oro Verde.** Once named "La Laguna" after the artificial lake at
Fodor'sChoice its center, this low-rise hotel has a relaxed, casual environment. This is
★ the place for animal lovers: ducks swim past your window, three resident alpacas munch on the grassy banks, and peacocks stroll through bushes heavy with pink and yellow roses. It's 2 km (1 mi) from the center of town, so take a taxi unless you're up for a 45-minute walk. The restaurant is famous for its fish—try the trout marinated in brandy. ⊠ *Av. Ordóñez Lazo* ☎ *07/831–200, 800/447–7462 in the U.S.* ☒ *07/832–849* ⊕ *www. oroverdehotels.com* ⇾ *80 rooms, 2 suites* ⚭ *Restaurant, coffee shop, pool, sauna, steam room, bar, airport shuttle* ▤ *AE, DC, MC, V.*

$$ 🏨 **Hotel El Dorado.** Convenient to most of the city's sights, this eight-story hotel is just two blocks from Parque Calderón. Rooms at the back of the hotel are quieter than on the street side. Enjoy a meal at the Inti Sumag restaurant or Chordeleg Café, or relax with a cocktail at the Samana piano bar. Buffet breakfast and airport transfers are included in the rate. ⊠ *Av. Gran Colombia 787, at Calle Luis Cordera* ☎ *07/ 831–390* ☒ *07/831–663* ⇾ *91 rooms* ⚭ *Restaurant, gym, sauna, steam room, bar, airport shuttle* ▤ *AE, DC, MC, V.*

$$ 🏨 **Mansión del Alcazar.** Fluffy down comforters top beds—some of them canopies—in rooms with filmy curtains covering windows that look onto an indoor courtyard with a trickling fountain. A hot water bottle slipped under your covers warms your bed at night. Crystal chandeliers, antique furniture, and art give you the feeling of what life was like hundreds of years ago in this carefully preserved colonial mansion two blocks from Plaza Abdón Calderó. Most rooms have only showers instead of full baths. A couple of rooms have windows looking onto an outdoor garden. ⊠ *Calle Bolívar 12–55, at Tarqui* ☎ *07/823–554 or 07/823–918* ☒ *07/823–889* ⇾ *10 rooms* ⚭ *Restaurant, bar* ▤ *AE, DC, MC, V* ⦿ *BP.*

$–$$ 🏨 **Hotel Santa Lucía.** In a beautifully restored building, Santa Lucía has attractive rooms, though their style is more modern than the building itself. Built by the first governor of the Azuay (Cuenca) province in 1859, it has been in the Vintimilla family for three generations and is in the center of the historic district. The family decided not to remove a large tree that was growing right in the middle of the courtyard. An American breakfast is included. The restaurant (¢–$$) has excellent service and food: Seabass in marinara sauce with assorted seafood; chicken in a lemon–herb sauce; and a number of risottos and gnocchis are some of the choices. ⊠ *Antonio Borrero 8–44 y Sucre* ☎ *07/828–000* 🖷 *07/842–443* ⊕ *www.santaluciahotel.com* 🛏 *22 rooms* ⚭ *Restaurant, bar* ▤ *AE, MC, V.*

$ 🏨 **Hotel Crespo.** This hotel overlooking the Río Tomebamba gives you the feeling of staying in a rambling country house. You climb a twisting wood stairway to the upper rooms, which have lovely views of the river. Scattered about are numerous sitting areas that add to the familiar, homey atmosphere. The restaurant serves excellent French cuisine. ⊠ *Calle Larga 793* ☎ *07/842–571* 🖷 *07/839–473* 🛏 *37 rooms, 3 suites* ⚭ *Restaurant, minibars, bar, business services, meeting rooms* ▤ *AE, DC, MC, V.*

¢ 🏨 **Hotel Inca Real.** Huddled around three covered courtyards, this sunny hotel is small, but has neat and cheerfully furnished rooms, original art, and unique lighting fixtures. ⊠ *Calle General Torres 840, between Calles Sucre and Bolívar* ☎ *07/823–636* 🖷 *07/840–699* 🛏 *30 rooms* ⚭ *Restaurant, bar, meeting room* ▤ *AE, DC, MC, V.*

¢ 🏨 **Las Casas de Guapdondélig.** This family-run inn, one block from the local Saturday market (known as Mercado 12 de Abril), occupies three former homes in a residential neighborhood on the south side of the city. It's popular with families. Rooms are simple and comfortable. From time to time, folk musicians enliven dinner in the restaurant. ⊠ *Calle Guapdondélig at Calle J. Roldos* ☎🖷 *07/861–917* 🛏 *22 rooms* ⚭ *Restaurant, indoor pool, sauna, steam room, bar* ▤ *AE, DC, MC, V.*

Nightlife & the Arts

Nightlife

Cuenca doesn't have a vivid nightlife. Locals usually stay home during the week, venturing forth only on weekends. **La Cantina** (⊠ Calle Presidente Borrero at Calle Córdova ☎ 07/832–339) is an attractive little bar next to Los Capulíes. Musicians play on weekends. German-owned **Wunderbar** (⊠ Calle Hermano Miguel at Calle Larga ☎ 07/831–274) is an intimate bar popular with locals. It's in an old building along the Escalinata, the wide stairway leading down to the river. For dancing check out **El Conquistador** (⊠ Av. Gran Colombia 665 ☎ 07/831–788).

The Arts

A good source for information on art events is the daily newspaper *El Mercurio*. **La Fundación Paul Rivet** (⊠ Av. Solano and 10 de Agosto ☎ 07/885–951) distributes a monthly newsletter of cultural events.

Plays are sometimes performed at **La Casa de la Cultura** (⊠ Calle Luis Cordero 718 ☎ 07/828–175).

Shopping

Cuenca's artisans produce fine ceramics, textiles, and silver and gold jewelry. Among its most important products is the Panama hat, whose name sticks in the collective craw of proud Ecuadorians. These finely made straw hats—also known as *toquillas*—got their name for the country to which they were first exported en masse. U.S. president Teddy Roosevelt wore one when he toured the Panama Canal, so the hats were forever associated with that Central American country.

The first hats were made by hand in the coastal towns of Jipijapa and Montecristi, and a really fine one can still take up to eight months to make. On a tour of **Homero Ortega & Sons** you'll see how palm leaf fibers are transformed into elegant headware. You'll also have the opportunity to buy one for as little as $10 up to $250. ⊠ *Av. Gil Ramirez Davalos 3–86* ☎ *07/834–045* 🖷 *07/834–045* ⊙ *Weekdays 9–5, Sat. 9–noon.*

If you're in the market for leather, **Concuero** (⊠ Calle Mariscal Lamar 1137) sells good-quality shoes, wallets, and handbags. **Fundación Jorge Moscoso** (⊠ Calle Presidente Córdova 614) has a limited but precious collection of antiques. **Kinara** (⊠ Calle Mariscal Sucre 770) stocks stylish gold and silver jewelry and shawls made of traditional ikat textiles in which the threads are knotted and dyed prior to weaving.

Original designs of ceramics, murals, and jewelry are for sale—browsers are welcome—at **Eduardo Vega's Workshop and Gallery.** Vega is Ecuador's most famous ceramicist and designer. The gallery not only sells Vega's beautiful designs but you'll get a really good cup of coffee here. Located on "El Turi" hill, known as the "Mirador de Turi," it's also the best spot for a spectacular view of Cuenca. ⊠ *Hermano Miguel 670* ⊙ *Mon.–Fr. 9–5 and Sat. 9:30–1:30.*

Ingapirca

FodorsChoice
★
70 km (42 mi) north of Cuenca.

Long before the Incas invaded the region in the latter half of the 15th century, the fierce and industrious Cañari people ruled Guapdondélig ("Plain as Wide and Beautiful as the Sky"), their name for the fertile highlands surrounding Cuenca. They built some stunning monuments, including the ancient city of Ingapirca.

An important religious and political center to the Cañaris, Ingapirca is perhaps better remembered for what the Incas built here after Tupac-Yupanqui conquered the Cañaris. The king left behind quite a legacy, including the name, which means "Wall of the Incas." The smaller stone structures, built completely without mortar, are thought to be Cañari temples to the moon, but the massive elliptical structure at the center is acknowledged to be a temple to the sun built by the Incas. A 10-minute hike away is La Cara del Inca, a natural rock formation said to resemble the face of an Inca chief.

There is a small museum at the entrance, built under the auspices of the Banco Central, which houses artifacts found at the ruins. The cozy restaurant on the hill overlooking the site serves excellent soups and local dishes in front of a fireplace. Getting to the ruins is half the fun. Buses

CloseUp

MARKET DAY IN THE ANDES

SUNDAY IS MARKET DAY IN villages near Cuenca. Buses leave regularly from Cuenca's Terminal Terrestre and getting there is half the fun. Drivers pick up anyone that waves them down. Young men lugging pots and pans jump on, leaving their wares piled in the aisle. Women carrying their babies wrapped in shawls drag burlap sacks filled with dried corn to their seats. Farmers taking livestock to the market hold roosters under their arms or strap piglets to the roof. (Larger pigs are more of a problem, and it's not unheard of to see the owner of a squealing sow trying to stuff it into the luggage compartment). By the time you arrive at your destination, the bus itself will seem like a market on wheels.

The largest village is Gualaceo, 38 km (24 mi) east of Cuenca. Well-dressed Cañari women in colorful polleras and jaunty straw or felt hats gather in the main square. Locals buy and sell clothing and kitchen items, but the majority of booths feature piles of fresh produce, sacks overflowing with grains, and barrels filled with spices.

The quietest of the Andean villages, the mining town of Chordeleg, is along a winding road about 5 km (3 mi) south of Gualaceo. The highlight of the market is handmade jewelry. Some complain that the quality of the gold and silver filigree has diminished, but good bargains can still be had. A ring with a startling amount of detail costs less than $5. Handicrafts, embroidered clothing, pottery, and mounds of jewelry, are sold in shops surrounding the tree-shaded square. About 24 km (15 mi) beyond Chordeleg is Sigsig, best known for its Panama hats.

–Wayne Hoffman

costing less than $2 depart from Cuenca's Terminal Terrestre at 9 and 1. Your return bus is likely to be filled with villagers transporting chickens and other livestock to market. The other option is to take a guided tour. Note that you might want to use a restroom before arriving. Those at the site leave much to be desired. ⊠ 5 km (3 mi) east of Cañaris ⊠ $2 ⊙ Daily 9–6.

Where to Stay & Eat

¢ 🏨 **Pousada de Ingapirca.** To spend more time at Ingapirca, consider a stay at this pousada. Rooms are simple and heated only by space heaters and fireplaces. If you want to see the countryside you can rent horses for $10 a day; for another $10 you can hire a guide, who will lead you along an old Inca trail. The restaurant is excellent. ⊠ 3 miles east of Cañaris, 42 mi north of Cuenca ☎ 07/290–670, 07/831–120 in Cuenca 🛏 8 rooms. ⚒ Restaurant ▭ No credit cards ⏀ BP.

Parque Nacional Cajas

32 km (20 mi) west of Cuenca.

A short drive from the sunny city of Cuenca are the cold, cloudy moors of Parque Nacional Cajas, where the average elevation is 10,500 feet.

The rugged terrain is the legacy left by glaciers as they retreated some 5 million years ago. Today the nearly 70,000 acres of this national park are home to Andean condors, hawks, and the elusive gray-breasted mountain toucan, as well as wolves, gazelles, and white-tailed deer. The area's 230 trout-filled lakes are accessible by boat, and fishing trips can be arranged through local tour operators and hotels.

Cajas is best explored with an experienced guide, because visitors can easily become disoriented in the stark landscape. A guide will point out the unique páramo vegetation and select the best place to set up camp each evening. Be prepared for strong sun, cold wind, and the possibility of rain. Sunglasses and sunscreen are necessities. There is a ranger station near the entrance where you can sometimes sleep for a small fee, although if the accommodations are full you'll have to make other plans.

Cuenca & the Southern Highlands A to Z

AIR TRAVEL

Cuenca's Aeropuerto Mariscal Lamar is 2 km (1 mi) from the city center, past the bus terminal. A cab from the airport to downtown costs around $3. Tame, ICARO, and Austro Aéreo fly daily between Cuenca, Guayaquil, and Quito.

🛪 Airlines **Austro Aéreo** ☎ 07/832-677 or 07/848-659. **ICARO** ☎ 07/802-700. **Tame** ☎ 07/843-222.

🛪 Airports **Aeropuerto Mariscal Lamar** ✉ Av. España ☎ 07/862-203.

BUS TRAVEL

From Cuenca's Terminal Terrestre, 1½ km (1 mi) northeast of the town center, there are daily departures to Quito (10 hours) and Guayaquil (6 hours), both less than $7. You can also catch buses to Ingapirca for less than $2.

You can reach Parque Nacional Cajas via buses that leave between 6 and 6:30 AM from the corner of Calles Bolívar and Colonel Talbot. Weekend trips can be crowded, so you may have to stand for the two-hour trip. The only bus back to Cuenca leaves around 3 PM; check with the driver for the exact time.

🚌 Bus Information **Terminal Terrestre** ✉ Av. España ☎ 07/827-061.

CAR TRAVEL

Cuenca is 472 km (293 mi) south of Quito via the Pan-American Highway. The drive from Quito is eight hours; from Guayaquil it's four hours. The former takes you along the Avenue of the Volcanoes, while the latter climbs through subtropical lowlands before beginning a dizzying mountain ascent—8,300 feet in just over 240 km (150 mi). There are services along the way but road conditions between Guayaquil and Cuenca are much better than from Quito. Flying is the better option.

MONEY MATTERS

Traveler's checks and credit cards are usually accepted at most hotels, restaurants, and shops in Cuenca.

TAXIS

Taxis are easy to find on the streets of downtown Cuenca. A trip almost anywhere in town should cost less than $2.

TOUR OPERATORS

For trips in and around Cuenca, try Ecotrek, Metropolitan Touring, or Seitur. Metrotours has tours in Cuenca.

🚩 Tour Companies **Ecotrek** ⊠ Calle Larga 7108, at Calle Cordero ☎ 07/842-531. **Metropolitan Touring** ⊠ Mariscal Sucre 662 ☎ 07/831-185 or 07/831-463. **Metrotours** ⊠ Calle Lagarta 6-96, at Borrero ☎🔛 07/837-000, 07/831-033, or 07/831-046 ⊕ www. metrotourscuenca.com. **Seitur** ⊠ Gran Colombia 20-109 ☎ 07/842-007.

VISITOR INFORMATION

The tourist office, a few blocks southeast of the main square, is open weekdays 8:30–5.

🚩 Tourist Information **Cuenca Tourist Office** ⊠ Calle Hermano Miguel 686, at Calle Presidente Córdova ☎ 07/839-337 or 07/839-338.

EL ORIENTE

Ecuador's slice of the Amazon basin accounts for roughly one-third of the country's landmass but just 4% of its population. One of the world's biodiversity hot spots, El Oriente is home to hundreds of colorful bird species, including macaws, toucans, and prehistoric-looking hoatzins. Jaguars, pumas, and peccaries are elusive, but you're sure to see howler monkeys, spider monkeys, or tamarins. Pink river dolphins are also easy to spot. An abundance of insects thrive under the jungle canopy, including workaholic leaf-cutter ants, society spiders, and enormous blue morpho butterflies. Myriad plant species coexist, and in some cases even cooperate, with the jungle animals. The giant kapok tree, El Oriente's tallest species, soars to nearly 200 feet above the jungle floor. Creeping vines cascade from strangler figs, which in turn envelop other species.

In this exuberant world, eight different indigenous peoples continue, to varying degrees, to live their traditional lifestyles. One group still lives a nomadic life and repels any attempts at rapprochement by outsiders. Others allow tourist groups to visit and share their tremendous knowledge of plants and animals.

Trips to El Oriente—especially in areas close to the Colombia border—should be arranged *only* with a tour operator who is familiar with the area and who keeps up with changing conditions. Independent travel to remote jungle areas is dangerous, and not recommended.

Macas

246 km (154 mi) northeast of Cuenca.

The pleasant town of Macas is the gateway to the southern Oriente, which is more heavily settled and has less primary rain forest than the northern sector. Nonetheless, there is still spectacular rain forest to be found here. You'll have to make arrangements with a tour guide if you want to fly here to explore the rain forest.

Kapawi

184 km (115 mi) east of Macas.

One of the most remote corners of Ecuador, this eastern jungle region near the Peru border is the territory of the Achuar people. Kapawi is actually the name of one of the Achuar villages.

Where to Stay

★ $$$$ ⊞ **Kapawi Ecolodge & Reserve.** This group of typical Achuar huts—no nails were used in construction—are equipped with modern amenities like electric lights and private baths. All-inclusive packages last four to eight days, but you must stay a minimum of four days and three nights, for a cost of $600. An extra day and night will cost you an extra $120. This is an excellent experience if you want to see wildlife and have some contact with the Achuar people. According to an agreement, the ecolodge will be transferred to the Achuar in 2011. For birders, Kapawi has a booklet mapping out trails and bird species nesting in the area. In 10 days it isn't unusual to see almost 400. All meals are included. Remember that airfare from Quito will cost you about $200. ⊠ *Kapawi* ☎ *04/228–5711, 800/327–9854 toll free in the U.S.* 🖨 *04/228–7651* ⊕ *www.kapawi.com* ➳ *20 rooms* ♿ *Dining room, bar* ▤ *AE, DC, MC, V.*

$$$$ ⊞ **Sacha Lodge.** A parrot clay lick and a butterfly farm in the nearby Yasuní Narional Park (close to the Colombian border) and a 43-meter (135-foot) observation tower built around a giant kapok tree at the lodge are added attractions at this rustic but comfortable thatch-roof lodge deep in the Amazon. Activities include birding and canoe trips on the Napo river. ⊠ *Julio Zaldumbinde 397 y Toledo* ☎ *02/256–6090, 800/327–3573 toll free in the U.S.* ⊕ *www.sachalodge.com.*

El Oriente A to Z

AIR TRAVEL

The El Oriente towns of Coca, Lago Agrio (officially known as Nuevo Loja), and Macas are just 40 minutes from Quito on Tame. Flights leave for Coca and Lago Agrio every day except Sunday, while flights depart for Macas on Monday, Wednesday, and Friday. There are also several small charter companies that specialize in jungle towns and other remote destinations; these are considerably more expensive.

🛈 Airlines & Contacts **Tame** ☎ 02/250–9382, 800/555–999 toll free in Ecuador.

BUS TRAVEL

The trip from Quito to Lago Agrio takes 8 hours by bus. Since Lago Agrio is near the Colombian border, it's best to consult a tour operator about safety in this area. The trip from Quito to Coca takes 9 hours. A journey from Cuenca to Macas takes 10–12 hours.

CAR TRAVEL

The long trip through lush cloud forests filled with giant tree ferns, orchids, and bromeliads is a wonderful opportunity to see transitional zones between the mountains and the rain forest. Be forewarned, however, that in some areas of El Oriente you will find yourself driving alongside ugly oil pipelines. The trip between Quito and Coca takes 8 hours. Misahuallí can be reached in 5–5½ hours by car. Since Macas is so remote, and the road sometimes becomes impassable, it is not wise to attempt to drive. No roads pass near Kapawi.

MONEY MATTERS
It is nearly impossible to change money in El Oriente. Don't count on finding a bank. Bring all the cash you will need.

TAXIS
Taxis from Quito can be hired to take you to the main towns of El Oriente; it's just a matter of negotiating the price. Remember, if you want a chauffeur, you'll have to pay his room and board in addition to the fare.

TOUR OPERATORS
In Coca, the family-run travel company Ejarsytur offers a variety of travel services and tours. Expediciones Dayuma, another reputable company, can assist you with travel in the region.

In Cuenca, Ecotrek will put you in contact with the Shuar people, who live to the east of Macas near the missionary town of Miazal.

🖪 Tour Companies **Ecotrek** ⊠ Calle Larga 7-108, Cuenca ☎ 07/834-677 or 07/842-531 🖨 07/835-387. **Ejarsytur** ☎ 06/880-251. **Expediciones Dayuma** ⊠ Dayuma Hotel, Misahuallí ☎ 06/571-513.

GUAYAQUIL & THE PACIFIC COAST

Change is everywhere you look in Guayaquil, the capital of Guayas Province, beginning with the airport, which is undergoing major renovation and should be completed in 2005. Ecuador's largest and most vibrant city, with a population of more than 2 million, was once one of South America's most attractive ports, but it was on a serious downward slide until the city revamped the waterfront with an ambitious project called *Malecón 2000*. The *malecón,* a promenade lined with museums, shops, restaurants and ongoing entertainment, fills residents with a sense of civic pride. Another attraction is the Historical Park. The Expoplaza convention center, next to the luxurious Colón Guayaquil Hilton, is attracting more international business and trade shows, and the World Trade Center is catching the attention of major corporations. In addition to being the jumping-off point for Galápagos Islands, Guayaquil is becoming a destination all its own.

Because it's about 55 km (35 mi) inland, Guayaquil doesn't catch ocean breezes, so during the stifling December–April rainy season *Guayaquileños* head en masse for the beaches along the Southern Coast. The blue waters teem with sailfish, albacore, wahoo, dolphin, and marlin, which attract world-class sport fishermen. Farther north on the coast is the splendid Parque Nacional Machalilla, from which you can take a boat to Isla la Plata, 24 km (15 mi) offshore. The island is called the poor man's Galápagos because you can see more than 20 species of the same sea and birdlife found in the Galápagos. If you're looking for a really splendid car trip—on a good highway—consider driving from Guayaquil up the Pacific coast 280 km (174 mi) to the eco-city of Bahía de Caráquez. There's lots to do along the way—you can lounge on the gorgeous beaches of Machalilla National Park, go deep-sea fishing in Salinas, explore the town of Manta where cruise ships dock, and visit the Indian village of Montecristi, where the original Panama hats are still made. Once you reach Bahia de Caráquez you can surf, watch for whales (June–Sept.), and help excavate an archaeological site at the Chirije beach resort. If you prefer not to drive, there is good bus service between towns along the coast (you can also fly to Manta from Quito; from there it's a 45-minute drive to Bahía de Caráquez).

Guayaquil

250 km (156 mi) southwest of Quito.

You couldn't find a nicer way to spend an evening than strolling along the Malecón, Guayaquil's lovely riverfront promenade. You'll be in good company, as locals love the landmark here. Most of the town's major sights are within a few blocks of the river.

Numbers in the text correspond to numbers in the margin and on the Guayaquil map.

a good walk

Start your morning walk west of the waterfront at the Parque de Centenario, at the center of which is a towering stone monument, commemorating the city's independence, that was erected in 1920. Just to the west is the **Museo Casa de la Cultura ❶** ☛, and beyond that the **Parque Histórico ❷**. Head east of the Parque de Centenario for five blocks, and then head south on to Calle Chimborazo until you reach **Parque Seminario ❸**, also known as "Parque de las Iguanas" because of the dozens of iguanas sunning themselves on the lawns. The imposing **Catedral Metropolitana ❹** dominates the west side of the park.

Stop to visit the **Museo del Municipal de Guayaquil ❺**, just southeast of Parque Seminario, and then head north two blocks along Calle Pichincha to reach the **Museo Nahím Isaías Barquet ❻**. Head east along Avenida Clemente Ballén between the imposing Palacio de Gobierno and the Palacio Municipal to reach the resplendent riverfront walk called **El Malecón ❼**. You can't miss the city's landmark, the Moorish-style **Torre del Reloj Público ❽**.

Stroll north along the Malecón to **La Rotonda ❾**, a semicircular monument commemorating the historic 1822 meeting between South America's two greatest heroes, Simón Bolívar and José San Martín. A block west of the monument is the **Museo Banco del Pacífico ❿**. At the northern end of the Malecón is the **Museo Antropológico y Arte Contemporáneo (MAAC) ⓫**. Just beyond the museum is Guayaquil's oldest neighborhood, **Las Peñas ⓬**, about 10 blocks north, so you may want to take a taxi. Las Peñas sits on a hillside and you'll have to climb 456 steps to reach El Mirador, the summit of Cerro Santa Ana and the small Santa Ana Chapel. Climb the stairs of the chapel to get a sweeping view of the malecón and the city. Guayaquil's oldest church, **Iglesia de Santo Domingo ⓭**, is three blocks from Las Peñas. Several blocks west of Las

558 <

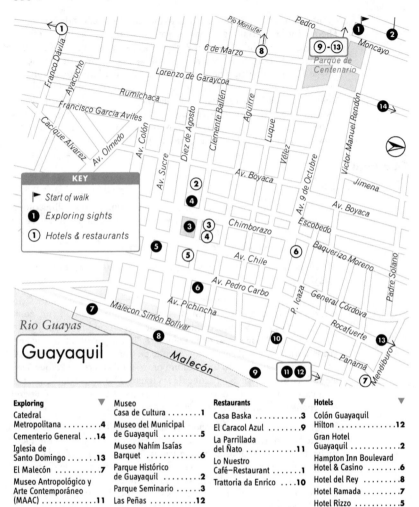

Peñas is Guayaquil's **Cementerio General** ⑭, also called Ciudad Blanca. The so-called White City is famous for its marble statues.

TIMING Most of Guayaquil's sights can be toured in a single day, as they are all along or close to the waterfront. You may want to split the tour between two days, as tropical temperatures may slow you down.

What to See

❹ **Catedral Metropolitana.** The twin-spired cathedral, which looms over the western edge of Parque Seminario, is actually one of the city's newer houses of worship. The gothic structure was dedicated in 1950. Vendors selling hand-carved rosaries and other items crowd the sidewalks outside. ✉ *Parque Seminario.*

★ ⑭ **Cementerio General.** Also called Ciudad Blanca, the General Cemetery is one of the city's most impressive sights. More than 200 mausoleums, all in elaborately carved white marble, line the neat paths. Because of a recurring problem with pickpockets, you may want to visit on a guided tour. ✉ *Av. Coronel, west of Las Peñas* ✑ *Free.*

⑬ **Iglesia de Santo Domingo.** Guayaquil's oldest church was founded by the Franciscans in 1548. Located near Las Peñas, the simple colonial structure has been rebuilt after being destroyed by pirate attacks. Locals also refer to it as the Iglesia de San Vicente.

❼ **El Malecón.** After years of neglect, Guayaquil's riverfront promenade has been transformed into one of the city's most pleasant attractions. As you stroll along the Río Guayas you can relax on benches in shady parks, or poke into numerous shops, restaurants, the contemporary art museum (MAAC), an IMAX theater, and a planetarium. Across the street from El Malecón is El Palacio Municipal, considered one of the country's best examples of neoclassic architecture. Beside the adjacent Palacio de la Gobernación is Parque Sucre, a sliver of greenery dedicated to war hero Mariscal Antonio José de Sucre. ⊕ *www.malecon2000.com* ◷ *7 AM–midnight; shops 10–9.*

⑪ **Museo Antropológico y Arte Contemporáneo** (MAAC). On exhibit here are paintings, ceramics, and unusual regional artifacts. Items on display include a monkey-shape vessel believed to be used in religious ceremonies 4,000 years ago, a statue of a figure covered with skin eruptions called "Peruvian wrinkles," and an *espejo shamanico* (shaman's mirror) made of crystal and encircled by copper. ✉ *Malecón, at foot of Cerro Santa Ana* ☎ *04/232–7402* ✑ *Free* ◷ *Tues.–Fri. 10–6, weekends 10–2.*

⑩ **Museo Banco del Pacífico.** Located just a block from the waterfront, the Pacific Bank Museum has rotating exhibits of archaeological discoveries, as well as a permanent collection of 19th-century South American art. ✉ *Calle P. Ycaza 113, at Calle Pichincha* ☎ *04/256–3744* ✑ *Free* ◷ *Tues.–Sat. 10–6.*

▶ ❶ **Museo Casa de la Cultura.** The Museum of Culture features prehistoric stone and ceramic artifacts discovered on the Isle of La Plata off the coast from Guayaquil. There's also an impressive collection of gold items dating from before the arrival of the Spanish. ✉ *Av. 9 de Oc-*

tubre 1200, at Calle P. Moncayo ☎ *04/230–0500* 🎫 *$1* ⊘ *Tues.–Fri. 10–6, Sat. 9–3.*

❺ Museo del Municipal de Guayaquil. While the Municipal Museum of Guayaquil has many interesting archaeological exhibits, the biggest draw is a collection of *tsantsas,* or shrunken heads. Artifacts from indigenous peoples include beadwork, featherwork, tools, and weapons. In the lobby is an unusual 8½-meter (28-foot) totem with 32 vertical figures. ⊠ *Av. Sucre, between Av. Chile and Av. Pedro Carbo* ☎ *04/251–6391* 🎫 *Free* ⊘ *Winter, Tues.–Sat. 9–4; summer, Tues.–Sat. 9–noon and 3–6.*

❻ Museo Nahím Isaías Barquet. The small Nahím Isaias Barquet Museum is located only a few blocks from the Malecón. Displays include examples of religious art from the colonial period. ⊠ *Calle Clemente Ballén and Pichincha* ☎ *04/232–9099* 🎫 *Free* ⊘ *Mon.–Sat. 10–5.*

★ ❷ Parque Histórico de Guayaquil. There are three sections to this park, which opened in 2002: the Architecture Zone, with colonial buildings dating to 1886 (they were restored and moved here); the Traditional Zone, where actors dressed in period costumes re-create life as it existed in the early 20th century; and the Endangered Wildlife Zone, with rare birds and animals. There are wooden walkways throughout and a small restaurant. This is a very pleasant way to spend a few hours; it's right on the edge of the rain forest. ⊠ *UPEC (Unidad de Proyectos Especiales Culturales), near the International airport.* ☎ *04/283–5356* ⊕ *www. parquehistorico.com* 🎫 *$3* ⊘ *Tues.–Sun. 9 to 4:30.*

❸ Parque Seminario. This lovely square, the heart of the city since it was inaugurated in 1895, is known by many different names. Because of the almost obligatory statue of a triumphant Simón Bolívar, many locals call it Parque Bolívar. A more common moniker is Parque de las Iguanas, as dozens of the scaly green creatures can be found lazing about on park benches and across the limbs of trees. The gardens, which still have a marvelous wrought-iron bandstand, are filled with 43 species of indigenous plants. ⊠ *Between Av. Clemente Baillén and Av. Diez de Agosto.*

⓬ Las Peñas. Until 2002, this neighborhood at the foot of Cerro Santa Ana (Santa Ana Hill) was a seedy barrio of ramshackle houses, where drugs dominated after dark. But from 2001 to 2002, the city poured $8 million into the neighborhood, transforming it in record time into one of the most charming parts of the city. Brightly painted houses, shops, and cafés climb Cerro Santa Ana (Santa Ana Hill). Old-fashioned street lamps light the way to the summit, where you can get an unparalleled view of the city. Perhaps the most amazing aspect of Las Peñas's transformation is that it was done without relocating the neighborhood's residents. Many of them benefited from business grants doled out by the city and now work as shopkeepers or manage cafés. The response from the community has been overwhelmingly positive and other cities around the globe are following Guayaquil's model.

❾ La Rotonda. Imposing marble columns form the backdrop for statues of the men who liberated most of the continent, Simón Bolívar and José de San Martín. The monument commemorates their first (and only) meeting, in Guayaquil in 1822. ⊠ *Malecón at Av. 9 de Octobre* ⌖ *Free.*

⑧ Torre del Reloj Público. The Moorish style clock tower, constructed in 1770, is one of the city's most enduring landmarks. Inside is a small exposition of photographs of Guayaquil dating from the early 20th century. ⊠ *El Malecón.*

Where to Stay & Eat

The majority of Guayaquil's nicer restaurants are clustered in the Urdesa neighborhood north of downtown, where you'll also find some of the city's most popular bars and dance clubs. Many restaurants close daily between 4:30 and 7:30, then reopen for dinner. Lodging rates vary dramatically depending on time of year—special promotions or apparently how many empty rooms the hotel has at the moment you call, so always ask whether discount rates are available.

$ ✕ El Caracol Azul. This downtown restaurant, specializing in Peruvian-style seafood, is popular with business executives. The interior of the nondescript building is surprisingly attractive, enlivened by a skylight and paintings by local artists. Start off with ceviche or *chicharrón de calamar* (deep-fried squid); then move on to a *langostino picante* (shrimp in a spicy cream sauce). ⊠ *Av. 9 de Octubre at Calle Los Ríos* ☎ *04/ 228–0361* ⊟ *AE, DC, MC, V* ⊙ *Closed Sun.*

$ ✕ Trattoria da Enrico. Tiny shuttered windows set into thick whitewashed walls reflect this restaurant's Mediterranean influence. The simple exterior doesn't prepare you for the aquarium in the dining room, which is set into the ceiling. Try the prosciutto and melon appetizer, then move on to the chicken with sour cream, vodka, and mushroom sauce. Musicians playing mandolins wander among the tables. ⊠ *Calle Bálsamos 504, at Calle Ebanos* ☎ *04/238–7079* ⊟ *DC, MC, V* ⊙ *Closed Tues.*

¢–$ ✕ Casa Baska. The owner peers out through a tiny window before opening the door to welcome you into this intimate Spanish restaurant across from Parque Seminario. The food, cooked up with a Basque flair, couldn't be better. Start with the broiled calamari, large enough to be worn as bracelets, then move on to the flavorful paella. You couldn't do better than end with the expertly prepared crème caramel. ⊠ *Av. Clemente Ballén 422* ☎ *04/253–4597* ⊟ *No credit cards.*

¢–$ ✕ Lo Nuestro Café Restaurant. Historic photos of Guayaquil crowd the walls of this restaurant in the Urdesa neighborhood. Guayaquil is known for its ceviche and Lo Nuestro has a good one, meant to be drenched in the fresh lime juice that accompanies it. ⊠ *Victor Emilio Estrado 903 at Higueras* ☎ *04/238–6398* ⊟ *DC, MC, V.*

¢ ✕ La Parrillada del Ñato. Several long grills make this barbecue restaurant appear as if it were designed to feed an army. It's a good thing, too, because legions of hungry carnivores fill the restaurant seven days a week to feast on racks of ribs, succulent steaks, and an array of other tasty meat dishes. ⊠ *Av. V. E. Estrada 1219, at Calle Costañera* ☎ *04/238– 7098* ⊟ *AE, DC, MC, V.*

$$$$ ✕⊞ Oro Verde. The chain's flagship hotel continues to be one of the top choices for business travelers. In addition to comfortable rooms and plenty of amenities, the hotel has a pool, health club, and even a casino. The lobby bar, with live music every night, draws locals. If you're hungry, head to the informal Spice Grill to sample the tasty Szechuan chicken salad. ⊠ *Av. 9 de Octubre at Calle García Moreno* ☏ *04/232–7999, 800/223–6800 in the U.S.* ☐ *04/232–9350* ⊕ *www.ororverdehotels. com* ↪ *192 rooms, 62 suites* ♢ *4 restaurants, pool, gym, sauna, steam room, bar, casino, business services, car rental* ⊟ *AE, DC, MC, V.*

$$ ✕⊞ **Gran Hotel Guayaquil.** This landmark hotel near Parque Seminario and most other downtown attractions shares a city block with the Catedral Metropolitana. Small but comfortable rooms with large windows let in lots of sun. The health club lets you play squash on two courts, relax in a sauna, or enjoy the terrace with a great view of the cathedral. ⊠ *Calle Boyaca at Av. 10 de Agosto* ☏ *04/232–9690, 800/334–3782 in the U.S.* ☐ *04/232–7251* ⊕ *www.cjhotels.com* ↪ *170 rooms, 10 suites* ♢ *3 restaurants, coffee shop, pool, gym, sauna, steam room, business services, travel services* ⊟ *AE, DC, MC, V.*

$$$–$$$$ ⊞ **Colón Guayaquil Hilton.** This majestic hotel outside the city center (next
FodorsChoice to the Expoplaza convention center) has a 10-story atrium lobby. It de-
★ livers everything you'd expect from a top-notch business hotel. The beautiful pool area is surrounded by palm trees. The Large Policentro Shopping Mall is nearby. ⊠ *Av. Francisco de Orellana* ☏ *04/268–9000* ☐ *04/268–9149* ⊕ *www.hilton.com* ↪ *273 rooms, 19 suites* ♢ *3 restaurants, minibars, pool, health club, hair salon, bar, business services, meeting rooms, airport shuttle, car rental, travel services* ⊟ *AE, DC, MC, V.*

$$$ ⊞ **Unipark Hotel.** Part of the Oro Verde chain, this comfortable hotel is within walking distance of most of the city's attractions. Across the street from the Parque Seminario, it gives you direct access to an 80-store shopping center. Several excellent restaurants are also on the premises, including a wonderful sushi bar called Unibar. Buffet breakfast is included. The best view is from a park-side room. ⊠ *Av. Clemente Ballén 406* ☏ *04/232–7100, 800/448–8355 in the U.S.* ☐ *04/232–8352* ⊕ *www. ororverdehotels.com* ↪ *138 rooms, 14 suites* ♢ *Restaurant, café, gym, sauna, bar* ⊟ *AE, DC, MC, V.*

$$–$$$ ⊞ **Hotel Ramada.** This popular hotel across from El Malecón, the riverfront, is within walking distance of Las Peñas. When the heat of tropical Guayaquil gets to be too much, you can sip a cocktail by the pool. Evenings find many guests slipping off to the casino. ⊠ *Malecón 606, at Orellana* ☏ *04/256–5555* ☐ *04/256–3036* ↪ *110 rooms, 5 suites* ♢ *Restaurant, indoor pool, bar, casino, business services, meeting rooms, airport shuttle* ⊟ *AE, DC, MC, V.*

$$ ⊞ **Hampton Inn Boulevard Hotel & Casino.** This small inn behind the
FodorsChoice beautiful San Francisco church is just a few blocks from the Malecon
★ and close to all the museums. Rooms are nice, and all have coffee makers and two phone lines. ⊠ *9 de Octobre 432, at Baquerizo Moreno,* ☏ *04/256–6700* ⊕ *www.hamptoninn.com* ↪ *95 rooms* ♢ *Restaurant, cable TV, in-room data ports, gym, casino, business services* ⊟ *AE, DC, MC, V.*

¢ ⊞ **Hotel del Rey.** Visiting soccer players love this pleasant hotel several blocks from Parque Guayaquil. The well-maintained rooms are a bit small, but this is one of the few moderately priced hotels in town that has exercise facilities. Breakfast is included. ⊠ *Calle Aguirre at Calle Andrés Marín* ☎ *04/245–3037 or 04/245–2053* 📠 *04/245–3351* 🛏 *47 rooms* ♨ *Restaurant, gym, sauna, bar* ▤ *DC, MC, V.*

¢ 🖭 **Hotel Rizzo.** A good budget option, this downtown hotel has comfortable rooms with balconies overlooking Parque Seminario. The staff is eager to help you in any way, whether it's to suggest a restaurant or give tips on nightlife. ⊠ *Av. Clemente Ballén 319, at Chimborazo* ☎ *04/232–5210* 📠 *04/232–6209* ♨ *Restaurant, café, minibars, pool, health club, casino, dance club* ▤ *MC, V.*

Salinas

141 km (88 mi) west of Guayaquil.

Guayaquileños flock to the popular, if sometimes overcrowded, beaches here on holidays and during the hot and humid rainy season. Deep-sea fishing is another draw. The continental shelf drops sharply to the ocean floor just 19 km (12 mi) offshore, providing a fertile feeding ground for Pacific sailfish, swordfish, and amberjack, as well as striped, blue, and black marlin. The biggest catches are made November through May, but fishing continues year-round. An excellent highway connects Salinas and Guayaquil.

Where to Stay

$$ 🖭 **Puerto Lucia Yacht Club.** If you need a place to anchor your 150-foot yacht, head to this beautiful resort on the Península Santa Elena. (You don't really need a yacht to stay here.) This is a great vacation destination for the entire family; it has everything from deep-sea fishing to rain-forest expeditions. The small suites have balconies overlooking the bay where you can watch the sun disappear into the ocean. For larger groups, two- and three-bedroom apartments are available. ⊠ *Av. C. J. Arosemena, Km 2.5* ☎ *04/220–6154, 877/426–3347 in the U.S.* ⊕ *www. puertolucia.com.ec* 🛏 *24 suites* ♨ *4 tennis courts, 3 pools, hot tub, beach, travel services* ▤ *AE, DC, MC, V.*

Sports & the Outdoors

The prime marlin season on the southern coast is from October through April. **Magellan Offshore Fishing Tours** (⊠ Salinas ☎ 04/247–83189, 877/426–3347 in the U.S. ⊕ www.magellanoffshore.com) arranges fishing tours on a private yacht called the *Hatteras Paper Moon*. **PescaTours** (⊠ Salinas ☎ 04/244–3365 or 04/277–2391 📠 04/244–3142 ⊕ www. pescatours.com.ec) organizes daylong charters for two to six people.

Machalilla National Park

Fodor'sChoice   *In Puerto López, 167 km (104 mi) northwest of Guayaquil.*
★

Come here for the sandy beaches, but be warned that riptides are common in this area, especially when the ocean is rough. Although the water is swimmable year-round, it is warmest during the rainy summer months (December–May). The 136,850-acre **Parque Nacional Machalilla** is in the extreme southwest corner of the state of Manabí, and was created in 1979 in an effort to halt the destruction of the country's remaining tropical dry forests. Unlike the lush greenery associated with rain forests, dry-forest vegetation includes kapok trees, prickly pear cactus, and strangler figs. The entrance fee is good for five days and includes access to Isla de la Plata, a 3,000-acre seabird sanctuary where red-footed, blue-footed, and masked boobies make their homes. The waters surrounding the island teem with flying fish, dolphins, and humpback whales that come from Antarctica to bear their young. There are rest rooms and changing facilities at the park. ⊠ *Visitor center is on the main street in Puerto López* ⊠ *$20.*

Where to Stay & Eat

¢ ✕ **Carmita's Restaurant.** Doña Carmita and her sister have a way with seafood. The signature dish at this simple beachfront eatery, among the best restaurants along the southern coast, is the zesty *pescado al vapor con vegetales* (lemony fish soup with vegetables). A wide variety of drinks, including German and Chilean wines, are available. ⊠ *Calle Malecón s/n, Puerto López* ☎ *05/604–148 or 05/604–149* ⊟ V.

$$ ✕⊞ **Hotel Atamari.** Papayas, palms, and flaming bougainvillea grow among the thatch-roof cottages of this hotel, which is perched on a rocky promontory overlooking the Ayampe Valley and the Pacific ocean, 28 km (17 mi) south of Puerto López. Trails by the hotel lead to a private beach where hundreds of birds and butterflies hover. Whale-watching season is June–October; from the cliff-top terrace you'll have the best seats in the house. The outdoor restaurant serves fantastic international cuisine, with an emphasis on seafood. ⊠ *Sector Ayampe, Puerto López* ☎ *04/278–0430, in Quito 02/222–8470* 🖷 *02/250–8369 in Quito* 🛏 *8 cottages, 4 suites* ⚭ *Restaurant, pool* ⊟ *AE, DC, MC, V.*

¢ ✕⊞ **Alandaluz Ecocultural Center.** The two- and three-story thatch-roof cabanas face several miles of sand beaches. About 15 minutes south of Puerto López, it is a favorite among tourists who come to get closer to nature. Many travelers come for a night and end up spending a week, lounging in hammocks and chatting at the open-air bar. The restaurant emphasizes vegetarian fare. ⊠ *Puerto López* ☎ *05/604–103, 02/250–5084 in Quito* 🖷 *02/254–3042 in Quito* 🛏 *38 rooms* ⚭ *Restaurant, bar* ⊟ *No credit cards.*

$ ⊞ **Mantaraya Lodge.** The adobe-style buildings that make up this lodge may remind you a bit of old Mexico. Nestled among the kapok trees of Parque Nacional Machalilla, the resort has its own guides to take you out on wilderness excursions. You can also join fishing, diving, and whale-watching trips aboard the *Mantarayas II and III.* Reservations are made through Advantage Travel in Quito. ⊠ *Puerto López* ☎ *02/246–2871, 800/327–3573 in the U.S.* 🖷 *02/243–7645* ⊕ *www.advantagecuador. com* 🛏 *15 rooms* ⚭ *Restaurant, cafeteria, pool, bar, travel services* ⊟ *AE, DC, MC, V.*

Sports & the Outdoors

FISHING **Advantage Travel** (⊠ El Telégrafo E10–63, at Calle Juan de Alcántara, Quito ☎ 02/246–2871) arranges fishing charters. If you're an experienced angler you'll be happier if you bring your own equipment. Otherwise, gear of dubious quality can be rounded up by the agency.

HORSEBACK RIDING
Trips to beautiful Los Frailes Cove can be arranged through **Pacarina** (✉ Puerto López ☎ 05/604–173) for less than $5 for a half-day trip. Pacarina also arranges overnight camping trips within Parque Nacional Machalilla. An excursion popular with birders is the seven-hour hike from Agua Blanca to San Sebastián, which passes through dry forest, cloud forest, and tropical rain forest—each climate with its own distinct species of flora and fauna. After a night camping outside San Sebastián, you can return to Agua Blanca on foot or by horse. The fee for this or other excursions in the area is less than $7 per day.

Bahia de Caraquez

14 km (23 mi) from Manta.

This beachfront port town, built by the Spaniards in 1624, has a delightful small-town resort vibe, with waterfront restaurants that serve delicious meals of organically grown shrimp and fresh crab. The Spaniards were not the first, however, to find this peninsula. A nation called the "Caras" arrived aboard balsawood sailing rafts around 1500 BC, and it's believed that Bahia de Caraquez was set up as a trading center—for shells and crafted ornaments, which were exchanged for gold, copper, and other goods from places as far away as Mexico and Chile. A large replica of a raft is in Bahia's Central Bank Museum, the **Casa de la Cultura** (✉ On the main street ☉ Daily 10–5 ☞ 75¢), which displays archaeological artifacts and costumes. Rafts were built with no nails and could hold 50 to 100 people.

This town with a population of 25,000 takes pride in being the first eco-city in Ecuador. There are few cars, as most transportation is by three-wheel cycles. An environmental learning center, started by Sra. Flor Maria Duenas, the owner of the small Casa Grande guest house, is an after-school center for children from underprivileged homes, where they learn the importance of recycling and environmental issues. Bahia's citizens envision their city as becoming a model of sustainability.

Just a short boat ride away from town is *Isla Corazon*, or Heart Island. First you'll stop at a welcome center to see a presentation at another island, then you get back on the boat to continue to Isla Corazon. The Island, which has 174 acres of mangroves, serves as a nesting place for frigate birds—males inflate what looks like a large red balloon to attract females during mating season. You can either walk along boardwalks to explore the forest or canoe around the island.

Where to Stay

$ ▦ **La Piedra.** This small oceanfront hotel gives you access to the beach. You can also tour the town in the hotel's horse-drawn carriage. ✉ *Av. Virgilio Ratti,* ☎ *05/690–780* ☎ *05/690–154* ☞ *42 rooms* ♨ *Restaurant, outdoor pool, volleyball, bar* ▭ *MC, V.*

¢ ▦ **Casa Grande.** This is the best place to stay in Bahia de Caraquez. There's a comfortable, friendly guest house with a living room decorated with paintings by the artist Eduardo Kingman, large rooms with picture windows and private baths, a sunny backyard, and home cooked meals. ✉ *Av.*

Fodor'sChoice
★

Bolívar 1004 and Riofrio, ☎ *05/692–097* 🖨 *05/692–088* ⊕ *www. bahiadolphin.com* 📡 *6 rooms* ⚭ *Dining room, pool* ▤ *MC, V.*

★ ¢ 🏨 **Chirije Ecolodge.** It's only 30 minutes from downtown Bahia de Caraquez, but you can only come at low tide, because you actually have to drive down along the beach before heading up a cliff again to get here. (The hotel knows about the tides a year ahead.) This cluster of comfortable, solar-powered, thatch-roof cabins (each fit for six people) is built on a cliff overlooking a beach, where you'll find little besides fishermen's huts and tiny red crabs. The lodge is also literally on top of an archaeological site: artifacts uncovered are placed in a small on-site museum and registered with the government. Pottery has been dated to 500 BC. If you stay here you'll be encouraged to help with the diggings—and if artifacts wash ashore, as they often do, to turn them in. ☎ *05/692–086* 🖨 *05/692–088* ⊕ *www.bahiadolphin.com* 📡 *5 cabins* ⚭ *Private baths, lounge, library* ▤ *MC, V.*

Guayaquil & the Pacific Coast A to Z

AIR TRAVEL

Guayaquil's international airport, Aeropuerto Simón Bolívar, is 6 km (4 mi) north of the city center; taxis to downtown should cost less than $4. From Guayaquil, Tame has flights to Quito and Cuenca, as well as to the Galápagos Islands of Santa Cruz and San Cristobal. They also fly between Quito and Manta. Austro Aéreo and ICARO fly& daily between Guayaquil, Cuenca, and Quito.

🛫 Airlines & Contacts **Austro Aéreo** ☎ 07/832–677 or 07/848–659. **ICARO Air** ☎ 04/263–0620, 800/883–567 toll-free in Ecuador. **Tame** ☎ 04/256–5806, 800/555–999 toll free in Ecuador.

🛫 Airport Information **Aeropuerto Simón Bolívar** ✉ Av. de las Américas ☎ 04/229–0005.

BUS TRAVEL

Guayaquil is 10 hours by bus from Quito and around 5 hours from Cuenca. The city's main bus station, Terminal Terrestre, is just north of the airport. You can take buses up the coast to various towns, all the way up to Bahia de Caraquez. The shortest route to Bahia de Caraquez is from Guayaquil, skipping Salinas—you can go directly northwest up the coast.

ENGLISH-LANGUAGE MEDIA

In Guayaquil, one of the few bookstores with English-language books is Librería Científica.

🛫 Bookstores **Librería Científica** ✉ Av. Luque 225, at Av. Chile.

MONEY MATTERS

Many banks in Guayaquil have ATMs where you can withdraw funds from your accounts back home. Try Banco del Pacífico and Citibank. Salinas and Manta also have ATMs.

🛫 Banks **Banco del Pacífico** ✉ Fco. P. Ycaza 200 ☎ 04/231–1744. **Citibank** ✉ Av. 9 de Octubre at Lorenzo de Garaicoa ☎ 04/256–3650.

TAXIS

Taxis throughout the Guayaquil are inexpensive. The average trip should cost $3. Most do not use meters, so be prepared to haggle.

TELEPHONES

In Guayaquil it's easiest to make phone calls at your hotel. You can also try the Emetel office. You can also make phone calls from pay phones in Salinas and Manta.

🔳 **Emetel** ⊠ Pedro Carbo y Aguirre and L. Urdaneta 426.

TOUR OPERATORS

Guides can be hired at the Parque Nacional Machalilla visitor center in Puerto López for less than $10 a day for up to 10 persons. Guided tours can also be arranged to the park through Advantage Travel in Quito.

🔳 Tour Companies **Advantage Travel** ⊠ El Telégrafo E10–63, at Calle Juan de Alcántara ☎ 02/246–2871, 800/327–3573 in the U.S. ⊕ www.advantagecuador.com. **Bahia Dolphin Tours** ⊠ Bolivar 1004 y Riofrio Bahia de Caraquez ☎ 05/692–088 ⊕ bahi-adolphin.com. **Conodros** ⊠ Santa Leonor M25, Solar 10, Via Terminal Terreste, Guayaquil ☎ 04/228–5711 ⊕ www.conodros.com.

VISITOR INFORMATION

Guayaquil's well-stocked tourist office is open weekdays 8:30–5.

🔳 Tourist Information **Guayaquil Tourist Office** ⊠ P. Icaza 203, at Pichincha, 4th fl. ☎ 04/256–1281.

THE GALÁPAGOS ISLANDS

Fodor'sChoice
★

A zoologist's dream, the Galápagos Islands afford a once-in-a-lifetime chance to witness animals found nowhere else on the planet. From the moment you step onto these dazzling shores you're confronted by giant tortoises basking in the sun, lava lizards darting between rocks, and frigates swooping overhead. No one who has walked among these unique creatures will ever forget the experience.

It is possible that indigenous coastal tribes were the first to discover the remote Galápagos Islands, a chain of rocky, highly active volcanic islands roughly 1,000 km (620 mi) off the coast of Ecuador; some think this is the explanation for legends among Ecuador's coastal peoples referring to "a land of fire across the sea." Less dramatic, perhaps, and certainly better documented, was the arrival of Fray Tomás de Berlanga, the Bishop of Panama, in 1535. His ship was stranded during a fact-finding mission to Peru and eventually drifted on strong currents to the Galápagos. Centuries later, English pirates used the remote archipelago as a place to rest and recoup after plundering the Ecuadorian and Peruvian coast. Many of the islands received their English names—some of which are still in use—during the patriotic tenure of these scurrilous buccaneers.

Naturalist Charles Darwin, the most famous visitor to the Galápagos, found inspiration for his ground-breaking treatise, *The Origin of Species,* among the strange and marvelous island creatures. "I never dreamed," he wrote in his memoirs, "that islands, about 50 or 60 miles apart, and most of them in sight of each other, formed of precisely the same rocks, placed under a quite similar climate, rising to a nearly equal height, would have been differently tenanted." He realized that slightly different conditions on each of the islands had caused animals and plants eventually to develop into completely different species.

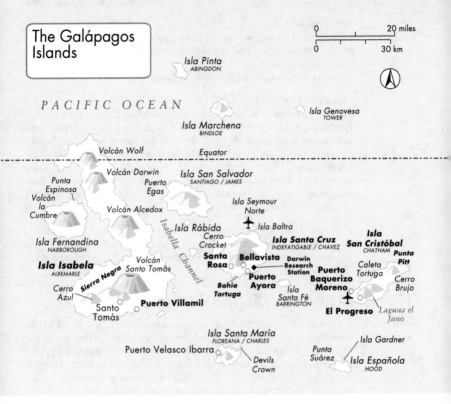

The Galápagos
Islands

PACIFIC OCEAN

Isla Pinta
ABINGDON

Isla Genovesa
TOWER

Isla Marchena
BINDLOE

Volcán Wolf   Equator

Volcán Darwin   Isla San Salvador
Punta   Puerto   SANTIAGO / JAMES
Espinosa   Egas
Volcán
la   Isla Seymour
Cumbre   Volcán Alcedox   Norte

Isabella Channel

Isla Rábida   Isla Baltra
Cerro
Isla Fernandina   Crocket   Isla Santa Cruz   Isla
NARBOROUGH   INDEFATIGABLE / CHAVEZ   San Cristóbal
Santa   Bellavista   CHATHAM   Punta
Volcán   Rosa   Darwin   Pitt
Isla Isabela   Santo Tomás   Research   Puerto   Caleta
ALBEMARLE   Station   Baquerizo   Tortuga
Cerro   Sierra Negra   Puerto   Moreno   Cerro
Azul   Ayora   Isla   Brujo
Bahía   Santa Fé
Santo   Puerto Villamil   Tortuga   BARRINGTON   El Progreso   Laguna el
Tomás   Juno

Isla Santa María
FLOREANA / CHARLES   Isla Gardner
Puerto Velasco Ibarra   Punta
Devils   Suárez   Isla Española
Crown   HOOD

Procreation, in one form or another, is always in progress on these islands. In January, male iguanas turn from drab to bright colors to attract females. February is the nesting season of the masked boobies. Waved
albatrosses begin their courtship dances in March. In April, tiny green
sea turtles begin breaking out of their eggs. Band-rumped storm petrels
make their first nests in May. In June, giant tortoises migrate from the
lowlands of Santa Cruz island in search of suitable places to lay their
eggs. July and August are the nesting seasons for the blue-footed boobies and Galápagos hawks. September and October are mating season
for penguins and fur seals. Sea lion pups are born in November, while
giant tortoises hatch in December.

The islands attracted only adventure seekers and odd recluses until well
into the 20th century. Tourism began in a limited fashion after the
Ecuadorian government declared the islands a national park in 1959.
Not even five decades later, the Galápagos must cope with 100,000 visitors each year. The delicate balance that exists on the Galápagos is difficult to overstate. Ecologists are concerned that the steadily increasing
number of tourists will prove destructive to the irreplaceable environment. The islands are particularly threatened by introduced animals—
goats, cats, pigs, dogs, and rats—which interrupt the islands' natural
food chain. While more than 250,000 giant tortoises once roamed the

islands, there are fewer than 15,000 today due to human hunting and newly introduced predators. Yet people are not the only ones to blame: El Niño currents also affect marine life, especially in unusually warm years, by raising water temperatures, sometimes as high as 40°C (104°F) and killing thousands of fish and destroying the food source for marine birds. The Charles Darwin Research Center based on Santa Cruz works to mitigate the effects of man-made and natural disasters and is dedicated to conserving the fragile ecosystem.

The best months to visit the Galápagos are generally May–June and November–December. Among the 13 principal islands, Santa Cruz and San Cristóbal are the most developed, each with a population of roughly 6,000 year-round residents. Of the two, Santa Cruz has more allure for visitors, with its dozen or so hotels, restaurants, and boutiques. The archipelago's four populated islands can be visited on a limited basis without guides, but the uninhabited islands can be seen only with a guide licensed through the Galápagos National Park Service. It's typical to book your own airfare and prearrange a one- to two-week package that includes guided visits to islands like Española and Isabela. A cruise of 10 days or longer is needed to reach the more remote northern islands or to climb either of Isabela's two accessible volcanic craters.

Santa Cruz

The most developed of the islands, Santa Cruz sits in the middle of the archipelago. Overlooking Academy Bay on the island's southern shore is the town of **Puerto Ayora,** with hotels, restaurants, shops, and even a few clubs.

Follow the main road east from Puerto Ayora to the **Charles Darwin Research Station** and its Van Straelen Visitor Center, which has an informative exhibit explaining the basics of Galápagos geology, ecology, and weather patterns. Self-guided trails lead to the station's giant tortoise pens, where you can see the only tortoises you're likely to encounter during your visit. ☎ 05/526–146 or 05/526–147.

Bahía Tortuga (Turtle Bay), 3 km (2 mi) southwest of Puerto Ayora, has a long, white-sand beach where marine iguanas sometimes strut along the water's edge. There are no facilities along the water, but if you walk from town (take the road to Bellavista and turn left past the bank) you'll pass a soda and beer stand at the top of a lava-rock staircase. Marine turtles drag their bulky shells up onto the beach to lay their eggs between November and February, with baby turtles hatching from June to July.

Near the small village of **Bellavista** you can explore amazing underground lava tubes. The mile-long tunnels, tall enough to walk through, were created when flowing lava cooled more quickly on the surface than below, forming a crust that enclosed an underground labyrinth. To reach the tunnels from Puerto Ayora, head north on the road to Bellavista; turn east at the cross street and walk about a mile until you find a farm with a sign that announces LOS TÚNELES. A small fee is collected by the owner, who also provides flashlights.

The road to **Santa Rosa**, 13 km (8 mi) beyond Bellavista, is lined with giant elephant grass, avocado and papaya trees, and boughs of yellow trumpet vines, all of which are in marked contrast to the dry, cactus-spotted lowlands. About 2 km (1 mi) beyond Santa Rosa look for a pair of giant sinkholes called **Los Gemelos** (The Twins), one on either side of the road.

The unattended **National Park Tortoise Reserve** is one of the few places in the archipelago where you can view giant Galápagos turtles in the wild. An unmarked track leads to the reserve from Santa Rosa. Along the way, keep alert for Galápagos hawks, Darwin finches, and short-eared owls. In Santa Rosa, a small restaurant across from the church sometimes rents horses that you are allowed to ride inside the reserve.

Where to Stay & Eat

If you prefer to sleep on land and take boat cruises during the day there are a few good options. However, most hotels and restaurants are working to upgrade their facilities, but many are still on the rustic side and some hotels have only cold running water and rooms often lack electrical outlets. If these things are important to you, be sure to ask before booking.

$$ ⨉ **Four Lanterns.** Expect to see diners sitting around long tables on the lantern-lit outdoor patio, enjoying lasagna, gnocchi, or cannelloni. The proprietor takes pride in her signature dish, *fettuccine mare e monte* (fettuccine with mushrooms and shrimp). An accepted piece of local wisdom is that all visitors eventually end up at the Four Lanterns. ⊠ *Av. Charles Darwin, Puerto Ayora* ☎ *No phone* ⊟ *No credit cards* ⊗ *No lunch.*

$$ ⨉ **La Garrapata.** This popular restaurant is run by the offspring of one of Galápagos's pioneer families. Its outdoor tables attract both tourists and locals. The menu, which is heavy on the seafood, also includes a few chicken and pasta dishes. Next door is the popular discotheque, La Panga, where salsa music plays until the lights go out or the last patron leaves. ⊠ *Av. Charles Darwin, Puerto Ayora* ☎ *05/526–266* ⊟ *MC, V* ⊗ *Closed Sun.*

$$ ⨉ **La Tolda Azul.** The first restaurant you'll encounter as you step off the boat in Port Ayora, this place has a small outdoor patio. The menu offers a wonderful selection of lobster dishes served in large portions; the grilled steaks are also good. ⊠ *Muelle Municipal, Puerto Ayora* ☎ *05/ 526–565* ⊟ *MC.*

$$ ⨉ **Narwahl.** With a gorgeous view of the island on a clear day, this hideaway in the highlands of Santa Cruz offers set meals that include a cocktail, soup or salad, and a dependably good entrée of chicken, fish, or beef. Vegetarian entrées are sometimes available. ⊠ *Road to Santa Rosa* ☎ *No phone* ⊟ *No credit cards.*

$$$$ ▦ **Finch Bay Hotel Galapagos.** A stay at this totally redone 4-star hotel (from 1960) can be combined with day cruises on the *Yacht Delphin*—which the hotel owns—or day tours that include snorkeling, diving, sea kayaking, hiking, mountain biking, and horseback trips along Santa Cruz's hillside paths. The highlands show a different side of the Galápagos. On kayaking trips behind the hotel you get a close-up look at sharks, sea turtles, rays, and a variety of birds. If you've never paddled a kayak you

can practice off the hotel's beach. Rates include a buffet breakfast. ⊠ *Santa Cruz Island at Punta Estrada* ☎ *02/246–4780, 800–527–2500 toll free in the U.S.* 🖷 *02/246–4702* ⊕ *www.metropolitan-touring.com* ⟟ *21* ♨ *Restaurant, bar, pool, beach* ⊟ *AE, D, MC, V.*

$$$$ 🏨 **Royal Palm Galapagos.** This small resort on Santa Cruz is the only five-star luxury hotel on the islands. Suites, villas, and rooms blend into the garden surroundings within a 500-acre property; all have the proper amenities of a mainland high-rise hotel. Features include an observatory with computerized telescopes for star gazing and a Galápagos Museum that focuses on the ecology and native species. Tours offered include horseback riding, diving, snorkeling, hiking, birding, sea kayaking, and wind surfing. You also are welcome at the Royal Palm Hotel's Airport VIP room in Baltra. An entire dinner here, without drinks, will run you about $25. ⊠ *20 minutes from Porto Ayora, Santa Cruz* ☎ *05/ 527–409* 🖷 *05/527–408* ⊕ *www.milleniumhotels.com* ⟟ *10 villas, 4 rooms, 3 suites* ♨ *Restaurant, pool, tennis court, health club, spa, library, bar, business center, meeting rooms* ⊟ *AE, D, DC, MC, V.*

$$–$$$ 🏨 **Hotel Angermeyer.** Sometimes called Hotel Silberstein—the family name of the ancestors who first opened a residence on the islands—this comfortable place has a pool with a waterfall and large, pleasant rooms. Dive tours are a specialty here; the hotel has 5-day packages for $695, including breakfast and dinner in the hotel and box lunches when out on dives. They also have rooms for travelers with disabilities. ⊠ *Av. Charles Darwin y Pequeros, Puerto Agora* ☎ *05/526–277* ⊕ *www. hotelangermeyer.com* ⟟ *22* ♨ *Restaurant, pool, travel services* ⊟ *AE, DC, MC, V.*

$$ 🏨 **Hotel Galápagos.** Covered with bougainvillea and other flowering plants, this casual hotel is a short walk to the Darwin Research Station. On the waterfront, it overlooks cruise ships bobbing in Puerto Ayora. Ocean-view rooms have cement floors covered by palm-frond mats. The restaurant serves healthy international dishes, and the seaside lounge has hammocks and a self-serve bar. The staff arranges scuba-diving excursions and day trips to surrounding islands. ⊠ *Av. Charles Darwin, Puerto Ayora* ☎🖷 *05/526–296 or 05/526–330* ⟟ *14 rooms* ♨ *Restaurant, bar* ⊟ *MC.*

San Cristóbal

The capital of Galápagos Province and the largest town on San Cristóbal, **Puerto Baquerizo Moreno** is a bit less tourist-oriented than Puerto Ayora. Two kilometers (1 mi) east of the port is **Frigatebird Hill,** where both great and magnificent frigates—two species of black seabirds famed for their courtship displays—make their nests. On a clear day it offers sweeping views of the bay.

El Progreso, one of San Cristóbal's first colonies, is a small village about 8 km (5 mi) east of Puerto Baquerizo Moreno at the end of one of the island's few roads (buses connect the two towns twice daily). From El Progreso you can rent a four-wheel-drive vehicle and explore the shores of **Laguna el Junco,** one of the archipelago's few permanent freshwater lakes, 10 km (6 mi) east.

CloseUp
SAN CRISTOBAL INTERPRETATION CENTER

NO MATTER HOW SHORT YOUR VISIT, *make time for the San Cristobal Interpretation Center, which covers the history of the* archipelago from its volcanic origins to the present. On the southwest side of the island in an area of lush vegetation and freshwater lakes just west of the provincial capital of Puerto Baquerizo Moreno, the center is at 730 meters (2,395 feet), surrounded by gardens and with sweeping views of the ocean.

The Center's aim: to explain the natural processes that have made Galápagos such a unique place, delineate efforts to protect and preserve the Islands, and serve as an education center for park personnel and naturalist guides. It also has an open-air theater for performances and dance and film festivals, which has made it the cultural center of the Galápagos. The three exhibits inside are Human History, covering events related to the discovery and colonization of the islands; Natural History, with illustrations of natural events and information on how different species arrived at the islands; and Conservation, an introduction to the struggles of the ecosystems and preservation efforts under way.

After viewing the exhibits, take a walk along winding paths leading from the Interpretation Center to Playa Punta Carola (about 35 minutes), a favorite of surfers, or on to Mann Beach for a swim and to Frigate Bird Hill, a nesting place for Frigate birds. Along the way are plants, lava lizards, and other endemic animals. Admission to the center—open daily 10–8—is included in your Galápagos Park tax.

Punta Pitt, at the northeastern tip of the island, is the only place in the Galápagos where you can view three species of boobies—masked, blue-footed, and red-footed—nesting together. Also found here are frigate birds, storm petrels, and swallow-tailed gulls. The site is accessible by motor launch from Puerto Moreno.

Where to Stay

$$ ⊞ **Hostal Orca.** You'll find this small hotel right on the beach, in the tiny village of San Cristóbal. Ask for a room on the second floor, with balconies overlooking the bay. The lively restaurant also has an ocean view. ⊠ *San Cristóbal* ☎ *05/520–233; 02/223–0552 in Quito* ➦ *20 rooms* ⌂ *Restaurant, beach, bar* ⊟ *MC.*

Isabela

Although Isabela is the largest island in the archipelago, it has very little tourism infrastructure. The handful of hotels are very basic, with only intermittent hot water. Sleepy **Puerto Villamil,** founded in 1897 as a center for extracting lime, is the focus of Isabela's tourist trade—nearby are several lagoons where flamingos and migratory birds can be viewed up close, as well as beaches with large populations of herons, egrets, and other birds. Isabela's other community is **Santo Tomás,** 18 km (11 mi) northwest.

You can climb Isabela's active volcano, 4,488-foot **Sierra Negra,** with a local guide. From Santo Tomás you can hire horses for the 9-km (5½-mi) trek to the volcano's rim. The view is awe-inspiring: the volcano's caldera—roughly 10 km (6 mi) in diameter—is the largest in the Galápagos and the second-largest in the world. A more ambitious trek, requiring adequate planning and equipment, is 3,600-foot **Volcán Alcedox.** The site can be reached only by boat, after which a 10-km (6-mi) trail climbs over rough terrain. You cannot traipse around the island without a guide, and you'll need one here. Your reward is stunning views and a chance to see the archipelago's largest population of Galápagos tortoises.

The Galápagos Islands A to Z

AIR TRAVEL
Tame flies once daily from Guayaquil to Baltra, a tiny island just north of Santa Cruz, and to San Cristóbal. The flight takes roughly three hours and costs $350–$400 round-trip. If you're a do-it-yourself type, to reach Puerto Ayora on Santa Cruz you can take a Tame bus from your hotel to the ferry and, once across the channel, hop on any bus for the 30-minute trip across the island.

Remember that all foreign visitors who enter the Galápagos must pay $100 (there's talk of increasing the fee, so inquire before your trip). You must pay in American cash—not traveler's checks—and the bills must be new, without markings or tears. The money is earmarked for training park rangers and funding conservation efforts.

MONEY MATTERS
Tour boats generally accept payments in dollars, traveler's checks, or credit cards.

TELEPHONES
Although telephone lines now connect the Galápagos with mainland Ecuador, service is poor. The larger cruise ships usually offer satellite telephone services for an additional fee.

TOUR OPERATORS
For tours of the Galápagos—which you book in Quito or Guayaquil—you can choose from a wide range of boats. Although they're the cheapest, economy vessels (typically converted fishing trawlers) are often poorly maintained and have guides with only a passing knowledge of English. It's better to stick with tourist-class or luxury vessels, which generally offer three-, four-, and seven-night tours. The price tag per person for a double cabin on a three-night, luxury-ship cruise can run $765–$1,300 in low season and $880–$1,600 in high season. Off-peak rates usually apply from May 1 to June 14, September 1 to October 14, and December 1 to 16. When you book, be sure to ask if the $100 park tax is included.

Boat tours mean dining and sleeping on board, with much of the sailing done at night to maximize time spent on the islands. Most of these vessels employ multilingual naturalists who are knowledgeable in marine sciences. At least once a day you'll have an opportunity to swim or snorkel. If you want to dive you should make arrangements beforehand, as it's not offered on all boats.

To save money, you can wait until you arrive on the islands and try to bargain for a cheaper boat fare. Operators of all vessel classes come to the airport selling last-minute tickets. The risk of doing this, however, is that you might not find an available boat, especially during peak seasons.

CRUISE SHIPS Except for two single cabins, the 293-foot M/V *Galápagos Explorer II* is an all-suites ship. Operated by Conodros (operators of the Kapawi jungle lodge), it has 50 cabins with two twin beds that can be converted to one king-size bed. There's a swimming pool and a piano bar, so you definitely won't feel as if you're roughing it.

Kleintours flagship in the Galápagos is the 300-foot M/V *Galápagos Legend*. It holds 90 passengers, and all cabins have ocean views. There's a pool, a lounge, and access to e-mail and telephones. Kleintours also operates two yachts, the 20-passenger M/Y *Coral* and the 22-passenger M/Y *Coral II*. Cruises on the yachts are for three, five, and eight days.

Metropolitan Touring's flagship is the 273-foot M/V *Santa Cruz,* which carries 90 passengers. It was built specifically for the Galápagos. The *Isabela II* is Metropolitan's 40-passenger luxury yacht. The 36-passenger *Delfin II*, a 724-foot yacht, runs cruises through the islands.

YACHTS Several companies offer a range of smaller yachts that can be chartered by individuals or groups. Costs range from $540 to $1,000 for three nights. Galápagos Galasam Tours operates eight yachts holding 10–16 passengers. Its newest, the luxurious *Catamaran Millenium,* is an 82-foot cruiser that carries diving gear on board. A seven-night cruise on the *Millenium* is $2,000 per person. Quasar Naútica has well maintained yachts, including the three-masted, ketch-rigged schooner *Alta.* Its most luxurious and fastest yacht is the *Parranda.* Angermeyer's Enchanted Expeditions also operates several yachts. TOPPSA is a last-minute booking agency; fares are quite inexpensive.

🚩 Tour Companies **Angermeyer's Enchanted Expeditions** ☎ 02/256-9960 in Quito, 800/327-3573 in the U.S. ⊕ www.angermeyer.com.ec. **Conodros** ☎ 04/228-5711 in Guayaquil, 800/327-9854 in the U.S. **Galápagos Galasam Tours** ☎ 04/230-6093 in Guayaquil ⊕ www.galasam-tours.com. **Kleintours** ☎ 02/243-0345 in Quito ⊕ www.kleintours.com. **Metropolitan Touring** ☎ 02/246-4780 in Quito, 800/527-2500 in the U.S. ⊕ www.metropolitan-touring.com. **Quasar Naútica** ☎ 02/244-6996 in Quito, 800/247-2925 in the U.S. ⊕ www.quasarnauticausa.com. **TOPPSA** ☎ 02/226-0651 for last-minute bookings in Quito, toll free from the U.S. 866/809-3145 ⊕ www.toppsa.com.

VISITOR INFORMATION

Tour reservations are typically booked through agencies in Quito, Guayaquil, or the United States. The tourist office has limited information about tours and guides.

🚩 Tourist Information **Santa Cruz Tourist Office** ✉ Av. Charles Darwin, Santa Cruz ☎ 05/526-174.

ECUADOR A TO Z

To research prices, get advice from other travelers, and book travel arrangements, visit www.fodors.com.

AIR TRAVEL

Quito and Guayaquil both serve as international gateways to Ecuador. American has daily flights from Miami to Quito and Guayaquil. Continental has daily flights from Houston to Quito and Guayaquil, as well as flights from Newark to Quito that stop in Bogota, Colombia. LanEcuador flies daily between Quito/Guayaquil and Miami or New York (JFK). Iberia has two flights per week from Madrid to Quito. KLM has four Amsterdam–Quito flights per week. Air France has three Paris–Quito flights per week.

There are no direct flights to Ecuador from Europe, Australia or New Zealand. Travelers can connect to Ecuador-bound flights in other South American countries or in the United States. Flights that originate in Houston fly to Quito in 6 hours; those that originate in Miami fly to Quito in 4½ hours and to Guayaquil in 4½ hours.

🛪 Airlines & Contacts **Air France** ☎ 0845/359-1000 in the U.K. ⊕ www.airfrance. com. **American** ☎ 02/226-0900 in Quito, 800/433-7300 in the U.S. ⊕ www. americanairlines.com. **Austro Aéreo** ⊠ Av. Colón at Av. Amazonas, Quito ☎ 02/256-4969 or 02/250-2706. **Continental** ☎ 02/255-7170 in Quito, 04/256-7241 in Guayaquil, 800/523-3273 in the U.S. ⊕ www.continental.com. **Iberia** ☎ 08456/012854 in the U.K. ⊕ www.iberia.com. **Icaro** ☎ 02/225-4891 in Quito, 04/229-4265 in Guayaquil, 07/802-700 in Cuenca. **KLM** ☎ 0870/507-4074 in the U.K. ⊕ www.klm.com. **LanEcuador** ☎ 02/256-3003 in Quito, 04/232-4360 in Guayaquil, 800/735-5526 in the U.S. ⊕ www.lanchile.com. **Tame** ⊠ Av. Amazonas 1354, at Av. Colón ☎ 02/250-9382, 02/250-9385, 800/555-999 toll free in Ecuador.

AIRPORTS

Aeropuerto Mariscal Sucre, Quito's international airport, is 8 km (5 mi) from downtown. Aeropuerto Simón Bolívar, Guayaquil's airport, is 5 km (3 mi) north of the city.

🛪 Airports **Aeropuerto Mariscal Sucre** ⊠ Av. Rio Amazonas ☎ 02/244-0080. **Aeropuerto Simón Bolívar** ⊠ Av. de las Américas ☎ 04/228-2100.

BUS TRAVEL

Major bus companies in Ecuador offer direct service operating between Quito, Cuenca, and Guayaquil. Buses run frequently throughout the country and are extremely cheap: The 2-hour ride from Quito to Otavalo costs $2; the 10-hour ride from Guayaquil to Quito is about $8. Crime on buses has been on the rise in the past few years, so keep a close eye on your valuables. Though they cost a bit more, consider using private bus companies such as Panamerican Internacional and Reytur. Their coaches are equipped with niceties such as air-conditioning and rest rooms.

🚌 Bus Information **Panamerican Internacional** ⊠ Av. Colón at Calle Reina Victoria, Quito ☎ 02/255-7133. **Reytur** ⊠ Calle Gangotena 158, Quito ☎ 02/256-5299 or 02/254-6674.

BUSINESS HOURS

Office hours are generally 8:30–5. Banks are open weekdays 9–6, and some are open Saturdays 9–1. Casas de cambio, which are much more efficient and less crowded, are open longer in the afternoon. Shops are open 9–6, closing for a few hours in the afternoon. Those catering to tourists don't close for lunch, but many are closed Saturday afternoon and all day Sunday.

CAR RENTAL

Car-rental offices outside Quito, Guayaquil, and Cuenca are virtually nonexistent. Renting a car in Ecuador can be quite expensive. The weekly rates can run higher than $300 for a compact car, and close to $375 for a four-wheel-drive vehicle. Inquire about deductibles for damage and theft, which can be quite high, before agreeing on a price. Examine the car carefully, and make sure it has a jack and spare tire.

CAR TRAVEL

Renting a car in the major cities is not advisable, as traffic is congested and, in Quito, parking spaces are impossible to find (Guayaquil has numerous parking garages). Outside of the major urban areas you'll find that only the major highways are paved. All roads can be treacherous in bad weather. In most parts of the country, a four-wheel-drive vehicle is a necessity. On the narrow mountain roads, bus drivers are notorious for making dangerous maneuvers, such as passing on curves. If you decide to drive, bring or rent a cell phone for emergencies.

EMERGENCY ASSISTANCE No emergency roadside service exists, although passing motorists will frequently stop to help with disabled vehicles. Ask your rental agency for emergency numbers and a list of garages in the area you're traveling.

GASOLINE Regular leaded gas, called *extra,* costs about $1.75 per U.S. gallon. Unleaded gas, called *super,* is roughly $2 per U.S. gallon.

PARKING Park your car at your hotel rather than leaving it on the street, where it is susceptible to theft. Larger hotels are more likely to have fenced parking lots.

CUSTOMS & DUTIES

You can import 1 liter of spirits, 300 cigarettes or 50 cigars, and reasonable amounts of perfumes, gifts, and personal effects. It is illegal to bring firearms, ammunition, drugs, fresh or dried meats, or plants and vegetables into the country.

There is a $100 fee to visit the Galápagos Islands. The airport departure fee is $25 when leaving Ecuador.

ELECTRICITY

In Ecuador, the electric current is 110 volts; North American–style two-pronged plugs are used. Areas outside of major cities are subject to frequent power surges.

EMBASSIES

The embassies for Canada and the United Kingdom are located near Parque La Carolina. The United States embassy is near Parque El Ejido.

🛂 Embassies **Canada** ✉ Av. 6 de Diciembre 2816, at Calle J. Ortón, Quito ☎ 02/254–3214. **United States** ✉ Av. 12 de Octubre and Av. Patria, Quito ☎ 02/256–2890. **United Kingdom** ✉ Calle González Suárez 111, Quito ☎ 02/256–0670.

FESTIVALS & SEASONAL EVENTS

Galápagos Days, celebrating the islands' statehood, is held on the second week in February. It features parades and all-out revelry throughout the islands. During Carnaval, Ecuadorians douse one another with buckets of water, water balloons, and squirt guns. Carnaval is most exuberant in the Cotopaxi Province—local dances and fairs are held in Saquisilí, Pujilí, Latacunga, and Salcedo.

Corpus Christi is observed in many mountain towns with fireworks displays. La Fiesta de San Juan enlivens highland towns, especially around Otavalo, on June 24. Otavalo also comes to life during La Fiesta de Yamor, a harvest festival held the first two weeks in September.

In Latacunga, September 24 is the Fiesta de la Mamá Negra, which honors Our Lady of Mercy with lively processions featuring costumed dancers. The Fiestas de Quito in the first week of December brings bullfights, art exhibitions, and outdoor concerts.

HEALTH

FOOD & DRINK   Food-borne illnesses are not serious problems in Ecuador. Avoid tap water to reduce the risk of contracting intestinal parasites. Drink only bottled water, which is available *con gas* and *sin gas* (with and without carbonation). Ask for drinks *sin hielo* (without ice). Avoid uncooked or unpeeled vegetables and fruits that may have been washed in tap water. Brush your teeth with bottled water in remote areas or budget hotels. At other hotels, ask if the water is purified; it often is. Eat at street stands at your own risk.

OTHER HAZARDS   Discuss malaria medications with your doctor if you're traveling to the rain forest or other isolated areas. In the Galápagos, the most serious threat you'll face is sunburn—do not underestimate the intensity of the equatorial sun. If you're prone to seasickness and you're planning a cruise around the archipelago, make sure to bring medications. At high altitudes, the sun is strong and altitude sickness can strike.

HOLIDAYS

New Year's Day; Easter; Labor Day (May 1); Battle of Pichincha (May 24); Simón Bolívar's birthday (July 24); Independence Day (Aug. 10); Columbus Day (Oct. 12); All Souls' Day (Nov. 2); Christmas.

LANGUAGE

Ecuador's two official languages are Spanish and Quechua, a language spoken by indigenous peoples in the highlands. English is the lingua franca of tourism, and although you will find many people in travel-related fields who speak excellent English, many people do not speak English. Learn a few phrases in Spanish before you go. In rural areas few people speak English, so bring along a phrase book if you don't speak Spanish.

MAIL & SHIPPING

Post offices throughout the country keep fairly standard hours. Most are open weekdays 9–5. First-class mail costs about 60¢ to the United States, 70¢ to Europe. You can expect mail to reach international destinations within two weeks.

MONEY MATTERS

Many goods and services—from taxi fares to textiles—are inexpensive by Western standards. Although international chain hotels are pricey, you can stay in perfectly nice places for less than $75.

Some sample prices are: a cup of coffee, 50¢; a bottle of beer, $1.50; a soft drink, 50¢; a bottle of wine, $8; a sandwich, $2; a 2-km (1-mi) taxi ride, 50¢; a city bus ride, 10¢; museum entrance, $1.

CURRENCY   The U.S. dollar is Ecuador's official currency—but the country also issues its own coins, equivalent to half dollars, quarters, dimes, nickels, and pennies. It has been reported that the dollar is easier to counterfeit than the former Sucre, so check your bills when receiving change.

PASSPORTS

Only a valid passport is required for U.S., Canadian, Australian, New Zealand, and British citizens for stays of up to 90 days.

SAFETY

Petty crime, such as pickpocketing, is a problem in Ecuador. Use the same precautions you would anywhere—avoid flashy jewelry and watches, hold purses and camera bags close to your body, and avoid handling money in public. Use extra caution in all crowded spaces, such as markets and plazas. In Quito, be especially wary in the streets and plazas of the Old City. Take taxis after dark, even if you are going only a few blocks.

TAXES

A few businesses add a surcharge of 3%–10% on credit-card purchases. Most hotels add a 20% surcharge to your bill. Some include this government tax when they quote prices, but others do not. Be sure to inquire when you book your room.

TAXIS

Taxis are a safe, convenient, and economical way to travel in Ecuador, even when you want to travel long distances. It's easy to negotiate a rate with a driver beforehand for a half- or full-day trip to your destination. A three-hour taxi ride, for example, should only cost about $20.

TELEPHONES

To call Ecuador from another country, dial the country code of 593, then the area code, then the local number. Include the "0" at the beginning of the area code only when calling long distance within the country.

Directory assistance, available only in Spanish, is available by dialing 104.

LOCAL CALLS   Coin-operated public phones are harder to find as more and more accept only phone cards. You can purchase phone cards in most shops and newsstands. Some stores now charge about 25¢ for a brief call on their private line; look for a sign in the window reading TELÉFONO or LLAMADAS.

Another alternative is placing a call from an office of Andinatel, the country's telephone company. Known as Emetel in the highlands and Pacifictel on the coast, it has offices in many towns and villages. Most are open daily 8 AM–9:30 PM.

LONG-DISTANCE CALLS To make collect or credit-card calls through an English-speaking operator, call AT&T, MCI, or Sprint.

🔋 **AT&T** ☎ 999-119. **MCI** ☎ 999-170. **Sprint** ☎ 999-171.

TIPPING

A tip of 5%–10% is appropriate for waiters in upscale restaurants. (A 10% surcharge often added to the bill is supposedly for service, although whether waiters actually receive it is questionable.) Porters and bellhops should receive the equivalent of 50¢ per bag. Guides expect $4–$8 per day for each person in a tour group, while drivers expect about $2. Taxi drivers don't expect tips.

VISITOR INFORMATION

For information about Ecuador, contact the embassy in Canada, the United Kingdom, or the United States, or Ecuador's Ministry of Tourism offices in Ecuador.

🔋 Tourist Information **Canada** ⊠ 50 O'Connor St., Suite 1311, Ottawa, Ontario K1P6L2 ☎ 613/563-8206. **United Kingdom** ⊠ 3 Hans Crescent, Flat 3B, London SW1X OLS ☎ 44171/584-1367. **United States** ⊠ 2535 15th St. NW, Washington, DC 20009 ☎ 202/234-7200

🔋 Ecuadorean Tourist Information **Ministry of Tourism** ⊠ Eloy Alfaro N32-300 Carlos Tobar Quito ☎ 02/250-7559 ⊕ www.vivecuador.com. **Coastal** ⊠ P. Ycaza 203 y Pichincha Guayaquil ☎ 04/256-8764. **Southern Andes** ⊠ Presidente Córdova y Benigno Malo ☎ 07/830-337. **Northern Region** ⊠ Ibarra García Moreno 744 Y Sánchez y Cifuentes ☎ 06/958-759. **Central Highland Region** ⊠ Av. Daniel León Borja y Pje. Municipal, Centro de Arte y Cultura Riobamba ☎☎ 03/941-213. **Amazon Region** ⊠ Calle Césalo Marin y 9 de Octubre, Ed. Center Shopping Carmelita ☎☎ 03/884-655.

WHEN TO GO

The high season revolves around national celebrations, especially Carnaval, Christmas, and Easter. During these peak periods hotel rooms become scarce and prices jump noticeably.

CLIMATE Ecuador's climate is remarkably varied, influenced by ocean currents, trade winds, and seasonal changes. The rainy season lasts from December to May and occasionally causes landslides and power outages. Weather in Quito is fairly constant, with warm sunny days giving way to very cool evenings. Guayaquil is muggy during the rainy season but is much cooler and drier the rest of the year than you might expect for an area so close to the equator. In the Galápagos Islands the weather is generally hot and humid January to April, with frequent afternoon showers. Cooler temperatures prevail the rest of the year, causing *garua,* the fine mist that envelopes the islands. The seas are roughest in September and October, when many cruise ships head for dry dock.

The following are the average daily maximum and minimum temperatures for Quito.

Jan.	69F	20C	May	69F	20C	Sept.	72F	22C
	46	8		47	8		45	7
Feb.	69F	20C	June	70F	21C	Oct.	70F	21C
	47	81		46	8		46	8
Mar.	69F	20C	July	71F	22C	Nov.	70F	21C
	47	8		44	7		46	8
Apr.	69F	20C	Aug.	71F	22C	Dec.	70F	21C
	47	8		44	7		46	8

PARAGUAY

7

Updated by
Jeffrey
Van Fleet

FROM THE SUBTLE CHARMS OF ASUNCIÓN, the laid-back capital, to the country's wild countryside and small colonial towns, Paraguay is a country full of surprises and little hideaways. Even the most seasoned travelers, however, scratch their heads when the subject is Paraguay. If the country enters their consciousness at all, it comes as an answer to the trivia question, "Which South American nations have no seacoast?" (Bolivia is the other.) But Paraguay is more than the answer to a stumper on a quiz show—this Rip Van Winkle of South American nations is now awakening from almost two centuries of slumber.

Decades of authoritarian rule left Paraguay behind while nearby Argentina and Brazil made rapid economic strides. The country has struggled since 1989—its first year of democracy—to make up for lost time. Although intent on catching up with its neighbors, Paraguay has not completely rubbed the sleep out of its eyes. Many marvel at the easy pace of life and the old-fashioned courtesies of the people. In the capital of Asunción, crowds are seldom a problem when you take in its architectural showplaces. In the wild countryside, you may stumble across villages where you're the only visitor.

A trip to the tranquil southern region of the *ruinas jesuíticas* (Jesuit ruins) transports you to a time when missionaries worked the fields alongside their indigenous Guaraní converts. Some of the world's best fishing can be had in rivers teeming with giant catfish. Anglers can test their skills as clouds of snowy egrets take flight and monkeys swing through trees along the banks. Vultures soar over the sun-scorched plains of the Chaco, an arid scrubland that covers half of Paraguay and is one of the most sparsely populated spots on earth, with less than one inhabitant for each of its 250,000 square km (97,500 square mi).

Paraguay's flamboyant history is one of a small country led by larger-than-life strongmen whose personal goals often conflicted with the needs of the people. The first president, José Gáspar Rodríguez de Francia, set the tone by calling himself "El Supremo." He preached a policy of complete self-sufficiency, forbidding trade and immigration, and set the stage for Paraguay's history of isolation. Then came the López family, father and son, the younger of whom, Francisco Solano, led Paraguay into the suicidal War of the Triple Alliance (1865–70) against Argentina, Brazil, and Uruguay; he lost half the country's territory and 80% of the male population and condemned Paraguay to a century of stagnation. A succession of presidents culminated in the 35-year authoritarian regime of General Alfredo Stroessner, toppled in a 1989 coup.

Although individual rights have been restored and free elections have been held, the transition has been lurching at best. As recently as March 1999, the assassination of vice-president Luis María Argaña demonstrated the government's tentative hold on power. Widespread corruption and smuggling (especially in the area around Ciudad del Este, which borders both Brazil and Argentina) continue to foment instability and undermine the rule of law. Since freedom of the press was restored, daily accounts of grievances against current officials fill the country's now-lively media. Dire financial straits in Argentina and Brazil, Paraguay's

If you have
3 days

Explore **Asunción's** tree-lined streets and colonial plazas, and spend your time here absorbing the city's mestizo heritage. Many of the capital's most interesting sights, including the Catedral and the Palacio de Gobierno, surround El Paraguayo Independiente, which runs west from Plaza Independencia to the port. Once you've finished exploring Asunción, venture outside the city, on a day trip, to **San Bernardino,** a rustic lakeside resort. A number of small towns en route offer chances to peruse indigenous handicrafts.

If you have
5 to 7
days

After a few days in **Asunción** and the surrounding area, head south to Paraguay's greatest attraction, the well-preserved ruins of about 30 17th-century Jesuit missions. Some Asunción tour operators offer a one-day marathon tour of the region. If you're bent on doing it all in one day, it's certainly feasible, if rushed. However, since it's a five-hour journey from Asunción, you're better off allowing at least two or three days for the journey—plus an additional day or two if you're an angler, so you can try your luck on the region's famous streams. If you've come all the way to Paraguay, it's worth your time to consider driving east from Asunción on Routes 2 and 7 and crossing the border at Ciudad del Este to see Iguazú Falls. (Don't stay in Ciudad del Estate overnight, however—it's not safe.) If you prefer just to head south, base yourself in the border town of **Encarnación** on your fourth and fifth nights and spend days checking out **Jesús, San Cosme y Damián,** and **Trinidad,** taking in Jesuit ruins and missions. Alternatively, stay overnight in **Villa Florida,** a must if you're an angler.

primary source of trade and tourism, have taken their toll here as well. It remains to be seen whether Paraguay's still-fragile democracy can withstand these challenges. The April 2003 election of president Nicanor Duarte, of the long-ruling Colorado party, brought the usual mix of hope and resignation that has accompanied such changes in the past.

Intrigued about joining the small number of people who have visited this developing destination? Realize that institutions and services catering to travelers are improving but are still in their infancy. Struggling museums are maintained more by enthusiasm than by government funds. On top of that, the highway system is underdeveloped and good accommodations are rare outside Asunción. But there's an upside to visiting one of the least-known countries on the continent: Paraguayans seem genuinely interested in finally becoming part of the international community. They'll start by lavishing attention on you, hoping you'll tell a few friends about their country once you get home.

About the Restaurants

A staple of Paraguayan dining is *parrillada*—barbecued meats served in large portions at restaurants called *parrillas*. Beef, including blood sausage and organ meats, is the mainstay, but pork and chicken are also common. *Puchero* is a meat, sausage, vegetable, and chickpea stew that's eaten in the cooler months. *Bori-bori* is a hearty soup with bits of meat, vegetables, and balls molded from cheese and corn. Paraguay's rivers abound with unusual fish, such as the *surubí*, a giant catfish. It's tastiest when served in a dish called *milanesa de surubí* (battered and deep-fried fillets). Another tasty option is the *dorado*, a ferocious predator resembling the salmon. Try it lightly grilled. A soup made from the fish's head and other leftovers is surprisingly delicious.

Usual accompaniments include salads (Paraguay's tomatoes are incredibly flavorful) and *palmitos* (hearts of palm), considered a delicacy. Other side dishes include *sopa paraguaya*, a kind of corn bread made with cheese, eggs, and onions, or *chipá-guazú*, a similar dish in which roughly ground corn is substituted for cornmeal. You also may be served boiled *manioc*, a white, fibrous root with a bland flavor. *Chipá*, a type of bread made from corn flour, ground manioc, and sometimes cheese, is baked in a clay oven called a *tatakua*. It is sold everywhere and is best eaten piping hot. Typical desserts include *dulce de leche*, a pudding made from slow-cooking milk and sugar; papaya preserved in syrup; and such fresh fruits as pineapple, banana, mango, and melon.

Cafés and bars usually sell snacks, mostly fried or grilled foods that can be prepared quickly. The most popular is *milanesa*, thin slices of batter-fried beef, chicken breast, pork, or fish. Other favorites are *empanadas*, envelopes of pastry filled with beef, pork, chicken, corn, or cheese; *croquetas*, sausage-shape minced meat or poultry that is rolled in bread crumbs and deep fried; and *mixtos*, ham-and-cheese sandwiches. Many cafés have a special of the day—*plato del día*—that's usually a good bargain. Paraguayan portions tend to be generous, so don't hesitate to share a dish.

Few Paraguayans are seen without their *guampa*, a drinking vessel made of a cow's horn, metal, or wood, from which they sip *tereré*, a cold infusion made from *yerba maté* tea. Maté is drunk hot throughout South America, but the cold version, often mixed with medicinal herbs, is more common in Paraguay. Pilsners, particularly the Baviera brand, are quite good. If you order beer in a restaurant, an enormous bottle is likely to be brought to your table in an ice bucket. Beer on tap is known as *chopp* (pronounced "shop"). Choose beer over the local wine whenever possible. In Asunción, society women fill the top hotels' tables for afternoon tea, and baby showers and parties for brides-to-be often take the form of teas. Espresso and often filtered coffee is served demitasse except at breakfast.

Asunción and the other larger cities have plenty of excellent restaurants, bars, and cafés, but in smaller towns the choices are few. If you're traveling along the highways you can expect to find a few good roadside restaurants serving grilled meat and fish.

Since restaurants sometimes close between meals, it's important to plan when to eat. Lunch can begin at 11:30, but 12:30 is more typical. Some restaurants stop serving lunch as early as 2. Dinner is often available at 7 PM, with restaurants staying open until 11. More sophisticated dining spots open at 8 PM and serve until shortly after midnight. On weekends and special occasions, dining hours are extended. Café hours are generally 7 AM–10 PM.

7

Colonial Architecture

In its colonial heyday, Asunción was the administrative center of southern South America. It still retains some of its pre-independence grandeur, but today the most compelling architectural attractions are the ruins of some 30 Jesuit missions in the southeast. Although Spanish missionaries came to what is now Paraguay in 1588, little remains of their earliest dwellings. What you'll find are fascinating traces of 17th-century *reducciónes* (literally, "reductions"). Here the Jesuits organized the indigenous Guaranís—a nomadic people—into farming communities, and worked with them side-by-side, providing vocational training and religious and secular education. You can do a mission tour in your own car—if you don't mind driving on unpaved or flooded roads and you can cope with motorists who don't obey traffic rules. The benefit of having your own car is that you can take it easy and spend a few days exploring. If you prefer not to drive, you can opt for a hurried day with an Asunción tour operator. The sites you'll see run the spectrum—from the well-preserved San Cosme y Damián, where many of the structures still serve the community, to the never finished, but intriguing, abandoned structures at Jesús.

Fishing

Paraguay's fishing is considered to be among the best in the world. Anglers come chiefly to catch dorado, spectacular fighters that leap high into the air when hooked, and surubí, giant catfish that take off like an express train when you reel them in. Dorado are generally between 9 and 27 pounds, although some weigh up to 40 pounds. Surubí weighing as much as 44 pounds are not uncommon, but the real trophies are more than 90 pounds. The top spots for anglers are in the southwest—Ayolas, on the Río Paraná, and Villa Florida, on the Río Tebicuary.

Handicrafts

The best-known Paraguayan craft is the delicate *ñandutí*, a type of spiderweb lacework. Patterns represent plants, animals, or scenes from local legends. Although ñandutí are traditionally made with white silk or cotton, colors are now being added to the designs. Both this and *ao p'oí*, a type of embroidery, are incorporated into items, such as tablecloths and place mats. Wood carvings, intricately decorated gourds, and figurines—including nativity figures—are reasonably priced mementos. Rustic leather items, such as suitcases, knapsacks, and briefcases, are long-lasting and only a fraction of the cost of Argentine goods. Plain white or colorful woven hammocks are another good buy. You'll be able to find all these crafts in stores in Asunción. Craftspeople in the town of Areguá, near Asunción on Lake Ypacaraí, make clay pots and other ceramics. In Luque, near the international airport, you can find Paraguayan harps, guitars, and fine silver filigree jewelry. The town of Itá, 37 km (23 mi) south of Asunción on Ruta 1, is famous for its ceramics, and is the place to come for distinctive black clay pottery.

WHAT IT COSTS In Dollars				
$$$$	**$$$**	**$$**	**$**	**¢**
AT DINNER over $20	$15–$20	$10–$15	$6–$10	under $6

Prices are for per person for a main course at dinner.

About the Hotels

The quality of lodgings has improved dramatically in Asunción in recent years, though sheer numbers of hotels remain small. Those that are here offer great value for the rates they charge. Be sure to ask for an air-conditioned room in summer. Outside Asunción, hotels are few and far between, as many villages are just a few hundred yards long and consist of little more than a handful of houses, a couple of general stores, a bakery, and, sometimes, a gas station.

WHAT IT COSTS In Dollars				
$$$$	**$$$**	**$$**	**$**	**¢**
FOR 2 PEOPLE over $180	$100–$180	$60–$100	$40–$60	under $40

Prices are for two people in a standard double room in high season, excluding tax.

Exploring Paraguay

Paraguay is divided into two distinct regions, separated by the Río Paraguay. The southeast region is distinguished by a subtropical climate, thick forests, and meandering rivers. It encompasses less than half of the country's territory but holds 98% of its population. Asunción, Ciudad del Este, Encarnación, and the Jesuit missions are all in the east. Paraguay is also the most inexpensive gateway to the famous Iguazú Falls. It can be reached from Ciudad del Este, directly east of Asunción, at the frontier where Paraguay, Argentina, and Brazil meet.

Paraguay's northwest, known as the Chaco, is a sparsely populated and largely unexplored expanse. This vast and desolate Paraguayan pampa, which abuts Bolivia, is used mostly by the lumber and cattle industries.

ASUNCIÓN

Asunción was founded on August 15, 1537—the Feast of the Assumption, or *Asunción* in Spanish. Take a step back and you'll see traces of the city that was once the colonial capital of southern South America. On the drive from the airport, taxis whisk by the magnificent mansions lining Avenida Mariscal López—a furtive glimpse through a doorway reveals a peaceful patio reminiscent of those in southern Spain. Remnants of Asunción's prosperous past can also be detected in the delicately decorated facade and balconies of Belle Epoque buildings that have survived the vagaries of fashion, although in some instances they've yielded to commercialism by leasing the ground floor to fast-food joints with blaring neon signs. Alongside the money changers and peddlers of fake Rolex watches who patrol the streets and plazas, indigenous women sell

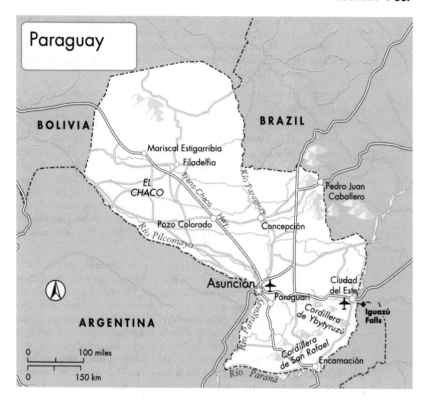

Paraguay

BOLIVIA

BRAZIL

Mariscal Estigarribia

Filadelfia

EL CHACO

Trans-Chaco Hwy.

Río Paraguay

Pedro Juan Caballero

Pozo Colorado

Concepción

Río Pilcomayo

Asunción

Paraguarí

Ciudad del Este

Cordillera de Ybytyruzú

Iguazú Falls

ARGENTINA

Cordillera de San Rafael

0   100 miles

0   150 km

Río Paraguay

Río Paraná

Encarnación

bundles of herbs and roots—centuries-old remedies for every ailment. Contrasting with the hustle and bustle of the nearby commercial center, the pristine columned government and legislative palaces overlook the Bay of Asunción as cool breezes rustle through flame trees in the riverside park.

Like most other Latin American cities, Asunción suffers from haphazard development and an inadequate infrastructure. But Paraguay's relative lack of development in the past few decades spared its capital some of the glaring excesses that characterize other cities on this continent. During the day the *centro* is packed. Rich and poor constantly rub shoulders, and air-conditioned sedans jostle at crossroads with packed buses. At night the wealthy drive to their elegant suburban homes, while street vendors lug their unsold wares back to the reclaimed swampland of the shantytowns near the river.

Exploring Asunción

The city is built on a rise overlooking a large bay formed by the Río Paraguay. The centro runs south–southeast from the bay for about 10 blocks to Teniente Fariña, and it stretches 17 blocks from Colón in the west to Estados Unidos in the east. Most hotels, restaurants, shops, and offices can be found in this rectangle. Except for the irregular coast along the river, Asunción's streets follow a standard grid. Downtown streets are narrow and generally have one-way traffic. Two major squares—Plaza de los Héroes and Plaza Uruguaya—provide cool resting places in the shade of jacaranda trees.

Numbers in the text correspond to numbers in the margin and on the Asunción map.

a good walk

Begin your walk on the northwest corner of **Plaza de los Héroes** ❶ ⌐, at the pink-domed **Panteón Nacional de los Héroes** ❷. Walk two blocks west on Palma, which runs along the north edge of the square, and turn right onto 14 de Mayo to find **Casa de la Independencia** ❸. Two blocks farther north on 14 de Mayo, at El Paraguayo Independiente, is **Casa de los Diputados** ❹. For a look at Paraguay's capitol, head two blocks west on El Paraguayo Independiente, which runs west toward the port; here you'll find the neoclassical, horseshoe-shape **Palacio de Gobierno** ❺, which is not open to the public. Across the street is **Manzana de la Rivera** ❻, Asunción's cultural center.

From the palace, retrace your steps to Avenida República and turn left. Walk east for three blocks to Plaza Independencia, around which most of Asunción's important public buildings lie. Facing the square from the north is the **Palacio Legislativo** ❼, and on the southeast corner is the **Catedral de Nuestra Señora de la Asunción** ❽. Behind the cathedral, heading toward the river, are shantytown neighborhoods that are best avoided. From the cathedral, walk two blocks east on Mariscal López and then two blocks south on Iturbe to the **Museo de Bellas Artes** ❾. Then head east down Estigarribia to **Plaza Uruguaya** ❿. If Asunción's crowds and pollution start to wear on you, take a walk across this plaza at dusk, when the shrill voices of creepers and critters hidden in the trees will remind you that, despite the urban environment, nature is never far away.

Save an afternoon for a trip to the **Jardín Botánico y Zoológico** ⓫. It's about a 15-minute taxi or bus ride from the centro. Also about 15 minutes from the city center is the **Museo del Barro** ⓬, the capital's modern art and ceramic museum, open only in the afternoon and early evening. Don't miss stopping in for a drink at the **Gran Hotel del Paraguay** ⓭, about 20 blocks from downtown.

TIMING & PRECAUTIONS

Asunción is a small city, so its centro can be easily explored in a day. Many of the attractions are free. Expect unbearably hot temperatures October through March, when you should plan outdoor activities for early morning and late afternoon. The rest of the year, Asunción has a pleasant, springlike climate. Few intersections in the heart of the city are governed by traffic lights, so be on guard crossing the street.

WHAT TO SEE

❸ **Casa de la Independencia.** This 1774 house with whitewashed walls, brick floors, and a lovely patio was once the secret meeting place of revolutionaries plotting to break away from Spain. They entered and left in the dead of night through the *callejón* (alleyway) in back. Relics from the May 1811 revolution, which secured Paraguay's independence, are displayed in this well-maintained museum, as are religious artifacts and furnishings depicting a typical colonial-era home. ⊠ *14 de Mayo at Presidente Franco* ☎ *021/493–918* ▣ *Free* ⊙ *Mon.–Fri 7–6:30; Sat. 8–noon.*

❹ **Casa de los Diputados.** Once a convent, then a much-needed blood bank during the Chaco War, then a military museum, then a cultural center, this Spanish colonial building now contains offices for members of Congress. ⊠ *14 de Mayo at El Paraguayo Independiente* ☎ *021/445–212* ▣ *Free* ⊙ *Weekdays 7:30–noon and 1:30–6, weekends 8–noon.*

❽ **Catedral de Nuestra Señora de la Asunción.** Inside the newly renovated seat of the Archdiocese of Asunción, portions of which date from 1687, are an enormous gilded altar and many 18th- and 19th-century religious statues and paintings. ⊠ *Plaza Independencia* ☎ *021/449–512* ▣ *Free* ⊙ *Daily 8–noon and 3–6.*

❸ **Gran Hotel del Paraguay.** This well-preserved mansion has an illustrious past as the former home of Madame Elisa Lynch, the Irish mistress of Paraguayan dictator Francisco Solano López. Now the oldest hotel in Asunción, and not quite where the action is, it's nonetheless surrounded by verandas and carefully tended tropical gardens. Duck inside to see the collection of 19th-century furniture and paintings and enjoy a cool cocktail at the bar. ⊠ *Calle de la Residenta 902* ☎ *021/200–051.*

⓫ **Jardín Botánico y Zoológico.** The government has improved maintenance at this once-neglected park (a trend that's catching on in other parts of the country as well). Besides plenty of plants and a small zoo, you'll find a fine example of a country house, once the home of President Francisco Solano López. It's now a museum with exhibits on Paraguayan wildlife, ethnology, and history. ⊠ *Gral Artigas and Primer Presidente* ☎ *021/291–255* ▣ *G6,000* ⊙ *Garden and zoo daily 7–6; museum weekdays 7–5, Sat. 7–noon and 1:30–5, Sun. 9–1.*

❻ **Manzana de la Rivera.** In a model for urban planners everywhere, the city of Asunción combined this *manzana* (block) of nine historic houses near the river into a pleasing cultural center. The oldest of these, the 1764 Casa Viola, the name by which many Asunceños refer to the complex, serves as a small city museum called the **Museo Memoria de la Ciudad.** The Casa Emasa, once a customs office, now houses **La Galería,** the center's art gallery. The 1914 art nouveau **Casa Clari,** the newest house, is the complex's café. ⊠ *Ayolas 129* ☎ *021/442–448* ▣ *Free* ⊙ *Weekdays 8 AM–9 PM, Sat. 10:30–8, Sun. 10:30–7.*

❾ **Museo de Bellas Artes.** The region's artistic legacy is displayed at the Museum of Fine Arts, which has a collection of paintings and sculpture by both Paraguayan and South American artists. Some of the country's most important documents are found in the museum's archive, but the records are geared toward scholarly research rather than tourist perusal. ⊠ *Mariscal Estigarribia at Iturbe* ☎ *021/447–716* ▣ *Free* ⊙ *Tues.–Fri. 7–7, Sat. 8–noon.*

⓬ **Museo del Barro.** Though billed as a modern art museum, the so-called Museum of Clay includes colonial and indigenous art, but is actually better known for its collection of pre-colonial Guaraní ceramics. ⊠ *Grabadores del Cabichu'í at Cañana* ☎ *021/607–996* ▣ *Free* ⊙ *Wed.–Sun. 3:30–8.*

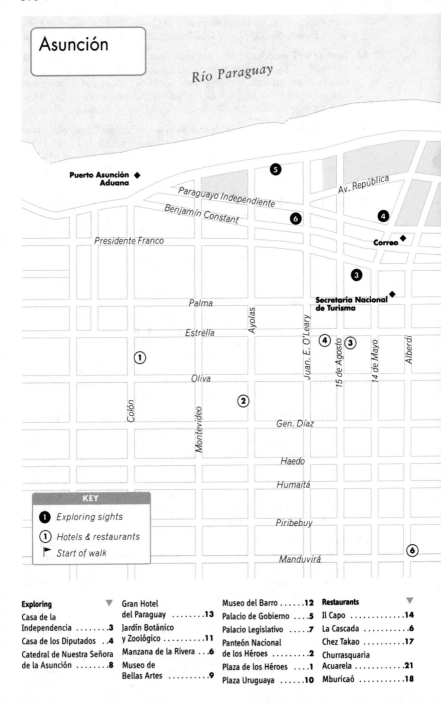

Asunción

Río Paraguay

Puerto Asunción ◆
Aduana

Paraguayo Independiente

Benjamín Constant

Av. República

Presidente Franco

Correo ◆

⑤

⑥

❹

❸

Secretaria Nacional
de Turismo ◆

Palma

Ayolas

Juan. E. O'Leary

Estrella

④ 15 de Agosto **③**

14 de Mayo

Alberdi

①

Oliva

Colón

Montevideo

②

Gen. Díaz

Haedo

Humaitá

KEY

❶ Exploring sights

① Hotels & restaurants

► Start of walk

Piribebuy

Manduvirá

⑥

Oliver's **8**
La Paraguayita **19**
La Pérgola Jardin **15**
Peter's Restaurant
en Casapueblo **20**
La Preferida **16**
Talleyrand **17**

Tio Lucas **8**

Hotels ▼

Apart Hotel
Mandu'Ará **11**
Asunción
Palace Hotel **1**

Chaco Hotel **9**
Excelsior Inn **6**
Granados Park Hotel **3**
Hotel Casino Yacht y Golf
Club Paraguayo **12**
Hotel Cecilia **15**
Hotel Excelsior **5**

Hotel Internacional
de Asunción **2**
Hotel Las Margaritas **4**
Hotel Preciado **13**
Hotel Presidente **7**
Sabe Center Hotel **10**

⑤ Palacio de Gobierno. The elegant horseshoe-shape Government Palace, with verandas and wide staircases, overlooks the bay. It's only open to the public on most holidays, but gives tours on Thursday and Friday if you arrange it one day in advance. ⊠ *El Paraguayo Independiente and Ayolas* ☎ *021/419–8220* 🖭 *Free.*

⑦ Palacio Legislativo. During the Francia dictatorship, Paraguayans were not permitted to view the exterior of this building, but today you can even tour the interior. Paraguay's constitution was proclaimed on the first floor of the Legislative Palace in 1870. The second floor was added in 1857, destroying the original symmetry of the single-story Jesuit design. Congress is scheduled to move into new modern quarters on the west side of the plaza in late 2003; it's not clear what this building will serve as after that. ⊠ *Plaza Independencia* ☎ *021/441–077* 🖭 *Free* ☽ *Weekday mornings.*

★ **② Panteón Nacional de los Héroes.** Nothing symbolizes Paraguayan history more than the National Pantheon of Heroes, a memorial to the fallen soldiers of the country's hopeless battles and disastrous wars. Construction began in 1864 under the regime of Francisco Solano López, who envisioned a chapel modeled after Les Invalides in Paris. López was soon to lead Paraguay into the catastrophic War of the Triple Alliance. The building was completed in 1936 after the Pyrrhic victory of the Chaco War against Bolivia. López is interred here, as are the remains of two of Paraguay's unknown soldiers. The wars still loom large in Paraguay's consciousness, but commemorative plaques placed on the walls by the old enemies—Argentina, Bolivia, Brazil, and Uruguay—illustrate that relations have improved. Two sentinels guard the eerily quiet memorial, a place of pilgrimage for every Paraguayan who visits Asunción. A 15-minute changing of the guard ceremony takes place Saturdays at 10 AM. ⊠ *Mariscal Estigarribia at Plaza de los Héroes* ☎ *No phone* 🖭 *Free* ☽ *Weekdays 6–5:30, weekends 6–noon.*

need a break?

Across from the Panteón Nacional de los Héroes is the doyenne of Asunción diners, the **Lido Bar** (Palma at Chile, 021/447–232). The counter loops around the room, painted tan with highlights of brown. Just pull up a stool and an army of pillbox hat-clad waitresses will dish up luscious ice cream and coffee. The icy air-conditioning feels so good that you'll hate to return to the sweltering heat outdoors. Order another slice of pie instead.

▶ **① Plaza de los Héroes.** This plaza, whose centerpiece is the Panteón Nacional de los Héroes, is the heart of Asunción. Since the subtleties of Paraguayan life are laid bare in its busy plazas, this is a good place to rest in the shade and watch the locals. Guaraní vendors sell feather headdresses and bows and arrows, artisans display their pottery, and traveling salespeople hawk anything from patent cures to miracle knife sharpeners. You can also climb onto a high chair for a shoe shine or have your picture taken with an old box camera. On public holidays the square is often the scene of live music and folk-dance performances. The plaza's northeast quadrant contains a monument to the victims of torture and execution under the Stroessner dictatorship. ⊠ *Nuestra Señora de la Asunción at 25 de Mayo.*

⑩ **Plaza Uruguaya.** So named to honor Uruguay for returning territory it seized in the bloody Chaco War initiated by Paraguay, the plaza is a pleasant respite from the city's heat. On one side is a covered market with a good selection of Latin American literature and on the other is the 1861 colonnaded **railway station,** shuttered since the discontinuation of rail service. In the terminal you can see a well-preserved old steam locomotive, the *Sapucaí,* no longer in use.

Where to Eat

A number of inexpensive lunch spots scattered throughout the centro serve fast food such as hamburgers and french fries. A few even offer regional specialties. Locals particularly favor **Pancholo's** (⊠ Mariscal López at Salaskín ⊠ Brasilia at Santiago ⊠ Mariscal López at Convención). **Biggest** (⊠ Estrella and 15 de Agosto) bustles with all the hubbub of a big city diner. The Victorian decoration at **San Roque** (⊠ Ayala at Tacuary) is a nice backdrop for the traditional food.

Brazilian

★ $ ✕ **Churrasquaría Acuarela.** A 10-minute taxi ride from centro, this enormous, 1,300-seat *rodízio*-style restaurant might just be the best value in town. Waiters traverse the dining room with skewers of grilled sausage, chicken, pork, and beef, slicing off as much as you want. You can mosey over to the buffet laden with salads, vegetables, and desserts. For something different, ask for *cupim,* a cut of meat taken from the hump of the Brahma cattle bred in Paraguay and Brazil. ⊠ *Mariscal López at Teniente Zotti* ☎ 021/601–750 ▤ AE, DC, MC, V.

Contemporary

$–$$ ✕ **La Cascada.** Dine alongside the lovely waterfall that flows from the foyer of the Hotel Excelsior into the refined, lower-level dining room. Asunción's elite comes here for the French- and Italian-influenced dishes with an emphasis on local fish, such as the surubí in shrimp sauce. The food is tasty, but overpriced in comparison with the many downtown alternatives. ⊠ *Chile 980* ☎ 021/495–632 ▤ AE, DC, MC, V.

$–$$ ✕ **Mburicaó.** Chef Rodolfo Angenscheidt honed his skills at the Parisian culinary landmark Maxim's before opening this contemporary restaurant, which has become a favorite of Asunción business executives. Specialties include innovative takes on South American and Continental favorites, including fresh Patagonian truffle risotto and surubí with mozzarella and tomato in puff pastry. The airy dining room overlooks a lush patio. ⊠ *Prof. A. González Riobbó 737, at Chaco Boreal* ☎ 021/ 660–048 ▤ AE, DC, MC, V.

¢–$ ✕ **La Pérgola Jardín.** Floor-to-ceiling mirrors, modern black-lacquer furniture, and live saxophone and piano music make this restaurant one of Asunción's most sophisticated dining spots. The service is efficient and friendly, and the ever-changing menu is contemporary. Warning: the piping-hot *pan de queso,* small cheese-flavored rolls, are irresistible. ⊠ *Perú 240* ☎ 021/214–014 ⚖ *Reservations essential* ▤ AE, DC, MC, V.

¢–$ ✕ **Oliver's.** This favorite executive lunchtime meeting place at the Hotel Presidente is known for its afternoon and evening buffets. Choose from all-you-can-eat dishes, such as goulash, pasta, and cold cuts, or order from an à la carte menu. ⊠ *Azara 128* ☎ *021/494–931* ▤ *AE, DC, MC, V.*

¢–$ ✕ **Peter's Restaurant en Casapueblo.** On weekday evenings, the three-course
Fodor'sChoice prix-fixe menu here is the best (and most mouth-watering) deal in town.
★ German émigré chef Peter Stenger uses natural ingredients, as in his fresh tomato soup with cheese and his filet mignon medallions on a bed of julienned seasonal vegetables. Pastas, steaks, and chicken dishes also win raves. The adjacent pub and disco attracts large crowds on weekends. ⊠ *Mariscal López at Mayor Rivarola* ☎ *021/610–447 or 021/609–663* ▤ *AE, DC, MC, V* ☉ *Closed Sun.*

¢–$ ✕ **Talleyrand.** Specialties at this local chain include duck à l'orange, sirloin steak, and surubí. The soft green color scheme and the hunting prints lend the dining rooms a refined colonial style. Talleyrand also has a location at Shopping del Sol. ⊠ *Mariscal Estigarribia 932* ☎ *021/441– 163* ⊠ *Av. Aviadores del Chaco, at Prof. D. E. González* ☎ *021/611– 697* ⌕ *Reservations essential* ▤ *AE, DC, MC, V* ☉ *Closed Sun.*

Italian

¢–$ ✕ **Il Capo.** Just opposite La Pérgola Jardín, this small eatery has whitewashed walls, wooden beams, and tile floors. The homemade pastas, like lasagna *con camarones* (with shrimp) and *melanzana alla parmegiana* (eggplant with tomato and Parmesan), are excellent, and the Italian wine list is reasonably priced. ⊠ *Perú 291* ☎ *021/213–022* ▤ *AE, DC, MC, V.*

¢ ✕ **Tío Lucas.** Glossy cream-and-black wallpaper and chic Thonet bentwood chairs give this corner eatery a crisp, modern look. The specialty here is pizza. ⊠ *25 de Mayo at Yegros* ☎ *021/447–114* ▤ *No credit cards* ☉ *Closed Sun.*

Japanese

★ $–$$ ✕ **Chez Takao.** A sushi bar (with an oversize Johnnie Walker case) is the centerpiece of this intimate Japanese restaurant, where a devoted clientele comes for the delicious sashimi, sushi, and tempura. Several "chef's suggestions" allow you to combine dishes, including grilled steak or chicken. The attentive staff works hard to ensure satisfaction. ⊠ *San Martín* ☎ *021/611–416* ▤ *AE, DC, MC, V.*

Paraguayan

$–$$ ✕ **La Preferida.** Rub shoulders with politicians and diplomats where the two chic dining areas (one of which is no-smoking at peak hours) are set with crisp linen tablecloths and elegant silver and glassware. The house specialty is surubí, served smoked or in a mild curry sauce. Try the excellent *lomo de cerdo à la pimienta* (peppered pork tenderloin)—ask for it if it's not on the menu. The Austrian owners have fine-tuned the service, so expect friendliness and efficiency. ⊠ *25 de Mayo 1005* ☎ *021/ 210–641* ▤ *AE, DC, MC, V.*

¢–$ ✕ **La Paraguayita.** Its shaded terrace makes this the best of the numer-
Fodor'sChoice ous parrillas that line Avenida Brasilia. Huge portions of perfectly bar-
★ becued beef and pork are accompanied by wonderfully seasoned sopa paraguaya and chipá-guazú. The chorizo sausages make a good starter,

especially when dunked in tangy *criollo,* a spicy onion, tomato, and garlic sauce. ✉ *Brasilia at Siria* ☎ *021/204–497* ⊟ *DC, MC, V.*

Where to Stay

Asunción's lodging situation has improved as new hotels have opened and older ones have finally been refurbished. Numbers are small, however. Accommodations vary from no-frills establishments costing less than $20 (G140,000) to luxury hotels running upwards of $200 (G1,400,000) a night. Since business travelers are usually the ones visiting the capital, rates usually drop on weekends and during the summer. Make sure your room has air-conditioning—you do not want to be without it during the hotter months, from December to March.

$$$$ ▦ **Hotel Casino Yacht y Golf Club Paraguayo.** This remodeled riverside resort 13 km (8 mi) southeast of Asunción has regained its reputation as one of South America's finest hotels. Some of the rooms, which are decorated with leather furniture, open onto verdant patios where hummingbirds nest in the foliage. You'll find plenty of recreational options here. ✉ *Av. del Yacht 11, Lambaré* ☎ *021/906–121 or 021/906–117* ▤ *021/906–120* ⊕ *www.hotelyacht.com.py* ⇱ *116 rooms, 12 suites* ⚘ *4 restaurants, 2 snack bars, minibars, 18-hole golf course, 14 tennis courts, pool, health club, hair salon, massage, spa, beach, fishing, boating, jet skiing, basketball, squash, soccer, volleyball, bar, casino, laundry service* ⊟ *AE, DC, MC, V* ¶ⓞ⧘ *BP.*

$$$ ▦ **Granados Park Hotel.** Replicating the sensibility of a grand old Latin American hotel, this place gives you colonial style with modern amenities. The attentive staff greets you in an opulent lobby filled with lush greenery. The modern rooms are much more subdued, decorated with carved wooden armoires and handicrafts. ✉ *Estrella and 15 de Agosto* ☎ *021/497–921* ▤ *021/445–324* ⊕ *www.granadospark.com.py* ⇱ *71 rooms* ⚘ *Restaurant, in-room data ports, in-room safes, minibars, pool, gym, hair salon, massage, sauna, bar, dry cleaning, laundry service, concierge, business services, meeting rooms, airport shuttle* ⊟ *AE, DC, MC, V* ¶ⓞ⧘ *BP.*

$$$ ▦ **Hotel Excelsior.** Regency-style fabrics, carved-wood furniture, and Oriental rugs make this one of the city's most elegant hotels, and a refurbishing has made the place gleam again. You'll sink into the carpeting in the huge, plush, brightly furnished rooms accented with wood carvings and Paraguayan art. The three-story Excelsior Mall is across the street. ✉ *Chile 980* ☎ *021/495–632* ▤ *021/496–748* ⊕ *www.excelsior.com.py* ⇱ *121 rooms, 12 suites* ⚘ *2 restaurants, room service, in-room data ports, in-room safes, tennis court, pool, gym, health club, hair salon, bar, piano bar, pub, dry cleaning, laundry service, dance club, business services, meeting rooms, airport shuttle* ⊟ *AE, DC, MC, V* ¶ⓞ⧘ *BP.*

$$ ▦ **Apart Hotel Mandu'Ará.** The suites in this hotel are popular with business travelers. Each suite includes a sitting room, a dining area, and a kitchenette. The furnishings differ markedly from room to room: "classic" rooms tend toward lots of carved wood, while "contemporary" rooms have more modern furnishings. Both types are equally plush. ✉ *Méx-*

ico 554   🖷🖷 *021/490–223*   ⊕ *www.manduara.com.py*   ⌗ *82 suites* ⚶ *Dining room, coffee shop, pool, gym, sauna, bar, laundry service, business services, meeting room, airport shuttle* ▤ *AE, DC, MC, V* ⍤⊙⍤ *BP.*

★ **$$**   ▦ **Sabe Center Hotel.** The sleek, orange-brick high-rise facing Plaza Uruguaya goes out of its way to impress: in the lobby, a giant chandelier shimmers above Oriental rugs, enormous urns, and a grand staircase. Rooms are less regal, but bright and comfortable. A breakfast buffet is included. ⊠ *25 de Mayo at México* 🕾 *021/450–093* 🖷 *021/450–101* ⊕ *www.sabecenterhotel.com.py* ⌗ *91 rooms* ⚶ *Restaurant, coffee shop, minibars, gym, bar, dry cleaning, laundry service, business services, meeting rooms* ▤ *AE, DC, MC, V* ⍤⊙⍤ *CP.*

$–$$ ▦ **Chaco Hotel.** Friendly, attentive service is the hallmark of this comfortable, if rather unremarkably decorated, lodging. The carpeted rooms are large, but the beds are small. A tasty breakfast is included in the rate. ⊠ *Caballero 285* 🕾 *021/492–066* 🖷 *021/444–223* ⊕ *www.hotelchaco.com. py* ⌗ *72 rooms* ⚶ *Restaurant, in-room data ports, minibars, pool, bar, laundry service, business services, meeting rooms* ▤ *AE, DC, MC, V* ⍤⊙⍤ *CP.*

$–$$ ▦ **Hotel Cecilia.** Priding itself on personalized attention, this hotel has won a devoted international clientele. Rooms are large, though slightly austere. The sixth-floor terrace has a pool with a terrific bay view. Adjacent to the hotel you'll find an excellent deli and pastry shop. ⊠ *Estados Unidos 341* 🕾 *021/210–365* 🖷 *021/497–111* ⊕ *www.uninet.com. py/cecilia* ⌗ *50 rooms* ⚶ *Restaurant, pool, gym, sauna, bar, laundry service, meeting rooms, airport shuttle* ▤ *AE, DC, MC, V* ⍤⊙⍤ *CP.*

$–$$ ▦ **Hotel Las Margaritas.** Cordial service and opulent, gleaming accommodations are the hallmarks of this lodging, which opened in January 2003. The lobby blooms with plants and works by indigenous artisans and paintings by Michael Burt, one of Paraguay's leading contemporary artists. Rooms come in one of three color schemes (green, light blue, or orange) and all harbor Burt paintings and Guaraní artwork. ⊠ *Estrella and 15 de Agostp* 🕾 *021/448–765* 🖷 *021/448–785* ⊕ *www.lasmargaritas.com.py* ⌗ *60 rooms, 17 suites* ⚶ *2 restaurants, grill, in-room data ports, in-room safes, minibars, pool, gym, sauna, billiards, bar, dry cleaning, laundry service, meeting rooms, airport shuttle* ▤ *AE, DC, MC, V* ⍤⊙⍤ *BP.*

FodorśChoice
★

$ ▦ **Excelsior Inn.** This hotel opened by the owners of the Hotel Excelsior lacks the frills of its pricier sibling. Rooms, many with hardwood floors, are pleasantly furnished with dark greens and golds. Each has an in-room data port—a rarity at this price range. ⊠ *Alberdi and Manduvirá* 🖷🖷 *021/496–743* ⊕ *www.excelsior.com.py* ⌗ *23 rooms, 1 suite* ⚶ *In-room data ports, minibars, laundry service, airport shuttle* ▤ *AE, DC, MC, V* ⍤⊙⍤ *BP.*

$ ▦ **Hotel Internacional de Asunción.** An abundance of greenery greets you as you enter this modern, 15-story hotel. The sleek black-and-white lobby has an executive bar where you can enjoy a cocktail. Many of the rather small rooms, which are redecorated every year, have views of the bay. Each contains a data port where you can plug in your laptop; if you didn't bring it along, the hotel's business center offers four terminals. ⊠ *Ayolas 520, at Oliva* 🕾 *021/494–114* 🖷 *021/494–383* ⊕ *www. hotelinternacional.com.py* ⌗ *70 rooms, 26 suites* ⚶ *Restaurant, snack bar, in-room data ports, in-room safes, pool, gym, massage, sauna, bar, business services, meeting room, airport shuttle* ▤ *AE, DC, MC, V* ⍤⊙⍤ *BP.*

$ ⊞ **Hotel Presidente.** Just two blocks from the Plaza de los Héroes, this comfortable lodging has conveniences usually reserved for more expensive establishments. All rooms have contemporary furnishings. Business travelers have access to fax machines and computers. Oliver's restaurant, in the plant-filled lobby, draws an executive crowd. ⊠ *Azara 128* 🖴 *021/494–931* ⊕ *www.hotelpresidente.net* 🛏 *44 rooms, 4 suites* ⌂ *Restaurant, minibars, bar, business services, meeting room* ⊟ *AE, DC, MC, V* ⦿ *BP.*

¢ ⊞ **Asunción Palace Hotel.** Built in the mid-19th century as a private residence for the López family, and transformed into a hospital during the War of the Triple Alliance, this beaux arts–style hotel is now a national landmark. It's certainly charming, though a few of the rooms are noisy. Others are quite nice and peaceful; ask to see one before taking it. All are simply furnished but this a good budget option. ⊠ *Colón 415* 🖀 *021/492–152* 🖴 *021/492–153* ✑ *aphotel@yahoo.com* 🛏 *25 rooms, 2 suites* ⌂ *Restaurant, refrigerators, bar; no TV in some rooms* ⊟ *DC, MC, V* ⦿ *BP.*

¢ ⊞ **Hotel Preciado.** Peace Corps volunteers in Asunción on business dub this place, just east of downtown, their favorite, and their presence here gives the hotel a youthful exuberance. High-ceiling rooms are simply furnished with two beds, a desk, and a chair, but are sparklingly modern. The low prices make this a solid budget bet. ⊠ *Azara 840* 🖀 *021/447–661* 🖴 *021/453–937* ✑ *hotelpreciado@hotmail.com* 🛏 *22 rooms* ⌂ *Dining room, minibars, pool, laundry service* ⊟ *AE, MC, V* ⦿ *BP.*

Nightlife & the Arts

Almost all of the information about nightlife in Asunción is in Spanish. Asunción's free biweekly arts and nightlife newsletter, *Tiempo Libre,* has cinema and theater listings. It's widely available in hotels and restaurants. The Friday editions of Asunción's daily newspapers, particularly *Última Hora,* also have excellent weekend arts and entertainment sections.

The Arts

Paraguay is renowned for its folk dancing. Traditional dances include the *chamamé,* performed by pairs to accordion music, and *la danza de las botellas,* literally "the dance of the bottles." A female dancer moves in time to the music while stacking six empty wine bottles on her head. Catch performances at **Noches del Paraguay** (⊠ Juan Domingo Perón and Cacique Lambaré 🖀 021/332–807). There's a show every night of the week, but Friday and Saturday are the most popular nights, so make reservations. Weeknight tickets are G5,000; weekends, G10,000.

Asunción's city cultural center, the **Manzana de la Rivera** (⊠ Ayolas 129 🖀 021/442–448), presents lectures, concerts, and movies many evenings. Spain has a network of active cultural centers throughout Latin America. Asunción's branch of the **Centro Cultural Español** (⊠ Tacuary 745 🖀 021/449–921) presents a mix of lectures, poetry readings, classical music concerts, and film screenings three or four nights a week. Most are free; a few have a nominal cover charge.

Nightlife

Asunción doesn't have the nightlife of other Latin American capitals, such as Buenos Aires or Rio de Janeiro, especially during the week. The scene picks up Thursday through Saturday when locals dress up to go out on the town. In many nightspots, you'll get turned away at the door if you're wearing jeans and T-shirts. Many upscale places cluster around Avenida Brasilia, Avenida España, and Avenida Mariscal López, about 2 km (1 mi) northeast of the centro. Most charge a small cover.

BARS   A visit to the friendly, semi-open air **Britannia Pub** (⊠Cerro Corá 851 ☎021/443–990) dispels the myth that Asunció has no expat population; they're all here. The always popular **Café Bohemia** (⊠ Senador Long and España) attracts young and old alike. As befits the name, **Café Literario** (⊠Mariscal Estigarribia 456 ☎021/491–640) draws aficionados of coffee, wine, books, quiet music, and animated conversation. **Faces** (⊠Brasilia 786 ☎021/225–360) is a good place to talk and have a drink. Just west of downtown, the nautical-theme **La Choppería del Puerto** (⊠Palma 1028 at Garibaldi ☎021/445–590) also has a pleasant sidewalk café. It is open 24 hours. **Mouse Cantina** (⊠Brasilia at Patria ☎021/228–794) gets a little loud at times. **Tequila Rock** (⊠Brasilia at Amistad ☎021/229–179), currently the trendiest of Asunción bars, caters to a twentysomething crowd.

CASINOS   Try your luck at slot machines, roulette, baccarat, and blackjack at the glitzy **Casino de Asunción** (⊠ España 151 and Sacramento, ☎ 021/603–160), open daily 2 PM–6 AM. The **Hotel Casino Yacht y Golf Club Paraguayo** (⊠ Av. del Yacht 11, Lambaré ☎ 021/906–043), which is about 13 km (8 mi) outside of town, offers all the standard casino games. The casino itself is open daily 9 PM–6 AM.

DANCE CLUBS   The most popular disco in Asunción is **Casapueblo** (⊠ Mariscal López and Mayor Rivarola ☎021/611–081), where you can dance all night to Latin rhythms. **Chaco's Pub** (⊠República Argentina 1035 ☎021/603–199) spins international disco music. Asunción's elite boogie the weekend nights away at **Coyote** (⊠Sucre 1655 at San Martín ☎021/662–816).

Sports & the Outdoors

Soccer

If you want to see Paraguayans get riled up, head to the **Defensores del Chaco** stadium in the suburb of Sajonia to catch a *fútbol* game. Cerro Porteño and Olimpia are two of the most popular teams. Matches are played on Sunday. Local newspapers publish current schedules.

Tennis

South American tennis tournaments, including zone matches of the Davis Cup, are held at the **Hotel Casino Yacht y Golf Club Paraguayo** (⊠ Av. del Yacht 11, Lambaré ☎ 021/906–043). If you're not a guest at the hotel, you can book a court at the **Club Internacional de Tenis** (⊠ Mademoiselle Lynch and Lilio ☎ 021/671–912).

Shopping

The best shopping in Asunción falls into two very distinct categories: handicrafts and electronics. Prices for both are among the lowest in South

America, though comparable to those of a large discount store in the United States.

Crafts Shops

Fodor's Choice
★

Paraguay's famous ñandutí, the delicate lacework, can be found everywhere in Asunción. One of the best shops for ñandutí is **Ao P'oí Raity** (⊠ F. R. Moreno 155 ☎ 021/494–475). For the best leather goods try **Casa Vera** (⊠ Mariscal Estigarribia 470 ☎ 021/445–868). **Folklore** (⊠ Mariscal Estigarribia at Iturbe ☎ 021/494–360) sells carved wood items. **Overall** (⊠ Caballero and Mariscal Estigarribia ☎ 021/448–657) is also well known for its selection of lace and woodwork. **Victoria** (⊠ Mariscal Estigarribia at Iturbe ☎ 021/450–148) sells ceramics and other items.

Craftspeople in the town of **Areguá,** near Asunción on Lake Ypacaraí, make clay pots and other ceramics. In **Luque,** near the international airport, you can find Paraguayan harps, guitars, and fine silver filigree jewelry.

Fodor's Choice
★

Constancio Sanabria (⊠ Av. Aviadores del Chaco 2852, Luque ☎ 021/662–408) is highly regarded for musical instruments.

Markets & Shopping Districts

Mercado 4, on Avenida Pettirossi, is a crowded market that overflows into neighboring streets. Its stalls are laden with produce, hammocks, and cage after cage of clucking chickens. The tables are set up before dawn, so get an early start to avoid the stifling heat and suffocating crowds. It is open all day, every day, except Sunday afternoons.

You can find lots of handicrafts west of **Plaza de los Héroes** between Palma and Estrella. For quality goods stick to the specialty stores. Hundreds of small shops here sell imported watches, electronics, cameras, and athletic shoes. Watch out for street vendors selling knock-offs such as "Rolec" watches.

Shopping Malls

For department-store items, try the three-story **Excelsior Mall** (⊠ Chile 901 ☎ 021/443–015). **Shopping del Sol** (⊠ Av. Aviadores del Chaco and Prof. D. E. González ☎ 021/611–780) has specialty shops, a cinema, and a children's play area. **Mariscal López Shopping** (⊠ Quesada 5050 ☎ 021/611–272) has stores selling clothing, books, and records, and computer terminals with free Internet access.

Side Trip from Asunción

San Bernardino

The popular holiday resort of San Bernardino, on the shores of Lago Ypacaraí, makes an excellent day trip from the capital. From December to March it's packed with weekenders enjoying the dark blue waters ringed by clean, white sand. Water sports are a popular pastime—windsurfing equipment can be rented at the beaches.

Looping back toward Asunción, the road passes through **Caacupé,** a mostly Catholic town where the Día de la Nuestra Señora de Los Milagros (Day of Our Lady of the Miracles) is celebrated on December 8. Hundreds of thousands make a pilgrimage to the basilica here.

✕⊡ **Hotel del Lago.** On the shores of Lago Ypacaraí, this low-key Spanish-style hotel offers simple, clean rooms with comfortable beds. The
rustic restaurant's forte is roast beef or pork, cooked in a wood-fire oven
and served with sopa paraguaya. ⊠ *Teniente Weiler and Carlos López*
☎ *0512/2201* ⤹ *23 rooms* ☆ *Restaurant, minibars, pool, laundry service, meeting room* ▤ *DC, MC, V* ⦿ *BP.*

¢ ⊡ **Hotel Pueblo.** The tranquillity of the forest surrounding this hotel is a
welcoming change from the noise and crowds of Asunción. Rooms are
simple but comfortable, and all have views of Lago Ypacaraí. Try the
restaurant for lunch, where you can order locally prepared surubí, sopa
paraguaya, and bori-bori. ⊠ *Calle 5 at Av. Mbocayá* ☎☎ *0512/2391*
⊘ *pueblo@telesurf.com.py* ⤹ *12 rooms, 6 suites* ☆ *Restaurant, minibars, pool, laundry service; no room phones* ▤ *AE, DC, MC, V* ⦿ *BP.*

Asunción A to Z

AIR TRAVEL

Aeropuerto Internacional Silvio Pettirossi (ASU) is 15 km (9 mi) northeast of downtown. The only U.S. carrier serving Paraguay is American,
which flies from Miami via São Paulo. Paraguay's national airline, TAM
Mercosur, likely the world's only airline that entertains departing passengers with harp music, does not fly directly to the United States, but
connects in São Paulo with the daily Miami flights of its affiliate TAM
Brazilian Airlines.

TAM Mercosur has daily service between Asunción and Ciudad del Este
(AGT), Concepción (CID), and Vallemí (VMI). South American carri-
ers that serve Asunción include Aerolíneas Argentinas, Bolivia's LAB,
Uruguay's Pluna, and Brazil's Varig.

🛪 Airlines **Aerolíneas Argentinas** ☎ 021/201-501. **American** ☎ 021/443-330. **LAB
Airlines** ☎ 021/441-586. **Pluna** ☎ 021/490-7128. **TAM Mercosur** ☎ 021/490-128.
Varig ☎ 021/490-128.

🛪 Airports **Aeropuerto Internacional Silvio Pettirossi** ☎ 021/645-600.

AIRPORTS & TRANSFERS

Taxis are the most practical means of getting to town, and they charge
a fixed rate of G84,000. The airport information desk can tell you the
exact rate. It can also arrange for an *omnibus special* whenever there
are six or more passengers. This costs G35,000 per person and will take
you to any address in downtown Asunción. Less conveniently, Bus 30A
leaves from the tollbooths on the road into the airport (about 200 yards
from the terminal). It departs for downtown Asunción every 15 minutes; the fare is G2,000.

BUS TRAVEL TO & FROM ASUNCIÓN

All intercity services leave from Terminal de Omnibus Asunción, located
east of downtown. The three major bus companies, La Encarnaceña, Pluma,
and Rápido Yguazú, also have information booths on Plaza Uruguaya.

🚌 Bus Companies **La Encarnaceña** ☎ 021/551-745. **Pluma** ☎ 021/445-024. **Rápido
Yguazú** ☎ 021/551-618 or 021/551-601.

🚌 Bus Terminals **Terminal de Omnibus Asunción** ⊠ República Argentina at Fernando
de la Mora ☎ 021/551-740.

BUS TRAVEL WITHIN ASUNCIÓN

Ever since the old yellow trams were retired, Asunción's bus service has improved. New local buses run every eight minutes. The fare is about 30¢. As in all big cities, watch your belongings carefully.

CAR RENTAL

You'll get the best rates in Asunción at Only Rent a Car, which has an office at the airport. Hertz and National are international companies that have offices in Asunción.

🏴 Rental Agencies **Hertz** ☒ Aeropuerto Internacional Silvio Pettirossi ☎ 021/645-600 ☒ Km. 4.5 Av. Eusebio Ayala ☎ 021/605-708. **National** ☒ Yegros 501 ☎ 021/492-157. **Only Rent a Car** ☒ Aeropuerto Internacional Silvio Pettirossi ☎ 021/646-083 Ext. 112 ☒ 15 de Agosto 520 ☎ 021/492-731.

CAR TRAVEL

Unless you plan to travel out of town, avoid renting a car—driving in Asunción can be a nerve-racking experience. Aggressive bus drivers, confusing routes, and never-ending road construction make even Paraguayans (who rarely follow traffic rules) nervous.

EMBASSIES

The United States embassy is open weekdays 7–3, although passport questions are not handled after 10:30. The British embassy is open weekdays 8–3. Australia, Canada, and New Zealand do not have diplomatic representation in Paraguay; contact their embassies in Buenos Aires.

🏴 **Australia** ☒ Villanueva 1400, Buenos Aires ☎ 11/4777-6580. **Canada** ☒ Tagle 2828, Buenos Aires ☎ 11/4808-1000. **New Zealand** ☒ Carlos Pelligrini 1427, Buenos Aires ☎ 11/4328-0747. **United Kingdom** ☒ Justo Román and Argaña, Asunción ☎ 021/614-814. **United States** ☒ Av. Mariscal López 1776, Asunción ☎ 021/213-728.

EMERGENCIES

🏴 Emergency Services **Ambulance** ☎ 141. **Fire** ☎ 132. **Police** ☎ 130.
🏴 Hospitals **Hospital Privado Francés** ☒ Brasilia at Insaurralde ☎ 021/295-250. **Hospital Privado San Lucas** ☒ Eusebio Ayala 2402 ☎ 021/553-914. **Hospital Privado Bautista** ☒ Argentina at Andrés Campos Cervera ☎ 021/600-171.

INTERNET

Connection times in Asunción's handful of cybercafés are surprisingly fast. While in the capital you can check your e-mail at Cyber Shop, which is open Monday to Saturday 8 AM–10 PM. An hour will set you back less than a dollar. Many hotels also offer Internet service to their guests.

🏴 Internet Cafés **Cyber Shop** ☒ Estrella 474 ☎ 021/446-290.

MAIL & SHIPPING

To mail letters and packages, go to the Dirección General de Correos, south of Plaza Juan de Salazar.

🏴 Post Offices **Dirección General de Correos** ☒ Alberdi and Benjamín Constant ☎ 021/498-112.

COURIERS Anything of value (or valuable looking) should be sent via a courier service. DHL, Asunción Express (the agent for FedEx), and Air Systems International (the agent for UPS) have offices in Asunción.

🏢 Courier Companies **DHL** ✉ Brasilia 355, Asunción ☎ 021/211-060. **FedEx/Asunción Express** ✉ Sargento Instrán and Primer Presidente, Asunción ☎ 021/297-475. **UPS/ Air Systems International** ✉ Independencia Nacional 821, Asunción ☎ 021/451-960.

RECEIVING MAIL You can have mail sent to Dirección General de Correos, the main post office, addressed to "Poste Restante." Make sure to bring identification when you pick it up. American Express will hold mail for members.

MONEY MATTERS

In Asunción, U.S. dollars are no problem to exchange. Cash is easier to exchange and earns a better rate than traveler's checks. Interbanco and Money Exchange change American Express traveler's checks for guaraníes, but the American Express office does not cash its own checks. Many places exchange Argentine pesos and Brazilian reales, but few deal with other currencies. You can change money and traveler's checks downtown at ABN Amro Bank and La Moneda or any of the *casas de cambio* (exchange houses) along Calle Palma and around the Plaza de los Héroes. Multibanco, just outside the customs exit at Aeropuerto Internacional Silvio Pettirossi changes cash dollars for guaraníes. You can also change money at major hotels, which have a less favorable rate. The money changers who call out "*¡Cambio dólares!*" offer decent rates during normal business hours but raise their rates evenings and weekends.

Machines on Paraguay's Infonet system of ATMs have an annoying habit of accepting either Plus- or Cirrus-linked cards, but rarely both. To be on the safe side, bring cards affiliated with both systems, and if you don't already use a four-digit password, contact your bank about changing your password to four digits—that's what will work here. The ATM at ABN Amro Bank *does* take both, as does the machine just beyond the customs exit at Aeropuerto Internacional Silvio Pettirossi, as well as those in most Esso gas stations.

🏦 Banks **ABN Amro Bank** ✉ Estrella at Alberi ☎ 021/419-0000. **Inerbanco** ✉ Oliva 349 ☎ 021/494-992. **American Express** ✉ Yegros 690 ☎ 021/490-111. **La Moneda** ✉ 25 de Mayo 127 ☎ 021/494-724. **Money Exchange** ✉ Palma 403 ☎ 021/453-277. **Multibanco** ✉ Aeropuerto Internacional Silvio Pettirossi ☎ 021/647-199.

SAFETY

Although Asunción has escaped the crime typical of other South American capitals, there is still a small amount of petty crime against tourists. As in any urban area, be aware of your surroundings and keep an eye on all valuables. Leave flashy jewelry and expensive watches in your hotel safe and keep laptops and cameras in an inconspicuous bag.

TAXIS

Asunción's yellow Mercedes taxis, operated by APTA, are an inexpensive way to get around the city. You can find one on the street, at any major hotel, or at one of the dozens of taxi stands around the city. Make sure your driver turns the meter on or you risk being charged an outrageous fare. A 30% surcharge is added after dark. It can be difficult to hail a taxi at night, so it's perfectly acceptable to ask your hotel or restaurant to call one for you.

🚖 Taxi Companies **APTA** ☎ 021/311-080.

TELEPHONES

Asunción has few telephone booths, per se. To make domestic or international calls, you can go to the downtown office of COPACO, the privatized national telephone company, which is open 6AM–midnight. Numerous private telephone offices let you make calls, too. Look for TELÉFONOS PÚBLICOS or CABINAS TELEFÓNICAS signs.

🖅 Telephone Offices **COPACO** ⊠ Oliva and 15 de Agosto ☎ 021/419–4452.

TIPPING

In upscale restaurants an appropriate tip is about 10% of the bill, more if the service is exceptionally good. In average places, round up the bill to the nearest G1,000. Round up taxi fares to the nearest G500, and give G3,000 to doormen who hail you a taxi. Give porters around G3,000 per bag. Leave the chambermaid G7,000 per day or about G40,000 per week. Gas-station attendants are tipped up to G500 for full service. Give ushers and checkroom and rest-room attendants G1,000.

TOUR OPERATORS

Many companies offer tours of Asunción and the surrounding region. Guided tours of the city start at G70,000, and trips to Areguá and other nearby destinations start at G30,000. Inter Express, Lions Tour, and VIP's Tour are three of the best.

🖅 Tour Companies **Inter Express** ⊠ Yegros 690 ☎ 021/490–111. **Lions Tour** ⊠ Alberdi 454, 1st fl. ☎ 021/490–591. **VIP's Tour** ⊠ México 782 ☎ 021/497–199.

VISITOR INFORMATION

Paraguay sees so few travelers that the friendly staff at Secretaria Nacional de Turismo (Senatur) seem grateful to see you. Stop in the main office near the Plaza de los Héroes weekdays 7–7 and Saturday 8–1 for pamphlets and maps—only a few are in English—or advice on hotels or restaurants. There's a branch office in the airport arrivals hall beyond the customs exit that is open daily 10–6. Lions Tour also has a desk at the airport with transportation, hotel, and tour information.

🖅 **Senatur** ⊠ Palma 468 at 14 de Mayo ☎ 021/494–110 🖷 021/491–230 ⊕ www.senatur.gov.py.

SOUTHERN PARAGUAY

The seven 17th-century Jesuit missions along the 405-km (253-mi) drive from Asunción to Jesús date from as far back as 1609, when the newly formed Compañía de Jesús (Society of Jesus) was granted permission by the Spanish crown to move the nomadic Guaraní people, threatened by slave traders from Brazil, into self-sufficient agricultural communities. The Jesuits also wanted, of course, to convert the Guaraní to Christianity. Each community, called a *reducción* (literally meaning "reduction"), had a population of about 3,000 Guaraní under the charge of two or three priests who taught them agricultural and other practical skills such as stonemasonry and metalwork. Each reducción was centered around a large plaza with a chapel, the priests' living quarters, and usually a school. The main buildings, most often constructed of red sandstone blocks, had terra-cotta-tile roofs, wide verandas, and covered walkways.

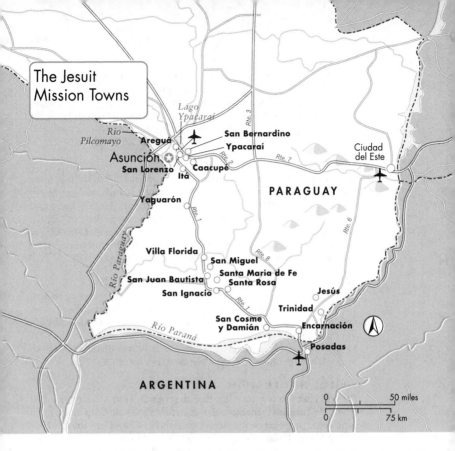

Under the tutelage of the Jesuits, the Guaraní excelled at wood carving, pottery, and calligraphy, and they proved to be particularly fine musicians. Performing mainly in church choirs and orchestras, they were able to adapt the complex European baroque counterpoint to their own traditional musical styles. The experiment, however, was so successful that the Spanish monarchs banned the Jesuits from their New World empire in 1767. The 100,000 Guaraní soon returned to their old way of life and the missions fell into disrepair.

Itá

37 km (23 mi) south of Asunción on Ruta 1.

Famous throughout Paraguay for its ceramics, Itá is the place to come for its distinctive black clay pottery. You'll pass a government-run handicraft exhibition before you reach town. On February 3 the town celebrates the Feast of St. Blas, the patron saint of Paraguay, with singing, dancing, a parade, and horse racing.

After Itá the countryside opens up into fruit orchards, sugarcane fields, and maize plantations.

Yaguarón

11 km (7 mi) south of Itá on Ruta 1.

Franciscan missionaries attempted to fill the void left after the Jesuits were expelled from the Spanish empire in 1767. They centered their efforts in Yaguarón but met with less success in maintaining the reducción communities established by their predecessors. The town's restored 18th-century **Iglesia de San Buenaventura** was the centerpiece of Paraguay's Franciscan missions. Inside you'll find brightly colored wooden statues carved by Guaraní artists. ☎ 053/332–213 ☒ *Free* ⊙ *Tues.–Sat. 8–11:30 and 2–5; Sun. 8–11:30.*

Yaguarón was also the home of José Gáspar Rodríguez de Francia, Paraguay's first dictator. The small **Museo del Doctor Francia** displays his portraits and belongings. ☎ 053/332–213 ☒ *Free* ⊙ *Mon.–Sat. 8–11:30 and 2–5; Sat. 8–11:30.*

Villa Florida

130 km (80 mi) south of Yaguarón on Ruta 1.

Farms give way to rolling grasslands as you approach Villa Florida, the grazing grounds of white Nelore cattle. Cowboys in wide-brim hats tend the herds on horses saddled in sheepskin, while goats stealthily graze in hibiscus- and bougainvillea-filled gardens outside tiny, rustic cottages along the Río Tebicuary. The river, which once marked the western border of the Jesuit mission area, now has several popular beaches; anglers know it well as a prime spot for catching dorado and surubí. The town is not particularly pretty, but there is a good selection of hotels and restaurants and magnificent sunsets over the water.

Fodor'sChoice
★

Where to Stay & Eat

¢ ✕⌨ **Hotel Centu Cué.** Comfortable bungalows scattered along the banks of the Río Tebicuary make up this isolated lodge frequented mainly by anglers in search of the one that didn't get away. Lounging on the 2-km (1-mi) private beach and taking a dip in the river are also a popular activities. At the nautical-theme restaurant, mounted heads of enormous fish and photos of proud fishermen with their catches may mock your day's accomplishments. What else would you eat here but dorado or surubí, grilled or in a casserole, caught just a few yards from the table? ☒ *7 km (4 mi) off Ruta 1 at Km 163, Desvío* ☎ *083/219* ⤴ *30 rooms, 5 cabins* ⟂ *Restaurant, beach, fishing, horseback riding, volleyball; no room phones* ☱ *No credit cards* ⎤ *FAP.*

Fodor'sChoice
★

¢ ✕⌨ **Hotel Nacional de Turismo.** Colonial-style rooms open onto a shady courtyard at this friendly hotel. Camping areas near the river have been set aside for fishing enthusiasts. The restaurant serves grilled meats and poultry; a must is the milanesa, made with freshly caught surubí. The chef is eager to please, and will be happy to prepare whatever you desire. Rates include a big breakfast. ☒ *Ruta 1, Km 162* ☎ *083/207* ⤴ *25 rooms* ⟂ *Restaurant, cafeteria, pool, volleyball, fishing, laundry service* ☱ *No credit cards* ⎤ *BP.*

$$ ⌧ **Estancia Santa Clara.** This ranch, 24 km (14 mi) north of Villa Florida, is downright plush compared to most of the other agriculture tourism lodgings in Paraguay. You can roll up your sleeves and rope steers, milk cows, pick vegetables, or bake bread if you really want a hands-on experience. You can also ride horses, hike bird-filled trails, or curl up in a hammock with a good book. Rooms in the rambling orange stucco house have vaulted wooden ceilings. Rates include all meals. ⌧ *Ruta 1, Km 141, Caapucé* ☎ *0981/405–020 (cell phone)* ☎☎ *021/605–729 in Asunción* ↷ *8 rooms* ⌂ *Dining room, pool* ⊟ *No credit cards* ¶⊙¶ *FAP.*

Sports & the Outdoors

Arrangements for everything from bait to boat charters can be made through the **Hotel Nacional de Turismo** (⌧ Ruta 1, Km 162 ☎ 083/207). Anglers should bring their own rod, line, and lures suitable for trolling, spinning, and live baiting. In nearby Desvío, **Hotel Centu Cué** (⌧ 7 km [4½ mi] off Ruta 1 at Km 163 ☎ 083/219) has one of the river's best fishing spots. The hotel sells fishing supplies.

Santa María

37 km (22 mi) south of San Miguel on Ruta 1.

You'll pass through San Miguel, where locals tempt you with handwoven woolen blankets, rugs, and ponchos, and San Juan Bautista, where quaint colonial houses line cobblestone streets, before you reach Santa María. Nearly 7,000 Guaraní lived here in the early 18th century, and some of the original houses have been restored. The **Museo Jesuítico** has some 70 Guaraní carvings and statues; the latter represent the life of Jesus. (The museum keeps no fixed hours; if the door is locked, you may have to ask around for the priest to let you in.) ⌧ *Santa María* ☎ *0781/ 222* ⌷ *G2,000.*

San Ignacio

18 km (11 mi) south of Santa Maria on Ruta 1.

The Jesuits established Paraguay's first mission in San Ignacio, and today the **Museo Jesuítico** displays the country's best collection of Guaraní wood carvings and other period artifacts, including gilded pulpits, door panels, and statues. A depiction of St. Paul pointing to new lands in need of salvation is most striking; at his feet are a number of carved faces with Guaraní features. The building itself, with its thick adobe walls, is believed to be the oldest in Paraguay. It dates from the establishment of the mission in 1609. ⌧ *Ruta 1 (look for the sign)* ☎ *082/2218* ⌷ *G3,000* ⊙ *Daily 8–noon and 2:30–5:30.*

Fodor'sChoice
★

Santa Rosa

19 km (12 mi) east of San Ignacio on Ruta 1.

The ringing of bells from the red sandstone bell tower, built in 1698, can still be heard in the town of Santa Rosa, one of the era's largest reducciónes. In the small **museum** you can see frescoes from the old altar of the local chapel called the Capilla de Nuestra Señora de Loreto.

You'll also find a group of centuries-old carvings representing the Annunciation. ☒ *Ruta 1 (look for the sign)* ☎ *0858/221* 💵 *G2,000* ⊙ *Mon.–Sat. 7:30–11:30 and 1:30–5:30.*

San Cosme y Damián

95 km (59 mi) southeast of Santa Rosa on Ruta 1.

Just as Ruta 1 reaches Coronel Bogado, a 25-km (15-mi) paved highway leads to the village of San Cosme y Damián, near the banks of the Río Paraná. Follow the signs along a dirt track to the red sandstone mission buildings, currently in use as a Jesuit school. They once held an astronomical observatory. Many original houses are still in use. ☒ *San Cosme y Damián* ☎ *No phone* 💵 *G2,000* ⊙ *Dec.–Mar., daily 7–7; Apr.–Nov. daily 7–5:30.*

Encarnación

27 km (17 mi) southeast of San Cosme y Damián on Ruta 1.

Encarnación was the site of the long-gone Itapúa mission, but you'd never know it today. Linked by bridge to the Argentine town of Posadas, Encarnación is a somewhat dreary border town that serves as a convenient stopping point for many a weary traveler. The town has seen an influx of Eastern European immigrants. Its most incongruous sight is the small, ornate Ukrainian Orthodox church on Plaza Artigas.

The **Museo de Arte Sacro,** a small museum in the center of town, is devoted to religious art. ☒ *Artigas and 14 de Mayo* ☎ *071/203–627* 💵 *Free* ⊙ *Mon.–Fri. 3–7.*

Where to Stay & Eat

¢–$ ✕🏨 **Encarnación Resort.** Amid spacious gardens, this hotel is a quiet 3 km (2 mi) away from town. The restaurant's menu has Paraguayan specialties, including milanesa, sopa paraguaya, and cassava. ☒ *Ruta 1, Km 361, Villa Quiteria* ☎ *071/207–248* 🖷 *071/207–267* ✉ *erhotel@itacom.com.py* 🛏 *102 bedrooms, 4 suites* ☖ *Restaurant, room service, minibars, tennis court, pool, soccer, volleyball, bar, meeting rooms, no-smoking rooms* ▤ *AE, DC, MC, V* ⋈ *BP.*

¢ ✕🏨 **Hotel Cristal.** This nine-story hotel has modern rooms decorated with original artwork. The restaurant, which fills up at lunch with local businesspeople, serves contemporary fare and local fish dishes. ☒ *Mariscal Estigarribia 1157* ☎ *071/202–371* 🖷 *071/202–372* 🛏 *85 rooms* ☖ *Restaurant, minibars, pool, meeting rooms; no room phones* ▤ *AE, MC, V* ⋈ *BP.*

Trinidad

 Fodor'sChoice ★ *28 km (17 mi) northeast of Encarnación.*

The area's most impressive **Jesuit ruins,** superior even to those of Argentina and Brazil, are at Trinidad. Unfortunately, restoration projects are frequently suspended while the government searches for funding. The red sandstone reducción, built between 1712 and 1764, stands on a hilltop, enabling its full size to be appreciated. After the expulsion of the Jesuits, much of it was destroyed by an unscrupulous local official who ripped out stones to build his own residence, causing the structure to collapse. Many of the church walls and arches remain intact, however, even though the roof is open to the elements. Note the elaborately carved doors and wall friezes depicting angels playing the clavichord, harp, and other musical instruments. The only building with a roof is the sacristy, with intricate relief work above the main entrance. Also surviving are the school and cloister foundations and a sandstone tower. The ruins here, as well as the uncompleted structure at nearby Jesús, are UNESCO World Heritage sites. ⊠ *Trinidad* 🕾 *No phone* 🖂 *G2,000* ⊙ *Dec.–Mar., daily 7–7; Apr.–Nov. daily 7–5:30.*

Where to Stay

¢ 🏨 **Tirol del Paraguay.** Built on a hillside 25 km (16 mi) from Encarnación, this hotel has spectacular views of the rolling countryside. Rustic rooms with reddish brick walls are furnished with sturdy wood furniture. Accommodations are in single-story bungalows that surround four swimming pools fed by natural springs, which are said to have therapeutic properties. (Some people come here to take the waters.) Rates include all meals. ⊠ *Ruta 6, 8 km (5 mi) from Trinidad, Capitán Miranda* 🕾 *071/202–388* 🖷 *071/205–555* 🛏 *56 rooms* ⌂ *Dining room, minibars, tennis, 4 pools, Ping-Pong, volleyball, laundry service, meeting room* ⊟ *MC, V* ⊺⊖⊺ *BP.*

Jesús

10 km (6 mi) north of Trinidad.

The Jesuits began construction of the hilltop **Church of Jesús del Tavarangue** a mere eight years before their expulsion from the New World. Though never finished, this is the most distinctive of the mission churches on this part of the continent. Moorish-style arches make up the building's three entrances and lead to what were to be three naves and three altars. Vegetation and earth have covered much of the nearby *reducción* community. Painstaking excavations, frequently suspended due to lack of funds, are under way. ⊠ *Ruta 6* 🕾 *No phone* 🖂 *G2,000* ⊙ *Dec.–Mar., daily 7–7; Apr.–Nov. daily 7–5:30.*

Southern Paraguay A to Z

AIR TRAVEL

Most people visiting southern Paraguay fly into Asunción's Aeropuerto Internacional Silvio Pettirossi. You can also fly to the eastern border town of Ciudad del Este. TAM Mercosur flies at least once daily from Asunción to Ciudad del Este's Aeropuerto Alejo García (AGT), 280 km (175 mi) from Encarnación.

Getting to Southern Paraguay from Argentina is another option. Aerolineas Aregentinas connects Buenos Aires with Aeropuerto Libertador San Martín (PSS) in Posadas, just across the border from Encarnación. 🛫 Airlines **Aerolineas Argentinas** ⊠ Posadas, Argentina 🕾 3752/433–340. **TAM Mercosur** ⊠ Ciudad del Este 🕾 061/506–030.

▣ Airports **Aeropuerto Alejo García** ⊠ Ciudad del Este ☎ 061/518-352. **Aeropuerto Libertador General San Martín** ⊠ Posadas, Argentina ☎ 3752/451-903.

BUS TRAVEL
Buses between Asunción and Encarnación leave frequently. The five-hour trip costs about G8,000. You can get off the bus along Ruta 1 to visit any of the Jesuit missions. When you are ready to leave you can flag down another, which will pick you up unless it is full. Rapido Iguazú has buses running between Asunción and Encarnación. La Encarnaceña runs the same route, as well between Encarnación and the ruins at Trinidad and Jesús.

▣ Bus Information **La Encarnaceña** ☎ 071/203-448. **Rapido Iguazú** ☎ 021/551-601.

CAR RENTAL
Your best bet is renting a car in Asunción. Remember that Paraguayan rental vehicles may not cross the border into Argentina.

CAR TRAVEL
Ruta 1, which runs from Asunción to Encarnación, is fairly well maintained, although there are occasional potholes. From Encarnación, the poorly maintained Ruta 6 stretches northeast for 280 km (175 mi) to Ciudad del Este, near the Brazil and Argentine border. This route takes you to Iguazú Falls. The missions are all near Rutas 1 and 6.

EMERGENCIES
▣ Emergency Services **Police** ☎ 441-111. **Ambulance** ☎ 204-800.
▣ Hospitals **Instituto Médico Privado** ⊠ J. L. Mallorquín 1629, Encarnación ☎ 071/203-615.

HEALTH
The heat is intense in southern Paraguay from October to March. Slather on plenty of sunscreen and a drink lots of water to avoid becoming dehydrated while touring the missions. Tap water is risky in this part of the country. Stick with the *agua purificada* (purified water).

MAIL & SHIPPING
Mail service is slow in southern Paraguay, so post letters and packages from Asunción if you'd like them to arrive back home before you do. In Encarnación, the Dirección General de Correos is near the Feria Municipal.
▣ Post Offices **Dirección General de Correos** ⊠ Capellán Molas 337, Encarnación.

COURIERS Anything of value (or valuable looking) should be sent via a courier service. Asunció Express, the agent for FedEx, has an office in Encarnación.
▣ Courier Companies **FedEx/Asunción Express** ⊠ Mariscal Estigarribia 987, Encarnación ☎ 071/200-716.

MONEY MATTERS
In Encarnación, try Guaraní Cambios for changing cash or traveler's checks. ABN Amro Bank in Encarnación has an ATM on the Infonet network that gives cash against Plus- and Cirrus-affiliated cards.
▣ Banks **ABN Amro Bank** ⊠ mariscal Estgarribia and Caballero, Encarnación ☎ 071/201-872. **Guaraní Cambios** ⊠ Mariscal Estigarribia 307, Encarnación ☎ 071/204-301.

SAFETY

Southern Paraguay is reasonably safe, but take the usual precautions. Always be aware of your surroundings and keep an eye on all valuables. As a border town of 50,000 people, Encarnación has instances of petty theft. Avoid Ciudad del Este unless you're going there to cross the border to see Iguazú Falls; crime has skyrocketed in Ciudad del Este in recent years.

TAXIS

Encarnación has good taxi service and even a few horse-drawn wagons that locals use as public transportation.

TELEPHONES

Make domestic and international calls at the COPACO office, just south of the bus terminal in Encarnación.

🚹 Telephone Companies **COPACO** ⊠ Mariscal Estigarribia and Mariscal López, Encarnación ☎ 071/204-033.

TOUR OPERATORS

In Encarnación, Euskal Viajes arranges trips to the Jesuit missions.

🚹 Tour Companies **Euskal Viajes** ⊠ Teniente González and Pereira, Encarnación ☎ 071/200-949.

VISITOR INFORMATION

The Secretaria Nacional de Turismo in Encarnación offers maps and other information about the area. It is officially open weekdays 8–noon but keeps erratic hours.

🚹 **Secretaria Nacional de Turismo** ⊠ Tomás Romero Pereira 126, Encarnación ☎ 071/203-508.

PARAGUAY A TO Z

To research prices, get advice from other travelers, and book travel arrangements, visit www.fodors.com.

AIR TRAVEL

Few international airlines fly directly to Asunción's modern but sleepy Aeropuerto Internacional Silvio Pettirossi. The best way to get to Paraguay is through another South American gateway. American flies from São Paulo, as does Paraguay's TAM Mercosur. Other South American carriers that serve Asunción include Aerolíneas Argentinas, Bolivia's LAB, Uruguay's Pluna, and Brazil's Varig.

BUS TRAVEL

Intercity buses are inexpensive, fast, and reliable. Long-distance buses—some with air-conditioning, reclining seats, and movies—race between the major centers. Bone-shaking local buses, known as *colectivos,* rattle between villages and along city streets. The 370-km (230-mi) journey from Asunción to Encarnación takes about five hours by bus and costs G70,000; the 330-km (205-mi) trip from Asunción to Ciudad del Este also takes five hours and costs G50,000.

BUSINESS HOURS

Remember that everything shuts down between noon and 3:30, except for department stores and the odd café.

BANKS & OFFICES Most banks are open weekdays 8:45–3. Casas de cambio are open weekdays 8:30–1 and 2:30–6, Saturday 8:30–1. Public offices operate weekdays 7–1, and businesses are open around 7:30 or 8 until midday and then reopen from 3 to 6.

MUSEUMS & Museum hours vary, but most are open weekdays 8–noon and 4–6 and
SIGHTS for a few hours on Saturday morning.

POST OFFICES Post offices are generally open weekdays 7–noon and 2:30–7:30.

SHOPS Most shops open weekdays 7–7, closing for a few hours for the siesta. Department stores and shopping centers are open weekdays 8–7:30.

CAR TRAVEL

Driving isn't easy in Paraguay—only 25% of the country's roads are paved and motorists tend to ignore traffic laws. On the plus side, there are fewer vehicles on the road here than in neighboring Argentina or Brazil.

GASOLINE Distances between gas stations can be long, so you should top off your tank regularly. Stations are normally open until midnight. Gasoline costs G3,500 per liter.

ROAD With a few exceptions, most roads outside of Asunción are unpaved,
CONDITIONS dangerously riddled with potholes, or closed altogether because of flooding. Beware of animals that wander onto the highways, particularly at night. On weekends and around public holidays, access roads into and out of the capital can be jammed with traffic.

RULES OF Your driver's license is valid here. Seat belts are mandatory. The speed
THE ROAD limit is 80 kph (50 mph) on highways and 40 kph (25 mph) in urban areas. Care should be taken at intersections in Asunción, as drivers rarely offer to give way.

CUSTOMS & DUTIES

Nonresidents may bring any personal-use items, plus 1 liter of spirits or two bottles of wine and 400 cigarettes. You cannot take sums of more than $10,000 into or out of Paraguay.

FESTIVALS

On February 3, the town of Itá celebrates the Feast of St. Blas, the patron saint of Paraguay, with folk dancing, popular music, and horse racing. On December 8, the Día de la Nuestra Señora de Los Milagros (Day of Our Lady of the Miracles) is celebrated in the town of Caacupé, where an effigy of Mary is paraded through the streets.

HEALTH

Although tap water is safe to drink in Asunción, drink agua purificada elsewhere. Order it *con gas* and *sin gas* (with and without carbonation).

Outside of Asunción, mosquitoes and snakes can be a problem. Bring plenty of mosquito repellent and, if you're cautious, a snake-bite kit.

HOLIDAYS
New Year's Day; Heroes Day (March 1); Holy Week (Palm Sunday through Easter Sunday, April 4–11 in 2004; March 20–27 in 2005; April 9–16 in 2006); Labor Day (May 1); Independence Day (May 14–15); Armistice of Chaco War (June 12); Founding of Asunción (August 15); Victory at Boquerón (September 29); Christmas.

LANGUAGE
Paraguay is South America's only officially bilingual country. About half the population speaks Guaraní as its first language. If you know some Spanish, do not hesitate to use it. In Asunción, the staff at more expensive hotels and restaurants are likely to speak English. Outside Asunción, it's unusual to find anyone who speaks anything but Spanish or Guaraní. There are some immigrant communities, mainly in the Chaco, where German is also spoken.

MAIL & SHIPPING
You can buy stamps from the Dirección General de Correos (post office), which you'll find in most towns, but to ensure that your mail will actually arrive you should post it from Asunción.

MONEY MATTERS
The Paraguayan guaraní (G) comes in bills of 1,000, 5,000, 10,000, 50,000, and 100,000 guaraníes, with coins in units of 100, and 500 guaraníes. At press time the exchange rate was about 6,900 guaraníes to the U.S. dollar.

It's practically impossible to change guaraníes outside Paraguay, so make sure you exchange them at the airport before leaving.

ATMS ATMs are still a bit of a novelty in Paraguay. You'll find them in the major cities, but not in smaller towns. Some machines on Infonet, the country's largest system, accept both Plus and Cirrus cards. Others accept one or the other.

PASSPORTS & VISAS
Citizens of the United Kingdom may enter Paraguay for 90 days with a valid passport. U.S., Canadian, Australian, and New Zealand citizens need to obtain a visa before arrival. Your application must be accompanied by your passport with at least six months' remaining validity, two passport-size photos, and two copies each of your bank statement and your return plane ticket or itinerary. Fees, payable in U.S. dollars, or the equivalent in local currency, are: U.S. citizens, $65; Canadians, $45; Australians and New Zealanders, no fee. There is no Paraguayan representation for Australia or New Zealand. Most travelers from those countries obtain their visas in another South American capital.
🛂 **Embassy of Paraguay** ✉ 151 Slater St., Suite 501, Ottawa, Ontario K1P 5H3 ☎ 613/567-1283 🖷 613/567-1679. **Embassy of Paraguay** ✉ 2400 Massachusetts Ave. NW Washington, DC 20008 ☎ 202/483-6960 🖷 202/234-4508.

SAFETY
Crime is rising in Paraguay, although you probably won't see any evidence of it during your trip. Paraguay's eastern tri-border region with

Brazil and Argentina, including the town of Ciudad del Este, has become increasingly dangerous—there has been a rise in extremist-group violence, and the town has become a haven for international terrorist groups. There's a general sense of lawlessness that pervades this part of the country, and the government exerts limited control here. It's not a problem if you pass through the border at Ciudad del Este to see the world-famous Iguazú Falls at the border—but it's better to see the Falls from Brazil or Argentina instead. Just don't stay in Ciudad del Este overnight.

TAXES

DEPARTURE TAX The departure tax is $18, payable in U.S. dollars or in guaraníes (about G123,000). American Airlines has begun to include the tax in the price of your ticket. Verify that you don't have to pay again.

VALUE-ADDED TAX A 10% nonrefundable value-added tax, known as IVA, is charged on all goods and services. It's included in the prices at bars and restaurants, but it's added to hotel bills. Watch for double-billing: IVA shouldn't be added to food-related bills charged to your room.

TELEPHONES

AREA & COUNTRY CODES Paraguay's country code is 595. To call Paraguay, dial the country code, then the area code, omitting the first 0.

LOCAL CALLS Local numbers in urban areas have six digits; a few in Asunción have seven digits. Rural numbers may carry as few as three or four digits. When calling between communities, precede the local number with the three- or four-digit area code. For local operator assistance, dial 010. For directory assistance, dial 112.

LONG-DISTANCE & INTERNATIONAL CALLS The privatized national telephone company, the Compañía Paraguaya de Comunicaciones (COPACO), has offices in most cities and towns where you can place local and international calls. Calls to the United States cost about G18,000 per minute during peak hours, G14,000 off-peak. Lines can become congested at peak hours. If you're calling from a hotel, be sure to hang up if there's no answer for about 20 seconds; otherwise, you'll be charged for a three-minute call.

🗐 Access Codes **AT&T** ☎ 008-11-800. **British Telecom** ☎ 008-44-800. **Canada Direct** ☎ 008-14-800. **MCI** ☎ 008-12-800. **Sprint** ☎ 008-13-800.

PUBLIC PHONES Paraguay has few phone booths, but numerous private telephone offices let you make calls. Look for TELÉFONOS PÚBLICOS or CABINAS TELEFÓNICAS signs.

TIPPING

An appropriate tip in upscale restaurants is about 10% of the bill, more if the service is exceptionally good. In average places, round up the bill to the nearest G1,000. Round up taxi fares to the nearest G500.

WHEN TO GO

Paraguay's relative lack of tourists means there aren't well-delineated high and low seasons. There are fewer good hotels in the country than elsewhere on the continent, so reservations are recommended year-round, especially in Asunción.

CLIMATE Traveling in Paraguay can be uncomfortable from December to March, when the sun beats down on the landlocked country. The heat is intense, so don't plan activities for the early afternoon (there's a daily siesta, anyway). The wettest months are December to April, the driest June to August. Torrential cloudbursts can quickly turn streets into torrents of muddy red water.

The following are the average daily maximum and minimum temperatures for Asunción.

Jan.	93F	34C	May	77F	25C	Sept.	80F	27C
	72	22		55	14		60	16
Feb.	93F	34C	June	72F	22C	Oct.	84F	29C
	72	22		55	13		62	17
Mar.	91F	33C	July	75F	24C	Nov.	88F	31C
	70	21		57	14		66	19
Apr.	82F	28C	Aug.	77F	25C	Dec.	91F	33C
	64	18		57	14		70	21

PERU

8

Updated by
Gregory
Benchwick,
Joan Gonzalez,
Holly Smith,
Mark Sullivan,
and Jeffrey
Van Fleet

THE STONE SANCTUARY OF MACHU PICCHU is what often springs to mind when someone mentions Peru. This incredible city, built more than a century before the arrival of Spanish conquistadors, is the most prominent example of how "The Land of the Inca" is a nation full of archaeological treasures. Its many historic sites are scattered among markedly different regions, each with a distinct character.

The arid desert coast is where you'll find the Nazca Lines, a mystery etched in the sand centuries before the Inca civilization appeared. North of Lima, ruins of vast, ancient cities and adobe pyramids are echoes of the sophisticated Moche and Chimú societies that thrived in the desert oases as early as 200 BC. In the mountains you'll find the monumental city of Cusco, once the capital of the Inca empire. The Colca Canyon, not far from Arequipa, is crisscrossed with Inca and pre-Inca agricultural terraces that are guarded by giant condors flying high overhead.

Although Peru is considered an Andean nation, more than half of its landmass is jungle. Here are the rain forests of the province aptly named Madre de Dios, or "Mother of God." It's remote, nearly untouched, but accessible to the adventurous. In the highland Ceja de Selva, or "Eyebrow of the Jungle," is the so-called "lost city of the Incas," Machu Picchu. Its vertiginous setting and stunning architecture make it one of the true wonders of the world. To the west the Andes form an impenetrable barrier of snowcapped peaks. Beyond them an utterly barren strip of coastal desert stretches for 2,000 km (1,240 mi), broken by dozens of narrow river valleys.

As a nation and a people, Peru has a strong character, not unlike the national drink called *pisco*, a heady brandy distilled in the coastal valleys south of Lima. Yet it isn't so difficult to tell from which part of the country a person might have come. The people of the Andes, often called *serranos*, tend to be introverted, with a melancholic side best expressed in their haunting music. Quite the opposite are the friendly and more lighthearted inhabitants of the coast. The *costeño* is quick with a joke but, like his beloved cuisine, *comida criolla* (creole food), has a piquant, teasing side to his nature.

Today, this nation of 26 million is focusing on its harsh economic realities. For the past three generations, millions of *campesinos* (peasants) have left the countryside for the cities. They built homes on the outskirts of Lima and other large cities, where they struggled to make a place for themselves. Unfortunately, there were not enough jobs to go around. The resulting crisis erupted in years of political violence that didn't end until the early 1990s.

President Alejandro Toledo, who took office in 2001, promised that one of his priorities is easing the poverty still gripping the nation. Peruvians, ever optimistic, stood firmly behind the former shoe-shine boy. However, Toledo has thus far been unable to come through on his election promises in a country where 55 percent of the 26-million-person population lives in poverty.

If you have
7 days   Arrive in **Lima,** where you can spend your first two days exploring the city's museums and markets. On your third day, fly to the colonial city of **Cusco** and take an afternoon tour of the city. The next day, head out into the countryside to see fascinating Inca ruins such as **Sacsayhuamán.** Take the morning train up into the mountains to **Machu Picchu,** the famed "lost city of the Incas." Spend the night and return to Cusco late the next afternoon. On your last day return to Lima.

If you have
10 days   Follow the same itinerary as the seven-day tour, but instead of returning to Lima, take the train from Cusco to **Puno.** Use this charming town as your base for exploring **Lake Titicaca** and the ruins of **Sillustani.** Fly back to Lima on your last day.

If you have
14 days   Follow the 10-day itinerary, but on the last day fly from Puno to the colonial town of **Arequipa.** Explore the town for two days, and then head to **Colca Canyon.** Return to Arequipa for the next day, and then fly back to Lima the next morning.

Exploring Peru

Peru can be divided roughly into three major geographical areas. The arid coastal desert extends the full length of the country. Within this narrow stretch are the Nazca Lines, a coastal marine park teeming with wildlife, verdant oases, rocky hills, and desert. Running through the country like a spine, separating desert from jungle, are the majestic Andes, with their snowcapped peaks, green valleys, and hidden ruins. To the east lies the world's widest river, the Amazon, and Peru's thick chunk of jungle.

About the Restaurants

The cost and quality of dining out in Peru can vary widely, but a modest restaurant may serve as splendid a meal as one with snazzier decor. Most smaller restaurants offer a lunchtime *menú,* a prix-fixe meal ($2–$5) that consists of an appetizer, a main dish, dessert, and a beverage. Peru is also full of cafés, many with a selection of delicious pastries. Food at bars is usually limited to snacks and sandwiches.

Top-notch restaurants serve lunch and dinner, but most Peruvians think of lunch as the main meal of the day, and many restaurants open only at midday. Served between 1 and 3, lunch is traditionally followed by a siesta, though the custom has largely died out. Dinner can be anything from a light snack to another full meal. Peruvians tend to dine late, between 7 and 11 PM.

Peruvians dress quite informally when they dine out, and often a jacket is sufficient for men even at the most expensive restaurants. A smart pair of slacks or a skirt is always appropriate for women. Shorts are frowned upon everywhere except at the beach, and T-shirts are appropriate only in very modest restaurants.

About the Hotels

Accommodations in Peru range from bare-bones rooms in private homes to suites in luxury hotels. They come with names such as *hostal, pensión, residencial,* and *hotel,* and though the implication is that the last is more upscale, this is not always the case. Rooms are more scarce during the high season (June through September), and if you're planning to visit during a festival, it's best to reserve in advance. Camping in Peru is limited to some beaches and a part of mountain and jungle treks. The only legal campsites are in some reserves, such as Manu National Park. Camping is pretty much required for those hiking the Inca Trail, but be careful and try to stay with a group.

WHAT IT COSTS In Nuevo Soles					
	$$$$	$$$	$$	$	¢
RESTAURANTS	over 65	50–65	35–50	20–35	under 20
HOTELS	over 500	375–500	250–375	125–250	under 125

Restaurant prices are per person, for a main course at dinner. Hotel prices are for two people in a standard double room, excluding tax.

LIMA

Founded along the banks of the Rimac River by Francisco Pizarro in 1535, Lima served as the capital of Spain's South American empire for 300 years. The "City of Kings" has a regal history that lingers on in its sophistication, the decaying beauty of its boulevards, and the liveliness of its intellectual life.

Exploring Lima

Most of Lima's colonial-era churches and mansions are found in the historic center, along the streets surrounding the Plaza de Armas. From El Centro, a highway called Paseo de la República whisks you south to residential areas like San Isidro, Miraflores, and Barranco. The charms of these neighborhoods are simpler—a tree-lined park, a bluff overlooking the sea, a wooden bridge filled with young couples.

Museums are more difficult to reach, as they are scattered around the city. Pueblo Libre, a neighborhood west of San Isidro, has two of the best, the Museo Arqueológico Rafael Larco Herrera and the Museo Nacional de Antropología, Arqueología, e Historia del Perú. In the other direction from San Isidro is the Museo de la Nación, in the residential area of San Borja. Monterrico, east of Miraflores, is the site of Lima's most popular museum, the glittering Museo de Oro.

Spend at least a day touring the sights in the historic center, with an additional day devoted to whichever museums strike your fancy. Bargain hunters should do some window-shopping in Miraflores. Take one evening to wander through laid-back Barranco, at one time a seaside retreat for wealthy *Limeños.* The café scene here is lively, attracting artists and those who would like to be.

Ancient Cities From every mountaintop, valley, or coastal plain in Peru you can almost hear the echoes of past civilizations. And just as each new archaeological discovery is thought, surely, to be the last, another ancient city reveals itself. The temples, palaces, shrines, and steep stone staircases of Machu Picchu are Peru's most famous, but there are extensive ruins throughout the country. North of Lima, 5 km (3 miles) from Trujillo is Chán Chán, the largest adobe city in the world and 1,759 km (1,092 mi) northwest of Trujillo, near Chachapoyas is Kuelap, called "The City of the Cloud People" because of the white skin of its former inhabitants. Kuelap was built on a mountaintop overlooking the Utcabamba River.

8

Caral, in the Supe Valley, is reportedly the oldest city in the Americas. It is 193 km (120 mi) north of Lima and 23 km (14 mi) inland from the Pacific Coast. It was settled around 2600 BC and is older than the pyramids of Egypt. The public area has a huge plaza surrounded by six mounds; the largest, Piramide Mayor, is 18 meters (60 feet) tall. An unusual find were 32 flutes made of condor and pelican wing bones. In 2002, Caral was put on the World Monuments Watch List due to heavy damage from wind erosion and looting.

Machu Picchu, Chán Chán, and areas of Kuelap and Caral are offered on tours, but other impressive sites, like Gran Pajaten in the Río Abiseo National Park on the eastern slope of the Andes, 402 km (250 mi) east of Trujillo, or Cota Coca, 40 km (25 mi) east of Machu Picchu, are difficult to reach and not quite ready for tourism. The Ríp Abiseo area was declared a National Park in 1983, not only to protect the overall area and the exceptionally preserved buildings, terraces, and roads of a pre-Hispanic civilization.

It isn't only ancient cities that are constantly being discovered or uncovered in Peru—in July 2002, Peruvian geologists found the perfectly preserved skeleton of a horse in the department of Arequipa 1,000 km (600 mi) south of Lima, proving that the horse existed in South America long before it was introduced by the Spaniards. The skeleton, on display in Peru's Natural History Museum in Lima, reveals that this early equine had a large head, thick neck, and short legs.

Peppers, Paiche & Potatoes From the Amazon to the Andes, the food you sample will be as varied as the landscapes you'll encounter. All the regions have one thing in common: the use of a small, thin *ají* pepper. The use of hot peppers is common in Latin America, especially Mexico, but Peruvian chefs strip the pepper of its veins and seeds and soak it or boil it in water to cool it down while retaining the flavor.

Peruvian cuisine is hard to define, as it has evolved from pre-Inca and Spanish colonial times and has been influenced by African, European, and Asian cooking. Fresh fish is found everywhere, including shrimp, lobster, piranha, *corvina* (a delicious sea bass), and *paiche* (a huge fish found in jungle lakes). Some of Peru's best dishes include *ceviche* (marinated fish with onions and peppers), *ají de gallina* (hen in a cream sauce), *lomo saltado* (sautéed beef with onions and peppers, served with fried potatoes and rice), *pachamanca* (a meat and vegetable stew), *anticuchos* (a shish kebab of marinated beef hearts), and *choclo* (Peru's version of corn on the cob). For dessert, try *suspiro a la limeña* (a rich, sweet pudding) and *mazamorra morada* (a fruity purple pudding).

Both Peru and Ecuador claim to have given the world the potato, and hundreds of varieties are grown here. Among the tastier recipes are *papas a la huancaina* (potatoes in spicy cheese sauce), *papas ocopa* (potatoes in spicy peanut sauce), and *carapulcra* (a stew of dried potatoes served over rice). Peru has wonderful fruit, such as *chirimoya* (custard apple) and *tuna* (cactus fruit).

Peru's national drink is the pisco sour, made from brandy. Peruvian beers aren't bad, either. In Lima, try Cristal and the slightly more upscale Pilsen Callao, both produced by the same brewery. In the south it's Arequipeña from Arequipa, Cusqueña from Cusco, and big bottles of San Juan from Iquitos. Tacama's Blanco de Blancos is considered the country's best wine.

Numbers in the text correspond to numbers in the margin and on the Lima maps.

El Centro

Almost all Lima's most interesting historic sites are within walking distance of the **Plaza de Armas** ❶ ▶, one of the grandest central squares in all South America. The lovely fountain in the center can be used as a slightly off-center compass. The trumpet of the bronze angel points due north, where you'll see the **Palacio de Gobierno** ❷. To the west is the neo-colonial **Municipalidad de Lima** ❸, while the **Catedral** ❹ and the adjoining Palacio Episcopal are to the east. Head north on Jirón Carabaya, the street running beside the Palacio de Gobierno, until you reach the butter-yellow **Estación de Desamparados** ❺, the municipal train station. Follow the street as it curves to the east. In a block you'll reach the **Iglesia de San Francisco** ❻, the most spectacular of the city's colonial-era churches. Plan to send some time here, as you'll want to explore the catacombs.

Follow Jirón Ancash one block east to reach Avenida Abancay, a major thoroughfare. One block south you'll see the imposing structure that corrals the country's congress. On the street that runs along the southern edge is the **Museo de la Inquisición** ❼, where you can explore one of the more gruesome aspects of the country's history. Head two blocks south to Jirón Ucayali, where a block west is the rather plain exterior of the **Iglesia de San Pedro** ❽. Just beyond, marvel at the facades of two of the city's finest private homes, **Casa Goyeneche** ❾ and **Casa Torre Tagle** ❿. There are two other stunning residences within a few blocks of the Plaza de Armas. **Casa Aliaga** ⓫ is a block north of the square on Jirón de la Union, which runs along the western side of the Palacio de Gobierno. **Casa Riva-Agüero** ⓬ is on Jirón Camaná, one block west and two blocks south of the square.

If you can't get enough of colonial-era churches, a cluster can be found south and west of the Plaza de Armas. From the Plaza de Armas, head one block west past the **Correo Central** ⑬ to the **Convento de Santo Domingo** ⑭, with the tomb of San Martín de Porras. Continue three blocks west to the **Santuario de Santa Rosa de Lima** ⑮, where locals pray to South America's first saint. Head south along bustling Avenida Tacna to the imposing **Iglesia de las Nazarenas** ⑯. From here, head four blocks east on Jirón Huancavelica to the **Iglesia de la Merced** ⑰. Walk a block west to Jirón Camaná, then two blocks south to the **Iglesia de Jesús, María y José** ⑱.

Up for a bit more walking? Head south on Jirón de la Unión to **Plaza San Martín** ⑲, one of the city's best-preserved squares. The neoclassical splendor of the Gran Hotel Bolívar presides over the western edge. Continue south on Jirón de la Unión, passing the Paseo de la República, until you reach the pretty green park called the Parque de la Exposición. Here, at what most people consider the gateway to the historic district is the **Museo de Arte Nacional** ⑳.

TIMING An unhurried visit to the historic district's main attractions takes a full day, with at least an hour devoted to both the Museo de Arte Nacional and the Museo de la Inquisición. Even if you're short on time, don't bypass the guided tour of the underground catacombs of the Iglesia de San Francisco. Also, spend some time just sitting on the cathedral steps, as the locals do.

As the locals begin to head home for the day, so should you. This neighborhood can be a bit dicey in the evening. If you find yourself on the street in the late afternoon, it's probably wise to take a taxi to your destination.

What to See

⓫ **Casa Aliaga.** Said to be the oldest colonial mansion in South America, the Aliaga House has been owned and occupied by the same family since Francisco Pizarro granted the land to Jerónimo de Aliaga in 1535. An impressive wooden staircase in the tree-shaded courtyard leads up to the elaborate rooms, many of which are decorated with colonial furnishings. Visitors must arrange trips in advance through Lima Tours. ⊠ *Jr. de la Unión 224, El Centro* ☎ *01/424–5110.*

➒ **Casa Goyeneche.** Although it strongly resembles nearby Casa Torre Tagle, the 40 or so years between them are evident. While the 1730 Casa Torre Tagle has a baroque style, the 1771 Casa Goyeneche has clearly been influenced by the rococo movement. Sadly, the house is not open to the public. ⊠ *Jr. Ucayali 360, El Centro.*

⓬ **Casa Riva-Agüero.** A matched pair of balconies with *celosías*—intricate wood screens through which ladies could watch passersby unobserved—grace the facade of this mansion dating from 1760. Ornately carved wooden balconies overlook the front and back courtyards of this typical colonial house. An interesting museum of folk art is on the second floor. ⊠ *Jr. Camaná 459, El Centro* ☎ *01/427–9275* ⊡ *Free* ☉ *Tues.–Sat. 10–12:30 and 2–7:30.*

➓ **Casa Torre Tagle.** Considered one of the most magnificent structures in South America, this mansion sums up the grace and elegance of the early 18th

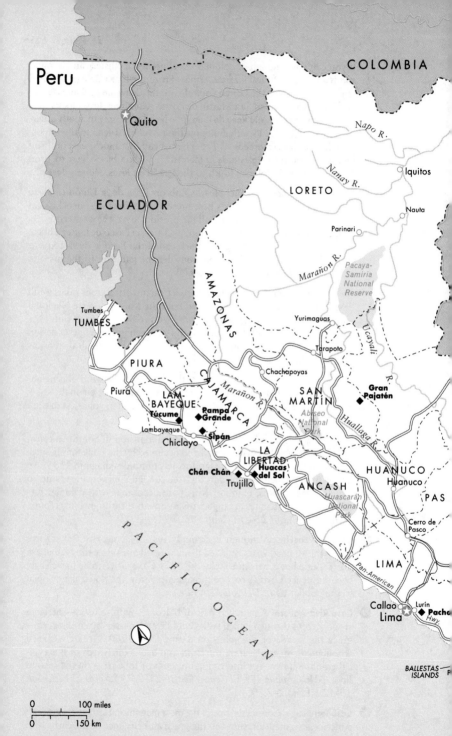

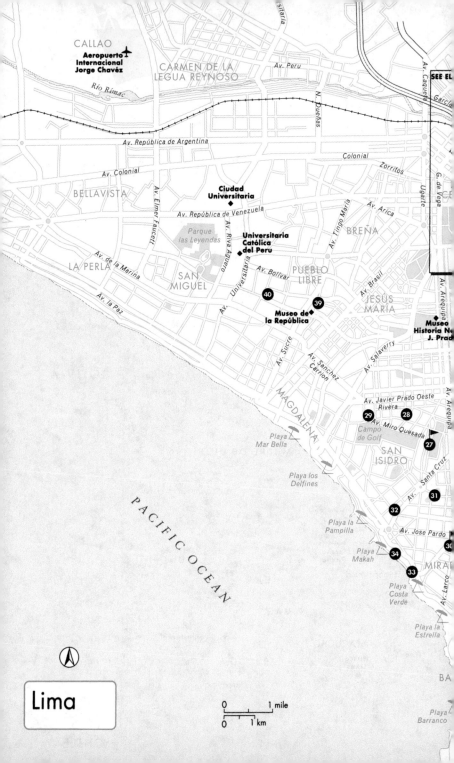

CALLAO

Aeropuerto Internacional Jorge Chavéz ✈

CARMEN DE LA LEGUA REYNOSO

Río Rímac

Av. Peru

Av. Caquetá

SEE EL

García

Av. República de Argentina

Av. Colonial

Colonial

Zorritos

G. de Vega

Ugarte

CE

BELLAVISTA

Ciudad Universitaria ◆

Av. Elmer Faucett

Av. República de Venezuela

Av. Arica

BREÑA

Av. Tingo María

Av. Riva Agüero

Universitaria Católica del Peru ◆

Av. Bolívar

Parque las Leyendas

PUEBLO LIBRE

Av. Brasil

Av. Arequipa

LA PERLA

Av. de la Marina

SAN MIGUEL

Av. Universitaria

🔘40

JESÚS MARÍA

Museo de la República ◆

🔘39

Museo Historia N J. Prad ◆

Av. la Paz

Av. Sucre

Av. Sanchez Carrion

Av. Salaverry

Av. Arequipa

MAGDALENA

Av. Javier Prado Oeste
Rivera

🔘29   🔘28

Av. Miro Quesada

Campo de Golf

🔘27

Playa Mar Bella

SAN ISIDRO

Av. Santa Cruz

Playa los Delfines

🔘31

🔘32

PACIFIC OCEAN

Playa la Pampilla

Av. Jose Pardo

🔘30

Playa Makah

🔘34

MIRA

🔘33

Av. Larco

Playa Costa Verde

Playa la Estrella

✦ (compass)

BA

Lima

0 _____ 1 mile
0 _____ 1 km

Playa Barranco

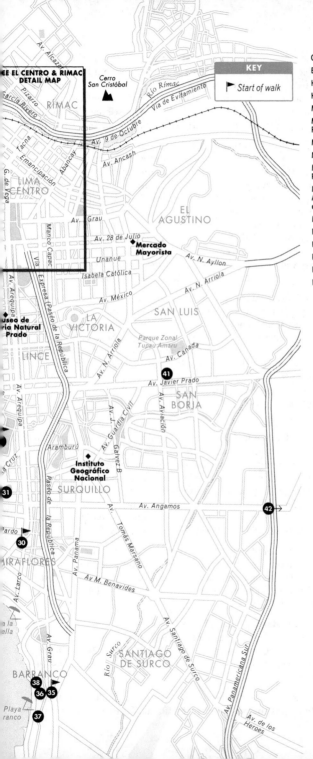

century. The coat of arms of the original owner, the Marquis of Torre Tagle, is still visible above the door. Flanked by a pair of elegant balconies, the stone entrance is as expertly carved as that of any of the city's churches. It currently serves as a governmental building and is not open to the public, but you can often get a peek inside. You might see the tiled ceilings, carved columns, or 16th-century carriage. ⊠ *Jr. Ucayali 363, El Centro.*

❹ Catedral. The layout for this immense structure was dictated by Francisco Pizarro himself, and his basic vision has survived even though earthquakes in 1746 and 1940 required it to be completely rebuilt. The first church on the site was completed in 1625. Inside are some impressive Baroque appointments, especially the intricately carved choir stalls. Because of changing tastes, the main altar was replaced around 1800 with one in a neoclassical style. At about the same time the towers that flank the entrance were added. A highlight of a visit to the church is seeing the chapel where Pizarro is entombed. There is also a small museum of religious art and artifacts. ⊠ *East side of the Plaza de Armas, El Centro* ☎ *01/427–9647* 🎫 *S/5* ⊗ *Mon.–Sat. 10–4:30.*

⓮ Convento de Santo Domingo. The 16th-century Convent of Saint Dominic clearly shows the different styles popular during the colonial era in Lima. The bell tower, for instance, has a Baroque base built in 1632, but the upper parts rebuilt after an earthquake in 1746 are more rococo in style. The church is a popular one, as it holds the tombs of the first two Peruvian saints, Santa Rosa de Lima and San Martín de Porres. The pair of cloisters in the convent are worth a look, as they are decorated with yellow-and-blue tiles imported from Spain in the early 17th century. ⊠ *Conde de Superunda and Camaná, El Centro* ☎ *01/427–6793* 🎫 *S/3* ⊗ *Mon.–Sat. 8:30–12:30 and 3–6, Sun. 9–12:30 and 3–6.*

⓭ Correo Central. Inaugurated in 1897, this regal structure looks more like a palace than a post office. You can certainly buy a stamp or send a package, but most people come here to admire the exuberance of an era when no one thought twice about placing bronze angels atop a civic building. A narrow passage filled with vendors splits the building in half. The Museo Postal y Filatélico, a tiny museum of stamps, is just inside the front entrance. ⊠ *Conde de Superunda, between Jr. de la Unión and Jr. Camaná, El Centro* ☎ *01/427–9370* 🎫 *Free* ⊗ *Mon.–Sat. 8–8, Sun. 9–2.*

❺ Estación de Desamparados. Inaugurated in 1912, Desamparados Station was the centerpiece for the continent's first railway. The building itself, using lots of glass to make use of the natural light, was based on styles popular in Europe. Trains no longer run from this station. ⊠ *Jr. Carabaya and Jr. Ancash, El Centro.*

⓲ Iglesia de Jesús, María y José. The 1659 Church of Jesus, Mary and Joseph may have a plain facade, but inside is a feast for the eyes. Baroque retables representing various saints grace the main altar. ⊠ *Jr. Camaná and Jr. Moquegua, El Centro* ☎ *01/427–6809* 🎫 *Free* ⊗ *Mon.–Sat. 7–noon, 3–8.*

⓱ Iglesia de la Merced. The first house of worship to be built in Lima, Our Lady of Mercy was commissioned by Hernando Pizarro, brother of the

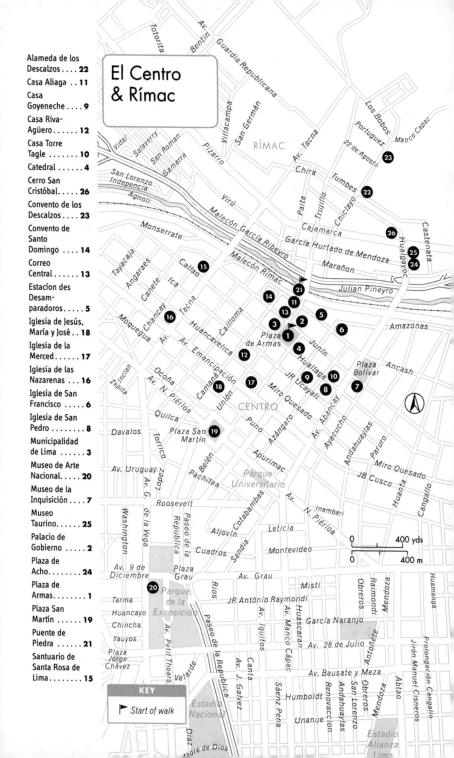

El Centro & Rímac

city's founder. He chose the site because it was here that services were first held in the city. The current structure, with an unusual Baroque facade, was finished in 1704. Inside are a series of retables that gradually change from Baroque to rococo styles. The intricately carved choir stalls, dating from the 18th century, have images of cherubic singers. ☒ *Jr. de la Unión at Jr. Miro Quesada, El Centro* ☏ *01/427–8199* ⬚ *Free* ☉ *Tues.–Sun. 8–12, 4–8.*

⑯ Iglesia de las Nazarenas. This rococo church has become the repository of the *Señor de los Milagros* (Lord of the Miracles). When an earthquake destroyed much of the city in 1655, a wall with an image of Christ remained standing. When it survived subsequent tremors in 1687 and 1746, people believed it to be miraculous. The church was built to house the now famous icon. Every year on October 18, 19, and 28 and November 1, purple-robed devotees carry an oil copy of the mural, resplendent in a gold frame, through the streets of Lima. ☒ *Jr. Tacna at Jr. Huancavelica, El Centro* ☏ *No phone* ⬚ *Free* ☉ *Daily 6:30–noon, 5–8:30.*

★ ☾ ❻ Iglesia de San Francisco. The Church of Saint Francis is the most visited in Lima, and with good reason. The 1674 structure is the best example of what is known as "Lima Baroque" style of architecture. The handsome carved portal would later influence those on other churches, including the Iglesia de la Merced. The central nave is known for its beautiful ceilings painted in a style called *mudejar* (a blend of Moorish and Spanish designs). On a tour, peruse the adjoining monastery's immense collection of antique texts, some dating back to the 17th century. But the best part of a tour is a visit to the vast catacombs. The city's first cemetery, these underground tunnels contains the bones of some 75,000 people. In many places the bones have been stacked in eerie geometric patterns. Tours are available in English. ☒ *Jr. Ancash 471, El Centro* ☏ *01/427–1381* ⬚ *S/5* ☉ *Daily 9:30–5.*

❽ Iglesia de San Pedro. The Jesuits built three churches in rapid succession on this corner, the current one dating from 1638. It remains one of the finest examples of early colonial religious architecture in Peru. The facade is remarkably restrained, but the interior shows all the extravagance of the era. The interior is richly appointed with a series of Baroque retables thought to be the best in the city. Don't miss the side aisle, where gilded arches lead to chapels decorated with beautiful hand-painted tiles. Many have works by Italians like Bernardo Bitti, who arrived on these shores in 1575. His style influenced an entire generation of painters. In the sacristy is *The Coronation of the Virgin,* one of his most famous works. ☒ *Jr. Ucayali at Jr. Azángaro, El Centro* ☏ *01/428–3010* ⬚ *Free* ☉ *Mon.–Sat. 7–noon and 5–8.*

❸ Municipalidad de Lima. Although it resembles the colonial-era buildings surrounding it, the City Hall was actually constructed in 1944. Step inside to see the stained-glass windows above the marble staircase. Running beside the building is a lovely pedestrian walkway called the Paseo Los Escribanos, or Passage of the Scribes, lined with inexpensive restaurants. On the south side of the building is the tourist information office. ☒ *West side of the Plaza de Armas, El Centro.*

㉕ Museo de Arte Nacional. Built in 1872 as the Palacio de la Expedición, this mammoth neoclassical structure now houses the National Museum of Art. It has a bit of everything, from pre-Columbian artifacts to colonial-era furniture to contemporary paintings. One of the highlights is the collection of 2,000-year-old weavings from Paracas. Make sure to leave time to wander around the extensive gardens outside. ⊠ *Paseo Colón 125, El Centro* ☎ *01/423–6332* ☞ *S/6* ⊗ *Thur.–Tue. 10–1 and 2–5.*

❼ Museo de la Inquisición. A massive mansion that belonged to the one of the first families to arrive in Lima served as the headquarters of the Spanish Inquisition. Visit the original dungeons and torture chambers, where stomach-churning, life-size exhibits illustrate methods of extracting information from prisoners. The residence later served as the temporary home of Congress, which found a permanent home in the neoclassical structure across the street. The guided tour lets you admire the beautiful building, especially the coffered ceilings dating from the 18th century. ⊠ *Jr. Junín 548, El Centro* ☎ *01/428–7980* ☞ *Free* ⊗ *Mon.–Sat. 9–5.*

❷ Palacio de Gobierno. Built on the site where Francisco Pizarro was murdered in 1541, the Palacio de Gobierno was completed in 1938. The neo-Baroque palace is the official residence of the president. The best time to visit is at noon, when soldiers in red-and-blue uniforms conduct an elaborate changing of the guard. Guided tours, which include visits to many of the rooms where the president conducts affairs of state, must be arranged at least two days in advance. To do so, bring your passport to the unmarked side door on Jirón de la Union, across from the statue of a conquistador on horseback. ⊠ *North side of the Plaza de Armas, El Centro* ☎ *01/426–7020* ☞ *Free* ⊗ *Weekdays 10–12:30.*

★ ▶ ❶ Plaza de Armas. This massive square has been the center of the city since 1535. Over the years it has served many functions, from an open-air theater for melodramas to an impromptu ring for bullfights. Huge fires once burned in the center for people sentenced to death by the Spanish Inquisition. Much has changed over the years, but one thing remaining is the bronze fountain unveiled in 1651. It was here that José de San Martín declared the country's independence from Spain in 1821. ⊠ *Jr. Junín and Jr. Carabaya, El Centro.*

⓳ Plaza San Martín. This popular plaza is unlike any other in the city. It is surrounded on three sides by French-style buildings—all of them an oddly appealing shade of pumpkin—dating from the 1920s. Presiding over the western edge is the Gran Hotel Bolívar, a pleasant place to stop for afternoon tea. Several restaurants on the periphery let you enjoy the view of the statue of San Martín in the center. ⊠ *Between Jr. de la Union and Jr. Carabaya, El Centro.*

⓯ Santuario de Santa Rosa de Lima. Inside the 17th-century Sanctuary of St. Rose, the tiny adobe cell that was her hermitage keeps alive the memory of the region's first saint. Here you'll find a well where every August 30 thousands of the faithful leave notes requesting that she hear their prayers. In the church next door is the Museo Etnográfico, where exhibits detail the lives of Peru's jungle peoples. ⊠ *Jr. Tacna and Conde de Superunda, El Centro* ☎ *01/425–0143* ☞ *Free* ⊗ *Tues.–Sun. 9–1 and 3 to 6.*

Rímac

In the beginning of the 17th century, the neighborhoods around the Plaza de Armas were bursting at the seams. The construction of the Puente de Piedra, which literally means "Stone Bridge," meant people were soon streaming over the Río Rímac. Among those who crossed the river were members of the upper classes who saw the newly christened Rímac as the perfect place to construct their mansions. It wasn't long before there were tree-lined promenades like the Alameda de los Descalzos and aquatic gardens like the Paseo de las Aguas. The neighborhood has fallen on hard times, but the faded facades are among the loveliest in the city.

a good tour

Like thousands of other people each day, you'll probably reach Rímac by crossing the historic **Puente de Piedra** ㉑ ▶. A few blocks north of the bridge is a strip of green called the **Alameda de los Descalzos** ㉒. You'll notice small churches like the Iglesia de Nuestro Señora de Patrocinio along on either side. At the far end of the alameda is a massive monastery called the **Convento de los Descalzos** ㉓.

As you head south, you'll probably notice another narrow park to the east. The Paseo de las Aguas, commissioned in 1770, is guarded at one end by a graceful arcade. The park, once a popular place for an evening promenade, has been badly neglected. A few blocks south of the Paseo de las Aguas is the city's bull ring, the **Plaza de Acho** ㉔. If you can't make it to a bullfight, get a peek inside the massive structure by visiting the adjacent **Museo Taurino** ㉕. Should you wish to get a bird's-eye view of the Plaza de Acho, as well as the rest of Rímac, hop in a taxi and head to the top of **Cerro San Cristóbal** ㉖.

TIMING & PRECAUTIONS

A tour of the sights won't take more than an hour or two, but know that Rímac is not a place where you want to walk; don't let that stop you from visiting, however. The best way to see the neighborhood is by taxi; hire one in the Plaza de Armas. Any driver will be happy to wait as you explore sights like the Convento de los Descalzos. Negotiate a price in advance.

What to See

㉒ **Alameda de los Descalzos.** The tree-lined Promenade of the Discalced Brothers, a reference to the monks at the nearby monastery, was constructed in 1610. A dozen marble statues representing the signs of the zodiac were added in 1858. On sunny afternoons ice-cream vendors blow little whistles as they pass. ⊠ *Northern end of Jr. Chiclayo, Rímac.*

㉖ **Cerro San Cristóbal.** Rising over the northeastern edge of Rímac is this massive hill, recognizable from the cross at its peak that is a replica of the one placed there by Pizarro. If the air is clear—a rarity in Lima—you'll see most of the city spread out below. It's not so easy to get here, but many tour companies include a visit here on their itineraries. ⊠ *Calle San Cristóbal, Rímac.*

㉓ **Convento de los Descalzos.** The rose-colored Monastery of the Discalced Brothers has been converted into a fascinating repository of colonial-era religious art. Room after room of this maze-like structure is filled with paintings dating back to the 16th century. There are four cloisters and two chapels, so it's easy to get lost here—in fact, it's practically guaranteed. A highlight is the Capilla de la Virgen Carmen, entered through a doorway decorated to resemble a bright blue Baroque church. Inside is an altar that gleams with gold leaf. The kitchen still contains antique wine-making equipment, and the pharmacy is filled with glass-stoppered bottles of unidentifiable liquids. English-speaking guides are available. ⊠ *Northern end of the Alameda de los Descalzos, Rímac* ☎ *01/481–0441* ☜ *S/5* ⊙ *Tues.–Sun. 10–6.*

㉕ Museo Taurino. Stuffed heads of several bulls stare down at you from the walls of the tiny Museum of Bullfighting. There are plenty of examples of the colorful costumes worn by the matadors, letting you see how styles have changed over the years. Perhaps most interesting are the posters from around the world. An 1899 advertisement from Barcelona shows women attending a bullfight in all their frills and finery. If there is no one around, the guard will let you see the Plaza de Acho. ⊠ *Jr. Hualgayoc 332, Rímac* ☎ *01/482–3360* ☜ *S/5* ⊙ *Tues.–Sun. 10–6.*

㉔ Plaza de Acho. Up until 1766, bullfights were held in the Plaza de Armas. They were moved across the river to this structure, which at the time was the largest bull ring in the world. It was originally octagonal, but in 1946 it was given its current circular shape. Matches were originally held on Sundays, but church leaders complained that attendance at services was getting sparse. ⊠ *Jr. Hualgayoc 332, Rímac* ☎ *01/481–1467* ☜ *S/5* ⊙ *Tues.–Sun. 10–6.*

▶ **㉑ Puente de Piedra.** Across the nearly dry Río Rímac is this 17th-century stone bridge, whose builders strengthened their mortar with thousands of egg whites. From the bridge is a nice view of the Palacio de Gobierno and other grand structures along the river's edge. ⊠ *Northern end of Jr. de la Union.*

San Isidro

Many frequent visitors to Lima find themselves drawn to the residential neighborhood of San Isidro. Like nearby Miraflores, it has plenty of boutiques selling designer goods, bars serving up the latest cocktails, and restaurants dishing out cuisine from around the world. What it lacks is the hustle and bustle. While strolling through Parque El Olívar you might be shocked to realize that there's not a single car in sight.

a good tour

Start in **Parque El Olívar** ㉗▶, a swath of green that runs through the center of San Isidro. Head north along any of the paths and you'll soon find yourself on Pancho Fierro, a block-long strip of cafés and restaurants. At the end you'll catch sight of the steeple crowning the Iglesia de la Virgen del Pilar. Go west on Avenida Victor A. Belaunde, then south on Avenida El Rosario. Soon you'll catch sight of the perfectly preserved pyramid that forms the centerpiece of the **Huaca Huallamarca** ㉘. Spend an hour or so clambering around the ruins, then continue south on Avenida El Rosario to Avenida El Golf, where you'll head west. After five blocks you'll reach the **Country Club Lima Hotel** ㉙, a lovely reminder of the city's glittering past. Stop for lunch here or double back to Parque El Olívar for an impromptu picnic.

TIMING &   Unless you have your own wheels, the best way to travel between San
PRECAUTIONS   Isidro's widely dispersed attractions is by taxi. Taking things at a leisurely
pace, this tour will take a few hours.

What to See

㉙ **Country Club Lima Hotel.** Two magnificent palms stand guard at the entrance to this 1927 hotel, widely regarded as the most elegant hotel in the city. If you're here in the afternoon, you might want to stop by for the English-style tea. ⊠ *Los Eucaliptos 590, San Isidro* ☎ *01/211–9000.*

㉘ **Huaca Huallamarca.** The sight of this flat-topped temple catches many people off guard. The structure, painstakingly restored on the front side, certainly seems out of place among the neighborhood's towering hotels and apartment buildings. The upper platform affords some nice views of San Isidro. There's a small museum with displays of objects found at the site, including several mummies. ⊠ *Av. El Rosario and Av. Nicolás de Rivera, San Isidro* ☎ *01/224–4124* 🎟 *S/5* ◷ *Tues.–Sun 9–5.*

▶ ㉗ **Parque El Olívar.** This was once an olive grove, so it's no surprise that you'll find an old olive press in this pretty park. The gnarled old trees, some more than a century old, still bear fruit. Yellow and red irises line the walkways, adding a splash of color. ⊠ *East of Av. La República, San Isidro.*

Miraflores

The seaside suburb of Miraflores has become the city's main destination for tourists, and it's easy to see why. Next to the relentless right angles of El Centro, the fan-like diagonals extending out from Ovalo José Pardo are a relief. For a complete change of place, wander through the neighborhood's flower-filled parks or along the cliffs overlooking the ocean. But Miraflores is also the city's cultural hub, which means there are plenty of boutiques, galleries, and museums, as well as bars, cafés, and restaurants. Some people who find themselves in Lima for a short time never leave this little haven.

a good tour

Any tour of Miraflores begins in **Parque Miraflores** ㉚ ▶, which sits like a slice of pie between Avenida José Larco and Avenida Diagonal. On the eastern side is the Parroquia Virgen Milagrosa, the neighborhood's largest church. The colonial-style building next door is the Municipalidad de Miraflores, where most governmental business takes place. Where you go next depends on your areas of interest. If you don't have time to venture outside the city to archaeological sites such as Pachacámac, head east along Avenida José Pardo then north on Miguel Grau to the towering temple of **Huaca Pucllana** ㉛. Continue east on Avenida José Pardo, then north on Avenida Santa Cruz to the **Museo Amano** ㉜. This tiny museum has one of the city's best collections of ancient artifacts.

More interested in shopping? Head south along Avenida José Larco, where you'll find many interesting shops. If antiques are your passion, take a detour a few blocks east to Avenida La Paz. At the tip of Avenida José Larco you'll find Larcomar, one of the city's best shopping centers. Cool off here with a pisco sour as you enjoy the ocean views. If you have romance on your mind, head south along Avenida Diagonal—also known as Avenida Oscar Benevidas—to reach **Parque del Amor** ③. You won't be alone, as this waterfront park attracts young lovers all day. If it's too crowded for your taste, stroll east to **El Faro de la Marina** ③, a lovely little lighthouse that dates back to the beginning of the last century.

TIMING & Good times to stroll Miraflores are mid-morning, when the heat is not
PRECAUTIONS yet overbearing, or mid-afternoon, when you can escape the sun by ducking into a bar or café. If shopping is your goal, arrive after sunset when things have cooled down. All the stores along Avenida José Larco stay open for early-evening window shoppers. About a half hour of walking will lead you to the ocean, where you'll want to spend another hour or so strolling along the cliff.

Miraflores is a very safe neighborhood, but keep your wits about you in the markets and parks. Pickpockets sometimes target tourists distracted by a street performer or a good bargain.

What to See

③ **El Faro de la Marina.** Constructed in 1900, this little lighthouse has steered ships away from the coast for more than a century. The classically designed tower is still in use today. ⊠ *Malecón Cisneros and Madrid, Miraflores.*

③ **Huaca Pucllana.** Rising out of a nondescript residential neighborhood is this mud-brick pyramid. The pre-Inca *huaca,* or temple, dates back to at least the 4th century. Archaeologists are still working on the site, and are usually happy to share their discoveries about the people who lived in this area hundreds of years before the Inca. A tiny museum highlights some of their recent finds. Knowledgeable guides are available in Spanish and English. ⊠ *Av. Larco Herrera at Elías Aguirre, Miraflores* ☎ *01/445–8695* ✒ *Free* ☉ *Daily 9–5.*

③ **Museo Amano.** Although it consists of only two rooms, this museum packs a lot into a small space. The private collection of pre-Columbian artifacts includes one of the best displays of ceramics in the city. Imaginative displays reveal how cultures in the northern part of the region focused on sculptural images, while those in the south used vivid colors. In between, around present-day Lima, the styles merged. A second room holds an impressive number of weavings, including examples from the Chancay people, who lived in the north between 1000 and 1500. Some of their work is so delicate that it resembles the finest lace. Call ahead, as you need an appointment to join one of the Spanish-language tours. ⊠ *Retiro 160, Miraflores* ☎ *01/441–2909* ✒ *Free* ☉ *Weekdays; by appointment only.*

③ **Parque del Amor.** You might think you're in Barcelona when you stroll through this pretty park. Like Antonio Gaudí's Parque Güell, the park that provided the inspiration for this one, the benches are decorated with broken pieces of tile. Here, however, they spell out silly romantic sayings like *Amor es como luz* ("Love is like light"). The centerpiece is a controversial statue of two lovers locked in a rather lewd embrace. ⊠ *Av. Diagonal, Miraflores.*

▶ ㉚ **Parque Miraflores.** What locals call Parque Miraflores is actually two parks. The smaller section is shady Parque Central, where you'll find frequent open-air concerts. Shoeshine boys will ask whether you need a *lustre* when you stop to listen to the music. The honking noise you hear is probably the ice-cream vendors that patrol the park on bright yellow bicycles. A friendly tourist information kiosk sits on the south side. Across a pedestrian street always full of local artists showing off their latest works is Parque Kennedy, where the babble from a lively crafts market fills the air each evening. A few sidewalk cafés are found on the eastern edge. ⊠ *Between Av. José Larco and Av. Diagonal, Miraflores.*

Barranco

With a bohemian feel found nowhere else in the city, Barranco is a magnet for young people, who come to carouse in its bars and cafés. A bit sleepy during the day, the neighborhood comes to life around sunset when artists start hawking their wares and its central square and bars begin filling with people ready to party. Founded toward the end of the 19th century, Barranco was where wealthy Limeños built their summer residences. The weather proved so irresistible that many eventually constructed huge mansions on the cliffs above the sea. Many of these have fallen into disrepair, but little by little they are being renovated into funky restaurants and hotels.

a good walk

To get your bearings, start in **Parque Municipal** ㉟▶, one of the prettiest parks in the city. To the south, the brick-red building with the tower is the Biblioteca Municipal, or Municipal Library. Stop by the tourist office on the ground floor to pick up a map of the neighborhood. To the north is the parish church called La Santisima Cruz. Across Avenida Pedro de Osma is a wonderful little museum called the **Museo-Galería Arte Popular de Ayacucho** ㊱. Continue down Avenida Pedro de Osma for about three blocks to the **Museo Pedro de Osma** ㊲. Backtrack to Parque Municipal, then head east to is Lima's own Bridge of Sighs, the **Puente de los Suspiros** ㊳. Directly below is the Bajada de Baños, lined with wonderful old houses. Head down this cobblestone street and soon you'll find yourself walking in the waves at Playa Barranquito. If it's late afternoon, you might want to watch the sunset from the deck of the elegant Costa Verde.

TIMING & PRECAUTIONS All the major sights in Barranco are within a block or two of Parque Municipal. Depending on how long you linger, the walk should take no more than a few hours. Don't walk down deserted streets, especially at night.

What to See

㊱ **Museo-Galería Arte Popular de Ayacucho.** Its unassuming facade makes it easy to miss this little gem. Inside you'll find one of the country's best collections of folk art. One especially interesting exhibit in the bright, airy gallery is an explanation of *cajones San Marcos,* the boxlike portable altars that priests once carried as they moved from village to village. Peasants began to make their own, placing scenes of local life inside. These dioramas, ranging in size from less than an inch to more than a foot wide, are still made today. ⊠ *Av. Pedro de Osma 423, Barranco* ☎ *01/ 247–0599* ◻ *Free* ☉ *Tues.–Sat. 9–6.*

★ 37 **Museo Pedro de Osma.** If there were not one piece of art hanging inside this museum, it would still be worth the trip to see the century-old mansion that houses it. The mansard-roofed structure—with inlaid wood floors, delicately painted ceilings, and breathtaking stained-glass windows in every room—was the home of a wealthy collector of religious art. The best of his collection is now permanently on display. The finest of the paintings, the 18th-century *Virgen de Pomato,* represents the earth, with her mountain-shape cloak covered with garlands of corn. The former dining room, in a separate building, contains some fine pieces of silver, including a lamb-shape incense holder with shining ruby eyes. ✉ *Av. Pedro de Osma 423, Barranco* ☎ *01/467–0141* 🎫 *S/10* ⏲ *Tues.–Sun. 10–1:30 and 2:30–6.*

35 **Parque Municipal.** Elegant swirls of colorful blooms make this park stand out from others in Lima. Here you'll find locals relaxing on the benches, their children playing nearby. At about 6 PM every evening you'll find artists who live in the nearby streets showing off their latest works. ✉ *Between Av. Pedro de Osma and Av. Grau, Barranco.*

★ 38 **Puente de los Suspiros.** The romantically named Bridge of Sighs is a lovely wooden walkway shaded with flowering trees. You won't have to wait long to see couples walking hand in hand. The bridge crosses over the Bajada de Baños, a cobblestone walkway that leads to Playa Barranquito. On the far side is La Ermita, a lovely little chapel painted a dazzling shade of red. ✉ *East of Parque Municipal, Barranco.*

Pueblo Libre

You may find yourself longing to linger in Pueblo Libre, which manages to retain a sense of calm not found elsewhere in the capital. Instead of hurrying past, residents often pause to chat with friends. This neighborhood northwest of San Isidro has two of the city's finest museums, the Museo Nacional de Antropología, Arqueología, e Historia del Perú and the Museo Arqueológico Rafael Larco Herrera.

What to See

39 Fodor'sChoice ★ **Museo Nacional de Antropología, Arqueología, e Historia del Perú.** The country's most extensive collection of pre-Columbian artifacts can be found at this sprawling museum. Beginning with 8,000-year-old stone tools, Peru's history comes to life through the sleek granite obelisks of the Chavín culture, the intricate weavings of Paraca peoples, and the colorful ceramics of the Moche, Chimú, and Inca civilizations. Fascinating are a pair of mummies from the Nazca region that are thought to be more than 2,500 years old; they were so well preserved that you can still see the grim expressions on their faces. Not all the exhibits are labeled in English, so you might want to hire a guide to negotiate your way around the museum's twin courtyards. ✉ *Plaza Bolívar, Pueblo Libre* ☎ *01/463–5070* 🎫 *S/10* ⏲ *Daily 9–5.*

40 Fodor'sChoice ★ **Museo Arqueológico Rafael Larco Herrera.** Fuchsia bougainvillea tumbles over the white walls surrounding Museo Arqueológico Rafael Larco Herrera, home of the world's largest private collection of pre-Columbian art. The oldest pieces here are crude vessels dating back several thou-

sand years. Most intriguing are the thousands of ceramic "portrait heads" crafted more than a millennium ago. Some owners commissioned more than one, allowing you to see how they changed over the course of their lives. The famous *sala erótica* reveals that these ancient artists were surprisingly uninhibited. Everyday objects are adorned with images that are frankly sexual and frequently humorous. As this gallery is across the garden from the rest of the museum, you'll be able to distance the kids from it if necessary. ⊠ *Av. Bolívar 1515, Pueblo Libre* 🕾 *01/461–1835* 🖃 *S/20* ⊘ *Mon.–Sat. 9–6, Sun. 9–1.*

Elsewhere in Lima

A few of Lima's most interesting museums are in outlying neighborhoods such as Monterrico and San Borja. The most convenient way to reach them is a quick taxi ride.

What to See

41 Museo de la Nación. If you know little about the history of Peru, a visit to this fortress-like museum is likely to leave you overwhelmed. The number of cultures tracked over the centuries makes it easy to confuse the Chimú, the Chincha, and the Chachapoyas. The three floors of artifacts end up seeming repetitious. The museum is more manageable if you have a specific interest, say, if you're planning a trip north to Chiclayo and you want learn more about the Moche people. Except for a pair of scale models of Machu Picchu, the pair of rooms dedicated to the Inca is disappointing. ⊠ *Av. Javier Prado Este 2465, San Borja* 🕾 *01/476–9878* 🖃 *S/6* ⊘ *Tues.–Sun. 9–5.*

42 Museo de Oro. All that glitters is not gold at this extremely popular museum. There's plenty of silver and other precious metals in this collection of Inca and pre-Inca treasures. When you see examples of how gold was used in these societies—from a mantle made of postage-stamp-sized pieces worn by a Lambayeque priest to an intricately designed sheet that once decorated an entire wall of the Chimú capital of Chán Chán—you can begin to imagine the opulence of these ancient cities. The museum has other interesting items, including a child's poncho of yellow feathers and a skull with a full set of pink quartz teeth. Upstairs are military uniforms and weapons. None of the displays are particularly well marked, either in English or Spanish, so you might want to see the museum as part of a city tour; it's a pretty good deal, as you'll save the cost of a taxi. At any rate, be prepared to pay one of the highest admissions of any of South America's museums. ⊠ *Alonso de Molina 1100, Monterrico* 🕾 *01/345–1271* 🖃 *S/30* ⊘ *Daily 11:30–7.*

FodorsChoice
★

Where to Stay & Eat

There's no need to get dressed for dinner in the capital. The heat and humidity dictate a casual dress code at all but the top restaurants. You will, however, get a few odd looks if you show up in shorts or with a baseball cap. Reservations are required if you hope for a table at a popular restaurant in Miraflores or San Isidro, especially on the weekend. Otherwise, you can simply show up at most places and be seated immediately. You may have to wait a few minutes at lunch if you have picked a place that is popular with business executives. Eating out in Lima need not cost a lot. One of the best deals is lunch in any of the hundreds of storefront restaurants scattered around the city. For a few bucks you get soup, a main dish, and even a dessert. How to pick among these no-name establishments? Just look for a crowd.

Lima isn't lacking in terms of lodging—you can't go far before you see the flurry of flags above a doorway indicating that international travelers are welcome. There are plenty of low-cost lodgings, but they are not clustered together as in many other cities. Budget hotels and most others are on quiet streets in the mostly residential neighborhoods of Miraflores, San Isidro, and Barranco. These areas are safe and secure, so you don't have to worry about taking a stroll during the day. Because many streets are deserted after dark, it's usually better to take a taxi at night. Travelers looking for something a little different should look at Barranco, which has a bohemian flavor. There are no big resorts here, just small hotels with a funky flavor. All of these neighborhoods are linked to El Centro by the Paseo de la República, so getting to the major sights is a snap.

El Centro

★ **$–$$** ✕ **L'eau Vive.** Calling to mind *The Sound of Music*, a group of nuns sings "Ave Maria" every night at this elegant eatery. You just might join them, as the French fare prepared by the holy sisters is simply heavenly. Trout baked in cognac is but one of the many dishes that bring locals back again and again. In a beautifully restored mansion directly across from Palacio Torre Tagle, the restaurant is worth a visit just for a peek inside the centuries-old rooms. The nuns, members of a French order, run the place as a charity, so all profits are given to the poor. ⊠ *Ucayali 370, El Centro* ☎ *01/427–5612* ▤ *AE, MC, V* ⊘ *Closed Sun.*

★ **¢–$** ✕ **Lima de Antaño.** Tucked into the courtyard of a beautiful colonial-era building, this is one of the prettiest restaurants in the historic district. Tables with chocolate-colored umbrellas are set beneath flower-covered colonnades. The food, creative takes on old recipes, is just as appealing. Start with a spinach salad tossed with bacon, walnuts, and slices of apples, then move on to roast pork with apple sauce made from scratch. For something special, order the *paríhuela*, a tasty seafood soup. The staff is eager to please, sometimes even running from the kitchen to deliver a dish while it's still hot. ⊠ *Jr. Ucayali 332, El Centro* ☎ *01/426–2372* ⊘ *Closed Sun. No dinner* ▤ *AE, DC, MC, V.*

$$$$ ▦ **Sheraton Lima Hotel & Casino.** The country's largest casino can be found in the lobby of downtown's most distinguished hotel. You might call it a landmark, except for the fact that its concrete facade makes it fade into the background. Perfectly serviceable rooms have subdued colors and surround an open atrium. This is a good choice for business travelers, as it has eight large meeting rooms and a convention center. Tourists appreciate that it's within walking distance of the city's historical district. The hotel is near the expressway, so it's also a short drive to San Isidro and Miraflores. ⊠ *Paseo de la República 170, El Centro* ☎ *01/315–5024* ▤ *01/315–5015* ☞ *438 rooms, 21 suites* ♨ *3 restaurants, coffee shop, bar, business services* ▤ *AE, DC, MC, V.*

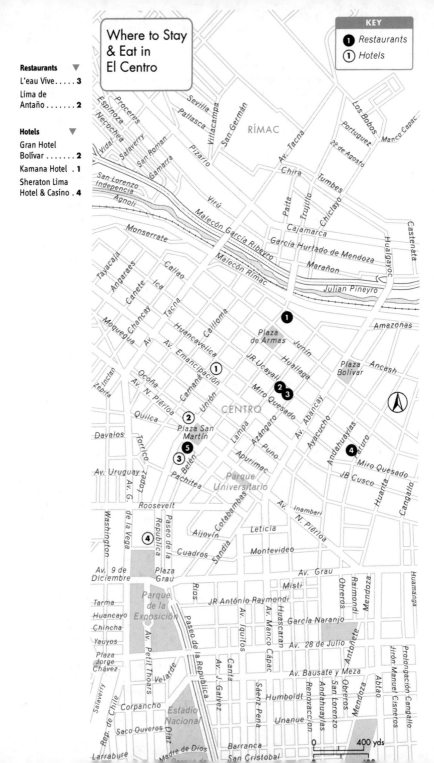

Where to Stay & Eat in El Centro

KEY
❶ Restaurants
① Hotels

★ **\$\$** 🖼 **Gran Hotel Bolívar.** Tastes may have changed since it was built in 1924, but this grand dame retains the sumptuousness of the days when guests included Ernest Hemingway. As you enter the marble-columned rotunda, your eyes are drawn upward to the magnificent stained-glass dome. Off to one side is the bar, which remains as popular as ever. The tables on the terrace are the perfect place to enjoy the best pisco sours in town. A grand staircase sweeps you up to the rooms, which retain lovely touches like parquet floors. Pull back the curtains for an unforgettable view of Plaza San Martín. ⊠ *Jr. de la Unión 958, El Centro* ☎ *01/ 619–7171* 🖷 *01/428–7674* ⊕ *www.granhotelbolivarperu.com* ⇥ *272 rooms, 5 suites* ⚬ *2 restaurants, bar* ▤ *AE, DC, MC, V.*

\$ 🖼 **Kamana Hotel.** Less than three blocks from the Plaza de Armas, this hotel puts you right in the middle of things. All the sights in downtown are a short walk away. The best part is that you don't have to pay a lot for this prime spot. Rooms are quite comfortable, and the locally made textiles make each feel a little different. Although rooms facing the street are sunnier, ask for an inside room if traffic noise bothers you. The improbably named café, Mr. Koala, specializes in Italian fare. ⊠ *Jr. Camaná 547, El Centro* ☎ *01/426–7204* 🖷 *01/426–0790* ⊕ *www. hotelkamana.com* ⇥ *44 rooms* ⚬ *Café, bar* ▤ *AE, DC, MC, V* ⲓ⚬ⲓ *CP.*

Miraflores

\$\$\$–\$\$\$\$ ✕ **El Rincón Gaucho.** The cowhides on the floors and the photos of prize heifers on the walls don't let you forget that this is the place for steaks. Even the menus are made of hand-tooled leather. The Argentine beef, always sliced to order, is on display just inside the front door. The best bet for the indecisive is the *parrillada,* a mixed grill of steaks, kidneys, livers, pork chops, chicken legs, and blood pudding. The order for two will satisfy three or four people. Although the restaurant overlooks the ocean, only a handful of tables have a view. ⊠ *Av. Armendariz 580, Miraflores* ☎ *01/447–4778* ▤ *AE, DC, MC, V.*

\$\$–\$\$\$\$ ✕ **Astrid y Gaston.** You can't help but watch the kitchen door at this el-
Fodor'sChoice egant restaurant, as each dish the waiters carry out is a work of art. Take
★ the eye-catching *pato asado con mil especies* (roast duck with 1,000 spices). The honey-brown breast is accompanied by a steamed pear and a pepper bubbling over with basil risotto. Other dishes, like the pasta with squid and artichokes, are just as astonishing. Make sure to peruse the wine list, one of the best in town. In a colonial-style building on a quiet street, the restaurant itself is lovely, with pumpkin-colored walls covered with original artwork. ⊠ *Cantuarias 175, Miraflores* ☎ *01/444– 1496* ▤ *AE, MC, V.*

★ **\$\$–\$\$\$** ✕ **Huaca Pucllana.** You feel like a part of history at this beautiful restaurant, which faces the ruins of a 1,500-year-old pyramid. Excavations are ongoing, so you can watch archaeologists at work as you enjoy the breezes on the covered terrace. Rough-hewn columns hold aloft the dining room's soaring ceiling. This is *novo andino* cuisine, which puts a new spin on old recipes. Yellow peppers stuffed with shrimp are a great way to start, while grilled scallops tossed with fried potatoes and covered with a spicy chili sauce are a work of art. Wash it all down with one of many pisco preparations. ⊠ *Av. General Borgoña, 2 blocks*

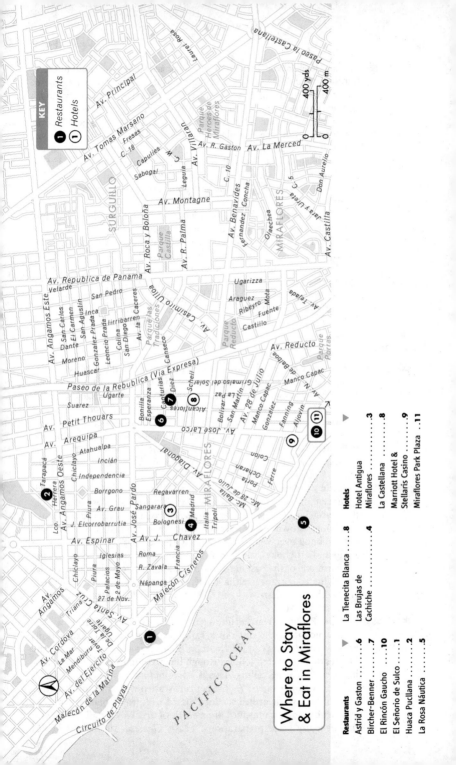

Where to Stay & Eat in Miraflores

KEY
- **1** Restaurants
- **①** Hotels

Restaurants
- Astrid y Gaston 6
- Bircher-Benner 7
- El Rincón Gaucho 10
- El Señorío de Sulco 1
- Huaca Pucllana 2
- La Rosa Náutica 5
- La Tienecita Blanca 8
- Las Brujas de Cachiche 4

Hotels
- Hotel Antigua Miraflores 3
- La Castellana 8
- Marriott Hotel & Stellaris Casino 9
- Miraflores Park Plaza ...11

north of Av. Angamos Oeste, Miraflores ☎ *01/445–4042* ⚞ *Reservations essential* 🍴 *AE, DC, MC, V.*

$–$$$ ✕ **La Rosa Náutica.** One of the most recognizable landmarks in Miraflores, La Rosa Náutica is at the end of a prominent pier. The blue slate roof of the rambling Victorian-style building is unmistakable. Take a seat in the gazebo-like dining room, where you'll have a view of the entire coast. Signature dishes include grilled scallops topped with a hearty cheese, but you might not be able to resist the succulent sea bass or the sole. The chef will prepare your selection *a su gusta.* For dessert, try the *crepes suchard* filled with ice cream and topped with hot fudge. ✉ *Espigón 4, Miraflores* ☎ *01/447–0057* 🍴 *AE, DC, MC, V.*

$–$$$ ✕ **El Señorío de Sulco.** It's no surprise that the food here is so good when you learn that owner Isabel Alvarez authored several cookbooks. The antique cooking vessels hanging on the walls reveal her passion for Peruvian cuisine. Start with *chupe de camerones,* a hearty soup combining shrimp and potatoes, then move on to *arroz con pato,* duck stewed in dark beer and seasoned with coriander. For dessert there's the meringue-topped *suspiro de limeña,* which literally means "sigh of a lady of Lima." Arrive early to watch the sun set over the ocean. ✉ *Malecón Cisneros 1470, Miraflores* ☎ *01/441–0389* 🍴 *AE, DC, MC, V* ⚞ *Reservations essential* ✆ *No dinner Sun.*

$–$$$ ✕ **Las Brujas de Cachiche.** Although the name conjures up a haunted house, The Witches of Cachiche is actually a modern space with huge windows, soaring ceilings, and lots of interesting modern art. The magic here is the cooking, which draws on Peru's traditional cuisines. Don't expect dishes like baby goat roasted with herbs to be just as they were handed down from *abuela,* as the chef often adds interesting touches from other cultures. The lunch buffet is a favorite of local business executives. The wine list offers several of the top South American vintages. ✉ *Bolognesi 460, Miraflores* ☎ *01/444–5310* 🍴 *AE, DC, MC, V* ⚞ *Reservations essential* ✆ *No dinner Sun.*

★ ¢–$ ✕ **Bircher-Benner.** In a colonial-style house painted a very appropriate shade of green, this vegetarian eatery is always packed. The food—like the fish-free cebiche made with mushrooms and sweet potatoes—is just that tasty. Peruvian dishes such as lomo saltado are expertly prepared. The menu has pages of fresh fruit salads, including a few with unusual ingredients, such as figs. If you want to take home some of this goodness, there's a little grocery just inside the front door. ✉ *Av. Diez Canseco 487, Miraflores* ☎ *01/444–4250* 🍴 *AE, DC, MC, V.*

$$$$ 🏨 **Miraflores Park Plaza.** Surprisingly few of the city's hotels are near the ocean, which is why this hotel is in such demand. If you think the views from your room are breathtaking, just head up to the rooftop pool overlooking the entire coastline. Rooms have sitting areas that make them as big as suites, and computer connections and fax machines that make them perfect for business travelers. Better suited for couples are the suites, which have hot tubs strategically placed beside the beds. Don't miss the Dr. Jekyll and Mr. Hyde bar, which has a hidden mezzanine for romantic rendezvous. ✉ *Malecón de la Reserva 1035, Miraflores* ☎ *01/242–3000* 🖷 *01/242–3393* ⊕ *www.mira-park.com* ⚑ *64 rooms, 17 suites* ♨ *2 restaurants, 2 bars, business services* 🍴 *AE, MC, V.*

$$$$ 🏨 **Marriott Hotel & Stellaris Casino.** This isn't a hotel—it's a small city. Just about anything you long for, whether it's a chocolate-chip cookie or a pair of diamond earrings, can be had in the shops downstairs. If not, there's the Larcomar shopping center across the street. The views are spectacular from the glass tower, which forever altered the skyline of Miraflores when it opened at the turn of the millennium. On clear days the entire coastline is visible. The only disappointment is the rooms, which are luxuriously appointed but lack the slightest hint that you're in Peru. The Stellaris Casino, one of the city's most glittery, is a winner. ⊠ *Malecón de la Reserva 615, Miraflores* ☎ *01/217–7000* 🖶 *01/217–7002* ⊕ *www.marriotthotels.com* 🛏 *288 rooms, 12 suites* ♨ *2 restaurants, bar, piano bar, casino. business services* ⊟ *AE, DC, MC, V.*

★ $$ 🏨 **Hotel Antigua Miraflores.** In a salmon-colored mansion dating back more than a century, this elegantly appointed hotel is perhaps the city's loveliest lodging. Black-and-white marble floors greet you as you stroll through the antiques-filled lobby. Up the wooden staircase are guest rooms with hand-carved furniture. Those in front have more character, while those in the newer section curve around a graceful fountain. Known for its impeccable service, the hotel sees repeat business year after year. The original art that adorns the dining room is for sale, so you may want to take home a souvenir of your stay. ⊠ *Grau 350, Miraflores* ☎ *01/241–6116* 🖶 *01/241–6115* ⊕ *www.peru-hotel* 🛏 *15 rooms* ♨ *Restaurant, bar* ⊟ *AE, DC, MC, V.*

★ $ 🏨 **La Castellana.** A favorite for years, this exuberantly neoclassical structure resembles a small castle. The foyer, where wrought-iron lanterns cast a soft glow, is a taste of what is to come. Beyond are lovely touches like stained-glass windows and a towering turret. All the wood-shuttered rooms are lovely, but especially nice are No. 10, which overlooks the sunny courtyard, and No. 15, which has a private balcony facing the front. The friendly staff goes above and beyond the call of duty, even helping with things like airplane reservations. This inn remains immensely popular, so reservations should be made far in advance. ⊠ *Grimaldo del Solar 222, Miraflores* ☎ *01/444–3530* 🖶 *01/446–8030* ⊕ *www.hotel-lacastellana.com* 🛏 *29 rooms* ♨ *Restaurant, bar* ⊟ *AE, DC, MC, V.*

San Isidro

$–$$$ ✕ **Matsuei.** Chefs shout out a greeting as you enter the teak-floored dining room of this San Isidro standout. Widely considered the best Japanese restaurant in town, Matsuei specializes in sushi and sashimi. If that's not your thing, the menu offers pages of fish dishes that are broiled, steamed, and fried. The tasty *kushiyaki,* one of the specialties, is a broiled fillet with a ginger-flavored sauce. There is plenty for vegetarians. Japanese eggplant is grilled to perfection and served with a sweet sesame glaze in the *goma nasu.* The building is shaded by a cluster of slender trees. ⊠ *Manuel Bañon 260, San Isidro* ☎ *01/422–4323* ⊟ *AE, DC, MC, V.*

$–$$ ✕ **El Cartujo.** With a tree-shaded park at its doorstep, El Cartujo feels
FodorsChoice miles away from the busy streets of San Isidro. Sit outside under honey-
★ color canopies or in the dining room dominated by a painting of the obscure order of monks that gave the place its name. The salads are ex-

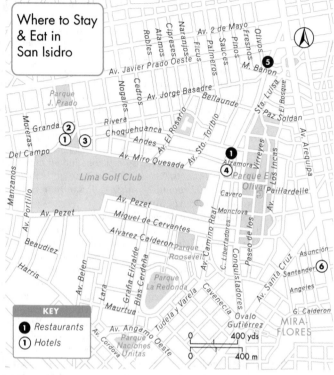

Where to Stay
& Eat in
San Isidro

KEY

❶ *Restaurants*

① *Hotels*

cellent; the *ensalada flamenco* has smoked salmon, plump olives, and buttons of caviar atop fresh greens. Save room for seafood, especially the sole stuffed with lobster or the sea bass topped with crab. There's a top-notch wine list, and the steward is happy to help you make the perfect selection. ⊠ *Calle Los Libertadores 108, San Isidro* ☎ *01/221–4962* ⚇ *Reservations essential* ☐ *AE, DC, MC, V.*

$$$$
Fodor'sChoice
★
🏨 **Country Club Lima Hotel.** Priceless paintings from the Museo Pedro de Osma hang in each room in this luxurious lodging. The hacienda-style hotel, dating from 1927, is itself a work of art. Just step into the lobby, where hand-painted tiles reflect the yellows and greens of the stained-glass ceiling. The air of refinement continues in the rooms, all of which are draped with fine fabrics. Many have private balconies that overlook the oval-shape pool or the well-tended gardens. Locals frequently come by for high tea in the atrium or traditional fare in the elegant restaurant. The outdoor terrace is perfect for romantic dinners. ⊠ *Los Eucaliptos 590, San Isidro* ☎ *01/211–9000* 🖷 *01/211–9002* 🛏 *75 rooms* ⚐ *Restaurant, business services* ☐ *AE, DC, MC, V.*

$$$$
🏨 **Libertador Hotel.** When you want to relax, this high-rise hotel knows how to accommodate you. The staff greets you in voices barely above a whisper as you stroll through the understated lobby. Although the hotel is in the heart of San Isidro's business district, the rooms are surprisingly

quiet. No bland furnishings here, as bright fabrics and original artwork make you doubt that this is a chain hotel. The top-floor restaurant, the Ostrich House, specializes in dishes made from that odd bird. The dining room has views of Club Lima Golf. ⊠ *Los Eucaliptos 550, San Isidro* ☎ *01/421–6666* 🖨 *01/442–3011* ⊕ *www.libertador.com.pe* 🖃 *53 rooms* ⚘ *2 restaurants, health club, bar, business services* ⊟ *AE, DC, MC, V.*

$$$$ ⊡ **Los Delfines.** It's not every day that a pair of dolphins greets you near the entrance of your hotel. Yaku and Wayra do just that in the lobby of this high-rise. Kids love to help feed them as their parents look on from the adjacent café. Although they're a bit on the small side, the rooms are bright and comfortably furnished, and many have sweeping views of the adjacent Club Lima Golf. Downstairs, the beautifully decorated Knossos restaurant serves up delicious Indian fare. ⊠ *Los Eucaliptos 555, San Isidro* ☎ *01/215–7000* 🖨 *01/215–7071* ⊕ *www.losdelfineshotel. com.pe* 🖃 *207 rooms, 24 suites* ⚘ *Restaurant, café, bar, casino, business services* ⊟ *AE, MC, V.*

★ $$$$ ⊡ **Sonesta Posada del Inca El Olívar.** Stretching along an old olive grove, this luminous hotel has one of the most relaxed settings in San Isidro. This is especially true as you avail yourself of the sundeck and pool on the top floor. Rooms are amply proportioned, especially those with private balconies overflowing with greenery. The clientele is mostly business travelers, so the rooms have computer connections and lots of space to spread out. Refined Italian cuisine is served at I Vitrali, where you're treated to a view of the park. Ichi Ban serves up a vast selection of sushi and sashimi. ⊠ *Pancho Fierro 194, San Isidro* ☎ *01/221–2121* 🖨 *01/221–2141* ⊕ *www.sonesta.com* 🖃 *134 rooms, 11 suites* ⚘ *2 restaurants, café, bar, business services* ⊟ *AE, DC, MC, V.*

★ $ ⊡ **Hotel San Blas.** The best deal in San Isidro—maybe in the entire city—is this little gem. Its price tag is below that of many budget hotels, while its amenities are equal to those of quite a few resorts. The bright, airy rooms are as big as suites and have niceties like modem connections and sound-proof windows. Jacuzzis turn the baths into spas. A well-equipped meeting room on the ground floor that accommodates 30 people opens out into a sunny patio. The café in the lobby is on call if you order up a midnight snack, even if it's three in the morning. ⊠ *Av. Arequipa 3940, San Isidro* ☎ *01/222-2601* 🖨 *01/222-0516* ⊕ *www.hotelsanblas.com. pe* 🖃 *30 rooms* ⚘ *Café, business center* ⊟ *AE, DC, MC, V.*

Nightlife & the Arts

Nightlife

Lima may not be the city that doesn't sleep, but it certainly can't be getting enough rest. Limeños love to go out on the town, as you'll notice on any Friday or Saturday night. Early in the evening they are clustered around movie theaters and concert halls, while late at night they are piling into taxis headed to the bars and clubs of Miraflores and Barranco. For more details on the city's cultural offerings, check newsstands on Fridays for the English-language *Lima Herald.* Ask at your hotel for a free copy of *Peru Guide,* an English-language monthly full of information on bars and clubs as well as galleries and performances. For the latest hot spots, peruse the Spanish-language *El Comercio.*

BARS When you're in Barranco, a pleasant place to start off the evening is **La Posada del Mirador** (⊠ Ermita 104 Barranco ☎ 01/477–9577). The bar has a second-story balcony that looks out to sea, making this a great place to watch the sunset. There's often a crowd at **Mochilero's** (⊠ Av. Pedro de Osma 135, Barranco ☎ 01/477–4506), in the hotel of the same name. Bands perform on the weekends. Miraflores lets you sample beers from around the world. If you're longing for a pint of Guinness, head to **Murphy's Irish Pub** (⊠ Schell 627 Miraflores ☎ 01/242–1212). The wood paneling and the well-worn dart board may convince you that you're in Ireland. If you prefer a good pilsner, try **Freiheit** (⊠ Lima 471, Miraflores ☎ 01/247–4630). The second-story establishment is a favorite among college students.

PEÑAS The most upmarket of the peñas is found in Barranco at **Manos Morenas** (⊠ Av. Pedro de Osma 409, Barranco ☎ 01/467–0421). Extravagantly costumed performers hardly seem to touch the ground as they re-create dances from around the region. The musicians, switching instruments half a dozen times during a song, are without equal. The place feels like a theme park, though, perhaps because of the long tables of picture-taking tourists. Vying for the tourist market is **La Candelaria** (⊠ Av. Bolognesi 292, Barranco ☎ 01/247–1314), which is immediately recognizable from the fiery torches flanking the front door. A series of small spaces leads to the main room, where the dancers have plenty of room to show off their steps. The facade may be dull, but the attitude is anything but at **De Rompe y Raja** (⊠ Jr. Manuel Segura 127, Barranco ☎ 01/247–3271). Slightly off the beaten path, this pená attracts mostly locals to its shows with *música negra*, a black variant of *música criolla*. In Miraflores, an older crowd heads to **Sachún** (⊠ Av. del Ejército 657, Miraflores ☎ 01/441–4465). The draw, it seems, are the sentimental favorites played by the band. **Zeñó Manué** (⊠ 2 de Mayo 598, Miraflores ☎ 01/444–9049) offers traditional folk shows most nights.

The Arts

GALLERIES Miraflores is full of art galleries that show the works of Peruvian and occasionally foreign artists. In the rear of the Municipalidad de Miraflores, the **Sala Luis Miró Quesada Garland** (⊠ Av. Larco Herrera and Calle Diez Canseco, Miraflores ☎ 01/444–0540) sponsors exhibits of sculpture, painting, and photography. **Trapecio** (⊠ Av. Larco Herrera 743, Miraflores ☎ 01/444–0842) shows works by contemporary Peruvian artists. In San Isidro, **Artco** (⊠ Calle Rouad and Paz Soldán, San Isidro ☎ 01/221–3579) sponsors cutting-edge art, sometimes involving different mediums such as painting and video.

MUSIC The Orquestra Sinfónica Nacional, ranked one of the best in Latin America, performs at the Museo de la Nación's **Auditoria Sinfónica** (⊠ Av. Javier Prado Este 2465, San Borja ☎ 01/476–9878). In the heart of Barranco, the **Centro Cultural Juan Parra del Riego** (⊠ Av. Pedro de Osma 135, Barranco ☎ 01/477–4506) sponsors performances by Latin American musicians. In the Municipalidad de Miraflores, the **Centro Cultural Ricardo Palma** (⊠ Av. Larco Herrera 770, Miraflores ☎ 01/446–3959), sponsors cultural events throughout the week, including films, poetry readings, and concerts. The **Instituto Cultural Peruano Norteamericano**

(✉ Av. Angamos Oeste and Av. Arequipa, Miraflores ☎ 01/446–0381) offers music ranging from jazz to classical to folk.

Shopping

On **Avenida La Paz** in Miraflores, crafts, jewelry, and antiques stores abound. The block-long, cobblestone, pedestrians-only street of **El Suche** has a wide variety of sweaters and crafts. Many upscale shops can also be found along **Avenida Benavides** and adjacent streets.

Lots of stores stock clothing made of alpaca, but one of the few to offer articles made from vicuña is **Alpaca 111** (✉ Av. Larco 671, Miraflores ☎ 01/447–1623 ✉ Larcomar Malecón de la Reserva and Av. José Larco, Miraflores ☎ 01/241–3484). This diminutive creature, distant cousin of the llama, produces the world's finest wool. It is fashioned into scarves, sweaters, and even knee-length coats. There are branches of the store in Hotel Los Delfines, Miraflores Park Hotel, and Sonesta Posada del Inca El Olívar. For beautiful pottery, head to **Antisuyo** (✉ Tacna 460, Miraflores ☎ 01/447–2557), which sells only traditional pieces from around the country. For one-of-a-kind pieces, **Coral Roja** (✉ Recavarren 269, Miraflores ☎ 01/447–2552) sells work made on the premises. The little red building is known for its original designs. The Brazilian firm **H. Stern** (✉ Museo de Oro Alonso de Molina 1100, Monterrico ☎ 01/345–1350) carries fine gold and silver jewelry with Peruvian designs. **Lanifico** (✉ Av. Alberto del Campo 285, San Isidro ☎ 01/264–3186) offers fine fabrics made from baby alpaca—wool from animals no older than two years old. For one-of-a-kind gifts, try **Migue** (✉ Av. La Paz 311, Miraflores ☎ 01/444—0333), where you'll find jewelers fashioning original pieces in gold and other precious metals.

Tiny *retablos* (boxes filled with scenes of village life) are among the eye-catching objects at **Raices Peru** (✉ Av. La Paz 588, Miraflores ☎ 01/447–7457) Inspired by Peru's proud past, Silvia Lawson has created a line of fine fabrics. The wonderful weaves at **Silvania Prints** (✉ Calle Diez Canseco 378, San Isidro ☎ 01/242–2871) are printed by hand on the finest cotton. Buy them already fashioned into everything from scarves to tablecloths.

Lima A to Z

AIRPORT

Aeropuerto Internacional Jorge Chávez is on the northwestern fringe of the city. A taxi to most places in the city should cost no more than $10. It is 10 km (6 mi) southeast and a 20-minute drive to El Centro, and a 30-minute drive to Miraflores and San Isidro.

🚩 Airport Information **Aeropuerto Internacional Jorge Chávez** ✉ Av. Faucett s/n ☎ 01/575-1712 international, 01/574-5529 domestic.

BUS TRAVEL

There's no central bus terminal in Lima. Buses generally depart for the northern regions along Avenida Alfredo Mendiola in San Martín de Porres. Buses to the southern regions line up along Avenida Carlos Zavala, while buses to the central part of the country can be found at Montevideo, Lima, and Nicolás Ayllon. Recommended bus companies in Lima include Cruz del Sur, Ormeño, and Tepsa.

🚍 Bus Information **Cruz del Sur** ✉ Jr. Quilca 531, El Centro ☎ 01/424-1005 or 01/424-0589. **Ormeño** ✉ Javier Prado Este 1059, San Isidro ☎ 01/472-1710. **Tepsa** ✉ Jr. Lampa 1337, El Centro ☎ 01/427-5642.

BUS TRAVEL WITHIN LIMA

Regular buses, the school-bus-size *micros,* and the van-size *combis,* offer frequent service. It is often difficult to tell where they are headed, so listen to the driver or ask before you board.

CAR RENTAL

Most rental agencies also offer the services of a driver, a good solution for those who want the freedom of a car without the hassle of driving on Lima's busy streets. The agencies below all have branches at Jorge Chávez International Airport that are open 24 hours.

🚗 Major Agencies **Avis** ✉ Av. Larco 1080, Miraflores ☎ 01/446-4533. **Budget** ✉ Moreyra 569, San Isidro ☎ 01/442-8703. **Hertz** ✉ Av. Cantuarias 160, Miraflores ☎ 01/447-2129. **National** ✉ Av. España 453, El Centro ☎ 01/433-3750.

CAR TRAVEL

Lima's main streets are in pretty good condition, but heavy congestion and the almost complete absence of traffic lights make driving a harrowing experience. Better to leave the hassle to a taxi driver. However, a car is a great way to see the sights outside the city. The highways surrounding the capital are reasonably well maintained. In the city, always park in a guarded lot. If you can't find one, hire someone who offers *"cuidar su carro"* ("to take care of your car"). Pay about S/5 when you return and find your car intact.

EMERGENCIES

🚨 Emergency Numbers **Fire** ☎ 116. **Police** ☎ 105. **Tourist Police** ☎ 01/225-8698 or 01/225-8699.

🏥 Hospital **Clinica Anglo-Americana** ✉ Av. Alfredo Salazar, San Isidro ☎ 01/221-3656. **Clinica Ricardo Palma** ✉ Av. Javier Pardo Este 1066, San Isidro ☎ 01/224-2224.
💊 Pharmacy **Farmacia Deza** ✉ Av. Conquistadores 144, San Isidro ☎ 01/441-5860. **Farmacia Fasa** ✉ Av. Benavides 487, Miraflores ☎ 01/475-7070 ✉ Av. Larco 129, Miraflores ☎ 01/619-0000. **InkaFarma** ✉ Av. Benavides 425, Miraflores ☎ 01/314-2020.

MAIL & SHIPPING

The Correo Central, the city's main post office, is in an incredibly ornate building just off the Plaza de Armas. It's open Monday through Saturday 8–8 and Sunday 9–1. There are also branches in Miraflores and San Isidro. It's best to send important packages from the Federal Express office in Miraflores or the DHL and UPS offices in San Isidro. DHL is open weekdays 8:30–1 and 2–9, Saturday 9–5, and Sunday 9–1. Federal Express is open weekdays 8:30–6. UPS is open weekdays 8–6:30.

📮 Post Offices **Centro** ✉ Av. Conde de Superunda, between Jr. de al Unión and Jr. Camaná ☎ 01/427-0370. **Miraflores** ✉ Av. Petit Thouars 5201 ☎ 01/445-0697. **San Isidro** ✉ Av. Libertadores 325 ☎ 01/422-0981.

🏢 Shipping Services **DHL** ✉ Calle Los Castaños 225, San Isidro ☎ 01/517-2500. **Federal Express** ✉ Martín Olaya 260, Miraflores ☎ 01/242-2280. **UPS** ✉ Av. Perez Aranibar 2107, San Isidro ☎ 01/264-0105.

MONEY MATTERS

Automatic teller machines have become ubiquitous in Lima. On Avenida José Pardo, the main commercial street in Miraflores, there's a bank on nearly every block. Banco Continental has branches all over Lima, but its ATMs accept only cards linked with Visa. Banco de Credito, Banco Santander, and Interbank accept all cards. Currency exchange offices include P&P, which has an office in Miraflores that is open weekdays 9:30–5. The company's downtown branch is also open Saturday 10–1. When exchanging money, you will usually be asked to show your passport.

🏢 Banks **Banco Continental** ✉ Av. Grau and Unión, Barranco ✉ Av. José Pardo and Jorge Chavez, Miraflores ✉ Av. Conquistadores and Conde de la Monclova, San Isidro. **Banco de Credito** ✉ Av. José Larco and Schell, Miraflores ✉ Av. José Pardo between Recavarren and Libertad, Miraflores. **Banco Santander** ✉ Carabaya and Ucayali, El Centro. **Interbank** ✉ Av. José Larco and Schell, Miraflores ✉ Jr. de la Unión and Huancavelica El Centro.

🏢 Currency Exchange **P&P** ✉ Av. Benavides 735, Miraflores ✉ Av. La Colmena 805, El Centro.

TAXIS

Locals warn you that hailing taxis on the street can be dangerous. In truth, robberies by cab drivers are rare. To be on the safe side, only use those taxis that are painted yellow and that have the driver's license prominently displayed. It's best to negotiate the fare before you get in. A journey between two adjacent neighborhoods should cost between S/4 and S/7, while longer trips should be about S/10. If you call a taxi, the price will be roughly double. Well-regarded companies include Taxi Metro, Taxi Seguro, and Taxi Móvil.

🏢 Taxi Companies **Taxi Metro** ☎ 01/437-3689. **Taxi Seguro** ☎ 01/438-7210. **Taxi Móvil** ☎ 01/422-6890.

TELEPHONES

Peruvian coins are used in public phones, but you can also make local or international calls with phone cards. Telefónica del Perú has branches throughout the city that sell phone cards. The main office is in El Centro near Plaza San Martín.

🏢 **Telefónica del Perú** ✉ Carabaya 933 El Centro ☎ 01/433-1616.

TOURS

Lima has many top tour operators with experienced English-speaking guides that can arrange local sightseeing as well as tours throughout the country. The most professional is Lima Tours, which offers tours of the city and surrounding area as well as the rest of the country. Other well-regarded companies include Condor Travel, Kinjyo Travel, Puma Tours, Setours, and Solmartour.

🏢 **Condor Travel** ✉ Av. Mayor Amando Blondet 249, San Isidro ☎ 01/615-3000. **Kinjyo Travel** ✉ Las Camelias 290, San Isidro ☎ 01/212-1111 ⊕ www.kinjyo.com.pe. **Lima Tours** ✉ Belén 1040, El Centro ☎ 01/619-6900 ⊕ www.limatours.com.pe. **Puma Tours**

✉ Bolognesi 147, Miraflores ☎ 01/441–1279 ⊕ www.pumatours.net. **Setours** ✉ Av. Comandante Espinar 229, Miraflores ☎ 01/446–9229. **Solmartour** ✉ Av. Grau 300, Miraflores ☎ 01/444–1313.

VISITOR INFORMATION

PromPerú, the national tourism organization, has English- and Spanish-language information for travelers. The two offices in San Isidro are open weekdays 9–6. An information booth at Jorge Chávez International Airport is open 24 hours. The most thorough information about Lima, as well as the rest of Peru, is available at South American Explorers. This nonprofit organization dispenses a wealth of information. You can also call ahead with questions, or just show up at the beautiful clubhouse in Miraflores and browse through the lending library or read through trip reports filed by members. It costs $50 to join, but you'll probably make up for that with discounts offered to members by hotels and tour operators.

🛈 **PromPerú** ✉ Calle 1 Oeste 50 13th floor, San Isidro ☎ 01/224–9355 ✉ Jorge Basadre 610, San Isidro ☎ 01/421–1627 ⊕ www.peru.org.pe. **South American Explorers** ✉ Calle Piura 135, Miraflores ☎ 01/445–3306 ⊕ www.saexplorers.org.

THE NORTH COAST

More than a thousand years ago, long before the Inca empire built Machu Picchu, civilizations flourished in the fertile river valleys of Peru's North Coast. Many of their carefully planned irrigation systems that turned the desert into productive agricultural land are still in use today. These early cultures are often referred to as the *Moche* or *Mochica*, a derivative of *Muchik*, an ancient language spoken on the North Coast.

The Spanish who settled these lands built their own cities—Trujillo, Chiclayo, and Lambayeque, among others—ignoring the spectacular agricultural and architectural achievements of earlier days. Although voracious *huaqueros*, or looters, have stolen many of the gold and silver treasures left in the ruins, archaeologists sifting through the sand still occasionally make unbelievable finds. The tomb of the Lord of Sipán, discovered intact in 1987, is the most famous example.

Trujillo

561 km (350 mi) northwest of Lima on the Pan-American Highway.

A lively metropolis that competes with Arequipa for the title of Peru's "Second City," Trujillo was founded in 1534. The Spanish named it in honor of conquistador Francisco Pizarro's hometown. More than any other city in Peru, Trujillo maintains much of its colonial charm, especially along Avenida España, which encircles the heart of the city. This thoroughfare replaced a 9-meter-high (30-foot-high) wall erected in 1687 to protect the city from pirates. A piece of the wall still stands at the corner of Estete and España. There are several Moche and Chimú archaeological sites in and around Trujillo, and the huge pyramids and ceremonial centers are some of the most impressive in all of northern Peru. Considered the cultural capital of Peru, the city is known for its many festivals, including an international ballet festival, a contemporary art biennial, and the *caballos de paso* (Peruvian pace horse) show. Consider coming to town for the Festival Internacional de la Primavera (International Spring Festival), held every year during the last week of September. Trujillo is also quite busy during the last week of January, when it holds the National Fiesta de La Marinera dance competition. These events provide glimpses of traditional *criollo* culture.

In the heart of the city is the broad **Plaza de Armas**, fronted by the 17th-century cathedral and surrounded by the *casonas* (colonial mansions) that are Trujillo's architectural glory. Locals say this is Peru's largest main plaza. In the center stands the Monument to Freedom, sculpted by the German sculptor Edmundo Moeller and unveiled in 1929.

Like most of the other restored colonial museums in Trujillo, **Casa Urquiaga** was saved by a bank whose offices now occupy part of the building. Visit this early 19th-century mansion on the Plaza de Armas, with its baroque patio and fine collection of pre-Colombian ceramics. The house was built in a neoclassical style and has lovely rococo furniture. ⊠ *Pizarro 446* ☎ *044/245–382* 💲 *Free* ☉ *Mon.–Sat. 9–1 and 5–7.*

Trujillo declared its independence from Spain on December 29, 1820, in the **Casa de la Emancipación**, which has an interesting scale model of Trujillo when it was a walled city. It is now owned by Banco Continental. There are rotating art exhibits here as well. ⊠ *Pizarro 610* ☎ *044/246–061* 💲 *Free* ☉ *Mon.–Sat. 9–1 and 5–7.*

The republican **Palacio Iturregui** is sometimes described as the most beautiful neoclassical home in South America. The mansion was built in 1842 by Juan Manuel Iturregui and has gorgeous Italian marble furnishings. It is now the private Club Central de Trujillo, and only the mansion's central plaza is accessible to visitors. ⊠ *Pizarro 688* 💲 *Free* ☉ *Weekdays 11–1 and 4–8.*

In this old colonial home is the **Museo de Arqueología,** with pottery and other artifacts recovered from tombs. You will find reproductions of the murals found at the Huaca de la Luna as well as some artifacts recovered from the site. The original house, called the Casa Risco, was built in the 17th century. ⊠ *Jr. Junín 682, at Jr. Ayacucho* ☎ *044/249–322* 💲 *S/5* ☉ *Mon. 9–2, Tues.–Fri. 9:30–1 and 3:30–7, weekends 9:30–4.*

Built in 1725, **Monasterio El Carmen** has valuable altarpieces and colonial art. ⊠ *Av. Colón at Av. Bolívar* 💲 *Free* ☉ *Museum Mon.–Sat. 9–1.*

A few artisan stalls and the town's old water distribution pump are nestled in the **Plazuela el Recreo,** a neat little square. ⊠ *Corner of Pizarro and Estete.*

⟳ The **Museo del Juguete,** or toy museum, has a large private collection of toys from all over the world. There are puppets and puzzles, as well as a large selection of pull-along toys. The toys from pre-Colombian Peru are especially interesting, as they give a seldom-seen view into the world of the ancient cultures that preceded the Inca. Regrettably, you can't play with any of the toys. ✉ *Independencia 713* ☎ *044/297–200* 💳 *S/4* 🕐 *Mon.–Sat. 10–6; closed Sun.*

Constructed of thick adobe and covered with white stucco, the **Casa del Mayorazgo de Facala** is a classic example of Trujillo colonial architecture. The open courtyard of this house dating from 1709 is surrounded by cedar columns and has a colonial carriage. Don't miss the Moorish-style carved-wood ceiling. ✉ *Pizarro 314* ☎ *044/256–600* 💳 *Free* 🕐 *Mon.–Sat. 9–1 and 5–7.*

In the northern sector of the city, the privately owned **Museo Cassinelli** is in, of all places, the basement of a gas station. Among the most spectacular objects in the 2,800-piece collection, which covers pre-Colombian ceramics that date from 1200 BC through the Inca period, are the Moche portrait vases. There are also whistling pots, which produce distinct notes that mimic bird calls. ✉ *Av. Nicolás de Piérola 607* ☎ *044/ 232–312* 💳 *S/5* 🕐 *Mon.–Sat. 9–1 and 3:30–6:30.*

Where to Stay & Eat

Fish dishes are ubiquitous in Trujillo. Ceviche made with fish or shellfish is extremely popular, as is *causa*, a cold casserole of mashed potatoes molded around a filling of fish, ají, and onions and topped with slices of hard-boiled egg. Tasty *cabrito al horno* (roast kid), *seco de cabrito* (stewed kid), and *shámbar*, a bean stew, are other local specialties.

★ **$–$$** ✕ **Las Bóvedas.** This quiet, elegant restaurant in the Hotel Libertador has a *bóveda*, or vaulted brick ceiling, and plant-filled wall niches. The house specialty is the local delicacy, shámbar, garnished with *canchita* (semipopped corn). ✉ *Independencia 485* ☎ *044/232–741* 🟰 *AE, DC, MC, V.*

★ **¢–$** ✕ **De Marco.** Right on the street, this noisy but cheery eatery, popular with locals and tourists for its excellent comida criolla and Italian dishes, has paneled walls with local artwork. Try the *tacu tacu*, a typical coastal dish of rice and beans, with seco de cabrito. Don't miss the homemade gelato. ✉ *Pizarro 725* ☎ *044/234–251* 🟰 *AE, DC, MC, V.*

¢–$ ✕ **El Mochica.** In a long, open hall with whitewashed walls and chandeliers, this traditional lunch spot is a satisfying stop—a typical meal starts with an industrial-size portion of spicy *ceviche de lenguado* (marinated sole), followed by rice smothered with *camarones* (shrimp) or *mariscos* (shellfish). ✉ *Bolívar 462* ☎ *044/224–247* 🟰 *AE, DC, MC, V.*

¢–$ ✕ **San Remo Restaurant.** Stained-glass windows greet you at this Italian ristoranti and pizzeria. The feel of provincial Italy runs throughout, with plates adorning the walls and a deer head at the entryway. The pasta-heavy menu also has meat and poultry dishes, as well as the town's best pizza. A decent wine list and good service burnish the evening. ✉ *Av. Húsares de Junín 450* ☎ *044/293–333* 🟰 *AE, DC, MC, V* 🕐 *No lunch.*

★ **$$–$$$** 🏨 **Hotel Libertador.** The former Hotel de Turistas on the Plaza de Armas has been splendidly renovated to retain its colonial elegance while adding modern amenities. The pool, surrounded by a garden filled with hummingbirds, is especially delightful. Rooms have artwork with pre-Colombian designs, locally tooled leather and wood furniture, and wrought-iron wall lamps. ✉ *Independencia 485* ☎ *044/232–*

741 or 800/537–8483 in U.S. 🖷 *044/235–641* ⊕ *www.libertador.
com.pe* ⇌ *73 rooms, 5 suites* ⌂ *Restaurant, café, room service, in-
room safes, minibars, cable TV, pool, gym, sauna, bar, laundry service, meeting rooms, free parking, some no-smoking rooms* ⊟ *AE, DC,
MC, V* ⦿ *BP.*

$$ 🖼 **El Gran Marques.** Minutes from the city center is this upscale busi-
ness hotel. A pool and lush gardens can be seen from most rooms. On
the roof you will find a mini-spa, sauna, and a small pool. Rooms have
soothing maroon carpets, wood furnishings, and paisley spreads. ⊠ *Díaz
de Cienfuegos 145, Urb. La Merced,* ☎ *044/249–366* 🖷 *044/249–161*
⊕ *www.elgranmarques.com* ⇌ *45 rooms, 5 suites* ⌂ *Restaurant, cafe-
teria, room service, minibars, cable TV, 2 pools, gym, hair salon, mas-
sage, sauna, spa, Ping-Pong, bar, laundry service, business services,
meeting rooms, car rental, free parking* ⊟ *AE, DC, MC, V* ⦿ *BP.*

$ 🖼 **Gran Hotel El Golf.** This low-slung lodging curves around a large pool
and is surrounded by landscaped gardens. Rooms, most with views of
the pool and gardens, have dark-wood furniture and rustic lamps. The
hotel is 10 minutes from the center of town and 15 minutes from the
airport. ⊠ *Los Cocoteros 500, El Golf* ☎ *044/282–515* 🖷 *044/282–
231* ⊕ *www.granhotelgolf.com* ⇌ *112 rooms, 8 suites* ⌂ *Restaurant,
cafeteria, room service, in-room safes, minibars, cable TV, 9-hole golf
course, 2 pools, gym, massage, sauna, bar, playground, laundry service,
meeting rooms, airport shuttle, free parking, some no-smoking rooms*
⊟ *AE, DC, MC, V* ⦿ *CP.*

Nightlife & the Arts

There are several art galleries near the Escuela de Bellas Artes (Calle
Húsares de Junín and Av. America Sur), and the Casa Urquiaga has ro-
tating art shows.

NIGHTLIFE **Chelsea** (⊠ Estete 675 ☎ 044/257–032) is a venerable men's club with
dancing on the weekends. A flying ghost adorns a wall of the studiously
funky **Haizea Pub** (⊠ Jr. Bolognesi 502 ☎ 044/392–961). There's live
music on the weekends. **Las Tinajas** (⊠ Pizarro 389 ☎ 044/296–272)
is a quiet, elegant evening spot in a converted casona. It is open only
Thursday through Sunday. **Luna Rota** (⊠ Av. América Sur 2119 ☎ 044/
228–877) has live criollo music most evenings. There is a discotheque
and casino downstairs. See plays and concerts at the **Teatro Municipal**
(⊠ Jr. Bolívar 753 ☎ 044/241–601). Consult local newspapers for
show times.

Shopping

Shop for ceramics along Avenida España, especially where it intersects
with Junín. Stalls display the locally made leather goods for which Tru-
jillo is famous, particularly shoes, bags, and coats. Don't hesitate to hag-
gle. Avoid this area after dark. For made-to-order boots or belts, check
out **Creaciones Cerna** (⊠ Bolognesi 567 ☎ 044/205–679). South of Huan-
chaco's Muelle Artesenal are several artisan stalls. Vendor's hock minia-
ture *caballitos de totora* and other kitsch. **Los Tallanes** (⊠ Jr. San Martin
455 ☎ 044/220–274) has a wide selection of artisanal goods. **Lujan**
(⊠ Obregoso 242 ☎ 044/205–092) makes stylized Peruvian jewelry.

Sipán

35 km (21 mi) south of Chiclayo.

The **Tumba del Señor de Sipán** (Tomb of the Lord of Sipán), saved from huaqueros in 1987 by renowned archaeologist Walter Alva, is within the Huaca Rajada, a pyramid near the town of Sipán. The trip here takes you past sugar plantations and through the fertile Chancay Valley to a fissured mud hill that is all that remains of the Huaca Rajada. The three major tombs in the smaller mound date from about AD 290 and earlier, and together they form one of the most complete archaeological finds in the Western Hemisphere. The tombs have been attributed to the Moche culture, who were known for their ornamental pottery and fine metalwork. The most extravagant funerary objects were found in the tomb, now filled with replicas placed exactly where the original objects were discovered. The originals are now on permanent display in the Museo Brüning and Museo Tumbas Reales de Sipán in Lambayeque. The Lord of Sipán did not make the journey to the Great Beyond alone—he was buried with at least eight living people: a warrior guard (whose feet were amputated to ensure that he didn't run away), three young women, two assistants, a servant, a child, a dog, and two llamas. The lord also got to bring gold and jewelry and hundreds of ceramic pots containing snacks for the long journey. It is best to stay in Chiclayo and visit the ruins early in the morning. The dig is ongoing, as other tombs are still being excavated. ☎ *No phone* 🎟 *S/7* ⊙ *Daily 9–4:30.*

A 15-minute drive east from Sipán is the 8th-century Moche capital **Pampa Grande,** a 6-square-km (2½-square-mi) archaeological complex that contains one of the largest pyramids ever built in the Andes, the 55-meter-high (178-foot-high) Huaca Fortaleza (Pyramid of Strength). Pampa Grande was constructed in the final years of the Moche empire. For unknown reasons the city was torched and abandoned near the beginning of the 9th century. ☎ *No phone* 🎟 *S/7* ⊙ *Daily 9–4:30.*

Chiclayo

219 km (131 mi) north of Trujillo.

A lively commercial center, Chiclayo is both prosperous and easygoing. Although it doesn't have much colonial architecture, it is surrounded by numerous pre-Columbian sites. The Moche and Chimú people had major cities in the area, as did the Lambayeque, who flourished here from about 700 to 1370. Tourists flocked here after the 1987 discovery of the nearby unlooted tomb of the Lord of Sipán. Chiclayo now provides a comfortable base from which to visit the tomb and other archaeological sites. The enormous **Cathedral,** dating back to 1869, is worth a look for its neoclassical facade on the Plaza de Armas. ⊠ *Plaza de Armas* 🎟 *Free.*

For a bit of fresh air, head to the **Paseo Las Musas.** The pedestrian walk borders a stream and has classical statues depicting scenes from mythology. ⊠ *La Florida and Falques.*

The closest beach to Chiclayo is in the port town of Pimentel, 14 km (8½ mi) west of Chiclayo. The beach itself is unattractive, but a pretty curved pier more than 100 years old is easy on the eyes.

Shopping

Fodor'sChoice ★ Chiclayo's **Central Market** on Avenida Balta is famed for its ceramics, weavings, and charms made by local *curanderos* (folk healers). Ask at any of the stalls for an evening session with a local shaman.

Lambayeque

12 km (7 mi) north of Chiclayo.

Lambayeque has some preserved colonial architecture and two notable museums. It is often called the "Cradle of Peruvian Liberty," because it was here, on December 27, 1820, that Peru declared its independence from the Spanish crown.

Fodor'sChoice ★ The Moche, Lambayeque, and other pre-Inca cultures such as the Cupisnique, Chavín, Moche, Chimú, and Sicán are explored at the **Museo Brüning.** Run by Walter Alva, who saved the marvelous tombs of Sipán, the museum has one of the finest archaeological collections in Peru. Among the highlights are the treasures taken from the Tomb of the Lord of Sipán; a group of ceramic frogs dating from 1200 BC; a small gold statue of a woman known as the Venus de Frías; and Moche and Sicán ceramics. The museum has excellent interpretive displays with text in Spanish. There is a small gift shop that sells replicas of the antiquities found at the Tomb of Sipán. ⊠ *Huamachuco and Atahualpa* ☎ *076/282–110* 🖃 *S/7, S/10 with guide* ☉ *Daily 9–5.*

★ The **Museo Tumbas Reales de Sipán,** offers a deeper look into the culture and everyday life of the Moche. The exhibits lay out where every jewel, ceramic, and other artifact was found in the Tomb of Sipán. Most of the Señor de Sipán artifacts are now found here. ⊠ *Av. Juan Pablo Vizcardo and Guzmán* ☎ *076/283–077* 🖃 *S/7* ☉ *Tues.–Sun. 9:30–1 and 4–8; closed Mon.*

Túcume

35 km (21 mi) northwest of Chiclayo.

With the decline of the Moche civilization, legend has it that a lord called Naymlap arrived in the Lambayeque Valley, and with his dozen sons founded the Lambayeque dynasty, whose cities included the immense pyramid complex of Túcume. Here you'll find the Huaca Larga, one of the largest adobe pyramids in South America. From the heights of the hill called El Purgatorio, see 26 giant pyramids and dozens of smaller ones spread across a desert sprinkled with hardy little *algarobo* (mesquite) trees. Late Norwegian explorer Thor Heyerdahl, of *Kon-Tiki* fame, directed the excavations of the pyramids. There is a small **Museo de Sitio** 1 km east of Túcume with a small collection of artifacts and some displays recounting the history of the nearby ruins. The museum's interesting architecture—it is made from mud, adobe, cane, and mesquite wood, resembling the chapels around Lambayeque—is the real draw. ☎ *076/800–052 or 074/422–027* ✉ *S/7* ⊘ *Daily 9–5.*

The North Coast A to Z

AIR TRAVEL

Aero Continente has daily flights to Trujillo and Chiclayo.

🛪 Airlines **Aero Continente** ☎ 01/242-4242 in Lima, 044/244-042 in Trujillo, 074/229-916 in Chiclayo, 073/325-635 in Piura, 072/523-892 in Tumbes, 877/359-7378 in the U.S.

BUS TRAVEL

Emtrafesa runs between Trujillo and Chiclayo, a three- to four-hour trip. Expreso de Chiclayo runs from Lima to Chiclayo. Other reputable companies include Cruz del Sur, Oltursa, Ormeño, and Tepsa.

🛪 Bus Information **Cruz del Sur** ✉ Jr. Quilca 531, in Lima ☎ 01/424-1005 in Lima, 044/261-802 in Trujillo, 074/225-058 in Chiclayo. **Emtrafesa** ✉ Av. Miraflores 127, Trujillo ☎ 044/243-981 in Trujillo, ✉ Av. Colón at Av. Bolognesi, Chiclayo ☎ 074/234-291 in Chiclayo. **Expreso Cruz del Sur** ✉ Av. del Ejército 285, Trujillo ☎ 044/26-1801. **Expreso de Chiclayo** ✉ Grau 653, Lima ☎ 01/428-5072 in Lima, 074/233-071 in Chiclayo. **Oltursa** ✉ Av. del Ejército 342, Trujillo ☎ 044/263-055. **Ormeño** ✉ Javier Prado Este 1059, Lima ✉ Carlos Zavala 177, Lima ☎ 01/427-5679 in Lima, 044/259-782 in Trujillo. **Tepsa** ✉ Paseo de la República 129, Lima ☎ 01/427-5642 in Lima, 044/205-017 in Trujillo, 074/234-421 in Chiclayo.

EMERGENCIES

🛪 Hospitals **Belén Hospital of Trujillo** ✉ Bolívar 350 ☎ 044/245-281. **Clinica del Pacifico** ✉ Av. José Leonardo Ortiz 420 Chiclayo ☎ 074/233-705.

🛪 Pharmacy **Boticas Fasa** ✉ Jr. Pizarro 512 Trujillo ☎ 044/899-028. **Max Salud** ✉ Corner 7 de Enero and Bolognesi Chiclayo ☎ 074/226-215.

TOURS

Condor Travel and Guía Tours both organize tours to the ruins around Trujillo. Sipán Tours is one of Chiclayo's best tour companies for trips to the Tomb of Señor Sipán.

🛪 **Sipán Tours** ✉ 7 de Enero 772, Chiclayo ☎ 074/229-053. **Piura Tours** ✉ Jr. Ayacucho 585, Piura ☎ 073/326-778. **Condor Travel** ✉ Jr. Independencia 553, Trujillo ☎ 044/254-763. **Guía Tours** ✉ Jr. Independencia 580, Trujillo ☎ 044/256-553 ⊕ www.geocities.com/guia_tours. **Trujillo Tours** ✉ Diego de Almagro 301, Trujillo ☎ 044/257-518. **Preference Tours** ✉ Calle Grau 427, Tumbes ☎ 072/524-757.

VISITOR INFORMATION

Most larger towns will have an iPerú or Mitinci tourist information office. These offices have informative maps and guides, will help you arrange accommodations, and will point out good local restaurants and attractions.

🛪 Tourist Information **iPerú** ☎ 01/574-8000 in Lima, 0800/42-579 throughout Peru ✉ Jr. Independencia 630, Trujillo ☎ 044/224-025 ✉ Av. Sáenz Peña 830, Chiclayo ☎ 074/236-700. **General information** ✉ Av. Ayacucho 733, Piura ☎ 073/303-208 ✉ Centro Civico, 2nd floor, 204, Tumbes ☎ 052/523-699.

THE SOUTH

Traveling south of Lima, the Pan-American Highway cuts through the desert with an occasional view of the Pacific Ocean. At first you might think this a wasteland, but then you'll spot a sudden patch of green— a thriving farm, a field of cotton, a patch of date palms. Add water to the desert and anything will grow. The highway leads to Pisco, 235 km (148 mi) south of Lima, which is mainly a jumping-off point for Paracas National Reserve and Chaco, where boats depart for the Ballestas Islands.

Paracas National Reserve

15 km (10 mi) south of Pisco.

Named for the blustering *paracas* (sandstorms) that buffet the west coast each winter, the Reserva Nacional de Paracas is Peru's first park for marine conservation. Settled atop a peninsular hook of land slightly southwest of Pisco, this 280,000-hectare (700,000-plus-acre) coastal park includes a conglomeration of mountains, desert, and islands. Thin dirt tracks lead to sheltered lagoons, rugged cliffs full of caves, and small fishing villages. The pristine surroundings and lonely feeling are misleading, however—a monument marks the spot where General José San Martín first stepped into Peru nearly 200 years ago.

Wildlife is everywhere in this stunning reserve, particularly bird colonies and sea creatures. Pelicans, condors, and red-and-white flamingos congregate and breed here; the latter, in fact, are said to have inspired the red-and-white independence flag General San Martín designed when he liberated Peru. On shore you can't miss the sound (or the smell) of the hundreds of sea lions, while in the water you might spot penguins, sea turtles, dolphins, manta rays, and even hammerhead sharks.

This is prime walking territory, where you can stroll from the bay to the **Julio Tello Museum,** and on to the fishing village of **Lagunilla** 5 km (3 mi) farther across the neck of the peninsula. Adjacent to the museum are colonies of flamingos, best seen June through July (and absent January through March, when they fly to Sierra). Hike another 6 km (4 mi) to reach **Mirador de Lobos** (Wolf Lookout) at Punta El Arquillo, along the cliffs overlooking a sea-lion colony, or to view the rock formation **La Catedral** (the Cathedral). Carved into the highest point in the cliffs above Paracas Bay, 14 km (9 mi) from the museum, is the **Candelabra.** Note that you must hire a guide to explore the land trails.

Minibus tours of the entire park can be arranged through local hotels and travel agencies for about S/15 for 5 hours. A taxi from Pisco to Paracas runs about S/14, or you can take a half-hour Chaco–Paracas–Museo *combi* to El Chaco for S/2.

Where to Stay

$$ **Hotel Paracas.** Opened in the 1940s for Lima's elite, this Mediterranean-style resort—the area's largest—lies behind a wide, half-circle park and dock that juts out into the deep-blue Paracas Bay. Air-conditioned rooms have wood furnishings, private bathrooms, and TVs. Larger suites and flower-bedecked bungalows are often booked by families. An extensive Sunday buffet (S/87) draws crowds, and nonguests can use the pool (S/7). It's a convenient base from which to launch trips into the reserve, tour local ruins, or head out for some fishing (bring your own gear). ⊠ *Av. Paracas 173* ☎ *034/221736, 01/447–0781 reservations in Lima* ⊟ *034/225379* ⊕ *www.hotelparacas.com* ↪ *95 rooms, 7 suites, 3 bungalows* ↧ *Restaurant, cafeteria, room service, some in-room safes, some mini-bars, some refrigerators, cable TV, 2 tennis courts, miniature golf, 2 pools, children's pool, beach, dock, boating, fishing, volleyball, 2 bars, shop, laundry service, meeting rooms, free parking* ⊟ *AE, DC, MC, V* ⚏ *CP.*

Ica

56 km (35 mi) southeast of Paracas.

Ica is a fertile patch of green in the middle of mountains of sand dunes where the sun is constantly shining. This was once the capital of the Naz-cas, a people noted for their 3rd- to 8th-century weavings and ceramics. Ica is now known for its gracious lifestyle and its high-stepping horses called *caballos de paso.*

Ica is in the heart of wine country. Chilean and Argentine wines may win all the awards, but some of the finer Peruvian labels hold their own in numerous competitions. The winery most convenient to visit is the **Bodega Vista Alegre** (⊠ Camina a la Tinguiña, Km. 205 ☎ 056/232919), about 3 km (2 mi) outside of town. About 8 km (5 mi) farther is the **Bodega Hacienda Tacama** (⊠ Camina a la Tinguiña s/n ☎ 056/228395), which produces some of Peru's best wines. Don't miss a chance to sample the Blanco de Blancos.

It's just a small, unmarked building on the Plaza de Armas, but the cluttered **Museo Cabrera** has regional cultural artifacts and more than 10,000 varieties of stones. The charismatic owner, Dr. Javier Cabrera, is a descendant of one of Ica's founders. Some of the rocks are etched with what might be pre-Columbian images of daily life and surgical techniques, possibly from a technologically advanced Stone Age civilization. ⊠ *Bolívar 170* ☎ *056/253576* ▨ *S/1 with guided tour* ⊗ *Mon.–Sat. 9–1 and 4:30–8:30.*

The quaint **Iglesia La Merced**, built in 1874, overlooks the Plaza de Armas. Peek in for a glimpse of the delicately carved wooden altars. ⊠ *Corner Libertad y Bolívar* ☎ *No phone* ▨ *Free* ⊗ *Mon.–Sat. 10–5.*

Inside the pretty, colonial-style **Iglesia El Señor de Luren** is a famous Christ image that is paraded around the city all night during local religious festivals. Legend has it that the statue, purchased for the church by a friar in 1570, was transported to Peru by boat. The captain threw it overboard in a storm, but it washed up on a beach near Paracas and was miraculously carried to Ica intact. The church stands slightly southeast of town. ⊠ *Cutervo y Ayacucho* ☎ *No phone* ▨ *Free* ⊗ *Mon.–Sat. 9–4.*

A vast and well-preserved collection on regional history—particularly from the Inca, Nazca, and Paracas cultures—is on display in the fascinating **Museo Histórico Regional.** Note the *quipas* (Inca counting strings), mysterious knotted, colored threads thought to have been used to count commodities and quantities of food. Head out back to view a scale model of the Nazca Lines from an observation tower. You can also buy maps (S/.50) and paintings of Nazca motifs (S/4). The museum is about 1½ km (1 mi) from town, so take a 20-minute walk, hop on Bus 17 from Plaza de Armas (S/2), or catch a *mototaxi* from the corner of the Plaza (S/2). ⊠ *Ayabaca s/n* ☏ *056/234383* 🖃 *S/7, plus S/.50 camera fee* ☉ *Mon.–Sat. 9–6:30, Sun. 9–2.*

Where to Stay & Eat

$$ ✕ **La Taberna.** In Bodega El Catador, this elegant restaurant serves exquisite local specialties at small, candlelit tables. Be sure to ask the waiter for his recommendations on the fine wines and pisco available. If you eat elsewhere, you can always stop by the bar for drinks and dancing to live Peruvian music. ⊠ *José Carrasco González, Km 296* ☏ *056/403263* 🖃 *AE, MC, V.*

¢ ✕ **El Otro Peñoncito.** Friendly and relaxed, this restaurant has Peruvian and international cuisine. The fettuccine *con ajo* (with garlic) is served with a spicy sauce similar to that used in the traditional *papa a la huancaina.* Milder fare, such as sandwiches and soups, is also served. ⊠ *Bolívar 255* ☏ *056/233921* 🖃 *DC, MC, V.*

$ 🏨 **El Carmelo Hotel & Hacienda.** At this colonial-style, slate-roof hotel 5 km (3 mi) from downtown Ica, rooms are in several buildings around a flower-filled courtyard. An inviting garden house has wicker furniture and a 19th-century wine press. ⊠ *Pan-American Hwy., Km 301* ☏ *056/232191* ⇆ *40 rooms* ⚅ *Restaurant, pool, bar, laundry service, travel services, free parking; no room phones, no room TVs* 🖃 *AE, MC, V.*

¢ 🏨 **Hostal Rocha.** Family-run, this operation provides guests with cooking and laundry facilities, hot water, and breakfast. Motorcycles are welcome, and you can grab a sand board for surfing the nearby dunes. ⊠ *Independencia 258* ☏ *056/232111* ⇆ *6 rooms* ⚅ *Dining room, kitchenettes (some), laundry facilities, travel services, free parking; no room phones, no room TVs* 🖃 *No credit cards.*

Huacachina

5 km (3 mi) southwest of Ica.

A 10-minute drive from downtown Ica will take you to the oasis of Huacachina, a patch of green amid towering sand dunes. In the 1920s, wealthy Peruvians flocked to this resort beneath the palm trees that crowd the shores of the lagoon. Locals come regularly to take a refreshing dip or ski down the dunes on "sandboards." The lagoon's sandy bottom reportedly makes swimming dangerous.

Where to Stay & Eat

$ ✕🏨 **Hotel Mossone.** A Spanish colonial–style courtyard lined with tall ficus trees is the focal point of this century-old mansion. Rooms look out onto gardens overflowing with flowers, which partially hide the small, secluded pool and playground. The relaxed bar and restaurant have splendid lake views, and if you like the food you can book a room with full board. The hotel provides free bicycles and sandboards for guests, but if you're staying elsewhere you can still stop in for excellent comida criolla, especially *papa a la huancaina* (potatoes with cheese sauce). ⊠ *Balneario de Huacachina* ☎ *034/213630, 01/442–3090 in Lima* 🖷 *034/236137* 🖄 *mossone@invertur.com.pe* 🛏 *53 rooms* 🖙 *Restaurant, pool, lake, bicycles, bar, playground, laundry service, travel services, free parking* 🖃 *AE, DC, MC, V.*

Nazca

Fodor'sChoice ★ *120 km (75 mi) southeast of Ica.*

A mirage of green in the desert, lined with cotton fields and orchards and bordered by crisp mountain peaks, Nazca has remained a quiet colonial town amid a cache of archaeological ruins. Set 598 meters (1,961 feet) above sea level, the town has a dry climate—scorching by day, nippy by night—that was instrumental in preserving centuries-old relics from Inca and pre-Columbian tribes. Overlooking the parched scene is 2078-meters (6,815-feet) Cerro Blanco, the highest sand dune in the world. In 1901 the area came to the world's attention when Peruvian archaeologist Max Uhle excavated sites around Nazca and rediscovered this unique culture. The area also has more than 100 cemeteries, where the humidity-free climate has helped preserve priceless jewelry, textiles, pottery, and mummies.

However, this area is most famous as the site of one of the world's greatest mysteries, the giant engravings—called the Nazca Lines—on the Pampas de San José, 20 km (12 mi) north of town. Discovered by scientist Paul Kosok in 1929, the motifs were made by removing the surface stones and piling them beside the lighter soil underneath. Figures, some measuring up to 300 meters (1,000 feet) across, include a hummingbird, a monkey, a spider, a pelican, a condor, a whale, and an "astronaut." Probably the most famous person to investigate the origin of the Nazca Lines was Kosok's translator, German scientist Dr. Maria Reiche, who studied the Lines from 1940 until her death in 1998.

Your best bet for exploring the area's archaeological sites and the Nazca Lines is on a set tour, which usually covers all the major areas. You can take a taxi to the *mirador* for around S/35, or catch a morning bus there for only 50¢ (then hitchhike back). Nazca Lines flights run S/104–S/180 depending on the season. Eager tour guides waiting at the bus stop in Nazca offer S/87 tours that include flights and a visit to the mummies at the Chauchilla cemetery.

Where to Stay & Eat

$ ✕ **La Taberna.** A fan slowly rotates above the churning bar crowd at this popular criollo restaurant, *the* watering spot in which to be seen. It's also one of the few places where you can leave your mark—literally—on walls decorated with a montage of international poems, art, and advice from former diners. Nightly Andean flute groups and local bands keep the place upbeat and relaxing. Ice-cold beer and per-

THE MYSTERY OF THE NAZCA LINES

ALL SORTS OF MYTHS *are attached to the mysterious Nazca Lines, for no one knows their purpose or origin. Only a few cultures dared to brave this barren desert 20 km (12 mi) from the town of Nazca, including the Paracas, who lived here from 200 BC to AD 600. The Nazca people also flourished here from 300 BC to AD 700, and migrants from Ayacucho took over the area about AD 630. Thus theories abound about how any—or all—of these groups might have used the Lines, if indeed they made them.*

Paul Kosok, an expert in ancient irrigation, was flying over the Nazca area on June 21, 1929, to document Inca irrigation patterns when he noticed the strange designs in the desert. He only spotted them because, coincidentally, the sunlight was at the southern hemisphere's winter equinox that day and highlighted the outlines of the designs. After Kosok told of his find, the area around Nazca was flooded with archaeologists and treasure hunters eager to figure out who had created the giant drawings—and see whether they had left valuables with them.

Dubbed the "Nazca Lines" by archaeologists for their proximity to town, the motifs were made by removing stones on the desert surface and piling them beside the lighter soil beneath. There are 11 major figures—including a hummingbird, a monkey, a spider, a pelican, a condor, and a whale—plus the mysterious "astronaut" and various triangles and trapezoids. Some measure up to 300 meters (1,000 feet) across and have been preserved for more than 2,000 years by an unusual combination of gentle, cleansing winds and arid climate.

Because the lines matched up to the sun at its equinox, Kosok maintained that the figures were some type of irrigation system marking the seasons. However, Kosok's

translator, German scientist Dr. Maria Reiche, had other ideas, which she explored from 1940 until her death at 95 in 1998. She theorized that the Lines were made by the Nazca people as part of a vast astronomical calendar noting the rainy season in the highlands, the source of the area's water supply, and seasonal changes in the regional climate. In 1976 she paid for the mirador (platform) 20 km (12 mi) north of town, from which the lizard, arbos (tree), and manos (hands) can be seen.

Other theories about the meaning of the Lines are that they are simply artwork meant to be seen from the air, based on ancient Nazca pottery and textiles depicting balloonists and local legends of flying men. Dr. Johan Reinhard proposed that because there are similar lines in Bolivia and Chile, they have to do with fertility rites throughout the Andes. British astronomer Alan Sawyer and scientist Georg A. von Breunig both proposed that since the Nazca and other local cultures were such excellent athletes, the Lines were running tracks for sports events. Henri Stirlin offered the explanation that the patterns represent local yarns and weaving motifs. Zsoltan Zelko deducted that the pampas were a map depicting the Tiahuanaco empire, and the designs are somehow part of the story.

Note that mid-morning is usually the best time to fly over the Lines, as earlier there is often a haze over the pampas, and later winds can make for a turbulent journey. The flight, which takes place in a small (and sometimes questionably rickety) propeller plane—and combines bright sunlight and strong fuel fumes with quick twists and turns, deep dives, and bumpy takeoffs and landings—is not for the queasy.

–By Holly Smith

fect pisco sours complement the delectable Peruvian spiced chicken, ceviche, and milder pasta choices. ✉ *Jr. Lima 321* ☎ *034/522322* ▱ *AE, MC, V.*

★ ¢ ✕ **El Griego Restaurant.** Huge portions of Peruvian specialties are served up to the backpacking crowd at this budget restaurant. It's all delicious, but go for the set almuerzo or one of the hearty soups. Top it off with a pisco sour in the evening. ✉ *Bolognesi 287* ☎ *No phone* ▱ *No credit cards.*

★ **$–$$** ✕▦ **Hotel Nazca Lines.** The former home of Maria Reiche, this historic hacienda set around a shaded, sunken courtyard with a pool is the perfect spot from which to explore local mysteries. Built in the 1940s, the hotel has long drawn international travelers and archaeologists, although the rooms have been updated over the decades to include air-conditioning, hot water, and sunny private patios. Attractive decorative touches such as charcoal sketches and wrought-iron headboards preserve the colonial feel. Delicious meals served on a tiled walkway beside the courtyard are worth the expense, and nonguests can use the pool for S/1.50. Nazca Lines tours, including 2–3 nights at the hotel and a scenic flight, run about S/870. ✉ *Jr. Bolognesi* ☎ *034/ 522293, 01/442–3090 in Lima* 🖷 *034/522112* ⤳ *34 rooms* ⚴ *Restaurant, lounge, tennis court, pool, bar, laundry service, travel services, free parking; no phones in some rooms, no TVs in some rooms* ▱ *AE, DC, MC, V.*

★ **$** ✕▦ **Hotel de la Borda.** In fragrant gardens and surrounded by cotton fields, this quiet 80-year-old hacienda 1½ km (1 mi) from the airport offers a taste of life on a coastal farm. Rooms with hot showers overlook a lush section of colorful blossoms. The excellent restaurant serves up local specialties, while the English-speaking staff can organize horseback rides, mountain-bike trips, or four-wheel-drive vehicle excursions. ✉ *Pan-American Hwy. S, Km 447* 🖷🖷 *034/522576* ⤳ *39 rooms* ⚴ *Restaurant, room service, 2 pools, horseback riding, mountain bikes, bar, laundry service, travel services, free parking; no room phones, no room TVs* ▱ *DC, MC, V.*

Arequipa

1,000 km (625 mi) southeast of Lima.

Arequipeños call their home "the white city" because of the *sillar* (a grayish-white local volcanic rock) used to construct most of its colonial buildings and churches. Dubbed the "Independent Republic of Arequipa," the city is beloved by its inhabitants, who are highly resentful of the notion that Peruvian life begins and ends in Lima. This main economic center for the south is also called the "Independent Republic of Arequipa" by its proud residents, who have made several attempts to secede from Peru and even designed the city's own passport and flag. Each August 15, parades, fireworks, bullfights, and dancing celebrate the city's founding. The combination of grace and conviviality has drawn many outsiders to move here, and the city's population has doubled in the last decade. Little wonder Arequipa received a designation as a World Cultural Heritage site by UNESCO.

FodorsChoice The city's crowning glory is the **Convento de la Santa Catalina,** founded
★ in 1579 a few blocks from what is now downtown's Plaza de Armas.
It was closed to the public for 400 years. About two dozen nuns live
here today; at the convent's height, there were 400 residents. Once inside its high walls, the nuns never left the 5-acre complex. Novices had
to pay to join the convent, and nuns were separated accordingly—the
higher the "contribution," the more luxurious the cell. Nuns (or their
slaves) prepared their own food in the tiny kitchens of each cell. It's a
good idea to hire a guide at the entrance (tip about S/10–S/20), but leave
some time to wander the twisting streets on your own. Also take time
to try the nuns' famous *torta de naranja* (orange cake) or another pastry in the small cafeteria midway through. ⊠ *Santa Catalina at Ugarte*
☎ *054/229798* 🎟 *S/14* ⊘ *Daily 9–5; last entry at 4.*

The colonial aristocracy left its mark in the fine mansions of downtown
Arequipa, many of which you may enter through high, arched portals.
Tall gateways were a 17th-century status symbol, designed to allow the
passage of an armored knight on horseback bearing an upright lance. A
particularly striking mansion open is open the public. **Casa del Moral**
(⊠ Moral 318 and Bolívar ☎ 054/213–171), a block from Santa Catalina,
has a stunning sillar portal carved in a mestizo design that combines puma
heads with snakes emerging from their mouths and a Spanish coat of arms.

Just off the Plaza de Armas, **La Compañía** (The Society) church consists
of a fine series of buildings in traditional Arequipa style. The 1525 church
is well worth seeing, and once inside you should also visit the **St. Ignatius** chapel and the former church sacristy, covered from floor to dome
with 17th-century paintings from the Cusco School. The former monastery,
now converted into shops, contains two cloisters with carved-stone pillars. They may be entered from General Morán or Palacio Viejo. ⊠ *General Morán at Alvarez Tomás* ☎ *No phone* 🎟 *Chapel 50¢* ⊘ *Church
daily 9–1 and 4–9, chapel Mon.–Sat. 9–1 and 4–9.*

Another religious center is **Monasterio de la Recoleta,** across the Chili River
from the city's colonial center. Founded in 1648, the Franciscan monastery
comprises a huge ancient library, a museum of the Amazon, a colonial-
art collection, and, of course, cloisters and cells. Guides are available
(tip about S/7). ⊠ *Recoleta 117* ☎ *054/270–966* 🎟 *S/7* ⊘ *Weekdays
9–12 and 3–5, Sat. 9–12.*

★ **Museo Santuarias de Altura.** This fascinating little museum at the Universidad Católica Santa Maria holds the frozen bodies of four young
girls who were apparently sacrificed more than 500 years ago by the
Inca to appease the gods. "Juanita," the first, was found in 1995 near
the summit of Mt. Ampato by local climber Miguel Zarate and an-
thropologist Johan Reinhard. When neighboring Volcán Sabancaya
erupted, the ice that held Juanita in her sacrificial tomb melted and she
rolled partway down the mountain and into a crater. English-speaking
guides will show you around the museum, and you can watch a video
detailing the expedition. No photographs are permitted. ⊠ *Samuel Velarde 305 Umacollo* ☎ *054/252554* ⊕ *www.mountain.org* 🎟 *S/10*
⊘ *Mon.–Sat. 9–1 and 3–5.*

Where to Stay & Eat

$ ✕ **El Conquistador Picantería.** You won't see any tourists at this tiny diner—but you will have the chance to rub shoulders (and perhaps share a pitcher of homemade sangria) with in-the-know locals who consider this the best food in Arequipa. Pork pie and pig's head salad are specialties, but you can also go for the white-vegetable soup or the ubiquitous relleno, too. ⊠ *Bayoneta 106* ☎ *054/286009* ▤ *No credit cards.*

★ ¢ ✕ **El Rincón Norteño.** Trujillo cuisine—seafood, grilled meats, and varying local specialties—is the specialty of this attractive, wood-paneled restaurant, but you can ask the friendly owners for recommendations that aren't on the menu. Sidle up to the wood-and-brick bar for a pisco, northern style, below photos of northern Peru. There are live folk music performances on weekend evenings. ⊠ *San Francisco 300-B* ☎ *054/ 215257* ▤ *No credit cards* ☽ *No dinner Sun.*

★ ¢ ✕ **Le Bistrot.** It's a streetside café straight out of Paris, with little tables, comfortable chatting seats, and end tables scattered with board games and international magazines. But everyone comes for the crêpes, served both filled and with sauce, as entrées and desserts. On the ever-changing menu, look for such crêpe specialties as the ham and asparagus; the spinach and mozzarella; or the lighter, buttery varieties drizzled with a berry sauce or sugar. If you're in the mood for more basic fare, try a baguette sandwich or a mixed salad. High-grade espresso drinks are served with such delicacies as chocolate gâteau. Look for the restaurant in the Alianza Francesa compound. ⊠ *Santa Catalina 208* ☎ *054/215579* ▤ *MC, V* ☽ *Closed Sun.*

★ ¢ ✕ **Mixto's Cebichería.** Above the glowing white Catedral, this lovely, romantic spot serves up some of Arequipa's best seafood dishes. Ceviche is, of course, the focus, but you'll also find shellfish empanadas and mixed stews. If you're averse or allergic to ocean fare, don't worry; the restaurant also serves pastas, salads, and grilled meats. If the weather is warm, ask for a table on the terrace above the Catedral entrance. ⊠ *Pasaje Catedral 115* ☎ *054/215325* ▤ *AE, MC, V.*

★ $$-$$$ ✕▦ **Hotel Libertador.** Amid beautiful, sprawling gardens, this 1940 Spanish colonial villa creates an oasis of Old Arequipa in the modern city. Hand-hewn sillar arches, wrought-iron window screens, and touches of Peruvian décor give this luxury hotel the intimate feel of an old family home. Breakfast on the terrace to absorb it all, then dip in a pool overlooking Volcán Misti and the Andean panorama. Nonguests can stop in the pub-style bar or splurge on the Continental delights at Restaurant Los Robles ($$). ⊠ *Plaza Bolívar, Selva Alegre* ☎ *054/ 221–5110* 🖷 *054/442–2988* ⊕ *www.libertador.com.pe* ↝ *92 rooms, 6 suites* ♨ *3 restaurants, room service, minibars, refrigerators, 4 tennis courts, pool, hot tub, massage, sauna, exercise equipment, gym, shops, bar, lounge, nightclub, Internet, baby-sitting, dry cleaning, laundry service, business services, meeting rooms, travel services, car rental, free parking* ▤ *AE, DC, MC, V.*

$ ✕▦ **La Posada del Puente.** Rose blossoms spill over the grounds of this FodorśChoice delightful hotel, set beside the Río Chili and overlooking Volcán Misti. ★ The pastel-colored rooms have charming art and antique furnishings, and two of the large suites have hot tubs. The cozy restaurant serves excellent pastas and a fine selection of Peruvian and Chilean wines. ⊠ *Bolognesi 101* ☎ *054/253132* 🖷 *054/253576* ⇱ *20 rooms, 4 suites* ⚴ *Restaurant, in-room hot tubs (some), refrigerators, bar, library, laundry service, travel services, free parking* ⊟ *AE, DC, MC, V.*

¢ ✕🖽 **La Casa de Melgar.** In a beautiful tiled courtyard surrounded by fragrant blossoms and dotted with trees is this 18th-century home. The magnificent double rooms have towering vaulted ceilings, as well as private baths with hot water. The single suite has an original cookstove from when this was a private house. The café serves light Continental and Peruvian meals. ⊠ *Melgar 108* ☎ *054/222459* ⊕ *www.lared.net.pe/lacasademelgar* ⇱ *6 rooms, 1 suite* ⚴ *Café, laundry service, free parking; no room phones, no room TVs* ⊟ *No credit cards.*

Fodor's Choice ★

Nightlife & the Arts

Young and gorgeous Arequipeños head to the **Blues Card Club** (⊠ San Francisco 319 ☎054/283387), where it's just S/12 cover for strong drinks and nightly live blues. **Déja Vu** (⊠ San Francisco 125 ☎ 054/2538757), open 10 PM to midnight, is a popular place to have a late meal of light Continental fare while watching eclectic films and listening to DJ-spun pop fare. At the **Forum Rock Café** (⊠ San Francisco 317 ☎ 054/202697) you can take your pick of six bars, enjoy live concerts, and dine among tropical furnishings. The **Instituto Cultural Peruano Norteamericano** (⊠ Melgar 109 ☎ 054/243–201) hosts evening concerts of traditional and classical music.

Shopping

Alpaca 21 (⊠ Jerusalén 115 ☎ 054/213425) sells high-quality clothing and accessories. **Anselmo's Baby Alpaca** (⊠ Portal del Flores ☎ no phone) carries sweaters, rugs, and wall hangings, and smaller woven items such as gloves, hats, and scarves. **Arte Peru** (⊠ Puente Bolognesi 147 ☎ no phone) is a virtual gallery of local antiques, including ceramics, jewelry, and carvings. In central Arequipa, **Claustros de la Compañía** (⊠ General Morán 118 ☎ No phone), is an old Jesuit compound where two dozen shops sell alpaca clothing, silver jewelry, and handmade crafts.

Colca Canyon

150 km (93 mi) north of Arequipa.

About five hours of rough driving from Arequipa takes you through the Reserva Nacional de Aguada Blanca (Aguada Blanca National Reserve), where herds of graceful, long-necked vicuñas graze, to the magnificent Colca Canyon, which slices a green and fertile trough through rocky, barren mountains. Said to be the deepest canyon in the world (twice as deep as the Grand Canyon), Colca Canyon is a place of rare beauty. Once you arrive, be on the lookout for immense Andean condors; the best place to spot them is from the Cruz del Condor overlook. Colca Canyon is also the site of a vast network of pre-Columbian agricultural terraces. Colca is, in its way, as impressive as Machu Picchu, especially since the terraces are still in use for growing grains such as *quinoa* and *kiwicha*. In the canyon's unspoiled Andean villages, Collaguas and Cabana people still wear their traditional clothing and embroidered hats.

The South A to Z

AIR TRAVEL TO & FROM THE SOUTH

Aero Continente has daily flights from Lima and Cusco to Arequipa. LanPeru has several daily flights between Lima and Arequipa. TANS Perú has one daily flight to Lima to Arequipa. Rodríguez Ballón Airport is 7 km (4½ mi) from Arequipa.

It's possible to fly over the Nazca Lines in small planes that originate in Lima, Pisco, Ica, and Nazca. Aero Condor and Aero Ica have 45-minute flights that leave from Nazca. Aero Paracas offers flights that originate in Lima, Pisco, and Nazca.

Airlines & Contacts **Aero Condor** ⊠ Juan de Arona 781, San Isidro, Lima ☎ 01/442-5215, 034/256230 in Ica, 034/522424 in Nazca ⊕ www.aerocondor.com.pe. **Aero Continente** ⊠ Av. Pardo 651, Miraflores, Lima ☎ 01/242-4260 ⊕ www.aerocontinente.com.pe ⊠ Portal San Agustín 113, Arequipa ☎ 054/204020. **Aero Ica** ⊠ Hotel Maison Suisse, Nazca ⊠ Tudela and Varela 150, Lima ☎ 01/440-1030. **Aero Paracas** ⊠ Santa Fe 270, Higuereta ☎ 01/271-6941 ⊠ Hotel Paracas, Pisco ⊠ Pan-American Hwy., Km 447 ☎ 034/522-688. **LanPeru** ⊠ Av. José Pardo 269, Miraflores, Lima, ☎ 01/213-8200 ⊕ www.lanperu.com ⊠ Portal San Augustín 109, Arequipa ☎ 054/201-100. **TANS Perú** ⊠ Av. Arequipa 5200, Miraflores, Lima ☎ 01/426-8480 ⊕ www.tansperu.com.pe.

Airport Information **Aeropuerto Nazca** ☎ 034/523854. **Rodríguez Ballón Airport** ☎ 054/443-464.

BUS TRAVEL

There is reliable, comfortable bus service throughout the region. From Lima to Ica it's 303 km (188 mi), and from Lima to Nazca it's 443 km (275 mi). The longest stretch, from Nazca to Arequipa, is a 566-km (351-mi) journey that takes at least 10 hours. Delays due to mud slides or sand drifts are common.

Ormeños has the most departures from Ica, and the expense is often worth the comfort.

Bus Information **Cruz del Sur** ⊠ Jr. Quilca 531, Lima ☎ 01/427-1311; ⊠ Av. Los Incas, Nazca ☎ 034/522484 ⊠ Av. El Sol 568, Puno ☎ 034/352451. **Ormeños** ⊠ Lambayeque 180, Ica ☎ 056/215600; ⊠ Av. Los Incas, Nazca ☎ 034/561432; ⊠ Av. San Francisco, Pisco ☎ 034/532764.

CAR TRAVEL

Depending on your appreciation of desert scenery, the trip south from Lima via the Pan-American Highway may strike you as beautiful or monotonous. Either way, the government has invested heavily in road repairs and the highway is in good condition.

The Touring and Automobile Club of Peru, in Arequipa and Ica, provides maps and details on routes.

Touring y Automóvile Club del Perú ⊠ Goyeneche 313, Arequipa ☎ 054/215-640 ⊠ Manzanilla 523, Ica ☎ 056/235061.

TOUR OPERATORS

Travel agencies in Lima offer three- to seven-day tours of Arequipa, Paracas, Ica, Nazca, and Lake Titicaca. Try Explorandes, Hirca Travel, Lima Tours, Peru Chasquitur, or Receptour.

From Arequipa, tours to Colca and Cotahuasi canyons can be arranged with local operators. Try Condor Travel Arequipa, G.A. Travel Expert, Santa Catalina Tours, or Transcontinental Tours. The Arequipa office of Lima Tours offers a two-day, one-night tour of Colca Canyon. Holley's Unusual Tours runs four-wheel-drive expeditions to area sites and ruins.

In Ica, Costa Linda and Pelican Travel Service offer tours of the city and can arrange trips to Paracas National Park and the Nazca Lines. Nazca-based Alegría Tours also has tours of pre-Columbian ruins in the area. Guided tours of Paracas National Park and the Ballestas Islands are offered by Ballestas Travel Service.

🖪 Fees & Schedules **Alegría Tours** ✉ Jr. Lima 168, Nazca ☎ 034/522985. **Ballestas Travel Service** ✉ San Francisco 249, Pisco ☎ 034/533095. **Condor Travel Arequipa** ✉ Av. Puente Bolognesi 120, Arequipa ☎ 054/218362. **Costa Linda** ✉ Prolongación Ayabaca 509, Ica ☎ 056/234251. **G.A. Travel Expert** ✉ Santa Catalina 312, Arequipa ☎ 054/247722. **Lima Tours** ✉ Belén 1040, Lima ☎ 01/424-5110 ✉ Santa Catalina 120, Arequipa ☎ 054/242271. **Pelican Travel Service** ✉ Independencia 156, Galerías Siesta, Ica ☎☎ 056/225211. **Santa Catalina Tours** ✉ Jerusalén 400-D, Arequipa ☎☎ 054/216991. **Transcontinental Tours** ✉ Puente Bolognesi 132, Arequipa ☎ 054/213843.

TRAIN TRAVEL

Three times a week, Peru Rail runs a train between Arequipa and Puno, via Juliaca. Be sure to request the safer, more comfortable—and heated—Pullman "Inka Service," which costs about S/100 each way. The trip takes about 11 hours.

🖪 Train Information **Peru Rail** ✉ Av. Tacna and Arica 201, Arequipa ☎ 054/215-350.

VISITOR INFORMATION

Information on all areas of Peru can be obtained from PromPerú. In Arequipa, the Oficina de Información Turística is helpful. The Tourist Office on La Merced is open weekdays 8:30–12:30 and 2:30–3:30; there's also an airport office. The Oficina de Información Turística in Ica, near the intersection of Avenidas Grau and Jirón Ayacucho and a block east of the Plaza de Armas, is open weekdays 8–3:30. The Tourist Office on Cajamarca is open weekdays 7:30–3. For information on Colca Canyon or Paracas National Park, contact the Lima-based Inrena.

🖪 **Inrena** ✉ Petirrojos 355, Urbanización El Palomar, San Isidro, Lima ☎ 01/441-0425. **Oficina de Información Turística** ✉ Portal de la Municipalidad 112, Plaza de Armas, Arequipa ☎ 054/211021. **Tourist Office** ✉ La Merced 117, Arequipa. **Inrena** ✉ Petirrojos 355, Ica ☎ 01/441-0425. **Tourist Office** ✉ Cajamarca 179, Ica. **PromPerú** ☎ 01/224-3125 or 01/224-3118 🖷 01/224-3323 ⊕ www.peru.org.pe.

PUNO & LAKE TITICACA

Legend has it that Manco Capac and Mama Ocllo, founders of the Inca empire, emerged from the waters of Lake Titicaca. Indeed, as one watches the mysterious play of light on the water and the shadows on the mountains, the myths seem tangible. This is the altiplano of Peru, the high plains, where the earth has been raised so close to the sky that the atmosphere takes on a luminous quality. Don't forget that at 12,550 feet above sea level, Puno will be a challenge to your system, so take it easy your first full day there.

Puno

975 km (609 mi) southeast of Lima.

Puno, the capital of the province of the same name, is the folklore capital of Peru. Traits of the Aymara, Quechua, and Spanish cultures who settled on the shores of the lake are evident in the art, music, dance, and dress of Puno's inhabitants, who call themselves the "Children of the Sacred Lake." Much of the city's character comes from the ongoing practice of ancient traditions: Every month there is a special observance, a parade, a festival, or a celebration. Each Sunday at 11 AM at the Plaza de Armas, a patriotic ceremony with bands and high-stepping young men in military uniforms takes place.

Puno is a small town, with a small-town friendliness. Most sites are between Pino Park and the Plaza de Armas, and restaurants and shops line pedestrian-only Jirón Lima, which connects the two. This is a place to enjoy wandering—and there is plenty to see and do in the surrounding area.

The focal point on the Plaza de Armas, the Baroque-style, 18th-century stone **Catedral** has carvings at the entrance of flowers and fruits, as well as mermaids playing an Andean guitar called the *charango*. It is rather plain on the inside, with its main decoration a gilt altar and paintings from the Cusco School. In back of the cathedral, on the corner of Deustua and Conde de Lemos, is the house where the viceroy Count Lemos stayed when he arrived for a visit in 1668. No visitors are allowed in the house, but you can gaze at its intricately carved wooden balcony from the street. ⊠ *Plaza de Armas,* ⊙ *Daily 8–12 and 3–5* ⊠ *Free.*

The iron ship **El Yavari**, built in England in 1862 and currently undergoing restoration, sits in Puno's port, 1 km (½ mi) east of the Plaza de Armas. Inside are a museum and bar, and future plans include day and night excursions on Lake Titicaca. ⊠ *Pier behind the Posada del Inca Hotel, at the end of Av. El Puerto* ☏ *051/369–329,* ⊕ *www.yavari.org.* ⊠ *Donation.* ⊙ *Daily 8–5.*

Where to Stay & Eat

★ ¢–$$ ✕**La Casona.** Walking into this restaurant along Puno's main street is like entering a museum. It's filled with antiques, with an especially interesting display of antique irons. The large space is divided into small, intimate rooms, and lace tablecloths give you the feeling of having dinner at great-grandma's. Try local fare, such as *lomo de alpaca* (alpaca steak) or one of their thick soups made with vegetables and meat or fish. Ask for the set menu and have a great meal for under US$5, and a pisco sour for under US$2. ⊠ *Av. Lima 517* ☏ *051/351–108* ⊟ *MC, V.*

¢–$ ✕**Apu Salkantay.** Even though it's a favorite with tourists and locals, you can usually manage to get a table. A fire is always burning in the wood stove and their set menu is a bargain. *Trucha ahumadas* (smoked trout), alpaca steaks, pizza and vegetarian dishes prepared with natural ingredients are also on the menu. Live folkloric music begins nightly at 8 PM. If the evening chill has your teeth chattering, across the street is Qori Chaska Artesanias (handicraft store) where you can pick up an inexpensive handknit alpaca sweater. ⊠ *Lima 425* ☏ *051/363–955* ⊟ *MC, V.*

★ **$$$** 🖼 **Libertador Hotel Isla Esteves.** A gleaming white low-rise hotel (just four stories), the Libertador is 5 km (3 mi) from Puno—40 minutes from the Juliaca (Puno) airport, and is the area's most luxurious lodging. On Isla Esteves, an island in Lake Titicaca, it is connected to the mainland by a causeway. In back of the hotel steps lead up to a small sitting area where you can watch the sun rise over Lake Titicaca. Play billiards in the game room, go to the discotheque, or relax in the piano bar. The gift shop has beautiful alpaca wool sweaters that are more expensive than in the street market, but the quality is excellent. Taxis are the only way to get to the center of town—about US $2 and usually a little cheaper on the return. You can catch a taxi around Parque Pino on Calle Lima. ⊠ *Isla Esteves* ☎ *051/367–780* 🖷 *051/367–879* ⊕ *www.libertador.com.pe* ➷ *126 rooms, 11 suites* ♧ *Restaurant, health club, bar, dance club* ⊟ *AE, DC, MC, V* ⑩ *BP.*

$$ 🖼 **Posada del Inca.** The warmth of Indian weavings, polished wood, and native art give character to this thoroughly modern Sonesta hotel on the shores of Lake Titicaca. It is 5 km (3 mi) from the center of town and has its own dock that extends out into the lake with the *El Yavari*, the world's oldest motorized iron ship anchored at the end. Hydrofoils to Copacabana and the Sun and Moon Islands on the Bolivian side of Lake Titicaca also leave from the Posada's dock. Eating in the hotel's restaurant is a pleasure, as large picture windows offer you a panoramic view of the lake. ⊠ *Sesqui Centenario 610, Sector Huaje* ☎ *051/363–672* ⊕ *www.posadas.com.pe* ➷ *62 rooms* ♧ *Restaurant, lounge, business services, meeting rooms* ⊟ *AE, DC, MC, V* ⑩ *BP.*

★ **$** 🖼 **Qelgatani.** The owner is always around to ensure your happiness at this small hotel on a quiet street about three blocks from the Cathedral and a five-minute walk from Jirón Lima. Rooms and private baths are large and have individual space heaters. A full breakfast in the friendly first-floor restaurant is included, and it is also open for lunch or dinner. Next door is Rey Travel Agency, where you can book tours or transfers or reconfirm your flights. ⊠ *Tarapacá 355* ☎ *051/366–172* 🖷 *051/351–052* ➷ *20 rooms* ♧ *Restaurant, coffee shop, travel services* ⊟ *AE, MC, V* ⑩ *BP.*

★ **¢** 🖼 **Pukara.** This hostal is just a few steps west of Jirón Lima, where all the action is, but the neighborhood is quiet, so you can get a good night's sleep. The hotel is casual and friendly, the staff speaks English, and all rooms, although small, have private baths with hot showers. Breakfast in the upstairs restaurant is included. An impressive, huge woven tapestry dominates the lobby. ⊠ *Libertad 328* 🖷🖷 *054/368–448* ➷ *10 rooms,* ⊟ *MC, V* ⑩ *BP.*

Shopping

Model reed boats, small stone carvings, and alpaca-wool articles are among the local crafts sold at Puno's **Mercado Artesanal** (Handicrafts Market) near the train station, two blocks east of Parque Pino around Calle Arbula and Avenida Los Incas. Don't be fooled by the market's shabby appearance—some of the country's highest-quality alpaca sweaters are sold here, and if you find you aren't dressed for Puno's chilly evenings, it's the place to buy a good woolen pancho for under US$10. A miniature reed boat is a nice souvenir to take home for your younger relatives. It's also interesting to stroll by the produce section and see the many varieties and colors of potatoes. There are no set hours, but the vendors start setting up their stands daily in the early morning and stay open all day, roughly 8–6. Make sure you know where your wallet or purse is while you're snapping a photo of the colorful market. **Artesanías Puno** (⊠ Lima 549 ☎ 051/351–261) sells a modest selection of locally made alpaca items.

Lake Titicaca

Divided by the border between Peru and Bolivia, Lake Titicaca draws visitors both for its scenery and for the vivid Quechua and Aymara cultures that still thrive on its shores. Surrounded by high, barren mountains, the lake is truly an inland sea whose opposite shores are often beyond view. Some 12,500 feet above sea level, Lake Titicaca is the largest lake in South America and the highest navigable lake in the world. The Bayhía de Puno, separated from the lake proper by the two jutting peninsulas of Capaschica and Chucuito, is home to the Uro people. The lakeshores are lush with totora reeds—valuable as building materials, cattle fodder, and, in times of famine, human food.

The Floating Islands

The most famous excursion from Puno is a trip to the Uros "floating islands," 8–24 km (5–15 mi) offshore. These man-made islands of woven totora reeds provide a fascinating look at a form of human habitation evolved over centuries. At the same time, the visit is a bit sad, with adults and runny-nosed children trying to sell you miniature reed boats and weavings. You can walk around the springy, moist islands; hire an islander to take you for a ride in one of his or her reed boats; see the islanders—Uro peoples who have intermarried with the Aymara—weaving and drying fish in the sun; and marvel at the microwave telephone stations on the islands of Torani Pata and Balsero.

Taquile & Amantani

These two lake islands are around an hour by launch from Puno. Unlike the floating islands, which are in the Bay of Puno, Taquile and Amantani are in Lake Titicaca proper and are surrounded by a vast, oceanlike panorama. The proud, Quechua-speaking people of Taquile, where the hills are topped with Inca and Tiahuanaco ruins, weave some of Peru's loveliest textiles. They still wear traditional dress and have successfully maintained the strong community ties and cooperative lifestyle of their ancestors, though there are signs that the island may be losing its unspoiled character under the weight of tourism. Amantani, also with pre-Columbian ruins, has a larger, mainly agrarian society, whose traditional way of life has stood up better to outside pressure. For a day visit to the islands, that take one of the agency tours that leave at around 7:30 AM and include a visit to one of the floating islands. If you want to make an overnight stay on Taquile or Amantani (which is recommended), travel instead on the slower local ferry, since there are sometimes problems with the agency services if you try to break your trip and continue the next day. Lodging costs about $4, and you stay in a local home. Nights can be cold and blankets inadequate, so you may wish to take along a sleeping bag. Bring your own water or water-purification tablets.

Chucuito

20 km (12 mi) southeast of Puno.

Chucuito is surrounded by hillsides crisscrossed with agricultural terraces. Be sure to take a look at the stone sundial that graces its main plaza, as well as at the local lakefront cottage industry: making reed boats for use on Titicaca.

Juli

On Lake Titicaca, 84 km (52 mi) southeast of Puno.

At one time this village may have been an important Aymará religious center, and it has served as a Jesuit training center for missionaries from Paraguay and Bolivia. Juli is considered a sort of altiplano Rome because of its disproportionate number of churches. Four interesting churches in various stages of restoration are **San Pedro Mártir, Santa Cruz de Jerusalén, Asunción,** and **San Juan de Letrán.** The latter has 80 paintings from the highly rated Cusco School and huge windows worked in stone.

Pomata

108 km (67 mi) southeast of Puno.

The main attraction in the small lakeside town of Pomata is the church of **Santiago Apóstol de Nuestra Señora del Rosario.** It was built in the 18th century of pink granite, and has paintings from the Cusco School and the Flemish School. Its mestizo baroque carvings and translucent alabaster windows are spectacular. Its altars are covered in gold leaf. Pomata is also famous for its fine pottery, especially for its Toritos de Pucará (bull figures).

Sillustani

30 km (19 mi) northwest of Puno.

High on a hauntingly beautiful peninsula in Lake Umayo is the necropolis of Sillustani. Twenty-eight stone burial towers represent a city of the dead that both predated and coincided with the Inca empire. The proper name for a tower is *ayawasi* (home of the dead), but they are generally referred to as *chullpas,* which are actually the shrouds used to cover the mummies deposited inside. This was the land of the Aymará-speaking Colla people, and the precision of their masonry rivals that of the Inca. Sillustani's mystique is heightened by the view it provides over Lake Umayo and its mesa-shape island, El Sombrero, as well as by the utter silence that prevails, broken only by the wind over the water and the cries of lake birds. On your way to the chullpas, keep an eye out for shepherds watching over their sheep and alpacas. Most of the chullpas date from the 14th and 15th centuries, but some were erected as early as AD 900. The tallest, known as the Lizard because of a carving on one of its massive stones, has a circumference of 28 feet. An unusual architectural aspect of the chullpas is that the circumference is smaller at the bottom than the top. To fully appreciate Sillustani, it is necessary to make the long climb to the top; fortunately, the steps are wide and it's an easy climb. You will be besieged at the site by young girls selling necklaces that are interesting, attractive, and inexpensive. If you take photos of mothers, children, and pet alpacas, a donation of a couple of soles will be much appreciated.

Puno & Lake Titicaca A to Z

AIR TRAVEL

You can arrange airport transfers to your hotel in Puno from the Aeropuerto Manco Cápac in Juliaca, a commercial and industrial center 50 km (31 mi) north of town. Make arrangements through a travel agency, take a taxi, or share a minibus.

Aero Continente has daily flights from Lima and Arequipa to Juliaca. LanPeru flies from Lima to Juliaca.

🛪 Airlines & Contacts **Aero Continente** ☎ 051/242-4242. **LanPeru** ☎ 051/367-227.

BOAT & FERRY TRAVEL

Crillón Tours in La Paz, Bolivia, is once again operating its hydrofoils all the way to Puno, eliminating the bus-hydrofoil combination between Peru and Bolivia. En route to Bolivia, the hydrofoil stops at the Uros floating islands and the Sun and Moon islands before continuing to Copacabana or to the Huatajata harbor. Passengers can stay overnight on Sun Island, at Copacabana, or at the Inca Utama Hotel & Spa at Huatajata harbor in Bolivia before continuing by bus to La Paz or returning to Puno. It's possible to go by bus from Puno to La Paz, but it takes more than 12 hours and involves a ferry crossing at the border. You can also take a bus from Juliaca, 50 km (31 mi) from Puno, around the top of the lake to La Paz, but it's a long, cold trip over rough roads. Make arrangements for the crossing to Bolivia through a travel agency in Puno or Lima or with Crillón Tours. The easiest and most pleasant way to cross the border between Peru and Bolivia is to book passage on the comfortable hydrofoils operated by Crillón Tours between Puno on the Peruvian side and Copacabana on the Bolivian side. Hydrofoils leave Puno Tuesday, Thursday, and Saturday, and from Copacabana to Puno on Wednesday, Friday, and Saturday. Once you make the crossing, you can choose to go from Copacabana to Sun Island to spend some time, then to Huatajata harbor to relax at the Inca Utama complex before returning via the same route to Peru, or go on to La Paz for a few days. Once in La Paz, LAB, the Bolivian airline, flies three times a week to Cusco, Peru, and daily between La Paz, Santa Cruz, and Miami, Florida.

🚢 Boat & Ferry Information **Crillón Tours** ✉ Av. Camacho 1223, La Paz ☎ 02/337-533 ⊕ www.titicaca.com.

TELEPHONES

In Puno, Telefónica del Peru is one of the best places to make calls.

☎ **Telefónica del Peru** ✉ Jr. Lima Puno ☎ 051/369-180.

TOUR OPERATORS

Excursions to the floating islands of the Uros as well as to Taquile and Amantani can be arranged through tour agencies in Puno. Most tours depart between 7:30 and 9 AM, as the lake can become choppy in the afternoon. You also can take the local boat at the Puno dock for about the same price as a tour, although boats don't usually depart without at least 10 passengers.

Allways Travel ⊠ Tacna 234 ☎ 051/355-552 ⊕ www.allwaystravelperu.com **Condor Travel** ⊠ Jr. Melgar 173 ☎ 051/352-632 🖶 051/355-794 ⊕ www.condortravel.com.pe. **Edgar Adventures** ⊠ Jr. Lima 328 ☎ 051/353-444 🖶 051/354-811. **Grace Tours** ⊠ Lima 385 ☎🖶 051/355-721. **Kontiki Tours** ⊠ Jr. Melgar 188 ☎🖶 051/353-473. **Receptour** ⊠ Lima 419, Suite 205 ☎ 051/352-391 🖶 051/369-941. **Rey Tours** ⊠ Tarapacá 399 ☎ 051/352-061. **Solmartour** ⊠ Jr. Libertad 229-231 ☎ 051/622-043. **Turpuno** ⊠ Lambayeque 175 ☎🖶 054/351-431.

VISITOR INFORMATION

Información Turística ⊠ Lima 582 and Ayacucho 682, Puno ☎ 051/364-976, 🖶 051/351-261. **Touring and Automobile Club of Peru** ⊠ Titicaca 531, Puno ☎ 051/352-432.

CUSCO & ENVIRONS

In a fertile valley in the Andes, 3,500 meters (11,500 feet) above sea level, lies Cusco, the southern capital of the Inca empire and today, arguably, the southern capital of tourism in the Western Hemisphere. While the name Inca originally applied only to the royal family, in particular the emperors (e.g., the Inca Pachacutec), today it describes the indigenous people as a whole. The Inca language was Quechua in this empire they called Tawantinsuyo, the four corners of the earth. Under the rule of the legendary Pachacutec, the Inca expanded that empire as far north and south as present-day Colombia and Argentina. But today's Cusco remained the Inca Qosqo, the "Navel of the World," the glittering capital from which all power emanated.

But not all was Inca in southern Peru, a point that gets lost in the tourist trek from one Inca ruin to the next. The presence not far from Cusco of Pikillacta, a pre-Inca city constructed by the Wari culture that thrived between AD 600 and 1000, is an indication that this territory, like most of Peru, was the site of sophisticated civilizations long before the Inca appeared on the scene. Then came Francisco Pizarro and the Spanish. After the 1532 conquest of the Inca empire, the new colonists overlaid a new political system and new religion onto the old. They also literally superimposed their architecture, looting former structures of their gold, silver, and stone, grafting their own churches, monasteries, convents, and palaces onto the foundations of the Inca sites. The result throughout the region is an odd juxtaposition of imperial and colonial, indigenous and Spanish. Traditionally clad Quechua-speaking women sell their wares in front of a part-Inca, part-colonial structure as a business executive walks by carrying on a cell-phone conversation. The two cultures coexist, but have not entirely embraced each other almost five centuries after the conquest.

Exploring Cusco

If you haven't booked a tour of Cusco through a travel agency, purchase a *boleto turístico* (tourist ticket) for S/36 (S/18 with an international student ID). Buy these at the lobby of the **Instituto Nacional de Cultura** (✉ Garcilaso and Heladeros ☎ 084/226–919), open Monday through Friday 8 to 5, Saturday 8 to 4, and Sunday 8 to 12. The ticket is valid for 10 days for one entry each to most main attractions in Cusco, including churches, convents, museums, and archaeological sites in the nearby Sacred Valley, a total of 16 locations in all. (Machu Picchu is *not* included.) This is the only way to visit any of the sites; individual admission prices are not assessed. The ticket takes the form of a color certificate that certifies that you visited each of the sites portrayed on its face. The reverse side shows a map, addresses, and opening hours. An alternative is the S/21 *boleto parcial* (partial ticket), valid for admission for one day only at Sacsayhuamán, Qenko, Puka Pukara, and Tambomachay, the four Inca ruins nearest Cusco.

Numbers in the text correspond to numbers in the margin and on the Cusco map.

a good walk

Most of Cusco's main attractions lie within its historic center, whose heart is the Haukaypata, more commonly known as the **Plaza de Armas ❶** ▶. In the eastern corner of the Plaza de Armas are remnants of an Inca wall, part of the Acllawasi (House of the Chosen Women). The palace of Pachacutec, who turned the Inca kingdom into an empire, once stood on what is now the western corner of the plaza. The **Catedral ❷** sits on the northeast side. Rivaling the cathedral in stature is **Iglesia de La Compañía ❸**, on the corner diagonally across the plaza. As you face the cathedral you will see to the right a steep, narrow street, Triunfo, now rebaptized with its original Quechua name of Sunturwasi. One block up on the right, where the street name changes to Hatun Rumiyoq, stands what is believed to have been the **Palacio de Inca Roca ❹**. Today the colonial building that rests on the Inca foundations is the **Museo de Arte Religioso del Arzobispado ❺**. Before heading up the hill to San Blas, a short detour on Choquechaca takes you to the **Museo Irq'i Yachay ❻**, a children's art museum. The street leads up to a steep, cobblestone hill known as the Cuesta de San Blas, the entry into the traditional artists' quarter of San Blas. Continue on the same street for one block to reach the **Plazoleta de San Blas ❼**. Also on the square is the **Museo Hilario Mendívil ❽**.

Backtracking again from the Plaza de Armas, the street to the left of the cathedral, called Cuesta del Almirante, will take you to a beautiful colonial mansion, the Palacio del Almirante, the site of Cusco's **Museo Inka ❾**. To the left of the modern fountain in the Plazuela del Tricentenario, in front of the mansion, is a 200-meter-long (656-foot-long) walkway with a fine view of the Plaza de Armas and central Cusco. Once again starting from the Plaza de Armas, follow the street named Santa Catalina Angosta along the Inca wall of the Acllawasi to the **Convento de Santa Catalina de Siena ❿**. A few blocks away is one of the most splendid examples of Inca architecture, the Temple of the Sun, known as **Qorikancha ⓫**, with a colonial church superimposed on it. West of the

Plaza de Armas, along the Calle del Medio, is the Kusipata, still commonly referred to by its former name, Plaza Regocijo. In the municipal building on the plaza sits the **Museo de Arte Contemporáneo** ⑫. Beyond it is the **Casa de Garcilaso** ⑬. Walk down Heladeros to Mantas to reach the church and monastery of **La Merced** ⑭. Follow Mantas to the **Plaza e Iglesia de San Francisco** ⑮. From here, through the attractive Arco Santa Clara, a colonial archway, Cusco's public market area begins. Ahead are **Iglesia Santa Clara** ⑯ and **Iglesia San Pedro** ⑰.

TIMING &
PRECAUTIONS
The city is compact, so you can visit most sites in a day. However, to fully enjoy Cusco, to have time inside the museums, and to adjust to the high altitude, you need at least two days. The churches close for a few hours in the middle of the day. Get a very early start, or split the walk in two. Most of the city's museums close on Sunday. Be street smart in the Cusco area, especially in the bustling Plaza de Armas, the San Pedro market area, and, particularly in the evenings, the pedestrian-only streets of San Blas. Stay alert, access your cash discreetly when you need it, and keep your valuables close. For further tips, *see* Safety *in* Smart Travel Tips A to Z.

What to See

⑬ **Casa de Garcilaso.** This is the colonial childhood home of Inca Garcilaso de la Vega, the famous chronicler of the Spanish conquest and illegitimate son of one of Pizarro's captains and an Inca princess. Inside the mansion, with its cobblestone courtyard, is the Museo de Historia Regional, with Cusqueña-school paintings and pre-Inca mummies—one from Nazca has a 1.5-meter (5-foot) braid—and ceramics, metal objects, and other artifacts. ⊠ *Heladeros at Garcilaso* ☎ *084/223–245* ☒ *Boleto Turístico* ☉ *Mon.–Sat. 8–5.*

❷ **Catedral.** The baroque-style cathedral is built on the foundations of the palace of the Inca Wirachocha. Construction began in 1550, using many stones looted from the site of the hillside Sacsayhuamán fortress, and ended a century later. It is considered one of the most splendid Spanish colonial churches in the Americas. Within its high walls are some of the best examples of the Cusqueña school of painting, including a Marcos Zapata painting of the Last Supper with a local specialty, cuy (guinea pig), as the main dish. The cathedral's centerpieces are its massive, solid-silver altar, and the enormous 1659 María Angola bell, the largest in South America, which hangs in one of the towers. The cedar choir has carved rows of saints, popes, and bishops, all in stunning detail down to their delicately articulated hands. Five chapels flank each side of the nave; the one dedicated to Nuestro Señor de los Temblores (Our Lord of the Earthquakes) contains a solid-gold crucifix that, legend has it, minimized damage to the chapel during a 1650 earthquake. There's non-Christian imagery here too: figures of pumas, the Inca representation of the earth, are carved on the enormous main doors. Normal access to the cathedral is not via those doors but through the adjoining Iglesia del Triunfo, the city's first Christian church. ⊠ *Haukaypata (Plaza de Armas)* ☎ *No phone* ☒ *Boleto Turístico* ☉ *Mon.–Wed. and Fri.–Sat. 10–11:30 and daily 2–5:30.*

Fodor's Choice
★

CUSCO

KEY

🚩 *Start of walk*

0   250 yards

0   250 meters

🔟 **Convento de Santa Catalina de Siena.** Still an active Dominican convent, Santa Catalina has a 1610 church with high and low choirs and a museum with religious art. Ironically, the site represents the change of one group of chosen women for another: the convent was built on the site of the Acllawasi, the house of some 3,000 Inca chosen women dedicated to teaching, weaving Inca ceremonial robes, and service to the sun. ⊠ *Santa Catalina Angosta s/n* ☎ *084/223–245* 🎫 *Boleto Turístico* 🕓 *Mon.–Thurs. and Sat. 9–5, Fri. 9–3:30.*

❸ **Iglesia de La Compañía.** The company referred to here is the Society of Jesus, the powerful Jesuit order that built this church on the foundation of the Inca Huayna Capac's palace in the late 17th century. Note the outstanding carved facade, the two Baroque towers and, inside, the Cusqueña-school paintings of the life of Jesuit patron St. Ignatius Loyola. During construction, the Archbishop of Cusco complained that the church would rival the cathedral a block away in beauty and stature. By the time the pope stepped in to rule in favor of the cathedral, it was too late; construction of the Compañía church was nearly complete. ⊠ *Haukaypata (Plaza de Armas)* ☎ *No phone* 🎫 *Free* 🕓 *Masses: Mon.–Sat. 7 AM, noon, and 6 PM, Sun. 7:30, 11:30 AM, and 6 and 7 PM.*

⑰ Iglesia San Pedro. Stones from Inca ruins were used to construct this church. Though spartan inside, San Pedro is known for its ornately carved pulpit. The vendors you see on the front steps are a spillover from the nearby central market. Though colorful, this neighborhood shopping area is not the safest for tourists—leave important belongings in your hotel room. ☒ *Santa Clara at Chaparro* ☎ *No phone* ⊠ *Free* ⊙ *Mon.–Sat. 7–11:30 and 6–7:30.*

⑯ Iglesia Santa Clara. This austere 1588 church, the oldest cloistered convent in Peru, was built in old Inca style, using stone looted from Inca ruins, finely hewn and tightly assembled. The inside is notable for its gold-laminated altar and thousands of mirrors. ☒ *Santa Clara* ☎ *No phone* ⊠ *Free* ⊙ *Daily 7–11:30 and 6–7:30.*

⑭ La Merced. Rebuilt in the 17th century, this monastery—with two stories of portals and a colonial fountain, gardens, and benches—has a spectacular series of murals that depict the life of the founder of the Mercedarian order, St. Peter of Nolasco. A small but impressive museum of the convent's treasures has, among other objects, the Custodia, a solid gold container for communion wafers encrusted with hundreds of precious stones. ☒ *Mantas 121* ☎ *084/231–831* ⊠ *S/3* ⊙ *Church: Mon.–Sat. 7–7:30 AM and 5–8 PM, Sun., 7–12 and 6:30–7:30 PM; museum: Mon.–Sat. 8–12:30 and 2–5:30.*

★ ❽ Museo Hilario Mendívil. In the home of famous 20th-century Peruvian religious artist Hilario Mendívil (1929–77), this gallery displays the maguey-wood and rice-plaster sculptures of the Virgin with the elongated necks that were the artist's trademark. Art has always been a family affair among this clan; Mendívil, himself the son of artists, began painting at age 10, and his wife, Georgina Dueñas, who died in 1998, also had an artistic flair. Their six children have continued the tradition since their father's death, and several budding painters and sculptors have sprung up in the fourth generation of Mendívils as well. ☒ *Plazoleta San Blas 634* ☎ *084/226–506* ⊠ *Free* ⊙ *Mon.–Sat. 8–8.*

★ ❾ Museo Inka. The draw of this archaeological museum is its collection of Inca mummies, but the entire facility is Cusco's best Spanish-language introduction to pre-Columbian Andean culture. The ceramics, vases, and textiles provide a much-needed reminder that civilizations thrived in this region before the Inca. The building was once the palace of Admiral Francisco Aldrete Maldonado, hence its common designation as the Palacio del Almirante (Admiral's Palace). ☒ *Ataúd at Córdoba del Tucumán* ☎ *084/237–380* ⊠ *S/5* ⊙ *Mon.–Fri. 8–5, Sat. 9–4.*

☸ ❻ Museo Irq'i Yachay. The museum's name translates as "Wisdom of the Young," and that it is. A rural-development venture, the Taller Móvil de Arte (Mobile Art Workshop), has collected children's artworks from remote Andean communities as part of an educational project to enhance young people's cultural awareness and sense of expression. ☒ *Choquechaca and Ladrillos* ☎ *084/223–390* ⊠ *Free* ⊙ *Wed.–Sun. 11–5.*

⑫ Museo de Arte Contemporáneo. Take a refreshing turn back toward the present in this city that wears its history on its sleeve. Yet even the modern-art museum, in the Cusco municipal hall, focuses on the past. Twentieth-century artists have put a modern-art spin on imperial and colonial themes. ⊠ *Kusipata s/n(Plaza Regocijo)* ☎ *084/240–006* ☒ *Boleto Turístico* ☉ *Mon.–Fri. 9–5:30.*

❺ Museo de Arte Religioso del Arzobispado. First the site of the Inca Roca's Hatun Rumiyoq palace, then the juxtaposed Moorish-style palace of the Marqués de Buenavista, the building reverted to the archdiocese of Cusco and served as the archbishop's residence. The prelate still lives in one wing of the building, which, with its elaborate gardens, doorways, and arcades is worth a look. But it now serves as the city's primary repository of religious art, mostly Cusqueña-school paintings, many by famed artist Marcos Zapata. A highlight of the collection of religious art is a series of 17th-century paintings that depict the city's Corpus Christi procession. ⊠ *Hatun Rumiyoq and Herejes* ☎ *084/ 222–781* ☒ *Boleto Turístico* ☉ *Mon.–Sat. 8–11:30 and 3–5:30.*

❹ Palacio de Inca Roca. Inca Roca lived in the 13th or 14th century. Halfway along the palace's side wall, nestled amid other stones, is the famous 12-angled stone, an example of masterly Inca masonry. There's nothing sacred about the 12 angles, other than that today the stone is the symbol that appears on every bottle of Cusqueña beer. Inca masons were famous for incorporating stones with many more sides than 12 into their buildings. Ask one of the shopkeepers along the street to point it out. ⊠ *Hatun Rumiyoq and Palacio Herrajes.*

▶ **❶ Plaza de Armas.** The imposing plaza is a direct descendant of imperial
Fodor'sChoice   Cusco's central square, which the Inca called the Haukaypata (the only
★   name indicated on today's street signs) and which extended beyond the area covered by the present-day square as far as the Plaza del Regocijo. According to belief, it was the exact center of the Inca empire, Tawantinsuyo, the Four Corners of the Earth. Eight *portales,* or covered arcades, now ring the plaza, one of Latin America's finest. Starting at the cathedral and going clockwise they bear religious or commercial names: Belén (Bethlehem); Carrizos (straw); la Compañía (Jesuits); Comercio (commerce); Confituría (preserves); Panes (breads); Harinas (flours); and Carnes (meats). Each Sunday morning sees a military parade on the cathedral side of the plaza that draws hundreds of spectators and, as a sign of the times in today's Peru, a few protesters.

⓯ Plaza e Iglesia de San Francisco. The plaza, though unimpressive, has an intriguing garden of native plants. The church has two sepulchers with arrangements of bones and skulls, some pinned to the wall to spell out morbid sayings. A small museum of religious art with paintings by Cusqueña-school artists Marcos Zapata and Diego Quispe Tito is in the church sacristy. ⊠ *3 blocks south of Plaza de Armas* ☎ *084/221–361* ☒ *S/1* ☉ *Mon.–Fri. 9–12 and 3–5.*

❼ Plazoleta de San Blas. The little square in San Blas has a simple adobe church with one of the jewels of colonial art in the Americas—the pulpit of San Blas, an intricately carved 17th-century cedar pulpit hewn from a single tree trunk and arguably Latin America's most ornate, dominated by the triumphant figure of Christ. ☎ *No phone* ✉ *Boleto Turístico* ⊙ *Church Mon.–Sat. 10–11:30 and 2–5:30.*

⓫ Qorikancha. The Temple of the Sun was built to honor Tawantinsuyos'

★ most important divinity and served as astronomical observatory and repository of the realm's gold treasure. (The temple's name translates as "Court of Gold.") If Cusco was constructed to represent a puma, then Qorikancha was positioned as the animal's loins. Some 4,000 priests and attendants are thought to have lived within its confines. Walls and altars were plated with gold, and in the center of the complex sat a giant gold disc, positioned to reflect the sun and bathe the temple in light. At the summer solstice, sunlight reflected into a niche in the wall where only the Inca were permitted to sit. Terraces that face it were once filled with life-size gold and silver statues of plants and animals. Much of the wealth was removed to pay ransom for the captive Inca Atahualpa at the time of the conquest, blood money that was paid in vain. In the 16th century, above its looted ruins, the Spanish constructed the Dominican church of Santo Domingo using stones from the temple, perhaps Cusco's most jarring imperial-colonial architectural juxtaposition. An ingenious restoration to recover both buildings after the 1953 earthquake lets you see how the church was built on and around the walls and chambers of the temple. In the Inca structures left exposed, you can admire the mortarless masonry, earthquake-proof trapezoidal doorways, curved retaining wall, and exquisite carving that exemplify the Inca artistic and engineering skills. A small museum just down the hill with an entrance on Avenida El Sol documents the history of the site. ✉ *Pampa del Castillo at Plazoleta Santo Domingo* ☎ *No phone* ✉ *Boleto Turístico* ⊙ *Daily 9–5:30.*

San Blas. Cusco's traditional old Bohemian quarter of artists and artisans is one of the city's most picturesque districts. Recently restored, its whitewashed adobe homes with bright blue doors shine anew. The Cuesta de San Blas (San Blas Hill), one of the main entrances into the area, is sprinkled with galleries that sell paintings in the Cusqueña-school style of the 16th through 18th centuries. Many of the stone streets are built as stairs or slopes (not for cars) and have religious motifs carved into them. Avoid wandering the pedestrian-only streets here at night, but if you choose to, travel with companions.

off the beaten path

COLCAMPATA – For the energetic, the 15-minute walk to Colcampata offers a tour through colonial neighborhoods in the heights above the city. Following Procuradores from the Plaza de Armas to Waynapata and then Resbalosa, you'll come to a steep cobblestone staircase with a wonderful view of La Compañía. Continuing to climb, you'll find the church of San Cristóbal, which is of little intrinsic interest but affords another magnificent panorama of the city. The church stands atop Colcampata, believed to have been the palace of the first Inca ruler, Manco Capac. The Inca wall to the right of the church has 11 niches in which soldiers may once have stood guard. Farther up the road, the lane on the left leads to a post-conquest Inca gateway beside a magnificent Spanish mansion.

Where to Stay & Eat

$ ✕ **Mesón de Espaderos.** You'll drink in the city's history as you dine on a rustic, second-floor terrace with stucco walls and high beamed ceilings above the Plaza de Armas. The *parrilladas* (barbecued meats) are the best in Cusco; the platter for one person is more than enough for two. But there's an ample salad bar if you're not feeling quite so carnivorous. ⊠ *Espaderos 105* ☎ *084/235–307* ⊟ *AE, DC, MC, V.*

$ ✕ **Pucará.** This is the best place in Cusco to sample regional dishes, which
Fodor'sChoice means it's always busy. The lunch specials are ample and reasonably priced.
★ The *ají de gallina* is outstanding but a bit heavy before an afternoon of sightseeing. On the lighter side, the fish dishes are served with a colorful assortment of vegetables. The homemade truffles are the perfect dessert. ⊠ *Plateros 309* ☎ *084/222–027* ⊟ *AE, MC, V.*

$ ✕ **Tunupa.** An endless buffet with platter after platter of dessert, free pisco sours, and a nightly show to boot make this upstairs venue a popular restaurant for sampling traditional Peruvian fare. Try the carpaccio *de lomo* (beef marinated in herbs, olive oil and Parmesan cheese) and top it off with a rich *suspiro a la limeña,* a sweet Peruvian mousse. ⊠ *Portal de Confiturías 233, Haukaypata (Plaza de Armas)* ☎ *084/252–936* ⊟ *AE, DC, MC, V.*

★ ¢–$ ✕ **Granja Heidi.** You won't offend the owner if you ask, "Are you Heidi?" but that's actually the name of the mule who resides on the nearby farm where Gudrun and Karl Heinz get much of the produce for this San Blas restaurant. Breakfast means crepes and farm-fresh yogurt. Lunch and dinner yield meat and vegetarian dishes, soups and stir fries. Try the *carapulcra* (dried potatoes served with a tangy, spicy sauce), and save room for the Nelson Mandela cake. (The owners are great admirers.) The service is the most attentive you'll find. ⊠ *Cuesta San Blas 525* ☎ *084/238–383* ⊘ *Closed Sunday.*

¢ ✕ **Al Grano.** Don't let the Andean tapestries and replica Inca stone wall fool you. This small restaurant off the Plaza de Armas specializes in Asian rice plates. It offers a fantastic selection of affordable dishes from India, Thailand, Malaysia, Sri Lanka, Vietnam, Myanmar, and Indonesia. You have a choice of eight prix-fixe dinners every evening, each including one of a rotating selection of entrées. The rich dessert cakes and brownies *are* Peruvian rather than Asian, however. ⊠ *Santa Catalina Ancha 398* ☎ *084/228–032* ⊟ *No credit cards* ⊘ *Closed Sunday.*

★ ¢ ✕ **Chez Maggy.** If you find the mountain air a little chilly, warm up in front of the open brick ovens that produce the café's great pizzas and calzones. (There actually is Peruvian cuisine on the menu, yet everyone comes here for the pizza.) There are two branches in Cusco within a block of each other. The tables are smaller and more intimate at the main location on Plateros, but you're sure to trade tales with other travelers around the corner at Procuradores 344, as seating there is at very long wooden tables. ⊠ *Plateros 344* ☎ *084/234–861* ⊟ *AE, DC, MC, V.*

$ ✕▦ **Sonesta Posada del Inca Valle Sagrado.** In the heart of the Sacred Val-
Fodor'sChoice ley is this 300-year-old former convent (monastery). The cobblestone
★ walkways are the perfect complement to the well-preserved colonial-era church on the grounds. A museum on the second floor of the main build-

ing has an extensive collection of pre-Inca ceramics. The rooms, with tile floors, wood ceilings, and hand-carved headboards, have balconies that overlook the gardens or the terraced hillsides. The restaurant has excellent regional fare and a popular Sunday lunch buffet. ⊠ *Plaza Manco II 123, Yucay* 🕾 *084/201–107, 01/222–4777 in Lima, 800/766–3782 in North America* 🖷 *084/201–345, 01/222–3031 in Lima* ⊕ *www. sonesta.com* 🖘 *65 rooms* ⟁ *Restaurant, bar, business services; no a/c* ⊟ *AE, MC, V.*

$$$$ 🏨 **Hotel Libertador Cusco.** Close enough, but a bit removed from the hubbub of the Plaza de Armas, this hotel on the tiny Plazoleta Santo Domingo was the last home of Francisco Pizarro, the first governor of Peru. The glass-covered lobby is a great place to relax with a mate de coca and soak in the antiques, fountain, and Cusqueño art that fills the lobby and courtyard. Rooms, decorated in Peruvian colonial style with views of patio gardens, all have central heating to keep out the chill. The plush bar makes a mean pisco sour. ⊠ *Plazoleta Santo Domingo 259* 🕾 *084/231–961* 🖷 *084/233–152* ⊕ *www.libertador.com.pe* 🖘 *254 rooms, 13 suites* ⟁ *Restaurant, café, bar, in-room data ports, in-room safes, minibars, hair salon, sauna, shops, laundry service, concierge, business services, meeting rooms; no a/c* ⊟ *AE, DC, MC, V* ⍟⍢ *BP.*

★ $$$$ 🏨 **Monasterio de Cusco.** One of Peru's loveliest hotels is in the restored 1592 monastery of San Antonio Abad, a national historic monument. Planners managed to retain the austere beauty of the complex—the lodging even counts the original chapel and its collection of Cusqueño art— and kept rooms simple and elegant with a mix of colonial and modern furnishings. At night the view of the stars from the main courtyard is truly serene. Eighty rooms can be pressurized much like an airplane cabin to duplicate conditions of those 1,000 meters (3,300 feet) lower than Cusco, the only such hotel system in the world, and an option for which you can pay a 25-percent premium. ⊠ *Palacio 136* 🕾 *084/240–696, 01/221–0826 in Lima* 🖷 *084/237–111, 01/440–6197 in Lima* ⊕ *www. orient-expresshotels.com* 🖘 *127 rooms, 6 suites* ⟁ *2 restaurants, café, in-room safes, minibars, bar, shops, laundry service, dry cleaning, concierge, business services, meeting rooms; no a/c* ⊟ *AE, DC, MC, V* ⍟⍢ *BP.*

$$ 🏨 **Hotel Savoy.** The Savoy, several blocks from the Plaza de Armas, has been acquired by the U.S. Howard Johnson's chain, but what other HoJo's offers you free *mate de coca* all day long? The mirrored colonial-style lobby introduces you to this hotel's conservative, yet friendly, style. Dark carved wood is everywhere: the front desk, the mailboxes, the elevators, the room doors, and the dressers and headboards inside the carpeted rooms. The rooftop Sky Room restaurant provides a panoramic view of the city. ⊠ *Av. El Sol 954* 🕾 *084/224–322* 🖷 *084/221–097* ⊕ *www. cusco.net/savoyhotel* 🖘 *114 rooms, 6 suites* ⟁ *Dining room, minibars, shop, bar; no a/c* ⊟ *AE, DC, MC, V* ⍟⍢ *BP.*

¢ 🏨 **Los Niños Hotel.** If you prefer lodging with a social conscience—and even if you don't—this is a great budget find; proceeds from your stay at "The Children's Hotel" provide medical and dental care, food, and recreation for 250 disadvantaged Cusqueño children who attend day care on the premises and cheerfully greet you as you pass through the courtyard. Rooms tend toward the spartan side, with painted hardwood floors but firm, comfy mattresses and an endless supply of hot water. A few other rooms as well as four apartments with shared bath, for longer stays, are down the street on Calle Fiero. The catch? The place is immensely popular. Make reservations weeks in advance. ⊠ *Meloq 442* 🕿🕿 *084/231–424* ⊕ *www.ninoshotel.com* 🛏 *20 rooms, 13 with bath* ⚭ *Café, laundry service, no smoking; no room TVs, no room phones, no a/c* ▭ *No credit cards.*

Nightlife & the Arts

The nights are chilly, the air is thin, and you need to rise early for your excursion tomorrow morning. So you'd anticipate no nightlife, right? You couldn't be more wrong. Cusco is full of bars and discos with live and recorded music, everything from U.S. rock to Andean folk. Though dance places levy a cover charge, there's usually someone out front handing out free passes to tourists—highly discriminatory, but in your favor, of course. Several restaurants also host live performances.

For a cold beer and satellite English-soccer broadcasts, try **Cross Keys** (⊠ Portal Confiturías 233, Haukaypata (Plaza de Armas) 🕿 084/229–227), a pub that will make London expats homesick. Challenge the regulars to a game of darts at your own risk. Reputed to be Cusco's first disco, dating all the way back to 1985, **Kamikase** (⊠ Kusipata 274 (Plaza Regocijo) 🕿 084/233–865) is a favorite gringo bar, though plenty of locals visit too, and has a mix of salsa, rock, and folk music for your dancing pleasure most evenings. **Mama Africa** (⊠ Portal de Panes 109, Haukaypata (Plaza de Armas) 🕿 084/245–550), Cusco's hottest reggae and hip-hop dance venue, is also part travel agency and cyber café.

Shopping

Cusco is full of traditional crafts and artwork and more modern handmade goods, especially clothing made of alpaca, llama, or sheep wool. Much of what you see is factory made, despite some sellers' claims to the contrary. Several enclosed crafts markets are good bets for bargains. Vendors will approach you relentlessly on the Plaza de Armas, and if you keep your eyes open and bargain hard, you may take home something special. The municipal government operates the **Centro Artesanal Cusco** (⊠ Tullumayo and El Sol 🕿 no phone), containing 340 stands of artisan vendors. Religious art, including elaborately costumed statues of the Virgin Mary, is sold at the shop at the **Galería Mendívil** (⊠ Plazoleta San Blas 🕿 084/226–506). In San Blas, the **Galería Mérida** (⊠ Carmen Alto 133 🕿 08/422–1714) sells the much-imitated ceramics of Edilberto Mérida. **Galería Latina** (⊠ San Agustín 427 🕿 084/246–588) is a reasonably priced crafts shop with many original pieces, tapestries, ceramics, and alpaca clothing among them. Triunfo is lined with crafts shops as far as San Blas. One of the best, **Taller Maxi** (⊠ Sunturwasi 393 (Triunfo) 🕿 no phone), sells dolls in historical and local costumes. You can even have one custom made. Also on display are *retablos* (wooden boxes) that show Cusco's most popular sites and alpaca jackets decorated with local weavings.

Side Trips from Cusco

Cusco is the gateway to some of Peru's greatest historical areas and monuments, such as Sacsayhuamán, on a hill that overlooks the city, or the southeastern sector of the Urubamba River Valley. Northwest of the city, the so-called Sacred Valley, an Inca breadbasket for centuries, is still marked with the footprints of its imperial past.

Sacsayhuamán

Dominating a hilltop north of the city is the massive complex of **Sacsayhuamán,** perhaps the most important Inca monument after Machu Picchu. Built of stones of astonishing size and weight—the largest is 361 tons—the center seems to have served both religious and military ends, with zigzag walls and cross-fire parapets that allowed defenders to rain destruction on attackers from two sides. Today only ruins remain of the original fortress city, which the Spanish tore down after crushing Manco Inca's rebellion in 1536 and then ransacked for years as a source of construction materials for the new Spanish city at Cusco. If you don't have a car, the easiest way to get here is to take a taxi. ☎ *No phone* 🎫 *Boleto Turístico* ☉ *7–6.*

Smaller archaeological sites around Sacsayhuamán include **Qenko,** 2 km (1 mi) away, a huaca with a small amphitheater where the mummies of nobles and priests were kept and brought out on sunny days for ritualistic worship. Continue 6 km (4 mi) to reach **Puka Pukara,** which some archaeologists believe was a fort and others claim was an inn and storage place used by the Inca nobility. Nearby **Tambomachay** is a huaca built on a natural spring. Perhaps a place where water, which the Incas considered a source of life, was worshiped, the huaca is almost certain to have been the scene of sacred ablutions and purifying ceremonies.

Urubamba Valley

Along the highway that runs southeast of Cusco to Sicuani are a number of lesser-known Inca sites. Despite the fact that they are easy to visit in one day by car, you may find that you have these magnificent ruins all to yourself, for they are off the traditional tourist circuit.

Tipón, 23 km (14 mi) southeast of Cusco, is one of the best surviving examples of Inca land and water management. It consists of a series of terraces crisscrossed by aqueducts and irrigation channels that edge up a narrow pass in the mountains. One theory is that the Incas used Tipón as an agricultural station to develop special crops. Unfortunately, the rough dirt track that leads to the complex is in wretched condition. If you visit, either walk up (about two hours each way) or go in a four-wheel-drive (about 45 minutes to the site and 30 minutes back). ☎ *No phone* 🎫 *Boleto Turístico* ☉ *Daily 7–6.*

About 9 km (5½ mi) down the highway from the Tipón turnoff stand the haunting ruins of **Pikillacta,** a vast city from the pre-Inca Wari culture, which existed between 600 and 1000. Like other Andean cultures, the Wari empire—which at its height stretched from near Cajamarca to the border of the Tiahuanaco empire based around Lake Titicaca—had a genius for farming in a harsh environment and built sophisticated urban centers such as Pikillacta. Wari's capital was at Ayacucho, but little is known about the empire. The rough ruins, once enclosed by a defensive wall whose remains are still evident, confirm the Incas' superiority in architecture and masonry. They are spread over several acres and include many two-story buildings. At the thatch-roofed excavation sites you can see uncovered walls that show the city's stones were once covered with plaster and whitewashed. Across the road lies a beautiful lagoon, Lago de Lucre. ⊠ *7 km (4 mi) south of Oropesa* ☏ *No phone* ☒ *Boleto Turístico* ☉ *7–6.*

The main attraction of the small town of **Andahuaylillas,** 8 km (5 mi) southeast of Pikillacta, is a small 17th-century adobe-towered church built by the Jesuits on the central plaza over the remains of an Inca temple. The contrast between the simple exterior and the rich, expressive, colonial Baroque art inside is notable: fine examples of the Cusqueña school of art decorate the upper interior walls. Traces of gilt that once covered the church walls are still visible. The church keeps no fixed hours. Ask around town for someone to let you inside. The town's name is a corruption of *Antawaylla,* Quechua for "copper prairie." ☏ *No phone* ☒ *Free.*

Sacred Valley of the Inca

In the time of the Tawantinsuyo, this area's pleasant climate, fertile soil, and proximity to Cusco made it a favorite with the Inca nobles, many of whom are believed to have had private country homes here. Inca remains lie throughout the length of the valley, which is filled with agricultural terraces and dominated by the archaeological remains of Pisac and Ollantaytambo.

The Sacred Valley of the Incas, along the Río Urubamba, begins at the town of Pisac, about 30 km (18 mi) northeast of Cusco. It ends 60 km (36 mi) northwest of Pisac at Ollantaytambo, where the cliffs that flank the river grow closer together, the valley narrows, and the agriculturally rich floodplain thins to a gorge as the Urubamba begins its abrupt descent toward the Amazon basin. (Machu Picchu is farther downriver, among the cloud forests on the Andean slopes above the Amazon jungle.)

At the valley's southern extreme, amid rugged sandstone cliffs, is Huambutío, a launching point for raft trips.

Fodor'sChoice
★

The road from Cusco leads directly to the town of **Pisac,** a colonial town where a mass in the Quechua language is held each week in a simple stone church. Various *varayocs* (mayors) attend in full ceremonial regalia. Many people come here for the popular Sunday market. From the market area you can rent a horse or take a taxi up the winding but well-maintained road to the nearby Inca ruins. Archaeologists think there was a fortress here to defend the empire from the fierce *Antis* (jungle peoples). The terraces and irrigation systems also support the theory that it was a refuge in times of siege. The fortress is a masterpiece of Inca engineering, with narrow trails that wind tortuously among and through solid rock. You may find yourself practically alone on the series of

CloseUp

HIKING THE INCA TRAIL

THE INCA TRAIL, a 50-km (31-mi) section of the stone path that once extended from Cusco to Machu Picchu, is one of the most popular hikes in South America. Nothing matches the sensation of walking over the ridge that leads to the Lost City of the Inca just as the sun is casting a yellow glow over the ancient stone buildings. U.S. historian Hiram Bingham announced his discovery of the Inca Trail in 1915. As with Machu Picchu itself, his discovery was a little disingenuous. Locals knew about the trail, and parts of it were used during the colonial and early republican eras. In fact, the Spanish used some of the roads constructed by the Inca when they were conquering the indigenous peoples. The trail begins outside the Sacred Valley town of Ollantaytambo at a place called Km 88. It takes you past ruins and through stunning scenery that starts in the thin air of the highlands and ends in cloud forests. The best months to make the four-day trek are May through September; rainy weather is more likely in April and October and a certainty the rest of the year.

You must use a licensed tour operator, one accredited by the Unidad de Gestión Santuario Histórico de Machu Picchu, the organization that oversees the trail, and which limits the number of hikers to 500 per day. (There are some 30 such licensed operators in Cusco.) Regulations require each agency to submit its group list to the Unidad five days in advance of departure. In practice this requirement is sometimes reduced to two days, especially in the low season, but advance reservations are essential any time of year. Groups may not exceed 16 people; for more than 9 a second guide is required. The trail closes for cleaning and maintenance at least one week each February, the lowest of the low season. If you've never been backpacking, try to get some practice before you set out.

You must be in decent shape, even if your agency supplies porters to carry your pack—current regulations limit your load to 20 kg (44 pounds)—as the trail is often narrow and hair-raising. As the mountains sometimes rise to over 4,200 meters (13,775 feet), you should be aware of the dangers of altitude sickness. Your gear should include sturdy hiking boots, a sleeping bag, clothing for cold, rainy weather, a hat, and a towel. Also bring plenty of sunblock and mosquito repellent. Toilet paper is another essential on this rustic trail with few comfort stations. Avoid cutting flowers and vegetation. There are seven well-spaced, designated campsites along the trail.

You'll cross several rivers and lakes as you ascend the trail using suspension bridges, log bridges, or causeways constructed by the Inca. You'll also encounter fantastic ruins almost immediately. The first is Llactapata, not far from the start of the trail. The best might be Phuyupatamarca, a beautifully restored site where you'll find ceremonial baths. The grand finale, of course, is Machu Picchu, the reason the trail was constructed in the first place. Your choice of operator will result in a "you get what you pay for" experience. Check closely what you get for the price. Several agencies, usually catering to a student clientele, offer trips for under S/700, and if you're up to carrying your own equipment and eating more basic rations they are fine options. Higher fees—and they range up to S/1,400—get you porters, more luxurious tents, and meals, and likely include rail transportation between Cusco and Ollantaytambo. All operators offer a 4-day/3-night package for the entire trail, as well as an abbreviated 2-day/1-night version beginning at Km 104.

—By Joan Gonzalez and Jeffrey Van Fleet

paths in the mountains that lead you among the ruins, through caves, and past the largest known Inca cemetery (the Inca buried their dead in tombs high on the cliffs).

From Pisac, the road passes through the quiet colonial towns of Calca, Yucay, and Urubamba before it reaches **Ollantaytambo,** a well-preserved Inca site. The fortress of Ollantaytambo, a formidable stone structure that climbs massive terraces to the top of a peak, was the valley's main defense against the Antis and was the site of the Incas' greatest victory against the Spanish during the wars of conquest. Below the fortress lies a complete Inca town, also called Ollantaytambo, still inhabited and with its original architecture and layout preserved.

To return to Cusco, take the road from Urubamba that climbs the valley wall to the town of **Chinchero.** Apparently one of the valley's major Inca cities, Chinchero has a colonial church that was built on top of the remains of an Inca palace, as well as immense agricultural terraces. A colorful Sunday market is frequented by tourists and locals.

MACHU PICCHU

34 – 47 *110 km (66 mi) northwest of Cusco.*

FodorśChoice
★

This mystical city, a three-hour-plus train ride from Cusco, is the most important archaeological site in South America, and one of the world's foremost travel destinations. The name itself conjures up the same magic as King Solomon's Mines or Xanadu, and Machu Picchu's beauty is so spectacular that the disappointed visitor is rare indeed. Its attraction lies in the exquisite architecture of the massive Inca stone structures and in the formidable backdrop of steep sugarloaf hills, with the winding Urubamba River—the Inca, who had a system of naming rivers by sector, called this portion of the river the Vilcanota—far below.

Ever since American explorer and Yale University historian Hiram Bingham, with the aid of local guides, "discovered" the Lost City in 1911, there have been debates about Machu Picchu's original function. Bingham himself speculated that the site was a fortress for defensive purposes, but the preponderance of religious structures here calls that theory into question. It was likely a small city of some 200 homes and 1,000 residents, with agricultural terraces to supply the population's needs and a strategic position that overlooked but could not be seen from the valley floor. Exactly when Machu Picchu was built is not known, but one theory suggests that it was a country estate of the Inca Pachacutec, which means its golden age was in the mid-15th century. Historians have discredited the romantic theory of Machu Picchu as refuge of the chosen Inca women after the conquest; analysis shows a 50/50 split of male and female remains found here.

Bingham erred in recognizing just what he had uncovered. The historian assumed he had stumbled upon Vilcabamba, the last real stronghold of the Inca, the hastily constructed fortress to which the puppet Inca Manco Capac II retreated after the battles at Sacsayhuamán and Ollantaytambo. (The actual ruins of Vilcabamba lie deep in the rain forest, forgotten and not uncovered until the 1960s. And, ironically, Bingham did stumble upon the real Vilcabamba two years before he announced his discovery, equally unaware of what he had seen.) But Machu Picchu shows no battle scars, despite Bingham's insistence that it was a citadel, or signs of having been constructed quickly the way history documents that Vilcabamba was. Bingham assigned his own English-language names to the structures within the city. Call it inertia, but those labels have stuck, even though archaeologists continue to debate the correctness of the Yale historian's nomenclature.

The site's belated discovery has led some academics to conclude that the Inca deserted Machu Picchu before the Spanish conquest. The reason for the city's presumed abandonment is as mysterious as its original function. Some archaeologists suggest that the water supply simply ran out. Some guess that disease ravaged the city. Others surmise it may have been something as basic as the death of Pachacutec, after which his estate was no longer needed. Whatever the purpose, whatever the reason, this "Lost City of the Inca" was missed by the ravaging conquistadors and survived untouched until the beginning of the 20th century, and the mystery and intrigue will certainly inspire you to devise your own theories.

Numbers in the text correspond to numbers in the margin and on the Machu Picchu map.

Within the Ruins

④ Upon entry, you first encounter the ☞ **House of the Terrace Caretaker.** Bingham surmised that Machu Picchu was divided into agricultural and urban sectors. As they did elsewhere in the empire, the Inca carved agricultural terraces into the hillsides here to grow produce and minimize erosion. Corn was the likely crop cultivated at Machu Picchu, though contemporary archaeologists wonder if the capacity and area of these terraces really could have supported a community of 1,000 residents. Absent are the elaborate irrigation systems seen at Inca ruins in the drier Sacred Valley. Machu Picchu's semitropical climate meant ample rain for most of the year.

㉟ About a 20-minute walk up to the left of the entrance, the **Caretaker's Hut** and **Funeral Rock** provide the quintessential vista overlooking Machu Picchu, one that you've seen in dozens of photos, and yet nothing beats seeing the view in person, especially if your schedule permits an early morning visit to catch the misty sunrise. Bodies of nobles likely lay in state at the site, where they would have been eviscerated, dried, and prepared for mummification.

㊱ Head back down the hill to the city itself; the **Dry Moat** separates the agricultural and urban sectors. After you enter the ruins through the terraces at the agricultural sector, you come to a series of 16 small, ritual **㊲** **Fountains** linked to the Inca worship of water.

㊳ Beyond the fountains is the round **Temple of the Sun,** a marvel of perfect Inca stone assembly. Here, on June 22 (the date of the winter solstice in the southern hemisphere), sunlight shines through a small,

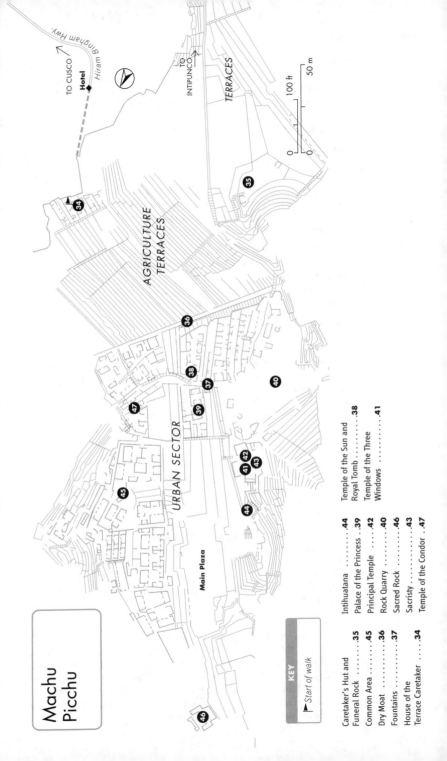

Machu Picchu

TERRACES

AGRICULTURE TERRACES

URBAN SECTOR

Main Plaza

TO CUSCO ↗
Hiram Bingham Hwy.

◆ **Hotel**

↑ TO INTIPUNCO

0 — 100 ft
0 — 50 m

trapezoid-shape window and casts light into the middle of a large, flat granite stone presumed to be an Inca calendar. Prediction worked from both directions too: looking out the window, astronomers sought the perfect view of the constellation Pleiades, revered as a symbol of crop fertility. Bingham dubbed the small cave below the temple the **Royal Tomb,** though no human remains were ever found here.

39 Adjoining the temple is a two-story building Bingham called the **Palace of the Princess.** Archaeologists have doubted the accuracy of the name.
40 Up a staircase, beyond the fountains and the temple, is a **rock quarry**
41 used by Inca masons. A stone staircase leads to the three-walled **Temple of the Three Windows**—the entire east wall is hewn from a single massive rock with trapezoidal windows cut into it. Further investigation has shown that there were really five original windows.

42 Another three-walled structure, the **Principal Temple** is so dubbed because its masonry is among Machu Picchu's best, a masterpiece of fitting together many-sided stones without mortar in true Inca fashion. A secondary
43 temple abuts the primary temple. Bingham called it the **Sacristy.** It was likely the place where priests prepared themselves for ceremonies.

44 Onward is a hillock that leads to the famous **Intihuatana,** the so-called "Hitching Post of the Sun." Every important Inca center had one of these vertical stone columns (called gnomons), but their function remains a mystery. They likely did double duty as altar and time measurement device to divine the growing seasons. The Spanish destroyed most of the hitching posts they encountered throughout the empire, deeming them to be objects of pagan worship. Machu Picchu's is one of the few to survive—partially survive at least. Shamefully, its top was accidentally knocked off in 2001 during the filming of a Cusqueña beer commercial on the site.

Cross a large grassy plaza toward an area of other buildings and huts.
45 Their less elaborate construction led Bingham to dub this the **Common Area.** Here you'll find the **Sacred Rock,** taking the shape in
46 miniature of the mountain range visible behind it. Little is known of its purpose.

47 A staircase leads to the **Temple of the Condor,** so named because the positioning of the stones resembles a giant condor, the symbol of heaven in the Inca cosmos. The structure's many small chambers led Bingham to dub it a "prison," a concept that did not likely exist in Inca society. ☎ No phone 🎫 S/72; S/36 with International Student Identity Card ☉ Daily 7–6.

Beyond the Ruins

Several trails lead from the site to surrounding ruins. A 45-minute walk southeast of the main complex is **Intipunku,** the Sun Gate, a small ruin in a pass through which you can see the sun rise at different times of the year. It is also the gateway to the **Inca Trail.** A two- or three-hour hike beyond the Intipunku along the Inca Trail will bring you to the ruins of **Huiñay Huayna,** a complex that climbs a steep mountain slope and includes an interesting set of ritual baths.

From the cemetery at Machu Picchu, a 30-minute walk along a narrow path leads to yet another example of Inca ingenuity and engineering skills: the **Inca Bridge,** built rock by rock up a hair-raising stone escarpment.

The **Huayna Picchu** trail, which follows an ancient Inca path, leads up the sugarloaf hill in front of Machu Picchu for an exhilarating, if challenging, trek. Climbers must register at the entrance to the path behind La Roca Sagrada (the Sacred Rock), where locals often pray.

At the top and scattered along the way are Inca ruins and the **Temple of the Moon.** The walk up and back takes at least two hours—more if you stay on the summit to enjoy the sun and drink in the marvelous view of Machu Picchu—and is only for the sure-footed. Bring insect repellent; the gnats can be ferocious.

Far below the ruins sits the slightly ramshackle, but thoroughly pleasant town of **Aguas Calientes,** sometimes called Machu Picchu Pueblo. But for the grace of Hiram Bingham, Aguas Calientes would be just another remote, forgotten crossroads. But 1911, and the tourist boom decades later forever changed the community. There are but two major streets—Avenida Pachacutec leads uphill from the Plaza de Armas, and Avenida Imperio de Los Incas isn't a street at all, but the railroad tracks; there's no vehicular traffic on the former except the buses that ferry tourists to the ruins. You'll have little sense of Aguas Calientes if you do the standard day trip from Cusco: train station, bus, ruins, bus, train station. But the town pulses to a very lively tourist beat with hotels, restaurants, Internet cafés, hot springs, and a surprising amount of activity even after the last afternoon train has returned to Cusco.

Aguas Calientes takes its name from the thermal springs, the **Aguas Termales,** that sit above town. Don't expect facilities and conditions to rival those at Baden Baden, but if you aren't too fussy, this can be a refreshing dip at the end of a hot day. ⊠ *Top of Av. Pachacutec* ☏ *No phone* ▨ *S/5* ⊙ *Daily 5 AM–9 PM.*

Where to Stay & Eat

¢–$ ✕ **Indio Feliz.** An engaging French-Peruvian couple manage the best restaurant in Aguas Calientes, and this pink bistro is possibly the only restaurant in town *not* to have pizza on its menu. Quiche lorraine, ginger chicken, and spicy *trucha macho* (trout in hot pepper and wine sauce) are favorites here, and are usually available as part of the more reasonably priced prix-fixe menu. Top it off with a fine coffee and apple pie or flan for dessert. ⊠ *Lloque Yupanqui 4* ☏ *084/211–090* ▭ *AE, MC, V* ⊙ *No dinner Sunday.*

¢–$ ✕ **Toto's House.** Long tables are set up in the center of the restaurant to accommodate the tour groups who flock here for the huge buffet lunch, and Toto's does it up big. Grab one of the smaller tables with a river view by the window or out on the front patio if you come on your own. Evenings are more sedate, with such dishes as ceviche and *chicharrón* (pork rinds and cabbage), all to the accompaniment of a folklore music show. ⊠ *Av. Imperio de los Incas Aguas Calientes* ☏ *084/211–020* ▭ *AE, DC, MC, V.*

$$$$ ✕🖾 **Machu Picchu Pueblo Hotel.** This stunningly beautiful ecolodge is
Fodor'sChoice in a high tropical cloud forest just off the twisting road leading up to
★ the ruins. The stone bungalows, none with the same design, have a
rustic elegance, with exposed beams and cathedral ceilings. Activities
include a one-day Inca Trail trek, bird-watching excursions, and orchid tours. Dining in the restaurant overlooking the surrounding hills
is first-rate—try the delicious *crema de choclo* (corn chowder). ⊠ *Av.
Imperio de los Incas s/n Aguas Calientes* ☎ *084/211–032, 01/610–
0404 in Lima* 🖷 *084/211–124, 01/422–4701 in Lima* ⊕ *www.
inkaterra.com* 🗺 *76 rooms, 9 suites* ⚭ *2 restaurants, dining room,
pool, spa, bar, shop, laundry service, travel services; no a/c* ▤ *AE, DC,
MC, V* ⦿⦿ *BP.*

$$$$ ✕🖾 **Machu Picchu Sanctuary Lodge.** If you can get a reservation, this hotel
at the entrance to Machu Picchu puts you closest to the ruins, a position
for which you admittedly pay dearly. Not only will you have the thrill of
watching the sun rise over the crumbling stone walls, but you'll have the
ruins to yourself after most of the tourists depart each afternoon. The lodge
has been completely renovated by Orient Express, which has taken over
the property. The restaurant has an excellent international menu that makes
it worth a special trip. ⊠ *Machu Picchu* ☎ *084/211–038, 084/241–777*
🖷 *084/211–053, 084/237–111* ⊕ *www.orient-expresshotels.com* 🗺 *29
rooms, 2 suites* ⚭ *Restaurant, snack bar, minibars, massage, bar, laundry service; no a/c* ▤ *AE, DC, MC, V* ⦿⦿ *FAP.*

Cusco, Machu Picchu & the Sacred Valley A to Z

*To research prices, get advice from other travelers, and book travel ar-
rangements, visit www.fodors.com.*

AIR TRAVEL

Aero Continente and its subsidiary Aviandina fly to Lima, Arequipa, and
Puerto Maldonado. LanPeru connects Cusco with Lima, Arequipa,
Juilaca, and Puerto Maldonado. TANS Perú flies to Lima and Puerto
Maldonado. TACA Peru flies to Lima.

🛂 Carriers **Aero Continente/Aviandina** ⊠ Portal de Carnes 254, Haukaypata (Plaza
de Armas) Cusco ☎ 084/243–031. **LanPeru** ⊠ Av. El Sol 627 Cusco ☎ 084/255–552.
Taca Peru ⊠ Av. El Sol 602 Cusco ☎ 084/249–921. **TANS Perú** ⊠ San Agustín 315 Cusco
☎ 084/242–727.

AIRPORTS

Cusco's Aeropuerto Internacional Teniente Alejandro Velasco Astete
(CUZ), about 15 minutes from the center of town, receives international
flights only from Bolivia. You'll likely arrive from elsewhere in Peru.

🛂 Airport Information **Aeropuerto Internacional Teniente Alejandro Velasco Astete**
⊠ Av. Velasco Astete s/n ☎ 084/222–622.

CAR RENTAL

If you want to explore the Sacred Valley by car, which is advised,
Cusco is the only place to rent a vehicle. However, you won't need or
want to drive in the city itself; heavy traffic, lack of parking, and narrow streets, many of them pedestrian only, make a car an unnecessary

burden. Avis has a branch here, as do local firms Explores Transportes and OSDI Rent-a-Car.

🏃 Agencies **Avis** ✉ Aeropuerto Velasco Astete ☎ 084/248–800. **Explores Transportes** ✉ Plateros 356 ☎ 084/261–640. **OSDI Rent-a-Car** ✉ Urb. Mateo Pumacahua B-10 ☎ 084/251–616.

EMERGENCIES

Most hotels have oxygen available for anyone having trouble with the altitude. The main hospital in Cusco is the Hospital Regional. Cusco's Tourist Police are part of the Policia Nacional and are specially trained to deal with visitor concerns.

🏃 Emergencies **Tourist Police** ✉ Monumento a Pachacutec, Av. Saphi s/n Cusco ☎ 084/249–654.

Policia Nacional ☎ 084/252–222. **Aguas Calientes** ☎ 084/211–178. **Ollantaytambo** ☎ 084/204–086. **Urubamba** ☎ 084/201–092.

🏃 Hospital **Hospital Regional** ✉ Av. de la Cultura s/n ☎ 084/227–661.

MONEY MATTERS

Take care of money exchange, traveler's checks, and ATM transactions in Cusco. A few hotels and shops outside the city do change dollars for soles, but at a less favorable rate than you can get at a Cusco bank.

Most banks will exchange U.S. dollars, the only real useful foreign currency here. Traveler's checks are becoming easier to change for soles in Cusco, but virtually no business accepts them as payment. Try the downtown branches of Banco de Crédito and Banco Wiese Sudameris. (The lines only look horrendous, they move quickly.) Casas de cambio bear a yellow MONEY EXCHANGE—TRAVELERS CHEQUE sign and populate the side of the Plaza de Armas opposite the cathedral and the first block of Avenida El Sol between Mantas and Almargo. Casas are open well into the evening, and rates are similar to those of banks, but they charge a two-percent commission. American Express and Diners Club both have offices in Cusco. An ATM in the luggage-claim area of Cusco's Velasco Astete airport gives cash against Plus, Cirrus, and American Express cards, as do those at Banco de Crédito offices.

🏃 Banks **American Express** ✉ Portal de Harinas 177, Haukaypata (Plaza de Armas), ☎ 084/235–241. **Banco de Crédito** ✉ Av. El Sol 189, ☎ 084/235–255. **Banco Wiese Sudameris** ✉ Maruri 315, ☎ 084/264–297. **Diners Club** ✉ Av. El Sol 615, ☎ 084/234–051.

TAXIS

Cusco's licensed taxis bear a black-and-gold checkered rectangle on each side. Fares are a standard S/2 within the central city and S/3 after 10 PM. "You should choose your taxi, rather than the driver choosing you," counsels one longtime hotel owner. Have your hotel or restaurant call a taxi for you if you are out late at night.

TELEPHONES

The area shares Peru's 084 area code. To call from abroad, drop the zero from the area code. To call within the region, dial only the six-digit number. Telefónica del Perú, the national telephone company, has an office in Cusco from which you can make international calls. Telefónica's Hola Perú phone cards can be used to place national or international calls from most telephones.

Telefónica del Perú (⊠ Av. El Sol 382 ☎ 084/221–231)

TOURS

There are many excellent tour operators and travel agents in Cusco, some also with offices in Lima that can help you with accommodations, transportation, and tours around Cusco. Several companies specialize in adventure tours, including Enigma, Explorandes, Mayuc, Peruvian Andean Treks, SAS Travel, and X-treme Tourbulencia. Globos de los Andes floats you above the Sacred Valley with accompanied hot-air balloon tours. Tranvía de Cusco offers a twist on the guided city tour using an old wooden streetcar, now motorized, departing several times daily from the Plaza de Armas.

🚩 Tour Operators **Enigma** ⊠ Garcilaso 132 ☎ 084/222–155. **Explorandes** ⊠ Garcilaso 316-A ☎ 084/620–717, 01/992–5060 in Lima ⊕ www.explorandes.com. **Globos de los Andes** ⊠ Q'apchik'ijllu 271 (Arequipa) ☎ 084/232–352 ⊕ www.globosperu.com. **Instinct** ⊠ Procuradores 50 ☎ 084/233–451 ⊕ www.instinct-travel.com. **Mayuc** ⊠ Portal de Confiturías 211, Haukaypata (Plaza de Armas) ☎ 084/232–666 ⊕ www.mayuc. com. **Peruvian Andean Treks** ⊠ Pardo 705 ☎ 084/225–701. **SAS Travel** ⊠ Portal de Panes 143, Haukaypata (Plaza de Armas) ☎ 084/237–292 ⊕ www.sastravelperu.com. **Tranvía de Cusco** ⊠ Parque Industrial G-1 ☎ 084/224–377. **X-treme Tourbulencia** ⊠ Plateros 358 ☎ 084/245–527 ⊕ www.x-treme_tourbulenicaperu.com.

TRAIN TRAVEL

The privatized Peru Rail's *Andean Explorer* departs from Cusco Monday, Wednesday, and Saturday at 8 AM for Puno, with a stop in Juliaca. The scenic journey takes 10 hours. The train arrives and departs from the Wanchaq Station on Pachacutec. The return trip from Puno also leaves at 8 AM on Monday, Wednesday, and Saturday. All trains make an exaggerated series of zigzag switchbacks, climbing elevation as they leave from Cusco before descending into the lower-altitude Sacred Valley. Trains stop at Poroy, Ollantaytambo, and Km 88, the start of the Inca Trail. Arrival is in Aguas Calientes, where you disembark to catch the buses up to the ruins. If you're using the Sacred Valley as your base, the Sacred Valley Railway, a Peru Rail subsidiary, operates a Vistadome train departing from Urubamba at 6 AM, and Ollantaytambo at 7, with arrival in Machu Picchu at 8:10. The return train leaves Machu Picchu at 5 PM, with arrival in Ollantaytambo at 6:20 and Urubamba at 7:10. Round-trip fare is S/190. Shuttle buses connect the Urubamba station to a few hotels in the valley.

Tourists are not permitted to ride the Tren Local, the less expensive, but slower train intended for local residents only.

🚩 Train Information **Asociación de Agencias de Turismo de Cusco** ⊠ Nueva Baja 424 Cusco ☎ 084/222–580. **Peru Rail** ⊠ Cusco (San Pedro) ☎ 084/233–551 ⊕ www. perurail.com ⊠ Cusco (Wanchaq) ☎ 084/238–722. **Sacred Valley Railway** ⊠ El Sol 803 Cusco ☎ 084/249–076 ⊕ www.sacredvalleyrailway.com ⊠ Av. Ferrocarril s/n Urubamba ☎ 084/201–071 ⊠ Pardo 329 Miraflores Lima ☎ 01/241–2645.

VISITOR INFORMATION

Cusco has three official tourist information offices. All provide information not just about the city, but also the surrounding Cusco department. The Dirección Regional de Industria y Turismo (DRIT) provides reliable information on the city and the surrounding area. A branch at the airport is open daily for all incoming flights. iPerú has helpful information on Cusco and the region and can provide assistance if you feel you've received inadequate service from a tourist establishment. An airport branch is open daily for all incoming flights. The Instituto Nacional de Cultura sells the 10-day boleto turístico, valid for admission to 16 museums and archaeological sites in the region. A private office of note is South American Explorers, a membership organization. Its $50 annual dues get you a quarterly magazine subscription and access to a wealth of information at its clubhouse here in Cusco, as well as in Lima and in Quito, Ecuador.

🚩 Tourist Information **Dirección Regional de Industria y Turismo** ✉ Mantas 117 Cusco ☎ 084/263–176 🕐 Mon.–Fri. 8–7, Sat. 8–12. **Instituto Nacional de Cultura** ✉ Garcilaso and Heladeros Cusco ☎ 084/226–919 🕐 Mon.–Fri. 8 to 5, Sat. 8–4, Sun. 8–12. **iPerú** ✉ Portal de Carrizos 250, Haukaypata (Plaza de Armas) Cusco ☎ 084/234–498 🕐 Daily 8:30–7:30. **South American Explorers** ✉ Choquechara 188 Cusco ☎ 084/245–484 🕐 May–Sept, Mon.–Fri. 9:30–5 and Sun. 9:30–1; Oct.–Apr., Mon.–Fri., 9:30–5.

MADRE DE DIOS

Do the math: 20,000 plant, 1,200 butterfly, 1,000 bird, 200 mammal and 100 reptile species (and many more yet to be identified). The national parks, reserves, and other undeveloped areas of the southern department of Madre de Dios are among the most biologically diverse in the world. The southern sector of Peru's Amazon Basin, most readily approached via Cusco, is famous among birders, whose eyes glaze over in amazement at the dawn spectacle of macaws and parrots visiting the region's famed *ccollpas* (clay licks); ornithologists speculate that the birds must ingest clay periodically to detoxify other elements in their diet. Madre de Dios also offers a rare chance to see large mammals, such as tapirs and, if the zoological fates smile upon you, jaguars. Groups such as the Nature Conservancy and Conservation International view the region as one of the world's natural arks, a place where the endangered Amazon rain forest has a real chance for survival. Animal and plant life may abound, but this is the least populated of Peru's departments in terms of human population: a scant 76,000 people reside in an area slightly smaller than South Carolina, and almost two-thirds of them in the sultry capital, Puerto Maldonado. Thoughtful conservation and planning here, coupled with keeping the humans at bay, has allowed the plant and animal population to thrive.

Madre de Dios began recorded history as part of the Inca empire, though far-off Cusco exerted limited control over this region the Inca called the Antisuyo, populated by indigenous forest peoples, the difficult-to-subdue Antis. The southern Amazon saw little incursion at the time of the Spanish conquest. The discovery in the late 19th century of the *shiringa,* known in the English-speaking world as the rubber tree, changed all that. Madre de Dios saw outside migration for the first time with the arrival of the *caucheros* (rubber men) and their minions staking out claims. The discovery of gold in the 1970s drew new waves of fortune seekers to the region. You can still see dreamers panning for gold in area rivers, hoping against hope to strike it rich.

Tourism and conservation have triggered the newest generation of explorers to the species-rich southern Amazon. Two areas of Madre de Dios are of special interest. One is around the city of Puerto Maldonado, including the Tambopata National Reserve and the adjoining Bahuaja-Sonene National Park; easily accessible, they offer lodges amid primary rain forest and excellent birding. Tambopata also exists for sustainable agriculture purposes: some 1,500 families in the department work to extract Brazil nuts from the reserve, an economic incentive to keep the forest intact, rather than cut it down for its lumber. The Manu Biosphere Reserve, directly north of Cusco, though more difficult and expensive to reach, provides unparalleled opportunity for observing wildlife in one of the largest virgin rain forests in the New World.

Puerto Maldonado

500 km (305 mi) east of Cusco.

Puerto Maldonado lies at the meeting point of the Madre de Dios and Tambopata rivers. It is a rough-and-tumble town whose main attraction is the municipal market, where you can buy freshly harvested *castañas* at a reasonable price. (Buying the Brazil nuts also gives the local people an economic incentive to protect the rain forest and the majestic castaña trees.) Maldonado is a convenient jumping-off point for visiting the rain forest.

Up the Tambopata River from Maldonado is the **Tambopata National Reserve,** a 3.8-million-acre "reserved zone" in which only environment-friendly activities are permitted. The area holds world records in the number of bird and butterfly species recorded by scientists and is the site of a *colpa* (clay lick) visited daily by hundreds of parrots and macaws.

Where to Stay

The listings below are for lodges comprised of wooden huts raised on stilts. All provide rustic but more than adequate accommodations. Rates include river transportation from Puerto Maldonado, guides, and meals. For properties where a minimum stay is indicated, the price category is based on the per-night cost.

$$$ ☒ **Tambopata Research Center.** A six-hour upriver boat journey from the Posada Amazonas lodge brings you to this Amazon base. Here you'll see several kinds of monkeys and other rain-forest wildlife, including hundreds of macaws and parrots at the nearby clay lick. The twin rooms at the lodge don't have private baths but instead share a separate room with four showers and another with four toilets. One current research project allows you to interact with macaws. The minimum stay is five days/four nights. *Reservations:* ☒ *Av. Aramburu 166, Miraflores, Lima* ☎ *01/421–8347, 877/905–3782 in the U.S.* 🖷 *01/421–8183* ☒ *Sunturwasi 350 (Triunfo), Cusco* ☎🖷 *084/232–772* ☒ *Are-*

quipa 401, Puerto Maldonado 🖼 *082/571–056* ⊕ *www.perunature. com* ⇗ *13 rooms with shared bath* ♻ *Dining room, bar; no a/c, no room phones, no room TVs* ⊟ *MC, V* ❚❘❙ *All-inclusive.*

$$ ⊞ **Explorer's Inn.** No place in the world tops this one for number of bird species (600, and 330 of those in one fortuitous day) sighted at a single lodge. Explorer's is managed by Peruvian Safaris, and accommodates tourists and visiting scientists in its thatched-roof bungalows. All can be seen navigating the lodge's 30 km (18 mi) of trails. The minimum stay is three days/two nights. *Reservations:* ⊠ *Alcanfores 459 Miraflores Lima* 🖼 *01/447–8888* 🖼 *01/241–8427* ⊕ *www.peruviansafaris.com* ⇗ *30 rooms* ♻ *Dining room; no a/c, no room phones, no room TVs.*

★ $$ ⊞ **Posada Amazonas.** This comfortable lodge is owned jointly by Rainforest Expeditions and the Ese'eja Native Community of Tambopata. The property defines "jungle chic," with mosquito nets over the beds and wide, screenless windows to welcome cooling breezes. A canopy tower provides a great view of the rain forest. Transportation to the lodge is usually by a combination of a thatch-roof truck and a large wooden boat with drop-down rain curtains. A visit to a local village is made en route. Packages include all transport, lodging, meals, and guides. The minimum stay is three days/two nights. *Reservations:* ⊠ *Av. Aramburu 166, Miraflores, Lima* 🖼 *01/421–8347, 877/905–3782 in the U.S.* 🖼 *01/421– 8183* ⊠ *Sunturwasi 350 (Triunfo), Cusco* 🖼 *084/232–772* ⊠ *Arequipa 401, Puerto Maldonado* 🖼 *082/571–056* ⊕ *www.perunature. com* ⇗ *30 rooms* ♻ *Dining room; no a/c, no room phones, no room TVs* ⊟ *MC, V* ❚❘❙ *All-inclusive.*

Manu Biosphere Reserve

FodorsChoice ★ *90 km (54 mi) north of Cusco.*

Readers of the British children's series *A Bear Called Paddington* know that the title character "came from darkest Peru." The stereotype is quite outdated, of course, but the Manu Biosphere Reserve, often called "the most biodiverse park on earth," will conjure up the jungliest Tarzanmovie images you can imagine. And the reserve really does count the Andean spectacled bear, South America's only ursid, and the animal on which Paddington was based, among its 200 mammals.

This reserve area half the size of Switzerland is Peru's largest protected area and straddles the boundary of the Madre de Dios and Cusco departments. Manu encompasses more than 4½ million acres of pristine primary tropical forest wilderness, ranging in altitude from 3,450 meters (12,000 feet) down through cloud forest and into a seemingly endless lowland tropical rain forest at 300 meters (less than 1,000 feet). Not surprisingly, this geographical variety shelters a stunning biodiversity, and a near total absence of humans and hunting has made the animal life here less skittish and more open to observation. The reserve's 13 monkey species scrutinize visitors with the same curiosity they elicit. White caimans sun themselves lazily on sandy riverbanks, while the larger black ones lurk in the oxbow lakes. And expect to see tapirs at the world's largest tapir ccollpa. Giant Orotongo river otters and elusive big cats such as jaguars and ocelots sometimes make fleeting appearances. But it's the avian life that has made Manu world famous. The area counts over 1,000 bird species, fully a ninth of those known. Some 500 species have been spotted at the Pantiacolla Lodge alone. Birds include macaws, toucans, roseate spoonbills, and 5-foot-tall wood storks.

Manu was declared a national park in 1973, and a biosphere reserve in 1977. Ten years later, UNESCO designated it a World Heritage Site. It is divided into three distinct zones. The smallest is the so-called "cultural zone" (Zone C), with several indigenous groups and the majority of the jungle lodges. Access is permitted to all, even to independent travelers in theory, though vast distances make this unrealistic for all but the most intrepid. About three times the size of the cultural zone, Manu's "reserve zone" (Zone B) is uninhabited but contains one of the lodges. Access is by permit only, and you must be accompanied by a guide from one of the 10 agencies authorized to take people into the area. The western 80 percent of Manu is designated a national park (Zone A). Authorized researchers and indigenous peoples who reside there are permitted in this zone; visitors may not enter.

A Manu excursion is no quick trip. Overland travel from Cusco, the usual embarkation point, takes up to two days, in a thrilling trip over the mountains and down into the lowland plains. A charter flight in a twin-engine plane to the small airstrip at Boca Manu shaves that time down to 45 minutes but adds a few hundred dollars onto your package price. From Boca Manu you'll still have several hours of boat travel to reach your lodge. The logistics of travel to this remote part of the Amazon mean you should allow at least five days for your excursion. A week is more manageable.

Where to Stay

$$$$ 🏠 **Manu Cloud Forest Lodge.** High in the cloud forest of Manu's cultural zone, this lodge sits on grounds blooming with orchids and overlooking the rushing Río Unión. Rooms are rustic and spartan, with beds and tables, but all have a private bath and plenty of hot water. The highly respected Manu Nature Tours operates the lodge. The minimum stay is three days/two nights. *Reservations:* ✉ *Av. Pardo 1046 Cusco* ☎ *084/ 252–721* 📠*084/234–793* ✉*Conquistadores 396, San Isidro, Lima* ☎*01/ 442–8980* ⊕ *www.manuperu.com* 📨 *8 rooms, 4 cabins* 🍴 *Dining room, bar, sauna, mountain bikes; no a/c, no room phones, no room TVs* 🚫 *AE, MC, V* 🍽 *All-inclusive.*

Madre de Dios A to Z

AIR TRAVEL

Starting in Lima and stopping in Cusco, Aero Continente, LAN Peru, and TANS Perú each have once-daily flights to Aeropuerto Padre Aldámiz (PEM), 5 km (3 mi) from Puerto Maldonado. All flights arrive and depart early in the morning. Several of the Manu lodges fly their passengers to the small airstrip at Boca Manu on a charter basis.

🛫 Carriers **Aero Continente** ✉ León Velarde 584 Puerto Maldonado ☎ 084/572–004. **LAN Peru** ✉ Puerto Maldonado. **TANS Perú** ✉ León Velarde 151 Puerto Maldonado ☎ 082/57–3861.

MONEY MATTERS

The Banco de Crédito on the Plaza de Armas in Puerto Maldonado changes U.S. dollars and traveler's checks for nuevo soles, and has an ATM machine that gives cash against Plus- and Cirrus-affiliated cards. Since trips into this area are usually booked through travel agents, you shouldn't need much extra cash beyond any tips you leave for the staff. Don't count on your lodge's cashing traveler's checks or accepting credit cards.

🏦 Banks **Banco de Crédito** ⊠ Arequipa 334 ☎ 082/571-001.

TOUR OPERATORS

Those who wish to reach the more isolated parts of Madre de Dios should contact one of the agencies that conduct camping trips in Manu Biosphere Reserve. They provide all equipment and food, but you must bring your own sleeping bag. One of the most experienced guide services, the Cusco-based Manu Expeditions, offers trips that last five to nine days. Manu Nature Tours, Pantiacolla, and Inkanatura Travel operate lodges in Manu. Inkanutura also manages lodges in the Tambopata National Reserve, as do Rainforest Expeditions and Peruvian Safaris. Another reliable agency, Hirca Travel, operates five- and nine-day trips to Manu.

🏢 Tour Companies **Hirca Travel** ⊠ Bellavista 518, Miraflores, Lima ☎📠 01/447-3807 ⊠ Retiro 128, Cusco ☎ 084/225-384. **Manu Expeditions** ⊠ Procuradores 50, Cusco ☎ 084/226-671.

VISITOR INFORMATION

The Dirección Regional de Industria y Turismo (DRIT) has an office in Puerto Maldonado and serves as the government tourist office. It provides reliable information on the city and Madre de Dios. A branch at the airport is open daily for all incoming flights. The Conservation Association of the Southern Rain Forest has details about parks in the region. Dirección de Areas Protegidas y Fauna Silvestre offers information about Manu National Park.

🏢 **Dirección Regional de Industria y Turismo** ⊠ Fitzcarrald 411 ☎ 084/571-164. **Conservation Association of the Southern Rain Forest** ⊠ Portal los Panes 123, Haukaypata (Plaza de Armas), Cusco ☎ 084/240-911. **Dirección de Areas Protegidas y Fauna Silvestre** ⊠ Petirrojos 355, Urbanización El Palomar, San Isidro, Lima ☎ 01/441-0425 ⊠ Urbanización Mariscal Gamarra 4-C, Apartado 1057, Cusco ☎ 084/223-633.

IQUITOS & ENVIRONS

Founded by Jesuit priests in the 1500s, Iquitos was once called the "Pearl of the Amazon." It isn't quite that lustrous today, but it's still a pleasant, friendly town on the banks of the Amazon River, situated in Peru's northeastern jungle. The jungle port, which sits near the confluence of the Río Nanay and the Río Amazonas, is only accessed by water and by air. Motor scooters outnumber cars, and the typical family transportation is a three-wheeler with a canvas top. When the river is high, the picturesque waterfront district of Belén actually floats; when the river is low, Belén is about a half-mile out and sits in mud. It rises and falls from season to season by as much as 50 feet. The region has cycled through booms and busts since the great rubber boom of the late 1800s. The boom lasted about 30 years and brought great richness to the region.

With the bust, the economy collapsed and remained stagnant for nearly 50 years. Iquitos, which had seen unprecedented growth and opulence during the rubber boom, became an Amazonian backwater overnight. The economy slouched along, barely sustaining itself with logging, exotic animal exports, and tobacco, banana, and Brazil-nut farming. In the early 1970s foreign interests began to explore the region for petroleum, and found it. The black gold, along with ecotourism and logging, have since become the backbone of the region's economy. While the main reason to drop into town is to explore the surrounding rain forest, given a chance, Iquitos will grow on you as you become accustomed to the humid climate and relaxed, easy ways of its citizens. A revamped riverwalk is the popular place for an evening stroll, followed by entertainment in the riverside plaza.

Iquitos

1,150 km (719 mi) northeast of Lima.

A sultry port town on the Río Amazonas, Iquitos is quite probably the world's largest city that cannot be reached by road. The city has some 350,000 inhabitants and is the capital of the vast Loreto Department. The area around Iquitos was first inhabited by small, independent Amazonian tribes. In the 1500s Jesuit missionaries began adventuring in the area, trying to Christianize the local population, but the city wasn't officially founded until 1757.

Where to Stay & Eat

¢–$ ✕ **El Mesón.** On the riverwalk, this restaurant serves ample portions of regional specialties. Try the delicious *paiche,* a giant fish found in jungle lakes. Tapestries and paintings depicting scenes from traditional Amazonian life adorn the walls. With good views of the Amazon and the easy-paced life of the paseo, this is an excellent sunset joint. ⊠ *Av. Malecón Maldonado 153* ☎ *094/231–857* ▭ *AE, MC, V, DC.*

¢–$ ✕ **Fitzcarraldo.** The colonial elegance of this riverwalk eatery shines
Fodor'sChoice through, from the antique firearms to the iron terrace chairs. The ex-
★ tensive menu has international essentials like pizza and pasta, but the Amazonian specialties are the real draw. Try the *chicharrón de lagarto* (crocodile nuggets), topping off the meal with a frothy *caipirinha* (a Brazilian drink with lime, sugar, and the sugar cane liquor cachaça). ⊠ *Napo 100, at El Boulevard* ☎ *094/243–434* ▭ *V, MC, AE, DC.*

★ $ ✕ **Gran Maloca.** This most elegant of the city's restaurants is in a lovely building encrusted with colorful *azulejos* (glazed tiles). The international fare is excellent, and the lobster and shrimp in pepper sauce is especially good. Try the *suri al ajo* (palm-tree grubs cooked in wine and garlic sauce) for an appetizer. They have an extensive wine and spirits list, with locally made fruit liqueurs. ⊠ *Sargento Lores 170* ☎ *094/ 233–126* ▭ *AE, DC, MC, V.*

★ $$$$ 🏨 **El Dorado Plaza Hotel.** This modern hotel, the best in Iquitos, richly deserves the praise it wins from guests. All rooms center around the grand entryway, which has a large fountain and a glass elevator. Behind the hotel you will find a pool with a swim-up bar. A bridge arches over the pool, leading you to the Jacuzzi. The rooms have all the modern conveniences and are equipped with soundproof glass to protect you from the incessant cacophony of central Iquitos. The hotel sits in the heart of the city on the Plaza de Armas. ⊠ *Napo 258* ☎ *094/222–555* 🖷 *94/ 224–304* ⊕ *www.eldoradoplazahotel.com* 🛏 *56 rooms, 9 suites* ⚂ *Restaurant, cafeteria, room service, in-room safes, minibars, cable TV, pool, health club, outdoor hot tub, 2 bars, shop, laundry service, business services, meeting rooms, airport shuttle, free parking* ⊟ *AE, MC, V* ⦿| *CP.*

★ $ 🏨 **Victoria Regia Hotel.** This modern, airy lodging has rooms dressed in cool colors that surround a courtyard with a small swimming pool. Rooms in the back are less noisy but darker. Most rooms have Impressionist and Expressionist prints adorning the walls, blond-wood furniture, and large, comfy beds. ⊠ *Ricardo Palma 252* ☎ *094/231–983 or 01/241– 9195* 🖷 *094/232–499* ⊕ *www.victoriaregiahotel.com* 🛏 *34 rooms, 8 suites* ⚂ *Restaurant, room service, in-room safes, minibars, cable TV, pool, bar, laundry service, business services, meeting rooms, airport shuttle, travel services* ⊟ *AE, DC, V, MC* ⦿| *CP.*

Into the Jungle

About 50 km (31 mi) from Iquitos you'll find primary rain forest, where the only intrusion from humans has been hunting and gathering. Sadly, even this light touch has had an effect, as hunting has all but eliminated large animals from the region. However, visitors are likely to see birds, monkeys, pink freshwater *bufeos* (dolphins), and caimans along the Amazon River and its tributaries. You're sure to spot large blue morpho butterflies.

It's interesting and worthwhile to visit the small villages of indigenous people. When the boat stops at these settlements, you'll usually find half the village waiting to trade handicrafts for whatever you have with you; items perpetually in demand include umbrellas, hammers, fishing hooks, flashlights, sewing supplies, lipstick, and clothing.

The best way to visit the jungle is with a prearranged tour with one of the many jungle lodges. All the lodges have highly trained naturalist guides. Among the activities offered at these lodges are nature walks, birding tours, nighttime canoe outings, fishing, and trips to indigenous villages. Some lodges have canopy walkways that take you into the seldom-explored rain-forest canopy.

Where to Stay

Rates for the rain-forest lodges near Iquitos include transportation, meals, and guided walks. Transportation to the lodges is either by *palm-caris* (large wooden boats with thatched roofs) or speedboats. Four lodges—Ceiba Tops, Explorama Lodge, ExplorNapo, and ExplorTambos—are owned and operated by Explorama Tours. For properties where a minimum stay is indicated, the price category is based on the per-night cost.

$$$$ 🏨 **Ceiba Tops.** Explorama's newest luxury lodge, with large picture windows overlooking the Amazon, is just 45 minutes downriver from Iquitos. After a jungle trek, plunge into the pool, take a nap in your

air-conditioned room, or relax with a book in a hammock. You can even take a hot shower before dinner. The restaurant has international cuisine and Peruvian wines. The hotel is on a 40-hectare private rain-forest reserve. All meals are included in the rate. ⊠ *Reservations: Av. de la Marina 340, Iquitos* ☎ *094/252–526, 800/707–5275 in the U.S.* 🖷 *094/252–533* ⊕ *www.explorama.com* ➾ *50 rooms, 3 suites* ⚴ *Restaurant, fans, pool, boating, fishing, hiking, bar, shop, airport shuttle, travel services, some no-smoking rooms; no room phones, no room TVs* ⊟ *MC, V, AE, DC* ⫣⚬⫢ *FAP.*

$$$$ ⊞ **Explorama Lodge.** Explorama's first lodge, built in 1964, is 80 km (50 mi) down the Amazon in pristine rain forest. Under palm-thatched roofs are several houses with a total of 60 rooms. Kerosene lamps light up the covered walkways between them. Many walks are offered, including one to the Seven Bridges Trail. The rooms are extremely simple, as they are in most jungle lodges, and the requisite mosquito nets ensure a night's sleep relatively free from bites. There are cold-water shower facilities. The minimum stay is two nights. ⊠ *Reservations: Av. de la Marina 340, Iquitos* ☎ *094/252–526, 800/707–5275 in the U.S.* 🖷 *094/252–533* ⊕ *www.explorama.com* ➾ *63 rooms with shared bath* ⚴ *Restaurant, boating, fishing, hiking, bar, airport shuttle, travel services, some no-smoking rooms; no room phones, no room TVs, no a/c* ⊟ *MC, V, AE, DC* ⫣⚬⫢ *FAP.*

$$$$ ⊞ **ExplorNapo.** The remote camp is set deep in the middle of the Sucusari
Fodor'sChoice Nature Reserve, 70 km (43 mi) up the Napo River and 1½ hours by
★ boat from the Explorama Lodge. There is a large canopy walkway here for exploring the seldom-seen upper-reaches of the Amazon, as well as an informative enthnological garden. Because of the distance, many people spend a night at the Explorama Lodge en route to ExplorNapo. Facilities are rustic, with kerosene lighting and separate cold-water shower facilities. There's a screened dining room, with occasional music performed by local people. This is a prime place for spotting wildlife, so guided walks and canoe trips are daily activities. The minimum stay is four nights. ⊠ *Reservations: Av. de la Marina 340, Iquitos* ☎ *094/252–526, 800/707–5275 in the U.S.* 🖷 *094/252–533* ⊕ *www.explorama.com* ➾ *30 rooms with shared bath* ⚴ *Restaurant, boating, fishing, hiking, bar, airport shuttle, travel services, some no-smoking rooms; no room phones, no room TVs, no a/c* ⊟ *MC, V, AE, DC* ⫣⚬⫢ *FAP.*

$$$$ ⊞ **ExplorTambos.** This very primitive lodge is a three-hour hike from ExplorNapo. There are no rooms here—you sleep on mattresses on platforms under mosquito netting. Visits here are usually an extension of trips to Explorama Lodge or ExplorNapo. Being the most remote lodge in the region, the chances of seeing wildlife are quite good. But this is definitely a place for serious explorers who don't mind a little discomfort. The minimum stay is four nights. ⊠ *Reservations: Av. de la Marina 340, Iquitos* ☎ *094/252–526, 800/707–5275 in the U.S.* 🖷 *094/252–533* ⊕ *www.explorama.com* ➾ *space for 16 people* ⚴ *Restaurant, boating, fishing, hiking, airport shuttle, travel services, some no-smoking rooms; no room phones, no room TVs, no a/c* ⊟ *MC, V, AE, DC* ⫣⚬⫢ *FAP.*

Iquitos & Environs A to Z

To research prices, get advice from other travelers, and book travel arrangements, visit www.fodors.com.

AIR TRAVEL

From Lima, Aero Continente has several flights a day to Iquitos. Taca Peru has daily flights to Iquitos, and TANS Perú has two flights a day between Iquitos and Lima. Aerocontinente offers round-trip flights from Miami on Sunday.

🛪 Carriers **Aero Continente** ☎ 094/243-489 in Iquitos, 01/242-4260 in Lima, 877/359-7378 in the U.S. **Taca Peru** ☎ 094/242-448 in Iquitos or 01/446-0033 in Lima. **TANS Perú** ☎ 094/231-071 in Iquitos, 01/575-3842 in Lima.

AIRPORTS

Iquitos's Aeropuerto Internacional Francisco Secada Vignetta is 8 km (5 mi) from the city center. There is a S/12 airport tax for domestic flights and a S/36 tax for international flights. A taxi to the airport should cost around S/10.

🛪 Airport Information **Aeropuerto Internacional Francisco Secada Vignetta** ☎ 094/260-151 in Iquitos.

EMERGENCIES

Some of the equipment in area hospitals may not be up-to-date, but doctors are knowledgeable.

🛪 **Clinica Adventista Ana Stahl** ✉ Av. de la Marina 285, Iquitos ☎ 094/252-518 or 094/252-535. **Hospital Regional de Iquitos** ✉ Av. 28 de Julio, Cuadra 15, Iquitos ☎ 094/252-743 or 094/251-882.

TOURS

In Iquitos, Amazon Tours and Cruises specializes in river cruises using boats with anywhere from 8 to 21 cabins. The longest and most comprehensive cruise includes a 6-day trip on the Amazon and a 10-day journey to Manaus, Brazil. All the boats have comfortable, air-conditioned cabins with private facilities. The boats stop at various points for nature hikes and visits to villages. International Expeditions has four of the most colorful and luxurious boats on the Amazon. Boats headed up the river to the Pacaya-Samiria National Reserve have accommodations for between 8 and 26 passengers. Cruises can be booked only from the company's offices in the United States. Jungle Exports and Cruceros also offer boat tours through the region. Emily Tours, Explorama Tours, Paseos Amazonicos, and Turismo Pacífico Iquitos arrange trips throughout the region.

🛪 Fees & Schedules **Amazon Tours and Cruises** ✉ Requeña 336, Iquitos ☎ 094/231-611 ⊕ www.amazontours.net ✉ 8700 W. Flagler St., Miami, FL 33174 ☎ 305/227-2266 or 800/423-2791. **Cruceros** ✉ Requena 336, Iquitos ☎ 094/231-611 in Iquitos, 01/265-9524 in Lima. **Emily Tours** ✉ Jr. Progreso 268-270, Iquitos ☎ 094/235-273. **Explorama Tours** ✉ Av. de la Marina 350, Iquitos ☎ 094/252-530, 800/223-6764 in the U.S. **International Expeditions** ☎ 800/633-4734 🖶 205/428-1714 ⊕ www.internationalexpeditions.com. **Jungle Exports** ✉ Puerto Masusa, Iquitos ☎ 094/231-870. **Paseos Amazonicos** ✉ Calle Pevas 246, Iquitos ☎ 094/233-110 🖶 094/231-618. **Turismo Pacífico Iquitos** ✉ Calle Ricardo Palma 180, Iquitos ☎ 094/231-627.

VISITOR INFORMATION

There are tourist information offices in downtown Iquitos and at the airport.

🚩 **iPerú** ✉ Airport ☎ 094/260-251. **Tourist Information Office** ✉ Napo 226 ☎ 094/235-621.

PERU A TO Z

To research prices, get advice from other travelers, and book travel arrangements, visit www.fodors.com.

AIR TRAVEL

The list of carriers flying between the United States and Lima continues to grow. American, Continental, Delta, LanChile, and LanPeru all have daily flights from several gateways.

Aero Continente, LanPeru, and Taca Peru are the principal airlines operating within Peru. Aero Condor operates charter flights throughout the country and scheduled flights between Lima and the Nazca Lines near Ica.

🚩 Airlines & Contacts **Aero Continente** 888/586-9400 in North America; ☎ 01/242-4242 in Lima, ⊕ www.aerocontinente.com. **American** ☎ 800/433-7300 in North America; 01/211-7000 in Lima; ⊕ www.aa.com. **Continental** ☎ 800/525-0280 in North America, 01/222-7080 in Lima; ⊕ www.continental.com.

Delta ☎ 01/440-4328. **LanChile** ☎ 800/735-5526 in North America; 01/241-5522 in Lima; ⊕ www.lanchile.com. **LanPeru** ☎ 800-735-5590 in North America; 01/221-3764 in Lima; 🖥 01/421-8914; ⊕ www.lanperu.com. **Taca Peru** ☎ 01/446-0033 or 01/446-0033; 🖥 01/241-7077 in Lima.

AIRPORTS

Lima's Jorge Chávez International Airport is the major international point of entry.

🚩 Airport Information **Jorge Chávez International Airport** ☎ 01/575-1434 ⊕ www.corpac.gob.pe.

BOAT & FERRY TRAVEL

Travel across Lake Titicaca from Peru to Bolivia is usually via hydrofoils operated by Crillón Tours, which run from Copacabana in Bolivia to Puno in Peru.

Passenger boats are the most important means of transportation in the jungle. If you visit a jungle lodge, your hosts will probably pick you up in an outboard-powered boat. Larger boats make 4- to 10-day cruises on the Amazon from Iquitos. You can also make arrangements for an excursion with a native guide in a wooden dugout called a *pecka-pecka,* the nickname coming from the sound of the small motor. On Lake Titicaca, small boats offer taxi service to the islands.

🚩 **Crillón Tours** ✉ Av. Camacho 1223, La Paz ☎ 02/337-533 🖥 02/391-039 ⊕ www.titicaca.com.

BUS TRAVEL TO & FROM PERU

Unless you're traveling with a group on a bus chartered by a reputable tour operator, travel between Peru and the neighboring countries of

Colombia, Ecuador, and Chile is not recommended. Whenever possible, travel and arrive at your destination during daytime. Petty theft is common at bus stations, and even the Pan-American Highway is not always in the best condition, especially during the December–March rainy season.

BUS TRAVEL WITHIN PERU

The intercity bus system in Peru is extensive, and fares are usually quite reasonable. Second-class buses (*servicio normal*) tend to be overcrowded and uncomfortable, while the more expensive first-class service (*primera clase*) is safer, more comfortable, and much more likely to arrive on schedule.

Alternative forms of public transportation are the *colectivos,* small vans that follow the same routes as the buses. They charge about twice as much but are usually much faster. The catch is that they often don't depart until they fill up.

BUSINESS HOURS

Hours vary from region to region, but office hours are usually from 8:30 AM to 5 PM Monday through Friday. Some businesses close for one to two hours for lunch, especially during the summer months.

CAR TRAVEL

If you decide to drive while in Peru, remember that most Peruvians see traffic laws as suggestions rather than commands. Outside cities, drive only during daylight hours, fill your gas tank whenever possible, and make sure your spare tire is in good repair. You may want to carry wooden planks to help you out of muddy spots on the road.

The major highways in Peru are the Pan-American Highway, which runs down the entire coast, and the Carretera Central, which runs from Lima to Huancayo. Most highways have no names or numbers; they are referred to by destination.

EMERGENCY SERVICES The Touring and Automobile Club of Peru will provide 24-hour emergency road service for members of AAA and affiliates upon presentation of their membership cards. Members of the American Automobile Association can purchase good maps at members' prices.

🚗 Emergency Services **Touring and Automobile Club of Peru** ✉ César Vallejo 699, Lince, Lima ☎ 01/221-2432.

RULES OF THE ROAD You can drive in Peru with a foreign license for up to six months, after which you will need an international driver's license. Speed limits are 25 kph–35 kph (15 mph–20 mph) in residential areas, 85 kph–100 kph (50 mph–60 mph) on highways. Traffic tickets range from a minimum of $4 to a maximum of $40. The police and military routinely check drivers at road blocks, so make sure your papers are easily accessible. Peruvian law makes it a crime to drive while intoxicated, although many Peruvians ignore that prohibition. If you are caught driving while under the influence, you will either pay a hefty bribe or spend the night in jail.

CUSTOMS & DUTIES

You may bring into Peru up to $1,000 worth of goods and gifts, which are taxed 20% (excluding personal and work items); everything there-after is taxed at a flat rate of 25%. You may also bring a total of three liters of liquor; jewelry or perfume worth less than $300; and 20 packs of cigarettes or 50 cigars.

Airport taxes are $25 for international and $4 for domestic flights. Be sure to keep your white entry paper that you filled out before arrival, as you will need it to check out of the country.

ELECTRICITY

To use electric-powered equipment purchased in the U.S. or Canada, **bring a converter and adapter.** The electrical current in Peru is 220 volts, 50 cycles alternating current (AC). An adapter is needed for appliances requiring 110 voltage. U.S.-style flat prongs are used.

If your appliances are dual-voltage, you'll need only an adapter. Don't use 110-volt outlets marked FOR SHAVERS ONLY for high-wattage appli-ances such as blow-dryers. Most laptops operate equally well on 110 and 220 volts and so require only an adapter.

EMBASSIES

Canada ⊠ F. Gerdes 130, Miraflores Lima ☎ 01/444-4015. **New Zealand** ⊠ Av. Na-talio Sánchez 125, Floor 12, Plaza Washington, Lima ☎ 01/433-4738. **United Kingdom** ⊠ Edificio El Pacífico, Arequipa, 5th block, Plaza Washington, Lima ☎ 01/433-4738 or 01/433-4839. **United States** ⊠ Encalada, Cuadra 16, Monterrico, Lima ☎ 01/434-3000.

HEALTH

FOOD & DRINK   The number of cases of cholera has dropped dramatically in recent years, but you should still take care. Even Peruvians tell you to stick to bottled water. Anything raw, including ceviche, should only be eaten only in the better restaurants, or ones that have been recommended. In Lima, you can buy solutions, such as Zonalin, to disinfect fresh fruit and vegetables.

Immunizations can help prevent some types of food- and water-borne diseases, such as for hepatitis A. Check with health authorities about which vaccinations they feel are necessary and which are only recom-mendations. Other possibilities include vaccinations for typhoid, polio, and tetanus-diphtheria. If you intend to travel in the jungle, you'll need a yellow fever vaccination and malaria prophylactics.

OTHER HAZARDS   *Soroche* (altitude sickness) hits most visitors to high-altitude cities such as Cusco and Puno. Headache, dizziness, and shortness of breath are common. When you visit areas over 10,000 feet above sea level, take it easy on your first day. Avoid alcohol and drink plenty of liquids. To fight soroche, Peruvians swear by *mate de coca,* a tea made from the leaves of the coca plant.

HOLIDAYS

New Year's Day; Easter holiday, which begins midday on Maundy Thursday and continues through Easter Monday; Labor Day (May 1); St. Peter and St. Paul Day (June 29); Independence Day (July 28); St.

Rosa of Lima Day (August 30); Battle of Angamos Day, which commemorates a battle with Chile in the War of the Pacific, 1879–81 (October 8); All Saints' Day (November 1); Immaculate Conception (December 8); Christmas.

LANGUAGE

Spanish is Peru's national language, but many indigenous languages also enjoy official status. Many Peruvians claim Quechua, the language of the Inca, as their first language, but most also speak Spanish. Other native languages include the Tiahuanaco language of Aymará, which is spoken around Lake Titicaca, and several languages in the rain forest. Wealthier Peruvians and those who work with tourists often speak English, but they are the exception. If you speak any Spanish at all, by all means use it. Your hosts will appreciate the effort, and any laughter that greets your words will be good-natured rather than mocking.

A word on spelling: since the Inca had no writing system, Quechua developed as an oral language. With European colonization, words and place-names were transcribed to conform to Spanish pronunciations. Eventually, the whole language was transcribed, and in many cases words lost their correct pronunciations. During the past 30 years, however, national pride and a new sensitivity to the country's indigenous roots have led Peruvians to try to recover consistent, linguistically correct transcriptions of Quechua words. As you travel, you may come across different spellings and pronunciations of the same name.

MAIL & SHIPPING

Airmail letters and postcards sent within the Americas cost S/2.70 for less than 20 grams; anything sent from Peru to the United States, Canada, the United Kingdom, Australia, or New Zealand costs S/3.30. Bring packages to the post office unsealed, as you must show the contents to postal workers. Mail service has been steadily improving, and a letter should reach just about anywhere in a week from any of the main cities, but for timely delivery or valuable parcels, use Federal Express, United Parcel, or DHL International.

The main post office (*correo*) in downtown Lima is open Monday–Saturday 8–8 and Sunday 9–1. Hours vary at the branches and in cities and towns outside Lima, but most are closed Sundays.

RECEIVING MAIL If you don't know where you will be staying in advance, you can have mail sent to you (mark the letters "poste restante") at Correo Central. American Express cardholders can receive mail at the company's Lima office. South American Explorers Club members can receive mail at the club address in Lima; the club will also forward mail for members.
🚩 **American Express** ✉ Belén 1040 ☎ 01/330–4481. **South American Explorers Club** ✉ Calle Piura 135, Miraflores, ☎ 01/445–3306. ✉ Choquechaca 188, No. 4, Cusco, ☎ 084/245–484.

MONEY MATTERS

You can safely exchange money or cash traveler's checks in a bank, at your hotel, or from *casas de cambio* (exchange houses). The rate for traveler's checks is usually the same as for cash, but many banks have a ceiling on how much they will exchange at one time. Stores, smaller hotels, and restaurants rarely accept traveler's checks. Major credit cards, especially Visa, are accepted in most hotels, restaurants, and shops in tourist areas.

CURRENCY   Peru's national currency is the nuevo sol (S/). Bills are issued in denominations of 5, 10, 20, 50, and 100 soles. Coins are 1, 5, 10, 20, and 50 céntimos, and 1, 2, and 5 soles.

PASSPORTS & VISAS
Visitors from the United States, Canada, the United Kingdom, Australia, and New Zealand require only a valid passport and return ticket to be issued a 60-day visa at their point of entry into Peru. For safety reasons, carry a copy of your passport while exploring, leaving the original in a secure place in your hotel room.

SAFETY
Be street-smart in Peru and trouble generally won't find you. Don't wear a money belt or a waist pack, both of which peg you as a tourist. Distribute your cash and any valuables (including your credit cards and passport) between deep front pockets, inside jacket or vest pockets, and a concealed money pouch. Do not reach for the money pouch once you're in public. If you carry a purse, choose one with a zipper and a thick strap that you can drape across your body; adjust the length so that the purse sits in front of you at or above hip level. Store only enough money in the purse to cover casual spending. If you must carry a camera bag, keep it close to your body; backpacks are best worn on your front. And at all times, avoid wearing flashy jewelry and wristwatches.

Many streets throughout Peru are not well lit, so avoid walking anywhere at night by yourself or even with a friend, and certainly avoid deserted streets, day or night. Always walk "with a purpose" as if you know where you're going, even if you don't—stay alert.

Use only "official" taxis: don't get into a car just because there's a taxi sign in the window, although it may be just a businessman on his way home with the hope of making some extra money. Especially at night, call a taxi from your hotel or restaurant.

TAXES
Peru's economy has stabilized after the chaos of the 1980s and '90s. Although the basics are reasonably cheap, anything that might loosely be called a luxury tends to be expensive. An 18% sales tax, known as *impuesto general a las ventas,* is levied on everything except goods bought at open-air markets and from street vendors. It is usually included in the advertised price of merchandise and should be included with food and drink.

Restaurants have been ordered to publish their prices—including taxes and a 10% service charge that is sometimes added on—but they do not always do so. They are also prone to levy a cover charge for anything from live entertainment to serving you a roll with your meal. It is best to check before you order. Hotel bills may also have taxes and a 10% service charge added on.

Airport taxes are $28 for international and $5 for domestic flights.

Telephones

For numbers anywhere in Peru, dial "103" for Telefónica del Perú. For assistance from an international operator to place a call, dial "108" or place your call through your hotel's front desk, which is usually more expensive. To place a direct call, dial "00" followed by the country and city codes.

COUNTRY & AREA CODES To call Peru direct, dial 011 followed by the country code of 51, then the city code, then the number of the party you are calling. (When dialing a number from abroad, drop the initial 0 from the local area code.)

INTERNATIONAL CALLS For international calls you should dial 00, then 1 for the United States and Canada or 44 for the United Kingdom. To make an operator-assisted international call, dial 108.

LOCAL CALLS Telefónica del Peru, the country's newly privatized telephone company, has invested a hefty sum in Peru's phone system. New, "intelligent" pay phones require a coin or phone card instead of the old token system. Unless you're making many calls, using coins is much easier than purchasing cards.

LONG-DISTANCE SERVICES To call another region within the country, first dial 0 and then the area code. Long-distance calls are easy to make from Lima and the coast, more difficult in the highlands, and sometimes impossible in the jungle. Hotels add hefty surcharges to long-distance calls made from rooms, so you may want to call from a pay phone.

AT&T, MCI, and Sprint access codes make calling long-distance relatively convenient, but you may find the local access number blocked in many hotel rooms. First ask the hotel operator to connect you. If the hotel operator balks, ask for an international operator, or dial the international operator yourself. One way to improve your odds of getting connected to your long-distance carrier is to travel with more than one company's calling card (a hotel may block Sprint, for example, but not MCI). If all else fails, call from a pay phone. To reach an AT&T operator, dial 171. For MCI, dial 190. For Sprint, dial 176.

🆔 Access Codes **AT&T Direct** ☎ 800/225-5288. **MCI WorldPhone** ☎ 800/444-4444. **Sprint International Access** ☎ 800/793-1153.

TIPPING

A 10% tip is sufficient in most restaurants unless the service has been exceptional. Porters in hotels and airports expect S/2–S/3 per bag. There is no need to tip taxi drivers. At bars, tip 20 céntimos–50 céntimos for a beer, more for a mixed drink. Bathroom attendants get 20 céntimos; gas station attendants get 50 céntimos for extra services such as adding air to your tires. Tour guides and tour bus drivers should get S/5–S/10 each per day.

VISITOR INFORMATION

Learn more about foreign destinations by checking government-issued travel advisories and country information. For a broader picture, consider information from more than one country.

Peru no longer has tourist offices in other countries. **PromPeru** (Comisión de Promoción del Peru) is Peru's official tourism information agency in Lima and it has an information Web site in English and Spanish, ⊕ www.peru.org.pe.

See the A to Z sections at the end of each chapter for area-specific visitor information.

WHEN TO GO
The tourist season in Peru runs from May through September, which corresponds to the dry season in the Sierra and Selva. The best time to visit is May through July, when the cool, misty weather is just beginning on the Costa, and the highlands are dressed in bright green under crystalline blue skies. June brings major festivals to Cusco, such as Inti Raymi (the Inca festival of the sun) and Corpus Christi. Other important festival months are February, which means Carnaval throughout Peru and Virgen de la Candelaria (Candlemas) celebrations in Puno, and October, when chanting, purple-clad devotees of El Señor de los Milagros (the Lord of the Miracles) fill the streets of Lima.

CLIMATE   When it's dry in the Sierra and the Selva, it's wet on the Costa, and vice versa. The Selva is hot and humid year-round, with endless rain between January and April. Friajes from Patagonia occasionally sweep through the southern rain forests of Madre de Dios, but the average daily minimum and maximum temperatures in the Selva are 20°C (69°F) and 32°C (90°F).

In the Sierra expect rain between October and April, and especially January through March. The rest of the year the weather is dry and the temperatures fickle. The sun can be hot, but in the shade it's refreshingly cool. Nights are chilly, and the temperature may drop to freezing. Temperatures during Cusco's dry months average 0°C (32°F)–22°C (71°F).

It never rains in the coastal desert, but a dank, heavy fog called the garua coats Lima from June through December. Outside Lima, coastal weather is clearer and warm.

The following are average daily maximum and minimum temperatures for Lima.

Jan.	27C	81F	May	25C	77F	Sept.	19C	66F
	21	70		19	66		15	59
Feb.	28C	82F	June	23C	73F	Oct.	21C	70F
	21	70		17	63		16	61
Mar.	29C	84F	July	18C	64F	Nov.	23C	73F
	23	73		15	59		17	63
Apr.	27C	81F	Aug.	18C	64F	Dec.	24C	75F
	22	72		15	59		18	64

URUGUAY

9

INDULGE IN A BEEF *PARRILLA*
at the Mercado del Puerto ⇨*p.717*

SADDLE UP (FIGURATIVELY SPEAKING)
at the Cowboy and Coin Museum
in Montevideo ⇨*p.718*

SERENADE YOUR SWEETHEART
on a cobblestone lane in romantic
Colonia del Sacramento ⇨*p.729*

EXPLORE A FANTASY IN THE SKY
at the gleaming, hilltop Casapueblo
Club Hotel in Punta Ballena ⇨*p.731*

JOIN THE SUN WORSHIPERS
at the beach town of Punta del Este ⇨*p.731*

Updated by
Michael de
Zayas

CONSIDERED THE MOST EUROPEAN of South American countries, Uruguay has a distinct cosmopolitan flair. That's not surprising, since about half of its population—largely of Spanish, Portuguese, and Italian descent—lives in the capital. Uruguay attracts international travelers (most of all neighboring Argentines) to the trendy boutiques and fashionable beaches of Punta del Este.

Uruguay's original inhabitants, the seminomadic Charrúa people, were attacked first by the Portuguese, who settled the town of Colonia in 1680, then by the Spanish, who in 1726 established a fortress at Montevideo. In 1811, José Gervasio Artigas mobilized the masses to fight against the heavy-handed influence of Buenos Aires. Though Artigas's bid for Uruguayan independence was unsuccessful, Uruguay finally became an autonomous state in 1825. On July 18, 1830—a date that gives the name to many a street—the country's first constitution was framed, and the *Republica Oriental de Uruguay* was formed.

Following a period of civil war, José Batlle y Ordóñez was elected president in 1903. Under his guidance, Uruguay became the first Latin American nation to grant voting rights to women and the first country to sever relations between church and state—a striking maneuver considering the Catholic Church's strong influence on the continent. Since then, except for a military-run government between 1973 and 1985, Uruguay has been one of the strongest democracies in South America.

The country takes pride in the number of world-famous artists it produces. Galleries here are full of works by masters such as sculptor José Belloni (1880–1965) and painters Joacquín Torres-García (1874–1949), Pedro Figari (1861–1938), and Pedro Blanes Viale (1879–1926). Uruguayans like to claim their country as the birthplace of the internationally renowned tango singer Carlos Gardel (1809–1935), although the Argentines and French also vie for this claim.

As in Argentina, the legendary gaucho is Uruguay's most potent cultural fixture, and it is difficult to pass a day without some reference to these cowboys who once roamed the country singing their melancholy ballads. Remnants of the gaucho lifestyle may still be seen on active ranches throughout the country.

About the Restaurants

Beef is the staple of the Uruguayan diet. It is cheap, abundant, and often grilled in a style borrowed from the gauchos, and known as *parrilla*. A meal in a *parrillada,* a Uruguayan steak house, should be on your agenda. Beef is also made into sausages, such as *chorizo* and *salchicha*, or is combined with ham, cheese, bacon, and peppers to make *matambre.* Seafood is also popular here—especially the *lenguado* (flounder), *merluza* (hake), and *calamar* (squid). Try the *raya a la manteca negra* (squid ray in blackened butter). If you are not up to a full meal, try the *chivito*, a hefty steak sandwich. Uruguayan wines under the Santa Rosa and Calvinor labels, a step up from table wine, are available in most restaurants. *Clericó* is a mixture of white wine and fruit juice, while *medio y medio* is part sparkling wine, part white wine.

9

If you have
5 days

Start your visit in **Montevideo** and spend a day exploring the city. Stop for lunch at one of the restaurants at the bustling Mercado del Puerto. The next morning, head to the jet-set beachfront resort of **Punta del Este,** where you'll spend the night. The two-hour ride to town should whet your appetite for a seafood lunch. After a few hours strolling or sunning on Punta's beaches, take the 10-minute boat ride to the pine-covered **Isla Gorriti** or the four-hour excursion around **Isla de los Lobos,** a sea lion sanctuary. On the third day head a few miles east to the hip community of **La Barra de Maldonado** and browse in the boutiques and antiques stores. After a few hours, head back west—to **Punta Ballena,** where the **Casapueblo** hotel-cum-sculpture will rejuvenate your spirits. Remain in Casapueblo overnight. On the fourth day, make the five-hour drive 180 km (113 mi) west from Montevideo to **Colonia del Sacramento.** Check out the Old City that evening and the next morning before returning to Montevideo.

If you have
more
than 5
days

Follow the itinerary described above, but take a few extra days to explore the **Atlantic coast** east of Punta del Este—past fishing towns and over to the wide beaches at **Rocha** and **Aguas Dulces.** Or add a few days to the end of the itinerary above by heading to the vast **grasslands** of the interior for a stay in an *estancia,* a working ranch. There's no need to rough it—most estancias have pools and good restaurants—for when you tire of living the life of a cowboy. It's best to arrange a stay through tour operators in Montevideo.

Lunch is served between noon and 3; restaurants begin to fill around 12:30 and are packed by 1:30. Many restaurants do not open for dinner until 8 PM and are rarely crowded before 10 PM. Most pubs and *confiterías* (cafés) are open all day. Formal dress is rarely required. Smart sportswear is acceptable at even the fanciest establishments.

	WHAT IT COSTS In U.S. Dollars				
	$$$$	**$$$**	**$$**	**$**	**¢**
AT DINNER	over $20	$15–$20	$10–$15	$6–$10	under $6

Prices are per person for a main course at dinner.

About the Hotels

Hotels here are generally clean and comfortable. Many include one or even two meals a day in their rates. You can save up to 30% in the same hotel by requesting a *habitación turística,* usually a bit plainer, smaller, and without a view, but with the same standards of cleanliness and service. *Hosterías* are country inns that not only offer modest rooms but which are open for dinner as well. Menus tend to be limited, though the food served is unfailingly hearty. Outside the cities hosterías are likely to be on the rustic side. Summer in Uruguay can be onerous, and many hotels and hosterías are not yet equipped with air-conditioning. Make sure you inquire when making a reservation.

One of the nicest ways to experience Uruguay's vast unspoiled countryside is to stay at an *estancia*. These ranches usually raise animals for the country's most-prized exports—wool, beef, and leather. Although some exist solely as tourist attractions, most estancias are fully operational. You may meet the *estancieros* (ranchers) and stay in quarters that date from the colonial period. The highlight is accompanying the gauchos while they herd cattle, shear sheep, or sit around a fire roasting up sausages for lunch.

Accommodations at estancias range from comfortable to luxurious, and meals are generally included. Some estancias have swimming pools and tennis courts, and most let you explore the countryside on horseback and swim in local rivers and lakes. All provide a chance to breathe the fresh air of the open range.

WHAT IT COSTS In U.S. Dollars				
	$$$$	**$$$**	**$$**	**$**	**¢**
FOR 2 PEOPLE	over $120	$80–$120	$40–$80	$20–$40	under $20

Prices are for two people in a standard double room in high season, excluding tax.

Exploring Uruguay

Uruguay is one of the smallest countries in South America, both in terms of area (it's roughly the size of England) and altitude (far from the Andes, there's nothing but gently rolling hills). In the sparsely developed country filled with vast ranches and farms, all roads lead to the capital of Montevideo. Here you'll find almost half the population. Montevideo's only cosmopolitan rival is Punta del Este, one of a handful of Atlantic Ocean resorts popular with well-heeled Brazilians and Argentines who can afford the region's variety of high-price fun (mornings and afternoons at Gucci, evenings at heady bars and discos).

MONTEVIDEO

Uruguay's only major metropolis, Montevideo has its share of glitzy shopping avenues and modern office buildings. But few visitors come here specifically in search of urban pleasures—in fact, Montevideans head to nearby Buenos Aires when they want to be someplace cosmopolitan. This city of 1½ million doesn't have the whirlwind vibe of Rio de Janeiro or Santiago, but it's a fine old city with sumptuous, if worn, colonial architecture, and a massive coastal promenade that often—as it passes fine beaches, restaurants, and numerous parks—recalls the sunny sophistications of the Mediterranean.

Legend has it that Montevideo was christened in 1516 when the Portuguese explorer Juan Diaz de Solís first laid eyes on a hill near the mouth of the harbor, and uttered the words "*Monte vide eu*" ("I see a hill"). Another theory has that Magellan, traveling along the coast from Brazil in 1520, counted off six hills from the Brazilian border and thus named the city Monte (mountain) vi (roman numeral six) de (from) eo (*este a*

Carnaval

Almost every town in Uruguay celebrates Carnaval, the weeklong festival that immediately precedes the beginning of Lent. The entire country participates in the *comparsas,* the festive mix of singing, dancing, drinking, eating, and general merrymaking.

Criollas

Also known as *jineteadas,* the Uruguayan-style rodeos called *criollas* are held all over the country, but the most spectacular one takes place in Montevideo's El Prado district every Easter. Gauchos (cowboys) from all over the country come to display their skill in riding wild horses.

9

Pious Processions

One of the most important is the Procession of Verdun in the Lavalleja region. Since 1901, thousands of believers have come here on April 19 to give thanks to the Virgin of the Immaculate Conception, who is believed to have appeared here. Many of the faithful climb a hill on their knees, arriving at the summit bruised and bleeding. The Festival of St. Cono, which takes place June 3 throughout the Florida region, attracts thousands of worshipers who come to pray to the icon of the Italian saint. Brought here by the region's first Italian settlers in 1885, the icon is believed to have the power to perform miracles.

Soccer

"Other countries have their history," Helenio Herrera, Uruguay's most famous soccer coach once said, "we have our fútbol." Indeed, *fútbol* is played anywhere there is space, by men of all ages. Try to attend a *clássico,* a match between Montevideo's two great rival professional teams, Nacional and Peñarol, played amid the screams and encouragement of passionate supporters at the capital's Estadio Centenario.

---

oeste, or east to west). Built along the eastern bank of the Río de la Plata (River of Silver), Montevideo takes full advantage of its location. When the weather's good, La Rambla, a 22-km (14-mi) waterfront avenue that links the Old City with the eastern suburbs, gets packed with fishermen, ice cream vendors, and joggers. Around sunset, volleyball and soccer games wind down as couples begin to appear for evening strolls. You'll always hear a melody in the air—often from a street musician playing tangos on his accordion.

Exploring Montevideo

Modern Montevideo expanded outward from the peninsular Ciudad Vieja, the Old City, still noted for its narrow streets and elegant colonial architecture. El Prado, an exclusive enclave a few miles north of the city center, is peppered with lavish mansions and grand parks. When you remember that these mansions were once summer homes for aristocratic Uruguayans who spent most of the year elsewhere, you'll get some idea of the wealth this small country once enjoyed.

Numbers in the text correspond to numbers in the margin and on the Montevideo map.

Ciudad Vieja

a good
walk

Begin at the **Plaza Independencia** ❶ ☞ at the eastern edge of the Old City. On the east side is the beautiful byzantine tower of the art deco Palacio Salvo. The **Palacio Estévez** ❷ is on the south side of the plaza. Cross the street on the west side of the plaza; this officially brings you into the Old City along the main artery, **Calle Sarandí.** Take your first left of Sarandí to **Calle Bacacay,** which is filled with bars, cafés, and little crafts shops. At the end of the block to the south is the **Teatro Solís** ❸. After a visit here, return to Calle Sarandí and head west a few blocks to **Plaza Matriz** ❹. Facing the plaza to the east is **El Cabildo** ❺, where the Uruguayan constitution was signed. On the opposite side of the square sits the oldest public building in Montevideo, **Iglesia Matriz** ❻. On the south side of the plaza is the Neoclassical building that houses the **Club Uruguayo** ❼. Walk a block north to **Calle Rincón,** a principal commercial and financial thoroughfare; banks are cheek by jowl among art galleries and antiques dealers. Walk two blocks west to the southeast corner of Calles Rincón and Misiones, where you'll find the **Bolsa de Montevideo,** Uruguay's stock exchange. At the northwest corner of the same intersection you'll find the **Casa de Rivera** ❽, where you can check out exhibits on Uruguay from colonial times to the 1930s. Two blocks west, down Rincón, is **Plaza Zabala** ❾. On the north side of the park you'll see the back of the ornate, fin-de-siècle **Palacio Taranco** ❿. From the entrance to the palace, head east one block and turn left (north) on Calle Zabala. Half-way down the street on your left is the colonial-era **Casa de Lavalleja** ⓫. At the corner of Zabala and Cerrito—the next block north and across the street and on the northwest side of the intersection—is a square-block-long parade of Corinthian columns that forms the monumental exterior of the **Banco de la Republica de Uruguay.** Finally, head two blocks west and then two blocks north to check out the wonderful **Mercado del Puerto** ⓬, a great place for a late lunch.

TIMING   This walk should take three to five hours. Ciudad Vieja is fairly compact, and you could walk from one end to the other in about 15 minutes. Take care at night, when the area is fairly deserted and feels a little sketchy.

WHAT TO SEE   **Casa de Lavalleja.** This Spanish neoclassical home was built in 1783 and ⓫ later became the home of General Juan A. Lavalleja, who distinguished himself in Uruguay's war for independence. This pristine colonial home with lovely wrought-iron balconies displays manuscripts and historical memorabilia. ⊠ *Calle Zabala 1469, Ciudad Vieja* ☎ *2/915–1028* ☜ *Free* ⊙ *Tues.–Fri. 1:30–6:30, Sun. 2:30–6:30.*

❽ **Casa de Rivera.** Once the home of General Fructuso Rivera, Uruguay's first president, the Rivera House was acquired by the government in 1942. Exhibits inside this pale yellow colonial house with an octagonal cupola document the development of Uruguay from the colonial period through the 1930s. ⊠ *Calle Rincón 437, Ciudad Vieja* ☎ *2/915–1051* ☜ *Free* ⊙ *Tues.–Fri. 1:30–6:30, Sun. 2:30–6:30.*

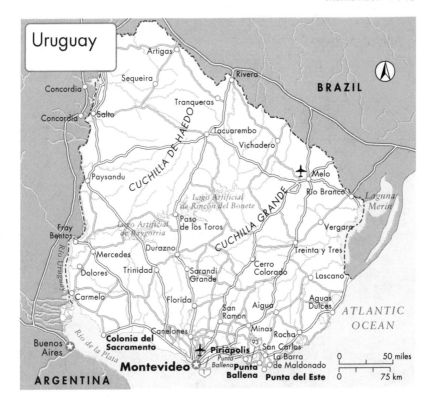

Uruguay

7 **Club Uruguayo.** Uruguay's most prestigious private social club, founded in 1878, is headquartered in this eclectic, three-story neoclassical national monument on the south side of Plaza Matriz. The club is open for tours (anytime) to the public, and friendly, English-speaking guides will happily show you up the marble staircases so you can marvel at the elegant salons. The club was formed for high society of European descent. Today its approximately 400 exclusive members gather for meals and to play bridge. ⊠ *Calle Sarandí 584, Ciudad Vieja* ☎ *No phone* ⊡ *Free* ⊗ *Daily 7 AM–10 PM.*

5 **El Cabildo.** The old City Hall is where the Uruguayan constitution was signed in 1830. This two-story colonial edifice houses an impressive collection of paintings, antiques, costumes, and rotating history exhibits. Fountains and statuary line the interior patios. English-speaking guides are available. ⊠ *Calle Juan Carlos Gómez at Calle Sarandí, Ciudad Vieja* ☎ *2/915-9685* ⊡ *Free* ⊗ *Wed.–Fri. 1:30–5:30, Sat. 11–4:30, Sun. 1:30–5:30.*

6 **Iglesia Matriz.** This cathedral, the oldest public building in Montevideo, has a distinctive pair of dome-cap bell towers that stand guard over the plaza below. Besides its rich marble interior, colorful floor tiling, stained glass, and dome, the Matriz Church is most notable as the final resting

Montevideo

Bahía de Montevideo

Estación Central
Gral. ARTIGAS
A.F.E

TO EL PRADO

Palacio
Legislativo

CENTRO

Banco de
Uruguay

CIUDAD
VIEJA

Río de La Plata

0   500 yards

0   500 meters

KEY

► *Start of walk*

place of Uruguay's most important political and military figures. ⊠ *Calle Sarandí at Calle Ituzaingó, Ciudad Vieja* ⊙ *Daily 9–7; mass Sundays 9–1.*

★ ⑫ **Mercado del Puerto.** The Port Market, housed in a train station of vaulted iron beams and colored glass that was never put into service, is where downtown workers meet for lunch during the week. The experience here— aesthetic, social, and gastronomical—is tough to top. The market shields dozens of stalls and eateries where, over large fires, the best *parrillas* (grilled beef) in the city are cooked. The traditional drink here is a bottle of *medio y medio* (champagne mixed with white wine). The market is also the site of huge, carousing celebrations on December 24 and December 31. ⊠ *Rambla 25 de Agosto, between Av. Maciel and Av. Pérez Castellano, across from the port, Ciudad Vieja* ☎ *no phone* ⊙ *Closed Sun. No dinner weekdays.*

② **Palacio Estévez.** On the south side of Plaza Independencia, Estévez Palace, one of the most beautiful old buildings in the city, was the seat of government until 1985, when the president's offices were moved to a more modern building. This building, unfortunately closed to the public, is used on occasion for ceremonial purposes. ⊠ *Plaza Independencia, Ciudad Vieja.*

⑩ **Palacio Taranco.** Built in 1908 atop the rubble of Uruguay's first theater, the ornate Taranco Palace, in the Ciudad Vieja, is representative of the French-inspired architecture favored in fin-de-siècle Montevideo. Even the marble for the floors was imported from France. Today you can survey that bygone glory in rooms filled with period furniture, statuary, draperies, clocks, and portrait paintings. A cultural center within has a calendar of performances and live music. ⊠ *Calle 25 de Mayo, 376, Ciudad Vieja* ☎ *2/915–1101* ▭ *Free* ⊙ *Tues.–Sat. 12:15–6, Sun. 2–6.*

▶ ① **Plaza Independencia.** Portions of Independence Square were once occupied by the *ciudadela*, a military fortification built originally by the Spanish but deemed militarily useless and destroyed in 1833. In the center stands a 30-ton statue of General Gervasio Artigas, the father of Uruguay and the founder of its 19th-century independence movement. At the base of the monument, two flights of polished granite stairs lead to an underground mausoleum that holds Artigas's remains. The mausoleum is a moving memorial: bold graphics chiseled in the walls of this giant space detail the feats of Artigas's life. Two uniformed guards, dressed in period uniforms, stand at solemn attention beside the urn in this uncanny, rarely visited vault. There's a changing of the guard Fridays at 12:30, and a parade at the mausoleum on Saturdays at 11:30 AM.

Looming over the north side of the plaza, the 26-story **Palacio Salvo** was the tallest building in South America when it was erected in 1927 (it's still the second tallest building in Uruguay). Today this gorgeous art deco edifice—one of the more beautiful skyscrapers in the world—is an office building and unfortunately closed to the public.

④ **Plaza Matriz.** The ornate cantilever fountain in the center of this tree-filled square (known to most as Plaza Constitución) was installed in 1871 to commemorate the construction of the city's first water system.

⑨ Plaza Zabala. At this charmed spot in the heart of the *ciudad vieja* it's easy to image the splendor of the old Montevideo. Around the fountain and flowers of the park is the turn-of-the-century Taranco mansion, and bank headquarters in—a refreshing sight in the Old City—renovated older buildings.

③ Teatro Solís. Named in honor of the discoverer of the Río de la Plata, Juan Diaz de Solís, the 1856 Solís Theater is famed for its fine acoustics. Sharing the building is the **Museo Nacional de Historia Natural** (National Museum of Natural History). Both are currently closed; the theater has been undergoing renovations since 1999, and isn't expected to reopen any time soon. ⊠ *Calle Buenos Aires 652, Ciudad Vieja* ☎ *No phone.*

Avenida 18 de Julio

Montevideo's main street has everything—shops and museums, cafés and plazas, bustling traditional markets and chrome-and-steel office towers. It runs east from Plaza Independencia, away from the Ciudad Vieja, passing through bustling Plaza Fabini and tree-lined Plaza Cagancha.

a good walk

Walk east from Plaza Independencia along Avenida 18 de Julio; three blocks up the street is the **Museo del Gaucho y la Moneda** ⑬ ▶, where you can learn about the country's cowboy history. Across the street is the beautiful **Plaza Fabini** ⑭. Continuing east, you'll pass through Plaza Cagancha before reaching the **Museo de Historia del Arte** ⑮, which you enter from the side of the tall, orange-brick city hall.

TIMING   It's a 30-minute walk from Plaza Independencia to the Palacio Municipal. To visit both sights on this tour, allow another 1½ hours for both. If shopping is your main interest, however, you may want to devote an entire afternoon to browsing and buying along the avenue.

WHAT TO SEE   **Museo del Gaucho y la Moneda.** The Cowboy and Coin Museum is in a
★ ▶ ⑬   rococo 19th-century mansion near Calle Julio Herrera y Obes, four blocks east of Plaza Independencia. Here you'll find articles from the everyday life of the gauchos, from traditional garb to the detailed silver work on the cups used for *mate* (an indigenous herb from which tea is brewed). Ancient South American and European coins are on the first floor. English tours are available with two days' notice. ⊠ *Av. 18 de Julio, 998, Centro* ☎ *2/900–8764* ⊠ *Free* ☉ *Weekdays 9–5.*

off the beaten path

MUSEO NACIONAL DE ARTES VISUALES – Parque Rodó has a little something for everyone—two amusement parks, a number of decent eateries, and the fascinating National Museum of Visual Arts, which has hosted exhibits from as far afield as China and Poland. Between December 5 and January 6, Parque Rodó is also the site of Montevideo's best *feria artesanal* (crafts fair). ⊠ *Av. T. Giribaldi at Av. J. Herrera y Reisig* ☎ *2/711–6054* ⊠ *Free* ☉ *Wed.–Sun. 4–8.*

⑮ Museo de Historia del Arte (MuHAr). In the **Palacio Municipal** (an ambitious name for this unremarkable brick city hall) you'll find the Museum of Art History, which has the country's best collection of pre-Columbian and colonial artifacts. You'll also find Greek, Roman, and Middle Eastern art, including ceramics, artifacts, and vitrines. On the street-level entrance is the **Biblioteca de Historia del Arte** (Library of Art History). ⊠*Calle Ejido 1326, Centro* ☎ *2/908–9252* 🖭 *Free* ☉ *Museum Tues.–Wed. and Fri.–Sun. 12:15–5:45, Th. 3:30–9. Library weekdays 9:30–4:30.*

⑭ Plaza Fabini. In the center of this lovely, manicured square is the Monumento del Entrevero, a large sculpture depicting a whirlwind of gauchos, *criollos* (mixed-blood settlers who are half native, half European), and native Uruguayans in battle. It's one of the last works by sculptor José Belloni (1882–1965). An open-air market with food and other items takes place here every morning. ⊠ *Av. 18 de Julio, Centro.*

El Prado

a good
walk

The district known as El Prado lies roughly 6 km (4 mi) north of Plaza Independencia. You could make the long uphill walk along the busy Avenida Agraciada, but it's a lot easier in a taxi. Start at the diminutive chapel of the **Sagrada Familia** ⑯ ▶ on Avenida Luis Alberto de Herrera. Nearby are numerous 18th- and 19th-century mansions. From there, take Avenida Millán north to the ornate **Museo de Bellas Artes** ⑰. After spending some time at the museum, head to the adjacent **Parque Prado** ⑱ and find a secluded spot for an afternoon picnic. Avenida Buschental, which bisects the park, takes you past El Rosedal, the lovely rose garden.

TIMING This walk should take about two hours. Allow an extra hour for a visit to the Museo de Bellas Artes. It is pleasant to walk along Avenida Buschental in fall and spring when the trees are in full color.

WHAT TO SEE **Museo de Bellas Artes.** The Museum of Fine Arts, known locally as the

⑰ Blanes Museum, is housed in an elegant colonial mansion that once belonged to Uruguay's foremost 19th-century painter, Juan Manuel Blanes. He was entirely self-taught and did not begin painting until he was in his fifties. His realistic portrayals of gauchos and the Uruguayan countryside compose the core of the museum's collection. ⊠ *Av. Millán 4015, El Prado* ☎ *2/336–2248* 🖭 *Free* ☉ *Tues.–Sun. 1–7.*

⑱ Parque Prado. The oldest of the city's parks is also one of the most popular. Locals come to see El Rosedal, the rose garden with more than 800 different varieties. Also in the park you'll find the statue called *La Diligencia,* by sculptor José Belloni. There's also a fine botanical garden. ⊠ *Av. Agraciada, El Prado* ☎ *2/336–4005* ☉ *Daily 7–7.*

▶ **⑯ Sagrada Familia.** Too tiny to require flying buttresses, the ornately Gothic Holy Family Church is complete in all other respects; a troop of gargoyles peers down at you, and the finely wrought stained-glass windows become radiant when backlit by the sun. ⊠ *Calle Luis Alberto de Herrera 4246, El Prado* ☎ *2/203–6824* ☉ *Mass weekdays 7 PM; Jan.–Feb., Sat. 7 PM and Sun. 8 PM.*

off the
beaten
path

PALACIO LEGISLATIVO – Almost 50 different types of native marble were used in the construction of the Legislative Palace, the seat of Uruguay's bicameral legislature. Free Spanish- and English-language tours are available when the congress is in session; passes are available inside at the information desk. ⊠ *Av. Agraciada at Av. Flores, El Prado* ☎ *2/200–1334* 🖭 *Free* ☉ *Weekdays 9–6; tours hourly 9–noon and 2–5.*

Where to Eat

Menus don't vary much in Montevideo—meat is always the main dish—
so the food may not provide a distraction from the blinding light (even
the most fashionable restaurant in Montevideo seems to be brightly illuminated). For an informal meal try one of the ubiquitous *parrillada
barbecues* (meat on a spit).

French

$ ✕ **Doña Flor.** Housed in a century-old home in the nearby suburb of Punta
Carretas, this quiet, elegant restaurant has a diverse menu heavily in-
debted to the French (the pâté is rich as butter and twice as smooth).
The house specialty is green lasagna with salmon. In summer, this location closes so the staff can give its full attention to a sister restaurant
in Punta del Este. ⊠ *Bulevar Artigas 1034, Punta Carretas* ☎ *2/708–
5751* ⚮ *Reservations essential* ▤ *AE, DC, MC, V* ⊗ *Closed Dec.–Apr.*

Swiss

$ ✕ **Bungalow Suizo.** The split-level dining area at this small, refined restau-
rant is subdued and intimate, with private tables tucked into quiet corners. Fondue is the specialty of the house, supplemented by various
cuts of beef. In summer the restaurant shuts down and the owner, chef,
and staff relocate to their other restaurant, Punta del Este. ⊠ *Calle
Sol 150* ☎ *2/601–1511 or 2/601–1073* ▤ *MC, V* ⊗ *Closed Dec.–Apr.
No lunch.*

Uruguayan

$ ✕ **La Casa Violeta.** Meats are the specialty at this beautiful restaurant
facing Puerto del Buceo, one of the prettiest spots in the city. Parrilla is
served in the method called *espeto corrido*—grilled meats are brought
to your table on a long skewer so you can slice off whatever you want.
There's also a good selection of salads. There's a big deck shaded with
umbrellas with attractive views of the port and surrounding homes.
⊠ *Rabmla Aremeña 3667 (corner of 26 de Marzo, Puerto del Buceo),
Pocitos* ☎ *2/628–7626* ▤ *AE, DC, MC, V* ⊗ *No lunch Mon.*

¢ ✕ **El Buzon.** This unassuming restaurant not far from the Palacio Legislativo serves excellent parrilla and inexpensive, homemade pastas.
The *pollo deshuesado* (boneless breast of chicken stuffed with ham and
mozzarella and served with mushroom sauce) is worth the trip. For dessert
try the *charlot* (vanilla ice cream with warm chocolate). ⊠ *Calle Hoc-
quard 1801 Centro* ☎ *2/200–9781* ▤ *DC, MC, V* ⊗ *No dinner Sun.*

¢ ✕ **Café Bacacay.** This small and smartly designed restaurant facing Theater Solís attracts a young, hip crowd. It serves a wide selection of international dishes. The owner takes special care in preparing the excellent
salads, such as the Bacacay (spinach, raisins, carrots, nuts, and hearts
of palm topped with croutons) or the Sarandí (lettuce, celery, chicken,
apples, carrots). ⊠ *Bacacay 1310, at Calle Buenos Aires, Ciudad Vieja*
☎ *2/916–6074* ▤ *AE, MC, V* ⊗ *Closed Sun.*

¢ ✕ **Meson Viejo Sancho.** What draws the post-theater crowds to this
friendly but plain restaurant near Plaza Cagancha are gargantuan portions of smoked pork chops and fried potatoes. ⊠ *Calle San José 1229
Centro* ☎ *2/900–4063* ▤ *MC, V* ⊗ *Closed Sun.*

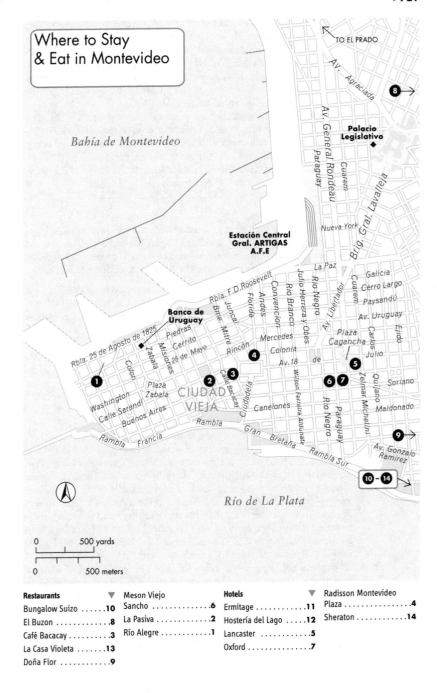

Where to Stay & Eat in Montevideo

Bahía de Montevideo

TO EL PRADO

Palacio Legislativo

Estación Central Gral. ARTIGAS A.F.E

Banco de Uruguay

CIUDAD VIEJA

Río de La Plata

0   500 yards

0   500 meters

Restaurants ▼
Bungalow Suizo **10**
El Buzon **8**
Café Bacacay **3**
La Casa Violeta **13**
Doña Flor **9**

Meson Viejo
Sancho **6**
La Pasiva **2**
Río Alegre **1**

Hotels ▼
Ermitage **11**
Hostería del Lago **12**
Lancaster **5**
Oxford **7**

Radisson Montevideo
Plaza **4**
Sheraton **14**

¢ ✕ **La Pasiva.** For an ice-cold beer, this popular *chopperia* (beer house) is a late-night favorite. The specialties are frankfurters (10 pesos), chivitos, and other bar food. In good weather you can socialize at the outdoor tables in Plaza Matriz. This Montevideo staple has franchises throughout the city, including a prominent location inside Plaza Fabini. ✉ *Calle Sarandí at Calle J.C. Gómez Ciudad Vieja* ☎ 2/915–7988 ⌂ *Reservations not accepted* ▭ *DC, MC, V.*

¢ ✕ **Río Alegre.** Pepe, the amiable proprietor of this restaurant in the Mercado del Puerto, will stuff you full of homemade chorizo and grilled provolone sprinkled with oregano. For a main course, *asado de tira* (short ribs) and *filete a la pimienta* (pepper steak) are good choices. ✉ *Calle Pérez Castellano at Calle Piedras Ciudad Vieja* ☎ 2/915–6504 ⌂ *Reservations not accepted* ▭ V ☉ *No dinner.*

Where to Stay

Many downtown hotels are grouped around the big three squares, Plaza Independencia, Plaza Fabini, and Plaza Cagancha. In the weeks before and after Carnaval in February, rooms become hard to come by. Otherwise, rooms are plentiful in summer, when beach-bound residents desert the city.

$$$$ 🏨 **Sheraton.** The city's biggest new hotel is removed from the Old City, and, decidedly modern, feels a world away. Attached to the flashy Punta Carretas shopping center, the hotel offers the comforts of a corporate luxury hotel only a five-minute walk from one of the city's many fine beaches. You will need a cab, however, to reach the majority of the city's sights. ✉ *Victor Soliño 349, Punta Carretas* ☎ 2/710–2121 ⊟ 2/712–1262 ⊕ *www.sheraton.com* ⇖ *207 rooms, 10 suites* ⌂ *Restaurant, room service, minibars, cable TV, golf privileges, tennis courts, indoor pool, gym, hot tub, sauna, spa, bar, casino, laundry service, concierge, Internet, business services, convention center, airport shuttle, car rental* ▭ *AE, DC, MC, V* ⍰ *BP.*

★ **$$** 🏨 **Ermitage.** This unprepossessing, sandstone-front building, overlooking the lovely Plaza Tomás Gomensoro, is a good, affordable choice if you want to be near the shore. It's in a calm residential zone a block from Pocitos beach and is also a 10-minute drive from the Old City. You'll find plenty of others sitting over a drink or playing cards in the wood-panel lobby—decorated with a large photo-mural of Playa Pocitos in 1928. Rooms are furnished with replicas of 1920s-style furniture and light fixtures—to reflect that gentler, more stylish era of city history. ✉ *Calle Juan Benito Blanco 783 Pocitos* ☎ 2/710–4021 or 2/711–7447 ⊟ 2/710–4312 ⇖ 90 *rooms* ⌂ *Restaurant, cable TV, laundry service* ▭ *AE, DC, MC, V* ⍰ *BP.*

★ **$$** 🏨 **Hostería del Lago.** On a beautiful lake about 12 km (7 mi) from downtown, this sprawling Spanish colonial hotel is the kind of place that encourages relaxation. Bask by the pool, play a few games of tennis, or head out on a horse for an afternoon of exploring the parkland. The split-level rooms, all the size of suites, have wood-beam ceilings and carpeted floors. ✉ *Av. Arizona 9637, Carrasco* ☎ 2/601–2210 ⊟ 2/601–2880 ⊕ *www.hosteriadellago.com.uy* ⇖ 70 *rooms* ⌂ *Restaurant, room service, tennis court, pool, horseback riding, playground, airport shuttle* ▭ *AE, DC, MC, V.*

$$ ☷ **Radisson Montevideo Plaza.** This luxurious glass-and-brick structure looking out over Plaza Independencia is Montevideo's top choice near the Ciudad Vieja. The café on the 24th floor is the best public space for views of the old and new city. ☒ *Plaza Independencia 759, Centro* ☎ *2/902–0111* ᐧ *2/902–1628* ⊕ *www.radisson.com/montevideouy* ◁ *190 rooms, 64 suites* ➺ *Restaurant, café, coffee shop, room service, minibars, cable TV, pool, gym, spa, bar, casino, shop, laundry service, Internet, business center, convention center, airport shuttle* ⊟ *AE, DC, MC, V* ⋈ *BP.*

$–$$ ☷ **Oxford.** Glass walls, broad windows, and mirrors give the small lobby an open but intimate feel, much like that of the hotel itself. The rooms at this English-style hotel are immaculately clean, the staff friendly and helpful. Despite its location near Plaza Cagancha, the hotel is remarkably quiet. ☒ *Calle Paraguay 1286, Centro* ☎ *2/902–0046* ᐧ *2/902–3792* ⊕ *www.oxford.com.uy* ◁ *64 rooms, 2 suites* ➺ *Cafeteria, minibars, cable TV, in-room safes, bar, Internet, business services, parking (fee)* ⊟ *AE, DC, MC, V* ⋈ *CP.*

$ ☷ **Lancaster.** Hidden behind tall poplars in a corner of Plaza Cagancha, this 11-story hotel in the heart of the city may be past its glory days, but it makes a fine budget lodging choice in the Centro. The rooms are sunny and large, with tall French doors that open out onto the square. ☒ *Plaza Cagancha 1334 Centro* ☎ *2/902–1054* ᐧ *2/908–1117* ◁ *78 rooms* ➺ *Cafeteria, minibars, cable TV, bar, laundry service* ⊟ *AE, DC, MC, V.*

Nightlife & the Arts

Nightlife

In Montevideo you'll find quiet, late-night bars, hip-hop clubs, and folk music shows. The entertainment and cultural pages of the local papers are the best sources of the latest information; particularly useful is the *Guía del Ocio,* a magazine inserted into the Friday edition of the daily newspaper *El País.* With few exceptions, bars and clubs come to life around 1 AM and do not close until it is time for breakfast.

DANCE CLUBS The retro set flocks to **Aquellos Años** (☒ Calle Beyrouth 1405, Pocitos), which has music from the '50s and '60s. You can hear live music and dance to house hits at **Mariachi** (☒ Gabriel Pereira 2964, Pocitos ☎ 2/709–1600). **Milenio** (☒ 25 de Mayo and Ciudadela, Ciudad Vieja), is popular with the MTV generation. **New York** (☒ Calle Mar Artico 1227 ☎ 2/600–0444) draws an older crowd. In front of Playa Ramirez in Parque Rodó, **W Lounge** (☒ Rambla Wilson s/n, Punta Carretas ☎ 2/712–5287) gets a large crowd on weekends. It transforms from a bar to a disco at 1 AM.

PUBS **Amarcor** (☒ Calle Julio Herrera y Obes 1231, Centro ☎ 2/900–1207) is popular with young artists, actors, and intellectuals. Also try **Perdidos en la Noche** (☒ Calle Yaguarón 1099 Centro ☎ 2/902–6733). **Riff Gallery Pub** (☒ Bul. España 2511, Centro ☎ no phone) is the only bar in the city devoted to jazz, with live shows on Thursday and Saturday. **The Shannon Irish Pub** (☒ Mitre 1318, Ciudad Vieja) in the Old City draws a young crowd. It has good rock music and an unpretentious vibe.

TANGO SHOWS **La Casa de Becho** (☒ New York, 1415, Centro ☎ 2/400–2717), the house that once belonged to Mattos Rodríguez, the composer of "La Cumparsita," has weekend shows for a younger crowd. You'll need reservations here. **Joven Tango** (⊠ Calle San José 1314, Centro ☎ 2/908–1550) is the best place in the city to learn tango. Shows are frequent; call for times.

The Arts

The **Servicio Oficial de Difusión Radio Elétrica (SODRE)** (⊠ Av. 18 de Julio 930, Centro ☎ 2/901–2850) hosts a season of classical concerts that runs from May to November. **Alliance Française** (⊠ Calle Soriano 1176, Centro ☎ 2/903–0473) has a series of plays and films. The **Instituto Goethe** (Goethe Institute; ⊠ Calle Canelones 1524, Centro ☎ 2/410–4432) has films and theater in German. The U.S.-sponsored **Alianza Artigas-Washington** (⊠ Calle Paraguay 1217, Centro ☎ 2/900–2721) host plays and concerts by foreign talent. The **Instituto Cultural Anglo-Uruguayo** (⊠ Calle San José 1426 ☎ 2/902–7634) hosts plays in English.

Shopping

Markets

Weekend *ferias* (open-air markets) are the best place for leisurely browsing among a warren of crafts stalls. Government regulations dictate that all ferias must close in the early afternoon, so make sure to arrive by 10 AM. **Feria Tristán Narvaja,** started over half a century ago by Italian immigrants, is Montevideo's top attraction on Sundays. (It's only open on Sundays, a day when all other markets, and much of the city, are closed.) Running off 18 de Julio at Calle Tristán Narvaja, a five- to 10-minute walk from the Old City and in the Centro district, the fair is plentifully stocked with secondhand goods. The Saturday morning market at **Plaza Biarritz** in the nearby neighborhood of Pocitos, sells crafts, clothes, and some antiques. **Plaza Cagancha,** between Avenida 18 de Julio and Calle Rondeau in Centro, has a crafts market every day except Sunday.

A fun market in Centro, a few blocks from the Palacio Municipal at the corner of Calle San José and Calle Yaguarón, is the **El Mercado de la Abundancia.** Inside is a tango dance center, four good choices for a fresh lunch time *parrillada,* and, downstairs, a crafts market from 8 AM–10 PM every day but Sunday.

Shopping Centers

There are three major shopping centers in Montevideo, offering everything from designer clothing to gourmet foods to art supplies. The original, called **Montevideo Shopping Center** (⊠ Av. Luis Alberto de Herrera and Calle General Galarza, Punta Carretas ☎ 2/622–1005) is near Parque Rodó. **Portones de Carrasco** (⊠ Avs. Bolívia and Italia Carrasco ☎ 2/601–1733) is a 2-story, 250-store indoor mall with a movie theater. **Punta Carretas Shopping Center** (⊠ Calles Ellauri and Solano Punta Carretas ☎ 2/701–0598), housed in a former prison, is the largest and most upscale mall in the city. It's a ten-minute cab ride from the Old City.

Specialty Shops

ANTIQUES Calle Tristán Narvaja north of Avenida 18 de Julio is packed with antiques shops. In the Old City, the streets north of Plaza Constitución are also lined with antiques stores. **El Rincón** (✉ Calle Tristán Narvaja 1747, Centro ☎ 2/400–2283) is one of the area's best antiques dealers. **El Galeón** (✉ Juan Gómez 1327, Centro ☎ 2/915–6139) sells antiques and rare books. The **Louvre** (✉ Calle Sarandí 652, Ciudad Vieja ☎ no phone), an antiques store, is the only source for handmade and painted trinket boxes—the perfect *recuerdos* (souvenirs).

GEMSTONES & JEWELRY
Amatistas Del Uruguay (✉ Calle P. Sarandí 604, Ciudad Vieja ☎ 2/916–6456) specializes in amethyst, topaz, and other gems. **Gemas de América** (✉ Av. 18 de Julio 948, Centro ☎ 2/902–2572) carries amethyst and topaz jewelry, agate slices, and elaborate objects made of precious gems. **La Limeña** (✉ Calle Buenos Aires 542, Centro ☎ no phone) has good prices on unset stones.

HANDICRAFTS
Ema Camuso (✉ Av. 8 de Octubre 2574, Centro ☎ no phone) offers a sophisticated and sporty line of hand-knit sweaters, all permanently on sale at factory prices. **Manos de Uruguay** (✉ Calle Reconquista 602, Centro ☎ 2/915–9522 ✉ Calle San José 111, Centro ☎ 2/900–4910 ✉ Montevideo Shopping Center, Punta Carretas ☎ no phone) has three locations with a wide selection of woolen wear and locally produced ceramics. **Tiempofunky** (✉ Bacacay 1307, Ciudad Vieja ☎ 2/916–8721) sells clothing, candles, lamps, soaps, and contemporary crafts and design items, on a pleasant street in the Old City.

LEATHER
Although Buenos Aires has more stylish choices, Montevideo is a good source for inexpensive leather. Shops near Plaza Independencia specialize in hand-tailored coats and jackets made out of nutria (fur from a large semiaquatic rodent). **Peleteria Holandesa** (✉ Calle Colonia 894, Centro ☎ 2/901–5438) carries leather clothing. **Péndola** (✉ Calle San José 1087, Centro ☎ 2/900–1524) has a particularly good selection of leather apparel. Try **Casa Mario** (✉ Calle Piedras 639, Centro ☎ 2/916–2356) for good leather clothes. Custom-made boots are available from **Damino Botas** (✉ Calle Rivera 2747, Centro ☎ 2/709–7823).

Montevideo A to Z

AIR TRAVEL

Uruguay's principal airport, Aeropuerto Internacional Carrasco (MVD), is 24 km (15 mi) east of Montevideo. It is regularly served by several South American airlines, such as Aerolíneas Argentinas, LanChile, and the Uruguayan/Brazilian airline Pluna-Varig. Large international carriers include Alitalia, American, Iberia, and United. A cab to downtown costs about 550 pesos. A city bus (marked Ciudadela) is cheap—about 26 pesos—but the drawback is that it takes an hour to reach downtown.

🛪 Airlines **Aerolíneas Argentinas** ☎ 2/601-4987. **Alitalia** ☎ 2/901-3076 or 2/908-5828. **American** ☎ 2/604-0133. **Iberia** ☎ 2/908-1032. **LanChile** ☎ 2/892-3877. **Pluna-Varig** ☎ 2/604-0306. **United** ☎ 2/604-0173.

🛪 Airports **Aeropuerto Internacional Carrasco** ☎ 2/604-0252.

BICYCLE TRAVEL

You won't see many bikes in the city, but biking is an especially fun way to explore the city's long coastal tract. Bicicletas de la Costa rents bikes and scooters for about 80 pesos an hour. The shop is located inside Club Nautilus.

🚲 Bike Rentals **Bicicletas de la Costa** ✉ J.M. Montero and Rambla Gandhi, Punta Carretas ☎ 099/177-356.

BOAT & FERRY TRAVEL

Buquebus operates hydrofoil service between Buenos Aires to the ports at Montevideo and Colonia. The trip takes less than three hours to Montevideo and less than four hours to Colonia. A round-trip ticket between Buenos Aires and Montevideo costs about 3,000 pesos. A package that includes a round-trip ticket between Buenos Aires and Colonia and a shuttle bus to or from Montevideo costs about 2,000 pesos.

🚢 Boat & Ferry Information **Buquebus** ✉ Terminal Tres Cruces, Bulevar General Artigas 1825, Centro ☎ 2/408-8120 📠 2/901-2555 ⊕ www.buquebus.com.

BUS TRAVEL

Montevideo's public buses are a great alternative to taxis, which can be difficult to find during peak hours. Buses crisscross the entire city 24 hours a day. You don't need exact change, and the price for any trip within Montevideo is only 13 pesos.

Colonia is serviced by several regional bus lines, including Cot and TURIL. The three-hour ride costs less than 400 pesos.

🚌 Bus Companies **Cot** ✉ Terminal Tres Cruces, Montevideo, Centro ☎ 2/409-4949 ✉ General Flores 440, Colonia ☎ 522/3121. **TURIL** ✉ Terminal Tres Cruces, Montevideo, Centro ☎ 2/402-1990 ✉ General Flores and Suárez, Colonia ☎ 522/5246.

🚌 Bus Terminals **Terminal Tres Cruces** ✉ Bulevar General Artigas 1825, Montevideo, Centro ☎ 2/409-8998.

CAR RENTAL

In Montevideo you can rent from several major international companies, including Avis, Budget, and Dollar, and from smaller companies, such as Inter Car and Multicar.

🚗 Rental Agencies **Avis** ✉ Av. Uruguay 1417, Montevideo ☎ 2/903-0303. **Budget** ✉ Av. General Flores 2211, Montevideo ☎ 2/203-7080. **Dollar** ✉ Av. J.B. Amorín 1186, at corner of Canelones, Centro, Montevideo ☎ 2/402-6427. **Inter Car** ✉ Colonia 926, Centro, Montevideo ☎ 2/902-3330. **Multicar** ✉ Colonia 1227, Centro, Montevideo ☎ 2/902-2555.

CAR TRAVEL

Because La Rambla, Montevideo's riverside thoroughfare, extends for dozens of miles, driving is a good way to see the city. Roads are well maintained and drivers obey the traffic laws—a rarity in South America. It's easy to rent a car, both downtown and at the airport.

EMBASSIES

The United States Embassy is open weekdays 9–1 and 2–5. The United Kingdom Embassy operates weekdays 9–1 and 2–5:15.

🏛 **Canada** ✉ Plaza Independencia 749, Ciudad Vieja ☎ 2/902-2030 📠 2/902-2029. **United States** ✉ Lauro Müller, No. 1776 [on the Rambla], Montevideo, Centro ☎ 2/203-6061 or 2/418-7777. **United Kingdom** ✉ Marco Bruto, No. 1073, Centro ☎ 2/622-3630 📠 2/622-7815.

EMERGENCIES

Contact Numbers Ambulance ☎ 105. **Fire** ☎ 104. **Pharmacy** ☎ 0900-2020. **Police** ☎ 109.

ENGLISH-LANGUAGE BOOKSTORES

The best place to find English-language print media is in one of the shops at the major hotels. However, a couple of stores in the Old City carry small selections of used books. The genteel owner of El Aleph lived for years in the United States and is helpful as a guide to Montevideo's literary culture. El Galeón is another bookstore with a large, dusty collection of interesting picks.

Bookstores El Aleph ⊠ Bartolomé Mitre 1358, corner of Sarandí, Ciudad Vieja ☎ 2/916-3687. **El Galeón** ⊠ Juan Gómez 1327, Ciudad Vieja ☎ 2/915-6139.

INTERNET

You'll find Internet cafés in major hotels and on Avenida 18 de Julio. They charge about $1 an hour. Babylon, in the back of the Galería de las Américas, is open weekdays 10–9 and Saturdays 6 PM–11 PM. Cybercafé, in Galería Uruguay, is open weekdays 8:30–10, Saturdays 9–9, Sundays 2–10. Playcenter is open daily 10–11 but can be distracting because it's inside an arcade.

Internet Cafés Babylon ⊠ 18 de Julio 1236, Centro ☎ 2/900-9361. **Cybercafé** ⊠ 18 de Julio, Centro ☎ 2/902-8497. **Playcenter** ⊠ 18 de Julio 862, Centro ☎ 2/900-4890.

MAIL & SHIPPING

The Correo Central, or Central Post Office, is the most reliable place to send and receive mail. It's open weekdays 9–5, Saturday 9–1. For packages, there are Federal Express and DHL offices downtown.

Post Offices Correo Central ⊠ Calle Buenos Aires 451, Centro ☎ 2/900-4034 ⊠ Av. Libertador 1440, corner of Av. Mercedes, Centro ☎ 2/902-0853.

Shipping Companies DHL ⊠ Calle Zabala 1377, Ciudad Vieja ☎ 2/604-1331. **Federal Express** ⊠ Calle Juncal 1351, Ciudad Vieja ☎ 2/628-0100.

MONEY MATTERS

Cambio Matriz, on Plaza Matriz, is a convenient place to change money. Bancomat, RED Banc, and Redbrou machines accept ATM cards on the CIRRUS network; you can withdraw both dollars and Uruguayan pesos.

Banks Cambio Matriz ⊠ Sarandí 556, Ciudad Vieja ☎ 2/915-0800.

SAFETY

Although Montevideo doesn't have the problems with crime that larger cities in South America do, it's best to watch your wallet in crowded markets, and to avoid walking down deserted streets at night. Most of Montevideo's residents stay up quite late, so the streets are usually full of people until 1 AM. The city bus authority discourages boarding empty buses at night.

TAXIS

All cabs have meters and the initial fare is roughly 20 pesos at flag fall and 15 pesos per ⅕ km (¹⁄₁₀ mi). You can hail taxis on the street with ease, or call one to pick you up at your hotel. A ride to the airport from the Old City costs about 500 pesos.

🚖 Taxi Companies **Radio Taxi Carrasco** ☎ 2/600-0416.

TELEPHONES

Telephone service in the city is convenient and dependable. Public telephones in downtown Montevideo accept either coins or magnetic phone cards. Phone cards are available in the following denominations: 25, 50, and 100 pesos. Unless you're planning on calling outside of Montevideo, the 25-peso card should be sufficient for about 10 local calls. Phone cards can be purchased at telecentros, kiosks, and small stores near public phones. Telecard, which uses a toll-free number, can be used from hotel rooms. Telecard is available in denominations of 100 and 200 pesos.

TOUR OPERATORS

Cecilia Regules Viajes, a travel agency with English-speaking agents, is open weekdays 8:30–8:30 and Saturday 9:30 to 5:45. The company can arrange everything from tours of the city to excursions to the country. Three-hour guided tours of Montevideo, as well as full-day guided tours of Colonia del Sacramento or Punta del Este, are offered by many travel agencies with English-speaking staffs. Passengers for these tours are collected from the major hotels starting at 8 AM. J. P. Santos Travel Agency is a reputable company.

🚌 Tour Agencies **Cecilia Regules Viajes** ✉ Bacacay 1334, Ciudad Vieja ☎ 2/916-3011 🖷 2/916-3012. **J. P. Santos Travel Agency** ✉ Calle Colonia 951, Centro ☎ 2/902-0397 🖷 2/902-0403.

VISITOR INFORMATION

The best source for city info is the city's own tourist information center, Información Turística de la Intendencia, set up in front of city hall. They have a knowledgeable staff, and brochures and maps. They are open weekdays 10–6, weekends and holidays 11-6. The Ministerio de Turismo—the national government's tourist center at Plaza Fabini—is open weekdays noon–6 in summer and weekdays 8–3 the rest of the year. The helpful kiosk at Terminal Tres Cruces, open weekdays 8–9 and weekends 9–9, supplies maps and other basic information.

🏛 **City Hall** ✉ 18 de Julio 1360, Centro ☎ 1950-1830. **Plaza Fabini** ✉ Calle Colonia 1021, Centro ☎ 2/900-1078 or 2/901-4340 🖷 2/901-6907 ⊕ www.turismo.gub.uy. **Terminal Tres Cruces** ✉ Bulevar General Artigas 1825, Centro ☎ 2/409-7399.

PUNTA DEL ESTE

Despite being a mere two hours east of Montevideo, Uruguay's highly touted Punta del Este is a world apart. Punta del Este (shortened to "Punta" by locals) and the handful of surrounding beachfront communities are, famously, jet-set resorts—places where lounging on white sand and browsing designer boutiques constitute the day's most demanding activities. For thousands of younger South Americans Punta del Este is also a party town. Here you can watch the sunrise from the balcony of an all-night disco.

Punta is underwhelming in the low season—the buildings are shuttered against the elements, their tenants gone elsewhere. In summer the city comes alive, lured out of dormancy by the smell of tourist dollars. Plan on a visit in either December or March (except during Holy Week, when prices skyrocket). During these two months the weather is superb, with an average daily temperature of 75°F, and the beaches are not unbearably crowded.

Piriápolis

98 km (61 mi) east of Montevideo.

In 1890, Francisco Piria, an Argentine born of Italian parents, purchased all the land, first established as a private residence, from the town of Pan de Azúcar to the Río de la Plata. Piria saw the touristic potential of the land and began developing "Piriápolis" to resemble a French coast town. Piriápolis is nowadays a laid-back beachfront enclave that lacks the sophistication—and the exorbitant prices—of nearby Punta del Este. Piriápolis has plenty of stores and restaurants, a casino, and the grand Argentino Hotel, the town's crown jewel, built in the old European tradition with spas and thermal pools.

Where to Stay & Eat

★ $$–$$$$ ×⊞ **Argentino Hotel.** This Belle Epoque–style structure, a national historic monument, clearly deserves the honor. Argentine president Baltasar Brum attended the groundbreaking in 1920; when completed a decade later the hotel was one of the biggest in South America. Elegantly furnished rooms have French doors and balustraded balconies overlooking the ocean. If this isn't stress-reducing enough, the hotel is renowned for its Piriavital health spa. ⊠ *Rambla de los Argentinos* 🕿 *43/422–572* ⊕ *www.argentinohotel.com* 🛏 *300 rooms, 56 suites* 🍴 *3 restaurants, room service, minibars, golf privileges, 4 tennis courts, 3 pools, health club, sauna, spa, basketball, volleyball, ice-skating, bar, casino, laundry service* ⊟ *AE, DC, MC, V.*

Colonia del Sacramento

★ *180 km (113 mi) west of Montevideo.*

It's hard not to fall in love with Colonia del Sacramento. The most picturesque town in Uruguay, and one of South America's most beautiful cities, Colonia possesses the best of an old colonial city, with wonderfully preserved architecture, rough cobblestone streets, and an easy grace and tranquillity evident in its people and pace. There are more bicycles than cars here, which adds to the serenity of this roughly six-by-six-block Old City that juts out on a small peninsula into the Río de la Plata.

Founded in 1680 by Portugal, the city was subject to wars and pacts between Portugal and Spain. The city's many small museums are dedicated to the story of its tumultuous history. The best place to begin a tour of the city is at the reconstructed **portón,** or city gate. Remnants of the old bastion walls lead to the river. A block farther is **Calle de los Suspiros,** a cobblestone street of one-story colonial homes that can rival any street in Latin America for sheer romantic effect. Clusters of bougainvillea flow over the walls, from which hang old lanterns. Art galleries and antiques shops line the street, which opens out to **Plaza Mayor,** a lovely square filled with Spanish moss, palm, and spiky, flowering *palo borracho* trees. On this square are three of the city's principal museums. The **Museo Portugués** documents the city's ties to Portugal. It's most notable for its collection of old map reproductions based on Portuguese naval expeditions. The museum is housed in a home built in 1720. The **Casa Rosada,** another 18th-century home, is filled with period furniture and clothing. Next door is the **Museo Municipal,** which has a collection of sundry objects related to the city's history housed in another early Portuguese settlement. Also near the plaza are the **San Francisco convent ruins,** dating from a 1683 construction. Towering above these surviving walls is the **faro** or lighthouse, built in 1857. You can climb to the top for a view of the Old City.

Where to Stay & Eat

¢ ✕ **La Bodeguita.** This hip restaurant with backyard tables overlooking the river serves incredibly delicious, crispy pizza, sliced into bite-size rectangles. ✉ *Calle del Comercio 167* ☎ *052/25329* ☐ *MC, V.*

¢ ✕ **Pulpería de los Faroles.** The specialties at this old stone house right off the Plaza Mayor are *lomo a los faroles* (beef with beans) and a fantastic selection of pastas. ✉ *Calle del Comercio 101* ☎ *052/25399* ☐ *AE, MC, V* ☉ *Closed Wed.*

$$$$ ✕▥ **Four Seasons Carmelo.** Serenity pervades this harmoniously deco-
Fodor's Choice rated resort an hour west of Colonia del Sacramento, reachable by car,
★ boat, or a 15-minute flight from Buenos Aires. Everything is done in a fusion of Asian styles—from tai chi classes at the incense-burning and bamboo-screen health club to bungalows (considered "standard rooms") with private Japanese gardens (and marvelous outdoor showers). In the evening torches illuminate the paths of the resort—through sand dunes. The hotel also offers free sunset cruises on the Río de la Plata. If you can't lodge here, try dining at the wonderful restaurant. ✉ *Ruta 21, km 262, Carmelo* ☎ *598/542–9000* 🖷 *598/542–9999* ⊕ *www.fourseasons. com/carmelo* 🛏 *24 duplexes, 20 bungalows* ⚒ *Restaurant, room service, in-room safes, minibars, cable TV, in-room VCRs, golf, 4 tennis courts, pool, health club, sauna, spa, massage, boating, jet ski, bicycles, horseback riding, Ping Pong, bar, video game room, casino, baby-sitting, children's programs, laundry service, Internet, business services, free airport shuttle* ☐ *AE, DC, MC, V.*

$$ ▥ **Hotel Plaza Mayor.** This lovely hotel with an impeccable location in the middle of the historic district (the Old City) dates from 1840. The simple rooms, many with high ceilings and beveled-glass doors, overlook a peaceful garden with a trickling fountain. ✉ *Calle del Comercio 111* ☎ *052/23193* 🛏 *8 rooms* ⚒ *Coffee shop, room service, minibars, hot tub, laundry service* ☐ *AE, DC, MC, V.*

★ $ ▥ **Posada de la Flor.** This place, which opened in early 2003, is on a quiet, dead-end street, and is arranged around a verdant courtyard. Second-floor rooms cost a few dollars more, but come with air-conditioners and cheery quilts. (Ask for the most spacious room, called "Nomeolvides," or "Forgetmenot.") A lovely third-floor terrace shaded with bamboo looks out over the river. The posada is a lovely five-minute walk to Plaza Mayor. If you arrive via the Buquebus ferry landing, the English-speaking owner, Roberto, will pick you up. ⊠ *Calle Ituzaingó 268* ☎ *052/ 30794* ⇨ *10 rooms* ⚫ *Laundry service, bar; no a/c in some rooms, no TV in rooms* ✉ *posadadelaflor@hotmail.com* ⊟ *AE, DC, MC, V* ⦿ *CP.*

Punta Ballena

25 km (15 mi) east of Piriápolis.

Built on a bluff overlooking the ocean that supposedly looks like a whale (*ballena*, in Spanish), Punta Ballena is hidden from vacationers passing on the main road—no cause for complaint from the resort's wealthy patrons. Inland, the **Arboretum Lussich** is a huge parkland perfumed with the scent of eucalyptus.

The main draw in Punta Ballena is **Casapueblo,** a hotel and museum perched at the tip of a rocky point with tremendous views of the Río de la Plata. This "habitable sculpture," as defined by its creator Carlos Páez Vilaró, defies architectural categorization. With allusions to Arab minarets and domes, cathedral vaulting, Grecian whitewash, and continuous sculptural flourishes that recall the traceries of a Miró canvas, this curvaceous 13-floor surrealist complex climbs up a hill and looks like nothing else in South America.

Begun in 1968, Casapueblo is a continually evolving work. Says the artist: "While there be a brick near my hands, Casapueblo will not stop growing." The spaces include an excellent series of galleries dedicated to his work. Here you can see photos of the artists with friends like Picasso and peruse copies of his books. One of Páez's books tells the true story of his son Carlos Miguel, who survived a plane crash in the Andes. The story was made into the 1993 film *Alive.* ⊠ *Punta Ballena* ☎ *42/578– 485* 🎫 *150 pesos* ⊙ *Daily 10–4.*

Where to Stay

★ $$$$ 🏨 **Casapueblo Club Hotel.** It would be hard not to feel like an artist in this whitewashed marvel. Merely riding the old-style iron elevators and walking through the sinuous hallways (there are no right angles here) is an experience. Spacious rooms have wood floors and handsome antique furniture. Each also has a different name—Paloma (Dove), for example, or Luna Negra (Black Moon)—that determines the design of the handmade tiles in your bathroom. The restaurant has a wide terrace with fine coastline views. ⊠*Punta Ballena* ☎*42/578–485* ⇨*72 rooms* ⚫*Restaurant, room service, minibars, cable TV, 2 pools, 2 health clubs, sauna, spa, bar, laundry service, Internet, business services* ⊟ *AE, DC, MC, V.*

Punta del Este

10 km (6 mi) east of Punta Ballena.

Half a century ago, the resort town of Punta del Este was a fishing village nearly covered by dunes. Its shores were first discovered by sunseekers escaping winter in North America. Its South American neighbors were soon to follow—today, it's so popular a beach resort that more than 100,000 Argentines flock to its beaches each January. (Punta is considered, during warm months, to be an annexation of Argentina.)

Punta del Este (East Point) marks the division of the Río de la Plata on the west from the Atlantic Ocean to the east. It also lends its name to the broader region encompassing Punta Ballena and La Barra de Maldonado, a trendy area of galleries and restaurants referred to simply as "La Barra." In Punta proper—the peninsular resort bounded by Playa Mansa and Playa Brava—the beach is the primary destination. In fact, if you are not into eating, drinking, and worshiping the sun, just about the only other attraction is the feria artesanal at Plaza Artigas.

Punta is circled by Rambla Artigas, the main coastal road that leads past residential neighborhoods and pristine stretches of beach. **Avenida Gorlero,** Punta's main commercial strip, runs north–south through the heart of the peninsula and is fronted with cafés, restaurants, and elegant boutiques bearing names such as Yves St. Laurent and Gucci.

You can take a boat from the marina to **Isla Gorriti,** a pine-covered island with a good restaurant. On the eastern side of Punta, and a couple of miles farther offshore, is **Isla de los Lobos,** home to one of the world's largest colonies of sea lions. The island can be viewed from tour boats that leave regularly from the marina.

Where to Stay & Eat

Restaurants come and go in Punta del Este. The better ones reopen from year to year, often transferring their operations from Montevideo for the summer. Year-round options—none of them spectacular—are generally found along Avenida Gorlero; they tend to be moderately priced and serve meat rather than seafood.

There are numerous hotels in and around Punta del Este, running the gamut from restored colonial mansions to modern high-rises. Rooms are mostly empty until January and February, when Punta teems with sunbathers and pleasure seekers. During these months lodgings are extremely difficult to come by, so book well in advance.

★ **$** ✕ **La Bourgogne.** A shaded terra-cotta terrace gives way to a breezeway with arched windows. This opens onto a large split-level dining room with antique sideboards. The food, served by impeccably clad waiters who go about their business with cordial authority, is prepared with only the finest and freshest of ingredients; the breads are baked on the premises (an adjoining bakery sells them by the loaf), and the herbs and berries are grown in the backyard garden. The desserts are sublime—the sampler is a good way to try them all. ✉ *Av. del Mar at Calle P. Sierra* ☎ *42/482–007* 🖷 *42/487–873* ⌖ *Reservations essential* ▭ *MC* ☾ *Closed May–Aug.*

¢–$ ✕ **Andrés.** Operated by a father and son, both of whom answer to Andrés, this small, unassuming restaurant on the Rambla Artigas, the oceanside promenade, offers fine dining at moderate prices. Most of the tables are outdoors under a canopy, so you can appreciate the excellent service while also enjoying the sea breeze. The fish Andrés (served in a white wine and tomato sauce), spinach or cheese soufflés, and grilled meats are exquisite. ⊠ *Parada 1, Edificio Vaguardia* ☎ *42/481–804* ▭ *AE, MC, V* ⊘ *Closed Mon.–Wed. No lunch Thur. or Fri. No dinner Sun.*

¢–$ ✕ **Yacht Club Uruguayo.** Loved by locals, this small eatery has a great view of Isla Gorriti. The menu includes a bit of everything, but the specialty is seafood. Perennial favorites are *brotola a la Roquefort* (baked hake with a Roquefort sauce) and *pulpo Provençal*, likely to be the most tender octopus you've ever eaten. ⊠ *Rambla Artigas between Calles 6 and 8* ☎ *42/441–056* ▭ *AE, DC, MC, V.*

¢ ✕ **Restaurante Ciclista.** This no-frills restaurant serves the best inexpensive meals in Punta. Choose from a menu of over 100 items, from soups to pastas. The *tortilla de papas* (potato pancake) is extremely hearty. ⊠ *Calle 20 at Calle 27* ☎ *42/440–007* ▭ *AE, DC, MC, V.*

$$$$ ▦ **Conrad Resort & Casino.** Spectacularly lit fountains and gardens, an abundant use of marble, and stunning art by Uruguayan painter Carlos Páez Vilaró make this one of Punta's most extraordinary resorts. Every room has a terrace with views of the beaches. Two of the floors cater to nonsmokers—an amenity virtually unheard of in this region. Of course, the most prominent draw is the Las Vegas–style casino—the country's best. Head to the blackjack tables, or try your luck at one of the nearly 500 slot machines. ⊠ *Rambla Claudio Williman at Parada 4, Playa Mansa* ☎ *42/491–111* 🖷 *42/489–999* ⊕ *www.conrad.com.uy* ⟿ *278 rooms, 24 suites* ⚐ *Restaurant, room service, minibars, in-room safes, cable TV, pool, bar, casino, laundry service, Internet, business services, no-smoking floors* ▭ *AE, DC, MC, V.*

$$$–$$$$ ▦ **L'Auberge.** In the heart of Parque del Golf, Punta's chicest neighborhood, this hotel can be spotted for miles around. An 18th-century stone water tower, which now contains guest rooms, rises from the hotel's double-wing chalet. Rooms are tastefully adorned with beautiful antiques; some even have working fireplaces. Some of Punta del Este's finest beaches are just a few blocks away, but the vast lawns and lovely terrace gardens create a world apart from the crowded beach. ⊠ *Barrio Parque del Golf* ☎ *42/482–601* 🖷 *42/483–408* ⊕ *www.lauberge.com.uy* ⟿ *40 rooms* ⚐ *Restaurant, tea shop, room service, minibars, in-room safes, cable TV, pool, hot tub, bar, laundry service, Internet, meeting rooms* ▭ *AE, DC, MC, V.*

$$$ ▦ **Hotel Salzburgo.** This delightful hotel occupies a white-stucco, three-story chalet with polished slate floors and exposed beams. Its rooms have ceiling fans, modern baths, and fine views framed by flower-filled window boxes. ⊠ *Calle Pedragosa Sierra at El Havre* ☎☎ *42/488–851* ⊕ *www.hotelsalzburgo.com* ⟿ *23 rooms* ⚐ *Cafeteria, minibars, in-room safes, cable TV, bar, laundry service, Internet, free parking* ▭ *AE, DC, MC, V.*

★ $–$$ ▦ **Palace Hotel.** Housed inside one of Punta's oldest structures—a three-story Spanish colonial masterpiece complete with an airy interior courtyard—this hotel is a stone's throw from the beach (at the end of the Gorlero shopping strip). The restaurant has one of the largest wine cellars in the country. ⊠ *Calle Gorlero at Calle 11* ☎ *42/441–919 or 42/441–418* 🖷 *42/444–695* ⟿ *47 rooms* ⚐ *Restaurant, room service, minibars, cable TV, in-room safes, laundry service, bar, Internet* ▭ *AE, DC, MC, V.*

Nightlife

Expect fast-paced evenings in bars and nightclubs that open as late as 1 AM and which only reach a fever pitch around sunrise. Most are open only during the high season and have a cover as steep as 800 pesos.

DANCE CLUBS Hop in a cab and head for **Gitane La Plage** (✉ Rambla Brava, Parada 12 ☎ no phone), on the road toward La Barra. The club is right on Playa Brava and has two dance floors, both of which play booming house music. In La Barra, **Space** (✉ Central La Barra ☎ no phone) occupies an enormous warehouse bursting with five different bars. Any taxi driver will know the way.

Sports & the Outdoors

GOLF **Club de Golf** (☎ 42/82127) charges a typical $70 greens fee for 18 holes of golf. You can play a round of golf at **Club de Lago** (☎ 42/78423), which has tennis courts as well.

HORSEBACK RIDING Mosey over to **Club Hípico Parque Burnett** (☎ 42/30765), an equestrian center on the distant outskirts of Punta, in Pinares, for an afternoon of trail riding. Montevideo-based **Estancias Gauchas** (✉ Bacacay 1334, Montevideo ☎ 2/916–3011 🖷 2/916–3012) offers various trips from Punta del Este to estancias where you can ride horses and take part in the gaucho life.

POLO From December 15 to February 28 there are several polo tournaments in Punta del Este, the most famous of which are the Medellín Polo Cup and the José Ignacio Tournament, attended by some of the best players from South America and Europe.

Shopping

An essential part of visiting Punta is exploring the colorful **Feria Artesanal** at the intersection of El Ramanso and El Corral. It's open weekends 5 PM–midnight all year; between Christmas and Easter it's open daily 6 PM–1 AM. Popular items include gourds for sipping mate (herb tea), and leather and silver crafts.

La Barra de Maldonado

5 km (3 mi) east of Punta del Este.

Gaily painted buildings give La Barra de Maldonado a carnival-like style. Here you'll find a handful of antiques dealers, surf shops, art galleries, and pubs that offer an afternoon's diversion. This is where young people come to do their eating, drinking, and dancing.

It's easy to get here from Punta del Este—drive east from the peninsula a few miles along coastal Ruta 10 until you cross over a cement camel-back bridge. Locals like to speed over this bridge to heighten the roller-coaster sensations of its wavy form. Just before you reach La Barra is Playa Verde, one of the area's finest beaches.

Where to Stay & Eat

★ $-$$ ╳🏨 **La Posta del Cangrejo.** From its stylish lobby to its relaxed lounge and restaurant, this hotel takes an informal approach to luxury. The Mediterranean theme—red tile floors and white stucco walls—complements the impeccably decorated rooms; each is furnished with hand-stenciled antiques and canopy beds and has views of either the beach or the small garden. The staff is warm and accommodating. The adjoining seafood restaurant is outstanding. ⊠ *La Barra de Maldonado* ☎ *42/470–021 or 42/470–271* 🖷 *42/470–173* ⊕ *www.netgate.com.uy/laposta* 🛏 *29 rooms* ⚐ *Restaurant, cable TV, in-room safes, pool, bar, laundry service, Internet* ▭ *AE, DC, MC, V.*

Punta del Este A to Z

AIR TRAVEL

Most people headed to the beach fly into Montevideo's Aeropuerto Internacional Carrasco (MVD). Some airlines fly from Buenos Aires directly to Punta del Este's Aeropuerto Internacional de Laguna del Sauce (PDP), about 24 km (15 mi) east of town.

🛪 Airlines **Aerolíneas Argentinas** ☎ 42/44343. **LAPA** ☎ 42/90840. **Pluna-Varig** ☎ 42/45292.

🛪 Airports **Aeropuerto Internacional Carrasco** ☎ 2/604–0252. **Aeropuerto Internacional de Laguna del Sauce** ⊠ Camino del Placer ☎ 42/59777.

BUS TRAVEL

Many bus lines travel daily between Montevideo's Terminal Tres Cruces and Piriápolis's Terminal de Omnibus, Maldonado's Terminal de Maldonado, and Punta del Este's Terminal Playa Brava. Two companies that serve the entire region are Copsa and Cot. There is frequent daily service from the Tres Cruces terminal in Montevideo to Colonia del Sacramento.

🚌 Bus Companies **Copsa** ☎ 42/89205. **Cot** ☎ 42/86810.

🚌 Bus Terminals **Terminal de Maldonado** ⊠ Roosevelt and Sarandí, Maldonado. **Terminal de Omnibus** ⊠ Misiones and Niza, Piriápolis. **Terminal Playa Brava** ⊠ Rambla Artigas and Calle Inzaurraga, Punta del Este.

CAR RENTAL

Renting a car is the simplest way to explore the coast. Agencies, such as Avis, Budget, and Dollar, are in downtown Punta del Este.

🚗 Rental Agencies **Avis** ⊠ Av. Gorlero and Calle 31 ☎ 42/442–020. **Budget** ⊠ Aeropuerto Laguna del Sauce ☎ 42/446–363. **Dollar** ⊠ Av. Gorlero 961 ☎ 42/443–444.

CAR TRAVEL

To get to Punta del Este from Montevideo, follow Ruta 1 east to the Ruta 93 turnoff. The road is well maintained and marked, and the trip takes about 1½ hours. It's a beautiful drive from Montevideo to Colonia del Sacramento, and it will take you about three hours on Ruta 1 east.

INTERNET

Internet cafés are ubiquitous in Uruguay; you won't have to travel far to find one. Cybermix is a café that offers Internet services.

🖥 Internet Cafés **Cybermix** ⊠ Av. Gorlero and Calle 30, Punta del Este ☎ 42/447–158.

MAIL & SHIPPING

Sending and receiving mail is easy and convenient—through the Correo Central in each town.

✉ Post Offices **Correo Central** ⊠ Gorlero and El Estrecho, Punta del Este ☎ 42/440–103.

MONEY MATTERS

American Express is a convenient place to change money. Bancomat and Redbrou ATMs—many are lined up along Avenida Gorlero in Punta del Este—accept cards on the Cirrus system. You can withdraw both U.S. dollars and Uruguayan pesos. There are plenty of ATM machines in Colonia del Sacramento as well.

🏦 Banks **American Express** ✉ Av. Gorlero 644 ☎ 42/442-555.

TELEPHONES

Public telephones in beach towns accept either coins only or magnetic phone cards only. Phone cards can be purchased at newsstands.

TOUR AGENCIES

Consider booking a package tour from Montevideo. It will be more difficult, not to mention costly, to arrange once you're in Punta del Este. For tours to Punta Ballena and La Barra de Maldonado, contact Cecilia Regules Viajes in Montevideo. Agencies along Calle Gorlero, such as Turisport, can assist with hotel bookings, transportation, and excursions.

🏢 Tour Agencies **Cecilia Regules Viajes** ✉ Calle Bacacay 1334, Local C, Montevideo ☎ 2/915-7308 or 2/916-3011 🖨 2/916-3012. **Turisport** ✉ Torre Verona building, Av. Gorlero and La Galerna, Punta del Este ☎ 42/445-500.

VISITOR INFORMATION

The Piriápolis Tourist Office provides hotel listings and maps for the town. The Punta del Este Tourist Office, with a main office north of Playa Mansa as well as a kiosk in Plaza Artigas, offers information about the community. The Maldonado Tourist Office provides info about the region, including Punta del Este. Colonia del Sacramento's tourist office is open weekdays 8–7 and weekends 9–noon.

🏢 **Colonia del Sacramento** ✉ General Flores and Rivera ☎ 52/2182. **Maldonado** ✉ Parada 1, Calle 31 and 18 Punta del Este ☎ 42/46510. **Piriápolis** ✉ Rambla de los Argentinos 1348 ☎ 43/22560. **Punta del Este** ✉ Rambla Artigas and Izaurraga ☎ 42/44069 ⊕ www.turismo.gub.uy.

URUGUAY A TO Z

To research prices, get advice from other travelers, and book travel arrangements, visit www.fodors.com.

AIR TRAVEL

Most international commercial flights land at Montevideo's Aeropuerto Internacional Carrasco, about 24 km (15 mi) east of downtown. A few fly from Buenos Aires directly to Punta del Este's Aeropuerto Internacional de Laguna del Sauce.

All Montevideo-bound flights are routed through Buenos Aires, São Paulo, or Rio de Janeiro. Flying times to Montevideo are 1 hour from Buenos Aires, 2 hours from São Paulo, and 2½ hours from Rio.

🛫 Airports **Aeropuerto Internacional Carrasco** ☎ 2/604-0252. **Aeropuerto Internacional de Laguna del Sauce** ✉ Camino del Placer ☎ 42/59777.

BOAT & FERRY TRAVEL

Ferries cross the Río de la Plata between Argentina and Uruguay several times daily. They travel to Montevideo or Colonia, where you can get a bus to Montevideo and Punta del Este. The best companies are Aliscafos, Buquebus, Ferry Lineas Argentina, and Ferry Tur.

🚢 Boat & Ferry Information **Aliscafos** ⊠ Av. Córdoba and Madero ☎ 1/313-4444. **Buquebus** ⊠ Av. Córdoba and Madero ☎ 1/313-4444. **Ferry Lineas Argentina** ⊠ Florida 780 ☎ 1/322-8421 or 1/394-8424. **Ferry Tur** ⊠ Florida 780 ☎ 1/322-8421 or 1/394-8424.

BUSINESS HOURS

BANKS In Montevideo, banks are open weekdays 1–5. In outlying areas banks are usually open during the morning only. Casas de cambio are open during regular business hours (9–5:30). Some are open later and on Saturdays and Sunday mornings.

POST OFFICES Most post offices are open weekdays 10–5, with shorter hours on Saturday, usually 10–2.

SHOPS Many shops stay open 9–7. In Montevideo and Punta del Este they may remain open until late in the evening. In smaller cities, it is common for shops to close at midday for an hour or two.

BUS TRAVEL

You can go almost anywhere in Uruguay by bus. Some are quite luxurious, with air-conditioning, movies, and snack service. Departures are frequent and fares low. Most companies are based in Montevideo and depart from its state-of-the-art Terminal Tres Cruces.

🚌 Bus Companies **Cita** ☎ 2/402-5425. **Coit** ☎ 2/401-5628. **Copsa** ☎ 2/409-9855. **EGA** ☎ 2/402-5164. **Rutas del Plata** ☎ 2/402-5129. **Rutas del Sol** ☎ 2/402-5451. **TTL** ☎ 2/401-1410.

CAR RENTAL

Rates are often higher in Uruguay than in the United States because of the value-added tax. For an economy-size car, expect to pay around $45 per day.

CAR TRAVEL

From Argentina, you can transport your car across the Río de la Plata by ferry. Alternatively, you can cross the Argentina-Uruguay border in three places: Puerto Unzue-Fray Bentos, Colon-Paysandu, or Concordia-Salto. From Brazil, you can cross the border either at Chuy, the Río Branco, Rivera, or via the bridge at Quarai-Artigas.

EMERGENCY For roadside assistance, contact the Autómovil Club Uruguayo. Expect
ASSISTANCE to pay $35 to enroll on the spot.

🚗 Automobile Clubs **Autómovil Club Uruguayo** ⊠ Libertador 1532, Montevideo ☎ 2/902-5792 ⊠ 3 de Febrero y Roosevelt, Punta del Este ☎ 42/20156.

GASOLINE Gas is expensive in Uruguay, and will cost you up to about 26 pesos per liter (there are almost four liters to a gallon, so that's 104 pesos per gallon). Stations operated by Shell, Esso, Texaco, and Ancap (the national petroleum company) are open Monday–Saturday until 9 PM or later. The Ancap station at Aeropuerto Internacional Carrasco is open daily 6 AM–11 PM.

ROAD CONDITIONS Roads between Montevideo and Punta del Este are quite good, as are the handful of major highways. In the countryside, roads are usually surfaced with gravel. If you want to leave the main roads, it's best to speak with locals about current conditions before setting off. Trips will often take longer than expected, so budget extra time. On the up side, country roads often have very little traffic and spectacular scenery.

RULES OF THE ROAD Uruguayans tend to drive carefully, but visitors from Argentina have the reputation of driving with wild abandon. Since almost all roads have only two lanes, keep an eye out for passing vehicles.

CUSTOMS & DUTIES
You may bring up to 400 cigarettes, 50 cigars or 500 grams of loose tobacco, and 2 liters of alcoholic beverages. Live animals, vegetable products, and products that originate from plant or animal products are not allowed into Uruguay. There is no limit on the amount of currency you can bring into the country.

ELECTRICITY
Uruguay runs on 220-volt power. The two-pronged plugs, such as those used in Europe, are standard here.

FESTIVALS & SEASONAL EVENTS
Carnaval overtakes Montevideo with parades, dancing in the streets, and general all-hours revelry. Semana Criolla, celebrated the week before Easter in the Montevideo suburb of Carrasco is an excellent way to observe traditional gaucho activities. Montevideo holds an annual cattle fair in August.

HEALTH
Cholera is almost unheard of in Uruguay, but you should still think twice before eating fresh fruits and vegetables. It's a good idea to avoid tap water, as pipes in many older buildings are made of lead. Almost everyone drinks locally bottled *agua mineral* (mineral water), which is available *con gas* or *sin gas* (with or without carbonation).

HOLIDAYS
New Year's Day; Three Kings' Day (January 6); Disembarkation of the 33 Exiles (April 19); Labor Day (May 1); Battle of Las Piedras (May 18); Artigas's Birthday (June 19); Constitution Day (July 18); Independence Day (August 25); Columbus Day (October 12); All Souls' Day (November 2); Christmas.

LANGUAGE
Spanish is the official language of Uruguay, though some descendants of early Italian and British settlers speak the language of their ancestors. Many Uruguayans speak at least a little English.

MAIL & SHIPPING

It costs about $1.80 to send a standard-size piece of international mail. To send a letter to Uruguay, simply give the name, address, and city on the letter or package. No specific postal codes are required.

MONEY MATTERS

The monetary system is pesos uruguayos. Given the instability of the currency, hotel and restaurant prices are quoted in United States dollars, indicated by a $ sign. Anything listed in pesos—such as admission prices—is indicated as such. Uruguayan bills come in $5, $10, $20, $50, 100, $200, $500, and $1,000 denominations. Coins are available in 50 centavos pieces (half a peso), $1, and $2.

All banks and exchange houses, which are plentiful in Montevideo, will change traveler's checks and cash. Most banks will also process cash advances from major credit cards, but expect a 5%–10% surcharge.

At press time the exchange rate was 26 Uruguayan pesos to the United States dollar, 19 pesos to the Canadian dollar, 44 pesos to the pound sterling, and 18 pesos to the Australian dollar.

WHAT IT WILL COST Relative to the dollar, prices in Uruguay have been cut in half in just two years. For years foreign visitors found Uruguay expensive compared to other South American countries. But with its economy tied so closely to Argentina's, Uruguay's peso dropped in value substantially relative to the dollar after an economic downturn in 2000. Although prices once were significantly more expensive in January and February, that's no longer the case. You'll find the quality of meals, hotels, and services quite good for the money.

Sample prices: cup of coffee, 20 pesos; bottle of beer, 30 pesos; soft drink, 20 pesos; bottle of house wine, 30 pesos; sandwich, 30 pesos; 1-km (½-mi) taxi ride, 20 pesos; city bus ride, 13 pesos.

PASSPORTS & VISAS

U.S. and British citizens need only a valid passport for stays of up to 90 days in Uruguay. Canadian citizens also require a tourist visa (C$37.50), available from the Consulate of Uruguay.

🔳 Consulates **Consulate of Uruguay** ✉ 30 Albert St., Suite 1905, Ottawa, Ontario K1P 5G4 Canada ☎ 613/234–2937.

SAFETY

Pickpockets are your biggest threat in the larger cities in Uruguay. Street crime has risen in recent years, particularly in Montevideo, so keep an eye on your purse or wallet. Crime in the countryside is practically nonexistent. As in the United States, call **911** for police, ambulance, and fire emergencies.

TAXES

DEPARTURE TAX To most foreign destinations you can expect to pay a $12 departure tax. If you're headed to Argentina, instead, you'll only pay $6.

VALUE ADDED TAX Throughout the country a value-added tax, called IVA, of 14% is added to hotel and restaurant bills. This tax is usually included in the rate. Almost all other goods and services carry a 23% IVA charge.

TELEPHONES

To call Uruguay from another country, dial the country code of 598, and then the area code. To call locally, dial the digits of the numbers without any prefix. In Montevideo, a local number has seven digits; in Punta it has six; in Colonia it has five. To dial domestically to another region, include the regional code and then the number. The Montevideo area code is 2; Punta's code is 42; Colonia's is 052.

LOCAL CALLS You can use coins or phone cards at public phones. Purchase phone cards at newsstands and other small businesses. You can also place calls at one of the offices of Antel, the national telecommunications company, though at a much higher rate.

TIPPING

In restaurants a flat 10% tip is considered adequate. For any other services, such as tour guides and valet services, a dollar tip is appreciated. Tips are optional for taxi rides.

WHEN TO GO

Between October and March the temperatures are pleasant—it's warm and the country is in bloom. Unless you are prepared to tangle with the multitude of tourists that overwhelm Punta del Este in January and February, late spring (October–December) is the most appealing season to lounge on the beach.

CLIMATE Uruguay's climate has four distinct seasons. Summer (January–March) can be hot and humid, with temperatures as high as 90°F. Fall (April–June) is marked by warm days and evenings cool enough for a light sweater. Winter (July–September) is cold and rainy with average temperatures generally below 50°F. Although it seldom reaches freezing, the wind off the water can give you quite a chill. Spring (October–December) is much like the fall, except that the trees will be sprouting, rather than dropping, their leaves.

The following are average daily maximum and minimum temperatures for Montevideo.

Jan.	83F	28C	May	64F	18C	Sept.	63F	17C
	62	17		48	9		46	8
Feb.	82F	28C	June	59F	15C	Oct.	68F	20C
	61	16		43	6		49	10
Mar.	78F	25C	July	58F	14C	Nov.	74F	23C
	59	15		43	6		54	12
Apr.	71F	22C	Aug.	59F	15C	Dec.	79F	21C
	53	12		43	6		59	15

VENEZUELA

10

Updated by
Jeffrey Van
Fleet

THE TURQUOISE WATERS OF THE CARIBBEAN gently lap at Venezuela's shores. Not so many years ago the 2,750-km (1,700-mi) coastline was the first glimpse of the country for almost all visitors. Christopher Isherwood, who arrived here on an ocean liner in 1950, wrote that "its mountains rose up sheer and solemn out of the flat sea, thrown into massive relief by tremendous oblique shafts of light from the rising sun. The gorges were deep in crimson shadow, the ridges were outlined in dazzling gold."

For natural beauty, Venezuela is a land of surprising diversity. In the Caribbean you'll find Los Roques, which has what is arguably the most spectacular snorkeling and diving in the region. Some of the islands that make up the archipelago virtually disappear with the high tide. Closer to the mainland is the lovely Isla Margarita, a popular destination for sun-seeking North and South Americans.

In the country's western reaches, snow glistens year-round in the northernmost fingers of the Andes. The longest and highest cable-car system in the world affords stunning views. The Río Orinoco, mustering its might from a million sources in Colombia and Brazil, meanders through the broad grasslands that cover about a third of the country. You'll spot brilliantly colored tropical birds that are found only here, including the rare jabiru stork. In the far southeast, flat-top mountains called *tepuis* tower over Parque Nacional Canaima. These same geological formations inspired Sir Arthur Conan Doyle's novel *The Lost World*. The park is also home to the world's highest waterfall, Angel Falls, which plummets over 2,647 feet into a bizarre landscape of inky black lagoons and plant life.

For hundreds of years Venezuela was grindingly poor, disregarded because it lacked the mineralogical riches of neighbors such as Peru and Ecuador. Then in 1914 huge deposits of oil were discovered in what was thought to be a barren region near Lago Maracaibo. Venezuela, one of the founding members of the Organization of Petroleum Exporting Countries (OPEC), would be the world's largest oil exporter for the next 50 years. Sleepy towns transformed into booming metropolises, and the country continued to grow with the energetic impatience of its youthful population (70% are under 35 years old).

Two failed coups in 1992 marred Venezuela's reputation as South America's most enduring democratic state. In an ironic twist, the 1998 elections saw the leader of the attempted takeovers, Hugo Chávez, swept into office. He won strong support from the poor for his promise of fairer wealth distribution, but has angered middle and upper classes over his populist policies. A 63-day nationwide strike calling for Chávez' ouster crippled the country and choked its lifeblood of petroleum in early 2003, ending with an uneasy impasse between the two sides.

About the Restaurants

Venezuela's larger cities boast a wide variety of restaurants, from Spanish *tascas* (Spanish-style casual restaurants with bars) to French bistros to Japanese sushi bars. But while you're here, you'll want to sample Venezuela's own unique cuisine. The national dish, *pabellón criollo*, consists of shredded beef or fish served with rice, black beans (*caraotas*),

Venezuela, at about 912,050 square km (355,799 square mi), covers a huge expanse of South America. You'll want to see quite a bit of it, as each far-flung region offers something unique. With careful planning, many of the country's high points can be experienced even during a short trip. Maximize a brief visit by contacting a tour operator—an agent knowledgeable about the region can arrange for accommodations, guides, and transportation.

If you have 7 days

If your port of entry is **Isla Margarita,** you'll want to spend a couple of days soaking up the sun and the lively beach-town atmosphere. On your third day, head to the paradisal archipelago of **Los Roques.** Some of the best snorkeling, diving, and bonefishing in the Caribbean await. On your fifth day, fly south to **Parque Nacional Canaima** and spend two days splashing in the waterfalls, hiking in the shadow of the majestic tepuis, and flying over famed Angel Falls.

10

If you have 10 days

If you enter the country through **Caracas,** spend at least two days exploring the capital's museums, historical sites, and fabulous restaurant scene. On your third day head south to **Los Llanos,** the vast grasslands, which offers the best wildlife this side of the Serengeti. Three full days of exploring the region by jeep or canoe will introduce you to anteaters, anacondas, and hundreds of species of wildly colored birds. When you return to Caracas, spend a couple of days winding your way along the magical Trans-Andina Highway toward **Mérida.** Take a day to ride the world's longest cable car to the glaciers of Pico Bolívar. Try one or more of the outstanding hiking, fishing, and horseback riding excursions in the area before heading back to Caracas on your last day.

---

fried plantains (*tostones*), and local white cheeses such as *queso de mano*. Venezuelans like beef, and restaurants that specialize in grilled meats (called *pardilleras* or *churrasquerías*) are popular with locals. If you visit during the Christmas season, try the holiday specialty called *hallaca,* a combination of chicken, corn, olives, and pork, wrapped in aromatic banana leaves.

Excellent fish and shellfish dominate in the coastal areas and on Isla Margarita, including grouper, snapper, mackerel, tuna, swordfish, lobster, crab, shrimp, and clams. In the Andean regions, treat yourself to rainbow trout.

Don't leave Venezuela without sampling at least one of these scrumptious, typical desserts: *bien me sabe* (coconut cake), *torta de guanábana* (a tart fruitcake), *merengón de nispero* (meringue cake), and the always popular *cascos de guayaba* (guava shells with white cheese). As a Caribbean nation, Venezuela excels at rum production (*ron* in Spanish). A small bottle of the dark Santa Teresa brand fits nicely in your pack to take home. Venezuela also produces some surprisingly good domestic wines, such as Viña Altagracia or the sparkling Pomar from Lara State in the northwest region of the country.

Lunch, the main meal of the day, begins at noon and lasts until about 3. Dinner is taken between 7 and 10 PM; don't count on being served much past 10:30 PM, except in the Las Mercedes district of Caracas, where some restaurants remain open until midnight. Some restaurants offer a prix-fixe meal at lunchtime known as the *menu ejecutivo*. This includes a *primero* (appetizer of soup or salad); a *segundo,* the main course; and *postre* (dessert). Espresso or *guayoyo,* a watery, American-style coffee, is included.

High-end restaurants frequently have dress codes, so inquire when making reservations. For most other dining establishments, a woman can't go wrong in an informal dress nor a man in a collared shirt with optional tie.

WHAT IT COSTS In Dollars				
	$$$$	**$$$**	**$$**	**$**	**¢**
AT DINNER	over $20	$15–$20	$10–$15	$6–$10	under $6

Prices are for a main course at dinner.

About the Hotels

Venezuela offers lodging options to suit almost every price range and comfort level—from the resort citadels of Caracas to the colorful, three-room posadas of the Gran Roque. Take in a view of the Andes from the window of a restored 17th-century monastery or from the cobblestone courtyard of a renovated coffee hacienda nestled in the cloud forest above Mérida. In Los Llanos, you can stay on a working cattle ranch or in the guest facilities of a biological field station. Those who seek adventure by day and comfort by night will relish the prime location and amenities offered by the Arekuna camp near Parque Nacional Canaima.

Luxury hotels rarely include meals when quoting rates, but many of the smaller lodgings in the Andes do include breakfast (and sometimes dinner) in their room rates. Remember that prices jump 10%–20% during holiday periods, particularly during Christmas, pre-Lenten Carnival, and Holy Week.

WHAT IT COSTS In Dollars				
	$$$$	**$$$**	**$$**	**$**	**¢**
FOR 2 PEOPLE	over $180	$100–$180	$60–$100	$40–$60	under $40

Prices are for a double room in high season, excluding tax.

Exploring Venezuela

North, south, east and west, Venezuela has an astonishing variety of landscapes. In the north is Caracas, a cosmopolitan if somewhat chaotic city—with its fair share of urban glories and woes. Sun-seeking travelers should waste no time in getting to the translucent waters of the Caribbean coast, specifically those around Isla Margarita and Los Roques. You might be surprised to see that the continent's mighty Andes take up such a prominent portion of Venezuelan territory, but for a taste of what the capital

10

Bird-Watching
With more than 1,300 species of birds, Venezuela is one of the world's top destinations for avid ornithologists. In Los Llanos, you will be awed by immense flocks of roseate spoonbills, giant egrets, green ibis, scarlet ibis, and jabiru storks. Hoatzins (primitive birds born with fingerlike claws on their wings) live in the brush that crowds the rivers crisscrossing the plains. In the Andean foothills, you may catch a glimpse of the brilliant red cock-of-the-rock, and in higher altitudes witness the magnificent soaring flight of Andean condors. On the Caribbean coast, numerous lagoons shelter flocks of pink flamingos.

Fishing
Los Roques is one of the top bonefishing destinations in the world, and many visitors come to Venezuela specifically to cast for the quick-running sport fish. You can catch *pavón*, huge peacock bass, in Los Llanos and in the Río Orinoco, where you may also enjoy the added thrill of angling for feisty piranha. Trout fishing is a popular diversion in the Andes, where local tour operators host a variety of expeditions to well-stocked, scenic lakes. A few restaurants will even fry up your catch.

History
Miles of skyscrapers and freeways might make you forget that Caracas is the repository of Venezuelan history. Colonial-era churches and houses populate the narrow streets of El Centro, the old city center. This district of the capital also sports many monuments to deified Venezuelan hero Simón Bolívar, often referred to as simply "El Libertador"—no other name seems necessary to designate the man who liberated the country and much of South America, and who gives the adjective to the country's official name, the Bolivarian Republic of Venezuela.

Shopping
Caracas is filled with hip clothing boutiques and shoe stores; the selection is interesting and the atmosphere fun, but prices are generally high. The Mérida region offers folkloric items, particularly pottery and wood carvings. Isla Margarita is a duty-free extravaganza where you'll find European clothing and leather goods, liquor, tobacco, and perfume. Hammocks are another favorite Isla Margarita purchase, well known for their fine craftsmanship and immense size. Although bargaining is not acceptable in city stores, prices at outdoor markets—and sometimes in smaller towns and villages—are negotiable.

Wilderness Expeditions
Venezuela has some of the world's largest national parks, which cover an amazing 15% of the country's landmass. Just one of its 43 national parks, Parque Nacional Canaima, is larger than Belgium. There are plenty of traditional treks available, from hiking in the Andes to boating on the Río Orinoco. Adventurous types can head to the Andes to bike to remote villages still inaccessible by car or paraglide over forest-covered canyons. Animal lovers should grab their cameras and head to Los Llanos, whose abundant wildlife earned it the title "the Serengeti of South America."

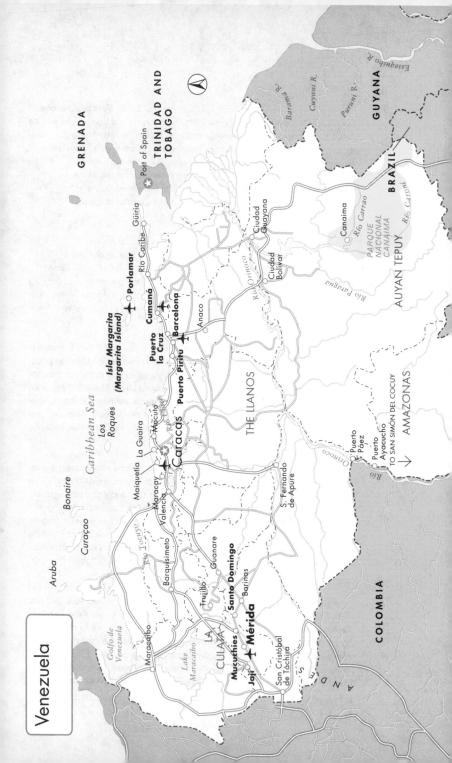

once was like, head to Andean towns such as Mérida, set against the sublime backdrop of the western mountains. The Orinoco River basin and Canaima National Park, itself the size of Belgium, occupy Venezuela's eastern sector. Deep in the south, is the jungly Amazonas, named, of course, for the hemisphere's largest river. Los Llanos, vast, wildlife-filled grasslands, sit in the center of it all.

CARACAS

On a wall facing the Plaza el Venezolano, Simón Bolívar is quoted as follows: SI SE OPONE LA NATURALEZA LUCHAREMOS CONTRA ELLA Y LA HAREMOS QUE NOS OBEDEZCA (If nature opposes us, we'll struggle against her and make her obey us). Nowhere in Venezuela is the legacy of Bolívar's defiant proclamation more apparent than in Caracas itself. Whether gazing at the city's sprawling skyline from the 17th-story window of a high-rise hotel or strolling in the shadows of looming concrete edifices, one wistfully dreams of what Caracas might have been like had its sudden growth spurt occurred during any other architectural moment than the 1970s. Reckless and desperate in its quest for modernity, Caracas, with a few notable exceptions, sacrificed elegance and grace for the unbridled visual of its charmless urban center.

What redeems Caracas is the Caraqueños themselves: a diverse, young, and lively population that colors the grimy streets of the capital with laughter, music, and unrestrained enthusiasm. The sophisticated tastes of the nearly 5 million inhabitants demand the endless parades of boutiques and fine restaurants that crowd commercial areas. The streets of the upscale Las Mercedes neighborhood, called London, Paris, and Madrid, are almost as chic as their namesakes. In the gargantuan cultural center of Bellas Artes, museums and concert halls erupt with the artistic accomplishments of Venezuela's past and present. Hip, fast-paced, and altogether cosmopolitan, Caraqueños still manage to retain a warmth and amiability you may not expect to encounter in a city this vast.

Although Caracas is a rambling metropolis, its places of interest can be explored comfortably in a day or two. Interesting museums and cultural centers, lively bars, and refined dining establishments are all connected by the city's clean, efficient subway system. The weather, too, facilitates exploring: At 3,000 feet above sea level, Caracas enjoys one of the world's most agreeable climates, with an average daily temperature of 24°C (75°F).

Be advised, however, that Caracas well deserves its reputation as a dangerous city. The main tourist areas are generally safe during the day, but always be on your guard. Even residents do not go out alone in most neighborhoods after dark, when muggings and other violent crimes are shockingly frequent. Taxis are the safest means of transportation after dark.

Exploring Caracas

Set amid rolling hills, Caracas lacks a single downtown area. However, the city can be divided into four principal areas of interest: El Centro

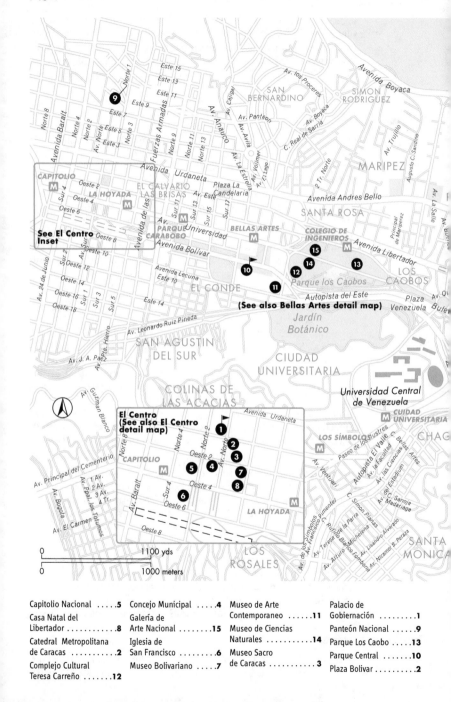

Caracas

Parque Nacional El Avila

Avenida Boyaca

ALTA FLORIDA

CHAPELLIN

EL PEDREGAL

Av. Murillo

Av. Maracaibo

Av. los Pinos

Av. los Chaguaramos

Av. Ppal. de la Castellana Eugenio Mendoza

Av. San Felipe

2A. Avenida

Tr. 4

Tr. 9

Tr. 3

4A. Avenida

Tr. 8

Av. San Juan Bosco

6A. Avenida

Tr. 7

Tr. 2

Tr. 6

LAS PALMAS

LA FLORIDA

Av. los Naranjos

Avenida los Mangos

Av. Nivaldo

Caracas Country Club

COUNTRY CLUB

ALTAMIRA

Av. las Palmas

Buenos Aires

Acacias

Av. J. B. Arismendi

Tr. 1

Av. El Bosque

Tr. 5

LA CAMPIÑA

Av. los Jabillos

C. Maturin

Av. El Saman

LA CASTELLANA

ito

las PLAZA VENEZUELA

var de

Sabana

Av. Ppal. del Country Club

CAMPO ALEGRE

Av. Blandin

SABANA GRANDE

C. 3A

3 Av. Tr.

C. J. F. Rivas

ALTAMIRA

SABANA GRANDE

Avenida

Grande

Av. Casanova

(Av. A. Lincoln)

Avenida Libertador

CHACAO

Av. Francisco de Miranda

CHACAO

BELLO CAMPO

Av. Sur de Altamira

Av. Bello Monte

CHACAITO

CHACAITO

Av. Tamanaco

Av. Venezuela

Av. Guaicaipuro

EL ROSAL

Av. Sorocaima

Distribuidor Altamira

Av. C. Orinoco

Av. Venezuela

C. Baruta

Autopista del Este - Francisco Fajardo

Av. Bello Monte

Av. Alameda

Av. El Retiro

C. las Mercedes

LOS GUARAMOS

C. Caicara

COLINAS DE BELLO MONTE

C. Jalisco

C. Madrid

C. Paris

Av. Ppal. las Mercedes

C. Londres

C. New York

Av. Rio de Janeiro

C. la Estancia

C. Blohm

Av. Baruta

LAS MERCEDES

CHULAVISTA

C. Estanques

Autopista Caracas-Baruta

Av. Dr. Nuñez Ponte

and its prerequisite Plaza Bolívar ringed by historic buildings; Parque Central and the surrounding Bellas Artes district; Las Mercedes with its many boutiques and restaurants; and the walled villas and apartment buildings of residential Altamira and La Castellana.

The main subway line runs across much of the city, supplemented by two short southern spurs. It's clean, safe, and great for traveling around Caracas. Buses confound first-time visitors because service is sporadic and routes are difficult to ascertain. *Por puestos*—the small vans that will pick you up and drop you off anywhere on their set routes—are fine for short point-to-point hops. Taxis, their progress often hampered during the day by gridlock, are the only other viable alternative for getting around downtown.

Numbers in the text correspond to numbers in the margin and on the Caracas maps.

El Centro

El Centro is the oldest part of Caracas, a city founded by Spanish conquistador Diego de Losada in 1567. Colonial buildings are clustered around the lush Plaza Bolívar. Numerous benches are almost always occupied by aged Venezuelans vehemently discussing the latest political events or admiring the passing Caraqueña girls. In the center is an imposing statue of Simón Bolívar, the hero of Venezuelan Independence best known as "El Libertador."

a good walk

Take the subway to the Capitolio station to reach the historic heart of Caracas, El Centro. It's a short stroll to Plaza Bolívar, where you'll find the **Palacio de Gobernación** ❶ ☛ on the north and the **Catedral Metropolitana de Caracas** ❷ and **Museo Sacro de Caracas** ❸ on the east. The **Concejo Municipal** ❹ is on the southern side of the plaza, across the street from the **Capitolio Nacional** ❺. Head south between the two buildings and you'll see the **Iglesia de San Francisco** ❻. Two blocks east is the tree-lined Plaza El Venezolano, ringed by the **Museo Bolivariano** ❼ and the **Casa Natal del Libertador** ❽, Bolívar's childhood home. Five blocks north of Plaza Bolívar is the imposing **Panteón Nacional** ❾.

TIMING Because of the concentration of sights in El Centro, you'll need only about two hours for the entire walk. With the exception of the Panteón Nacional, which is a 15-minute stroll from Plaza Bolívar, all of the buildings are within a few minutes of each other. You'll need to add time, of course, if you want to tour any of the museums. Keep in mind that museums are closed in the middle of the day and all day Monday. While this area is safe for exploring in the day, after dusk it gets rougher.

WHAT TO SEE   **Capitolio Nacional.** Venezuela's Congress is housed in the neoclassical
★ ❺   National Capitol, a pair of buildings constructed on the site of the 17th-century convent of the Sisters of the Conception. President Guzmán Blanco, who ordered the disbanding of all convents, razed the original building in 1874. On the site he built the Federal and Legislative palaces. The paintings in the oval Salón Elíptico by Venezuelan artist Martin Tovar y Tovar are quite impressive, especially those on the ceiling. The bronze urn in the room contains the 1811 Declaration of Independence. (In deference to decorum, you must tuck in your shirt when you enter this room.)

⊠ *Av. Norte 2 at Av. Oeste 2, El Centro* ☎ *Free* ☉ *Daily 9–12:30 and 3–5* Ⓜ *Capitolio.*

⑧ Casa Natal del Libertador. The birthplace of Simón Bolívar is a pilgrimage site for Venezuelans, who honor him as "El Libertador." The house has very little to offer about the great man himself but is a lovely example of a spacious and airy old colonial house in the midst of downtown's hustle and bustle. Monumental wall paintings by Tito Salas in the front room that retell the stories of Bolívar's heroic battles are well worth a look. ⊠ *Av. Universidad at Av. Norte 1, El Centro* ☎ *0212/ 541–2563* ☎ *Free* ☉ *Tues.–Fri. 9–noon and 2:30–5, weekends 10–1 and 2:30–5* Ⓜ *Capitolio.*

② Catedral Metropolitana de Caracas. With its original facade unaltered since it was built at the end of the 17th century, the Metropolitan Cathedral towers over Plaza Bolívar. The main altar is a magnificent Baroque creation gilded with more than 300 pounds of gold leaf. Don't miss the Bolívar family chapel on the right-hand side. ⊠ *Plaza Bolívar, El Centro* ☎ *0212/862–1518* ☎ *Free* ☉ *Tues.–Sun. 8–1 and 3–6* Ⓜ *Capitolio.*

④ Concejo Municipal. This graceful colonial building, set around a manicured courtyard, is considered the cradle of Venezuelan statehood. On

July 5, 1811, the National Congress met here and approved the Declaration of Independence. Today the building houses the **Museo Criollo,** which exhibits a permanent collection of works by noted Venezuelan painter Emilio Boggio (1857–1920) and scale-model miniatures by Raúl Santana that depict every imaginable aspect of Venezuela's early culture. ⊠ *Plaza Bolívar, El Centro* ☎ *0212/545–6706* ≣ *Free* ⊙ *Tues.–Fri. 9:30–11 and 2:30–5, weekends 10–4* Ⓜ *Capitolio.*

❻ Iglesia de San Francisco. Filled with richly gilded altars, this church dating from 1593 was the site of Simón Bolívar's proclamation as "El Libertador" (the Liberator) and of his massive funeral 12 years after his 1830 death. It remains the loveliest example of colonial architecture in Caracas. ⊠ *Av. Bolsa at Av. San Francisco, El Centro* ☎ *0212/484–5172* ≣ *Free* ⊙ *Daily 7–noon and 3–6* Ⓜ *Capitolio.*

Fodor'sChoice ★

❼ Museo Bolivariano. Next to Casa Natal, this museum in a fine old colonial house exhibits countless documents, flags, and other memorabilia from Venezuela's war for independence from Spain. ⊠ *Av. San Jacinto at Av. Trapsos, El Centro* ☎ *0212/545–9828* ≣ *Free* ⊙ *Tues.–Fri. 9–noon and 2:30–5, weekends 10–1 and 2:30–5* Ⓜ *Capitolio.*

★ **❸ Museo Sacro de Caracas.** The Museum of Religious Art of Caracas, a former sacristy and ecclesiastical prison built in 1844 adjoining the cathedral, now houses ornate religious statues and lavish costumes from the colonial era. Especially noteworthy in the first salon is the ornate silver canopy made to cover the statue of Our Lady of the Rosary. Downstairs you'll find an intriguing, albeit rather macabre, common grave where remains of the religious are interred in sealed niches. ⊠ *Plaza Bolívar, El Centro* ☎ *0212/861–6562* ≣ *Free* ⊙ *Tues.–Sun. 10–5* Ⓜ *Capitolio.*

⌐ **❶ Palacio de Gobernación.** The art deco–style Government Palace, built in 1935, now houses political offices and a ground-floor gallery with rotating exhibits of international and Venezuelan art. ⊠ *Plaza Bolívar, El Centro* ☎ *0212/564–3080* ≣ *Free* ⊙ *Tues.–Sat. 10–6* Ⓜ *Capitolio.*

★ **❾ Panteón Nacional.** Five blocks north of Plaza Bolívar, the striking National Pantheon's exquisite marble interior holds the remains of 138 Venezuelan political and historical figures, including Simón Bolívar. The walls and ceilings are graced with murals depicting some of the most famous battles for independence. ⊠ *Av. Norte, El Centro* ☎ *0212/ 862–1518* ≣ *Free* ⊙ *Tues.–Fri. 9–noon and 2:30–5, weekends 10–noon and 3–5* Ⓜ *Capitolio.*

Bellas Artes

The cultural center of Caracas, Bellas Artes hosts almost all the major exhibitions and performances that visit Venezuela. This zone encompasses the giant twin towers of Parque Central and the museums of Parque Los Caobos.

a good walk

Begin your walk at the Bellas Artes Metro station. When you reach street level, look for the two tall glass towers to the south. Walk toward the towers and you'll reach a gargantuan slab of cement known as the **Parque Central ⑩** ⌐. At the eastern end of this complex is the **Museo de Arte Contemporáneo ⑪**. Crossing the pedestrian bridge will bring you to the

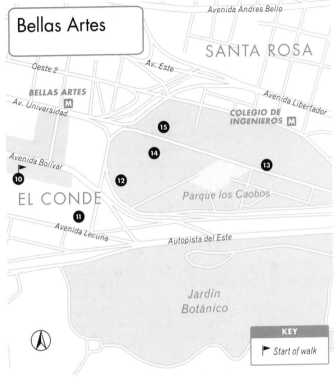

Bellas Artes

Complejo Cultural Teresa Carreño , where you can check out its underground bookstore and coffee shop. A short stroll north brings you to the entrance of the immense **Parque Los Caobos** ⑬, where you'll find the **Museo de Ciencias Naturales** ⑭ and the **Galería de Arte Nacional** ⑮.

TIMING Visiting all of the sights of Bellas Artes will take half a day. Allow an hour and a half to visit the museums on weekdays, a bit more on weekends, when they tend to be crowded. All museums are closed on Monday.

WHAT TO SEE **Complejo Cultural Teresa Carreño.** World-class ballet, opera, and classi-
⑫ cal concerts are regularly presented at this modern cultural center named for Venezuela's most famous classical pianist. Hanging from the theater roof is the kinetic sculpture "Yellow Pendants" by Venezuelan artist Jesús Soto. Adjacent to the complex is a bookstore and the Teatro Ateneo de Caracas, home of a popular movie theater screening art films. ⊠ *Plaza Morelos, Bellas Artes* ☎ *0212/574–9122* Ⓜ *Bellas Artes.*

⑮ **Galería de Arte Nacional.** Known around town as the "GAN," the interesting National Art Gallery, across the circular Plaza Morelos from the Museum of Natural Science, displays more than 4,000 works of art from Venezuela's proud past. It shares a building with the **Museo de Bellas Artes,** which exhibits a random selection of art from all around the globe. The top floor is a terrace offering views over Parque Los Caobos and much of Caracas. ⊠ *Plaza Morelos, Bellas Artes* ☎ *0212/ 578–1818 for the gallery, 0212/578–1816 for the museum* 🖭 *Free* ⊙ *Tues.–Fri. 9–5, weekends 10–5* Ⓜ *Bellas Artes.*

off the beaten path

PARQUE NACIONAL EL ÁVILA – The mountains of Parque Nacional El Ávila rise some 3,300 feet over the northern edge of Caracas, then slope down its other side directly into the Caribbean. The national park is a favorite destination for weekend hikers, as its southern side is crisscrossed with trails. Novices prefer the daylong hike that leads to Pico Ávila, while more experienced hikers take the two-day trek to Pico Naiguatá. The park is easily accessible from the Altamira neighborhood in eastern Caracas. If you don't feel like hiking you can ride up in a cable car.

San José de Galipá, a settlement on the coastal side of Mount Ávila, makes a nice destination if you've been hiking all morning. Horses are available there for further exploring. The town's cool climate makes it perfect for growing flowers to sell in Caracas.

⑪ **Museo de Arte Contemporáneo de Caracas Sofía Imber.** This excellent contemporary art museum displays paintings by Picasso, Miró, and Bacon. There are also 3-D works by renowned Venezuelan artist Jesús Soto. Housed on the edge of the Parque Central complex, this is one of the best collections of modern art in South America. ⊠ *Parque Central, Bellas Artes* ☎ *0212/573–8289* 🖭 *Free* ⊙ *Tues.–Sun. 10–6* Ⓜ *Bellas Artes.*

FodorsChoice ★

⑭ **Museo de Ciencias Naturales.** The Museum of Natural Science includes archaeological, botanical, and zoological displays (stuffed animals against rather dismal backdrops). The pre-Columbian displays, however, are particularly interesting, as are the overviews of early-American life, such as demonstrations of the farming methods of indigenous peoples. ⊠ *Plaza Morales, Bellas Artes* ☎ *0212/577–5786* 🖭 *Free* ⊙ *Mon.–Fri. 9–5, weekends 10:30–6* Ⓜ *Bellas Artes.*

▶ ⑩ **Parque Central.** Don't be surprised by the lack of greenery in this so-called park. This vast expanse of concrete holds some of the city's finest museums. ⊠ *Av. Bolívar and Calle Sur 4, Bellas Artes* Ⓜ *Bellas Artes.*

⑬ **Parque Los Caobos.** One of the city's oldest parks, Parque Los Caobos has towering mahogany trees planted to celebrate Venezuela's independence. The lovely old fountain, ringed by bronze sculptures, is a taste of the Caracas of a century ago. ⊠ *Av. México, Bellas Artes* Ⓜ *Bellas Artes.*

Where to Eat

Caracas has one of the busiest and most varied restaurant scenes in Latin America, from the linen-covered tables of fine French restaurants to the counters at fast-food joints. Although dining out in Caracas is more expensive than in the rest of the country, the variety of restaurants is impressive. Many upstart restaurants vanish as quickly as they appear, but there are a few dozen establishments that have endured. Casual attire is appropriate for all but the more upscale restaurants.

American

$$$-$$$$ ✕ **Lee Hamilton's Steak House.** Billing itself as the only restaurant in
Fodor'sChoice Caracas serving real American cuts of beef, this steak house has stood
★ the test of time, remaining a favorite among business executives since 1958. One of the most popular dishes here is the delectable steak tartare. ✉ *Av. San Felipe and Av. El Bosque, La Castellana* ☎ *0212/261–0511* ▭ *AE, MC, V.*

Continental

$$-$$$ ✕ **Café L'Attico.** With soft lights glimmering on brass bar rails, this time-honored Caracas institution echoes the atmosphere of a neighborhood pub. Strategically placed large-screen TVs categorize L'Attico as a sports bar, but the large menu of freshly prepared specialties gives it a flavor that is altogether more sophisticated. Don't miss the Belgian waffles at the Sunday brunch, they're out of this world. ✉ *Av. Luis Roche at 1a Transversal, Altamira* ☎ *0212/265–8555* ▭ *AE, MC, V* Ⓜ *Altamira.*

French

$$-$$$ ✕ **Lasserre.** For more than 30 years Venezuelans have enjoyed the finest in classical French food here. House specialties include the hard-to-find *lapa*, a small tropical boar cooked to perfection in a rich red-wine sauce, and *pabon*, an exquisite freshwater peacock bass. The Grand Marnier soufflé, which must be ordered in advance, is a great finishing touch. Enjoy a glass of wine from the top-notch cellar as you listen to the live piano music. ✉ *Av. Tercera, between 2a and 3a Transversals, Los Palos Grandes* ☎ *0212/283–4558* ▭ *AE, D, MC, V* ☾ *Closed Sun.*

Italian

$-$$ ✕ **Da Guido.** This casual, family-style restaurant with hams hanging from the ceiling and colorful murals depicting the Italian countryside is filled with locals who enjoy its classic dishes and affordable prices. Owner Eliseo Peserico and his friendly waiters have been serving up delicious veal parmigiana, gnocchi, ravioli, and fettuccine for more than 30 years. ✉ *Av. Mariscal Francisco Solano 8, Sabana Grande* ☎ *0212/763–0937* ▭ *AE, MC, V* Ⓜ *Plaza Venezuela.*

$-$$ ✕ **La Romanina.** This superb Italian eatery near Plaza La Castellana serves great pizzas cooked over burning logs in a brick oven. The pizza topped with salmon and cream cheese is one of the favorites. The decor is nothing fancy—just simple pine tables—but the service is friendly and hospitable. ✉ *Av. Ávila, La Castellana* ☎ *0212/267–6739* ▭ *AE, MC, V* Ⓜ *Altamira.*

Japanese

$$-$$$ ✕ **Taiko.** Next door to the French Embassy in an ultra-hip neighborhood, this chic restaurant serves excellent Japanese dishes ranging from hibachi-grilled meats and seafood, udon noodle soups, and lightly fried tempura to fresh sushi and sashimi. The modern, industrial decor is softened by touches of wood, rock, and the pleasant buzz of satisfied diners. ✉ *Calle La Trinidad, near Calle Madrid, Las Mercedes* ☎ *0212/993–5647* ▭ *AE, MC, V.*

Where to Stay & Eat in Caracas

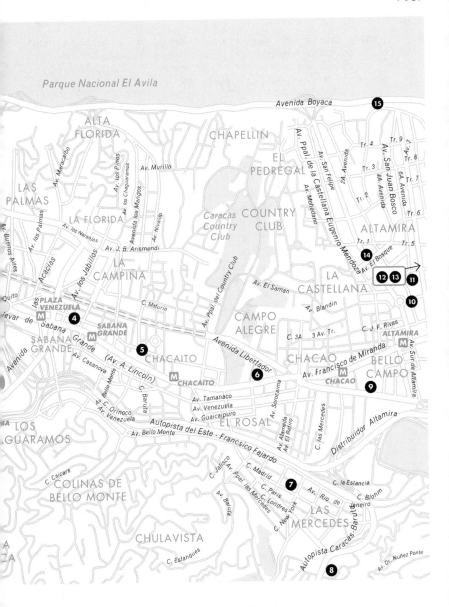

Spanish

Spanish

$$$ ✕ **Casa Farruco.** One of several excellent Spanish restaurants scattered around the neighborhood of La Candelaria, this warm and welcoming place feels more like Seville than Caracas. The menu is dominated by seafood dishes—the squid plate comes with a cream sauce that should not be missed. ⊠ *Av. Este 2,, La Candelaria* ☎ *0212/572–9343* ⊟ *AE, MC, V* Ⓜ *Parque Carabobo.*

Venezuelan

★ **$$–$$$** ✕ **Tarzilandia.** Lush tropical vegetation filled with parrots, tree frogs, and turtles has been part of the experience at this Caracas landmark since it opened in 1950. On the menu are exotic Venezuelan dishes: turtle pie, shrimp mixed with tropical fruit, and delectable grilled steaks and seafood. The mango flambé à la mode seems much-loved. ⊠ *Av. San Juan de Bosco at Decima Transversal, Altamira* ☎ *0212/261–8419* ⊟ *AE, MC, V* ☉ *Closed Mon.*

Where to Stay

Most of the top hotels in Caracas, including those belonging to international chains, are south and east of the city center, in the upscale neighborhoods of Altamira and Las Mercedes. Prices tend to be much higher than in the rest of the country. The area around Sabana Grande has a cluster of more economical accommodations. Avoid the cheap hotels in the capital; most double as brothels and rent by the hour.

$$$–$$$$ 🏨 **Hilton Caracas.** This complex in the heart of the financial district, a favorite for international business travelers, is like a city unto itself. You have your pick of restaurants and bars, as well as plenty of facilities. Although the rooms look bland, they have great views of the nearby Parque Los Caobos. ⊠ *Av. Libertador at Av. 25 Sur, Bellas Artes* ☎ *0212/503–5000, 800/221–2424 in the U.S.* 🖷 *0212/503–5003* ⊕ *www.hiltoncaracas.com.ve* 🖘 *738 rooms, 27 suites* ⚬ *2 restaurants, in-room data ports, in-room safes, minibars, room service, 2 tennis courts, 2 pools, health club, hair salon, massage, sauna, bar, shops, baby-sitting, playground, dry cleaning, laundry service, concierge, business services, meeting rooms, car rental, travel services, no-smoking rooms, free parking* ⊟ *AE, D, MC, V* Ⓜ *Bellas Artes.*

★ **$$$–$$$$** 🏨 **Tamanaco Inter-Continental.** A permanent part of the Caracas social scene, this venerable hotel sits on a bluff above the southeastern section of the city. The oldest of the city's luxury hotels, this pyramid looming over the Las Mercedes neighborhood is exceptionally well maintained. Its most stunning facility, a free-form pool, loops around any which way but not rectangularly. You can take a dip after working out at the health club or playing a few games on the tennis courts. The bar, El Punto, has long been a gathering site of choice for the city's elite and influential. Rooms are spacious and eminently well appointed. ⊠ *Av. Principal de Las Mercedes, Las Mercedes* ☎ *0212/909–7111, 800/327–0200 in the U.S.* 🖷 *0212/909–7116* ⊕ *caracas.venezuela.intercontinental.com* 🖘 *486 rooms, 55 suites* ⚬ *4 restaurants, in-room data ports, in-room safes, minibars, 3 tennis courts, pool, health club, hair salon, sauna, spa, 3 bars, concierge, dry cleaning, laundry services, business services, meet-*

ing rooms, car rental, travel services, no-smoking rooms, free parking ⊟ *AE, D, MC, V.*

$$$ ⊞ **Embassy Suites.** This 20-floor tower in the financial district caters to the needs of business travelers. The soaring atrium, which lets in lots of sun, is a great place to relax over breakfast. The suites all have separate living rooms. ⊠ *Av. Francisco de Miranda and Av. El Parque, Campo Alegre* ☎ *0212/276–4200* ⊟ *0212/266–6556* ⊕ *www. embassysuitescaracas.com* ⟲ *224 suites* ⟳ *Restaurant, in-room data ports, in-room safes, minibars, pool, health club, hair salon, hot tub, 2 bars, shops, laundry service, concierge, business services, meeting rooms, travel services, no-smoking floors, free parking* ⊟ *AE, D, MC, V.*

★ $$$ ⊞ **Hotel Ávila.** This international-style hotel, built by American industrialist Nelson Rockefeller in 1942, is so bedecked with flowers and vines that the hustle-bustle of the city seems deceptively distant. All of the spacious rooms have balconies, many of which command a resplendent view of Mt. Ávila. The poolside dining area, attractively furnished with white wicker, is one of the details that make the Ávila the city's most charming larger hotel. ⊠ *Av. George Washington, San Bernardino* ☎ *0212/ 551–5155* ⊟ *0212/552–3021* ⊕ *www.viajes-venezuela.com/hotelavila* ⟲ *113 rooms* ⟳ *Restaurant, 7 tennis courts, pool, health club, hair salon, bar, playground, laundry service, concierge, travel services, free parking* ⊟ *AE, MC, V* ⦿❘ *BP.*

$$ ⊞ **Continental Altamira.** Within walking distance of the Plaza Altamira, this hotel is a favorite of travelers on a mid-range budget. Although the hotel is slightly dated on the outside, the interior is modern and nicely furnished. Most rooms have balconies overlooking the tree-lined Avenida San Juan Bosco. ⊠ *Av. San Juan Bosco, Altamira* ☎ *0212/261–0644* ⊟ *0212/261–0131* ⊕ *www.hotel-continental.org* ⟲ *80 rooms, 2 suites* ⟳ *Restaurant, in-room safes, minibars, pool, bar, laundry service, meeting rooms, free parking* ⊟ *AE, D, MC, V* Ⓜ *Altamira* ⦿❘ *BP.*

$$ ⊞ **Shelter Suites.** This tastefully decorated hotel across the street from the massive Centro Sambil shopping complex has spacious rooms with views of Parque Nacional El Ávila from its balconies. Many rooms have hot tubs. There's live music in the bar every night. ⊠ *Av. Libertador, Chacao* ☎ *0212/265–3860* ⊟ *0212/265–7861* ⟲ *82 rooms* ⟳ *Restaurant, bar, laundry service, meeting room, free parking* ⊟ *AE, MC, V* Ⓜ *Chacao.*

$–$$ ⊞ **Savoy.** This hotel not far from Bulevar de Sabana Grande is a great budget option. You can relax in the small patio restaurant or retire to your comfortable, quiet room. The atmosphere is casual and not particularly fancy, but the friendly environment facilitates meeting fellow travelers. ⊠ *Av. Francisco Solano López at Av. Las Delicias, Sabana Grande* ☎ *0212/762–1971 or 0212/762–1979* ⊟ *0212/761–7154* ⟲ *95 rooms* ⟳ *Restaurant, in-room data ports, minibar, laundry service, meeting room, travel services, free parking* ⊟ *AE, D, MC, V* Ⓜ *Chacaíto.*

Nightlife & the Arts

Nightlife

Monday must be the only night Caraqueños get any sleep, because Tuesday seems to be the unofficial start of the weekend. By Saturday the whole population appears to be out on the town. As in much of Latin

America, the nightlife doesn't really get swinging until close to midnight. The trendy Las Mercedes neighborhood, packed with cafés, restaurants, bars, and dance clubs, is the place to be on Friday and Saturday. Although Caracas is generally pretty casual, clubs often require men to wear jackets. Take a taxi after dark no matter where you go or how short the distance.

BARS In Las Mercedes, **Auyama** (⊠ Calle Londres, Las Mercedes ☎ 0212/991–9489) is a popular place for a cocktail before heading to the clubs. It also serves reasonably priced food. **Weekends** (⊠ Av. San Juan Bosco at La Segunda Transversal, Las Mercedes ☎ 0212/261–3839) is where you can challenge locals to a game of pool. Tasty Tex-Mex items are available. In La Candelaria, any of the Spanish-style tapas bars are a great place to enjoy a beer. One of the best is **El Pozo Canario** (⊠ Calle Alcabal, La Candelaria ☎ 0212/572–6180).

DANCE CLUBS Salsa and merengue are more popular in Venezuela than in any other South American country, which means that both types of music can be found in almost any club in the city. Many begin the night playing pop, then switch to salsa and merengue when the crowd gets warmed up. The dance floors immediately fill with young couples gyrating hip to hip.

The most popular salsa club is **El Maní Es Así** (⊠ Calle El Cristo at Av. Francisco Solano López, Sabana Grande ☎ 0212/763–6671), which is always packed with a crowd covering a wide age range. **Latino's** (⊠ Centro Comercial Los Chaguaramos, Los Chaguaramos ☎ 0212/693–6695) is a more upmarket salsa club where jackets and ties are not out of place. The crowd is relatively young and definitely affluent. At **O'-Gran Sol** (⊠ La Calle Villaflor between Av. Casanova and Sabana Grande, Sabana Grande ☎ 0212/761–1796), you can enjoy live music Thursday, Friday, and Saturday nights.

The Arts
Theater and other types of performances are popular nighttime diversions. For current listings, pick up a copy of the English-language newspaper *The Daily Journal* at any newsstand.

FILM The **Cinemateca Nacional de Venezuela** (⊠ Edificio José Vargas, Av Este 2, ☎ 0212/576–2336) hosts film screenings, usually the latest or the classics of Latin American cinema, several evenings a week.

MUSIC The campus of Universidad Central de Venezuela, **Aula Magna** (☎ 0212/578–1132) has concerts by the Venezuelan Symphony Orchestra on Sunday at 11 AM. This impressive concert hall features a ceiling full of colorful "acoustic clouds" designed by Alexander Calder. The **Teatro Ateneo de Caracas** (⊠ Plaza Morelos, Bellas Artes ☎ 0212/571–3664) hosts chamber music and operatic concerts between September and April. **Teatro Teresa Carreño** (⊠ Plaza Los Caobos, Bellas Artes ☎ 0212/571–7279), the center for cultural events in Venezuela, has the best-known national and international musicians and theater groups.

THEATER **Teatro Nacional** (⊠ Av. Lacuna, Bellas Artes ☎ 0212/482–5424) has a roster of cultural events.

Sports & the Outdoors

On a continent where soccer is nearly a religion, Venezuela's obsession with baseball is a notable exception. The popularity of the sport is due in large part to the thriving professional winter league, where North American players such as Johnny Bench, Pete Rose, and Darryl Strawberry all honed their skills. Atlanta Braves slugger Andres Galarraga, born in Caracas, is a hero in his hometown. The stadium at the **Universidad Central de Venezuela** (✉ Ciudad Universitaria ☎ 0212/572–2211) is the best venue for baseball or soccer. Tickets can be purchased at the gate on the day of the game. Arrive early on weekends.

Shopping

Caraqueños are style-conscious, which accounts for the city's numerous modern shopping centers. Jewelry (especially gold) and leather goods (including shoes, handbags, and luggage) are some of the best bargains in Caracas, but don't expect a steal. Prices are often high in the wake of sobering inflation.

Markets

One of the most popular markets is the Thursday-morning **Mercadito de Chacao,** where you can stroll through the stands overflowing with fruits and vegetables. It's a block from Avenida Francisco de Miranda in the Chacao district. The **Mercado Guacaipuro,** open Tuesday, Thursday, and Saturday, is known for its produce as well as its fresh fish. You'll find it on the corner of Avenidas Andrés Bello and Libertador.

Shopping Centers

Caracas is home to two of the most gargantuan shopping centers on the continent. **Centro Sambil** (✉ Av. Libertador, Chacao ☎ 0212/267–9302), the largest mall in South America, is a five-level behemoth packed with more than 500 shops, restaurants, theaters, and even amusement park rides. The **Central Comercial Ciudad Tamanaco** (✉ Calle La Estancia, Las Mercedes ☎ 0212/271–7435), east of Las Mercedes in the suburb of Chuao, attracts crowds with its upstairs cinemas, fast-food restaurants, and swanky boutiques.

Las Mercedes has its own sprawling shopping complex, **Paseo de Las Mercedes** (✉ Av. Principal de Las Mercedes, Las Mercedes ☎ 0212/991–7242). **El Recreo** (✉ Paseo El Recreo ☎ 0212/762–7228) is the newest of the large-scale malls and boasts the best food court in the city.

Shopping Districts

With the growing popularity of shopping malls, traditional shopping districts have suffered a decline. One area that continues to draw crowds is the **Bulevar de Sabana Grande.** Once a main traffic thoroughfare, this is a bustling promenade where Caraqueños converge to browse in the tiny shops or chat over a *marrón grande* (large coffee) in one of the many cafés that line the streets. On weekends, browse among the endless rows of stalls or take in performances by mimes, musicians, or even flame-swallowers. The area can be crowded, so be wary of pickpockets.

Besides its restaurants and clubs, **Las Mercedes** is overflowing with fancy boutiques and fashionable shops. The most exclusive are often tucked into side streets. Avoid its main strip, Avenida Principal de Las Mercedes, which has an overwhelming collection of cheap clothing stores.

Specialty Shops

In addition to the gold peddlers who roam the downtown streets, there are more reputable (and more expensive) dealers in Caracas. Inside the Central Comercial Ciudad Tamanaco is **Muzo Gemologists** (⊠ Calle La Estancia, Las Mercedes ☎ 0212/959–3995), which has displays of gemstones, crystals, and rough stones. A reputable gem dealer in the Central Comercial Ciudad Tamanaco mall is **Diamoro** (⊠ Calle La Estancia, ☎ 0212/955–0988). **H. Stern** (☎ 0212/992–7313 Tamanaco Inter-Continental, 0212/571–0520 Caracas Hilton), one of South America's largest gem dealers, sells all grades of gems at outlets in the Tamanaco Inter-Continental and the Caracas Hilton.

Side Trips from Caracas

El Hatillo

★ On the southern outskirts of Caracas is the hillside village of El Hatillo, a destination well worth the 30-minute taxi ride. Its narrow stone streets are lined with 17th-century buildings housing dozens of shops and boutiques, galleries, and restaurants. Here you'll find unique handicrafts and indigenous artifacts, original artwork and rare antiques, from all over Venezuela. The restored village is clearly intended for tourists, but it somehow has managed to preserve its colonial style.

Colonia Tovar

Colonia Tovar, 65 km (40 mi) west of Caracas, is an intriguing mountain village colonized by German immigrants in the 1840s. Because it remained isolated until the 1930s, the community retained a German character as authentic as any you'll find in the Black Forest. Given its cooler climate, you'll quickly forget that this breezy mountain retreat is so close to the Caribbean. The real joy is hiking in the surrounding hills or spending an evening in one of the village's jovial inns indulging in hearty German foods.

Parque Nacional Los Roques

Fodor'sChoice An archipelago composed of some 350 tiny islands sprinkled in the dazzling Caribbean, Parque Nacional Los Roques is a 30-minute (propeller-aircraft) flight north from Caracas. Only one of those islands, Gran Roque, boasts a bona fide town, tiny as it is. A few others have private weekend retreats or fishermen's shacks, while most are completely uninhabited. Some are so small they disappear at high tide. The sandy beaches of Parque Nacional Los Roques are uncommonly white, even by uncompromising Caribbean standards. The crystalline waters reveal thriving coral reefs that are home to more than 300 species of fish.

As a national park since 1976, Parque Nacional Los Roques is subject to strict federal regulations that protect it from overdevelopment. New construction is prohibited on any of the islands. Every structure on Gran Roque—which enjoys fresh water from a desalinization plant and electricity from a generator—existed before the archipelago became a national park. Many have been extensively remodeled and are meticulously maintained as *posadas* (small inns), colorfully painted and adorned with brilliant flowering plants. A handful of bars and eateries make up the rest of the businesses. A mid-19th-century lighthouse, its windmill-like appearance revealing its Dutch heritage, overlooks the town from a small hill nearby.

Los Roques is considered one of the finest locales for hooking snapper and other types of fish. You can head out in powerboats or in *peñeros* (local fishing boats). Sea kayaking is also popular, and some of the islands have emerged as premier sailboarding destinations. More sedate pastimes include scuba diving and snorkeling. Sunbathing, however, remains the most popular activity.

WHERE TO STAY & EAT Approximately 60 posadas line the sandy roads of Gran Roque. Most have two to six rooms with private or shared bath and a common dining area. Except during the peak season you should have no difficulty finding lodging on the island.

$$$ 🏨 **Posada Mediterráneo.** Italian-born innkeeper Elena Battani's heritage
Fodor's Choice is evident throughout this exquisite posada, from the simple furnishings
★ of the rooms to the white stone staircase leading to the rooftop terrace hung with sun-shaded hammocks. Join her for a chat at the rustic wooden dining table on her flowering vine-laden front patio. ⊠ *Isla Gran Roque* 🕿 *0237/221–1130* ⊕ *www.posadamediterraneo.com* ⇗ *6 rooms* ⚱ *Dining room, in-room safes, fishing; no room phones, no room TVs* ⊟ *AE, MC, V* ⭘ *FAP.*

Caracas A to Z

AIR TRAVEL TO & FROM CARACAS
Caracas is served by Aeropuerto Internacional Simón Bolívar (CCS), about 25 km (16 mi) from downtown in the coastal area of Maiquetía.

Major U.S. carriers serving Venezuela are American, Continental, and Delta. Venezuela's Aeropostal flies to Caracas from Miami. Air France, British Airways, Iberia, KLM, and Lufthansa fly from their respective hubs in Europe. A number of domestic regional airlines fly throughout Venezuela. Among them are Aereotuy, Avior, Laser, and Santa Barbara. Most domestic flights stop in Caracas.

Upon landing, you can expect to be issued a free tourist visa, valid for a stay of up to three months.

🛪 International Airlines **Aeropostal** 🕿 0212/708-6211. **Air France** 🕿 0212/283-5855. **American** 🕿 0212/267-9111. **British Airways** 🕿 0212/263-7011. **Continental** 🕿 0212/359-2600. **Delta** 🕿 0212/958-1111. **Iberia** 🕿 0212/267-9733. **KLM** 🕿 0212/285-3432. **Lufthansa** 🕿 0212/267-4767.

🛪 Domestic Carriers **Aereotuy** ⊠ Av. Abraham Lincoln and Bulevar de Sabana Grande, Edificio Gran Sabana, Sabana Grande 🕿 0212/761-6247. **Avior** ⊠ Aeropuerto Nacional Simón Bolívar 🕿 0231/202-5811. **Santa Barbara** ⊠ Calle 3B, Edificio Tokay, La Urbina 🕿 0800/865-2636 in Venezuela.

🛪 Airports **Aeropuerto Internacional Simón Bolívar** 🕿 0231/352-2222.

AIRPORTS & TRANSFERS

The trip into town from the airport is via a busy four-lane highway and takes between 30 and 45 minutes, depending upon your destination in Caracas. Cab fare to downtown Caracas costs about Bs25,000. The official fare is posted next to the taxi stand outside the international terminal.

Robberies of tourists by drivers of unofficial cabs are all too common. To be on the safe side, take a taxi from the dispatcher outside the international terminal.

BUS TRAVEL TO & FROM CARACAS

There are two inconveniently located and slightly unsavory public bus terminals serving Caracas. For travel to destinations west of the city, buses leave from Terminal La Bandera. The Terminal del Oriente serves destinations to the eastern part of the country.

Far more convenient—and much safer—is the *servicio especial* (special service) offered by Aeroexpresos Ejecutivos. All buses depart from the company's own clean, quiet terminal in the Bello Campo district. Two other reliable private companies are Expresos del Oriente and Expresos Alianza. 🔢 Bus Companies **Aeroexpresos Ejecutivos** ✉ Av. Principal de Bello Campo ☎ 0212/ 266-3601 or 0212/266-1295. **Expresos Alianza** ✉ Terminal de Occidente ☎ 0212/462- 0546. **Expresos del Oriente** ✉ Terminal de Oriente ☎ 0212/462-5371.

BUS TRAVEL WITHIN CARACAS

Clean, air-conditioned buses leave all Metro stops for areas outside the reach of the subway system. The cost is Bs300. If used within four hours of purchase, it's also valid for a one-way ride on the Metro. Smaller public buses called *carritos* connect all parts of the city, but they are no quicker in heavy traffic.

CAR RENTAL

Should you decide to rent a car, major rental chains are located in the airport and downtown. 🔢 Local Agencies **Avis** ✉ Hotel Tamanaco Intercontinental Av. Principal de Las Mercedes ☎ 0212/959-5822 ✉ Aeropuerto Internacional Simón Bolívar ☎ 0231/355- 1190. **Budget** ✉ Calle Lourdes and Av. Nueva Granada ☎ 0212/283-4778 ✉ Aeropuerto Internacional Simón Bolívar ☎ 0231/355-2799. **Hertz** ✉ Hotel Tamanaco Intercontinental Av. Principal de Las Mercedes ☎ 0212/905-0430 ✉ Aeropuerto Internacional Simón Bolívar ☎ 0231/396-0004.

CAR TRAVEL

Heavy traffic, a lack of parking, and the city's baffling layout combine to render Caracas a driving nightmare for residents, let alone visitors. If you can avoid it, do not rent a car to explore the city.

EMBASSIES & CONSULATES

The Australian embassy is open for consular services Monday–Thursday, 8 AM–4:45 PM. The Canadian embassy, in the same building as its Australian counterpart, offers services to its citizens Monday–Friday 8–noon. The New Zealand consulate offers consular services Monday–Friday 8–noon. The British embassy serves its citizens Monday–Friday 12–4:30. The U.S. Embassy opens for consular services Monday–Friday 1–4.

🇦🇺 **Australia** ✉ Av. Francisco de Miranda at Av. Sur Altamira ☎ 0212/263-4033. **Canada** ✉ Av. Francsco de Miranda at Av. Sur Altamira ☎ 0212/264-0833. **New Zealand** ✉ Av. Libertador at Av. Francsco de Miranda Chacao ☎ 0212/277-7965. **United Kingdom** ✉ Edificio Las Mercedes, Av. La Estancia, Chuao ☎ 0212/993-4111 or 0212/993-5280. **United States** ✉ Calle F at Calle Suapure, Colinas de Valle Arriba ☎ 0212/977-0553 or 0212/977-2011.

EMERGENCIES

Dial 171 for police, ambulance, fire, or any emergency in the metropolitan area.

Pharmacies in different neighborhoods take turns staying open all night; spot them by the sign *turno,* or consult local newspapers for lists of open *farmacias* (pharmacies).

A reputable private clinic with an English-speaking staff is the Clínica El Ávila in Altamira.

🏥 Hospitals **Clínica El Ávila** ✉ Av. San Juan Bosco at 6a Transversal, Altamira ☎ 0212/276-1111.

ENGLISH-LANGUAGE MEDIA

The American Bookshop on Plaza Altamira Norte carries new and used books of all kinds, including books about Venezuela. *The Daily Journal,* an English-language newspaper, hits the newsstands Monday through Saturday and is a lively, terrific source of news that pulls no punches in its coverage of Venezuelan politics.

📚 Bookstores **American Bookshop** ✉ Av. San Juan Bosco at 1 Av. Transversal ☎ 0212/263-5455.

HEALTH

In Caracas and other large cities, food in reputable hotels and restaurants should be safe. Avoid raw fruits and vegetables, uncooked fish, and tap water. Bottled water is readily available throughout the country.

INTERNET

Internet cafés dot the city. Expect to pay Bs2,000 per hour of computer access. Try Galileos Internet in the Edificio El Conde of the Parque Central office complex, or CANTV Net in the Centro Sambil shopping center.

💻 Internet **CANTV Net** ✉ Nivel Acuario, Centro Sambil, Chacao ☎ 0212/263-0881. **Galileos Internet** ✉ Edificio El Conde, Nivel Bolívar, Parque Central, Bellas Artes ☎ 0212/571-0942.

MAIL & SHIPPING

A main branch of Ipostel, the country's postal system, is located near the Capitolio Metro stop. It is open weekdays 8–6, Saturday 8–2. A far more reliable way to send anything, however, is by an overnight service. DHL has several offices downtown, including one in the Tamanaco Inter-Continental. FedEx and Transvalcar Air Courier (the agent for UPS) have offices in Caracas.

📮 Post Offices **Ipostel** ✉ Edificio Sur, Centro Simón Bolívar, El Centro.

🛪 Overnight Services DHL ✉ Av. Chicago and Av. Milán ☎ 0212/205-6000 ✉ Av. Principal de Las Mercedes, Las Mercedes ☎ 0212/909-8226. **FedEx** ✉ Av. Milán ☎ 0212/205-3333. **Transvalcar Air Courier/UPS** ✉ Av. Principal de la Urbina and Calle 10, La Urbina ☎ 0212/204-1455.

MONEY MATTERS

Italcambio, the largest of the *casas de cambio* (exchange houses), is permitted to exchange cash dollars and American Express traveler's checks denominated in dollars for bolívares, but not vice-versa. (Most banks will not exchange currency, and none will accept traveler's checks.)

You can use your ATM card in some machines to obtain bolívares, but it is impossible to obtain dollars here. Gauge your cash spending needs accordingly to avoid being stuck at the end of your trip with local currency that is impossible to change back. The black market is prevalent, but engaging in transactions carries stiff penalties and is dangerous.

🛪 Currency Exchange Offices **American Express** ✉ Centro Comercial Ciudad Tamanaco, Calle La Estancia, Las Mercedes ☎ 0212/959-1011. **Thomas Cook** ✉ Maso Tours, Av. Francisco de Miranda, Torre Provincial B, 11th floor, Chacao ☎ 0212/264-6466.

🛪 Italcambio Exchange Houses **Italcambio** ✉ Edificio Belmont, Av. Luis Roche, Altamira, Caracas ☎ 0212/263-7110 ✉ Centro Comercial Sambil, Av. Libertador, Chacao, Caracas ☎ 0212/265-7645 ✉ Aeropuerto Internacional Simón Bolívar, Maiquetía, Caracas ☎ 0231/355-1080.

SAFETY

Pickpocketers and muggers, sometimes violent, are serious problems for residents and visitors alike. Most downtown areas, including those popular with tourists, are generally safe during the day. Note that even residents do not go out alone on foot in most neighborhoods after dark. Use taxis at night, even if you are traveling a short distance.

When visiting the city, don't wear expensive clothing or flashy jewelry, and don't handle money in public. It's a good idea to keep your money in a pocket rather than a wallet, which is easier to steal. On buses, in the Metro, and in crowded areas, hold purses or camera bags close to your body; thieves use knives to slice the bottom of a bag and catch the contents as they fall out.

Avoid all political demonstrations. They're common in Caracas and occasionally result in clashes between demonstrators and police.

SUBWAY

The safe, speedy Metro system traverses the city between Palo Verde in the east and Propatria in the west, with connecting north–south lines from Capitolio and Plaza Venezuela. One-way tickets, which can be purchased in all stations, are Bs260, Bs300, or Bs350, depending on distance traveled. Save your ticket; you'll need it to exit the turnstile out of the station. If you plan to use the Metro frequently, opt for the convenience of a *multi abono* card (Bs2,500), valid for 10 rides anywhere on the system. These cards save you the hassle of waiting in long lines for individual tickets. (The stations' automated ticket vending machines are frequently out of order.) Route maps are posted at ticket booths and inside each car, but not on the platforms. The Metro operates daily 5:30 AM–11 PM. Cars get very crowded during the 6–9 AM and 5–8 PM rush hours.

TAXIS

Licensed taxis have yellow license plates and carry secured signs that say *libre* (free) on the roof, while *pirata* (pirate) varieties have signs that are obviously detachable. When selecting a taxi off the street, settle only on official cars—tales of robbery by pirata drivers are legion—and agree on the rate before you depart. Unless you are traveling only a couple of blocks, Bs5,000 is a standard fare anywhere in the central city area between Capitolio and Altamira. Note that fares increase by as much as 50% at night and on weekends. Once en route, don't be surprised if your driver cuts corners and ignores stop signs and red lights as he maneuvers through downtown traffic. Many larger hotels have their own taxi companies. Ask your hotel or restaurant to call you a taxi if you go out at night.

TELEPHONES

You can make long-distance calls with a credit card at the state-run telephone company CANTV. You can also purchase phone cards for use in public phones at many shops and newsstands.

▉ Telephone Companies **CANTV** ✉ Centro Sambil, Nivel Acuario, Chacao ☎ 0212/263-7783.

TOUR OPERATORS

Lost World Adventures specializes in tailoring an independent travel itinerary around your interests. The founder of this U.S.-based company once lived in Venezuela, so he knows his way around. The company also leads small-group expeditions of 7 to 11 days throughout Venezuela—they'll set you up to travel from the Andes to Angel Falls and everywhere in between—and several other Latin American countries.

A reputable tour operator in Caracas is Orinoco Tours, centrally located on Bulevar de Sabana Grande. This well-run company, which often offers rates much lower than competitors, specializes in ecotourism in Venezuela.

▉ Tour Companies **Lost World Adventures** ✉ 220 Second Ave., Decatur, GA 30030 ☎ 404/373-5820 or 800/999-0558 🖷 404/377-1902 ⊕ www.lostworldadventures. com. **Orinoco Tours** ✉ Edificio Galerías Bolívar, Piso 7, Bulevar de Sabana Grande, Sabana Grande ☎ 0212/761-7712 🖷 0212/761-6801 ⊕ www.orinocotours.com.

VISITOR INFORMATION

The Instituto Nacional del Turismo (INATUR), Venezuela's semi-privatized tourism agency, has information offices on the 35th floor of the Edificio Conde in the Parque Central office complex, open Mon.–Fri. 8 AM–12:30 PM and 2–5 PM. A branch in the arrivals hall at the Aeropuerto Internacional Simón Bolívar is open daily 6 AM–10 PM. Signs at both offices still show the agency's former name, Corpoturismo.

▉ Tourist Information **INATUR** ✉ Edificio Conde, Bellas Artes ☎ 0212/574-2220, or 0800/462-8871 in Venezuela ⊕ www.inatur.gov.ve ✉ Aeropuerto Internacional Simón Bolívar ☎ 0231/507-8607.

THE CARIBBEAN COAST

Sometimes referred to as La Ruta del Sol (the Route of the Sun), the 563-km (350-mi) stretch of highway along the Caribbean Coast from Caracas to Puerto La Cruz and Cumaná is at once picturesque and treacherous. Seldom far from the water's edge, most of the Autopista del Oriente (Eastern Highway) follows the myriad loops and twists of the natural shoreline, beside unspoiled bays and isolated hamlets.

Much of the coastline is protected from development, but small posadas are occasionally nestled among the palm trees along the shore. Sprawling resorts line the broad beaches near Puerto La Cruz and Cumaná.

Río Chico

167 km (103 mi) east of Caracas.

The main reason to stop in this town is **Playa Colorada,** Río Chico's well-maintained beach. It's lined with palm-thatch bars and restaurants.

Parque Nacional Laguna de Tacarigua, about 18 km (11 mi) northeast of Río Chico, is surrounded by mangrove forests. In the late afternoon it comes alive as thousands of white herons and scarlet ibis return to settle down for the night. At the park's entrance is a fishing dock with a very rustic bar where you can drink and dance with the locals.

Puerto Píritu

110 km (70 mi) east of Río Chico.

The streets of this sleepy port town are lined with well-preserved colonial mansions with wood-shuttered windows and intricately carved eaves. The highlight, though, is Píritu's 2-km (1-mi) ribbon of sparkling white sand. Restaurants and hotels are clustered at regular intervals along Puerto Píritu's shoreline drive, Bulevar Fernández Padilla.

Barcelona

41 km (25 mi) east of Puerto Píritu.

Capital of the state of Anzoátegui, Barcelona was founded more than 300 years ago by settlers from the eastern coast of Spain. Today it is the site of the region's largest airport. Although it's a bit rough around the edges, Barcelona's colonial-era vibe makes it a pleasant alternative to the resort-town style of its neighbors.

On the corner of Plaza Boyacá, the city's tree-lined main square, is the **Iglesia de San Cristóbal,** a stunning church built in 1748.

Even more impressive than the town's church is the adjacent Palacio del Gobierno (Palace of the Government), built in 1671. Today it houses the **Museo de la Tradición,** which has rotating exhibits of colonial and religious art. ⊠ *Plaza Boyacá* ☎ *0281/277–3481* 🎫 *Free* ☉ *Daily 9–12:30 and 3–5.*

Puerto La Cruz

12 km (7 mi) east of Barcelona.

The region's main tourist hub, Puerto La Cruz has attractive waterways lined with marinas and expensive villas. Visitors flock to the maze of shops and restaurants along Paseo Colón, a busy thoroughfare that runs along the beach. At night, the crowds move to the bars and dance clubs in town.

Although Puerto La Cruz's own beaches are dangerously polluted, its main attractions are the alluring islands of nearby Parque Nacional Mochima. At the eastern end you'll find boats to the national park that charge Bs12,000–Bs40,000 for round-trip service. Puerto La Cruz is also a jumping-off point for ferries to Isla Margarita, which depart from the western end of Paseo Colón.

Where to Stay & Eat

$ ✕ **Porto Vecchio.** This lively restaurant on Paseo Colón, one of the best eateries in eastern Venezuela, has a faithful clientele that drops in for the house specialty—excellent pastas with fish and shellfish. Don't miss the delicious veal. ⊠ *Paseo Colón 117, at Calle Boyacá* ☎ *0281/265–2047* ▤ *AE, D, MC, V.*

$$$ ▦ **Hotel Hesperia Puerto La Cruz.** This expansive hotel at the end of the Paseo Colón is next to the marina where the boats take off for excursions to the nearby islands. Spacious rooms overlook the lush gardens and pool. ⊠ *Paseo Colón* ☎ *0281/265–3611, 800/558–6625 in the U.S.* 🖷 *0281/265–3117* ⊕ *www.hoteles-hesperia.es* ⤳ *220 rooms* ⚬ *2 restaurants, minibars, pool, hair salon, dive shop, snorkeling, boating, bar, shops, meeting room, car rental, travel services* ▤ *AE, D, MC, V.*

$$$ ▦ **Punta Palma Hotel.** Built at the end of the bay, this hotel has an enviable view of Puerto La Cruz. Most of its colorfully decorated rooms have balconies and overlook the pool, marina, and small private beach. ⊠ *Prolongación Av. La Península, Cerro El Morro* ☎ *0281/281–1211* 🖷 *0281/281–8277* ⊕ *www.puntapalma.com* ⤳ *154 rooms, 25 suites* ⚬ *3 restaurants, snack bar, in-room safes, 4 tennis courts, 2 pools, sauna, marina, 2 bars, shops, baby-sitting, laundry service, business services, meeting room, car rental, travel services* ▤ *AE, D, MC, V.*

Nightlife

You won't have to look far to find bars and dance clubs in Puerto La Cruz, as all are along Paseo Colón or adjacent streets. A popular part of the scene is the vibrant **Harry's Pub** (⊠ Calle Bolívar 53 ☎ 0281/265–3605), a casual watering hole with an interesting mix of young locals and seasoned wayfarers.

Sports & the Outdoors

FISHING Boat owners throughout the region will take you fishing in their small wooden peñeros. Bargain for the best price—the going rate is about $5 per person for a half-day excursion. Located in the Hotel Caribbean Inn, **Amerinda Tours** (⊠ Calle Freites ☎ 0281/267–0693) charters deep-sea boats for serious anglers. The friendly staff at **Macite Turismo** (⊠ Centro Comercial Paseo Mar, Calle Sucre at Paseo Colón ☎ 0281/265–5703) offers full-day trips to Isla Tortuga for barracuda fishing. The price is Bs200,000, including meals.

WATER SPORTS In Puerto La Cruz, **Explosub** (✉ Paseo Colón ☎ 0281/267–3256) offers snorkeling and scuba diving trips, as well as excursions to Parque Nacional Mochima. If you are not already an experienced diver, Explosub also offers certification classes. In neighboring El Morro, **Odisea** (✉ Av. Américo Vespucio ☎ 0281/281–2222) rents sailboats, windsurfers, and pedal boats at the Hotel Doral Beach.

Mochima

50 km (30 mi) east of Puerto La Cruz.

Beyond the town of Santa Fe you'll reach the turnoff for Mochima, the launching point for boat trips to the tranquil beaches of **Parque Nacional Mochima,** which encompasses hundreds of small islands. Contract a *peñero* (boat operator) to take you to any of the nearby beaches, where you can spend a relaxing morning or afternoon lazing around in the sun. It's about $10 per person, but the rate is negotiable.

Cumaná

75 km (47 mi) east of Puerto La Cruz.

The oldest European settlement on South America's mainland, Cumaná was founded by the Spanish in 1521. Most of its colonial buildings were destroyed by a string of earthquakes that devastated the town. After the last major earthquake, in 1929, the **Iglesia de Santa Inés** was rebuilt a few blocks south of Plaza Bolívar. Inside are a few items from the colonial period. One block south of Plaza Bolívar, the **Ateneo de Cumaná** (✉ Calle Antonio ☎ 0293/431–1284) hosts dance and opera evenings in addition to periodic exhibits of contemporary and colonial art.

Overlooking Cumaná from its hilltop perch, **Castillo de San Antonio de la Eminencia** is one of two forts commissioned in the 1680s to protect what was at the time the world's largest salt deposit. The four-point fort was built entirely of coral and outfitted with 16 guns. The fort **Castillo de Santiago de Araya,** is on treeless Araya Peninsula. Ferries leave daily from Cumaná's harbor for the 90-minute trip.

It's estimated that **Cueva del Guácharo,** Venezuela's largest cave, has at least 9 km (5½ mi) of subterranean passageways. Groups are led into the dank caverns by guides who tote kerosene lanterns so as not to upset the light-sensitive *guácharos*—a nocturnal species of fruit-eating birds. Visitors are not allowed to bring anything inside, including purses, flashlights, or cameras. To reach the cave from Cumaná, take Highway 9 south toward Caribe for about 65 km (40 mi) and follow the signs. ✉ *Parque Nacional El Guácharo* ☎ *0281/478–4445* 💰 *Admission* 🕙 *Daily 8–4.*

Where to Stay & Eat

★ $$$ 🏨 **Hesperia Cumanagoto.** Attention to the smallest of details makes this beachfront hotel among the finest hotels outside of Caracas. Large wrought-iron perches holding colorful macaws border the open-air, Mediterranean-style lobby, which has a terra-cotta floor and plenty of old-world charm. Bars and restaurants take full advantage of the Caribbean breezes with outdoor seating. The generously proportioned rooms have terraces overlooking the beautiful pools and gardens below. ☒ *Final Av. Universidad* ☎ *0293/430–1400* ⊟ *0293/452–1877* ⊕ *www. hoteles-hesperia.es* ⤳ *150 rooms, 13 suites* ⚭ *4 restaurants, golf course, tennis court, 2 pools, gym, spa, hair salon, massage, sauna, 2 bars, shops, business services, meeting rooms* ⊟ *AE, D, MC, V.*

$–$$ ✕⊡ **Hotel Turístico Los Bordones.** This hotel on the outskirts of town, popular among Venezuelans, has a relaxed, family-friendly vibe. When you're not enjoying the pool, you can take advantage of the secluded beach just a pebble's throw away. An on-site travel office can arrange snorkeling and windsurfing jaunts. Polinesia, the hotel's restaurant, is considered the best in town for fresh seafood. ☒ *Av. Universidad* ☎ *0293/451–3111* ⊟ *0293/451–5377* ⤳ *114 rooms, 3 suites* ⚭ *3 restaurants, 2 tennis courts, pool, car rental, travel services* ⊟ *AE, D, MC, V.*

The Caribbean Coast A to Z

AIR TRAVEL TO & FROM THE CARIBBEAN COAST
Several regional airlines fly regularly between the domestic terminal of Aeropuerto Internacional Simón Bolívar in Caracas and the coastal towns of Barcelona and Cumaná. Aeropostal, Avior Express, and Santa Bárbara serve both airports. Aeroposal and Avior fly between Barcelona and Isla Margarita, while Avior flies between Cumaná and Isla Margarita. Santa Barbara connects Barcelona and Cumaná with Mérida.

Barcelona's Aeropuerto José Antonio Uzcátequi (BLA) is 3 km (2½ mi) south of the city. The Aeropuerto Antonio José de Sucre (CUM) in Cumaná is 4 km (2 mi) southeast of the city.

🛪 Airlines **Aeropostal** ☒ Aeropuerto José Antonio Uzcátequi, Barcelona ☎ 0281/277–1735 ☒ Aeropuerto Antonio José de Sucre, Cumaná ☎ 0293/467–1429. **Avior** ☒ Aeropuerto José Antonio Uzcátequi, Barcelona ☎ 0281/274–9545. **Santa Barbara** ☒ Aeropuerto José Antonio Uzcátequi, Barcelona ☎ 0251/443–0662 ☒ Aeropuerto Antonio José de Sucre, Cumaná ☎ 0293/467–2933.

BOAT & FERRY TRAVEL
Conferry shuttles passengers and cars six times daily between Puerto La Cruz on the mainland and Punta de Piedras, 25 km (16 mi) west of Porlamar. It also offers twice-daily service between Cumaná and Punta de Piedras. Gran Cacique serves Margarita six times daily from both Cumaná and Puerto La Cruz. Naviarca operates two ferries a day between Cumaná and Punta de Piedras.

Purchase tickets at least two hours in advance for all ferries, particularly on weekends and holidays. Crossings take from two to four hours and cost $10–$25 per passenger and $20–$40 per car.

🛥 Boat & Ferry Companies **Conferry** ☒ Terminal Los Cocos, Puerto La Cruz ☎ 0281/267–7847 ☒ Terminal Puerto Sucre, Cumaná ☎ 0293/431–1462. **Gran Cacique** ☒ Terminal Los Cocos, Puerto La Cruz ☎ 0281/263–0935 ☒ Terminal Puerto Sucre, Cumaná

☎ 0293/432-0011 ⊕ www.grancacique.com. **Naviarca** ⊠ Terminal Puerto Sucre, Cumaná ☎ 0293/431-5577.

BUS TRAVEL

There are daily buses from Caracas to Barcelona, Puerto La Cruz, and Cumaná. One-way fare for each is about Bs24,000. Connect to local buses to reach smaller towns, such as Río Chico or Puerto Píritu.

Por puestos are another option. These minibuses carry up to 15 people and travel set routes between the Terminal de Oriente in Caracas and the Caribbean Coast. Drivers shout the names of cities they serve and leave the terminal when full. Expect to pay Bs32,000 between Caracas and Puerto La Cruz and about Bs9,600 between Puerto La Cruz and Cumaná.

CAR RENTAL

Inside the airport terminals at Barcelona and Cumaná are dozens of car-rental agencies. Rates are high, as an economy car rents for as much as Bs160,000 per day.

CAR TRAVEL

A car is a nice option for this part of the country, as you can travel at your own pace and stop at beautiful beaches along the coastal route. The often-congested Autopista del Oriente connects Caracas with Barcelona, Puerto La Cruz, Cumaná, and smaller towns beyond. It has plenty of roadside services.

MAIL & SHIPPING

In Barcelona, Cumaná, and Puerto La Cruz, you can post letters and packages at the centrally located post offices.

🚩 Post Offices **Barcelona** ⊠ Carrera Bolívar at Calle San Félix. **Cumaná** ⊠ Calle Paraíso at Calle Juncal. **Puerto La Cruz** ⊠ Calle Freites at Calle Libertad.

MONEY MATTERS

Italcambio, the largest of the *casas de cambio* (exchange houses), is permitted to exchange cash dollars and American Express traveler's checks denominated in dollars for bolívares, but not vice-versa. (Most banks will not exchange currency, and none will accept traveler's checks.)

You can use your ATM card in some machines to obtain bolívares, but it is impossible to obtain dollars here. Gauge your cash spending needs accordingly to avoid being stuck at the end of your trip with local currency that is impossible to change back. The black market is prevalent, but engaging in transactions carries stiff penalties and is dangerous.

🚩 Banks **Banco Unión** ⊠ Calle Libertad at Calle Freites, Edificio Banco, Puerto La Cruz ☎ 0281/264-9857.

🚩 Italcambio Exchange House **Italcambio** ⊠ Centro Comercial Paseo del Mar Paseo del Mar, Puerto La Cruz ☎ 0281/265-3993.

TELEPHONES

You can purchase phone cards at many shops and newsstands for local and long-distance calls from public phones. You can also make long-distance calls with a credit card at the state-run telephone company CANTV.

🚩 Telephone Offices **CANTV** ⊠ Calle Freites at Calle Bolívar, Puerto La Cruz.

TOUR OPERATORS
In Puerto La Cruz, Macite Turismo can arrange local fishing and boating expeditions, as well as more far-flung tours to Canaima, the Orinoco River, and Los Roques. Oventour, at the Gran Hotel Hesperia, operates a fleet of deluxe coaches and smaller vans for city tours of Puerto La Cruz and longer trips into the interior.

🔃 Tour Companies **Macite Turismo** ⊠ Centro Commercial Paseo Mar, Calle Sucre at Paseo Colón ☎ 0281/265–5703. **Oventour** ⊠ Gran Hotel Hesperia, Av. Paseo Colón ☎ 0281/265–3690.

VISITOR INFORMATION
Coranztur, the Anzoátegui state tourism corporation, has offices in Barcelona and Puerto La Cruz. The Sucre tourism corporation has an information office in Cumaná.

🔃 Tourist Information **Coranztur** ⊠ Av. 5 de Julio at Calle Las Flores Barcelona ☎ 0281/275–0474 ⊠ Paseo Colón at Calle Maneiro, Puerto La Cruz ☎ 0281/268–8170. **Información Turística** ⊠ Calle Sucre 49, Cumaná ☎ 0293/432–2403.

ISLA MARGARITA

Venezuelans are enormously fond of the island they call the "pearl in the Caribbean." Its status as a duty-free port and proximity to the mainland make it the top vacation spot for Venezuelans. Its miles of white sandy beaches, glittering hotels and restaurants, and vibrant nightlife, as well as 16th-century forts and national parks, have transformed Isla Margarita into a newly popular destination for other travelers.

Isla Margarita is split into two sections linked by an 18-km (11-mi) spit of sand. Most of the island's 350,000 residents occupy the more developed eastern half, especially the bustling city of Porlamar and the adjoining Pampatar. Others are found in the much smaller city of La Asunción, the capital of the region that also encompasses the neighboring islands of Coche and Cubagua.

Direct flights from Caracas and other Venezuelan cities, as well as scheduled or charter flights from a number of North American and European cities, make Isla Margarita an easy destination. Ferries from Puerto La Cruz, Cumaná, and La Guaira also travel to the island. Roads on Isla Margarita are good, which means a car is the easiest way to venture out on your own. Taxis and vans serve as public transportation throughout the island.

Porlamar

Porlamar, with about a third of Isla Margarita's population, is the island's center of commerce. Since it was granted free-port status in 1973, its boutique-lined avenues have been mobbed with tourists in search of tax-free bargains. Many of the goods found here are no cheaper than on the mainland, however. Porlamar is also the most cosmopolitan city on Isla Margarita, boasting countless restaurants, bars, clubs, and casinos.

A few blocks east of shady Plaza Bolívar is the **Museo de Arte Contemporáneo Francisco Narváez,** named after the native Margariteño sculptor whose works also can be viewed on the grounds of the Bella Vista Hotel. Here you'll find a permanent collection of Narváez's works, plus a rotating exhibit of national and international artworks. ⊠ *Calle Igualdad at Calle Fraternidad* ☎ *0295/261–8668* ⊠ *Free* ☉ *Tues.–Fri. 9–5.*

The mangrove forests of **Parque Nacional Laguna de la Restinga** cover the 20-km (12-mi) thread of sand that makes up the tenuous link between the main part of the island and the Península de Macanao. Here you'll find a variety of colorful birds, such as the scarlet ibis. The park has an unspoiled beach and a sprinkling of fishermen's huts where you can buy the catch of the day.

☺ In Boca del Río, 50 km (30 mi) west of Porlamar, stands the **Museo Marino de Margarita,** a museum whose eight exhibit halls serve as a repository for Venezuela's astounding variety of marine life. As aquariums go, this is a small facility, but you can find everything from barracudas to flying fish. Many of the exhibits focus on the history of sea exploration in northern South America. ☎ *0295/291–3231* ⊠ *Bs2,000* ☉ *Dec.–Apr, daily 9–5:30; May–Nov., daily 9–4:30.*

Where to Stay & Eat

★ $$–$$$ ✕ **Bahía.** With large bay windows overlooking the beach, this place has a long-standing reputation for serving fine Spanish-style seafood dishes. Expect strolling musicians while you struggle to decide between the tasty paella and the succulent crab. Best of all, the prices are quite reasonable. ⊠ *Av. Raúl Leoni* ☎ *0295/261–4156* ⊟ *MC, V.*

$–$$ ✕ **Cocody.** Not far from Playa Bella Vista, this restaurant pairs exquisite French cuisine with fine wines in romantic elegance. You can also dine under the palms on the open-air terrace overlooking the beach. ⊠ *Av. Raúl Leoni* ☎ *0295/261–8431* ⊟ *AE, MC, V.*

$–$$ ✕ **Poseidón.** The god of the sea serves top-quality seafood artfully presented with a local touch, and is among the most exclusive—and best— in Isla Margarita. The restaurant has a tropical fish aquarium. ⊠ *Centro Comercial Jumbo, Av. 4 de Mayo* ☎ *0295/269–6555* ⊟ *AE, MC, V.*

$–$$ ✕ **Sevillana's.** As this pleasant Spanish restaurant specializes in expertly prepared fish and shellfish, it's no surprise the paella is the standout. The colonial-style interior, all leather and wood furnishings, is complemented by the ever-present sound of flamenco music. Enjoy colorfully dressed performers demonstrating traditional dances from Seville nightly at 9 and 11:30. ⊠ *Av. Bolívar, Bella Vista district* ☎ *0295/263–8258* ⊟ *AE, DC, MC, V.*

¢–$ ✕ **Lucky.** As an alternative to ubiquitous seafood, this Chinese restaurant dishes up Cantonese specialties, including a savory Peking duck. If you're a vegetarian you'll be pleased with the selections as well. ⊠ *Av. Santiago Mariño* ☎ *0295/264–2991* ⊟ *AE, MC, V.*

$$$–$$$$ ▥ **Hilton Margarita.** Close to the sands of Playa Moreno, this venerable hotel offers a great location—only five minutes from the center of the city. The upper-floor rooms in the white tower are spacious and have balconies overlooking the sea, but you'll probably spend most of your time lying by the lovely pool, playing a few matches on the lighted tennis courts, or heading out for waterskiing. The Vegas-style casino is one

of the city's top nightspots. ☒ *Calle Los Uveros, Costa Azul* ☎ *0295/ 262–3333, 800/221–2424 in the U.S.* 🖷 *0295/262–0810* ⊕ *www. hilton.com* ↝ *269 rooms, 11 suites* ⚲ *3 restaurants, room service, in-room safes, minibars, 2 tennis courts, pool, health club, hair salon, massage, sauna, snorkeling, boating, jet skiing, parasailing, waterskiing, 2 bars, dance club, shops, baby-sitting, playground, dry cleaning, laundry service, business services, meeting room, airport shuttle, car rental, travel services, no-smoking rooms* ⊟ *AE, D, MC, V.*

$$ 🏨 **Hotel Bellavista.** The first seafront hotel in the area, this imposing property has reigned over the beach since 1955. It offers exclusive access to its own well-maintained section of the beach. ☒ *Av. Santiago Mariño* ☎ *0295/261–7222 or 0295/261–4157* ⊕ *www.hbellavista.com* ↝ *293 rooms, 12 suites* ⚲ *4 restaurants, 2 pools, shops, playground, meeting rooms, car rental* ⊟ *AE, MC, V.*

$$ 🏨 **Marina Bay.** On the Costa Azul, this gleaming white hotel wraps around the lushly landscaped pool area, where you can swim up to the floating bar protected by palm trees. A walkway leads to the sugary sands of Playa Moreno. The casino is crowded until the wee hours of the night. ☒ *Calle Abancay at Calle Trinitarias* ☎ *0295/267–1487* 🖷 *0295/262– 7419* ⊕ *www.hotelmarinabay.com* ↝ *170 rooms* ⚲ *3 restaurants, tennis courts, pool, 2 bars, casino, dance club, business services, meeting rooms* ⊟ *AE, MC, V.*

¢ 🏨 **Hotel María Luisa.** The comfortable rooms are only one reason this hotel is so popular with vacationing Venezuelans. Note also the intimate poolside patio and prime location on Playa Bella Vista. It's near restaurants, bars, and shops. ☒ *Blvd. Raúl Leoni* ☎🖷 *0295/261– 0564* ↝ *98 rooms* ⚲ *Restaurant, snack bar, pool, beach, bar, laundry service* ⊟ *AE, MC, V.*

Nightlife

Porlamar hot spots come and go with alarming frequency, but one place that seems to have settled in for the time being is **Señor Frog's** (☒ Av. Bolívar, Costa Azul ☎ 0295/262–0451), the mustard-yellow Mexican restaurant that transforms itself into the city's liveliest dance club at night.

A sports bar, the **Dugout** (☒ Av. 4 de Mayo ☎ 0295/263–9752) fills up with an energetic crowd cheering for their favorite major-league teams. Salsa or merengue gets the crowds dancing at **Dady's Latino** (☒ Av. 4 de Mayo ☎ 0295/265–9405). **Woody's Pub** (☒ Av. 4 de Mayo ☎ 0295/263– 2062) attracts a young, energetic crowd intent on dancing the night away.

Shopping

Although Isla Margarita is a major destination for Venezuelan day-trippers taking advantage of the duty-free prices, real bargains are hard to find. Your best bets are liquor and jewelry. Aside from the less expensive shops along Bulevar Guevara and Bulevar Gómez, shoppers are attracted to boutiques along Avenidas Santiago Mariño and 4 de Mayo. More and more shoppers are heading to the ubiquitous malls that are taking over the island. One of the most popular is the massive **Jumbo Mall** on 4 de Mayo. The stadium-size **Centro Sambil,** has 137 stores and is the offspring of its mammoth parent shopping center in Caracas.

El Valle del Espíritu Santo

5 km (3 mi) north of Porlamar.

Founded as the capital of the island in 1529, El Valle del Espíritu Santo has a splendid pink-and-white church honoring the Virgen del Valle, patron saint of eastern Venezuela. Pilgrims journey here year-round, but especially on her feast day in early September. The stained-glass windows of the **Santuario de la Virgen del Valle**, a twin-towered chapel on the main plaza, are worth a visit. A small museum open most afternoons contains the thousands of tokens, jewelry, and holy medals left by supplicants.

La Asunción

5 km (3 mi) north of El Valle.

From the mountains in the center of the island there are striking views as the road slowly descends to La Asunción, the small capital of the region. The sleepy little town, ignored by the bargain-hunting throngs, is the opposite of the bustling Porlamar. A handful of pretty colonial buildings are found around La Asunción's tree-covered Plaza Bolívar. Built in 1568, the **Catedral de Nuestra Señora** is one of the oldest churches in Venezuela. Of particular interest is its three-tiered tower—the country's only surviving example of a colonial church tower. Overlooking the main square, the **Castillo de Santa Rosa,** with its famous dungeon, is one of seven fortifications constructed by the Spanish to guard against pirate attacks.

Parque Nacional Cerro El Copey, along the road between Porlamar and La Asunción, has the highest point on the island. The mountain soars to 3,109 feet. From here you can often spot the smaller islands of Coche and Cubagua.

Pampatar

10 km (6 mi) northeast of Porlamar.

Northeast of Porlamar, this coastal town was founded nearly 500 years ago. Its strategic importance is clear when you visit the **Castillo de San Carlos de Borromeo** on the waterfront in the center of town. Constructed entirely of coral, the fort was built by the Spanish in 1662 after the original was destroyed by the Dutch. The port town is now known more for its myriad yachts and the fortnightly ferries that set sail for nearby Trinidad. In the center of town is the **Iglesia Santísimo Cristo,** which features a bell tower with an outside staircase—an architectural oddity found on several churches on Isla Margarita.

A giant Ferris wheel leads you to the island's largest amusement park, **Diverland** (⊠ Av. Jóvito Villalba, Pampatar ☎ 0295/262–1854). There are 16 attractions, including a roller coaster and water slide.

Where to Stay

$$$ 🏨 **Hesperia Playa El Agua.** With a soaring atrium lobby, this place is tucked away on the north side of the island near Pedro González. It has the is-

land's only 18-hole golf course and an almost deserted stretch of beach right behind it, so there are plenty of outdoor activities to indulge in here. A sumptuous buffet breakfast is included in the rate. ☒ *Av. 31 de Julio* ☎ *0295/249–0433* 🖷 *0295/249–0466* ⊕ *www.hoteles-hesperia. es* ⇆ *355 rooms, 42 bungalows* ♿ *2 restaurants, in-room safes, refrigerators, golf course, 3 tennis courts, 5 pools, health club, massage, spa, 2 bars, shops, meeting rooms, car rental, travel services* ▤ *AE, D, MC, V* ⊙⧵ *All-inclusive.*

$$$ 🖭 **Lagunamar.** This vast complex just north of Pampatar spans a huge swath of coastline. There's plenty to keep sun-worshipers busy, from waterskiing to windsurfing to relaxing by one of the pools. Meals are included in the rate, with dining options ranging from a poolside café to a glittery Italian restaurant. ☒ *Vía Agua de Vaca, Playa Guacuco* ☎ *0295/262–0711, 800/858–2258 in the U.S.* 🖷 *0295/262–1045, 305/ 460–8961 in the U.S.* ⊕ *www.lagunamar.com.ve* ⇆ *216 rooms, 190 suites* ♿ *5 restaurants, cafeteria, in-room safes, refrigerators, 6 tennis courts, 9 pools, gym, hot tub, massage, beach, windsurfing, jet skiing, racquetball, 3 bars, casino, shops, laundry service, meeting rooms, travel services* ▤ *AE, DC, MC, V.*

$ 🖭 **Flamingo Beach Hotel.** At this all-inclusive hotel on the beach, a glass elevator whisks you up to rooms overlooking the ocean. The pink interior is not the prettiest, but the range of water sports available makes it a fun place to stay. Sumptuous breakfast and dinner buffets are served on a deck with lovely views. ☒ *Calle El Cristo, Sector La Caranta* ☎ *0295/267–1487* 🖷 *0295/267–7419, 305/599–1946 in the U.S.* ⇆ *160 rooms* ♿ *3 restaurants, in-room safes, tennis court, pool, gym, sauna, beach, snorkeling, windsurfing, boating, bar* ▤ *AE, MC, V.*

Sports & the Outdoors

Easily the most famous beach on the island, palm-lined **Playa El Agua** is a remarkable stretch of fine white sand that runs along the coast just north of Pampatar. For much of its 4-km (2-mi) length, restaurants and bars lure sunbathers with blaring salsa music and ice-cold beers.

Isla Margarita A to Z

AIR TRAVEL TO & FROM ISLA MARGARITA

Most major domestic carriers have daily service from Caracas, Cumaná, Valencia, and Maracaibo to Isla Margarita's Aeropuerto Internacional del Caribe (PMV), 29 km (18 mi) south of Porlamar.

Aeropostal flies directly from New York and Miami to Isla Margarita. Aserca operates its single international route between Miami and Isla Margarita. Aereotuy flies between Porlamar and Los Roques.

🛪 Airlines **Aeropostal** ☎ 800/284-6637. **Aereotuy** ☎ 0212/761-6247 🖷 0212/762-5254.
🛪 Airports **Aeropuerto Internacional del Caribe** ☎ 0295/269-1438.

BOAT & FERRY TRAVEL

Conferry shuttles passengers and cars six times daily between Puerto La Cruz on the mainland and Punta de Piedras, 25 km (16 mi) west of Porlamar. It also offers twice-daily service between Cumaná and Punta de Piedras. Gran Cacique serves Margarita six times daily from both

Cumaná and Puerto La Cruz. Naviarca operates two ferries a day between Cumaná and Punta de Piedras.

Purchase tickets at least two hours in advance for all ferries, particularly on weekends and holidays. Crossings take from two to four hours and cost Bs16,000–Bs40,000 per passenger and Bs32,000–Bs64,000 per car.
🛥 Boat & Ferry Companies **Conferry** ⊠ Terminal Los Cocos, Puerto La Cruz ☎ 0281/267-7847 ✉ Terminal Puerto Sucre, Cumaná ☎ 0293/431-1462 ⊕ www.conferry.com. **Gran Cacique** ⊠ Terminal Los Cocos, Puerto La Cruz ☎ 0281/263-0935 ✉ Terminal Puerto Sucre, Cumaná ☎ 0293/432-0011 ⊕ www.grancacique.com. **Naviarca** ⊠ Terminal Puerto Sucre, Cumaná ☎ 0293/431-5577.

BUS TRAVEL TO & FROM ISLA MARGARITA
Unión Conductores de Margarita makes the 12-hour road/boat trip from Caracas to Isla Margarita for less than Bs32,000.
🚌 Bus Information **Unión Conductores de Margarita** ⊠ Terminal de Oriente, Caracas ☎ 0212/541-0035 ✉ Calle Maneiro, Porlamar ☎ 0295/263-7987.

CAR RENTAL
At Aeropuerto Internacional del Caribe near Porlamar, Hertz is a good option. In downtown Porlamar, try Beach Car Rental.
🚗 Local Agencies **Beach Car Rental** ⊠ Calle Tubores, Porlamar ☎ 0295/261-7753. **Hertz** ⊠ Aeropuerto Internacional del Caribe ☎ 0295/269-1237.

CAR TRAVEL
Renting a car is a great way to explore Isla Margarita, and it's one of the best ways to reach the more secluded stretches of sand off the beaten track. The island's roads are in good condition.

CONSULATES
The United Kingdom maintains an honorary consulate in Pampatar.
🏛 Consulates **United Kingdom** ⊠ Av. Principal B-14, Urbanización Playas del Angel, Pampatar ☎ 0274/262-4655.

MAIL & SHIPPING
Mail letters from the branch of Ipostel in Porlamar.
📮 Post Offices **Porlamar** (Calle Arismendi and Calle San Nicolás).

MONEY MATTERS
Italcambio, the largest of the *casas de cambio* (exchange houses), is permitted to exchange cash dollars and American Express traveler's checks denominated in dollars for bolívares, but not vice-versa. (Most banks will not exchange currency, and none will accept traveler's checks.)

You can use your ATM card in some machines to obtain bolívares, but it is impossible to obtain dollars here. Gauge your cash spending needs accordingly to avoid being stuck at the end of your trip with local currency that is impossible to change back. The black market is prevalent, but engaging in transactions carries stiff penalties and is dangerous.
🏦 Banks **Banco Unión** ⊠ Av. 4 de Mayo, Edificio Banco Unión, Porlamar ☎ 0295/265-8631.
💱 Italcambio Exchange House **Italcambio** ⊠ Centro Comercial Jumbo, Porlamar ☎ 0295/265-9392.

TELEPHONES

You can purchase phone cards at many shops and newsstands for local and long-distance calls from public phones. Also, you can make long-distance calls with a credit card at the state-run telephone company CANTV.

🗐 Telephone Office **CANTV** ✉ Blvd. Guevara Porlamar ☎ 0295/264-5059.

VISITOR INFORMATION

Corpotur has offices at the international airport near Porlamar and in Los Robles, between Porlamar and Pampatar.

🗐 Tourist Information **Corpotur** ✉ Aeropuerto Internacional del Caribe, Porlamar ☎ 0295/269-1438 ✉ Centro Artesanal Gilberto Machini, Av. Jóvita Villalba, Los Robles ☎ 0295/262-2322.

MÉRIDA & THE ANDES

As you begin your ascent into the Andes, the changes are swift and unmistakable. Winding your way along the Trans-Andina Highway, you pass stone-strewn fields sprouting wheat and coffee and tile-roof hamlets clinging to hillsides before reaching the *páramo*, the arid region above the timberline. After hitting an altitude of 13,146 feet at Paso Pico El Aguila (Eagle Peak Pass), the highway descends past towns such as Apartaderos, San Rafael de Mucuchíes, and Mucuchíes before reaching the capital city of Mérida.

Mérida

622 km (422 mi) southwest of Caracas.

Mérida is cradled in a valley by the two arms of the Andes, yet this is anything but a sleepy mountain village. This is a city whose spirit is decidedly young, hip, and bohemian. Home of one of Venezuela's largest universities, the Universidad de los Andes, Mérida has all the pleasures of an academic center, including eclectic bookstores, lively coffeehouses, and an arts scene that ranges from refined and traditional to wild and spontaneous.

Founded in 1558, Mérida grew up around the **Plaza Bolívar,** a bustling center that attracts artisans hawking their wares during the day and flocks of young couples in the evening. Facing the main square is the embellished baroque facade of the **Catedral Metropolitana.** Although construction began in 1787, the cathedral wasn't completed until 1958. Its geometric designs make this one of Venezuela's most striking churches.

Dedicated to the artist responsible for the famous stone chapel in nearby San Raphael de Mucuchíes, the **Casa de Cultura Juan Félix Sánchez** (Juan Felix Sánchez Cultural House) hosts exhibitions of paintings and sculptures by regional artists. This lovingly restored colonial house is found on Plaza Bolívar, opposite the cathedral. ✉ *Plaza Bolívar* ☎ *0274/252-6101* 🎟 *Free* 🕙 *Weekdays 8:30–noon and 2:30–6:30, weekends 9–5.*

The **Museo de Arte Colonial** (Colonial Art Museum) houses a rich collection of religious art from the 16th to 19th centuries. ✉ *Av. 4 at Calle*

20 ☎ 0274/252–7860 ✉ Bs5,000 ⊗ Tues.–Fri. 8–noon and 2–6, weekends 8:30–12:30.

The **Museo Arqueológico** (Archaeological Museum) has the region's finest collection of figurines, ceramics, and tools from the pre-Hispanic cultures that once dominated this part of the Andes. ⊠ Av. 3, Edificio Rectorado ☎ 0274/240–2344 ✉ Bs5,000 ⊗ Tues.–Fri. 8–11 and 2–5:30, weekends 1–6.

The **Museo de Arte Moderno** (Modern Art Museum) contains an excellent permanent collection of works by some of Venezuela's most heralded contemporary painters. It faces Parque Reloj de Beethoven (Beethoven's Clock Park), which holds a well-known clock that ushers in the hour with music from the great composer. ⊠ Centro Cultural Tulio Febres Cordero, Av. 2 at Calle 21 ☎ 0274/252–9664 ✉ Free ⊗ Weekdays 9–noon and 3–6, weekends 10–5.

<table>
<tr><td>

need a break?
</td><td>

At least once during your sojourn in Mérida, head to **Heladería Coromoto** (Av. 3 No. 28–75, ☎ 0274/252–3525, open Tues.–Sun. 2–10) for a scoop of ice cream with the flavor of *chicharrón* (fried pork skin). Proprietor Manuel S. da Oliviera holds a proud place in the *Guinness Book of Records* for producing the most flavors (725 and counting). Dare your companions to sample the sausage or smoked trout, and order for yourself a cone topped with rose petal, ginger, or plain old strawberry.
</td></tr>
</table>

FodorsChoice
★

Five blocks east of Plaza Bolívar is Parque Las Heroínas, where you can catch the **Teleférico de Mérida.** Built in 1957 by French engineers, it is the longest and highest cable-car system in the world. In under an hour, the Teleférico ascends in four breathtaking stages to the 15,634-foot Pico Espejo, a mountain peak 892 feet taller than Switzerland's Matterhorn.

The 13-km (8-mi) journey carries you to four stations—Barinitas, La Montaña, La Aguada, and Loma Redonda—before reaching Pico Espejo, where you'll be treated to a great view of Pico Bolívar, Venezuela's highest peak, at 16,428 feet. The first car departs around 7 AM, the last around noon. Head out early in the day to beat the clouds that often obscure the views by late morning. Dress appropriately for the snowy heights, as the temperature change can be quite dramatic, and evaluate carefully your ability to make the trip if you have high blood pressure or a heart condition. The Loma Redonda stop houses a medical station for passengers having trouble with the altitude. Along the way, you'll encounter restaurants, coffee shops, bars, souvenir stores, and an Internet café to let the folks back home know what lofty heights you've reached. Reservations are mandatory during the high season which lasts from Christmas to Easter, and during that time must be procured at least the day prior from the ticket office on Parque Las Heroínas, or via phone or fax. Your reservation will carry a specific departure time, and you're expected to show up an hour in advance to secure your place. The system is much more flexible the rest of the year. ⊠ Parque Las Heroínas ☎ 0274/252–5080 ⊟ 0274/252–9174 ⊕ www.telefericodemerida.com ✉ Baranitas to Loma Redonda Bs18,000;

Loma Redonda to Pico Espejo Bs4,000 ☉ *Dec.–Apr., daily 7–12; May–Nov., Wed.–Sun. 7:30–12.*

off the
beaten
path

LOS NEVADOS – From Lomas Redonda, the second-highest point on the Teleférico, you can hire donkeys, mules, or horses for a descent to Los Nevados, a secluded mountain village that was once a garrison for Spanish conquistadors. Following an initial sharp ascent through a thick forest called the Bosque de los Coloraditos, you'll begin a four- to five-hour ride down a rocky path followed by pre-colonial indigenous peoples. Weary and winded, you finally come upon the red-tile roofs of Los Nevados. There are unpretentious accommodations in local posadas. For the return trip, take a four-wheel-drive vehicle back to Mérida. This route takes you through tiny hamlets, past generations-old farms, colonial ruins, and some of the most spectacular scenery in the Andes.

Where to Stay & Eat

For an inexpensive meal, head to the top floor of the **Mercado Principal de Mérida** on Avenida Las Américas. Six different kitchens surround the common dining area. All serve up heaping portions of *comida típica* (traditional fare) for just a few dollars.

$–$$ ✕ **Miramelindo.** This intimate restaurant is noted for its succulent Basque cuisine. The exquisitely prepared entrées include *pargo a la champaña* (snapper in champagne) and *muslo de pollo al ron* (chicken drumstick in rum). ⊠ *Calle 29 at Av. 4* ☎ *0274/252–9437* 🖃 *AE, V.*

¢–$ ✕ **El Oso Polar.** A quick cab ride from the center of town delivers you to one of Mérida's most popular restaurants. Everything from theater posters to graffiti adorns the walls; the menu is equally varied. Try the *pollo durazno* (chicken with apricot and yogurt sauce) or the spinach and cheese soufflé. ⊠ *Pedregosa Alta at La Gran Parada* ☎ *no phone* 🖃 *No credit cards* ☉ *Closed Mon.*

★ **¢–$** ✕ **Restaurant El Puntal Andino.** This comfortable restaurant, popular with locals, serves up Venezuelan standards, such as *pabellón criollo* (shredded beef, black beans, egg, cheese, rice, and fried bananas). Try the trout, prepared seven different ways. ⊠ *Parque Las Heroínas* ☎ *0274/244–7532* 🖃 *No credit cards.*

★ **$$$** ✕🍽 **Estancia San Francisco.** The cherry-red facade of the main building is your first clue that this hotel is out of the ordinary. At this country inn you can catch trout in a private lagoon and have the chef cook it up for dinner with freshly baked *arepas* (thin biscuits). Little extras like the down pillows and comforters, cushy bathrobes, and cozy fireplaces make this deluxe mountain retreat worth every bolívar. All the two-level suites feature spectacular views of the valley; the more luxurious three-bedroom chalets have their own kitchens. ⊠ *Carretera Via La Culata, 10 km (7 mi) northwest of Mérida* ☎ *0274/244–8838* 🖷 *0274/974–4000* ⊕ *www.estancia.com.ve* ⇌ *20 suites, 12 chalets* ⚘ *Restaurant, fishing, bicycles, horseback riding, bar, recreation room, baby-sitting, laundry service, meeting room, helipad; no a/c* 🖃 *AE, MC, V* 🍽 *MAP.*

$$ 🍽 **El Tisure.** From the window of your room in this colonial-style building you may be able to glimpse the dome of the Catedral Metropolitana. In addition to a superb location in the center of town, El Tisure offers elegant furnishings and a whirlpool bath in every room. ⊠ *Av. 4 Bolívar 17–47* ☎ *0274/252–6072* 🖶 *0274/262–6061* 🖃 *33 rooms* ♨ *Restaurant, cafeteria, health club, hot tub, sauna, spa, bar, laundry service, business services; no a/c* ▤ *AE, MC, V.*

★ $ 🏨 **Hotel Belensate.** Expect to be pampered amid the rolling hills of a former sugarcane plantation. This Mediterranean-style lodging has open-air dining in lush gardens and a gorgeous Romanesque swimming pool. The friendly owners have added a small playground. ⊠ *Urbanización La Hacienda* ☎ *0274/266–2963* 🖶 *0274/266–2823* ⊕ *www. hotelbelensate.com* 🖃 *84 rooms, 7 cabins* ♨ *Restaurant, pool, bar, shops, laundry service, meeting room, travel services; no a/c* ▤ *AE, DC, MC, V.*

¢ 🏨 **Posada Luz Caraballo.** Facing the leafy Plaza Sucre, this homey inn is a great budget option. The simple yet cheerful rooms all have beds piled high with cozy plaid blankets. The lobby lounge features a fireplace for cold nights in the mountains. ⊠ *Av. 2 Lora 13–80* ☎ *0274/252–5441* 🖶 *0274/252–0177* ⊕ *www.andes.net/luzcaraballo* 🖃 *36 rooms* ♨ *Restaurant, laundry service; no a/c* ▤ *No credit cards.*

Nightlife & the Arts

In the towns of the Andes, hotel bars are often the only choice for after-dark excitement. Many host performances by local musicians, particularly on weekends. In Mérida, the enthusiastic crowds of young people at **Birosca Carioca** (⊠ Calle 24 at Av. 2 ☎ no phone) swing into the wee hours with live salsa, reggae, and hip-hop.

Sports & the Outdoors

FISHING Anglers flock to Mérida, where the mountains are liberally sprinkled with small lakes stocked with rainbow and brown trout. In remote reaches, hooking a 15-pound trophy is commonplace. Getting there, however, isn't always easy. Fishing season runs between March 30 and September 30.

HIKING Mérida is the base for three- to seven-day treks into the Andes. Rocky trails trod during the early 19th century by armies struggling for independence from Spain make for good hiking. **Montaña Adventures** (⊠ Av. Las Américas ☎ 0274/266–2867 🖶 0274/266–1448) arranges multiday excursions to El Tisure, the secluded village of Los Nevados, and Paso Pico El Aguila. Another company offering trekking in the region is **Páramo Tours** (⊠ Centro Commercial Oasis, Piso 2, Viaducto Campo Elias, Mérida ☎ 0274/244–8855).

Shopping

The 433 stalls of the **Mercado Principal de Mérida** (⊠ Av. Las Américas at the Viaducto Miranda bridge) offer everything from *flores* (flowers) to *recuerdos* (souvenirs). Begin your morning by sampling traditional Andean *pasteles* (pocketlike pastries) filled with pork, chicken, or beef. You can take home a *cuatro* (traditional four-string guitar) or a hand-loomed blanket from any of the dozens of shops that crowd the top two floors. Excellent handicrafts by local artists are found at **La Calle Mayor** (☎0274/252–7552) on the third floor of the Mercado Principal de Mérida.

Mucuchíes

52 km (30 mi) east of Mérida.

The Trans-Andina Highway brings you to Mucuchíes, founded in 1596 on the site of a pre-colonial village. (You'll spot the prefix *mucu—* meaning "place of" in the indigenous language—at the beginning of the names of many Andean villages. Here it refers to "Place of Cold.") The starkly beautiful landscape—scrub-filled fields and barren hillsides—includes half a dozen pristine lakes. The nearby town of San Rafael de Mucuchíes is the site of the renowned **Capilla de Juan Félix Sánchez,** built by the reclusive, iconoclastic local artist for whom it is named. As he single-handedly built this stone chapel, in honor of the Virgin of Coromoto, Juan Félix came to be greatly loved throughout this region.

Where to Stay & Eat

★ $ ✗▦ **Los Balcones de la Musui.** You reach this colonial-era hacienda, which clings to a mountain ridge, via a steep road that takes you literally into the clouds. When it's clear, which is virtually every morning, the view from each of the cozy rooms is breathtaking. Colorful hammocks slung on the lower-level patio command the same view. A two-hour hike takes you to the Aguas Termales de la Musui, a local hot spring where you'll catch sight of the Humboldt glacier. The restaurant ($–$$) serves food worth going out of your way to sample; don't pass up the trout. ✉ *Carretera Trasandina, near Mucuchíes* ☎ *0414/974–4846* 📠 *0274/ 266–1346* ✎ *balconesmusui@cantv.net* 🛏 *12 rooms, 6 cabins* ⚘ *Restaurant, bar; no a/c* ▤ *MC, V.*

$ ✗▦ **Hotel Carillón.** Resting against the hillside, this hacienda-style hotel is surrounded by gardens overflowing with flowers. Enormous porches with views of the countryside are held up by squat white columns. Enormous suites are luxurious, with inlaid hardwood floors and elegantly carved furniture made on the premises. The sumptuously decorated restaurant ($$$$) serves French cuisine so superb that even Caraqueños think it worth the trip to the Andes. ✉ *Trans-Andina Hwy.* ☎ *0274/ 882–0160* 🛏 *16 rooms* ⚘ *Restaurant, room service, recreation room, meeting room; no a/c* ▤ *AE, D, MC, V.*

¢–$ ▦ **Cabañas Xinia y Peter.** This tranquil refuge near Tabay is run by a Venezuelan-German couple who work hard to make you feel at home. Every detail is perfect, from the fresh flowers on the tables to the thick comforters piled on the beds. The four tile-roof cabins have handcrafted furnishings and fully equipped kitchens, making them perfect for an extended stay. The staff can arrange for horseback, fishing, and hiking tours. The place is popular, so reservations are necessary at both the hotel and the restaurant. ✉ *La Mucuy Baja, Tabay* ☎ *0414/742–1833* 📠 *0274/ 283–0214* ⊕ *www.andes.net/cabanasxiniaypeter* 🛏 *3 cabins* ⚘ *Restaurant, airport shuttle, travel services; no a/c* ▤ *No credit cards* ⏹ *MAP.*

Santo Domingo

86 km (50 mi) east of Mucuchíes.

The road to Santo Domingo passes through the páramo, an eerily beautiful region above the timberline where the most typical vegetation is the *frailejon* (espeletia), a grayish-green plant whose leaves are covered by velvety hairs that protect it from the harsh sunlight penetrating the thin mountain air. Craggy peaks pierce the skies above steely blue lagoons reflecting the flight of soaring condors. Along the way you'll drive through the town of Apartaderos, famous for its delicious cured hams.

About 10 km (6 mi) past Apartaderos, the Trans-Andina Highway leads you to the incredible views from the 14,000-foot **Paso Pico El Aguila** (Eagle Peak Pass), Venezuela's highest roadway. Paso Pico El Aguila marks the spot where Simón Bolívar and his army crossed the Andes in 1813 on their way to fight for independence from the Spanish. Near a statue commemorating this triumphant crossing sits a café serving fresh trout and steaming cups of *calentado* (a regional drink made with liquors and herbs).

Where to Stay & Eat

$ ✕🏨 **La Trucha Azul.** The soothing sounds of rushing water from the small rivers meandering through the grounds make the Blue Trout a special place. Graceful plazas surround the tile-roof buildings containing charming rooms with exposed beams and roaring fireplaces. The elegant restaurant ($–$$) with whitewashed walls and dark-wood furnishings serves excellent local trout. The staff can arrange horseback riding excursions. ✉ *Trans-Andina Hwy., Santo Domingo* 🕿 *0274/898–8066* 🖷 *0274/898–8067* ⊕ *www.latruchaazul.com* ⬦ *56 rooms, 40 villas* ⚿ *Restaurant, café, fishing, horseback riding, bar, dance club, recreation room, playground, travel services; no a/c* ▭ *AE, D, MC, V.*

$$ 🏨 **Los Frailes Inn.** A popular destination for Venezuelan honeymooners, this inn—a converted 17th-century monastery—overflows with colonial charm from the squat bell tower to the fountain gracing the courtyard. Each room is uniquely and exquisitely decorated with rich woods and sumptuous fabrics. The attention to detail is also evident in the intimate dining area and bar. After a full day of fishing or horseback riding in the area, curl up in the reading room on one of the wide, comfortable couches set by the fireplace. ✉ *Trans-Andina Hwy., Santo Domingo* 🕿 *0274/263–773, 800/606–9111 in the U.S.* 🖷 *0212/907–8140, 305/751–3315 in the U.S.* ⬦ *48 rooms* ⚿ *Restaurant, bar, travel services; no a/c* ▭ *AE, D, MC, V.*

Fodor'sChoice ★

Shopping

Roadside stands in the Andes are festooned with tourist-attracting trinkets, most of which come from Ecuador, Peru, and even Guatemala. If you're seeking folk art from Venezuela, visit **La Casa Del Páramo** (✉ San Isidro 29, Apartaderos 🕿 0274/898–0132). Fine wood carvings, pottery, stained glass, and hand-painted clothing—all bearing the signatures of their artists—are attractively displayed in the rooms surrounding a lovely courtyard filled with flowers. The prices are reasonable, to boot.

> **off the beaten path**
>
> **MUCUBAJÍ –** With five beautiful lakes and several waterfalls, this section of Parque Nacional Sierra Nevada is the ideal area in which to get to know the páramo. The well-designed and informative displays at the visitor center introduce you to the flora and fauna of

the region. Travel on foot or horseback along the clearly marked scenic trails to Pico Mucuñuque, which soars to 13,800 ft. While you're enjoying the mountain air, remember that there isn't much of it. Keep your pace slow and take time to smell the frailejones. Mucubají is 2 km (1 mi) from Apartaderos on the road to Barinas.

Jají

35 km (22 mi) west of Mérida.

Tiny Jají bewitches visitors with babbling fountains, colorful gardens, and whitewashed colonial buildings. Founded in the late 16th century, Jají was completely restored in the 1960s in an effort to draw tourists to the region. In the charming central square, local artisans work wonder with clay, wood, fiber, and wool.

Where to Stay

★ $ ⊞ **Hacienda El Carmen.** Nestled in a cloud forest, this century-old coffee hacienda is in itself worth the hour-long drive from Mérida. Fronted by cobblestone patios, the open-air dining room serves delicious grilled meats and, naturally, some of the best coffee around. Adding to its charm, the hacienda is still a working plantation where you can watch coffee beans being picked and then processed by antique machinery. Reservations are required. ⊠ *2 km (1 mi) west of Jají* ☎ *0414/639–2701* ⓐ *0274/263–5852* ⊕ *www.haciendaelcarmen. com* ➩ *17 rooms* ⚹ *Restaurant, hiking, horseback riding, recreation room, meeting room, airport shuttle; no a/c, no room TVs* ⊟ *AE, MC, V* ⵔ *BP.*

¢–$ ⊞ **Posada Papá Miguel.** This beautifully constructed colonial-era house not far from Jají dates from 1750 and has been described as a "marvelous surprise in this quaint mountain village." A local band often plays Andean music. A sugar-processing mill nearby is open to the public. ⊠ *Calle Piñango, Mesa de los Indios* ☎ⓐ *0274/252–2529* ⊕ *www.andes. net/papamiguel* ➩ *14 rooms* ⚹ *Restaurant, horseback riding, meeting room; no a/c* ⊟ *AE, MC, V* ⵔ *MAP.*

Mérida & the Andes A to Z

AIR TRAVEL TO & FROM MÉRIDA & THE ANDES

Mérida's Aeropuerto Alberto Carnevali (MRD), five minutes by taxi from the city center, is served by Aeropostal, Avior, and Santa Barbara with 12 flights daily from Caracas.

🛪 Airlines **Aeropostal** ⊠ Aeropuerto Alberto Carnevali, Mérida ☎ 0274/263–6307. **Avior** ⊠ Centro Comercial Canta Claro, Av. Las Américas ☎ 0274/244–2563. **Santa Barbara** ⊠ Aeropuerto Alberto Carnevali, Mérida ☎ 0274/262–0381.

🛪 Airports **Aeropuerto Alberto Carnevali** ☎ 0274/263–9330.

BUS TRAVEL TO & FROM MÉRIDA & THE ANDES

There are morning and evening departures from Terminal de Occidente in Caracas to Terminal Antonio Paredes in Mérida. The grueling 10- to 13-hour trip costs less than Bs40,000. Purchase your ticket at least a day in advance at the station. Expreso Alianza and Expreso Mérida are two reputable companies that service the route.

🚌 Bus Companies **Expreso Alianza** ✉ Terminal Antonio Paredes ☎ 0212/541-1975. **Expreso Mérida** ✉ Terminal Antonio Paredes ☎ 0212/541-1975. 🚌 Bus Terminals **Terminal Antonio Paredes** ✉ Av. Las Américas ☎ 0274/266-1193.

BUS TRAVEL WITHIN MÉRIDA & THE ANDES

Buses from Mérida's Terminal Antonio Paredes head to all the smaller mountain towns along the Trans-Andina Highway, including Jají, Apartaderos, and Mucuchíes.

CAR RENTAL

Budget and Davila are reputable agencies at Mérida's Aeropuerto Alberto Carnevali. With either agency, expect to pay close to Bs160,000 per day for the smallest car.

🚗 Local Agencies **Budget** ☎ 0274/263-1758. **Davila** ☎ 0274/263-4510.

CAR TRAVEL

The Trans-Andina Highway is one of the most scenic routes in the country, with wonderful towns along the way where you'll be tempted to stop. The spectacular 12-hour journey from Caracas begins on Highway 51 west to Valencia. From here, follow the road to Barinas, where the ascent of the Andes begins.

CONSULATES

The United Kingdom maintains an honorary consulate in Mérida.

🏛 Consulates **United Kingdom** ✉ Edificio Don Chabelo, Urbanización Humboldt, Mérida ☎ 0274/266-2022.

MONEY MATTERS

Italcambio, the largest of the *casas de cambio* (exchange houses), is permitted to exchange cash dollars and American Express traveler's checks denominated in dollars for bolívares, but not vice-versa. (Most banks will not exchange currency, and none will accept traveler's checks.)

You can use your ATM card in some machines to obtain bolívares, but it is impossible to obtain dollars here. Gauge your cash spending needs accordingly to avoid being stuck at the end of your trip with local currency that is impossible to change back. The black market is prevalent, but engaging in transactions carries stiff penalties and is dangerous.

🏦 Banks **Banco Unión** ✉ Av. Bolívar and Calle 4, Mérida ☎ 0274/252-7218. 🏦 Italcambio Exchange House **Italcambio** ✉ Aeropuerto Internacional Alberto Carnevalli, Mérida ☎ 0274/263-2977.

SAFETY

The center of Mérida is relatively safe during the evening, but as in any tourist destination, be aware of your surroundings and avoid unnecessary displays of wealth. Being a university town, the city sees its share of political demonstrations. Avoid such scenes.

TELEPHONES

You can purchase phone cards at many shops and newsstands for local and long-distance calls from public phones. Also, you can make long-distance calls with a credit card at the state-run telephone company CANTV.

🛈 Telephone Office **CANTV** ✉ Av. 7, Calle 25–26, Mérida ☎ 0274/251–0666.

TOUR OPERATORS

Travel through this Andean region can be arranged according to your own desires and interests through the U.S.-based Lost World Adventures or through its partner in Mérida, Montaña Adventures. Another reputable Mérida-based company is Natoura Adventure Tours.

🛈 Tour Companies **Lost World Adventures** ✉ 220 Second Ave., Decatur, GA 30030, ☎ 404/373–5820 or 800/999–0558 🖷 404/377–1902 ⊕ www.lostworldadventures.com. **Montaña Adventures** ✉ Av. Las Américas, Edificio Las Américas, Mérida ☎ 0274/266–2867 🖷 0274/266–1448. **Natoura Adventure Tours** ✉ Calle 24, Mérida ☎ 0274/252–4216.

VISITOR INFORMATION

There is a state tourism office, Cormetur, near the airport in Mérida. Some staff members speak English. The Institute of National Parks, Inparques also has an office in Mérida that can assist you with camping permits.

🛈 Tourist Information **Cormetur** ✉ Av. Urdaneta at Calle 45, Mérida ☎ 0274/263–0814 ⊕ www.merida.com.ve. **Inparques** ✉ Calle 19, between Av. 5 and 6, Mérida ☎ 0274/252–9876.

ELSEWHERE IN VENEZUELA

Los Llanos

Known as the "Serengeti of South America," Los Llanos is an alluring destination for anyone interested in wildlife. Covering nearly a third of Venezuela's total area, the sprawling grasslands of Los Llanos are just a short flight away from Caracas—through San Fernando de Apure or Barinas—but they feel a world away from the bustling capital. The air sings with birdcalls instead of car horns, and the unpaved roads are more likely to carry iguanas searching for a sunny spot than commuters looking for a parking space.

Los Llanos (literally "The Plains") has two distinct seasons, each offering opportunities to see a wide variety of animals and birds. From May to November, the plains are inundated with water and crisscrossed by powerful rivers, forcing land animals to scramble for higher ground as the rains unleash their fury. Flooding submerges the smaller roads, making it a bit more difficult to get around. This is the best time, however, to observe the large river otters, and to see clusters of capybaras and troops of howler monkeys gather in small patches of gallery forest. This is also the time when Los Llanos cools off; daytime temperatures hover above 90°F, but the evenings are comfortably mild.

With the end of the rainy season in December, the landscape begins a dramatic transformation. Standing water quickly evaporates in the heat of the tropical sun, revealing the bright greens, yellows, and golds of the grasses. By the end of the dry season in April, the mighty rivers have

CloseUp

THE "SERENGETI OF SOUTH AMERICA"

THE FIRST ANIMALS YOU'LL NOTICE are the scary ones. In Los Llanos, the vast grasslands that make up nearly a third of Venezuela, roadside pools teem with crocodiles—both the endangered Orinoco caiman and the more common (and larger) spectacled caiman, which locals call "babas." Anacondas, some more than 20 ft long, slither across your path. If you're lucky you'll spot an elusive puma—and if you're really lucky, it'll be far away.

But there's much more to see in Los Llanos, often called the "Serengeti of South America." Bird lovers will delight in spotting dozens of species—majestic hawks to diminutive burrowing owls, well-camouflaged herons to brightly colored tanagers. Spoonbills and storks, flycatchers and kingfishers, parrotlets and cormorants abound in this isolated region, and since the landscape is perfectly flat and sparsely wooded, they're all easy to see. The most spectacular of these is the scarlet ibis; when hundreds of them return home to roost at sunset, they cluster so closely together that they seem to turn entire trees bright red.

During the dry season you can catch sight of giant anteaters lumbering across plains punctuated by knee-high termite mounds. The rainy season finds the tree branches filled with sun-worshiping iguanas that occasionally lose their grip and tumble into the waters below. The splash attracts the attention of nearby crocodiles. No matter what time of year you visit you'll see hundreds of capybaras, furry brown mammals that are equally comfortable on land or in water. Weighing more than 100 pounds when fully grown, they're the world's largest rodents—but unlike their cousins they're completely adorable. Think of them as a bizarre cross between guinea pigs and hippos and you'll get a sense for how they move, either sniffing around for

food with their wide snouts or dog-paddling across a pond in single file.

A guided excursion is the best—and safest—way to observe wildlife in this remote region. A naturalist at one of the many lodges will take you out in a jeep or a converted pick-up truck, driving along dirt roads and across patches of parched earth to get as close to animals as possible. At first you'll need help spotting the yellow eyes of the crocodiles lurking beneath the water's surface or hearing the distinctive cry of the howler monkeys feeding in the trees. But once you get the hang of it, you'll find you can see an amazing variety of animals at close range, without binoculars. Often you can get out of the jeep and walk right among them.

But boating down the Río Apure, or one of the mighty river's tributaries, is the only way to see what the rest of Los Llanos has to offer. Freshwater dolphins will jump and play around your boat as you drift downstream watching the egrets build their nests in the branches above the water. You might want to stop on a sandbar to do some fishing—for piranha. Catching these hungry little creatures is a fast-paced sport. Baiting a hook with chunks of raw meat, you toss a line (no rods are necessary) into the deceptively calm water. Schools of piranha gather immediately, leaping out of the water in a frenzy to grab the bait with their jagged teeth. The trick here is to yank on the line before the bait disappears, which can happen in seconds. With some practice, you'll be able to catch enough of the salad-plate-size fish for dinner. Just brace yourself for the boat ride back to your lodge; the river won't seem so tranquil now that you know the water is infested with these little carnivores.

–Wayne Hoffman

become trickles, and only a few pools remain. Temperatures soar to over 110°F during the day, but it's worth enduring the heat, as the dry season is the best time to view wildlife. Four-wheel-drive vehicles can head in almost any direction across the parched landscape, bringing you to where the animals have gathered around the few remaining pools of water.

Spanish settlers established the first cattle ranches in Los Llanos in 1548, and within 200 years the expansive ranches, known as hatos, had spread across the region. Today, amid the more exotic wildlife, thousands of cows still roam the range, driven by cowboys known as llaneros. The best way to see Los Llanos is to stay at one of the half dozen hatos set up to accommodate guests. Sometimes you can eat dinner with the llaneros in the dining hall or head out with them for a cerveza in one of the little towns that dot the region.

Although sparsely populated, Los Llanos is considered by many to be the cultural heart of Venezuela. It's no coincidence that the traditional music of Venezuela—called *joropo*—was born in Los Llanos. Locals still gather after dark to listen to these lilting folk songs, sung over the sounds of maracas, harps, and miniature guitars called cuatros. In outdoor bars with dirt floors, couples dance while joropo bands alternate rousing tunes that celebrate the bravery of the llaneros with ballads that recount the difficult lives these cowboys must endure.

Where to Stay & Eat

$$$$ ✕▥ **Estación Biológica El Frío.** Besides being a working ranch, this place also functions as a biological research center. So in addition to the wildlife that exists across the region, Hato El Frio also houses animals that are the subject of conservation efforts and biological studies, from tortoises to pumas. Want to see a caiman up close? Accompany one of the biologists in residence when they head out for the daily feeding. You may even get a chance to hold one of the crocodile hatchlings. These knowledgeable—and English-speaking—scientists take you on twice-daily excursions in trucks or boats, answering any questions about the varied flora and fauna. There's also ample opportunity to mingle with the llaneros, whose quarters are a short distance away. The cowboys and researchers work closely together, frequently coming together for an outdoor barbecue or a night out in the local village. They won't mind if you tag along.

Facilities are basic but comfortable. Fans and a cool breeze make it comfortable enough for sleeping, even in the summer. There is no hot water, but even the "cold" water in these sun-drenched grasslands is warm enough for bathing. The dining hall doubles as a lounge, and there is a small library, a few board games, and a television with a slew of videos for passing the time on rainy mornings or quiet nights. Meals are hearty and always fresh, as the ranch produces its own eggs, meats, and dairy products. You can bet that the fruit that made your juice was still on the tree that morning.

Trips to Hato El Frio must be arranged through a travel agent such as the Caracas-based Orinoco Tours. The tour company can also arrange for a car to transfer you from the airport in the town of San Fernando de Apure, two hours away. ⊠ *145 km (90 mi) west of San Fernando de Apure* ☎ *0414/743–5329 or 0212/761–7712* 🖷 *0247/882–1228* ⊕ *www.orinocotours.com* ⊕ *www.elfrioeb.com* 🛏 *10 rooms* ♻ *Dining room, fans, airport shuttle; no a/c, no room phones, no room TVs* ❙⊘❙ *All-inclusive.*

Parque Nacional Canaima

Here, in Venezuela's remote southeast, is a surreal landscape of pink beaches and black lagoons, where giant waterfalls plunge from the summits of prehistoric table-top mountains called *tepuis,* formations that harbor some of the most unusual life on earth. A trip to Venezuela is not complete without a visit to these mist-enshrouded plateaus that inspired Sir Arthur Conan Doyle's *The Lost World.*

This unique region is protected by Parque Nacional Canaima, which covers an area the size of Belgium. Most of the park is extremely remote, so the only way to see it is by boat or plane. Most people head to Canaima to see **Angel Falls,** the world's tallest waterfall. This spectacular torrent of water plummets 2,647 feet—more than twice the height of the Empire State Building, and 15 times higher than Niagara Falls—from atop the giant Auyantepuy mesa. Indigenous people knew the falls as "Kerapa kupai merú," (the fall to the deepest place.) But this natural phenomenon acquired its English-language moniker after its sighting by barnstorming U.S. pilot Jimmy Angel, who crash-landed on Auyantepuy's vast surface in 1937 while in search of gold. Angel, his wife, and two companions spent 11 days descending on foot from the tepui back to civilization and told the world of his "discovery." Angel's ashes were scattered over the falls after his 1956 death. His plane was retrieved from the top of the summit in 1970 and placed on exhibit in the nearby town of Maracay.

The eastern half of Parque Nacional Canaima is crossed by a road, and this region is referred to as the Gran Sabana. Three- to four-day excursions to the Gran Sabana are made in four-wheel-drive vehicles and will carry you to waterfalls, indigenous villages, and vantage points that provide breathtaking views of the tepuis. These round-trip excursions generally begin in Ciudad Bolívar or Ciudad Guayana, working slowly south toward Santa Elena de Uairén. The especially adventurous can hire a Pemón guide and scale a large tepui called Roraima, an undertaking that requires a minimum of five days. At the top, you find yourself in an unearthly lunarlike landscape.

Where to Stay & Eat

$$$$ ✕▦ **Arekuna.** This self-contained luxury camp is on the bank of the Río Caroni, just outside the boundaries of Parque Nacional Canaima. After a full day of land and water excursions, enjoy a glorious sunset from the hilltop dining area before retiring to a stylish cabaña, where attention to detail is evident in the hand-painted sinks and the curious figures carved into the walls. All of the building materials are produced locally and the entire camp is powered by solar energy. Most importantly, the hotel is staffed by extremely personable, multilingual guides who create a fun, informative atmosphere. Packages for this 90-person facility, including round-trip airfare, lodging, meals, and guided excursions, start at $375 per couple, and are arranged through charter airline Aerotuy. ✉ *Parque Nacional Canaima* ☎ *0212/761–6247 or 0212/761–6231* 🖷 *0212/762– 5254* ⊕ *www.tuy.com* ⚓ *30 rooms* ⚐ *Dining room, bar, laundry service; no a/c, no room phones, no room TVs* ◎ *All-inclusive.*

Amazonas

Venezuela's largest region is Amazonas, an ironic name given that virtually the entire area lies within the watershed of the mighty Río Orinoco and not the Amazon. Amazonas contains two gargantuan national parks that together cover an area of almost 48,000 square km (30,000 square mi), feature varied flora and fauna, and comprise the homeland of many native peoples, most notably the Yanomami. Tourist facilities in this vast area are limited to a small number of lodges that are connected to the outside world through the region's only sizable town, Puerto Ayacucho.

Where to Stay & Eat

$$$$ ✕🛏 **Yutajé Camp.** This camp in the Manapiare Valley, just east of Puerto Ayacucho, appeals to families who prefer the comfort of real beds, private baths, and sit-down meals. Built and run year-round by José Raggi, the camp has a 5,000-foot airstrip and accommodations for about 30. During the day you trek through the jungle in search of howler monkeys, or float down a river to view spectacular waterfalls. A two-night package from Caracas, including air and meals, runs about $450 per person. *Reservations* ✉ *Alpi Tours, Av. Sucre, Centro Parque Boyacá, Torre Centro, Piso 1, Oficina 2, Caracas,* ☎ *0212/283–1433* 🖷 *0582/285–6067* ⚐ *Dining room; no a/c, no room phones, no room TVs* ◎ *All-inclusive.*

Elsewhere in Venezuela A to Z

AIR TRAVEL

To reach Los Llanos, take one of the daily flights from Caracas to San Fernando de Apure, Barinas, and Guanare. Aereotuy flies regularly between Caracas and Canaima and Ciudad Bolívar. To reach Amazonas, you can fly daily from Caracas to Puerto Ayacucho, the region's only tourist hub. Aereotuy connects Ciudad Bolívar with Puerto Ayacucho once weekly.

🛪 Airlines **Aerotuy** ✉ Edificio Gran Sabana, Blvd. de Sabana Grande Sabana Grande Caracas ☎ 0212/761–6231.

BUS TRAVEL

Cities such as Barinas and San Fernando de Apure in Los Llanos are accessible by bus from Caracas and other major cities. Amazonas is not as accessible by bus. You can get to Puerto Ayacucho from Caracas via San Fernando de Apure, but it's at least a 16-hour trip. Most visitors fly into the region instead. There is no bus service at all to Canaima.

MONEY MATTERS

Italcambio, the largest of the *casas de cambio* (exchange houses), is permitted to exchange cash dollars and American Express traveler's checks denominated in dollars for bolívares, but not vice-versa. (Most banks will not exchange currency, and none will accept traveler's checks.)

You can use your ATM card in some machines to obtain bolívares, but it is impossible to obtain dollars here. Gauge your cash spending needs accordingly to avoid being stuck at the end of your trip with local currency that is impossible to change back. The black market is prevalent, but engaging in transactions carries stiff penalties and is dangerous. Take care of cash matters before arriving in these remote regions.

TELEPHONES
Communication with the outside world at the remote lodges is via cell phone or radio.

TOUR OPERATORS
The savvy staff of Lost World Adventures specializes in tailoring an independent travel itinerary around your interests. The founder of this U.S.-based company once lived in Venezuela, so he knows his way around. The company specializes in small-group expeditions throughout Venezuela and other South American countries.

A reputable tour operator in Caracas is Orinoco Tours, centrally located on Bulevar de Sabana Grande. The company specializes in ecotourism in Venezuela, including the Amazonas, Llanos, and Parque Nacional Canaima. Also in Caracas, Alpi Tour specializes in adventure tourism to the Amazonas and other regions.

🚩 Tour Companies **Alpi Tour** ✉ Av. Sucre, Centro Parque Boyacá, Piso 1, Oficina 2, Caracas ☎ 0212/284-1433 ⊕ www.alpi-group.com. **Lost World Adventures** ✉ 220 Second Ave., Decatur, GA 30030 ☎ 404/373-5820 or 800/999-0558 🖷 404/377-1902 ⊕ www.lostworldadventures.com. **Orinoco Tours** ✉ Edificio Galerías Bolívar, Bulevar de Sabana Grande ☎ 0212/761-7712 🖷 0212/761-6801 ⊕ www.orinocotours.com.

VENEZUELA A TO Z

To research prices, get advice from other travelers, and book travel arrangements, visit www.fodors.com.

AIR TRAVEL
Major U.S. carriers serving Venezuela include American, Continental, and Delta. Venezuela's Aeropostal flies to Caracas from Miami. Air France, British Airways, Spain's Iberia, the Netherlands' KLM, and Germany's Lufthansa jet in from their respective hubs in Europe. Most fly into Aeropuerto Internacional Simón Bolívar, located about 25 km (16 mi) from downtown Caracas in the coastal area of Maiquetía. A few scheduled flights and many charters fly directly to the Caribbean island of Isla Margarita.

A number of regional airlines provide regular service throughout Venezuela. Among them are Aeropostal, Aereotuy, Avior, and Santa Barbara. Bad weather or periodic disruptions in fuel flow can cause flight cancellations. Allow some flexibility in your itinerary, and do not plan out-country air travel for the very end of your stay in Venezuela.

🚩 Airlines in Venezuela **Aereotuy** ✉ Av. Abraham Lincoln, Bulevar de Sabana Grande 174, Edificio Gran Sabana, Piso 5, Caracas ☎ 0212/761-6247, 0212/761-6231, or 0212/761-

8043. **Avior** ✉ Aeropuerto Nacional Simón Bolívar ☎ 0231/202–5811. **Santa Barbara** ✉ Calle 3B, Edificio Tokay, Piso 2, La Urbina, Caracas ☎ 800/865–2636.

BUSINESS HOURS

BANKS & OFFICES Banks are open weekdays 8:30–3:30. Watch for special bank holidays—which are numerous—when all branches are closed.

MUSEUMS & SIGHTS Most museums are open from Tuesday through Sunday, 9–noon and 2–5.

SHOPS Stores are open weekdays 9–1 and 3–7; on Saturday, they tend to stay open from 9 to 7. On Sunday, most shops are closed.

BUS TRAVEL TO & FROM VENEZUELA

Buses connect the Brazilian town of Manaus to the Venezuelan town of Santa Elena de Uairén, a trip that takes six hours and costs Bs24,000.

BUS TRAVEL WITHIN VENEZUELA

Almost all of Venezuela can be traversed by bus, the least expensive and often most agreeable way to see the country. Your best bet is using the private carriers, usually referred to as *rápidos* (express buses). Private companies typically accept reservations and offer comforts such as assigned seats, air-conditioning, toilets, and on-board attendants.

CAR TRAVEL

Although the Venezuelan highway system is still a work in progress, more than 80% of the country's roads are paved. Driving can get you places you wouldn't otherwise get to see. However, Venezuelans often drive as if the traffic rules are merely suggestions. It's important to drive defensively. Avoid using your car at night, when poorly lit roadways and erratic drivers make things especially dangerous.

EMERGENCY ASSISTANCE The major rental agencies will tow your car in an emergency. Towing services can be found under *grúas* in the telephone book.

GASOLINE Oil-rich Venezuela has among the world's cheapest gas prices. A liter of leaded gas (*plomo*) cost Bs70, but cast a vote for the environment and opt for unleaded (*sin plomo*) instead, still inexpensive at Bs90, but still a novelty outside the big cities. The national oil company, Petroleos de Venezuela (PDV), operates 24-hour stations on major highways. Shell, Texaco, and others also have stations.

PARKING Theft of a car's contents, as well as the car itself, is a major problem in Venezuela, especially in Caracas and other major urban centers. Never leave anything of value in your car and park in enclosed or guarded lots when possible.

CUSTOMS & DUTIES

Persons entering Venezuela may bring in duty-free up to 400 cigarettes and 50 cigars, 2 liters of liquor, and new goods such as video cameras and electronics up to $1,500 in value if declared and accompanied by receipts. Plants, fresh fruit, dairy products, and pork are prohibited.

ELECTRICITY

Venezuela operates on a 110 volt, 60-cycle system, with a single-phase AC current.

FESTIVALS

During February's Carnaval the entire country goes on a Mardi Gras–like binge; in Caracas, nearly everyone vacates the city and heads for the beach. Also in February, Mérida celebrates its Feria del Sol (Festival of the Sun) with bullfights and open-air salsa and merengue performances. In mid-March Paraguachí on Isla Margarita celebrates the Feria de San José. In the week before Easter, the country celebrates Semana Santa (Holy Week). El Hatillo hosts an annual music festival in late October or early November with classical and pop performances. On September 24, Jají celebrates the Feast of St. Michael the Archangel with music, dance, and much fanfare.

HEALTH

In Caracas and other large cities, food in reputable hotels and restaurants should be safe. A sudden change of diet, however, can result in an upset stomach, which is often misinterpreted as a form of food poisoning. Avoid raw fruits and vegetables, uncooked fish, and tap water. Bottled water is readily available throughout the country, as are good beer and a wide variety of safe soft drinks.

Pharmacies in different neighborhoods take turns staying open all night; you can spot them by the sign *turno*, or consult local newspapers for lists of open *farmacias* (pharmacies).

HOLIDAYS

New Year's Day; Holy Thursday and Good Friday (April 8–9 in 2004; March 24–25 in 2005; April 13–14 in 2006); Proclamation of Independence Day (April 19); Labor Day (May 1); Battle of Carabobo (June 24); Independence Day (July 5); Simón Bolívar's birthday (July 24); Columbus Day (October 12); Christmas Eve and Day.

LANGUAGE

Spanish is the official language of Venezuela, but many words in common usage are unique to the country, especially regarding foods. For instance, Venezuelans call a banana a *cambur*; a watermelon a *patia*; a papaya a *lechosa*; and a passion fruit a *parchita*.

MAIL & SHIPPING

The state-owned postal service, Ipostel, is slow and not very reliable—it can take up to a month for a letter to arrive in the United States or Europe. It costs Bs400 to send a letter domestically and Bs1,500 internationally.

MONEY MATTERS

In hopes of stemming the flight of dollars from Venezuela during the 2003 emergency, the government implemented rigid currency controls, which had been relaxed slightly at this writing. The exchange rate of the Venezuelan currency, the bolívar, is fixed at 1,600 to the U.S. dollar. Italcambio, the largest of the *casas de cambio* (exchange houses), is permitted to exchange cash dollars and American Express traveler's checks denominated in dollars for bolívares, but not vice-versa. (Most banks will not exchange currency, and none will accept traveler's checks.)

ATMS You can use your ATM card in some machines to obtain bolívares, but it is impossible to obtain dollars here. Gauge your cash spending needs accordingly to avoid being stuck at the end of your trip with local currency that is impossible to change back. The black market is prevalent, but engaging in transactions carries stiff penalties and is dangerous.

BLACK MARKET Given Venezuela's currency restrictions at press time, there will be no shortage of dealers approaching you quietly about changing money in public places, but the so-called *mercado negro* is officially illegal and a dangerous risk for robbery.

CREDIT CARDS In major cities, credit cards are generally accepted at upscale hotels, restaurants, and some shops, with Visa and Master Card being the most widely used. Many businesses accept American Express as well, but Diner's Club is a distant fourth. However, carrying cash is advisable when traveling in more remote areas.

CURRENCY The bolívar is the official unit of currency. Bolívars (Bs) come in bills of 500, 1,000, 2,000, 5,000, and 10,000. Coins come in 10-, 20-, 50-, 100-, and 500-bolívar denominations. At press time, the exchange rate was a fixed, government-regulated Bs1,600 to the U.S. dollar.

WHAT IT WILL COST Venezuela is a relatively inexpensive country in which to travel, although the prices are greatly inflated in Caracas and on Isla Margarita. The best hotels cost up to $250 per double, while budget lodgings go for as low as $25. Going to the theater can cost from Bs8,000 to Bs80,000 for special shows or featured artists. Movies are still a bargain at Bs5,000. Nightlife ranges greatly in price; some of the best clubs charge upward of Bs8,000 for a cocktail.

Sample Prices: Cup of coffee, Bs1,000–Bs2,000; bottle of beer, Bs3,000; soft drink, Bs1,000-Bs2,000; bottle of wine, Bs6,000 (at a liquor store); sandwich, Bs3,000–Bs8,000; crosstown taxi ride, Bs5,000; city bus ride, Bs400; museum entrance, Bs2,000, though the majority of museums in the country are free.

PASSPORTS & VISAS
Australian, British, Canadian, New Zealand, and United States citizens who fly to Venezuela are issued 90-day tourist cards, free of charge, immediately upon arrival with presentation of a passport that has at least six months' remaining validity. Keep the flimsy second copy of the tourist card you receive when you arrive; you'll need it to leave the country. Procure a visa in advance from a Venezuelan embassy abroad if you plan to arrive overland. Most land immigration posts charge $3 to $5 for a tourist card.

SAFETY
Crime, both petty and violent, is prevalent in Caracas, but much less so in other parts of Venezuela. Use common sense wherever you travel.

Always be aware of your surroundings and avoid unnecessary displays of wealth.

Political demonstrations are common in Caracas, as well as in Mérida with its large student population, and there's always the potential for such gatherings to turn violent. It is illegal for foreigners to engage in anything deemed "political activity." **Steer clear of such scenes.**

TAXES
At hotels, foreigners must pay a 10% tourist tax. You will find it added to your bill.

DEPARTURE TAX The airport departure tax for international flights leaving Venezuela is $36 or the bolívar equivalent.

SALES TAX Venezuela has a non-refundable 16.5% sales tax, known as the IVA, which is added to the price of all articles except basic foodstuffs and medicine.

TELEPHONES
All telephone numbers have seven digits. Area codes begin with a "0" followed by a three-digit number, the first of which is a 2. Use the zero only for long-distance calls from other parts of Venezuela, not for calls from other countries. An "0414" code designates a mobile phone number.

To call a Venezuelan number from another country, dial the international access code, the country code of 58, and then the area code. Be prepared for frequent busy signals.

LOCAL CALLS A three-minute local call costs Bs400. Public pay phones accept phone cards, available in denominations of 2,000, 3,000, and 5,000 bolívars at kiosks and newsstands marked TARJETA INTELLIGENTE (smart card). To speak with a local directory assistance operator, dial 113.

LONG-DISTANCE & INTERNATIONAL CALLS International calls are extremely expensive: The average international rate per minute is $3.50 to the United States and $10 to Europe. Hotels typically add as much as 40% to the rate, so avoid calling from your room. Call from a CANTV office or use a public phone.

You can reach an English-speaking long-distance operator by dialing 122. To use a calling card or credit card, or to place a collect call, use the various international access numbers from your home country.

🛈 Access Codes **AT&T** ☏ 800/11-120. **Australia Direct** ☏ 800/11-610. **British Telecom** ☏ 800/11-440. **Canada Direct** ☏ 800/11-100. **MCI** ☏ 800/11-140. **New Zealand Direct** ☏ 800/11-640. **Sprint** ☏ 800/11-110.

TIPPING
Restaurants usually add 10% to the bill for service, but you are expected to tip an additional 10%. Tipping hotel porters, hair stylists, and guides up to 10% is customary. Taxi drivers do not expect a tip unless they carry suitcases.

VISITOR INFORMATION
One good source of Venezuela travel information is the U.S.-based Venezuelan Tourism Association.

🛈 Tourist Information **Venezuelan Tourism Association** ✍ Box 3010, Sausalito, CA 94966 ☎ 415/331-0100 🖷 415/332-9197.

WHEN TO GO
The most popular time to visit is between December and April, during Venezuela's dry season. During holidays an influx of tourists pushes prices higher and makes it more difficult to find accommodations. During the rainy season from May to October—when there is still plenty of good weather—crowds are rare and hotel prices drop significantly.

CLIMATE Caracas and much of Venezuela boast a year-round mild climate, temperatures ranging between 65°F and 75°F during the day and rarely dropping below 55°F at night. Expect it to be somewhat chillier in the higher altitudes of the Andes, so bring a sweater. Some coastal areas are hotter and more humid, but you can usually depend on a cool breeze blowing in off the ocean.

The following are the daily maximum and minimum temperatures for Caracas.

Jan.	79F	26C	**May**	81F	27C	**Sept.**	82F	28C
	60	16		66	19		64	18
Feb.	80F	27C	**June**	80F	27C	**Oct.**	81F	27C
	62	17		65	18		64	18
Mar.	81F	27C	**July**	80F	27C	**Nov.**	82F	28C
	62	17		65	18		62	17
Apr.	80F	27C	**Aug.**	84F	29C	**Dec.**	80F	27C
	64	18		65	18		61	16

ADVENTURE & LEARNING VACATIONS

11

Whether it's an active vacation you're craving or the chance to be immersed in some of Earth's most splendid natural environs, South America has it all. Explore the Amazon by riverboat or from a jungle lodge; trek, ski, or climb the Andes; raft some of the world's most challenging rivers or kayak over peaceful lakes; fish for peacock bass or saber-toothed payara; take part in a research project in a national park or an indigenous village; investigate the remains of ancient cultures, or join a bird-watching or photo safari.

Updated by
Joyce Dalton

THESE DAYS, MORE TRAVELERS THAN EVER are seeking trips with an active or adventure component, and tour operators are responding with an ever-increasing selection of exciting itineraries. Choosing a tour package carefully is always important, but it becomes even more critical when the focus is adventure or sports. You can rough it or opt for comfortable, sometimes even luxurious, accommodations. You can select easy hiking and canoeing adventures or trekking, rafting, and climbing expeditions that require high degrees of physical endurance and technical skill. Study multiple itineraries to find the trip that's right for you. Below are selected trip offerings from some of the best adventure tour operators in today's travel world. Wisely chosen, special-interest vacations lead to distinctive, memorable experiences—just pack your curiosity along with the bug spray.

For additional information about a specific destination, contact the country's tourist office (often attached to the embassy) or the **South American Explorers Club** (⌧ 126 Indian Creek Rd., Ithaca, NY 14850 ☎ 607/277–0488 or 800/274–0568 ☎ 607/277–6122 ⊕ www.saexplorers. org). This company is a good source for current information regarding travel throughout the continent. The Explorers Club also has offices in Quito, Lima, and Cuzco.

Choosing a Trip

With hundreds of choices for special-interest trips to South America, there are a number of factors to keep in mind when deciding which company and package will be right for you.

- **How strenuous a trip do you want?** Adventure vacations commonly are split into "soft" and "hard" adventures. Hard adventures, such as strenuous treks (often at high altitudes), Class IV or V rafting, or ascents of some of the world's most challenging mountains, generally require excellent physical conditioning and previous experience. Most hiking, biking, canoeing/kayaking, and similar soft adventures can be enjoyed by persons of all ages who are in good health and are accustomed to a reasonable amount of exercise. A little honesty goes a long way—recognize your own level of physical fitness and discuss it with the tour operator before signing on.

- **How far off the beaten path do you want to go?** Although many trips described in this chapter might seem to be headed into uncharted territory, tour operators carefully check each detail before an itinerary goes into a brochure. While you won't be vying with busloads of tourists for photo ops, you'll probably run into occasional small groups of like-minded travelers. Journeys into truly remote regions typically involve camping or the simplest of accommodations, but they reward with more abundant wildlife and locals who are less accustomed to the clicking of cameras. Ask yourself if it's the reality or the image of roughing it that appeals to you. Stick with the reality.

- **Is sensitivity to the environment important to you?** If so, then determine if it is equally important to the tour operator. Does the company protect the fragile environments you'll be visiting? Are some of the company's profits designated for conservation efforts or put back into the communities visited? Does it encourage indigenous people to dress up (or dress down) so that your group can get great photos, or does it respect their cultures as they are? On ecotourism programs, check out the naturalist's credentials. A string of degrees can be less important than familiarity with the area.

- **What sort of group is best for you?** At its best, group travel offers curious, like-minded people with whom to share the day's experiences. Do you enjoy a mix of companions or would you prefer similar demographics—for example, age-specific, singles, same sex? Inquire about the group size and the qualifications of accompanying guides. If groups aren't your thing, most companies will customize a trip just for you. Responding to a renewed interest in multigenerational travel, many tour operators offer designated family departures, with itineraries carefully crafted to appeal both to children and adults.

- **The client consideration factor—strong or absent?** Gorgeous photos and well-written tour descriptions go a long way in selling a company's trips. But the "client consideration factor" is important, too. Does the operator provide useful information about health (suggested or required inoculations, tips for dealing with high altitudes)? A list of frequently asked questions and their answers? Tips for photography under destination-specific conditions? Recommended readings? Equipment needed for sports trips? Packing tips when baggage is restricted? Climate info? Visa requirements? A list of client referrals? The option of using your credit card?

- **Are there hidden costs?** Make sure you know what is and isn't included in basic trip costs when comparing companies. International airfare is usually extra. Sometimes, flights within the country you are visiting are additional. Is trip insurance included? How much does it cost and what situations are covered? Are airport transfers included? Visa fees? Departure taxes? All excursions? Gratuities? Equipment? Meals? Bottled water? Many factors affect the price, and the trip that looks cheapest in the brochure could well turn out to be the most expensive. Don't assume that roughing it will save you money, as prices rise when limited access and a lack of essential supplies on-site require costly special arrangements.

Tour Operators

Below is contact information for all tour operators mentioned in this chapter. For international tour operators, we list both the tour operator and their North American representative, so you can contact whichever company is easier for you. For example, Exodus is represented in North America by G.A.P. Adventures, and Sherpa Expeditions is represented by Himalayan Travel. While the list below hardly exhausts the number of reputable companies, these were chosen because they are established firms that offer a good selection of itineraries. Such operators are usually the first to introduce great new destinations, forging ahead before luxury hotels and air-conditioned coaches tempt less hardy visitors.

Only the most adventurous companies have discovered the numerous attractions, particularly in the realm of ecotourism, of Guyana and Suriname. Although a lack of infrastructure outside the capital cities precludes chapters on these countries for this edition, both nations are places of great natural beauty, with historical sites and varied cultures. You'll find several listings for Guyana and Suriname in this chapter. Except for Clipper Cruise Line, which functions as both a cruise line and tour operator, listings for cruise ships are in the section, "Ocean Cruises."

Abercrombie & Kent ⊠ *1520 Kensington Rd., Oak Brook, IL 60523* ☎ *630/954–2944 or 800/323–7308* 🖷 *630/954–3324* ⊕ *www. abercrombiekent.com.*

Adventure Associates ⊠ *13150 Coit Rd., Suite 110, Dallas, TX 75240* ☎ *972/907–0414 or 800/527–2500* 🖷 *972/783–1286* ⊕ *www. metropolitan-touring.com.*

Adventure Life ⊠ *1655 S. 3rd St. W, Suite 1, Missoula, MT 59801* ☎ *406/541–2677 or 800/344–6118* 🖷 *406/541–2676* ⊕ *www. adventure-life.com.*

Adventures on Skis ⊠ *815 North Rd., Westfield, MA 01085* ☎ *413/568–2855 or 800/628–9655* 🖷 *413/562–3621* ⊕ *www.adventuresonskis.com.*

Amazon Tours & Cruises ⊠ *275 Fontainebleau Blvd., Suite 173, Miami, FL 33172* ☎ *305/227–2266 or 800/423–2791* 🖷 *305/227–1880* ⊕ *www. amazontours.net.*

American Alpine Institute ⊠ *1515 12th St., Bellingham, WA 98225* ☎ *360/671–1505* 🖷 *360/734–8890* ⊕ *www.aai.cc.*

Amizade ⊠ *920 Pitt Union, Pittsburgh, PA 15260* ☎ *412/648–1488 or 888/973–4443* 🖷 *412/648–1492* ⊕ *www.amizade.org.*

Andes Adventures ⊠ *1323 12th St., Suite F, Santa Monica, CA 90401* ☎ *310/395–5265 or 800/289–9470* 🖷 *310/395–7343* ⊕ *www. andesadventures.com.*

Angel-Eco Tours ⊠ *53 Remsen St., Suite 6, Brooklyn, NY 11201* ☎ *888/ 475–0874* 🖷 *212/656–1240* ⊕ *www.angel-ecotours.com.*

Arun Treks & Expeditions ⊠ *301 E. 33rd St., Suite 3, Austin, TX 78705* ☎ *512/407–8314 or 888/495–8735* 🖷 *512/495–9037* ⊕ *www. aruntreks.com.*

Backroads ⊠ *801 Cedar St., Berkeley, CA 94710* ☎ *510/527–1555 or 800/462–2848* 🖷 *510/527–1444* ⊕ *www.backroads.com.*

BikeHike Adventures ✉ 597 Markham St., Toronto, Ontario M6G 2L7 Canada ☎ 416/534–7401 or 888/805–0061 🖷 416/588–9839 ⊕ www.bikehike.com.

Clipper Cruise Line ✉ 7711 Bonhomme Ave., St. Louis, MO 63105 ☎ 314/727–2929 or 800/325–0010 🖷 314/727–6576 ⊕ www.clippercruise.com.

Colorado Mountain School ⌖ Box 1846, Estes Park, CO 80517 ☎ 970/586–5758 or 888/267–7783 🖷 970/586–5798 ⊕ www.cmschool.com.

Country Walkers ⌖ Box 180, Waterbury, VT 05676 ☎ 802/244–1387 or 800/464–9255 🖷 802/244–5661 ⊕ www.countrywalkers.com.

Earthquest ✉ 2400 NW 80th St., Suite 114, Seattle, WA 98117 ☎ 206/334–3404 🖷 206/706–0302 ⊕ www.earthquestadventure.com.

Earth River Expeditions ✉ 180 Towpath Rd., Accord, NY 12404 ☎ 845/626–2665 or 800/643–2784 🖷 845/626–4423 ⊕ www.earthriver.com.

Earthwatch ✉ 3 Clocktower Pl., Suite 100, Maynard, MA 01754 ☎ 978/461–0081 or 800/776–0188 🖷 978/461–2332 ⊕ www.earthwatch.org.

Ecotour Expeditions ⌖ Box 128, Jamestown, RI 02835 ☎ 401/423–3377 or 800/688–1822 🖷 401/423–9630 ⊕ www.naturetours.com.

ElderTreks ✉ 597 Markham St., Toronto, Ontario M6G 2L7, Canada ☎ 416/588–5000 or 800/741–7956 🖷 416/588–9839 ⊕ www.eldertreks.com.

Equitours ⌖ Box 807, Dubois, WY 82513 ☎ 307/455–3363 or 800/545–0019 🖷 307/455–2354 ⊕ www.equitours.com.

Exodus ✉ 9 Weir Rd., London SW12 OLT, England ☎ 02086/730–859 🖷 02086/730–779 ⊕ www.exodus.co.uk.

Explore Bolivia ✉ 2510 N. 47th St., Suite 207, Boulder, CO 80301 ☎🖷 303/545–5728 ⊕ www.explorebolivia.com.

Far Horizons ⌖ Box 91900, Albuquerque, NM 87199 ☎ 505/343–9400 or 800/552–4575 🖷 505/343–8076 ⊕ www.farhorizons.com.

Field Guides ✉ 9433 Bee Cave Rd., Building 1, Suite 150, Austin, TX 78733 ☎ 512/263–7295 or 800/728–4953 🖷 512/263–0117 ⊕ www.fieldguides.com.

Fishing International ⌖ Box 2132, Santa Rosa, CA 95405 ☎ 707/542–4242 or 800/950–4242 🖷 707/526–3474 ⊕ www.fishinginternational.com.

FishQuest! ✉ 3375 Highway 76 West, Hiawassee GA 30546 ☎ 770/971–8586 or 888/891–3474 🖷 770/977–3095 ⊕ www.fishquest.com.

Fly Fishing And ⌖ Box 1719, Red Lodge, MT 59068 ☎ 406/446–9087 ⊕ www.flyfishingand.com.

Focus Tours ✉ 103 Moya Rd., Santa Fe, NM 87508 ☎ 505/466–4688 🖷 505/466–4689 ⊕ www.focustours.com.

Frontiers ⌖ Box 959, Wexford, PA 15090 ☎ 724/935–1577 or 800/245–1950 🖷 724/935–5388 ⊕ www.frontierstrvl.com.

Galápagos Network ✉ 6303 Blue Lagoon Dr., Suite 140, Miami, FL 33126 ☎ 305/262–6264 or 800/633–7972 🖷 305/262–9609 ⊕ www.ecoventura.com.

G.A.P. Adventures ✉ 19 Duncan St., Suite 401, Toronto, Ontario M5H 3H1 Canada ☎ 416/260–0999 or 800/465–5600 🖷 416/260–1888 ⊕ www.gapadventures.com.

Geo Expeditions ✉ 67 Linoberg St., Sonora, CA 95370 ☎ 209/532–0152 or 800/351–5041 🖷 209/532–1979 ⊕ www.geoexpeditions.com.

Geographic Expeditions ✉ *2627 Lombard St., San Francisco, CA 94123* ☎ *415/922–0448 or 800/777–8183* 🖷 *415/346–5535* ⊕ *www. geoex.com.*

Hidden Trails ✉ *202–380 West 1st Ave., Vancouver, BC V5Y 3T7 Canada* ☎ *604/323–1141 or 888/987–2457* 🖷 *604/323–1148* ⊕ *www. hiddentrails.com.*

Himalayan Travel ✉ *8 Berkshire Pl., Danbury, CT 06810* ☎ *203/743–2349 or 800/225–2380* 🖷 *203/797–8077* ⊕ *www.himalayantravelinc.com.*

Inca ✉ *1311 63rd St., Emeryville, CA 94608* ☎ *510/420–1550* 🖷 *510/ 420–0947* ⊕ *www.inca1.com.*

International Expeditions ✉ *One Environs Park, Helena AL 35080* ☎ *205/428–1700 or 800/633–4734* 🖷 *205/428–1714* ⊕ *www. internationalexpeditions.com.*

International Mountain Guides ✍ *Box 155, Ashford, WA 98304* ☎ *360/ 569–2604* 🖷 *360/569–0824* ⊕ *www.mountainguides.com.*

Joseph Van Os Photo Safaris ✍ *Box 655, Vashon Island, WA 98070* ☎ *206/463–5383* 🖷 *206/463–5484* ⊕ *www.photosafaris.com.*

Journeys International ✉ *107 Aprill Dr., Suite 3, Ann Arbor, MI 48103* ☎ *734/665–4407 or 800/255–8735* 🖷 *734/665–2945* ⊕ *www. journeys-intl.com.*

KE Adventure Travel ✉ *1131 Grand Ave., Glenwood Springs, CO 81601* ☎ *970/384–0001 or 800/497–9675* 🖷 *970/384–0004* ⊕ *www. keadventure.com.*

Ladatco Tours ✉ *3006 Aviation Ave., Suite 4C, Coconut Grove, FL 33133* ☎ *305/854–8422 or 800/327–6162* 🖷 *305/285–0504* ⊕ *www. ladatco.com.*

Latin American Escapes ✍ *PMB 421, 712 Bancroft Ave., Walnut Creek, CA 94598* ☎ *925/935–5241 or 800/510–5999* 🖷 *925/945–0154* ⊕ *www.latinamericanescapes.com.*

Lindblad Expeditions ✉ *720 5th Ave., New York, NY 10019* ☎ *212/765–7740 or 800/397–3348* 🖷 *212/265–3770* ⊕ *www.expeditions.com.*

Maxim Tours ✉ *50 Cutler St., Morristown, NJ 07960* ☎ *973/984–9068 or 800/655–0222* 🖷 *973/984–5383* ⊕ *www.maximtours.com.*

Moguls ✉ *6707 Winchester Cir., Boulder, CO 80301* ☎ *303/440–7921 or 888/666–4857* 🖷 *303/440–4160* ⊕ *www.moguls.com.*

Mountain Madness ✉ *4218 SW Alaska, Suite 206, Seattle, WA 98116* ☎ *206/937–8389 or 800/328–5925* 🖷 *206/937–1772* ⊕ *www. mountainmadness.com.*

Mountain Travel-Sobek ✉ *6420 Fairmount Ave., El Cerrito, CA 94530* ☎ *510/527–8100 or 888/687–6235* 🖷 *510/525–7710* ⊕ *www. mtsobek.com.*

Myths and Mountains ✉ *976 Tee Ct., Incline Village, NV 89451* ☎ *775/832–5454 or 800/670–6984* 🖷 *775/832–4454* ⊕ *www. mythsandmountains.com.*

Nature Expeditions International ✉ *7860 Peters Rd., Suite F-103, Plantation, FL 33324* ☎ *945/693–8852 or 800/869–0639* 🖷 *954/693–8854* ⊕ *www.naturexp.com.*

Naturequest ✉ *30872 S. Coast Hwy., Box 185, Laguna Beach, CA 92651* ☎ *949/499–9561 or 800/369–3033* 🖷 *949/499–0812* ⊕ *www. naturequesttours.com.*

Oceanic Society Expeditions ⊠ *Fort Mason Center, Bldg. E, San Francisco, CA 94123* ☎ *415/441–1106 or 800/326–7491* 🖷 *415/474–3395* ⊕ *www.oceanic-society.org.*

Quark Expeditions ⊠ *980 Post Rd., Darien, CT 06820* ☎ *203/656–0499 or 800/356–5699* 🖷 *203/655–6623* ⊕ *www.quarkexpeditions.com.*

Remote Odysseys West (ROW) ⟟ *Box 579, Coeur d'Alene, ID 83816* ☎ *208/765–0841 or 800/451–6034* 🖷 *208/667–6506* ⊕ *www.rowinc.com.*

Rod & Reel Adventures ⊠ *32617 Skyhawk Way, Eugene, OR 97405* ☎ *541/349–0777 or 800/356–6982* 🖷 *541/338–0367* ⊕ *www.rodreeladventures.com.*

Sherpa Expeditions ⊠ *131A Heston Rd., Hounslow TW5 0RF U.K.* ☎ *44/20-8577–2717* 🖷 *44/20-8572–9788* ⊕ *www.sherpa-walking-holidays.co.uk.*

Society Expeditions ⊠ *2001 Western Ave., Suite 300, Seattle, WA 98121* ☎ *206/728–9400 or 800/548–8669* 🖷 *206/728–2301* ⊕ *www.societyexpeditions.com.*

South American Journeys ⊠ *9921 Cabanas Ave., Tujunga, CA 91042* ☎🖷 *818/352–8289 or 800/884–7474* ⊕ *www.southamericanjourneys.com.*

Southwind Adventures ⟟ *Box 621057, Littleton, CO 80162* ☎ *303/972–0701 or 800/377–9463* 🖷 *303/972–0708* ⊕ *www.southwindadventures.com.*

Swallows and Amazons ⟟ *Box 771, Eastham, MA 02642* ☎ *508/255–1886* 🖷 *508/240–0345* ⊕ *www.swallowsandamazonstours.com.*

The World Outdoors ⊠ *2840 Wilderness Pl., Suite F, Boulder, CO 80301* ☎ *303/413–0938 or 800/488–8483* 🖷 *303/413–0926* ⊕ *www.theworldoutdoors.com.*

Tours International ⊠ *12750 Briar Forest Dr., Suite 603, Houston, TX 77077* ☎ *281/293–0809 or 800/247–7965* 🖷 *281/589–0870* ⊕ *www.toursinternational.com.*

Travcoa ⊠ *2350 SE Bristol St., Newport Beach, CA 92660* ☎ *949/476–2800, 800/992–2003, 800/563–0005 in Canada* 🖷 *949/476–2538* ⊕ *www.travcoa.com.*

Tucan ⊕ *www.tucantravel.com.* This Australia-based company is represented in the United States by Himalayan Travel ⊠ *8 Berkshire Pl., Danbury, CT 06810* ☎ *203/743–2349 or 800/225–2380* 🖷 *203/797–8077* ⊕ *www.himalayantravelinc.com.*

Ultimate Ascents International ⊠ *3535 28th St., Boulder, CO 80301* ☎ *303/443–2076* 🖷 *303/443–2778* ⊕ *www.ultimateascents.com.*

Victor Emanuel Nature Tours ⊠ *2525 Wallingwood Dr., Suite 1003, Austin, TX 78746* ☎ *512/328–5221 or 800/328–8368* 🖷 *512/328–2919* ⊕ *www.ventbird.com.*

Wilderness Travel ⊠ *1102 9th St., Berkeley, CA 94710* ☎ *510/558–2488 or 800/368–2794* 🖷 *510/558–2489* ⊕ *www.wildernesstravel.com.*

Wildland Adventures ⊠ *3516 N.E. 155th St., Seattle, WA 98155* ☎ *206/365–0686 or 800/345–4453* 🖷 *206/363–6615* ⊕ *www.wildland.com.*

WorldTrek Expeditions ⊠ *220 E. Palmdale St., Tucson, AZ 85714* ☎ *520/807–0706 or 800/795–1142* 🖷 *520/807–0749* ⊕ *www.adventurebiketours.com.*

Zegrahm Expeditions ⊠ *192 Nickerson St., No. 200, Seattle, WA 98109* ☎ *206/285–4000 or 800/628–8747* 🖷 *206/285–5037* ⊕ *www.zeco.com.*

CRUISES

Antarctica Cruises

Founded to promote environmentally responsible travel to Antarctica, the **International Association of Antarctica Tour Operators** (☎ 970/704–1047 ⊕ www.iaato.org) is a good source of information, including suggested readings.

Season: November–February.
Location: Most cruises depart from Ushuaia, Argentina.
Cost: From $3,790 for 11 days from Ushuaia.
Tour Operators: Clipper Cruise Line; Galápagos Network; Geographic Expeditions; Inca; Lindblad Expeditions; Mountain Travel-Sobek; Quark Expeditions; Society Expeditions; Wilderness Travel; Zegrahm Expeditions.

From Ushuaia, the world's southernmost city, you'll sail for two days through the Drake Passage and then on to the spectacular landscapes of Antarctica. Accompanied by naturalists, you'll travel ashore in small inflatable crafts called Zodiacs to view penguins and nesting seabirds. Some cruises visit research stations, and many call at the Falkland, South Orkney, South Shetland, or South Georgia Islands. Some companies, such as Mountain Travel-Sobek and Wilderness Travel, partially trace the route of the explorer, Sir Ernest Shackleton. Expedition vessels range from luxury ships with ice-strengthened hulls to polar-research vessels that have been refitted to take on passengers. On certain Quark Expeditions itineraries you can travel aboard an icebreaker that carries helicopters for aerial viewing. This company has made two circumnavigations of Antarctica, a 21,000-km (13,000-mi) journey lasting almost three months, and may offer this trip again.

Galápagos Cruises

Season: Year-round.
Location: Galápagos Islands.
Cost: From $1,124 for four days from Guayaquil.
Tour Operators: Adventure Associates; Galápagos Network; Inca; International Expeditions; Lindblad Expeditions; Nature Expeditions International; Oceanic Society Expeditions; Travcoa; Wilderness Travel; Wildland Adventures.

Isolated in the Pacific some 950 km (600 mi) west of South America, the Galápagos Islands' abundant wildlife inspired Charles Darwin's theory of evolution by natural selection. Even today, about two-thirds of the birds and most reptiles on this barren archipelago are found nowhere else. Following a flight from Guayaquil, Ecuador, you'll board a comfortable vessel and spend four to eight days visiting various islands where your ship's naturalists will lead guided nature walks. You'll find the animals and birds quite unafraid, but strict rules for shore visits are enforced. You'll be required to follow established pathways, stay with your guide, and not give food or water to any wildlife. Pathways are rough and often rocky, but the pace is not hurried. Most operators include time for swimming or snorkeling with the sea lions. Vessels vary from small yachts to the 100-passenger M/V *Galápagos Explorer II*. Some companies combine the Galápagos with stays in the Amazon or Andes; almost all include time in Quito and/or Guayaquil. Numerous companies offer Galápagos cruises; the above operators were chosen for the variety of programs they offer and for the number of departures. The character of your trip will probably depend less on the number of islands visited than on the quality of the naturalists who are leading you around.

Ocean Cruises

Season: October–April.

Locations: Some Caribbean cruises include ports of call in South America and a partial navigation of the Amazon River. An increasing number of ships have created itineraries traveling exclusively along the Atlantic and Pacific coasts of South America. You can opt for a circumnavigation of the continent (about 50 days) or choose one or more segments. Brazil, Argentina, and Chile are especially popular. Some itineraries include the Falkland Islands. Typical port calls include Devil's Island, French Guiana; Belém, Fortaleza, Salvador, and Rio de Janeiro, Brazil; Punta del Este and Montevideo, Uruguay; Buenos Aires and Ushuaia, Argentina; Punta Arenas, Puerto Montt, Valparaíso, and Arica, Chile; Callao, Peru; Guayaquil, Ecuador; Cartagena, Colombia; and Caracas, Venezuela.

Cost: Prices vary according to the ship, cabin category, and itinerary. Figure from about $150 to several hundred dollars per day.

Cruise Companies: The following operators offer cruises calling at various South American ports. Several have itineraries that include the Amazon. **Abercrombie & Kent** (☎ 800/323–7308 ⊕ www.abercrombiekent.com). **Celebrity Cruises** (☎ 800/437–3111 ⊕ www.celebrity.com). **Clipper Cruise Line** (☎ 800/325–0010 ⊕ www.clippercruise.com). **Crystal Cruises** (☎ 800/446–6620 ⊕ www.crystalcruises.com). **Holland America Line** (☎ 877/724–5425 ⊕ www.hollandamerica.com). **Orient Lines** (☎ 800/333–7300 ⊕ www.orientlines.com). **Princess Cruises** (☎ 800/774–6237 ⊕ www.princess.com). **Radisson Seven Seas Cruises** (☎ 800/285–1835 ⊕ www.rssc.com). **Royal Olympic Cruises** (☎ 800/801–6086 ⊕ www. royalolympiccruises.com). **Seabourn Cruise Line** (☎ 800/929–9391 ⊕ www.seabourn.com). **Silversea Cruises** (☎ 800/722–9955 ⊕ www. silversea.com).

Patagonia Coastal & Lake Cruises

Cruising the southern tip of South America reveals some of Earth's most spectacular scenery: fjords, glaciers, lagoons, lakes, narrow channels, waterfalls, forested shorelines, fishing villages, penguins, and other wildlife. While many itineraries include a one- or two-day boating excursion, the companies listed below offer multiple nights aboard ship.

Argentina & Chile

Season: October–April.

Locations: Chilean fjords; Puerto Montt and Punta Arenas, Chile; Tierra del Fuego and Ushuaia, Argentina.

Cost: From $930 for four days from Punta Arenas.

Tour Operators: Abercrombie & Kent; Clipper Cruise Line; Inca; International Expeditions; Latin American Escapes; Maxim Tours; Tours International; Travcoa.

Take a cruise around Cape Horn, South America's southern trip, then northward along the fjords of Chile's western coast, for unsurpassed natural vistas. Aboard Clipper Cruise Line's 122-passenger vessel, you'll also call at Chiloé Island and the Falkland Islands. With Abercrombie & Kent, the Cape Horn cruise is followed by days savoring the mountain scenery of Chile's Torres del Paine National Park and Argentina's Bariloche. Inca's 16-day itinerary combines four sailing days with time in Torres del Paine and Buenos Aires. Tours International offers several options, ranging from four to seven days, for cruising around Patagonia and the fjords. After spending days in Argentina's Lake District and two national parks, Travcoa's guests board the *M/V Mare Australis* for a multiday glacier sail. Latin American Escapes, Maxim Tours, and International Expeditions also use this vessel.

River Cruises

Stretching 6,300 km (3,900 mi), the Amazon is the world's longest river. From its source in the Peruvian Andes, the river and its tributaries snake through parts of Bolivia, Ecuador, Colombia, and Brazil before emptying into the Atlantic. The Amazon nourishes thousands of species of birds, mammals, and plants. Whatever your style of travel, there's a boat plying the river to suit your needs. Sleep in a hammock on the deck of a thatch-roof riverboat or in the air-conditioned suite of an upscale vessel.

Brazil

Season: Year-round.

Locations: Anavilhanas Archipelago; Lago Janauári Ecological Park; Manaus; Río Branco; Río Negro.

Cost: From $1,050 for seven days from Manaus.

Tour Operators: Ecotour Expeditions; Maxim Tours; Nature Expeditions International; Southwind Adventures; Swallows and Amazons; Travcoa.

River journeys along the Brazilian Amazon typically begin in Manaus. Some itineraries combine three or four cruising days with visits to Rio, others savor life on the river for the entire 7 to 15 days. You'll explore tributaries by small boats, take jungle walks, and visit indigenous villages. Accommodations range from deck-side hammocks to luxurious wood-panel cabins. With Swallows and Amazons, you'll also do some beach and forest camping. A highlight of all trips is the "Meeting of the Waters," where the dark waters of the Rio Negro join the lighter waters of the Amazon.

Peru

Season: March–December.
Locations: Iquitos to Tabatinga; Pacaya-Samiria National Reserve; various Amazon tributaries.
Cost: From $635 for four days from Iquitos.
Tour Operators: Amazon Tours & Cruises; International Expeditions; Ladatco Tours; Maxim Tours; Tours International.

Peru vies with Brazil as a destination for Amazon cruises. Many itineraries sail from Iquitos to *tres fronteras,* the spot where Peru, Brazil, and Colombia meet. Along the way, there's time for jungle hikes and visits to river towns and indigenous communities. You can expect to see monkeys, sloths, numerous bird species, freshwater dolphins, and butterflies. Ladatco and International Expeditions visit Pacaya-Samiria National Reserve, known for 350 species of birds, 130 types of animals, and 22 varieties of orchids. These operators utilize classically styled riverboats carrying 22 to 29 passengers in air-conditioned cabins with private baths. Tours International and Amazon Tours & Cruises favor the *M/V Río Amazonas* with 21 air-conditioned cabins, some with private baths. On Maxim Tours' vessels, you also get air-conditioning and a private bath.

LEARNING VACATIONS

Cultural Tours

Some travelers want a quick look at a country's major sights, while others prefer to immerse themselves in the culture. This could mean studying the archaeological remains of great civilizations, learning about the lives and customs of indigenous peoples, or trying your hand at local crafts. Other options include language studies or mastering the intricacies of the tango.

Argentina

Season: Year-round.
Locations: Buenos Aires; northwest Argentina.
Cost: From $336 for five days from Buenos Aires.
Tour Operators: Latin American Escapes; Maxim Tours; Tours International.

With the three companies above, you can learn the tango, the daring dance that Buenos Aires made famous. You'll take both private and group lessons before trying your skill on the dance floors of world-famous tango bars. Latin American Escapes and Maxim Tours also offer trips to northern Argentina, where you see striking geological formations and visit Indian villages and colonial towns and observe local handicrafts.

Bolivia

Season: March–November.
Locations: Cochabamba; Inkallajta; Lake Titicaca; Potosí; Sucre; Tiahuanaco; Uyuni Salt Flats.
Cost: From $1,295 for 11 days from La Paz.
Tour Operators: Abercrombie & Kent; Adventure Life; Amizade; Explore Bolivia; Far Horizons; Focus Tours; G.A.P. Adventures; Maxim Tours; Myths and Mountains; Wildland Adventures.

Far Horizon's 16-day program focuses on Bolivia's archaeology from the Andes to the Amazon; you visit a number of remote sites. Explore Bolivia uses four-wheel-drive vehicles to traverse the unique landscapes of the Salar de Uyuni; on the 10-day trip you also check out the old mining town of Oruro and the colonial city of Potosí. With Wildland Adventures, you combine highlands and Amazonian sightseeing. Adventure Life focuses on Potosí, Uyuni, and villages near Sucre, and spends two nights at a working hacienda. Myths and Mountains offers a program that explores the medicinal heritage of the Kallawaya people, and a Maxim Tours departure studies Bolivian textile traditions. For an in-depth experience, join an Amizade work project where you'll help renovate a community building (accommodations are in dormitories).

Brazil

Season: Year-round.
Locations: Amazon; Olinda; Ouro Prêto; Salvador.
Cost: From $1,390 for 14 days from Santarém.
Tour Operators: Amizade; G.A.P. Adventures; Maxim Tours; Swallows and Amazons.

If your interest is learning about other cultures, consider Swallows and Amazons' eight-day trip along the Rio Vaupes, during which you visit various indigenous groups—or choose the company's programs focusing on the Yanomami and Tucano people. Following 10 days in Venezuela, G.A.P. Adventures moves on to the Brazilian Amazon, then works its way down the coast to Rio, exploring such points as São Luis, Fortaleza, Recife, and Salvador along the way. Maxim Tours lets you determine the number of days you'd like in the architectural and historical gems of Ouro Prêto, Olinda, and Salvador. To add a rewarding dimension to your trip, consider an Amizade work project in the Brazilian Amazon where you'll help construct a children's health clinic.

Chile

Season: Year-round.
Locations: Atacama Desert; Colchagua Valley; Easter Island; Santa Cruz.
Cost: From $1,550 for seven days from Santiago.
Tour Operators: Abercrombie & Kent; ElderTreks; Far Horizons; Focus Tours; Frontiers; Myths and Mountains; Travcoa; Zegrahm Expeditions.

In the Pacific Ocean 3,680 km (2,300 mi) west of the Chilean mainland, remote Easter Island is famed for its *moais,* nearly 1,000 stone statues whose brooding eyes gaze over the windswept landscape. ElderTreks, Far Horizons, Frontiers, Travcoa, and Zegrahm Expeditions are among the tour operators who will take you there. Far Horizons' departure is timed for the annual Tapati festival. For a cultural experience of another sort, Abercrombie & Kent and Focus Tours will show you the archaeological sites and ancient petroglyphs of the Atacama Desert. While based on a working farm, let cowboys introduce you to their version of the wild west or visit Chilean vineyards and join a harvest festival; both trips are with Myths and Mountains.

Ecuador

Season: Year-round.
Locations: Throughout Ecuador.
Cost: From $425 for seven days from Quito.
Tour Operators: G.A.P. Adventures; Myths and Mountains; Zegrahm Expeditions.

Centuries ago, Spaniards settling in Ecuador were given vast land grants on which many built elegant haciendas. With Zegrahm Expeditions, you'll stay on these grand estates, experiencing their cultural history and fine art. Myths and Mountains' "The Road Not Traveled" program stays in private homes where you'll share meals and conversation with the proprietors. This company's "Shamans of Ecuador" travels through jungles and highlands, meeting with shamans and learning about their rituals and healing practices. If fluency in Spanish is your goal, consider G.A.P. Adventures' weeklong language program in Quito. You'll live with an Ecuadorean family and receive 25 hours of one-on-one tutoring.

Peru

Season: Year-round.
Locations: The Amazon; Chán Chán; Cuzco; Machu Picchu; Sipan.
Cost: From $495 for seven days from Cuzco.
Tour Operators: Far Horizons; G.A.P. Adventures; Geo Expeditions; Inca; International Expeditions; Maxim Tours; Myths and Mountains; South American Journeys; Southwind Adventures; Tours International.

Since virtually all tours to Peru include visits to Cuzco and Machu Picchu, the emphasis here will be on other noteworthy sites or activities. Chán Chán, one of the largest pre-Columbian cities yet discovered, and Sipan, where archaeologists unearthed the most spectacular tomb in the Western Hemisphere, are highlights in itineraries offered by many of the above operators. Southwind Adventures leads an archaeological exploration of the ruins, tombs, and fortress of Kuelap. Myths and Mountains' specialty tours focus on Andean weaving and crafts and on Inca rituals. South American Expeditions runs workshops devoted to yoga, Andean music, cooking, weaving, writing, and the beliefs and practices of the Chachapoya people. With G.A.P. Adventures you can perfect your Spanish at a language school in Cuzco. International Expeditions presents an Amazon rain forest workshop for students, designed to acquaint young people with the diversity of life in this unique environment.

Scientific Research Trips

Joining a research expedition team gives you more than great photos. By assisting scientists, you can make significant contributions toward a better understanding of the continent's unique ecosystem. Flexibility and a sense of humor are important assets for these trips, which often require roughing it.

Argentina

Season: March–October.
Locations: Ischigualasto Provincial Park; Parque Provincial Ernesto Tornquist.

Cost: $1,445 for 10 days from Bahía Blanca.
Tour Operator: Earthwatch.

In Earthwatch's Triassic Park program you'll prospect for dinosaur fossils, excavate and map the finds, then collect and catalog them. Another program lets you aid researchers in trapping, tagging, and observing some little-known carnivores: the pampas fox, the hog-nosed skunk, and the grison (a South American cousin of the badger).

Brazil
Season: Year-round.
Locations: Baía Norte; Bananal Island; Pantanal.
Cost: From $1,695 for 14 days from Florianópolis.
Tour Operator: Earthwatch.

Earthwatch has three projects in Brazil. In and around a marine reserve, you'll work aboard a rigid-hull inflatable boat to determine the habits and habitat needs of *tucuxi* dolphins. The Amazon Turtles project helps identify and protect turtle nesting sites and explores the creatures' behavioral ecology and responses to environmental variables. In the Pantanal, the largest freshwater wetland on the planet, help a multinational team of scientists collect data on vital links in the Pantanal food web, thus accelerating the conservation process.

Chile
Seasons: January–May; October–November.
Locations: Navarino Island; Toltén basin.
Cost: $1,495 for 15 days from Valdivia.
Tour Operator: Earthwatch.

Join a Chilean professor and veterinarian to survey the endangered river otter's habitat; trap and identify prey; and track individual otters using radiotelemetry. In Chile's far south, on Navarino Island, you'll find the rufous-legged owl, a species whose habitat is threatened. Help assess the distribution, abundance, and habitat needs of this owl.

Ecuador
Season: December–January.
Location: Loma Alta Ecological Reserve.
Cost: From $1,695 for 14 days from Guayaquil.
Tour Operator: Earthwatch.

Ecuador contains more than half of South America's bird species. You'll help survey a remote tropical forest to track seasonal shifts in bird populations and perform such tasks as setting up and checking mist nets. Volunteers have the chance to interact with the local community and participate in village events.

Guyana
Seasons: February–March; November.
Location: Rupununi River.
Cost: $2,385 for nine days from Miami.
Tour Operator: Oceanic Society Expeditions.

Based at Karanambo Ranch and owned and operated by Diane McTurk—who is widely known for her work rehabilitating orphaned giant otters—Oceanic Society Expeditions' volunteers help document the distribution and abundance of giant otters along the Rupununi River. Individual otters are identified and their behavior recorded.

Peru
Season: Year-round.
Location: Amazon.
Cost: From $1,695 for 12 days from Puerto Maldonada.
Tour Operators: Earthwatch; Oceanic Society Expeditions.

With Oceanic Society Expeditions you can assist in a study of the Amazon's two species of river dolphins. Identify individual dolphins, record their behaviors and vocalizations, and plot their location from your base aboard a 76-foot boat. With Earthwatch, take part in a study of macaws at Tambopata Research Center or join members of a team in conducting water analysis and identifying and preserving fish and other river wildlife.

Suriname
Season: March–May.
Location: Galibi Nature Reserve.
Cost: $2,190 for nine days from Miami.
Tour Operator: Oceanic Society Expeditions.

The coastal area round the Galibi Nature Reserve is a prime nesting site for green, olive ridley, and leatherback turtles. Aid researchers in monitoring the turtles' nesting activities, collect biological data, measure the turtles' length and width, and patrol the beaches at night and in the early morning.

THE OUTDOORS

Amazon Jungle Camping & Lodges

Because the Amazon and its tributaries provide easy access to remote parts of the jungle, river transport often serves as the starting point for camping and lodge excursions. Many jungle lodges can also be reached by small planes using dirt or grass airstrips. Accommodations range from hammocks to comfortable rooms with private baths. Nature walks, canoe trips, piranha fishing, and visits to indigenous villages are typically part of rain forest programs led by naturalists or indigenous guides. Numerous Amazon itineraries are available, so study several companies' offerings to choose an appropriate trip.

Bolivia
Season: Year-round.
Locations: Madidi National Park; Noel Kempff Mercado National Park.
Cost: From $700 for four days from La Paz.
Tour Operators: Focus Tours; Latin American Escapes; Maxim Tours; Wildland Adventures.

With some 525 bird species, 91 types of mammals, 18 reptile species, and numerous fish, Neol Kempff Mercado National Park offers an abundance of wildlife and rain forest experiences. All of the companies mentioned above have programs here. Latin American Escapes and Maxim Tours also arrange travel to Madidi National Park, which has monkeys, capybaras, caimans, and countless species of birds and butterflies. The lodge, reached by a five-hour dugout canoe journey, is owned and operated by an indigenous community.

Brazil
Season: Year-round.
Locations: Rio Negro and its tributaries.
Cost: From $1,395 for eight days from Manaus.
Tour Operators: Focus Tours; International Expeditions; Maxim Tours; Naturequest; Swallows and Amazons.

Most jungle adventures here begin with a boat trip up the Rio Negro, the main tributary of the Amazon. Naturequest has created a rustic jungle lodge and riverboat safari combination. With International Expeditions, you explore the rain forest and watery byways from your base at remote Uakari Lodge's cluster of floating cabañas. Focus Tours' program focuses on the rain forest, rivers, and wildlife of the Alta Foresta region. Maxim Tours offers short stays at the comfortable Pousada dos Guanavenas or the more rustic Amazon Lodge. Swallows and Amazons built Over Look Lodge, with eight private bedrooms and shared baths, exclusively for its clients.

Ecuador
Season: Year-round.
Location: Amazon basin.
Cost: From $720 for five days from Quito.
Tour Operators: Adventure Life; ElderTreks; Galápagos Network; G.A.P. Adventures; Latin American Escapes; Inca; Ladatco Tours; Maxim Tours.

Scientists estimate that the Ecuadorean Amazon has 1,450 species of birds and as many as 20,000 varieties of plants. Operators use several comfortable lodges: Sacha Jungle Lodge, a cluster of cabanas nestled deep in the rain forest; La Selva Lodge, a group of cabins overlooking the waters of Lago Garzacocha; and Kapawi, a pioneering ecolodge on the Pastaza River where the majority of staff are indigenous Achuar people.

Peru
Season: March–December.
Location: Amazon basin.
Cost: From $567 for four days from Iquitos.
Tour Operators: Amazon Tours & Cruises; Ecotour Expeditions; Inca; International Expeditions; Journeys International; Latin American Escapes; Naturequest; Southwind Adventures; Tours International; Wildland Adventures.

At Tambopata Macaw Research Center, you'll witness hundreds of macaws and parrots returning each morning to nibble bits of clay from a riverside ledge. Other popular destinations include Manu Biosphere

Reserve, where you take canoe trips on lakes inhabited by giant river otters; Explorama Lodge, reached by boat from Iquitos; the even more remote ExplorNapo Camp, or the Amazon Center for Environmental Education and Research, where an elevated walkway allows you to see wildlife from the forest canopy.

Bird-Watching Tours

When selecting a bird-watching tour, ask questions. What species might be seen? What are the guide's qualifications? Does the operator work to protect natural habitats? What equipment is used? (In addition to binoculars, this should include a high-powered telescope, a tape recorder to record and play back bird calls [a way of attracting birds], and a spotlight for night viewing.)

Argentina

Season: October–December.
Locations: Altiplano; Chaco; Pampas; Patagonia; Yungas Forest.
Cost: From $2,800 for 14 days from Buenos Aires.
Tour Operators: Field Guides; Focus Tours; Victor Emanuel Nature Tours.

More than 1,000 types of birds inhabit this vast country. Depending on the trip, you should see diverse species, including the red-tailed comet, Andean condor, crested gallito, snowy sheathbill, and hooded grebe. Punta Tambo, in Patagonia, has the world's largest colony of Magallanic penguins. The operators listed above offer itineraries that cover both the northern and southern regions.

Bolivia

Seasons: October; July.
Locations: Andes; Madidi National Park; Noel Kempff Mercado National Park.
Cost: From $3,850 for 20 days from Santa Cruz.
Tour Operators: Field Guides; Focus Tours; Victor Emanuel Nature Tours.

Thanks to its varied geography, Bolivia has some 1,300 bird species. Up to 213 species have been recorded by one tour group on a single day. Manakins, guans, eagles, macaws, toucans, and hummingbirds are among the birds found in Noel Kempff Mercado Park, while the Andean condor and the endemic rufous-faced antpitta are two of the species viewable at higher elevations.

Brazil

Seasons: February; June–November.
Locations: Amazon; Northeast; Pantanal; Southeast.
Cost: From $1,750 for seven days from Manaus.
Tour Operators: Field Guides; Focus Tours; Swallows and Amazons; Victor Emanuel Nature Tours.

Bird habitats in Brazil range from coastal rain forests to cloud forests to open plains. The Pantanal, a vast area of seasonally flooded grassland, has the hyacinth macaw, bare-faced curassow, epaulet oriole, and nacunda nighthawk, while the golden parakeet is but one of many exotic species inhabiting the Amazon. Brazilian avian life is so rich that

Victor Emanuel Nature Tours runs five different programs here and Field Guide offers seven.

Chile

Seasons: October–November; February.
Locations: Atacama Desert; Lake District; Patagonia.
Cost: From $3,998 for 11 days from Miami.
Tour Operators: Field Guides; Focus Tours; International Expeditions; Victor Emanuel Nature Tours.

Chile spans a number of distinctive vegetational and altitudinal zones, ensuring a varied and abundant avian population. Almost 300 species are found here, including lesser and puna rheas, Chilean tinamou, tawny-throated dotterel, rufous-legged owl, white-sided hillstar, Chilean woodstar, and Megellanic woodpecker. Many species have very local distribution, so you can only find them in these particular regions.

Ecuador

Season: Year-round.
Locations: Amazon basin; Andes; Galápagos Islands.
Cost: From $2,250 for 10 days from Quito.
Tour Operators: Field Guides; South American Journeys; Victor Emanuel Nature Tours.

Some birders describe one of Ecuador's nature reserves as "one of the birdiest places on earth." In each region, from the Amazon to the Andes to the Galápagos, you'll find hundreds of distinct species. Common sightings include sword-billed and giant hummingbirds, quetzals, bearded guans, cock-of-the-rock, and plate-billed mountain toucans. Attesting to Ecuador's excellent birding, both Field Guides and Victor Emanuel Nature Tours offer seven different programs here. South American Journeys' programs are based at Kapawi Lodge in the Amazon.

Peru

Season: Year-round.
Locations: Amazon basin; Andes.
Cost: From $3,350 for 12 days from Lima.
Tour Operators: Field Guides; Tours International; Victor Emanuel Nature Tours.

With habitats ranging from the Amazon to the Andes, Peru has many kinds of birds, including white-bearded, blue-backed, and wire-tailed manakins. There are also almost 60 species of antbirds, as well as black-spotted bare-eyes, harpy eagles, and cock-of-the-rock. Some of the continent's rarest and most spectacular birds, including the elusive black-necked red-cotinga, inhabit the country's forests.

Suriname

Season: January.
Locations: Brownsberg Nature Reserve; Central Suriname Nature Reserve.
Cost: From $3,100 for 12 days from Paramaribo.
Tour Operators: Field Guides; Victor Emanuel Nature Tours.

Although Suriname has a good system of nature reserves, it remains one of South America's lesser-known destinations. Those willing to rough it, including spending some nights in rustic accommodations, are rewarded with sightings of harpy eagles, guans, macaws, and forest falcons. Suriname has the largest display site of the Guianan cock-of-the-rock, with 30 or more males in full display.

Venezuela

Season: Year-round.
Locations: Andes; Gran Sabana; Henri Pittier National Park; Los Llanos.
Cost: From $1,350 for nine days from Caracas.
Tour Operators: Angel-Eco Tours; Field Guides; Victor Emanuel Nature Tours.

With topography ranging from cloud forests to the Andes Mountains, the *tepuis* (mountains with sheer sides and flat tops), saline lagoons, grasslands, and a number of national parks, Venezuela offers an abundance of birding opportunities. More than 500 species are found in Henri Pittier National Park alone. Depending on the program you select, you could spot harpy eagles, amethyst-throated and orange-throated sunangels, velvet-browed brilliants, white-tipped quetzals, agami herons, or even the rare great antpitta. Field Guides and Victor Emanuel Nature Tours have regularly scheduled birding packages in Venezuela, while Angel-Eco Tours creates customized itineraries in Henri Pittier National Park.

Natural History

Many operators have created programs that provide insight into the importance and fragility of South America's ecological treasures. The itineraries mentioned below take in the deserts, glaciers, rain forests, mountains, and rivers of this continent, as well as the impressive variety of its wildlife.

Argentina & Chile

Season: October–March.
Locations: Buenos Aires; Lake District; Patagonia; Santiago.
Cost: From $2,638 for 17 days from Buenos Aires.
Tour Operators: ElderTreks; Geo Expeditions; Geographic Expeditions; Ladatco Tours; Myths and Mountains; Nature Expeditions International; Southwind Adventures; Travcoa; Wildland Adventures; Zegrahm Expeditions.

The southern tip of Argentina and Chile, commonly referred to as Patagonia, has long been a prime ecotourism destination, and nature lovers will find no lack of tour offerings for this region. You'll view the glaciers of Los Glaciares National Park, the soaring peaks of Torres del Paine, and the fjords of the Chilean coast. Many itineraries include some hiking and, often, a one- to three-day cruise.

Bolivia

Season: Year-round.
Locations: Andes; Eastern Lowlands; Lago Uru-Uru; Noel Kempff Mercado National Park; Torotoro National Park.

Cost: Custom tours with cost determined by number of participants and length of itinerary.
Tour Operator: Focus Tours.

With years of experience designing custom itineraries for nature enthusiasts, Focus Tours offers nine different programs in Bolivia. At Torotoro National Park, you'll visit a region that's considered a trove for both paleontologists and naturalists—dinosaur tracks measuring 20 inches long have been discovered here, and Noel Kempff Mercado National Park's 2.4 million acres contain 525 bird, 91 mammal, and 18 reptile species, plus numerous plants.

Brazil

Season: Year-round.
Locations: Caraça National Park; Iguaçu Falls; Pantanal; Serra da Canastra National Park.
Cost: From $595 for four days from Campo Grande.
Tour Operators: Ecotour Expeditions; ElderTreks; Focus Tours; International Expeditions; Latin American Escapes; Maxim Tours; Southwind Adventures; Zeghram Expeditions.

The Pantanal is Earth's largest freshwater wetlands. Most operators are based at Refúgio Caiman, which offers comfortable lodgings and a staff of naturalists who lead excursions by truck, boat, on horseback, and on foot. Storks, tropical birds, anteaters, caimans, capybaras, and possibly jaguars are among the wildlife you might see. Some programs also spend time in Rio and at Iguaçu Falls. Zegrahm Expeditions' 17-day itinerary takes in several national parks.

Ecuador

Season: Year-round.
Locations: Amazon; Cotacachi-Cayapas Ecological Reserve; Cotopaxi National Park; Pasochoa Protected Forest; Pululahua National Reserve.
Cost: From $2,295 for 12 days from Quito.
Tour Operators: ElderTreks; Southwind Adventures.

It's the smallest Andean country, but Ecuador is impressively scenic and culturally diverse in both the historical sense and in terms of the kinds of people who live here. Pululahua Natural Reserve encompasses five distinct ecological zones within its boundaries. Southwind Adventures' 10-day program covers several reserves and parks whose ecosystems represent glacier-clad peaks, tropical rain forests, and the Lake District's páramo. The Amazon portion utilizes either Kapawi or Sacha Lodge. After allocating time for Quito, Cotopaxi National Park, and a train ride through the Andes, ElderTreks' itinerary includes ancient ruins and hikes in national parks and the Mindo Cloud Forest.

Guyana

Season: Year-round.
Locations: Iwokrama Field Station, Georgetown, Kaieteur Falls; Karanambo Ranch.
Cost: From $1,325 for eight days from Georgetown.

Tour Operators: G.A.P. Adventures; Latin American Escapes; Oceanic Society Expeditions.

With some half-dozen different natural history itineraries in Guyana, Latin American Escapes covers a good part of the country, including rain forest sites, Amerindian villages, and Kaieteur Falls. One trip focuses on wildlife. G.A.P. Adventures' 11-day trip includes Kaieteur and Orinduik Falls, Amerindian villages, canoeing, a night in a hammock camp, visits to rain forest field stations, and time in the capital, Georgetown. Oceanic Society Expeditions divides its 15-day venture between Guyana—with days at Karanambo Ranch (a giant otter rehabilitation center), Kaieteur Falls, and Georgetown—and neighboring Suriname for visits to its capital, Paramaribo, and two nature reserves.

Peru
Season: March–December.
Locations: Tambopata-Candamo Reserve.
Cost: From $1,185 for eight days from Lima.
Tour Operators: Adventure Life; Southwind Adventures; Tours International.

Covering 3.7 million acres, the Tambopata-Candamo Reserve is primarily known for its Macaw Research Center, where a huge nutrient-rich clay lick attracts hundreds of parrots, parakeets, and macaws. The reserve has some 500 bird species, 11 varieties of monkeys, and various mammals, including ocelots and jaguars.

Suriname
Seasons: February–April; August–October.
Locations: Awara'an; Brownsberg Nature Park; Central Suriname Nature Reserve; Galibi Nature Reserve; Paramaribo.
Cost: From $2,150 for nine days from Paramaribo.
Tour Operators: Mountain Travel-Sobek; Oceanic Society Expeditions.

Suriname may be small, but its boundaries encompass a rich biodiversity. More than three-quarters of its land is covered in primary (original growth) rain forest, and at 4 million acres, the Central Suriname Reserve, a World Heritage site, is the largest tropical reserve in the world. With Mountain Travel-Sobek you hike jungle paths, travel rivers in motorized dugout canoes, and meet people who have settled in this region. While in the capital, Paramaribo, Ocean Society Expeditions' participants meet with personnel of STINASU (The Foundation for Nature Conservation) before heading into the interior and Brownsberg Nature Park.

Venezuela
Season: Year-round.
Locations: Canaima; Gran Sabana; Los Llanos; Mérida; Orinoco Delta.
Cost: From $750 for four days from Caracas.
Tour Operators: Angel-Eco Tours; G.A.P. Adventures; Southwind Adventures.

Besides 1,250 species of birds and 250 kinds of mammals, Venezuela also has mountains, tropical forests, mesas, and waterfalls. Southwind

Adventures visits Andean communities, hikes near Lake Mucubají, flies over Angel Falls, and spends two days on a ranch. G.A.P. Adventures' 14-day trip takes in Angel Falls, the sandstone mesas, or *tepuis*, of the Gran Sabana, and meets with local people of the Orinoco Delta. Angel-Eco Tours offers ecology-focused packages. One visits the historical city of Mérida, the Mif[fí] highlands, the abundant wildlife of Los Llanos, and Hato El Cedral, while others include in-depth stays at comfortable, though somewhat rustic, camps in Canaima National Park (Angel Falls) or along the Orinoco River. The company designs custom itineraries in Henri Pittier National Park, and has a two-day river cruise and bird-watching jungle journey on the Orinoco.

Overland Safaris

While definitely not for everyone, an overland adventure is sure to take you far from the beaten path. It's also a great way to immerse yourself in a number of cultures and landscapes. Expect to travel by truck, bus, train, boat, or even custom-built expedition vehicles. Occasionally, you may find yourself in lodges or inns, but most of the time you'll be sleeping outdoors. Know that you're expected to help pitch tents, cook, and do other chores. The camaraderie that evolves often sparks lifelong friendships. This type of trip generally attracts an international mix of physically fit adventurers between 18 and 50. The age at which a doctor's certification is required before you're accepted on the trip varies depending on the outfitter.

Season: Year-round.
Locations: Throughout South America.
Cost: From $45 per day, depending on location, trip length, and mode of transport. International airfare and a "kitty" for such expenses as camp food and park entrance fees are extra.
Tour Operators: Exodus; G.A.P. Adventures; Tucan.

These companies offer trips that cover most of South America, and which range from 20 to 171 days. Itineraries are typically composed of short segments, which you can combine into a longer trip, if you wish. Most programs visit between three and nine countries.

Photo Safaris

A benefit of photo tours is the amount of time spent at each place visited. Whether the subject is a rarely spotted animal, a breathtaking waterfall, or villagers in traditional dress, you get a chance to focus both your camera and your mind on the scene before you. The tours listed below are led by professional photographers who offer instruction and hands-on tips.

Antarctica
Season: November–December.
Locations: Antarctic Peninsula; South Georgia Island; South Shetland Islands.
Cost: From $5,995 for 19 days from Santiago.
Tour Operator: Joseph Van Os Photo Safaris.

A voyage aboard the *Professor Multanovskiy,* with only 46 participants, visits the most prolific wildlife habitats at each location, and allows maximum time ashore. Photograph seabird colonies, king penguin colonies, albatross nesting areas, elephant and fur seals, and colonies numbering close to 100,000 penguins and other birds. All this, plus the spectacular landscapes of Antarctic.

Brazil

Season: May.
Locations: Iguaću Falls; Pantanal.
Cost: $3,795 for 15 days from São Paulo.
Tour Operator: Joseph Van Os Photo Safaris.

The Pantanal, Earth's largest freshwater wetland, is sparsely populated by humans but abundantly populated with animals. From small boats and other vehicles, you can photograph jabiru storks, caimans, capybaras, marsh deer, giant anteaters, and, with luck, the camera-shy jaguar. Joseph Van Os Photo Safaris spends six days at a private ranch in the Pantanal, as well as time in Cuiabá (with photo shoots at two zoos) and at Iguacú Falls.

Chile

Season: November.
Location: Easter Island.
Cost: $1,995 for nine days from Santiago.
Tour Operator: Joseph Van Os Photo Safaris.

The mysterious *moai* (stone monoliths) of Easter Island are as evocative a subject as any photographer could want. What inspired the statues' construction, how the stones, which weigh up to 80 tons, were transported from quarry to final location, and what the forms signify remain mysteries. A professional photographer will help you understand the subtleties of lighting and other factors that will enable you to create memorable images.

Peru

Season: June–August.
Locations: Cuzco; Machu Picchu.
Cost: From $2,180 for eight days from Lima.
Tour Operators: South American Journeys; Southwind Adventures.

Arguably the most photographed site in South America, Machu Picchu inspires more than the usual vacation photos. A professional photographer helps you determine the best angles and lighting for your images of the world's most famous Inca site. On Southwind Adventures' "Inca Visions–The Art of Seeing," photographer Karen Gordon Schulman helps you deepen your knowledge and skill in photographing festivals, markets, archaeology, and the natural world. South American Journeys offers two photo workshops. One is led by landscape photographer Efrain Padro and Leslie Spurlock, who specializes in indigenous cultures; photographer Don Gale accompanies the second departure.

SPORTS

Bicycling

Argentina & Chile

Season: October–April.
Locations: Lake District; Patagonia.
Cost: From $1,395 for nine days from Santiago.
Tour Operators: Backroads; Latin American Escapes; Southwind Adventures.

Excursions follow a moderately challenging route around the waters and valleys of Chile's Lake District, a region of glacier-clad peaks and volcanic cones. You'll mountain-bike through two or more national parks, pedaling an average of 40 km (25 mi) per day on unpaved roads. At night you relax at comfortable inns and hotels.

Bolivia

Season: July–August.
Locations: Altiplano; Lake Titicaca vicinity.
Cost: From $1,395 for seven days from La Paz.
Tour Operator: Explore Bolivia.

Bolivia is thought of as the end-all-be-all of South American mountain biking, and it's easy to see why. With Explore Bolivia, you first take acclimatization rides near La Paz, then move on to Lake Titicaca for a circuit of its circumference and a night's camping on its shores. With 6,480 meters (21,260 feet) Mt. Illimani in view, you continue along river valleys, rugged canyons, and ancient villages.

Ecuador

Season: June–December.
Locations: Lake District; Valley of the Volcanoes.
Cost: From $950 for five days from Quito.
Tour Operators: Latin American Escapes; World Trek Expeditions; Southwind Adventures.

Using 21-speed mountain bikes, your Southwind Adventures trip follows backcountry roads around Ecuador's Lake District, visiting Otavalo communities and crossing a 3,200-meter (10,500-foot) pass. You'll also hike in Intag Cloud-Forest Reserve. With World Trek Expeditions, bike through forests, villages, in the shadows of Cotopaxi volcano, and into the volcanic crater of Pululahua. Latin American Escapes' moderate to challenging high altitude biking expedition visits Cotopaxi National Park, crater lakes, and Indian markets.

Peru

Season: April–December.
Locations: Amazon basin; Andes; Cuzco.
Cost: From $1,595 for nine days from Lima.
Tour Operators: BikeHike Adventures; Southwind Adventures; World Trek Expeditions.

All of the above operators visit Machu Picchu. BikeHike Adventures uses fat tire all-terrain mountain bikes to explore a network of backcountry roads and dirt trails. With World Trek Expeditions, you descend 12,000-foot mountain paths and ride along jungle tracks. There's white-water rafting and hot-air ballooning. On Southwind Adventures' Andean trip you use a 21-speed mountain bike to visit ancient ruins and market towns, and to cross passes up to 13,615 feet.

Canoeing, Kayaking & White-Water Rafting

White-water rafting and kayaking can be exhilarating experiences. You don't have to be an expert paddler to enjoy many of these adventures, but you should be a strong swimmer. Rivers are rated from Class I to Class V according to difficulty of navigation. Generally speaking, Class I to III rapids are suitable for beginners, while Class IV and V rapids are strictly for the experienced. Canoeing, of course, is a gentler river experience.

Bolivia

Season: Year-round.
Locations: Lake Titicaca; Río Tuichi.
Cost: From $705 for five days from La Paz.
Tour Operator: Explore Bolivia.

Explore Bolivia has put together two quite different adventures for water-lovers. Its five-day itinerary explores Lake Titicaca by sea kayak, visiting Inca ruins, taking in the splendid mountain scenery, and camping by secluded bays; your route circumnavigates the Island of the Sun. If rafting is your thing, consider the 12-day Tuichi River expedition. After a two-day drive, followed by a two-day trek through the Yungas valley and along an old rubber tapper trail, your river experience begins. The rapids gradually progress from Class II to IV.

Brazil

Season: Year-round.
Location: Amazon.
Cost: From $1,100 for eight days from Manaus.
Tour Operator: Swallows and Amazons.

Following a day's journey along the Rio Negro, you overnight in a small rain forest lodge owned by Swallows and Amazons. The following day, you set out by boat for Jau National Park for six days of canoeing, hiking, fishing, swimming, and visiting with the local river people. Accommodations are nil—you camp in the rain forest or on the beach each night.

Chile

Season: September–May.
Locations: Patagonia; Río Futaleufú.
Cost: From $1,300 for seven days from Puerto Montt.
Tour Operators: Earth River Expeditions; Geographic Expeditions; Latin American Escapes.

Chile has both scenic fjords for sea kayaking and challenging rivers for white-water rafting. With Geographic Expeditions and Latin American Escapes, sea kayakers can explore the fishing villages, glaciers, and wildlife of Patagonia. For the experienced rafter, the Class V Río Futaleufú offers many challenges. Its sheer-walled Inferno Canyon includes such well-named rapids as Infierno and Purgatorio. Earth River's Río Futaleufú program includes a Challenge Cirque, a unique course in which you undergo physical challenges, such as rock climbs and harness and zip-line traverses over rapids (hooked in, you slide over the river on the metal line). This company also offers a kayaking journey over a chain of three lakes. Access is by float plane.

Ecuador

Season: Year-round.
Locations: Amazon basin; Cuyabeno Reserve; Río Upano.
Cost: From $950 for six days from Quito.
Tour Operators: Adventure Life; Earthquest; Earth River Expeditions; Latin American Escapes; Mountain Travel-Sobek; Remote Odysseys West (ROW).

The Class III–IV Río Upano's rapids have become synonymous with world-class rafting. Experience these "big volume" rapids on 6- to 11-day adventures with Earth River Expeditions, Latin American Escapes, Mountain Travel-Sobek, or ROW. Earthquest explores the Cuyabeno Reserve by dugout canoe (a native-made canoe cut from tree trunks), hiking on old hunting trails, and sleeping in hammocks under thatch-roof shelters. Adventure Life leads a kayaking journey along the Shiripuno River, paddling three to six hours per day; you also hike and meet the Huaorani people. Latin American Escapes also offers the chance to kayak with whales in Machalilla National Park.

Peru

Season: May–October.
Locations: Colca Canyon; Cotahuasi Canyon; Río Apurímac; Río Tambopata.
Cost: From $1,968 for 10 days from Arequipa.
Tour Operators: Earth River Expeditions; Latin American Escapes.

The moderate-to-difficult rapids of the Class III–IV Río Tambopata lead to the Tambopata-Candamo Reserve, while the wilder ride of the Class IV–V Río Apurímac cuts through gorges and canyons under towering Andean peaks. Cotahuasi Canyon rafting takes you through Class IV and V whitewater on the Andes' western slopes. For serious rafters, the Class V Río Colca is one of the deepest and most inaccessible river canyons in the world. ROW organizes a 12-day Colca Canyon expedition. Latin American Escapes has itineraries on each of these rivers.

Venezuela

Season: Year-round.
Locations: Los Roques; Río Karuai.
Cost: From $1,300 for six days from Caracas.
Tour Operator: Earthquest.

Only three hours by air from Miami, Venezuela is a popular choice for water sports enthusiasts. With Earthquest, you can choose between a sea kayaking experience among the islands of Los Roques archipelago, with ample opportunity for snorkeling, diving, and swimming—or opt for a 14-day sea kayak and dugout canoe adventure along the Karuai River. You view exotic flora and fauna, visit local villages, and make a fly-over of Angel Falls.

Fishing

Argentina & Chile

Season: November–April.
Locations: Chiloé Island; Lake District; Patagonia.
Cost: From $1,695 for five days from Puerto Montt.
Tour Operators: Earthquest; Fishing International; FishQuest; Fly Fishing And; Frontiers; Rod & Reel Adventures.

For anglers, Argentina and Chile are the southern hemisphere's Alaska, offering world-class trout fishing in clear streams. An added bonus is the availability of landlocked salmon and golden dorado, known as the "river tiger." Bilingual fishing guides accompany groups, and accommodations are generally in private lodges.

Brazil

Season: Year-round.
Location: Amazon.
Cost: From $2,650 for nine days from Manaus.
Tour Operators: Fishing International; FishQuest; Rod & Reel Adventures.

While pirapitinga, pirarucú, jancundá, matrincha, arapá, and many other exotic fish inhabit the Amazon, it is the legendary peacock bass that anglers describe as the "ultimate adversary." Depending on the trip, your base will be a fishing camp, a five-star resort, or a comfortable live-aboard yacht.

Venezuela

Season: Year-round.
Locations: Lake Guri; Los Roques; Rí Caura; Río Chico.
Cost: From $1,152 for five days from Puerto Ordaz.
Tour Operators: Fishing International; FishQuest; Frontiers; Rod & Reel Adventures.

Venezuela has an enviable reputation for both saltwater and freshwater fishing. Los Roques, an archipelago that's a short flight from Caracas, offers exciting bonefishing, while Río Chico is known for tarpon and snook. Guri Lake and Río Caura are top spots for peacock bass, some of them exceeding 15 pounds. Other challenges are the payara, described as "a salmon with a bad attitude," giant catfish, and the fierce aymara.

Hiking, Running & Trekking

South America's magnificent scenery and varied terrain make it a terrific place for trekkers and hikers. The southern part of Argentina and Chile, known as Patagonia, and Peru's Inca Trail are especially popular. Plenty of tour operators offer hiking and trekking trips to these regions, so study several to determine the program that's best for your ability and interests. The trips outlined below are organized tours led by qualified guides. Camping is often part of the experience, although on some trips you stay at inns and small hotels. Itineraries range from relatively easy hikes to serious trekking and even running.

Argentina & Chile

Season: November–March.
Locations: Atacama Desert; Lake District; Patagonia.
Cost: From $1,845 for eight days from Santiago.
Tour Operators: Adventure Life; Andes Adventures; Backroads; Country Walkers; Geographic Expeditions; KE Adventure Travel; Mountain Travel-Sobek; Southwind Adventures; Wilderness Travel; Wildland Adventures.

Patagonia may be the most-trekked region in South America; most companies above at least offer standard Patagonia excursions. Highlights include moderate to vigorous excursions in Torres del Paine or Glacier National Park and over the Patagonian Ice Cap. Adventure Life's program lets you overnight in igloo-shape tents at EcoCamp in Torres del Paine. In addition to its hiking trip, Andes Adventures offers an 18-day running itinerary with runs covering as much as 31 km (19 mi) per day. Other options include an Atacama Desert trek with Geographic Expeditions or KE Adventure Travel (the latter includes an ascent of Licancabur volcano) or Backroads' Lake District walk.

Bolivia

Season: April–October.
Locations: Cordillera Apolobamba; Cordillera Quimsa Cruz; Cordillera Real; Lake Titicaca; Uyuni.
Cost: From $1,030 for seven days from La Paz.
Tour Operators: American Alpine Institute; Explore Bolivia; KE Adventure Travel; Latin American Escapes; Mountain Madness; Sherpa Expeditions; Southwind Adventures; Wildland Adventures.

Bolivia's majestic mountain ranges offer some challenging treks. The extreme altitude makes the going even tougher, so operators allow time for acclimatization in La Paz before heading to higher ground. On some trips, you'll be accompanied by llamas that tote your gear. Camping is likely to be part of the experience.

Brazil

Season: Year-round.
Locations: Amazon basin; Pico da Neblina National Park.
Cost: From $2,400 for 15 days from Manaus.
Tour Operators: KE Adventure Travel; Swallows and Amazons.

For an up-close jungle experience, join Swallows and Amazons for 10 days of trekking and camping in Jau National Park, during which you walk an average of six hours daily through thick vegetation, then relax at night in a jungle camp. The company also runs two treks in Pico da Neblina National Park to the base of Mount Pico da Neblina. KE Adventure Travel's 15-day trip in this same region includes an ascent of the 3,013 meters (9,885 feet) mountain, known in English as the "Mountain of the Mists."

Ecuador

Season: Year-round.
Locations: Galápagos; Highlands.
Cost: From $1,890 for eight days from Quito.
Tour Operators: Country Walkers; KE Adventure Travel; Mountain Travel-Sobek; Southwind Adventures.

Two mountain ranges slice through Ecuador, making for some great trekking. Here you'll find the Avenue of Volcanoes, one of the largest concentrations of volcanoes in the world. Treks lead to glacier-clad peaks, national parks, and cloud forests. On Mountain Travel-Sobek's "Hiking the Haciendas" journey, you'll overnight in elegant estates, some dating to the 16th century. Country Walkers' program hikes in both the highlands and the Galápagos Islands, while Southwind Adventures focuses on the highlands. KE Adventure Travel's 16-day arduous trek traverses mountain forests and páramo grasslands, crossing several 3,962 meters (13,000 feet) passes.

Guyana

Season: Year-round.
Locations: Kaieteur Falls; Potaro River.
Cost: From $775 for five days from Georgetown.
Tour Operator: Latin American Escapes.

The majority of Guyana's interior is pristine rain forest, explored by few travelers. Latin American Escapes' overland journey travels from Georgetown, the capital, by bus and Jeep to the Potaro River. Trekking through forest, you'll make your way to a camp site at Waratuk Falls before continuing on to Tukiet camp at the base of a mountain—for splendid views of a gorge and time for swimming. Ascend the mountain for a panoramic view of Kaieteur Falls.

Peru

Season: May–September.
Locations: The Blanca, Huayhusah, and Vilcabamba mountain ranges; Inca Trail; Mount Ausangate; Mount Salcantay.
Cost: From $2,325 for 16 days from Lima.
Tour Operators: Andes Adventures; Country Walkers; Geographic Expeditions; Journeys International; KE Adventure Travel; Mountain Travel-Sobek; Sherpa Expeditions; Southwind Adventures; Wilderness Travel; Wildland Adventures.

The Inca Trail, stretching from the Urubamba valley to Machu Picchu, has become one of South America's most popular destinations for trekkers. The 45-km (28-mi) mountain trail is mostly level but the altitude makes it challenging. All of the above companies offer Inca Trail treks. Some also lead more difficult Andean treks at altitudes in excess of 5,181 meters (17,000 feet). In addition to treks, Andes Adventures has three running programs in Peru, including a 44-km (27.5-mi) marathon and a circuit around Mount Ausangate.

Venezuela

Season: Year-round.
Locations: Mt. Roraima; Sierra Nevada National Park.

Cost: From $2,995 for 10 days from Caracas.
Tour Operators: KE Adventure Travel; Southwind Adventures; Swallows and Amazons.

Trekkers often head to 2,810-meter (9,220-foot) Mt. Roraima, rumored to be the setting of Arthur Conan Doyles's *The Lost World*. All tour operators above organize treks here, including a nontechnical ascent of the summit. With KE Adventure Travel and Southwind Adventures, your trip includes an overflight of Angel Falls. The latter company also offers a strenuous six-day trek through the Sierra Nevadas, covering 69 off-the-beaten-path km (43 mi).

Horseback Riding

Argentina
Season: November–April.
Locations: Alto Ongamira; Lake District; Patagonia.
Cost: From $525 for eight days from Alto Ongamira.
Tour Operators: Equitours; Hidden Trails.

Few countries have a greater equestrian tradition than Argentina. Equitours introduces you to the country's gaucho culture at a 15,000-acre *estancia* (cattle ranch). You ride through the grasslands and beech forests of Lanin National Park and spend several nights camping. Hidden Trails offers three itineraries in Argentina. You can explore the forests, mountains, and lakes of northwestern Patagonia, which includes some camping, or set out each day from your base at an *estancia* in the Lake District or from Alto Ongamira.

Brazil
Season: Year-round.
Locations: Highlands; Pantanal.
Cost: From $1,075 for eight days from Campo Grande.
Tour Operator: Hidden Trails.

Observe the flora and fauna as you ride through the vast Pantanal on a "Wildlife Safari Ride." Enjoy picnics, camping, and ranch stays, plus sightseeing and a show in Rio. Hidden Trails also has an eight-day "Southern Cross Fazenda Ride" where you journey along high plains at elevations reaching 1,676 meters (5,500 feet). Meet local ranchers and gauchos and, perhaps, participate in a local rodeo.

Chile
Season: October–April.
Locations: Atacama Desert; Lake District; Patagonia; Río Hurtado Valley.
Cost: From $1,695 for seven days from Punta Arenas.
Tour Operators: Equitours; Hidden Trails; Latin American Escapes.

On Equitours' 10-day "Patagonia Glacier Ride" you cross the pampas to Torres del Paine National Park, a region of mountains, lakes, and glaciers. Nights are spent camping or in lodges. Latin American Escapes has a five-day journey, accompanied by gauchos, in the scenic Lake District. Hidden Trails has three itineraries: you can opt for a ride in southern Chile through lonely valleys, along historic mule trails created by gold diggers, and into the Andes; join a Lake District program that passes through rain forests, over mountain passes, and past isolated pioneer farms; or take an Atacama Desert adventure, during which you ride over the crusted salt of the Salar de Atacama and across expanses of sand, visiting ancient ruins and petroglyphs. Most trips involve camping.

Ecuador
Season: Year-round.
Location: Andes.
Cost: From $1,050 for 10 days from Quito.
Tour Operators: Equitours; Hidden Trails.

Journeying into the heart of the Eucadorean Andes, Hidden Trails' "Cloud Forest to Highlands" program takes you on rides through bamboo forests, desert-like landscapes, mountain slopes, and canyons. A second itinerary rides along ancient Inca trails and colonial routes, as well as the Avenue of Volcanoes, during which you visit village markets and overnight in centuries-old haciendas. Equitours offers a hacienda-to-hacienda ride through the Zuleta Valley and Cotopaxi National Park. This company also has an "Andean Mountain Ride," where daily you amble through pine forests and canter over grasslands and the *páramo* (above the tree line, at altitudes up to 11,000 feet) from your base at a comfortable hacienda located about three hours' drive from Quito.

Peru
Season: April–November.
Locations: Arequipa; Cuzco; Machu Picchu.
Cost: From $2,100 for 11 days from Cuzco.
Tour Operators: Equitours; Hidden Trails.

Astride Peruvian Paso horses, a breed dating back to the colonial era and originating from Spanish Andalusians, you'll explore the terraces of the Sacred Valley of the Incas and the ancient city of Machu Picchu on programs offered by both of the operators above. You'll also mingle with descendants of the Incas and learn about their culture. Hidden Trails has a second itinerary that flies over the Nazca lines (more than 300 geometric and animal figures etched some 1,000 years ago on the desert's surface) and visits the region around Arequipa before moving on to Cuzco. Dinner with a major breeder of Peruvian Paso horses is a special offering of this departure.

Mountaineering

Antarctica
Season: January.
Location: Mount Vinson.
Cost: $26,000 for 17 days from Punta Arenas.
Tour Operator: Mountain Madness.

If you have a solid mountaineering background and you're accustomed to cold weather camping, this could be the ultimate mountaineering adventure. You get to base camp by taking a short flight from Patriot Hills.

Via the Branscomb Glacier, make your way to 4,897 meters (16,067 feet) Vinson Massif and establish three additional camps. Although the climb itself is considered technically moderate, extreme temperatures, as low as -40F, make this a serious challenge.

Argentina & Chile

Season: December–February.
Locations: Mount Aconcagua, Cerro Torre, and Fitzroy, Argentina; Torres del Paine National Park, Chile.
Cost: From $3,395 for 23 days from Mendoza.
Tour Operators: American Alpine Institute; Arun Treks & Expeditions; Colorado Mountain School; KE Adventure Travel; Mountain Madness; Ultimate Ascents.

At 6,960 meters (22,835 feet), Argentina's Mount Aconcagua, in central Argentina near the Chilean border, is the highest peak in the world outside of Asia. Though some routes are not technically difficult, Aconcagua is quite demanding physically and requires the use of ice axes, crampons, and ropes. All of the above operators offer climbs of Aconcagua, some via the more difficult Polish glacier route. Frequent high winds and ice make the Polish glacier route very demanding and only for those with extensive mountaineering experience at high altitudes. Mountain Madness has a circumnavigation of Aconcagua, going in via the Polish traverse under the glacier, summiting, then descending through the Horcones Valley. American Alpine Institute also organizes ascents of several peaks in Patagonia.

Bolivia

Season: June–September.
Location: Cordillera Real.
Cost: From $2,100 for 11 days from La Paz.
Tour Operators: American Alpine Institute; Arun Treks & Expeditions; Colorado Mountain School; KE Adventures; Mountain Madness.

Stretching for 160 km (100 mi), Bolivia's Cordillera Real has some of the continent's finest and most varied alpine climbing. Large crevasses and a 40- to 45-degree glacial face will challenge you even if you have lots of experience. Twenty-two mountains are 5,791 meters (19,000 feet) or higher. The highest, Illimani, soars to 6,462 meters (21,201 feet). You can also attempt ascents of Antisana, Huayna Potosí, Illliniza Norte and Sur, and Pequeno Alpamayo. In addition to climbs, Mountain Madness operates a glacier mountaineering course in Bolivia.

Ecuador

Season: May–February.
Locations: Antisana; Carihuairazo; Cayambe; Chimborazo; Cotopaxi; Cubilche; Illiniza Sur.
Cost: From $1,875 for nine days from Quito.
Tour Operators: American Alpine Institute; Arun Treks & Expeditions; Colorado Mountain School; KE Adventures; Mountain Madness.

With challenges for all levels of ability, Ecuador's volcanoes have become a major destination for climbers and would-be climbers. Question operators carefully to match the trip to your ability level. All of the companies above organize climbs of 6,267-meter (20,561-foot) Chimborazo and 5,897-meter (19,347-foot) Cotopaxi. American Alpine Institute offers six different climbing itineraries in Ecuador, while Mountain Madness' 20-day trip includes climbs for a total of four volcanoes. They also operate a 19-day climbing course in Ecuador, designed for beginners and intermediates, with stays in huts and haciendas.

Peru

Season: June–July.

Locations: Alpamayo; Chopicalqui; Huascarán; Ishinca; Pisco Oeste; Toclararju; Tscara; Urus.

Cost: From $2,700 for 16 days from Lima.

Tour Operators: American Alpine Institute; Arun Treks & Expeditions; Colorado Mountain School; KE Adventures; Mountain Madness; Ultimate Ascents.

Considered one of the world's most beautiful mountains, Alpamayo's pyramid-shape peak soars to 5,947 meters (19,512 feet). Strong snow- and ice-climbing skills are necessary for this climb. Huascarán, Peru's highest mountain, has two extinct volcanic summits separated by a deep saddle. Prerequisites for Huascarán include high-altitude climbing experience and the ability to scale 45-degree ice with a full pack. Advanced beginners can handle some Peruvian peaks.

Multisport

Multisport trips grow in popularity every year. Innovative itineraries combine two or more sports, such as biking, fishing, canoeing, hiking, horseback riding, kayaking, rafting, and trekking.

Argentina & Chile

Season: November–April.

Locations: Lake District; Patagonia; Río Futaleufú, Chile.

Cost: From $1,595 for eight days from Puerto Montt, Chile.

Tour Operators: BikeHike Adventures; Earth River Expeditions; Hidden Trails; Latin American Escapes; Maxim Tours; Mountain Travel-Sobek; Naturequest; The World Outdoors.

Whether you choose the Lake District or Patagonia, the scene for your active vacation will be one of great beauty. Both regions offer superb trekking, kayaking, horseback riding, and biking. If you want to try serious rafting, consider one of the Río Futaleufú trips, such as those run by Earth River Expeditions and Mountain Travel-Sobek, which include rafting along with hiking, biking, and sea kayaking.

Bolivia

Season: Year-round.

Locations: Altiplano; Cordillera Real; Lake Titicaca.

Cost: From $1,625 for nine days from La Paz.

Tour Operators: Explore Bolivia; Naturequest.

Bolivia's diverse topography means the chance to enjoy many outdoor sports. Naturequest's eight-day itinerary includes sea kayaking, mountain biking, and hiking along ancient trails. You make nature expeditions into the jungle and explore Inca ruins. After sightseeing in La Paz and the ruins of Tiahuanaco with Explore Bolivia, you kayak on Lake Titicaca, then trek and mountain bike in the Altiplano and the Cordillera Real.

Brazil

Season: Year-round.
Locations: Minas Gerais; Pico da Neblina National Park.
Cost: From $1,695 for nine days from Belo Horizonte.
Tour Operators: BikeHike Adventures; Swallows and Amazons.

BikeHike's nine-day adventure starts off with a three-day trek through the Cipó mountain range, followed by kayaking, horseback riding, and a 21-meter (70-foot) rappel down a waterfall. Nights are spent in farmhouses and camping. Swallows and Amazons' multisport trips include mountain biking, canyoning, snorkeling, and trekking in several locations.

Ecuador

Season: Year-round.
Locations: Amazon basin; Andean Highlands; Antisana Ecological Reserve; Cotopaxi National Park; Galápagos.
Cost: From $1,295 for nine days from Quito.
Tour Operators: Adventure Life; Backroads; BikeHike Adventures; Latin American Escapes; The World Outdoors.
Backroads runs an 11-day biking and hiking itinerary in the highlands, plus snorkeling and kayaking in the Galápagos. BikeHike Adventures has a 15-day mountain biking, hiking, sea kayaking, and horseback riding adventure covering the high altiplano and the rain forest of the Amazon basin; and a 9-day biking, sea kayaking, horseback riding, and hiking trip in the Galápagos. For a 13-day highlands and Galápagos hiking, biking, sea kayaking, snorkeling, and horseback riding adventure, try The World Outdoors. Latin American Escapes offers a Galápagos program of kayaking, snorkeling, hiking, and horseback riding—an 8-day trip that includes volcano biking in Bellavista Cloud Forest Reserve, Class III white-water rafting on the Río Blanco or Río Toachi, and a 3-day alpine trek at elevations up to 4,572 meters (15,000 feet) in Antisana Ecological Reserve.

Peru

Season: Year-round.
Location: Andes.
Cost: From $1,795 for 12 days from Lima.
Tour Operators: Backroads; BikeHike Adventures; KE Adventure Travel; The World Outdoors.

Peru's Andes offer splendid scenery and interesting archaeological sites. What better way to see it all than by horseback, mountain bike, raft, or on foot? Itineraries range from moderately easy to challenging and run from 8 to 14 days. Many programs include Cuzco and Machu Picchu, and some include rock climbing. On all trips you visit village markets and relish endless vistas.

Venezuela

Season: Year-round.
Location: Andes.

Cost: From $2,095 for 12 days from Caracas.
Tour Operator: BikeHike Adventures.

Enjoy Venezuela's snow-capped mountains, cloud forests, and páramo tropical highlands as you bike and hike along backcountry roads and hidden trails and raft down rushing rivers. Such travel virtually guarantees interaction with village people and gives you some insight concerning their traditions.

Skiing

When ski season's over in the northern hemisphere, it's time to pack the gear and head for resorts in Argentina or Chile.

Argentina
Season: June–September.
Locations: Bariloche; Las Leñas.
Cost: From $2,679 for seven days from Miami.
Tour Operators: Adventures on Skis; Ladatco Tours; Moguls.

Argentina's Bariloche, an alpine-style resort town nicknamed "Little Switzerland," is 13 km (8 mi) from the slopes of Cerro Catedral. This ski area offers more than 64 km (40 mi) of trails accessed by 33 lifts. Another option is Las Leñas, with 56 km (35 mi) of downhill trails and a vertical drop of 1,219 meters (4,000 feet). Appealing especially to the expert skier, Las Leñas has served as summer training ground to several Olympic ski teams. The price above includes air fare from Miami, accommodations, daily breakfast, transfers between town and the slopes, and a six-day ski pass.

Chile
Season: June–September.
Locations: Portillo; Termas de Chillán; Valle Nevado.
Cost: From $1,971 for seven days from Miami.
Tour Operators: Adventures on Skis; Ladatco Tours; Moguls.

A short drive from Santiago, Valle Nevado has more than 300 acres of groomed runs and a 792-meter (2,600-foot) vertical drop. Near the base of Mount Aconcagua, the highest mountain in the western hemisphere, is Portillo, with lots of slopes and trails. Also nearby, Termas de Chillán, 483 km (300 mi) south of Santiago, has fine downhill runs plus a network of forest tracks for cross-country skiers. The rate above includes air fare from Miami, accommodations, seven days of unlimited lift passes, breakfast and dinner daily, and transfers.

UNDERSTANDING SOUTH AMERICA

A CONTINENT OF TREASURES

PORTUGUESE VOCABULARY

SPANISH VOCABULARY

PAST AND PRESENT exist side by side in South America. Smartly dressed business executives brush shoulders with women clad in traditional costumes that have changed little since the colonial conquests. Centuries-old cathedrals with dazzling facades are reflected in sleek glass skyscrapers. Gleaming Volvos and BMWs share streets with dusty oxcarts and men on horseback. The continent has its eyes fixed on the future but can't help but cast a wistful glance at the past.

It's these sharp differences that make South America such a fascinating destination. Choose nearly any major city as a base and you have an amazing array of activities nearby. In Rio de Janeiro, for example, you can spend a splendid morning sunbathing on the beach at Ipanema, then visit the historic Palácio Catete in the afternoon. In Buenos Aires you can pass the day exploring the ornate churches surrounding the Plaza de Mayo before heading off for an evening of tango in the city's picturesque waterfront district. In Santiago you can start your day on the slopes of the trendy ski resort of Valle Nevado and end it with a glass of wine at a country inn dating from colonial times.

A handful of South American sights have been popular for years, but trailblazing travelers are discovering that other destinations have just as much, if not more, to offer. The Galápagos Islands off the coast of Ecuador have fascinating fauna, but so does Los Llanos, the vast savannas that cover more than a third of Venezuela. Called the "Serengeti of South America," the region is teeming with wildlife ranging from fearsome caimans to cuddly capybaras. At sunset, endless flocks of brilliantly colored scarlet ibises fill the skies as they return home to roost. Machu Picchu in Peru attracts busloads of picture-snapping tourists, but head to Ingapirca in Ecuador and you may find yourself alone

at its awesome Inca temple. The city-size cruise ships that head up the mighty Amazon would never fit through the icy fjords navigated by smaller ships that ply the waters around windswept Tierra del Fuego. Sailing through the fabled Avenue of the Glaciers at dawn is an experience you're not likely to forget.

A Short History

South America was inhabited for thousands of years before it was "discovered" by Europeans. Archaeologists have determined that a 12,500-year-old village near the town of Monte Verde in southern Chile could be the oldest in the Americas, essentially rewriting the first chapter of human history in the hemisphere. (The actual age of the site is the subject of heated debate in archaeological circles.) Other societies nearly as old have been uncovered all over the continent. One of the most venerable was the Chinchorros, who inhabited the western coast more than 8,000 years ago. This nomadic people had already perfected the process of mummifying their dead 5,000 years ago—thousands of years before the Egyptians.

Most of the tribes of South America were small and loosely organized, making them easy targets. The first invaders did not come from Europe but from elsewhere in South America. Pushing outward from their empire in what is now Peru, the Incas dismantled existing cultures, forcing indigenous peoples to give up their language and their rituals. Only fierce resistance from other native peoples, such as the Mapuches in what is now southern Chile, halted the expansion of the Inca empire.

The Inca empire had spread over much of the western edge of the continent by the time Christopher Columbus first stepped foot on the mainland in 1498. Spain was eager to develop an overseas empire at that time, so it didn't wait long to send others to explore and colonize this new territory. In 1531, conquistador Francisco Pizarro sailed south from Panama with some 180 men and 27 horses. Two years later he had conquered the entire Inca empire, accomplishing in South America what Hernán Cortés had already done in Mexico. One of Pizarro's officers, Pedro de Valdivia, conquered northern Chile in 1541, giving Spain control of the west coast of the continent from Panama to central Chile.

The Portuguese, meanwhile, were busy on the eastern coast laying claim to Brazil. Unlike the situation in the rest of South America, however, the colonization of Brazil was gradual and relatively peaceful. While Spanish conquistadors were seeking the gold of legendary El Dorado, wood was the first natural resource exploited by the Portuguese. Then came sugar, which gave rise to vast plantations along the coast—and to the importation of millions of African slaves to do the backbreaking labor. Afterward came gold and diamonds, opening up the land in the interior. Coffee followed, and with it the appearance of planters on the red earth of southeastern Brazil.

Many Spaniards and Portuguese came here to make a quick fortune and return to Europe as soon as possible. Their expeditions, however, often included farmers and craftsmen who wished to begin life anew in the Americas. What these settlers encountered instead was an oppressive feudal system that evolved apace with such glittering colonial cities as Lima, Quito, and Ouro Prêto. For three centuries colonists labored under European rule, but between 1808 and 1826 the New World empires built by Spain and Portugal began to crumble—often due to political and economic factors similar to those that had precipitated the revolution in Great Britain's North American colonies.

Although each country had its own revolutionary heroes, two men stand out as leaders in South America's struggle for independence. The first is Venezuelan general Simón Bolívar, a man of tremendous vision whose courageous battles freed Bolivia, Colombia, Ecuador, Peru, and Venezuela. The second is José de San Martín, the Argentine general who helped win independence for Chile and Peru. Streets and plazas all over the continent are named for the two heroes. One of the most moving monuments, La Rotonda in the Ecuadoran city of Guayaquil, memorializes the historic meeting between the two. Brazil, on the other hand, won its independence from Portugal in 1822 without bloodshed and changed from colony to monarchy to republic fairly easily.

Inspired by the American and French revolutions, eager patriots in the Southern Hemisphere established republican governments. Unfortunately, the new nations were ill prepared for the task. Most lacked the broad popular base necessary to enforce their fragile constitutions. A disheartening number of civil wars, coups d'état, and upheavals have shaken South America's nations since they gained independence. Down through the centuries, power has been seized by charismatic leaders such as Argentina's Juan Perón–although wife Eva was the real power behind the throne—and Paraguay's Alfredo Stroessner.

Things do change, however, and the 1990s brought democratic rule (albeit fragile in some cases) to the entire region. One of the most notorious dictators, General Augusto Pinochet of Chile, was brought down in 1990. Impassioned international debate followed his 1999 arrest in London, but Chilean courts have ruled him mentally unfit to stand trial for human rights abuses occurring during his regime. Colombia continues to grapple with a two-decade-old problem of drug trafficking and its pervasion into many levels of society. The new millennium saw the election of populist leftist leaders in Brazil, Ecuador, and Venezuela, the latter of which endured a two-month nationwide strike in early 2003 in an attempt to force embattled President Hugo Chávez from office.

PORTUGUESE VOCABULARY

English	Portuguese	Pronunciation
Basics		
Yes/no	Sim/Não	**see**ing/nown
Please	Por favor	pohr fah-**vohr**
May I?	Posso?	**poh**-sso
Thank you (very much)	(Muito) obrigado	(**mooy**n-too) o-bree **gah**-doh
You're welcome	De nada	day **nah**-dah
Excuse me	Com licença	con lee-**ssehn**-ssah
Pardon me/what did you say?	Desculpe/O que disse?	des-**kool**-peh/o.k. **dih**-say?
Could you tell me?	Poderia me dizer?	po-day-**ree**-ah mee dee-**zehrr**?
I'm sorry	Sinto muito	**seen**-too **mooy**n-too
Good morning!	Bom dia!	bohn **dee**-ah
Good afternoon!	Boa tarde!	**boh**-ah **tahr**-dee
Good evening!	Boa noite!	**boh**-ah **noh**ee-tee
Goodbye!	Adeus!/Até logo!	ah-**deh**oos/ah-**teh loh**-go
Mr./Mrs.	Senhor/Senhora	sen-**yor**/sen-**yohr**-ah
Miss	Senhorita	sen-yo-**ri**-tah
Pleased to meet you	Muito prazer	**mooy**n-too prah-**zehr**
How are you?	Como vai?	**koh**-mo **vah**-ee
Very well, thank you	Muito bem, obrigado	**mooy**n-too **beh**-in o-bree-**gah**-doh
And you?	E o(a) Senhor(a)?	eh oh sen-**yor**(**yohr**-ah)
Hello (on the telephone)	Alô	ah-**low**

Numbers		
1	um/uma	oom/**oom**-ah
2	dois	**doh**ees
3	três	**treh**ys
4	quatro	**kwa**-troh
5	cinco	**seen**-koh
6	seis	**seh**ys
7	sete	**seh**-tee
8	oito	**oh**ee-too

9	nove	**noh**-vee
10	dez	**deh**-ees
11	onze	**ohn**-zee
12	doze	**doh**-zee
13	treze	**treh**-zee
14	quatorze	kwa-**tohr**-zee
15	quinze	**keen**-zee
16	dezesseis	deh-zeh-**seh**ys
17	dezessete	deh-zeh-**seh**-tee
18	dezoito	deh-**zoh**ee-toh
19	dezenove	deh-zeh-**noh**-vee
20	vinte	**veen**-tee
21	vinte e um	**veen**-tee eh **oom**
30	trinta	**treen**-tah
32	trinta e dois	**treen**-ta eh **doh**ees
40	quarenta	kwa-**rehn**-ta
43	quarenta e três	kwa-**rehn**-ta e **treh**ys
50	cinquenta	seen-**kwehn**-tah
54	cinquenta e quatro	seen-**kwehn**-tah e **kwa**-troh
60	sessenta	seh-**sehn**-tah
65	sessenta e cinco	seh-**sehn**-tah e **seen**-ko
70	setenta	seh-**tehn**-tah
76	setenta e seis	seh-**tehn**-ta e **seh**ys
80	oitenta	ohee-**tehn**-ta
87	oitenta e sete	ohee-**tehn**-ta e **seh**-tee
90	noventa	noh-**vehn**-ta
98	noventa e oito	noh-**vehn**-ta e **oh**ee-too
100	cem	**seh**-ing
101	cento e um	**sehn**-too e **oom**
200	duzentos	doo-**zehn**-tohss
500	quinhentos	key-**nyehn**-tohss
700	setecentos	seh-teh-**sehn**-tohss
900	novecentos	noh-veh-**sehn**-tohss
1,000	mil	meel
2,000	dois mil	**doh**ees meel
1,000,000	um milhão	oom mee-lee-**ahon**

Colors

black	preto	**preh**-toh
blue	azul	a-**zool**
brown	marrom	mah-**hohm**
green	verde	**vehr**-deh
pink	rosa	**roh**-zah
purple	roxo	**roh**-choh
orange	laranja	lah-**rahn**-jah
red	vermelho	vehr-**meh**-lyoh
white	branco	**brahn**-coh
yellow	amarelo	ah-mah-**reh**-loh

Days of the Week

Sunday	Domingo	doh-**meehn**-goh
Monday	Segunda-feira	seh-**goon**-dah **fey**-rah
Tuesday	Terça-feira	**tehr**-sah **fey**-rah
Wednesday	Quarta-feira	**kwahr**-tah **fey**-rah
Thursday	Quinta-feira	**keen**-tah **fey**-rah
Friday	Sexta-feira	**sehss**-tah **fey**-rah
Saturday	Sábado	**sah**-bah-doh

Months

January	Janeiro	jah-**ney**-roh
February	Fevereiro	feh-veh-**rey**-roh
March	Março	**mahr**-soh
April	Abril	ah-**breel**
May	Maio	**my**-oh
June	Junho	gy**oo**-nyoh
July	Julho	gy**oo**-lyoh
August	Agosto	ah-**ghost**-toh
September	Setembro	seh-**tehm**-broh
October	Outubro	owe-**too**-broh
November	Novembro	noh-**vehm**-broh
December	Dezembro	deh-**zehm**-broh

Useful Phrases

Do you speak English?	Fala inglês?	**fah**-lah een-**glehs**?
I don't speak Portuguese.	Não falo português.	nown **fah**-loh pohr-too-**ghehs**
I don't understand (you)	Não lhe entendo	nown ly**eh** ehn-**tehn**-doh

I understand	Eu entendo	**eh**-oo ehn-**tehn**-doh
I don't know	Não sei	nown say
I am American/ British	Sou americano (americana)/inglês (inglêsa)	sow a-meh-ree-**cah**-noh (a-meh-ree-**cah**-nah)/een-**glehs** (een-**gleh**-sa)
What's your name?	Como se chama?	**koh**-moh seh **shah**-mah
My name is . . .	Meu nome é . . .	mehw **noh**-meh eh
What time is it?	Que horas são?	keh **oh**-rahss **sa**-ohn
It is one, two, three . . . o'clock	É uma/Saõ duas, três . . . hora/ horas	eh **oom**-ah/**sa**-ohn oomah, **doo**-ahss, **trehys oh**-rah/**oh**-rahs
Yes, please/No, thank you	Sim por favor/ Não obrigado	seing pohr fah-**vohr**/ nown o-bree-**gah**-doh
How?	Como?	**koh**-moh
When?	Quando?	**kwahn**-doh
This/Next week	Esta/Próxima semana	**ehss**-tah/**proh**-see-mah seh-**mah**-nah
This/Next month	Este/Próximo mêz	**ehss**-teh/**proh**-see-moh mehz
This/Next year	Este/Próximo ano	**ehss**-teh/**proh**-see-moh **ah**-noh
Yesterday/today tomorrow	Ontem/hoje amanhã	**ohn**-tehn/**oh**-jeh/ ah-mah-**nyan**
This morning/ afternoon	Esta manhã/ tarde	**ehss**-tah mah-**nyan**/ **tahr**-deh
Tonight	Hoje a noite	**oh**-jeh ah **noh**ee-tee
What?	O que?	oh **keh**
What is it?	O que é isso?	oh **keh** eh **ee**-soh
Why?	Por quê?	pohr-**keh**
Who?	Quem?	**keh**-in
Where is . . . ?	Onde é . . . ?	**ohn**-deh eh
the train station?	a estação de trem?	ah es-tah-**sah**-on deh train
the subway station?	a estação de metrô?	ah es-tah-**sah**-on deh meh-**tro**
the bus stop?	a parada do ônibus?	ah pah-**rah**-dah doh **oh**-nee-boos
the post office?	o correio?	oh coh-**hay**-yoh
the bank?	o banco?	oh **bahn**-koh
the hotel?	o hotel . . . ?	oh oh-**tell**
the cashier?	o caixa?	oh **kahy**-shah
the museum?	o museo . . . ?	oh moo-**zeh**-oh
the hospital?	o hospital?	oh ohss-pee-**tal**
the elevator?	o elevador?	oh eh-leh-vah-**dohr**

the bathroom?	o banheiro?	oh bahn-**yey**-roh
the beach?	a praia de . . . ?	ah **prahy**-yah deh
Here/there	Aqui/ali	ah-**kee**/ah-**lee**
Open/closed	Aberto/fechado	ah-**behr**-toh/feh-**shah**-doh
Left/right	Esquerda/direita	ehs-**kehr**-dah/dee-**ray**-tah
Straight ahead	Em frente	ehyn **frehn**-teh
Is it near/far?	É perto/longe?	eh **pehr**-toh/**lohn**-jeh
I'd like to buy . . .	Gostaria de comprar . . .	gohs-tah-**ree**-ah deh cohm-**prahr** . . .
a bathing suit	um maiô	oom mahy-**owe**
a dictionary	um dicionário	oom dee-seeoh-**nah**-reeoh
a hat	um chapéu	oom shah-**peh**oo
a magazine	uma revista	**oo**mah heh-**vees**-tah
a map	um mapa	oom **mah**-pah
a postcard	cartão postal	kahr-**town** pohs-**tahl**
sunglasses	óculos escuros	**ah**-koo-loss ehs-**koo**-rohs
suntan lotion	um óleo de bronzear	oom **oh**-lyoh deh brohn-zeh-**ahr**
a ticket	um bilhete	oom bee-lyeh-teh
cigarettes	cigarros	see-**gah**-hose
envelopes	envelopes	eyn-veh-**loh**-pehs
matches	fósforos	**fohs**-foh-rohss
paper	papel	pah-**pehl**
sandals	sandália	sahn-**dah**-leeah
soap	sabonete	sah-bow-**neh**-teh
How much is it?	Quanto custa?	**kwahn**-too **koos**-tah
It's expensive/cheap	Está caro/barato	ehss-**tah** kah-roh/bah-**rah**-toh
A little/a lot	Um pouco/muito	oom **pohw**-koh/**mooy**n-too
More/less	Mais/menos	**mah**-ees/**meh**-nohss
Enough/too much/too little	Suficiente/demais/muito pouco	soo-fee-see-**ehn**-teh/deh-**mah**-ees/**mooy**n-toh **pohw**-koh
Telephone	Telefone	teh-leh-**foh**-neh
Telegram	Telegrama	teh-leh-**grah**-mah
I am ill.	Estou doente.	ehss-**tow** doh-**ehn**-teh
Please call a doctor.	Por favor chame um médico.	pohr fah-**vohr** shah-meh oom **meh**-dee-koh
Help!	Socorro!	soh-**koh**-ho
Help me!	Me ajude!	mee ah-**jyew**-deh

Fire!	Incêndio!	een-**sehn**-deeoh
Caution!/Look out!/ Be careful!	Cuidado!	kooy-**dah**-doh

On the Road

Avenue	Avenida	ah-veh-**nee**-dah
Highway	Estrada	ehss-**trah**-dah
Port	Porto	**pohr**-toh
Service station	Posto de gasolina	**pohs**-toh deh gah-zoh-**lee**-nah
Street	Rua	**who**-ah
Toll	Pedagio	peh-**dah**-jyoh
Waterfront promenade	Beiramar/ orla	behy-rah-**mahrr**/ **ohr**-lah
Wharf	Cais	**kah**-ees

In Town

Block	Quarteirão	kwahr-tehy-**rah**-on
Cathedral	Catedral	kah-teh-**drahl**
Church/temple	Igreja	ee-**greh**-jyah
City hall	Prefeitura	preh-fehy-**too**-rah
Door/gate	Porta/portão	**pohr**-tah/porh-**tah**-on
Entrance/exit	Entrada/saída	ehn-**trah**-dah/ sah-**ee**-dah
Market	Mercado/feira	mehr-**kah**-doh/**fey**-rah
Neighborhood	Bairro	**buy**-ho
Rustic bar	Lanchonete	lahn-shoh-**neh**-teh
Shop	Loja	**loh**-jyah
Square	Praça	**prah**-ssah

Dining Out

A bottle of . . .	Uma garrafa de . . .	**oo**mah gah-**hah**-fah deh
A cup of . . .	Uma xícara de . . .	**oo**mah **shee**-kah-rah deh
A glass of . . .	Um copo de . . .	oom **koh**-poh deh
Ashtray	Um cinzeiro	oom seen-**zehy**-roh
Bill/check	A conta	ah **kohn**-tah
Bread	Pão	**pah**-on
Breakfast	Café da manhã	kah-**feh** dah mah-**nyan**
Butter	A manteiga	ah mahn-**tehy**-gah

Cheers!	Saúde!	sah-**oo**-deh
Cocktail	Um aperitivo	oom ah-peh-ree-**tee**-voh
Dinner	O jantar	oh **jyahn**-tahr
Dish	Um prato	oom **prah**-toh
Enjoy!	Bom apetite!	bohm ah-peh-**tee**-teh
Fork	Um garfo	**gahr**-foh
Fruit	Fruta	**froo**-tah
Is the tip included?	A gorjeta esta incluída?	ah gohr-**jyeh**-tah ehss-**tah** een-clue-**ee**-dah
Juice	Um suco	oom **soo**-koh
Knife	Uma faca	**oo**mah **fah**-kah
Lunch	O almoço	oh ahl-**moh**-ssoh
Menu	Menu/ cardápio	me-**noo**/ kahr-**dah**-peeoh
Mineral water	Água mineral	**ah**-gooah mee-neh-**rahl**
Napkin	Guardanapo	gooahr-dah-**nah**-poh
No smoking	Não fumante	nown foo-**mahn**-teh
Pepper	Pimenta	pee-**mehn**-tah
Please give me	Por favor me dê	pohr fah-**vohr** mee **deh**
Salt	Sal	sahl
Smoking	Fumante	foo-**mahn**-teh
Spoon	Uma colher	**oo**mah koh-ly**ehr**
Sugar	Açúcar	ah-**soo**-kahr
Waiter!	Garçon!	gahr-**sohn**
Water	Água	**ah**-gooah
Wine	Vinho	**vee**-nyoh

SPANISH VOCABULARY

English	Spanish	Pronunciation

Basics

English	Spanish	Pronunciation
Yes/no	Sí/no	see/no
Please	Por favor	pore fah-**vore**
May I?	¿Me permite?	may pair-**mee**-tay
Thank you (very much)	(Muchas) gracias	(**moo**-chas) **grah**-see-as
You're welcome	De nada	day **nah**-dah
Excuse me	Con permiso	con pair-**mee**-so
Pardon me	¿Perdón?	pair-**dohn**
Could you tell me?	¿Podría decirme?	po-dree-ah deh-**seer**-meh
I'm sorry	Lo siento	lo see-**en**-to
Good morning!	¡Buenos días!	**bway**-nohs **dee**-ahs
Good afternoon!	¡Buenas tardes!	**bway**-nahs **tar**-dess
Good evening!	¡Buenas noches!	**bway**-nahs **no**-chess
Goodbye!	¡Adiós!/¡Hasta luego!	ah-dee-**ohss**/**ah**-stah-**lwe**-go
Mr./Mrs.	Señor/Señora	sen-**yor**/sen-**yohr**-ah
Miss	Señorita	sen-yo-**ree**-tah
Pleased to meet you	Mucho gusto	**moo**-cho **goose**-to
How are you?	¿Cómo está usted?	**ko**-mo es-**tah** oo-**sted**
Very well, thank you.	Muy bien, gracias.	**moo**-ee bee-**en**, **grah**-see-as
And you?	¿Y usted?	ee oos-**ted**
Hello (on the telephone)	Diga	**dee**-gah

Numbers

1	un, uno	oon, **oo**-no
2	dos	dos
3	tres	tress
4	cuatro	**kwah**-tro
5	cinco	**sink**-oh
6	seis	saice
7	siete	see-**et**-eh
8	ocho	**o**-cho

9	nueve	new-**eh**-vey
10	diez	dee-**es**
11	once	**ohn**-seh
12	doce	**doh**-seh
13	trece	**treh**-seh
14	catorce	ka-**tohr**-seh
15	quince	**keen**-seh
16	dieciséis	dee-**es**-ee-**saice**
17	diecisiete	dee-**es**-ee-see-**et**-eh
18	dieciocho	dee-**es**-ee-**o**-cho
19	diecinueve	**dee-es**-ee-new-**ev**-ah
20	veinte	**vain**-teh
21	veinte y uno/ veintiuno	**vain**-te-**oo**-noh
30	treinta	**train**-tah
32	treinta y dos	train-tay-**dohs**
40	cuarenta	kwah-**ren**-tah
43	cuarenta y tres	kwah-**ren**-tay-**tress**
50	cincuenta	seen-**kwen**-tah
54	cincuenta y cuatro	seen-**kwen**-tay **kwah**-tro
60	sesenta	sess-**en**-tah
65	sesenta y cinco	sess-**en**-tay **seen**-ko
70	setenta	set-**en**-tah
76	setenta y seis	set-**en**-tay **saice**
80	ochenta	oh-**chen**-tah
87	ochenta y siete	oh-**chen**-tay see-**yet**-eh
90	noventa	no-**ven**-tah
98	noventa y ocho	no-**ven**-tah-**o**-choh
100	cien	see-**en**
101	ciento uno	see-**en**-toh **oo**-noh
200	doscientos	doh-see-**en**-tohss
500	quinientos	keen-**yen**-tohss
700	setecientos	set-eh-see-**en**-tohss
900	novecientos	no-veh-see-**en**-tohss
1,000	mil	meel
2,000	dos mil	dohs meel
1,000,000	un millón	oon meel-**yohn**

Colors

black	negro	**neh**-groh
blue	azul	ah-**sool**
brown	café	kah-**feh**
green	verde	**ver**-deh
pink	rosa	**ro**-sah
purple	morado	mo-**rah**-doh
orange	naranja	na-**rahn**-hah
red	rojo	**roh**-hoh
white	blanco	**blahn**-koh
yellow	amarillo	ah-mah-**ree**-yoh

Days of the Week

Sunday	domingo	doe-**meen**-goh
Monday	lunes	**loo**-ness
Tuesday	martes	**mahr**-tess
Wednesday	miércoles	me-**air**-koh-less
Thursday	jueves	hoo-**ev**-ess
Friday	viernes	vee-**air**-ness
Saturday	sábado	**sah**-bah-doh

Months

January	enero	eh-**neh**-roh
February	febrero	feh-**breh**-roh
March	marzo	**mahr**-soh
April	abril	ah-**breel**
May	mayo	**my**-oh
June	junio	**hoo**-nee-oh
July	julio	**hoo**-lee-yoh
August	agosto	ah-**ghost**-toh
September	septiembre	sep-tee-**em**-breh
October	octubre	oak-**too**-breh
November	noviembre	no-vee-**em**-breh
December	diciembre	dee-see-**em**-breh

Useful Phrases

Do you speak English?	¿Habla usted inglés?	**ah**-blah oos-**ted** in-**glehs**
I don't speak Spanish	No hablo español	no **ah**-bloh es-pahn-**yol**
I don't understand (you)	No entiendo	no en-tee-**en**-doh

I understand (you)	Entiendo	en-tee-**en**-doh
I don't know	No sé	no seh
I am American/ British	Soy americano (americana)/ inglés(a)	soy ah-meh-ree-**kah**-no (ah-meh-ree-**kah**-nah)/ in-**glehs(ah)**
What's your name?	¿Cómo se llama usted?	koh-mo seh **yah**-mah oos-**ted**
My name is . . .	Me llamo . . .	may **yah**-moh
What time is it?	¿Qué hora es?	keh **o**-rah es
It is one, two, three . . . o'clock.	Es la una. . . . Son las dos, tres	es la **oo**-nah/ sohn lahs dohs, tress
Yes, please/ No, thank you	Sí, por favor/ No, gracias	**see** pohr fah-**vor**/ no **grah**-see-us
How?	¿Cómo?	**koh**-mo
When?	¿Cuándo?	**kwahn**-doh
This/Next week	Esta semana/ la semana que entra	**es**-teh seh-**mah**-nah/ lah seh-**mah**-nah keh **en**-trah
This/Next month	Este mes/ el próximo mes	**es**-teh mehs/ el **proke**-see-mo mehs
This/Next year	Este año/el año que viene	**es**-teh **ahn**-yo/el **ahn**-yo keh vee-**yen**-ay
Yesterday/today/ tomorrow	Ayer/hoy/mañana	ah-**yehr**/oy/mahn-**yah**-nah
This morning/ afternoon	Esta mañana/ tarde	**es**-tah mahn-**yah**-nah/ **tar**-deh
Tonight	Esta noche	**es**-tah **no**-cheh
What?	¿Qué?	keh
What is it?	¿Qué es esto?	keh es **es**-toh
Why?	¿Por qué?	pore **keh**
Who?	¿Quién?	kee-**yen**
Where is . . . ?	¿Dónde está . . . ?	**dohn**-deh es-**tah**
the train station?	la estación del tren?	la es-tah-see-**on** del **train**
the subway station?	la estación del Tren subterráneo?	la es-ta-see-**on** del trehn soob-tair-**ron**-a-o
the bus stop?	la parada del autobus?	la pah-**rah**-dah del oh-toh-**boos**
the post office?	la oficina de correos?	la oh-fee-**see**-nah deh koh-**reh**-os
the bank?	el banco?	el **bahn**-koh
the hotel?	el hotel?	el oh-**tel**
the store?	la tienda?	la tee-en-dah
the cashier?	la caja?	la **kah**-hah

the museum?	el museo?	el moo-**seh**-oh
the hospital?	el hospital?	el ohss-pee-**tal**
the elevator?	el ascensor?	el ah-**sen**-sohr
the bathroom?	el baño?	el **bahn**-yoh
Here/there	Aquí/allá	ah-**key**/ah-**yah**
Open/closed	Abierto/cerrado	ah-bee-**er**-toh/ser-**ah**-doh
Left/right	Izquierda/derecha	iss-key-**er**-dah/dare-**eh**-chah
Straight ahead	Derecho	dare-**eh**-choh
Is it near/far?	¿Está cerca/lejos?	es-**tah sehr**-kah/**leh**-hoss
I'd like . . .	Quisiera . . .	kee-see-ehr-ah
a room	un cuarto/una habitación	oon **kwahr**-toh/**oo**-nah ah-bee-tah-see-**on**
the key	la llave	lah **yah**-veh
a newspaper	un periódico	oon pehr-ee-**oh**-dee-koh
a stamp	un sello de correo	oon **seh**-yo deh koh-**reh**-oh
I'd like to buy . . .	Quisiera comprar . . .	kee-see-**ehr**-ah kohm-**prahr**
cigarettes	cigarrillos	ce-ga-**ree**-yohs
matches	cerillos	ser-**ee**-ohs
a dictionary	un diccionario	oon deek-see-oh-**nah**-ree-oh
soap	jabón	hah-**bohn**
sunglasses	gafas de sol	**ga**-fahs deh sohl
suntan lotion	loción bronceadora	loh-see-**ohn** brohn-seh-ah-**do**-rah
a map	un mapa	oon **mah**-pah
a magazine	una revista	**oon**-ah reh-**veess**-tah
paper	papel	pah-**pel**
envelopes	sobres	**so**-brehs
a postcard	una tarjeta postal	**oon**-ah tar-**het**-ah post-**ahl**
How much is it?	¿Cuánto cuesta?	**kwahn**-toh **kwes**-tah
It's expensive/cheap	Está caro/barato	es-**tah kah**-roh/bah-**rah**-toh
A little/a lot	Un poquito/mucho	oon poh-**kee**-toh/**moo**-choh
More/less	Más/menos	mahss/**men**-ohss
Enough/too much/too little	Suficiente/demasiado/muy poco	soo-fee-see-**en**-teh/deh-mah-see-**ah**-doh/**moo**-ee poh-koh
Telephone	Teléfono	tel-**ef**-oh-no

Telegram	Telegrama	teh-leh-**grah**-mah
I am ill	Estoy enfermo(a)	es-**toy** en-**fehr**-moh(mah)
Please call a doctor	Por favor llame a un medico	pohr fah-**vor ya**-meh ah oon **med**-ee-koh
Help!	¡Auxilio! ¡Ayuda! ¡Socorro!	owk-**see**-lee-oh/ ah-**yoo**-dah/ soh-**kohr**-roh
Fire!	¡Incendio!	en-**sen**-dee-oo
Caution!/Look out!	¡Cuidado!	kwee-**dah**-doh

On the Road

Avenue	Avenida	ah-ven-**ee**-dah
Broad, tree-lined boulevard	Bulevar	boo-leh-**var**
Fertile plain	Vega	**veh**-gah
Highway	Carretera	car-reh-**ter**-ah
Mountain pass, Street	Puerto Calle	poo-**ehr**-toh **cah**-yeh
Waterfront promenade	Rambla	**rahm**-blah
Wharf	Embarcadero	em-bar-cah-**deh**-ro

In Town

Cathedral	Catedral	cah-teh-**dral**
Church	Templo/Iglesia	**tem**-plo/ee-**glehs**-see-ah
City hall	Casa de gobierno	kah-sah deh go-bee-**ehr**-no
Door, gate	Puerta portón	poo-**ehr**-tah por-**ton**
Entrance/exit	Entrada/salida	en-**trah**-dah/sah-**lee**-dah
Inn, rustic bar, or restaurant	Taverna	tah-**vehr**-nah
Main square	Plaza principal	plah-thah prin-see-**pahl**
Market	Mercado	mer-**kah**-doh
Neighborhood	Barrio	**bahr**-ree-o
Traffic circle	Glorieta	glor-ee-**eh**-tah
Wine cellar, wine bar, or wine shop	Bodega	boh-**deh**-gah

Dining Out

A bottle of . . .	Una botella de . . .	**oo**-nah bo-**teh**-yah deh
A cup of . . .	Una taza de . . .	**oo**-nah **tah**-thah deh
A glass of . . .	Un vaso de . . .	oon **vah**-so deh
Ashtray	Un cenicero	oon sen-ee-**seh**-roh
Bill/check	La cuenta	lah **kwen**-tah
Bread	El pan	el pahn
Breakfast	El desayuno	el deh-sah-**yoon**-oh
Butter	La mantequilla	lah man-teh-**key**-yah
Cheers!	¡Salud!	sah-**lood**
Cocktail	Un aperitivo	oon ah-pehr-ee-**tee**-voh
Dinner	La cena	lah **seh**-nah
Dish	Un plato	oon **plah**-toh
Menu of the day	Menú del día	meh-**noo** del **dee**-ah
Enjoy!	¡Buen provecho!	bwehn pro-**veh**-cho
Fixed-price menu	Menú fijo o turistico	meh-**noo** **fee**-hoh oh too-**ree**-stee-coh
Fork	El tenedor	el ten-eh-**dor**
Is the tip included?	¿Está incluida la propina?	es-**tah** in-cloo-**ee**-dah lah pro-**pee**-nah
Knife	El cuchillo	el koo-**chee**-yo
Large portion of savory snacks	Raciónes	rah-see-**oh**-nehs
Lunch	La comida	lah koh-**mee**-dah
Menu	La carta, el menú	lah **cart**-ah, el meh-**noo**
Napkin	La servilleta	lah sehr-vee-**yet**-ah
Pepper	La pimienta	lah pee-me-**en**-tah
Please give me	Por favor déme	pore fah-**vor** **deh**-meh
Salt	La sal	lah sahl
Savory snacks	Tapas	**tah**-pahs
Spoon	Una cuchara	**oo**-nah koo-**chah**-rah
Sugar	El azúcar	el ah-**thu**-kar
Waiter!/Waitress!	¡Por favor Señor/Señorita!	pohr fah-**vor** sen-**yor**/sen-yor-**ee**-tah

INDEX